A

GENEALOGICAL DICTIONARY

OF

THE FIRST SETTLERS OF NEW ENGLAND,

SHOWING

THREE GENERATIONS

OF

THOSE WHO CAME BEFORE MAY, 1692,

ON THE

BASIS OF FARMER'S REGISTER.

BY

JAMES SAVAGE,

FORMER PRESIDENT OF THE MASSACHUSETTS HISTORICAL SOCIETY AND EDITOR OF WINTHROP'S
HISTORY OF NEW ENGLAND.

WITH TWO SUPPLEMENTS

IN FOUR VOLUMES.

VOL. III.

Originally Published
Boston, 1860-1862

Reprinted with
"Genealogical Notes and Errata,"
excerpted from
*The New England Historical
and Genealogical Register,*
Vol. XXVII, No. 2, April, 1873,
pp. 135-139

And

*A Genealogical Cross Index
of the Four Volumes
of the Genealogical Dictionary
of James Savage,*
by O. P. Dexter, 1884.

Genealogical Publishing Co., Inc.
Baltimore, 1965, 1969, 1977, 1981, 1986, 1990, 1994, 1998

Library of Congress Catalogue Card Number 65-18541
International Standard Book Number: 0-8063-0962-8
Set Number: 0-8063-0759-5

ADVERTISEMENT.

CONTRARY to my intention, this third volume is larger than the second, and I fear that the fourth, of which nearly one half is already printed, may not be confined in fewer pages than the present. My apology will, probably, be accepted by all subscribers, for it was most reasonable that each volume should begin with a *new* letter.

Often I have been desired to explain the marks, as *, and others, set before the baptismal names in so many instances. They are exactly copied from Farmer's Register, and seemed to me appropriate. They are hereunder described.

§ shows, that the man was Governor or President.

† " that he was Deputy Governor.

‡ " that he was an Assistant, or Counsellor.

* " that he was a Representative.

‖ " that he belonged to the Ancient and Honorable Artillery Company of Massachusetts.

GENEALOGICAL DICTIONARY

OF THE

FIRST SETTLERS OF NEW ENGLAND.

KATES. See Cates.

KATHERICK. See Carthrick.

KEAIS, SAMUEL, New Hampsh. m. 4 Feb. 1696, Mary, wid. of John Hoddy, had Samuel, b. 11 Apr. 1697; and William, 27 Aug. 1699.

KEATS, RICHARD, Boston 1677, bricklayer.

KEAYNE, ‖ BENJAMIN, Boston 1638, only s. of Robert, b. in London, came with his f. when his age was rat. perhaps two or more yrs. too low, freem. 6 Sept. 1639, ar. co. 1638, m. bef. 9 June 1639, Sarah, d. of Gov. Thomas Dudley, had only ch. Ann; liv. some short time at Lynn, was a maj. went home, in disgust with his w. a. 1645, and repud. her; d. 1668. She had been disciplin. Nov. 1646 for irreg. prophesy. and was excom. in Oct. 1647, and sadly degrad. but was made the w. of one Pacey. Ann, wh. was well provid. for in will of gr.f. K. mak. the chief gent. here to assist his w. "to dispose of her for her future educ. unto some such wise and godly mistress or fam. where she may have her carnal disposition most of all subdu. and reform. by strict discipline; and also that they would show like care and assist. in seasona. time to provide some fit and godly match, proportiona. to her est. and condit. that she may live comforta. and be fit to do good in her place, and not to suffer her to be circumvent. or to cast away hers. upon some swagger. gent. or other, that will look more after the enjoy. what she hath, than live in the fear of God, and true love to her," m. 11 Dec. 1657, Edward Lane, a merch. from London, and, next, to Nicholas Paige; but she

seems ill to have repaid the pious care of her gr.f. and d. 30 June 1704.
Her gr.f. took care, that her mo. " Sarah Dudley, now Sarah Pacey, may
have no part" of the prop. thus giv. to the d.   The unhappy w. of K.
d. Nov. 1659.   See Winth. I. 314 and II. 4.   JOHN, Hingham, d. 14
Jan. 1650, of wh. no more is kn. but that his name appears sometimes
Cane.   * ‖ ROBERT, Boston, merch. of the Merch. Taylors' comp. of
London, came in the Defence, 1635, aged 40, with w. Ann, 38 ; and s.
Benjamin, 16; perhaps, however, some of these yrs. are designedly
wrong.   In 1624 he had been one of the Undertakers, wh. encourag. the
Plymouth Pilgrims, and of his pub. spirit no doubt can be felt by any
wh. reads his will, begun 1 Aug. 1653, and for some yrs. extend. of wh.
a very short abstr. is seen in Geneal. Reg. VI. 89 and 152.   He was
freem. 25 May 1636, rep. 1638 and 9, one of the found. of ar. co. hav.
been "train. up in milit. discip. from his younger yrs." in London Artill.;
d. 23 Mar. 1656, and his wid. m. 16 Oct. 1660, Samuel Cole.   WILLIAM,
Boston, had w. Agnes, wh. join. the ch. 31 May 1646.

   KEBY, or KEBBY.   See Kibby.

   KEDALL, KEDELL, or KEEDELL, is a strange name of two maids that
m. very reput. at Watertown, viz. Mary, 11 Jan. 1655, Thomas Whitney ;
and Bethia, 3 Nov. 1666, Theophilus Phillips ; and long and large inq.
has been foil. as to their origin.

   KEDEN, BENJAMIN, Boston 1661, serv. of Rice Jones.

   KEELER, * JOHN, Norwalk, s. of Ralph, m. 18 June 1678, Mehitable,
d. of John Rockwell, had Eliz. b. 19 Mar. 1679; John, 26 Dec. 1682;
and, perhaps, others ; was rep. 1698.   RALPH, Hartford, had a lot in
1640, tho. not orig. propr. there had Rebecca, b. 9 Feb. 1651 ; and Eliz.
wh. may have been b. at Norwalk; beside an elder d. wh. m. Thomas
Moorhouse, wh. was not nam. in the will of 20 Aug. 1672, when he
calls his age 59 yrs. and the Ct. of pro. correct. the oversight in her
favor.   With the first sett. of Norwalk he plant. there, was freem. 1668,
had John, Ralph, Samuel, and Jonah, wh. d. 1676 ; and d. 1672, betw.
20 Aug. and 10 Sept.   He had m. Sarah, wid. of Henry Whelpley.
RALPH, Norwalk, perhaps the eldest s. of the preced. freem. 1675, had
Sarah, wh. m. 7 Dec. 1702, Nathan Olmstead, as may be guess. from
Hall, 194.   Prob. he had other ch.   * SAMUEL, Norwalk, br. of the
preced. was in the gr. Narragansett fight, 19 Dec. 1675, m. 10 Mar.
1682, Sarah, d. of Mark Sension, or St. John, had Samuel; and prob.
more; was rep. 1701.   WALTER, Norwalk 1651, perhaps a nonentity.

   KEELEY, EDWARD, New Haven, a propr. in 1685, may be he, wh.
came from London, 1635, in the Hopewell, Capt. Bundocke, aged 14.

   KEEN, or KEAN, ARTHUR, Boston, d. Mar. or Apr. 1687, his will
being of 21 Mar. in that yr. pro. 14 Apr. foll.   It ment. w. Jane, to wh.

he gave all his est. for her life; s. John and d. Sarah Pierce, wh. was w. of William, m. 13 July 1666, equal sh. of remainder. JAMES, Braintree 1645, was capt.   JOHN, Boston 1662, mariner, and in few yrs. innholder, may be that passeng. in the Confidence from Southampton, 1638, aged 17, with Martha, 60, wh. may have been his mo. Eliz. Martha, Josias, and Sarah, prob. his br. and sis.   JOSIAH, Duxbury, m. Hannah, d. of John Dingley, had John, b. 1661; Josiah; Matthew; and Hannah. The last m. 1695, Isaac Oldham of Scituate.   WILLIAM, Salem 1638, of wh. Felt says, he had in that yr. a gr. of ld. and nobody else tells any thing.

KEENY, KENY, or KEENEY, ALEXANDER, Wethersfield, freem. 1667, d. 1680, leav. Alexander, 18; Thomas, and Sarah, tw. 16; Joseph, 14; Lydia, 11; Ebenezer, 8; and Richard, 6. His wid. Alice d. 1683. JOHN, New London, s. of William, freem. 1670, m. Oct. 1661, Sarah, d. of William Douglas, had Susanna, b. Sept. 1662; John, William, and Hannah.   WILLIAM, Gloucester, by w. Agnes had Susanna; Mary; and John, b. a. 1640; rem. to New London a. 1651; in 1662 was aged a. 61, and his w. 63; he d. 1675. Susanna m. Ralph Parker; and Mary m. Samuel Beebe. This name is *not* bec. Kinne.

KEEP, JOHN, Springfield 1660, freem. 1669, m. 31 Dec. 1663, Sarah Leonard, had Sarah, b. 1666; Eliz. 1668, d. young; Samuel, 1670; Hannah, 1673; and Jabez, wh. was, with his mo. tak. by the Ind. 20 Mar. 1676, when the f. was k. as were the mo. and ch. soon after.   The Commander of the forces on Conn. riv. Maj. Savage, in despatch of 28 Mar. tells the story.   SAMUEL, Springfield, s. of the preced. m. 1696, Sarah Colton, had twelve ch.

KEESE, JOHN, Portsmouth, R. I. m. 18 Sept. 1682, Ann, d. of Shadrach Manton, had Alice, b. Aug. 1683; William, 26 Oct. 1685; Patience, 27 June 1690; John, 14 Mar. 1693; Shadrach, 5 Oct. 1695; Ann, 26 Oct. 1698; and he d. 10 Dec. 1700.

KEET, FRANCIS, Northampton, had come from the E. part of the Col. on serv. in Philip's war, was at the Falls fight, 19 May 1676; m. Hannah, d. of John French, had Francis, John, and, perhaps, Thomas.

KEETCH, JOHN, Boston, by w. Hannah had Mary, wh. d. 1 Jan. 1656, says the rec.

KEISAR.   See Keysar.

KEITH, JAMES, first min. of Bridgewater, bred at one of the coll. in Aberdeen, came a. 1662, was ord. early in 1664, when he was under 21 yrs. d. 23 July 1719, in 76th yr.   In the solemn induct. a part was born by Rev. Increase Mather, perhaps the youngest min. in the assemb.; yet in the Magn. III. 4, with heedlessness, strange even in Cotton Mather, his third classis, " of such MIN. as came over to N. E. after the reëstabl. of the Episc. ch. gov." in Eng. among all the veterans is crowd. in our Keith; wh. might be less, could not be more than 18 yrs. Ever honor. should be his name for oppos. to the design of putting to d. the child of king Philip. His first w. was Susanna, prob. d. of deac. Samuel Edson, and his sec. 1707, was Mary Williams of Taunton, wid. of Thomas; and all his ch. were by the first. Of one d. as I presume, the m. is found at Taunton in the rec. of Jonathan Howard and Susannah K. 8 Jan. 1689. Progeny of his s. James, Joseph, Samuel, Timothy, John, and Josiah, is scatt. thro. most of the U. S. At Bridgewater alone in 1810, this name count. 200. Of his ds. Margaret m. a Hunt; and Mary m. Ephraim Howard. JAMES, Bridgewater, s. of the preced. by w. Mary had James, b. 1696; Mary, 1698; Gershom, 1701; Israel, 1703; Faithful, 1704; Esther, 1707; Jane, 1709; and Simeon, 1712; rem. to Mendon 1719. JOHN, Bridgewater, br. of the preced. m. 1711, Hannah, d. of Samuel Washburn, had John, b. 1712; James, 1716; Israel, 1719; Hannah, 1721; Kezia, 1723; Daniel, 1725; Susanna, 1727; Zephaniah, 1730; Joseph; and Mary; and d. 1761. His wid. d. 1766. * JOSEPH, Bridgewater, br. of the preced. m. Eliz. d. of Edward Fobes, had Ann, b. 1695; Susanna, 1697; Joseph, 1699; Jemima, 1701; Eleazer, 1703; Abigail, 1705; Ephraim, 1707; Ichabod, 1709; Martha, 1711; Mary, 1713; and Eliz. 1715; was rep. 1726, and made his will 1730; and his wid. made hers 1759. JOSIAH, Bridgewater, br. of the preced. m. 1703, Mary, d. of Samuel Lothrop, had Margaret, b. 1704; Joseph, 1706; William, 1708; Mark, 1710; Sarah, 1712; Mary, 1714; Daniel, 1716; Jane; Silence; and Phebe; and rem. to Easton. SAMUEL, Bridgewater, br. of the preced. m. 1703, Bethia, d. of Edward Fobes, had Constant, b. 1703; Amos, 1705; Samuel, 1707; Bethia, 1710; Susanna, 1714; Ebenezer, 1716; Robert, 1718; Jane, 1720; and Benjamin, 1723, and d. 1750. TIMOTHY, Bridgewater, br. of the preced. m. 1710, Hannah, d. of Edward Fobes, had Timothy, b. 1711; Abiah, 1712; Nathan, 1714; and Hannah, 1718. His w. d. 1765; and he d. 1767, in 83d yr. says Mitchell, from whose work all of this fam. is tak. Four at Harv. and three at the other N. E. coll. had been gr. in 1829.

KELLEN, KILLIN, or KELLING, JAMES, Charlestown, m. 12 Dec. 1679, Hannah Trarice, perhaps d. of John, had James, b. 10 May foll. Samuel, 1 Oct. 1682; and Margaret, 25 Oct. 1684.

KELLOGG, * DANIEL, Norwalk 1655, by first w. wh. is unkn. to us, had Mary, b. 1663, wh. m. 1680, Joseph Platt of Milford; and Rachel, Feb. 1664, wh. m. Abraham Nichols; and he m. 1665, Bridget, d. of John Bouton, as sec. w. had Sarah, Feb. 1666, wh. m. Daniel Brinsmead; Eliz. Aug. 1668 (but I find confus. in Hall, 187), wh. d. young; Daniel, 7 May 1671; Samuel, Feb. 1674; Lydia, Apr. 1676; Benjamin and

Joseph, tw. Mar. 1678, of wh. Benjamin d. bef. Nov. 1703; was rep. 1670, and six of seven yrs. aft.; and d. 1688. DANIEL, Norwalk, eldest s. of the preced. had Daniel, b. 7 Mar. 1691; John, a. 1701; Benjamin, 1704; Joanna, 1706; and Eliasaph, July 1709; and the f. d. that yr. Whether he had more than one w. or wh. was mo. of his ch. I find not. JOSEPH, Farmington, weaver, freem. 1654, had John, bapt. 29 Dec. 1656; and Martin; rem. 1659 to Boston, had Edward, b. 1 Oct. 1660, but next yr. sold his prop. in B. and went to Hadley; where his first w. Joanna d. 14 Sept. 1666, and he m. 9 May foll. Abigail, d. of Stephen Terry. Beside these ch. he had Samuel, 1662; Joanna, 8 Dec. 1664, wh. m. 29 Nov. 1683, John Smith of H.; and Sarah, 1666; all by first; and by sec. w. had Stephen, 1668; Nathaniel, 8 Oct. 1669; Abigail, 1671; Eliz. 1673; Prudence, 1675; Ebenezer, 1677; Jonathan, 1679; Daniel, 1682, d. in 2 yrs.; Joseph, 1684; and Ephraim, 1687, d. young. All the ds. were m. In the Falls fight he was a lieut. and command. the men of H. He d. 1707, then hav. fourteen adult ch. As they scatt. so much, I give the places of resid. of most of the eleven s. John, wh. had ten ch. liv. at Hadley; Martin was at Hatfield, and Deerfield; Edward had nine ch. b. at Hadley, and then rem. to Brookfield; Samuel, sett. at Hartford, had nine ch.; Stephen, in Westfield, had eleven ch.; Nathaniel, at Hadley and Amherst, had eight or nine ch.; Ebenezer, and Jonathan sett. at Colchester; Joseph, wh. had no ch. was at Hatfield. Ano. JOSEPH, call. jr. was at Hadley in 1678, old eno. to take o. of fidel. in Feb. 1679. JOSEPH, Norwalk, s. of the first Daniel, m. 25 Nov. 1702, Sarah, d. of John Plum of Milford, had Eliz. b. 5 Oct. 1703; Sarah, 5 Apr. 1706; Joseph, 26 Sept. 1707; Rachel, 15 July 1710; Hannah, 1 Aug. 1712; and his w. d. 17 Aug. foll. but the same page of Hall, in the next line, says he m. Mary, wid. of Andrew Lyon, on 17 Aug. 1712, wh. must be a mistake for 10 Oct. and this was less than eight wks. aft. d. of first w.; and had David, 28 Sept. 1715; and Benjamin, 26 Sept. 1717; and d. a. 1721. MARTIN, Hatfield, s. of the first Joseph, m. 10 Dec. 1684, Ann, d. of Samuel Hinsdale, had Martin, b. 26 Oct. 1686; and Ann, 14 July 1689; by sec. w. Sarah, d. of the first John Dickinson of Hadley, wid. of Samuel Lane, had Joseph, 8 Nov. 1691; Joanna, 8 Feb. 1693; Rebecca, 22 Dec. 1695; and Jonathan, 17 Dec. 1698. He, with ch. Martin, Joseph, Joanna, and Rebecca, were tak. 29 Feb. 1704, by the Fr. and Ind. when they destroy. Deerfield (where he had liv. some yrs.) and carr. to Canada, and long kept. prison. but all came back, exc. Joanna, wh. m. an Ind. ch. and bore him childr. NATHANIEL, Farmington 1653, had been one of the sett. at Hartford 1640, tho. not orig. propr. had, perhaps, Eliz. b. 1652; Joseph, 1653; and Nathaniel, bapt. 29 Oct. 1654, wh. all d. early, and he d. aft. short resid. at F.

1 *

NATHANIEL, Hadley, s. of Joseph of the same, m. 28 June 1692, Sarah, d. of Samuel Boltwood, had Nathaniel, b. 22 Sept. 1693, and prob. others; rem. to Amherst, and d. 30 Oct. 1750. SAMUEL, Hatfield, perhaps br. of first Joseph, m. 24 Nov. 1664, Sarah, wid. of Nathaniel Gunn, d. of Robert Day, had Samuel, b. 1669; Nathaniel, 1671; Ebenezer, 1674; and Joseph, 1676, wh. was k. with his mo. 19 Sept. 1677 by the Ind. wh. carr. young Samuel off to Canada, whence he came back. He m. 1679, Sarah Root of Westfield, had John, b. 1680; and Thomas, 1681; wh. both d. at H. unm. over 70 yrs. of age; and Sarah, 1684. The elder s. Nathaniel, and Ebenezer sett. at Colchester, and perhaps, Samuel too. SAMUEL, Hartford, s. perhaps, of Joseph the first, had Samuel, b. 1688; Margaret, Jan. 1690; Abraham, 1692; John; Isaac; Jacob; Benjamin; Joseph; and Daniel. SAMUEL, Norwalk, s. of the first Daniel, m. 6 Sept. 1704, Sarah, d. of John Platt, had Sarah, b. 26 Sept. 1705; Samuel, 23 Dec. 1706; Mary, 29 Jan. 1709; Martin, 23 Mar. 1711; Abigail, 19 Jan. 1713; Lydia, 30 Oct. 1715; Gideon, 5 Dec. 1717; and Epenetus, 26 June 1719. STEPHEN, Westfield, s. of Joseph of Hadley, by w. Lydia had Lydia, b. 24 Jan. 1697; Moses, 26 Oct. 1700, d. young; Abigail, 27 Dec. 1702; Daniel, 16 Dec. 1704; Ephraim, 2 July 1707; Mercy, 30 Oct. 1709; Noah, 13 Feb. 1712; Silas, 7 Apr. 1714; Amos, 13 Sept. 1716; and d. 5 June 1722. Twenty of this name had, in 1829, been gr. at the N. E. coll. Large acco. of the descend. of Silas, fifth s. of Stephen bef. ment. wh. was the fifth s. of Joseph the first, may be seen in Geneal. Reg. XII. 202–6.

KELLOND, THOMAS, Boston, merch. recent. from Eng. had warrant, in May 1661, from our Gov. Endicot, for pursuit that was fruitless of the regicides, Whalley and Goffe; m. Abigail, d. of Capt. Thomas Hawkins, wid. of Samuel Moore, had Susanna, b. 21 Oct. 1665; John, 2 June 1667, d. young; John, again, 13 Feb. 1669, d. young; Thomas, 18 July 1670, d. young; Samuel, 11 Sept. 1671; Eliz. 14 Aug. 1673; Thomas, again, 29 Aug. 1674; John, again, 15 June 1678; and Richard, 26 Sept. 1681; d. 12 July 1686, and his wid. m. third h. Hon. John Foster, wh. she outliv. 2 Mass. Hist. Coll. VIII. 68, 105; Hutch. I. 243, 330; and Hutch. Coll. 334, where is the very curious docum. call. their return. THOMAS, Boston, by w. Eliz. had Eliz. b. 6 Aug. 1687, d. soon; Eliz. again, 5 Dec. 1689; Mary, 4 July 1697; and Thomas, 4 Mar. 1699.

KELLY, ABEL; Salem, freem. 2 June 1641, rem. to where I kn. not. BENJAMIN, a freem. of Mass. 1669, I can assign to no town with confid. DAVID, Boston, by w. Eliz. had David, b. 18 Dec. 1647; and Samuel, 1653, and ano. Samuel, 9 Oct. 1657. He d. 1662, and his wid. Eliz. had admin. the childr. being refer. to. She m. 4 Aug. 1663, Robert Smith.

DAVID, Portsmouth, and Newbury, mariner, was, prob. s. of the preced. HENRY, Lancaster, was freem. 1668, if the printer have not mistak. the name, that, perhaps, was intend. for Kerley. JOHN, Newbury, among the first sett. came, says Coffin, from Newbury in ·Berks, 1635, had Sarah, b. 12 Feb. 1641; and John, 2 July 1642, d. 28 Dec. 1644. JOHN, Newbury, only s. of the preced. m. 25 May 1663, Sarah, d. of Richard Knight, had Richard, b. 28 Feb. 1666; John, 17 June 1668; Sarah, 1 Sept. 1670; Abiel, 12 Dec. 1672; Rebecca, 15 May 1675; Mary, 24 May 1678; Jonathan, 20 Mar. 1681; Joseph, 1 Dec. 1683; and Hannah, 17 Nov. 1686. He was freem. 1669, and d. 21 Mar. 1718. His s. John by his sec. w. Eliz. Emery, beside seven other ch. had John, b. 8 Oct. 1697, liv. at Atkinson, d. 27 Apr. 1783, wh. was f. of Col. Moses, wh. d. 2 Aug. 1824, aged 86, and of Rev. William, H. C. 1767, first min. of Warner, and f. of John, the assid. secr. of the N. H. Hist. Soc. and Reg. of Prob. for Rockingham. A John K. was adm. freem. of Conn. 1658; but of his resid. I learn not. RENALD, or REGINALD, Pemaquid, took o. of fidel. 1674. * ROGER, Isle of Shoals 1668, m. at Exeter, 29 Sept. 1681, Mary, d. of William Holdridge of Salisbury, was rep. at the first gen. Ct. in Boston says Farmer, under the new chart. 1692. Twelve of this name had, in 1829, been gr. at the N. E. coll.

KELSEY, JOHN, Hartford, s. of William, freem. 1658, m. Phebe, d. of Nicholas Disbrow, rem. to Killingworth; was lieut. d. 1709, leav. w. Hannah, ch. John, Joseph, Josiah, and three ds. ws. of Joseph Wilcoxson, Nathaniel Parmelee, and John Lane. MARK, Windsor, perhaps br. of the preced. m. 8 Mar. 1659, Rebecca Hoskins, had Rebecca, b. 2 Jan. foll. and John, wh. d. young. His w. d. 28 Aug. 1683, and within four mos. he took sec. w. Abigail Atwood, wh. d. 28 Mar. 1713. STEPHEN, Hartford, s. of William, m. 15 Nov. 1672, Hannah, eldest d. of John Ingersoll, first of Westfield, not "Higginson of Wethersfield," as Hinman, p. 151, says, and repeats, 261; had Hannah, b. 1675; Stephen, 20 Sept. 1677; John, 20 Jan. 1680; Daniel, 14 Sept. 1682; William, 19 Feb. 1685; James, 21 Aug. 1687; and Charles, 15 June 1692; and d. 30 Nov. 1710. * WILLIAM, Cambridge 1632, freem. 4 Mar. 1635, rem. to Hartford, thence, a. 1663, to Killingworth, but at H. the only ch. b. were Abigail, in Apr. 1645; Stephen, 7 Nov. 1647; and Daniel, 1650; but, no doubt, others were omit. in the rec. or were earlier b. at C. was rep. in 1671, when the rec. is Callsey, but oft. it is Kelse, Kelso, Kelsea, Kelsa, or Kelsy.

KELSON, THOMAS, Reading.

KEMBLE, or KEMBALL. See Kimball.

KEMPE, EDWARD, Dedham, freem. 13 Mar. 1639, prob. was of Wenham 1651, and aft. a blacksmith, and d. 17 Dec. 1668, at Chelmsford, to wh. he rem. 1655. His will of 27 Dec. preced. names only d. Esther,

w. of Samuel Foster, and her s. Samuel, and his own kinsm. Samuel of Groton. ROBERT, Dedham 1639, adm. with w. of the ch. that yr. as was Esther on 6 Mar. 1646. SAMUEL, Billerica 1659, aft. prob. at Andover, and at Groton, where the fam. widely extend. by w. Sarah had Jonathan, b. 6 Apr. 1668; Mehitable, 4 Jan. 1673; and Bethia, 9 July 1683. WILLIAM, Duxbury, is call. in the custom ho. certif. from Southampton, Apr. 1635, a serv. passeng. in the James, arr. at Boston, 3 June foll. But I presume there is intentional carelessness in the *number* of passeng. and as Thomas Thacher is not nam. this man's name may be miscall.; had William; and d. Sept. 1641, leav. wid. Eliz. admix. WILLIAM, Dover 1664, of wh. no more is kn. WILLIAM, Duxbury, s. of the first William, m. Patience, d. of Rev. Thomas Thacher.

KEMPSTER, DANIEL, Cambridge, freem. 1647. Abigail, perhaps his d. more prob. his w. d. 22 Oct. 1657. His will, of 27 Sept. 1665, pro. 2 Apr. 1667, names no w. nor ch.

KEMPTHORNE, DANIEL, Cambridge, is in the list of credit. of James Astwood "for keeping his sons," 1653. SIMON, Charlestown, perhaps s. of Daniel, m. Mary, d. of Robert Long, had Sarah, b. 1656, wh. d. 21 Oct. 1671. Early in July 1656 he brot. from Barbados, as master of the ship Swallow, two women, the first Quakers in this Col. for wh. he was blam. by the Court of Assist. and he d. a. 1657. His wid. d. 14 Jan. 1675.

KEMPTON, EPHRAIM, Scituate, perhaps br. of Manasseh, is includ. in the list of those able to bear arms, 1643, with Ephraim jr. but his name is eras. bec. no doubt, he was too old or infirm, and he d. 5 May 1645. We kn. not when he came, but it was after 1627, as may clearly be infer. for he is not ment. in the div. of cattle that yr. EPHRAIM, Scituate, prob. s. of the preced. b. in Eng. m. 28 Jan. 1646, Joanna Rawlins, d. of Thomas, had Joanna, b. 29 Sept. 1647; Patience, 2 Oct. 1648, d. soon; Ephraim, 1 Oct. 1649; Manasseh, 1 Jan. 1652; and d. 1655. His wid. d. 31 Mar. next yr. Deane, 299, is deficient in dates. EPHRAIM, Boston, gunsmith, prob. s. of the preced. m. 7 Nov. 1673, Patience, d. of Elder Thomas Faunce, had rem. 1677 to Salem, but, perhaps, went to Plymouth late in life, and his wid. is one of the instances, well authentica. (as very few are) of much exceed. 100 yrs. of age. Her memory was accurate, if not happy, for she saw the head of Philip, the gr. Ind. king, upon a pole at Plymouth, where it remain. over twenty yrs. from his fall, and said, that a wren used to make her nest in the skull, where she hatch. her young every yr. * MANASSEH, Plymouth, one of the "old comers," prob. in the Ann, 1623, tho. the name in the div. of lds. is print. Faunce, stand. next to John F. but the infreq. bapt. name encourages this conject. and in the div. of cattle, 1627, he had sh. with Julian, his w. sis. of Gov. Bradford, wid. of George Morton; was rep. 1639, at the first assemb. in the Col. and for nine yrs. more ; was one of the first purch. with Gov. B. of Dartmouth, and d. 14 Jan. 1663 ; and the rec. adds : "He did much good in his place, the time God lent him." His wid. d. 19 Feb. 1665, in 81st yr. See Russell's Guide to Plymouth, appx. XI.

KEN, ROBERT, Reading, among early sett.

KENDALL, FRANCIS, Woburn 1640, m. 24 Dec. 1644, Mary Tidd, had John, b. 2 July 1646 ; Thomas, 10 Jan. 1649 ; Mary, 20 Jan. 1651 ; Eliz. 15 Jan. 1653 ; Hannah, 26 Jan. 1655 ; Rebecca, 2 Mar. 1657 ; Samuel, 8 Mar. 1659 ; Jacob, 25 Jan. 1661 ; and Abigail, 6 Apr. 1666 ; was freem. 1647 ; in 1700 sw. he was a. fourscore yrs. old. His w. d. 1705, and his will was pro. soon aft. his d. 1708. Mary m. Israel Read ; Eliz. m. James Pierce ; Hannah m. William Green, as his sec. w. ; Rebecca m. Joshua Eaton ; and Abigail m. 24 May 1686, William Read. JACOB, Woburn, s. of the preced. m. 2 Jan. 1684, Persis Hayward, had Persis, b. 24 Aug. 1685 ; Jacob, 12 Jan. 1687 ; Joseph, 17 Dec. 1688 ; Jonathan, 2 Nov. 1690, d. very soon ; Daniel, 23 Oct. 1691. His w. d. 19 Oct. 1694 ; and he m. 10 Jan. foll. Alice Temple, had Ebenezer, 9 Nov. 1695 ; John, 19 Jan. 1697 ; Sarah, 18 July 1698 ; Esther, 20 Nov. 1699 ; Hezekiah, 26 May 1701 ; Nathan, 12 Dec. 1702 ; Susanna, 27 Oct. 1704 ; Phebe, 19 Dec. 1706 ; David, 28 Sept. 1708 ; Ebenezer, again, 5 Apr. 1710 ; Alice, 31 Jan. 1712 ; Abraham, 26 Apr. 1712, accord. to the strange rec. ; and Jacob, 22 Apr. 1714. JOHN, Cambridge 1647, d. 21 Mar. 1661. His d. Eliz. m. 26 June 1647, Morris Somes of Gloucester. JOHN, Woburn, eldest ch. of Francis, m. 29 Jan. 1668, Hannah, d. of Thomas Bartlett, had Mary, b. 1 Sept. 1671 ; Lydia, 23 Apr. 1674 ; Francis, 4 Dec. 1678, d. soon. By sec. w. Eliz. Comey, prob. d. of David, m. 29 Mar. 1681, had Francis, again, 11 Apr. 1682 ; John, 7 Oct. 1684 ; David, 14 Nov. 1686 ; Eliz. 23 Feb. 1689 ; Jonathan, 28 Nov. 1690 ; and Rebecca, 22 Mar. 1693 ; and he had third w. Eunice, wid. of Samuel Carter, d. of John Brooks. He was freem. 1678. ROBERT, Mass. 1640. Felt. SAMUEL, Woburn, s. of Francis, m. 13 Nov. 1683, Rebecca, d. of Isaac Mixer, had Samuel, b. 13 Aug. 1684 ; Isaac, 13 Sept. 1686 ; Joshua, 14 Mar. 1689 ; Rebecca, 6 July 1691, d. soon ; and his w. d. 25 Oct. foll. He m. 30 Mar. 1692, Mary, d. of William Locke, had Mary, b. 3 Feb. 1693 ; Rebecca, 26 Jan. 1695 ; Abigail, 31 Mar. 1697 ; Ebenezer, 16 May 1700 ; Ruth, 23 Apr. 1703 ; and Tabitha, 22 Jan. 1707 ; rem. to Lancaster, and his will, says Barry, was pro. 1749. THOMAS, Lynn, br. of Francis, freem. 1648, had one s. wh. d. young and ano. d. beside the eight foll. : Eliz. b. 17 Feb. 1643 ; Rebecca, 10 Feb. 1645 ; Mary, 24 Dec. 1647 ; Hannah, 29 Jan. 1650 ; rem. to Reading, had Sarah, 22

June 1653; Abigail, 30 Nov. 1655; Susanna, 27 June 1658; and Tabitha, 5 Nov. 1660; was deac. and d. 22 July 1681. His wid. Rebecca d. 17 July 1703, aged 85. Rebecca m. 1665, James Boutell of R.; Mary m. Abraham Bryant; Hannah m. 13 Nov. 1667, a serg. whose name is lost to me. THOMAS, Woburn, s. of Francis, by w. Ruth, m. 1673, had Ruth, b. 17 Feb. 1675; Thomas, 19 May 1677; Mary, 27 Feb. 1680; Samuel, 29 Oct. 1682, f. of Rev. Samuel, H. C. 1731, of New Salem; Ralph, 4 May 1685; Eliezer, 16 Nov. 1687; Jabez, and Jane, tw. 10 Sept. 1692; and a s. d. at b. 16 Dec. 1695, and the w. d. two days aft. He m. sec. w. 30 Mar. 1696, Abigail Broughton, wh. d. 31 Dec. 1716, and he d. 25 May 1730. One of this name suffer. d. at Cambridge for the suppos. crime of witchcraft, acc. Hale, 18 and 19. In 1828 eight of this name had been gr. at Harv. and three at other N. E. coll.

KENNARD, JOHN, Haddam, a. 1674, m. Rebecca, d. of Jared Spencer of the same, and d. Feb. 1689, leav. John, 6 yrs. old; and Eliz. 2. His wid. m. John Tanner.

KENNEDY, ALEXANDER, Plymouth, by w. Eliz. had Hannah, b. 1678; Eliz. 1682; Joanna, 1685; William, 1689; Sarah, 1693; Annable, 1698; and John, 1703. Descend. are at Middleborough.

KENNET, RICHARD, Boston, d. 1 Apr. 1693. His wid. Susanna had admin. I suppose he was an apothecary.

KENNICUT, ROGER, Malden, m. Nov. 1661, Joanna Sheperson, had Joanna, b. Jan. 1664; Lydia, Jan. 1667; and John, Oct. 1669; was freem. 1670, but sold his est. 30 Jan. 1679, he and his w. then call. of Swanzey.

KENNISTON, or KINISTON, ALLEN, Salem 1638, or earlier, for Dorothy K. his w. is by Felt ment. 1636, but in 1638 a gr. of ld. was made to him, was freem. 18 May 1642, and d. 1648; his will, made 10 Nov. of that yr. was pro. in the mo. foll. CHRISTOPHER, Portsmouth, m. at Exeter, 4 Dec. 1677, Mary Mushamore. Perhaps he was s. of William. JOHN, Dover 1663, Greenland 1675, was k. by the Ind. and his ho. burn. 16 Apr. 1677. Belkn. I. 81. WILLIAM, Dover 1646-71.

KENNY, or KENNEY, ANDREW, Malden, by w. Eliz. had Samuel, b. 28 Oct. 1690. HENRY, Salem 1653, had John, bapt. Sept. 1654; Mary, 3 July 1659; Sarah, 29 June 1662; and, perhaps, others. HENRY, Salem, perhaps s. of the preced. m. 14 May 1691, Priscilla Lewis, had Jemima, b. 14 Feb. 1693; Priscilla, 29 Oct. 1696; Dinah, 9 Dec. 1698; and Mary, 5 Apr. 1701. JOHN, Salem, had Hannah, bapt. 8 Mar. 1657, wh. prob. d. young, as his will names only w. Sarah; and he d. 1670, says Felt. RICHARD, New Hampsh. 1680. THOMAS, Gloucester 1664. Gibbs.

KENRICK, KENERICK, oft. KENDRICK, CALEB, Boston 1652. ELIJAH, Cambridge, s. of John, m. Hannah, d. of deac. John Jackson of the same, had Margaret, b. 29 Jan. 1669; Hannah, 5 Aug. 1670; Ann, 3 July 1672; John, 7 July 1675; Elijah, 11 May 1678; and Ebenezer, 12 Feb. 1680; and d. 24 Dec. foll. His wid. m. 20 Jan. 1683, John Hyde. * GEORGE, Scituate 1634, freem. 1635, join. the ch. with w. 9 Apr. 1637, had Deborah, bapt. 25 Nov. 1638, d. in few wks.; Joseph, b. Feb. 1640; was rep. 1642 and 4, rem. to Rehoboth 1645, says Deane, but more prob. to Boston, where is rec. the b. by w. Jane of Joseph; and Deborah, 16 Aug. 1646. His s. Isaac d. 13 Jan. 1676. JOHN, Boston 1639, adm. 11 Aug. of that yr. into the ch. so that he had come, prob. the former yr. if not earlier, and there is no slight reason to think he came with Mather in the James from Bristol, 1635; by w. Ann, sis. prob. of Robert Smith, from London, had Hannah, bapt. 9 Feb. 1640, wh. d. soon; John, 3 Oct. 1641; Elijah, 21 Jan. 1644, then six days old, d. soon; Elijah, again, or Elisha, as the false rec. has it, 18, bapt. 19 Oct. 1645; and Hannah, again, 20 Mar. 1652, wh. m. 10 Apr. 1674, Jonathan Metcalf. He liv. after 1652, when 'he sold his est. in Boston proper, in that part of B. call. Muddy riv. now Brookline, where his w. d. 15 Nov. 1656; but rem. 1658 to Cambridge vill. now Newton, there d. 29 Aug. 1686, aged 80, if we may reckon from his will of 21 Jan. 1684, call. hims. a. 78. His wid. Judith d. says Roxbury rec. 23 Aug. 1687. JOHN, Ipswich, or Rowley, m. 12 Nov. 1657, Lydia Cheny. JOHN, Newton, s. of John of Boston, by w. Esther had Mercy, b. 1 July 1673; Grace, 10 Sept. 1674; Maria, 28 Jan. 1676; Esther, 25 Sept. 1677; Sarah, 26 Feb. 1679; Hannah, 15 Dec. 1680; Ann, 4 Nov. 1682; Abigail, 12 Nov. 1684; Mary; John, 6 Jan. 1690; Eliz. 9 Feb. 1693; Caleb, 8 Mar. 1695; and Margaret, 15 Jan. 1697; of wh. all but Abigail and John are nam. with gr.s. John Lyon, in his will, made the yr. of his d. He serv. as selectman nine yrs. was freem. 1690, d. 30 Sept. 1721; and his wid. d. 1723, in 70th yr. He was ancest. of late John K. Esq. THOMAS, Rehoboth, m. 17 June 1681, Mary Perry, had Jehiel, b. 23 Mar. 1682; and Mary, 2 Jan. 1684. Some descend. make the first syl. end with d.

KENT, JAMES, Newbury, br. of Richard jr. freem. 1669, had only s. John, b. 1641, possib. in Eng. d. 12 Dec. 1681. JOHN, Dedham 1652, freem. 1654, but of wh. no more is learn. JOHN, Charlestown, by w. Hannah Grissell, wh. d. 9 Jan. 1696, had Hannah, b. 2 July 1667; Mary, 3 Feb. 1670; Joshua, 15 June, bapt. 7 July 1672, d. soon; Joshua, again, 5, bapt. 6 July 1673; Joseph, 13, bapt. 17 Oct. 1675; Samuel, 23 Mar. 1678, d. at 25 yrs.; Ebenezer, b. 18 Aug. 1680; and Lydia, 16 July 1683. JOHN, Newbury, s. of James, freem. 1669, m. 24

Feb. 1665, Mary Hobbs, had John, b. 8 Apr. 1665, d. soon; Sarah, 1 Aug. 1666, d. soon; Sarah, again, 30 Aug. 1667; John, 23 Nov. 1668, d. young; John, again, 16 July 1675, d. under 28 yrs.; James, 3 Sept. 1679; and Mary, wh. d. 17 Mar. 1703; and he d. 30 Jan. 1718, in 77th yr. John, Newbury, perhaps s. of Richard the first, m. 13 Mar. 1666, Sarah Woodman, had Mary, b. 10 Sept. 1668, d. young; Richard, 25 June 1670, d. young; Richard, again, 17 Jan. 1673; Mary, again, 24 Oct. 1674; Emma, 20 Apr. 1677; Hannah, 10 Sept. 1679; Rebecca, 20 Feb. 1684; and James, 5 Mar. 1686. Coffin says, Emma K. a wid. but of wh. is unkn. d. 10 Jan. 1677. JOHN, Suffield, s. prob. of John, m. 9 May 1686, Abigail, d. of William Dudley, had Mary, b. 26 Jan. 1687, d. in few wks.; John, 26 Jan. 1688; Abigail, 28 Sept. 1690; Deborah, 22 Aug. 1693; Dudley, 23 Oct. 1695; Mary, again, 29 Oct. 1697, d. soon; Daniel, 14 Dec. 1698; Abner, 7 June 1701; Elisha, 9 July 1704; and by sec. w. Abigail Wenchell, had Joseph, 26 Feb. 1710; Noah, 28 Apr. 1714; and Experience, 4 Mar. 1717; and d. 11 Apr. 1721, leav. wid. with those ten ch. of wh. Elisha, Y. C. 1729, was a min. whose s. Moses, Y. C. 1752, was f. of the Hon. James, LL. D. the disting. jurist, late Chancellor of N. Y. JOSEPH, Dedham, br. of John, as I guess from the equal bequests in the will of Eliz. Hardier. See Geneal. Reg. XIII. 12. JOSEPH, Charlestown, s. of John, d. 30 May 1753, in 79th yr. as the gr.stone asserts, when he was prob. under 78. JOSHUA, Dedham 1643, prob. br. of first John, adm. of the ch. Nov. 1644, went home, and came again, 1645, bring. two brs. it is said, but, perhaps, only one; freem. 1646; by w. Mary had Lydia, b. 17, bapt. 28 Feb. 1647; went, with w. again to Eng. that yr. his reasons not well satisfy. his friends in the ch. but came, again, in Oct. 1648, prob. dishearten. by the convuls. of his nat. ld.; that yr. had Sarah, b. 27 Mar. bapt. 7 Apr. 1650; and Mary, bapt. 14 Dec. 1651. JOSEPH, New Hampsh. 1689. OLIVER, Dover 1648, d. a. 1670, leav. wid. Dorothy. RICHARD, Ipswich 1634, came that yr. with ano. of the same chr. and surname, perhaps a cous. in the Mary and John, freem. 4 Mar. 1635, rem. with first sett. to Newbury 1635, left in Eng. Sarah, and other ds. of wh. one, Rebecca, had m. in Eng. Samuel Scallard, and aft. his d. she came, and, perhaps, brot. d. Mary, wh. m. 4 Dec. 1656, John Rolfe; and the mo. m. Oct. 1647, John Bishop; but here, says Coffin, he had John, b. 20 July 1645; and he d. 11 June 1654. RICHARD, Newbury 1635, came the yr. bef. in the Mary and John, br. of James, had w. Jane, wh. d. 26 June 1674, and he m. 6 Jan. 1675, Joanna, wid. of Nicholas Davison of Charlestown, and d. 25 Nov. 1689, without ch. but gave his est. to his neph. John. SAMUEL, Gloucester, perhaps s. of Thomas of the same, b. prob. in Eng. by w. Frances had

Sarah, b. 14 Aug. 1657 ; Mary, 19 Dec. 1658 ; Samuel, 26 Oct. 1661 ; and John, 28 Apr. 1664; was prob. of Brookfield 1673–5, Suffield 1678, and back again to G. freem. 1681; but the same yr. of Suffield then pt. of Springfield, there his w. d. 10 Aug. 1683, and he d. 2 Feb. 1691. SAMUEL, Suffield, s. of the preced. m. 1 Nov. 1683, Priscilla, d. of William Hunter, had Samuel, b. 8 Dec. 1685 ; Thomas, 3 Apr. 1688; John, 24 Aug. 1690, d. young ; and Josiah, 1692 ; he m. 1696, sec. w. Martha, had Martha, wh. d. soon ; as did her mo. and he m. 1700, third w. wid. Esther Phelps, had Martha, 1703 ; Daniel, and Mary, tw. 1704; beside two, Benjamin, and Priscilla, of whose date we hear not.   He d. 1740, in his will of 1737 names the five surv. s. and three ds.   STEPHEN, Newbury, br. of the first Richard, came, says Coffin, 1635 ; but if so, he went home, and came again 1638, in the Confidence from Southampton, with w. Margery, and four or five serv.   In his case is observa. how readily the officers of the custom-ho. acquiesc. in false statem. to avoid the arbitra. orders of the Lords of Trade and Planta. for his age is mark. 17, that of his w. 16, and George March, serv. 16 ; beside Hugh March, 20 ; Anthony Sadler, 9 ; Nicholas Wallington, a poor boy, without any yrs. ; and Rebecca Kent, 16, call. serv. perhaps to increase the delus.   He was older, prob. for he was sw. a freem. 22 May 1639 ; had Eliz. b. 1 Mar. 1642, d. at 11 yrs. ; Hannah, 20 Mar. 1644; Stephen, 6 Mar. 1648; Rebecca, 3 Aug. 1650; David, 26 May 1657 ; and Mary. He had three ws. Ann, the sec. d. 3 May 1660 ; and he m. 9 May 1662, Eleanor, wid. of William Scadlock of Saco ; and rem. to Haverhill, thence to Woodbridge, N. J.   Hannah m. 19 Sept. 1669, Isaac Toppan, and d. 10 Dec. 1688; Rebecca m. 12 Aug. 1667, John Farnham the first of Andover.   THOMAS, Gloucester 1643, d. 1 Apr. 1658 ; and his wid. d. 16 Oct. 1671.   THOMAS, Gloucester, perhaps s. of the preced. m. 28 Mar. 1659, Joan, d. of Thomas Penny, had Thomas, b. 31 Mar. 1660 ; Mary, 22 Jan. 1662; Mercy, and Joan, tw. 24 Feb. 1665, d. both in 6 days; Joan, again, 5 Aug. 1666 ; and John, 2 Jan. 1677 ; was of Brookfield 1671, freem. 1690. ‖ WILLIAM, Boston 1662, m. Mary, wid. of John Mears ; of ar. co. 1667, its ensign 1673, d. 9 July 1691.   Seven of this name had, in 1834, been gr. at Harv. and nine at other N. E. coll.

KERLEY, CARSLEY, or CARLSLY, EDMUND, of Ashmore, Co. Dorset, near Shaftsbury, husbandman, emb. in the Confidence, 24 Apr. 1638, aged 22, at Southampton ; but we kn. no more of him.   HENRY, Lancaster, s. of William, b. a. 1632, brot. prob. by his f. to Hingham, m. 2 Nov. 1654, Eliz. d. of John White, had Henry, b. 1658; William, 1659 ; Joseph, 1669 ; and prob. other ch. freem. 1668 ; but in 1676, aft. his w. (a sis. of famous Mary Rowlandson, the w. of the min.) with the two last nam. ch. were k. by the Ind. 10 Feb. at the assault (in wh.

Mrs. R. as she has relat. was tak.) he m. 18 Apr. 1676, Eliz. How at Charlestown, went to Marlborough, and there spent the rest of his days, was a capt. and his depon. against Andros, 27 Dec. 1689, with Thomas How, is giv. in Revo. in N. E. Justif. 35.   See Willard's Hist. of Lancaster, 27, 8, and 38.   WILLIAM, Hingham 1637, of Sudbury a. 1641, rem. to Lancaster, freem. 1647; in his old age m. sec. w. 16 May 1664, Rebecca, wid. of Thomas Josselyn, and d. 14 July 1670, leav. William, and Henry, bef. ment.   His will of 26 July 1669 adds nothing to our acquaint. with his fam.   WILLIAM, Sudbury, eldest s. prob. of the preced. by wh. he was, perhaps, left in Eng. came in the Confidence from Southampton 1638, call. of Ashmore, with Edmund, bef. ment. wh. may have been uncle or br. rem. to Marlborough, freem. 1666; by w. Jane had Mary, b. at S. 4 May 1667; Sarah, 23 Jan. 1669; and Hannah, 8 Jan. 1671; was an ens. d. at Marlborough, 4 Jan. 1684.   I suppose the name is mispr. Kerby in Geneal. Reg. VIII. 241.

KESKEYS, HENRY, Boston, by w. Ruth had Henry, b. 3 May 1656.

KETCHAM, EDWARD, Ipswich 1635, freem. 9 Mar. 1637, may reasona. be thot. progenit. of all of the name, in our country, and therefore I regret the more that we are ign. of the circumstances of his migrat. and subseq. resid.   By conject. it seems to me, that EDWARD of Stratford, wh. d. bef. 1678, was his s. whose d. Rebecca m. 14 Feb. 1678, Thomas Taylor of Norwalk.   An Edward K. m. Mary, d. of Richard Harcutt, but prob. he was of L. I. yet may have been the Stratford man, wh. in his will of June 1655 names three ds. Mary, Hannah, and Esther. HENRY, Ipswich 1638, perhaps s. of the preced.   * JOHN, Ipswich 1648, prob. s. of Edward, rem. to that pt. of L. I. call. Setauket, now Brookhaven, constable, stood up for the jurisdict. of Conn. was honor. 1662, with a commiss. to make his neighb. swear, and rep. 1664.   In 1668 he rem. to Newtown, there was a man of influence to his d. 1697.   Riker, 89. JOSEPH, Norwalk 1672, possib. s. of the preced. or gr.s. of Edward, m. 3 Apr. 1679, Mercy, d. of deac. Henry Lindall of New Haven, had Nathaniel, b. 23 Jan. 1680; and Sarah, 19 Feb. 1672; was in town serv. 1701.   SAMUEL, Newtown, L. I. 1655, prob. br. of John, was of Setauket, freem. of Conn. 1664, and with Edward, wh. may, also, have been br. at Huntington, 1672.

KETTLE, JOHN, Gloucester, by w. Eliz. d. of the first William Allen of Salem, had Eliz. b. 15 Feb. 1658; Mary, 5 Mar. 1660; Samuel, 2 Apr. 1662; and James, 20 Mar. 1665.   Prob. from him is deriv. the name Kettle Cove at the adjoin. town of Manchester.   JOHN, Charlestown, eldest s. of Richard of the same, was, perhaps, of Portsmouth 1663.   He m. first, Sarah, d. of Edmund Goodenow, had John (wh. m. 11 Sept. 1688, Abigail, d. of Richard Austin, and d. at C. 17 Mar. 1691,

aged 30) ; Sarah, b. in Sudbury, 8 Mar. 1663 ; and Joseph. He had a
sec. w. Mr. Wyman says, Eliz. d. of Samuel Ward the sec. wh. was carr.
away from Lancaster in 1676, says Frothingham, 82 ; and by her had
only Jonathan, b. at L. 24 Nov. 1670. JONATHAN, Charlestown 1677,
youngest br. of the preced. m. 30 Mar. 1676, Abigail, d. of James
Convers, wh. d. 25 Jan. 1691, aged 33, had Jonathan, b. 1677, wh. d.
soon, and he d. 18 Dec. 1720. His other ch. Ann, b. 1679 ; Jonathan.
1681 ; and Abigail, 1684, were bapt. 29 Mar. 1685, when he join. tc
the ch. ; and he had aft. James, 1686 ; and David, 1689, d. the same yr.
JOSEPH, Charlestown, elder br. of the preced. freem. 1670, m. 5 July
1665, Hannah, d. of William Frothingham, had Hannah, wh. d. 26 June
1666 ; Hannah, again, d. 5 Sept. 1669 ; Richard, bapt. 1 May 1670 ;
Esther, 29 Jan. 1671, d. 25 May 1678 ; Hannah, 27 Oct. 1672, d.
young ; Joseph, 31 Jan. 1675 ; Eliz. 18 Mar. 1677 ; Esther, again, 13
Feb. 1679 ; William 6 Feb. 1681 ; Mary, 25 Mar. 1683 ; Benjamin, 7
Sept. 1684 ; Rebecca, 7 Jan. 1687 ; and Hannah, again, 7 July 1689.
His s. Richard d. 7 Dec. 1690 ; and his w. d. 15 Sept. 1693 ; he was
chos. deac. 1695 ; m. for sec. w. Dorothy, wid. of Thomas Hett, wh. d.
11 Dec. 1710, in her 60th yr. and he d. 5 Apr. 1711. NATHANIEL,
Charlestown, br. of the preced. by first w. Hannah, m. 13 June 1669,
wh. d. 19 Nov. 1670, had only Nathaniel ; m. 30 Oct. 1672, Hannah, d.
of James Kidder, both unit. with the ch. 22 Mar. 1685, and on 29 of
same had bapt. Nathaniel, James, Samuel, Hannah, and Sarah ; Rebecca, 30 Jan. 1687 ; Rachel, b. 10, bapt. 14 Apr. 1689 ; Union, 15
Mar. 1691 ; and Richard, 10 Dec. 1693. He had three others, wh. d.
bef. bapt. was one of the constables, 1690, and d. 1723. PETER, came
in the Abigail, 1635, aged 10, from London ; but who can tell, whether
he grew to manhood, where he liv. wh. he m. or when he d. ? RICHARD,
Charlestown 1633, butcher, freem. 4 Mar. 1635, by w. Esther, d. of
Samuel Ward, had Hannah, bapt. 29 Oct. 1637, m. 21 Jan. 1657, John
Call ; John, b. 6, bapt. 8 Dec. 1639 ; Joseph, 15, bapt. 21 Feb. 1641 ;
Samuel, 19 Nov. 1642 ; Nathaniel, 11 Oct. 1644 ; Jonathan, 1646.
Perhaps we may doubt the ch. rec. of Budington, 247, of the date,
25 July 1633, giv. the adm. of "Richard Kettle and Esther his
w." as a *modern* interpolat. in its latter clause, bec. the Boston ch. rec.
of 26 Jan. 1634 has this entry, "Esther Ward, our br. Atherton Hough's
maid serv." for evid. of her adm. and the dism. on 17 July 1642 reads,
"Our sis. Esther Ward, now w. to Richard Kettle of Charlestown hath
letter of recommenda. gr. unto her to the ch. at C." Possib. he had two
ws. nam. Esther, but it is less prob. than that the Charlestown ch. rec.
was enrich. with a postlimin. addit. It must always be rememb. that we
have not orig. ch. rec. of early yrs. in either Boston or Charlestown ch.
but only copies, made prob. betw. 1650 and 1670, of both. He was usu-

ally call. serg. and d. 28 June 1681, aged 71. Esther, his w. d. 2 or 5 July 1679. ROBERT, Gloucester 1653, perhaps br. of John, wh. was three yrs. older. SAMUEL, Charlestown, s. of Richard, m. 11 July 1665, Mercy Hayden, d. of James, wh. d. 19 Oct. 1692, aged 45; and he m. 3 May 1694, Mary, wid. of Nathaniel Frothingham, d. of Thomas Hett; and by the first had Mary, bapt. 1 May 1670, tho. b. 8 Oct. 1666; and Mercy, 18 May 1679; freem. 1670, was one of the tythingmen 1680, d. 20 Dec. 1694. His wid. d. 5 June 1710, aged 62 yrs.

KEY, JOHN, Dover, had James, tak. a. 1690 by the Ind. and soon k. Magn. VII. 69. But he and ano. John, call. jr. perhaps his s. were prison. from Piscataqua, at Quebec, 1695.

KEYES, ELIAS, Sudbury, s. of Robert, m. 11 Sept. 1665, Sarah, d. of John Blandford, had Elias, b. 15 Nov. 1666; James, 13 Sept. 1670; Sarah, 11 Apr. 1673; and Thomas, 8 Feb. 1675; perhaps, also, John. PETER, Sudbury, perhaps s. of Robert, by w. Eliz. had, prob. John, b. 1664, wh. was one of the found. of the ch. at Shrewsbury; and, perhaps, others, bef. or aft. Esther, 12 Feb. 1668. ROBERT, Watertown 1633, by w. Sarah had Sarah, b. 26 May 1633; Rebecca, 17 Mar. 1638; Mary, 17 June 1639, d. soon; Mary, again, Feb. 1642, d. soon; Elias, 20 May 1643, bef. ment. rem: to Newbury, there had Mary, again, 16 June 1645, may have ret. to Watertown, perhaps had Peter, and others; and he d. 16 July 1647. His wid. m. Nov. 1658, John Gage; Mary m. 16 Feb. 1664, Benjamin Cady of Andover. SOLOMON, Newbury, m. 2 Oct. 1653, Frances Grant, had Hannah, b. 12 Sept. 1654; Sarah, 24 Aug. 1656; Mary, 26 Sept. 1658; Jane, 25 Oct. 1650; and Judith, 16 Sept. 1662; rem. to Chelmsford, there he had Solomon, bapt. 25 June 1665; and was tythingman 1679. His d. Jane m. 17 May 1680, Samuel Cleveland. His gr.s. Solomon was disting. by personal courage, as is seen at Lovewell's fight, in Hoyt's Antiq. Researches, 218, 274; and he was k. 8 Sept. 1755, when the Fr. and Ind. under Baron Dieskau were defeat. Five of this name had, in 1826, been gr. at Dart. Sometimes it was writ. as sound. Kies.

KEYSAN, or KEZAN, JOHN, Haverhill, m. Hannah, d. of John Davis of Dover, but date, or other partic. is unkn.

KEYSER, or KEASUR, GEORGE, Lynn, a tanner, freem. 14 Mar. 1639, rem. to Salem, m. Eliz. d. of Edward Holyoke, had Elizur; George, b. May 1657; and Edward, 20 June 1659. His w. d. 24 June 1659, and the last ch. foll. in Nov. aft.; and he d. 1676, or by ano. acco. Sept. 1690, aged 73. Elizur foll. the same trade. JOHN, Haverhill 1682, a tanner, s. of George, took o. of fidel. 28 Nov. 1677, had s. John, George, and Timothy. THOMAS, Lynn 1638, perhaps br. of George, by w. Mary, had Rebecca, b. Nov. 1640; and Thomas, both bapt. 15 June

1645, in her own right, when the girl is call. a. 4 yrs. and 7 mos. and the boy 2 yrs. and 5 wks.; Timothy, bapt. 15 Feb. 1646, a. 5 days old, at Boston, where he was merch. and shipmaster, act. that yr. in both capacit. on the detesta. voyage to Africa for steal. nat. See Winth. II. 243, 379.

KIBBY, KIBBE, or KIBBEE, ARTHUR, Salem, fisherman, or mariner, by w. Abigail, d. of William Ager of the same, had Abigail, b. 4 Jan. 1659; Arthur, 6 Jan. 1660; William, 14 Sept. 1661; and, perhaps, tw. Mary; tho. she is not on town rec. yet the rec. of ch. has "Mary, William, Abigail, and Arthur, childr. of Abigail *Kippins*, bapt. 13 Apr. 1662;" but, perhaps, the name of this last ch. may be on the town rec. Eliz. Other ch. were Joseph, also on both rec. the town for b. mark. 23 Feb. but not the yr. and the ch. for bapt. giv. 23 May 1666; and the same has Hannah, 23 Aug. 1668, while that of the town has among b. Hannah, 28 June 1669; Sarah, 31 May 1670; and Jerusha, 19 Apr. 1670. Errors are easi. found in rec. of the elder days; but it is not *necessary* in this case to charge wrong on either town or ch. He prob. d. early in 1685, for his inv. is of 29 June. EDWARD, Boston 1645, a sawyer, liv. at Muddy riv. had Reuben, bapt. 30 June 1653; and Eliz. b. 27 Jan. bapt. 4 Mar. 1655, both at Roxbury, in right of their mo. Mary, a sis. of the ch. at B. wh. she join. 29 Nov. 1645, says the rec. and had bapt. on 30th James, a. 3½ yrs. old, and Elisha, a. 10 mos. 10 days. Morse adds to these four more, as, prob. Joshua; Rebecca, 1 May 1657; Edward; and, perhaps, Hannah. His wid. Grizzle had admin. 15 Aug. 1661. One Rachel K. d. at Dorchester 16 July 1657. ELISHA, Salem, m. Rachel Cook, had John, b. 1 Feb. 1668; Edward, 2 Feb. 1670; Elisha, 2 Mar. 1673, d. young; and James, 27 Dec. 1675; rem. to Enfield 1682, then pt. of Springfield, had Isaac, the first male ch. in E. b. 21 Mar. 1683; and Rachel, 17 Apr. 1688; and he may have had others bef. He d. 3 Apr. 1735, and tradit. with its aptness to exagger. made him 97; but, in 1693, he calls hims. a. "48 yrs." Perhaps he was s. of the preced. or of the foll. ‖ HENRY, Dorchester, tailor, freem. 18 May 1642, ar. co. 1644, d. 10 July or Aug. 1661. JAMES, Dorchester, s. of Edward, rem. to Cambridge, by w. Hannah had Mary, b. 1668; Ann, 1670; James, 1674; and Eliz. b. 13, bapt. 14 Aug. 1681. But this last was by sec. w. Sarah, d. of Andrew Stephenson, m. 23 Oct. 1679 as wid. of John Lowden. JOSEPH, Salem, m. Abigail, d. of William Anger. JOSHUA, Sherborn, by Morse, the autocrat of S. regard. as s. of Edward, m. 24 May 1688, at Woburn, Mary Comy, d. of David, had Edward; Sarah, b. 1708; and Joshua, 2 June 1712. His w. d. 9 July foll. and he d. 1731. WILLIAM, Hull 1642.

KIDBY, JOHN, Duxbury 1640. LEWIS, Boston 1640, fisherman.

Kidd, James, Dover 1657, took o. of fidel. 30 Nov. 1677; was of Exeter 1688.

Kidder, Edward, by Eaton call. one of the first sett. of Reading, but I kn. no more, unless, as is prob. he were the man (as Eaton is liberal in count. first) wh. bound hims. at Wrexham, in Co. Denbigh, 28 July 1675 to serv. four yrs. in Boston Theophilus Yale of Chester, in Eng. as a shoemak. Ephraim, Billerica, s. of James the first, m. 1 Aug. 1685, Rachel, eldest d. of Simon Crosby, had Joseph; Ephraim, b. 26 Apr. 1688; and Rachel, 1 Apr. 1691; Alice, 8 Feb. 1693; Hannah, and Dorothy, tw. b. at Medford 2 Sept. 1696; Thomas, 3 Aug. 1700; Benjamin, 3 Aug. 1702; and Richard, 10 May 1705; his w. d. 14 Sept. 1721; and he d. 25 Sept. 1724. James, Cambridge 1649, s. of James, b. a. 1626, at East Grinstead, Co. Sussex, by w. Ann, d. of Elder Francis Moore, m. 1649, had Hannah, b. 1 Mar. 1650; Dorothy, 1651; James, 3 Jan. 1654; John, 1655; Thomas, 1 Mar. 1657; all bapt. as Mitchell's Reg. test. without giv. dates; Nathaniel, bapt. 27 Feb. 1659; Ephraim, b. 31 Aug. 1660, bapt. 26 May 1661; and dism. to ch. at Billerica, there had Stephen, 26 Nov. 1662; Enoch, 16 Sept. 1664; Samuel, 7 Jan. 1666; Sarah, 1 June 1667; and Joseph, 30 Nov. 1670; and d. a. 1683. Descend. it is common. said, may be found in every state of this Union. Dorothy m. 6 June 1673, the sec. Jonathan Hyde; and Sarah m. 30 Jan. 1690, George Brown. James, Billerica, eldest s. of the preced. m. 23 Sept. 1678, Eliz. Bunn, had James, b. 27 June 1679; John, 27 Jan. 1681; Joseph, 21 Apr. 1683; Eliz. 30 Mar. 1686; Hannah, 25 Apr. 1689; and Samuel, 2 Mar. 1691; and his w. d. 10 Aug. foll. John, Chelmsford, br. of the preced. m. 3 Sept. 1684, Lydia Parker, had Ann, b. 12 Sept. 1685; John, 23 Dec. 1687; and Thomas, 13 Oct. 1690. Nathaniel, Newton, perhaps s. of James the first, d. 1690. Samuel, Cambridge, s. of James, m. 23 Dec. 1689, Sarah, d. of John Griggs, had Sarah, b. 17 Aug. 1690; Francis, 1692; Samuel, 1694, d. at 24 yrs.; James, 1696, d. at 18 yrs.; John, 1701; and Joseph, 1704, d. in 21st yr. and the f. d. 4 July 1724. Stephen, Berwick 1633, in the employm. of Mason the Patentee. See in Belkn. I. 425, let. of Ambrose Gibbons. Stephen, Charlestown, s. of the first James, by w. Mary had Stephen, bapt. at Boston, 31 Oct. 1697, d. soon; others, of wh. some earlier, were Ann; Sarah; Eliz.; Mary, bapt. 21 Oct. 1694; Stephen, 21 June 1696, d. soon; Isaac; John; and Abigail. His w. d. 17 Sept. 1722, and he d. 5 July 1748. Thaddeus, Marblehead 1674. Thomas, Watertown, prob. br. of the sec. Stephen, was freem. 1690. Four of this name had, in 1834, been gr. at Harv. and four at other N. E. coll.

Kilbourn, or Kilborne, Abraham, Glastonbury, youngest s. of the first John, m. 26 Oct. 1699, Sarah, d. of John Goodrich, had Samuel, b. 25 Jan. 1701; Sarah, 20 May 1702; and Abraham, 12 Apr. 1708; and d. 9 Mar. 1713. EBENEZER, Glastonbury, br. of the preced. m. 20 Sept. 1692, Grace, d. of Peter Bulkley, had Grace, b. 25 June 1693; Ebenezer, 27 Mar. 1696; Eleazer, 26 July 1698; Josiah, 5 June 1702; Daniel, 5 May 1705; Margaret, 3 Oct. 1707; Sarah, 13 Apr. 1710; and George, posthum. 24 Apr. 1712; and d. 17 Dec. 1711, prob. sudden, certain. without will. GEORGE, Roxbury 1636, freem. 13 May 1640, in the ch. rec. is call. serv. rem. to Rowley, by w. Eliz. had Mary, b. 3 May 1649; Joseph, 1 Feb. 1652; Jacob, 12 Jan. 1655, one of the flower of Essex in Lothrop's comp. k. by the Ind. 18 Sept. 1675, at Bloody brook; Samuel, 11 Sept. 1656; Isaac, 26 Jan. 1659; and Eliz. 1 Feb. 1663. He was s. of Thomas, bapt. at Wood Ditton, Co. Cambridge, 12 Feb. 1612. GEORGE, Glastonbury, s. of John, m. 16 May 1689, Abigail, d. of Thomas Atwood, had George, b. 14 Sept. 1690, d. at 21 yrs.; Israel, 5 May 1692, d. in few wks.; Abigail, 5 Sept. 1696; Hezekiah, 24 June 1700, Y. C. 1720; and Pelatiah, 7 Feb. 1704, Y. C. 1724. His w. d. 8 Feb. 1740; and he 8 Feb. of the next yr. ISAAC, Rowley 1691, s. of George of the same, m. 24 July 1684, Mary Cheny, d. of the sec. John of Newbury, had Eliz. b. 10 Apr. 1685; Martha, 25 Nov. 1687; Mary, 17 Mar. 1697; John, 12 May 1700; and Isaac, 15 Oct. 1707; and d. 19 Dec. 1713. He was b. deaf and dumb. JACOB, Rowley, br. of the preced. was a soldier, it is said, in the Ind. war; perhaps was never m. but d. in the serv. * JOHN, Wethersfield 1647, s. of Thomas, b. in Eng. came in the Increase with his f. 1635, by w. Naomi, wh. d. 1 Oct. 1659, had John, b. 15 Feb. 1651; Thomas, 1653; and Naomi; and by w. Sarah, perhaps d. of John Brownson of Hartford, had Ebenezer, b. 1665; Sarah; George, 1668; Mary; Joseph, a. 1672; and Abraham, 1675. He was rep. 1660, 1, and 2; made his will 24 Sept. 1688, but liv. many yrs. aft. at Glastonbury, and d. 9 Apr. 1703; and his wid. d. 4 Dec. 1711. Of all these ch. exc. Mary, the m. is kn. Naomi m. 30 Oct. 1679, Thomas Hale; Sarah m. 16 Dec. 1684, Joseph Crane. JOHN, Glastonbury, s. of the preced. m. 4 Mar. 1674, Susanna, d. of William Hills of Hartford, had Susanna, b. 4 Feb. 1675, d. at 10 yrs.; John, 30 Oct. 1676; Ebenezer, 10 Mar. 1679; Jonathan, 17 Sept. 1681; Benjamin, 30 Mar. 1684; David, 25 Feb. 1688; and Abraham, 25 Aug. 1691. His w. d. Oct. 1701, aged 50; and he m. 12 May 1702, Eliz. d. of John Mitchell; and d. 25 Nov. 1711, and his wid. d. 8 June 1718. JOSEPH, Rowley 1691, s. of George, m. 1678, Frances Trumbull, perhaps d. of the first John of the same, had Joseph, b. 20 Oct. 1678, d. soon; Ann, 28 Nov. 1680; Joseph, 16 Jan. 1684; George, 21 Jan. 1687; Mary, 22 Sept. 1689; Eliz. 22 June 1692; and Abigail, 14 July

1694, and he d. 5 Mar. 1723. JOSEPH, Glastonbury, s. of the first John, m. 4 June 1696, Dorothy, d. of Samuel Butler, had Dorothy, b. 17 Apr. 1697; Joseph, 9 July 1700; Jonathan, 17 Mar. 1703; James, 13 Apr. 1707; and his w. d. 19 Aug. 1709. He m. 29 June 1710, Esther, d. of Jacob Gibbs, and had Benjamin, 27 July 1711; Esther, 4 Aug. 1713; Eliz. 19 Oct. 1716; and Mary, 9 Feb. 1720. He d. at Litchfield (of wh. he was an early sett. 1721) but the date is unkn. for his will of 1737 was pro. seven yrs. later. SAMUEL, Rowley, s. of George, m. 12 Nov. 1682, Mary, d. of William Foster, had Hannah, b. 2 Oct. foll.; Samuel, 20 July 1687; David, 12 Mar. 1689; Mary, 21 July 1696; Jedediah, 20 Apr. 1699; and Eliphalet, 1706; and d. 22 Apr. 1722. THOMAS, Wethersfield, from Wood Ditton, in Co. Cambridge, came to Boston in the Increase, 1635, aged 55, with w. Frances, 50; and ch. Margaret, 23, as the custom-ho. rec. imports, but she was bapt. 23 Sept. 1607; Lydia, 22, but bapt. 14 July 1616, and that age might have suit. better an elder sis. Eliz. bapt. 12 May 1614, wh. did not come; Mary, 16; Frances, 12, bapt. 4 Sept. 1621; and John, 10, bapt. 29 Sept. 1624. He d. bef. 25 Dec. 1640, when ment. of the lds. of Frances the wid. is found. She d. Nov. 1650. Margaret m. Richard Law, the gr.f. of Gov. Law; Lydia m. Robert Hayward or Howard of Windsor; Mary m. John Root; and Frances m. Thomas Uffoot; and the three first nam. had ch. but the last none. To the dilig. fondness of Payne Kenyon K. of Litchfield, Esq. in 1847, were we indebt. for a copious memor. of predecess. and descend. in 140 pages, wh. is multipl. threefold in 1856. THOMAS, wh. came in the Elizabeth, from Ipswich, 1634, aged 24, with w. Eliz. 20, was eldest s. of the preced. bapt. 30 Nov. 1609, sent by the f. in adv. to make prepar. for the fam. migrat. but no more is kn. of him, so that it is not improb. that soon aft. his f. arr. he went home. THOMAS, Hartford, s. of the first John, m. Hannah, d. of William Hills, had Thomas, b. a. 1677; John; Mary, 1686; Naomi, 1693; and Samuel, 1696. Prob. the last three d. young, for they are not nam. in settlem. of the est. aft. his d. 1712.

KILBY, CHRISTOPHER, Boston, by w. Sarah had Nathaniel, b. 20 Mar. 1694; Miriam, 5 Dec. 1696; John, 24 Aug. 1699; Rebecca, 27 Dec. 1701; Samuel, 2 Oct. 1706; Sarah, 10 July 1708; and Mary, 18 Nov. 1712. EDWARD, Boston, m. 9 May 1662, Eliz. wid. of Edward Yeomans, d. of Thomas Josselyn. JOHN, Boston, perhaps br. of Christopher, by w. Rebecca had Eliz. b. 15 Sept. 1686; John, 24 Dec. 1688; Sarah, 8 Mar. 1692; Christopher, 9 Dec. 1693, prob. d. soon; Richard, 2 Jan. 1695; William, 6 Apr. 1698; Catharine, 10 Feb. 1700; Rebecca, 30 Mar. 1702; Christopher, again, 25 May 1705; Nicholas, 28 July 1708; and Ebenezer, 25 June 1711.

KILCUP, ‖ ROGER, Boston, perhaps s. of William, freem. 1690, m. 4 July 1695, Abigail, d. of Joseph Dudson, had Dudson, was of ar. co. and d. 1 Oct. 1702, aged 52. I presume his wid. m. 11 Oct. 1704 Ezekiel Lewis. WILLIAM, Boston 1649, in few yrs. was of Charlestown with w. Grace, and call. a sieve-maker; may have had d. Sarah m̐. to Richard Wilson bef. Aug. 1654, tho. in Geneal. Reg. VIII. 277, a differ. conject. is giv.

KILHAM, KILLAM, KELHAM, or KEELUM, AUSTIN, or AUGUSTINE, Salem 1637, had then, says Felt, a gr. of ld. but was of Dedham soon after, and may have short time liv. at Ipswich; by w. Alice had Lot, b. 11 Sept. 1640; and Sarah, 4 Jan. 1642; was freem. 2 June 1641. He was of the ch. at Wenham bef. 1655, when he rem. to Chelmsford. ‖ DANIEL, Wenham, ar. co. 1645. DANIEL, Wenham, s. of the preced. freem. 1680. JOHN, Dedham 1654; perhaps was of Brookfield 1690, and his fam. in poverty. LOT, Salem 1670, s. of Austin, went to Enfield, d. 26 Oct. 1683, being the first d. in the town. He had James, and prob. other ch.

KILTON, ROBERT, is on the list of Gallop's comp. in Phips's crusade against Quebec 1690, but of what town he was inhab. or of any thing else a. him, we are ign. yet of THOMAS in the comp. of Capt. Withington of Dorchester in the same disastr. expedit. our kn. is no larger. See the Hist. of D. 256.

KIMBALL, sometimes KEMBALL, BENJAMIN, Rowley 1664, prob. s. of Richard, had been, 1659, perhaps of Exeter, m. Apr. 1661, Mary, d. of Robert Hazeltine, had Ann, b. 22 Dec. foll. was freem. 1682. CALEB, Ipswich 1665, s. prob. youngest of Richard, had w. Hannah, and ch. Caleb, Ann, Eliz. Abigail, Mary, Robert, and Benjamin, was k. by the Ind. 18 Sept. 1675, with the flower of Essex, under capt. Lothrop at Bloody brook. EBENEZER, Rowley 1691. EPHRAIM, Wenham, freem. 1690. GILES, Charlestown 1656, br. of Thomas, d. at Boston, 1 Aug. 1659. HENRY, Watertown, prob. br. of Richard the first, came in the Elizabeth, 1634, from Ipswich, aged 44, with w. Susanna, 35; ch. Eliz. 4; and Susan, 1 and ½; and serv. Richard Cutting, 11; freem. 2 May 1638; had John, b. 5 Mar. 1638, d. soon; Mary, 26 Nov. 1641; Richard, 13 Oct. 1643; and John, again, 25 Dec. 1645; and d. 1648, his inv. being of 22 July. His wid. m. again, and d. 19 Aug. 1684. Eliz. m. Capt. Thomas Straight, and Susanna m. John Randall, both of W. HENRY, Ipswich 1640, eldest s. of Richard, perhaps sett. first at Watertown, and from Ipswich rem. and may have been the blacksmith of Boston, 1657, wh. had w. Mary, that outliv. him, and had admin. of his est. Jan. 1676; and s. Timothy finish. the settlem. of est. aft. d. of his mo. He was a man of large business. HENRY, Charlestown, m. 13 Nov.

1656, Sarah, that I presume to be d. of John Fownell, wh. d. 10 Aug. foll. He m. sec. w. Mary, d. of Thomas Brigden, had Zechary, Mary, Sarah, and Henry. JOHN, Newbury, m. 25 Feb. 1665, Mary Hobbs, had Mary, b. 19 July 1667 ; and John, 15 Oct. 1668, and the f. d. same mo. JOHN, Boston, carpenter, or cooper, perhaps both, s. of Thomas of the same, d. prob. at New York, where he made his will, 10 May 1695, in wh. he gave his w. Eliz. his lds. and houses for her life, aft. to his sis. Sarah Knight for her life, and aft. to Eliz. d. of Richard Knight of Boston. JOHN, Watertown, prob. s. of Henry of the same, m. 19 Jan. 1668, Hannah, d. of Thomas Bartlett, had Hannah, b. 11 July 1671, d. young; Susanna, 18 July 1675 ; John, 3 Aug. 1678; and Hannah, again, 8 June 1681 ; was freem. 1690, was a cooper, and d. 7 June 1714 ; and his wid. d. 22 Nov. 1715. JOHN, Amesbury, took o. of fidel. 20 Dec. 1677, and was made freem. 1690. JOHN, Boxford, freem. 1690. RICHARD, Watertown, prob. br. of Henry of the same came from Ipswich, O. E. 1634, aged 39, in the Elizabeth, with w. Ursula; ch. Henry, 15 ; Richard, 11 ; Mary, 9 ; Martha, 5 ; John, 3 ; and Thomas, 1 ; and serv. John Laverick, 15 ; was freem. 6 May 1635; rem. 1638 to Ipswich, there had more ch. and d. 1675, leav. Henry, Richard, Mary, Thomas, Benjamin, Eliz. Caleb, Sarah, and ano. d. w. of John Severns. He is call. by Thomas Scott (a passeng. with w. and fam. in the same sh.) br. and this may mean, that one m. a sis. of the other, or they m. sis. but in this case not, I judge, the mere ch. relationsh. See Scott. It is said, that two of his s. Thomas and William, were k. by the Ind. in 1675 ; but I suppose Caleb was one. A William K. of capt. Oliver's comp. was wound. 19 Dec. 1675, in the gr. battle of Narraganset, but he was of Boston, and serv. as substitute for his master, John Clear. An Eliz. K. aged 13, was passeng. in the same sh. with Henry and Richard; but on the custom-ho. list is not insert. as ch. of either, but under the care of Thomas Reyner. RICHARD, Bradford, s. of Richard, b. in Eng. long liv. in Ipswich, but was of B. when freem. 1685. SAMUEL, Wenham, freem. 1682. SAMUEL, Boston, mariner, perhaps eldest s. of Thomas of the same, may have been a soldier in Moseley's comp. in Dec. 1675, and d. 1684, on ret. voyage and his f. took admin. THOMAS, Charlestown 1653, merch. by w. Eliz. Trarice, perhaps eldest d. of Nicholas, had John, b. 1 July 1656, rem. to Boston, and had Sarah, 19 Apr. 1666 ; Rebecca, 12 July 1668; Henry, 14 Mar. 1670, and Eliz. 8 Sept. 1671. He was bur. on Copp's hill, d. 29 Jan. 1689, was b. 15 Jan. 1622. Sarah m. Richard Knight of Boston, and attain. no little celebr. as skil. in trade and observant of manners. See Knight. THOMAS, Ipswich, s. of Richard, an early sett. of that pt. of Rowley, that aft. was call. Bradford, k. by the Ind. 3 May 1676, when his w. and five ch. Joanna, Thomas, Joseph, Priscilla, and John, were tak. prison. carr. a. forty miles into the wilderness, and allow. to come home 13 June foll. THOMAS, Dover 1660. This name is spell. oft. Kemble. Ten had, in 1834, been gr. at Harv. and twenty two at other coll. in N. E.

KIMBERLY, ABRAHAM, New Haven, s. of Thomas, had Mary, bapt. 24 July 1659 ; and fam. tradit. says, went to S. Carolina, and there was k. by the Ind. ELEAZER, Glastonbury, s. of Thomas, said to be the first male b. in New Haven, was in 1661 sch.master at Wethersfield, and contin. in that employm. at intervals till 1689 ; was freem. 1667, and in 1696 succeed. Col. John Allyn, as Secr. of the Col. and so cont. to his d. Feb. 1709. He left s. Thomas, and four ds. refer. to in his will, two m. and two, Eliz. and Ruth, unm. THOMAS, Dorchester 1635, had w. Alice, with wh. he rem. to New Haven 1639 ; his est. was then small. His w. by wh. he had Eleazer, bapt. 17 Nov. 1639 ; and Abiah, 19 Dec. 1641 ; beside five or six others, bef. or aft. d. 1659, at New Haven ; he m. ano. w. and rem. to Stratford, there d. 1673 ; in his will of 11 Jan. of that yr. he names his s. Thomas, Abraham, Nathaniel, and Eleazer, w. Mary, and sev. ds. Of these Hannah was b. so late as 1656 ; Abiah m. a Boardman, and she and three ch. are refer. to in his will ; and Mary m. Nathaniel Hayes, prob. and her 3 ch. Nathaniel, Eliz. and Mary, are nam. in it. THOMAS was freem. 1669, had w. Hannah, and with Nathaniel, propr. at New Haven 1685 ; but T. had no ch. and it is said Nathaniel left s. of the same name. Great var. in spell. of this name occurs both at D. and New Haven ; Kinnersly, Kimerly, Kemmerly, and even with C. for first let. are found. At New Haven the fam. is perpet. with repute, and four had been gr. at Yale in 1829.

KIME, WILLIAM, Dover 1668–71.

KIMWRIGHT, GEORGE, Dorchester, m. a. 1653, the wealthy wid. of John Holland, rem. to Cambridge, a. 1664 ; but I doubt the spell. of the surname.

KINCAID, DANIEL, New Hampsh. came, 1689, prob. from Scotland.

KIND, ARTHUR, Boston, by w. Jane had Sarah, b. Nov. 1646 ; James, wh. d. 9 July 1654 ; Mary, wh. d. 27 Oct. 1655 ; James, again, 29 Oct. 1655 ; Nathaniel, May 1658 ; Thomas, 26 Sept. 1659 ; Mary, 27 Apr. 1662 ; and William, 26 Feb. 1665.

KING, ALEXANDER, Wickford, R. I. 1674. BENJAMIN, Northampton, s. of John of the same, m. 16 May 1700, Mary, d. of Abel James, had Elisha, b. 11 Nov. 1717, the only ch. and he d. 20 Jan. foll. His wid. m. 1721, Jonathan Graves. CLEMENT, Marshfield, by Miss Thomas, in Geneal. Reg. VIII. 192, is favor. with w. Susanna, wh. d. or was bur.

19 June 1669; but whose s. or whose d. when b. or m. is not to be easi.
kn. A later report, in the same vol. 229, makes the d. of w. occur.
thirty yrs. aft. DANIEL, Lynn 1647, a merch. b. a. 1601, d. 28 May
1672. His will of 7 Feb. preced. pro. 26 June foll. names w. and ch.
Daniel, Hannah, w. of John Blaney, Eliz. Redding, and Sarah, w. of
Ezekiel Needham. His wid. Eliz. wh. had been wid. Corwin, says
Lewis, d. 26 Feb. 1677 or 8. His est. was very good. DANIEL,
Charlestown 1658, s. prob. of the preced. was, perhaps, of Salem 1676,
but intermed. at Lynn, m. 11 Mar. 1663, Tabitha Walker, had Richard
b. 1 Mar. 1668; Tabitha, 6 Jan. 1670; John; Sarah, 11 Apr. 1672;
Eliz. 19 Mar. 1674. John has a date, giv. by Felt, but as it is inconsist. with the one that precedes him, it is mark. here as the other may
be erron. DAVID, Westfield, br. of Benjamin, by w. Abigail had David,
b. 1702; Thankful, 1704; Moses, 1706; Stephen, 1708; Benjamin,
1710; Aaron, 1714; Asahel, and Eldad, tw. 1718, of wh. the first nam.
d. soon; and Gideon, 1722; rem. to a new planta. now Sheffield, and d.
1730. In his will he nam. all the ch. exc. Asahel. EDWARD, Windsor,
an Irish serv. had gr. of ld. 1663, liv. on Long Isl. when he d. 1702;
had two ds. nam. Mary Hilliard and Saray Cady, req. adm. on his est.
Their h.'s names are not found. Perhaps there were other ch. FEAR-
NOT, Westfield, s. prob. of •John of Weymouth, m. 14 May 1677,
Mary, d. of Ambrose Fowler, had Mary, b. 7 Mar. 1678; Eliz. 12
May 1680; Abigail, 15 Feb. 1683; Experience, 1 May 1684, d. in 10
days; Deborah, 3 Mar. 1686; Ebenezer, 3 Sept. 1687; and John, 30
Sept. 1690; and d. 1 Feb. 1703. GEORGE, freem. of Mass. 18 Apr.
1637, came in the Hercules, 1634, and by Farmer is set down at Newbury, but he must soon have rem. for Coffin names him not. HENRY,
came in the James from Southampton, 1635, is call. a laborer, but I
hear no more of him. HEZEKIAH, Weymouth, by w. Mary had Mary,
b. 10 Oct. 1679; and Samuel, 20 Apr. 1686; and prob. others. ISAAC,
Weymouth, a soldier in capt. Johnson's comp. in the gr. Narraganset
fight, 19 Dec. 1675, when he was wound. Prob. he is call. Hezekiah
in that list of Geneal. Reg. VIII. 242. JAMES, Suffield, d. 1722, leav.
James, b. bef. he went thither; William, 1679; Annis, 1681; Benoni,
1685; Joseph, 1687; and Mary, 1692. JOHN, Northampton, is by
Hinman said to have come at the age of 16 in 1645, liv. at Hartford,
and 5 yrs. aft. m. Sarah Holton, d. of John; but part of this is erron.
for he m. 18 Nov. 1656, Sarah, d. of William Holton, wh. of course, was
sis. not d. of John; had John, b. July 1657; William, 28 Mar. 1660;
Thomas, 14 July 1662; Samuel, 6 Jan. 1665; Eleazer, 26 Mar. 1667,
wh. d. at 32 yrs. unm.; Joseph, 23 Mar. 1669, d. next yr.; Sarah, 3
May 1671; Joseph, again, 8 May 1673; Benjamin, 1 Mar. 1675;

Thankful, Sept. 1679 ; David, 1677, or 1681 ; and Jonathan, 25 Apr. 1683 ; and his w. d. 8 May foll. ; was rep. 1679 and 89 ; m. sec. w. Sarah, wid. of Jacob Mygatt, d. of William Whiting, was a capt. and d. 3 Dec. 1703. Sarah m. 22 Dec. 1692, Ebenezer Pomeroy ; and Thankful m. 1704, Samuel Clapp. JOHN, Weymouth, by w. Esther had Fearnot, b. 29 June 1655 ; John, 12 Apr. 1659, d. soon ; John, again, 25 Dec. 1661 ; Esther, 28 Sept. 1664 ; and Patience, 4 Oct. 1668. Perhaps he was s. b. in Eng. of an elder JOHN of the same, wh. had Mary, b. 15 June 1639 ; and Abigail, 14 Mar. 1641, whose sec. or third w. made her will, 14 June 1652, in wh. her s. Joseph Barker, and d. Sarah Hunt are refer. to ; and this younger John may be the officer in the Ind. war, 1691, ment. by Niles in his Hist. 3 Mass. Hist. Coll. VI. 227. JOHN, Salem, s. perhaps of William of the same, m. Sept. 1660, Eliz. d. of Thomas Goldthwait of the same, had John, b. Oct. 1661 ; Samuel, May 1664 ; William, June 1669 ; Eliz. Feb. 1672 ; Jonathan, 1675 ; Thomas, 1678, d. at 2 yrs. ; Hannah, 15 Apr. 1681 ; and Mary, 28 Mar. 1687. JOHN, Northampton, eldest s. of John of the same, freem. 1690, m. 4 Nov. 1686, Mehitable, d. of Medad Pomeroy, had Mehitable, b. 13 Mar. 1690 ; Experience, 17 Apr. 1693 ; Medad, 26 Mar. 1699 ; Catharine, 17 Aug. 1701 ; John, 1 Apr. 1704 ; tw. ch. 1 June 1706, both d. soon ; and Thankful, 18 Feb. 1709, d. in few days. He d. 20 Mar. 1720 ; and his wid. d. 8 Nov. 1755, in her 90th yr. JOSEPH, Northampton, br. of the preced. m. 3 June 1696, Mindwell, d. of Medad Pomeroy, had Sarah, b. 10 Mar. 1697 ; Esther, 1 Jan. 1700, d. young ; Eunice, 12 Mar. 1703 ; Mindwell, 15 Mar. 1705 ; Phineas, 27 Sept. 1707 ; Joseph, 24 Nov. 1709 ; Thankful, 9 Feb. 1712 ; and Simeon, 28 Oct. 1714 ; he m. sec. w. 30 Aug. 1733, Mindwell Porter, and d. 3 Dec. 1734. JONATHAN, Northampton, youngest br. of the preced. m. 3 Apr. 1711, Mary French, perhaps d. of Thomas of Deerfield, had Jonathan, b. 25 Jan. 1712 ; Abigail, 1 Dec. 1713 ; Charles, 3 July 1716 ; Mary, 31 May 1718 ; Beriah, 2 Oct. 1721 ; Seth, 18 Apr. 1723 ; Oliver, 20 Apr. 1726 ; rem. to Bolton, and had Gideon, 24 Aug. 1729. See Hinman, 280. MARK, Charlestown 1658, by w. Mary, adm. of the ch. 20 Nov. 1659, had Mark ; beside Mary, b. 28 Mar. preced. both bapt. 27 Nov. of that yr. ; two ch. bapt. 6 May 1660, whose names are not found ; Hannah, 18 Dec. 1664, d. soon ; Hannah, again, 4 Mar. 1666 ; and Samuel, 19 Nov. 1671. * PETER, Sudbury 1654, deac. and rep. 1689 and 90, d. 27 Aug. 1704. Prob. he had ch. of wh. one may have been Peter, freem. 1690. PHILIP, Weymouth 1672. His d. Mary m. John Leonard. RALPH, Lynn 1648, m. 2 Mar. 1664, Eliz. Walker, had Ralph, b. 13 Aug. 1667 ; Daniel, 10 Oct. 1669 ; Sarah, 25 Nov. 1671 ; Richard, 3 May 1677 ; and Mary, 28

July 1679; freem. 1680, was capt. and d. 1689. RICHARD, prob. of Salem, had d. and his wid. m. Richard Bishop of Salem, to wh. in her right was gr. admin. of est. of K. as early as 1635. Felt. ROBERT, came in the Confidence from Southampton, 1638, aged 24, a serv. but we kn. no more. SAMUEL, Plymouth 1643, had Samuel, b. 29 Aug. 1649; and Isaac, 24 Oct. 1651. SAMUEL, Weymouth, by w. Experience had Susanna, b. 6 May 1659; Eliz. 23 Sept. 1662; Experience, 6 Oct. 1664; Sarah, 31 Jan. 1666; and Samuel, 1 Mar. 1671; was freem. 1681. Ano. Samuel, at Weymouth, or the same, had Abigail, b. 20 Apr. 1681. SAMUEL, Northampton, br. of Benjamin, m. 1690, Joanna, wid. of Thomas Alvord, had Eliakim, b. 19 Feb. 1692; Samuel, 19 Nov. 1693; Jemima; and tw. ch. 31 July 1699, wh. both d. soon; and he d. 3 Oct. 1701; and his wid. m. 1702, Deliverance Bridgman. THOMAS, Sudbury, and Lancaster, by w. Ann, wh. d. 24 Dec. 1642, had Thomas, b. 4 Dec. 1642, d. 3 Jan. 1645. The f. also, d. soon, for his inv. was tak. by Capt. John Coolidge and Hugh Mason, 23 Apr. foll. Possib. he was that youth of 15, wh. came from Ipswich at the same time, in 1634, with the other Thomas a few yrs. older, but in a differ. ship, the Elizabeth. THOMAS, Watertown 1640, prob. in the Frances from Ipswich, 1634, aged 19, came with so many, wh. sat down at that place, but first was, prob. at Hampton; by w. Mary had Thomas, b. 6 Mar. 1641; Mary, 2 Feb. 1643; and d. 7 Dec. 1644. His wid. m. 9 Mar. 1645, James Cutler. THOMAS, perhaps s. of the preced. in 1676 was of Marlborough. THOMAS, Scituate, came in the Blessing, from London, 1635, aged 21, in comp. with William Vassall, unit. with the ch. 25 Feb. 1638, but did not rem. next yr. with the pastor and his many friends; by w. Sarah had Rhoda, b. 11 Oct. 1639; George, 24 Dec. 1642, wh. it is thot. d. young; Thomas, 21 June 1645; Daniel, 4 Feb. 1648; Sarah, 24 May 1650; and John, 30 May 1652, d. in few wks.; and his w. d. 6 June aft. He next m. 31 Mar. 1653, Jane, wid. of Elder William Hatch, wh. d. 8 Oct. foll. had third w. Ann; but ch. of the first w. only are heard of; was Rul. Elder, and d. 1691; his will is of this date. Rhoda m. 8 Oct. 1656, at Boston, John Rogers of S. THOMAS, Scituate, s. of the preced. was a deac. had two ws. one prob. Mary, d. of the first William Sprague of Hingham, wh. must have been sec. w. for in 1669 he m. Eliz. d. of Thomas Clap of S. He had sev. ch. of wh. Daniel was of Marshfield; and Sarah m. Elisha Bisby, jr. says Deane. In the same sh. with him came Susanna, aged 30, wh. may have been aunt. THOMAS, Sudbury, m. 26 Dec. 1655, Bridget Davis. THOMAS, Taunton, d. 30 Mar. 1713, aged 70, says gr.stone. He may be that Weymouth inhab. wh. by w. Mary had John, b. 29 Aug. 1670; Mary, 12 June 1673; and, perhaps, had ch. aft. rem. to T. THOMAS,

Hatfield and Hartford, br. of Benjamin, m. 17 Nov. 1683, Abigail, d. of
Jedediah Strong, had Thomas, b. at Northampton, 3 Dec. 1684, d.
young; Abigail, 1687; and Mary, 1691, both at Hatfield; beside
Thomas; and Robert; both at Hartford, where, aft. d. of his first w.
1689, he'm. 1690, Mary, d. of Robert Webster, wh. d. 27 Sept. 1706.
He had third w. and d. 26 Dec. 1711, and his wid. d. 2 Jan. foll. WIL-
LIAM, Salem, came from London in the Abigail, 1635, aged 28, freem.
25 May 1636, wh. is inconsist. in trifling degree with Felt, wh. says he
had gr. of ld. 1637, and was freem. aft. it; had there bapt. Mehitable,
on 25 Dec. 1636; John, 1 Nov. 1638; and Deliverance, 31 Oct. 1641.
In his case, we find not the w. in the valua. list of ch. mem. as was
commonly the much more natural occurr. but he seems to have been the
superior polemic, if not devotee; as, in the antinom. perversity of 1637,
he was one of the five men in S. requir. to be disarm. for the public
safety; and in the more violent ragings of spiritual insubordin. 1659, his
Christian kindness to the Quakers expos. him to whip. and banishm.
From the latter he was restor. on repent. 1661. WILLIAM, Isle of
Shoals, d. 28 May 1664, leav. William. WILLIAM, Boston, wh. by w.
Sarah, d. of George Griggs, had William, b. 6 Nov. 1655, is, perhaps,
f. of that man, honor. by Dunton in 1686, wh. d. 1690. The wid. of
William m. bef. July 1662, Roger Burgiss, and d. 1664. WILLIAM,
Northampton, br. of Benjamin, m. 1686, Eliz. d. of Henry Denslow of
Windsor, and had William, b. 7 Sept. 1687; Daniel, 17 Oct. 1689;
Josiah, 27 Aug. 1693; John, 11 June 1697; Eleazer, Dec. 1701; and
Eliz. 15 June 1707. He d. 20 Sept. 1728; and his wid. d. 27 May
1746, aged 80. Of the gr. fam. of Kings at N. a hundred and fifty yrs.
since, near all are extinct. A Winifred K. was m. at Boston, 15 Jan.
1657, to Joseph Benham of New Haven, but her f. is not kn. Seven
of this name, Farmer saw, had, in 1829, been gr. at Harv. and twenty-
two at other coll. of N. E. and Union and N. J.

KINGMAN, EDWARD, Weymouth, a soldier of capt. Johnson's comp.
1675, in the Narraganset campaign. * HENRY, Weymouth, freem. 3
Mar. 1636, rep. 1638 and 52; his w. Joan d. 11 Apr. 1659; s. Henry,
perhaps eldest, d. May 1660. In his will of 24 May 1666, he calls his
age 74, or thereabouts, ment. s. Edward, Thomas, John, and ds. Holbrook; Davis, w. of Tobias, m. 13 Dec. 1649; and Barnard; of wh. the
last was d. leav. five ch. JOHN, Weymouth, s. of the preced. by w. Eliz.
had John, b. 30 Apr. 1664; Henry, 11 May 1668; Samuel, 28 May
1670; Eliz. 9 July 1673; Deliverance, 12 Mar. 1676; Susanna, Mar.
1678, d. soon; and Susanna, again, 12 Apr. 1679; was freem. 1666,
rem. to Bridgewater, and d. 1690. THOMAS, Weymouth, br. of the
preced. by w. Rebecca had Rebecca, b. 2 July 1664, d. young; Hannah,

1 June 1666; Thomas, 11 Feb. 1671; John; and four others; was freem. 1681. Of the orig. stock descend. have been num. and reput.

KINGSBURY, ELEAZER, Dedham, s. of Joseph of the same, was freem. 1690. EPHRAIM, Haverhill, perhaps s. of Henry of the same, k. by the Ind. 2 May 1676, prob. unm. HENRY, Ipswich 1638, came, with w. Margaret and two or more ch. in the Talbot, one of the fleet of Winth. 1630; is No. 25 on the list of mem. in the ch. of Boston, and his w. 26, against her name being writ. "dead since," that means, I presume, to refer to the *orig.* MS. lost aft. the third or fourth yr. Of him we learn no more, but possib. his liv. at I. 1648. Winth. Appx. A. 41 and 45. HENRY, Ipswich, call. hims. 54 yrs. old in a depon. of 1669, with w. Susanna, by wh. he had Susanna, wh. m. 29 Jan. 1663, Joseph Pike; John; James, perhaps; Joseph, b. a. 1656, and other ch. prob. Samuel, and Thomas; may be the s. of the preced. liv. at I. 1660, at Rowley 1662, and she d. at Haverhill, 21 Feb. 1679, and he d. there 1 Oct. 1687. Perhaps he had Ephraim. JAMES, Haverhill, perhaps s. of Henry, or of Thomas, took o. of fidel. 28 Nov. 1677, had m. 6 Jan. 1674, Sarah, d. of Matthias Button, rem. later to Conn. and in 1730 was of Plainfield. * JOHN, Watertown, freem. 3 Mar. 1636, rem. that yr. to Dedham, of wh. he was rep. 1647. From his will, of 2 Dec. 1659, pro. 16 Oct. foll. we find that his w. was Margaret, only ch. John, br. Joseph, and his s. John, and kinsmen Henry K. of Ipswich, and Thomas Cooper of Seaconk, all, with other childr. of br. Joseph to be favor. with parts of his est. JOHN, Dedham, perhaps s. of the preced. d. bef. mid. life, and his wid. Eliz. d. of Thomas Fuller, m. 17 Sept. 1672, Michael Metcalf, third of the same. JOHN, Rowley 1667, s. prob. of Henry the sec. cannot be the man (yet was prob. his f.) ment. by Coffin, wh. says he had by w. Hannah, John, b. at Newbury, 8 Apr. 1689, for this s. of Henry d. at Haverhill, 23 Jan. 1671, leav. one s. John, b. 28 July 1667, and one d. as in Geneal. Reg. VI. 346; and his wid. Eliz. m. 11 Dec. 1672, Peter Green, and d. five yrs. aft. JOSEPH, Dedham, br. of the first John of the same, freem. 2 June 1641, by w. Milicent had Mary, b. 1 Sept. 1637; Eliz. 14 Sept. 1638; Joseph, 17 Feb. 1641; John, 15 of some mo. not stat. 1643; Eleazer, 17 May 1645; and prob. others, of wh. one may have been Sarah, wh. d. 24 Jan. 1646. JOSEPH, Wrentham, s. perhaps of the preced. by w. Mary, had Eliz. b. 14 May 1670; Eleazer, 12 May 1673; Hannah, 26 July 1675; Mary, 19 July 1680; and prob. one or more intermed. when rec. of the town were lost. His w. d. 31 July 1680; and he m. 7 Sept. 1681 ano. Mary, was freem. 1682. JOSEPH, Haverhill, s. of Henry the sec. m. 2 Apr. 1669, Love Ayers, as fam. tradit. tells, and had Joseph, Nathaniel, Mary, Eliz. and Susanna, with wh. it adds, that he rem. a. 1708 (when his employer, capt. Simon Wainwright had been k. by the Ind.) to Norwich, there d. 1741. NATHANIEL, Dedham, freem. 1677, was, perhaps, s. of Joseph of the same, m. Mary, d. of John Bacon of the same. SAMUEL, Haverhill, prob. s. of the sec. Henry, m. 5 Nov. 1679, Huldah Corliss, and d. 26 Sept. 1698, she surv. THOMAS was br. of the first Henry perhaps, but I have knowl. of no more, exc. that he agreed to emb. with him. See Winth. II. 340. THOMAS, Haverhill, s. perhaps of the preced. sw. fidel. 1677, was more prob. s. of the sec. Henry, m. 29 June 1691, wid. Deborah Eastman, and, next, 19 Jan. 1703, Sarah Haines, wh. outliv. him, but no ch. by either is kn. Two of this name had been gr. at Harv. in 1834, and twelve at other N. E. coll.

KINGSLEY, or KINSLEY, ELDAD, Rehoboth 1663, s. of John of Dorchester, aid. that yr. Rev. John Myles in form. first Bapt. ch. of Mass.; m. Mehitable, d. of Roger Morey in 1662, and had John; Samuel; Jonathan; Mary, b. 7 Oct. 1675; and Nathaniel, 5 Feb. 1679, and d. 28 Aug. 1679. Professor K. the late venerab. and well belov. of New Haven, was of the seventh generat. from the first John, thro. Eldad. ENOS, Northampton, br. prob. of the preced. m. 15 June 1662, Sarah, d. of Edmund Haynes of Springfield, had John, b. 1664, d. soon; Sarah, 1665; John, again, 1667; Haynes, 1669, d. at 20 yrs.; Ann; Samuel, 1675; Remember, 1677, d. soon; and Hannah, 1681; was freem. 1680, and d. 9 Dec. 1708. JOHN, Dorchester 1635, came prob. with some friend of Mather, and was here bef. him; at least was one of the seven pillars on format. of the new ch. for him, 23 Aug. 1636, and was the last surviv.; had Freedom; Eldad. b. 1638; Enos; Edward; and Renewal, 19 Mar. 1644; rem. to Rehoboth, aft. 1648, when he was in office, and 1658; there liv. and suffer. the Ind. hostil. of wh. in a letter of supplicat. for relief, under date of 5 May 1676, most sad pict. is giv. It is print. in Trumbull, Col. Rec. II. 445. His will, of 2 Nov. 1677, ment. on y 3 ch. Edward, Enos, and Freedom; but a d. prob. then d. had m. John French of Northampton. Perhaps ano. d. m. Timothy Jones. One John, perhaps the same, of R. was bur. 6 Jan. 1679, and Mary, prob. his w. 29 of the same mo. JOHN, Dorchester, s. of Stephen, m. a d. of William Daniels, perhaps nam. Alice, had Susanna, b. 1671. This w. d. 14 Jan. 1674, and 16 Mar. foll. he m. Mary Maury or Morey, and he and w. d. 1679. JOHN, Milton, m. Abigail, d. of James Leonard, had Abigail; Mary, b. 1676; John; Stephen; Samuel; and Eliz. and d. 1698, leav. the w. and ch. here nam. SAMUEL, Billerica, freem. 1651, m. Hannah, d. of Capt. Richard Brackett, d. 21 May 1662; and his wid. and her f. were admors. SAMUEL, Braintree, prob. s. of Stephen, by w. Hannah had Hannah, b. 27 July 1656; Eliz. 22 Nov. 1657; and Mary, 3 Mar. 1659, possib. this may be the ch. that d. 26 Mar. 1658, as

near that time in the yr. the count. is easi. mistak. in rec. He may be
the same as the preced. I think. A Samuel, perhaps his s. was b. 1662,
and in the next generat. of Bridgewater, m. Mary, d. of John Washburn. * STEPHEN, Dorchester, perhaps br. of John, freem. 13 May 1640,
rep. 1650, rem. to Braintree, there had Mary, b. 30 Aug. 1640 ; ord. rul.
Eld. of the ch. that was gather. 17 Sept. 1639. He rem. final. to Milton,
was rep. 1666, and in his will of 27 May, pro. 3 July foll. in 1673,
provides for s. John, three s.-in-law, Henry Crane, Anthony Gulliver,
and Robert Mason, beside a s. and two ds. ch. of his s. Samuel,
prob. dec.

KINGSNOTH, or KINGSWORTH, HENRY, Guilford 1639, sign. the cov.
for settlem. of 1 June, m. Mary, d. of John Stevens of the same; d.
1668, and his wid. m. 2 June 1669, John Collins as his sec. w.

KINGSMILL, WILLIAM, a Quaker, punish. at Boston with 15 stripes,
wh. did not, however it might reasonab. be anticipat. prevent him from
renounc. his errors.

KINNICUT. See Kennicut.

KINSMAN, or KINGSMAN, ROBERT, Ipswich 1635, came the yr.
preced. in the Mary and John, had soon aft. a gr. of ld. m. a d. of
Thomas Boreman, and d. Jan. 1665. * ROBERT, Ipswich, s. of the
preced. freem. 1674, m. Rebecca, eldest d. of Andrew Burley of the
same, was a warm oppon. of Andros, rep. 1692. Revo. in N. E.
Justif. 14.

KIRBY, HENRY, a soldier, 1676, serv. in Turner's comp. on Conn. riv.
wh. may be the Salem freem. 1677, spell. in the list Kirrey, unless, as
seems more prob. that be intend. for Skerry. JOHN, Middletown,
whither Dr. Field thot. he rem. from Boston, and Hinman made him of
Hartford 1645 ; but bef. the sett. of M. he had been at H. and Wethersfield, and at Plymouth 1643 ; had Eliz. b. at Hartford, 8 Sept. 1646 ;
and at Wethersfield, Hannah, 1649 ; John, and Eunice, tw. 18 Dec.
1651. He own. an est. at Rowington, near Kenilworth in Warwicksh.
His s. John was k. by the Ind. 1676; and he d. Apr. 1677, his will
bears date 6, and was pro. 27 of that mo. He left wid. Eliz. and ch.
Mary, then w. of Emanuel Buck, aged 32; Hannah, w. of Thomas
Andrews, 27 ; Esther, w. of Benajah Stone, 25 ; Sarah, w. of Samuel
Hubbard, 23 ; Joseph, 21 ; Bethia, 18 ; Susanna, 13 ; and Abigail, 11 ;
beside Eliz. w. of David Sage, wh. was dec. Susanna m. Abraham
Cruttenden. JOSEPH, Middletown, only surv. s. of the preced. went to
Carolina, but at the end of some yrs. came home poor, had lawsuit with
other heirs a. est. of his f. RICHARD, Lynn, rem. 1637 to Sandwich,
by w. Jane had Increase, and prob. Abigail, tw. b. Feb. 1650, of wh.
Abigail was bur. the same, and Increase, the next mo. and the mo. and

her s. Richard were bur. in Mar. of that yr. He was imprison. as a Quaker 1658, may have tak. o. of fidel. at Dartmouth 1684, where he m. 2 Nov. 1678, Abigail Rowland of D. perhaps as sec. or third w. By former w. Patience he had at D. Sarah, b. 1 May 1667; John, 2 Mar. 1673; and Robert, 10 Mar. 1675. Perhaps he was of Oyster Bay, L. I. 1685. ROBERT, Dartmouth 1684, or near that time. WILLIAM, Boston, by w. Eliz. had Eliz. b. 20 Dec. 1640, wh. d. 12 July 1642. He was the executioner 1657 and 8, liv. in 1667, may be that freem. of 1647, print. Kerley.

KIRGE, JOSEPH, is the un-Eng. name, giv. to one of "the flower of Essex," wh. fell at Bloody brook under capt. Lothrop, 18 Sept. 1675, wh. prob. should be King.

KIRK, HENRY, Dover 1665. THOMAS, Boston, merch. from. London, or as Sir Thomas Temple wrote, then here, capt. of a sh. was sent with Thomas Kellond, bear. warrant from Gov. Endicott, 1662, to arrest in Conn. the regicides Whalley and Goffe. Hutch. I. 215. 3 Mass. Hist. Coll. VIII. 325. Full report from their search, a curious paper, is in Hutch. Coll. 334. ZECHARIAH, Boston 1686, m. Abigail, d. of Joshua Rawlins.

KIRKEETE, KARKEET, or CARKEET, WILLIAM, Saco, d. 1662, leav. prop. by inv. of £134. The name seems strange, yet one *William* K. of Lynn, wh. may have come from Saco, by w. Lydia had Robert, b. at Salem 11 Nov. 1697.

KIRKHAM, THOMAS, Wethersfield 1648, had Samuel, and, perhaps, other ch. but not on rec. The name is various. spelt, sometimes with initial C.

KIRMAN, * JOHN, Lynn 1632, freem. 4 Mar. 1633, rep. 1635.

KIRTLAND, or KERTLAND, now commonly KIRKLAND, JOHN, Saybrook, by tradit. call. one of the first sett. but may not reasona. be thot. among the inhab. of first 30 or 40 yrs. was s. of Nathaniel of Lynn, m. 18 Nov. 1679, Lydia, d. of lieut. William Pratt, had John, b. 11 July 1681; Priscilla, 1 Feb. 1683; Lydia, 11 Oct. 1685; Eliz. 27 June 1688; Nathaniel, 24 Oct. 1690; Philip, 28 May 1693; Martha, 11 Aug. 1695; Samuel, 19 Jan. 1699; Daniel, 17 June 1701; and Parnell, 16 Oct. 1704; was a lieut. and d. 20 Jan. 1716. He was made heir by John Westall to all his good est. exc. £500 by him, h. of K.'s aunt, reserv. for her. The ninth of these ch. Daniel, Y. C. 1720, first min. of third ch. at Norwich, call. Newent (thro. affect. for the town of that name in the N. W. part of Gloucestersh.) had tenth ch. Samuel, the celebr. missiona. to the Ind. of the six nations, wh. was f. of the more disting. John Thornton K. the ever hon. Presid. of Harv. Univ. NATHANIEL, Lynn, came in the Hopewell, capt. Bundock, from London,

1635, aged 19, call. of Sherington, in Co. Bucks, near Olney, went to L. I. with first sett. there, but aft. few yrs. came back to L. there by w. Parnell had Ann, b. 16 Apr. 1658 ; John, Aug. 1659 ; Hannah, 15 Apr. 1662 ; Eliz. 20 Mar. 1664 ; Martha, and Mary, tw. 15 May 1667 ; and he d. Dec. 1686. Hannah m. 20 Feb. 1679, William Pratt of Saybrook. NATHANIEL, Lynn, prob. s. of the preced. b. at Southold, L. I. m. 20 Jan. 1675, Mary Rand, had Nathaniel, b. 3 May 1677 ; Mary, 1 Feb. 1680 ; Priscilla, 9 Apr. 1683 ; and Eliz. 22 June 1685. His wid. m. 24 Apr. 1690, Dr. John H. Burchsted. PHILIP, Lynn, came in the Hopewell, capt. Bundock, from London, 1635, aged 21, call. on the custom-ho. rec. of Sherington near Olney in Co. Bucks, was prob. br. of Nathaniel first ment. and went with him to sett. L. I. and came back sooner than he, was a shoemak. Lewis says ; by w. Alice had Mary, b. 3 or 8 June 1640 ; Sarah, 27 Sept. 1646 ; Susanna, 8 Mar. 1652 ; Hannah, and Ebenezer, tw. 12 June 1654. He had elder br. John, whose resid. is unkn. and d. bef. July 1659, and his wid. Alice m. Evan Thomas of Boston, wh. in favor of the childr. made convey. of est. in tr. 24 Apr. 1661. Sarah m. 5 Oct. 1664, John Davis. PHILIP, Lynn, perhaps s. of the preced. perhaps of the first Nathaniel, m. 14 Oct. 1679, Ruth Pierce.

KIRTSHAW, JOHN, Newtown, L. I. 1655.

KISKEYES, or KESKEYS, HENRY, Boston, m. 7 Aug. 1656, Ruth, d. of Richard Graves, had Henry, b. 3 May 1657, mispr. in Geneal. Reg. X. 68.

KITCHELL, ROBERT, Guilford 1639, had w. Margaret, s. Samuel; Hannah, wh. m. 12 Nov. 1656, Jeremiah Peck ; and Sarah, d. May 1657 ; was giv. power, in 1665, to hold court at G. but next yr. rem. to N. J. where he was disting. and is call. in hist. the benefact. of Newark. His wid. rem. to Greenwich, there d. 1679. SAMUEL, Guilford, s. of the preced. was ensign 1665, m. 11 Mar. 1657, at New Haven, Eliz. d. of John Wakeman, had Sarah, b. the same yr. ; Eliz. b. 1 Feb. bapt. 13 Mar. 1659 ; and Abigail, 10, bapt. 11 Aug. 1661 ; but then liv. at New Haven ; may have had more ch. at G. In July 1667, unit. with Bruen and others, he purch. large tract from Ind. in and around Newark, N. J.

KITCHEN, JOHN, Salem 1640, freem. 28 Feb. 1643, shoemak. by w. Eliz. had there bapt. Eliz. and Hannah, 12 Mar. 1643, wh. were not, prob. tw. but the f. was not earlier of the ch. ; Joseph, 20 Apr. 1645 ; John, 28 June 1646, d. soon ; Mary, 23 Apr. 1648 ; John, again, 21 Mar. 1652 ; and Robert, 15 Apr. 1655 ; was chos. sealer of leather, 1655, and d. 1676. ROBERT, Salem, s. of the preced. merch. and shipowner, d. 28 Oct. 1712, in 56th yr. says gr.stone ; and his s. Robert, a student at H. C. d. 20 Sept. 1716.

KITCHERELL, KETCHERWELL, KETCHERING, or KECHERELL, sometimes with the first let. C., JOSEPH, Charlestown 1636, perhaps the same,
whose w. perhaps, or sis. Sarah on adm. there by the ch. 30 Nov. 1643,
is spell. Kitcherin, and for wh. Felt shows, in Salem, gr. of ld. 1639,
and adm. to the ch. in the same yr. I doubt he was not many yrs. at
either place, being mark. in the ch. rec. as drown. as in Essex Inst. Coll.
I. 39, where the c is mistak. for t. SAMUEL, Hartford, by w. Martha
had Martha; Samuel, and Hannah, b. 4 Jan. 1646; and d. 1650. His
wid. m. 2 Jan. 1651, Anthony Dorchester of Springfield, where Samuel
d. 9 June 1651, and Hannah d. 29 Apr. 1658, and Martha m. 1 Dec.
1659, Abel Wright.

KITTREDGE, JOHN, Billerica 1661, or earlier, the ancest. of the many
thousands of the name in our ld. came, it is said, in youth with his mo.
was a farmer; had John, b. 24 Jan. 1666; James, 28 Mar. 1668;
Daniel, 23 July 1670; Jonathan, 1674, d. 1696; and Benoni, 1677,
posthum. for the f. d. 18 Oct. 1676. Much do I regret, that of those
five s. our informat. is confin. to JOHN, Billerica, s. of the preced. m. 3
Aug. 1685, Hannah, perhaps d. by sec. w. of William French, had six s.
and five ds. and d. 27 Apr. 1714. He was, says Farmer, the first of
the fam. with that prefix, Dr. wh. has since been so freq. with his
progeny, of wh. three at Harv. and nineteen at other N. E. coll. had
been gr. in 1834.

KNAPP, AARON, Taunton 1643, may have been f. of Eliz. wh. m. 17
Feb. 1674, Nicholas Stoughton; and beside had Mary, bapt. at Roxbury, 20 Nov. 1659; and he d. bef. 1676. Baylies, II. 267, 278.
CALEB, Stamford, s. of Nicholas, freem. 1670, made his will 11 Dec.
1674, d. soon. He names w. Hannah, and ch. Caleb, wh. was b. 1661;
John, 1664; Moses; Samuel; Sarah; and Hannah. JAMES, Watertown 1652, s. of William the first, b. in Eng. m. Eliz. d. of John
Warren, had Eliz. b. 21 Apr. 1655; and James, 26 May 1657, wh. d.
26 Sept. foll. In the autumn of 1671, at Groton, where he then liv. his
w. suffer. terrib. by witchcraft, if the trifling story in the Magn. VI. 67,
is good for any thing. JOHN, Watertown, br. of the preced. m. 25 May
1660, Sarah Young, had John, b. 4 May 1661; and Sarah, 5 Sept.
1662; and sev. others, for his will of 22 Jan. 1696, pro. 27 Apr. foll.
tho. it names not either of these, wh. were, perhaps, d. ment. wid. Sarah,
and ch. Henry, Isaac, John, Daniel, and Abigail. JOHN, Taunton, m.
7 Oct. 1685, Sarah Austin. Possib. he was s. of the preced. JONA-
THAN, Fairfield, s. of the first Roger, d. young, for his inv. is of 1 Feb.
1676. JOSHUA, Greenwich 1670, s. of Nicholas, m. 9 June 1657, at
Stamford, Hannah Close, had good est. by inv. of 1685, tho. he d. 27
Oct. 1684, leav. ch. Hannah, aged 25; Joshua, 22; Joseph, 20; Ruth,

18; Timothy, 16; Benjamin, 10; Caleb, 7; Jonathan, 5. His wid. m. John Bowers. MOSES, Greenwich 1670, br. of the preced. prob. youngest, but perhaps was only a ld. holder, and never liv. at G. but at Stamford as early as 1667, and there his f. gave him ld. by his will; m. a. 1669, Abigail, d. of Richard Wescoat. Whether he had ch. I am not advis. but he was liv. certain. at S. up to 1701, perhaps later. NICHO-LAS, Watertown, may have come in the fleet with Winth. and Saltonstall 1630, by w. Elinor had Jonathan, wh. was bur. 27 Dec. 1631; Timothy, b. 14 Dec. 1632; Joshua, 5 Jan. 1635; Caleb, 20 Jan. 1637; Sarah, 5 Jan. 1639; Ruth, 6 Jan. 1641; and Hannah, 6 Mar. 1643; rem. to Stamford, there, I suppose, had Moses, and Lydia. His w. Elinor d. 16 Aug. 1658, and he m. 9 Mar. foll. Unity, wid. of Peter Brown, wh. had been wid. of Clement Buxton; d. Apr. 1670. His will of 15 of that mo. names four s. Caleb, Joshua, Moses, Timothy; and four ds. Sarah, Hannah, Lydia, and Ruth. Sarah m. 6 Sept. 1667, Peter Disbrough; and Ruth m. 20 Nov. foll. Joseph Ferris. ROGER, New Haven 1643–7, Fairfield 1656–70, and prob. later, had made his will 21 Mar. 1673, nam. w. Eliz. and ch. Jonathan, Josiah, Lydia, Roger, John, Nathaniel, Eliz. and Mary, some of wh. were minors, and his inv. is of 20 Sept. 1675. ROGER, Fairfield, s. of the preced. d. 1691, but no acco. is found of his fam. THOMAS, Sudbury, m. at Watertown, 19 Sept. 1688, Mary, d. of John Grout, and d. beyond sea, leav. wid. and ch. Sarah, aged 9 yrs. and Mary, 6, when admin. was issu. 28 May 1697. * TIMOTHY, Stamford, s. perhaps eldest, of Nicholas, rep. for Rye 1670, was of Greenwich, liv. 1697. In that century a single *p* was used. WILLIAM, Watertown 1636, d. 30 Aug. 1658, "aged a. 80 yrs." Perhaps he came as early as Nicholas; and had, in his will of 1655, not nam. any w. but refer. to ch. of wh. sev. were brot. by him from Eng. and to gr.ch. His ch. were William; Mary; Eliz.; John, b. 1624; James, 1627; Ann; and Judith. Mary m. Thomas Smith; Eliz. m. in Eng. a Buttery; Ann m. Thomas Philbrick, but d. bef. her f. wh. in his will names her childr.; and Judith m. Nicholas Cady. WILLIAM, Watertown, s. of the preced. by w. Mary had prob. Joseph, beside Priscilla, b. 10 Nov. 1642; and by w. Margaret had Judith, b. 2 Mar. 1653; Eliz. 23 July 1657; and, perhaps, others; left wid. Priscilla, wh. had been wid. of Thomas Akers, and s. John. Three of this name had, in 1829, been gr. at Harv. and as many at other N. E. coll.

KNEELAND, JOHN, Boston, one of the found. of the Scots' Charit. Soc. 1657, by w. Mary had Mary, b. 6 Oct. 1659, d. next yr.; Hannah, 18 July 1663; Mary, again, 13 Apr. 1666; John, 9 Nov. 1668; Solo-mon, 7 Feb. 1671; and Ruth, 30 July 1673. He d. at Roxbury, 11 Aug. 1691, aged 59. PHILIP, Lynn 1637. Several of this name have been gr. at Harv. of wh. William, 1751, was nine yrs. a tutor, and Presid. of M. M. S. d. 2 Nov. 1788, aged 56.

KNELL, KNEALE, or KNILL, JOHN, Charlestown, perhaps s. of Nicholas, rem. to Boston, had w. Eliz. wh. bec. third w. of Nathaniel Bachiler of Hampton, 23 Oct. 1689. Ch. of K. were John, b. 13 May 1679, bapt. 12 Sept. 1680; Hannah, bapt. 1 May 1681; and Richard, b. 26, bapt. 27 May 1683. NICHOLAS, Stratford 1650, m. Eliz. wid. of Thomas Knowles of New Haven, had John, b. 24 Oct. 1651, d. soon; Eliz. 3 May 1653; Isaac, Feb. 1655; John, again, 17 Dec. 1657; by the governm. was grant. in 1668, 50 acres, and as much more next yr.; and d. Apr. 1675. His will names only w. and the two s. He seems to have been a man of some conseq. has Mr. prefix, and the ment. in town rec. of his d. calls him "that aged benefact. of the country." PHILIP, Charlestown, perhaps br. of John, by w. Ruth, m. 5 Oct. 1666, as wid. Allen, had Ruth, b. 6, bapt. 10 July 1670; Eliz. 15, bapt. 26 Apr. 1674; and Philip, 4 July 1675, bapt. the same day. His wid. petitn. the Gov. and Counc. 30 Oct. 1697, for redress in the case of her serv. Sambo, impress. under 21 yrs. of age. His will, made at the age of 51 or 2 yrs. 18 Feb. 1689, was not pro. bef. 15 Oct. 1699.

KNIGHT, or KNIGHTS, ALEXANDER, Ipswich 1635, had kept an inn at Chelmsford, Eng. says Vincent in his Hist. of the Pequot war. Perhaps we may be justif. in think. he came in the Defence, but could not obtain license to emb. being a subsidy man; we kn. at least, that in that sh. that yr. came from London, Sarah K. aged 50; and Dorothy, 30, of wh. one might be w. and the other sis. or d. APSIA, Charlestown 1637, if the force of Frothingham, 57 and 88, can render such a name credible. Without sight of the MS. I should indulge the license of modest conject. to make it Apphia. BENJAMIN, Newbury; s. of the sec. John of the same, m. Abigail, d. of Henry Jaques, had Benjamin, b. 8 Feb. 1693; Isaac, 15 Jan. 1695; Abigail, 15 Apr. 1697; Daniel, 4 Dec. 1699, d. young; Daniel, again, 11 Jan. 1702; and George, 31 Jan. 1704. CHARLES, Salem, a soldier of Gardner's comp. wound. in the gr. Narraganset fight, 19 Dec. 1675. DANIEL, York 1640, perhaps in Ind. war rem. to Lynn, d. 29 Oct. 1672. He may have been inf. s. of Jacob. EZEKIEL, Salem, if the gr. of ld. 1637, wh. Felt ment. drew him thither, but most of his days was of Braintree, by w. Eliz. wh. was bur. 28 Apr. 1642, had Ezekiel, b. 1 Feb. 1641, d. at 7 mos. * EZEKIEL, Wells 1645, prob. had w. and ch. in early life, and may be the same as the preced. was commiss. i. e. rep. 1661, at York, much betrust. in public serv. and aft. 1662 m. Mary, d. of Gov. Theophilus Eaton, wid. of Valentine Hill of Dover, formerly of Boston; and, next, the wid. of John Lovering, and she d. bef. 29 June 1675, when he present. a bill for support. of the childr. of L. and he d. 1687. His will of 18 Apr. in that yr. pro. 16 Sept. foll. made Mr. Shubael Dummer, capt. Job Alcock, and Mr. John Bass excors. but its provis. was very plain; all est. to w. for her life, and of remaind. two parts to s. Ezekiel, and one to d. Eliz. Wentworth of Dover, wh. is believ. to have been w. of Ezekiel W. FRANCIS, Pemaquid 1648. GEORGE, Hingham, came, 1638, in the Diligent, with w. and ch. from Barrow, a parish of Co. Suffk. near Bury St. Edmunds. GEORGE, Scarborough, d. 1671, in his will of 5 Apr. of that yr. gives to w. Elinor, s. Nathan, and d. Eliz. His wid. m. Henry Brooking, as perhaps I may be justif. for conject. by the dark passage in Geneal. Reg. IX. 220. GEORGE, Hartford 1671, d. 1699, his inv. being of 15 June that yr. leav. wid. Sarah, sev. ds. but no s. JACOB, Lynn, s. of William, m. 25 Dec. 1668, Sarah Burt, had Sarah, b. 28 Nov. 1670, d. within 13 mos.; Daniel, 25 Oct. 1672; Eliz. 4 Aug. 1677. His w. Sarah, d. 14 Feb. 1682, and he m. 18 Sept. foll. Hannah Rand. JOHN, Dorchester 1634, with prefix of resp. prob. rem. but may have been that John wh. d. in a town not ment. 4 Nov. 1634. JOHN, Newbury, came from Southampton, 1635, in the James; was a tailor of Romsey in Hants, adm. freem. with his br. Richard 25 May 1636, had w. Eliz. wh. d. 20 Mar. 1645, and by her, or a former w. had John, b. 1622. His next w. was Ann, wid. of Richard Ingersoll of Salem, and he d. May 1670. JOHN, Watertown 1636, a maulster, not in my opin. the freem of 1636, as Bond thot. was among orig. proprs. of Sudbury 1642, prob. the freem. of 10 May 1643, was of Woburn 1653, first signer of a petit. for ch. liberty. JOHN, Newbury, s. of John of the same, b. in Eng. m. 1647, Bathshua, d. of Richard Ingersoll of Salem, had John, b. 16 Aug. 1648; Joseph, 21 June 1652; Eliz. 18 Oct. 1655; Mary, 8 Sept. 1657; Sarah, 13 Apr. 1660; Hannah, 22 Mar. 1662, d. young; Hannah, again, 30 Aug. 1664; Richard, 26 July 1666; Benjamin, 21 Aug. 1668; and Isaac, 31 Aug. 1672, wh. d. at 18 yrs.; was freem. 1671, and d. 25 Feb. 1678, in 56th yr. and his wid. d. 25 Oct. 1705. Eliz. m. 25 Feb. 1674, Cutting Noyes; Mary m. 13 Jan. 1681, Timothy Noyes; and Hannah m. 31 Mar. 1684, James Noyes. JOHN, Charlestown 1653, s. of John, a cooper, was prob. b. in Eng. m. 25 Apr. 1654, Ruhamah Johnson, had Ruhamah, b. 29 Jan. 1655, d. at two wks.; Eliz. 3 June 1656; John, 4 Nov. 1657; Ruhamah, again, 16 Feb. 1659; and Abigail, bapt. 25 Nov. 1660; but I kn. not, whether he had others of sec. or third w. tho. it seems prob. In the ch. rec. of adm. 1667, Abigail K. is call. d. of sis. Stower's, and that may indicate, but not exclusive. a maiden; for "goodman John K." comes in few mos. aft.; and on 23 Sept. 1677 is found "Mary K. the w. of our br. John K. He m. 19 Dec. 1678, wid. Mary Clements, as fourth w. and she d. 12

July 1682, and, again, " 9 Jan. 1680, Mary K. w. of our br. John K."
and finally, " 9 Mar. 1684, Sarah K. w. of our br. John K. by dism.
from Boston first ch." as Budington's valua. list, pp. 248, 9 and 50 show.
So that we might take the last two, or even three to belong to John the
younger and leave eno. But five ws. this man had. From the will of
ano. John of Charlestown, no doubt his f. made 14 Feb. 1673, of wh.
we see not the day of pro. but find the inv. of 1 June 1674, we find no
other relat. nam. but Eliz. and Abigail, ds. of his s. John, s.-in-law
Robert Peirce of Woburn, and the w. his own d. Mary, and makes
overseer, his friend and br. (but this means only, I judge, the ch. relationsh.) John Chickering wh. was the physician. For his third w. this
John of C. took, 22 June 1668, Mary Bridge, wh. d. Oct. 1678. In
spite of his five ws. he liv. to ripe age, for in 1679 he was call. 46 yrs.
old, and his fourth w. 52 ; and his will, made 28 Nov. 1701, was pro. 13
Dec. 1714. JOHN, Lynn, had Martha, b. 11 Aug. 1657. JOHN,
Northampton, freem. 1676. JOHN, Charlestown, not s. of John of the
same, by w. Persis had Persis, bapt. 2 May 1669, d. young ; Mary, 31
July 1670; Persis, again, 17 Mar. 1672 ; John, 23 Nov. 1673 ; Samuel,
12 Sept. 1675 ; perhaps sev. more, and some of these may belong to the
other John of C. for, Mr. Wyman assures me, no John of C. had w.
Persis. ·JOHN, Newbury, eldest br. of Benjamin, m. 1 Jan. 1672, Rebecca, d. of Rev. James Noyes, had James, b. 3 Sept. 1672 ; Rebecca,
27 Apr. 1674; John, 3 Apr. 1676; Sarah, 25 Feb. 1679 ; Eliz. 13 Apr.
1681 ; Joseph, 9 Oct. 1683 ; and Nathaniel, 22 Dec. 1688. JOHN,
Woburn, not s. of the first John of Charlestown, m. 2 Mar. 1681, Abigail,
eldest ch. of John Craggin, had Abigail, b. 27 Dec. 1681 ; John, 31 Jan.
1684, d. next yr. ; John, again, 3 Mar. 1686 ; Benjamin, 20 Mar. 1688, d.
under 10 yrs. ; Samuel, 27 Sept. 1690 ; Ebenezer, 20 Aug. 1695 ; Rebecca, 14 May 1698 ; Benjamin, 20 Oct. 1700 ; and Amaziah, 14 Dec.
1703. JOHN, Dover, perhaps s. of Richard of the same, m. Leah, wid.
of Benedictus Tarr, it is said, but no more is kn. of him, exc. that his
inv. was brot. in 17 June 1700. JONATHAN, Salem 1670, m. prob. at
Woburn 31 Mar. 1663, Ruth Wright, and had Jonathan ; Ebenezer ;
Enos ; Ruth ; and Deborah ; and he d. 17 Jan. 1683. He was prob. s.
of the first Philip. A John, with w. Mary, and Joseph, with w. Hannah, early at Watertown, are ment. by Bond, but no issue is found in
his vol. JOSEPH, Woburn, freem. 1652, had Sarah, b. 8 Mar. 1651 ;
Samuel, 8 Sept. 1652, d. next yr. ; Hannah, 25 Mar. 1654; John, 16
Jan. 1656 ; Eliz. 7 Apr. 1658 ; Mary, 6 June 1660, d. at 10 mos. ;
Dinah, 4 July 1661; Samuel, again, 18 Mar. 1663 ; Mary, again, 12
Dec. 1672, d. in few mos. ; Joseph, 12 Dec. 1673 ; Edward, 31 Aug.
1677 ; Isaac, 24 Feb. 1680, d. next mo. ; James, 22 Apr. 1681, d. next

day; Ruth, 7 May 1682; Ebenezer, 24 Aug. 1684; and Amos, 19 May 1687; but most prob. by more than one w. and quite prob. by two Josephs. The senr. d. 13 Aug. 1687, and his wid. Hannah d. 13 Jañ. 1695. JOSEPH, nam. by Thomas Spaule of Boston, in his will of 23 Feb. 1671, as the h. of testator's d. Mary, and hav. childr. and to her and them mak. resid. devise aft. that to his own w. dur. wid. I guess was of B. JOSEPH, Newbury, br. of Benjamin, freem. 1684, m. 31 Oct. 1677, Deborah, prob. d. of sec. Tristram Coffin, had Judith, b. 23 Oct. 1678; John, 20 Jan. 1680, d. at 16 yrs.; Joseph, 16 Feb. 1682, d. within two yrs.; Deborah, 26 Apr. 1684; Sarah, 3 Nov. 1686; Eliz. 18 Apr. 1690; Joseph, again, 16 Feb. 1692; Mary, 3 Sept. 1693; Tristram, 9 June 1695; John, again, 10 Dec. 1696; and Stephen, 9 Oct. 1699; was ens. and d. 29 Jan. 1723. JOSEPH, Woburn, freem. 1676, perhaps s. of first Joseph, wh. m. 4 Apr. 1699, Martha Lilly, in his will of 16 Jan. 1733 names w. Martha, and ds. Martha, Ruth, Rebecca, Hannah, Mary, and Dorothy. MAUTLYN, or MACKLIN, Boston 1643, had w. Dorothy. MICHAEL, Woburn, m. 20 Oct. 1657, Mary Bullard, had Mary, b. 14 Oct. 1658; Jonathan, 23 Mar. 1662; Joshua, 20 Jan. 1665; Lydia, 29 Sept. 1674; and he had been adm. freem. 1654. PHILIP, Charlestown, had w. Margery, ch. Jonathan, Philip, Rebecca, Eliz. and Mary; wh. at his d. were of the ages respectiv. a. 26, 23, 17, 13, and 11; but he had rem. long bef. to Topsfield, or near it, and d. Nov. 1668. PHILIP, Wenham 1669, s. of the preced. was of Salem 1670. RICHARD, Newbury, prob. younger br. of the first John, came with him from Southampton in the James, 1635, call. in the custom-ho. rec. tailor of Romsey, in Hants, m. says Coffin, Agnes Coffley, wh. d. 29 Mar. 1679, had Rebecca, b. 7 Mar. 1643; Sarah, 23 Mar. 1648; Ann; and Eliz. He was sw. freem. 25 May 1636, was deac. and d. 4 Aug. 1683, in 81st yr. RICHARD, Weymouth 1637, ment. by Winth. II. 348, may be he wh. was rec. an inhab. of Boston early in 1642, a slater, being adm. of the ch. a few days bef. and, perhaps, s. of a wid. Sarah, adm. in May 1639; freem. 18 May 1642, by w. Dinah had Samuel, b. 9 Jan. bapt. 12 Feb. 1643, and bur. 25 Sept. foll.; Joseph, 15, bapt. 18 May 1645; and by w. Joanna had Joanna, b. 24 Jan. 1653; James, 1 Feb. 1655; but it may be very diffic. to disting. him from others of the name. RICHARD, Hampton, perhaps Portsmouth, 1643, was, perhaps, of Dover 1659, or bef. 1668, of Boston, a merch. RICHARD, Boston, by w. Joanna had James, wh. d. 27 Sept. 1652; Sarah, b. 6 Nov. 1656; and Mary, 25 Jan. 1659. RICHARD, Newport 1648, next yr. chos. Gen. Sergent, whatever that may mean, and many yrs. bot. ld. of Ind. on the contin. 1665 in conjunct. with Henry Hall of Westerly. He had eldest s. John of Norwich, as from law papers I learn; and this may imply, that he had other ch. RICHARD, Boston 1673, bricklayer, was call. to

serve in Philip's war on Conn. riv. in capt. Turner's comp. Perhaps
he m. Sarah Kimball, and had d. Eliz. to wh. her uncle John Kimball
gave est. This Richard was bred a carver, but m. a w. of superior
mind, Sarah, d. of Thomas Kemble, or Kimball, of Charlestown. They
had only ch. Eliz. wh. m. John Livingston of New London, and outliv.
him. Some proof of the mother's literary skill is furnish. by her journal
of travels in 1704 from Boston to New York and back, publish. so late
as 1825 by Theodore Dwight, Esq. She had rem. aft. the d. of her h.
to Norwich, and thence to New London, where she d. 25 Sept. 1727.
See Caulkins's Hist. 372. RICHARD, Newbury, s. of the sec. John of
the same, m. Eliz. d. of Henry Jaques, had Henry, b. 6 July 1697; and
Eliz. 11 Mar. 1702. ROBERT, Hampton 1640, rem. to Boston, had, by
first w. Samuel, b. 1642, wh. prob. d. young. He m. Ann, the young
wid. of Thomas Cromwell, the rich privateersman, I presume early in
1650, and may thereafter have spent a yr. or more in Maine, but had
Edward, b. 5 Feb. 1652; and Martha, 1 Sept. 1653; beside James, in
1654, wh. prob. d. soon; and he d. 27 June 1655; his will of 8 May
preced. gave all to w. with care of only ch. Edward and Martha.
ROBERT, Marblehead 1648, may be he wh. d. at Cambridge 29 Oct.
1652; but nothing more is kn. ROBERT, Kittery 1647, rem. to York,
d. 1676, his will of 23 June, pro. 24 Aug. of that yr. ment. s. Richard,
liv. in Boston. ROGER, Portsmouth 1631, among the people sent by
Mason the patentee. Belkn. I. 425. His d. Mary m. John Bruster or
Brewster of Portsmouth. SAMUEL, Roxbury, m. 16 Oct. 1685, Sarah,
perhaps d. of Abraham Howe of the same, had Mehitable, b. 9 Sept. 1686, d.
under 17 yrs.; Samuel, wh. d. 20 May 1689; and Ebenezer, Feb. 1694.
THOMAS, Salem 1661, a mason, perhaps s. of Walter. TOBY, Newport
1638. WALTER, Salem 1626, had been here in 1622, and is now sent
over by the Dorchester people to strengthen Conant; perhaps was of
Duxbury 1638; in 1653 giv. evidence a. something that occur. in 1622,
perhaps only hearsay, he call. his age 66. WILLIAM, Salem, a mason,
had gr. of ld. 1637, yet seems rather to belong to Lynn, freem. 2 May
1638, had John, Ann, Francis, Hannah, all by sec. w. Eliz. Jacob,
Daniel, Eliz. and Mary, and d. 5 Mar. 1656. From Lewis was this
acco. deriv. by Farmer; yet there is evid. that he had John and Francis,
Joanna, and Mary only, all brot. from Eng. and that the s. both went
home, and there Francis d. without issue; but John aft. serv. the
parliam. cause in the civil war, obt. possessn. of est. in Eng. that was
his f.'s m. and d. in that country. His will, of 2 Dec. 1653, provides
for div. of est. among the ch. of both ws. ea. nam. and to eldest s. Jacob
doub. portion. The inv. was ret. when the will was pro. 28 June 1655.
WILLIAM, Topsfield, came, perhaps, in 1638, tho. by no means can I

agree with Farmer in mak. him freem. on 2 May of that yr. imply of course that he had come as early as 1637, when the prefix of resp. is wanting to this name next yr.; however it may be that he came not bef. 1639, in wh. yr. he had gr. of 200 acres at Ipswich, to the outlying farmers of wh. town, in 1641, at the place call. New Meadows, he began to preach. This was 8 or 9 yrs. bef. the incorp. by its present name, nor was a ch. allow. to be gather. there bef. 1645, as Winth. II. 254, tells, so that prob. K. was discourag. at least bef. 1648 we kn. he went home. Mather, putting him into his first classis of min. found no Christian name for him, yet as above twenty others of the same list show the same deficiency, we may be sure, he did not much inquire. Of this name, had, in 1834, eight been gr. at the var. N. E. coll. yet none at Harv.

KNOCKER, GEORGE, and THOMAS, misprint. thus in Geneal. Reg. III. 80 for Knower of Charlestown.

KNOLLYS, *HANSERD*, Dover, was b. it is said, 1598 at Cawkwell in Co. Lincoln, bred at the Univ. of Cambridge, ord. 29 June 1629, as a priest by the Bp. of Peterborough, renounc. the ch. of Eng. in 1636, and in 1638 came to N. E. tho. some Eng. books say a yr. earlier. On arr. at Boston, he was refus. permis. of resid. thro. suspic. of antinom. taint, so that he went to N. H. jurisdict. and in 1641 home, reach. London 24 Dec. See Winth. I. 326; II. 27. Yet Brook's Lives of the Purit. III. sub voce, with Crosby's Hist. of Bapt. I. 334, furnish. more favora. views of his charact. and even Mather's Magn. III. 6 refers to the d. of the "goodman in a good old age;" while in our times an Assoc. in Eng. of the Bapt. Commun. honors the confessor by adopt. the title of the Hanserd Knollys' Soc.

KNOTT, GEORGE, Sandwich 1637, perhaps rem. thither from Lynn, d. 1, bur. 3 May 1648, leav. wid. Martha, s. Samuel, and d. Martha, wh. he wish. Thomas Dunham to m. as in his nuncup. will of that date express. but she m. 18 Nov. 1650, Thomas Tobey. JAMES, a soldier on Conn. riv. 1676, under capt. Turner. RICHARD, Marblehead 1678, a surg. with prefix of resp.

KNOWER, GEORGE, Charlestown 1631, may have come in the fleet with Winth. liv. on the Malden side, d. 13 Feb. 1675, leav. prop. to w. Eliz. s. Jonathan, b. 1645, and d. Mary Mirable. He, or rather his w. (for the men were too timid) unit. in the petit. 28 Oct. 1651, to the Gen. Court, in favor of Rev. Mr. Matthews. Frothingham, 81, 85, 126. In his will of 3 Dec. 1674 he calls hims. a. 67 yrs. of age. He ment. in it ano. d. w. of Joses Bucknam. JONATHAN, Malden, freem. 1690, spell. Knohre, was s. of the preced. by w. Sarah, d. of John Winslow, had Sarah, b. July 1680; Jonathan, 1682; Thomas, 24 Nov. 1685, d. soon;

Eliz. 22 Apr. 1688, wh. d. in few wks.; John, 22 Mar. 1689; John, again, 22 May 1690; and Thomas, again, 28 Apr. 1694. JOSEPH, Mass. 1639. Felt. SAMUEL, Malden, by w. Eliz. had Samuel, b. 28 Dec. 1690; is in Geneal. Reg. VI. 336 an error, for the f.'s name is Kenny. This name is, also, falsely spell. Knowlton in Vol. X. 163 of the same valu. periodic. tho. it is right in Vol. VI. 336. THOMAS, Charlestown, perhaps br. of George, was punish. 1632, and went home I suppose, but came again in 1635, then call. 33 yrs. with Nell (as I judge the name print. Moll) 29; and Sarah, 7; thot. to be w. and d. in the Abigail, bear. the clk.'s designat. at the London custom-ho. Knore; and d. Nov. 1641. His inv. is on our rec. as that of Thomas Knocker.

KNOWLES, ‡ALEXANDER, a freem. of Mass. 7 Dec. 1636, whose resid. is unkn. to me; but in few yrs. he rem. to Fairfield, there was in good esteem; and was chos. an Assist. of the Col. of Conn. 1658. He d. Dec. 1663, in his will ment. s. John and Joshua, d. Eliz. Ford, w. of Thomas, and her five ch. and, perhaps, ano. d. at Milford. ELEAZUR, Stratford, s. of Thomas of New Haven, was one of the orig. project. of the new town of Woodbury, and of the early sett.; by w. Mary had Thomas, b. 26 Dec. 1683; Isaac, d. young; Mary, 22 Mar. 1687; Ann, 5 Jan. 1689; Samuel, 15 Apr. 1691; Isaac, again, 28 July 1696; and Eliz. 30 Mar. 1698; and d. 31 Jan. 1731. His wid. d. 24 Oct. 1732. HENRY, Warwick, on list of freem. 1655, in 1644, was of Portsmouth, R. I. and had, I suppose, m. a d. of Robert Potter of Warwick; and 1671 was in his 62d yr. 6 Jan. when, I judge, his will was made, by wh. he names s. John, William, and Henry, ds. Mary, wh. had m. 9 Nov. 1668, Moses Lippit, and Martha, w. of Samuel Eldredge; and at Kingstown, or into Narraganset, that disput. territory, prob. all the brs. and sis. were gather. HENRY, Kingstown, s. of the preced. m. Alice, d. of Thomas Fish, had no ch. but in his will of 1726, names sis. Martha Eldredge, and sev. neph. and nieces. JOHN, Watertown, the sec. min. of that town, was b. in Lincolnsh. bred at Magdalen Coll. Cambridge, where he was matric. a pensioner July 1620, sign. without final s. had his B. A. Jan. 1623, O. S. and M. A. 1627, with last letter, and was chos. a fellow of Catharine Hall, 9 July 1627, tho. Mather says, of Emanuel in his common heedless way. He was not prob. a sett. min. bef. com. over to us in Aug. 1638; he join. with the ch. at Boston 15 Aug. of next yr. hav. m. prob. in Eng. the wid. of Ephraim Davis; in Mar. foll. was dism. to go to aid Phillips at W. and there was ord. 9 Dec. 1640 as pastor, went on a mission, 1642, to Virginia, back next yr. was freem. 1650, and next yr. went home, and for some time preach. at Bristol, was silenc. by the act of 1662, and dur. the plague of London, 1665, was there with w. Eliz. On the d. of Presid. Chauncy, 1672, he was propos. to succeed him as head of Harv. Coll. tho. in Mather's Hist. we should not look to discov. any thing like it, for that writer is very sparing of his facts in the chap. devot. to this life, III. 216, and in the first classis insert. him without bapt. name. He had at W. by w. Eliz. Mary, b. 9 Apr. 1641; Eliz. 15 May 1643; and Hannah, wh. are found to be his ch. the first two by a gift in will of Edward How to ea. and Hannah, by her petit. aft. com. back hither in 1681, calls hers. his ch. represent. injury by desert. of her and her ch. by h. Benjamin Eyre, and pray. for divorce, 17 Nov. 1685. He d. 10 Nov. 1685, at gr. age. JOHN, Fairfield, s. of Alexander, freem. 1664, d. 1673, nam. in his will of 1 Nov. in that yr. ch. John, Joshua, Sarah, Eliz. and Rebecca, and refer. to his br. Joshua, as hav. tak. for his own testator's s. Joshua. JOHN, Eastham, s. of Richard, m. 28 Dec. 1670, Apphia, d. of Edward Bangs, had Edward, b. 7 Nov. 1671; John, 10 July 1673; and Deborah, 2 Mar. 1675. His wid. m. Joseph Atwood. JOHN, Hampton, took o. of alleg. Dec. 1678. JOHN, Warwick, eldest s. of the first Henry, had no ch. d. 16 Dec. 1716, had made his will Dec. 1714. JOSHUA, Fairfield, br. of John of the same, freem. 1658, was liv. in 1673. RICHARD, Cambridge 1638, by w. Ruth had James, b. 17 Nov. 1648; may be he that d. at Hampton 1 Feb. 1682. RICHARD, Plymouth, had Samuel, b. 17 Sept. 1651; rem. to Eastham, had Mehitable, 20 May 1653; Barbara, 28 Sept. 1656; and, perhaps, Mercy and others bef. or aft. Mercy m. 5 Feb. 1668, Ephraim Doane; Barbara m. 13 June 1677, Thomas Mayo. SAMUEL, Eastham, s. of the preced. m. Dec. 1679, Mercy, d. of Hon. John Freeman, had James, b. 13 Aug. 1680; Mercy, 13 Sept. 1681; Samuel, 15 Jan. 1683; Nathaniel, 15 May 1686; Richard, July 1688, Rebecca, Mar. 1690; John, Apr. 1692; Ruth, Nov. 1694; Cornelius, Oct. 1695; and Amos, 1702. THOMAS, New Haven 1645, was d. leav. Eleazer and Thomas, bef. 1648. His wid. Eliz. m. Nicholas Knill of Stratford. WILLIAM, Kingstown, s. of the first Henry of Warwick, d. 1727, and his wid. Alice d. 1730. His will, made 6 Oct. 1721, names w. Alice, ds. Rose Wilson, Martha Sherman, Mary Chase, and Alice Screvin, and s. Henry, William, Daniel, Robert, and John.

KNOWLTON, ABRAHAM, Salisbury 1677, prob. s. of the first John. BENJAMIN, Springfield, m. 1676, Hannah Mirick, had Mary, b. 1677; Benjamin, 1679; Sarah, 1682; Mercy, 1685, d. young; Joseph, 1687; and Mercy, again, posthum. He d. 19 Aug. 1690. JOHN, Ipswich, freem. 2 June 1641, d. a. 1654, leav. w. Margaret, ch. John, Abraham, and Eliz. JOHN, Ipswich, s. of the preced. freem. 1680, liv. then at Wenham. JONATHAN, Malden, by w. Sarah had Eliz. b. 22 Apr. 1688. NATHANIEL, Ipswich, freem. 1683, was a man of conseq. SAMUEL,

Wenham, freem. 1680. THOMAS, Ipswich 1648, br. of the first John, m. 24 Nov. 1668, Hannah Green, was deac. and prison-keep. d. 3 Apr. 1692. WILLIAM, Hingham 1635, was, Felt thot. the bricklayer, wh. d. at Ipswich 1644, found. of a respecta. fam. and in my opin. the Hingham name, giv. Nolton, by Lincoln, means, that same Norton, wh. was of Ipswich.

KNOX, JOHN, Watertown, by w. Hannah had Sarah, bapt., 26 Dec. 1686; John, 3 Feb. 1689; and James, 17 May 1690.

KOLDOM, the older spell. of Coldham, wh. see.

KOSTLO, JOHN, . . . by w. Sarah had Sarah, b. 8 Mar. 1663; and John, 6 Aug. 1666.

KOWDALE, EDWARD. See Cowdall.

LACOCK, LAWRENCE, Boston 1644, ship carpenter, had w. Alice.

LACY, LAWRENCE, Andover, had Lawrence, b. 1683. Abbot, 39. He was "the first person she afflict." as poor Eliz. Johnson was driv. to confess. in the sad delus. of 1692. MORGAN, Saco a. 1660.

LADD, DANIEL, Ipswich, came in the Mary and John, 1634, by tradit. call. s. of Nathaniel, was one of the first townsmen of Salisbury, a. 1639, but, perhaps, not long there, and bec. perman. inhab. of Haverhill aft. b. of one or two ch. By w. Ann he had Eliz. b. 11 Dec. 1640; Daniel, 26 Sept. 1642; Lydia, 8 June 1645; the three being on rec. at S.; Mary, 14 Feb. 1647; Nathaniel, 10 Mar. 1652; Ezekiel, 16 Sept. 1654; and Sarah, 4 Nov. 1657. Both he and his w. were liv. 1678. Eliz. m. at Haverhill, 14 May 1663, Nathaniel Smith. Part of the fam. tradit. that Nathaniel, f. of Daniel was from Dartmouth, in Devon, may be reasona. eno. at least it bears no inherent improb. as the more fondly desir. clause of the story does, that he was one of the first comers to Plymouth; for that phrase belongs only to those wh. arr. in the yrs. 1620, 1, and 3, of wh. was no. Ladd; and minute inquiry even shows, there was nobody in either of the three passeng. lists with that bapt. name. * DANIEL, Haverhill, eldest s. of the preced. m. 24 Nov. 1668, Lydia Singletary, was rep. 1693, and 4. EZEKIEL, Haverhill, br. of the preced. took o. of fidel. 28 Nov. 1677. JOHN, m. at Woburn, 12 June 1678, Eliz. Fifield. JOSEPH, Portsmouth, R. I. whose will of 1669 names ch. Joseph, William, Daniel, Mary, and Sarah. NATHANIEL, Exeter, s. of the first Daniel, erron. said to be from Scotland, or Devonshire (perhaps tradit. thot. these adjoin. towns), m. 1678, Eliz. Gilman, was mort. wound. 11 Aug. 1691 at Maquoit, left w. and seven ch. His gr.s. capt. Daniel fell in bat. with the Ind. 12 Aug. 1746 at Concord, N. H. SAMUEL, Ipswich, s. of the first Daniel, m. a d. of George Corliss.

LAHORNE, ROWLAND, Plymouth 1636, Charlestown 1649, had w. Flora.

LAIGHTON, or LEIGHTON, DANIEL, Newport, perhaps s. of John of the same, by w. Rebecca had Thomas, b. 2 Mar. 1666; Daniel, 28 Oct. 1667; Rebecca, 24 Feb. 1669; Jeremy, 21 Dec. 1670; Adam, 5 Nov. 1672; Eliz. 12 Mar. 1674; and Mary, 31 Aug. 1675. EZEKIEL, Rowley 1691, s. of Richard. GEORGE, Portsmouth, R. I. 1638, freem. there 1655; m. Eliz. d. of Thomas Hazard of the same. JOHN, Ipswich 1648, may have been ten·yrs. bef. at Newport. JOHN, Kittery, s. of William, m. ·13 June 1686, Honor, d. prob. of the first Tobias Langdon, had Eliz. ḅ. 30 May 1691; Mary, 7 May 1693; William, 9 Sept. 1696; John, 27 May 1699; Tobias, 17 Nov. 1701; and Samuel, 22 Nov. 1707; was sheriff of the Co. of York, and d. 10 Nov. 1724, and his wid. d. 21 Nov. 1737, in 75th yr. JOHN, Rowley 1691, s. of Richard. RICHARD, Rowley 1643. His will, of 1682, names ch. John, Ezekiel, Mary, and Sarah, of wh. Mary m. prob. Francis Spofford of the same. SAMUEL, Lynn, prob. s. of Thomas, m. 14 Feb. 1680, Sarah, d. perhaps of the first Samuel Graves, had Eliz. b. 30 Oct. 1681; Samuel, 10 Feb. 1683, d. at two days; and, perhaps, others. * THOMAS, Lynn, freem. 14 Mar. 1639, rep. 12 yrs. betw. 1646 and 61, had Thomas, Margaret, Samuel, Rebecca, and Eliz. THOMAS, Saco 1645, had John, wh. m. 1665, Martha, d. of Robert Booth. Folsom. THOMAS, Dover 1648, d. 22 Jan. 1672, in his 68th yr. leav. only s. Thomas; Mary, wh. m. Thomas Roberts, jr.; Eliz. wh. m. John Hall; and Sarah. His wid. Joanna m. 16 July 1673, Job Clements, outliv. him and d. 15 Jan. 1704, in 88th yr. THOMAS, Portsmouth, R. I. 1638, freem. there 1655, perhaps was br. of George. THOMAS, Dover, only s. of Thomas of the same, freem. 1672, m. a d. of Hatevil Nutter, had Thomas, Eliz. and John; and d. bef. 1711. Eliz. m. Philip Cromwell, and, next, Philip Chesley. THOMAS, Lynn, perhaps s. of the first Thomas, freem. 1680, m. 28 Dec. 1670, Sarah Redknap, had Thomas, b. 15 Oct. 1671; Sarah, 16 Sept. 1673; Joseph, 14 Oct. 1675; and Margaret, 13 June. 1677; his w. d. 26 Feb. 1680, and he m. 2 Dec. foll. Hannah Silsbee or Silsby, wh. might easi. be rec. for Libby. WILLIAM, Kittery, m. bef. 1650, Catharine, d. of Nicholas Frost, had John, b. May 1661; and Eliz. a. 1663, wh. d. young; and he d. Sept. 1666. His inv. of 6 June foll. was of £308, 16, 6; and the wid. m. Joseph Hammond, outliv. him, and d. 1 Aug. 1715. One Laighton, common. in the earlier day, spelt conform. to sound, Layton, was k. by the Ind. near Swanzey, on the first hour of outbreak of Philip's war, 24 June 1675. In our day the name is usual. Laughton or Leighton, and it is very difficult to trace.

LAKE, HENRY, Salem 1649, a currier, perhaps the same wh. was of Dorchester 1658, br. of Thomas of the same. JAMES, Mass. 1647. Felt. Perhaps only a trans. one. JOHN, Boston 1643, a tailor, freem.

1644, by w. Mary, sis. of Matthew and Richard Coy, had Caleb, b. 27 May, bapt. 1 June 1645, but prob. d. young; and the f. d. 6 Aug. 1677, leav. wid. Lucy, and gave her some of his est. resid. to John and Mary, ch. of his br. but ment. no ch. of his own. His will of 4 of the same mo. as Hammond in his Diary tells, was writ. by Richard Sharp of Boston, wh. d. the next day, so one day bef. testat. and Lake's wid. d. 13 May foll. JOHN, Boston, perhaps neph. of the preced. d. 1691, unm. LANCELOT, Boston 1695, a physician, of wh. nothing is kn. but that he m. 6 May 1708, wid. Catharine Child, and 3 Mar. foll. in his will, pro. 3 Oct. 1715, gave her all his est. He d. 17 Sept. and, I presume, it was a doubt in the mind of the wid. whether the est. would amount to the few shillings of expense. His gr.stone was lately found in the cemetery of King's Chapel. THOMAS, Dorchester, freem. 2 June 1641, d. 27 Oct. 1678; his w. Alice, wh. was ten yrs. older, hav. d. 7 days bef. Oft. the name was writ. yet prob. not by hims. Like, or Leake. His will, made aft. d. of his w. names no ch. but gives his prop. to br. Henry, and equal. to childr. of br. H. exc. that Thomas should have £5 more. THOMAS, Boston, where he own. lds. bef. his resid. an emin. merch. came from London to New Haven, there m. Mary, d. of Stephen Goodyear, the dep.-gov. of that col. had Stephen, b. 13 Feb. 1650; Mary, 27 July 1653, d. in few wks.; Thomas, 9 Feb. 1657; Mary, again, 1 May 1659, d. soon; Edward, 28 June 1661, d. soon; Edward, again, 15 July 1662, d. soon; Ann, 12 Oct. 1663; John, 22 Feb. 1666; Nathaniel, 18 July 1668; Rebecca, 6 July 1670; and Sarah, 14 Sept. 1671. He purch. 1654, from John Richards, half of Arousick isl. in the Kennebeck, and many yrs. held a trad. house there, was freem. 1671, selectman, had large transact. with the Ind. by wh. he was k. 14 or 16 Aug. 1676, being on a visit. He had made his will dur. a sickness so long bef. as 27 Jan. 1664, from wh. we learn, that he was br. of John, that his w. had sis. Lydia, and not much more. His est. was large; and his s. Thomas enjoy. it at London, where he d. 22 May 1711, at the Middle Temple; and his d. Ann, w. of Rev. John Cotton at Hampton, m. 17 Aug. 1686, next, of Rev. Increase Mather, wh. she surv. d. at Brookline, 29 Mar. 1737. WILLIAM, Salem 1665, a cooper, perhaps s. of Henry, allow. 1674, to sell beer and cider, as was his wid. Ann in 1681. Of Mrs. Margaret L. at New London 1646, and many yrs. aft. at Ipswich [see Geneal. Reg. VI. 165], much hard labor has been expend. by Miss Caulkins to learn her derivat. and m. but in vain. She d. says Felt, 1672, leav. two ds. Hannah, w. of John Gallop; and Martha, w. of Thomas Harris.

LAKEMAN, * WILLIAM, rep. of the Isle of Shoals 1692, says Farmer.

LAKIN, JOHN, Reading, br. prob. younger of William, was driv. from Groton, I suppose, dur. the Ind. war, but had, by w. Mary, Sarah, b. 4

Feb. 1662; William, 12 May 1664; Abigail, 13 Mar. 1667; Joseph, 14 Apr. 1670; Benjamin, 6 Nov. 1672; and Josiah, 14 Sept. 1675; and prob. went back to G. where he was ens. and had been of the first sett. d. 21 Mar. 1697. His f. was s. of William, and d. in Eng. says Butler, and his wid. m. William Martin; but his name is not giv. Three of the s. perhaps all, had fam. He had a d. Mary, elder than any of these ch. m. 18 July 1674, Henry Willard; and Sarah m. a. 1691, Benjamin Willard. Thomas, is, by Farmer, mistak. for the foll. William, Groton, freem. 1670, d. 10 Dec. 1672, in 90th or 91st yr. Tradit. more credib. than common makes him bring the gr.ch. William and John, perhaps at the same time with William Martin of Reading, wh. m. their mo. yet it does not tell the name of their f. nor whether the mo. m. in Eng. to Martin, nor whether the gr.f. had w. on this side of the water, nor when or whence he came. Shattuck, 95, borrows the tradit. of Butler in Hist. of G. 273, that he emigr. in his old age from Redington. But this must be mistake, as there is no such place in Eng. Prob. the parish of Ridlington is meant. That is a small parish in the hundred of Martinsley, Co. Rutland, 2 and ¼ ms. from Uppingham; or more likely the native seat of the Lakins may have been the smaller parish of the same name in the hundred of Tunstead, Co. Norfk. 4 and ¼ ms. from North Walsham. If he came with Martin his old age should not be thot. of; for he pass. above thirty yrs. here. William, Reading, br. of John, by w. Lydia, d. of the first Abraham Brown, had William, b. 6 May 1655; John, 3 Jan. 1658; and Jonathan, 28 June 1661; rem. to Groton and had Abraham, 10 Jan. 1664, d. soon; William, May 1665; Abraham, again, 11 Sept. 1667; and Elias, 8 Jan. 1669; was freem. 1672, unless (wh. is not prob.) it was he, not his gr.f. in 1670; lieut. 1673; and d. 22 Feb. 1700. Great list of descend. appears in Butler's valua. Hist. of G.

LAMB, ABEL, Cambridge, perhaps s. of Thomas of Roxbury, in the employm. of William French, was bur. 16 Oct. 1649. ABIEL, Roxbury, s. of Thomas, was one of brave capt. Johnson's comp. Dec. 1675, had bapt. there s. Harbottle, 28 Feb. 1675; Abiel, b. 23 Dec. bapt. 4 Jan. 1680; Jonathan, b. 11 Nov. 1682; and Samuel, bapt. 12 Apr. 1685; but I kn. not his w. and suspect, that he liv. over the line of the town, for the town rec. has not one of these b. He rem. to Framingham, then pt. of Sudbury, a. 1695, was constable 1700, selectman 1701, and d. bef. 1710. CALEB, Roxbury, mariner, br. of the preced. m. 30 June 1669, Mary, d. of Joseph Wise, had Thomas, b. 26 Apr. bapt. 15 May 1670; Caleb, 29, bapt. 31 Dec. 1671; Joseph, 11, bapt. 16 Nov. 1673; Mary, 13 Apr. 1678, d. soon; Jeremiah, 24, bapt. 25 May 1679; Mary, again, 7, bapt. 13 Mar. 1681; Eliz. bapt. 4 Mar. 1683 (but the town rec. has, erron. I suppose, John, b. 5 Apr. 1683); John,

29, bapt. 30 Mar. 1684; and Eunice, bapt. 22 Nov. 1685, of wh. is no
ment. in the town rec. that supplies Huldah, b. 31 Jan. 1688. He
d. Barry thinks, a. 1697. DANIEL, Springfield, prob. s. of John, freem.
1690, had a fam. and d. 1692. EDWARD, Watertown 1633, had w.
Margaret; ch. Hannah, b. 27 Dec. 1633; Mary, 10 Sept. 1635, d.
soon; Samuel, 3 Apr. 1637; Mary, again, 30 Apr. 1639; John, and
Increase, tw. 13 Feb. 1640, d. both in a wk.; and rem. to Boston, there
had Eliz. bapt. 27 Aug. 1648, a. 11 days old. His wid. m. Samuel
Allen. Coll. Rec. III. 216 and IV. pt. I. p. 31. JOHN, Springfield
1653, prob. s. of Thomas, came 1630, with his f. had John, b. 1654, d.
soon; John, and Thomas, tw. 1655, of wh. John d. at 21 yrs.; Joanna,
1657; Sarah, 1660; Samuel, 1663; Daniel, 1666; Mary, 1669, d.
young; Abigail, 1670; and Joshua, 1674. He for sec. or third w. in
1688 m. Lydia, wid. of John Norton, wh. bef. was wid. of Lawrence
Bliss, and d. of deac. Samuel Wright, and d. 28 Sept. 1690. His ds.
Joanna, wh. m. Samuel Stebbins, and Sarah d. aft. m. but bef. him;
Thomas, and Joshua, prob. rem. to Stonington; at least they at S. have
no ch. on rec.; Samuel and Daniel liv. at S. JOHN, New London
1664–9, was offer. in the latter yr. to be made freem. in Nov. 1677
lost a s. by being struck by a mill-wheel, as told in Bradstreet's Journ.
He perhaps was in 1712 in that pt. made Groton. JOSHUA, Roxbury,
s. of Thomas, m. Mary, d. of John Alcock, had Joshua, bapt. 7 Mar.
1675; Dorothy, 8 June 1679; George, 27 Mar. 1681; John, 22 Apr.
1683, d. soon; Eliz. b. 2 Mar. 1684, d. soon; John, again, 3, bapt. 8
Feb. 1685, d. at four mos.; and Samuel, 9, bapt. 11 Apr. 1686. He
was a merch. purch. of Sir William Berkeley, lands at Roanoke in
Virg. wh. he sold 1677, and d. 23 Sept. 1690. His wid. d. 9 Oct. 1700.
Dorothy, m. Rev. Dudley Woodbridge, first min. of Simsbury, and, also,
his successor, Rev. Timothy Woodbridge. SAMUEL, Springfield, freem.
1690. THOMAS, Roxbury, came, 1630, in the fleet. with Winth. brot.
w. Eliz. and two ch. Thomas, and John, req. adm. 19 Oct. had Samuel,
b. in Oct. bapt. that yr. at Dorchester, bef. the ch. at R. was gather. and
was freem. 18 May foll. had Abel, fourth s. b. Oct. 1633; Decline, the
first d. b. Apr. 1637, wh. m. 7 Dec. 1666, Stephen Smith; and Benjamin, the sixth ch. Oct. 1639, d. soon, as did his mo. both bur. on 28 Nov.
Barry calls this last ch. of Eliz. Caleb; but the ch. rec. is copious, and
explicit to the contra. The town rec. said Benjamin, b. 27 Nov. but a
modern hand eras. that, and wrongful. ins. Caleb. Such violat. of the
vestal purity of rec. is less rare than might be expect. He m. 16 July
1640, Dorothy Harbottle, " a godly sis. of the ch." had Caleb, b. 9 Apr.
1641; Joshua, 27, bapt. 28 Nov. 1642; Mary, bapt. 29 Sept. 1644; and
Abiel, 2 Aug. 1646. The f. d. 28 Mar. preced. and apostle Eliot notes

(on the bapt.) his "not long afore leav. his childr. to the Lord to be their f." and his wid. m. 2 Feb. 1652, Thomas Hawley. See Winth. II. 339, 40. Mary m. Thomas Swan. WILLIAM, Boston 1668, d. 1685.

LAMBERT, EZRA, Salem, fisherman, tak. by the French 1689. FRANCIS, Rowley, freem. 13 May 1640, by w. Jane had John; Ann; brot. from Eng. prob. with other ch. and here had Jonathan, b. 1639; Gershom, 1643; and Thomas, 1645; and d. 1648. His will of 26 Sept. 1647 names all but Thomas. GERSHOM, Rowley, s. of Francis, prob. d. unm. his will, early in 1664, nam. no w. nor ch. but only brs. John, Thomas, Thomas Wilson, aunt Rogers, sis. Ann Wilson, and some other relat. beside br. Thomas Nelson, made excor. GERSHOM, Stonington, possib. s. of Francis, m. Deborah, d. of John Frink, had John, b. 10 May 1687; perhaps rem. to New London, there had Gershom, bapt. 14 Aug. 1692. JESSE, Milford 1680, m. 10 May 1688, Deborah, d. of William Fowler the sec. had Rachel, whose date of b. is not seen, tho. she must have been young, if m. (as the Hist. of Ancient Woodbury tells) 30 Dec. 1703; Martha, wh. d. at 20 yrs. unm.; Richard, d. young; Sarah; Jesse, b. 20 Apr. 1693;. Deborah, d. unm.; Eliz. and David, 1700. He had sec. w. Joanna, and d. 1718. Much idle tradit. and wild geneal. accomp. the introd. of this name in Cothren, 607. JOHN, Lynn, a fisherman, a. 1644, Salem 1663, at Lynn again till d. 28 Oct. 1676. JOHN, Saybrook, m. 15 Jan. 1668, Mary Lews. JOHN, Hingham, rem. says Deane, to Scituate, there had John, b. 1693. MICHAEL, Lynn 1647, had w. Eliz. wh. d. Oct. 1657, and he m. 1659, Elinor, wid. of Strong Furnell, had Michael, and Mary, b. 23 Jan. 1662; and, perhaps, by third w. Moses, 27 Apr. 1673; and d. 18 Aug. 1676. MICHAEL, Stonington, perhaps s. of the preced. m. 19 Apr. 1688, Eliz. Starke. RICHARD, Salem 1637, had then gr. of ld. and, perhaps, d. Esther, wh. m. 8 Oct. 1659, Jeremiah Bootman. RICHARD, Salem, perhaps s. of the preced. not possib. the same, was k. by the Ind. 18 Sept. 1675, at Bloody brook, with the flower of Essex, under capt. Lothrop. ROBERT, Boston, came from Dartmouth, in Devon, it is said, was among the found. of the first ch. of Bapt. in Boston 1665. THOMAS, Dorchester 1637, may be ill. spell. of Lombard. THOMAS, Rowley, s. of Francis, m. Edna Northend, had Thomas, b. 1678; Nathan, 1681; and two ds. WILLIAM, came in the Susan and Ellen, from London, 1635, aged 26; but where he sat down is unkn.

LAMBERTON, GEORGE, New Haven 1641, prob. merch. from London, was one of the chief inhabs. employ. 1643 in project. a sett. at Delaware, but resist. by the Swedes, wh. vindica. their right; by w. Margaret had Mercy, bapt. 17 Jan. 1641; Desire, 13 Mar. 1642; and Obedience, 9 Feb. 1645; went in Jan. 1646 for Eng. in the sh. of 80 tons, " cut out of the ice 3 miles," with Mr. Gregson, the w. of dep.-gov. Goodyear, and others, wh. was never heard of. Johnson, in his W. W. P. and Winth. II. 266, well relate the matter; but Mather, Magn. I. 25, has prov. the gr. superiority result. from tradit. of a story told 50 yrs. aft. to the contempo. narrat. By tak. the " dimensions " of the sh. in the air, Mather's worthy corresp. could make her a. 150 tons. His readers admit, that benefits of similar measure the ecclesiast. hist. gain. in his everyday life. He left wid. wh. m. dep.-gov. Stephen Goodyear, and, perhaps, ds. Eliz. wh. m. 1654, Daniel Sillevant; Desire, m. 1659, Thomas Cooper, jr. of Springfield; Hannah m. Samuel Wells; and, next, Col. John Allyn; and Obedience, wh. m. 1676, Samuel Smith. Yet it is not sure, that these were his ds. and possib. ano. fam. may have come, for at Jamaica, L. I. was a THOMAS, 1686.

LAMBSHEAD, THOMAS, Marblehead 1666. Felt. Sis. L. was of the sec. ch. in Boston 1673.

LAMPHEAR. See Landfear.

LAMPREY, LAMPHREY, LAMPER, or LAMPRELL, HENRY, Boston 1,652, a cooper, by w. Julian had Mary, b. 8 Mar. 1653; and Mary, again, 19 Mar. 1657; but elder ch. he had, perhaps bef. com. Henry, Daniel, and Eliz. He prob. rem. to Hampton, or Exeter, perhaps both in differ. times, was of gr. jury 1684, when was, also, a David L. there. In 1678 he, and Benjamin, and Daniel took the o. of alleg. HENRY, the s. not the f. I suppose, m. 24 July 1686, Eliz. Mitchell.

LAMSON, BARNABAS, Cambridge 1635, had brot. Joseph, prob. other ch. perhaps all those nam. in his will, Geneal. Reg. II. 104, wh. distrib. them to near friends in the ch.: Mary, Sarah, Barnaby, Martha, and Joseph. He d. bef. 1642. Mary m. Philip Cook; Joseph was of C. 1658. BARNABAS, Salisbury 1652, is thot. to be the s. of the preced. JOHN, Ipswich, freem. 27 May 1674; if I may venture to assume, that the name print. in Col. Rec. V. 536, as likewise Mr. Paige's list, Lumpson, is wrong. JONATHAN, New Haven, s. of Thomas, was a propr. 1685. JOSEPH, Malden, s. perhaps, more prob. gr.s. of the first Barnabas, serv. in Philip's war, Mar. 1676, then aged 18, under capt. Turner, on Conn. riv. was freem. 1690; by w. Eliz. Mitchell, m. 12 Dec. 1679, wh. d. 10 June 1703, had Eliz. b. 24 Oct. 1680; Joseph, 28 July 1684; John, 15 Apr. 1687; Eliz. again, 29 Aug. 1689; William, 25 Oct. 1694; Caleb, 12 June 1697; and Hannah, 9 Oct. 1699. He had sec. w. Hannah, wid. of Thomas Welsh; and a third, Dorothy Mousal, outliv. him. His will, of 16 July 1722, was produc. 19 Sept. foll. SAMUEL, Reading, among early sett. was freem. 1677, d. 1692; where Samuel jr. might be his s. THOMAS, New Haven, d. 1664, in his will names only two ch. Jonathan, wh. was bapt. 2 Mar. 1645, and Zubah, wh. m. 5 May 1670, Joshua Wills of Windsor. WILLIAM, Ipswich, freem. 17 May 1637, d. 1 Feb. 1659, leav. w. Sarah, and eight ch. whose names are not seen. His wid. m. 10 Apr. 1661, Thomas Hartshorn of Reading. Of this name, that oft. in early rec. has its mid. letter *b*, or *p*, two had, in 1834, been gr. at Harv. and four at other N. E. coll.

LANCASTER, or LANKASTER, HENRY, Dover 1634, testif. in 1682, that he kn. Walford of Portsmouth 50 yrs. bef. It may be the same as Langstaff. JOSEPH, Salisbury, by w. Mary had Joseph, b. 25 Feb. 1666; Mary, 8 Sept. 1667 ; and Thomas, 15 Mar. 1669 ; rem. to Amesbury, freem. 1690. WALTER, Fairfield 1654, had lds. perhaps never occup. but rem. soon. WILLIAM, Providence, did not rem. in 1676.

LANCLON, easi. mistak. for Langdon, wh. may be refer. to.

LAND, EDWARD, Duxbury 1666.

LANDDIER, CHARLES, Dover 1672. It seems an unus. name, but may not be impossib.

LANDER, JOHN, Portsmouth or Kittery 1639, a fisherman, d. bef. 1646. Belkn. I. 28. THOMAS, Lynn, came in the Abigail, from London, 1635, aged 22 ; rem. 1637 to Sandwich; there had John, b. 2 Jan. 1651. WILLIAM, Marshfield 1643, d. 1648. It seems to be oft. spell. with a *u* in the first syl.

LANDFEAR, or LAMPHEAR, GEORGE, Westerly, R. I. 1669, had Richard, Shadrach, John, Theodosius, Seth, and ds. of wh. one was w. of Eber Crandall; Mary, w. of Peter Button ; Sarah, wh. m. 21 Mar. 1708, James Covey; and Eliz. wh. m. 12 Jan. 1710, James Pendleton ; and he d. 6 Oct. 1731. RICHARD, Westerly 1679, perhaps s. of the preced. by w. Mary had Amie, b. 22 June 1715; Lucy, 9 July 1718 ; Esther, 21 Feb. 1721 ; Zerviah, 12 Oct. 1724; and Jerusha, 25 Jan. 1727. SETH, Westerly, br. of the preced. by w. Sarah had Eliz. b. 10 Aug. 1715 ; and Elisha. SHADRACH, Westerly, br. of the preced. m. 15 June 1696, Experience Reed, had Oliver, Ann, Experience, Prudence, Mary, Solomon, John, and Hezekiah. THEODOSIUS, Westerly, br. of the preced. m. 22 Jan. 1708, Rachel Covey, had Theodosius, b. 31 Jan. 1709 ; James, 22 Nov. 1710; Joshua, 23 Nov. 1712; Abigail, 27 Mar. 1715; Susanna, 14 Dec. 1716 ; Nathaniel, 22 Mar. 1718 ; Mary, 14 Dec. 1721 ; Samuel, 23 Dec. 1723; Stephen, 5 Feb. 1726 ; Jabez, 25 Mar. 1731 ; and Joseph, 20 Sept. 1736.

LANDON, JAMES, Boston, or Charlestown, memb. of the first Bapt. ch. 1670. Mr. Wyman thinks this name was Lowden.

LANE, AMBROSE, Portsmouth 1648–50, then call. (as from its orig. settlem. it had been), Strawberry bank, shipmaster, was, perhaps, br. of Sampson, wh. mortga. to him that yr. all his prop. for £1,000. ANDREW, Hingham 1635, s. of William, was call. feltmaker, by w. Tryphena had Mary, Abigail, and Andrew, all bapt. in Aug. 1646; John, 30 Jan. 1648; and with this s. I pause to expose many errors. To him is giv. s. Samuel, b. 16 Mar. 1678 by w. Mehitable Hobart. Sorry am I to obs. that in the Geneal. Reg. XIII. 91, the statem. that "John, bapt. in Norton, 30 June 1648, m. Mehitable Hobart," labors under such incongru. It says that Andrew and Tryphena had seven childr. when the names of nine are kn. No s. Samuel had he, no Mehitable Hobart can be found for that John to m. and he could not be bapt. at Norton that day, for the town was not begun to be sett. till many yrs. aft. nor could he be bapt. anywhere else in N. E. on 30 June 1648, wh. was not Sunday, but Friday. Beside those four ch. we find Ephraim, bapt. Feb. 1650; Deborah, 20 June 1652; Joshua, 20 Aug. 1654; Caleb, 17 July 1657; and Hannah, 17 Oct. 1658; and he d. 1 May 1675. His wid. d. 2 June 1707, "a. 95 yrs. of age," says the town rec. All the ds. were m. Abigail m. perhaps, John Low, first, but certain. 27 Dec. 1665, Daniel Stodder, and Deborah m. 30 Dec. 1674, William Sprague; but whether the date of Mary, wh. m. William Orcutt, were earlier or later in m. than her sis. Abigail, is uncert.; and Hannah m. Thomas with a surname utterly illegib. in the orig. and plain. false in the copy of Prob. reg. All the s. and the hs. of the ds. gave, 27 July 1675, to their mo. acquit. of the est. of dec. for her life, wh. has signa. of each, but Orcutt's is by ⊙ mark, and the h. of the youngest d. might as well have used a bear's claw to write his. ANDREW, Hingham, s. of the preced. freem. 1677, by w. Eliz. had John, b. 13 Oct. 1673; Eliz. 20 Nov. 1675; Andrew, 8 Feb. 1678; Bethia, 10 Aug. 1680; Isaac, 8 Apr. 1683; Jonathan, 27 Dec. 1685; and Solomon, 12 Jan. 1694, wh. d. at 21 yrs. He d. 4 Dec. 1717, and his wid. d. 12 Nov. 1727. DANIEL, New London 1652, m. Catharine, wid. of Thomas Doxy, rem. 1661 to L. I. was one of the grantees of Brookhaven 1666. EBENEZER, Hingham, s. of George, m. 27 Dec. 1688, Hannah, whose surname is uncert. had Sarah, b. 24 Dec. 1692; Ebenezer, 11 Dec. 1694; Peter, 25 May 1697; and Susanna. He had serv. in brave capt. Johnson's comp. in Philip's war. EDWARD, Boston, a merch. came in the Speedwell, from London 1656, aged 36, hav. bot. 1651, est. of Robert Harding, m. 11 Dec. 1657, Ann, d. of Benjamin Keayne, had Ann, b. 5 Oct. 1660, d. 27 June foll.; and Edward, 20 Feb. 1662. He next yr. sold est. at Malden to Richard Dexter, and liv. not long aft. His wid. m. Nicholas Paige. EPHRAIM, Hingham, s. of Andrew, serv. in Philip's war, with Johnson's comp. m. late in life, 20 Feb. 1701, Susanna, d. of Ephraim Huet of Scituate, had Ephraim, b. July 1703; and his w. d. 15 May 1708. For sec. w. he took, 29 Dec. foll. Eliz. youngest d. of Jeremiah Beal, and had Jeremiah, 8 June 1710; d. 1 Dec. 1715, and his wid. d.

30 July foll. GEORGE, Hingham 1635, br. of Andrew, b. in Eng. by
w. Sarah had Sarah, bapt. Mar. 1638; Hannah, 24 Feb. 1639; Josiah,
23 May 1641; Susanna, 23 June 1644; John; Eliz.; Ebenezer, bapt.
25 Aug. 1650; Mary, b. 11, bapt. 17 Apr. 1653; and Peter, 23, bapt.
27 July 1656; freem. 1672, d. 4 June 1689. His wid. d. 26 Mar.
1696. Sarah m. 31 Oct. 1655, James Lewis of Barnstable; Hannah
m. Dec. 1665, Thomas Humphrey of Dover; Susanna m. 23 Dec.
1665, William Roberts; Eliz. m. Walter Pore; and Mary m. an Ellis.
GEORGE, Portsmouth, freem. 1672. ISAAC, Middletown 1669, m. 5
Nov. of that yr. Hannah, only d. of Nathaniel Brown, had Hannah,
b. 27 Mar. 1671; Eliz. 24 Jan. 1673; Eleanor, 9 Apr. 1674; Isaac,
and John, tw. 22 Dec. 1675, both d. soon; John and Sarah, tw. 28 Feb.
1677, both d. soon; Sarah, again, 29 Sept. 1678; Samuel, 24 Nov.
1679, d. soon; John, again, 10 Jan. 1681; Nathaniel, 29 June 1682, d.
soon; Isaac, 5 Nov. 1683; Benoni, 13 Feb. 1685, d. at 4 yrs.; Mary,
25 Apr. 1687, d. soon; Mary, again, 20 Aug. 1688, d. soon; Abigail, 8
Apr. 1690, d. very soon; and Nathaniel, again, 28 Mar. 1694, d. at 8
yrs.; and the f. wh. in Oct. 1704 call. his age 65, d. 18 July 1711.
JAMES, Boston, carpent. had come from Plymouth in O. E. with s.
Francis, not long bef. mak. his will, 2 Oct. 1662, pro. same mo. Such
is the opin. natural. deriv. from refer. to his s. James and w. Dousabel,
remain. at home, and subseq. action of Ct. *JOB, Rehoboth 1644,
was in Eng. in June 1647, when his kinsm. Thomas Howell, of Marsh-
field, made his will, nam. him to be excor. but he declin. that trust, yet
aft. some yrs. came back, and sett. at Malden, freem. 1656, had by w.
Sarah, wh. d. 19 May 1659, Rebecca, b. Apr. 1658, d. young. He m.
Sept. 1660, Hannah, or Ann, d. of Rev. John Reyner, had John, b.
Oct. 1661; Ann, Sept. 1662, d. in few wks.; Jemima, 19 Aug. 1666;
Dorothy, 24 July 1669; and Rebecca, again, 6 Apr. 1674; rem. to
Billerica, was rep. 1676, 9, and for Malden 1685, and under the new
chart. in 1692. His will is of 28 Sept. 1696, and he d. 23 Aug. foll.
His wid. d. 30 Apr. 1704. From the will we learn that he had other
ds. Mary, w. of William Avery, wh. with ch. Mary and Sarah, are
rememb.; Eliz. w. of Robert Avery (m. 13 Apr. 1676), with her d.
Rachel; ano. Ann, w. of James Foster of Dorchester; and Sarah, w. of
Samuel Fitch; and that Jemima m. Matthew Whipple; and Dorothy
m. 24 Nov. 1693, Edward Sprague. JOHN, Milford 1640, perhaps, or
soon aft. had good est. freem. 1665, d. 1669, leav. will made that yr.
JOHN, Boston 1674, cordwainer. JOHN, Hingham, s. of George, 1674,
carpent. m. 18 June 1674, Mehitable Hobart, whose f. is unkn. had
Samuel, b. 16 Mar. 1678; Priscilla, 15 Mar. 1680; Mary, 3 Apr.
1682; and Asaph, 21 July 1685. JOHN, Hingham, s. of Andrew,

m. 21 Jan. 1680, Sarah, d. of Jeremiah Beal, had Sarah, b. 12
Dec. 1683; Hannah, 22 Aug. 1685; Rachel, 23 May 1688; and
Susanna, 4 Dec. 1690. His w. d. 13 Dec. 1693, and he m. 18 Nov.
1697, Tabitha, d. of John Stodder, had Tabitha, 11 Sept. 1698; and
his w. d. 2 Mar. 1707; and he d. 12 Mar. 1730. JOHN, Falmouth
bef. 1690. * JOHN, Billerica, only s. of Job of the same, m. 20 Mar.
1680, Susanna, d. of the sec. John Whipple of Ipswich, had Susanna, b.
24 Feb. 1682; Job, 19 Dec. 1884, d. in few wks.; Mary, 15 May
1686; Jemima, 27 June 1688, d. in few days; Job, again, 22 June
1689; John, 20 Oct. 1691; Martha, 1 Oct. 1694; James, 12 Aug.
1696; and Joseph, 18 Feb. 1699; freem. 1690, was major, rep. 1702;
his w. d. 4 Aug. 1713, and he d. 17 Jan. 1715. JOSHUA, a soldier
under capt. Turner in Mar. 1676, on Conn. riv. from E. part of the
Col. was aft. at Falmouth. JOSIAH, Hingham, s. of George, by w.
Mary had only Mary, b. 26 Sept. 1671, and the mo. d. in 5 days.
Next, he m. 9 May 1672, Deborah, d. of Thomas Gill, had Josiah, b.
27 Jan. 1675; George, 22 June 1677; Deborah, 21 Nov. 1679; Sarah,
12 Feb. 1682; Thomas, 29 May 1684; Peter, 21 Dec. 1687, d. next
day; Peter, again, 2 Mar. 1690, d. at 3 mos.; Peter, again, 15 July
1691; and Ruth, 26 July 1696, d. young. ROBERT, Stratford 1665–85.
He may be the man, by Field, 107, said to be from Derbysh. and an
early sett. but with no more precise date, at Killingworth. SAMSON,
Portsmouth 1631, one of Mason's men, said to have come from Teign-
mouth in Devon, purch. 1646 the est. that had been Thomas Wanner-
ton's and was then call. master of the Neptune of Dartmouth, in 1650
mortga. the est. and his other prop. includ. a ship on the stocks to
Ambrose L. bef. ment. and prob. went home. SAMUEL, Hadley, had
been a soldier, 1676, from the E. under capt. Turner, m. 11 Dec. 1677,
Sarah, d. of the first John Dickinson of H. had Samuel, and Sarah, rem.
to Suffield, there had Mary, b. 7 May 1684; John, 3 Apr. 1686; and
Eliz. and he d. a. 1690, leav. these five ch. and his wid. m. 27 Feb.
1691, Martin Kellogg. WILLIAM, Dorchester 1641, from whose will,
made 28 Feb. 1651, pro. 6 July 1654, we learn that he had s. Andrew,
and George, both of Hingham, d. Mary Long, and Eliz. w. of Thomas
Rider, beside ds. whose bapt. names are not seen, ws. of Nathaniel
Baker, and of Thomas Lincoln of Hingham. WILLIAM, Boston 1651,
freem. 1657, by w. Mary had Samuel, b. 23 Jan. 1652; John, 5 Feb.
1654; and Mary, 15 May 1656, says rec. in Geneal. Reg. IX. 312.
His w. d. 2 May 1656, by G. R. X. 220; and he m. 21 Aug. foll.
Mary, d. of Thomas Brewer of Roxbury, had Sarah, 15 June 1657;
William, 1 Oct. 1659; and Eliz. 3 Feb. 1662. I testif. that both the
extr. in Geneal. Reg. that are so inconsist. are truly tak. from what pur-

ports to be the rec. in Boston, and both in the same handwrit. But the age was not, I think, quite so credul. as to receive for "*absolute verity*" assert. that the mo. d. thirteen days bef. her last ch. was b. Possib. the recorder might have intend. 22 instead of 2 May. Instances of such carelessness are oft. seen. WILLIAM, Boston, s. of the preced. m. 21 June 1680, Sarah Webster, d. of Thomas of Hampton. Six of this name had, in 1834, been gr. at Harv. and seven at other N. E. coll.

LANESON, JACOB, Weymouth, by w. Susanna had Abigail, b. 11 Nov. 1680; and Susanna, 24 Dec. 1683.

LANFEAR. See Landfear.

LANG, JOHN, Portsmouth, m. a d. of William Brooking.

LANGBURY, GREGORY, Pemaquid, took o. of fidel. 1674. JOHN, a soldier, k. 19 May 1676 at the Falls fight. As he was of Turner's comp. he was from the E.

LANGDEN, THOMAS, New Haven 1650, a taverner, wh. had w. and one s. at least. Being censur. and fined, more than once, for not restrain. the drink or speech of his guests, he prob. gave up his premises, hired of Richard Malbon, one of the Ct. and, perhaps, went home. The name was, in the reg. of births, *ll* for final *n* at first, but has been alter.

LANGDON, BENJAMIN, Boston 1674, s. of John the first, by w. Phebe had John, b. 20 May 1678. DAVID, Boston, by w. Martha had David, b. 20 Sept. 1685; Samuel, 13 Nov. 1686; Jonathan, 2 Jan. 1688; Mary, 4 Apr. 1698; Martha, 23 Nov. 1701; and Sarah, 7 Feb. 1704; and he d. 21 Jan. 1725, in 75th yr. JOHN, Boston 1648, sailmaker, had Sarah; Benjamin; Abigail, b. 25 Aug. 1660; and, perhaps, others. Sarah m. 1664, Thomas Randall of Marblehead. JOHN, Farmington, join. the ch. there 7 Feb. 1653, was a deac. m. the wid. of Thomas Gridley. JOHN, Boston, by w. Eliz. had Eliz. b. 1686; Josiah, 28 Jan. 1687; Ephraim, 25, bapt. 26 Jan. 1690; Mary, bapt. 15 Nov. 1691; Joanna, 22 Oct. 1693; Nathaniel, 14 Sept. 1695; Margaret, b. 23, bapt. 29 Aug. 1697; John, b. 17 Oct. 1698; and Margaret, again, 10 Aug. 1703. He d. 6 Dec. 1732, aged 82. JOSEPH, Farmington, perhaps s. of John of the same, had Sarah, Joseph, John, and Samuel, all bapt. 6 June 1697, in right of his w. wh. join. the ch. on Sunday preced. See Geneal. Reg. XII. 37, and correct the misspell. PHILIP, Boston, br. of the sec. John of the same, a mariner, by w. Mary had Philip; Susanna, b. 23 Oct. 1677; John, 22 Aug. 1682; James, 15 Aug. 1685; Samuel, 22 Dec. 1687; Mary, 24 Mar. 1690; and Paul, 12 Sept. 1693. He d. 11 Dec. 1697, and his wid. d. 14 Feb. 1717. Samuel, was f. of Rev. Samuel, D. D. b. 12 Jan. 1723, H. C. 1740, min. of the first ch. at Portsmouth, made Presid. of H. C. 1774–80, injur. compel. to resign, d. min. at Hampton Falls, 29 Nov. 1797. TOBIAS, Portsmouth, 1662, had w. Eliz. and prob. sev. ch. d. 27 July 1664. TOBIAS, Portsmouth, perhaps s. of the preced. m. 17 Nov. 1686, Mary Hubbard, had Eliz. b. 17 Nov. 1687; Tobias, 11 Oct. 1689; Martha, 7 Mar. 1692; Richard, 14 Apr. 1694; Joseph, 28 Feb. 1696; Mark, 15 Sept. 1698; Samuel, 6 Sept. 1700; William, 30 Oct. 1702; and John, 28 May 1707. John, the youngest ch. was f. of John, b. 1740, d. 18 Sept. 1819, hav. serv. as ch. mag. of the State call. Presid. two yrs. and Gov. six yrs. and sat twelve yrs. in Senate of U. S. Six of this name had, in 1826, been gr. at Harv. and eight at the other N. E. coll.

LANGER, HENRY, Boston 1645, by w. Ann had Susanna, b. 16 Jan. 1646. RICHARD, Hingham 1636, very aged, when he made his will, 20 Feb. 1660, pro. 2 May 1661, in wh. he refers to ds. Dinah and Eliz. wh. should rec. ea. 4s. from his d. Margaret, w. of Thomas Lincoln, to whose eldest s. Joshua, the testat. gave his lds. at H.

LANGFORD, JOHN, Salem, mov. in from ano. town ,but wh. is unkn. tho. prepond. of prob. is in favor of Sudbury. He was freem. 1645, yet his name is not among ch. memb. in Salem, down to 1650; but there he was liv. 1689, as, Farmer says, is shown by Revo. in N. E. Justif. 41. Mr. Felt assures me, there was a Francis Lingford of Essex Co. in 1663; and possib. he may have been of the same fam. RICHARD, writ. Lanckford, Plymouth 1632.

LANGHORNE, or LONGHORNE, RICHARD, Rowley 1649, d. 1669. THOMAS, Cambridge 1644, by w. Sarah, d. of Bartholomew Green, had, beside Thomas, wh. was b. 26 Aug. 1647, bur. 5 Apr. 1648, Sarah, 26 Feb. 1649; Eliz. and Mary, bapt. all as the precious reg. of matchless Mitchell proves, but at dates not giv.; Samuel, 9 Dec. 1660; Mercy, 11 May 1662; and Patience, 3 Apr. 1664. He was the town drummer, and d. 6 May 1685, aged, says the gr.stone, a. 68 yrs. Mary d. 27 Mar. 1654, b. as the rec. says in one place, in Sept. in ano. in Mar. preced.

LANGLEY, ABEL, Rowley 1651. DANIEL, Boston 1689, mariner, went, with others, that yr. to take a piratical vessel in Vineyard Sound, of wh. in Geneal. Reg. II. 393, is acco. JOHN, Hingham, m. Jan. 1666, Sarah, d. of Thomas Gill, was a soldier in the comp. of brave capt. Johnson of Roxbury, Dec. 1675, an innhold. 1695. Of his ch. I kn. only Sarah, b. 15 Mar. 1668, wh. m. Nov. 1686, Jonathan May of H. WILLIAM, Lynn, freem. 14 Mar. 1639, in 1677 was, I think, of Charlestown. But it may be well to see Longley.

LANGMEAD, RICHARD, Boston perhaps, mariner, d. 1660, leav. w. Ellen, wh. had admin. 18 June 1661.

LANGSTAFF, HENRY, Portsmouth 1631, or soon aft. sent over by Mason, the patentee, was of the gr. jury 1643, and at Dover 1648, had

Sarah, wh. m. Anthony Nutter, also Henry; and d. by a fall, says Pike's Journ. 18 July 1705, near 100 yrs. old.

LANGTON, LANCKTON, or LANKTON, GEORGE, Springfield 1646, m. a'sec. w. 29 June 1648, Hannah, wid. of Edmund Haynes, had Esther (strangely call. s. in the rec. pr. in Geneal. Reg. IX. 171), b. 22 Aug. 1649, and no more ch. but had formerly been at Wethersfield, and by first w. had there or in Eng. sev. ch.; rem. a. 1658, to Northampton, there d. 29 Dec. 1676. His will ment. s. John, ds. Pritchet, Corbee, Hanshet [wh. was Deliverance, w. of Thomas], Hannum [wh. was Esther, w. of John], and gr.s. Samuel. * JOHN, Farmington 1650, s. of the preced. b. prob. in Eng. was rep. 1668, deac. and d. 1689; had four ch.: John, wh. d. 1683, leav. John; Samuel, wh. was bapt. 13 Feb. 1653, and liv. with his gr.f. at N.; Joseph, bapt. 1660, liv. at F.; and Eliz. JOSEPH, Ipswich 1648, may have been s. of Roger. ROGER, Ipswich, freem. 4 Mar. 1635. His inv. of 24 Jan. 1672 may seem to prove, that he d. that winter. SAMUEL, Northampton, s. of John, m. 1676, Eliz. wid. of Praisever Turner, was freem. 1681, and d. 11 Aug. 1683, leav. John, and Samuel. His wid. took third h. David Alexander.

LANGWORTH, ANDREW, Newport 1656, m. a. 1661, Rachel, d. of Samuel Hubbard.

LAPHAM, JOHN, Malden, m. Aug. 1671, a Hollis, and I find no more of him. JOHN, Providence, m. 6 Apr. 1673, Mercy, d. of Francis Mann of the same, had Mary, b. 1 Mar. 1673; John, 13 Dec. 1677; and William, 29 Nov. 1679. He was call. 45 yrs. old in 1680. THOMAS, Scituate 1635, join. Lothrop's ch. 24 Apr. 1636, m. 13 Mar. 1637, Mary, d. of Nathaniel Tilden, had Eliz. bapt. 6 May 1638; Mary; Thomas, b. 1643; Lydia; Rebecca, 1645; Joseph, 1648; in wh. yr. the f. d. hav. made his will 15 June 1644, in wh. the four elder ch. are nam. and w. made extrix. Lydia m. 1666, Samuel Bates of Hingham. THOMAS, Marshfield, elder s. of the preced.

LAPTHORNE, STEPHEN, Scarborough 1640.

LARAN, JOHN, Jamaica, L. I. 1656.

LARGE, JERVICE, Scituate, a serv. of Samuel Hinckley, brot. prob. from Co. Kent, was bur. 9 Aug. 1636. JOHN, Branford 1672, perhaps came over from L. I. may be the man wh. m. at Saybrook, 1 Nov. 1659, Phebe, d. of Thomas Lee, and possib. was s. of William. WILLIAM, Hingham 1635, rem. with w. to Cape Cod, perhaps further.

LARGIN, HENRY, Boston, by w. Ann had Susanna, b. 16 Jan. 1646; and by w. Alice had Joseph, b. 23 Nov. 1653, wh. d. in few wks. JOHN, a soldier, from the E. under capt. Turner, at Hatfield, 1676.

LARKHAM, MORDECAI, Beverly 1681, has num. descend. it is believ. writ. the name Larcom. THOMAS, Dover 1640, was a cause, or occasion of trouble, tho. so popular for a time that the people call. their town aft. that from wh. he came, Northam, near Barnstable, in Devon; but he went off in 1642, d. at home 1669, in 68th yr. His s. George, bred at Trinity Coll. Cambridge, was min. of Cockermouth, in Cumberland, eject. 1662, d. 26 Dec. 1700, in 71st yr.

LARKIN, || EDWARD, Charlestown 1638, by w. Joan had John, b. 10 Mar. 1640; Sarah, 4 Sept. 1641; but ano. rec. says Eliz. b. 5 Sept.; Thomas, 18 Oct. 1644; and, I presume, Edward; certain. Sarah, again, 12 Mar. 1648; was freem. 13 May 1640, ar. co. 1644. He d. bef. mid. life, prob. and the wid. m. John Pentecost; and she d. 27 Jan. 1686, aged 70. * EDWARD, Newport, in the list of freem. 1655, was rep. 1663. He was of Westerly, in the same Col. 1669; and by w. Eliz. d. of the first Henry Hall, had Edward and John, prob. also Roger, and d. Hannah to dwell there ten yrs. later. EDWARD, Westerly, s. of the preced. m. Mary, d. of Nicholas Cottrell, had Stephen, Nicholas, David, Eliz. Penelope, Tabitha, Edward, John, Samuel, and Lydia. EDWARD, Charlestown, perhaps s. of the first Edward, m. 1 Nov. 1688, Mary Walker, had Edward, wh. d. 18 Nov. 1689; John, bapt. 7 Sept. 1690; Mary, 10 Sept. 1693; John, again, 17 Feb. 1695; Edward, again, 13 Sept. 1696; Joanna, 19 Mar. 1699; and Samuel, 26 Oct. 1701. JOHN, Charlestown, perhaps br. of the first Edward, by w. Joan had Hannah, b. 16 Mar. 1643, wh. m. 15 Feb. 1665, John Newell, outliv. him, and d. 10 Dec. 1704. JOHN, Charlestown, s. prob. of first Edward, m. 9 Nov. 1664, Joanna, d. of deac. Robert Hale, had Joanna, wh. d. 3 June 1673; Edward, John, and Robert, bapt. at once, 4 July 1675, of wh. Robert d. in few wks.; Joanna, again, 12 Mar. 1676; Sarah, 2 Dec. 1677; and he d. 17 Feb. 1678. ROGER, Westerly, perhaps s. of the first Edward of the same, m. Hannah, d. of the sec. James Babcock of the same; but I kn. no more. THOMAS, Charlestown, s. of Edward, shoemak. m. 13 Sept. 1666, Hannah Remington, wh. d. 9 Nov. 1673, and 18 June foll. m. Eliz. d. of Francis Dowse, wid. of Samuel Miles, had Thomas, wh. d. 20 May 1676; and Thomas, again, bapt. 9 Sept. and d. 8 Nov. 1677; and d. hims. 10 Dec. foll. of smallpox. Gladly would we receive better notes of this very num. fam. If the stocks spring from Edward alone, or not, is not kn. to me. At Salem, in 1668, was Mordecai, but unless he be the same as Larcom, of him I hear nothing, exc. that he sign. that yr. petit. against imposts.

LARRABEE, BENJAMIN, Falmouth, s. of Isaac, a milit. man, recov. the prop. of his f. wh. with his fam. had been forc. to fly from the war, m. Deborah, d. of John Ingersoll, had Benjamin, b. 1700; and he d. 1733. See Willis, II. 27. GREENFIELD, Saybrook, had (by his w.

suppos. to have been a Brown of Providence) Greenfield, b. 20 Apr. 1648; John, 23 Feb. 1650; Eliz. 23 Jan. 1653; Joseph, Mar. 1655, d. young; and Sarah, 3 Mar. 1658. GREENFIELD, Saybrook, s. of the preced. m. Alice, d. of Thomas Parke of New London. ISAAC, Falmouth a. 1680, being driv. off by the Ind. went to Lynn, says Willis; had Benjamin, b. 1666, at Casco, bef. ment.; beside Samuel, and Thomas. In Maine the name spread much. WILLIAM, m. at Malden Nov. 1655, Eliz. perhaps d. of George Felt; was freem. 1690. Sometimes this name is pervert. to Leatherby, as very oft. it was sound.

LARY, CORNELIUS, Exeter, took o. of fidel. 30 Nov. 1677.

LASKIN, HUGH, Salem 1636, freem. 22 May 1639, d. Mar. 1659.

LATCOME, WILLIAM, a passeng. in the Hercules 1634, as print. in Geneal. Reg. IX. 267, wh. may be error for Larcom, or Larkham; but nothing can be kn.

LATHAM, * CARY, Cambridge, m. Eliz. d. of John Masters, and prob. wid. of Edmund Lockwood, had Thomas, b. Nov. 1639; Joseph, 2 Dec. of a yr. to be supplied by conject. as the rec. is defic.; rem. early to New London, where he was of active serv. rep. 1664, and aft. to 70. He had there Eliz. wh. m. 25 Jan. 1678, John Leeds; Jane, m. Hugh Hubbard; Lydia, m. John Packer; and Hannah, wh. m. prob. John Lockwood. He d. 1685. JOSEPH, New London, s. of the preced. took w. Mary at Newfoundland, there had Cary, b. 14 July 1668, and at New London ten more ch. at his d. in 1706 leav. seven s. one d. LEWIS, Newport, of wh. we kn. no more, but that his d. Frances m. Jeremiah Clark, and was mo. of Gov. Walter and others; but it may be that he never came to our shores. ROBERT, Cambridge, perhaps br. of Cary, liv. two yrs. or more with Rev. Thomas Shepard, rem. to Marshfield, where he was constable 1643, thence to Plymouth, where he m. Susanna, d. of John Winslow, in 1649, and had Mercy, b. 2 June 1650; bef. 1667 rem. to Bridgewater, had s. James, Chilton, Joseph, Eliz. Hannah, and Sarah. Mitchell thinks him s. of William. Hannah m. Joseph Washburn. THOMAS, New London, s. of Cary, m. 15 Oct. 1673, Rebecca, d. of Hugh Wells, had only ch. Samuel; and his wid. m. 24 June 1676, John Packer. Groton side of the harbor of New London was the resid. of the fam. still perpet. there. WILLIAM, Plymouth, came in the Mayflower, 1620, serv. to Gov. Carver, only a youth, and, in 1627, had sh. in the div. of cattle, being in the lot with Gov. Bradford, yet was never nam. as one of the Mayflower's comp. in 1620 when he was a boy under Carver's charge, and for the div. of lds. in 1624, with ano. serv. of C. may have help. John Howland to count four heads. By the discov. of Bradford's Hist. his right to passage in the first sh. is prov. He was of Duxbury 1637–9, and Marshfield 1643, and 8, and in Bradford we see, that aft. so long resid. here, he went home to Eng. thence to the Bahamas, and d. of starvation. Of one Latham, in our country, there is idle tradit. that he was brot. up with Charles I. but no benefit or evil of the companionsh. is boasted.

LATHROP. See Lothrop.

LATTIMORE, or LATIMER, CHRISTOPHER, Marblehead 1648, in 1663 sold dwel.-ho. to Robert Hooper, but was there liv. 1674. HUGH, Marblehead, perhaps s. of the preced. m. 1669, Mary, d. of William Pitt. JOHN, Wethersfield, had Rebecca, b. 1646 ; Naomi, 1648; Abigail, 1649 ; John, 1650 ; Elisheba, 1652 ; Jonathan, 1655 ; and Bezaleel, 1657 ; all with w. Ann nam. in his will 1662, when he d. Eliz. m. Thomas Hollister of W. ROBERT, New London, mariner, a. 1660, m. prob. at Boston, Ann, wid. of Matthew Jones, and d. of George Griggs, had Robert, b. 5 Feb. 1664 ; and Eliz. 14 Nov. 1667 ; and he d. 1671. Eliz. m. Jonathan Prentiss. ROBERT, New London, s. of the preced. d. 2 Nov. 1728, leav. John, perhaps H. C. 1703 ; Robert ; Jonathan ; Samuel ; and Peter.

LATTING, LETTEN, or LETTIN, JOSIAH, Huntington, or Oyster Bay, L. I. 1685, was s. prob. of Richard. RICHARD, Concord, had Josiah, b. 20 Feb. 1641 ; and ano. s. on 12 Sept. 1643 ; but the rec. gives not the name ; rem. to Fairfield, and thence in few yrs. to L. I. a. Huntington. In 1663 he was order. to depart for not submit. to jurisdict. of Conn. and in Nov. 1672 was by New York denounc. for disloyal speech against the Duke.

LAUGHTON, THOMAS, Boston 1660.

LAURENSON, JAMES, and JOHN, Newtown, L. I. 1686, were prob. of Dutch descent.

LAURIE, FRANCIS, Salem, of wh. the Hist. Coll. of Essex Inst. II. 15, gives all that I have learn. that his will of 6 Nov. 1665, pro. June foll. ment. s.-in-law John Neal and w. Mary, and gr.ch. Jeremiah, John Jonathan, Joseph, and Lydia. But conject. is bold eno. to suggest, that the same man is intend. where Felt, II. 447, places the graveyard " on the hill above Francis Lawe's ho. ; " and there is no doubt of the soundness of the conject. after turn. to the artic. Lawes in this volume ; but whose reading, Felt's or Patch's should be prefer. must be left to ano. eye to decide. GILBERT, Boston 1686, went to preach that yr. in abs. of Moody, at Portsmouth, was prob. a Scotchman, and may be presum. to have gone home in 1689.

LAVENUKE, STEPHEN, a Frenchman, m. 25 Sept. 1672, Mary Dival, perhaps French also, had Isabella, b. 22 Dec. 1673 ; Judith, 1677, wh. d. 22 Apr. 1758 ; and Stephen, in 1678, wh. d. 1 Jan. 1764.

LAVERICK, JOHN, perhaps at Watertown, as serv. of Richard Kimball, came at the age of 15, in the Elizabeth from Ipswich, 1634.

LAVERS, GEORGE, and JACOB, Portsmouth 1683, petitioners to the
king against Gov. Cranfield that yr. Belkn. I. 473.

LAW, ANDREW, Hingham 1654, had Joshua, Josiah, and Caleb, is by
Farmer erron. giv. I suppose, for Lane, wh. see. JOHN, Concord, m. 5
Mar. 1660, Lydia, d. of Roger Draper, had John, b. 1661; Thomas,
1663; Stephen, 1665; and Samuel. JONATHAN, Milford 1667, freem.
1669, perhaps only s. of Richard, m. Sarah, d. of George Clark, senr.
by her had Jonathan, b. 6 Aug. 1674, H. C. 1695, wh. was Ch. Just. 16
yrs. and a disting. Gov. of Conn. LYMAN, Gravesend, L. I. 1650.
Thompson. * RICHARD, Wethersfield 1638, may, therefore, have first
been at Watertown, m. Margaret, eldest d. of Thomas Kilbourne, had
Abigail, Jonathan, and Sarah, and prob. more ch.; rem. early to
Stamford, may have been rep. in New Haven Ct. certain. was, aft. the
union, in Conn. 1665, 6, 9, and 72. His d. Abigail m. Jonathan Sellick; and Sarah m. John Sellick. WILLIAM, Rowley 1643. Pro. rec.
show that he was d. 1669, leav. w. Faith and four ch. Fifteen of this
name, oft. in old rec. hav. *es* final, had, in 1829, been gr. at the N. E.
coll. most at Yale.

LAWES, FRANCIS, Salem, a weaver, b. at Norwich, Eng. emb. at Ipswich 8 Apr. arr. at Boston 20 June 1637, with w. Lydia, aged 49, one
ch. Mary, and two serv. Samuel Lincoln, 18; and Ann Smith, 19. He
was freem. 2 June 1641, and d. a. 1666. Mary m. John Neal, and,
next, Andrew Mansfield. See Laurie.

LAWRENCE, BENJAMIN, Charlestown, sec. s. of George of Watertown, m. in Boston, 4 July 1689, Mary Clough, perhaps d. of John, had
John, bapt. 22 Nov. 1696; Abigail, 30 Oct. 1698; William, and Eliz.
tw. 14 July 1700, both d. soon; Eliz. again, 4 Oct. 1702; Benjamin, 10
Sept. 1704; and Mary, 28 Feb. 1707; but all these by sec. w. Ann,
wid. of Benjamin Phillips, wh. he m. 3 Feb. 1696, wh. d. 11 Jan. 1716,
aged only 37, says Bond, wh. is a strange error, for she bore her first ch.
to former h. above 36 yrs. bef. On 18th Nov. of the same yr. he took
third w. Ann, wid. of Nathaniel Adams, d. of Nathaniel Coolidge of
Watertown; and she d. 28 Dec. 1718, aged 47, so that 9 July foll. he
could take his fourth w. Eliz. Bennett, wh. outliv. him, and he d. 26 Nov.
1738, aged 75. DANIEL, Charlestown, tw. br. of the preced. a painter,
m. 19 June 1689, Sarah, d. of Edward Counts, wh. prob. brot. him no
ch. and d. in few yrs.; serv. in the army, and was in the garrison at
Brookfield tak. by the Ind. in the assault, 27 July 1693, but was recov.
got back to Charlestown, there by w. Hannah Mason, m. Nov. 1695, had
Daniel, bapt. 9 Aug. 1696; Samuel, 22 May 1698, at Mather's ch. in
Boston; Hannah, 26 Feb. 1700, at C.; Sarah, 29 Mar. 1702, d. soon;
Lydia, 30 Jan. 1704; and Sarah, again, 3 Feb. 1706. His w. d. 27
Aug. 1721, aged 56, and he m. 23 Aug. foll. Maud, d. of the Hon. James

Russell; and d. 20 Oct. 1743. DAVID, New Hampsh. 1683, d. 1710, leav. wid. Mary, ch. Joseph, David, and Phebe, and gr.ch. David, and Jonathan. ENOCH, Groton, s. of John of the same, m. 6 Mar. 1677, Ruth, wid. of John Shattuck, d. of John Whitney, had Nathaniel, b. 21 Feb. 1678; Daniel, 7 Mar. 1681; Zechariah, 16 July 1683; and Jeremiah, 1 May 1686; d. at gr. age 28 Sept. 1744. GEORGE, Watertown, m. 29 Sept. 1657, Eliz. d. prob. of Benjamin Crispe, had Eliz. b. 30 Feb. says the rec. mean. perhaps 28, 1659; Judith, 12 May 1660; Hannah, 24 Mar. 1662; John, 25 Mar. 1664, k. by accid. at ten yrs.; Benjamin, and Daniel, tw. 2 May 1666; George, 4 June 1668; Sarah; Mary, 4 Dec. 1671; Martha; and Grace, 3 June 1680. His w. d. 28 May 1681, and he m. 16 Aug. 1691, Eliz. perhaps wid. of Joseph Holland, had Joseph; and Rachel, and Patience, tw. 14 July 1694. He d. 21 Mar. 1709. Eliz. m. 29 Jan. 1679, Thomas Whitney; Judith m. John Stearns; Hannah m. prob. Obadiah Sawtell; Sarah m. Thomas Rider; Mary m. 5 Apr. 1689, John Earle, and, next, Michael Flagg; Martha m. 29 Nov. 1697, John Dix; and Grace m. an Edes. GEORGE, Watertown, s. of the preced. by w. Mary had Mary, b. 15 Feb. 1697; George, 3 June 1698; Eliz. 9 Oct. 1700; John, 20 Feb. 1704; David, 16 July 1706; Sarah, 20 Jan. 1709; William, 20 May 1711; and Ann, 1 Mar. 1714, and he d. 5 Mar. 1736. HENRY, Charlestown 1635. Frothingham, 84. A wid. Christian wh. Bond thot. to be his, d. 3 Mar. 1648. ISAAC, Norwich, s. of the first John, m. 19 Apr. 1682, Abigail, d. of John Bellows. JOHN, Watertown, freem. 17 Apr. 1637, by w. Eliz. had John, b. 14 Mar. 1636; Nathaniel, 15 Oct. 1639; Joseph, Mar. 1642, d. at 2 mos.; Joseph, again, 30 May 1643; Jonathan, perhaps his tw. br. d. soon; Mary, 16 July 1645; Peleg, 10 Jan. 1647; Enoch, 5 Mar. 1649; Samuel; Isaac; Eliz. 9 May 1655; Jonathan, again; and Zechariah, 9 Mar. 1659; all at W. exc. Eliz. b. at Boston, wh. may however have been ano. John's. He rem. a. 1662 to Groton, and his w. d. there 29 Aug. 1663; and he m. 2 Nov. 1664, Susanna, d. of William Batchelor of Charlestown, had Abigail, b. 11 Jan. 1666, prob. d. young; and Susanna, 3 July 1667. He d. 11 July 1667, and his wid. rem. to Charlestown, there d. 8 July 1668. His will, of 24 Apr. 1667, provides for w. and ch. as well as all the ch. of the former w. exc. John, and Peleg, wh. may have been bef. provid. for by deeds. His wid. in her will, names f. and mo. Batchelor, sis. Rachel Atwood, and Abigail Austin, and both her own ch. but in the will of gr.f. only Susanna, her d. is nam. so that we may infer, that Abigail was dec. bef. Feb. 1670, when his will was made. Mary m. 25 Aug. 1663, Indigo Potter, so shortly bef. the dec. of her mo. that her f. notic. it in his will. JOHN, Charlestown, s. of the preced. by w. Susanna had Hannah, b. 22

Feb. 1659; Abigail, a. 1661; Sarah; David; and John, bapt. aft. his
mo.'s 2d m. at her req. 24 Apr. 1681, as she join. the ch. 6 Mar. bef.
then wid. of the first Thomas Tarbell. He d. 1672, his inv. was tak. 17
June; and his wid. m. 15 Aug. 1676, Thomas Tarbell. JOHN, Newtown, L. I. one of the patentees of Hempstead 1644, was there in
1655; but was first of Ipswich, came at the age of 17 with his mo.
Joan Tuttle, and sixteen other Tuttles, in the Planter, from London,
1635, hav. certif. from St. Albans, Co. Herts; after the conq. of New
York, rem. thither and was an alderman, mayor of the city, judge of the
Sup. Ct. of the Prov. d. 1699. He had Joseph, John, Thomas, Martha,
Susanna, and Mary, wh. were all m. but none left issue to reach
maturity exc. this last, whose h. was William Whittingham. JOHN, Boston, m. 8 Feb. 1654, Eliz. Atkinson, had Eliz. b. 9 May 1655, but wh.
the w. was, or his parentage, is unkn. Perhaps he was the pub. executioner, appoint. 1669, serv. many yrs. complain. of inadequacy of support by loss of employm. JOHN, Boston, of that pt. call Muddy riv.
now Brookline, m. 30 Sept. 1657, Sarah, d. of Thomas Buckminster, or
by rec. Buckmaster. JOHN, Wrentham, by w. Sarah, wh. d. 25 Mar.
1684, had Mary, b. 16 Mar. 1682. JOHN, Hadley, br. of Daniel, m.
1684, Sarah Smith, d. of Samuel of Hadley, had John, b. 1686, d. next
yr.; Mary, 1688; Deliverance, 1693; and Sarah, 1694. He was k. by
the Ind. 1694 at Brookfield, whither he had recent. rem. His wid. m.
1705, Ebenezer Wells of Hatfield. NATHANIEL, Groton, s. of John,
freem. 1672, m. 13 Mar. 1660, Sarah, d. of John Morse of Sudbury,
had Nathaniel, b. 4 Apr. 1661; Sarah, 1 Jan. 1663, d. soon, both at S.;
Hannah, 3 July 1664; John, 29 July 1667, wh. d. at Lexington, 12
Mar. 1746; Mary, 3 Mar. 1670; Sarah, again, 16 May 1672; Eliz. 6
Sept. 1674, d. next yr.; Eliz. again; and Deborah, 24 Mar. 1683; and
by sec. w. Hannah had Hannah, again, 26 Apr. 1687; Mary, again, 16
Oct. 1690; and Jonathan, 14 June 1696; and d. 14 Apr. 1724. As in
his will of 4 Aug. 1718, no w. is nam. it may seem prob. that she was d.
His s. John of Lexington, blacksmith, had Amos, youngest of ten ch.
whose third s. Samuel was f. of Amos, Luther, William, Abbot, the min.
of the U. S. at the Court of London, and Samuel, all disting. in our day
for pub. serv. and private munif. NICHOLAS, Charlestown 1648, may
have been that br. of first John, design. by his will. NICHOLAS, Dorchester, s. of Thomas, by w. Mary had Patience, b. 13 June 1658, d.
young; and he d. 1685; in his will of 26 Jan. pro. 21 May of that yr.
gives his w. Mary, and eldest s. without nam. him, and calls the ch.
Mary, Rebecca, Nicholas, and Benjamin. PELEG, Groton, br. of Nathaniel, m. 1668, Eliz. d. of John Morse, had Eliab, b. 9 Jan. 1669;
Samuel, 16 Oct. 1671; Eleazer, 28 Feb. 1674; Eliz. wh. d. 10 Oct.

1685; Jonathan, 29 Mar. 1679; Abigail, 6 Oct. 1681; Jeremiah, 3
Jan. 1687, d. soon; Joseph, 12 June 1688; Daniel; and Susanna; and
d. 1692. RICHARD, Branford 1646, had Bethia, and Esther, both bapt.
at New Haven, 1 June 1651, wh. are not found on the rec. of b. at B.
but others are, Eleazer, b. 17 Jan. 1652; Eldad, 15 July 1655, d. soon;
and Sarah, 27 May 1657. He sign. the agreem. for rem. to New Jersey
1665, and was estab. at Passaic, June 1668. ROBERT, Falmouth 1680,
m. Mary, wid. of George Munjoy, d. of John Phillips of Dorchester,
was a man of distinct. lieut. of the town, k. at the tak. May 1690, by the
Fr. and Ind. and his wid. had third h. Stephen Cross, 1690, at Boston.
Willis, I. 212. THOMAS, Hingham 1638, m. Eliz. d. of James Bates of
Dorchester, had Nicholas, b. at H.; Mary and Eliz. at D. d. 5 Nov.
1655, and his wid. rem. to Dorchester with her ch. Nicholas, bef. ment.;
Mary, wh. m. 28 Oct. 1658, Thomas Maudesley, and Eliz. m. 31 Dec.
1658, William Smead. THOMAS, Milford 1639, an orig. sett. d. 1648.
THOMAS, Newtown, L. I. 1656, may have been of Stamford 1670, was
br. of John and William of Newtown, and much engag. in the politics
of N. Y. 1689, d. 1703. Acco. of him and both brs. with large genealog.
details is in Riker's Ann. of N. 281–290. THOMAS, Brookfield, br. of
Daniel, was k. by the Ind. 27 July 1693. WILLIAM, Duxbury 1643.
At D. he m. a d. of Francis Sprague. WILLIAM, Newtown, L. I. 1645,
may be the youth wh. was emb. in the Planter at London, 1635, aged
12, with elder br. John and Thomas, bef. ment. liv. first at Ipswich with
his mo. was a man of gr. energy, d. 1680, had childr. by two ws. and
his wid. m. Sir Philip Carteret, Gov. of N. J. Seven of this name had
been gr. at Harv. and six at other N. E. coll. in 1834.

LAWSON, CHRISTOPHER, Exeter 1639, rem. to Boston, by w. Eliz.
had Thomas, b. 4 May 1643; and Mary, 27 Oct. 1645; was a cooper,
rem. to Maine bef. 1665, there purch. Swan isl. in Kennebeck riv. from
the Ind. and was an import. man. Sullivan, 290; Holmes, I. 349;
Folsom, 128; Williamson, II. 172. Yet so ill did he agree with his w.
that their mut. complaints came to the Gen. Ct. 1669. DEODATE,
Scituate, s. of Rev. Thomas of Denton, Co. Norfk. Eng. is first heard
of at Martha's Vineyard 1676, had been bred to divinity, I presume,
but kn. nothing, for even Cotton Mather, tho. he gives him a place
among his contempo. fellow serv. in Hecatompolis, felt unable to intro-
duce him into either of his three classes; liv. aft. few yrs. at Boston,
join. with our third, or Old South, ch. (had it been the sec. wh. then was
taught by the Mathers, f. and s. his name would have found, as it should,
room in the Magnalia, III.). He took the o. of freem. 1680, was call.
to preach 1683 at Salem vill. now Danvers, where no ch. was yet form.
but George Burrows had taught the people above two yrs. and they

would have ord. Lawson in the latter pt. of 1686; but hav. lost his first w. and her d. Ann, he luckily for him went to sett. at Scituate sec. ch. of wh. he was third min. and dism. in 1698 for hav. been abs. more than two yrs. gone home. At Boston, by w. Jane he had Deodate, b. 1682; and he had sec. w. Deborah Allen, m. 6 May 1690, by wh. he had at S. Deborah, b. 1694; and Richard, 1696. Deane, 195; Calamy, II. 629. HENRY, Mass. prob. came 1630, and d. early in 1631. JAMES, Dartmouth, sw. fidel. 1684. JOHN, Boston 1690, had Ann, bapt. 10 Nov. 1700; Sarah, 29 Mar. 1702; and John and Savil, 16 July 1704, the rec. at Mather's ch. being "tw. of John, lately d." ROGER, Boston, mariner, 1690.

LAWTON, GEORGE, Portsmouth, R. I. had Isaac, b. 11 Dec. 1650; George; perhaps Job; and certain. Robert; but no more can be learn. of him exc. that his d. Ruth m. 10 Feb. 1681, William Wodell; and Mercy m. 19 Jan. 1682, James Tripp; prob. he d. 5 Oct. 1693; at least, one George then d. and the rec. adds, " his s. Job d. 8 Oct. 1697." GEORGE, Portsmouth, R. I. perhaps s. of the preced. m. 17 Jan. 1678, Naomi Hunt, had Eliz. b. 15 Nov. foll.; George, 30 Apr. 1685; Robert, 4 Oct. 1688; Job, 22 Jan. 1693; and d. 11 Sept. 1697. His wid. m. 11 Oct. 1701, his br. Isaac. ISAAC, Portsmouth, R. I. s. of the first George, m. 3 Mar. 1674, Eliz. d. of Peter Talman, had Eliz. b. 16 Feb. foll.; Sarah, 25 Oct. 1676; Ann, 25 Apr. 1678; Isaac, 21 May 1681; Mary, 3 Apr. 1683; Ichabod, 12 Mar. 1685; Thomas, 25 Apr. 1687; Susanna, 3 Apr. 1689; Job, 28 Apr. 1691; Ruth, 9 Apr. 1694; and John, 2 Sept. 1696. His w. d. 20 May 1701, and he m. 11 Oct. foll. Naomi, wid. of his br. George; and she d. 3 Jan. 1720. * JAMES, Suffield, s. of John, had Jacob, wh. was sev. yrs. rep. and, from caprice, adopt. in his business as a lawyer the name of Christopher Jacob L. JOHN, Newtown, L. I. 1656, may be the one wh. m. at Boston 21 Sept. 1659, wid. Joanna Mullins; and had sec. w. perhaps that Mary, d. of Matthew Boomer, or some such name, wh. next m. 3 June 1678, Gideon Freeborn as his sec. w. at Portsmouth, R. I. JOHN, Suffield, had James, Benedicta, Mary, and, perhaps, others, d. 19 Dec. 1690; and his wid. Benedicta d. 18 Nov. 1692. Both of the ds. were m. 1683. ROBERT, Portsmouth, R. I. s. perhaps youngest, of George the first, m. 16 Feb. 1681, Mary, d. of Gershom Wodell or Waddell, had Mary, b. 20 Feb. 1682; George, 1 Sept. 1685; Eliz. 12 Sept. 1688; Robert, 5 Jan. 1696; and d. 25 Jan. 1706; and his wid. d. 14 Jan. 1731. THOMAS, prob. of Portsmouth, R. I. may have been an early sett. for his ds. Eliz. m. 25 July 1657, Peleg Shearman of that place; Sarah m. 1 Aug. 1667, George Sisson; and Ann m. 26 May 1669, Giles Slocum.

LAY, EDWARD, Hartford 1640, rem. to Saybrook 1648, on E. side, or

Lyme, d. bef. 1657, or perhaps rem. to Portsmouth, R. I. where in 1679 he was liv. 71 yrs. old. JOHN, Saybrook 1648, perhaps br. of the preced. was on the side of the riv. incorp. 1667, as Lyme, in his will of 16 or 18 Jan. 1675, two days bef. he d. calls hims. aged, names s. John, and James, by former w. and Peter and John of his present w. Abigail, ds. Abigail, Susanna, and Eliz. John, and, perhaps, others of these ch. were b. in Eng. James, one of the s. d. a. 1683; and the wid. Abigail d. 1686. JOHN, Lyme, s. of the preced. b. in Eng. prob. was badly wound. in the gr. swamp fight, 19 Dec. 1675, had w. Sarah, and ch. Sarah, b. 4 Feb. 1665; Rebecca, 9 Sept. 1666; Edward, 26 Jan. 1668; Catharine, 11 Feb. 1672; Abigail, 9 Sept. 1673; Marah, 21 Mar. 1678; Eliz. 18 Dec. 1681; John, 25 Mar. 1683; and Phebe, 13 Jan. 1685; and d. 13 Nov. 1696, aged 63; and his wid. d. 12 June 1702. Possib. this Lyme name may be the same as Laigh or Lee. * ROBERT, Lynn 1638, rem. to Saybrook, prob. 1647, in Dec. of this yr. was m. had Phebe, b. 5 Jan. 1651; and Robert, 6 Mar. 1654; was freem. 1657, rep. 1666; his w. Sarah d. 21 May 1676, aged a. 59, and he d. 9 July 1689, aged 72. Phebe m. 1667, John Denison of Stonington. ROBERT, Saybrook, s. of the preced. m. 22 Jan. 1680, Mary Stanton, had Robert, b. 27 Jan. 1681; Sarah, 19 Feb. 1683; Mary, 3 Oct. 1685; Thomas, 10 May 1688; Samuel and Temperance, tw. 25 July 1691, of wh. Samuel d. soon; Samuel, again, 18 Feb. 1695; Phebe, 14 Aug. 1698; and Dorothy, 3 June 1701. WILLIAM, Boston, by w. Mary had Susanna, b. 6 Aug. 1690. It is spelt Ley, sometimes, and, also, Lee.

LAYLAND. See Leland.

LAYTON. See Laighton.

LAZELL, HENRY, Barnstable 1637, of wh. no more is heard. ISAAC, Hingham, s. of John, m. 20 Jan. 1686, Abigail, or Abiah, d. of John Leavitt, had Abiah, b. 26 June 1687; and Isaac, 6 Sept. 1690; and d. 18 Oct. foll. I think, in Phips's sad exped. against Quebec. The wid. had admin. 28 Apr. 1691, and m. Isaac Johnson. ISRAEL, Hingham, youngest br. of the preced. m. 6 July 1698, Rachel, d. of Daniel Lincoln, had Isaac, b. 30 Aug. 1701; Israel, 8 Jan. 1704; Daniel, 1 Feb. 1706; and Jonathan, 19 Mar. 1708. JOHN, Hingham 1647, m. 29 Nov. but ano. rec. says 22 Dec. 1649, Eliz. d. of Stephen Gates, had John, bapt. 8 Sept. 1650, d. under 15 yrs.; Thomas, b. 15, bapt. 19 Sept. 1652; Joshua, 17 Nov. 1654, bapt. 6 May foll.; Stephen, b. 6 or 10, bapt. 19 Oct. 1656; Eliz. 28 Feb. bapt. 21 Nov. 1658, wh. d. at 18 yrs.; Isaac, b. 10 or 15 July 1660; Hannah, 31 Aug. 1662; Mary, 2 Sept. 1664; Sarah, 29 Nov. 1666; John, again, 25 Apr. 1669; and Israel, 24 Sept. 1671; was freem. 1678. His will, of 2 Sept. 1695, pro. 16 Jan. 1700, ment. four s. liv. beside gr.ch. Joshua, s. of his s. Joshua, and the two ch. Isaac and Abiah, s. and d. of his s. Isaac, both the f.'s dec. The ds. are nam. Hannah Turner, Mary Burr, and Sarah, wh. m. 17 Apr. 1693, Peter Ripley. JOHN, Hingham, tenth ch. of the preced. m. 26 Mar. 1696, Deborah Lincoln, had John, b. 23 Jan. foll. and Joshua, 29 Dec. 1703. JOSHUA, Hingham, br. of the preced. d. 12 Feb. 1688, and his wid. Mary, wh. he m. " the last of Jan." 1681, had admin. on his est. 28 Apr. 1691. Their ch. were Eliz. b. 20 Dec. 1681; Martha, 23 Feb. 1683; Joshua, 15 Nov. 1686; and Simon, 12 Sept. 1688. STEPHEN, Hingham, br. of the preced. by w. Sarah had Lydia, b. 20 Sept. 1688, d. next yr.; Phebe, 23 Feb. 1690; Stephen, 29 Jan. 1691; Lydia, again, 26 Nov. 1693; Mary, wh. d. 28 Dec. 1698; and Mary, again, 11 May 1700; beside ano. whose name is not found, unless it be that Israel, bapt. 2 Oct. 1692. He d. 16 Jan. 1718, in his will of 9 of that mo. pro. 4 Mar. foll. speak of his *five* ch. THOMAS, Duxbury, m. 26 Apr. 1685, Mary Allen, rem. to Plympton, Falmouth, C. C. and Windham, says Windsor. Early this name seems Lassell, or Lasell.

LEA, JOHN, a youth, aged 13, came 1634, in the Francis, from Ipswich, prob. as serv. to William Westwood. WILLIAM, a youth of 16, came in the Planter, 1635, from London. Possib. this may be the same as Lee.

LEACH, AMBROSE, Boston 1648, is spok. of in Hutch. Coll. 298, and, in 1663, was concern. in Narraganset, or the King's Province. BENJAMIN, Bridgewater, s. of Giles, m. 1702, Hepzibah, d. of Joseph Washburn, had Ann, b. 1703; Joseph, 1705; Mary, 1708; Sarah, 1711; Benjamin, 1713; Ichabod, 1716; Jerathmeel, and Benanuel, tw. 1718; Nokes, 1720; Susanna, 1722; Hannah, 1725; Phebe; Nathan; and Eunice. DAVID, Bridgewater, br. of the preced. by w. Hannah had Mercy, b. 1693; Hannah, 1696; Ephraim, 1699; Experience, 1702; David, 1706; Mehitable, 1711; and Abigail, 1714; and he d. 1757. EBENEZER, Bridgewater, br. of the preced. m. 1707, Prudence Stetson of Scituate, may have had Lydia and possib. others. EDMUND, New Haven 1647-9 and may be longer. GILES, Weymouth 1656, but rem. to Bridgewater bef. 1665 says Mitchell, wh. ment. that he m. Ann Nokes, 1656 (but Weymouth rec. says, 20 Jan. 1657), had Sarah, b. 1656 (but rec. says, 13 Nov. 1657); Eliz.; Samuel, 1662; David; John; Ebenezer; Benjamin; and, perhaps, others, add. that Sarah m. John Aldrich; and Eliz. m. 1693, John Emerson. JOHN, Salem 1637, then had, says Felt, gr. of ld. was br. of Lawrence, d. Dec. 1658. He gave his small prop. to his neph. Richard's s. John. JOHN, Salem 1637, s. of Lawrence, had gr. of ld. says Felt, that yr. and there bapt. John, 3 Sept. 1648; John, and Sarah, tw. Nov. 1648; Rachel, 6 Apr. 1651; Sarah, again, 6 June 1652; Eliz. 27 Nov. 1653; Mary, 3

Sept. 1654; Richard, 15 June 1656; Remember, and Hannah, 3 Nov. 1661; was, prob. the freem. 1681. Mary m. 2 Mar. 1681, Thomas Field. JOHN, Beverly 1671, may have been s. of the preced. or of other s. of Lawrence. JOHN, Bridgewater, s. of Giles, by w. Alice had John, b. 1695; Giles, 1697; Stephen, 1698; Abiel, 1700; Ebenezer, 1702; Mehitable, 1704; Timothy, 1707; Nehemiah, 1709; Solomon, 1712; and Jesse, 1714; and d. 1744. LAWRENCE, Salem 1629, came in one of the fleet with Higginson, req. adm. 19 Oct. 1630, and 18 May foll. was sw. freem. d. June 1662, aged 82, or 85, leav. all his est. to wid. Eliz. wh. d. 1674. Of his s. beside John, and Robert, herein ment. Clement liv. in Eng. and Richard d. here 1647, leav. s. John and Robert. RICHARD, Salem 1639, m. Ann Fuller, freem. 1665, lieut. 1675, and capt. two yrs. aft. d. 1687, leav. sev. ch. of wh. I only kn. that Hannah was bapt. 2 June 1662; and Sarah m. 7 Feb. 1667, Joseph Herrick. ROBERT, Charlestown 1637, where Mary unit. with the ch. 9 Sept. 1639, might be thot. his w. but Felt gives him gr. of ld. at Salem 1637; and the freem. of 1644 was mem. of neither of the chs. in those towns, yet he is said to be s. of Lawrence, and to have d. bef. his f. However, we may presume there was one at ea. and he of Charlestown was householder in 1658 and 78, chos. tythingman 1679, and d. 22 May 1688, aged a. 80, says the rec. ROBERT, and SAMUEL were inhabs. of Manchester, and in favor of that small town petit. for relief, in 1686, from expense of support. worship. See Geneal. Reg. X. 322. SETH, Bridgewater, m. Mary, d. of Thomas Whitman. The name was freq. A Margaret, aged 15, was passeng. in the Planter, ano. Margaret, 22, in the Susan and Ellen, both from London 1635. SAMUEL, Bridgewater, s. of Giles, m. Mary, d. of Nicholas Byram, had Samuel, Josiah, Seth, and Elijah. THOMAS, New London 1680, m. Abigail, d. of Richard Haughton, wh. d. soon aft. her ch. Sarah was b. 7 July 1684. By two other ws. he had ten ch. more bef. 1719.

LEADBETTER, HENRY, Dorchester, m. 18 Mar. 1660, Sarah, d. of Thomas Tolman, had Sarah, b. 31 Dec. 1660; Catharine, 1662; Henry, 1664; Deliverance, 1667; Increase, 1672; Ebenezer, 1676; and Israel, 1678; was freem. 1671, and constable 1673; and d. 20 Apr. 1722. His wid. Relief d. 7 July 1743, aged 92. She had been wid. of Timothy Foster, and first of John Dowse, being d. of John Holland. Sarah m. 1684, Henry Withington; and Catharine m. 29 May 1684, Ephraim Payson. Of the s. Henry, and Israel were m. as well as the foll. INCREASE, Dorchester, s. of the preced. had w. Sarah, wh. d. 16 June 1734, aged 53 yrs. and he d. 10 Nov. 1737.

LEADER, GEORGE, Kittery, submit. to Mass. 1652. JOHN, Boston, s. of Thomas of the same, by w. Abigail had Rebecca, b. 10 Apr. 1652;

Abigail, 29 May 1653; and Thomas, 19 Nov. 1654; and he d. bef. his f. RICHARD, Lynn 1645, superintend. of iron works, tried copper mine in Endicott's farm at Salem, meet. ill success, went, 1650, to Berwick, had gr. of exclus. use of the Little riv. to erect mills, and was a magistr. Winth. II. 356; Belkn. I. 56; Lewis, 96; Sullivan, 326. In 1654 he was call. of Strawberry bank. SAMUEL, Boston 1670, s. of Thomas, excor. of his will. THOMAS, Dedham 1640. His w. Susanna was rec. of the ch. 10 Apr. 1641 ; he rem. to Boston 1647, his sec. w. Rebecca d. 16 Dec. 1653, and he d. 28 Oct. 1663. His will of 17 of that mo. proves, that he had third w. Alice, s. Thomas, dec. and that he well provid. for his wid. with three ch. of Thomas, and his other s. Samuel.

LEAGER, LEGARE, or LEGER, JACOB, Boston, tailor, freem. 2 June 1641, had Hannah, b. 14 Nov. 1655; and d. 24 Feb. 1664, leav. wid. Ann, d. of William Blake of Dorchester, his sec. w. wh. m. a Hallowell, and d. Bethia, wh. m. Fearnot Shaw. His will of 10 Nov. 1662, pro. 19 Mar. foll. provid. for w. and ds. Bethia and Hannah.

LEAMAN, SAMUEL, Charlestown, by w. Mary had Joanna, b. 28 May 1676, d. soon; Nathaniel, d. young; Rebecca, d. young; and Eliz. 13 Nov. 1684. Eaton calls him one of the first sett. of Reading.

LEAR, or LEARE, JOHN, Salem 1658. TOBIAS, Portsmouth 1665, m. Eliz. d. prob. eldest, of Henry Sherburne, and d. a. 1681, leav. Tobias, wh. may have been of Newcastle 1727. A Mrs. L. d. at Portsmouth 1775, in 105th yr. Tobias, H. C. 1783, priv. Secr. of Washington, d. Oct. 1816.

LEARNED, LARNED, or LARNET, sometimes LARNIT, and LERNET, BENONI, Chelmsford, s. of Isaac the first, m. at Sherborn, 10 June 1680, Mary, d. of Thomas Fanning of Watertown, had Thomas, b. 11 Feb. 1682; Benjamin, 15 Aug. 1685 or 6 ; Mary, 10 Oct. 1688; and the mo. d. four days aft. By sec. w. Sarah More he had Hannah, 10 Sept. 1690; Sarah, 31 May 1692; Eliz. 28 Apr. 1694; John, 2 May 1696; Tabitha, 19 Mar. 1698; Abigail, 4 July 1700; Thankful, 1 Aug. 1702 ; Edward, 2 Dec. 1705 ; and Bathsheba, 3 May 1708. He was deac. and d. 10 Apr. 1738; his w. Sarah d. 25 Jan. 1737; and, in the short interval, a third w. Sarah is giv. him by Morse. ISAAC, Woburn, only s. of William, b. in Eng. freem. 1647, m. 9 July 1646, Mary, eldest ch. of Isaac Stearns, had Mary, b. 7 Aug. 1647; Hannah, 24 Aug. 1649; William, 1 Oct. 1650; rem. to Chelmsford, there had Sarah, 28 Oct. or 15 Nov. 1653 ; Isaac, 16 Sept. or 5 Oct. 1655, and Benoni, 4 Dec. 1656, bapt. Dec. 1657; was a selectman, and d. 27 Nov. or 4 Dec. 1657. His wid. m. 9 June 1662, John Burge, and d. next yr.; Mary m. Moses Barron ; Hannah m. 1666, Joseph Farwell; and Sarah m.

Jonathan Barrett. Isaac, Chelmsford, s. of the preced. serv. at the Narraganset fight, 19 Dec. 1675, as a soldier in Davenport's comp. and was then wound.; m. 23 July 1679, Sarah, d. of John Bigelow, had Isaac, b. 10 May 1680; Sarah, 16 Mar. 1682; Abigail, 11 Mar. 1684; Mary, 12 Apr. 1686; William, 12 Feb. 1688; Ebenezer, Sept. 1690; Samuel, 4 Oct. 1692; Hannah, 16 Sept. 1694; Eliz. 27 July 1696; Moses, 29 Apr. 1699; and Martha, 2 May 1702; and he d. 15 Sept. 1737. William, Charlestown 1632, may have come two yrs. bef. but is first heard of in join. the ch. with his w. Goodith in Dec. being the first· adm. since the separat. from Boston ch.; was freem. 14 May 1634, selectman 1636, and in the same office first at the sett. off of town of Woburn to wh. he rem. 1641. In the gr. trouble of 1637 he was on the side of moderat. so far as to disappr. the banishm. of Wheelwright. He d. says the rec. 1 Mar. but Frothingham, wh. may have reason, says 5 Apr. 1646. A wid. Sarah says the rec. d. 24 Jan. 1661, at Malden, and I find admin. 2 Apr. foll. on est. of wid. Jane (but no doubt the same person), of M. yet I am wholly unable to guess wh. would have been the h. unless she were a sec. w. of William, or we presume the rec. of adm. into the ch. means only to designate her as his w. without giv. a name. This to me seems the best solution.

Leathers, Edward, Dover 1665. Perhaps he was common. regard. as of Gipsey blood.

Leavenworth, David, and Thomas, Woodbury, as Cothren, in his Hist. p. 612, tells by aid of tradit. came a. 1690 from Germany; and that David was drown. in youth; and of Thomas, nothing. But one of my Hartford correspond. refers to the State archives as contain. a docum. of 11 June 1684, by Grace L. wid. of Woodbury, and my own suspic. is that the German derivat. should be some centuries earlier.

Leaver, Thomas, Rowley 1643, town clk. m. Damaris, d. of James Bayley of the same; and we hear no more, but that he d. 27 Dec. 1683, leav. prob. Thomas, and, perhaps, others; certain. Prudence, b. 1 Jan. 1645, wh. m. 11 Oct. 1671, Benjamin Gage, as his sec. w. and, next, 6 Apr. 1674, Samuel Stickney.

Leavitt, Aratus, Hampton, s. of Thomas, m. Ruth, d. of Thomas Sleeper, wh. d. 10 Jan. 1726; and he d. 14 Jan. 1739. Hezron, Hampton, s. of Thomas, m. 25 Sept. 1667, Martha, d. of Anthony Taylor, had Lydia, b. 5 Aug. 1668; John, 24 Nov. 1670; James, 31 Jan. 1673, d. soon; Moses, 30 Jan. 1674; Thomas, 8 May 1677, d. young, prob.; and James, again, 1686. Israel, Hingham, s. of John, m. 10 June 1677, Lydia, d. of Abraham Jackson of Plymouth, had John, b. 6 July 1678 (wh. d. 29 July 1749, leav. John, wh. d. 13 Apr. 1797, in 86th yr.); Israel, 1 Aug. 1680; Solomon, 24 Feb. 1682;

Elisha, 16 July 1684; Abraham, 27 Nov. 1686; Sarah, 8 Feb. 1689;
Lydia; Hannah, 30 June 1693; and Mary, 18 Feb. 1696; and he d.
26 Dec. 1696, not 1699, as the gr.stone says. His wid. m. Preserved
Hall. She and all the ch. were liv. July 1708. * JOHN, Dorchester
1634, rem. to Hingham, freem. 3 Mar. 1636, was rep. 1656, 64, a deac.
d. 20 Nov. 1691, aged 83. By w. Sarah, wh. d. 26 May 1700, he prob.
had John; Hannah, bapt. 7 Apr. 1639; Samuel, Apr. 1641; Eliz. 28
Apr. 1644; Jeremiah, 1 Mar. 1646; Israel, 23 Apr. 1648; Moses, b.
12 Aug. 1650; Josiah, 4, bapt. 8 May 1653; Nehemiah, 21 Jan. bapt.
24 Feb. 1656; Sarah, b. 22 Feb. 1659; Mary, 12 June 1661; Hannah,
the sec. 20 Mar. 1664; and Abigail, 9, bapt. 15 Dec. 1667. His will,
of 30 Nov. 1689, ment. these exc. John (and of him names the w. wh.
was m. to Joseph Turner) and Jeremiah, of the s. and first Hannah, and
Eliz. of the ds. wh. were d. (and of Eliz. names the s.). Sarah m. 17
Apr. 1678, Nehemiah Clap of Dorchester; and aft. him Samuel Howe;
Hannah 2d m. 25 Oct. 1683, Joseph Loring; and Abigail m. 20 Jan.
1686, Isaac Lazell. But the two elder ds. wh. were d. had m. viz.:
Hannah, 29 July 1659, to John Lobdell, and d. 23 Apr. 1662; and
Eliz. m. 25 Mar. 1667, Samuel Judkins. Moses went to Exeter bef.
1683. JOHN, Exeter, or Dover, 1645. JOHN, Hingham, s. of John of
the same, m. 27 June 1664, Bathsheba, d. of the Rev. Peter Hobart,
and d. bef. his f. His wid. m. Joseph Turner. JOSIAH, Hingham, br.
of the preced.; was freem. 1679; m. 20 Oct. 1676, Margaret, d. of
Humphrey Johnson, had Josiah, b. 28 July 1679; Joseph, 23 July
1681; Margaret, 20 Oct. 1683; Jeremiah, 21 Aug. 1685; Joshua, 1
Aug. 1687; David, 16 Aug. 1691; Asaph, 31 July 1695; Hezekiah,
17 Sept. 1697; and Mary, 7 Oct. 1699; every one, with his w. nam. in
his will, 2 Aug. 1708. He d. 14 Sept. foll. and his wid. d. 12 June
1739. Joshua, his s. was early at Suffield, where his est. in 1734, was
div. among 5 ch. MOSES, Exeter, s. of the first John, m. 26 Oct. 1681,
Dorothy, d. of Rev. Samuel Dudley, had John; Dudley; Daniel;
Stephen; Joseph; and seven more, whose names are not kn. NEHE-
MIAH, Hingham, br. of the preced. by w. Alice had Mary, b. 19 Aug.
1693, d. next mo.; ano. ch. d. 18 Oct. 1694, whose name was prob.
Jacob; Daniel, 30 May 1697; and Abigail, 10 Dec. 1699. * SAMUEL,
Exeter, br. of the preced. had James, was rep. 1684. THOMAS, Exeter
1639, may have been br. of the first John, bef. 1644 rem. to Hampton,
and d. 28 Nov. 1696; leav. says Farmer, s. Hezron, Aratus, b. 1646;
John; Thomas; James, 1652, d. young; Isabel; Jemima; and Heriah;
but the order is unkn. His w. Isabel d. 19 Feb. 1700. His name is
used as a grantee, with John Wheelwright and two others in that
enormous forgery of the deed of the whole S. and E. part of the Prov-

ince of N. H. with the Isle of Shoals from Indian sachems 17 May
1629, certain. more than seven yrs. bef. the principal W. came to this
country, and near nine yrs. bef. that honest purch. by W. of all the lds.
for 30 ms. betw. the gr. riv. Merrimack and Piscataqua. Nor can any
evid. be discov. prob. bef. the gen. conflagrat. of this globe, that L. was
here a single yr. earlier than W.

LE BLONDE, JAMES, Boston 1689, prob. a Huguenot, whose w. Ann
unit. 1690, with Mather's ch. had there bapt. James, 20 Apr. 1690, d.
soon; James, again, 7 June 1691; Ann, 9 Apr. 1693, d. soon; Peter, 6
Jan. 1695; Gabriel, 6 Mar. 1698; Ann, again, 15 Dec. 1700; Phil-
lippa, 23 Apr. 1704; Marian, 10 Mar. 1706; and Alexander, 4 Sept.
1709.

LECHFORD, ‖ THOMAS, Boston, a lawyer from one of the Inns of
Court at London, came 1637, left here, aft. vain attempt to earn bread,
and being ar co. 1640, in the same sh. with Hugh Peter, Thomas Welde,
and John Winthrop, the younger. He got his book thro. the press
almost two yrs. bef. Welde's, and Cotton says he d. shortly aft. its pub.
I think he design. this as evid. of the displeasure of heaven; but the
date may be adm. however erron. the construct. of it.

LECK, LECKE, or LEEKE, AMBROSE, Wickford 1674.

LEDDRA, WILLIAM, Boston, convict. Sept. 1660, of being a Quaker,
next yr. for return. sentenc. on 9th and hang. 14 Mar. An excel. letter
to the w. of his bosom upon the day bef. execut. is preserv. Sewel,
Hist. I. 336, 459. 65, 8. Hutch. I. 202, calls him Ledea.

LEE, ABRAHAM, Dover 1680, a man of some skill in natural science,
m. 21 June 1686, Esther, wid. of Henry Elkins, and d. of Major Richard Waldron, was k. with the f. of his w. by the Ind. 27 June 1689.
His wid. m. Richard Jose, sheriff of the Prov. outliv. him, and d. in the
Isl. of Jersey, says the pedigree of W. in Geneal. Reg. V. 182. ED-
WARD, Hartford 1648, is by me thot. the same as Lay. HENRY, Manchester 1650, was br. of Thomas of Ipswich, and prob. rem. to Boston
1656. JOHN, Ipswich 1640, had, it is said, come a. 1635, from London,
had John, b. a. 1639; and Joseph, late in 1643; d. 1671. Fam. tradit.
makes him m. on our side of the water, yet tells not the name of the w.
but gives him four ds. three without names, of wh. one m. a Patch; one a
Hunkins; ano. a Tuttle, and exact acco. of the other is, that she was
call. Ann, d. unm. 28 Sept. 1691. On the same evid. it is shown, that
orig. the name was Leigh, and the s. of this man agr. to change it.
JOHN, Saco 1645, was of the gr. jury that yr. but in Dec. 1647, was d.
or rem. JOHN, Farmington 1653, d. 1690, had w. Mary, d. of Stephen
Hart, and ch. John, b. 11 June 1659, bapt. 22 July 1660; Mary, b. 14
Aug. 1664; Stephen, 2 Apr. 1667; Thomas, 1671; David, 1674; and

Tabitha, 1677. His wid. m. 1691, Jedediah Strong, as his third w.;
Mary m. Stephen Upson, 28 Dec. 1682 ; Tabitha m. Preserved Strong of
Northampton, s. of her mo.'s h. ; and they rem. to Coventry, whither, also,
her br. David rem. aft. some yrs. at N. JOHN, Westfield, s. of Walter,
was in the Falls fight, 1676, m. 9 Dec. 1680, Sarah Pixley, prob. d. of
William, had John, b. 8 July 1683, d. within two wks. as did the mo. in
one. By sec. w. Eliz. d. of Dennis Crampton, m. 1686, had John, again,
2 Aug. 1687 ; Eliz. 14 Dec. 1689 ; Sarah, 24 Apr. 1692 ; Abigail, 28
Oct. 1694 ; Ruth, 1 Apr. 1697 ; Joanna, 1702 ; Samuel, 1704 ; and
Margaret, 1707 ; and d. 13 Nov. 1711. His wid. was Sarah, and she
with s. John were admors. JOHN, Boston, s. of the first John, by fam.
tradit. is call. a surg. in the navy, and said to have m. and had fam. two
s. and two ds. but no names or dates are giv. and unhap. no illustr. of
this obscurity can be got from rec. of Boston, so that acquiesc. in the
result of the authority, that in this branch the name bec. extinct, is easy.
JOHN, Farmington, s. prob. of John of the same, had John, and Jonathan, both bapt. 28 Nov. (not 27) 1686; Mary, 4 May 1690; Eliz.
5 Feb. 1693 ; Samuel, 1 Apr. 1694; and Hezekiah, 6 June 1687.
JOSEPH, Ipswich, s. of John of the same, m. Mary, eldest ch. of Henry
Woodhouse of Concord, had Woodis, b. 17 Oct. 1679, d. soon; Joseph,
16 Oct. 1680 ; Mary, 14 July 1682; Ann, 17 May 1684; Henry, 16
May 1686; John, 10 Sept. 1688, d. in three mos.; Woodis, again, 18
Dec. 1689 ; and Hannah, 10 Apr. 1691, d. next mo. He rem. to Con-
cord, where his w. d. and he m. 15 Nov. 1697, Mary, wid. of Edmund
Wigley, d. of John Miles, wh. d. 25 Nov. 1708. He took third w. 28
Jan. 1713, wid. Mary Fox, and d. 4 Nov. 1716. His wid. m. Daniel
Hoar. His s. Joseph, Henry, and Woodis largely and honora. perpet.
the name. JOSEPH, Manchester 1684. JOSHUA, Boston, m. 14 Dec.
1688, wid. Mary Engs. NATHANIEL, Westfield, s. of Walter, m. Abigail Warner, d. of Daniel of Farmington, had Daniel, b. 1698, d. young ;
Nathaniel, 1700, d. bef. his f. but had two s. wh. then were liv. ; Abigail,
1702, d. young; Margaret, 1705; Daniel, again, 1707; Hezekiah, 1710,
d. young; tw. ch. 1711, both d. soon; and a d. 1717, wh. d. soon; and
he d. 26 Apr. 1745. ROBERT, Plymouth 1636, was, prob. from London,
adm. freem. 3 Jan. 1637, may have been short time in 1638 at Lynn ;
had w. Mary, and ch. Ann and Mary, was liv. 1654. Either he or his
w. was br. or sis. of John Atwood or his w. wh. left them part of their
est. See Geneal. Reg. IV. 173, and V. 260. Mary m. 26 Oct. 1651,
John Howland, jr. SAMUEL, Boston, may seem only a trans. visitor, as
he is call. of Virginia in the rec. of his m. 2 Aug. 1655, to Eliz. Rowland of B. yet tho. the h. has prefix of resp. I regret to remark, that the
w. is equally unkn. Yet perhaps he was the Malden man, wh. had

Eliz. b. Nov. 1670; and she may have m. 24 May 1690, Jonathan Howard. SAMUEL, Bristol, b. in London 1623, bred at Magdalen Coll. Oxford, there creat. M. A. 14 Apr. 1648, and, in violat. of their rights, made, 9 Apr. 1651, one of the Proctors of the Univ. See Wood's Fasti Oxon. II. 164. He came over hither 24 June 1686, arr. 22 Aug. as in Sewall's Almanac, and bec. the sett. min. of B. 8 May 1687; preach. at the pub. fast in Boston 17 June 1691, and emb. for home, on the voyage was tak. by a French privateer, carr. into St. Maloes, there d. in prison the same yr. Mather, III. 223, makes some amends for the brevity of his narrat. by the praise of its subject. But Baylies follows Eliot in more sober estimate of him. Rebecca, his d. was third w. of John Saffin. In a letter to her h. 19 July 1710, Mather, wh. aft. some yrs. was m. to her sis. Lydia, shows, in an extraord. manner, exceed. never by him unless in his intemper. address to Gov. Joseph Dudley, his harshness of admonit. and resolution to govern. Ano. d. Catharine was w. of Henry Howell, aft. of Stephen Sewall; and this connex. was assoc. with one of the principal causes of the many miseries that afflict. the latter days of Cotton Mather. See 4 Mass. Hist. Coll. II. 122. SAMUEL, Malden, freem. 1671, d. Aug. 1676, aged 36, m. 4 Nov. 1662, Mercy Call, d. of Thomas. He may have had Mercy to m. 2 Dec. 1686, Richard Wicks; and his wid. m. 25 Oct. 1677, John Allen. STEPHEN, Westfield, s. of Walter, m. 23 Dec. 1691, Eliz. Woodward, d. of John, had Thomas, b. 5 Nov. 1692; and Samuel, 9 May 1695. He rem. to Lebanon. THOMAS, Ipswich 1648, br. of Henry, and John, d. 1662, aged a. 82. *THOMAS, Lyme, came a. 1641 with his mo. and two sis. Phebe, and Jane, the f. whose name was Thomas, hav. d. as the tradit. was, on the voyage, of smallpox. The surv. came from Boston to Saybrook, tho. the f. of the mo. by the same authority, is call. Brown of Providence. This s. must have been *very* young, for Lyme rec. gives him ch. up to 22 Dec. 1692, and his first, John, by w. Sarah Kirkland, was b. 21 Sept. 1670; Thomas, 10 Dec. 1672; Sarah, 14 Jan. 1675; and aft. this w. d. 21 May 1676, he took 13 July foll. sec. w. Mary, perhaps d. of Balthazar De Wolf, and had Phebe, b. 14 Apr. 1677; Mary, 23 Apr. 1679; Eliz.; William, 10 Apr. 1684; Stephen; Hannah; and four more ch. one of wh. d. young. He was ensign, rep. 1676, and d. 30 May 1705, and his wid. Mary bec. sec. w. of sec. Matthew Griswold. His sis. Jane m. June 1659, Samuel Hyde of Norwich; and Phebe m. 1 Nov. 1659, perhaps, John Large of Saybrook. WALTER, Windsor, freem. of Conn. 1654, rem. to Northampton 1656, thence, a. 1665 to Westfield, there d. 9 Feb. 1718, at gr. age. His ch. were John, b. 2 Jan. 1657; Timothy, 8 Aug. 1659, d. soon; Stephen, 5 Mar. 1662; and Nathaniel, 25 Dec. 1663; all at N.; this last rec. at Westfield, but, perhaps, some yrs. aft. b.; Mary, 15 Jan. 1665, rec. at Springfield, prob. bef. he was fix. at W.; Eliz. 28 Feb. 1667, d. young; Hannah, 9 Jan. 1668; and Abigail, 11 Dec. 1670. His w. d. 29 Feb. 1696; and he m. 1705, sec. w. Hepzibah, wid. of Caleb Pomeroy, wh. d. 18 Nov. 1711. Oft. the spell. is Laigh, and it may sometimes be Lay, wh. see. Twenty-four of this name had been gr. in 1834, at the N. E. coll. of wh. one half at Harv.

LEEDS, BENJAMIN, Dorchester, s. of Richard, freem. 1670, m. 17 Sept. 1667, Mary, d. of William Brimsmead, had Benjamin, d. 13 Mar. 1718, aged 80. It would be pleasant to kn. what means the insert. of this name among freem. 1680. He had sec. w. wh. d. 10 Aug. 1692; and again m. 11 Aug. 1696, Abigail Knight, wh. d. 29 June 1712. No ch. by either of the last two ws. is kn. and all of the name in our vicin. are descend. of his br. JOHN, New London 1674, mariner, from Staplehoe, Co. Kent, call. hims. 39 yrs. old in Sept. 1680, m. 25 Jan. 1678, Eliz. d. of Cary Latham, had John, bapt. 13 Mar. 1681; Eliz. 16 Oct. 1681; William, b. 3 Mar. bapt. 20 May 1683; Gideon; and Thomas, both bapt. aft. d. of f. 1 Aug. 1697. He liv. on Groton side, where William liv. 1712. JOHN, Watertown, had, says Bond, Eliz.; John; Edward; Joseph; Abigail; and Deborah, bapt. 19 Jan. 1688; but he could not name the w. JOSEPH, Dorchester, br. of Benjamin, rem. a. 1661 to Northampton, m. 8 Nov. of that yr. Miriam, d. of capt. Aaron Cook, had Miriam, b. 1663; one, in 1664; Joseph, 1665; wh. all d. young; Joanna, 1667; Miriam, again, 1670; John, 1672, d. soon; John, again, 1674; Joseph, 1675, d. soon; Benjamin, 1677; was in the Falls fight, 19 May 1676, and next yr. went back to his nat. town, there had Samuel, 1679; Eliz. 1684; and Rebecca, 1687; d. 28 Jan. 1715, aged a. 77. His wid. Miriam d. 23 Aug. 1720. RICHARD, Dorchester, emb. Apr. 1637 at Great Yarmouth, Co. Norf k. aged 32, with w. Joan, 23, and a ch. whose name is not found in the Eng. rec.; had a gr. of ld. that yr. at Salem, says Felt, but did not cont. there, had Benjamin and Joseph, tw. b. 14 July 1637, bapt. 4 Apr. 1639; freem. 1645, a select-man 1653; constable 1664, d. 18 Mar. 1693, aged a. 98, says the inscript. over his gr. whereas his declarat. in 1637 would prove him to be 88. The fond exaggera. of his days is seen in the will, made a few days bef. d. pro. 1 Apr. foll. begin. with this language: "being by the patience of God near an hundred yrs. old." It names only s. Joseph, and Benjamin; d. Hannah Clap, w. of Samuel, wh. was bapt. 16 Feb. 1640; d.-in-law Miriam, w. of Joseph, and gr.s. Joseph.

LEEK, PHILIP, New Haven, took o. of fidel. 1644, had Philip, b. 26 Aug. 1646; Eleazer, bapt. 12 Sept. 1647, wh. is call. Ebenezer at the Pro. Court distribut. of the est. of his f.; Thomas, 21 Jan. 1649, wh.

was a propr. 1685; Mary, perhaps 15 June 1651, but the town rec. much more reliab. says she was b. 16 June 1652; and Joanna, b. 22 Jan. bapt. 28 Mar. 1658; and d. May 1676. Mary m. 9 Mar. 1675, John Davis; and Joanna m. 6 Feb. 1678, Henry Stephens.

LEES, EDWARD, Guilford, perhaps s. of Hugh, m. at Saybrook, 7 Nov. 1676, Eliz. Wright, was a propr. 1685. HUGH, Saybrook 1648, liv. there 1664. WILLIAM, Norwalk, prob. s. of the preced. but the dilig. annalist, Hall, names not w. or ch. exc. Deborah, wh. m. 9 Mar. 1710, John Scrivener; yet shows him there 1672–87.

LEETE, ‡ * ANDREW, Guilford, s. of Gov. William, freem. 1670, rep. 1675, an Assist. 1678, m. 1 June 1669, Eliz. d. of Thomas Jordan, had William, b. 24 Mar. 1671; Caleb, 10 Dec. 1673; Samuel, 1677; Dorothy, 1680; Abigail, 1683; and Mercy, 1685; and was a propr. 1685. His w. d. 4 Mar. 1701, and he d. 31 Oct. 1702, all the ch. then liv. JOHN, Guilford, br. of the preced. said to be the first Eng. male ch. b. in the town, freem. 1671, was a propr. 1685; m. 4 Oct. 1670, Mary, d. of William Chittenden, had Ann, b. 5 Aug. 1671; John, 4 June 1673; Joshua, 7 July 1676; Sarah, 16 Dec. 1677; Pelatiah, 26 Mar. 1680; Mehitable, 10 Dec. 1683; Benjamin, 26 Dec. 1686; and Daniel, 23 Dec. 1689, d. young. He d. 25 Nov. 1692; and the wid. d. 9 Mar. 1712. § † ‡ WILLIAM, Guilford, sign. the planta. covenant of 1 June 1639, was an Assist. of N. H. col. 1643 to 57, dep.-gov. 1658, Gov. 1661 to 65; on the union with Conn. bec. an Assist. to 1669, then dep.-gov. to 1676, when, on d. of Gov. Winthrop, he was chos. to that office, and so by ann. elect. till his d. at Hartford, 16 Apr. 1683. He was oft. a Commissr. of the Unit. Col. of N. E. from 1655 to 79. Of three ws. I presume the first w. Ann, wh. d. 1 Sept. 1668, or rather was bur. that day, was mo. of all the ch.: John, b. a. 1639; Andrew; William; Abigail; Caleb, 24 Aug. 1651, d. at 21 yrs.; Graciana, 22 Dec. 1653; Peregrine, 12 Jan. 1658, d. young; Joshua, d. 22 Feb. 1660, prob. very young; and Ann, 15 Mar. 1662. Abigail m. 26 Oct. 1671, Rev. John Woodbridge of Killingworth, and Ann m. 9 or 19 Nov. 1683, John Trowbridge, and, next, 1696, Ebenezer Collins; and Graciana liv. long, infirm in body and mind. His sec. w. Sarah m. 1671, had been wid. of Henry Rotherford, d. 10 Feb. 1674. Mary, the third w. wid. of Rev. Nicholas Street, wh. outliv. him but a few mos.; had been w. of Gov. Francis Newman. * WILLIAM, Guilford, youngest surv. s. of the preced. freem. 1671, rep. 1677, d. 1 June 1687, leav. wid. Mary, wh. m. Stephen Bradley, and d. Mary, 11 Jan. 1672, wh. m. 1 Aug. 1691, James Hooker.

LEETH, JOHN, Boston, by w. Hannah had Martha, b. 31 Aug. 1654. It may be the same as Leathe.

LEFFINGWELL, sometimes in old rec. read LEPPINGWELL, or LAP-PINGWELL, MICHAEL, Woburn, had Hannah, b. 4 Jan. 1643, d. in few wks.; Hannah, again, 6 Jan. 1646; Sarah, 10 Mar. 1647; Thomas, 13 Jan. 1649; Ruth, 2 Jan. 1650; Michael, 8 June 1651, d. in a wk.; Rachel, 4 Mar. 1653; Abigail, 24 May 1655; Esther, 16 May 1657; and Tabitha, 8 May 1660; and he d. 22 Mar. 1687. Geneal. Reg. VII. 284, gives from Boston copy of rec. differ. dates. * THOMAS, Saybrook 1637, prob. on the E. side of the riv. had Rachel, b. 17 Mar. 1648; Thomas, 27 Aug. 1649; Jonathan, 6 Dec. 1650; Joseph, 24 Dec. 1652; Mary, 10 Dec. 1654; and Nathaniel, 11 Dec. 1656; was one of the purch. of the tract from the Ind. 1659, now includ. Norwich and sev. other towns, and with the first sett. of N. its rep. 1662, and many foll. yrs. was an active partisan, when he was lieut. in Philip's war. THOMAS, Woburn, s. of Michael, m. 11 May 1675, Sarah Knight, wh. d. 16 Aug. 1691, and he m. 15 Jan. foll. Hannah Duntlin.

LEGAT, or LEGGETT, JOHN, Hampton 1640, Exeter 1642, clk. of the writs, kept sch. in ea.; at H. in 1649; m. 1644, Ann, Thomas Wilson's wid.

LEGAREE, FRANCIS, Boston 1690, a Huguenot goldsmith, with two s.

LEGGE, JOHN, Salem 1631, serv. of John Humfrey, •came in the fleet with Winth. liv. at Marblehead, was freem. 6 May 1635, d. 1674. JOHN, Marblehead, s. perhaps of the preced. freem. 1680, had Samuel, wh. was a mariner of Boston in 1671; and John of M. 1691.

LEGROVE, NICHOLAS, Salem 1668.

LEIGH, JOHN, a soldier in Moseley's comp. Dec. 1675, of wh. I see no more. JOSEPH, Ipswich 1651. Perhaps it is the same as the name of like sound, Lee. THOMAS, Roxbury, neph. of capt. Thomas Brattle, d. 20 July 1694, aged 30.

LEIGHTON. See Laighton.

LEISTER, or LISTER, EDWARD, a youth from London, in the employm. of Stephen Hopkins, came in the Mayflower, 1620. But we kn. no more of him, exc. his punishm. for fighting a duel with ano. youth from London, and Bradford, wh. calls him Litster, 4 Mass. Hist. Coll. III. 455, says, he went to Virg. and there d.

LELAND, EBENEZER, Sherborn, s. of Henry, by w. Deborah had Deborah, b. 16 Aug. 1679; Ebenezer, 14 Jan. 1681; Timothy, 22 Feb. 1684; James, 22 Sept. 1687; Susanna, 1690; Patience, 1695; Martha, 8 Sept. 1699; Isaac, 19 Apr. 1702; Sibella, 1708; and Amariah, 11 Dec. 1710; but by a sec. w. Patience Sabin, were the last five. His third w. was Mary Hunt. In Oct. 1742 admin. of his est. was giv. to his s. Timothy. ELEAZER, Sherborn, younger br. of the preced. had w. Sarah, m. 13 July perhaps of the yr. 1690, but no ch. and d. 5 Dec.

1703, tho. he made his will, in wh. no name is found but that of the w.
16 Oct. 1691. HENRY, Dorchester 1653, s. of the first Hopestill, rem.
to Medfield, had by w. Margaret Badcock, or Babcock, sis. of Robert
(wh. in fam. tradit. he is vainly reckon. to have brot. perhaps with her
first born, from Eng. 1652), Hopestill, bapt. at D. May 1653, d. soon ;
Hopestill, again, 15 Nov. 1655 ; Experience, 16 May 1656 ; Ebenezer,
2 or 25 Jan. 1658 ; and Eleazer, 16 June 1660 ; with w. Margaret are
nam. the four ch. in his will of 27 Mar. pro. 8 June 1680. He was of
that pt. of M. wh. bec. Sherborn. Experience m. it is said, 1672, John
Colburn of Dedham. HOPESTILL, Weymouth, in very recent time
ascertain. to be the ancest. of all the numer. tribe, deriv. thro. only s.
Henry, wh. was bef. thot. the progenit. of our side of the water. Perhaps he had sev. ds. beside Experience, wh. m. the first Thomas Holbrook, in Eng. He d. at Medfield 1655, aged 75. Morse exults in his
honor, as "one of the most ancient, if not the most ancient," that ever
came to our country, yet presumes the time of his com. was 1624,
when he, of course, could not be over 43 yrs. old. Even if he puts his
arr. a dozen yrs. too early, as to me seems prob. he borders on presumpt.
in clos. with assert. " no monum. inscript. in N. E. but his will date back
to 1580." Surely one dozen, if not two, of the first score of yrs. comers
to N. E. includ. Elder Brewster and Gov. Dudley, must have been b.
as early as this venerab. head of the Lelands. HOPESTILL, Sherborn,
eldest s. of Henry, had two ws. Abigail Hill, m. 5 Nov. 1678, d. 5 Oct.
1689 ; and Patience Holbrook ; and ch. Henry, b. 22 Feb. 1680 ; Hopestill, 4 Aug. 1681 ; Abigail, 17 Feb. 1684 ; John, 11 Oct. 1687 ; William, 11 Feb. 1692 ; Eleazer, 8 Apr. 1695 ; Joseph, 9 May 1698 ;
Isaac, 2 June 1701 ; Joshua, 5 May 1705 ; and Margaret, 25 Dec.
1708. In his will, of 18 Aug. 1729, the day bef. he d. pro. 13 Oct.
foll. he names w. Patience, and all the ch. exc. John, and Eleazer. His
wid. d. 5 Oct. 1740.

LELLOCK, JOSEPH, Boston, found in the *sec.* copy of rec. to have, by
w. Joanna, b. to him s. Martin, 22 Nov. 1658. As this seem. to me
almost an impossib. name, occurr. in no other place of county, town, or ch.
rec. I spent a good time in vain attempt to find it or any *such* from
wh. the pervers. might have orig. but on the older copy could not
discern it, nor do I believe it was ever in the true lost rec. This instance
justifies my caution to all interest. in similar inquiries, and to courts of
law, not to accept certif. *copies*, but to call for *orig.* rec.

LEMON, LEAMOND, or LEMOND, sometimes LEMAN, JOSEPH, Charlestown, came in youth from Eng. where he was b. a. 1662, m. 12 June
1690, Mary Bradley, had Joseph, bapt. 26 June 1692, wh. was f. of
Joseph, H. C. 1735. ROBERT, Salem 1637, by w. Mary had there

bapt. Grace, and Mary, 7 Apr. 1639; Martha, 22 Mar. 1640; John, 27 Mar. 1642; Eliz. 17 Dec. 1643; John, 12 Oct. 1645; and Hannah, 7 July 1650, wh. m. 28 June 1668, Samuel Beadle; was freem. 27 Dec. 1642, when the name is rec. Leoman or Looman. His wid. m. 19 Nov. 1674, Philip Cromwell. SAMUEL, Groton, m. Mary, d. of William Longley, had Samuel, b. 29 Apr. 1667. He was driv. I presume, to live at Charlestown, and there was impress. into Moseley's comp. in Dec. 1675, or volunteer. to have his revenge.

LENOX, RALPH, New Haven, had John, b. 1655; but some doubt is felt a. this name.

LENTHALL, *ROBERT*, Weymouth 1637, not pleas. the governm. of our col. he was forbid. to be ord. went to Newport next yr. where his name is spell. Lintell, when adm. a freem. 1640, kept a sch. but was glad to go home 1642. See Lechford; Callender, 62; Winth. I. 287.

LENTON, LAWRENCE, Ipswich 1673. Felt.

LEONARD, ABEL, Springfield 1678, s. of John, m. 4 Mar. 1687, Mary Remington, had Mary, b. 16 Dec. 1687; and Sarah, 8 Oct. 1689, both d. young; and he d. 10 Mar. 1690, and his wid. m. Samuel Bedurtha. BENJAMIN, Springfield, freem. 1690, br. of the preced. was there 1678. He m. 9 Feb. 1680, Sarah Scott, had John, b. 12 July 1681; Benjamin 3 Oct. 1683, d. young; Nathaniel, 6 Oct. 1685; Ebenezer, 26 Jan. 1687; Margaret, 1689; Sarah, 23 Mar. 1691; Martha, 23 Oct. 1695; Kezia, 25 Nov. 1697; Abel, 27 Aug. 1700; Benjamin, again, 17 Aug. 1702; and Rachel, Jan. 1706. He d. 21 Dec. 1724; and his wid. d. 2 Dec. 1751. BENJAMIN, Taunton, s. of the first James, m. 15 Jan. 1679, Sarah Thrasher, perhaps d. of Christopher, had Sarah, b. 21 May 1680; Benjamin, 25 Jan. 1684; Hannah, 8 Nov. 1685, d. young; Jerusha, 25 Jan. 1689; Hannah, 8 Dec. 1691; Joseph, 22 Jan. 1693; and Henry, 8 Nov. 1695. ELKANAH, Middleborough, s. of Thomas, d. 29 Dec. 1714, leav. s. Elkanah, a man of distinct. GEORGE, Taunton, s. of Thomas, highly disting. as the gr. propr. m. 4 July 1695, Ann Tisdale, had George, b. 4 Mar. 1698; Nathaniel, 9 Mar. 1700, H. C. 1719; Abigail, 16 Dec. 1703; and Ephraim, 16 Jan. 1706, wh. was f. of the famous Daniel, H. C. 1760, antagonist of John Adams in the questions of allegiance, Ch. J. of Bermuda, d. at London 27 June 1829; and d. 5 Sept. 1716. HENRY, Lynn, had w. Mary in 1650, it is said, and ch. perhaps one or more b. in Eng. Samuel, Nathaniel, and Thomas, but certain. at L. Henry, b. 14 June 1656, d. next yr.; Sarah, 26 June 1663; Mary, 13 Jan. 1666, d. next yr.; was aged 37 in 1655, freem. 1668, of Rowley, perhaps, 1674, when certain. his three s. engag. there in iron works; rem. it is thot. to N. J. where the iron works (in wh. he had been engag. at Lynn, Braintree, and Taunton at sev. times, tho. chief. at

L.) now under the governm. of Carteret, promis. better. ISAAC, Bridge-water, s. of Solomon, by w. Deliverance had Hannah, b. 1680, and prob. Isaac, Deliverance, Joseph, and others, as Mitchell thinks. JACOB, Weymouth, br. of the preced. had Abigail, b. 1680; and Susanna, 1683; rem. to Bridgewater, and had Experience; Mary; Sarah, 1699; Solomon; and Jacob, 1702, d. young. In his will, 1716, ment. w. Susanna. JAMES, Providence 1645, Taunton 1652, from Pontypool, Monmouthsh. s. of Thomas, wh. came not, with his br. Henry inspect. iron works, at Lynn and Braintree; had Thomas, b. a. 1641; James, a. 1643; Abigail; Rebecca; Joseph, a. 1655; Benjamin; Hannah, wh. d. 25 Feb. 1675; and Uriah, 10 July 1662; beside John, wh. d. says fam. tradit. a. 20 yrs. old; the first two, perhaps in Eng. He had sec. w. Margaret, wh. bore him no ch. d. bef. 1691, and his wid. d. a. 1701. Baylies, Hist. of Plymouth, II. 268; III. 120. His d. Hannah m. 24 Jan. 1678, Isaac Deane. JAMES, Taunton, s. of the preced. by first w. Hannah, wh. d. 25 Feb. 1674, had Eunice, b. 25 Nov. 1668; Prudence, 24 Jan. 1670; Hannah, 2 Oct. 1671; and James, 1 Feb. 1673, d. within 2 yrs. He m. next, 25 Oct. 1675, Lydia, d. of Anthony Gulliver of Milton, wh. d. 24 July 1705, had James, again, 11 May 1677; Lydia, 10 Mar. 1679; Stephen, 14 Dec. 1680; Abigail, 30 Jan. 1683; Nathaniel, 18 Mar. 1685; Seth, 3 Apr. 1686; Sarah, 6 Sept. 1688; Mehitable, 24 Oct. 1691; and Eliz. 19 Apr. 1694. He m. third w. Rebecca, and had Ebenezer, 28 Aug. 1708, wh. d. young. He was a capt. and d. 1 Nov. 1726, in 84th yr. and his wid. d. 3 Apr. 1738, in 76th yr. JOHN, Springfield 1639, m. 4 Sept. 1640, Sarah Heald, had John, b. 1641, d. young; Joseph, 1 Jan. 1643, d. soon; Joseph, again, 20 Mar. 1644; Sarah, 13 Oct. 1645; Mary, 14 July 1647; Martha, 15 Feb. 1649; Lydia, 1 Aug. 1650; John, again, 10 July 1652, d. young; Benjamin, 5 July 1654; Abel, 22 May 1656; Josiah, 2 Jan. 1658; Hannah, 19 Dec. 1659; Rebecca, 26 Mar. 1661; Deborah, 15 Oct. 1663; and Rachel, 8 Nov. 1665; and he was k. by the Ind. early in 1676; and his wid. m. 21 Feb. 1677, Benjamin Parsons; and, again, in 1690, the worshipful Peter Tilton; and she d. at S. 23 Nov. 1711, 71 yrs. aft. first m.; but it is not kn. that she had any more ch. than those fifteen she bore to L. Eight ds. and four s. were m. Sarah m. John Keep; Mary m. 10 Nov. 1665, Samuel Bliss; Martha m. 8 June 1670, Benjamin Wait; Lydia m. 18 Mar. 1675, John Dumbleton; Hannah m. 24 Apr. 1676, Daniel Denton; Rebecca m. 1 Dec. 1681, Thomas Miller; and Rachel m. 17 Mar. 1685, Thomas Hancox. JOHN, Bridgewater, s. of Solomon, by w. Sarah had John, Enoch, Moses, Josiah, Joseph, and Sarah; and d. 1699. JOHN, Taunton, s. of Thomas, m. Mary, d. of Philip King, had Thomas. JOSEPH, Taunton, s. of the first James, m.

15 Dec. 1679, Mary Black of Milton, had Mary, b. 2 Oct. 1680; Experience, 18 Mar. 1682; Joseph, 28 Jan. 1684; Mehitable, 22 Aug. 1685; Edward, 2 Nov. 1688; William, 26 Mar. 1690; and Silence; and he d. 18 Oct. 1692, in his 38th yr. JOSEPH, Springfield, eldest s. of John, had five or six ws. and ch. perhaps not by all; Mary, b. Feb. 1674, d. at two 'yrs.; Samuel, 16 May 1677; John, 12 Sept. 1679, d. next mo.; Joseph, 1 Jan. 1681; and his first w. Mary d. the same mo. By sec. w. Eliz. m. 29 Mar. 1683, wh. d. 6 July 1689, he had Mercy, 6 Nov. 1683, d. in few days; Ebenezer, 15 Mar. 1685, d. young; Mehitable, 5 Sept. 1686, d. young; and Eliz. 14 Jan. 1689; and by third w. Rebecca Dumbleton, m. 1 Mar. 1693, had Ebenezer, 16 Jan. 1694; was freem. 1690, and d. 1716. JOSIAH, Springfield, youngest br. of the preced. was in the Falls fight, 1676, m. 19 Dec. 1678, Sarah Dumbleton, d. of John, had Josiah, b. 21 Oct. 1680; Sarah, 16 Sept. 1682; Abel, 1685; and Mary, 12 Mar. 1687, and d. 13 Feb. 1689, and his wid. m. Thomas Root. PHILIP, Marshfield, br. of the first Henry and James, was s. of Thomas of Pontypool, in Wales, had w. Lydia, wh. d. 13 Nov. 1707, and only d. Phebe, wh. m. 6 Nov. 1694, Samuel Hill of Duxbury, whither he rem. and d. 5 July 1708. RICE, Rehoboth 1644, had Rachel, b. 26 Jan. 1674; Sarah, 16 Mar. 1676; and his w. Sarah was bur. 16 Mar. foll. SAMUEL, Bridgewater, s. of Solomon, sett. the est. of his f. 1686, wh. says Mitchell, was the first in Plymouth; tho. I do not kn. what he means by the phrase. He rem. to Worcester. SAMUEL, Taunton, s. of Thomas, m. 17 Apr. 1701, Catharine, d. of Thomas Deane, had four s. wh. were all deac. and five ds. d. 13 Apr. 1745. SOLOMON, Duxbury 1637, rem. to Bridgewater 1645, had Solomon, Samuel, John, Jacob, Mary, and Isaac. He d. 1686, leav. wid. Mary. His d. Mary m. 24 Dec. 1673, John Pollard. * THOMAS, Taunton, eldest s. of the first James, b. prob. in Eng. m. at Plymouth, 21 Aug. 1662, Mary Watson, prob. d. of George, had Mary, b. 2 Aug. 1663; Thomas, 22 Jan. 1666; John, 18 May 1668; George, 18 Apr. 1671; Samuel, 1 Feb. 1674; Elkanah, 15 May 1677; James, 17 Dec. 1679, d. young; Seth, 28 Apr. 1682, d. at six mos.; Phebe, 3 Mar. 1684, d. next yr.; and Eliz. 15 July 1686; and he d. 24 Nov. 1713, in 72d yr. His wid. Mary d. 1 Dec. 1723, in 81st yr. THOMAS, Taunton, s. of the preced. had w. Joanna, but I kn. no more. URIAH, Taunton, youngest s. of the first James, m. 1 June 1685, Eliz. d. of Thomas Caswell, had Uriah, b. 10 Apr. 1686; William; James; Seth; Jonathan; and Margaret. Eight of this name had, in 1834, been gr. at Harv. eight at Yale, and fourteen at other N. E. coll.

LEONARDS, THOMAS, freem. of Conn. 1658; but his resid. is unkn.

LEONARDSON, JACOB, Newtown, L. I. 1655. Thompson.

LESTER, ANDREW, Gloucester, an early sett. freem. 1643, then call. Lister, by w. Barbara had Daniel, b. 15 Apr. 1642; Andrew, 26 Dec. 1644; Mary, 26 Dec. 1647; and Ann, 24 Mar. 1651; rem. that yr. to New London, where his w. d. 2 Feb. 1654. By sec. w. Ann he had Timothy, b. 4 July 1662; Joseph, 15 June 1664; beside Benjamin, whose date is not giv. He d. aft. 14 Oct. 1669, when the two elder s. were propos. for freem. Ann m. 3 May 1670, Nathaniel Millet of Gloucester.

LETHERLAND, or LITHERLAND, WILLIAM, Boston, might rather be insert. here than Lytherland, where Farmer first plac. the name. Still hav. resolv. not to differ from his work without manifest reason, there it may still be seen.

LETHERMORE, JOHN, freem. of Mass. 6 May 1635, whose resid. is uncert. perhaps at Watertown; but Bond names him not.

LETTIS, or LETTICE, THOMAS, Plymouth 1638, may be that passeng. in the Elizabeth, 1635, from London, aged 23, in the custom-ho. rec. call. Lettyne. His will, of 1678, pro. 25 Oct. 1681, names w. Ann, wh. d. 3 July 1687, in 80th yr. He had Thomas, wh. d. 3 Nov. 1650, and prob. no other s. Of his ds. Ann m. Samuel Jenney; Eliz. m. 18 Oct. 1655, William Shurtleff; and on 18 Nov. 1669, Jacob Cook, and, third, on 1 Jan. 1689, Hugh Cole; and Dorothy m. 12 Dec. 1665, Edward Gray; and, next, Nathaniel Clarke. WALTER, at Newport, in Jan. 1649, was stab. by capt. George Wright, as in a letter of Roger Williams is told, 3 Mass. Hist. Coll. IX. 280.

LEVENS, or LEAVENS, ANDREW, Hadley, s. of John, was on serv. in Philip's war from Roxbury, but stopp. tho. we kn. not that he had ever any fam. in H. 1678. JOHN, Roxbury, freem. 4 Mar. 1634, came, 1632, with w. Eliz. in the William and Francis, leav. London 9 Mar. Rev. Thomas Weld being the attraction prob. of him and some other Roxbury people in that sh. His w. d. aft. very long illness, says the ch. rec. or was bur. 10 Oct. 1638; and he m. 5 July 1639, Rachel Wright, " a godly maid," had John, b. 27 Apr. 1640; James, 16, bapt. 24 Apr. 1642; Peter, and Andrew, 11, bapt. 15 Sept. 1644, the ch. rec. adds " twin ch. of John L. in the 63d yr. of his age, a *double* blessing"; but Peter d. in Jan. foll.; beside Rachel, bapt. in Aug. 1646; and next yr. 15 Nov. he d. of palsy. JOHN, Roxbury, s. of the preced. a carpent. m. 7 June 1665, Hannah Woods, had Hannah, b. 17 Oct. 1666, and his w. d. a wk. aft. aged 28. I presume he rem. to Stratford, there got w. Eliz. had Peter, 15 Nov. 1677; and James, 14 Oct. 1679, b. there, but caus. the rec. to be made at R. whither he came back, and had John, 10 Dec. 1681; Joseph, 15 Nov. 1683; Rachel, 10 or 15 Dec. 1685; and Benjamin, 15 Apr. 1692.

LEVER, or LEVAR, RICHARD, a soldier, from the E. under capt.
Turner, at Hadley 1676.

LEVERETT, ‖ HUDSON, Boston, s. of Gov. John, m. 1661, Sarah, d. of
Bezaleel Payton, had John, b. 25 Aug. 1662, H. C. 1680; Bezaleel, 1
Sept. 1664, d. young; Sarah, 6 June 1667, d. young; all bapt. 8 May
1670, in right of the mo.; and Thomas,.bapt. 7 June 1674; was of ar.
co. 1658, but never adm. a freem. His w. d. 7 June 1679, and in a yr.
or two he had w. Eliz. wh. outliv. him, but had no ch. and d. at Roxbury
16 Dec. 1714. He d. in summer of 1694; .and Hutch. I. 323, in note
indicates his character. But his first w. undoubted. was a woman of
great worth, form. the heart and mind of her admira. eldest ch. the
eighth presid. of H. C. (in wh. off. he d. 3 May 1724), wh. had been
active in civ. life, as speaker of the Ho. and one of the Judges of the
Sup. Ct., aft. long preparat. as student in divinity, and a teacher in the
coll. For him, and his able classm. Rev. William Brattle. the degr. of
B. D. was introd. 1692 for the first and last time, in conjunct. with the
first S. T. D. then bestow. on Increase Mather, the head of the Inst.
Great was the reput. of the Coll. dur. his presid. care; but he expend.
his private fortune for its good; and from an inadequate salary irregul.
paid, left his childr. in poverty. Cotton M. wh. ought to have been
chos. (as he confident. deem. the will of heaven), instead of L. yet
express. gratitude for his attent. to his s. the gr. of 1723; but in a letter
to Hollis, soon aft. the Presid. d. next yr. stigmatiz. him, as " an infamous
drone." For the effect of the preposterous falsehood on the London
friend of the Coll. see Hollis's note in the invalua. Hist. of the Univ. I.
343; and we kn. that the number of students, was more than double in
the last seven or ten yrs. of the rule of Leverett to what the same
period of Increase Mather exhibits. Allowance should be made, however, for such failing in Cotton Mather's expression of his pious ma-
lignity, bec. the next Presid. of Harv. aft. I. Mather, and the six yrs. of
Willard's substitu. was this same Leverett, wh. stood two yrs. younger
in the Coll. Catal. than the ambitious and ambiguous author of the
Magnalia. Tenderness was shown by Rev. Dr. Colman, the correspond.
of Hollis, wh. preach. a fun. sermon two days aft. the d. of M. for he
kind. kept back the knowl. of the posthum. attack on his friend L.
Indeed the charge was so absurd, and the reputa. of its inventor for
studied looseness of language, had so long been establish. that Colman
would, on such an occasion, have been thot. blameworthy for point. out
the darkness of the ingratitude, and the equally loathsome and ludicrous
cowardice of the calumny. § † ‡ * ‖ JOHN, Boston, s. of Thomas, the rul.
Elder, b. in Eng. (no doubt, at Boston) 1616, brot. prob. 1633, by his
f. at the same time with Cotton, Gov. Haynes, and other men of emin.

arr. 4 Sept. join. to the ch. 14 July 1639 under the spiritual teacher, wh. he had always heard from his b.; freem. 13 May foll. m. Hannah, eldest d. of Ralph Hudson, had Hudson, bef. ment. b. 2, bapt. 10 May 1640; John, bapt. 4 July 1641, four days old (but the town rec. differs much), d. young; Hannah, b. 16, bapt. 23 Apr. 1643, d. young, but aft. Sept. 1651, nam. then in the will of her gr.mo. Hudson; and his w. d. perhaps the same yr. He m. next, Sarah, perhaps d. but perhaps sis. of Major Robert Sedgwick, wh. long outliv. him, d. 2 Jan. 1705, had John, b. 17, bapt. 22 Mar. 1646, d. young; Sarah, 12, bapt. 16 July 1648, d. soon; Sarah, again, 2, bapt. 19 Aug. 1649, d. soon; Eliz. 26 Apr. bapt. 4 May 1651; Ann, 23, bapt. 28 Nov. 1652; Sarah, again, bapt. 20 Aug. 1654, d. soon; Mary, 12 Feb. bapt. 16 Mar. 1656; Hannah, again, b. prob. in Eng. dur. his agency; Rebecca, 5, bapt. 11 Dec. 1664; John, 20 Aug. 1668, d. young; Sarah, again, 30 June, bapt. 3 July 1670, d. young; and Sarah, again, being the fifth of this name, 15, bapt. 22 June 1673. No man in our country ever fill. more import. offices, nor with happier repute. He was rep. 1651, and some yrs. again, speaker in 1663 and 4, maj.-gen. 1663, as success. to Denison, Assist. 1665 to 71, dep.-gov. 1671 to 3, and, on the d. of Bellingham, Gov. 1673 to his own d. 16 Mar. 1679, aged 62. He had been sent agent for the Col. late in 1655 to Eng. whither his w. foll. him in June 1657, and there he cont. for the first yr. aft. the restor. of Charles II. reach. Boston on 19 July 1661. In Aug. 1676, the king knighted him by a special grant, and he had sense enough to keep the letter secret for his descend. His will, made the day bef. he d. wh. was by the afflict. disease of stone, gave all his est. to w. but names as deserv. provis. three unm.-ds., neph. Isaac Addington, the s. of his sis. Ann, and her three ds. Ann Moseley, Rebecca Davenport, and Sarah Townsend; desires his gr.s. John to be brot. up to learning, as was most felicitous. accompl. and on the d. of his w. the prop. to go to s. Hudson $\frac{1}{4}$, and $\frac{3}{4}$ to six ds. Of these Eliz. m. June 1668, Elisha Cooke; Ann m. John Hubbard; Mary m. Paul Dudley, s. of Gov. Thomas, and next, Penn Townsend, wh. had been h. of her cous. Sarah Addington; Hannah m. 12 Sept. 1689, Thomas Davis, but she may first have been w. of an Allen; Rebecca m. 3 Nov. 1691, James Lloyd; and Sarah, the youngest, m. 17 Apr. 1718, Nathaniel Byfield as his sec. w. His wid. Sarah d. 2 Nov. 1704, in her 75th yr. C. Mather wrote an Elegy; but this was bef. her gr.s. was chos. Presid. of H. C. THOMAS, Boston, came in the Griffin, arr. from London 4 Sept. 1633, hav. in July preced. resign. his place as one of the aldermen of the borough of Boston, Co. Lincoln, with w. Ann, ds. Jane and Ann, and prob. s. John; was soon made rul. Elder, and selectman, in ea. place contin. till his d. wh. occur. 3 Apr. 1650. On the day preced.

by verbal will he gave all his est. to his w. wh. d. 16 Oct. 1656, made
her will the day preced. from the silence of wh. we judge Jane was d.
Ann m. Isaac Addington. But he had thirteen ch. as by the Registry of
the borough, certif. copy of wh. was sent to Gov. L. by a friend, as follows: John, bapt. 16 Aug. 1612; Jane, 9 Aug. 1613; Jane, again, 6
Dec. 1614; John, again, 7 July 1616; Thomas, 30 July, 1618; Ann, 8
Jan. 1619; James, 28 June 1621; Sarah, 26 Sept. 1622; Mary, 5 Feb.
1623; Jabez, 6 Sept. 1627; Israel, 25 Sept. 1628; Elisha, 3 July 1630;
and Nathaniel, 12 Apr. 1632; and we may believe that all but the 3d,
4th, and 6th d. young. A perfect Memoir of his fam. is cont. in Geneal.
Reg. IV. 121; and a Pedigree in the same work XII. 289, that is quite
deficient in accurate dates. Four of this name at Harv. and five at
other N. E. coll. had been gr. in 1834.

LEVERICH, LEVERAGE, LOVERIDGE, or LEVERIDGE, CALEB, Newtown, L. I. 1664, that yr. made freem. of Conn. by w. Martha, wid.
of Francis Swaine, had John, Mary, and Eleanor, and so by s. John
the head of large and reput. progeny, d. 1717, aged 79; was eldest
s. of Rev. William. ELEAZER, Newtown, L. I. 1662, br. of the preced.
m. Rebecca, d. of Nicholas Wright, but had no ch. HENRY, a tailor,
came from Southampton, 1635, in the James, call. of Salisbury, Co.
Wilts, arr. at Boston 3 June; but I kn. no more. WILLIAM, Sandwich,
came with Wiggin, 1633, arr. 10 Oct. in the James from London, but
went from Salem, where they land. to Dover, being engag. for that
planta. but in 1635 came to Boston, and join. our ch. 9 Aug. soon aft.
was at Duxbury, and a lot was, in 1637, laid out for him, but in 1639 or
40 was estab. at Sandwich, and yrs. aft. employ. by the Commissrs. of
the Unit. Col. to instruct the Ind. on Cape Cod, thence rem. 1653 to
Oyster Bay and with early sett. to Huntington, L. I. there was in 1664
made freem. of Conn. and contin. until 1670, and at Newtown 1674, d.
not, as oft. said, in 1692, but 1677. Riker, 98.

LEVETT, CHRISTOPHER, an explorer of the coast of Maine 1623 and
4, whose valua. work, print. at London 1628, is repub. in 3 Mass. Hist.
Coll. VIII. 159. See Hubbard, 186. He may be the man, call. capt.
at Salem in June 1630, when Winth. arr. and, perhaps, was here again
in 1632, and carrying letters from here, they were expos. by his d. upon
the voyage, to unfriendly eyes at home.

LEWISTON, DANIEL, York, k. by the Ind. 20 Aug. 1694. JOHN,
Billerica, a. 1679, a Scot, whose five young ch. and the mo. of his w.
were k. by the Ind. 5 Aug. 1695, and one d. carr. away by them. Memoir of Billerica, 13, as cit. by Farmer.

LEWIS, DANIEL, Westerly, R. I. 1679, perhaps was s. of John of the
same, m. Mary Button, d. prob. of Peter, and in his will of 1 Feb.

1718, names eldest s. John, Jonathan, Mary, Dorcas, Daniel, and Hannah. DAVID, Westerly, br. of the preced. m. Eliz. d. of the sec. James
Babcock. DAVID, Salem, d. prob. June 1662, for Samuel Archard of
S. was order. to admin. in behalf of the country, so that perhaps he was
only trans. EDMUND, Lynn, was first at Watertown, rem. a. 1643, not,
as Lewis has it, 1640, came in the Elizabeth, from Ipswich 1634, aged
33, with w. Mary, 32; and two ch. John, 3 yrs. and Thomas, 9 mos. had
James, b. 15 Jan. 1636; and Nathaniel, 25 Aug. 1639, b. at W. beside
a ch. bur. 6 Nov. 1642, 10 days old, and had two more ch. b. at L.
where he d. 1651. His will, of 18 Jan. pro. 25 Feb. 1651, names w.
extrix. and s. John and Thomas. His wid. Mary d. 7 Sept. 1658.
EDWARD, Barnstable, s. of the first George, b. perhaps in Eng. (yet
Mr. Hamblen thinks him the s. recorded as Ephraim, and I think, tho.
his authority is great, he must be wrong here, for the will names both);
m. 9 May 1661, Hannah, d. of the first Henry Cobb of the same,
common. call. Elder C. had Hannah, b. 24 Apr. 1662; Eleazer, b. 26
June 1664; John, 1 Jan. 1666; and Thomas, Mar. 1669. *EZEKIEL,
Boston, merch. s. of William of Farmington, by his sec. w. Mary, d. of
famous master Ezekiel Cheever, in honor of wh. he was nam. and in
imitat. of wh. after leav. coll. he bec. an instructor, first at Westfield,
soon serv. as his gr.f.'s assist. at the Boston gr. sch. was selectman, rep.
1723, and oft. aft. He m. 18 Mar. 1702, Mary Breadon, had Mary, b.
21 Jan. 1703; and his w. d. next mo. He next m. 11 Oct. 1704, Abigail
Kilcup, wh. I judge to have been wid. of Roger, had Abigail, 12 June
1706; William, 28 Nov. 1707, d. young; Sarah, 21 May 1710, prob. d.
young; Eliz. 22 Aug. 1712; Hannah, 14 Sept. 1714, prob. d. young;
and Ezekiel, 15 Apr. 1717, H. C. 1735; and d. 14 Aug. 1755, above
80 yrs. old. Most of my details are deriv. from a very careful correspond. as mark. in Geneal. Reg. VIII. 48. FRANCIS, Boston 1663, a
boatman. GEORGE, Plymouth, and Scituate, where he join. the ch. 20
Sept. 1635, a clothier, was from East Greenwich, in Kent, bef. 1633,
and rem. to Barnstable bef. 1641, had in Eng. m. Sarah Jenkins, by her
had sev. ch. b. there, as Mary, wh. m. 14 Nov. 1643, John Bryant;
prob. George; and Thomas; perhaps Edward; Jabez, wh. d. unm.;
and James, but at S. had John, b. 2, bapt. 11 Mar. 1638; and at B. had
Ephraim, 23, bapt. 25 July 1641; and Sarah, 2, bapt. 11 Feb. 1644;
but we know not the date of his d. yet it was prob. aft. 1663, for his will
was brot. forward 3 Mar. 1664. It names w. Mary, s. Ephraim,
George, Thomas, James, Edward, John, and d. Sarah. John was k. by
the Ind. unm. 26 Mar. 1676, under capt. Pierce. His d. Mary, wh. had
m. 14 Nov. 1643 John Bryant of Scituate, and had seven ch. was d.
seven yrs. bef. her f.; and Sarah m. 26 Dec. 1663, James Cobb, and,

next, 23 Nov. 1698, Jonathan Sparrow. He had, in 1658, with Richard
Foxwell, purchas. lds. at Scarborough, but both soon came back.
GEORGE, Barnstable, s. of the preced. b. in Eng. prob. m. Dec. 1654,
Mary, d. of Bernard Lumbard, had George, b. Sept. 1655; Mary, 9
May 1657; Sarah; 12 Jan. 1660; Hannah, July 1662; d. at 5 yrs.;
Melatiah, 13 Jan. 1664; Bathshua, Oct. 1667; Jabez, 10 June 1670;
Benjamin, 22 Nov. 1671; Jonathan, 25 July 1674; John, 1 Dec. 1676;
and Nathan, 26 July 1678; and he d. 20 Mar. 1710. GEORGE, Casco,
bef. 1640 had gr. of ld. Mr. Willis, in Vol. I. 37 and 174, conject. that
he was s. of the first ment. George; but in my opin. he was older, and
may have been s. of Thomas, tho. he d. without issue male, Willis thinks.
He liv. and d. at Falmouth, had s. John, to wh. were gr. 100 acres as
early as 1657; and Philip; beside four ds. Ann, wh. m. James Ross;
Susanna, m. Thomas Cloice or Cloyse; Mary, b. at F. 1654, m. first,
Thomas Skillings, sec. Jotham Lewis, and third, a Wilkins, was liv. at
Salem 1732; and Hannah, m. James Darling. GEORGE, Barnstable,
eldest s. of George the sec. of the same, by w. Eliz. had Thankful, bapt.
16 Sept. 1683, and I find no more of him. ISAAC, Boston, perhaps s.
of John of Charlestown, freem. 1690, m. 25 May 1680, Mary Davis,
had Mary, b. May 1681; Isaac, 21 Aug. 1683; Joseph, 16 Nov. 1685;
John, 25 Feb. 1688; Eliz. 12 Feb. 1689; and Abraham, posthum. 9 June
1691; and he d. at Malden 3 Apr. preced. Yet it must be obs. that this
Isaac, is by Lewis, in Hist. of L. 108, made s. of *William* of Roxbury;
and the hist. asserts that his gr.f. Nathan was gr.s. of this person.
But Court rec. as brot. out in the invalua. Hist. of Watertown by Bond,
p. 125, show the contra. ISRAEL, Westerly 1679, br. of Daniel, m. Jane,
d. of sec. James Babcock, had Israel, b. 22 June 1695; Benjamin, 8
June 1697; Jane, 21 May 1700; and Ann, 13 July 1704. JABEZ,
Barnstable, s. of George the sec. by w. Experience had John, bapt. in
her right, 14 Nov. 1697, wh. prob. d. soon; and John, again, May 1698.
JAMES, Barnstable, s. of the first George, perhaps b. in Eng. was selectman and lieut. m. 31 Oct. 1655, Sarah Lane, d. of George of Hingham,
had John, b. 29 Oct. 1656, bapt. 27 Sept. foll.; Samuel, 10 Apr. 1659;
Sarah, 4 Mar. 1661; James, 3 June 1664; Susannah; and Ebenezer;
and he d. 4 Oct. 1713, in 82d yr. Sarah m. 6 Jan. 1685, Thomas
Lincoln; and next, 20 Feb. 1699, Robert Waterman. JAMES, a soldier,
k. at Hatfield by the Ind. 25 Aug. 1675. Ano. JAMES, was of Westerly
1679, s. of John sen. that was there ten yrs. earlier, m. Sarah, d. of the sec.
James Babcock. JAMES, Boston, freem. 1684, with prefix of respect.
JOHN, Charlestown 1634, freem. 1646, by w. Margaret had John, b. 12,
bapt. 14 Sept. 1638; Joseph and Mary, tw. bapt. 29 Mar. 1640; Samuel, 24, bapt. 27 June 1641; Eliz. b. 10 Sept. 1642; Sarah, 24 Dec.

1647; liv. on Malden side, there w. d. 10 Mar. 1649, and he m. 10 Apr. 1650, Mary Brown, perhaps d. of Abraham the first of Watertown, had Abraham, b. 10 Dec. 1650; Jonathan, 4 Jan. d. 10 Feb. 1652; Mary, Jan. 1653; Hannah; Isaac; and Trial, posthum. Jan. 1658. He d. 16 Sept. preced. His wid. m. a Cutler. Mary m. 30 Nov. 1675, Samuel Penfield; Eliz. m. Bryant Borden; and Sarah m. Joseph Brabrook. JOHN, Scituate, by Deane call. br. of the first George, was of Tenterden in Co. Kent, and came in the Hercules, 1635, with w. Sarah and one ch. as the vicar of T. and the mayor certify for him. He rem. in few yrs. to Boston, where his w. d. 12 July 1657. JOHN, New London 1648, common. noted as sen. because, beside other ch. of whose b. none is seen on rec. he had s. John; was freem. bef. 1669; and d. 8 Dec. 1676. JOHN, br. of George of Barnstable, was, very early, perhaps 1638, at Yarmouth, but not long contin. may be the same as the preced. JOHN, Lancaster, freem. 1665. JOHN, Falmouth, eldest s. of George of the same, took a deed from Cleves 1657. Willis, I. 68. In 1674 he kept an inn, and rem. aft. the begin. of Philip's war to the W. prob. was liv. 1683. JOHN, Lynn, s. of Edmund, b. in Eng. m. 17 June 1659, Hannah, d. of capt. Thomas Marshall, had John, b. 30 Mar. 1660; Hannah, 25 Feb. 1662; Thomas, 2 June 1663; Mary, 24 Feb. 1666; Benjamin, 27 Apr. 1667; Samuel, 25 July 1675, d. soon; Abigail, 16 May 1679; Ebenezer, 16 July 1681; and Eliz. 7 Apr. 1684. He may have been the freem. of 1684, but certainly not, as Farmer, foll. the lead of Lewis in his Hist. gave it, 1646. JOHN, Boston, butcher, m. 22 Nov. 1659, Alice, wid. of Nathaniel Bishop, d. of James Mattock, who, in his will, refers to her, had Samuel, b. 12 Jan. 1662; Joseph, 4 Feb. 1663; and Benoni, 25 Jan. 1665. Ano. JOHN of Boston is call. mariner in 1669. JOHN, Portsmouth, perhaps s. of Philip of the same, m. Martha, d. of William Brooking, and she next m. a Rendall, prob. had John, James, and Philip, nam. in their gr.f.'s will of 1 Nov. 1700. JOHN, Saybrook, d. prob. 1670, for in June of that yr. inv. was rend. says the rec. by Lord, his admor. JOHN, Westerly 1669, had John, Daniel, James, David, Israel, and Samuel. JOHN, Windsor, had Samuel, b. 6 Aug. 1677; Mary, 18 Dec. 1679; Eliz. 1682; Sarah, 1684; and John, 1694. JOHN, New London, s. of John of the same, m. 1677, Eliz. Huntley, d. 1717, leav. wid. Eliz. and s. John, wh. liv. at Lyme. JOHN, Hingham, m. Nov. 1682, Hannah, d. of Daniel Lincoln. JOHN, Lynn, s. of John of the same, m. Sarah, wid. of John Jenks, d. of William Merriam, was prob. freem. 1690, call. junr. and at the same time were adm. lieut. John and Thomas L. of L. of wh. the latter may have been br. but the unnamed milit. officer must have been uncle. JOHN, Westerly, s. of John of the same, by w. Ann had Joseph, b. 16 Oct. 1683; Sarah,

17 Aug. 1687; Mary, 4 May 1689; Ann, 6 Jan. 1691; Abigail, 20
May 1693; John, 13 June 1698; William, 1 Feb. 1702; and Jerusha,
11 Jan. 1707. JOSEPH, Swansey, by w. Mary, had Joseph, b. 6 Jan.
1672; Sibill, 18 Mar. 1674; and he was bur. 24 June 1675, prob. k.
that day by the Ind. JOSEPH, New London 1666, may have been s. of
John of the same, perhaps of Windsor 1675, and d. at Simsbury 1680,
m. Eliz. eldest d. of John Case of S. a. 1674, had Eliz. b. 20 Mar.
1675; Joseph, 15 Mar. 1677; and John, posthum. 8 Jan. 1681. His
wid. m. 1684, John Tuller. NATHANIEL, New London 1666, perhaps
br. of the preced. NATHANIEL, Lynn, s. of Edmund, rem. I suppose,
to Swansey, there by w. Mary had Nathaniel, b. 17 July 1673, wh. d.
20 Aug. 1676; and Mary, b. 4 Dec. 1677; and he d. 13 Oct. 1683.
NATHANIEL, Farmington, s. of William of the same, m. 25 Nov. 1699,
Abigail, d. of David Ashley of Westfield, had prob. others bef. or aft.
or both, beside Noadiah, b. 27 Apr. 1708; but I have gather. no more
of him. * PHILIP, Portsmouth 1665, prob. of Dover 1672, rep. 1680,
at the first assemb. under Provinc. gov. His will was of 1 Nov. 1700.
PHILIP, Falmouth 1669, s. of George of the same, was, in 1676, a soldier
of Turner's comp. serv. on Conn. riv. PHILIP, Farmington, s. of the
sec. William, propos. as freem. 1669, had 100 acres given 1675 by his
gr.f. William at F. with wh. I suppose he liv. as both their names are
sign. to memor. from Hadley, against imposts, some yrs. earlier, but liv.
chief. at Hartford until he rem. to Fairfield. ROBERT, Newbury, came
from Bristol to Salem, says Coffin, and d. aft. rem. to N. 4 Mar. 1644.
His inv. is of 6 July 1644. I suppose he emb. in the Blessing at London, 1635, aged 28, with, perhaps, w. Eliz. 22; and the custom-ho. list,
that there may be no mistake, repeats the names in a few lines. ROB-
ERT, Charlestown, spelt Luist in the rec. by w. Rebecca had Robert,
bapt. 11 Feb. 1683; Thomas, 5 Apr. 1685; and David, 30 Jan. 1687;
perhaps rem. to Boston. SAMUEL, Malden, perhaps s. of John, by w.
Sarah had Hannah, b. 12 Dec. 1689; and he d. 1 Feb. 1699. SAMUEL,
Farmington, s. of William of the same, freem. 1676, by w. Eliz. had
Hannah, bapt. 4 Oct. 1691, his w. hav. join. the ch. Sunday preced.; and
Samuel, 29 May 1692, and he d. 1725. SAMUEL, Westerly, s. of John
of the same, by w. Joanna had Samuel, Jonathan, and d. Joanna Tanners
as nam. in his will of 5 Aug. 1734. THOMAS, Saco, bef. 1630 had prob.
ranged the coast to ascertain the most agreeable spot for his patent, was
assess. £3 quarterly for support of min. d. bef. 1640. Willis, I. 16.
Belkn. I. 9. THOMAS, Lynn, s. of Edmund, m. 11 Nov. 1659, Hannah
Baker, d. perhaps, of Edward, had Edward, b. 28 July 1660; and
Thomas, 29 Apr. 1668, was freem. 1690. THOMAS, Barnstable, s. of
the first George, b. prob. in Eng. m. 15 June 1653, Mary Davis, d.

possib. of the first Dolor D. had James, b. 31 Mar. 1654; Thomas, 15
July 1656; Mary, 2 Nov. 1659; and Samuel, 14 May 1662; rem. to
Swansey, of wh. he was one of the first sett. and was a selectman there,
by w. Hannah had Samuel, again, 23 Apr. 1673; and Hepzibah, 15
Nov. 1674. THOMAS, Northampton, had Mary, b. 1663; Esther, 1665;
and Thomas, 1666. On 11 Jan. 1667, Thomas d. but it is not certain
wh. of the two, prob. it was the ch. was then taken. No more is heard
of the fam. WALTER, Wethersfield 1648. * WILLIAM, Cambridge,
1632, came in the Lion, with Wadsworth, Talcot, Goodwin, Olmstead,
and others, arr. at Boston 16 Sept. and adm. freem. 6 Nov. foll. rem.
1636 to Hartford, and was of orig. proprs. selectman 1641, rem. a. 1659
to Hadley, for wh. he was rep. 1662, for Northampton 1664; his w.
Felix d. 1671, at H. and he finally rem. a. 1675 to Farmington, there d.
1683, at gr. age. His only ch. was William, b. in Eng. and the mo. is
call. Felix. WILLIAM, Roxbury, in absurd fam. tradit. by wh. Farmer
was misled, oft. made the same as the foregoing, adm. freem. 18 May
1642, brot. it is said, John, b. 1 Nov. 1635; and Christopher, 1636,
both in Eng. and the town rec. has Lydia, b. 25 Dec. 1640; and Josiah,
28 July 1641; so careless was that keeping, that we willingly miss the
later ch. Perhaps he rem. to Boston 1644, and contin. to worship with
apostle Eliot; at least we find at R. bapt. Isaac, 14 Apr. 1644; tho. a
rec. is found of his b. 15 Apr.; Mary, 2 Aug. 1646; and Hannah, 18
Mar. 1649; and may be that propr. of Lancaster 1654, wh. d. 3 Dec.
1671. His will of 21 Nov. preced. names w. Amy, who with Isaac, are
made excors. Other ch. were John, Lydia, Mary, and Hannah. WIL-
LIAM, Farmington, s. of the first William, b. in Eng. m. 1644 (in
conform. with a contr. betw. his f. and Mary Whitehead of Windsor, w.
of Richard, mo. prob. of) Mary Hopkins prob. d. of William, Esq. a
few yrs. earlier of Stratford, had Mary, b. 6 May 1645; Philip, bapt.
13 Dec. 1646, bef. ment.; Samuel, b. 18 Aug. 1648, bef. ment.; Sarah;
Hannah; William, bapt. 15 Mar. 1657, d. 1737; Felix, 12 Dec. 1658;
Ebenezer, sett. at Wallingford; John, 1665, d. at 19 yrs.; and James,
1667; liv. at Jamaica, L. I. d. 1728. He m. 22 Dec. 1671, sec. w. at
Boston, Mary, d. of celebr. Ezekiel Cheever, had Eliz. b. 1672, d.
young; Ezekiel, 1674, H. C. 1694; Nathaniel, 1 Oct. 1676, wh. d. 24
Feb. 1752; Abigail, 1678; Joseph, bapt. 14 Mar. 1680; and Daniel,
16 July 1682. The last two d. young. He had milit. office in the war,
ranks from serg. to capt. and d. 1690, when of his 16 ch. 13 were liv.
Mary m. Benjamin Judd; Sarah m. Samuel Boltwood of Hadley;
Hannah, m. first, Samuel Crowe of Hadley, had two ch. and sec. in
1676, Daniel Marsh; and Felix m. Thomas Selden of Hadley. Sometimes the terminat. is es, but it would be vain to attempt to disting.

Thirteen of this name had been gr. at Harv. and thirty-four at other N. E. coll. in 1834.

LEY, HENRY, Boston, by w. Mary had Richard, b. 27 July 1657. JOSHUA, Boston, by w. Mary had Benjamin, b. 18 Feb. 1691.

LIBBEY, ANTHONY, Scarborough 1676, rem. a. 1685 to Portsmouth. JAMES, HENRY, DAVID, MATTHEW, DANIEL, and SAMUEL, Scarborough 1676, were brs. of the preced. and s. of JOHN, who, as well as John jr. prob. first b. of the fam. was there 1663, and there the name has cont. The f. d. 1683; in his will of 9 Feb. of that yr. admir. for its brevity, naming only "two younger s. Matthew and Daniel." He came, it is said, from Broadstairs, in the Isle of Thanet, Co. Kent. Of the ch. James m. 9 June 1698, Mary, d. of Isaac Hanson wh. prob. liv. at Portsmouth.

LIDGETT, ‖ CHARLES, Boston, s. of Peter, ar. co. 1678, call. col. 1689, in Hutch. I. 374, at the overthrow of Andros, whom he favor. d. at London, says Sewall, 13 July 1698. PETER, Boston, a rich merch. partner in many voyages with John Hull, was freem. 1673, when it is spell. Lydgett, 'had w. Eliz. Scammon, and ch. Eliz.; Charles, b. 29 Mar. 1650; and Jane; d. 26 Apr. 1676. His wid. m. 1680, Hon. John Saffyn as his sec. w.; and Eliz. m. John Usher, stationer of Boston, afterwards lieut.-gov. of New Hampsh. Abstr. of his will, 10 Feb. 1671, pro. 5 May 1676, is in Geneal. Reg. XIII. 139.

LIGHT, HENRY, New Hampsh. d. a. 1677. JOHN, Salisbury, by w. Dorothy had Joseph, b. 21 Apr. 1676, rem. to New Hampsh. 1676, had Mary, 20 Mar. 1678; Robert, 15 Sept. 1680; John, 8 Feb. 1682 and Dorothy, 28 Apr. 1685.

LIGHTFOOT, FRANCIS, Lynn, freem. 8 Dec. 1636, said to have come from London, d. 1646. His will of 10, pro. 29 Dec. in that yr. dispos. of his small prop. by mak. w. Ann extrix. but names br. John of London, sis. Isabel L. liv. at Frieston, Co. Lincoln, wh. may be 4 miles E. from Boston, and five or six friends, the most, if not all, in the mo. country. JOHN, Boston 1653. Haz. II. 210. WILLIAM, Marblehead 1674.

LILFORD, or LILFORTH, FRANCIS, Rowley 1643, drown. 15 Nov. 1672. THOMAS, Rowley 1643, perhaps br. of the preced. rem. to Haverhill 1654, had w. Eliz. and was freem. 1666. It may reward investigat. whether that passeng. in the Susan and Ellen, from London 1635, aged 13, whose name appears Ann Lieford, were not a sis.

LILLY, EDWARD, Boston 1670, a cooper. GEORGE, Reading, m. 15 Nov. 1659, Hannah, but the rec. did not ins. surnames, had Hannah, b. 25 Oct. 1660; John, 5 Dec. 1662; beside others prob. and d. 1691. JOHN, Concord, by w. Dorothy had Israel, b. 30 July 1660. JOHN,

Woburn, by w. Hannah had John, b. 3 June 1691; Hannah, 13 Sept. 1694; Sarah, 11 Nov. 1696; Rebecca, 9 Mar. 1699; Susanna, 13 Oct. 1702; Phebe, 21 Feb. 1705. LUKE, Marshfield 1643. SAMUEL, Boston 1686, merch. at whose grave, I suppose, in 1689, occurr. the indecent dispute about the burial serv. of wh. Increase Mather had fine acco. from his gossipp. corresp. Joshua Moody in let. of 8 Feb. as in Hutch. I. 356. SAMUEL, Boston 1682, perhaps s. of the preced. had Theophilus, bapt. 24 Aug. 1690; Samuel, 5 June 1692; Mehitable, 4 Feb. 1694; Eliz. 1 Mar. 1696; Edward, 27 Feb. 1698; and Abigail, 19 Nov. 1699. SAMUEL, Reading, freem. 1691. Oft. the name is Lilley.

LINCOLN, BENJAMIN, Hingham, youngest s. of Thomas, the cooper, m. 6 Jan. or as the old Hobart rec. says, 6 Feb. 1667, Sarah, d. of the first John Fearing, had John, b. 5 Jan. 1668; Margaret, 7 Oct. 1669, d. at 14 yrs.; Benjamin. 16 Jan. 1672; Thomas, 12 Dec. 1674, d. within 9 mos.; Jeremiah, 1 Apr. 1682; and Jonathan, 28 Sept. 1684, d. within 3 yrs. He was a maltster, freem. 1677, and d. 27 Sept. 1700. His s. Benjamin had col. Benjamin, f. of Benjamin, the soldier friend of Washington, wh. d. 9 May 1810. His s. Benjamin, H. C. 1777, wh. d. 18 Jan. 1788, by w. Mary, younger of the two ds. of the celebr. James Otis, had Benjamin, H. C. 1806; and James Otis, H. C. 1807. CALEB, Hingham, s. of Thomas, the husbandman, m. 8 May 1684, Rachel, d. of James Bates, had Ruth, b. 11 Feb. 1685; Rachel, 4 June 1688; Ann, 15 Sept. 1690; Silence, 26 Dec. 1692; and Luke, 27 Mar. 1695. His w. d. 10 Nov. 1696, and he m. 2 Sept. 1698, Hannah Jackson, and he d. Nov. 1721, unless this date belong to a neph. of the same name. DANIEL, Hingham 1644, a young man of wh. we are not sure that he was a relat. of any earlier person bearing this surname, by w. Susanna, wh. d. 20 Feb. 1704, had Susanna, b. 14 May 1654; Daniel, 22 Feb. 1657, d. young; Hannah, 10 Sept. 1659; Daniel, again, a. 1662; Sarah, 7 Sept. 1664; Ephraim, 26 May 1667; and Rachel, 27 June 1671; and he d. 19 Mar. 1699. In his will, of 16 Sept. 1692, he names w. the four ds. and two s. as liv. Three of the ds. were then m. viz.: Susanna, on 1 Oct. 1675, to Robert Waterman; Hannah, 17 Nov. 1682, to John Lewis; and Sarah, 1 Apr. 1687, to Nathaniel Nichols, and she d. at Pembroke, 1748. DANIEL, Hingham, s. of the first Samuel, m. 23 Jan. 1678, Eliz. d. of Thomas Lincoln, the husbandman, had Obadiah, b. 21 Apr. 1679; Hezekiah, 26 Dec. 1681; Eliz. 26 Feb. 1689; and Martha, 13 Feb. 1695. DANIEL, Hingham, s. of the first Daniel, m. 16 Apr. 1687, Sarah Nichols, had Moses, b. 25 Feb. 1688, d. 1772; Sarah, 15 Apr. 1690; Susanna, 19 Dec. 1693; Leah, 9 Sept. 1695; Daniel, 28 Feb. 1698; Joshua, 1 Jan. 1702; and Eliz. June 1703. DAVID, Hingham, s. of the

sec. Stephen, m. 4 Jan. 1693, Margaret Lincoln, perhaps d. of Benjamin,
had Eliz. b. 8 Oct. 1693; David, 8 Feb. 1695; Sarah, 24 Oct. 1696, d.
at two yrs.; Matthew, 2 Sept. 1698; Isaac, 18 Jan. 1702, H. C. 1722,
first of the name in the catal.; Job, 16 Mar. 1710; and Margaret, wh.
d. 26 Sept. 1711. He d. 9 Oct. 1714, and his wid. d. 23 Aug. 1716.
From him, beside Isaac, are derived Abner, H. C. 1788; Levi, H. C.
1789; and Rev. Calvin, H. C. 1820. EPHRAIM, Hingham, younger s.
of the first Daniel, by w. Mary had Mary, b. 28 Nov. 1714; Ephraim,
3 Feb. 1717, d. 1795; and Susanna, 27 June 1721. He d. 1762, aged
95. JAMES, Hingham, br. of David, m. 28 Feb. 1711, Deborah, eldest
d. of the sec. Samuel L. had James, b. 2 Nov. 1711, d. next mo. as did
his w. He had sec. w. Joanna, wh. d. 4 Jan. 1726, and he d. 3 May
1731. JOHN, Taunton, s. of Thomas, the miller, had John, b. 11 Oct.
1665; and Thomas, 15 Sept. 1667; but I kn. no more of him or his
progeny. JOSEPH, Hingham, br. of Benjamin, freem. perhaps 1670, m.
14 June 1682, Prudence, d. of Andrew Ford of Weymouth, wh. d. 26
Nov. 1695, had Joseph, b. 13 Mar. 1683; Israel, 17 Apr. 1685; Nehemiah, 4 May 1688; and Elisha, 2 Oct. 1692. He m. 27 Feb. 1696,
Sarah, wid. of Hopestill Bisbee, but prob. had no ch. for his will, of 5
Mar. 1715, names her as his w. but only the four ch. of the former. He
d. 18 Mar. 1716. JOSHUA, Hingham, br. of Caleb, perhaps the freem.
of 1670, m. 20 Apr. 1666, Deborah, d. of Joshua Hobart, had Peter, b.
6 June 1667, d. at one yr.; Joshua, 9 May 1669; Peter, again, 19 Jan.
1671; Jacob, 5 Mar. 1673, d. next mo.; Deborah, 31 Aug. 1674;
Margaret, 14 May 1677; Caleb, 9 Oct. 1678; Jacob, 21 Mar. 1681;
Solomon, 25 Nov. 1682; and Isaac, 14 Nov. 1684; his w. d. Nov.
1684; and a ch. prob. the last, d. 29 Dec. 1689; and he d. 2 Apr.
1694. MORDECAI, Hingham, s. of the first Samuel, rem. to Scituate,
by w. Sarah there had Mordecai, b. 24 Apr. 1686; Abraham, 13 Jan.
1689; Isaac, 21 Oct. 1691; and Sarah, 29 July 1694. ROBERT, Boston 1646, laborer, whose w. Ann unit. with the ch. 9 May 1647; liv. at
Rumney Marsh, or Winisemet, d. 6 May 1663. SAMUEL, Hingham,
came from the city of Norwich, with Francis Lawes, of Salem, a weaver,
prob. his apprent. 1637, but the old Cushing MS. says, he was of old
Hingham, aged 18, went, perhaps, on reach. his majority, to H. where
liv. his br. Thomas, a weaver, also, by w. Martha had Samuel, bapt. 25
Aug. 1650; Daniel, 1 or 2 Jan. 1653, bef. ment.; Mordecai, b. 19, bapt.
24 June 1655, d. soon; Mordecai, again, 14 June 1657; Mary, b. 27
Mar. 1662; Thomas, 20 Aug. 1664; Martha, 11 Dec. 1667; a d. 13
Aug. 1669; prob. d. without a name; Sarah, 17 June 1671; and Rebecca, 11 Mar. 1674; and he d. 26 May 1690. His wid. d. 10 Apr.
1693. Mary m. 3 Jan. 1684, Joseph Bates; Rebecca, m. 14 May 1695

John Clark of Plymouth; Martha d. unm. 13 Feb. 1741. SAMUEL, Taunton, br. of John, had Samuel, b. 1 June 1664; Hannah, 24 Mar. 1666; Thomasin, 27 Oct. 1667; Eliz. 24 Apr. 1669; Ebenezer, 15 Oct. 1673; Rachel, 16 Sept. 1677; John, 15 Sept. 1679; and Thomas, 1683. SAMUEL, Hingham, s. of the first Samuel, was a soldier in Philip's war, serv. in cavalry attach. to Johnson's comp. for Narraganset campaign, Dec. 1675, m. 29 Apr. 1687, Deborah, d. of William Hersey, had Deborah, b. 15 June 1689; Samuel, 1 Feb. 1691; Jedediah, 2 Oct. 1692; Mary, 18 Sept. 1694; Rebecca, 11 Aug. 1697; Elisha, 3 Sept. 1699; Lydia, 14 Sept. 1701; Abigail, 11 Jan. 1704; and Susanna, 18 Apr. 1706. Jedediah, wh. d. at more than 90 yrs. is progenit. of very num. public men, as thro. s. Enoch, f. of the disting. Levi, H. C. 1772, of Worcester, wh. was f. of Levi, H. C. 1802, Gov. of Mass. and of Enoch, Gov. of Maine, as thro. s. William of Solomon, the glad historian of his nat. town. STEPHEN, Hingham 1638, came that yr. from Wymondham, a town a. 9 ms. from Norwich, bring. mo. w. and s. Stephen, but prob. not in the Diligent, that arr. 10 Aug. of that yr. or Cushing, wh. was careful to note his fellow-passeng. would have told us so; had Sarah, b. 22 Mar. 1642; and his w. wh. name is unkn. d. next mo.; the d. d. 4 Nov. 1649, and he d. 11 Oct. 1658. His will, made 3 days bef. ment. his mo. Joan, Susanna, d. of his br. Thomas, and gives part of his est. to mo. but most to only ch. STEPHEN, Hingham, only s. of the preced. b. in Eng. m. Feb. 1660, Eliz. d. of Matthew Hawke, had Eliz. b. 3 Nov. 1660; Mary, 27 Dec. 1662; Stephen, 9 Nov. 1665; David, 22 Sept. 1668, bef. ment.; Bethia, 29 Oct. 1670; Abigail, 7 Apr. 1673; Margaret, 30 June 1677, and James, 26 Oct. 1681, bef. ment. was freem. 1680, and d. 17 Sept. 1692, and his wid. d. 4 Nov. 1713. Eliz. m. 4 Jan. 1693, Ephraim Marsh; Mary m. 11 Jan. 1688, Enoch Whiton; Bethia m. 16 Apr. 1701, John Lane; and of the other two ds. no rec. of m. or d. is found. STEPHEN, Hingham, s. of the preced. never m. was ens. town clk. and d. 27 Dec. 1717. THOMAS, Hingham 1636, the weaver, elder br. of the first Samuel, was two yrs. or more at Watertown and Charlestown, having, says the Cushing MS. come with Nicholas Jacob, a relat. in 1633; had gr. of lds. in 1635, and house lot gr. 3 July 1636, so that he would be judged a first sett. with Hobart, and may have been the freem. of Mar. 1638 or of 18 May 1642. His first w. Susanna d. Mar. 1641, and he had ano. w. Mary, who, by one report, prob. erron. outliv. him, and d. 2 Sept. 1675, leav. no ch. His will is without date, but well pro. provides for w. gives small legacy to br. Samuel, larger to Samuel, and Daniel, s. of that br. and smaller to ea. of the other liv. ch. exc. Rebecca, latest b. wh. may render prob. that it was made bef. she was b. THOMAS, Hingham, the miller, prob. came 1635, certain. had house lot 3 July 1636, brot. sev. ch. perhaps two or three, rem. a. 1652 to Taunton, where he took sec. w. 10 Dec. 1665, Eliz. Streete, prob. wid. of Francis. He, in his will of 28 Aug. 1683, call. hims. "eighty yrs. or thereabouts," pro. 5 Mar. foll. he ment. with these ch. of former w. Thomas, John, Samuel, Sarah, Mary, and s.-in-law Joseph Willis, perhaps h. of Sarah, and Sarah's s. Thomas. In Geneal. Reg. VI. 188, it is print. Linton. THOMAS, Hingham, the cooper, s. of Thomas, in O. E. had gr. in the town 1636, more likely, in my judgment, than either of the preced. to have been the freem. of Mar. 1638, had, bef. com. from Eng. m. 1630, a d. of Andrew Lane, had two ch. of wh. one d. and the other, Sarah, was brot. and d. soon aft. arr. and here had Thomas, bapt. 6 May 1638; Joseph, 22 Nov. 1640, bef. ment.; Benjamin, 7 May 1643, bef. ment.; Deborah, 3 Aug. 1645; and Sarah, 6 Oct. 1650, d. young. His w. wh. name is unkn. d. 13 Feb. 1683, and he d. 28 Sept. 1691. His will, of 13 July 1688, names the four liv. ch. Deborah m. 13 June 1678, as sec. w. Samuel Thaxter. Tradit. brings him from West of Eng. where he left br. John. This may seem not improb. if we substitute E. for W. The name belong. to Co. Norf'k. or the adj. Co. Lincoln. THOMAS, Hingham 1638, the husbandman, br. of the first Stephen, prob. younger, had gr. of ld. 1638, came, says the Cushing MS. in 1638 from Wymondham, Co. Norf'k. with Jeremiah Moore, perhaps is the freem. of 18 May 1642, had w. Margaret, d. of Richard Langer, and ch. Caleb, bapt. 8 Oct. 1643, d. soon; Joshua and Caleb, tw. 2 Mar. 1645, of wh. the latter, I think, liv. not long; Susanna; Mary, b. 10, bapt. 23 Apr. 1648; Sarah, 29 Sept. bapt. 6 Oct. 1650; Thomas, 26 Dec. 1652; Eliz. and Ruth, b. 19 Nov. 1664. He d. 16 Aug. 1692; but his will, of 24 May 1681, names the w. and eight ch. His d. Susanna m. 16 May 1666, to Joseph Barstow of Scituate; Mary m. 5 Jan. 1675, Francis Barker of Duxbury; Sarah m. 6 May 1675, Thomas Marsh; Eliz. m. 23 Jan. 1678, Daniel Lincoln, bef. ment.; and Ruth, m. Jan. 1685, Samuel Gill. It seems very curious, that at our Hingham, within the first three yrs. of its sett. should be found four heads of fams. nam. Thomas Lincoln, and yet at Hingham in O. E. where this fam. name was quite freq. not one Thomas occurs in the rec. from 1600 to 1663 incl. neither as f. nor s. among ms. 15 in number, of wh. 8 were of males, nor among 28 bur. nor among 62 bapt. Clearly the other parishes of Co. Norf'k. had the name of bapt. in greater abund. for males of this surname. THOMAS, Taunton, s. of Thomas, the miller, of Hingham, b. in Eng. had Mary, b. 12 May 1652; Sarah, 25 Sept. 1654; Thomas, 21 Apr. 1656; Samuel, 16 Mar. 1658; Jonah, 7 July 1660; Hannah, 15 Mar. 1663; d. Constant, 16 May 1665; Eliz. 24 Apr. 1669; and Mercy, 3 Apr. 1670. Constant m. 13 July 1687, William Briggs; Hannah m. 23 Dec. 1689,

Daniel Owen; and Eliz. m. 17 Oct. 1693, William Briggs, as sec. w.
THOMAS, Hingham, eldest s. of Thomas, the cooper, was a carpenter, m.
18 Feb. 1663, Mary, d. of Thomas Chubbuck, wh. d. 12 June 1690,
without ch. it is thot. He m. 13 Nov. foll. Lydia, d. of Rev. Peter
Hobart, had Lydia, b. 29 Sept. 1691, d. young; Mary, 24 June 1693, d.
in few wks.; Thomas, 3 July 1695; Lydia, again, 16 Oct. 1696, d.
young; and Josiah, 10 Apr. 1699, wh. was a deac. and liv. to 23 Jan.
1774. He was freem. prob. 1672, a lieut. and capt. d. 28 Nov. 1708;
and in his will of 18 Dec. 1700, names only w. Lydia and her two s.
THOMAS, Hingham, youngest s. of Thomas, the husbandman, m. 6 Jan.
1685, Sarah, d. of James Lewis of Barnstable, had Sarah, b. 21 Oct.
1685; Susanna, 19 Sept. 1688; Thomas, 30 Aug. 1692, d. at 3 mos.;
Ebenezer, 9 Apr. 1694; and Mary; and d. 28 Sept. 1698; and his
wid. m. 20 Feb. foll. Robert Waterman. THOMAS, Taunton, eldest s.
of Thomas of the same, m. 14 Nov. 1689, Susanna Smith; but my
kn. ends here. WILLIAM, Roxbury, a soldier in the comp. of his townsman, the brave capt. Johnson, was wound. 19 Dec. 1675, in the gr.
Narraganset battle, and d. soon aft. Twenty of this name had, in 1834,
been gr. at Harv. two at Yale, and four at other coll. of N. E.

LINDALL, LYNDALL, or LINDALE, HENRY, New Haven 1646, sometimes spell. Lindon, was a deac. d. late in 1660 or early in 1661, his inv.
being in Feb. of this yr. had Mary, bapt. 19 July 1646, wh. m. 14 Sept.
1666, John Hoyt of Norwalk; Sarah, 29 Oct. 1648; Hannah, b. 7,
bapt. 12 Jan. 1651; Rebecca, b. 20 Oct. 1653, wh. m. 3 Dec. 1674,
John Fitch of Norwalk; Grace, 31 Mar. bapt. 6 Apr. 1656; and
Mercy, 18 Dec. 1658, bapt. 30 Jan. 1659, wh. m. 3 Apr. 1679, Joseph
Ketchum of Norwalk. JAMES, Duxbury 1640, a propr. of Bridgewater 1645, had Abigail, wh. m. capt. Samuel Wadsworth; d. 1652, as
did his w. Mary soon aft. His will of 10 Aug. names two minor ch.
(commit. by the Ct. to care of Constant Southworth) Abigail, and Timothy,
wh. was b. 3 May 1642, says the fam. bible tradit. wh. carries other less
definite matters, as that he was from the North of Eng. and had James,
Caleb, and Joshua, wh. d. of the plague bef. he came over. JAMES,
Boston, was a soldier in Oliver's comp. and wound. in the terrib. day of
Narraganset, tho. hav. been press. in the first of the mo. he had hir. a
substit. By w. Susanna he had Eliz. b. 16 July 1680; and James, 28
May 1684. His will, made 12 June foll. names the two ch. and made w.
extrix. * TIMOTHY, Salem, merch. s. of the first James, freem. 1678, m.
7 Feb. 1673, Mary, d. of Nathaniel Verin, had Mary, b. 7 Apr. 1674;
James, 1 Feb. 1676, wh. was deac. kept the fam. tradit. in bible and d.
1753; Timothy, 3, bapt. 4 Nov. 1677; Nathaniel, b. 4 Nov. 1679;
Abigail, 15 Sept. 1681; Sarah, 4 Mar. 1683; Caleb, 5 Feb. 1685;

Rachel, 3 Dec. 1686 ; and Verin, 2 Feb. 1690, wh. was k. by the Ind. at Haverhill, 29 Aug. 1708. He was rep. 1683 and 92, and d. 6 Jan. 1699, and his wid. d. 7 Jan. 1732, aged 83. Timothy, his s. H. C. 1695, was oft. rep. from 1717, speaker 1720 and 1, of the counc. 1727–30, d. 25 Oct. 1760,.the last surv. of his class ; had two ws. Bethia Kitchen, m. May 1714, d. 20 June 1720 ; and Mary, wh. d. 8 Feb. 1767, aged 80 yrs. From him, thro. his gr.mo. the late lieut.-gov. Winthrop derived his mid. name.

LINDON, or LYNDON, AUGUSTINE, Boston, mariner, 1652, by w. Jane had Samuel, prob. b. Mar. 1653, and both mo. and ch. d. that same mo. ; his w. Eliz. d. at Charlestown, 29 June 1657, and he m. third w. Dec. 1658, Phebe, wid. of William Franklin, was freem. 1660, and an iron-monger in 1672 at B. JOHN, New Haven, prob. a workman at the ironworks, d. 1667 ; no w. or ch. is heard of, and his inv. was £13 only.

LINDSAY, or LINSEY, CHRISTOPHER, Lynn 1630 perhaps, d. 19 Apr. 1669, and his wid. Margaret d. 30 Dec. foll. leav. s. John, and Eleazer. DANIEL, came Apr. 1637 in the employm. of Samuel Dix, from the city of Norwich, but I kn. no more of his master or him. ELEAZER, Lynn, s. of Christopher, m. Aug. 1668, Sarah, d. of Hugh Alley, had Sarah, b. 12 May 1669 ; Eleazer, 25 Mar. 1671 ; Mary, 22 July 1673, perhaps d. young ; John, Aug. 1675 ; Abigail, 10 Nov. 1677 ; Mary, again, 10 Mar. 1680 ; and Ralph, 15 Dec. 1684, was freem. 1691. JOHN, Lynn, br. of the preced. m. 6 June 1667, Mary, d. of Hugh Alley, had John, b. 15 Feb. 1668 ; Samuel, May 1669 ; Eleazer, 19 Feb. 1671 ; Nathan-iel, 16 Apr. 1672 ; Sarah, 2 Mar. 1675 ; Mary, 28 Nov. 1677 ; Mar-garet, 25 Feb. 1680 ; and Benoni, 2 Jan. 1681, d. in few days, as did the mo. on the day of his b. and in July 1682, he m. Amy Richardson ; was freem. 1690. Descend. contin. at Lynn.

LINES, LOINES, or LINE, BENJAMIN, New Haven, youngest s. of Ralph, a propr. 1685. GABRIEL, freem. of Conn. 1656, most prob. d. or rem. soon. HENRY, New Haven, s. of John of Badby, 2 ms. from Daventry, 13 from Northampton, Co. Northampton, had John, b. 1656, d. young, it is thot. ; Joanna, b. 20, bapt. 24 Oct. 1658 ; Samuel, 16 Jan. bapt. 4 Mar. 1660 ; and Hopestill, 6, bapt. 10 Nov. 1661 ; and he d. 1663, leav. wid. JOHN, Isle of Shoals, wh. d. a. 1675, I think was a fisherman, for his excors. were of Dartmouth, in Devonsh. JOSEPH, New Haven, br. of Benjamin, a propr. 1685. RALPH, New Haven, perhaps br. of Henry, may have had Samuel, freem. 1670 ; Ralph, b. 1652 ; and certain. John, 1655 ; Joseph, 1657 ; and Benjamin, 1659 ; the three last s. bapt. 1661 ; perhaps other ch. ; was freem. bef. 1669. He and the four s. are in the list of proprs. 1685, spell. Loines, but in the rec. of b. Lines. ROGER, Jamaica, L. I. 1656. SAMUEL, New

Haven 1687, perhaps s. of Ralph of the same, had w. Mary, d. of John Thompson the sec. of the same.

LING, BENJAMIN, Charlestown 1636, went to New Haven, prob. with Gov. Eaton, had his est. laid out 1640, was a freem. with prefix of respect, liv. in what is now East Haven, d. 27 Apr. 1673, leav. no ch. but giv. good prop. to some friends, and large to w. Joanna, wh. m. 3 Nov. foll. col. John Dixwell, the regicide, and d. in a few wks.

LINN. See Lynn.

LINNELL or LYNNELL, oft. print. LINNETT or LYNNETT, DAVID, Barnstable, perhaps s. of Robert, b. in Eng. m. 9 Mar. 1653, Hannah Shelley or Shilley, had Samuel, b. 15 Dec. 1655; Elisha, 1 June 1658; and Hannah, 15 Dec. 1660, wh. m. 3 Aug. 1681, the sec. Dolor Davis; beside Jonathan. JOHN, Barnstable, wh. was s. possib. of the preced. or of Jonathan, of wh. we kn. from Hamblen only that he was a sett. of B. bef. 1700, and may have been a br. of David, or of John, m. Ruth Davis, had Thankful, b. 12 Nov. 1696, bapt. 17 Sept. 1699; Samuel, b. 16 Nov. 1699; John, 15 June 1702; Bethia, 14 May 1704; Joseph, 12 June 1707; Hannah, 10 July 1709; and Jabez, 30 July 1711. JONATHAN, Eastham, s. perhaps youngest, of David, by w. Eliz. had David, b. 28 Jan. 1694; Eliz. 17 Apr. 1696, d. at 18 yrs.; Abigail, 1 July 1699; Jonathan, 4 Aug. 1701; Thomas, 12 Oct. 1703; Elisha, 15 Feb. 1707; and d. 27 July 1725. ROBERT, Scituate, with his w. under let. of dism. from ch. in London, join. this 16 Sept. 1638, rem. to Barnstable next yr. had Bethia, bapt. 7 Feb. 1641; left wid. and sev. ch. and prob. gr.ch. The wid. in 1669, says Deane, complain. that part of the prop. giv. her by her h. was kept back by his s. Robert, so we may, I think, infer, that she was not the mo. His d. Hannah, m. 15 Mar. 1649, John Davis; Mary m. 15 Oct. 1649, Richard Child; and Abigail m. 27 May 1651, Joshua Lombard. Of Experience, wh. m. 20 Aug. 1689, Jabez Davis, we may conject. that she was his cous. THOMAS, Hampton 1643. Deane made the last let. of this name t.

LINSLEY, JOHN, Guilford 1650, or earlier, rem. long bef. 1667 to Branford, when John jr. was there.

LINTON, RICHARD, prob. at Gov. Cradock's planta. Medford 1630, and Watertown 1638, one of the first sett. of Lancaster, 1643, d. 30 Mar. 1665. His est. was small, and very little is kn. of him but that his d. Ann m. Lawrence Waters of Lancaster.

LIPPET, or LIPPIT, JOHN, early a townsman of Providence, and aft. freem. at Warwick 1655, had, perhaps, Nathaniel, certain. John, Moses, and Joseph, prob. Rebecca, wh. m. 2 Feb. 1665, Joseph Howard, and next, 19 Mar. 1669, Francis Budlong; yet Joseph and Nathaniel d. perhaps early. JOHN, Warwick, s. of the preced. m. 9 Feb. 1665, Ann

Grove, had John, b. 10 Nov. foll. and Moses, 17 Feb. 1668. He d. early, and his wid. m. 21 Feb. 1671, Edward Searle, jr. Moses, perhaps of Kingston, s. of the first John, m. 9 or 19 Nov. 1668, Mary, d. of Henry Knowles, was, I presume, of Wickford, as the Conn. favorers name their claim to the Narraganset country. His will of 1700, tho. he did not d. bef. 6 Jan. 1705, ment. s. Moses, then a minor, ds. Mary, w. of John Burlingame; Martha, w. of Thomas Burlingame; and Rebecca w. of John Lippet.

LIPPENCOT, BARTHOLOMEW, Dover 1658. RICHARD, Dorchester, freem. 13 May 1640, rem. to Boston 1644, by w. Abigail had Remembrance, bapt. 19 Sept. 1641, at D. and at B. had John, b. 6, bapt. 10 Nov. 1644; Abigail, 17, bapt. 24 Jan. 1647, d. in few wks. In a few yrs. he disagr. with his brethr. of the ch; who cast him out from their communion, 6 July 1651, tho. only for his conscientious scruples, and soon aft. he went home, where more liberty was encouraged by Cromwell than our people liked.' There he had Restore, b. at Plymouth, 3 July of yr. not ment. in the fam. geneal. but prob. 1653; and at some other town in Devonsh.; Freedom, 1 Sept. prob. 1655; Increase, 5 Dec. 1657; and Jacob, 11 May 1660; in 1663 came again over the ocean, and at R. I. had Preserved, 25 Feb. 1663, wh. d. at three yrs. In few yrs. more he rem. to New Jersey, and at Shrewsbury in that Col. he was a patentee of the chart. 30 May 1669, and his descend. have cont.

LISCOME, or LISCOM, NICHOLAS, Marblehead 1663. Felt. Perhaps he had gr. of ld. 1637, and is the man whose name is by Felt, I. 169, print. Listen, wh. seems a very uncommon surname, and the mistake might easi. arise by reading c as t, wh. in the old engross. hand it so much resembles as to have a thousand times been so tak. Possib. the modern fam. of Luscome at Salem may thus be derived. See Lyscom.

LISLE. See Lyall.

LISTER, ANDREW. See Lester.

LITCHFIELD, EXPERIENCE, Scituate 1671, s. of Lawrence of the same, k. by accid. 1673. JOSIAH, Scituate, s. prob. of Lawrence, m. 1671, Sarah, d. of Rev. Nicholas Baker, had Hannah, b. 24 Dec. 1672, Sarah, 25 Sept. 1674; Josiah, 10 Jan. 1677; Nicholas, 7 Feb. 1680; Experience, 25 May 1683; Judith, 25 Apr. 1687; and Samuel, 4 Feb. 1690. His gr. gr.s. Joseph, Br. Univ. 1773, d. 28 Jan. 1828, in 78th yr. and gr. gr. gr.s. Paul, H. C. 1775, d. 5 Nov. 1827, in 76th yr. says Farmer, and both were min. LAWRENCE, Barnstable 1640, thot. to be progenit. of all of this name in N. E. rem. aft. 1643, and in 1646 is found at Scituate, had d. Dependence, b. 15 Feb. that yr.; and, perhaps, Josiah, 1647; but at B. had d. Remember (wh. Deane says, m. a Lewis of Barnstable, but I doubt his accuracy); and s. Experience, bef.

ment. He d. 1650 at S. and his wid. Judith, perhaps d. of William Dennis of Scituate, m. that yr. William Peaks.

LITTLE, EPHRAIM, Marshfield, s. of Thomas, m. 1672, Mary Sturdevant, of wh. we kn. not the f. had Ephraim, b. 1673, H. C. 1695, min. of Plymouth; Ruth, 1675, d. soon; David, 1681; John, 1683; Ann; and Mary; and, perhaps, other ch. He d. 24 Nov. 1717, aged 68, and his wid. d. 10 Feb. foll. aged 66. GEORGE, Newbury 1640, a tailor from London, m. Alice Poor, had Sarah, b. 8 May 1652, d. at 6 mos.; Joseph, 22 Sept. 1653; John, 28 July 1655, d. at 17 yrs.; Moses, 11 Mar. 1657; Sarah, again, 24 Nov. 1661; his w. d. 1 Dec. 1680; and he m. 19 July 1681, Elinor, wid. of Thomas Barnard of Amesbury (who outliv. him a short time), and d. 27 Nov. 1694. ISAAC, Marshfield, br. of Ephraim, by w. Bethia, wh. d. 3 Sept. 1718, had Thomas, b. 15 Dec. 1674, H. C. 1695; Dorothy, 11 Aug. 1676, d. at 6 mos.; Isaac, 21 Feb. 1678; Bethia, 9 Dec. 1681, d. young; ano. d. 27 Nov. 1683, prob. liv. not many days; Charles, 15 Oct. 1685; Nathaniel, 12 Apr. 1690; and William, 27 Feb. 1692, H. C. 1710; and d. 29 Dec. 1699, by one acco. but Miss Thomas says, 1712. George, an officer of distinct. in the U. S. navy, was of this branch. JONAS, Scituate 1663, of wh. I kn. no more. JOSEPH, Newbury, s. of George of the same, m. 31 Oct. 1677, Mary, d. of Tristram Coffin, had Judith, b. 19 July 1678; Joseph, 23 Feb. 1680, d. young; George, 12 Jan. 1682; Sarah, 23 Oct. 1684; Enoch, 16 Dec. 1685; Tristram, 7 Apr. 1688; Moses, 5 May 1690; Daniel, 13 Jan. 1692; and Joseph, again, 27 Dec. 1693. MOSES, Newbury, br. of the preced. m. Lydia, d. of Tristram Coffin, had John, b. Jan. 1680; Tristram, 9 Dec. 1681; Sarah, 28 Apr. 1684; Mary, 13 Jan. 1687; Eliz. 25 May 1688; and Moses, 26 Feb. 1691; and d. 8 Mar. 1691. His youngest ch. Moses, liv. to 19 Oct. 1780. RICHARD, New Haven, freem. 1670, a propr. 1685. SAMUEL, Marshfield, s. perhaps youngest of Thomas, m. 18 May 1682, Sarah Gray, and for sec. w. 5 Dec. 1698, Mary Mayhew. THOMAS, Plymouth 1630, m. 19 Apr. 1633, Ann, d. of Richard Warren, rem. to Marshfield 1650, where his s. Ephraim was b. 17 May of that yr. Beside him and Isaac, both bef. ment. he had Thomas, k. at Rehoboth fight 1676, and Samuel, and, perhaps, ds. certain. Hannah, m. 15 Jan. 1662, Stephen Tilden of M.; Mercy, m. 1666, John Sawyer; Ruth; and Patience, as giv. by Miss Thomas; and he d. 12 Mar. 1671. THOMAS, Cambridge, had d. Patience, said on rec. at Boston to have m. at Weymouth 11 Nov. 1657, Joseph Jones of Hingham, and any thing else is not kn. Twelve of this name had, in 1829, been gr. at Harv. eight at Dart. and nine at other coll. of N. E.

LITTLEFIELD, ANTHONY, Wells, s. of Edmund, took the o. of submiss. to Mass. 1653. DANIEL, Wells, m. Mary, d. of capt. Roger Hill, and num. descend. prosper there. EBENEZER, Newton, s. of John, by w. Lydia had Jemima, b. 19 Aug. 1697; Ezra, Mar. 1699, d. young; Ebenezer, 2 May 1701, liv. very long; Pelatiah, 12 Oct. 1703; Lydia, 15 Feb. 1706; Jerusha, 15 Apr. 1708; Praisever, 5 Mar. 1710; Susanna, and Ephraim, tw. 21 Nov. 1712; and Sybil, 1 Nov. 1714; his w. d. 12 Oct. 1717, and he d. 9 Apr. or by ano. acco. Jan. 1728. EDMUND, Exeter 1639, rem. to Wells in or bef. 1645, was there a man of distinct. as commiss. with Ezekiel Knight and Thomas Wheelwright, is call. "old Edmund L." d. 11 Dec. 1661, by his will of that date, gave good provis. to w. Ann, to eldest s. Francis, and other s. Anthony, Thomas, John, and youngest Francis, to ds. Eliz. Wakefield, Mary Barrett, and Hannah L. His inv. show. £588, 13, 4. The h. of Eliz. was, I presume, John W. and of Mary was John B. * FRANCIS, Wells, eldest s. of the preced. had been of Dover 1648, a leader in support of Mass. cause, rep. 1660, had tak. the o. 1653, with Francis, jr. Anthony, and Thomas, prob. his s. as may have been John. His d. Sarah m. John Wells, wh. came from Ipswich. A very curious story is told, that the parents of this man, in Eng. of wh. he was the eldest s. suppos. him d. as they in many yrs. heard not of him, call. ano. s. by the same name, wh. came over to Wells, in the time a little bef. the Commissnrs. of Mass. 1668, reinstated affairs, and they made him an officer. Of the value of the tradit. I judge not, but refer to Maine Hist. Coll. I. 262; Hubbard, 600; and Hutch. I. 266. FRANCIS, Woburn, had Mary, b. 14 Dec. 1646; and his w. Jane d. 6 days aft. JOHN, Dedham 1650, by w. Mary had Rebecca, b. 26 Mar. 1651; Experience, 7 or 17 Dec. 1659; John, 5 Oct. 1664; and Ebenezer, 13 Oct. 1669; was freem. 1671, liv. in that part which was incorp. as Wrentham. His w. d. 13 Jan. 1675, and he rem. JAMES, Wells, k. by the Ind. May 1690. JOHN, Wells 1656, constable 1661, made a lieut. in 1668 by the Commissnrs. who created Francis, jr. ensign; so that we may reckon him older, if a br. or superior in influence, if not. His d. Mary m. Matthew Austin. THOMAS, Dover 1648, aft. at Wells, sw. to Mass. in 1653, was there still in 1680, to sw. alleg. to the k. In the Bevis, from Southampton 1638, came Annis L. with six ch. she 38 yrs. old.

LITTLEHALE, RICHARD, came in the Mary and John, 1634, and prob. was first sett. at Ipswich, thence at Newbury, m. 15 Nov. 1647, Mary Lancton, had twelve ch. says Coffin, but he names only John, b. 27 Nov. 1650, wh. was a soldier in Lothrop's comp. " the flower of Essex," k. 18 Sept. 1675; and adds, that he d. at Haverhill, 18 Feb. 1664. Mirick says he was clk. of the writs. His wid. m. 6 Apr. 1665, as his third w. Edmund Bridges. No doubt some of his ch. spread the name.

LIVEEN, JOHN, New London, where it was common. writ. Living, came from Barbados, 1677, with w. Alice, wh. had by former h. John, and Nicholas Hallam; d. 19 Oct. 1689; in his will, made that day, unhappi. gave large part of his prop. to the min. which caus. long controversy in the law, and appeal to the k. in Council. His wid. wh. brot. (the s. said), most of the est. d. 1698.

LIVERMORE, JOHN, Watertown, was prob. s. of Peter of Little Thurlow, in the W. of Co. Suff'k. came in the Francis from Ipswich 1634, aged 28, but with no w. or ch. yet it is thot. that w. foll. from Eng. with d. Hannah, b. 1633; went to Wethersfield, where he own. lds. in 1640, but was, in 1639, of New Haven, then sign. the coven. with fam. count. four, there had bapt. Samuel, 15 Aug. 1641; Daniel, 8 Oct. 1643; a d. 1 June 1645; and Mary, 12 Sept. 1647; beside Eliz. and Sarah, but sold, 7 May 1650, to Theophilus Higginson, his ho. and ld. and rem. back to Watertown. By w. Grace at W. he had Edmund, wh. d. soon aft. b. 24 May 1659. Hannah m. 14 May 1655, John Coolidge; but in Bond may be seen other date, as 14 Nov. and also 14 Feb. foll. one under Coolidge, the other under Livermore; and wh. of the three dates is correct may be matter of dispute; Sarah m. James Townsend of Charlestown; and Martha m. 15 July 1682, Abraham Parker, jr. of Chelmsford. His will, of 10 Jan. 1683, was pro. 16 June 1684; he had d. 14 Apr. preced. aged 78; and the will of his wid. of 19 Dec. 1690, was pro. 16 June foll. Both ment. ch. and gr.ch. JOHN, Watertown, eldest s. of the preced. by w. Hannah had John, b. 21 Mar. 1668, d. at 15 yrs.; Hannah, 27 Sept. 1670; Sarah, 18 Feb. 1672; Joseph, 27 Jan. 1675; Daniel, 8 June 1677; James, 13 Feb. 1680; Mary, and Martha, tw. 11 Apr. 1684; and John, 8 July 1690. He m. sec. w. Eliz. wid. of Samuel Allen, d. of capt. John Grout, and his will, of 20 Oct. 1714, was pro. 25 Feb. 1719. SAMUEL, Watertown, s. of John the first, freem. 1671, m. 4 June 1668, Ann, d. of Matthew Bridge, had Ann, b. 29 Mar. 1669, d. young; Grace, 28 Sept. 1671; Samuel, 27 Apr. 1673; Daniel, 3 Feb. 1675; Thomas, 5 Jan. 1677; Jonathan, 19 Apr. 1678; Matthew, 12 Feb. 1680, d. young; John, 27 Feb. 1681; Abigail, 9 Oct. 1683; Nathaniel, 29 Dec. 1685; Lydia, 26 July 1687; and Ann, 1690. He d. Dec. of that yr. and his wid. m. Oliver Wellington, and d. 28 Aug. 1727, aged 81. His will, of 5 Dec. 1690, pro. 16 June foll. made w. and s. Samuel excors. THOMAS, Charlestown, by w. Mary, had John, bapt. 21 Aug. 1687; and Thomas, 16 Dec. 1688. Seven of this name had, in 1834, been gr. at Harv. and nine at other N. E. and Princeton coll. of wh. three were mem. of the U. S. Congress. In early rec. it may easi. be mistak. for Lethermore.

LIVINGSTON, JOHN, Boston 1659, then adm. of the Scots' Charit. Soc.

LLOYD, EDWARD, Charlestown, spell. sometimes with single l, by w. Hannah had Hannah, bapt. 18 June 1682; Edward, b. 28 Dec. 1684,

bapt. 4 Jan. foll. ; Eliz. bapt. 6 Jan. 1689 ; and Martha, 11 June 1693.
JAMES, Boston, merch. prob. from Bristol, as fam. tradit. said, had come
a. 1670 to Newport, but 1673 was fix. at B. m. Griselda, d. of Nathaniel
Sylvester of Shelter Isl. and d. 1693. He m. for sec. w. 3 Nov. 1691,
Rebecca, d. of our Gov. John Leverett. His s. Henry, of Queen's Co.
L. I. was f. of James, a disting. physician of Boston, b. 1728, d. Mar.
1810, whose s. James, H. C. 1787, a U. S. senator, d. 1831, without
issue. WALTER, came in the Hopewell, capt. Babb, in the aut. of 1635,
aged 27 ; but where he sat down is unkn.

LOBDELL, or LOBDEN, ISAAC, Hull 1658, may have sev. yrs. bef.
been at Plymouth, freem. 1673. I have seen it stated that his w. was
Martha, d. of Samuel Ward. JOHN, Hull, perhaps br. of the preced.
m. 29 July 1659, Hannah, d. of John Leavitt, wh. d. 23 Apr. 1662, and
he d. 1673, the same yr. in wh. he was freem. and Nathaniel Bosworth,
call. his f.-in-law, had admin. of his est. wh. was good. JOSHUA, Milford, s. of Simon of the same, liv. there 1713, prob. had fam. NICHO-
LAS, Hingham 1636, had that yr. gr. of ld. ; but Lincoln, 44, spells
the name Lobdin. NICHOLAS, Charlestown, by w. Eliz. had Nicholas,
bapt. 18 Nov. 1688; Eliz. 8 Sept. 1689. SIMON, Milford, Hartford
1655, freem. 1657, rem. to Springfield, there from 1666 to 74, was pris.-
keep. and had Eliz. b. 1669 ; and Joshua 1671, rem. to M. and there
had Rebecca, bapt. 1677, and, perhaps, other ch. Lambert is, perhaps,
wrong by thirty yrs. in mark. him of Milford 1645. Eliz. possib. his
sis. m. at Boston 1651, Jonathan Burt of Springfield ; and Ann, ano. sis.
perhaps m. 3 Jan. 1660, Samuel Terry of S.

LOCKE, EBENEZER, Woburn, s. of William, m. 18 Oct. 1697, Susanna, d. of Israel Walker, had Ebenezer, b. 28 Apr. 1699, and she d.
13 June foll. ; he m. again, 14 Oct. 1701, Hannah, d. of David Mead,
had Samuel, 24 Aug. 1702 ; Josiah, 15 Mar. 1705 ; Joshua, 21 Aug.
1709 ; Nathan, 20 Mar. 1713 ; and Hannah, 11 Apr. 1716; and he d.
24 Dec. 1723. His wid. d. 24 July 1739. EDWARD, Hampton, s. of
John of the same, m. Hannah, d. of Francis Jenness, had Francis, b. 18
July 1694 ; Samuel, 4 Sept. 1698 ; Edward, 28 May 1701 ; Prudence,
30 May 1707; James, 4 Oct. 1709; and Thomas, 10 June 1713.
JAMES, Woburn, br. of Ebenezer, m. 5 Dec. 1700, Sarah, d. of Richard
Cutter, had Hannah, b. 11 July 1701 ; James, 17 June 1703 ; Ruhamah,
23 Apr. 1705 ; Sarah, 5 July 1707 ; Phebe, 15 Aug. 1709 ; Rebecca,
11 Nov. 1711 ; Mary, 12 Oct. 1713 ; and Jonathan, 17 Jan. 1717 ; and
d. 11 Dec. 1745. JAMES, Hampton, s. of John of the same, had, prob.
James. JOHN, Dover 1645, rem. to Hampton, m. a. 1652, Eliz. d. of
William Berry, had John ; Eliz. ; Nathaniel, b. 1661 ; Alice ; Edward ;
Tryphena ; Rebecca ; Mary ; William, 17 Apr. 1677 ; James ; and

Joseph; was k. by the Ind. 26 Aug. 1696. JOHN, Woburn, br. of
Ebenezer, m. 29 or 31 May 1683, Eliz. Plimpton, d. of Thomas of Sudbury, had Thomas, b. 20 Mar. 1684, d. in 3 days; Mary, 1 Apr. 1685;
John, 14 May 1686; Thomas, again, 5 Apr. 1688; a d. without name,
11 June 1693; Abigail, 2 Apr. 1694; and Peter, 10 Sept. 1698, wh.
d. young. His w. d. 23 Feb. 1720, aged 61; and he m. 30 Nov. foll.
Mary, wid. of Nathaniel Wyman, d. of Increase Winn, and he d. Apr.
1756, and his w. near the same time. JOHN, Hampton, s. of John of the
same, had John, Richard, and Jethro. JOSEPH, Woburn, br. of Ebenezer,
had three ws. and by the first, Mary, wh. d. Apr. 1707, had, perhaps,
Mary; Abigail; Lydia; Sarah, b. 14 July 1696; Joseph, 19 Mar.
1699; Eliz. 15 Mar. 1703; and Huldah, 28 June 1705. He m. Margaret, d. of Israel Mead, and had Margaret, 6 May 1710; Joanna, 2
Feb. 1712; and all these were bapt. 26 Oct. 1712 at Lexington, near
the bounds of wh. was most of his est.; Ruth, 9 May 1714; and
Stephen, 26 Jan. 1718. His 3d w. Hannah Pierce, m. 5 Nov. 1743, d.
10 Apr. 1747; and he d. 1754. JOSEPH, Hampton, s. of John of the
same, by w. Salome, had Salome, b. 20 Oct. 1710; Joseph, 27 Apr.
1716; Eliz. 1 Dec. 1718; Mary, 1 May 1720; Ann, 25 Mar. 1723;
Abigail, 6 Nov. 1725; and Jeremiah, 4 Aug. 1728. NATHANIEL,
Hampton, s. of John of the same, m. 22 Jan. 1689, Dorothy or Deborah,
d. of Jasper Blake, had, says tradit. nineteen ch. but the names of only
a dozen are ment. and some of them rather doubtful, viz.: John, b. 1689;
Dorothy, 1691; Tryphena; Eliz. 1694; Rachel, 12 Dec. 1695; Nathaniel, 18 Oct. 1698; Samuel, 1702; Jonathan, 22 Dec. 1705; Deborah; Joseph; Abijah; the six last all bapt. at once, it is said; and
Timothy; and d. 12 Nov. 1734. SAMUEL, Lexington, s. of William,
had w. Ruth, wh. d. 14 Dec. 1714, and 2d w. Mary Day of Ipswich, by
wh. was his only ch. Samuel, b. 5 July 1718, and no more is told, but
that this s. had good est. from his f. and spent it. WILLIAM, Woburn,
is prob. that ch. of 6 yrs. brot. over by Nicholas Davis, in the Planter
1635, from London, where prob. he was b. 13 Dec. 1628, no doubt liv.
first at Charlestown, m. 27 Nov. 1655, Mary, d. of William Clark of
Watertown, wh. d. 18 July 1715, had William, b. 27 Dec. 1657, d. in 2
wks.; William, again, 18 Jan. 1659; John, 1 Aug. 1661; Joseph, 8
Mar. 1664; Mary, 16 Oct. 1666; Samuel, 14 Oct. 1669; Ebenezer, 8
Jan. 1674, bef. ment.; James, 14 Nov. 1677; and Eliz. 4 Jan. 1681;
was deac. and d. 16 June 1720. Mary m. 30 Mar. 1692, Samuel Kendall; and Eliz. m. 14 Oct. 1700, James Markham. WILLIAM, Woburn,
s. of the preced. m. 29 May 1683, Sarah, d. of Francis Whitmore, had
William, b. 28 June 1684; Francis, 25 July 1690; Daniel, 9 July
1693; by 2d w. Abigail Hayward, m. 8 June 1698, wh. outliv. him, he

had Ebenezer; and Abigail, 22 June 1710, was deac. and d. 8 July
1738. WILLIAM, Portsmouth, s. of John of Hampton, m. 23 Nov. 1699,
Hannah Knowles, had Jonathan, b. 15 Mar. 1702; William; Abigail;
Hannah, d. young; Patience, 1710; Sarah; Elijah; Elisha; Eliphalet,
d. young; Jemima, 20 Jan. 1721; and Hannah, again, 1724; prob. was
of Portsmouth some yrs. but deac. at Rye, there d. 22 Jan. 1768. Rev.
Samuel, H. C. 1755, s. of Samuel, wh. was s. of Ebenezer, bef. ment. b.
23 Nov. 1731, early call. to be Presid. from 1770 to 1773, was a fine
scholar, but by untoward circumstances requir. to resign his office, d. 15
Jan. 1778, of apoplexy.

LOCKHART, GEORGE, Falmouth 1688, by Sir Edmund Andros made
comm. of the fort, seiz. by the patriots on the Revo. as partaker of his
tyranny. Willis, I. 196.

LOCKWOOD, DANIEL, Fairfield 1667, third s. of Robert of the same,
freem. 1669, d. early in 1691, leav. wid. and three ch. Daniel, aged 22;
Abigail, 17; and Mary, 10. His s. Daniel d. 1698, leav. large est. for
so young a man. EDMUND, Cambridge, came, prob. in the fleet with
Winth. as he req. 19 Oct. 1630, to be made free, when he bears the
prefix of respect, and was adm. 18 May foll. when the prefix is omit.;
was a man of good repute, constable, and on the finance Comtee. 1632
for the Col. d. 1635, leav. wid. Ruth, as strange. reads Mass. Rec. I.
134, when her name was Eliz. and ch. (perhaps more than one) John,
b. Nov. 1632, tho. the rec. calls the parents, Edward and Eliz. "Elder
childr." by order of Ct. 2 June 1635, to be dispos. of, leaves no doubt
of a former w. Perhaps the wid. was d. of John Masters, wh. in
his will, 19 Dec. 1639, leaves handsome sum to his gr.ch. John L. She
m. Cary Latham. EDMUND, Stamford 1651, perhaps s. of the preced.
on d. of his br. John without issue in 1683, had his est. and d. 31 Jan.
1693, leav. ch. John, Daniel, Edmund, Mary, and Abigail, of wh. John
was old eno. to be tax. in 1687. EPHRAIM, Norwalk, br. of Daniel, m.
8 June 1665, Mercy, d. of Matthias Sension, had John, b. 19 Mar.
1666; Daniel, 13 Aug. 1668; Sarah, 3 Nov. 1670; Ephraim, 1 May
1673; Eliphalet, 27 Feb. 1676, Joseph, 1 Apr. 1680; and James, 21
Apr. 1683; all nam. in his will of 13 Jan. 1685, pro. same yr. Sarah
m. May 1695, John Platt. GERSHOM, Greenwich 1672, fifth s. of Robert, was liv. there 20 yrs. later, and had been there 3 yrs. bef. but we
kn. of him only, that he had Gershom. JOHN, New London, prob. s. of
the first Edmund, m. (said a wild tradit.) a d. of Cary Latham, wh.
might have been his uterine sis. d. 1683, without issue, and his prop. fell
to br. Edmund. * JONATHAN, Stamford, eldest s. of Robert, by w.
Mary had Jonathan, Robert, Gershom, Joseph, John, and, perhaps,
some ds. but he was not long at S. hav. sold his est. there 1665, and in

five yrs. aft. is call. of Greenwich, was rep. 1671, 3, 4, and 6, and a lieut. JOSEPH, Fairfield, sec. s. of Robert, m. the only ch. of Robert Beacham, had Robert, Susanna, John, and Sarah, all nam. in will of gr.f. RICH-ARD, Maine, was 40 yrs. old when he gave evid. in 1672. ROBERT, Watertown, perhaps br. of Edmund, of whom, in 1635, he was excor. freem. 9 Mar. 1637, by w. Susanna had Jonathan, b. 10 Sept. 1634; Deborah, 12 Oct. 1636; Joseph, 6 Aug. 1638 ; Daniel, 25 Mar. 1640 ; Ephraim, 1 Dec. 1641; Gershom, 6 Sept. 1643; rem. to Fairfield aft. 1645, but bef. 1652 ; d. 1658. His wid. Susanna m. Jeffry Ferris, and was d. May 1661. All the ch. bef. nam. exc. Deborah, partook of his est. and four others, John, Abigail, Sarah, and Mary, perhaps all b. at Fairfield. Abigail m. John Barlow of Fairfield ; and Mary m. Jona-than Huested of Greenwich. Eleven of this name had been gr. at Yale 1834.

LOFT, RICHARD, a maltster, from Kent, Eng. d. here 1690. By his will of 25 Apr. pro. 24 May in that yr. he gave all his prop. to wid. Eliz.

LOGYN, or LOGAN, ALEXANDER, Charlestown, one of the Scots' Charit. Soc. 1684, by w. Susanna had Alexander, bapt. 3 May 1685 ; John, same day; James, 29 July 1687 ; Jonathan, 28 Mar. 1690; Eben-ezer, 13 Nov. 1692; Isaac, 10 Nov. 1695. JACOB, a propr. at Water-town 1642, says Bond, wh. tells no more.

LOHUN, WILLIAM, Swansey, had Nathaniel, b. 2 Feb. 1675 ; and was k. by the Ind. 24 June foll.

LOKER, JOHN, Sudbury, had, bef. 1652, m. Mary Draper.

LOLLENDINE, JOHN, Dunstable, an orig. sett. a. 1673, contin. a house-holder 1699.

LOMBARD, LUMBORT, or LUMBART, BENJAMIN, Barnstable, youngest s. of Thomas the first, m. 19 Sept. 1672, Jane Warren, prob. d. of Na-thaniel, wh. d. 27 Feb. 1683, had Mercy, b. 2 Nov. 1673 ; Benjamin, 27 Sept. 1675; and Hope, 26 Mar. 1679 ; and he m. 19 Nov. 1685, sec. w. Sarah Walker, had Sarah, 29 Oct. 1686; Bathshua, 4 May 1687 ; Mary, 17 June 1688 ; and Samuel, 15 Sept. 1691. His w. d. 6 Nov. 1693, and he m. 24 May foll. wid. Hannah Whetstone, had Temperance, 25 May 1695 ; and Martha, 28 Dec. 1704. BERNARD, s. of Thomas, b. in O. E. took the o. of freem. in Mass. 1 Apr. 1634, when he was, perhaps, of Dorchester, but soon went to Scituate, where he may have been earlier, but with his w. join. the ch. 19 Apr. 1635, thence to Barn-stable, with Lothrop, hav. then Joshua, and Mary, bapt. at S. 8 Oct. 1637, not 57 as in Geneal. Reg. XII. 249, the former, perhaps, b. in Eng. but at B. where he was ensign 1652, had Martha, bapt. 3 Nov. 1639, not, as in Geneal. Reg. XII. 249, perhaps d. soon, for in Col. Rec. is Martha, b. 19 Sept. 1640, tho. we may suspect error in this ; and

Jabez, 4 July 1641; yet Col. Rec. makes this b. 1 July 1642. When he d. I kn. not, but presume it was aft. 1664. Mr. Hamblen discov. that he was b. 1607 or 8. Mary m. 1 Dec. 1654, George Lewis, jr.; and Martha m. 1 July 1657, John Martin. DAVID, Springfield 1676, s. of John, had Mary, b. 1677; Margaret, 1679; Abigail, 1682; John, 1685; David, 1690; Ebenezer, 1692; and Joseph, 1696; beside two that d. soon; and he d. 17 Aug. 1716. JABEZ, Barnstable, s. of Bernard, m. 1 Dec. 1660, Sarah, d. of Martha Derby, had a s. b. 18 Feb. 1662, d. very soon; Eliz. June 1663; Mary, Apr. 1666; Bernard, Apr. 1668; John, Apr. 1670; Matthew, 28 Aug. 1672; Mehitable, Sept. 1674; Abigail, Apr. 1677; Nathaniel, 1 Aug. 1679; and Hepzibah, Dec. 1681. JEDEDIAH, Barnstable, s. of Thomas the first, m. 20 May 1668, Hannah Wing, had Jedediah, b. 25 Dec. 1669; Thomas, 22 June 1671; Hannah, Aug. 1673, and Experience, Apr. 1675 or 77. JOHN, Springfield 1646, m. at New Haven, 1 Sept. 1647, Joanna Pritchard, had John, b. 1648, d. at 24 yrs.; David, 1650, bef. ment.; and Nathaniel, 1654, d. young; and he d. 15 May 1672. This name was at S. writ. Lumbard, as sound. JONATHAN, Barnstable, s. of the first Joshua, m. 11 Dec. 1683, Eliz. Eddy, d. perhaps of Zechariah, had Jonathan, b. 20 Nov. 1684; Alice, 19 Oct. 1686; Ebenezer, 1 Feb. 1688; and Abigail, 12 July 1691. JOSHUA, Barnstable, s. perhaps of Bernard, prob. b. in Eng. but may be more prob. of Thomas, m. 27 May 1651, Abigail, d. of Robert Linnell, had Abigail, b. 6, bapt. 11 Apr. 1652; Mercy, 15 June 1655; Jonathan, 28 Apr. 1657; and Joshua, 16 Jan. 1661. JOSHUA, Barnstable, s. prob. of the preced. m. 6 Nov. 1682, Hopestill Bullock, had Mercy, b. 16 Mar. 1684; Hopestill, 15 Nov. 1686; Joshua, 5 Aug. 1688; Samuel, 1 June 1690; Abigail, 20 Jan. 1692; Mary, 22 Nov. 1697; Eliz. 22 Apr. 1700; and Jonathan, 16 Apr. 1703; and d. Oct. 1724. RICHARD, Scituate 1640, was of Tenterden, Co. Kent, and went home that yr. says Deane. THOMAS, Dorchester, came, prob. bringing Bernard, and two other ch. in the Mary and John 1630, req. to be made freem. 19 Oct. of that yr. and was adm. 18 May foll. rem. in few yrs. perhaps to Scituate first, but to Barnstable by 1640, had Jedediah there, bapt. 19 Sept. 1641; and Benjamin, not 5 (as in Geneal. Reg. XII. 249) but 27 Aug. 1643. That he had other ch. of wh. one or two must have been b. in Eng. is plain eno. from his will of 23 Mar. 1663, in wh. while he names these, he ment. that he formerly gave prop. to s. Barnard; Joshua; Joseph, b. a. 1638; and s.-in-law Edward Colman, wh. m. 27 Oct. 1648, his d. Margaret; provides for w. Joyce, and s. Caleb. Perhaps he had, also, younger d. Jemima, wh. may have made a runaway match with Joseph Benjamin at Boston, 10 June 1661; and liv. many yrs. aft. her f. at New London. THOMAS, Barnstable, perhaps br.

perhaps s. of Bernard, m. 23 Dec. 1665, Eliz. Darby or Derby, had Sarah, b. Dec. 1666; Thomas; Eliz.; Mary; Hannah; Jabez; Rebecca; Bethia; Bathshua; and Patience, given by Mr. Hamblen from the rec. Geneal. Reg. XII. 249, with so many inconsist. dates that we kn. not wh. may be correct. In Col. Rec. we read, "Joseph, Benjamin, and Jeremiah, 10 June 1671," wh. perhaps, means that they d. or were bur. that day at B.

LOMMAKS, NATHANIEL, Dover 1672 to 88, was s. of Edward. See Loomis.

LONDON, JOHN, Windsor, was a soldier in Philip's war. Trumbull, Coll. Rec. II. 396, 9. The Conn. counc. of war (for his com. from the army without license in Jan. 1676, calumn. the officers, and report. many notorious lies), sent him to prison, but he was soon releas. on acknowledg. of his offence, and promise to do good service. He was engag. in the work of befooling Sir Edmund Andros in 1680 about the regicide Goffe, and swore, in N. Y. 20 Apr. 1680, where A. was then Gov. that G. was, in Apr. 1678, liv. at Hartford, and that James Richards, wh. was the oldest mem. of the Counc. and the richest man in the Col. was agt. of G. and that if he, L., discov. the matter it would tend to his ruin; and much other preposterous stuff he testif. All wh. trifling was, with the letter of Andros to Conn. Gov. and their reply, print. in 1855. See the curious matter in Conn. Hist. Coll. III. 284, et seq. showing how the letter of Gov. Andros from New York, of 18 May, was receiv. on 10 June, twenty-three days from date, and travel. almost six miles a day. Perhaps Gov. Leete was innocent of the deception, but he must have been blind, or deaf, or both, not to have suspect. the contrivance, and distrust. the agent.

LONG, ABIEL, Newbury, s. of Robert of the same, m. 27 Oct. 1682, Hannah, d. of Mr. Joseph Hill, had Abiel, b. 24 July 1683, d. in few wks.; Hannah, 6 Nov. 1684; and Benjamin, 1 Sept. 1691; and d. 13 Apr. 1743, aged 94. JOHN, Charlestown, s. of the first Robert of the same, b. in Eng. brot. by his f. had two ws. of wh. the first, Abigail Norton, d. of Francis, wh. d. 21 Apr. 1674, had John, b. 17 Feb. 1656; Mary; and Abigail; all bapt. 6 May 1660; the s. may have d. young, as we find, consistent with rec. of d. of his w. Eliz. 29 July 1678, and child of smallpox, a gr.stone of John, 10 Nov. 1678; Robert, b. 7, bapt. 14 Feb. 1664; Norton, b. 17, bapt. 20 May 1666; a former Norton, b. 21 Aug. 1662, hav. d. 12 July 1664; Abigail, 6 Dec. 1668; Sarah, 26 Feb. 1671; and Isaac; 1 Jan. 1675; and by his sec. m. 10 or 16 Sept. 1674, wh. was Mary, d. of Increase Nowell, and wid. of Isaac Winslow, had Isaac, bapt. 6 June 1675, d. young; Catharine, bapt. 3 June 1677; Samuel; and Mary, b. 31 Mar. bapt. 3 Apr. 1681, wh. m. 7 May 1700, Rev. Simon Bradstreet. He kept the gr. ordinary, as had his f. and the wid. aft. his d. 20 July 1683, retain. the care of it until 1711, when she gave it to Samuel, wh. next yr. sold that "great house" built 1629 for the Gov. and Comp. and wh. above 80 yrs. for the three generat. had been the "Long" tavern. The wid. d. aft. 14 Apr. 1720, the date of will. Mary, the ch. by first w. m. 23 Jan. 1677, Henry Sanford; Catharine m. 24 May 1694, William Wellstead. JOSEPH, Dorchester 1660, s. of Mary, the w. of Joseph Farnsworth, by her former h. for wh. in F.'s will, as also for his br. Thomas, good provis. was made. By w. Mary, whose surname is not kn. m. 3 Feb. 1662, he had Mary, and d. 26 Aug. 1676. His wid. m. Thomas Litchfield, from wh. she was divorc. and d. a. 1703. The d. Mary, on the same authority, I learn, had m. Henry Straight of Greenwich, R. I. JOSHUA, Charlestown, youngest s. of first Robert of the same, H. C. 1653, has nothing, not even date of d. to be learn. but he was liv. 1659, when f. made his will. MICHAEL, Charlestown, eldest br. of the preced. came with his f. had by w. Joan (wh. d. 19 Jan. 1692, aged 74, says the gr.stone) Samuel; Hannah, b. 29 Dec. 1657; and Deborah, 1, bapt. 2 Oct. 1659, d. under 19 yrs.; and he d. 12 Jan. 1689, aged a. 78. NICHOLAS, aged 19, came in the Blessing, 1635, from London, but no more can be told of him; and equal. ign. are we of Ellen L. a serv. of Samuel Andrews, aged 20. PHILIP, Ipswich 1648, rem. to Boston, m. prob. as sec. w. Ann, wid. of Thomas Constable, had Joseph, b. 16 or 20 Aug. 1652. His d. Sarah m. 1656, Benjamin Briscoe; and he had ano. d. In 1656, he was of Edgartown, on the Vineyard; in Oct. 1658 made his will, bound to sea, and d. next yr. as may be infer. from the pro. of the will, 13 Nov. 1659. RICHARD, Weymouth 1635. RICHARD, Salisbury, by w. Ann, d. of Joseph French of the same, had Eliz. b. 30 Oct. 1680; William, 25 June 1682; Richard, 3 Jan. 1684; Susanna, 30 Nov. 1685; Joseph, 6 Jan. 1688; Sarah, 13 Oct. 1689; Eleanor, 16 Jan. 1691; and Sarah, 13 Jan. 1693. ROBERT, Plymouth, was passeng. in the Ann, 1623, had sh. in the div. of ld. but was rem. bef. 1627, when the div. of cattle was made, unless he d. in the interval. Morton's Memor. Davis's Ed. 379. ‖ ROBERT, Charlestown, came in the Defence from London, 1635, aged 45, with w. no doubt his sec. Eliz. 30, says the custom-ho. rec. but prob. 33, and ten ch. Michael, 20; Sarah, 18; Robert, 16; Eliz. 12; Ann, 10; Mary, 9; Rebecca, 8; John, 6; Zechary, 4; and Joshua, 9 mos.; had here Hannah, b. 2, bapt. 12 Mar. 1637; Ruth, bapt. 3 June 1639; Deborah, 10 Aug. 1642; and was freem. 25 May 1636. He had been an innholder at Dunstable, Co. Bedford, 30 ms. from London, therefore well kn. to Rev. Zechariah Symmes, rector in that ch. (in whose honor, perhaps, he call. one of his s.) ar. co. 1639, was a selectman, kept the inn, and d. 9 Jan. 1664, leav. good est. His will, made 10 July 1658, names his wid. wh. liv. to 29 May 1687, aged 84, and eleven ch. being all those he brot. exc. Robert, wh. had d. near seven yrs. bef.; beside Ruth, and Deborah. The regist. of Dunstable, Eng. wh. ment. the bapt. of his s. Zechary, 20 Oct. 1630, relates also, that a Sarah was bur. 12 Dec. 1631, so she was not his d. Sarah m. Abraham Hill; Eliz. m. James Parker; Ann m. 24 Oct. 1643, James Convers; Mary m. Simon Kempthorne; Rebecca m. 17 July 1656, Elias Rowe; and Hannah m. 22 Oct. 1657, Henry Cookery. His will also names gr.s. Samuel L. wh. was s. of Robert. ROBERT, Charlestown, sec. s. of the preced. b. in Eng. had Samuel, b. 23 Apr. 1647; d. under mid. age, and his wid. Eliz. m. Jacob Green. ROBERT, Newbury, m. 1647, Alice Stevens, had Mary, b. 24 Feb. 1649; Abiel, 19 Feb. 1650; Susanna, 4 Nov. 1656; Shubael, 14 Apr. 1661; Martha; John; and Rebecca; was freem. 1645, deac. and d. of small-pox, 27 Dec. 1690; and his wid. d. in three wks. Mary m. 1664, John Cloyes; Susanna m. Stephen Blandford of Sudbury; as Coffin, in Hist. of N. tells. SAMUEL, Ipswich 1648, may have been br. of Philip. SAMUEL, Charlestown, s. of the sec. Robert, by w. Eliz. had Robert, and d. early in Nov. 1671. His will, of 22 Aug. bef. pro. 19 Dec. foll. made w. extrix. and f. Jacob Green and uncle John L. overseers, directs only ch. Robert to be brot. up to letters, and provides for un-born ch. SHUBAEL, Newbury, s. of Robert of the same, m. 26 Aug. 1695, Hannah Merrill, had Robert, b. 20 May 1696; Abigail, 3 Jan. 1698, d. in few days; Abigail, again, 31 Jan. 1699; and John, 2 Nov. 1701. THOMAS, Hartford 1665, had Joseph, b. 22 Jan. 1668; and William, 4 Feb. 1670. THOMAS, Roxbury, had Thomas, b. 26 Nov. 1688. Per-haps he was br. of Joseph of Dorchester. ZECHARY, Charlestown, s. of Robert of the same, b. in Eng. came with his f. m. 24 Sept. 1656, Sarah Tidd, had Sarah, b. 22 July 1657; Zechary; Mary; and Eliz. all bapt. 21 June 1668; Deborah, 23 Oct. 1670; John, 31 Aug. 1673; his w. d. 3 July 1674, and he m. Mary, d. of Rev. Jonathan Burr, wh. brot. him Jonathan, bapt. 8 Oct. 1676; and d. 2 Aug. 1681; and he had third w. Sarah Moore, by wh. he had Sarah, bapt. 13 May 1683; Rob-ert, 28 Dec. 1684; and Eliz. 20 Mar. 1687; and he d. 28 Mar. 1688. His wid. m. 24 Sept. 1690, capt. Caleb Stanley of Hartford. ZECHARY, Charlestown, s. prob. of the preced. by w. Eliz. Checkley, d. prob. of Anthony, had Zechary, bapt. 9 July 1693. Three of this name, in 1834, had been gr. at Harv. and eight at the other N. E. coll.

LONGBOTTOM, JAMES, Newport 1660, was one of the purchasers of Misquamicut, or Ascomicut, now Westerly. R. I. Hist. Coll. III. 251, and R. I. Col. Rec. I. 450.

LONGDON, ANDREW, New London, had been bef. 1643 on the riv. Conn. d. a. 1680, without ch. ANTHONY, perhaps of Hartford 1647. This is diverse from Langdon.

LONGFELLOW, NATHAN, Newbury, s. of William, m. 28 May 1713, Mary Green, liv. at Hampton Falls, had Jonathan, b. 1714; Samuel, 8 May 1717, d. soon; Ann, 2 Aug. 1719 ; Jacob, 20 July 1722; Sewall, 6 Oct. 1724, d. at 10 yrs.; Abigail, 5 Feb. 1728 ; Nathan, 8 June 1729 ; and Green, 3 Apr. 1731, posthum. for f. d. 15 Jan. preced. STEPHEN, Newbury, elder br. of the preced. m. 25 Mar. 1713, Abigail, d. of Rev. Edward Tompson of Marshfield, wh. d. 10 Sept. 1778, had William, b. 10 Sept. 1714; Ann, 24 Apr. 1716 ; Edward, 29 Apr. 1718; Sarah, 8 Jan. 1721 ; Stephen, 7 Feb. 1723 ; Samuel, 12 Mar. 1725 ; Abigail, 23 May 1727, d. next yr. ; Abigail, again, 10 Nov. 1729, d. at 21 yrs.; Eliz. 18 Aug. 1732, d. in few days ; and Nathan, 17 Jan. 1736, d. in 10 mos. He was a lieut. and selectman, and d. 17 Nov. 1764, at Byfield. WILLIAM, Newbury, b. a. 1651, in Co. Hants, came in youth to N. m. 10 Nov. 1678, Ann, d. of Henry Sewall, then 16 yrs. old, had William, b. 25 Nov. 1679; Stephen, 10 Jan. 1681, d. under 3 yrs.; Ann, 3 Oct. 1683 ; Stephen, again, 22 Sept. 1685; Eliz. 3 July 1688; and Nathan, 5 Feb. 1690. He went, in 1687, Judge Sewall says, to Eng. to obtain his patrimony in Yorksh. widely remote from his birthplace; and aft. his return was ensign of the comp. emb. in the wild project of Sir William Phips against Quebec, and with nine others perish. by shipwreck, on the return in Oct. at Anticosti, as Coffin, 155, takes from Sewall's Diary, whose first report was Cape Breton. His wid. m. 11 May 1692, Henry Short. Five of this name had been, in 1834, gr. at Harv. and Bowd.

LONGHORN. See Langhorn.

LONGLEY, JOHN, Groton, s. of William, by w. Hannah had William, b. 12 Mar. 1669; Margaret, 28 Oct. 1671 ; and Mary, 10 Jan. 1673; fled in the Ind. war, I presume, to his native town, there had Nathaniel, 1 July 1676. RICHARD, Lynn 1636, had William, and Jonathan. See Lewis, Ed. 2d, p. 91. WILLIAM, Lynn, s. of the preced. from Eng. perhaps ; yet in 1661 he was able to prove there was no Richard, but he was the person to wh. in the partition of lds. in 1638, was gr. by name of Richard. See the blind story in Geneal. Reg. VII. 188. He may be that freem. of 14 Mar. 1639 call. Langley, was clk. of the writs 1655, by w. Joanna (who soon aft. his d. m. Benjamin Crispe, outliv. him, and by her will, of 1698, gave to two Shattucks, her gr.ds.) had Sarah, b. 15 Oct. 1660, but he had elder ch. John ; Ann ; Mary ; Eliz. wh. m. James Blood, and d. bef. her f. ; and William ; beside Lydia, wh. may have been younger. He rem. to Groton, there d. 29 Nov. 1680; in his will of 6 days bef. pro. Apr. foll. names four ds. Mary, w.

of Samuel Lemont or Leman; Hannah, w. of Thomas Tarbell, jr.; Lydia, w. of James Nutting; and Sarah; beside two s. John and William. Sarah m. 17 June 1679, Thomas Rand of Charlestown, whither, in Ind. war, he prob. rem. WILLIAM, Groton, s. of the preced. by w. Lydia, wh. he m. 15 May 1672, had Lydia, b. 1 Mar. 1674; William, 17 Feb. 1676; and other ch. beside Joseph, 6 Jan. 1687; was town clk. six yrs. and with w. and four or five ch. k. by the Ind. 27 July 1694. His s. John was carr. to Canada, and ransom. aft. five yrs.

LOOK, THOMAS, Lynn, had Thomas, b. June 1646; Sarah, 12 Mar. 1648; Jonathan, July 1651; Mary, July 1654; and Eliz. May 1656. Jonathan was of Topsfield 1684. THOMAS, Nantucket, s. of the preced. m. Eliz. Bunker, sis. I think, of William, not d. as the Nantucket Mirror of 22 Mar. 1856, makes it, had Experience, b. 22 Nov. 1672; Eliz. 28 Nov. 1675; Jane, 24 Dec. 1680; and others; rem. to the Vineyard, where the name was perpet.

LOOKER, or LUKER, ‖ HENRY, Sudbury, ar. co. 1640, was freem. 10 May 1643. JOHN, Sudbury, freem. 1646, by w. Mary had Mary, b. 28 Sept. 1653, and he d. 18 June preced. Mary m. 14 Dec. 1670, Jonas Prescott. MARK, Newport 1644, a freem. there 1655, was an old mem. of the Bapt. ch. and rul. elder, d. Dec. 1676.

LOOMAN, or LOOMER, STEPHEN, New London 1687, d. 1701, and his wid. m. Caleb Abell of Norwich. He left ch. as Miss Caulkins, in her elabor. Hist. of that town ment.

LOOMIS, LOOMAS, LOOMYS, LOMES, LOOMAX, LUMAX, LUMMUS, or LUMMIS, DANIEL, Windsor, s. of John the first, m. 23 Dec. 1680, Mary, d. of Josiah Ellsworth, had Daniel, b. 15 Nov. 1682; Josiah, 1684; Job, 21 Jan. 1686; John, 11 Oct. 1688; Mary, 15 Jan. 1691; Isaac, 23 Aug. 1694; Abraham, 13 Dec. 1696; Benjamin, 7 Feb. 1699; and Benajah, 20 Jan. 1702; and d. 25 June 1740. DAVID, Windsor, br. of the preced. had Lydia, b. 21 Oct. 1693; David, 2 Dec. 1694; Aaron, 5 Sept. 1696; Hepzibah, 2 Dec. 1698; Eliakim, 27 July 1701; Eliz. 26 Sept. 1704; Richard, 1 Jan. 1707; and Hannah, 2 Aug. 1709. EBEN-EZER, Windsor, youngest s. of the first Nathaniel, m. 15 Apr. 1697, Je-mima Whitcomb, had Ebenezer, b. 15 July 1698, d. young; Jemima, 9 Dec. 1702, d. at 2 yrs.; Abigail, 31 Oct. 1706; and Jane, 22 Nov. 1708. The f. d. Oct. foll. and his wid. d. 10 Dec. 1712. EDWARD, Ipswich 1648, came in the Elizabeth from London, 1635, aged 27, but in the same mo. at London, we find Edward Lummus emb. in the Susan and Ellen, aged 24, wh. was, I think, the same person, and playing a delusion upon the custom-ho. officers. He had four s. Jonathan and Samuel wh. liv. in Ipswich; Edward, wh. went to N. J.; and Nathaniel of Dover; and a d. wh. m. John Sherring. See Lommaks. Prob. the

descend. adher. to the spelling, Lummus. HEZEKIAH, Windsor, s. of
Nathaniel the first, m. 30 Apr. 1690, Mary Porter, had Noah, b. 1 Apr.
1692; Mary, 15 Nov. 1694; Hezekiah, 7 Nov. 1697; Solomon, 14
July 1700 ; Joanna, 4 Dec. 1702 ; Jonah, 1 Apr. 1705 ; Eliz. 13 Aug.
1708; and Ann, 20 Feb. 1710.　JAMES, Windsor, s. of the sec. Joseph,
had Mindwell, b. 28 Dec. 1697 ; James, 27 Jan. 1700; Henry, 14 Sept.
1701; Matthew, 25 Oct. 1703 ; Eunice, 1 May 1705 ; Hannah, 19 Apr.
1707 ; Mary, 3 Jan. 1709, d. soon ; Mabel, 20 May 1710, d. at 3 mos. ;
Nathaniel, 15 Feb. 1712 ; and Lois, 26 Oct. 1715.　* JOHN, Windsor, s.
of the first Joseph, b. in Eng. m. 3 or 6 Feb. 1649, Eliz. d. of Thomas
Scott of Hartford, had John, b. 9 Nov. 1649 ; Joseph, 7 Nov. 1651 ;
Thomas, 3 Dec. 1653 ; Samuel, 29 June 1655, d. young; Daniel, 16
June 1657 ; James, 19 Sept. 1659, d. young; Timothy, 27 July 1661;
Nathaniel, 8 July 1663 ; David, 30 May 1665, d. young; Samuel,
again, 12 Aug. 1666 ; Isaac, 31 Aug. 1668, d. at 20 yrs. soon aft. his f.;
Eliz. 8 May 1671 ; and Mary, 7 Aug. 1673, d. in few mos.; was rep.
1666 and 7, 75–7, liv. some time a. 1652 at Farmington, but went back ;
was deac. and d. 2 Sept. 1688.　Nine of the ch. outliv. him and Eliz. m.
4 Feb. 1692, John Brown.　JOHN, Hatfield, s. prob. of Joseph the second, by w. Mary had John, b. 19 Oct. 1670, d. soon ; John, again, 1676 ;
and Mary, 1677 ; liv. at H. until 1683 or later, and rem. to Windsor.　There Stiles gives him sec. w. 30 Aug. 1705, Esther, d. of the first
Cornelius Gillett, I presume, and ch. John, 12 Feb. 1707 ; Esther, 13
Sept. 1708; Sarah, 26 Sept. 1710; Damaris, 1 Dec. 1712 ; John, 21
Sept. 1713; and Abel, 3 Aug. 1716.　JOHN, Windsor, eldest s. of the
first John, had Mary, b. 20 Mar. 1673 ; Eliz. 31 Dec. 1677 ; Deborah,
1680 ; Zechariah, Nov. 1681 ; Ezekiel, Oct. 1683 ; Ephraim, Nov.
1685, d. young ; Rebecca, Dec. 1687 ; and Ruth, 28 Jan. 1690 ; beside
John, 28 Mar. 1692.　He was deac. and m. 1696, Sarah, wid. of Isaac
Warner.　JOSEPH, Windsor, was not first at Dorchester perhaps, and
the fam. tradit. that he came in the Mary and John is wrong; and more
likely is it, tho. no evidence is found, that he accomp. Rev. Ephraim
Huet, in 1638, and brot. s. Joseph, John, Thomas, Samuel, and Nathaniel, beside ds. Mary, w. of John Skinner, wh. when wid. m. 13 Nov.
1651, Owen Tudor ; Eliz. wh. m. 20 May 1641, Josiah Hull ; and one
wh. m. Nicholas' Olmstead.　His w. d. Aug. 1652, and he d. 1658.
JOSEPH, Windsor, s. of the preced. b. in Eng. m. 17 Sept. 1646, Sarah
Hill, had Sarah, b. 22 July 1647, d. young ; Joseph, 15 July 1649 ; John,
1 Oct. 1651 ; Mary, 3 Aug. 1653.　His w. d. 23 of the same mo. and
by sec. w. Mary Chauncy, m. 28 June 1659, had Sarah, again, 1 Apr.
1660, d. young ; Hannah, 2 Feb. 1662 ; Matthew, 4 Nov. 1664 ; Stephen,
1 Sept. 1668 ; James, 31 Oct. 1669 ; Nathaniel, 8 Aug. 1673 ; and

Isaac, 28 Oct. 1677; was freem. 1654, and d. 26 June 1687, when nine of the ch. were alive. JOSEPH, Windsor, s. of the preced. m. 10 Apr. 1681, Lydia, d. of John Drake, had Joseph, b. 8 Oct. 1684; Caleb, 10 Oct. 1686, both d. at 5 mos.; Lydia, 17 Feb. 1688; Rachel, 12 Jan. 1693; Enoch, 23 Mar. 1695; and Damaris, 29 July 1699, d. in few yrs. In Hist. of W. 679, Stiles gives to ano. JOSEPH, s. of John the first, Hannah, and Ann, b. 10 Jan. 1678; Joseph, 13 Feb. 1681; Joseph, 28 Nov. 1682; Grace, 17 Mar. 1685; Lydia, 15 Apr. 1686, wh. d. at 16 yrs.; and Sarah, 8 Jan. 1693. JOSIAH, Windsor, s. of the first Nathaniel, m. 23 Oct. 1683, Mary Rockwell, prob. d. of Samuel, had Mary, b. 18 Jan. 1685; Josiah, 23 Jan. 1688; Abigail, 10 Aug. 1691; Caleb, 23 Dec. 1693; Ephraim, 2 May 1698, d. young; and Nathaniel, Oct. 1700. MATTHEW, Windsor, s. of the sec. Joseph, m. 6 Jan. 1687, Mary Gaylord, prob. d. of John of the same, had Mary, b. 31 Oct. foll. MOSES, Windsor, br. of Hezekiah, m. 27 Apr. 1694, Joanna Gibbs, d. prob. of Samuel of the same, had Moses, b. 24 June 1696; Joanna, 22 Sept. 1699, d. at 13 yrs.; Catharine, 19 Dec. 1702; Thankful, 5 Mar. 1709; and Joanna, again, 17 Jan. 1713. NATHANIEL, Dover, s. of Edward, there liv. from 1672 to 88. NATHANIEL, Windsor, br. of the 2d Joseph, b. in Eng. freem. 1654, m. 24 Nov. 1654, Eliz. d. of John Moore, had Eliz. b. 7 Aug. 1655; Nathaniel, 20 Mar. 1657; Abigail, 27 Mar. 1659; Josiah, 17 Feb. 1661; Jonathan, 30 Mar. 1664; David, 11 Jan. 1668; Hezekiah, 21 Feb. 1669; Moses, 15 May 1671; Mindwell, 20 July 1673; Ebenezer, 22 Mar. 1675; Mary, 5 Jan. 1680; and Rebecca 10 Dec. 1682. He d. 19 Aug. 1688, when it is thot. all the ch. were liv. His wid. m. John Case, long outliv. him, and d. 23 July 1728, aged 90. Abigail m. 22 Nov. 1677, Josiah Barber of Simsbury, not Brown, as Stiles has it; and he makes Mindwell m. Oct. 1696, Jonah Brown. Stiles gives him, for sec. w. 23 Dec. 1680, that young woman, that in my opin. clear. belongs to prob. his eldest s., NATHANIEL, Windsor, m. 23 Dec. 1680, Eliz. d. of Josiah Ellsworth. NATHANIEL, Windsor, prob. s. of the first John, m. 28 Nov. 1689, Ruth Porter, had Nathaniel, b. 7 Mar. 1695, Charles, 20 Feb. 1697. NEHEMIAH, Westfield, s. of the first Samuel, m. 3 Jan. 1694, Thankful, d. of Nathaniel Weller, had Isaac, b. 29 July 1695, d. in few wks.; Nehemiah, wh. d. 24 Jan. 1727; Abigail, 4 May 1701; Nathaniel, 19 Aug. 1703; Rachel, 26 Mar. 1706, d. in few days; Thankful, 3 May 1710, d. in few mos.; and he d. 4 Feb. 1740; and his wid. d. 23 Feb. 1748. SAMUEL, Farmington, perhaps s. of Joseph the first, b. in Eng. freem. 1654, m. 27 Dec. 1653, Eliz. d. of Thomas Judd, had Samuel, and Eliz. rem. to Windsor, there had Ruth, b. 14 June, bapt. 22 July 1660; Sarah, 3 Feb. 1663; Joanna, 22 Oct. 1665; Benjamin, 11 Feb. 1668; Nehemiah, 15 July 1670; William, 18 Mar.

1672; rem. to Westfield, there had Philip, 22 Feb. 1675; and Mary, 16 Aug. 1678; he was a lieut. and d. 1689. Eliz. m. 1673, the sec. Thomas Hansett; and Ruth m. Benjamin Smith of Farmington; and their mo. was liv. 1716. SAMUEL, Westfield, eldest s. of the preced. m. 14 Apr. 1678, Hannah, d. of the first Thomas Hansett, had Samuel, b. 28 Apr. 1681; James, 25 Feb. 1683, d. next yr.; James, 8 Oct. 1686, d. young; Hannah, 29 Jan. 1691; Deliverance, 13 May 1694, d. within 3 yrs.; and Joshua, 21 July 1696, d. at 4 yrs.; and he d. 6 Nov. 1711. SAMUEL, Windsor, s. of the first John, m. 2 July 1688, Eliz. White, d. of Daniel of Hatfield, had Eliz. b. and d. next yr.; Samuel, 28 Feb. 1690, d. at 2 wks.; Samuel, again, 17 July 1692, not 1695, as Stiles tells; Isaac, 28 Dec. 1693; Jacob, 25 Feb. 1695, not 1692, as in Stiles; Azariah, 2 May 1700; Eliz. 13 Nov. 1702; Sarah, 7 Mar. 1705; Caleb, 20 Sept. 1707; and Daniel, 20 Feb. 1709. He had rem. some yrs. bef. to Colchester, there was deac. 1702, and his w. d. Feb. 1736. A sec. w. m. 25 Oct. 1738, wid. Eliz. Church, d. 10 Aug. 1751, aged 78 yrs. and he d. 20 May 1754, near 88. STEPHEN, Windsor, br. of Matthew, m. 1 Jan. 1691, Esther Colt, had Martha, b. 15 Nov. foll.; Stephen, 21 July 1693; Hannah, 13 Apr. 1703; Israel, 6 Aug. 1705; Amos, 12 Aug. 1707; Mary, 26 Mar. 1709; and Sarah, 16 Apr. 1711. THOMAS, Windsor, s. of the first Joseph, b. in Eng. freem. 1654, m. 1 Nov. 1653, Hannah Fox, had Thomas, b. 29 Oct. 1654, d. soon; Thomas, again, 17 Mar. 1656; Hannah, 8 Feb. 1658; and Mary, 16 Jan. 1660. His w. d. 25 Apr. 1662, and he m. 1 Jan. 1663, Mary, d. of Thomas Judd, had Eliz. 21 Jan. 1664; Ruth, 16 Oct. 1665; Sarah, 1 Feb. 1668; Jeremiah, 3 July 1670, d. at 2 yrs.; Mabel, 27 Oct. 1672; Mindwell, 6 Aug. 1676; and Benjamin, 20 May 1679. His w. d. 8 Aug. 1684, and he d. 28 Aug. 1689, when nine of these ch. were liv. Mary m. 3 Apr. 1679, Michael Taintor of Branford; and Stiles says, Ruth m. 29 Oct. 1691, Joseph Colt; and Sarah m. Wakefield Dibble. THOMAS, Salem 1668, sign. the petitn. against impost that yr. THOMAS, Hatfield, s. of the first John, m. 31 Mar. 1680, Sarah, eldest d. of Daniel White of the same, had John, b. 1 Jan. 1681; Thomas, 20 Apr. 1684; and d. 12 Aug. 1688. His wid. m. 12 Nov. 1689, John Bissell. THOMAS, Windsor, s. of the first Thomas, m. 17 Dec. 1682, Hannah Porter, had Mary, b. 2 Sept. 1683; Hannah, 9 Oct. 1685; Thomas, 16 Mar. 1688; Joshua, 6 Nov. 1692; Sarah, 22 Jan. 1695; Jabez, 29 Jan. 1697; Ruth, 27 Dec. 1698; and Gershom, 9 Apr. 1701. His w. d. 1 Jan. 1739; and he d. I suppose, 19 Apr. 1746. TIMOTHY, Windsor, s. of the first John, m. 20 Mar. 1689, Rebecca Porter, had Timothy, b. 22 Feb. 1691; Ichabod, 25 Jan. 1693; Lois, 15 Aug. 1695, d. next yr.; Ann, 15 June 1698; Rebecca, 24 May 1700; Uriah, 8 May 1703;

and Obadiah, 4 Aug. 1705.   Ten of this name had, in 1834, been gr. at the N. E. coll. chief. at Yale.

LOPER, JAMES, Nantucket 1672, was the first person, says Macy's Hist. 28, that undertook the catching of whales there.   See large extr. in Geneal. Reg. XIII. 311.   But Felt, II. 223, says, that his petitn. in 1688, for a patent for making the oil, asserts that he had been engaged 22 yrs.

LORD, JOHN, Hingham 1637, may be the man wh. d. at Watertown, 28 Apr. 1669, as Bond says.   JOHN, Kittery, was of the gr. jury 1651. JOHN, Hartford, s. of Thomas, b. in Eng. had first w. Rebecca, d. of Francis Bushnell of Guilford, wh. d. bef. 1647, and he m. 15 May 1648, Adrian Bayc, the surname prob. being (with profuse expense) Baysey; but he soon abandon. her, and in Sept. 1651, an order of the Court for secur. her apparel and a bed is found in Trumbull, Col. Rec. I. 224. He had fled in debt to Virginia, and there wrote a letter to his creditor's neph. Richard, Feb. 1664, wh. is print. by Porter, p. 11, that serves to show him little changed; and he was nam. in his mo.'s will, 1670. JOHN, Watertown, d. 23 Apr. 1669.   NATHAN, or NATHANIEL, Kittery, freem. 1652.   In some rec. the name is Lawd.   Farmer thot. him f. of that capt. Samuel, the ancest. of sev. fam. of this name in the parts adjacent, of wh. one descend. is Rev. Nathan, Presid. of Dart. Coll. * RICHARD, Cambridge 1632, s. of Thomas, who, perhaps, had sent him to look out the most desirable place for his friends, Gov. Haynes and Rev. Thomas Hooker, was freem. 4 Mar. 1635, but next yr. rem. with Hooker and his f. to Hartford, and Gov. Haynes soon foll.   He was an orig. propr. and one of the earliest sett. capt. of the first troop in the Col. rep. 1657 to 61, and is nam. in the Union chart. of 1662, but bef. it was brot. over, d. at New London, 17 May 1662, in 51st yr. if the fig. be well decyph. from the honorab. inscript. on a crumbling sandstone monu.   See Caulkins's Hist. of New London.   Porter says he d. 1664, but he says also, he was rep. to his d. and the latest yr. of his serv. was 1661; and Goodwin makes his d. 10 May 1662, only a week diff. from Caulkins.   His wid. was Sarah; the ch. Richard, b. 1636; Sarah, 1638; and Dorothy.   He was the capt. relied on, in conjunct. with John Pyncheon, for secur. the persons of the regicides, Goffe and Whalley, that they might be brot. to justice in Eng. as Sir Thomas Temple wrote to Secr. Morrice.   His loyalty in this went beyond his judgment.   See 3 Mass. Hist. Coll. VIII. 326.   Sarah m. Joseph Haynes.   * RICHARD, Hartford, s. of the preced. m. 15 Apr. 1665, Mary, d. of Henry Smith of Springfield, had only Richard, b. 1 Feb. 1670, was rep. 1669, and oft. aft.; but was lost at sea 1685.   His wid. in 1686 m. Dr. Thomas Hooker, and d. 17 May 1702.   He left large est. and his s. m. 14 Jan. 1692, Abigail, d. as was said, of William Warren, and had ten ch.   But great reach of investigat. leaves this m. uncert. * ROBERT, Ipswich, freem. 3 Mar. 1636, rep. 1638, was clk. of the courts, marshal, town clk. and reg. of deeds, Coffin thot.; m. Mary Waite, had Thomas, b. 1633; Robert, a. 1634; Samuel, 1640 ; Joseph, d. young; Nathaniel, d. 1658 ; and ds. Abigail, wh. m. 26 Feb. 1666, Jacob Foster; Hannah ; and ano. wh. m. a Chandler; and he d. perhaps 12 May 1650. A wid. Catharine L. wh. had gr. of ld. at I. 1641, may have been his mo. and it was prob. his s. wh. d. 11 Nov. 1696. ROBERT, Boston, by w. Rebecca (d. I suppose, of Christopher Stanley by Susanna his w. who aft. m. William Phillips, and in her will calls Rebecca her d. in 1650), had Robert, b. Apr. 1651; Thomas, 18 May 1653, d. soon ; and d. as Farmer thot. in Charlestown, 13 July 1678. Perhaps, as he came in the same sh. with Stanley and his w. he may be s. of the first Thomas by Porter call. sea capt. but we kn. nothing more of *him*, exc. that his mo. in her will, 1670, names him, unless he were that Robert of London, sued in 1675, by his neph. Richard. SAMUEL, Charlestown, perhaps s. of Robert of Ipswich, by w. Eliz. had Joshua; Robert; and Eliz. all bapt. 21 May 1676; Nathaniel, 30 May 1680; and his w. d. and he m. 16 Dec. 1684, Rebecca Eddington, d. 27 May 1696, in 56th yr. says the gr.stone. THOMAS, Hartford, came in the Elizabeth and Ann, 1635, from London, aged 50, with w. Dorothy, 46; and ch. Thomas, 16; Ann, 14; William, 12; John, 10; Robert, 9; Annie, 6 ; and Dorothy, 4; call. at the London custom-ho. a smith; but that may have been a godly deception. His eldest s. Richard, had been sent over three yrs. bef. and Thomas stopped at Boston, or Cambridge a yr. or more, but was an orig. propr. and among first sett. at H. Date of his d. is not ascert. His wid. Dorothy, wh. d. 2 Aug. 1676, made her will 8 Feb. 1670, in wh. she names ch. of her dec. s. Thomas; d. Ann, w. of Thomas Stanton; William ; John ; Robert; Amie, w. of John Gilbert; gr.s. Richard, bef. ment.; and gr.ch. Hannah ; Dorothy ; and Margaret, ch. of d. Dorothy, w. of John Ingersoll. THOMAS, Wethersfield, s. of the preced. b. in Eng. was a physician and surg. for whose serv. the Gen. Ct. made liberal contr. in 1652, as in Trumbull, Col. Rec. I. 234, appears, correct. stat. by Hinman, 47; but he mistakes in call. him the earliest on the rec. He was also employ. as sch.master; by w. Mary had Hannah, b. 1656; Mary, 1659 ; and prob. Sarah; beside Dorothy, the first b. 17 Aug. 1653. He d. a. 1661, and his wid. m. an Olmstead. THOMAS, Boston, m. 23 Sept. 1652, Hannah Thurston, but of h. or w. no more is kn. and it may be that he did not inhab. at Boston, but came here only to be m. by Bellingham. At least no issue is kn. THOMAS, Charlestown, s. of Robert of Ipswich, there liv. sev. yrs. and rem. with w. Alice, d. of Robert Rand of C. a. 1666, d. 4 June 1713, aged 80. His wid. Alice (by wh. he had Nathaniel and Mary, tw. bapt. 4 Nov. 1666; Eliz. 23 Aug. 1668;

Joseph and Benjamin, tw. 25 Sept. 1670 ; Joseph, again, 23 June 1672, H. C. 1691; min. for 20 yrs. at Dorchester, S. C. aft. at Chatham, Mass.; and Abigail, 26 July 1674) d. 11 Aug. 1721, in her 88th yr. and s. Thomas d. 11 Nov. 1749, in 86th yr. THOMAS, Saybrook, s. of William, was propound. for freem. 1672. WILLIAM, Salem 1636, a cutler, said to have been b. a. 1590, freem. 6 Sept. 1639, was constable next yr.; perhaps had w. Mary, d. 14 Jan. 1673, wild tradit. says in his 96th yr. WILLIAM, Salem 1670, perhaps s. of the preced. had William. His wid. Abigail, extrix. of his will, m. 5 Oct. 1674, Resolved White. WILLIAM, Saybrook, s. of the first Thomas, by him brot. from Eng. 1635, had William, b. Oct. 1643 ; Thomas, Dec. 1645 ; Richard, May 1647; Mary, May 1649 ; Robert, Aug. 1651; John, Sept. 1653 ; Joseph, Sept. 1656; Benjamin ; Daniel; James; Samuel; and three more ds. 14 ch.; and d. 17 May 1678. WILLIAM, Haddam, eldest s. of the preced. d. 4 Dec. 1696, leav. s. William, aged 16; Jonathan, 11 ; Nathaniel, 9 ; John, 3 ; and ds. Mary, 18 ; Sarah, 14 ; Hannah, 7 ; and Dorothy, 7 mos. in Mar. aft. Of this name, five had been gr. at Harv. nineteen at Yale, and eight at other N. E. coll. in 1834.

LORING, BENJAMIN, Hingham or Hull, s. of the first Thomas, freem. 1673, m. 8 Dec. 1670, Mary, d. of Matthew Hawkes, had Benjamin, b. 1671; John, 1674 ; Mary, 1676 ; Samuel, 1680 ; and Matthew, 19 Oct. 1684. He d. 10 Mar. 1716, his w. hav. d. 17 July 1714. CALEB, Plymouth, s. of the sec. Thomas, m. 7 Aug. 1696, Lydia, d. of Edward Gray, had Caleb, b. 7 June 1697, d. early; Hannah, 7 Aug. 1698 ; Ignatius, 27 Dec. 1699 ; Polycarpus, 1702 ; rem. to Plimpton, there had Caleb, again, 2 Oct. 1704, d. at 19 yrs.; Lydia, 1706, d. soon ; Jacob, 15 May 1711, d. at 16 yrs. ; Joseph, 25 July 1713, d. at 16 yrs.; John, 15 Nov. 1715; Thomas, 14 Apr. 1718 ; and Lydia, 23 Aug. 1721. CALEB, Hingham, s. of the first John of the same, m. 24 June 1714, Eliz. Baker, had Caleb, b. 1715, d. soon ; and his w. d. 19 Sept. of the same yr. He m. 15 Feb. 1719, Susanna Coxe, had Caleb, b. 1720, d. soon ; Susanna, 1 June 1721 ; Sarah, 25 Mar. 1723 ; and this w. d. 8 Apr. foll. He m. 3d w. 6 Feb. 1732, Rebecca Lobdell, had Rebecca, 29 Dec. 1733 ; Caleb, again, 1736 ; Joshua, Dec. 1737 ; Rachel, 1740 ; Israel, 30 Aug. 1741 ; Joseph, July 1743 ; Mary, 1745 ; Cromwell, 1747, d. at 7 yrs.; and Celia, 1749. Of this branch is Charles G. L. the disting. advocate at the Boston bar. DANIEL, Boston, br. of the preced. m. 2 Feb. 1699, Priscilla Mann, had Sarah, b. 15 Nov. 1701, d. next yr.; Daniel, 5 Oct. 1703, d. at 18 yrs.; Isaac, 30 Nov. 1705 ; Nathaniel, 10 Feb. 1708 ; and Priscilla, 15 Jan. 1713. DAVID, Barnstable, s. of the sec. Thomas, m. 20 July 1699, Eliz. wid. of Thomas Allyn, d. of John Otis, had Solomon, b. 19 Mar. 1701 ; David, 17 Aug.

1704; Eliz. 10 June, 1708; Lydia, 29 Mar. 1711; and Mary, 19 Apr. 1714. ISAAC, Boston, s. of the first John, m. 5 Aug. 1691, Sarah Young, had Sarah, b. 26 Aug. 1693; Ruth, 19 Dec. 1696; Isaac, 20 Apr. 1699; William, 23 Dec. 1700; Mary, 5 Feb. 1702; and two more ds. wh. d. inf. ISRAEL, Sudbury, br. of the preced. m. 25 May 1709, Mary, d. of Nathan Hayman, had John, b. 27 Apr. 1710; Eliz. 16 Nov. 1712; Mary, 14 Sept. 1716; Jonathan, 29 Aug. 1719; Nathan, 27 Nov. 1721; Sarah and Susan, tw. 10 Nov. 1724; and all these ds. were m. JACOB, Hingham, br. of the preced. m. 9 Feb. 1709, Sarah Lewis, had only Sarah, b. 9 Nov. 1723; and he m. sec. w. 8 May 1728, Hannah Jacobs, had Jacob, 25 June 1729; Israel, 26 Mar. 1731; Zechariah, 13 Aug. 1733; Peter, 27 Aug. 1735, d. next yr.; and Hannah, 6 Nov. 1737. * JOHN, Hull, s. of Thomas, b. in Eng. m. 16 Dec. 1657, Mary, d. of Nathaniel Baker, had John, b. 19 Sept. 1658, d. at 20 yrs.; Joseph, 10 Mar. 1660; Thomas, 11 Mar. 1662; Sarah, 1 Jan. 1664, d. at 14 yrs.; Isaac, 22 Jan. 1666, sett. at Boston; Mary, 4 Feb. 1669; Nathaniel, 5 Mar. 1670; Daniel, 8 Feb. 1672, both sett. at Boston; Rachel, 28 Feb. 1674, d. at 2 yrs.; Jacob, 21 Apr. 1676; Israel, 29 Mar. 1678, d. soon, as did the mo. 13 July 1679. He m. 22 Sept. foll. wid. Rachel Buckland, d. prob. of John Wheatley of Braintree, had John, again, 28 June 1680; Israel, again, 15 Apr. 1682, H. C. 1701, d. 9 Mar. 1772, for sixty-six yrs. the min. of Sudbury; Sarah, again, 6 June 1684; and Caleb, 2 Jan. 1689; was freem. 1673; rep. under new chart. 1692; his w. d. 20 Sept. 1713; and he d. 19 Sept. foll. Mary m. Thomas Jones. JOHN, Hingham, s. of the preced. m. 2 Sept. 1703, Jane, d. of Samuel Baker, had John, d. soon; John, again, d. soon; John, third, b. 15 Jan. 1708; Jane, 7 Oct. 1709; Nicholas, 1 Sept. 1711; Thomas, 30 Aug. 1713; Solomon, 12 Jan. 1715; and Rachel, 17 Oct. 1717. JOSEPH, Hingham, br. of the preced. m. 25 Oct. 1683, Hannah Leavit, d. of John, and sec. of the name (the first, wh. was w. of John Lobdell, hav. d. near two yrs. bef. this was b.) had Joseph, b. 28 Sept. 1684; Nehemiah, 17 June 1686; and Joshua, 21 Sept. 1688. He d. early, and his wid. m. 25 Aug. 1693, deac. Joseph Esterbrook of Lexington. JOSIAH, Hingham, br. of Benjamin, m. 1662, Eliz. d. of John Prince, the rul. elder of Hull, had Jane, 9 Aug. 1663; Josiah, 22 Nov. 1665; Samuel, 12 July 1668, d. at 6 yrs.; Job, 26 Feb. 1670, sett. at Rochester; Eliz. 6 Apr. 1672, d. unm. Jan. 1743; Jonathan, 24 Apr. 1674, sett. at Boston, d. 15 Oct. 1752. He d. 14 Feb. 1713, and his wid. d. 13 May 1727, in 88th yr. NATHANIEL, Boston, s. of the first John, m. 13 Dec. 1699, Susanna Butler, had Susanna, b. 15 Oct. 1700; Joseph, 23 Oct. 1706, d. soon; Rachel, Dec. 1710, d. young; Nathaniel, 11 June 1713; and Thomas, 20 Aug. 1715. THOMAS, Hingham, freem. 3 Mar. 1636, came from Axminster, Co. Devon, says the fam. tradit. with w. wh. was Jane Newton, and ch. Thomas, and John, the latter b. 22 Dec. 1630, and they left their home 22 Dec. 1634, stopped first at Dorchester, but it could not be long, for his house lot was drawn at H. 18 Sept. aft. emb.; had bapt. there Isaac, on 22 Jan. 1640, d. next mo. by scald.; Josiah, 9 Jan. 1642; Joshua, 1643, d. soon; and Benjamin, 17 Nov. 1644; was early a deac. rem. to Hull, d. 1 Apr. 1661; and his wid. d. 25 Aug. 1672. THOMAS, Hull, s. of the preced. b. in Eng. freem. 1673, same day with younger br. John, m. 1657, Hannah, d. of Nicholas Jacob, had Hannah, b. 9 Aug. 1664; Thomas and Deborah, tw. 15 Mar. 1668; David, 15 Sept. 1671; Caleb, 9 June 1674; Abigail, 1678, d. soon; and he d. 1679. His wid. m. Stephen French, and d. 20 Oct. 1720. The d. Hannah m. Rev. Jeremiah Cushing, and next, 1706, John Barker, and Deborah m. 20 May 1687, John Cushing. THOMAS, Hull, s. of the first John, m. 10 Jan. 1687, Leah, d. of Benjamin Buckland, had Jael, b. 11 Sept. 1688; Sarah, 13 Nov. 1690; and Benjamin, 1 Oct. 1692. THOMAS, Hingham, s. of the sec. Thomas, m. 19 Apr. 1699, Deborah, d. of Hon. John Cushing, had Thomas; Joshua, b. 1701; Nathaniel, 21 Aug. 1704; Benjamin, 12 Oct. 1708; beside Hannah, and Deborah. He had early sett. at Duxbury where he was lieut. and d. 5 Dec. 1717. Winsor adds that his wid. d. 30 Nov. 1755, in 78th yr. Descend. of the first Thomas are found, by scores, in many parts of the U. S. Thirteen of the name had been gr. at Harv. in 1834, and eight at the other N. E. coll.

LORPHELIN, PETER, Boston, a Frenchman, put in the pillory 1679, for clip. money, prob. went away as soon as he could.

LOTHROP, LATHROP, LOTHORP, or LOWTHROP, LAWTHROP, ‡ * BAR-NABAS, Barnstable, s. of Rev. John, m. Plymouth rec. says, 3 Nov. or as ano. report is, 1 Dec. 1658, Susanna, d. of Thomas Clark, had John, b. 7 Oct. 1659, d. bef. 7 yrs.; Abigail, 18 Dec. 1660; Barnabas, 22 Mar. 1663; Susanna, Feb. 1665; Nathaniel, 23 Nov. 1669; Bath-shua, 25 June 1671; Ann, 10 Aug. 1673; Thomas, 7 Mar. 1675, d. at 7 mos.; Mercy, 27 June 1676, d. at one yr.; Thankful, bapt. 16 Sept. 1683; James, 30 Mar. 1684; and Samuel, 14 June 1685; was six yrs. a rep. also an Assist. of the Col. of Plymouth, named a counsellor in the new Province Chart. by Increase Mather, and rechosen; m. sec. w. 15 Nov. 1698, Abigail, wid. of Joseph Dudson, d. of Robert Button, and d. 1715, in 79th yr. BENJAMIN, Barnstable, br. of the preced. b. prob. in Eng. rem. to Charlestown, had w. Martha, and ds. Martha, b. 3 Nov. 1652; Hannah, 15 Sept. 1655; and Benjamin; all bapt. 5 Aug. 1660; Mary, bapt. 9 June 1661; Sarah, b. 10, bapt. 17 Apr. 1664, d. soon; Eliz. bapt. 21 May 1665; Rebecca, 14, bapt. 18 Nov. 1666; Mercy, 17, bapt. 18 Dec. 1670; and John, 15, bapt. 21 July 1672, d. young. Of

the ds. Martha m. 2 Dec. 1669, John Goodwin, and was mo. of the four
ch. wh. plagued Cotton Mather; Mary m. 21 May 1679, William Brown;
and Hannah m. 21 Aug. 1679, Henry Swain; was a householder 1658
and 1678, aft. the gr. Ind. war, when he was a soldier in capt. William
Turner's comp. 1676 at Hatfield, unless that soldier was his neph. s. of
Joseph, as seems more prob. the same being in the list call. jr. d. 3 July
1691. HOPE, Barnstable, s. of Joseph, m. 17 Dec. 1696, Eliz. d. prob.
of Meletiah or of John Lothrop, had Benjamin, b. 18 Dec. 1697; and
John, 3 Oct. 1699. *JOHN*, Scituate, the first min. was bred at Oxford, if
the tradit. may be trusted, but prob. he was there only for a short time,
preached, perhaps, at Egerton, in Kent, but certain. in London, where
Bp. Laud caus. him to be impris. for it, for two yrs. in wh. time his w. d.
by whom he had all his ch. exc. these by sec. w. Barnabas, bapt. at S. 6
June 1636; Abigail, wh. was bapt. at Barnstable, 3 Nov. 1639, the first
in that ch.; Bathshua, bapt. 27 Feb. 1642; John, 9 Feb. 1645; and
two, wh. d. soon aft. b. 30 July 1638 and 25 Jan. 1650. On liberat.
from prison he embark. for Boston 1634, hav. fellow-passeng. Rev.
Zachary Symmes, celebr. Ann Hutchinson, and many others, arr. in
Sept. and 27th of that mo. went to S. there m. sec. w. Ann, wh. long
outliv. him, dying 25 Feb. 1688. On 18 Jan. 1635, the ch. at S. were
gather. for enjoy. the benefit of his services, as in Deane's Hist. 167, is
told, but the author. ment. that the centenn. anniver. would occur on 7
Jan. 1835, deduct. eleven days, whereas the true anniver. requir. addit.
of ten days, must have been 28 of the mo. He rem. to Barnstable with
a large part of his flock, 11 Oct. 1639, and was held in honor to his d. 8
Nov. 1653. His will, made 10 Aug. bef. provides for w. the eldest s.
Thomas, and Benjamin, beside John, wh. was in Eng. and ds. Jane and
Barbara. Jane m. 8 Apr. 1635, says her f. Samuel Fuller; Barbara m.
19 July 1638, ... Emerson; and Abigail m. 7 Oct. 1657, James
Clark. It is much regretted that no better acco. of this eminent confessor is obtaina. than a descend. of our days compil. in 2 Hist. Coll.
I. 163, for in Mather nothing but his name in the list is giv. Ch. beside
those already nam. were his sec. and third s. Samuel and Joseph, both
brot. from Eng. JOHN, Barnstable, youngest s. of the preced. m. 3 Jan.
1672, at Plymouth, Mary Cole, junr. had John, b. 5 Aug. 1673; Mary,
27 Oct. 1675; Martha, 11 Nov. 1677; Eliz. 16 Sept. 1679; James, 3
July 1681; Hannah, 13 Mar. 1683; Jonathan, 14 Nov. 1684; Barnabas, 22 Oct. 1686; Abigail, 23 Apr. bapt. 12 May 1689; and Experience, 7 Jan. bapt. 10 May 1692; and, perhaps, others; and he d. 17
Sept. 1727, in 85th yr. wh. proves that he was b. at Barnstable, unless
fig. err. JOHN, Norwich, s. of Samuel the first, m. 15 Dec. 1669, Ruth,
d. of Robert Royce. * JOSEPH, Barnstable, s. of the first John, b. in

London, perhaps, certain. in Eng. m. 11 Dec. 1650, Mary Ansell, had a ch. b. 19 Nov. 1651, bur. next day; Joseph, 3 Dec. 1652, d. at 24 yrs.; Mary, 22 Mar. 1654; Benjamin, 25 July 1657; Eliz. 18 Sept. 1659; John, 28 Nov. 1661, d. at two yrs.; Samuel, 17 Mar. 1664; John, again, 7 Aug. 1666; Barnabas, 24 Feb. 1669; Hope, 15 July 1671; Thomas, 6 Jan. 1674; and Hannah, 23 Jan. 1676, d. at 5 yrs. He was rep. 1667, and for eleven yrs. aft. Mary m. 16 Jan. 1674, Edward Crowell; and Eliz. m. 29 Dec. 1680, Thomas Fuller. MARK, Salem 1643, rem. to Duxbury, and thence to Bridgewater 1656, d. a. 1686. He had Eliz. Mark, Samuel, and Edward. Eliz. m. Samuel Packard the sec. of the same; Mark perish. in the abortive expedit. of Phips 1690, prob. unm. but left a will, and his br. Edward d. without issue. Descend. are, it is said, num. MELETIAH, Barnstable, s. of Thomas, m. 20 May 1667, Sarah, eldest d. of Thomas Farrar of Lynn, had Thomas, b. 22 Aug. 1668; Tabitha, 3 Apr. 1671; Isaac, 23 June 1673; Joseph, 15 Dec. 1675; Eliz. 23 Nov. 1677; Ichabod, 20 June 1680; Shubael, 20 Apr. 1682; and Sarah, 5 Mar. 1684. He d. 6 Feb. 1712, and his wid. d. 23 May foll. in her 64th yr. SAMUEL, New London, s. of Rev. John, b. in Eng. one of the first sett. 1648, had m. at Barnstable, 28 Nov. 1644, as his f. tells, Eliz. Scudder (sis. I suppose, of John), had John, bapt. at Boston, in right of his mo. 7 Dec. 1645. This discov. of the meaning of our ch. rec. wh. is strange. confused, aft. being by me some three or four yrs. given over, may encourage other explorers not to despair. He was of high esteem, rem. to Norwich 1668, had by w. Abigail, m. 1692 (wh. long outliv. him, and was 100 yrs. old 13 Jan. 1733, when in her room, at the ho. of her s. a sermon was preach.) no ch. of course, as she was sixty yrs. old when m. By the first w. were nine ch. five ds. and the other s. were Samuel, 1650; Israel, 1659; and Joseph, 1661; as ment. by Miss Caulkins in her Hist. of N. Of the five ds. I kn. only Eliz. wh. m. 15 Dec. 1669, Isaac Royce of New London; and Ann, wh. m. William Hough, sec. of N. and d. 19 Nov. 1745. He d. 19 Feb. 1701. SAMUEL, Barnstable, s. of Joseph, is said to have m. Hannah, d. of Thomas Adgate, but more prob. m. 1 July 1686, Hannah, d. of John Crocker, had Mary, b. 19 Oct. 1688; Hannah, 11 Nov. 1690; Abigail, 10 Aug. 1693; Benjamin, 16 Apr. 1696; Joseph, 10 Nov. 1698; and Samuel, 28 Apr. 1700. * ‖ THOMAS, Salem, freem. 14 May 1634, ar. co. 1645, lieut. and capt. rep. 1647, 53, and 64, and for Beverly 1672 and more yrs. where he was one of the found. of the ch. 1667; tho. no acc. is kn. of his w. or ch. my conject. makes him the same who was capt. in the fight at Bloody brook, 18 Sept. 1675, near Deerfield, k. by the Ind. with almost every man of his comp. call. "the flower of Essex." He left, perhaps, no ch. but his wid.

Bethia, d. of Daniel Rea, m. Joseph Grafton, as his sec. w. and next, m. deac. William Goodhue. THOMAS, Barnstable, eldest s. of Rev. John, b. in Eng. join. his f.'s ch. 14 May 1637, m. 11 Dec. 1639, Sarah, wid. of Thomas Ewer of Charlestown, d. of William Larned, had Mary, bapt. 4 Oct. 1640; Hannah, b. 18 Oct. 1642; Thomas, bapt. 7 July 1644; Meletiah, 22 Nov. 1646; and Bethia, 22 July 1649, wh. m. July 1668, John Hinckley; Mary m. Dec. 1656, the first John Stearns, as his sec. w. and next, 6 May 1669, capt. William French, both of Billerica, and 3d in 1684, Isaac Mixer of Watertown, as his 3d w. He sw. in a depon. of 4 Apr. 1701, that he was "a. 80 yrs. of age." THOMAS, Barnstable, perhaps youngest s. of Joseph, unless Meletiah were his f. m. 23 Apr. 1697, Experience, d. of James Gorham, had a s. b. 10 Jan. 1698, d. next mo.; Deborah, 21 Apr. 1699; Mary, 4 Apr. 1701; James, 9 Aug. 1703; Thomas, 8 July 1705; Ansel, a. 1707; Joseph, 8 Dec. 1709; and Seth, Mar. 1712. Five of this name, varying only bet. *a* and *o* in the first syl. had been gr. at Harv. in 1834, seventeen at Yale, and two at other N. E. coll.

LOUD, SOLOMON, a soldier from the E. was at Northampton in Turner's comp. 1676.

LOVE, JOHN, Boston 1635, prob. only transient resid. ‡ JOHN, New Hampshire, made a couns. 1692. Belkn. I. 124. THOMAS, Boston, m. 23 Sept. 1652, Hannah Thurston.

LOVEJOY, JOHN, Andover, m. 1 June 1651, Mary, d. of Christopher Osgood, wh. d. 15 July 1675, was freem. 1673, had sec. w. m. 23 Mar. 1678, Naomi Hoyt, d. of John the first of Salisbury, and d. 7 Nov. 1690. Beside Benjamin, wh. d. in serv. as a soldier, early in 1689, at Pemaquid, he had John; William; Christopher, wh. m. 26 May 1685, Sarah Russ, and d. 1737, in 78th yr.; Joseph; Nathaniel, wh. m. 21 Mar. 1694, Dorothy Hoyt, and d. 1758, aged 84; and Ebenezer, wh. m. 11 July 1693, Mary Foster, and d. 1759, in 86th yr. Mary, wh. m. 4 July 1670, Joseph Wilson; Sarah, wh. m. 23 May 1678, William Johnson; Ann, wh. m. 26 May 1685, Jonathan Blanchard; and Abigail, wh. m. 9 Apr. 1691, Nehemiah Abbot, were, I presume, his ds. JOHN, Andover, s. of the preced. m. 12 Jan. 1677, Hannah Prichard, and d. 14 July 1680. JOSEPH, Andover, br. of the preced. m. 26 May 1685, Sarah Prichard, had Joseph, wh. d. 2 Mar. 1698, and prob. other childr. was freem. 1691, and d. 1737, aged 76. WILLIAM, Andover, br. of the preced. m. 29 Nov. 1680, Mary Farnum, had Caleb, wh. d. 26 Apr. 1691, and prob. other ch. was freem. 1691, and d. 1748, in 91st yr.

LOVELAND, LOVEMAN, or LOVENAM, JOHN, Hartford, d. 1670, had w. and possib. ch. but no more is kn. Perhaps the fam. was perpet. at Glastonbury. ROBERT, Boston 1645, a witness then to deed from

Bendall to Yale, may have rem. to Conn. was tax. at New London 1666 ; had four yrs. bef. a lawsuit with Bigot Eggleston of Windsor, about hides to be tanned; and a wid. Lovenam pursued a remedial action for trespass 1649. THOMAS, Wethersfield 1670, propos. for freem. that yr. had gr. of ld. 1673, perhaps ten yrs. aft. was of Hartford.

LOVELL, ALEXANDER, Medfield 1649, m. 30 Oct. 1658, Lydia Albee, d. of Benjamin of the same. ANDREW, Barnstable, prob. s. of the first John, had liv. at Scituate, where his d. Deborah was b. 6 May 1689 ; and at B. had Silas, 16 May 1690 ; Mary, 17 Nov. 1693 ; Jonathan, 27 Mar. 1697 ; Thankful, 6 Oct. 1699 ; Joseph, 10 Oct. 1707 ; and Jane, 14 May 1715. DANIEL, Boston 1640, liv. with his mo. in the part wh. bec. Braintree. JAMES, Weymouth, by w. Jane had Deborah, b. 8 Jan. 1665; James, 7 Mar. 1667 ; Hannah, 29 Sept. 1668; a s. 29 Dec. 1670; Mary, 5 Jan. 1674; John, 19 Apr. 1675 ; Eliz. 22 Sept. 1679 ; and Joseph, 25 Oct. 1684. Perhaps he rem. to Barnstable. JAMES, Barnstable, s. prob. of the first John, m. Mary, perhaps d. of Jabez Lombard, had Mary, b. Oct. 1686 ; Jacob, Aug. 1688, both bapt. 17 Apr. 1691; James, Aug. bapt. 18 Sept. 1692 ; Mercy, May, bapt. 7 July 1695; Martha, bapt. 27 June 1697 ; Rebecca, Feb. bapt. 9 Apr. 1699 ; Lazarus, Nov. 1700, bapt. 30 Mar. foll.; Lydia; John; and Sarah, whose dates Mr. Hamblen could not give ; and I suppose the one he gives for the m. is wrong. JOHN, Weymouth, perhaps elder br. of James of the same, by w. Jane, d. of William Hatch of Scituate, who in his will of 5 Nov. 1651, names her and gr.s. John L. wh. d. young; had, also, Eliz. wh. d. 21 Jan. 1657 ; Phebe, b. 19 May 1656; John, again, 8 May 1658; Eliz. 28 Oct. 1660 ; James, 23 Oct. 1662 ; William, 24 Feb. 1665; Andrew, 28 June 1668, bef. ment.; Jane, 28 July 1670 ; and prob. rem. to Barnstable, where Phebe m. Nov. 1679, Thomas Bumpas ; and Eliz. m. Oct. 1684, Thomas Ewer. JOHN, Lynn, had Zacheus, wh. d. 28 Dec. 1681, unless the rec. means that date for the f. JOHN, Barnstable, s. of John of the same, m. 1688, Susanna Lombard, had Abigail, b. 25 Oct. 1688 ; Susanna, Sept. 1692 ; Joshua, Oct. 1693 ; Eliz. Nov. 1696; Ann, Nov. 1698; and John, 13 Aug. 1700, d. at 4 mos. ROBERT, the freem. of Mass. 2 Sept. 1635, was, I think, then of Weymouth, and may have brot. John, the first above ment. and here had James. THOMAS, Ipswich 1647, currier, had been at Salem, perhaps in 1640, and was one of the selectmen at I. 1681. He came from Dublin 1639, had Alexander, b. 29 May 1657, d. at 2 yrs.; and Nathaniel, 28 Mar. 1658; was in 87th yr. of his age in 1707. Ano. THOMAS of Ipswich, call. junr. may not have been s. of the preced. d. 2 Jan. 1710, leav. wid. Ann, and ch. John, Thomas, Eliz. Perkins, Hannah Dutch, and Mary Downton. WILLIAM, Dorchester 1630, was a capt. of a small vessel, coasting in the neighbor. seas, from wh. perhaps, Lovell's isl. in Boston harb. got its name. Harris, 62 ; Winth. I. 174. WILLIAM, Barnstable, s. of John, m. 24 Sept. 1693, Mehitable, d. prob. of Jabez Lombard, had Eliz. b. Aug. 1694; Jerusha, Sept. 1696 ; Elinor, 10 Sept. 1698, perhaps d. young; Abia, 12 Sept. 1700 ; Beulah, 7 Feb. 1704; and Eleanor, 17 May 1707. He d. 21 Apr. 1753, in 90th yr. Of this name, eight had, in 1829, been gr. at Harv. and two at other N. E. coll.

LOVERING, JOHN, Watertown, freem. 25 May 1636, was from Dedham, Co. Essex, a selectman 1636 and 7, d. early, made a nuncup. will 9 Nov. but of what yr. is uncert. from the abstr. of it in Geneal. Reg. III. 79, in wh. he gave all his prop. to his w. but said, also, that, aft. her, £100 should be giv. to his br. that had childr. and £20 to the ch. Who that br. was, or whether he was on this side of the sea, is unkn. Barry says, and Bond confirms, that his wid. Ann, in 1644, m. Rev. Edmund Brown of Sudbury. JOHN, Dover 1657, had prob. liv. bef. at Ipswich, was drown. 1668 or 9, leav. sev. young ch. His wid. who had, perhaps, been wid. of Valentine Hill, m. Ezekiel Knight, and d. bef. 29 June 1675. Descend. are in that neighb. MARK, Salem 1668. THOMAS, Watertown, s. of William in Oldham, Co. Suff'k. came a. 1663, had w. Ann, but no ch. His will, of 13 Aug. 1692, was pro. 27 Feb. foll. and his br. Daniel, aft. d. of w. claim. the est.

LOVETT, ALEXANDER, Medfield 1678, had his ho. burn. by the Ind. DANIEL, Braintree 1662, m. Joanna, d. of Robert Blott, rem. to Mendon with early sett. was freem. 1673 ; but at B. had, prob. all his ch. James, b. 8 July 1648 ; Mary, 7 Mar. 1652 ; Martha, 7 June 1654 ; Hannah, 30 Mar. 1656 ; perhaps others, but his w. perhaps, was d. bef. the will of her f. in 1662. JOHN, Salem 1639, had that yr. gr. of ld. by w. Mary had there bapt. Simon, Joseph, and Mary, on 8 Sept. 1650, his w. unit. that yr. with the ch.; Bethia, 13 June 1652 ; and Abigail, Mar. 1655 ; prob. also, John, perhaps others, for the name has much prevail. there ; dwelt on Beverly side, d. 5 Nov. 1687, in 76th yr. JOHN, Mendon, perhaps s. of Daniel, d. 26 July 1668. THOMAS, Boston 1645, own. a lot, bounding on Christopher Lawson, look. prob. to the common.

LOVEWELL, JOHN, Boston 1660, of wh. we kn. nothing exc. that he was witness that yr. to will of Thomas Rawlins. JOHN, Dunstable 1690, had John, b. 14 Oct. 1691, more celebr. than any youth of his time, for serv. and sagac. in Ind. warf. k. at Pequawket 8 May 1725 ; Hannah ; Zaccheus, 22 July 1701, wh. was col. of a N. H. regim. in the last French war, 1759 ; and Jonathan, 14 May 1713, a preach. rep. and judge. See Farmer and Moore's Coll. I. 57, and III. 64 ; Belkn. I. 208 and 319 ; Fox, Hist. of D. 246. He, with the comm. exagger. of his age, is said popularly to have been 120 yrs. old, and prob. was near 100 at his d. a. 1754.

LOW, or LOWE, AMBROSE, Hingham, m. Feb. 1688, Ruth Andrews. ANDREW, New Haven 1639, m. Joan, wid. of Henry Peck, d. 1670, in his will of that yr. gave some prop. to four ch. of his w. by her former h. and ment. only s. Andrew, wh. was then in Eng. ANTHONY, Boston, s. of John, a wheelwright, rem. aft. 1654 to Warwick, had w. Frances, and s. John, perhaps other ch. He was afterwards of Swansey, when his ho. had been burned at W. in Mar. 1676, and in July aft. performed good service for the famous capt. Church. ARTHUR, Marshfield, s. of John of the same, m. 1714, Eliz. perhaps d. of Daniel Crooker, had Hannah, b. 1717; Eliz. 1720; and Jeremiah, 1735. FRANCIS, belong. we kn. not where, but, as he trav. the road from Swansey to Boston, was k. by lightning 15 July 1685, says an old diary. JOHN, Boston 1637, a wheelwright, had w. Eliz. and d. 1 Dec. 1653. His s. Anthony is bef. ment. JOHN, Sudbury 1641. JOHN, Hingham, m. Feb. 1650, Eliz. Stodder, d. of John the first, and Sept. 1659, Hannah Lincoln, wh. perhaps, d. in few yrs. and he m. 25 Sept. 1679, Ruth, d. of Thomas Joy. Perhaps there were at H. two; but one may have had the three ws. By the first w. he had John, b. 3 Apr. 1655; and Eliz. to ea. of wh. in the will of gr.f. S. 20 Nov. 1661, a legacy is giv.; also Tabitha, b. 7 Jan. 1653, wh. d. next yr. JOHN, Concord, by w. Lydia had John, b. 7 Mar. 1661. JOHN, Ipswich, s. prob. of Thomas, m. 10 Dec. 1661, Sarah, d. of John Thorndike. JOHN, Marshfield, whose f. is not nam. by Miss Thomas, m. Eliz. d. of Arthur Howland, had Arthur, b. 1665; and Hannah, 1670; and he was k. by the Ind. 1676 at Rehoboth. JOHN, Warwick, s. of Anthony, m. 3 Mar. 1675, Mary, d. of Zachary Rhoades. JOSEPH, Charlestown, a soldier of Moseley's comp. in the gr. battle of Narraganset 19 Dec. 1675. RICHARD, Rye 1663, one of the first sett.; and, perhaps, a merch. of Salem 1672. ROBERT, Boston 1649, vintner. THOMAS, Ipswich 1644, d. 8 Sept. 1677, leav. Thomas, John, and sev. ds. Descend. are very num. WILLIAM, Kittery, was of the gr. jury 1662.

LOWDEN, JOHN, Charlestown, s. of Richard, m. 29 May 1662, Sarah, d. of Andrew Stephenson, had John and Richard, both bapt. 29 Mar. 1668; Andrew, 2 Aug. 1668; Mary, 22 Jan. 1671; Sarah, 16 Nov. 1673; Joseph, 27 Feb. 1676; and by w. Eliz. had Eliz. bapt. 13 Mar. 1687; was freem. 1668. RICHARD, Charlestown 1638, freem. 18 May 1642, by w. Mary had John, b. 10, bapt. 16 May 1641; Jeremy, b. 8 Mar. 1643, bur. 11 mos. aft.; Mary, 24 Feb. 1645; Samuel, wh. d. Sept. 1682, in 33d yr.; Eliz. bapt. 23 Sept. 1656; and Martha, b. 6

Apr. 1659. His w. Mary d. 6 Oct. 1683, aged 65; and he d. 12 July 1700, in 88th yr. Martha m. John Call.

LOWELL, ancient. writ. LOWLE, BENJAMIN, Newbury, s. of John the first, m. 17 Oct. 1666, Ruth, d. of Edward Woodman, had Ruth, b. 4 Sept. 1667; Eliz. 16 Oct. 1669; Benjamin, 5 Feb. 1674; Sarah, 15 Mar. 1676; Mary; Joseph, 12 Sept. 1680; and John, 25 Feb. 1683; was freem. 1669. JOHN, Newbury, came 1639, it is said, with his f. Percival, and brot. ch. by his w. Mary, b. in Eng. John, Peter, Mary, and James, beside an apprent. Richard Dole; had here Joseph, b. 28 Nov. 1639; was freem. 2 June 1641; had sec. w. Eliz. Goodale, wh. bore Benjamin, 12 Sept. 1642, bef. ment.; Thomas, 4 June 1644, prob. d. young, not nam. in the will of f.; and Eliz. 16 Feb. 1646; and d. 10 July 1647, being town clk. that yr. His will is of 29 June preced. The wid. d. Apr. 1651; and d. Eliz. m. 1 Jan. 1667, as his sec. w. Philip Nelson of Rowley. JOHN, Boston, a cooper, b. in Eng. s. of the preced. m. 3 Mar. 1653, Hannah, d. of George Proctor of Dorchester, had John, b. 26 Aug. 1655, d. young; Mary, 7 Jan. 1658; and aft. d. of his w. he rem. to Scituate, there m. 24 Jan. 1659, Eliz. d. of Richard Sylvester, had John, b. 7 Apr. 1660; Joseph, d. soon; Patience, 7 Oct. 1662; and Eliz. wh. d. soon; beside Ruth, 11 July 1665. He m. third w. 1666, Naomi, sis. of his sec. rem. to Rehoboth, there had Phebe, d. soon; Margaret, 20 Oct. 1667; Samuel, 1 Aug. 1669, d. soon; Samuel, again, 30 Jan. 1671; Eliz. again, 1 Mar. 1674; William, 3 Jan. 1677, d. soon; Mehitable, 7 Jan. 1678; Benjamin, 5 Nov. 1679; and Nathaniel, 25 Feb. 1681. He came back to B. and had Ebenezer, in 1675, tho. the b. is not ent. on the rec. very deficient that yr. as the clk. with his f. and two brs. was occup. in milit. service of Philip's war, and there d. 7 June 1694. His wid. Naomi admin. the est. His s. Ebenezer was a shoemaker, f. of Rev. John, H. C. 1721, ord. at Newbury, 19 Jan. 1726, wh. was f. of John, H. C. 1760, disting. as a judge, and f. of sev. great benefact. of the commonw. JOSEPH, Boston, a cooper, br. of the preced. m. 8 Mar. 1660, Abigail, d. of George Proctor of Dorchester, had Joseph, b. 1 Aug. 1661, d. soon; Hannah, 31 Jan. 1663; Joseph, again, 9 Nov. 1665; Abigail, 4 Feb. 1667, d. soon; James, 27 Mar. 1668; Abigail, again, 9 Mar. 1671; and Samuel, 13 July 1678. PERCIVAL, Newbury, merch. came from Bristol, 1639, bring. s. John and Richard; his w. Rebecca d. 28 Dec. 1645, and he d. 8 Jan. 1665. Fam. tradit. says he was eldest s. of Richard, wh. m. a Percival, and drew his descent thro. eight generat. by the eldest s. of ea. from Walter of Yardley, in Co. Worcester. PERCIVAL, Newbury, s. of Richard, m. 7 Sept. 1664, Mary Chandler, had Richard, b. 25 Dec. 1668, wh. liv. to 29 May 1749; Gideon, 3 Sept. 1672; Samuel, 13

Jan. 1676; and Edmund, 24 Sept. 1684. RICHARD, Newbury, br. of John of the same, came with his f. 1639, bring. w. but no ch. that is kn. had Percival, bef. ment. b. 1639; and Rebecca, 27 Jan. 1642. His w. d. that yr. and by sec. w. Mårgaret he had Samuel, 1644; and Thomas, 28 Sept. 1649; and d. 5 Aug. 1682, aged 80, says Coffin. Fifteen descend. of the first Percival have been gr. at Harv. and it is noted, that four have, at diff. times, been of the corpo. of the Univ.

LOWGIE, or LOUGEE, John, came at the age of 16, in the Confidence of London, from Southampton 1638, ẁith Grace, perhaps his sis. as serv. of John Stephens of Caversham, Oxfordsh. This name is preserv. in N. H. but the tradit. of the fam. derives it from a John, wh. came from the Isle of Jersey, seventy yrs. later.

LUCAR, MARK, Newport, among freem. 1655.

LUCAS, THOMAS, Plymouth, had John, b. 15 July 1656; Mary, 15 Mar. 1658; Benoni, 30 Oct. 1659; Samuel, 15 Sept. 1661; and William, 13 Jan. 1663; and was k. by the Ind. in Philip's war. WILLIAM, Middletown, m. 12 July 1666, Esther Clark, perhaps d. of John of New Haven, wh. d. 15 Apr. and he d. 20 Apr. 1690, leav. William, b. 26 Apr. 1667; John, 14 Oct. 1669; Mary, 5 Dec. 1672; Thomas, 1676; and Samuel, 15 Apr. 1682. A Mr. L. with prefix of respect was of New Haven 1643, with fam. of six, of wh. no more is heard. He prob. was one of the London associates who soon went home. A Lucas fam. of good est. in N. E. is of French descent, but came not early across the ocean, the first emigr. Augustus writ. of hims. " I m. 6 Jan. 1696, at St. Malo, in Bretagne."

LUCE, or LUCY, HENRY, Rehoboth 1668. THOMAS, Charlestown, had Samuel, b. 1644, says Farmer, to wh. I can ȧdd nothing, but that he prob. rem. soon. The name abounds at the Vineyard. One LUCY, at Portsmouth, m. Mary, d. of William Brooking, and had Benjamin.

LUCKIS, or LUCKIN, WILLIAM, Marblehead 1648. Dana, Hist. Disc. 7.

LUDDEN, BENJAMIN, Weymouth, perhaps s. of James, by w. Eunice, d. I think, of John Holbrook, had d. Abia, b. 22 Dec. 1679; a s. whose name is not kn. 13 Mar. 1681; and James, 9 Nov. 1689. JAMES, Weymouth, had Mary, b. 17 Dec. 1636; Sarah, 15 Nov. 1639, d. soon; Sarah, again, 5 June 1642; and John, so late as 13 Jan. 1657, by w. Alice, wh. may have been mo. of the others. Perhaps this man was the guide, in Oct. 1632, in honor of wh. Gov. Winth. then travelling on foot from Plymouth to W. named a fording place in the North river. But the rec. in Geneal. Reg. IX. 171, calls him Laddon. In the note on p. 146 of the Hist. of Boston, attention is drawn to this name. Diligent as the writer is, his meaning may be misunderstood, when, aft. printing the name Ludham, at the foot, tho. in the text above, and in his

Index, with me he adopts Luddam, yet, for change of sec. *d* to *h* he says, "I follow Prince, wh. follow. or used Winth. *in the original.*" As the last three words are print. in Italics it might seem, that an insinuation was intend. that I had not used or follow. the orig. A candid reader need not be distressed with such a suspicion, or presume that Mr. Drake *believ.* such a thing; for the venerable MS. in its original ink is accessib. and here more plain than often it appears. Winth. wrote the name twice in the same short sentence, the first time, as it was print. by me, and the sec. as giv. in Webster's Ed. of 1790, with *h* aft. double *dd*. I was content with one form. Prince struck a mid. course, and the historian of Boston might learn from inspection, that the petty deviation from the orig. is seen in the scrupulous annalist, Hale's Ed. 407, and not in the annotator of Winth. Nobody would blame Winth. for spelling the name two ways in one sentence, nor Prince for so slight variance from both; nor quarrel with Secr. Porter in transcrib. the copy that Webster print. for obeying the *latter* form of Winthrop's writing of the name with an *h*, nor with me for accepting the *earlier* form, without that letter. After inspection of the ancient MS. Mr. Drake would observe that his criticism was more than unnecessary ; and his readers may excuse the error by inferring that instead of the open, bold Roman types, the natural overflow of his benignant impulses sought the more modest Italic character of censure. JOHN, Weymouth, wh. may have been s. of the preced. was a soldier on Conn. riv. under capt. Turner, in Mar. 1676. This name is not rare in the W. part of Mass.

LUDDINGTON, WILLIAM, Charlestown 1642, liv. in the part wh. bec. Malden, by w. Ellen had Mary, b. 6 Feb. 1643 ; had, also, Matthew, 16 Dec. 1657, d. next mo.; rem. to New Haven, but the time is unkn. there had William ; Henry, wh. d. 1676 ; Hannah ; John ; and Thomas ; and d. at the East Haven iron works, 1662. His wid. m. George Rose. His inv. calls him of Malden, but the fam. was perpet. at New Haven, by WILLIAM, prob. the eldest surv. s. wh. m. Martha, perhaps d. of George Rose, had Henry ; Elinor ; and William, b. 25 Sept. 1686. By sec. w. m. 1690, Mercy Whitehead, he had Mercy, b. 31 May 1691 ; Hannah, 13 Mar. 1693 ; John, 31 Jan. 1695 ; Eliphalet, 28 Apr. 1697 ; Eliz. 1699, d. young ; Dorothy, 16 July 1702 ; and Dorcas, 16 July 1704. The name is very rare of any other stock certain. but in the spring of 1635 a Christian L. aged 18 embark. at London, on board the Hopewell.

LUDECAS, or LEUDECOES, DANIEL, Dover 1659. His w. d. 1 Nov. 1662 ; and he d. in 1664.

LUDKIN, AARON, Charlestown, prob. s. of George or William, but may have been younger br. of them, or otherwise relat. came, we may

LUDLOW. 129

be sure, from Norwich, Eng. own sev. pieces of ld. in our Hingham, sold by him in 1671. His w. Hannah, d. perhaps, of George Hepbourne, was rec. into the ch. Apr. 1650, yet I find not in Budington's valua. list his adm. tho. he was chos. deac. Feb. 1672. Nor is the acco. much better of ch. for we hear only of Hannah, w. of Samuel Dowse, join. the ch. 15 June 1673. He d. 26 Mar. 1694, in 76th yr. and his wid. Hannah, d. of Richard Miller, wh. had been wid. of Nathaniel Dade, and of John Edmunds, he had m. 22 May 1684, and she d. 13 Dec. 1717, if the gr.stones are correct. GEORGE, Hingham, one of the first drawers for house lots, 1635, came from Norwich, Co. Norf'k. with w. and s. freem. 3 Mar. 1636, rem. to Braintree, there d. 22 Feb. 1648. ‖ WILLIAM, Hingham, perhaps br. of the preced. a locksmith, b. at Norwich, aged 33, and his w. Eliz. aged 34, with one ch. and one serv. Thomas Howes, as we learn from the declar. 8 Apr. 1637, came that season from Ipswich, arr. at Boston, 20 June, freem. Mar. foll. in Boston his d. Esther was bur. Oct. 1645, ar. co. 1651, chos. constable 8 Mar. and drown. 27 Mar. 1652, leav. wid. Eliz. and two ch.

LUDLOW, GEORGE, a gent. with prefix of respect, req. adm. 19 Oct. 1630 as freem. was, perhaps, kinsman of Roger L. then one of the Assist. and may have accomp. him in the Mary and John to Dorchester, but prob. went home in the spring of the foll. yr. for it may be infer. from Col. Rec. of 1 Mar. that a petit. from Eng. had been receiv. to wh. his attent. was to be request. by the Gov. and Council. HENRY, Huntington, L. I. adm. freem. of Conn. 1664; may have been s. of Roger, but we kn. nothing of it. ROGER, Dorchester, came in the Mary and John from Plymouth, May 1630, an Assist. chos. at the last gen. court in London, 10 Feb. 1630, and first attend. at the first Assist. court in Charlestown, Aug. foll. in 1634 was made dept.-gov. but left out next yr. hav. infirmity of temper. He rem. 1635, to Windsor, and in the civil line was chief of a commiss. of eight from Mass. with unlimit. power, 1636, for some time; was engag. in the Pequot war; and the first dept.-gov. of the Col. of Conn. rem. to Fairfield a. 1639, and early in 1641 bot. from the Ind. the territ. on E. side of Norwalk riv. was employ. in 1646 for reduc. their laws to a system, and was Commissnr. 1651, 2, and 3 in the congr. of the Unit. Col. of N. E. but went off next yr. to Virg. in some disgust, and there pass. the residue of his days, under a maledict. for carrying away the town rec. wh. was a charge long aft. refut. by find. the vol. in town. He had a ch. b. at W. but the rec. does not tell the name; and his d. Sarah m. Rev. Nathaniel Brewster of Brookhaven. That the habit. heedlessness of Mather, II. 33, made his name William, is less matter of surprise than that Farmer was blinded by the blunder. Its origin was prob. reading Mr. as abbrev. for William.

LUDWELL, JOHN, a passeng. aged 50, in the Confidence from South-ampton 1638, but no more is kn. of him.

LUFKIN, HUGH, Salem 1654, says Farmer, and I can add nothing. THOMAS, Gloucester, perhaps s. of Hugh, by w. Mary had Joseph, b. 16 Nov. 1674; Ebenezer, 18 May 1676; Abraham and Isaac, tw. 14 and 16 Feb. says the rec. without ment. of the yr. but it adds (as we might expect), d. same mo.; and Thomas, 9 Apr. 1682. The name is spell. Lovekin or Loufken. Lufkin is a name at Dedham, in Old Eng.

LUGG, or LUGGE, JOHN, Boston 1637, by w. Jane had Eliz. b. 7 Mar. 1638, bapt. 24 Mar. 1639, the mo. aft. his w. join. to the ch.; Mary, b. Aug. 1642, but the rec. of her bapt. 25 Sept. adds, "a. 4 days old;" and John, 4 Aug. 1644, a. 2 days old; and he d. 1647. He is, I presume, the man wh. Felt enumer. among Salem people, as John Luff, hav. gr. of ld. 1637, because that name never occurs elsewhere except in the list of passeng. to pass for N. E. in the Mary and John, who took the o. of supremacy and alleg. 24 Mar. 1634. Final letters are easily mistaken; and very many of such grants were ineffect. In the will of Samuel Hagborne of Roxbury, 24 July 1643, are giv. " unto my br. Lugg four bushels of corn, and my suit of apparel." His d. Mary m. 11 Feb. 1659, Nathaniel Barnard. Possib. there were both Luff and Lugg with common name of John, but it appears very unlikely.

LUIN, HENRY, Boston, by w. Sarah had Sarah, b. 20 Aug. 1636; Eliz. 27 Mar. 1638; and Ephraim, 16 Jan. 1640.

LUKE, GEORGE, Charlestown, by w. Hannah had George, bapt. 6 Mar. 1687.

LULL, THOMAS, Ipswich, freem. 1672.

LUM, JOHN, Southampton, L. I. 1641, perhaps liv. in 1673, when John Knowles of Fairfield writes the name in his will Loom.

LUMBARD, or LUMBART. See Lombard.

LUMMUS. See Loomis.

LUMPKIN, * RICHARD, Ipswich, from Boxted, in Essex, was freem. 2 May 1638, and rep. the same yr. d. 1642, prob. without ch. His wid. m. deac. Simon Stone of Watertown, and d. 1663, in her will of 25 Mar. in that yr. ment. no ch. by either h. but gives her prop. to h. Stone, to kinsmen John and Daniel Warner, and Thomas Wells. See Geneal. Reg. VIII. 71. WILLIAM, Yarmouth 1643, by w. Thomasine had Thomasine, b. 1626, wh. m. Samuel Mayo of Barnstable; and John Sunderland for sec. h.; perhaps Hannah, wh. prob. m. John Gray; ano. d. m. an Eldridge; but no s. and d. 1671. His will, of 23 July 1668, names his w. Thomasine.

LUND, THOMAS, Boston, merch. brot. from London 1646, power from

certain citizens of L. to collect debts. THOMAS, Dunstable, an early
sett. and selectman, had Thomas, b. 9 Sept. 1682 ; Eliz. 29 Sept. 1684;
and William, 19 Jan. 1686. His s. Thomas left descend. but was k. by
the Ind. 5 Sept. 1724. See Belkn. I. 207 ; and Fox, Hist. of D. for
inscript. to him and seven more on the monum.

LUNDALL, THOMAS, Dover 1658.

LUNERUS, ... a German or Polish doctor in Boston, wh. m. 1
July 1652, wid. Margaret Clemens. In 1654, by our Gen. Ct. rec. it
appears, that he was to determine when an offender should be whipp.
he, the offend. being then too ill. I trust the adv. of the physician was
on the side of mercy, for the poor Scotch prisoner, a waif from the civil
war in G. B. d. soon aft.

LUNT, DANIEL, Newbury, eldest s. of Henry, m. 16 May 1664, Hannah, d. of Robert Coker, had Hannah, b. 17 May 1665 ; Daniel, 1 May
1667 ; Henry, 23 June 1669 ; John, 10 Feb. 1672; Sarah, 18 June
1674 ; Mary, 24 July 1677 ; his w. d. 29 Jan. 1679, and he m. Mary,
wid. of Samuel Moody, had Joseph, 4 Mar. 1681; Ann, 28 Jan. 1683 ;
and Benjamin, 15 Mar. 1686; was freem. 1683, and k. by the Ind. 27
June 1689, at the ho. of maj. Waldron in Dover. HENRY, Newbury
1635, one of the passeng. in the Mary and John, who took the o. of
supremacy and alleg. 26 Mar. 1634, first sat down, perhaps, at Ipswich,
freem. 2 May 1638, by w. Ann had Sarah, b. 8 Nov. 1639 ; Daniel, 17
May 1641, bef. ment. ; John, 20 Nov. 1643 ; Priscilla, 16 Feb. 1646 ;
Mary, 13 July 1648 ; Eliz. 29 Dec. 1650; and Henry, 20 Feb. 1653;
and he d. 10 July 1662. In his will, made two days bef. pro. 30 Sept.
foll. the w. and seven ch. are well provid. for. His wid. m. 8 Mar.
1665, Joseph Hills. HENRY, Newbury, s. of the preced. by w. Jane
had Skipper (if Coffin is right), b. 29 Nov. 1679 ; Mary, 16 Jan. 1682;
Abraham, 10 Dec. 1683; John, 1 Feb. 1686 ; William, 4 July 1688 ;
Daniel, 1 Jan. 1691; Jane, 9 Nov. 1693 ; and Samuel, 26 Mar. 1696.
JOHN, Newbury, br. of the preced. m. 19 Nov. 1668, Mary Skerry, had
John, b. 22 Oct. 1669 ; Eliz. 12 Oct. 1671 ; and Henry, 22 Feb. 1674 ;
and d. 17 Sept. 1678, unless Coffin is mistak. for one John L. m. 26 Oct.
1696, Ruth, wid. of the third Joseph Jewett, d. of Thomas Wood, wh.
long outliv. him. THOMAS, Newbury, m. 17 Jan. 1679, Opportunity, d.
of Stephen Hoppin of Dorchester.

LUPTON, CHRISTOPHER, Southampton, L. I. 1673, may have been s.
of Thomas. THOMAS, Norwalk 1654, one of the first sett. and adm. to
be freem. 1664, but was not actually accounted so in 1669 ; had two ch.
but we learn not their names from Hall, the dilig. histor. and, perhaps,
they d. young. On p. 61, his Peter Lupton should be Clapton, or Clap-
ham. He was liv. 1687, but a wid. L. is ment. next yr. She was prob.
his, and was Hannah, d. of Thomas Morris of New Haven, m. in 1652.

LUSCOMB, HUMPHREY, Boston 1686, was a major, d. 10 June 1688, and prob. his w. or d. had d. 1 Feb. 1687, as Sewall marks. WILLIAM, Salem 1686, a cooper, perhaps had w. and fam. for the name has cont. there.

LUSHER, ‡ * ‖ ELEAZER, Dedham 1637, one of the found. of the ch. 1638, freem. 13 Mar. 1639, was of ar. co. 1638, as one of the founders, rep. 1640, for many yrs. aft. Assist. 1662 to his d. capt. in 1644, and head of the regim. later; had for sec. w. Mary, wid. of John Gwin of Charlestown, but not any ch. is kn. unless Samuel, wh. d. says the rec. 28 Dec. 1638 were one. He has high charact. in Wonder Work. Provid. and d. 3 or 13 Nov. 1672. His will was made 23 Sept. 1672, as in our Vol. VII. at the Reg. is kn. and his wid. 26 Jan. foll. made her will, both pro. together 6 Feb. aft.

LUSON, or LEUSON, JOHN, Dedham 1637, one of the found. of the ch. freem. 13 Mar. 1639, d. May 1661, his will of 15 Feb. preced. in wh. he dispos. of his est. names no ch. nor near relat. exc. Thomas, Robert, and Susan, ch. of Robert L. in Old Eng. late dec. to wh. a legacy is giv. to be equal. div. within two yrs. aft. the d. of his w. Martha. Also he names kinswo. Ann, w. of William Barstow of Scituate, but he gave the larger part of his est. to his neighb. Thomas Battelle, special. remembr. his ch. John and Mary.

LUTHER, HEZEKIAH, Swansey, had Edward, b. 27 Apr. 1674. JOHN, Taunton 1639, by Baylies, I. 286, numb. as one of the purch. yet may have been of Gloucester 1647. SAMUEL, Rehoboth 1662, was sec. Bapt. min. at Swansey, ord. 22 July 1685, d. 1717. He had Experience, b. 3 Mar. 1675. That town of R. sent many in the mad expedit. of Phips against Quebec, 1690, of wh. one was SAMUEL, perhaps s. of the preach. Progeny in that quarter is very much diffused. Benedict, Hist. I. 426. SAMUEL, Norwich 1675. A capt. of a vessel trading to Delaware, from Boston, of this name, in 1644, was k. by the Ind. in that riv. See Winth. II. 203, 237.

LUX, JOHN, Saco 1664, had there d. Mary, and s. Joseph, I presume by first w. for he had lately m. Mary, wid. of Gregory Jeffries, wh. in her will of 8 Sept. of that yr. provid. for her s. John by former h. with proviso, that if he d. bef. 17 yrs. of age, Mary and Joseph Lux should have that portion; and I presume that he liv. many yrs. aft. as I find JOHN, Boston, mariner, in 1676 styled junr. as if there were an elder of that name. WILLIAM, Exeter, sw. alleg. to Mass. 14 July 1657.

LUXFORD, JAMES, Cambridge, by w. Eliz. had Eliz. b. Sept. 1637; and Reuben, Feb. 1641. REUBEN, Cambridge, s. of the preced. m. 22 June 1669, at Lancaster, w. Margaret, had Margaret, b. 27 July 1673; was freem. 1674. His w. d. 31 Aug. 1691. STEPHEN, Haddam, d. 1676, leav. w. but no ch.

LYALL, LYSLE, LISLE, LIOLL, or LOYAL, FRANCIS, Boston 1637, a barber surg. of some importance, adm. of the ch. 29 Sept. 1639, and, in my judgment, may be that freem. of 13 May 1640, whose name is print. Seyle by Paige, in Geneal. Reg. III. and Shurtleff, in Col. Rec. as it had been in Winth. Hist. Vol. II. Appx. of Ed. 1826; by w. Alice had Joseph, b. 10 Oct. 1638, bapt. 6 Oct. 1639, d. 10 Feb. 1640 ; Benjamin, 1, bapt. 5 Jan. 1640, bur. Mar. 1 foll.; Mary, bapt. 14 Feb. 1641, four days old, when the rec. of the town perverse. says she was b. that day ; and Joseph, again, 14, bapt. 26 Mar. 1642. He went to Eng. with Leverett, Bourne, Stoughton, and others, to serve in the cause of Parliam. and bec. surg. in the life guard of the Earl of Manchester, whence he had the wisdom, like most of his townsmen, to come back in 1645. See Winth. II. 245. Snow's Hist. 118. Farmer said, that his s. Joseph was a lawyer, wh. may be less prob. than that he was of ar. co. 1668, wh. also, I doubt. His d. Mary m. Freegrace Bendall, and to him was giv. in conjunct. with Joseph, admin. 1 Nov. 1666, on est. of Alice, wh. prob. outliv. her h.

LYDE, ALLEN, Portsmouth, m. 3 Dec. 1661, Sarah Fernald, had Allen, b. 29 July 1666, perhaps other ch. and d. a. 1671. ALLEN, Portsmouth, s. of the preced. had Allen, b. 15 Nov. 1691 ; and Francis, 28 Sept. 1695. EDWARD, Boston, m. 4 Dec. 1660, Mary, d. of Rev. John Wheelwright, had Edward, and d. bef. June 1663. The name in the rec. of the m. is Loyd. The wid. m. Oct. 1667, Theodore Atkinson. Wheelwright, in his will, provides for the gr.s. EDWARD, Boston, s. of the preced. m. 29 Nov. 1694, Susanna, d. of capt. George Curwen, and for sec. w. m. 22 Oct. 1696, Deborah, d. of Hon. Nathaniel Byfield, had Byfield, H. C. 1722; but strange. is the name giv. James in Judge Sewall's Diary, print. in Geneal. Reg. VI. 76.

LYE, ROBERT, Lynn 1638. Lewis says descend. remain.

LYFORD, FRANCIS, Boston, a mariner, m. a. 1670, a d. of Thomas Smith, and rem. to New Hampsh. and there m. 21 Nov. 1681, Rebecca, d. of Rev. Samuel Dudley. The name is perpet. JOHN, Plymouth 1624, came that yr. prob. in the Charity with Edward Winslow, bring. w. and ch. prob. four, soon bred disturbance, and was forced to leave ; went to preach to the fishermen at Nantasket, and next at Cape Ann, and thence, Felt thinks, he accomp. Conant, 1626, to Naumkeag ; but a. 1627 rem. with some adherents to Virg. and there d. soon, it is thot. A reasona. conject. is, that he had w. Ann and ch. Ruth and Mordecai left at Nantasket, and that his wid. Ann, wh. d. July 1639, had m. Edmund Hobart of Hingham. Ruth, in 1641, and Mordecai, next yr. give to him discharge, as their stepfather, of certain tobacco and other chattels, in the will of their f. John, giv. to them. Ruth m. 19 Apr. 1643,

James Bates. MORDECAI, Hingham 1642, s. of John, of whom I would gladly kn. more.

LYMAN, BENJAMIN, Northampton, s. of John of the same, had Medad; Joseph, b. 22 Aug. 1699; Benjamin, 6 Dec. 1701, d. young; Benjamin, again, 4 Jan. 1704; Aaron, Apr. 1705; Eunice, 1708; Hannah, 1709; Caleb, 1711; William, 12 Dec. 1715; Daniel, 1717; Elihu; and Susanna. CALEB, Northampton, youngest s. of John, much disting. for bold and brief campaign against Ind. 1704, of wh. Penhallow and Hutch. II. 146, give the story; rem. to Boston, d. without issue. JOHN, Hartford, s. of Richard the first, b. in Eng. brot. by his f. in the Lion, Nov. 1631, by w. Dorcas, in a tradit. of little value, call. d. of Rev. Ephraim Huit (wh. in his will names no such, and she was d. of John Plum of Wethersfield), m. 12 Jan. 1655, had Eliz. b. at Branford, 6 Nov. foll. and rem. early to Northampton, there had Sarah, b. 1658; John, 1660; Moses, 1663; Dorothy, 1665; Mary, 1668; Ephraim, 1670, d. soon; Joseph, 1671, d. at 21 yrs.; Benjamin, 1674; and Caleb, 1678, bef. ment. was in the Falls fight 1676, then an ens. freem. 1690 perhaps, and d. 20 Aug. 1690, 66 yrs. old, says the gr.stone truly, for he lack. a mo. of 67. JOHN, Northampton, eldest s. of the preced. m. 19 Apr. 1687, Mindwell, wid. of John Pomeroy, d. of the first Isaac Sheldon. MOSES, Northampton, s. of the first John, by w. Ann, m. 1686, had Ann, b. 1688; Moses, 1690; Martha, 1695; Bethia, 1698; beside four, wh. d. young; was freem. 1690, and d. 1702. RICHARD, Roxbury 1631, b. at High Ongar, where he was bapt. 30 Oct. 1580, came with Eliot, in the Lion, bring. says the ch. rec. "Phillis, bapt. 12 Sept. 1611, at H. O. Richard, bapt. 24 Feb. 1618; Sarah, bapt. 8 Feb. 1621; John, b. Sept. 1623; and ano." kn. now to be Robert, b. Sept. 1629; and it goes on to tell how he went to Conn. "when the gr. removal was made," and suffer. greatly in loss of his cattle; was freem. 11 June 1633, and among the orig. proprs. of Hartford, where he d. 1640. His will, of 22 Apr. in that yr. is the first in the valu. work of Trumbull, Coll. Rec. I. 442, 3, foll. by the Inv. His wid. Sarah d. not long aft. All the ch. are nam. in the will, and Phillis is call. w. of William Hills. RICHARD, Windsor, eldest s. of the preced. b. in Eng. m. Hepzibah, d. of Thomas Ford, and had Hepzibah, Sarah, Richard, Thomas, Eliz. and John, all b. at W. bef. 1655, when he rem. to Northampton, there had Joanna, 1658, d. soon; and Hannah, 1660. He d. 3 June 1662, and his wid. m. John Marsh of Hadley, wh. thereupon rem. to N. Hepzibah m. 6 Nov. 1662, Josiah Dewey; Sarah m. 1666, John Marsh, jr.; Eliz. m. 20 Aug. 1672, Joshua Pomeroy; and Hannah m. 20 June 1677, Joseph Pomeroy. RICHARD, Northampton, eldest s. of the preced. m. 1675, Eliz. Cowles, d. of John of Hatfield, had Samuel, b. 1676; Richard, 1678; John, 1680; Isaac, 1682;

Jonathan, 1684; Eliz. 1686; David, 1688; and Josiah; and rem. to Lebanon, 1696, where he had Ann, 1698. ROBERT, Northampton, youngest s. of the first Richard, b. in Eng. m. 5 Nov. 1662, Hepzibah, d. of Thomas Bascom, had Sarah, b. 1664; John, 1664; Thomas, 1666, all of wh. d. young; Samuel, d. bef. manhood; Thankful, 1671; Hepzibah, 1674; Preserved, 1676; Wait, 1678, d. at 19 yrs.; and Experience, 1680. Two of his ds. were m. He was freem. 1684, liv. his last ten yrs. in "distract. condition," giving time sole. to fishing or hunting, and perish. as tradit. goes, on a hill in N. still nam. Robert's hill, but the date of d. is not found on rec. THOMAS, Northampton 1678, br. of the third Richard, m. that yr. Ruth, wid. of Joseph Baker, d. of William Holten, had Thomas, Mindwell, Ebenezer, Eliz. Noah, and Enoch; was freem. 1690, and rem. to Durham. Noah was f. of Gen. Phineas. Forty-seven of this name, says Farmer, had been, in 1834, gr. at the N. E. coll. of wh. thirteen were clerg. and three mem. of Congr. and of those, twenty-eight were of Yale, only six of Harv.

LYNDE, BENJAMIN, Boston, s. of Simon, stud. at the Middle Temple, and bec. a barrister bef. he came home, m. 22 Apr. 1699, Mary, d. of Hon. William Brown, had Benjamin, b. 5 Oct. 1700, H. C. 1718 (wh. was made Ch. Just. of the Sup. Ct. of Mass. and d. 3 Oct. 1781); and William, 27 Oct. 1714, H. C. 1733, a merch. at Salem; was sw. as one of the judges of the Sup. Ct. 25 July 1712, aft. Ch. Just. of Mass. and d. 28 Jan. 1745; and his wid. d. 12 July 1753. JOHN, Malden, by w. Mary had Thomas, b. 24 Oct. 1685; Ann, 13 Aug. 1687; Abigail, 4 Dec. 1689; Samuel, 29 Nov. 1690; and, perhaps, his w. d. 22 Dec. foll. He by sec. w. Eliz. had Dorothy, 20 Dec. 1692; Joanna, 22 Feb. 1697; Mehitable, 11 Mar. 1698; and his w. d. 19 Jan. 1699. He was a capt. and d. 17 Sept. 1723, prob. a. 75. ‡ * ‖ JOSEPH, Charlestown, s. of the first Thomas of the same, freem. 1671, rep. 1674, 9, and 80, ar. co. 1681, a patriot in the Committee of Safety 1689, made by Mather and king William in the Chart. of 1691, a counsel. but left out at the first elect. by the people, m. 24 Mar. 1665, Sarah, d. of Nicholas Davison, had Nicholas, b. 1665, d. soon; Sarah, 5 Dec. 1666, bapt. 13 Jan. foll.; Margaret, 24, bapt. 30 Jan. 1669; Joseph, 15, bapt. 21 May 1671, wh. was lost at sea, 16 Oct. 1694; Nicholas, again, 2, bapt. 14 July 1672, H. C. 1690, d. at Jamaica, Oct. 1703; Ann, bapt. 26 July 1674; Joanna, 4, bapt. 9 July 1676; and Thomas, 1678, wh. was lost at sea with his br. Joseph. His w. d. 13 Dec. 1678, aged 31; and his sec. w. was Emma, wid. of John Brakenbury, and d. of John Anderson, wh. d. 1 Sept. 1703; and his third w. was Mary, wid. of Hon. Adam Winthrop, 13 Mar. 1706, wh. d. 30 Oct. 1715; was lieut. col. and d. 29 Jan. 1727, aged, says Judge Sewall, a. 90. JOSEPH, Malden,

s. of the sec. Thomas, freem. 1678, d. 2 Jan. 1736, aged 83, says the
gr.stone; by w. Eliz. d. of Peter Tufts, had Mary, b. 30 Apr. 1686, d.
in few days; Joseph, 1687, d. 13 Feb. 1688; Ann, 29 May 1688;
Joseph, 2 Sept. 1690; perhaps others; certain. Mary, again, 25 Aug.
1692; Sarah, 12 Nov. 1694; Rebecca, 14 July 1696; and Thomas, 21
Apr. 1702. NATHANIEL, Saybrook, s. of Simon, m. 1683, Susanna, d.
of dep.-gov. Francis Willoughby, had Susanna, b. 6 Aug. 1685, d. at 4
mos.; Samuel, 29 Oct. 1689; Nathaniel, 22 Oct. 1692; Eliz. 2 Dec.
1694; and four others; and d. 5 Oct. 1729. SAMUEL, Charlestown, s.
of Thomas, by w. Rebecca had Thomas, b. and d. 1678; and Rebecca,
bapt. 19 Feb. 1682, when the mo. join. the ch. as a wid. but when the f.
d. is unkn. SAMUEL, Boston, br. of Nathaniel, was a merch. and freem.
1690, d. Dec. 1697. ‖ SIMON, Boston 1650, b. in London, June 1624,
s. of Enoch, wh. d. there 23 Apr. 1636, and of Eliz. wh. long surv. m.
22 Feb. 1653, Hannah, d. of John Newgate, had Samuel, b. 1 Dec.
1653, bef. ment.; Simon, 26 Sept. 1655, d. soon; John, 8 Nov. 1657;
Nathaniel, 22 Nov. 1659, bef. ment.; Eliz. 25 Mar. 1662; Benjamin, 22
Sept. 1666, H. C. 1686, bef. ment.; Hannah, 19 May 1670; and Sarah,
25 May 1672; beside John; Joseph; Enoch, wh. was bapt. 1 Feb. 1674;
and James, wh. all d. young; was of ar. co. 1658, and d. 22 Nov. 1687;
and his wid. d. 20 Dec. 1689. He was bred to trade in Holland, and
aft. com. to B. and here resid. sev. yrs. went to London, and sometime
was engag. there, and partook in 1672 of design for planting near
Stonington, as land speculat. The d. Eliz. m. George Pordage;
Hannah had three hs. but no ch. and d. 9 Aug. 1725; and Sarah m.
her cous. Nathaniel Newgate, or Newdigate, as in Eng. it was writ.
* THOMAS, Charlestown 1634, freem. 4 Mar. 1635, rep. 1636, 7, 45,
and sev. yrs. more, selectman 14 yrs. and a deac. d. 30 Dec. 1671, in
77th yr. By first w. he had Thomas, b. in Eng. where prob. she d.;
and Mary, wh. prob. was brot. over in 1635, by John Winth. jr. in
the Abigail, then aged 6 yrs.; beside six others, wh. d. bef. him, one
being Henry, wh. d. 9 Apr. 1646; and by sec. w. Margaret, wid. of
Thomas Jordan, and d. of John Martin, had Joseph, b. 3, bapt. 5 June
1636; Sarah, bapt. 14 Apr. 1639; Hannah, 2, bapt. 8 May 1642;
William; and Samuel, 14 Oct. 1644. This w. d. 3 Aug. 1662, and he
m. 6 Dec. 1665, Rebecca, wid. of capt. Nicholas Trerice, wh. long outliv.
him, and d. 8 Dec. 1688. His will, made only ten days bef. he d. with
a codic. of a single day bef. ment. w. Rebecca, s. Joseph, Samuel, and
Thomas, s.-in-law Robert Pierpont, ds. Hannah Trerice, and Mary
Wicks of Succonessett. The inv. was of good amount. Mary m. a
Wicks; Hannah m. 1663, John Trerice; and Sarah m. 18 Feb. 1657,
Robert Pierpont of Roxbury. THOMAS, Malden, s. of the preced. b. in

Eng. freem. 1645, had Thomas, b. 25 Mar. 1647 or 8; Eliz. 20 Apr. 1650; Joseph, 13 Dec. 1652; and, perhaps, other ch. d. 15 Oct. 1693, aged 78; his w. Eliz. aged 81, hav. d. six wks. bef. Eliz. m. 26 Aug. 1670, Peter Tufts. THOMAS, Charlestown, prob. s. of the preced. by w. Mary had Mary, bapt. 18 May 1684. Betw. the fams. of Boston and of Charlestown, under this patronym. no relat. is discov. Oft. the spell. in var. rec. is Lind, Linds, and even Lines. Six had, in 1834, been gr. at Harv. and five at Yale.

LYNN, or LYME, HENRY, Boston 1630, prob. came in the fleet with Winth. wh. speaks of his dissatisfact. with our governm. I. 61, by w. Sarah had Sarah, b. 20 Aug. 1636; Eliz. 27 Mar. 1638; Ephraim, 16 Jan. 1640; and Rebecca, 15 Feb. 1646, all of wh. she, as wid. Lynn, hav. m. Hugh Gunnison, brot. to bapt. 23 May 1647. The ch. rec. indicates the age of ea. of them, and these dates, exc. for the youngest, concur; but this is said to be 5 yrs. and a. 3 mos. and we may therefore believe the rec. of b. to be monstrous. incorrect. He was of York 1640, prob. and in 1645 went to Virginia, carry. most of his prop. there d. soon, for his w. and four ch. only £4. 18. 10. remain. aft. debts paid. Joanna, perhaps his d. m. 19 July 1660, William Williams.

LYON, GEORGE, Dorchester 1666, freem. 1669, of wh. no more is kn. but that in 1678 he join. the new ch. gather. at Milton. HENRY, Milford 1646, was of Fairfield 1652, where he m. the only d. of William Bateman. JAMES, Roxbury, had Ann, b. 4 Mar. 1683. JOHN, Salem 1638, when, Felt says, he had gr. of ld. liv. prob. on Marblehead side in 1648. JOHN, Roxbury, eldest s. of the first William, m. 10 May 1670, Abigail, d. of John Polley, had John, b. 14 May 1673; William, 15 Sept. 1675; Joseph, 10 Feb. 1678; Benjamin, 1680, d. soon; Abigail, 12 July 1682; Benjamin, again, 18 Dec. 1684; Bethia, 20 Oct. 1690; Ebenezer, 10 Mar. 1693; Nehemiah, 23 July 1695; and Hannah, 22 Apr. 1698, d. Dec. foll. and he and his w. were bur. says the rec. in one grave 15 Jan. 1702. He had intermed. liv. at Dorchester, and was freem. 1690. ┼JOSEPH, Roxbury, s. of the first William, was a soldier of Turner's comp. Mar. 1676, m. 23 Mar. 1681, Mary, d. of John Bridge, had Mary, b. 9 Jan. foll. d. soon; Joseph, 4 July 1684; and, perhaps, rem. for no more occurs of them in the rec. unless he be that one wh. d. 19 June 1724, but said to be in 47th yr. by the inscript. wh. may be erron. ┊ Gen. Reg. VII. 331. PETER, Dorchester, freem. 1649, had Mary, b. 4 Nov. 1650; Elkanah or Elhanan, 23 Sept. 1652; Nathaniel, 28 Dec. 1654; Susanna, 25 Mar. 1658; Ebenezer, 20 Feb. 1661; and, perhaps, others. His sec. w. Hannah or Ann, was d. of Thomas Tolman, and d. 26 Nov. 1689. PETER, Dorchester, freem. of 1690, may have been s. of the preced. RICHARD, Cambridge, sent by

Sir Henry Mildmay as tutor for his s. William at Harv. a. 1644 or 5, and, perhaps, went home with him aft. gr. 1647; but prob. assist. Presid. Dunster in his revision of the N. E. version of the Psalms, of wh. the first Ed. was pr. at Cambridge 1640. Tradit. had magn. his service into translation, tho. the melody of the verse was not exquisite. RICHARD, Fairfield 1649, recommend. to be freem. 1664, but not qualif. bef. 1669. SAMUEL, Roxbury, s. of the first William, had, says the ch. rec. Ebenezer, bapt. 29 Sept. 1678, and, I suppose, rem. to Rowley, but came back, and the rec. of the town says, by w. Deliverance had Margaret, b. 24 Aug. 1685; and by w. Maria, wh. d. 25 Apr. 1704, had John, b. 7 days bef. unless this refers to his neph. Samuel, as seems likely; and he d. 7 Apr. 1713. THOMAS, Fairfield 1654-70, may be the soldier under capt. Turner, in the Falls fight, k. by the Ind. aft. his victory, 19 May 1676. THOMAS, Roxbury, sec. s. of first William, m. 10 Mar. 1669, Abigail Gould, had Thomas, b. 4 Sept. foll. if the rec. be good; Sarah, 26 Aug. 1672; both bapt. 20 Apr. 1673; Jonathan, 24 June, bapt. 23 Aug. 1674, d. in Oct. of next yr.; Jonathan, again, 25 Aug. 1676, whose bapt. I find not; Esther, 13 Oct. 1678, bapt. 8 June 1679; Mehitable, 17 Mar. bapt. 24 Apr. 1681; Ann, wh. d. soon, in 1683; Jonathan, d. soon; Eliphalet, 20 Sept. 1687; and Ann, again, 28 Apr. 1689, d. at 4 yrs. ‖ WILLIAM, Roxbury, came 1635, aged 14, in the Hopewell, capt. Babb, prob. under charge of Isaac Heath, a passeng. with his fam. in the same sh. m. 17 June 1646, Rachel, d. of Thomas Ruggles, had John, b. 10 Apr. 1647; Thomas, 8 Aug. 1648; Samuel, 10 June 1650, all bef. ment.; William, 12, bapt. 18 July 1652; Joseph, 30 Nov. bapt. 3 Dec. 1654, when the ch. rec. calls him John; Sarah, bapt. 8 Mar. 1657, whose b. I find not in the town rec.; Jonathan, 5 Sept. 1666, wh. d. bef. ano. Jonathan, b. late in 1668, or early in 1669; was of ar. co. 1645, freem. 1666, and d. 21 May 1692; and his wid. d. 4 Aug. 1694. ⁄WILLIAM, Roxbury, s. of the preced. m. Sept. 1675, Sarah Dunkin, perhaps d. of Samuel, had William, b. 9 Dec. 1677; Samuel, 20 Sept. 1679; Hannah, 11 Aug. 1681; Benjamin, 29 Mar. 1683, d. in few days; Mehitable, 24 Mar. 1684; his w. d. 9 Feb. 1689, and by w. Deborah he had David, 31 Oct. 1692; Martha, wh. d. soon; and Jacob, 4 June 1696; and d. 10 Aug. 1714. His wid. Deborah d. 12 Mar. 1717. Thirteen of this name, says Farmer in MS. had, in 1829, been gr. at the coll. of N. E. and Union, and N. J.

LYSCUM, or LISCOM, ‖ HUMPHREY, Boston, ar. co. 1678. He was a merch. of whose est. admin. was giv. 23 June 1688, by Sir Edmund Andros, calling him major, to Abigail Kellond, his mo.-in-law, and on her resign. next mo. it was giv. to his br. Thomas. JOHN, Lynn, by w. Abigail had Samuel, b. 16 Sept. 1693.

LYTHERLAND, LETHERLAND, or LITHERLAND, WILLIAM, Boston 1630, came, no doubt, in the fleet with Winth. in the employm. of Owen Roe of London, wh. was one of the comp. of adventur. to Mass. who never came here, but was made memb. of the High Court of Justice, so call. for condemnat. of the king, and affixed his seal, as one of the regicides, to the warrant for execut. L. joined our ch. 24 Nov. 1633, and bec. I suppose, freem. 4 Mar. foll. when the name in the list is Netherland; was a supporter of Mrs. Hutchinson's opinions, for wh. he was disarm. and went off to R. I. was many yrs. town clk. of Newport, had w. Margaret, but whether any ch. is unkn. to me. In 1684, he was call. to give testim. as to the purch. from the Ind. on first com. to sett. here, and then call. his age 74. See 2 Mass. Hist. Coll. IV. 203. ZIBION, or more prob. ZEBULON (both names being used in the rec. of b. tho. the former more frequent and latest), Boston, by w. Rachel had Margaret, b. 4 July 1670; William, 5 Mar. 1673; and Deborah, 2 Oct. 1678.

MACCALLOM, or MAKCALLOM, MALCOLM, Boston, 1657, one of the first mem. of the Scots' Charit. Soc. In Drake's Hist. 455, by error of one letter, the name is made Maktallome.

MACCANE, WILLIAM, Wrentham, by w. Ruth had William, wh. was k. by casualty in youth; Mary, b. 1 Feb. 1670; Sarah, 10 Aug. 1671; and Deborah, 23 May 1674; prob. others.

MACCARTY, FLORENCE, Boston 1686, butcher, was one of the found. of the first soc. for Episcop. worship in N. E. by w. Eliz. had Eliz. b. 25 Dec. 1687; Thomas, 5 Feb. 1689; William, 3 Feb. 1691; and by w. Sarah had Esther, 1 July 1701; and Margaret, 29 Mar. 1702, if the rec. be thot. right. He d. 13 June 1712, at Roxbury, and a third w. Christian, with his s. William admin. the est. wh. was compet. ‖ THADDEUS, Boston, by w. Eliz. had Charles, wh. d. 25 Oct. 1683, aged 18; Francis, b. 21 Mar. 1667; Thaddeus, 12 Sept. 1670; Margaret, 25 Sept. 1676, and Samuel, bapt. at Roxbury, 3 Nov. 1678. He was of ar. co. 1681, d. at B. 18 June 1705, aged 65; and his wid. Eliz. d. 7 June 1723, aged 82. A Thomas, H. C. 1691, wh. was d. 1698, Hutch. I. 392, 3, and a Charles, badly wound. in the exped. 1690, against Quebec, are of unkn. descent.

MACARTER, MAKARTA, MAGARTA, or MECARTA, JOHN, Salem, m. 27 Jan. 1675, Rebecca Meacham, d. perhaps of Jeremiah, had John, b. 13 Jan. 1676; Rebecca, 4 Feb. 1678; Jeremiah, 9 Sept. 1679; Peter, 1 Nov. 1681; Andrew, 6 June 1684; James, 17 Nov. 1686; all bapt. 16 Nov. 1687; Isaac, 3 June, bapt. 28 Sept. 1689; and Rebecca, again, b. 6 Feb. 1691.

MAC CLARY, or McCLARY, JOHN, Haverhill 1655, was a Scotchman, possib. one of the wretched prisoners at Dunbar, or Worcester, shipped over here for sale; but not the ancest. of a disting. fam. in N. H. wh. had been of the Protestant defenders of Londonderry, and emigr. from Ireland, so late as 1725.

MACCOOME, or MACOMB, ALEXANDER, Boston 1659, one of the Scots' Charit. Soc. that yr.

MACCULLOCK, or McCULLOCK, ALEXANDER and THOMAS, Boston 1684, were of the Scots' Charit. Soc.

MACDANIEL, or MAGDANIEL, DENNIS, Boston, by w. Alice had Dennis, b. 25 Nov. 1671; and Eliz. 7 May 1674. JOHN, Boston, m. 17 May 1658, Eliz. Smith, had John, b. 13 Sept. 1659; Eliz. 3 Sept. 1661; Martha and Mary, tw. 14 Sept. 1663; Michael, 26 July 1666; William, 21 Sept. 1671; and Mary, again, 11 Oct. 1674. NEAL, Newton 1678.

MACDOWALL, STURGIS, Boston, of the Scots' Charit. Soc. 1684. See Drake, 455, where all the early mem. are giv.

MACE, WILLIAM, Warwick, I presume, as one of this name m. Sarah, d. of Samuel Gorton.

MACGINNIS, DANIEL, Woburn, m. 10 Feb. 1677, Rose Neal, had Rose, b. 19 Nov. 1677; rem. to Billerica 1679, but in W. had Edmund, 23 Mar. 1685.

MACK, JOHN, Salisbury, m. 5 Apr. 1681, Sarah Bagley, had John, b. 29 Apr. 1682.

MACKANEER, ALEXANDER, perhaps of Boston, yet it is not cert. His inv. of 5 Dec. 1670, shows £123. 9.

MACKAY, ARCHIBALD, Newton, prob. s. of Daniel of the same, by w. Margaret had Hannah, b. 24 Feb. 1694; William, 25 Dec. 1695; John, 22 Sept. 1698; Nathaniel, 5 Jan. 1702; Abigail, 6 Jan. 1705; Edward, 21 July 1706; Eliz. 20 Feb. 1712, d. at 4 yrs.; Nehemiah, 14 Feb. 1715; and Mary, 14 Jan. 1721. DANIEL, Newton, by w. Sarah had Mary, b. 25 Sept. 1673; Jacob, 14 Mar. 1675; Hannah, 29 Mar. 1677; and Ebenezer, 20 Oct. 1680; beside Archibald, bef. either of these, and perhaps others. He was a Scotchman, and Jackson supposes he came from Roxbury, but in that town I never find the name so early.

MACKINTOSH, JOHN, Dedham, m. 5 Apr. 1659, Rebecca, d. of the first Michael Metcalf, wh. d. bef. him, and by ano. w. had William, bapt. 25 Nov. 1665, prob. other ch.; d. 1691, in his will, made 13 Aug. pro. 28 Oct. foll. ment. w. Jane, and ch. William and Rachel.

MACKLATHLIN, MACLOTHLIN, MACKLATHIN, or MEGLATHLIN, ROBERT, Brookfield, perhaps a Scotch prisoner of O. Cromwell's field of triumph, either at Dunbar or Worcester, sent to our country to be sold for yrs. may have m. at B. a d. of the first John Warner, as Mr. Judd infer. from the fact that one of two orphan ds. of M. aft. the destruct. of B. appears at Hadley, 1685, nam. Joanna, and m. that yr. Samuel Smith of H. and ano. d. m. at H. 1699, a man whose name is not plain on rec.

MACLOUD, MORDECAI, Lancaster 1658, was with w. and two ch. k. by the Ind. 22 Aug. 1675. Willard, 26, 28.

MACKMALLEN, or MACKMILLION, ALISTER, Salem, a. 30 yrs. old in Nov. 1661, perhaps had w. Eliz. and d. Eliz. His d. perhaps m. 17 Dec. 1677, Henry Bragg, and his wid. perhaps m. 4 Nov. 1679, John Baxter, both at Salem.

MACKMAN, JAMES, Windsor, m. 1690, Eliz. d. of Thomas Stoughton, had no ch. d. 18 Dec. 1698. He was a merch. left good est. and his wid. m. John Eliot of Windsor. Sometimes this is spell. Mackmin, never Markham, as Hinman, 153, gives it.

MACOMBER, or MACUMBER, JOHN, Taunton 1643 (Baylies, II. 267), had Thomas, b. 30 July 1679; William, 31 Jan. 1684; beside prob. John, as the rec. shows, that John sen. m. 7 Jan. 1686, Mary Badcock. THOMAS, Marshfield, m. 20 Jan. 1677, Sarah Crooker, d. of Francis. WILLIAM, Duxbury 1643, was there 1638, possib. br. of the preced. may have rem. to Marshfield, where Sarah, perhaps his d. m. 6 Nov. 1666, William Briggs; rem. aft. to Dartmouth, there was liv. 1686. This name has been well diffus. various. spell.

MACOONE, MACKOON, or MACOUNE, JOHN, Cambridge, m. 8 Nov. 1654, Deborah Bush, wh. d. 20 Feb. 1665, had Hannah, b. 31 Oct. 1659; Deborah, 31 Dec. 1661; Eliz. 31 Jan. 1663, d. at one yr.; and Sarah, 15 Feb. 1664; he m. 14 June 1665, Sarah Wood, had John, 14 June 1666; Daniel, 18 Feb. 1669; Eliz. 17 Jan. 1670; Margaret, 20 Feb. 1672; and Peter, 21 Feb. 1674. Sometimes the rec. confus. the name of w. JOHN, Westerly 1669, in his will of 15 Dec. 1732, names w. Ann, eldest s. John, other ch. Daniel; Rachel, wh. m. 17 Apr. 1721, James Hall; Mary, wh. m. a Larkin; Abigail, wh. m. a Brown; William, and Joseph. JOHN, Westerly, s. of the preced. in his will of 2 Apr. 1754, ment. w. Patience, ch. William, Samuel, Lois, and Sarah. JOSEPH, Westerly, br. of the preced. had w. Jemima, and d. bef. 1750.

MACRANNEY, WILLIAM, Springfield, m. 1685, Margaret, d. of John Riley.

MACKRENEL, JAMES, a soldier under capt. Turner, and so kn. to be from Boston or Charlestown, k. at Northampton, 14 Mar. 1676, by the Ind.

MACREST. See Makrest.

MACUMMORE, JOHN, Newport 1639.

MACWORTH, ARTHUR, Casco 1636, one of the most respect. sett. of the early time, m. Jane, wid. of Samuel Andrews; but prob. he had w. perhaps ch. bef. that union, when he liv. at Saco, whither Willis thinks he came with Vines 1630, and where he serv. on gr. jury 1640. He d. 1657, leav. Arthur, John, and sev. ds. of wh. all would not be ch. of the wid. Jane, wh. d. at Boston 1676, tho. it may be difficult to discrimin. those she bore to Andrews and to him. See Willis, I. 32, 75, 165. His d. Rebecca m. Nathaniel Wharff of the same.

MACY, FRANCIS, m. Sarah, d. of Jeremiah Norcross of Watertown, but I kn. not whether he was ever in our country, and Bond, 376, was uncert. whether his name was Merry or Massey. * GEORGE, Taunton 1643, was lieut. in Philip's war, rep. 1672 six yrs. d. 17 Aug. 1693, leav. sev. ds. (of wh. one was prob. Eliz. wh. m. 15 May 1672, John Hodges; ano. might be Rebecca, m. 18 Mar. 1690, Benjamin Williams) but no s. Baylies, I. 287. JOHN, Nantucket, s. of Thomas, m. Deborah, d. of the first Richard Gardner, and she next m. Stephen Pease. * THOMAS, Newbury, came, it is said, from Chilmark, Co. Wilts, freem. 6 Sept. 1639, m. Sarah Hopcot, wh. d. 1706, aged 94, rem. to Salisbury, had Sarah, b. 9 July 1644, d. young; Sarah, again, 1 Aug. 1646; Mary, 4 Dec. 1648; and Thomas, 22 Sept. 1653 ; was rep. 1654, rem. to Nantucket a. 1659, being there one of the first sett. had six ch. and d. 19 June 1672, in 74th yr. Coffin's Newbury; Holmes's Ann.; Macy's Nantucket, 13–18. His d. Sarah m. 11 Apr. 1665, William Worth; Mary m. 11 Apr. 1669, William Bunker; and Bethia m. 30 Mar. 1670, Joseph Gardner.

MADDOCKS, MADDOCK, MATTOCKS, or MADDOX, EDMUND, Boston, m. 14 Jan. 1652, Rebecca Munnings, had Mary, b. 4 Jan. 1656; and John, 12 Mar. 1657. HENRY, Saco 1653, sw. fealty that yr. to Mass. rem. to Boston, had w. Rachel, and d. Rachel, b. 24 July 1673, d. soon; and again, Rachel, b. 2 Sept. 1677. HENRY, Watertown, m. 21 May 1662, Mary, only d. of Roger Wellington, had only ch. John, b. 16 May 1663 ; and his wid. m. 16 Sept. 1679, John Coolidge. JAMES, Lynn, came, it is said, from Bristol 1642, and d. at Newbury. JOHN, Boston, perhaps elder br. of the preced. came in the Planter, from London, early in 1635, call. a sawyer, aged 43, was at Lynn, and last at Newbury, there d. 24 Apr. 1643. JOHN, Watertown, s. of Henry of the same, m. 23 June 1689, Ruth, d. of Caleb Church, had Ruth, b. 13 or 19 Feb. 1691; John, 22 Jan. 1693; Mary, 4 Dec. 1694; Sarah, 22 Dec. 1696 ; Henry, 18 Oct. 1698 ; Caleb, 29 Aug. 1700 ; and Joanna, 4 Oct. 1702. He d. 1 Feb. aft. and his wid. m. 25 July 1705, Joseph Child.

MADER, ROBERT, Boston, freem. 1643, of wh. I kn. no more, but that, on join. with the ch. 16 Apr. of that yr. he is termed serv. to our br. William Franklin.

MADIVER, JOEL, Casco, s. of Michael, driv. by Ind. war, 1676, to Boston, there by w. Rebecca had Mercy, b. 12 Aug. 1677; ret. aft. the peace; and in the third war was k. by the French, Aug. 1703. His s. Joel liv. at Falmouth. MICHAEL, Casco, was in the part call. Perpoodick, now Cape Elizabeth, aft. 1658. See Willis, I. and II. But he own. ld. on W. side of the Spurwink riv. wh. makes the E. bound of Scarborough, and there first liv. His inv. Aug. 1670, was small. He m. a wid. Carter. See Southgate, 74. Oft. this name is found Madeford, and in Geneal. Reg. III. 194, becomes Madinde, and in V. 264, Maddine.

MAGOON, MAGOUN, McGOWN, or MAKOON, ELIAS, Duxbury, s. of John the first, by w. Hannah had David, b. 1 Nov. 1703; Mary, 24 Mar. 1705; and Elias, 9 Oct. 1707; Recompence; and Ruth; but perhaps his sec. w. Ruth was mo. of this last. He liv. in that part wh. was made Pembroke 1712, and d. 1727. His will of 13 Aug. pro. 25 Sept. of that yr. names w. Ruth and the s. and ds. s.-in-law John Clark, perhaps h. of Mary. Of this stock was the late eminent shipbuilder of Medford. HENRY, Dover 1657–83, at Exeter took the o. of alleg. 1677, had s. Alexander and John. JAMES, Duxbury, eldest s. of John of Scituate, by w. Sarah had James, b. 25 Mar. 1697; Thomas; Isaac, wh. prob. d. young; and Sarah. He d. 1705, and his wid. Sarah admin. the est. bef. close of wh. a. 1720, James was d. His wid. Sarah m. 23 Nov. 1710, Stephen Bryant. JOHN, Scituate, bef. 1662, was among freeholders 1666, had m. at Hingham, and had a d. b. 1663, whose name is not ment. but was, perhaps, Hannah; James, 25 June 1666; and at S. had John, b. 1668; Elias, 1673; and Isaac, 1675. His will, of 20 May 1697, pro. 27 June 1712, names w. Rebecca, eldest s. James, the other three s. and d. Hannah Lovell. JOHN, Marshfield, s. of the preced. prob. had John, and, perhaps, others. JONATHAN, Hingham 1657.

MAGSON, RICHARD, Boston 1634, in the employm. of James Everill, as the ch. rec. of his adm. 2 Oct. ment. but no more is kn.

MAGVARLOW, MACVARLO, or MACFARLO, PURDY, Hingham, m. July 1667, Patience Russell, had sev. ch. of wh. prob. was Margaret, wh. m. 26 May 1690, David Stodder.

MAHOONE, DERMIN or DORMAN, Boston 1646, of wh. I hear nothing but that by w. Deiner, or Dinah, he had Daniel, b. 4 Dec. 1646; and Honor, 29 Oct. 1648; and his w. Dinah d. 8 Jan. 1657.

MAINE, or MAYEN, EZEKIEL, Stonington 1670, offered to be freem. 1673. EZEKIEL, Stonington, s. of the preced. m. 14 Jan. 1689, Mary Wells. JOHN, Boston, in a petn. to Andros and the counc. 1687, says that 30 yrs. since he had purch. ho. and lds. at what is now North Yarmouth, and when the Ind. burnt his ho. and k. two of his s.-in-law, he

and w. and rest of his fam. hardly esc. 3 Mass. Hist. Coll. VII.
176. But he was of York in 1681, when his name is writ. with a *y* as
he took o. of alleg. and he d. at B. 27 Mar. 1699.

MAJOR, GEORGE, Newbury, from Isle of Jersey, says Coffin, took w.
Susanna 21 Aug. 1672, had Hannah, b. 18 May 1673; and George, 20
Nov. 1676.

MAKEPEACE, ‖ THOMAS, Dorchester 1636, came with a large fam.
ar. co. 1638, m. 1641, for his sec. w. Eliz. wid. of Oliver Mellows, had
Joseph, bapt. 20 Sept. 1646, wh. prob. d. bef. his f. rem. some yrs. later
to Boston, and there d. In his will of 30 June 1666, he names eldest s.
Thomas, to wh. he had bef. giv. ho. and ld. in Eng. where he then liv.
and William; eldest d. Hannah, w. of Stephen Hoppin; Mary, w. of
Lawrence Willis; Esther, w. of John Brown of Marlborough; and
Waitawhile, w. of Josiah, not (as Geneal. Reg. V. 402, has it) Thomas
Cooper, nine ch. of Hoppin, whose mo. was Opportunity, four of Brown,
and two of Cooper. WILLIAM, Boston, s. prob. of the preced. m. 23 May
1661, Ann Johnson, rem. I suppose, to Taunton, for there the name was
long kept up.

MAKREST, BENONI, Salisbury, by w. Lydia Fifield, m. 12 Sept. 1681,
had Samuel, b. 3 Sept. 1682, d. at 2 mos.; Joseph, 28 Aug. 1683;
Benjamin, 16 Nov. 1685; Lydia, 27 Mar. 1688; and Mary, 15 Apr.
1690; and he d. 7 Aug. 1690, leav. wid.

MALBON, JOHN, Salem 1629, supposed to have skill in iron works,
came in the fleet with Higginson, and prob. went home next yr. ‡ RICH-
ARD, New Haven, an early Assist. but not, as Mather, II. cap. 12, careless. writes, in 1637. See Winth. II. 95 and 353. The d. against wh.
her f. called for the perilous animadv. was nam. Martha. He rem. or
perhaps went home in 1648 or 9, and it had been better, if he had gone
earlier. He was d. bef. May 1661.

MALINE, or MELLEN. See Melyen.

MALINS, ROBERT, Newport, m. 1 Jan. 1675, Patience, d. of Peter
Easton, had Mary, b. 21 Oct. foll.; and Robert, 22 Jan. 1677; and d.
26 Aug. 1679, and my report is that w. d. the same day, ea. aged 30,
tho. she was only 24.

MALLARD, ‖ THOMAS, Boston, ar. co. 1685, perhaps rem. to N. H.
where the name occurs.

MALLORY, JOHN, New Haven, s. of the first Peter, had John, b. 6
Sept. 1687; Eliz. 1 May 1691; Rebecca, 15 Sept. 1693; Mabel, 19
Dec. 1695; Silence, 13 Oct. 1698; John, 1 Mar. 1701; and Obedience,
11 Apr. 1704. JOSEPH, New Haven, br. of the preced. m. Mercy, d.
of Thomas Pinion, had Mercy and Thankful, tw. b. Aug. 1694; Abigail,
Aug. 1696; Joseph, 5 Nov. 1698; Benjamin, 5 Nov. 1701; and Han-

nah, 1 Sept. 1709. PETER, New Haven, sign. the planta. cov. 1644, had Rebecca, b. 18 May 1649; Peter, 27 July 1653; Mary, Oct. 1655, d. soon; Mary, again, 28 Nov. 1656; Thomas, 15 Apr. 1659; Daniel, 25 Nov. 1661; the last three bapt. 12 July 1663, not 11 (wh. was Saturday), as the eminent. untrustworthy ch. rec. tells; John, 10 May 1664, bapt. I suppose, next Sunday, not Tuesday 17, by the wretch. rec.; Joseph, b. 1666; Benjamin, 4 Jan. 1669; Samuel, 10 Mar. 1673; and William, 3 Sept. 1675. PETER, New Haven, s. of the preced. m. 27 May 1678, Eliz. eldest d. of James Trowbridge, had Peter, b. Apr. 1679, d. young; Caleb, 3 Nov. 1681; Peter, again, Aug. 1684, d. young; Eliz. 27 Apr. 1687; Judith, 2 Sept. 1689; Benjamin, 3 Apr. 1692; Stephen, 12 Oct. 1694; Ebenezer, 29 Nov. 1696; Zechariah, 2 May 1699; Abigail, 5 Aug. 1701; Zipporah, 15 Dec. 1705; and Peter, again, 1 Mar. 1708. THOMAS, New Haven, br. of the preced. m. 26 Mar. 1684, Mary Umberfield, had Thomas, b. 1 Jan. 1685, wh. d. 21 July 1783, of course 98 yrs. 6 mos. and 9 days old, magnif. up to "one hundred and one yrs." in Cothren; and Daniel, 2 Jan. 1687, was a propr. as also were his f. and brs. Peter, Daniel, and John in 1685; but he d. 15 Feb. 1691. Oft. the sec. syl. has e, sometimes a.

MALONE, or MALOON, HENDRICK, Dover 1660. LUKE, Dover 1670, m. 20 Nov. 1677, Hannah Clifford, perhaps d. of John, first of the same, had Sarah, b. 1679; Joseph; Samuel; Luke; Eliz.; and Nathaniel; but dates are not seen, and order of b. is unkn.

MALTBY, JOHN, New Haven, m. Mary, d. of Richard Bryan of Milford, had John, and Mary, was lost at sea, as in 1676 was conclud. and 10 June of that yr. his inv. of only £58. was brot. in; yet he has the prefix of respect, and he was prob. a valua. man. Mary m. Rev. John Fordham. WILLIAM, Branford 1667, in 1673 was cornet of the New Haven troop, and left descend.

MANCHESTER, STEPHEN, Portsmouth, R. I. m. 13 Sept. 1684, Eliz. d. of Gershom Wodell.

MANLY, RALPH, Charlestown, prob. came in the fleet with Winth. and d. Sept. 1630. WILLIAM, Weymouth, by w. Rebecca had Sarah, b. 5 Oct. 1675; in Mar. foll. was soldier in Turner's comp. outliv. the camp, and had Thomas, 11 July 1680; and by w. Sarah had Rebecca, 6 Mar. 1687; perhaps he rem. to Boston, and was freem. of 1690.

MANN, ABRAHAM, Providence 1676, was one of the few that did not rem. in Philip's war. He took o. of alleg. May 1671. FRANCIS, Providence, of wh. I can only learn, that his d. Mary m. 6 Apr. 1673, John Lapham. JAMES, Newport, freem. 1653. JOHN, Boston 1670, a baker, by w. Mary had Joseph, b. 30 June 1672. JOSIAH, a soldier prob. from Boston or Charlestown, under capt. Turner, 1676, at Hadley.

NATHANIEL, Boston 1670, perhaps br. of Josiah, by w. Deborah had William, b. 19 Feb. 1672. RICHARD, Scituate 1646, by Deane, 309, was reckon. a youth in Elder Brewster's fam. who could claim to have come in the Mayflower, 1620; but I reject that supposition, for the per-. son who had share with Brewster's lot in the div. of cattle, 1627, was not Mann, but More. See Davis's Morton, 382; and Bradford gives the Mayflower Richard More to be count. with the other heads, to Brewster, six in number, at the div. of lds. He had Nathaniel, b. 1646, and d. a. 1656; Thomas, 15 Aug. 1650; Richard, 1652; and Josiah, 1654. The last was prob. that soldier of wh. no more is kn. Of Nathaniel, Deane says he liv. in S. left no fam. gave est. 1680, to his brs. Thomas and Richard, yet refers to his Appx. II. in wh. no more is found. But he may have been short time of Boston. Thomas saw hard fighting and was badly wound. in the Rehoboth day, when Pierce was ambushed; but liv. to have four s. and three ds. of wh. descend. are yet seen. Richard had three s. and four ds. I can feel no doubt, that this Mann should be More, or Moore. See that name. SAMUEL, Dedham 1642. SAMUEL, Wrentham, only s. of William, had engag. to keep the sch. in Dedham one yr. for £20. "to be pd. in corn at the current price," and contin. sev. yrs. in that honora. employm. m. 13 by rec. or 19 May 1673, Esther, d. of Robert Ware of Dedham, wh. d. 3 Sept. 1734; and was freem. 1678; ord. 13 Apr. 1692, in the place former. part of D. where he had preach. many yrs. and d. 22 May 1719. His ch. by the Wrentham rec. were Mary, b. 7 Apr. 1674; Samuel, 8 Aug. 1675; Theodore, 8 Feb. 1681; Thomas, 24 Oct. 1682; Hannah, 12 June 1685; Beriah, 30 Mar. 1687; Pelatiah, 2 Apr. 1689; Margaret, 21 Dec. 1691; and Esther, 26 June 1696; beside wh. were Nathaniel, and William, b. aft. the sett. was brok. up by Philip's war, and bef. his return, i. e. Mar. 1676 and Aug. 1680. All these six s. and five ds. were m. Of this fam. most have writ. but a single n in the name. THOMAS, Rehoboth, had w. Rachel, wh. d. June 1676, and a ch. at the same time. He m. 9 Apr. 1678, Mary Wheaton, had Rachel, b. 15 Apr. 1679; Mary, 11 Jan. 1681; Bethia, 12 Mar. prob. 1683. WILLIAM, Cambridge 1634–52, came, it is said, from Kent, b. 1607, youngest of eleven ch. m. 1643, Mary Jarrad, or perhaps Garrard, had share in the Shawshin div. 1652, but possib. was of Providence 1641, as Farmer has it; yet he could not long have cont. there. He had by first w. Samuel, bef. ment. b. 6 July 1647, H. C. 1665; and m. 11 June 1657, sec. or third w. Alice Teel, and d. 7 Mar. 1662. In his will of 10 Dec. preced. nam. no ch. but Samuel. Six of this name had, in 1819, been gr. at Harv. and nine at other N. E. coll.

MANNERING, EDWARD, Scarborough 1663. JOSEPH, a passeng. in

the William and Francis from London, 1632, emb. in Mar. and reach. Boston 5 June, with Edward Winslow; but no connex. with him is kn. nor indeed is this name heard of for many yrs. except by judgm. of Court, 4 Mar. 1634, it was found that he had not paid £5. on acco. of wh. Joseph Twitchell had been charg. Several whom we know to have been on board· that ship could not have obt. leave from governm.

MANNING, GEORGE, Boston 1653, shoemaker, perhaps an orig. propr. 1640, of Sudbury, m. 15 July 1653, Mary Harraden; and ano. rec. tells that he m. 13 Mar. 1655, Hannah, wid. of .William Blanchard, d. of James Everill, had George, b. 24 Nov. 1655; Eliz. 19 Mar. 1657, d. young; Mary, 15 Dec. 1659, d. young; Eliz. again, 13 Oct. 1661; James, 6 Mar. 1663; Hannah, 20 Apr. 1665; Mary, again, 3 Nov. 1666; Sarah, 19 Mar. 1668; John, 11 Oct. 1671; and Joseph, 6 Nov. 1674. ‖ JOHN, Boston, merch. ar. co. 1640, by w. Abigail, wh. d. 25 June 1644, had John, b. 25 May 1643; and Mary, 3 June 1644; and by w. Ann, d. of Richard Parker, wh. join. our ch. 15 May 1647, had Ann, b. 12, bapt. 21 Mar. 1652 (tho. the same rec. in Geneal. Reg. IX. 250, by repetit. in ano. line on the same page, adds a day); and Ephraim, 10 Aug. 1655. Ann m. 1669, John Sandys. A JOHN, at Ipswich so early as 1634, I kn. no more of. But there the name was much diffus. and so, I believe, it was at Norwich, Eng. whence came many puritans to our country. Of ano. JOHN, in Maine, inv. of £115. was ret. 5 Oct. 1674. NICHOLAS, Ipswich, prob. s. of Richard, had command of a vessel at Salem 1677, in 1681 had w. Eliz. was in 1688 appoint. by Andros a Judge in the remotest E. part of his jurisdict. near Kennebec, and as one of his adher. was next yr. imprison. Willis, I. 187. RETURN, Boston, m. at Hingham, Dec. 1664, Sarah Hobart, prob. d. of Edmund the sec. of the same, had d. Mary rememb. in the will of gr.f. Hobart, but whence he came I find not. At Boston he had Sarah, b. 7 Apr. 1669; and Rebecca, 21 Sept. 1670, and, perhaps, rem. RICH-ARD, Ipswich, by w. Anstis had Nicholas, b. 23 June 1644; Richard, 22 June 1646; Anstis, 8 Jan. 1655; Margaret, 9 Oct. 1656; Jacob, 25 Dec. 1660, wh. was of Salem, and d. 24 May 1756; Thomas, 11 Feb. 1665; and Sarah, 28 Aug. 1667, wh. m. 8 Dec. 1686, John Williams of the same. Descend. are num. * SAMUEL, Billerica, s. of the sec. William, freem. 1670, was selectman 1680, rep. 1695 and 6, town clk. 6 yrs. d. 22 Feb. 1711, aged 66. THOMAS, Ipswich 1636, perhaps elder br. of Richard, d. a. 1668, aged 74. THOMAS, Swansey, m. 28 Oct. 1674, Rachel Bliss, perhaps d. of Jonathan. THOMAS, a soldier of Ipswich, perhaps s. of Thomas the first, or more prob. gr.s. k. with the "flower of Essex" under Lothrop, 18 Sept. 1675, at Bloody brook, Deerfield. WILLIAM, Cambridge 1634, freem. 13 May 1640, brot. from Eng. William, and prob. other ch. perhaps Timothy, wh. d. 8 Nov. 1653, was one.

His w. Susanna was bur. 16 Oct. 1650, but when he d. is not ascert. WILLIAM, Cambridge, s. of the preced. b. in Eng. freem. 10 May 1643, by w. Dorothy had Hannah, b. 21 June 1642; Samuel, 21 July 1644, bef. ment.; Sarah, 28 Jan. 1646 ; Abigail, 15 Jan. 1648, d. at 4 mos.; John, 31 Mar. 1650, wh. d. of smallpox, 25 Nov. 1678; and Mary. He was selectman 1667, and many yrs. aft. sent, 1670, to Eng. to induce Urian Oakes to come over to be presid. of the coll. says tradit. with more wildness than might have been expect. of Cambridge people, wh. kn. that vacancy did not occur by d. of Chauncy until 1672. The gr.stone that tells his d. 14 Mar. 1691, aged 76 yrs. may be truer, but I suspect some exagger. in that for his w. Dorothy, when it makes her 80 yrs. at the d. 26 July 1692. Sarah m. 11 Apr. 1671, Joseph Bull of Hartford; and Mary m. 21 Oct. 1674, Rev. William Adams of Dedham. In the coll. of N. E. and N. J. fourteen had been gr. 1834, of wh. ten were of Harv. From Ormsby, in Co. Norfk. came, in 1637, aged 17, Ann M. as serv. of Henry Dow, says the rec. of his declar. bef. embar. as found at Westminster Hall.

MANSFIELD, ANDREW, Lynn 1639, had been at Boston 1636, came from Exeter, in Devon, it is said, bring. s. Andrew, b. 1630; and, I sup̄ pose, w. Eliz. d. of Rev. William Walton, wh. d. 8 Sept. 1673, aged above 80 yrs. by wh. prob. he had other ch. as, perhaps, ea. of these foll. Joseph; John, wh. d. 16 Oct. 1671; Robert, wh. d. 16 Dec. 1666; Samuel; and Eliz. This last m. 10 June 1675, Joshua Witt; and he d. 1692, in 94th yr. The will of his w. of 20 Apr. 1667, pro. 26 Nov. 1673, is abstract. in Essex Inst. Hist. Coll. II. 125. * ANDREW, Lynn, s. of the preced. b. in Eng. was rep. 1680-3, Lewis says; by w. Bethia had Bethia, b. 7 Apr. 1658, d. at 14 yrs.; Mary, 7 Mar. 1660, d. next yr.; Lydia, 15 Aug. 1662 ; Deborah, 1 Jan. 1667 ; and Daniel, 9 June 1669. He had sec. w. 4 June 1673, Mary, wid. of John Neale, d. of Francis Lawes, wh. d. 27 June 1681 ; and he m. 10 Jan. 1682, Eliz. Conant. ANDREW, Lynn, freem. 1691, may have been s. of the preced. or of Robert. DANIEL, Lynn, s. of the sec. Andrew, was freem. 1691. JOHN, Boston, s. of Sir John, came in the Regard, 1634, sent out by charity, with his fam. as Winth. I. 150, tells. His wid. mo. d. that yr. in London, at the ho. of Robert Keayne, whose w. was a d. and Eliz. the w. of Rev. John Wilson was ano. but he seems to have done little here beside worrying his brs. Wilson and Keayne, in the will of the last, most curious details being relat. for wh. see Geneal. Reg. VI. 156. Yet K. gave something to the two ch. and their f. seems to have held on a long time, dying at Charlestown 1674. JOHN, Lancaster, s. of the preced. bec. a propr. in 1654, had 500 acres giv. by his Aunt Ann Keayne, as Rev. John Wilson of Medfield testif. 11 Feb. 1675. JOHN, Lynn, perhaps younger br. of the first Andrew, came in the Susan and

Ellen, from London, 1635, aged 34, freem. 1643, may be the one wh. d. 1671,⁻ above designa. as perhaps s. of Andrew. JOHN, Charlestown 1658. JOHN, Hingham, freem. 1684, in his will of 19 Feb. 1689, pro. 20 Aug. foll. names only w. Eliz. wh. was, perhaps, d. of Joseph Farnsworth of Dorchester, and two ch. Mary, and John, b. 15 Nov. 1656, wh. had m. Sarah Neal. JOHN, Windsor, m. 13 Dec. 1683, Sarah, d. of Samuel Phelps, had John, b. 1684, d. at 6 yrs.; Sarah, 1686; Samuel, 1687; Mary, 1689, and, perhaps, more. JOSEPH, Lynn, s. of the first Andrew, prob. b. in Eng. by w. Eliz. had Joseph, b. 20 Mar. 1661, and may have had other ch. earlier. She d. 25 Feb. 1662; and he was call. sen. as Felt notes from the rec. when his d. Deborah d. 14 Feb. 1678. JOSEPH, New Haven, s. of Richard, prob. b. in Eng. had Mary, b. 1658; Martha, 1660; and, perhaps, others; is in the list of freem. 1669, and propr. in 1685; in the Index of Trumbull, Col. Rec. II. is nam. incorrect, wh. is very seldom seen. JOSEPH, Lynn, s. of the first Joseph, m. 1 Apr. 1678, Eliz. d. of Isaac Williams of Salem, had Eliz. b. 6 Feb. 1679; tw. b. 25 Oct. 1680, d. soon; Joseph, 18 Aug. 1681; and Sarah, 22 Jan. 1684; freem. 1691. * MOSES, New Haven, s. of Richard, b. in Eng. was a very valua. man in town business 1673, lieut. and capt. in the Ind. war, rep. 1676 and 7, a propr. in 1685, had Samuel, H. C. 1690, wh. kept the gr. school at New Haven some yrs. bec. a merch. and d. 1701, perhaps bef. his f. PAUL, Salem, sign. the petitn. against imposts 1668. RICHARD, New Haven 1643, perhaps earlier, d. 10 Jan. 1655, leav. wid. Gilian, wh. m. Alexander Field, and ch. Moses, and Joseph, bef. ment. ROBERT, Lynn 1642, may have been s. of the first Andrew, or more prob. his br. b. in Eng. wh. d. 1666. SAMUEL, Lynn, perhaps s. of the first Andrew, m. 3 Mar. 1674, Sarah Barsham, had Andrew, b. 4 Jan. 1675; Sarah, 6 Nov. 1676; and Bethia, 13 Mar. 1679; and he d. 10 Apr. foll. * SAMUEL, Springfield, rep. 1680, 3, and 4. THOMAS, Lynn 1642. One of this fam. name came in the Regard 1634, who was from Exeter, Eng. and was not found to be a desirab. inhab. as ment. by Winth. I. 150. In 1834 four had been gr. at Harv. six at Yale, and one at Amherst coll.

MANSIR, MANSER, or MANSUR, ROBERT, Charlestown 1678, a householder, of wh. I kn. no more.

MANSON, may or may not be found in N. E. bef. 1692, but as yet he has been sought in vain. Yet in the Blessing, from London, 1635, there was brot. a Thomasin M. aged 14, wh. may have foll. her f.

MANTON, EDWARD, Providence, s. of Shadrach of the same, m. 9 Dec. 1680, Eliz. d. of John Thornton, freem. 1655, sw. alleg. May 1682. He was the only s. of the three, that had a s. to perpet. the name, and of his three s. two d. infs. while his s. Daniel, at the age of 16, it is said, was the only male on this side of the sea with this surname. He left eight s. and three ds. all of wh. m. and had s. and ds. SHADRACH, Newport 1668, sw. alleg. 1 June of that yr. had, beside two other s. Edward; and Ann, wh. m. 18 Sept. 1682, John Keese.

MANWARING, ‖ NATHANIEL, is by Whitman call. of ar. co. 1644, but his resid. is unkn. OLIVER, New London 1664, in the tax list of 1666 his name is spell. Mannering, but the Col. Rec. of 1669, when he was offer. for freem. recovers his right; m. Eliz. d. of Richard Raymond, but Miss Caulkins in ano. place calls her Hannah, had Hannah, Eliz. Prudence, and Love, all bapt. 1671; Richard, 13 July 1673; Judith, Apr. 1676; Oliver, 2 Feb. 1679; Bathsheba, 9 May 1680; Ann, 18 June 1682; and Mercy, whose bapt. is not found, nor the b. of any one; but of the five preced. the last we may be content with dates of bapt. He d. 3 Nov. 1723, aged 90, when all those ch. were liv. and the eight ds. m. tho. Miss Caulkins gives not the names of any one exc. Love, wh. m. John Richards; and it is said Eliz. m. 7 July 1686, Peter Harris. PHILIP, New Hampshire 1683.

MAPES, JOHN, aged 21, came from Ipswich in the Francis, 1634; but this name is so very rare in our country, that unless he d. in few yrs. we can hardly mistake in suppos. he was of L. I. where in 1662 goodman Mapes of Southold, was allow. to be made freem. of Conn. Perhaps he had first been of Salem, at least Dickinson, who was at the same time with him at Southold, had liv. at Salem some yrs. JOSEPH, Setauket, L. I. 1655, says Thompson's Hist. He may be the same or THOMAS, wh. is by Wood, in his Hist. placed at Southold 1640.

MARBLE, JOHN, Boston, by w. Judith, had John, b. 10 Nov. 1646. JOSEPH, Andover, m. 30 May 1671, Mary Faulkner, prob. d. of Edmund, had Deborah, wh. d. 30 June 1673; and prob. other ch. JOSEPH, Andover, perhaps s. of the preced. m. 23 Apr. 1695, Hannah Barnard, unless this m. were by the bef. ment. of a sec. w. NICHOLAS, Gloucester 1658. SAMUEL, Andover 1660, m. 26 Nov. 1675, Rebecca Andrews, prob. for sec. w. WILLIAM, Charlestown, or Malden, by w. Eliz. had Mary, b. 10 Apr. 1642; but perhaps he rem. for Frothingham, in his list of 1658, does not include the name, nor do we see it among ch. memb. tho. he was freem. 1654.

MARCH, GEORGE, Newbury, brot. by Stephen Kent, in the Confidence, as a serv. from Southampton, 1638, aged 16, and he may be thot. to be that freem. 1666, at Boston, whose name in Geneal. Reg. is print. Marg, wh. ano. eye, almost as practised as Paige's, made Marcy, for thus Farmer's correspondent instruct. him. GEORGE, Newbury, s. of Hugh, freem. 1683, m. 12 June 1672, Mary, d. of John Folsom of Exeter had George, b. 6 Oct. 1674; John, 18 Aug. 1676; Mary, 28 Aug. 1678,

d. bef. 3 mos.; Stephen, 19 Sept. 1679, d. bef. 5 yrs.; James, 19 June 1681; Israel, 4 Apr. 1683; Sarah, 6 July 1685; Stephen, again, 16 Nov. 1687; Henry, 31 July 1794, perhaps; George, again, 24 Apr. 1698; and Jane, 8 May 1699; beside Hugh, prob. the eldest, a serg. k. by the Ind. at Pemaquid, 9 Sept. 1695, as Judge Sewall tells in Coffin's Newbury, 161. His wid. m. 28 June 1707, Joseph Herrick, as his third w. Hugh, Newbury, br. prob. of the first George, came in the Confidence, 1638, from Southampton, aged 20, as serv. of Stephen Kent, a carpenter, by w. Judith, wh. d. 14 Dec. 1675, had George, b. 1646; Judith, 3 Jan. 1653; Hugh, 3 Nov. 1656; John, 10 June 1658; and James, 11 Jan. 1664. He m. 29 May 1676, Dorcas Blackleach, wh. d. 22 Nov. 1683; and he m. third w. 3 Dec. 1685, Sarah Healy, and d. 12 Dec. 1693, aged 73; and his wid. d. 25 Oct. 1699. Hugh, Newbury, s. of the preced., m. 29 Mar. 1683, Sarah, d. of Caleb Moody, had Sarah, b. 27 Apr. 1684; Henry, 22 Sept. 1686; Samuel, 2 Mar. 1689; Eliz. 27 Oct. 1691; Hannah, 4 Sept. 1694, d. next mo.; Daniel, 30 Oct. 1695; Mehitable, 3 Jan. 1703; and Trueman, 14 Nov. 1705. He was a capt. James, Newbury, br. of the preced. was a lieut. by w. Mary had Benjamin, b. 23 Nov. 1690; Nathaniel, 2 Sept. 1693; and Tabitha, 20 June 1696; rem. prob. to Salisbury, there had Judith, 13 May 1698. John, Charlestown 1638, prob. had w. Rebecca, and Edward, his s. d. 4 Oct. 1638; as did John, ano. ch. 2 May 1641; on 15 May of next yr. he join. to the ch. and on 18th was adm. freem. perhaps had more ch. was there a householder 1658. John, Newbury, s. of the first Hugh, m. 1 Mar. 1679, Jemima True, had Judith, b. 21 Mar. 1682; Mary, 2 Apr. 1684; Joseph, 8 May 1687; John, 26 Sept. 1690; Abigail, 4 Sept. 1693; Hugh, 8 Jan. 1696; and Eliz. 6 Sept. 1698; was a sturdy soldier, capt. in Phips's diastrous exped. against Quebec 1690, and more happy, as a major, in defence of Falmouth 1703. See Penhallow, and Willis, II. 8. Two of this name had, in 1834, been gr. at Harv. and four at other N. E. coll.

MARCHANT. See Merchant.

MARDEN, RICHARD, New Haven 1646, took o. of fidel. next yr. and soon rem.

MARGERUM, or MARGORUM, RICHARD, Salem 1655, was not, perhaps, a perman. inhab. See Essex Inst. Hist. Coll. I. 67.

MARGESON, EDMUND, a single man, came in the Mayflower, as one of the passeng. to Plymouth, Dec. 1620, d. early in 1621.

MARGIN, RICHARD, Dover 1659, m. at Andover, 21 May 1660, Rebecca, prob. d. of William Holdridge of Haverhill.

MARINER, JAMES, Falmouth 1686, by Willis, I. 212, was suppos. to have come from Dover, prob. had ch. at F. wh. in his age he left there, and was of Boston 1731, aged 80.

MARION, BENJAMIN, one of Gallup's comp. in the sad expedit. against Quebec, 1690. ISAAC, Boston, s. of the first John of the same, by w. Phebe had Mary, b. 4 Dec. 1682. JOHN, Watertown, cordwainer, m. Sarah, d. of John Eddy, was freem. 1652, had Mary, bur. 24 Jan. 1642, aged 2 mos.; John, b. 12 May 1643; Isaac, 20 Jan. 1653*; Samuel, 1655; rem. to Boston, was selectman 1693, and d. 7 Jan. 1705, aged 86. || JOHN, Cambridge, prob. s. of the preced. rem. to Boston, m. Ann, d. of John Harrison, had John, b. 30 May 1683, d. soon; John, again, 17 Aug. 1684, d. young; Joseph, 10 Aug. 1686; John, 29 Aug. 1687, d. soon; and John, again, 28 June 1689; freem. 1679; was deac. selectman 1698, and of ar. co. 1691. SAMUEL, Boston, s. of the first John, but of him I learn from Sewall in his Diary, of the sad manner of d. of his w. Hannah 4 Apr. 1688; and from the rec. that by her he had John, b. 25. Dec. 1681; Hannah, 23 June 1685; and Mary, 18 June 1687. He m. a sec. w. Mary, and had Samuel, 8 June 1689; Catharine, 15 Sept. 1690; Edward, 2 Dec. 1692; Isaac, 8 Mar. 1694; Eliz. 21 Nov. 1695; Joseph, 18 Dec. 1698, prob. d. young; Joanna, 10 May 1701; John, 5 Apr. 1703; and Joseph, again, 22 July 1705. It is sometimes spell. Merion.

MARK, or MARKS, JOHN or other name begin. with J. of Middleborough, d. July 1675, of a wound by the Ind. Hubbard's Ind. Wars, 133. PATRICK, Charlestown 1677, by w. Sarah had Mary, bapt. 20 Jan. 1689, aged 18, the mo. hav. been adm. to that rite 10 Apr. 1687, aged a. 50. ROGER, Andover, a soldier of maj. Appleton's comp. wound. by the Ind. at the gr. fight 19 Dec. 1675 (Hubbard, 84), lost his w. Sarah 22 Dec. 1690, by smallpox.

MARKHAM, DANIEL, Cambridge, m. 3 Nov. 1669, Eliz. d. of Francis Whitmore, had James, b. 16 Mar. 1675, perhaps freem. 1674, rem. to Middletown and m. Patience, d. of William Harris. JAMES, Cambridge, s. of Daniel, m. 14 Oct. 1700 (but Parsons, in Geneal. Reg. XIV. 67, says 1699), Eliz. youngest ch. of the first William Locke, rem. to Middletown, had James, b. 22 Nov. 1701; Eliz. 18 Jan. 1704; William, 28 Jan. 1706; John, 28 Dec. 1708; Mary, 14 May 1710; Abigail, 22 July 1712; Martha, 18 June 1714; Hannah, 6 Sept. 1716; and Nathaniel, 27 Feb. 1719; and d. 8 June 1731. His wid. d. 25 (but Parsons, appeal. to the testimo. of the gr.stone, says 17) Sept. 1753. JEREMIAH, Dover 1659. NATHANIEL, Watertown, freem. 1682, was, perhaps, f. of that Nathaniel of Charlestown, whose d. 26 Sept. 1673, is noted by Farmer. WILLIAM, Hadley, of the first sett. but bef. that had William, wh. was k. by the Ind. with capt. Beers at Northfield, 4 Sept. 1675, and ds. Priscilla and Lydia; at H. had John, b. 1661, d. at less than 3 yrs.; and Mercy, 1663, d. young; was freem. 1661, in 1681, 15 Oct. sw. he was in 60th yr. and d. a. 1689. Priscilla m. a. 1675,

Thomas Hale; Lydia m. 1682, Timothy Eastman, and her descend. nam. Smith, now enjoy the ancient homestead of Markham, wh. had much est. from Nathaniel Ward of H. wh. he call. uncle. Of this name the writing is sometimes Marcum and Marcam.

MARLO, MORLEY, or MARLOW, EDWARD, Hartford 1667. THOMAS, Westfield, m. 8 Dec. 1681, Martha, d. of the first Abel Wright, had Martha, b. 7 Sept. 1682 ; Thomas, 14 Sept. 1684 ; Mary, 30 Oct. 1686 ; Abel, 18 Jan. 1689; Eliz. 23 June 1691 ; Thankful, 28 Feb. 1693 ; Mary, again, 14 Nov. 1695 ; John, 1 May 1699 ; and Ebenezer, 22 Mar. 1701. The fam. may be still at W. but the name long since bec. Morley. WILLIAM, a soldier under capt. Turner in Mar. 1676.

MARRETT, AMOS, Cambridge, s. of John of the same, m. 12 Nov. 1681, Bethia Longhorn, wh. d. 20 Nov. 1730, in. 70th yr. had Amos, and, perhaps, others ; and he m. 22 Nov. 1732, Ruth Dunster, prob. a wid. d. 17 Nov. 1739. He was lieut. and his s. Amos m. 21 Sept. 1732, Mary Dunster, perhaps d. of her, who a few wks. aft. m. the f. JOHN, Cambridge, s. of Thomas of the same, was brot. by his f. from Eng. when 5 yrs. old, m. 20 June 1654, Abigail Richardson, had Thomas, b. 15 Dec. 1655 : John, 13 Dec. 1656, wh. d. 7 Mar. 1658 ; Amos, 25 Feb. 1658 ; Susanna, 19 Jan. 1660 ; John, again, 29 Jan. 1662, d. late next yr. ; John, again, bapt. 6 June 1664; and Abigail, 19 Aug. 1666, as by Mitchell's Reg. compar. with Harris, is made out ; beside Hannah, 17 Aug. 1668, d. soon; Edward, 2 Aug. 1670; Mary, 7 Mar. 1672 ; and Lydia, 22 Feb. 1674; was freem. 1665, own. est. at Watertown, as early as 1642. Mary m. 10 Dec. 1702, Joseph Hovey, wh. d. at Cambridge, giv. her by will of 28 June 1735, all his prop. and bec. sec. w. 27 Jan. 1737, of Nathaniel Parker of Newton ; and Abigail m. 27 Apr. 1687, Timothy Rice. NICHOLS, or NICHOLAS, Salem 1636, was of Marblehead 1648, says Coffin, and b. 1613. THOMAS, Cambridge 1635, freem. 3 Mar. 1636, brot. with him from Eng. s. John, bef. ment. ; Susanna ; Thomas ; and Abigail ; beside w. Susanna ; and had, also, Hannah, wh. may have been b. at Cambridge, and d. unm. 9 Dec. 1668 ; and he d. 3 June 1664, aged 75. His will of 15 Oct. preced. ment. his aged w. four liv. ch. (being all, exc. Susanna, wh. had m. George Barstow, and d. not long aft. him) beside ch. of George Barstow, dec. other gr.ch. Lydia, Amos, John, and Jeremiah Fisher ; also Thomas, Amos, Susanna, and John Marrett, wh. all appear to me ch. of John. Abigail had m. 17 Nov. 1641, Daniel Fisher of Dedham. The wid. d. 23 Feb. 1665. His name in Col. Rec. is Marryott ; but in the town rec. slightly chang. at any time from this adopt. here, wh. is the uniform spell. of the ch. rec. THOMAS, New London 1666, may have been s. of the preced.

MARRIOTT, JOHN, Marblehead 1674.

MARSH, * ALEXANDER, Braintree, was freem. 1654, m. 19 Dec. 1655, I judge, Mary, d. of Gregory Belcher, was rep. under new chart. 1692; d. 7 Mar. 1698, aged a. 70 says gr.stone. His will of 19 Mar. 1697, pro. 31 Mar. 1698, ment. w. Bathsheba, s. John, ds. Rachel, Phebe, Ann, w. of Samuel French, beside gr.d. Mary French, s.-in-law Dependence French, and Samuel Bass. His s. John was then a minor, and f. I believe, of John, H. C. 1726. His wid. d. 8 Jan. 1723, aged a. 82, says the gr.stone at Dorchester. * DANIEL, Hadley, s. of John of the same, m. 1676, Hannah, wid. of Samuel Crow, d. of William Lewis of Farmington; was freem. 1690, rep. under the new chart. in 1692, and oft. aft. d. 1725, aged 72. He had ch. but their respective names and dates are not given to me, other than of Joseph, H. C. 1705, wh. was min. of Braintree, and d. 8 Mar. 1726, and had Joseph, H. C. 1728, yet I find that Elisha, H. C. 1738, first min. of Westminster, and Perez, H. C. 1748, a physician of Dalton, were also his gr.ch. EPHRAIM, Hingham, s. of Thomas, m. Jan. 1682, Eliz. Lincoln. EZEKIEL, Salem, s. of John of the same, sign. petitn. against imposts 1668. GEORGE, Hingham 1635, freem. 3 Mar. 1636, d. 2 July 1647, w. Eliz. surv. His will, made the same day, provides for her, s. Thomas and Onesiphorus, ds. Eliz. Turner, and Mary Page. Rev. John, of Wethersfield, H. C. 1761, S. T. D. was a descend. JOHN, Charlestown 1638, d. 1 Jan. 1666, in his will made that day, names w. Ann, and her gr.ch. Sarah Bicknor, s. Theophilus, and his s. John, d. Frances Buck, and her childr. JOHN, Salem, had gr. of ld. 1637, but tho. I find neither his nor his wife's name in Felt's valua. list of early ch. memb. yet I doubt not that he came in the Mary and John, 1634; and at S. his ch. bapt. were Zechary, 30 Apr. 1637; John, 9 May 1639; Ruth, 5 May 1641; Eliz. 13 Sept. 1646; Ezekiel, 29 Oct. 1648; Bethia, 1 Sept. 1650; Samuel, 2 Oct. 1652; Susanna, 7 May 1654; Mary, 14 Sept. 1656; Jacob, 10 Apr. 1659; and a d. 12 June 1664, whose name is not found. His will, of 20 Mar. 1674, pro. 26 Nov. foll. names w. Susanna, s. Zechary, Samuel, Jacob, Ezekiel, Benjamin, and d. Bethia. JOHN, Hartford 1636, m. Ann, d. of Gov. John Webster, with him rem. 1659 or 60 to Hadley; but bef. rem. had Joseph, bapt. 24 Jan. 1647, d. soon; Joseph, again, 15 July 1649; John, Samuel, Jonathan, Daniel, Hannah, and Grace. His w. d. 9 June 1662, and he m. 1664, Hepzibah, wid. of Richard Lyman of Northampton, d. of Thomas Ford, and rem. to N. and had Lydia. He d. 1688. Grace m. 16 Jan. 1672, Timothy Baker. By will, 1676, of his br. Joseph at Braintree, Co. Essex, est. was giv. to these ch. and obt. by suit at law, so that I presume he came from that part of Eng. JOHN, Hartford, eldest s. of the preced. m. 1666, Sarah,

d. of Richard Lyman, and of the w. of his f. freem. 1670, d. 1727.
JOHN, Boston 1672. JONATHAN, Milford 1649, rem. to Norwalk, one
of the first sett. 1655, but not nam. aft. 1659, nor do we kn. whether he
had w. or ch. * JONATHAN, Hadley, br. of Daniel, m. 1676, Dorcas,
wid. of Azariah Dickinson, had Jonathan, H. C. 1705, wh. bec. min. of
Windsor; was freem. 1690, rep. 1701, d. 1730, aged 80. ONESI-
PHORUS, Hingham, s. of George, m. 6 Jan. 1655, Hannah Cutter, had
ONESIPHORUS, b. 5 Nov. foll.; Hannah, 28 June 1657 ; was freem.
1672, and of Haverhill, I think, in 1690, at least of the same name one
had there so call. his s. SAMUEL, New Haven, had Mary, b. 1648;
Samuel, 12 Feb. 1650; Comfort, 22 Aug. 1652 ; all bapt. 20 Mar.
1653 ; Hannah, b. 22 July 1655, bapt. next mo. but not on the day
ment. in the ch. rec.; Eliz. 27 Dec. 1657, bapt. Feb. foll. on a day not
truly giv. in ch. rec. ; John, 2 May 1661, bapt. next Sunday, prob. for the
careless ch. rec. gives a false date ; a ch. without a name, 1 Apr. 1663 ; and
prob. rem. * SAMUEL, Hatfield, br. of Daniel, m. 1667, Mary Allison ;
was freem. 1690, rep. 1705 and 6, d. 1728, leav. sev. ch. THOMAS,
Hingham, s. of George, b. in Eng. m. 22 Mar. 1649, Sarah, d. of John
Beal, and d. 2 Aug. 1658, leav. four ch. nam. in his will, Thomas;
Sarah; Ephraim, b. 11 July 1655 ; and Mary, 22 Feb. 1658. His s.
John, b. 20 Feb. 1654, prob. d. young. His wid. m. 1 Sept. 1662,
Edmund Sheffield of Braintree. ZECHARY, Salem, s. of John of the
same, was freem. 1680. Ten of this name had, in 1834, been gr. at
Harv. eleven at Yale, eleven at Dart. and six at other N. E. coll.

MARSHALL, BENJAMIN, Ipswich, s. of the first Edmund, m. 1677,
Prudence Woodward, had Edmund, Ezekiel, John, and four ds. d. 1716.
CHRISTOPHER, Boston 1634, single man on join. the ch. late in Aug. of
that yr. freem. 6 May 1635, was of Cotton's party in the great schism of
1637, but not disarm. as a dangerous heretic, so that he was, perhaps,
a student of divinity, and certain. m. here, for his d. Ann was bapt. 13
May 1638, at our ch. adhered to Wheelwright at Exeter, and, with him,
had dism. Jan. 1639, from our ch. prob. went home in 1640 or 1, and
may be that man wh. Calamy says was partly educ. by our Rev. John
Cotton, min. of Woodkirk, in Yorksh. and d. Feb. 1673, aged 59.
DAVID, Windsor, s. of capt. Samuel, m. 9 Dec. 1686, Abigail Phelps, d.
prob. of Samuel, had Abigail, b. 9 Jan. 1687; Hannah, 8 Dec. 1689;
and David, 14 Apr. 1692, wh. d. at 33 yrs. EDMUND, Salem 1636, had
there perhaps by w. Milicent, bapt. Naomi, 24 Jan. 1637 ; Ann, 15
Apr. 1638; Ruth, 3 May 1640; Sarah, 29 May 1642 ; Edmund, 16
June 1644 ; and Benjamin, 27 Sept. 1646 ; was freem. 17 May 1637,
and rem. either to Ipswich or Newbury. EDMUND, Newbury, a shipwright, perhaps s. of the preced. had Edmund, b. 5 Oct. 1677 ; and

John, 7 July 1682; but may have had older ch. bef. liv. at N. and possib. rem. to Suffield, there had Martha, 1685; and Eliz. 1689; for certain it is, that one of the name there liv. and d. by his will, made in 1721, tho. not pro. until a long time aft. ment. these ch. with others, John, Benjamin, Mary, and Abigail. EDWARD, Warwick, by w. Mary had Edward, b. 10 Apr. 1658; John, 12 May 1660; Thomas, 1 Mar. 1663; Mary, 1 July 1666; Charles, 28 June 1668; and Martha, 16 Mar. 1670. EDWARD, Reading, by Mr. Eaton numb. among early sett. may be the same who was freem. at Malden, 1690. ELIAKIM, Boston, s. of Thomas the shoemaker, rem. to Stratford, and in 1665, sold his est. in B. but came back in few yrs. was of Lothrop's comp. in Philip's war, and k. at Bloody brook, 18 Sept. 1675. ELIAKIM, Windsor, s. of capt. Samuel, m. 23 Aug. 1704, Sarah Liet of Guilford, if that be correct name in Stiles, 693, had Dorothy, b. 1 Oct. 1705; Sarah, 27 June 1709, prob. d. soon; Sarah, again, 29 Jan. 1711; Mary, 14 Mar. 1715; and Eliakim, 15 July 1720, d. in few days. FRANCIS, Boston, master mariner, came in the Christian from London, 1635, aged 30, was liv. in 1659. JAMES, Windsor 1640, was from Exeter, in Devon, did not long cont. and, per- haps, was the man, expect. in vain, to sett. at New Haven 1643, where his est. was val. at £1,000, his fam. of five heads, and his lot, transf. to Richard Mansfield. He sold his W. est. and may be that "rich merch." referred to in Winth. I. 150. JOEL, Hartford 1682, perhaps s. of Thomas of the same. JOHN, Duxbury, had been of Leahorn, in Co. Kent, s. and heir of Sybil Marshall, by wh. descript. in Nov. 1631, he enters into contr. of m. with Mary, eldest d. of Rev. Ralph Partridge of Sutton, near Dover, to wh. and his br. Jervase P. citizen and cord- wainer of Lond. as trust. he made convey. of est. in Co. Kent, as jointure of his w. if she outliv. him. This instr. with a bond in the penal sum of £200 to secure, &c. are rec. in Vol. III. of our Suff'k. Reg. of Deeds; but it is curious, that these docum. were not rec. here bef. Jan. 1661, some yrs. aft. d. of the Rev. Ralph, wh. in his will notices Robert and John, s. of his d. Mary M. JOHN, Providence 1639. JOHN, Boston, came, perhaps, in the Hopewell, capt. Babb, from London 1635, aged 14, by w. Sarah had John, b. 10 Dec. 1645; Thom- as, 11 May 1656; Benjamin, 15 Feb. 1661; and Christopher, 18 Aug. 1664. JOHN, Billerica 1659, freem. 1683, had John, wh. was prob. the freem. at Billerica 1690. JOHN, Boston, a mariner from Barnstaple, Co. Devon, d. 1662; and his br. Thomas of Alwington, in Devon, took admin. of his est. in Eng. and in 1670, claim. and obt. the assets from John Sweete, who was admor. here. JOHN, Boston, by w. Ruth had Mary, b. 2 Jan. 1661; John, 2 Oct. 1664 (who was a mason of Brain- tree, kept that valua. Diary, formerly quoted oft. by Dr. T. M. Harris,

who procured it for the Hist. Soc. as Fairfield's); Thomas, 6 Feb.
1666; Samuel, 14 July 1669; and Joseph, 14 Apr. 1672; was prob.
the freem. of 1671, and d. Nov. 1672. His wid. Ruth m. Daniel Fairfield. JOHN, Braintree, s. of the preced. m. 12 May 1690, Mary, wid.
of Jonathan Mills, d. of Edmund Sheffield, had Deborah. In the Diary,
sub. 25 Dec. 1700, John writes "br. Thomas came to Boston to visit,
aft. being abs. 17 yrs. and ½, tarried three wks. and ret." Whence he
came for this visit to his nat. town, must be inq. but can hard. be answ.
JOHN, Greenwich 1672. JOHN, Boston 1681–4, had an office under
the Col. governm. with salary of £13. a yr. may have been freem. 1690,
and d. 1694. JOHN, Windsor, youngest s. of capt. Samuel, by w. Abigail, wh. d. 29 Feb. 1698, had Abigail, b. 10 Dec. 1693, wh. d. in few
wks.; and Hannah, 16 Apr. 1695. NOAH, Northampton, d. 15 Dec.
1691. PETER, Newbury, with prefix of respect, by w. Abigail had
Thomas, b. 1 July 1689; and Ruth, 31 Dec. 1690; perhaps rem. to
Boston. RICHARD, Taunton, m. 11 Feb. 1676, Esther Bell. ROBERT,
Salem 1637, perhaps soon rem. to New Hampsh. as one of the name d.
there in 1663. ROBERT, Plymouth, s. of John, gr.s. of Rev. Ralph
Partridge, m. 1659, Mary, d. of John Barnes, had John; Robert, b. 15
Aug. 1663; and, perhaps, more. ROBERT, Boston 1668, merch. may
be the same as the preced. or not. SAMUEL, Windsor, s. of Thomas the
shoemaker of Boston, b. in Eng. was a tanner, by Stiles, in Hist. 692, is
made to own lot a dozen yrs. too early, and rep. in 1637, magistr. in
1638, when he never gain. either of those honors. Thomas was mistak.
for this Samuel, wh. m. 6 May 1652, Mary, only ch. of David Wilton,
not Wilson, as Geneal. Reg. V. 229 prints the name, had Samuel, b. 27
May 1653; Lydia, 13 Feb. 1656; Thomas, 23 Apr. 1659, d. soon;
David, 24 July 1661; Thomas, again, 18 Feb. 1664; Mary, 8 May
1667, d. at nine yrs.; Eliakim, 10 July 1669; John, 10 Apr. 1672;
and Eliz. 27 Sept. 1674. He was freem. 1654, and in the war against
Philip had short but most honor. serv. On 30 Nov. he was made a
capt. in place of Benjamin Newbury, who was disabled, for the project.
winter campaign, and on 19 Dec. 1675, in the great swamp fight, the
hardest ever kn. in N. E. he was k. with many of the men under him.
His wid. d. 25 Aug. 1683. Lydia m. 24 Sept. 1676, Joseph Hawley of
Northampton, where the oldest s. liv. while the others cont. at W.
SAMUEL, Barnstable, by w. Sarah had Sarah, wh. d. 2 Aug. 1690, and f.
and mo. had d. the mo. preced. SAMUEL, Charlestown, freem. 1690,
says the rec. but Budington has not giv. his name among ch. memb.
SAMUEL, Northampton, eldest s. of the brave capt. Samuel, m. 1675,
Rebecca, d. of capt. Benjamin Newbury of Windsor, had Mary, b. 1676,
d. soon; Samuel, 1679; Abigail, 1682; Sarah, 1685; Preserved, 1691;

Lydia; and Mercy; was freem. 1690. SAMUEL, Boston 1681, had w. Ruth, freem. 1691. *THOMAS, Dorchester 1634, freem. 6 May 1635, rem. it is thot. to Windsor; was rep. in Mar. and Apr. 1638; but no more is kn. with certainty. In Stiles, Hist. 698, he is said to m. 2 Mar. 1637, Mary Drake, wh. may have been d. of the first John; and we might suppose, from the same line, the same man m. 10 May 1660, Bethia Parsons, but the darkness is palpable, upon the same page, where he teach. that Thomas Maskell m. that day that same woman; and great distrust springs up, when we see him, p. 735, give the same woman, the same day, to Thomas Haskell. *THOMAS, Boston, shoemaker, or ferryman, or both, call. widower on adm. to the ch. 31 Aug. 1634; freem. 4 Mar. 1635, had brot. from Eng. prob. s. Thomas and Samuel, ds. Sarah and Frances; and here by sec. w. Alice had Eliakim, b. 1 Mar. 1637, yet not bapt. until 15 Apr. 1638, no doubt on acco. of the antinom. quarrel in the ch. for acting with the major part of wh. in support of Wheelwright, he was requir. in Nov. 1637 to surrender his arms; but like most of the rest, thus abused, regain. high esteem, was selectman 1647–58, deac. and rep. 1650, and d. perhaps 1665. Frances m. 16 July 1652, Joseph Howe; and Sarah m. James Penniman. Great indulgence must be granted to investigat. a. this name, for ano. THOMAS, Boston 1643, a tailor, adm. of the ch. 17 Feb. 1644, had Thomas, bapt. 7 Jan. 1644, 5 days old; freem. in May of same yr. prob. and in June foll. was excom. I think he went to New Haven, aft. recov. in 1646, the favor of his former fellow-worshippers. *‖ THOMAS, Reading, came, prob. in the James from London 1635, aged 22, had Hannah, b. 7 June 1640; Samuel, 1 Sept. 1643, d. in one wk.; Abigail; Sarah, d. young; Thomas and Rebecca, tw. 20 Feb. 1648; Eliz.; Sarah, again, 14 Feb. 1655; was freem. 1653, a lieut. and aft. very long deliberat. by me, is thot. to be that man of Lynn, always call. capt. who there had Joanna, 14 Sept. 1657; John, 14 Feb. 1660; Ruth, 14 Aug. 1662; and Mary, 25 May 1665; was of ar. co. 1640, and, perhaps, freem. 4 June 1641; certain. rep. 1659, 60, 3, 4, 7, and 8; d. 23 Dec. 1689; and his wid. Rebecca d. Aug. 1693. Hannah m. at Lynn, 17 June 1659, John Lewis; Sarah m. 15 July 1674, Ebenezer Stocker; and Mary m. 7 Apr. 1685, Edward Baker. Lewis seems to me, to have confus. f. and s. and to have misled Farmer. See p. 92 of Lewis, Ed. 2d. But for what John Dunton, in Life and Errors, says of this capt. hav. been one of Cromwell's soldiers, I am compell. to suspect, that the author mistook his jolly host, or that the veteran designedly impos. on him. THOMAS, Salem 1657. THOMAS, Middletown 1669, then offered as freem. may have had Thomas, Joel, and Mary, wh. m. 27 July 1665, John Catlin, but it is not certain. THOMAS, d. at Northampton,

3 June 1663, but we are sure he was only a casual visitor. Thomas, Andover, ought to have more told of him than is found in Farmer, that he d. Jan. 1708, almost 100 yrs. old, and that Joanna d. there in May foll. aged a. 100. Perhaps it was his d. Mary wh. m. 6 July 1659, Robert Russell. Thomas, Charlestown 1684, who gains this place, as does he of Salem 1657, on authority of Barry. Thomas, Hartford, had sis. Mary, wh. m. John Catlin, but who was their f. is not ascert. He had Mary, b. 10 May 1670; John, 24 Feb. 1672; William, 21 Apr. 1674; Thomas, 3 Oct. 1676; Eliz. 23 Oct. 1678; Sarah, 27 Mar. 1681; and Benjamin, 22 Feb. 1684; and d. 1692. His s. Thomas, a mariner, m. aft. the date of his will, 15 Feb. 1697, Mary Chantrel of Boston, spinster, and she had it pro. 19 Sept. 1700, as his wid. in wh. he gave memo. to his sis. Eliz. spinster, and bro. Benjamin, and uncle John Catlin, all of Hartford, as he also styles hims. but all resid. to his beloved fr. M. C. Thomas, Windsor, s. of capt. Samuel, m. 3 Mar. 1686, Mary Drake, d. prob. of John of the same, had Thomas, b. 14 Jan. 1687, d. young; Mary, 21 Feb. 1689; Samuel, 23 July 1691; Thomas, 6 Feb. 1694; Rachel, 12 Apr. 1696; Catharine, 11 Apr. 1699; John, 3 Apr. 1701; Noah, 24 Apr. 1703, d. young; Daniel, 1705; Benjamin, 8 Aug. 1707, d. in few mos.; and Eunice, 3 May 1709. William, Salem 1638, had then, says Felt, gr. of ld. He prob. came in the Abigail, 1635, from London, aged 40. William, Charlestown, m. 8 Apr. 1666, Mary. d. of William Hilton, wh. d. 15 July 1678, aged a. 33, had William, and Mary, bapt. 4 Feb. 1672, she hav. join. the ch. a few days bef.; John, 20 Apr. 1673; Edward, 16 Apr. 1676; and by sec. w. Lydia had Samuel, bapt. 31 Aug. 1684; Hannah, 25 Sept. 1687. Twelve of this name had, in 1834, been gr. at N. E. coll. half of them at Harv. three at Yale, and two at Dart.

Marshcroft, Mashcroft, or Mascroft, Daniel, Roxbury, m. 23 May 1665, Mary, d. of John Gorton, prob. liv. in some other place, there had Eliz. until d. of the f. of his w. aft. wh. I find in the rec. of R. Hannah, b. 6 May 1677; but perhaps he rem. again to some neighb. town, and had Samuel, brot. to bapt. with Mehitable, 3 Feb. 1684, when we see in rec. of b. only that of the d. 28 Feb. bef. He had also Mary, whose b. is not kn. but she d. 8 June 1688; and he d. perhaps bef. mid. age, and his wid. d. 30 June 1703. Eliz. m. at R. 18 Mar. 1700, Samuel Spencer; and Hannah m. 15 July 1701, Samuel Frost. But both the hs. were, I suppose, of ano. town.

Marshfield, Josiah, Springfield, s. of Samuel, m. 22 Sept. 1686, Rachel, d. of Jonathan Gilbert, had six ch. b. at S. was freem. 1690, and aft. 1700 rem. to Hartford, there had a s. b. 17 Mar. 1704. * Samuel, Springfield, s. of Thomas, b. in Eng. m. 18 Feb. 1652, Esther, d.

of deac. Samuel Wright, had Mercy, b. 10 June 1653 ; Thomas, 6 Sept. 1654, both of wh. d. young; Sarah, 2 Feb. 1656; Samuel, 1659, d. young; Hannah, 1661 ; and Abilene, 2 Apr. 1664. His w. d. next day, and he m. 28 Dec. 1664, Catharine, wid. of Thomas Gilbert, d. of Samuel Chapin, and had been wid. first of Nathaniel Bliss, had Josiah, 29 Sept. 1665 ; Esther, 6 Sept. 1667 ; and Margaret, 3 Dec. 1670 ; was a propr. of Westfield 1666, but never liv. there; rep. 1680, 3, and 4, sheriff of the Co. and d. 8 May 1692. Sarah m. 1676, William Holton, jr.; Hannah m. Joseph Bedurtha; Abilene m. Thomas Gilbert; Esther m. Ephraim Colton; and Margaret m. Ebenezer Parsons. THOMAS, Windsor, may be thot. to have rem. with Warham, from Dorchester, but no certainty is reach. by inquir. unless the conject. be adopt. that he and first Thomas Marshall were the same person. The first that can positive. be learn. is by a letter from him, as Marshfield, to Samuel Wakeman, 6 May 1641, on p. 12 of our Vol. I. of Reg. of Deeds, strange as the place is, where an extr. is insert. by Gov. Winth. and next yr. he withdrew from the country, as by Conn. Rec. 14 Oct. 1642, when the Court appoint. trustees to manage his est. for use of the creditors. Perhaps he was lost at sea, but at least no more was ever heard of him. His wid. and fam. rem. to Springfield, the ch. being Samuel, bef. ment. ; Sarah, wh. m. Thomas Miller, and ano. d.

MARSTON, * BENJAMIN, Salem, s. of John, m. Sarah, d. prob. of Hilliard Verin, rep. 1696, was, I presume, f. of Benjamin, H. C. 1689, a man of distinct. EPHRAIM, Hampton, s. of Thomas, m. 19 Feb. 1678, Abigail, d. of John Sanborn, took o. of alleg. 1678, as also did, in the same town, the same yr. ISAAC, JAMES, and WILLIAM, who, perhaps, were his brs. or cous. of wh. ISAAC m. 23 Dec. 1669, Eliz. d. of John Brown, had Caleb, b. 19 July 1672; Abigail, 25 Dec. 1673, d. in six mos. ; Eliz. 30 Apr. 1675 ; Mary, 18 Apr. 1677 ; Sarah, 6 Nov. 1680 ; Abigail, again, 7 May 1682 ; and Bethia, 6 July 1687. JACOB, Andover, m. 7 Apr. 1686, Eliz. Poor, had Jacob, wh. d. 31 Mar. 1688 ; and John, wh. d. 20 Nov. 1700. Prob. Mary, wh. m. 1 Dec. 1680, Stephen Parker, was his sis. and possib. Hannah, wh. m. 2 Jan. 1689, Benjamin Barker; and Sarah, wh. m. 24 May 1692, James Bridges, all at Andover, may have been. JAMES, Hampton, s. prob. of Thomas, by w. Dinah Sanborn had Abigail, b. 17 Mar. 1679, wh. m. 5 Aug. 1701, John Prescott of H. and d. 14 Nov. 1762 ; and Ann, 16 Feb. 1681, wh. m. 30 Dec. 1702, Nathaniel Prescott, and d. 30 Dec. 1761. JOHN, Salem, came 1637, aged 20, as serv. of wid. Mary Moulton, from Ormsby, Co. Norf'k. was a carpenter, freem. 2 June 1641, had bapt. John, 12 Sept. 1641 ; Ephraim, 10 Dec. 1643 ; Manasseh, 7 Sept. 1645 ; Sarah, 19 Mar. 1648; Benjamin, 9 Mar. 1651, bef. ment.; Hannah,

Apr. 1653; Thomas, 11 Oct. 1655; Eliz. 30 Aug. 1657; and Abigail, 10 Apr. 1659. He d. 19 Dec. 1681, aged 66, says the gr.stone. JOHN, Barnstable, m. 1 July 1657, Martha, d. of Bernard Lombard, had John, b. a. 15 June 1658; and George, a. 4 Oct. 1660; rem. to Swansey, there, by w. Joan, had Melatiah, 31 Aug. 1673. JOHN, Andover 1667, perhaps was f. of Jacob, and Mary, Hannah, and Sarah, above ment. and of John; but means of certainty are beyond our reach, and all we know is that he had w. Martha, was freem. 1691, and that his d. Sarah m. 24 May 1692, James Bridges of A. JOHN, Salem, prob. s. of the first John, had w. Mary, wh. d. 25 May 1686, aged 43, by the inscript. on the gr.stone; but I kn. no more of him, than that he was freem. 1671. JOHN, Andover, prob. s. of John of the same, m. 28 May 1689, Mary Osgood, d. of Christopher, had John, wh. d. 25 Jan. 1694; John, again, 13 May 1699; and, perhaps, others. His w. d. 5 Apr. 1700, hav. suffer. in the delus. of 1692, imprisonm. as a witch. * MANASSEH, Salem, br. of Benjamin, was a blacksmith; freem. 1677; capt. rep. 1691, d. 1705. ROBERT, Hampton 1636. * THOMAS, Salem 1636, freem. 2 June 1641, rem. to Hampton as one of the first sett. was h. of Mary, d. of William Estow of H. and prob. f. of Ephraim, perhaps of Isaac, James and William, as well as of Mary, wh. m. 1 Jan. 1681, the sec. William Sanborn, unless one or more were ch. of William; rep. 1677. WILLIAM, Salem 1637, perhaps br. of Thomas, had gr. of ld. that yr. but was of Hampton 1640, and back to S. in few yrs. had there bapt. Hannah, Sarah, and Eliz. all on 10 Apr. 1659; Deliverance, Aug. 1663; rem. to Newbury, yet prob. for short time, and so to Hampton, again, where he was freem. 1666; there d. 30 June 1672, acc. Coffin, who says his w. was Sabina, d. of Robert Page, and that he left five ch. Thomas, William, John, Tryphena, and Prudence Cox. WILLIAM, Hampton, s. of the preced. m. Rebecca Page, had Mary, wh. m. 6 Mar. 1695, James Prescott.

MARTIN, ABRAHAM, Hingham 1635, a weaver, at Rehoboth 1643. His will was pro. 9 Sept. 1669. AMBROSE, Weymouth 1638, Concord 1639, had Joseph, b. 8 Nov. 1640; and Sarah, 27 Oct. 1642. Winth. I. 289. ANTHONY, Middletown, m. 10 or 11 Mar. 1661, Mary, d. of Richard Hall, had Mary, b. 1 Jan. foll. d. soon; John, 17 Mar. 1663; Mary, Mar. 1667; and Eliz. 3 Aug. 1671; and d. 16 Nov. 1673, leav. wid. CHARLES, York, 1680, sw. alleg. next yr. CHRISTOPHER, Plymouth, a pilgr. of the Mayflower, was of Billericay, in Co. Essex, came with w. two serv. Solomon Prower, and John Langemore. All d. shortly, the serv. Solomon bef. land. 24 Dec. 1620, and the h. 8 Jan. foll. EDWARD, Boston 1679. EMANUEL, Salem, sign. petitn. against imposts, 1668. GEORGE, Salisbury, blacksmith, by w. Hannah, wh. d. soon, had

Hannah, b. 1 Feb. 1644; m. 11 Aug. 1646, sec. w. Susanna, d. of Richard North, had Richard, 29 June 1647; George, 21 Oct. 1648; John, 26 Jan. 1651; Esther, 7 Apr. 1653; John, again, 2 Nov. 1656; Abigail, 10 Sept. 1659; William, 11 Dec. 1662, d. very soon; and Samuel, 29 Sept. 1667. Hannah m. 4 Dec. 1661, Ezekiel Worthen; and Esther m. 15 Mar. 1670, John Jameson. ISAAC, Rehoboth 1643. JOHN, Charlestown 1638, freem. 13 May 1640, by w. Rebecca had Sarah, bapt. 9 Sept. 1639; Mary, 14 Mar. 1641; John, 1 May 1642; and by w. Sarah had Mehitable, b. 1 Oct. 1643. JOHN, Dover 1648, of the gr. jury 1654, m. Esther, d. of Thomas Roberts, was freem. 1666, but in 1673 was in Jersey. JOHN, Barnstable, m. 1 July 1657, Martha d. of Bernard Lombard, had John, b. June 1658; George, Oct. 1660; and Desire, 1 Jan. 1663. He rem. to Martha's Vineyard. JOHN, Chelmsford, freem. 1665. JOHN, Marblehead 1674. JOHN, Swansey, had John, b. 15 Mar. 1675, and the Col. Rec. transcr. of Swansey rec. gives him by w. Joan, d. Joanna, 15 Feb. 1683. JOHN, Rehoboth, m. 27 June 1681, Mercy Billington, d. of Francis, as I infer, had John, b. 10 June 1682; Robert, 9 Sept. 1683. JOHN, Middletown, s. prob. of Anthony, had w. Eliz. wh. d. 26 July 1718. His ch. were John, wh. d. young, 14 Mar. 1687; Nathaniel, b. 17 Mar. 1688; Eliz. 24 Sept. 1689; John, 4 Apr. 1692; Ebenezer, July 1694; Daniel, Oct. 1697; Hannah, 23 May 1699; and Mary, 31 May 1701. JONATHAN, Farmer, in MS. says, was of New Hampsh. and freem. 1668, of wh. I find not the evid. MICHAEL, Boston, mariner, m. 12 Sept. 1656, Susanna, d. of Mr. Edward Holyoke of that pt. of Boston call. Rumney marsh. RICHARD, Casco 1646, m. a wid. Atwell, perhaps was of Scarborough, freem. 1658, d. early in 1673, his will of 11 Jan. being pro. in Apr. of that yr. In it he teaches us that he had w. Dorothy, s.-in-law Robert Corbin and his w. Lydia, and gives to Benjamin Atwell, wh. prob. had m. ano. d. perhaps dec. for he also gives to gr.ch. Joseph Atwell, and this Joseph, in 1679, then only eight yrs. old, is call. only heir. He brot. from Eng. two ds. of wh. Lydia m. Robert Corbin, and possib. the other was Mary, execut. at the age of 22, in Boston, for murder of her illegit. ch. as told in Winth. II. 302. See also, Willis, I. 134. RICHARD, Boston, merch. m. 1 Feb. 1654, Sarah, d. of John Tuttle of the same, had Mary, b. 7 June 1655; Sarah, 2 July 1657; and m. a. 1660, sec. w. Eliz. d. of John Gay of Dedham, had John, b. 2 Aug. 1661; Richard, 24 Mar. 1663; Eliz. and Mary, tw. 15 Apr. 1665, perhaps both d.; Eliz. again, 25 July 1667; Abigail, 14 Nov. 1669; and a posthum. ch. Lydia, 8 Feb. 1672. He d. betw. 19 July, the date of a deed to serve for his will, and 6 Nov. 1671, when admin. was giv. to his w. Perhaps he came in the Elizabeth and Ann, from London, 1635, aged 12, and may have been br. of John of B. RICHARD, Charlestown, a capt. d. 2 Nov. 1694, aged 62, and his wid. Eliz. d. 7 Jan. 1726, aged 84, say the gr.stones; but he had prob. not liv. there most of his days, for the list of house-holders in 1678, Frothingham, 183, tho. it gives the prefix of respect, tells not the bapt. name, but indicates barely Mr. Martin's, and there is reason to think it did not mean either John's or Thomas's, and Coffin authorizes the conject. that he was of Newbury, had Richard, b. 8 Jan. 1674. A former w. Eliz. d. 6 Oct. 1689 ; and the sec. m. 28 Nov. foll. was wid. of Joshua Edmonds. ROBERT, freem. of Mass. 13 May 1640, was, perhaps, of Weymouth then, soon rem. to Rehoboth 1643, and Swansey. ROBERT, New Haven, had Mary, bapt. perhaps 24 May 1646 ; John, 28 May 1648 ; and Stephen, perhaps 13 May 1652, but for the first and last wrong days are giv. in the rec. of ch. Geneal. Reg. IX. 361. SAMUEL, Wethersfield 1646, went to New Haven, and m. the wid. Bracey, but this may have been bef. his perman. sett. at W. at least in the ch. seating 11 Mar. 1647, at N. H. br. and sis. M. are ment. Her name was Phebe, d. of Mr. Bisby of London, who provid. for her and ch. buying est. at W. He had s. Samuel ; and, perhaps, Richard ; went to London 1652, soon ret. serv. in Philip's war as a lieut. and in Oct. 1677, had a gr. of 50 acres " to him and his heirs forever, prohibit. him the sale of the same, or any alienation thereof from his heirs," showing us that his courage was valued higher than his thrift. He d. 15 Sept. 1683. SAMUEL, Andover, m. 30 Mar. 1676, Abigail Norton, had Samuel, wh. d. 1 Feb. 1683 ; was an ens. and d. 16 Nov. 1696. SOLOMON, Gloucester, ship-carpenter, came in the James, I presume, 1635, from London, aged 16, m. 21 Mar. 1643, Mary, d. of Henry Pindar, had Samuel, b. 16 Apr. 1645 ; and Mary, 9 Jan. 1648. His w. d. 9 Feb. foll. and he m. 18 June next, wid. Alice Varnum of Ipswich, perhaps rem. to Andover, at least sold his G. est. in Mar. 1651, and next yr. was freem. of A. THOMAS, Charlestown 1638, freem. 22 May 1639, perhaps rem. to Cambridge, there by w. Alice Ellet, m. 1 June 1650, had Abigail, b. 22 Aug. 1653 ; may have been of New London 1666, hav. prefix of respect, at least was not householder at Charles-town 1658. THOMAS, Boston, mariner, m. 1670, Rachel, d. of John Farnham. THOMAS, Marlborough 1675, freem. 1690. WILLIAM, Read-ing 1641, one of the earliest selectmen, freem. 1653, perhaps rem. to Groton, there d. 23 Mar. 1673, his w. Mary, wh. had been wid. Lakin, hav. d. 14 Aug. 1669, made provis. of his will dated 6 Mar. bef. pro. 1 Apr. aft. more liberal. To his w's. ch. William and John Lakin, to the ch. of William L. and to sis. Allen and her childr. exc. Hannah, are bequests, to three neighbs. release of debts, and £10. is giv. to the town for purch. of a bell for the meeting-house. Fifteen of this name, says

Farmer, MS. had, in 1834, been gr. at the coll. of N. E. but as at Harv. was none, I think he may have includ. those who spell. the last syl. with *y*, two being early at Harv. with this form, as very oft. in some rec. are the preced. found. Uniform use of that letter prob. belongs only to the New Hampsh. fam.

MARTYN, EDWARD, New Hampsh. 1674, may have been s. of John of Dover. ‡ * RICHARD, Portsmouth, was one of the found. of the first ch. there 1671, rep. 1672 and 9, speaker of the ho. and a couns. of the Prov. 1680, d. 2 Apr. 1694. He had Richard, b. 10 Jan. 1660, H. C. 1680; Eliz. 1662; Hannah, 1665; Michael, 3 Feb. 1667; John, 9 June 1668; and Elias, 18 Apr. 1670. He m. sec. w. Mary, wid. of John Denison, d. of Hon. Samuel Symonds of Ipswich, and third w. was Mary, wid. of Samuel Wentworth. RICHARD, Portsmouth, s. of the preced. was a sch.-master, and preach. but prob. did not wish for sett. but d. 6 Dec. 1690.

MARTUGAL, SAUNDERS, sw. 9 May 1667, as freem. of Conn. if Trumbull has correct. giv. the odd name in Col. Rec. II. 58. What town he liv. at is unkn. but in 1669, as this name is not among the freem. of any town, it may be thot. he was d. or rem.

MARVIN, JOHN, Lyme, eldest s. of the sec. Reynold, m. 7 May 1691, Sarah, d. of Henry Graham or Grimes, had Sarah; Mary; John, b. 9 Aug. 1698; Eliz.; Joseph, 1703; Benjamin; Mehitable; and Jemima; and d. 11 Dec. 1711. His wid. m. Richard Sears, and d. 14 Dec. 1760, aged 90. JOHN, Norwalk, s. of the sec. Matthew, m. 22 Mar. 1704, Mary Beers, had John, b. 22 July 1705; Nathan, 4 Mar. 1708; Seth, 13 July 1709; David, 24 Aug. 1711; Eliz. 23 Oct. 1713; Mary, 20 Dec. 1716; and Elihu, 10 Oct. 1719. His w. d. 17 Apr. foll. and on 27 Apr. 1721, he m. Rachel, d. of Matthias St. John, and had Hannah, 4 Dec. 1722; Joseph, 20 May 1724; Rachel, 24 Dec. 1725, d. in two days; Benjamin, 14 Mar. 1728, d. in three days; Rachel, again, 27 Mar. 1729; Sarah, 18 May 1733, d. in three days; and Ann, 7 Sept. 1741. * MATTHEW, Hartford 1638, an orig. propr. came in the Increase, 1635, from London, aged 35, a husbandman, with w. Eliz. 31, and ch. Eliz. in the custom-ho. rec. call. 31, prob. by error for 11; Matthew, 8; Mary, 6; Sarah, 3; and Hannah, 6 mos. He was one of the orig. grantees of Norwalk, and sett. there 1653, rep. next yr. At Hartford he had Abigail, b. bef. 1641; Samuel, bapt. 16 Feb. 1648; and Rachel, 30 Dec. 1649; and d. 1687. Eliz. m. John Olmstead, surv. him and made her will 15 Oct. 1689; Mary m. 11 Oct. 1648, Richard Bushnell of Saybrook, and in 1680, deac. Thomas Adgate as sec. h. had ch. by ea. and d. 29 Mar. 1713, aged 84; Sarah m. 4 Oct. 1648, William Goodrich of Wethersfield; Hannah m. Jan. 1654, Thomas Seymour; Abigail m. 1 Jan. 1657, John Bouton; and Rachel

m. Samuel Smith. * MATTHEW, Norwalk, s. of the preced. b. in Eng.
freem. 1664, by w. Mary had Matthew; Sarah; Samuel; Hannah;
John, b. 2 Sept. 1678; and Eliz.; beside others, for in 1672 he counted
six ch. was rep. 1694 and 7. Of the ch. our acco. is imperfect, as so
frequent. found in the third generat. Matthew m. Rhoda, d. of Mark
St. John, and had one d. Mary, b. 7 Oct. 1689, and he d. 1691; Sarah m.
Jan. 1681, Thomas Betts; Samuel was rep. 1718, and left descend. by
s. Samuel, and Matthew, and had also Josiah; Hannah m. Epenetus
Platt; John is bef. ment.; and Eliz. m. 6 Nov. 1700, Joseph Platt. I
think Mary M. wh. m. Daniel Benedict of N. may be a d. RENOLD,
REYNOLD, REINOLD, REGINALD, or RAINOLD, Hartford 1639, not an
orig. propr. was prob. younger br. of the first Matthew, rem. to Farmington, soon aft. to Saybrook, freem. 1658, d. 1662, betw. 13 May, the
date of his will, and 28 Oct. that of his inv. in that yr. leav. only Reynold, and Mary, perhaps both b. in Eng. to enjoy good est. Mary m.
William Waller of S. * REYNOLD, Lyme, s. of the preced. prob. b. in
Eng. freem. 1658, was deac. rep. 1670, 2, 3, 4, and 6 in wh. yr. he d.
By w. Sarah, d. of George Clark, he had John, b. 1665; Reynold,
1669; and Samuel, 1671; beside Mary and Sarah, whose dates are
unkn. as also all else, exc. that Mary m. Richard Ely of Saybrook.
The gr.stone tells of his milit. rank. His wid. m. Joseph Sill or Scill,
the disting. soldier, surv. him and was liv. 28 May 1702. Descend. are
very num. REYNOLD, Lyme, s. of the preced. by w. Phebe had Phebe,
b. 3 Dec. 1696; Reynold, Jan. 1702; Lydia, 12 Jan. 1704; Esther, 3
Apr. 1707; and his w. d. 21 Oct. foll. In 1708 he m. Martha, d. of
Thomas Waterman of Norwich, had Martha, b. 3 Apr. 1710; Elisha, 26
Sept. 1711, d. young; James, 26 May 1713; Sarah, 8 Mar. 1716;
Elisha, again, 8 Mar. 1718; and Miriam, Mar. 1720. He was deac.
and capt. and d. 18 Oct. 1737. From him, thro. his ninth ch. desc.
Theophilus R. Marvin, Esquire, of Boston. * SAMUEL, Lyme, br. of
the preced. m. 5 May 1699, Susanna, d. of Henry Graham, or Grimes,
had Samuel, b. 10 Feb. 1700; Zechariah, 27 Dec. 1701; Thomas, 4
Mar. 1704; Matthew, 7 Nov. 1706; Abigail, 13 Sept. 1709; Eliz. 1
June 1712; Nathan, 21 Nov. 1714; Nehemiah, 20 Feb. 1717; Mary,
and a tw. s. wh. both d. soon; was rep. 1711 and 22, and d. 15 Mar.
1743. THOMAS, Newbury, d. 28 Nov. 1651, Coffin tells, and tells no
more. In a hundred yrs. from 1747, eight of this name had been gr.
at Yale.

MASCALL, or MASKELL, JOHN, Salem, there had bapt. John, 23 Feb.
1651; Stephen, 13 Mar. 1653; Mehitable, 3 June 1655; Thomas, Aug.
1657; James, 26 May 1662; and Nicholas, 5 June 1664; was freem.
1678, or possib. 1671, where the name is Maskor in the list. ROBERT,
Boston 1640, in the fam. of William Pierce, went home and had letters

of dism. from our ch. 5 July 1646, to ch. at Dover, Eng. THOMAS, Windsor, where it is writ. Maskell, m. 10 May 1660, Bethia Parsons (his claim to her seem. to me better than Thomas Haskell's or Thomas Marshall's, yet see Stiles, 698 and 735), had Bethia, b. 6 Mar. 1661 ; Thomas, 19 Mar. 1662, d. soon; Abigail, 17 Nov. 1663; Thomas, again, 2 Jan. 1666 ; John, 19 Nov. 1667 ; Eliz. 19 Oct. 1669 ; and he d. 1671. His wid. m. 8 Aug. 1672, John Williams. Hinman, 52, 53, and 153 means one only.

MASON, ARTHUR, Boston, m. 5 July 1655, Joanna, d. of Nicholas Parker, had Ann, b. 10 Aug. 1656, d. at 1 yr.; Mary; Abigail; David, 24 Oct. 1661 ; Joanna, 26 Mar. 1664 ; Arthur, 16 Apr. 1666, d. soon ; Alice, 26 June 1668; Arthur, again, 18, bapt. 31 Jan. 1674; Jonathan, bapt. 23 Apr. 1676, d. at Dorchester, 9 Mar. 1723 ; and Lucy, or, as rec. of bapt. is, Lois, 11 Aug. 1678. It is somewhere said, that he came 1639, and I will not controvert it; but he was only 77 at his d. 4 Mar. 1708. The w. had d. 2 Jan. 1708. He was a constable, and well dispos. to magnify his office, for amusing proof of which see Hutch. I. 254; wrote his name with *ss*. Mary m. Nov. 1678, Rev. John Norton of Hingham; Joanna m. a Perry; Alice m. Samuel Shepard; his s. Arthur, wh. was a mariner, m. 26 June 1701, Mary, d. of Sampson Stoddard, wh. d. 19 Sept. 1746. DANIEL, Watertown, youngest s. of Hugh of the same, stud. for a profess. and went as surg. of a vessel from Charlestown, of wh. James Ellson of that town was master, in 1678 or 9, was captur. as tradit. tells, by an Algerine corsair, and prob. d. in Barbary. DANIEL, Stonington 1673, s. of major John, rem. that yr. to New London or Norwich, m. a wife for wh. he had obt. liberty to come to Roxbury to her relations in the early spring of 1676, and for this yr. to dwell there, his s. Daniel was bapt. at R. 9 Apr. in that yr. and aft. her ret. prob. she d. and he at Hingham, m. Oct. 1679, Rebecca Hobart. He was that yr. sch.master at Norwich, rem. thence to Lebanon, and finally to Stonington, there d. 1736. EDMUND, Watertown, a propr. 1642. EDWARD, one of the early sett. at Wethersfield, of wh. no more is kn. exc. that in 1640, aft. d. his inv. of a good est. is found in the rec. but no fam. is heard of. ELIAS, Salem, had there bapt. Sarah, and Mary, 23 May 1647 ; Hannah, 14 Jan. 1649 ; Martha, 18 May 1651 ; and Elias, 29 May 1653. His will of 1 May 1684, pro. 13 June 1688, ment. w. Eliz. and no ch. but Sarah, w. of John Robinson, with gr.ch. John ; and Mary, w. of George Cox, with gr.ch. George. Emma, a wid. of Eastwell, Co. Kent, who came in the Hercules, 1635, and had gr. of ld. 1637, at Salem, may have been his mo. tho. no ch. in the ship's list of passeng. is giv. HENRY, Scituate 1643, perhaps rem. to Dorchester, and may be the freem. of 1650, aft. 1656 a brewer in Boston, wh. d. 1676, and in his will of 6 Oct. of that yr. pro. next mo.

ment. w. Esther, d. of the first Abraham Howe, no ch. and cous. i. e. niece Mary, d. of Joseph Eliot. HENRY, Boston, serv. to James Everell, d. 10 Nov. 1653. * HUGH, Watertown, a tanner, came in the Francis, from Ipswich, Co. Suff'k. 1634, aged 28, with w. Esther, 22, freem. 4 Mar. 1635, had Hannah, b. 23 Sept. 1636; Eliz. 3 Sept. 1638, d. young; Ruth, bur. 17. Dec. 1640; Mary, b. 18 Dec. 1640; John, 1 Jan. 1645; Joseph, 10 Aug. 1646; Daniel, 19 Feb. 1649, 'prob. H. C. 1666; and Sarah, 25 Sept. 1651; was rep. 1644, 5, 60 and oft. later to 1676 and 7; in 1652 a capt. and d. 10 Oct. 1678, and his wid. d. 21 May 1692. Hannah m. 17 Oct. 1653, Joshua Brooks of Concord; Mary m. 20 May 1668, Rev. Joseph Estabrook; and Sarah m. the same day capt. Andrew Gardner of Muddy riv. Of ano. HUGH we may be led to inq. the resid. by the passage in Drake's Hist. of Boston, 418, of expedit. into the Ind. country, 1676, by one of this name, when we may justly presume, that our Watertown rep. was too old for such severe duty. JACOB, Boston, s. of Ralph, prob. the instrument maker, of wh. Judge Sewall notes the d. 9 Feb. 1695, by w. Rebecca had Eliz. b. 29 July 1671, d. soon; Eliz. again, 23 Apr. 1676; Hannah, 25 May 1678; Jacob, 23 Apr. 1680; Rebecca, 24 Aug. 1681; and Joseph, 9 Feb. 1684. JOHN, the patentee of N. Hampsh. by whose pub. spirit, tho. he never came in person to our country, so much was effect. in its sett. that he well deserves ment. in this work, d. 26 Nov. 1637, leav. only ch. Jane to inherit his vexatious principality. She m. John Tufton, Esquire, had John, wh. d. without issue, as is told by Farmer, and Robert, who took the name of Mason. † ‡ * JOHN, Dorchester, tho. thot. by some to have come 1630, with Winth. prob. came early in 1632, was in Dec. of that yr. sent as lieut. with 20 men against a pirate at the E. for wh. in July foll. he was paid £10, and bec. capt. in Nov. aft. was first on the list of freem. 4 Mar. 1635, and disting. then by title of capt. rep. 1635 and 6, and this yr. rem. with Warham to Windsor, of great serv. in milit. and civ. life, finished the Pequot war, in 1637, being in chief com. rep. 1637 to 41, then Assist. to 59, then dep.-gov. for eight yrs. maj.-gen. and commiss. for the Congr. of N. E. 1647, 54, 5, 6, 9, and 61. From Windsor he rem. 1647 to Saybrook, thence to first sett. of Norwich 1659. By first w. wh. d. at W. we kn. not of any ch. but he took sec. w. in July 1639, nam. Peck, and had, perhaps, Isabel; certain. Priscilla, b. Oct. 1641; Samuel, July 1644; John, Aug. 1646; Rachel, Oct. 1648; Ann, June 1650; Daniel, Apr. 1652; and Eliz. Aug. 1654; and d. at N. 30 Jan. 1672, in 72d yr. All that the diligence of Prince, the annalist, could gather to prefix to his Hist. of the Pequot war may be read in 2 Mass. Hist. Coll. VIII. 122; and later inq. adds little; yet in Sparks's Amer. Biog. Vol. III. of 2d Series, is a copious biogr. of the great capt. writ. with much felicity, by the Rev. George E. Ellis. Isabel m. 17 June 1658, John Bissell of Windsor; Priscilla m. 8 Oct. 1664, Rev. James Fitch; Eliz. m. 8 May 1671, Thomas Norton; Rachel m. 12 June 1678, Charles Hill, as his sec. w. and of the other d. we are not told. Thro. Daniel, the youngest s. the late Hon. Jeremiah deriv. descent. JOHN, Portsmouth, R. I. 1655, was, perhaps, of Westerly in 1669. JOHN, Watertown, an early sett. perhaps elder br. of Hugh, was a capt. d. 10 Oct. 1678, in 73d yr. by the gr.stone. JOHN, Dedham, s. of the first Robert, m. 5 May 1651, Mary, d. prob. of John Eaton, had Hannah, bapt. 15 July 1655; John, 23 Aug. 1657; and ano. d. 25 Aug. 1661. JOHN, Salem, bricklayer, 1661, may be he wh. m. at Charlestown 30 Jan. 1659, Ann Colliham. JOHN, Concord, wh. d. 10 Mar. 1667, had m. 11 Dec. 1662, Hannah Ramsden, and his ch. were John, b. 14 May 1664, and Hannah. ‡ * JOHN, Norwich, s. of famous major John, freem. 1671, rep. 1672 and 4, in Philip's war was a capt. had bef. been a merch. dangerous. wound. in the great Narragansett fight, 19 Dec. 1675, chos. an Assist. in May 1676, but 18 Sept. foll. d. of his wounds, leav. wid. Abigail, and ch. John, and Ann. John, the s. furnish. to Prince the Hist. of the Pequot war in MS. by his gr.f. JOHN, Dorchester, a tanner, was s. of Sampson, m. Content, d. of John Wales, d. 18 Mar. 1683, aged 26, says the inscript. on his gr.stone; he was brot. up by John Gornell, and had part of his est. JOHN, Hartford, d. 19 Feb. 1698, leav. good est. for these ch. Mary, then aged 20; Hannah, 17; John, 13; Joseph, 10; Abigail, 7; Jonathan, 4; and Lydia, 1. JOHN, Boston, merch. came a. 1678, from London, m. Sarah, d. of Robert Pepper, had Sarah, b. 25 Aug. 1681; Susanna, 19 Mar. 1687; Samuel, 31 July 1689; Jonathan, 4 Jan. 1692; Abigail, 12 Apr. 1693; Benjamin, 23 Dec. 1695; and John, 1 Nov. 1697. He d. betw. 12 July 1698, the date, and 29 Sept. foll. when pro. of his will was made. His s. Benjamin is counted the progenit. of the late Hon. Jonathan of U. S. senate. Ano. JOHN, of Boston had w. Prudence, and ch. a few yrs. later. JOHN, Cambridge vill. now Newton, s. of Hugh of Watertown, freem. 1690, was a lieut. selectman, by w. Eliz. eldest d. of lieut. John Hammond, had John, b. 22 Jan. 1677; Eliz. 10 Nov. 1678; Abigail, 16 Dec. 1679; Samuel, 22 Jan. 1690; Hannah, 26 Jan. 1696; and Daniel, 10 Nov. 1698; w. d. 1714, and he d. a. 1720. JOSEPH, Portsmouth, in 1667, convey. his est. to br. Robert of Sulham, Co. Berks, in tr. for his three ds. JOSEPH, Watertown, s. of Hugh, m. 5 Feb. 1684, Mary, d. of John Fiske, had Mary, b. 2 May 1685; Esther, 8 July 1686; Joseph, 2 Oct. 1688; and Sarah, 17 Nov. 1691; was freem. 1690, and d. 22 July 1702. His wid. d. 6 Jan. 1725. NICHOLAS, Saybrook 1648, may be thot. f. of that NICHOLAS, wh. m. at S.

11 May 1686, Mary, d. prob. of William Dudley. One Nicholas, perhaps from the E. was at Northampton, a soldier, 1676, in capt. Turner's comp. NOAH, Rehoboth 1675, was, perhaps, s. of Sampson. His w. Martha d. 6 Feb. 1676, and he m. at Taunton, 6 Dec. 1677, Sarah Fitch, had Noah, b. 17 Dec. 1678; John, 28 Nov. 1680; Mary, 12 Dec. 1682. RALPH, Boston, came in the Abigail, from London, 1635, was a joiner of Southwark, aged 35; with w. Ann, 35, the age perhaps careless. insert. and ch. Richard, 5; Samuel, 3; and Susan, 1; had here Zuriel, b. 11 Apr. 1637; John, 15 Oct. 1640; Jacob, 12 Apr. 1644; and Hannah, 23 Dec. 1647. But his will of 11 Jan. 1673, pro. 23 Jan. 1679, names only aged w. and the ch. Richard, Samuel, Susanna, John, and Jacob. Susanna m. 14 Dec. 1659, William Norton. RICHARD, Boston, prob. s. of the preced. m. 20 Nov. 1660, Sarah, d. of Henry Messenger, had Sarah, b. 3 Sept. 1661; Jacob, 17 Oct. 1662; Simeon, 23 Mar. 1664; and John, 9 Mar. 1671. ROBERT, Roxbury, where his w. d. Apr. 1637, rem. to Dedham, there d. 15 Oct. 1667. His s. John, Robert, and Thomas, who may all have been b. in Eng. had admin. of his est. ROBERT, Boston, by w. Sarah, d. of Robert Reynolds, had Robert; Sarah, b. 20 Aug. 1657; Nathaniel, 23 Dec. 1659; Philip, 16 July 1662; and Eliz. 29 July 1669. He was freem. 1673. ROBERT, Medfield 1664, s. of Robert of Dedham, m. Abigail, d. prob. of John Eaton. ‡ ROBERT, Portsmouth, gr.s. of the patentee, nam. by the king, a couns. of the Prov. in 1680, d. 1688, leav. s. John Tufton M. and Robert Tufton M. to keep up the righteous but useless claim. ROBERT, Roxbury, m. 18 Nov. 1680 or 2, Eliz. Chandler, wh. d. 1688, had Robert, b. 12, bapt. 20 Jan. 1684; Eliz. wh. d. 1686; and John, bapt. 3 July 1687, d. in few days. ROGER, Hartford 1670, then propound. for freem. SAMPSON, Dorchester 1651, shoemaker, had prob. Sampson, wh. serv. in Philip's war; and John, b. a. 1656; was of Rehoboth 1657, Swansey 10 yrs. later; a Bapt. wh. aft. his rem. permit. his s. John to be offer. for bapt. 23 Sept. 1660, by John Gornel, tho. hims. was in his judgm. oppos. to that ordin. admin. to childr. and he liv. to Sept. 1676. See Bliss, 48. Of this man, Benedict, in Hist. I. 427, speaks, I believe, tho. he calls him Samuel, when he relates, that he was a soldier on the Parl. side, in the great civil war, in the army bec. a Bapt. and here was one of the chief founders with Myles, of the ch. at Swansey, the first in Mass. He had, perhaps, s. Samuel, inhab. of Rehoboth many yrs. later, and others, as Sampson, Joseph, and Noah. SAMUEL, Boston, s. of Ralph, b. in Eng. m. 29 May 1662, Mary, d. of John Holman of Dorchester, had Mary, b. 19 Apr. 1663; Ann, 4 July 1665; Thomas, 6 Dec. 1668; Samuel, 18 Apr. 1671; John, 29 Jan. 1674; and Joseph, 24 Nov. 1678. He was freem. 1669. ‡ SAMUEL, Stonington,

s. of major John, had w. Eliz. and ch. Ann, Sarah, Eliz. and Harriet; was lieut. in 1673 ; Assist. in 1683.   SAMUEL, Hingham, m. June 1670, Judith Smith.   SAMUEL, Rehoboth, s. prob. of Sampson, m. 2 Mar. 1682, Eliz. Miller, had Samuel, b. 9 June 1683.   ‡ STEPHEN, one of the first couns. nam. in the new chart. wh. William and Mary allow. Increase Mather to fill, was a merch. of London, prompt in friendship for us, tho. he never came to N. E. yet Hutch. II. 15, supposes him " from mere respect and gratitude " to be insert.   At the first elect. our people were not prevented by respect and gratitude from leav. him out, as they did sev. others of the creatures of Mather.   One Stephen, however, is put into Whitman's list of ar. co. 1686, but I doubt the correctn.   THOMAS, Watertown 1637, perhaps rem. to Hartford bef. 1651, and thence in 1656 to North-ampton, had w. Clemence, and only ch. Samuel, wh. was k. by the Ind. 25 Aug. 1675, and he d. 1 Dec. 1678.   His wid. m. 2 Dec. 1679, deac. Thomas Judd, and d. 22 Nov. 1696.   THOMAS, Dedham 1642, prob. s. of the first Robert, b. in Eng. m. 23 Apr. 1653, Margery Partridge, had John, b. 3 Nov. 1655 ; and Mary, 8 Feb. 1658, liv. in that pt. wh. bec. Medfield, and was k. by the Ind. 21 Feb. 1676.   His ho. was burn. I presume, at the same time.   Sev. of his descend. have been gr. at Harv. and the number at all the N. E. coll. 1834, was twenty-seven, fourteen of wh. at H. C. among them Thaddeus, 1728, d. in 92d yr. 1 May 1806.

MASSEY, JEFFREY, Salem, one of the first mem. of the ch. there, freem. 14 May 1634, was clk. of the market 1642, d. 1677, aged a. 84 ; had John, b. 1631, wh. by Dr. Bentley was call. the first b. male of the town ; but Felt differs from that judgment, tho. the cradle in wh. he was rocked was long admired, and perhaps acknowl. as proof.   JOHN, Salem, s. of the preced. freem. 1668, had Jeffrey, bapt. 30 July 1665 ; and John, perhaps older ; beside Sarah, b. a. 1669, wh. m. Miles Ward. He kept the ferry to Beverly, in wh. office his s. John, who perhaps in 1687 liv. at Roxbury, and by w. Sarah, d. of Thomas Wells of Ipswich, had Ann, b. 11 Oct. of that yr. succeed. 1701, and the sen. d. 1 Sept. 1710.

MASSON.   See Mason.

MASTERS, ABRAHAM, Cambridge 1639, prob. s. of John, but may have been gr.s.   GILES, Boston, d. 29 Feb. 1688.   He prob. had liv. here but very short day, and with no sympathy towards our people, as in Sewall's Diary he is describ. merely as " the king's attorney."   JOHN, Cambridge, perhaps came in the fleet with Winth. freem. 18 May 1631, with prefix of respect, a man of skill and enterprise, d. 21 Dec. 1639, and Jane, his w. d. five days aft.   His will, made two days only bef. he d. abstract. in Geneal. Reg. II. 180, names d. Sarah Dobyson, or Dobson, but we kn. nothing of her or her h. ; d. Lydia Tabor, perhaps w. of Philip; gr.ch. John Lockwood, prob. by his d. Eliz. s. of Edmund; Abraham and Nathaniel Masters, whom I judge to be s. and gr.s. and gives residue of est. to d. Eliz. w. of Cary Latham. NATHANIEL, Beverly 1659, seems to be s. of Abraham, and gr.s. of the preced. None of this fam. was of Cambridge, when the Shawshin div. of ld. was made in 1652.

MASTERSON, NATHANIEL, York, s. of Richard, had liv. early at Salem, at Boston 1660, and at sev. other places, with Rev. Ralph Smith, his f.-in-law, was marshal or sheriff in 1665, imprison. by the royal commiss. for upholding the right of Mass. and restored to his office by Leverett and the other agents of Mass. 1668, when the people return. to alleg. under our Col. Hubbard, 593. RICHARD, Plymouth 1630, came prob. the yr. preced. a deac. of the "goodly company of the Pilgrims at Leyden" bef. the d. of Rev. John Robinson, 1625, chos. prob. 1620, when Gov. Carver, Elder Brewster, and Samuel Fuller, wh. had, I suppose, all been predeces. in that office, emb. for N. E. in the Mayflower. He brot. w. Mary, nam. Goodall, of Leicester, in the docum. at Leyden, as m. 26 Nov. 1619; ch. Nathaniel, bef. ment. and Sarah, wh. m. John Wood, or Atwood. The wid. m. Rev. Ralph Smith. It has been doubted, whether the deac. ever came to this country, but the doubt relies, I suppose, mainly on the negative fact of ment. of him being hardly found, and yet we kn. from Bradford, that he d. at P. in the gr. sickness 1633. In 1649, Mary Smith, their mo. gave to Nathaniel M. and his sis. Sarah, w. of Atwood, her right in "a ho. in Leyden, in Holland, sometime appertain. to my dec. h. Richard Masterson."

MATHER, ATHERTON, Dorchester, s. of Timothy, rem. to Windsor, there m. 20 Sept. 1694, Rebecca, d. of Thomas Stoughton, and by her had William, b. 2 Mar. 1698; and Jerusha, 18 July 1700; his w. d. 1704, and by sec. w. Mary he had Joshua, 26 Nov. 1706; Richard, 31 Mar. 1708; Mary, 2 Mar. 1711; rem. to Suffield, there had Thomas, 5 Apr. 1713; Eliakim, 10 July 1715; and Catharine, 5 Jan. 1718, wh. d. at 15 yrs.; and he d. 9 Nov. 1734. COTTON, Boston, eldest s. of Increase, freem. 1680, when he was only 17 yrs. old, so that he came forward with strange rapidity (hav. join. the ch. of his f. 31 Aug. 1679), wh. is the more striking, as his f. was never adm. freem. that we find; and if his course at coll. were full one, he must have ent. at $11\frac{1}{2}$ yrs. Yet more than two or three have been min. in Boston younger than he; but with less sagacity than his f. he was ord. at 2d ch. collea. with him 13 May 1685; disting. as a scholar above most of his contemp. but kn. in mod. days chiefly as author of the Magn. in seven books, London 1702, a work of no little value, and more curious than valuable, d. 13 Feb. 1728. He m. 4 May 1686, Abigail, d. of John Phillips of Charles-

town, wh. d. 28 Nov. or as town rec. says, 1 Dec. 1702, hav. borne to
him nine ch. of wh. five d. young, three bef. bapt. and he m. 18 Aug.
1703, Eliz. d. of Dr. John Clark, wid. of Richard Hubbard, mariner,
with a good est. had six more ch. of wh. Rev. Samuel, b. 30 Oct. bapt.
3 Nov. 1706, H. C. 1723, attained no humble share of celebrity; and
she d. 18 Nov. 1713. He next m. 5 July 1715, Lydia, d. of Rev. Samuel Lee, wid. of John George, wh. long surv. On 3 Jan. preced. he
had writ. to Colman, saying he had "no manner of prospect of return.
unto" the married state; tho. "I have no doubt foolishly eno. been
ready to fall into this weakness." Hardly any more curious letter can
be found in the Geneal. Reg. See V. 60. In less than a yr. aft. his m.
with this d. of Lee, her sis. Catharine, by sudden death of her h. Henry
Howell, was left with two ch. of two and three yrs. of age, to wh. in
evil hour, M. was appoint. guardian, and suffer. much anxiety in conseq.
See 4 Mass. Hist. Coll. II. 122. Twelve of his ch. with dates of bapt.
and names, are in the appendix to Rev. Chandler Robbins's Hist. of the
2d ch. but six of them are by the sec. w. In the pious labor of his s.
Rev. Samuel, on the biography of his f. he is more copious than exact.
The most agreeable of all the copious writings of Mather, will, perhaps,
be found in some apologues design. to magnify the merits of his f. in
obtain. the new chart. for wh. however, little favor was found in the
mind of Calef. They may be seen in 3 Mass. Hist. Coll. I. 126, 133.
But his epistolary exercises are most frequent. refer. to, and they are
very num. As the sample of his style, and also highly illustrat. the
politics of the day, that his f. was too much engag. in for the larger
part of his life, the reader will glad. turn to the letters in 1 Mass. Hist.
Coll. III. admonish. Gov. Dudley by f. and s. each, as if in rivalry,
more venomous than the other. ELEAZER, Northampton, s. of Richard,
was the first min. at N. ord. 18 June 1661, m. 29 Sept. 1659, Esther,
youngest d. of Rev. John Warham, had Eunice, b. 2 Aug. 1664; Warham, 7 Sept. 1666, H. C. 1685; and Eliakim, 22 Sept. 1668; and d.
24 July 1669, only 3 mos. aft. his f. His wid. m. Rev. Solomon Stoddard, success. of her h. outliv. him, and d. 10 Feb. 1736, in her 92d yr.
Eunice m. Rev. John Williams, and was k. by the Ind. the day aft. the
capt. of Deerfield by them and their French allies, 29 Feb. 1704;
Eliakim d. bef. mature age; but the other ch. freem. of Mass. 1690, aft.
some yrs. preach. and many yrs. teach. sch. sat down at New Haven,
was judge of Pro. Ct. and there d. 12 Aug. 1745. INCREASE, Boston,
youngest br. of Eleazer, hav. tak. at Harv. his A. B. went at 18 yrs. of
age to his br. Samuel at Dublin, and studied there for his A. M. in
1658, preached in sev. places, as Co. Devon and Isle of Guernsey, leav.
the latter aft. the restorat. but. ret. at the end of Aug. 1661, to N. E.

and on 8 Sept. utter. his first sermon on our side of the water in that ch. where he serv. above 60 yrs. tho. he was not ord. until 27 May 1664. He was chos. Presid. of the coll. 1685, and fill. the office until 1701, when the increase of dissatisfact. long prevail. at his refusal to give up his pulpit in Boston, and reside at Cambridge, compell. his resigna. Next yr. he fear. the glory of N. E. was depart. and that the coll. under direct. of Willard of the O. S. ch. should " become a nursery, not of plants of renown, but of degenerate plants, who will forsake those holy principles of truth," &c. &c. But his talents had new scope in the intermed. time, for in the last dangerous yr. of Sir Edmund Andros, he was sent in disguise, on board a ship, to intercede with king James, and sail. 7 Apr. 1688, being absent from his coll. duties, on political engagem. until 14 May 1692, when Sir William Phips the Gov. of his own nominat. land. with him, bring. the new chart. of William and Mary. Unhappi. the desire to manage state affairs ever aft. possessed him, and lessen. his usefulness, beside embitter. his life. He d. 23 Aug. 1723, and was bur. 29, with the greatest marks of esteem and affection. He m. 6 Mar. 1662, Mary, sometimes spell. Maria, d. of famous John Cotton, wh. d. 4 Apr. 1714 ; had Cotton, H. C. 1678, bef. ment. b. 12, bapt. 15 Feb. 1663 ; Maria, 7, bapt. 19 Mar. 1665 ; Eliz. 6 Jan. bapt. 3 Feb. 1667 ; Nathaniel, H. C. 1685, 6, bapt. 11 July 1669, whose great promise of disting. talents was cut off 17 Oct. 1688, at Salem ; Sarah, 9, bapt. 12 Nov. 1671 ; Samuel, H. C. 1690, 28, bapt. 30 Aug. 1674 ; Abigail, 13, bapt. 20 Apr. 1677 ; Hannah, 30 May, bapt. 16 July 1680 ; Catharine, 14, bapt. 17 Sept. 1682, d. within 9 mos. ; and Jerusha, 16, bapt. 20 Apr. 1684. He m. sec. w. 1715, Ann, d. of Thomas Lake, wid. of Rev. John Cotton of Hampton, wh. outliv. him, and d. at Brookline, 29 Mar. 1737, in 74th yr. All the ds. exc. her wh. d. in infancy were m. and of the six, all but Hannah had ch. Maria m. Bartholomew Green, and next, Richard Fifield, surv. him, and d. 24 Nov. 1746 ; Eliz. m. July 1696, William Greenough, and next, 6 Oct. 1703, Josiah Byles, and d. 20 Aug. 1745 ; her only ch. was Mather B. a min. of celebr. in Boston, wh. resembled, in some points, his uncle Cotton ; Sarah m. 1691, Rev. Nehemiah Walter of Roxbury ; Abigail m. Newcomb Blake, and next, 1727, Rev. John White of Gloucester ; Hannah m. 28 Jan. 1698, John Oliver, and d. 2 Dec. 1706 ; and Jerusha m. 8 Mar. 1710, Peter Oliver, and d. 30 Dec. foll. her d. Jerusha d. 5 days aft. A ridic. mistake of ano. Jerusha, niece of this, tho. not b. bef. her death, mystified the geneal. of the late Gov. Smith of Conn. Samuel, the third s. went to Eng. was sett. as min. at Witney, in Oxfordsh. made some preparat. for an abridg. of his br. Cotton's Magnalia, wh. from many judicious omissions it is regret.

15 *

that he had not complet. and published. His copy is in the library of the Mass. Hist. Soc. JOSEPH, Dorchester, s. of Timothy, m. 2 or or 20 June 1689, Sarah Clap, had Catharine, b. a. 1690, and he d. a. 1691. NATHANIEL, Dorchester, s. of Richard, b. at Toxteth, near Liverpool, Eng. went some yrs. aft. his gr. at Harv. to Eng. had the living at Barnstable, 1656, by presentat. of Oliver Cromwell, it is wildly said, meaning, perhaps, by his recommend. for eccles. patronage had ceased; ejected in 1662, preach. at Rotterdam, aft. some yrs. was at Dublin, success. to his br. Samuel, whence he sent contrib. for relief to the suffer. in Philip's war 1676, and last in London, d. 26 July 1697, hav. serv. at the altar 47 yrs. in Eng. Holland, Ireland, and Eng. again. RICHARD, Dorchester, s. of Thomas, b. 1596, of an ancient fam. as his gr.s. Cotton in Magn. III. c. 20, assures us, at Lowton, in the parish of Winwick, Lancash. was employ. in teach. a sch. some yrs. bef. going to the Univ. but at length, on 9 May 1618, was ent. of Brazen Nose Coll. Oxford, yet soon call. to Toxteth, where he had taught the sch. preach. his first sermon 30 Nov. of the same yr. There most faithful. he serv. 15 yrs. and was then suspend. for non-conform. and feeling the true sense of his office, resolved on expatriat. In disguise he emb. at Bristol in the James, arr. 17 Aug. 1635, aft. peril in the remarka. storm two days bef. and on 25 Oct. with w. Catharine join. the ch. of Boston. He had m. 29 Sept. 1624, that d. of Edmunt Holt, Esquire, of Bury, in Lancash. had Samuel, b. 13 May 1626, H. C. 1643; Timothy; Nathaniel, 20 Mar. 1630, H. C. 1647, bef. ment.; and Joseph, wh. d. in childhood; aft. com. to N. E. had Eleazer, 13 May 1637, H. C. 1656; and Increase, 21 June 1639, H. C. 1656, bef. ment. He was a man of excel. discretion, of less learning, it is prob. than his ambitious s. Increase, and less brilliancy, it is clear, than his eccentr. gr.s. the never dying author of Magnalia, but in true serv. as min. happier than either, and better than both. He was sett. at D. 23 Aug. 1636; his w. d. 1655, and he m. 26 Aug. 1656, Sarah, wid. of his great friend John Cotton, and d. 22 Apr. 1669. A few days bef. he had met a great indignity, in being refus. adm. with sundry others, sent by an ecclesiast. council, met at Boston, to attempt conciliat. in the first ch. there, as John Hull, one of the aggriev. mem. relates in his Diary, p. 229 of the Vol. pub. by the Antiq. Soc. of Worcester. The wid. made her will 3 May 1670, but did not d. for six yrs. His life, written by Increase, print. 1670, is condensed in the Magn. the author of wh. could never be scrupulous in use of materials; and of course he shows that he had not resort. to the MS. of the journal of his gr.f. Yet the slight extracts from the interesting work, caused a desire for the orig. wh. in Young's Chron. was print. from the autogr. 210 yrs. aft. its date. RICHARD, Dorchester, s. of Timothy, m. 1 July 1680,

Catharine, d. of Joseph Wise of Roxbury, had Timothy, b. 20 Mar. 1681 ;
Eliz. 20 Nov. 1682 ; Samuel, 23 Jan. 1684 ; and Joseph, 29 Jan. 1686.
He had sett, at Lyme, and d. 17 Aug. 1688. Goodwin calls his w. Eliz.
wh. seems wrong. SAMUEL, Dorchester, eldest s. of the first Richard,
b. in Eng. freem. 1648, aft. large preparat. here for his profess. went
home, preach. in Eng. Scotland, and Ireland, sett. in Dublin, was made
a fellow of Trinity Coll. there, says fam. tradit. m. a sis. of Sir John
Stevens, and d. 29 Oct. 1671. SAMUEL, Windsor, eldest s. of Timothy,
preach. some time at Deerfield, and on destruct. of that town by the
Ind. 1675, went down with the surv. people to Hatfield, and there preach.
and elsewhere, but was call. from preach. at Branford to be ord. at W.
1682, bef. wh. he had m. Hannah, d. of Gov. Treat, wh. d. 8 Mar. 1708,
had Samuel, b. 1677, H. C. 1698, a physician, wh. d. 6 Feb. 1746 ;
Hannah, Sept. 1682, d. next yr. ; John ; Joseph ; and Azariah, 29 Aug.
1685, a min. wh. d. at Saybrook, 11 Feb. 1737 ; Ebenezer, 3 Sept.
1687 ; Joseph, 6 Mar. 1689 ; Eliz. 2 Jan. 1691 ; Nathaniel, 30 May
1695 ; Benjamin, 29 Sept. 1696 ; and John. He was one of the first
Trustees of Yale Coll. and d. 18 Mar. 1728. The s. kept up the
name to our times. TIMOTHY, Dorchester, s. of Richard, b. in Eng. m.
Catharine, d. of Humphrey Atherton, had Samuel, b. 5, bapt. 7 Sept.
1651, H. C. 1671, bef. ment. ; Nathaniel, bapt. 30 Jan. 1653, prob. d.
very soon, wh. may explain the fail. of entry of b. ; Richard, 22, bapt.
25 Dec. 1653, bef. ment. (of course not bapt. on Wednesday, 2 Nov. of
that yr. as print. in Geneal. Reg. XIII. 280) ; Catharine, 6, bapt. 13
Jan. 1656 ; Nathaniel, again, 2, bapt. 5 Sept. 1658 ; Joseph, 25, bapt.
26 May 1661 ; and Atherton, 4 Oct. 1663, bef. ment. ; and he d. 14
Jan. 1685, by falling from a scaffold in his barn, says Blake's Ann. His
wid. Eliz. wh. he had m. 20 Mar. 1680, d. 20 Feb. 1710, aged 70 yrs.
Of the eleven male descend. of famous Richard, bred at Harv. as above
enum. ten were of the seventeenth cent. and the other had his A. B. a
hundred and thirty yrs. since. From 1705 to 1837 eighteen have been
gr. at Yale.

MATSON, JOHN, s. of the first Thomas, m. 7 Mar. 1660, Mary, d. of
William Cotton, had Ann, Amey or Emma, b. 12 Mar. 1662 ; John, 26 Jan.
1665 ; Mary, 22 Dec. 1666 ; and Abigail, 19 Oct. 1668. JOHN, Simsbury 1690, a gr.s. of first Thomas, had serv. his apprent. at Windsor.
THOMAS, Boston 1630, gunsmith, came prob. in the fleet with Winth. as
among the early mem. of the ch. he is ent. as rec. by commun. of chh.
from a ch. in London, tho. at a later day, 17 July 1636, he was fully rec.
yet had been adm. freem. 4 Mar. 1634 ; by w. Ann, wh. was sis. of Abigail, the first w. of Theodore Atkinson, had Thomas, bapt. 27 Oct. 1633 ;
John, 10 July 1636 ; rem. to Braintree, hav. been disarm. as one of the

recusant friends of Wheelwright, in Nov. 1637, there had Joshua, 23
July 1640; and Abigail, perhaps eldest of all; was a milit. officer aft.
the relig. heats were assuaged; d. aft. 1666. THOMAS, Boston, s. of the
preced. m. 14 Aug. 1660, wid. Mary Read, had Thomas and Hannah,
was freem. 1666, then titled jun. prison-keep. 1674, for sev. yrs.; d.
1690. By deeds of Theodore Atkinson, first of the name, in Apr.
1675, Thomas jr. John, Joshua, and Abigail, ch. of his w.'s sis. and
Thomas and Hannah, ch. of that Thomas jr. and Ann, John, and Mary,
ch. of John the sec. s. of first Thomas, are indicat. for us.

MATTHEWS, BENJAMIN, Dover 1659, was s. of Francis, and had s.
Francis. DANIEL, Boston, mariner, m. Mary, d. of James Neighbours,
was first serg. in the comp. of Moseley for the Narraganset serv. Dec.
1675. FRANCIS, Portsmouth 1631, of the men sent over by Mason,
was of Exeter 1639 to 46, rem. to Dover, prob. d. 1647, when, perhaps,
his wid. Thomasine (with childr. Benjamin, Walter, and Martha, wh. m.
first a Snell, and next, a Browne), was on the est. he purchas. 1640 of
William Beard. Descend. wh. write the name Mathes are num. and
respect. HUGH, Newbury, m. 28 Aug. 1683, Mary Emerson, had
John, b. 26 Feb. 1688; Judith, 30 Apr. 1689; Joanna, 19 Apr. 1690;
Hugh, 15 May 1691, d. soon; and Hugh, again, 19 May 1696.
* JAMES, Charlestown 1634, prob. rem. bef. 1639 to Yarmouth, where
he had Samuel, b. 1 May 1647; Sarah, 21 July 1649; Esther, 8 Jan.
1651; prob. others; and was rep. 1664. JOHN, Roxbury, had Gershom,
b. 25 July 1641, perhaps bapt. but the rec. of ch. prior to Dec. is lost;
and Eliz. 14, bapt. 22 Oct. 1643. Ellis, in his Hist. 123, follow. the
erron. suppos. of Farmer, a. his rem. to Springfield, and adds that he
was excomm. for drunken. Now that censure was on 1 May 1659,
many yrs. later than his namesake was at S. but then he ought to have
turned over the ch. vol. very little, and seen that he was restor. to his
honora. relation 29 Dec. 1660. He was freem. 18 May 1642, when
the Col. rec. spells it Mathis. JOHN, Rehoboth, perhaps rem. to Springfield, m. 1644, Pentecost Bond, had two ch. wh. d. one Sarah, bur. 7
Jan. 1650, and the w. was k. by the Ind. 5 Oct. 1675. He was fined
two or three times for drunken. but that frailty would not fully prove
his ident. with the preced. He m. sec. w. and had s. wh. d. young, and
he d. 25 Apr. 1684. JOHN, Boston 1645, a tailor. JOHN, Charlestown,
m. 7 Jan. 1659, Margaret Hunt, and he d. 28 June foll. JOHN, Marlborough, Barry thinks, in 1681, m. Mary, d. of Jonathan Johnson, had
Lydia, b. 16 Mar. 1691, d. at 15 yrs.; Ruth, 9 May 1693; John, 18 Jan.
1695; and Daniel, Mar. 1697. His w. d. 22 June 1710, and he m.
1713, Sarah Garfield. *MARMADUKE*, Malden, was s. of Matthew of
Swansea, in Glamorgansh. and in his 18th yr. matric. 20 Feb. 1624, at

All Souls, Oxf. came to Boston, in a sh. from Barnstable, 21 Sept. 1638, and his w. Catharine join. to our ch. 6 Feb. foll. He preach. at Yarmouth 1639 to 43, for in Aug. of this latter yr. his w. was dism. from our ch. to that of Y.; was adm. freem. of Plymouth Col. 1641, had Manasseh, bapt. 24 Jan. 1641, by Lothrop, at Barnstable, but came to Hull a. 1644; some yrs. later taught at Malden, where his troubles are copious. detail. by Frothingham, in Hist. of Charlestown; he had there been ord. but, against the good will of the hearers, he was forced to depart, was then employ. at Lynn and other places, finally went home, and Calamy says he d. at his nat. place, a. 1683. MORDECAI, H. C. 1655, was, I presume, s. of the preced. and, as no more is heard of him, prob. he went to Eng. ROGER, Dorchester, had gr. of ld. Feb. 1635, but prob. soon rem. SAMUEL, Jamaica, L. I. 1656. Thompson. WALTER, Isle of Shoals, s. of Francis, was constable there 1658, rem. to Dover, had w. Mary, and d. 1678, leav. s. Samuel, ds. Susanna Young and Mary Senter. His will of 15 Apr. was pro. 25 June, as Mr. Quint finds.

MATTHEWSON, JAMES, is by Farmer, put into the list of earliest sett. of R. I. but I have found nothing to add, exc. that at Providence he took the engagem. of alleg. to Charles II. in May 1666, and prob. had Ruth, wh. m. 1 Apr. 1686, Benjamin Whipple. JOSEPH, wh. m. 19 Feb. 1715, Sarah, d. of the sec. Valentine Whitman, is call. s. of Daniel. Yet wh. Daniel was, or where he liv. I find not.

MATTOCKS, DAVID, Braintree, freem. 1650, had w. Sarah, and d. Eliz. wh. was decrepid, one s. and d. at Roxbury bef. 14 May 1654, when his inv. was dated, and his d. d. 4 July 1655. The wid. m. 2 May 1656, Thomas Rawlins of Boston. JAMES, Boston, a cooper, came from Bristol, perhaps bef. 1635 (at least his d. Alice was then w. of Nathaniel Bishop), join. the ch. in Feb. 1639, and was made freem. 13 Mar. foll. Perhaps all his ch. were b. in Eng. In his will, made 21 Jan. 1667, wh. is on the latest page in Vol. I. of Suff k. Reg. he names s. Samuel, and ds. Alice, w. of John Lewis, wh. had been wid. of Nathaniel Bishop, and Mary, w. of Samuel Brown, m. 9 July 1661. RICHARD, New Haven, m. 1669, Grace Todd, but it is not certain that he was resid. long. He had desert. his w. bef. 1686, when her f. d. SAMUEL, Boston, s. of James, m. 30 Mar. 1653, Constance, d. of Richard Fairbanks, had Samuel, b. 15 Oct. 1659; James, 27 Oct. 1662; Constance, 10 Sept. 1665; Zaccheus, 15 Sept. 1668; John, 14 Sept. 1669; Eliz. 18 Aug. 1670; Mehitable, 7 Nov. 1672; and Mary, 13 Nov. 1673. Maddox is very easily confound. with this name, as well as Maddock, and I dare not, in some cases, disting.

MATTOON, HUBERTUS, or HERBERT, Kittery 1652, when he submit. to jurisdict. of Mass. prob. rem. to Saco bef. 1683. Folsom, 174.

PHILIP, a soldier from the E. part of the Col. in the spring of 1676, was in Turner's comp. and took part in the Falls fight, then sett. at Springfield, m. Sarah, d. of John Hawkes of Hadley, had Margaret, b. 1678; Philip, 1680·; John, 1682; Isaac, 1684; Sarah, 1687; rem. to Deerfield, there had Eleazer, 1689; Gershom, 1690; Nathaniel, 1693; Ebenezer, 1695; and Mary, posthum. 1697. He d. 30 Dec. 1696, and his wid. m. Daniel Belden, as third w. and d. 17 Dec. 1751, in 95th yr. Of his s. Philip, with w. Rebecca, d. of Godfrey Nims, and only ch. were k. at the sec. destruct. of D. by the Ind. and Fr. 29 Feb. 1704; John sett. at Wallingford; Isaac and Nathaniel at Northfield; Eleazer at Amherst, but was first at N.; and Gershom at Lebanon; Ebenezer d. at 21 yrs. The late Hon. Ebenezer, Dart. Coll. 1776, was gr.s. of Eleazer. RICHARD, or ROBERT, Exeter, prob. s. of Hubertus, sw. fidel. 14 July 1657, m. Jane, d. of Edward Hilton junr. was k. by the Ind. 23 July 1706, with his s. Hubertus. Belkn. I. 172.

MAUDE, *DANIEL*, Boston, came in the James, from Bristol, 1635, in comp. with Richard Mather, was bred at Emanuel, Cambr. where he had his A. B. 1606, and A. M. 1610, kept the sch. for some yrs. join to our ch. 25 Oct. 1635, freem. 25 May foll. yet without prefix of respect; for sec. w. m. Mary Bonner, a wid. with four ch. went to Dover, there was first min. on sett. found. 1642 to his d. in 1655. His will was of 17 Jan. in that yr. He left no ch. by either of his ws.

MAUDSLEY, ‖ HENRY, Braintree, came in the Hopewell, capt. Babb, in the autumn of 1635, aged 24, had Mary, b. 29 Sept. 1638; Samuel, 14 June 1641; and, perhaps, others; ar. co. 1643; freem. 1646; we kn. not the name of his w. nor any more item. Dr. Harris claims him for Dorchester 1630, but without suffic. warrant, that I can discov. yet he had gr. of a houselot 1637. JOHN, Dorchester, freem. 14 Mar. 1639, by w. Eliz. had Joseph, b. 1638, as print. in Geneal. Reg. V. 244, tho. I think the s. call. Joseph in the rec. may have been John; and whether any more, or when that w. d. is unkn.; d. 1661, bef. 4 Oct. the date of his inv. but by w. Cicely's will of 28 Nov. foll. are nam. s. John, d. Eliz. and s. Thomas. This Cicely, wh. may seem to be the same as w. Eliz. d. 3 Dec. 1661. JOHN, Windsor, s. of the preced. m. 10 or 14 Dec. 1664, Mary, d. of Benjamin Newbury, had Benjamin, b. 13 Oct. 1666; Margaret, 4 Feb. 1668, d. young; Joseph, 21 Dec. 1670; Mary, 3 May 1673; and Consider, 21 Nov. 1675; was freem. 1666, lieut. in Philip's war, rem. to Westfield 1677, bec. freem. of Mass. May 1678, there had John, 21 Aug. 1678, d. at 12 yrs.; Comfort, 3 Dec. 1680; Margaret, again, 22 May 1683; Eliz. 17 Nov. 1685; Hannah, 3 Apr. 1690, wh. d. 1708; and he went back to Windsor, there d. 18 Aug. 1690. All the five s. were liv. 1706; but Comfort d. 1711. Benjamin,

Joseph, Consider, and John ea. had fam. at Westfield, but in 1719, a few yrs. bef. his d. Joseph rem. to Glastonbury. SAMUEL, Dorchester, s. of Henry, a cooper, rem. early to Boston, and in the way of trade visit. Jamaica and other parts of the W. I. where the adventurous spirit was excited and schooled, perhaps by Sir Henry Morgan and associate buccaneers, the result of wh. was, his bring. home to Boston two prizes from some unment. enemy. An explanat. of this may be, that the prizes (wh. were command. by Dutchmen) had been engag. in irreg. or piratical business. He m. Ann, eldest d. of the first Isaac Addington, and sis. of the Hon. Isaac, had Samuel, b. 18 Apr. 1671; Rebecca, 1673; and Mary. He was a capt. in Philip's war, showed gallant spirit, had great success in destroy. the Ind. by some was thot. to take too great delight in that exercise, and d. Jan. 1680. The s. d. young, and the wid. in 1684 contemplat. m. with Nehemiah Pierce, made deed of trust in favor of the ds. of wh. Rebecca m. 22 Jan. 1695, James Townsend, and Mary m. William Webster of·Boston. THOMAS, Dorchester, s. of the first John, m. 28 Oct. 1658, Mary, d. of Thomas Lawrence of Hingham, had prob. that John, wh. the rec. says d. 27 Oct. 1661, unless Increase were earlier; Mary, b. 31 Dec. 1660, d. 4 Dec. next yr.; Thomas, 12 Mar. 1667, wh. d. 12 Apr. 1749; Eliz. 19 Feb. 1669; Unite, 5 May 1671, wh. was a soldier in Withington's comp. for the crusade against Quebec 1690; Ebenezer, 4 Sept. 1673; John, 9 Apr. 1676; Nathaniel, 28 Oct. 1678; and Joseph, 17 Apr. 1681; and d. 22 Oct. 1706. His will of 4 Oct. preced. names Increase, s. of his eldest dec. s. Increase. The wid. d. Apr. 1723. The name was spell. with many variat. as Mawdesly, Modesly, Madesly, but long has been fixed at Moseley, yet liable to be much mistak. as in Geneal. Reg. VI. 268, print. Moreley.

MAULE, or MAULD, THOMAS, Salem 1669, a shopkeep. from Eng. came, he says in his book, via Barbadoes, was whip. for ill words, being a Quaker, in May of that yr. m. 1670, Naomi Lindsay; perhaps as sec. w. had Mary, d. of George Keyser of the same, and in 1695 punish. again, for "Truth held forth, &c." Still, he show. great fondness for Salem, and in his will, a. 1723, left a bequest to its use, of wh. part was to be applied to support the writing-school. He had s. John, and third w. Sarah, wh. surv.

MAURY. See Morey.

MAVERICK, ANTIPAS, Isle of Shoals 1647, attend. bef. Commissrs. of Mass. and submit. to her jurisdict. Nov. 1652, was of the gr. jury of the Col. 1654, was d. bef. 24 Apr. 1682, when adm. of his est. was gr. to Edward Gilman and Stephen Paul, in behalf of their ws. His d. Abigail m. Edward Gilman. ‖ ELIAS, Charlestown 1632, was of the ch. in Feb. of next yr. and freem. 11 June, liv. at Winnesemet, then pt.

of Boston, now Chelsea, m. Ann, d. of a wid. Eliz. Harris, wh. bec. the
w. of deac. William Stetson, had John, b. 13, bapt. 27 Feb. 1636; Abigail, 10, bapt. 14 Aug. 1637; Eliz. 2 June 1639, d. young, prob.;
Sarah, 20 Feb. 1641, d. young perhaps; Elias, 17 Mar. 1644; Peter;
Mary; Ruth; Paul, 10 June 1657; and Rebecca, 1 Jan. 1660; was of
ar. co. 1654, and d. a. 1684. His will, of 19 Oct. 1681, pro. 6 Nov.
1684, provides for w. s. Elias, Peter, Paul, gr.s. Jotham, s. of s. John,
wh. therefore, I presume, was d.; James, s. of s. Peter, wh. was prob.
d.; and ds. Abigail, wh. had m. 4 June 1655, Matthew Clark; Sarah
Walton; Mary Way; Ruth Smith; and Rebecca Thomas; beside f.-in-
law deac. Stetson, and Ruth Johnson, then liv. with testator, ch. of his
d. Eliz. wh. m. 15 Oct. 1656, John Johnson, wh. had rem. to Haverhill;
and nam. Elias and Paul excors. ELIAS, Boston, s. of the preced. m. 8
Dec. 1669, Margaret Sherwood, wh. join. the ch. of Charlestown in
Aug. 1675, wh. may rend. it prob. that he liv. on the est. of his f. or
near it, had Elias, b. 4 Nov. 1670; Margaret, and Eliz. bapt. 22 Aug.
1675; Abigail, 24 Sept. 1676; Samuel, 14 Aug. 1687; and was freem.
1690. JOHN, Dorchester, came in the Mary and John, 1630, from Plymouth, with collea. Warham, desir. to be adm. freem. 19 Oct. and is
first on the list of those wh. took the o. 18 May 1631, d. 3 Feb. 1636,
while prepar. to accomp. his friends, wh. rem. to Windsor, perhaps, tho.
Blake's Ann. say he would have contin. with Mather. He was in
60th yr. and much do I regret the ill success of inq. for his place of
educ. or any acco. of his early days. All that we get from the veracious
annals of Clap, wh. was by his f. commit. to the care of M. when the
youth had leave to come to N. E. is, that he liv. 40 miles off. On what
author. he is said to have d. at Boston, I kn. not. JOHN, Boston, possib.
s. of the preced. as Farmer thot. but to me it seems very improb. by w.
Jane had John, b. 18, bapt. with his sis. Jane or his mo. 30 Apr. 1653:
and Dorothy, 23, bapt. 28 Jan. 1655. Perhaps his w. d. soon aft. as
well as s. John, and by sec. w. Rebecca he had John, again, 28 July
1662. JOHN, Boston, s. of Elias the first, m. 9 Apr. 1656, Catharine
Skipper, had Jotham, b. 30 Mar. 1660; Eliz. 17 Oct. 1662; Sarah, 20
June 1665; Ann, 21 Sept. 1671; Skipper, 4 May 1674; and Catharine, 18 Sept. 1676. When he d. is not told; but his wid. I presume, m.
8 Sept. 1680, John Johnson. MOSES, Salem, perhaps br. of the first
Elias, freem. 3 Sept. 1634, tho. Felt ins. his name with w. in the list of
ch. memb. under 1637, and so he must believe that he had been accept.
in ano. town, had Rebecca, bapt. 7 Aug. 1639; Mary, 14 Feb. 1641, d.
at 15 yrs.; Abigail, 12 Jan. 1645; Eliz. 3 Dec. 1646, d. soon; Samuel,
19 Dec. 1647; Eliz. again, 30 Sept. 1649, wh. m. 6 Apr. 1665, Nathaniel Grafton; Remember, 12 Sept. 1652; Mary, again, 6 Sept. 1657;

and a s. wh. name is not in the rec. 20 Mar. 1663; beside Sarah, wh. is not found in the rec. He liv. on Marblehead side, was one of the found. of the ch. 24 May 1684, and d. 28 Jan. 1686, aged 76, wh. date, Farmer says, Dana mistook. His w. Remember, d. of famous Isaac Allerton (but in Geneal. Reg. VIII. 270, she is call. Sarah, and possib. he had both to w. tho. it seems not prob.) d. aft. 1652, and he m. 22 Oct. 1656, Eunice, wid. of Thomas Roberts. His d. Rebecca m. 3 June 1658, John Hawkes of Lynn, and d. soon aft. b. of s. Moses, next yr. His will, pro. 30 Mar. 1686, names w. and Moses, the only surv. ch. of his d. Rebecca; four ch. of his dec. d. Abigail, viz.: Samuel Ward, Abigail Hinds, Mary Dollabar, and Martha Ward; and four liv. ds. viz.: Eliz. Skinner; Remember Woodman; Mary, w. of Archibald Ferguson; and Sarah, w. of John Norman. PAUL, Boston, s. of the first Elias, m. Jemima, d. of lieut. John Smith, had Moses, b. 8 Feb. bapt. at Charlestown, 11 Sept. 1681; Jotham, 28 Oct. 1683; John, 14 Aug. 1687, one yr. old. PETER, Boston, elder br. of the preced. m. Martha, d. of Robert Bradford, had Martha, b. 8 Feb. 1671; and James. SAMUEL, Boston, found here on Noddle's isl. by the Mass. comp. in 1630, hav. built a little fort with four small pieces of artil. so that we may be sure he was here in 1629, perhaps came in 1628, too late for liability to expense of the expedit. of Endicott against Morton. He desir. adm. 19 Oct. 1630, into the comp. but did not take the freeman's o. until 2 Oct. 1632. Against all probabil. he is call. s. of Rev. John by a writer of more animation than exactness, in Hist. of E. Boston; and even the careful Hist. of Dorchester, 404, confident. says the same. For his habit of hospitality, he was requir. in the spring of 1635, to change his resid. and move to the peninsula, but that tyranny was not enforced, and in the autumn of the same yr. he went to Virg. to buy corn, was absent almost a yr. He was one of the king's Commissrs. 1665, and in a depon. 9 Dec. 1665, sw. he was 63 yrs. old. Of his fam. only w. Amias, d. Mary, and s. Nathaniel, and Samuel are kn. Nathaniel, wh. was a merch. in a conveyance by his f. and mo. 1650, of the isl. to some creditors, is styled heir of Noddle's isl. and he join. in the security. But we never hear more of him. Mary m. 8 Feb. 1656, John Palsgrave, and next, 20 Sept. 1660, Francis Hooke. She, in a petitn. to Andros, a few wks. bef. his overthrow, tells a strange story a. her elder br. defraud. his f. of the title to Noddle's isl. wh. had above seventeen yrs. been own. by Col. Samuel Shrimpton, under sale from Sir Thomas Temple. It may be, that, as Shrimpton was oppos. to Sir Edmund A. tho. one of his council, that this was a contrivance to get rid of him. See Geneal. Reg. VIII. 334. SAMUEL, Boston, s. of the preced. m. 4 Dec. 1660, Rebecca, d. of Rev. John Wheelwright of Wells, had Mary, b. 2 Oct. 1661; and Hannah, 25 Oct. 1663 ; and he d. 10 Mar. 1664, and some unusual proceed. in few days by creditors that the "est. be not conceal. or convey. away " may be seen in Col. Rec. IV. part II. 145, and Geneal. Reg. XII. 155. His br.-in-law Francis Hooke was appoint. admor. 1666, in Maine. So that Eliot, in Biog. Dict. mistook, saying he was the last nam. of four Royal Commissnrs. in the Warrant of 25 Apr. 1664 to hear all complaints and settle every thing in the Col. of N. E. respective of the doings under wh. most copious details are in Hutch. I. 229–57. Strange. is he miscall. s. of the Rev. John in Josselyn, 252. His wid. m. 12 Mar. 1672, William Bradbury. But ano. SAMUEL of Boston, wh. by w. Martha had Samuel, b. 16 Mar. 1671, may have been s. of John, tho. it is very improb. as the Dorchester min. is never report. to have had any s. and he, I infer from both Moses and Samuel sign. 1668 the petitn. from Marblehead against imposts, was, perhaps, s. of Moses, and of a differ. tribe from the royal commissnr.

MAWER, WILLIAM, Boston 1636, liv. at Mount Wollaston, but rem. I think, bef. 1640.

MAWNEY, MOSES, Narraganset, a Huguenot, wh. escap. from France, soon aft. 1685, and as Potter in his Hist. tells, sat down in that part now East Greenwich, prob. bring. w. and ch. of wh. two are nam. Peter and Mary. Mary m. in New York. PETER, Providence, s. of the preced. m. Mary, d. of the sec. Pardon Tillinghast, had, as we learn from the will of their gr.f. without any indicat. of order, Sarah, Amey, Lydia, Mary, John, b. Aug. 1718, and Peter. By a sec. w. whose name Potter has not giv. he says there were three, perhaps nam. Eliz. Mercy, and Pardon, but the want of precision is unavoid. The name is one of the perversions that the Huguenots suffer. in change of their alleg. since in France it was spell. Le Moine.

MAWRY, MOURIE, MOREY, or MOWRY, * ROGER, Salem, freem. 18 May 1631, serv. as neatherd for the town 1637 ; may have had w. Eliz. in 1641, but in few yrs. rem. to Providence, and was among the list of freem. there 1655, when he kept an inn, and was rep. 1658.

MAXCY, ALEXANDER, a soldier of Gallup's comp. for the sad expedit. 1690, of Phips against Quebec.

MAXFIELD, CLEMENT, Dorchester 1658, came with his w. from Taunton, but they had yrs. bef. been memb. of Dorchester ch. had m. Mary Denman, prob. d. of John, constable 1664, had Samuel, and, perhaps, John; d. 3 Feb. 1692, and his wid. d. 31 May 1707, in 86th yr. JAMES, Boston, a cordwainer in 1675. JOHN, Salisbury 1652, was of Gloucester 1679 ; but this may be the Mayfield of Lynn in Felt's list, Geneal. Reg. V. 339, wh. m. Rebecca Armitage. See that. JOHN, Salisbury, by w. Eliz. had John, b. 23 Oct. 1680 ; Timothy, Oct. 1682 ;

Mary, 10 Jan. 1685; Margery, 5 Nov. 1686; Nathaniel, 1 Mar. 1689; Joseph, 4 Mar. 1692; Eliz. 18 Jan. 1695; and William, 4 Sept. 1699; and d. sudden. 10 Dec. 1703. SAMUEL, Dorchester, m. Mary, d. of Thomas Davenport, had John; Ebenezer, b. 20 Nov. 1675; Mary; and Mehitable. His wid. Mary d. 1707.

MAXSON, or MAGGSON, * JOHN, Westerly, perhaps s. of Richard, was rep. 1685, may have been f. of a min. wh. serv. the seventh day Bapt. congrega. (as ment. by Callender) at Westerly 1738; and d. 17 Dec. 1720, aged 82. Descend. have been num. He m. Mary Mosher, had John, b. 1666; Joseph, 1672; Dorothy; Jonathan; Hannah; and Mary. His w. d. 2 Feb. 1718, aged 77. RICHARD, Newport 1638, of wh. no more is kn. but that he was a blacksmith.

MAXWELL, JAMES, Boston 1684, a memb. of the Scots' Charit. Soc. was doorkeep. for the Gen. Court 1693. The name may be the same as Maxfield. JOHN, the freem. of 1669, may have then been of Andover.

MAY, ELEAZER, Roxbury, s. of Samuel, m. early, and by w. Sarah had Eleazer, b. 21 June 1687; Samuel, 26 Dec. 1688, d. the same day, and his w. d. ten days aft. He was k. by the Ind. 29 Apr. foll. ‖ GEORGE, Boston, m. 6 Oct. 1656, Eliz. d. of William Franklin, was an iron-monger, ar. co. 1661, freem. 1665. JOHN, Roxbury, writ. Mayes and Mays in the early rec. of town and ch. but Maies in Col. rec.; came as early as 1640, or bef. with w. and prob. ch. John and Samuel, freem. 2 June 1641, d. 28 Apr. 1670, aged 80 yrs. His nuncup. will, made four days bef. pro. next day, names s. John and Samuel; and his w. Sarah d. 4 Mar. foll. This was not that w. he brot. from Eng. for in the rec. of ch. Eliot had writ. under 18 June 1651, " sis. Mayes d. a very gracious and savoury christian," nor was she that Sarah rec. by dism. from Dorchester ch. as the same hand notes "an aged woman join. here 29 Apr. 1660." Farmer was inform. that he was of Mayfield, Co. Sussex. JOHN, Roxbury, s. of the preced. b. in Eng. freem. 1660, m. 19 Nov. 1656, Sarah, d. of the first Daniel Brewer, had Mary, b. 7 Nov. 1657, bapt. 29 May 1659, but in the rec. writ. Sarah by mistake; Sarah, 8, bapt. 11 Sept. 1659; Eleazer, 12, bapt. 16 Feb. 1662, d. soon; John, 19, bapt. 24 May 1663; Mehitable, 6, bapt. 7 May 1665; Naomi, 20, bapt. 26 May 1667; Elisha, 20, bapt. 21 Mar. 1669; and Ephraim, 23, bapt. 25 Dec. 1670; and d. 11 Sept. 1671, aged a. 40, hav. been blind sev. mos. His will, pro. 11 Oct. foll. names the seven liv. ch. Mary, m. 4 Nov. 1676, John Ruggles; Sarah m. 24 Feb. 1680, Samuel Williams; Ephraim d. in minority, but admin. of his est. was giv. 13 Nov. 1690, to capt. Nathaniel Stearns; and Elisha perhaps rem. to a dist. JOHN, Roxbury, s. of the preced. m. 2 June 1684, Prudence, d. of John Bridge, had John, b. 12 Apr. 1685, d. soon; a s. 23 Feb. 1686, d. the

same day; John, again, 23 Nov. 1686; Samuel, 8 Jan. 1689, d. at 8
yrs.; Ebenezer, 19 Oct. 1692; Prudence, 29 Nov. 1694; Hezekiah, 14
Dec. 1696; Sarah, 29 Oct. 1698; Nehemiah, 28 June 1701; Mehitable, 27 Feb. 1703; Eleazer, 9 July 1705; and Benjamin, 1 Mar.
1708; was freem. 1690, a deac. and his descend. are very wide. diffus.
Fam. tradit. antedat. his b. seven yrs. and gave him 7 s. 4 ds. His w.
d. 26 Sept. 1723, and he d. 24 Feb. 1730. JONATHAN, Hingham, m.
Nov. 1686, Sarah, d. of John Langley of the same, had Mary, b. 3 Nov.
1687, and no more. He d. of smallpox, 22 Nov. 1690, a soldier in the
lamenta. expedit. of Phips against Quebec. SAMUEL, Roxbury, s. of
the first John, b. in Eng. freem. 1660, m. 7 June 1657, Abigail Stansfull
if the copy of rec. furnish. me spell correct. so strange a name, had
Abigail, b. 22, bapt. 29 May 1659; Jonathan, 4, bapt. 7 Feb. 1664;
Joanna, 7, bapt. 11 Mar. 1666; Eleazer, 6, bapt. 8 Mar. 1668; John,
17, bapt. 19 June 1670; Gideon, 25 Jan. bapt. 4 Feb. 1672, d. in few
wks.; and Experience, a d. 28, bapt. 31 Aug. 1673; and he d. 17 July
1677. THOMAS, Malden, one of Moseley's comp. in 1675 for Narraganset campaign. Four of the name had, in 1834, been gr. at Harv.
and eight at other N. E. coll.

MAYBEE, HENRY, Newtown, L. I. 1656. Thompson. NICHOLAS,
Windsor, was bur. 1 Mar. 1667, with very small est. and neither w.
nor ch.

MAYER, HENRY, Boston, butcher, by w. Alice had Joseph, b. 13 Mar.
1686; and by w. Hannah had Patience, 17 May 1698. ROBERT, Boston, by w. Hannah had Hannah, b. 16 Sept. 1683. THOMAS, Hingham
1638, came from Co. Norf.'k that yr. in the Diligent.

MAYFIELD, JOHN, Lynn, m. Rebecca, d. of Godfrey Armitage of the
same, had Benoni, b. Mar. 1666.

MAYHEW, *JOHN*, Chilmark, s. of the sec. Thomas, labor. all his
short life in teach. the Ind. chiefly on the Vineyard, d. 3 Feb. 1689, in
37th yr. leav. s. Experience to carry on the work on larger scale, b.
1674, d. 29 Nov. 1758, wh. m. 12 Nov. 1695, at Barnstable, Thankful,
d. of Gov. Hinckley, and f. of an illustr. line, Joseph, H. C. 1730;
Nathan, H. C. 1731; Zechariah, a missiona. to the Ind. wh. d. 6 Mar.
1806 in 89th yr.; and Jonathan, H. C. 1744, one of the most disting.
divines of our country, premature. tak. from his serv. at the age of 44
by d. at Boston 9 July 1766. JOHN, New London, mariner, was from
Devonsh. m. 25 Dec. 1676, Joanna, d. of Jeffrey Christophers, had
John, b. 15 Dec. 1677; Wait, 4 Oct. 1680; Eliz. 8 Feb. 1683; Joanna;
Mary; and Patience; and d. 1696. His s. John serv. as one of the
pilots for the fleet of Sir Hovenden Walker, in the abortive expedit.
1711, against Quebec, and was sent to Eng. to give evid. of the cause of

its failure, should any inquiry ever be instit. See Hutch. II. 197.

* *THOMAS*, Watertown, b. early in 1591, came in the Griffin, 1633, if we might so infer from the fact of his tak. his o. as freem. 14 May 1634, when Gov. Haynes and Gov. Brenton, besides Cotton, Hooker, and Stone, passeng. in that ship were adm. But that infer. would be wrong, for in Col. Rec. I. 95, is a report sign. by him and two other gent. for sett. out the bounds betw. Watertown and the new town, 6 Mar. 1632, and in July 1633, he was appoint. admor. of Ralph Glover, while Cotton and fellow-passeng. did not arr. bef. Sept. next, so that he must have been here in 1631, and he serv. as a merch. at Southampton, Eng. as Bond relates, and here as rep. 1636–44 exc. 42, was active in trade, first at Medford, aft. at W. but was induced to rem. to the Vineyard a. 1647, where he was propr.'s Gov. and preacher to the Ind. above 33 yrs. d. 1681, six days only bef. being 90 yrs. old. It is indistinct. pronounc. by tradit. that first w. wh. d. in Eng. had been Martha Parkhurst, and sec. was prob. brot. with him, Grace, wid. of Thomas Paine of London, and by her he had Hannah, b. 15 June 1635; Bethia, 6 Dec. 1636; and Mary, 14 Jan. 1640. It is not kn. that he had any s. but Thomas wh. he, as b. of the former w. brot. from Eng. but some uncert. is felt as to the relat. of f. and I do not concur with Bond, 857, in mak. Jane the last w. of Thomas the elder, but think her wid. of the s. nor do I believe that it was the s. wh. was, in 1647, chos. by Thomas Paine, then 15 yrs. old, as, with his w. Grace, guardians for him. *THOMAS*, Nantucket, s. of the preced. b. in Eng. serv. with his f. at the Vineyard, being the first min. bef. rem. to N. m. Jane Paine, perhaps d. of Grace, w. of his f. had Matthew, a teacher of much celebr. in the Ind. cause, wh. d. 1710; Thomas, wh. was a judge; and John, bef. ment. He was on board of that ship of wh. Garrett was master, from Boston to London in Nov. 1657, with Davis, Ince, and Pelham, young scholars, the hope of the country, fellow-passeng. never heard of, so proper. lament. by Gookin, as in his Hist. Coll. may be read. He sail. from B. the same day in ano. ship for London. His wid. Jane m. Richard Sansom.

MAYNARD, DAVID, Westborough, s. of sec. John of Sudbury, by w. Hannah, wh. d. 1725, had Keziah, b. 1703; David, 1704; Ruhamah, 1706; Jonathan, 1708; Martha, 1710; Jesse, 1712; Jotham, 1714; Ebenezer, 1716; Nathan; Hannah; and Mercy; and he d. a. 1757. JOHN, Cambridge 1634, rem. to Hartford, there was exempt, 1646, from watch, prob. for infirm. m. aft. May 1648, Editha, wid. of Robert Day, whose s. John rec. the prop. of Maynard by his will, as he had no ch. and d. not long aft. JOHN, Duxbury 1643. JOHN, Sudbury 1640, an orig. propr. freem. 1644, was one of the petitnrs. for gr. of Marlborough in 1656, and d. 10 Dec. 1672. He had two ws. if not more; by first

was b. John, but of what date is unkn. and, perhaps, others; he m. says
Barry, 1646, Mary Axdell or Axtel, had Zechary, b. 7 June 1647;
Eliz. 26 May 1649; Lydia; Hannah, 30 Sept. 1653; and Mary, 3 Aug.
1656. Hannah d. prob. young, as she is not nam. in his will of 4 Sept.
1672, in wh. he calls John eldest s. but makes w. with Zechary excors.
calls Eliz. w. of Joseph Graves; and Lydia, w. of Joseph Moore; and
the youngest d. unm. but she m. Feb. 1674, Daniel Hudson of Lancaster, and d. in 1677. Perhaps the first w. was d. of Comfort Starr,
and the sec. may have been m. a doz. yrs. later than Barry tells. JOHN,
Dorchester or Boston 1648, a carpenter, freem. 1649, m. wid. Eliz. Pell
(that had bef. been wid. of Nathaniel Heaton), and d. 4 Oct. 1658, leav.
her once more a wid. JOHN, Sudbury, eldest s. of the first John of the
same, perhaps brot. by his f. from Eng. m. 5 Apr. 1658, Mary, d. of
Stephen Gates of Lancaster, had John, b. 1661; Eliz. 1664; Simon,
1666, d. young; Simon, again, 1668; David, 1669, bef. ment.; Zechariah, 1672; Hannah; Sarah, 1680; Lydia, 1682; and Joseph, 1685;
all b. at Marlborough, where he was freem. 1685, and d. leav. wid.
Sarah, perhaps 1711. JOHN, Marlborough, eldest s. of the preced. by
w. Lydia, d. of Richard Ward, had John, b. 1690; Daniel, 1692;
James, 1694; Mary, 1696; Reuben, 1698; Abigail, 1701; Phineas,
1703; Bethia, 1705; and Hezekiah, 1708; was freem. I think, 1690,
tho. the rec. says sen. when his f. was alive, and hav. once sworn in
1685, needed not to go through the solemnity again, yet it was, perhaps,
thot. good to swear double in those times. He d. 15 May 1731, and his
wid. d. 10 Jan. 1740. JOSEPH, Marlborough, youngest s. of the sec.
John of Sudbury, m. 1707, Eliz. Price, had Persis, b. 1713; Eliz. 1716;
and Benjamin, 1721. His w. d. 1732, at Worcester. SIMON, Marlborough, br. of David, by w. Hannah had Hannah, b. 1694; Simon,
1696; Eliz. 1698; Tabitha, 1701; Elisha, 1703; Eunice, 1705;
Ephraim, 1707; and Benjamin, 1709; and d. 19 Jan. 1747; and Hannah, his wid. d. 5 Apr. 1748. WILLIAM, New London, came from
Hampsh. Eng. m. 15 Nov. 1678, Lydia, d. of John Richards, had William, b. 16 Nov. 1680; and eight more ch. of wh. three were under age
when he d. 1711. ZECHARY, Sudbury, s. of the first John of the same,
m. 1678, Hannah, not d. of John Cooledge, as Barry, 323, says, but d.
of John Goodrich of Wethersfield, had Zechariah, b. 30 Apr. 1679;
John, 26 Jan. 1681; Hannah, 25 Jan. 1683; Jonathan, 8 Apr. 1685;
David, or Daniel, 22 May 1687; Eliz. 3 Jan. 1692; Joseph; Moses;
and Abigail, 13 May 1700. His w. d. 1719, and he d. 1724. This
name is spell. with many variat.

MAYNE, or MAYEN. See Maine.

MAYO, DANIEL, Eastham, s. of the sec. John, had Bethia, Sarah,
Daniel, Jeremiah, Margery, Mary; and d. a. 1715. JAMES, Eastham,

br. of the preced. had Gamaliel, Joseph, James, and prob. Jonathan, by first w. and by the sec. Sarah, m. 1702, had Sarah, b. 14 Jan. 1703; Henry, 3 May 1705; and John, 11 Oct. 1707; and d. 1708. JOHN, Barnstable, min. collea. with Lothrop, came in 1638 prob. as he was sw. freem. 3 Mar. 1640, and ord. 15 Apr. foll. brot. from Eng. ch. Hannah, Samuel, John, Nathaniel, and, perhaps, Eliz. wh. may, however, have been b. on this side of the water; rem. to Eastham 1646, thence, discourag. at E. drawn to Boston, where he was inst. 9 Nov. 1655, first min. of the sec. or N. ch. and Michael Powell ord. ruling eld. the same day; dism. 1673, in advanc. age, aft. hav. more than twenty yrs. had joint. serv. with Increase Mather, he went to Barnstable, there, and at Eastham and Yarmouth liv. the short resid. of his days with one or ano. ch. and d. at Y. May 1676, leav. wid. Thomasine, wh. d. 26 Feb. 1682, but we kn. not whether she had been his first w. in Eng. The agreem. 15 June 1676, for settlem. of the small est. betw. wid. ch. and gr.ch. is on rec. His d. Hannah m. 1642, Nathaniel Bacon; and Eliz. m. Joseph Howes of Yarmouth. JOHN, Eastham, s. of the preced. b. in Eng. m. 1 Jan. 1651, Hannah Reycraft, if Col. Rec. has the name right, had John, b. 15 Dec. 1652; William, 7 Oct. 1654; James, 3 Oct. 1656, bef. ment.; Samuel, 2 Aug. 1658; Elisha, 7 Nov. 1661; Daniel, 24 Jan. 1664, bef. ment.; Nathaniel, 2 Apr. 1667; Thomas, 24 June 1670, d. soon; and Thomas, again, 15 July 1672. He d. a. 1706, the only s. wh. outliv. the f. His will, of June 1702, was pro. 4 Nov. 1706. JOHN, Roxbury, came in 1633, a young ch. brot. by Robert Gamblin, jr. as s. of his w. by former h. m. 24 May 1654, Hannah, d. of John Graves, had Hannah, b. 24 Apr. 1657, d. soon; John, 15, bapt. 20 Feb. 1659; Hannah, again, 16, bapt. 24 Feb. 1661; Rebecca, 30 June, bapt. 3 July 1664, d. at 21 yrs.; Joseph, 11, bapt. 13 Jan. 1667; Mehitable, 6 Jan. bapt. 28 Feb. 1669; Thomas, 16, bapt. 20 Nov. 1670; Benjamin, 29, bapt. 31 Mar. 1672, d. in Oct. foll. as did also Thomas, the predeces.; Thomas, again, 12, bapt. 16 Nov. 1673; yet the town rec. makes this last b. 12 Dec. 1676. He d. 28 Apr. 1688, but his will of 9 Feb. preced. was kept back until 11 June 1691, perhaps to avoid the Andros jurisdict. upon pro. business. It names the w. Hannah, wh. d. 5 Oct. 1699, aged 63; and the five liv. ch. Hannah m. 2 Mar. 1680, Isaac Morris; and Mehitable m. 23 July 1695, Thomas Thurston. *JOHN, Hingham, s. of the sec. John, m. 14 Apr. 1681, Hannah, d. of maj. John Freeman, had Hannah, b. 8 Jan. 1682; Samuel, 16 July 1684; John; Mercy, 23 Apr. 1688; Rebecca; Mary, 26 Oct. 1694; Joseph, 22 Dec. 1696; and a. 1700 rem. to Harwich, there had Eliz. 1706; was rep. oft. and he d. 1 Feb. 1726. JOHN, Roxbury, s. of John of the same, m. 8 July 1685, Sarah Burden, had Rebecca, b. 14 May 1686, d. at 2 mos.;

Sarah, 9 June 1688, d. in 3 wks. He was deac. and d. 25 Feb. 1733.
JOSEPH, Newbury, m. 29 May 1679, Sarah, prob. d. of Henry Short,
had Sarah, b. 9 July foll.; and Thomasine, 10 June 1689, as Coffin
gives the dates. JOSEPH, Roxbury, br. of John the sec. m. 10 Mar.
1692, Eliz. d. of John Holbrook, had Rebecca, b. 26 Dec. foll. d. young;
Eliz. 17 Mar. 1696; and his w. d. 7 Feb. 1735. * NATHANIEL, Eastham, s. of Rev. John, b. in Eng. m. 13 Feb. 1650, Hannah, d. of Gov.
Thomas Prence, had Thomas, b. 7 Dec. foll.; Nathaniel, 16 Nov. 1652;
Samuel, 12 Oct. 1655; Hannah, 17 Oct. 1657; Theophilus, 17 Dec.
1659; and Bathshua, 1662; was rep. 1660, and he d. 1662. His wid.
m. Jonathan Sparrow. NATHANIEL, Eastham, s. of the preced. m. 28
June 1678, Eliz. d. of Robert Wickson or Wixam, had Nathaniel, b.
July 1681; Bathsheba, 23 Sept. 1683; Alice, 29 Apr. 1686; Ebenezer, 13 July 1689; Hannah, Jan. 1692; Elisha, 28 Apr. 1695; and
Robert, 20 Mar. 1698. He took sec. w. 10 June 1708, Mercy, wid. of
Nathaniel Young, and d. 30 Nov. 1709. NATHANIEL, Eastham, s. of
the sec. John of the same, by first w. whose name is not ment. had Rebecca, b. Apr. 1697; William, Aug. 1699; and Robert, June 1701;
and he m. sec. w. 28 Oct. 1703, Mary Brown, had Mary, 1704; Mehitable, 1705; Ann, 1707; Priscilla, 1708; Phebe, 1709; Lydia; and
Hannah; and d. 1716. SAMUEL, Barnstable 1640, s. of Rev. John, b.
in Eng. a mariner, one of the purchas. of Oyster Bay, L. I. Apr. 1653,
had his vessel seiz. for intercourse with the Dutch, then our enemies,
by Thomas Baxter, under a R. I. authority, but obtain. restit. with
decree for £150 dams. By w. Thomasine, d. of William Lumpkin of
Yarmouth, had Mary, 1645; Samuel, 1647, bapt. together, 3 Feb. 1650
(his w. hav. join. Lothrop's ch. 20 Jan. preced.); Hannah, 20 Oct.
1650; Eliz. 22 May 1653; and at Boston, whither he had rem. Nathaniel, 1 Apr. 1658; and Sarah, 1660; and he d. 1663. Admin. of
his est. was giv. 26 Apr. 1664, to his f. at Boston, his wid. declining
the tr. Mary m. 16 July 1664, Jonathan Bangs; and Eliz. m. 1674,
Rev. Samuel Treat. SAMUEL, Eastham, s. of the first Nathaniel, had
Samuel, b. 1690; Jonathan; Rebecca; and Mercy; and d. 29 Oct. 1738.
SAMUEL, Eastham, s. of the sec. John of the same, had Ann, Martha,
Eliz. and Content. THOMAS, Eastham, s. of the first Nathaniel, m. 13
June 1677, Barbara, d. of Richard Knowles, had Thomas, b. 3 Apr.
1678; Theophilus, 31 Oct. 1680; Mary, Aug. 1683; Maria, 19 Jan.
1685; Ruth, Jan. 1688; Judah, 25 Nov. 1691; Lydia, 12 June 1694;
Richard, 13 Jan. 1696; and Israel, 12 Aug. 1700; and d. 22 Apr.
1729. THOMAS, Eastham, youngest s. of the sec. John of the same,
had Mary, and, Mr. Hamblen thinks, Mercy, Hannah, and Noah.
THOMAS, Roxbury, s. of John of the same, m. 4 May 1699, Eliz. d. of

John Davis, had Hannah, b. 4 Apr. 1700 ; Mary, 22 Oct. 1702, d. at 16 yrs.; Sarah, 30 May 1705; Eliz. 22 Sept. 1707 ; John, 17 Sept. 1709 ; Rebecca, 21 Oct. 1711 ; Thomas, 23 Sept. 1713 ; Abigail, Sept. 1715 ; Joseph, 13 June 1717, d. within 4 wks.; Mary, again, 20 Feb. 1719 ; Joseph, again, 28 Feb. 1721 ; and Mehitable, 12 Apr. 1724 ; and he d. 26 May 1750. WILLIAM, Eastham, s. of the sec. John of the same, d. 1691, and his wid. d. next yr.; had, as Hamblen thinks, Thankful and Mercy.

MAYSANT, WILLIAM, Branford 1646 and 8, then own. ld. prob. rem. for no more is kn.

McDONALD, JOHN, Boston 1657.

McDOUGALL, ALISTER, Boston 1658.

McEWEN, or MEKUNE, McCUNE, or MECUNE, GERSHOM, Stratford, youngest s. of Robert, m. Jan. 1737, Martha, d. of Samuel Picket, had Mary, b. Apr. 1738 ; Robert, June 1743 ; Sarah, Apr. 1747 ; and Samuel, Dec. 1749. JOHN, Stratford, eldest br. of the preced. m. Oct. 1727, Rebecca, d. of Daniel Picket, had Eliz. b. Mar. 1729 ; Daniel, Nov. 1730, wh. d. unm.; Nathan, Feb. 1733, d. at 5 yrs.; Rebecca, Sept. 1737, d. next yr.; Nathan, again, Nov. 1740 ; and John, Feb. 1745. The two youngest s. were m. ROBERT, Stratford 1686, a Scotchman, came in the Henry and Francis, a sh. of 350 tons, charter. by the laird of Pitlochie, as Whitehead, in Hist. of Perth Amboy tells, or in the Caledonia (by ano. rep.) a man of war of 50 guns, to transport covenanters releas. from the tolbooths of Edinburgh, Glasgow, and Sterling, on condition of transporta. to the colonies. No little of historic interest attaches to this colony that land. their precious freight at Perth Amboy. McEwen hims. wh. by tradit. is deriv. from Dumfries, explains: "In June 18, 1679, I was in an engagem. in Scotland, at Bothwell brigg, then of the age of 18 yrs. The 5th of Sept. 1685 we set sail to come to America, and land. at Amboy 18 Dec. and 18 Feb. foll. I came to Stratford." Here he was a tailor, made leather breeches for men, stays and mantys for women ; and he says he m. 20 June 1695, Sarah Wilcockson, d. of Timothy, as the rec. says, noting the m. of 2 June, and of b. of two first ch. his own writ. agrees very near. with rec. John, 20 or 23 Sept. 1697 ; and Eliz. wh. he calls Betty, 7 Nov. 1699. Other ch. were Robert, 7 Mar. 1702 ; Sarah, 5 Nov. 1704 ; Timothy, 11, bapt. 27 Apr. 1707 ; and Gershom, b. 7 Apr. 1711 ; and the f. d. Feb. 1740. Of fellow-passeng. I presume very few (I hear with certain. of only one), came to N. E. and concur. reports say more than one third d. on the voyage to N. J. Not a few, Whitehead says, went back to Scotland, prob. aft. the revo. of 1688. ROBERT, Stratford, s. of the preced. m. Aug. 1727, Mary, d. of Abel Birdsey, had Comfort, b.

Sept. 1728; Sarah, Nov. 1730; Hezekiah, Oct. 1732; and Eunice, 9
Aug. 1740. TIMOTHY, Stratford, br. of the preced. m. Aug. 1736, Abi-
gail, d. of John Hurd, had Ruth, b. Sept. 1737; Ephraim, Dec. 1739;
Abijah, Sept. 1742; Phebe, Apr. 1745; Ann, July 1747; perhaps Wil-
liam, said to have been lost at sea; George, June 1752; and Charity,
Nov. 1754; and he d. Feb. 1788.

MEACHAM, ISAAC, Enfield, weaver, s. prob. of Jeremiah the first, liv.
many yrs. at Salem, m. 28 Dec. 1669, wid. Deborah Perkins, had
Deborah, b. 15 Dec. 1670, d. next yr.; Isaac, 13 Nov. 1672; Jeremiah,
13 Nov. 1674; Israel, 28 Sept. 1676, wh. both d. without ch.; Ebenezer, 21 Feb. 1678; Ichabod, 11 Aug. 1679; Deborah, again, 8 Apr.
1681; and John, 11 June 1682. He rem. next yr. from S. and at E.
had Mary, 1684; Joseph, 18 Feb. 1686, H. C. 1710, the first min. of
Coventry 1713; and Benjamin, 1687; and d. 1692. JEREMIAH, Salem
1660, a fuller, m. Deborah, d. of John Brown of Watertown, had prob.
Isaac, and Jeremiah, beside ds. Rhoda, wh. m. a West, and d. bef. her f.
leav. Samuel; Sarah, wh. m. 4 Feb. 1668, Joseph Boyce or Boyes;
Hannah, wh. m. 16 Feb. 1668, William Gill; Bethia, wh. m. Sept.
1672, George Hacker; and, perhaps, Rebecca, wh. m. 27 Jan. 1675,
John Macarty. He d. 1695, aged 81, and his will was pro. 12 Apr.
of that yr. JEREMIAH, Salem, s. of the preced. m. 3 Jan. 1673, Mary
Trask, prob. d. of Henry, had Jeremiah, b. 21 Dec. 1673. JOHN,
Salem, m. 28 May 1697, Mary, d. of William Cash.

MEADE, MEADES, or MEDE, DAVID, Cambridge vill. perhaps s. of
Gabriel, m. at Watertown, 24 Sept. 1675, Hannah Warren, perhaps d.
of David, had Hannah, b. 17 Sept. 1676; and David, 1678; rem. to
Billerica, freem. 1683; rem. to Woburn, there had John, 14 Aug. 1685;
Sarah, 24 Oct. 1688; Susanna, 11 Oct. 1690; and, perhaps, rem. again.
Hannah m. 14 Oct. 1701, Ebenezer Locke. GABRIEL, Dorchester,
freem. 2 May 1638, d. 12 May 1666, in 79th yr. as was suppos. His
will, of 18 Jan. 1654, pro. 17 July 1667, names w. Johanna, wh. prob.
was a sec. w. s. David, and four ds. Lydia, Experience, Sarah, and
Patience. Lydia m. 19 Oct. 1652, James Burgess; Experience m. 4
Dec. 1663, Jabez Heaton; Sarah m. 30 Nov. 1664, Samuel Eddy; and
Patience m. 28 Apr. 1669, Matthias Evans, all, I think, of Boston. He
had also s. not nam. in the will, Israel, b. 1639, wh. liv. at Watertown
some yrs. but rem. to D. in Aug. 1674, and, perhaps, later to Woburn.
ISRAEL, Woburn, prob. s. of the preced. m. 26 Feb. 1669, Mary, d. of
wid. Mary Hall, had Margaret, b. 20 Jan. 1676; Mary, 10 Feb. 1682;
Ruth, 10 Aug. 1684; Ebenezer, 10 May 1686, and, perhaps, some
earlier. Margaret m. Joseph Locke, as sec. w. JAMES, Wrentham, by
w. Judith had Grace, b. 11 Dec. 1692; and James, 9 Oct. 1694; and

his w. d. that same day. JOHN, Greenwich, prob. s. of Joseph, propound. for freem. 1670. * JOSEPH, Stamford 1657, rem. to Greenwich, was freem. 1662, rep. 1669–71. NICHOLAS, Charlestown 1680, had by w. Eliz. wh. join. the ch. 6 Mar. 1681, Susanna, bapt. 13 Mar. 1681; Eliz. 14 Aug. 1681, and, perhaps, rem. RICHARD, Roxbury 1663, freem. 1665, had Richard, a mariner, wh. d. bef. 15 Feb. 1679, when the f. took admin. on the est. but that s. was, I think, not b. at R. The f. m. 6 Nov. 1678, Mary, a sec. w. and d. I believe, 21 Feb. 1689. * WILLIAM, Gloucester 1641, one of the selectmen 1647, rem. to New London, bef. Oct. 1653, when he was rep. but never aft. tho. liv. 1669. WILLIAM, Roxbury, br. of Richard, had w. Rebecca, and d. 29 Oct. 1683, and his wid. 8 days aft. His will, made the day of his d. if the rec. be right, pro. 2 Nov. foll. names only br. Richard, w. Rebecca, and s.-in-law Joseph Stanton, tho. undutiful. The wid. made her will 5, pro. 15 Nov. foll. Nineteen of the name had, in 1834, been gr. at the coll. of N. E. of wh. only one was of Harv.

MEADER, JOHN, Dover 1653, by w. Abigail, had Eliz. b. 26 Mar. 1665; John; Sarah, 11 Jan. 1669; and Nathaniel, 14 June 1671, wh. was k. by the Ind. 23 Apr. 1704, and, perhaps, Nicholas. Sarah m. 16 Mar. 1692, Edward Wakeham. Belkn. I. 168; and Niles, in 3 Mass. Hist. Coll. VI. 254. NATHANIEL, Dover, s. of the preced. by w. Eleanor had Lydia, b. 25 Aug. 1696; Daniel, 3 Nov. 1698; Nathaniel, 8 Mar. 1700; Eliz. 3 Apr. 1702; and Eleanor, posthum. 3 June 1704. NICHOLAS, Dover, perhaps br. of the preced. by w. Lydia had Keziah, b. 23 June 1709; Samuel, 15 Jan. 1711; Nicholas, 9 Oct. 1712; John, 8 Oct. 1715; and Daniel, 6 Nov. 1718.

MEADOWS, PHILIP, Roxbury, m. Apr. 1641, Eliz. d. of Stephen Iggulden or Iggleden, had Hannah, b. 1 Feb. 1643. Perhaps he rem. for no more is found of him in the rec.

MEAKINS, or MEEKINS, JOHN, Hartford, is in the list of freem. 1669, d. 1706, leav. wid. Mary, ds. Mary Belden, Sarah Spencer, beside Rebecca, and Hannah, unm. when his will of 1702 was made, and three s. John, Joseph, and Samuel. Of these John was a lieut. d. 1739, aged 76; Samuel was a lieut. d. 1733, in 60th yr. The wid. wh. may have been his sec. w. was d. of John Biddle, and she d. 1725, in 78th yr. THOMAS, Boston 1633, came prob. in the Griffin, adm. with w. Catharine of Boston ch. 2 Feb. foll. then call. " serv. to our br. Edmund Quincy," freem. 9 Mar. 1637, prob. d. in few yrs. and his wid. went to live at Roxbury, with s. Thomas, there d. " an aged woman," as Eliot writes " mo. of br. Meakins," 3 Feb. 1651. * THOMAS, Braintree, s. of the preced. b. in Eng. came, no doubt, with his f. and mo. 1633, " serv. to our br. Edmund Quincy," as on adm. to the ch. 30 Mar. foll. he is call. was freem. 25

May 1636, had Joseph, bapt. 5 May 1639, at Boston, and at Braintree, Sarah, b. 24 Apr. 1641; and Thomas, 8 June 1643; was rep. 1644; rem. to Roxbury, there had Hannah, bapt. 13 Mar. 1647; and John, 28 Jan. 1649, d. in May foll. and his w. Sarah d. in childbed, 21 Jan. 1651, says the ch. rec. wh. adds " she was a gracious woman, and left a good savor behind her." The Braintree rec. ment. that " Helen M. was drown. 3 Dec. 1638;" and she may have been ch. but more prob. sis. of this man. He rem. to Hadley, with sec. w. Eliz. m. says rec. of R. 14 Feb. 1651 (unless this be antedat.) wh. d. 1683 without ch. and he d. 10 Dec. 1687. He had ds. Mary, I suppose, b. at Braintree, wh. m. at H. Nathaniel Clark of Northampton, bore him two ds. and in 1669 m. John Allis of Hatfield; and Hannah, w. of Joseph Belknap, wh. d. 26 Dec. 1688, to share his prop. acc. his will, with heirs of his only s. THOMAS, Hatfield, s. of the preced. m. Mary, d. of Thomas Bunce of Hartford, had Sarah, b. 1666; Mary, 1670; John, 1672; Thomas, 1673; and Mehitable, 1675; and he was k. by the Ind. 19 Oct. of that yr. His. wid. m. next yr. John Downing.

MEANE, or MEANS, JOHN, Cambridge, by w. Ann had John, b. 3 Feb. 1638, wh. d. 10 Aug. of the yr. foll.; Sarah, Feb. 1640; Mary, 3 Apr. 1644; John, again, posthum. 19 Sept. wh. was bur. 21 Oct. 1646; but the f. d. or was bur. 19 Mar. bef. The wid. m. John Hastings, outliv. him, and d. 10 June 1667, acc. Harris, Epit. 170, but her inv. tak. 3 Apr. 1666, says she d. 25 Mar. preced. Her d. Sarah m. 10 Apr. 1655, Walter Hastings, s. of John, but not, as Harris, Epit. 35, makes him, also, of Ann Meane, and she d. 27 Aug. 1673; Mary m. 12 Nov. 1661, Samuel Hastings, s. of John.

MEARS, JÁMES, Boston, feltmaker, s. of Robert, by w. Eliz. had Eliz. b. 1 Aug. 1668; Edward, 22 Mar. 1670; Robert, 29 Jan. 1672; Oliver, 3 Dec. 1673; Hannah, 28 Jan. 1677, d. soon; Hannah, again, 2 June 1678; John, 12 May 1680; Nathaniel, 7 Oct. 1682, d. soon; and Nathaniel, again, 26 Sept. 1683. In 1704 he sold the ld. on wh. the French, or Huguenot, chapel was soon built, wh. in 1748 was sold to the relig. soc. that symboliz. with Rev. Andrew Croswell, and in 1785 pass. into the hands of Roman Catholics, where on 2 Nov. 1788 was for the first time in Boston held the performance of the mass. There the pious services of Rev. Father Matignon, and of the blessed Cheverus, aft. a Cardinal, and Archbp. of Bordeaux, were giv. to a very small congrega. JOHN, Boston, br. of the preced. d. 12 Nov. 1663, under mid. age, leav. wid. Mary, and posthum. s. John, b. 28 Dec.; had made his will 26 Sept. bef. as in Geneal. Reg. XII. 153. Ano. JOHN, of Boston, by w. Lydia had John, b. 5 July 1678. ROBERT, Boston, tailor, came in the Abigail, 1635, from London, aged 43, with w. Eliz. 30; Samuel, wh. prob. d. soon; and John, 3 mos.; and his w. Eliz. join. our ch. 24 July 1636; had Stephen, b. 25 Dec. or earlier, bapt. same mo. 1637, Samuel, 7, bapt. 13 June 1641; and James, 3, bapt. 31 Mar. 1644. His will, of 20 Feb. 1667, pro. 10 Sept. foll. ment. w. Eliz. ch. Samuel, and James, and gr.ch. John, s. of John, dec. SAMUEL, Boston, s. of the preced. by w. Mary had Stephen, b. 21 Nov. 1665; Eliz. 9 Apr. 1668; Samuel, 22 May 1671; and Mary, 26 Nov. 1673.

MEASURE, or MASUER, * WILLIAM, New London 1664, m. that yr. Alice, wid. of John Tinker, rem. to Lyme bef. 1671, was rep. 1676, d. 24 Mar. 1688, and admin. of his est. was giv. 26 June of that yr. to Alice, his wid. by Sir E. Andros.

MECOCK, MEACOCK, MAYCOCK, or MECOKE, PETER, Newtown, L. I. 1656. His wid. Mary m. Thomas Case of Fairfield, bef. 1661. THOMAS, Milford 1658, rem. to Guilford 1667, was a propr. 1685.

MEDBURY, JOHN, Swansey, by w. Sarah had Benjamin, b. 5 Mar. 1682 or 3.

MEECH, JOHN, Charlestown, rec. says, was there 1629, but no more is ever heard. Young's Chron. 375.

MEEK, RICHARD, Marblehead 1668.

MEEKER, MECAR, or MEAKER, ROBERT, New Haven, m. 1651, Susan Turberfield, rem. to Fairfield, bef. 1670. WILLIAM, New Haven 1657, sued Thomas Mulliner that yr. for slander in bewitching his pigs.

MEER, or MEERS, THOMAS, Salem, d. Sept. 1674, of wh. we kn. only that his br. John was made admor.

MEGAPOLENSIS, JOHN, s. of a min. of the same name, came in the sum. of 1642, aged 39, with w. 42, to New York from Holland, and was first employ. by the patroon, Van Rensselaer, up the river, but soon aft. is found at the city, and lastly on L. I. While at Albany, he wrote 1644, his acco. of the Maquas, or Mohawks. He had Hellegord, Dirck, Jan, and Samuel, of the ages respectively, 14, 12, 10, and 8, that is, I imagine, at the time of arr. Samuel was sent to H. C. 1657, stud. there 3 yrs. thence to Leyden Univ. where he was adm. M. D. was licens. as min. came back to New Amsterdam, and was the dominie, yet of such good capac. for worldly affairs, that Gov. Stuyvesant made him one of the Commissrs. for adjust. the terms of surrender of that Prov. 1665, to the Eng.

MEIGS, JOHN, Weymouth, s. of Vincent, b. in Eng. had John, b. 29 Feb. 1642, rem. prob. to Rehoboth 1643, next to New Haven, a. 1647, not long aft. a. 1654, to Guilford, thence, last, a. 1662, to Killingworth, where both he and s. John are in the list of freem. 1669, d. 4 Jan. 1672. He had only one s. four ds. Mary, w. of William Stevens; Concurrence, w. of Henry Crane; Trial, w. of Andrew Ward; and Eliz. w. of Richard Hibbell, wh. had d. bef. her f. He was a tanner, had large est. and some books, of wh. one was a Latin and Greek Dict. JOHN, Guilford, s. of the preced. m. 1665, Sarah Wilcoxson, had Sarah, b. 14 Feb. 1668; John, 10 Nov. 1670; a s. Janna, 21 Dec. 1672; Ebenezer, 19 Sept. 1675; Hannah, 25 Feb. 1678; Esther, 10 Nov. 1680; and Mindwell, 1682. He had sec. w. Lydia, perhaps wid. of Isaac Cruttenden, and d. 9 Nov. 1713. His s. John, with his f. were proprs. 1695, at G. MARK, New Haven 1646 or 7, br. of the first John, being rather wild, rem. to L. I. and is not ment. again. VINCENT, New Haven 1646, prob. carr. thither by s. John, he being an old man, hav. only two ch. kn. to us, rem. to Guilford, and again rem. d. at what is now Killingworth, Dec. 1658, his will of 2 Sept. being pro. 2 Dec. of that yr. A slight fam. acco. is in Geneal. Reg. IV. 91, very imperf. better than nothing, but not much. Early the name is Meggs always.

MELBY, NATHANIEL, Hull, freem. 1680, seems to me a wrong name. I never heard of it in N. E.

MELCHER, EDWARD, Portsmouth 1684, d. 1695. The name remains in N. H.

MELLEN, MELIN, MELLING, or other var. ISAAC, New Haven 1657, rem. soon aft. 1664, prob. to Virginia. JACOB, New Haven, br. of Isaac. See Melyen. JAMES, Malden, s. of Richard, m. a. 1658, Eliz. d. of Richard Dexter, had Eliz. b. 4 Sept. 1659; Mary, 8 July 1661, d. soon; James, 14 Apr. 1663; Mary, again, 1664; Richard, 24 Apr. 1665; John, 17 Sept. 1666; Sarah, 27 Nov. 1668; Thomas, 11 May 1670; William, 22 Aug. 1671; and he d. bef. 15 June 1680, when adm. of his est. was giv. to his wid. Eliz. wh. m. that yr. Stephen Barrett. JOHN, perhaps of Watertown, s. it may be, of James, m. Eliz. wid. of John Gale, d. of Henry Spring, wh. in his will of 29 June 1695, names her, when Barry thinks the h. may have been d. RICHARD, Weymouth, freem. 7 Sept. 1639, rem. to Charlestown, there had James, b. 4 June 1642, bef. ment. unless the date be wrong, as on the rec. is the name Mellers, wh. deceiv. Farmer, making him think it was a real new name. See Geneal. Reg. I. 194 and IV. 269. He had, also, at Weymouth, if the date be right, Sarah, 4 Apr. 1643; prob. Mary, and, perhaps, others. Of no fam. in the land is the investigat. more difficult, the spell. more various, the dates more perverse, the deficiencies more num. SAMUEL, Fairfield, d. bef. 1659, and John Ufford of Milford had admin. It may be that this gent. was Dutch, from Monhados, now New York. SIMON, Boston, on Winnisemet side, perhaps s. of Richard, by w. Mary had Simon, b. 25 Sept. 1665; rem. to Malden, had Thomas, Aug. 1668; Richard, 2 Mar. 1672; Mary; James, a. 1682; and John, b. in Watertown, 29 Jan. 1686; rem. to

Sherborn, and d. 19 Dec. 1694. From him, thro. Thomas, descend. Prentiss, H. C. 1784, disting. as first Ch. J. of Maine. Seven of this name had been gr. at Harv. in 1834, and two at Bowd.

MELLOWS, or MELLHOUSE, ABRAHAM, Charlestown, adm. of the ch. with w. Martha, and s. Edward in 1633, freem. 14 May 1634, d. as early as 1639, leav. six ch. says Felt, and Frothingham asserts, that he adventur. £50. in the comp. wh. I presume, means bef. com. from Eng. His will was brot. into Court in June 1639. EDWARD, Charlestown, s. of the preced. b. in Eng. came prob. with his f. and mo. freem. 4 Mar. 1634, constable 1637 ; by w. Hannah had Hannah, bapt. 22 Nov. 1636 ; Mary, 21 July 1638 ; Martha, 26 Oct. 1640, wh. d. 25 Feb. 1643 ; Edward ; Eliz. 5 Mar. 1644 ; and Abraham, 22 June 1645 ; was town clk. and selectman five yrs. d. 5 May 1650, since wh. none of the name is kn. at C. His wid. m. 24 June 1651, Joseph Hills. JOHN, Boston, s. of Oliver, b. in Eng. by w. Martha had John, b. 8 Apr. 1647, d. soon ; Martha, 8 Feb. 1654 ; Eliz. 15 Dec. 1656 ; Elisha, 16 Nov. 1659 ; Oliver, 3 Apr. 1662 ; Joseph, 6 Dec. 1664 ; Sarah, 16 Oct. 1667 ; Mary, 19 Mar. 1670 ; John, again, 5 Mar. 1676 ; and by w. Sarah had Elisha, again, 16 Mar. 1681 ; but perhaps there were two of the same name (not discrim. by the rec.) to have these ch. ; was freem. 1671, had gr. of ld. in the Stonington country. OLIVER, Boston 1634, with w. Eliz. adm. of our ch. 20 July, freem. 3 Sept. foll. disarm. in 1637, as one of the support. of Wheelwright, had Samuel, bapt. 7 Dec. 1634 ; Martha, 6 Mar. 1636 ; and Mary, 26 Aug. 1638 ; soon aft. d. at Braintree, and there prob. had liv. His wid. m. 1640 or 1, Thomas Makepeace of Dorchester. Martha m. 13 Sept. 1655, Joseph Waters ; and Mary, same day, m. Emanuel Springfield.

MELVILLE, DAVID, Barnstable 1691, merch. rem. to Eastham, there by w. Mary, d. of Rev. Samuel Willard, had Thomas, b. 25 July 1697 ; Mary, 31 July 1699 ; Abigail and Eliz. tw. 28 May 1702 ; and David, 17 Oct. 1704.

MELVIN, JOHN, Charlestown, by w. Hannah, wh. d. 27 May 1696, aged 41, had John, b. 29 Aug. 1679, bapt. 13 Feb. 1681, the w. being adm. of the ch. two wks. bef. ; Hannah, 15, bapt. 21 Aug. 1681 ; Robert, 13, bapt. 20 Jan. 1684 ; James, 20 Mar. 1686 ; Jonathan, 29 May, bapt. 3 June 1688 ; David, 29 Oct. bapt. 2 Nov. 1690 ; and Benjamin, bapt. 24 Feb. 1695.

MELYEN, MELYNE, or MALINE, ISAAC, New Haven, br. of Jacob, whose f. (always call. Mr. without name of bapt. as on list of those sw. to fidel. 7 Apr. 1657) had prob. brot. them both from Holland or New York ; but of this s. the last ment. is 1663, and whether he had w. and fam. or not is unkn. It must be very easy to distinguish this fam. from the numerous Mellens. JACOB, New Haven, took o. of fidel. with his f. (wh. had been there seat. in the ch. as early as 1655, prob. a Dutchman from New York), m. 1662, perhaps, Hannah, d. of George Hubbard, but aft. 1663, had rem. to Boston, was a leather seller, constable sev. yrs. bef. and aft. 1695, he had been chos. guardian 27 July 1693, by his neph. Riderus, call. hims. s. of Isaac, late of Virg. planter. His will, of 27 Sept. 1706, pro. 26 Dec. foll. speaks of his advanced age and infirm.; names w. Hannah and only two ch. Samuel, H. C. 1696, and Abigail Tilley, w. of William, aft. of Hon. Samuel Sewall, Ch. J. and explains his act in giv. equal. to s. and d. bec. for his liberal educ. he had expend. £300. This s. SAMUEL stands the lowest in the class, being ninth in the mod. catal. but in the old catal. of the Magnalia, the class contain. but eight. I found at the State House a letter from Samuel (teach. the gram. sch. 1700 at Hadley) to Cotton Mather, beg. his aid in restoring him to a higher rank; but the consequence was, that Mather had his cous. Roland Cotton insert. in the catal. as second next aft. Gov. Vaughan, and poor Melyen took nothing but one peg lower by his motion. So that he had shown greater discret. in keep. quiet, than in ask. the patronage of his Boston friend. His wid. d. Nov. 1717. SAMUEL, Fairfield, perhaps br. of Jacob, and uncle of the preced. had d. bef. 1660.

MENDAM, MENDALL, or MENDON, RICHARD, Kittery 1663, may have been s. of, if not the same as, the foll. ROBERT, Duxbury 1638, or earlier, sold, in 1639, ho. and ld. rem. to Kittery bef. 1647, and 1652 submit. to Mass. was constable that yr. and in 1666 was of the gr. jury. WILLIAM, Braintree 1667.

MENDLOVE, MARK, Plymouth 1637, Duxbury 1640. WILLIAM, Plymouth 1633. Yet in 1643 the name is not seen.

MENTOR, THOMAS, a soldier, k. 18 Sept. 1675, by the Ind. at Bloody brook, with " the flower of Essex," under Lothrop.

MEPHAM, MAPHAM, or MIPHAM, JOHN, Guilford 1639, one of the seven pillars at found. of ch. in 1643, and d. 1647, leav. only ch. John, wh. was rememb. in the will of Timothy Baldwin that m. his mo. in 1649, and wh. had third h. Thomas Tapping. JOHN, Southampton, L. I. 1673, print. Mepdam in a valua. paper, 3 Mass. Hist. Coll. X. 88, was prob. s. of the preced.

MERCER, THOMAS, Boston, d. 28 May 1699. In his will, of 8 Apr. 1698, he names w. Eliz. and their ch. William, the eldest, Thomas, and Sarah. Perhaps he had, in 1665, been of Sheepscot. Sullivan, 287. TIMOTHY, Windsor 1649, of wh. all we kn. is he was fined that yr. A Lucy M. came in the Defence, 1635, aged 19, from London.

MERCHANT, or MARCHANT, JOHN, Braintree, whose w. Sarah d. 3 Dec. 1638, rem. I think, soon to R. I. and 2 June 1639 was allow. inhab. of

Newport. Perhaps he was aft. of Yarmouth, there had Mary, b. 20 May 1648; Abijah, 10 Jan. 1651. WILLIAM, Watertown 1639, by w. Mary had Mary, b. 24 Mar. 1642, and rem. to Ipswich, there d. 4 Sept. 1668.

MEREDITH. See Ameredith. JONAH M. was one of the soldiers in Gallup's comp. in the doleful serv. 1690.

MERIAM, GEORGE, Concord, freem. 2 Jan. 1641, by w. Susannah had Eliz. b. 8 or 11 Nov. 1641; Samuel, 21 July 1642; Hannah, 14 July 1645; Abigail, 15 July 1647; Sarah, 17 July 1649; and Susanna. His w. d. 8 Oct. 1675, and he d. 29 Dec. aft. One of the ds. d. 10 Aug. 1646. JOHN, Boston, freem. 1647, by w. Sarah had Samuel, bapt. 9 Dec. (yet ano. rec. says b. 14, perhaps for 4) 1655; Sarah, 25 Apr. 1658; Thomasine, 23 Sept. 1660; and Mary, 24 May 1663; was selectman 1681. JOHN, Concord, s. of Joseph, freem. 1677, m. Mary Cooper, says Shattuck, was, perhaps, of Lexington 1679. He had John, it is said. JOHN, Concord, freem. 1690, may have been s. of William the first, and possib. of Hampton, there tak. o. of alleg. Dec. 1678. JOSEPH, Concord, br. of George, freem. 14 Mar. 1639, had Joseph, b. prob. in Eng. and John, 9 July 1641, bef. ment. and had d. 1 Jan. bef. He had other ch. as by his will of 29 Dec. 1640, speaking of sons and ds. and leav. care of all to w. Sarah, appears in Geneal. Reg. II. 184. JOSEPH, Concord, s. of the preced. prob. b. in Eng. m. 12 July 1653, Sarah, d. of Gregory Stone of Cambridge, had Sarah, b. 2 Aug. 1654; Lydia, 3 Aug. 1656; Joseph, 1658; and prob. other ch.; was freem. 1650. JOSEPH, Lynn, s. of the first William, m. 19 Aug. 1675, Sarah Jenkins, had Joseph, b. 10 July 1676; Benjamin, 23 Apr. 1678; Sarah, 26 Feb. 1681; Eliz. 2 July 1683; and, perhaps, others; was freem. 1691. * ROBERT, Concord, br. of George, freem. 13 Mar. 1639 (the day bef. his br. Joseph), was town clk. 1654–76, rep. 1655–8, deac. d. 15 Feb. 1682, aged 72, leav. no ch. His will of 10 Dec. bef. pro. 4 Apr. foll. names w. Mary, brs. Joseph and George, and their ch. and the wid. d. 22 July 1693, aged 72. SAMUEL, Lynn, perhaps s. of William, m. 22 Dec. 1669, Eliz. Townsend, may have rem. to Concord, there bec. the freem. of 1690. SAMUEL, Charlestown, by w. Mary had Samuel, bapt. 4 Jan. 1691; Catharine, 26 Apr. 1691; Edward, 11 June 1693; and Isaac, 11 Nov. 1694. WILLIAM, Concord 1645, freem. 1649, then, perhaps, of Boston, but in short time of Lynn, had w. Sarah, and ch. Joseph, William, and John, all bef. ment. however inadequate. d. 1689. WILLIAM, Lynn, s. prob. of the preced. by w. Eliz. had Eliz. b. 8 Nov. 1654; John, 13 Sept. 1657, d. young; Sarah, 3 June 1660, d. next yr.; Rebecca, 21 Oct. 1662; Sarah, again, 14 Sept. 1665; William, 8 Mar. 1668; John, again, 25 Apr. 1671; his w. d. and he m. 11

Oct. 1676, Ann Jones, wh. d. 29 July foll. He, or the s. of the same
name, was freem. 1691. He wrote his name Mirriam. Three had, in
1834, been gr. at Harv. and six at other N. E. coll.

MERING, JOSEPH, a soldier at Hatfield 1676, in Turner's comp. from
the E.

MERLAN, JOHN, Hampton 1649.

MERRELLS, THOMAS, Hartford, had Thomas, bapt. 1 Nov. 1646.
Perhaps the name was Merrill.

MERRICK, JAMES, Marblehead 1668. JOHN, Hingham, d. 2 July
1647, leav. John, and prob. wid. Eliz. wh. sold est. there in 1649, to
Thomas Thaxter. JOHN, Boston, perhaps s. of the preced. m. 3 Apr.
1655, Eliz. d. of Thomas Wyborne, had Deborah, nam. in the will of her
gr.f. JOSEPH, Eastham, s. of William, m. 1 May 1684, Eliz. Howes,
had Eliz. b. 1 Jan. 1685; Mary, 7 July 1687; Joseph, 8 Mar. 1690;
William, 26 Jan. 1693; and Isaac, 12 Aug. 1699. STEPHEN, Eastham,
s. of William, m. 28 Dec. 1670, Mercy, d. of Edward Bangs, had
Stephen, b. 26 Mar. 1673. THOMAS, Springfield, by tradit. said to have
come from Wales thro. Roxbury, and reach. S. in 1636; but there is evidence that he was of Hartford early in 1638. He was very young, if he
left, as is said, his native land in 1630; and no trace is seen at R. of him,
or of f. or mo. br. or sis. nor can the name be found there bef. 1649. At
S. he m. 14 July 1639, Sarah, d. of Rowland Stebbins, wh. was the third
m. in that town, of any Eng. had Thomas, b. 12 Feb. 1641, the third b.
of the town rec. d. young; Sarah, 1643; Mary, 1645, d. soon; Mary,
1647; and Hannah, 10 Feb. 1650. In 1653 he m. Eliz. Tilley, had
Eliz. b. 1654, d. young; Miriam, 1656, d. at 28 yrs.; John, 1658; Eliz.
again, 1661; Thomas, 1664; Tilley, 1667; James, 1670; and Abigail,
1673; was freem. 1665, and d. 7 Sept. 1704. Five of his ds. and four
s. were m. John, Thomas, and James liv. at S. John had 13 ch. of wh.
nine liv. and Jonathan, Y. C. 1725, was one of them; Thomas had seven
ch. and James seven, of wh. was Noah, Y. C. 1731, first min. of Wilbra-
ham; Tilley had one s. and four ds. liv. chiefly at Brookfield, but d.
1732, at S. WILLIAM, Duxbury 1640, was one of the orig. proprs.
of Bridgewater, early rem. to Eastham, by w. Rebecca had William, b. 15 Sept. 1643; Stephen, 12 May 1646; Rebecca, 28 July
1648; Mary, 4 Nov. 1650; Ruth, 15 May 1652; Sarah, 1 Aug. 1654;
John, 15 Jan. 1657; Isaac, 6 Jan. 1661; Joseph, 1 June 1662; and
Benjamin, 1 Feb. 1665; was an ens. and d. a. 1688. Mary m. 23 May
1667, Stephen Hopkins. WILLIAM, Eastham, eldest s. of the preced.
m. 23 May 1667, Abigail, d. of Giles Hopkins, had Rebecca, b. 28 Nov.
1668; and William, 1 Aug. 1670; and d. 20 Mar. foll. Of this name,
that is frequently giv. Mirrick or Myrick, four had, in 1828, been gr. at
Harv. and three at Yale.

MERRILL, or MERRILLS, ABEL, Newbury, s. of Nathaniel, m. 10 Feb. 1671, Priscilla, d. of Aquila Chase, had Abel, b. 28 Dec. foll.; Susanna, 14 Nov. 1673; Nathan, 3 Apr. 1676; Thomas, 1 Jan. 1679; Joseph, 12 July 1681; Nathaniel, 6 Feb. 1684; Priscilla, 13 July 1686; and James, 27 Jan. 1689. ABRAHAM, Newbury, br. of the preced. m. 1 Jan. 1661, Abigail, d. perhaps, of John Webster of Ipswich, had Abigail, b. 13 Aug. 1665; Mary, 5 July 1667; Prudence, 26 Apr. 1669, d. young; Hannah, 9 Jan. 1671; John, 15 Oct. 1673; Jonathan, 19 Jan. 1676; David, 20 Feb. 1678; Sarah, 9 Oct. 1679; Susanna, 6 Dec. 1681, d. in few days; and Prudence, again, 1 Oct. 1683. DANIEL, Newbury, br. of the preced. m. 14 May 1667, Sarah Clough, had John, b. 7 Oct. 1674; Sarah, 15 Oct. 1677; Ruth, 7 Feb. 1681; Moses and Martha, tw. 3 Sept. 1683; and Stephen, 16 Sept. 1688; and by w. Esther had three more ch.; was freem. 1683 or 4, his name being in the list of both yrs. JEREMIAH, Boston, by w. Sarah had Jeremiah, b. 22 Aug. 1652; and Sarah, 14 Aug. 1655. JOHN, Newbury, one of the first sett. freem. 13 May 1640, d. 12 Sept. 1673; by w. Eliz. wh. d. 14 July 1682, had Hannah, b. in Eng. wh. m. 24 May 1647, Stephen Swett; and d. 4 Apr. 1662. JOHN, Hartford, prob. s. of Nathaniel of Newbury, had a lot, Porter says, in 1657, was made freem. next yr. m. Sarah, d. of the first John Watson of the same, had Sarah, b. 10 Sept. 1664; Nathaniel, 15 Jan. 1667; John, 7 Apr. 1669; Abraham, 21 Dec. 1670; Daniel, 15 June 1673; Wolterton, 28 June 1675; Susanna, 20 May 1677; Abel, 25 Jan. 1680; Isaac, 11 Mar. 1682; and Jacob, 27 Mar. 1686. He had much of est. of Gregory Wolterton, for wh. he gave one of his s. that name; was deac. and d. 18 July 1712, when the eight s. were liv. Sarah m. 22 Sept. 1687, Samuel Kellogg; and Susanna m. John Turner. These hs. join. with the s. in partit. of the prop. In early rec. the name in Conn. had final s. but it is reject. by all the num. descend. NATHANIEL, Newbury, br. of the first John, m. Susanna Jordan, had Nathaniel, b. 1638; John, bef. ment. wh. was prob. oldest; Abraham; Susanna; Daniel, 20 Aug. 1642; Abel, 20 Feb. 1644; and d. 16 Mar. 1655. His will of 8 Mar. pro. 27 of same, ment. w. and the six ch. all under 21 yrs. made Nathaniel excor. with overseers. NATHANIEL, Newbury, s. of the preced. m. 15 Oct. 1661, Joanna Kenney, had John, b. 16 Feb. 1663; Nathaniel, 8 Feb. 1665; Peter, Aug. 1667; Hannah, 12 July 1672; and Mary, 18 Sept. 1675; and he d. 1 Jan. 1683. Seven of this name had, in 1834, been gr. at Harv. and twenty at the other N. E. coll.

MERRIFIELD. See Merryfield.

MERRIMAN, * NATHANIEL, New Haven, had Nathaniel; Hannah, b. 1651; Grace, 1653; Sarah, 1655; Eliz. 1657; Abigail, perhaps 18

Apr. 1659 ; John, last of Feb. 1660 ; Mary ; the last three bapt. prob. 24 June 1660, or 27 Jan. foll. wrong dates in the Geneal. Reg. IX. 361, driving me to conject.; and Caleb, b. May, bapt. 25 June 1665. He was one of the first sett. of Wallingford, its rep. 1674, lieut. and late in 1675 capt. of the dragoons of the Co. and contin. propr. at New Haven, but d. at W. 13 Feb. 1694, aged 80.

MERRITT, EZEKIEL, Newport 1639. HENRY, Scituate, his w. join. the ch. in Apr. 1637, d. last of Nov. 1653; his inv. is of 24 Jan. leav. Henry, wh. Deane thinks, d. young, without fam. and John, wh. left num. descend. JAMES, Boston 1655. JOHN, Scituate 1643, perhaps earlier, was br. of Henry. JOHN, a soldier, k. by the Ind. at Bloody brook with "the flower of Essex" under capt. Lothrop, 18 Sept. 1675. JOHN, Marblehead, perhaps s. of Nicholas, was freem. 1684. JOHN, Scituate, had w. Eliz. and d. 5 June 1740, in his 80th yr. and his wid. d. 13 Apr. 1746, aged 82. NICHOLAS, Marblehead 1648, or earlier, in his will of 17 July 1685, pro. 9 Dec. 1686, names his ch. Martha Owens, Rebecca Chin, helpless d. Mary, John, James, Samuel, and Nicholas. SAMUEL, Marblehead, s. of the preced. sign. the petitn. 1669, against imposts. WILLIAM, Duxbury, constable 1647.

MERROW, or MERO, HENRY, Woburn, m. 19 Dec. 1660, Jane Wallis, had ch. b. 14 Sept. 1662 ; prob. was most of his days of Reading, freem. 1677, d. 1685 ; had, I suppose, John and Samuel, as Mr. Eaton gives their names among early sett. at R.

MERRY, CORNELIUS, Northampton, an Irishman, had gr. of ld. 1663, m. Rachel Ballard, had John, wh. d. soon ; John, again, b. 1665 ; Sarah, 1668; Rachel, 1670 ; Cornelius ; Leah ; and, perhaps, others ; was in the Falls fight, and aft. the war rem. John, the s. went to L. I. Cornelius at Hartford, had nine ch. b. 1702–18. JOHN, Boston, by w. Constance had Jonathan, b. 3 Sept. 1663. JOSEPH, Haverhill 1640, perhaps rem. to Hampton, thence to Edgartown a. 1678, had w. Eliz. there, and d. 5 Apr. 1710, in 103d yr. says tradit. A d. of his was w. of Timothy Hilliard of Hampton 1669. WALTER, Boston, shipwright, had whf. and dwell. and warehouse conven. for his trade, at the point bearing his name, later call. N. Battery ; by w. Rebecca, adm. of our ch. 29 Dec. 1633, and he the 9th Feb. foll. had Jeremiah, bapt. 15 Dec. 1634, d. soon ; Rebecca, 18 Dec. 1636; and Jeremiah, Jan. 1638, d. soon, and his w. d. perhaps not long aft. He m. sec. w. Mary Dolens or Dowling, 18 Aug. 1653, had Sylvanus, 8 Apr. 1655, d. soon; and Walter, 3 June 1656; was freem. 4 Mar. 1634, and was drown. 28 Aug. 1657. His wid. m. 13 Nov. 1657, Robert Thornton of Taunton. There Walter contin. to reside with his mo. By momenta. forgetfulness, that Walter is oft. writ. Waters, this man was, by Farmer, brot. in again as an inhab. by name Merry Waters. WALTER, Taunton, s. of the preced. m. 17 Feb. 1683, Martha Cotterill, wh. liv. not long; and he m. 31 Jan. 1686, Eliz. Cunnill.

MERRYFIELD, HENRY, Dorchester 1641, by w. Margaret had John, Eliz. and Ruth, all bapt. 15 Apr. 1649; Hannah, 7 Apr. 1650; Mary, 18 Apr. 1652; Abigail, 3 Aug. 1656; Benjamin, 12 Dec. 1658; Martha, 28 Apr. 1661; and Henry, 31 July 1664. JAMES, Boston, of wh. I kn. only that he d. 1690. JOHN, Dorchester, s. of Henry, d. bef. mid. age, leav. ds. Sarah and Hannah.

MERWIN, MILES, Milford, where Lambert reports him in 1645, had Eliz.; John; Abigail; Thomas; Samuel, b. 21 Aug. 1656; and Miles, 14 Dec. 1658; Daniel, 1661, d. young; Martha and Mary, tw. 23 Jan. 1666; Hannah, 1667; and Deborah, 1670; all the first six nam. in the will of his aunt Abigail, wid. of Rev. John Warham, wh. had bef. been wid. of John Branker, made in 1684, when he calls hims. 60 yrs. old, but in 1692 says a. 70. He d. 23 Apr. 1697, aged a. 74, in his will of 18 May 1695, names third w. Sarah and all the s. liv. four in number, and sev. gr.ch. The inv. 12 May 1697, names six ds. by the surnames of their hs. His first w. wh. name is untold, d. 10 July 1664; his sec. w. was Sarah, wid. of Thomas Beach, wh. d. 1670. Eliz. m. a Canfield; Abigail m. a Scofield; Martha m. James Prince; Mary m. a Hull; Hannah m. Abel Holbrook; and Deborah m. a Burwell. MILES, Milford, s. of the preced. m. 20 Sept. 1681, Hannah, wid. of Samuel Miles, had Ann, b. 17 Jan. foll. at New Haven, prob. others. SAMUEL, New Haven, elder br. of the preced. m. 1682, Sarah, d. of William Wooden. THOMAS, Norwalk, soon aft. 1672, a propr. 1685, s. of the first Miles, may have had ch. for the name was there diffus. in the third generat. Six of this name have been gr. at Yale.

MESSER, EDWARD, New Hampsh. 1689. Kelly.

MESSINGER, ANDREW, Norwalk 1672, may have been as early as 1639 at New Haven, in 1687 had good est. but no ment. of him aft. is found. EBENEZER, Boston, youngest s. of Henry, by w. Rose had Ebenezer, b. 30 Mar. 1688; and Henry, 8 July 1689. EDWARD, Windsor, had Dorcas, b. 1650; Nathaniel, 1653; but no more is heard of him. Dorcas m. Peter Mills. ‖ HENRY, Boston, by w. Sarah had John, b. 25 Mar. bapt. in right of his w. 25 Apr. 1641; Sarah, 12 Mar. 1643, a. 6 days old; Simeon, 23 Mar. 1645, a. 4 days old; Henry; Ann, bapt. 20 Jan. 1650, a. 13 days old; Rebecca, b. 26 June 1652; Lydia and Priscilla, tw. 22 Nov. 1656, prob. both, certain. the latter, d. young; Thomas, 22 Mar. 1661; and Ebenezer, 25 Oct. 1665. He was a joiner, ar. co. 1658, freem. 1665, perhaps a short time, a. 1656, at Jamaica, L. I. for one of that name is ment. in Thompson's Hist. The will, of 15 Mar. 1678,

gives little light on fam. and his est. was not apprais. bef. 30 Apr. 1681,
but Ann, d. of John, was, by the wid. in her will of 24 June 1697, consid.
Sarah m. 20 Nov. 1660, Richard Mason. HENRY, Boston, s. of the
preced. a joiner, m. Mehitable, d. of Stephen Minot, by his w. Truecross,
and d. not long aft. left no ch. His will, of 17 Nov. 1686, was pro. by
his w. extrix. 5 May aft. She m. Edward Mills. JOHN, Boston, br.
perhaps eldest, of the preced. by w. Martha had John, b. 2 Jan. 1670;
Joshua, 2 Jan. 1671; Sarah, 1 Oct. 1672; and Ann; and prob. d. at
mid. age. His wid. m. 5 Sept. 1689, Jeremiah Fitch. NATHAN, Windsor, prob. s. of Edward, tho. rec. calls him Nathaniel, m. 5 Apr. 1678,
Rebecca, eldest ch. of Mark Kelsey, had Hannah, b. Sept. 1682;
Nathan, 17 Apr. 1684, d. in few mos.; Rebecca, 11 Feb. 1686;
Joseph, 2 Sept. 1687; John, 24 Nov. 1689; Return, 4 Aug. 1691; and
Nathan, again, 1693. ‖ SIMEON, Boston, s. of the first Henry, ar. co.
1675, by Bethia, d. of Robert Howard, the notary of Boston, had Bethia,
b. 24 May 1668; and Mary, 25 Mar. 1672. THOMAS, Boston, br. of
the preced. by w. Eliz. d. of John Mellows of the same, had Eliz. b. 23
Mar. 1687, d. young; Sarah, 17 Apr. 1688; Thomas, 18 Jan. 1691;
Eliz. 7 Oct. 1692; Henry, 28 Feb. 1695, H. C. 1717, misprint. in
Geneal. Reg. IX. 59; and Ebenezer, 2 June 1697.

METCALF, frequently MEDCALF in early rec. ELEAZER, Wrentham,
s. of the sec. Michael, m. 9 Apr. 1684, Meletiah Fisher, had Eleazer,
b. 30 May 1685, d. young; Michael, 21 May 1687; Samuel, 15 Jan.
1689; Ebenezer, 8 Jan. 1691; Jonathan, 9 Apr. 1693; Meletiah, 21
Apr. 1695; Timothy, 2 July 1697; Martha and Mary, tw. 27 Aug.
1699; and Eleazer, again, 21 Nov. 1701; was deac. and d. 14 May
1704. JOHN, Medfield, s. of the first Michael, b. in Eng. m. 22 Mar.
1647, Mary, d. of Francis Chickering, had John, b. 21, bapt. 26 Mar.
1648; Michael, 20, bapt. 25 Aug. 1650; Mary, 9, bapt. 24 Oct. 1652;
these all at Dedham; but at M. we kn. not that we name all, when
enumer. Joseph, 22 Nov. 1658; and Hannah, 13 Oct. 1664. He was
freem. 1647, and d. 27 Nov. 1675, unless this date belong to his eldest s.
JOHN, New Haven 1645, a brickmaker, may have been s. or br. of
Stephen, as a. the yr. 1647, he rem. JONATHAN, Dedham, s. of the sec.
Michael, m. 10 Apr. 1674, Hannah, d. of John Kenrick, had Jonathan,
b. 16 Mar. 1675; John, 20 Mar. 1678; Ebenezer, 14 Feb. 1680;
Joseph, 2 or 11 Apr. 1682, H. C. 1703, min. of Falmouth; Timothy, 18
Nov. 1684, d. at 11 yrs.; Eleazer, 14 Feb. 1687; Hannah, 10 Apr.
1689; Nathaniel, Apr. 1691; Mehitable; and Mary; was freem. 1683
or 4, his name being ins. ea. yr. and he d. 27 May 1727, and his wid. d.
23 Dec. 1731. * JOSEPH, Ipswich, freem. 4 Mar. 1635, rep. in Sept. of
that yr. and oft. aft. d. 21 July 1665, aged 60. By his will, we learn

that his w. was Eliz. his s. Thomas, b. in Eng. prob. and gr.ch. Joseph, Mary, and Eliz. but perhaps this had d. soon. His wid. m. 8 Nov. 1670, Edward Beacham. JOSEPH, Ipswich, s. of Thomas, prob. by w. Rebecca, had Jacob, b. 8 June 1685, prob. d. soon; and Abigail, 29 Mar. 1686. MICHAEL, Dedham, b. 1586, at Tatterford, in Co. Norfolk, was a dornock weaver at Norwich, and free of the city, where all his ch. were b. m. 13 Oct. 1616, Sarah, had Michael, b. 13 Nov. 1617, d. soon; Mary, 14 Oct. 1618, but the geneal. of the fam. in Reg. VI. 173, says 14 Feb. 1619; Michael, again, 29 Aug. 1620; John, 5 or 15 Sept. 1622, bef. ment.; Sarah, 10 Sept. 1624; Eliz. 4 Oct. 1626; Martha, 27 Mar. or Oct. 1628; Thomas, 27 Dec. 1629 or 30; Ann, 1 Mar. 1631 or 34, d. soon; Jane, 24 Mar. 1632; and Rebecca, 5 Apr. 1635; his w. was b. at a village near Norwich, he says, 17 June 1593, but possib. the figures have been mistaken, as in the examin. one week bef. the sail. of the ship, call. I think, the Rose, of Yarmouth, from Yarmouth, Apr. 1637, he calls hims. 45 yrs. of age, and w. 39. "From the relig. tyranny" exercised by Wren, then Bp. of Norwich, he felt forced to esc. even at the expense of separ. from his fam. for a time, and emb. at London, 17 Sept. 1636, for N. E. but was sadly tormented by equal tempests on the water, and the ship at Christmas put back to Plymouth; and so far was this a happiness that in Apr. foll. he had license for the whole fam. to come; only 8 ch. are ment. in the custom-ho. docum. but I can hardly doubt that the name of John was casually overlook. At Boston he arr. "three days bef. mid. sum. with w. nine ch. and a serv." wh. was Thomas Comberbach, aged 16, I presume in one of the three ships ment. by Winth. as coming in, from Ipswich, 20 June. He may have been br. of Joseph; was freem. 13 May 1640, or 18 May 1642, and, perhaps, swore on both days, tho. more prob. it is a fault of the Secr. as in the list appears. His w. d. 21 Feb. 1645, and he m. 13 Aug. foll. Martha, wid. of Thomas Pigg, or Pidge; and he d. 27 Dec. 1664. A very curious docum. his engagem. aft. 70 yrs. of age to keep the town sch. in 1656, is giv. in Geneal. Reg. X. 282. His will, made six wks. bef. gives to eight ch. Michael being d. and ea. of the ds. m. Martha hav. then a sec. or third h. to gr.ch. Michael, s. of Michael, and gr.ch. William Brignall, s. of d. Martha, wh. was a mem. of Roxbury ch. by her first h. and to Martha Bullard, d. of his w. Mary m. 24 Nov. 1642, Henry Wilson; Sarah m. Robert Onion, as his sec. w. the first hav. d. in Apr. 1643; Eliz. m. 15 Sept. 1648, Thomas Bancroft of Reading; Martha m. William Brignall, next, 2 Aug. 1654, Christopher Smith as the Geneal. Reg. VI. 173, says, tho. I doubt its correctness, for Christopher Smith in 1668, is nam. in his will by Jonathan Fairbanks as h. of his d. Mary, and third h. . . . . . Stow; Jane m. 1654, Samuel Walker, (tho. strong doubts of error in the name are felt) of Rehoboth; and Rebecca m. 5 Apr. 1659, John Mackintosh. MICHAEL, Dedham, eldest s. of the preced. b. in Eng. m. 2 or 12 Apr. 1644, Mary, d. of John Fairbanks, says the Metcalf geneal. bef. ment. but perhaps by mistake, had Michael, b. 21 Jan. 1645; Mary, 15 Aug. 1646; Sarah, 7 Dec. 1648; Jonathan, 21 Sept. 1650; and Eleazer, 20 Mar. 1653, bef. ment. was freem. 1645, and d. (ten yrs. bef. his f.) 24 Dec. 1654. Mary m. 10 Dec. 1668, John Ware; and Sarah m. 4 June 1677, Robert Ware. MICHAEL, Dedham, s. of the preced. m. 17 Sept. 1672, Eliz. not, I think, as Goodwin has it, d. but wid. of the sec. John Kingsbury, d. of Thomas Fuller, both of the same, had Michael, b. 9 May 1674; Mary, 3 Oct. 1676; Thomas, 3 Jan. 1679; Sarah, 26 Apr. 1682; Eleazer, 12 Feb. 1685; Hannah, 17 Apr. 1687; Daniel, 25 June 1691; and Eliz.; was freem. 1690, and d. 2 Sept. 1693. His wid. d. 24 Oct. 1732. STEPHEN, New Haven 1639, a brickmaker, aft. 1647 prob. rem. was in good repute. * THOMAS, Dedham, youngest s. of the first Michael, b. in Eng. m. 12 Sept. 1656, Sarah Paige, had Sarah, b. 3 Mar. 1658; Mary, bapt. 25 Nov. 1660; Samuel, b. 17 Oct. 1661, d. soon; Thomas; 22 Sept. 1665, d. soon; Samuel, again, 17 Sept. 1668; Thomas, again, 7 or 21 May 1671; John, 20 Sept. 1675; and Judith, 25 Nov. 1677, d. at 5 yrs. The w. d. and he m. 2 Dec. 1679, Ann Paine of Rehoboth, was freem. 1653, deac. and rep. 1691, d. 16 Nov. 1702. Sarah m. 23 Nov. 1676, Samuel Whiting, and d. 1702. THOMAS, Ipswich 1648, s. of Joseph the first, b. in Eng. I suppose, had Mary, b. 23 June 1658; Joseph, 27 Jan. 1661; Thomas, 4 Dec. 1667; beside prob. Eliz. nam. in the will of gr.f. He was freem. 1674. Of the mo. of these ch. we kn. nothing; but she may have d. and one Thomas of Ipswich, a widower, m. 1685, wid. Lydia Davis. Still more uncertainty is felt unless we give him ano. w. for the wid. of Thomas M. nam. Abigail, d. at I. 5 May 1727, aged 88 yrs. An earlier Thomas of Ipswich is found by Mr. Felt to be inhab. there 1638. · THOMAS, Dedham, s. of the first Thomas, m. 24 Nov. 1696, Sarah, d. of William Avery, the sec. of the name, had Sarah, b. 26 Apr. 1698, d. in few wks.; Samuel, 9 Apr. 1699, d. at 14 yrs.; Thomas, 30 Dec. 1701; and Sarah, 1 Dec. 1703; and he d. 12 Dec. 1704; and his wid. m. 6 Apr. 1709, Joseph Wight, and d. 1748. Two of this name had, in 1829, been gr. at Harv. and seven at the other N. E. coll. It is oft. in old rec. writ. as no doubt it was sound. Medcalf.

METHUP, with five variations, DANIEL, Watertown, m. 25 or 27 Mar. 1664 (Bond gives both dates) Bethia, perhaps d. of Anthony Beers, had Bethia, b. 24 Feb. 1665; Mary, 13 Sept. 1666; Daniel, 10 May 1668; Robert, 31 Aug. 1671; Isaac, 22 Dec. 1672; Sarah, 14 Feb. 1675;

Abigail, 2 June 1678; and Hannah, 31 July 1681. He d. 24 Feb. 1717, and his wid. d. 22 Feb. 1722. Dissatisf. with all the forms of this name, Bond inq. if it be not pervers. of Maddock.

MEW, ELLIS, New Haven, took o. of fidel. 1654, is one of the freem. 1669, by w. Ann, d. of William Gibbons, had Ann; and Dodd, 135, tells no more. In his list of deaths is Ann, only ch. 1681, and Ann, wid. Feb. 1704. But he might have added, that the h. and f. d. 1681; and in 1685 his heirs appear, as proprs. without discrimin. as he had not long been d.

MICO, JOHN, Boston 1689, merch. m. 20 Aug. of that yr. Mary, d. of Thomas Brattle, and d. Oct. 1718. His wid. d. 22 Dec. 1733.

MIDDLEBROOK, JOSEPH, Concord, went with Rev. John Jones to Fairfield 1644, in 1670 was propr. there, call. sen. and prob. d. in Nov. 1686, the inv. of his est. being 22 of that mo. He m. Mary, wid. of Benjamin Turney the first, had s. of the same name with hims. and d. Phebe, w. of Samuel Wilson, the only heirs.

MIDDLECOTT, ‡ RICHARD, Boston, came from Warminster, Co. Wilts, bring. s. Edward, m. here sec. w. Sarah, wid. of Tobias Payne, wh. had been wid. of sec. Miles Standish, and d. of John Winslow, had Mary, b. 1 July 1674, bapt. 2 May 1675; Sarah, 2 June 1678; and Jane, 16 Sept. 1682; was freem. 1690; nam. one of the counc. in the new Chart. by Mather, and left out at the first popul. elect. d. 1704. His wid. d. 1728. Mary m. Henry Gibbs; and next, Othniel Haggett of Barbadoes; Sarah m. 26 Mar. 1702, Louis Boucher; and Jane m. 7 Jan. 1703, Elisha Cooke, jr.

MIDDLETON, JAMES, Dover 1658, rem. to Maine 1665. THOMAS, L. I. 1661. Thompson. WILLIAM, Boston, by w. Eliz. had Eliz. b. 11 Feb. 1673; Abigail, 22 Mar. 1680; Alice, 4 July 1684; and Joanna, 8 Nov. 1687. He d. 3 Mar. 1699, aged 74, as says the gr.stone found, Oct. 1850, in the wall of the tower of the Old South ch.

MIGHILL, EZEKIEL, Rowley 1691, s. of Thomas of the same. JOHN, Suffield, was, perhaps, s. of Thomas of Rowley, d. 1702, leav. John, Thomas, Nathaniel, and Nicholas, but no d. is nam. SAMUEL, Rowley, s. of Thomas, was, perhaps, b. bef. com. to our country, m. 21 Nov. 1657, Eliz. d. of Abraham Toppan of Newbury, was tax. in 1691, STEPHEN, Rowley, s. prob. youngest, of Thomas of the same, m. Sarah d. of Rev. Samuel Phillips, had Nathaniel, b. 1684; and two ds. * THOMAS, Roxbury, with w. Ellen was adm. of the ch. perhaps as early as 1637, at least the name is ent. prior to that of Rev. John Miller, wh. he accomp. from Roxbury to Rowley 1639, was deac. of the ch. gath. 3 Dec. 1639, freem. 13 May 1640, rep. 1648; had Samuel, possib. b. in Eng. but more prob. not; Thomas, at Rowley, 29 Oct. 1639, H. C.

1663; John; Ezekiel, 1642; Timothy, 1644; Nathaniel, 1646; Stephen, 1651; and two ds. of wh. one was Mary. *THOMAS*, Scituate, s. of the preced. preach. some yrs. m. at Roxbury, 8 Nov. 1669, Bethia, d. perhaps, of Joseph (more prob. of Daniel) Weld, and had d. Eliz. bapt. 30 Apr. 1671; and Hannah, 22 Mar. 1674; bef. going to S. and there had Mary, b. 1683; Samuel, 1685, H. C. 1704; and Grace, 1688; was ord. over the sec. ch. at S. 15 Oct. 1684, and d. 26 Aug. 1689. Deane. His s. Samuel taught the gr. sch. at Hadley, perhaps aft. at Milton, m. and liv. some yrs. at Hartford, but was poor, went back to Hadley, d. at S. Hadley, 11 Apr. 1769, long support. by the town.

MILBURNE, *WILLIAM*, Saco, was the min. 1685, acc. Folsom, 137, prob. d. at Boston, Aug. 1699.

MILBURY, or MILLBURY, HENRY, York 1680, had a fam. for the will of William Dixon gave something to his childr. and he may have m. a d. of Dixon. RICHARD, York 1680, perhaps s. of the preced. sw. alleg. 1681, as did Henry.

MILDMAY, WILLIAM, s. of Sir Henry of Graces, in Essex, H. C. 1647, tho. sent by his f. with a tutor from Eng. Richard Lyon, is ranked lowest in his class, yet had his A. M. in regul. course. Sir Walter, of the same fam. was founder, in the time of Queen Eliz. of Emanuel Coll. at the Univ. of Cambridge, wh. supplied N. E. in its early days, as Farmer remarks, with some of the chief lights that illumin. its chhs. and well may be added the venerab. Gov. Bradstreet.

MILES, BENJAMIN, Dedham, s. of Samuel, freem. 1678. JOHN, Concord 1637, freem. 14 Mar. 1639, by w. Sarah had Mary, b. 11 Feb. 1640, and, perhaps, no other ch. His w. d. 18 July 1678, and he m. Susanna, wid. of John Rediat, had John, b. 20 May 1680; Samuel, 19 Feb. 1682; and Sarah, 25 May 1686; d. 28 Aug. 1693, hav. made his will two yrs. bef. in wh. are ment. ch. of both ws. His wid. m. 10 Nov. 1698, William Wilson of Billerica. Sarah m. 10 May 1705, Edward Putnam of Salem. JOHN, New Haven, s. of the first Richard, m. 11 Apr. 1665, Eliz. d. of John Harriman of the same, had Eliz. b. 21 Dec. foll.; John, 9 Jan. 1668; Mary, 10 Mar. 1670; Richard, 21 Mar. 1672; and Samuel, 6 Apr. 1674. His w. d. 3 Déc. 1674, and he m. 2 Nov. 1680, Mary, d. of Joseph Alsop of the same, had Hannah, 20 Aug. 1681; Daniel, 20 Sept. 1683; and Joseph. He was a capt. made his will 28 Nov. 1700, but liv. to 7 Nov. 1704; and the wid. d. 16 Oct. 1705; freem. 1669, lieut. in 1675, and propr. in 1685. *JOHN*, Boston, min. of the first Bapt. ch. rem. 1683 to Swansey. JOHN, Concord, s. of the first John, m. 16 Apr. 1702, Mary, d. of Dr. Jonathan Prescot, had John, b. 24 Dec. 1704; Jonathan, 13 Feb. 1706; Mary, 18 Oct. 1709; Eliz. 16 Nov. 1714, d. young; James, 1 Aug. 1719; and Benjamin, 26

Nov. 1724; and d. 23 Aug. 1725. JOSEPH, Kittery, submit. 1652, to jurisdict. of Mass. JOSEPH, Salem, arraign. as a Quaker 1659, may have been the passeng. wh. took the o. of supremacy and alleg. 26 Mar. 1634, to pass for N. E. in the Mary and John, tho. it may be he was his s. for we hear not where the passeng. sat down. * RICHARD, Milford 1639, New Haven 1643, then had 7 in his fam. of wh. Samuel was bapt. at M. 12 Apr. 1640, being the first in that town; but at New Haven, Hannah, Oct. 1642; and John, Oct. 1644; but the days of both are unkn. as tho. Hannah's is giv. in print. 7, it is wrong, in that most valua. list, with so many other errors, furnished by the scrupulous Henry White of that city. Aft. spend. in ea. day of a whole week, not a few hours, in compar. that rec. as thus publish. I wrote to ask explana. of the discrepancies and errors, and obtain. full ansr. The town clk.'s entries may be relied on, in opposit. to those of the ch. that, I am happy to say, is contra. to com. experience. Take p. 359 of Geneal. Reg. IX. where names of 80 bapt. are giv. and only one half are true, 27 being positiv. false, and 13 more deficient in days. Two ch. of Rev. William Hooke are correct. enter.; but of two of John Davenport, the s. of the pastor, one is. clea. wrong, 19 Nov. 1666, wh. was Monday. We kn. that ordin. was never allow. on a week day. He d. 7 Jan. 1667. In his will of 28 Dec. 1666, names w. Catherine, eldest s. Richard, and to other ch. without nam. makes div. In 1651 he was rep. His wid. was, no doubt, a sec. or third w. for in the will wh. was pro. 13 June 1667, aft. provid. for his ch. he gave residue to her, bec. she had considerable, when he m. her, part of wh. belong. to her childr. by former h. Of the ds. Martha m. 20 Oct. 1650, George Pardee; Mary m. 12 Dec. 1654, Jonathan Ince, and next, 22 Oct. 1661, Rev. Thomas Hanford; and Ann m. 3 Nov. 1664, Samuel Street, min. of Wallingford. RICHARD, New Haven, wh. sw. fidel. 1654, then call. jr. may have been s. of the preced. but we kn. no more. RICHARD, Boston, by w. Experience had Eliz. b. 22 Dec. 1664; and Richard, 10 Oct. 1667. SAMUEL, Dedham 1642, freem. 1645, by w. Frances had Samuel, bapt. 29 Mar. 1646, d. next mo.; Benjamin, 13 Apr. 1651, bef. ment.; Eliz. 5 Dec. 1652; and Rebecca, 17 May 1657. SAMUEL, Boston, m. 16 Oct. 1659, Eliz. d. of Francis Dowse, had Samuel, b. 27 Apr. 1662. SAMUEL, New Haven, freem. 1669, wh. d. 24 Dec. 1678, was s. of the first Richard. By first w. had John, b. 29 Jan. 1664, wh. d. young. He m. sec. w. 9 Apr. 1667, Hannah, d. of the sec. Benjamin Wilmot, had Samuel, b. and d. 1668; Abigail, 3 Jan. 1670; Samuel, again, 15 July 1672; Stephen, 5 Dec. 1674; and Theophilus, 17 Mar. 1677; the last four were liv. at his d. His wid. m. Miles Merwin, jr. SAMUEL, Concord, s. of the first John of the same, m. 28 Jan. 1706, Sarah Foster, had Samuel, b. 20 Mar. 1707; Joseph, 8 Aug. 1709; Sarah, 1 Sept. 1711; Ezekiel, 26 Dec. 1713; Esther, 10 Sept.

1716; Martha, 18 Mar. 1719; Nathan, 14 Jan. 1721; Reuben, 12 Dec. 1723; and Charles, 28 June 1727. Whether some of the foregoing should be spell. Mills, or whether others should be brot. in here from that platoon, I have vain. labor. to ascert. In the old rec. we may find the same man, often, in or under differ. names.

MILK, or MILKE, JOHN, Salem, authoriz. chimney sweep. 1663.

MILLARD, JOHN, Rehoboth, a tanner, had a s. of the same name, perhaps bef. 1658. Baylies, II. 208. THOMAS, Boston, had a lot for five heads, gr. him at Mount Wollaston 1639.

MILLER, ABRAHAM, Charlestown, had Susanna, bapt. 12 June 1692. He was, perhaps, s. of James, the Scotchman. ABRAHAM, Northampton, youngest s. of William of the same, m. 1 Jan. 1700, Hannah, d. of Elder Preserved Clapp, had John, b. 4 Feb. 1701; Abraham, 29 Nov. 1702; Jonathan, 12 Mar. 1704, d. young; Roger, 22 July 1705; Hannah, 24 Oct. 1707; Wait, 26 July 1711; Zebediah, 6 Nov. 1713; William, 21 Sept. 1716; and Seth, 25 June 1719. Both the last nam. d. soon; and he d. 7 Feb. 1727. His wid. m. 1729, lieut. John Parsons, and d. 8 Nov. 1758. ALEXANDER, Dorchester 1637, freem. 2 May 1638, was never m. that we hear of, or at least no ch. is ment. ANDREW, Enfield, an early sett. d. 1708, aged 60, had David, wh. m. 1713, Hannah Miller, and d. 1715. * ANTHONY, Dover, was rep. 1674–6. EBENEZER, Northampton, s. of William of the same, m. 1688, Sarah, d. of Samuel Allen of the same, had Mary, b. a. 1689; John, 12 Jan. 1692, d. young; Ebenezer, 15 Aug. 1696; Jonathan; Hannah, 20 Aug. 1700; Joseph, 4 June 1705; Aaron, 6 Nov. 1708; Patience; and John, again; and d. 23 Dec. 1737. His will, of 1735, names w. the five s. and two ds. liv. and childr. of d. Patience. EPHRAIM, Kittery, bef. 1690, had, beside Samuel, Martha, wh. m. John Wentworth of Dover, and Mary, wh. m. Ephraim Wentworth. GEORGE, Easthampton, L. I. 1660. Thompson. HUMPHREY, Reading, by Mr. Eaton ins. among early sett. m. at Cambridge, 12 Sept. 1677, Eliz. Smith, had not issue kn. to me. JAMES, Charlestown, perhaps s. of Richard, m. 25 Nov. 1673, Hannah, d. of John George, who join. the ch. 15 Apr. 1677, and was then bapt. had James, b. 19 Dec. 1674; Hannah, 16, bapt. 22 July 1677; Elinor, bapt. 16 May 1680; •James, again, b. 1, bapt. 5 Feb. 1682; Richard, 13, bapt. 19 Oct. 1684; Eliz. 27 Dec. 1686, bapt. 2 Jan. foll.; John, b. 27 Aug. 1688; Mary, 6, bapt. 15 June 1690; and Ruth, 31 Dec. 1693, bapt. 7 Jan. foll. and he d. 10 Jan. 1705, aged a. 64. His wid. d. 11 Dec. 1733, aged 78. He d. 2 Aug. 1676, Farmer says, tho. a doubt arises as to the justness of the date, exc. for that of d. of his first b. ch. None of this name was ever heard of at C. a short time prior, certain. no householder in 1658. Yet in Dec. 1676 a James is adm. of the ch. and freem. in May foll. and in Mar. of next yr. two Jameses are among the householders, prob. mov. in from neighb. town, one of wh. was selectman 1690, and ano. perhaps the Scotchman, whose s. was prob. the other, for his d. was 14 July 1690, and his w. Mary join. to the ch. 5 Aug. 1677, being bapt. that day, with her eight ch. James, Mary, Robert, Job, Abraham, Isaac, Mercy, and Jane. The rec. of his f.'s d. 1 Aug. 1688, calls him "sen. an aged Scotchman, above 70." Still ano. JAMES, prob. not of Charlestown, a soldier, was k. by the Ind. 4 Sept. 1675, near Northfield, with his capt. Beers. JAMES, Norwalk 1671, of wh. we hear no more, exc. that he liv. at Rye nine yrs. aft. *JOHN*, Dorchester 1636, by some thot. not by me, perhaps s. of Richard the first, had sh. in 1637, says Harris, of the lds. in the neck, now South Boston; but he was rather of Roxbury, in my opinion, for there is rec. of his d. Mehitable, b. 12 July 1638, and with w. Lydia, he belonged to Eliot's ch. of wh. he was an elder, was bred at Gonville and Caius Coll. Cambridge, where he took his A. B. 1627, freem. 22 May 1639, without the prefix of respect; brot. from Eng. John, b. Mar. 1632, perhaps had there other ch. or aft. coming here, may have had at Roxbury, or at Rowley, some not ment.; went to be min. 1639 at Rowley, and was also the first town clk. there, where he had Lydia, b. 2 Feb. or 12 Apr. 1640, as the numerals are read both ways, contin. only two or three yrs. and he was invit. to go on the mission of 1642 to Virg. but declin. it, and soon aft. accept. the call to Yarmouth, Cape Cod; yet he can hardly have been long resid. there. At Roxbury, again he was liv. had Susanna, b. 2 May, by Yarmouth rec. but by R. 24, bapt. 29 Aug. 1647, who d. at Charlestown, unm. 14 Oct. 1669; Eliz. 13 Oct. 1649; perhaps preach. where any tempo. want existed. His w. d. at Boston, 7 Aug. 1658, and he d. at Groton, 12 June 1663. His s. John took admin. of his est. 3 July foll. His d. Mehitable m. John Crow of Yarmouth; Lydia m. a Fish of Sandwich; Faith m. 3 Aug. 1664, Nathaniel Winslow of Marshfield, and d. 9 Nov. 1729; Eliz. m. Samuel Frost of Billerica; Hannah m. 22 May 1666, Joseph Frost of Charlestown; and Mary, the youngest I suppose, m. 8 Nov. 1677, John Whittemore of Charlestown. JOHN, Dover 1647, was, perhaps, of Kennebec 1665, as in Sullivan, 287, and sw. alleg. to the k. 1681. *JOHN, Yarmouth, s. of Rev. John, b. in Eng. m. 24 Dec. 1659, Margaret, d. of the first Josiah Winslow, had Lydia, b. 18 May 1661; Rebecca, 7 Nov. 1663; Hannah, 19 Apr. 1666; Margaret, 19 Apr. 1668; Mehitable, 14 May 1670; John, 20 Feb. 1673; Margaret, again, 2 Mar. 1675; Susanna, 26 July 1677; Josiah, 27 Oct. 1679; and John, again, 16 Oct. 1681. He was rep. 1671-82; and of his ds. we find m. of the first three, viz.: Lydia, 29 Dec. 1681, to Jacob Cook; Rebecca, 15 Feb. 1682, to Thomas Clark; and Hannah, 12 Feb. 1690, to Joseph Hall. JOHN, Rehoboth 1643, may have gone

from Dorchester, but not so prob. as that he was f. of John, Ichabod,
and Robert, who all appear there in div. of lds. 1668. His w. Eliz. was
bur. 18 Apr. 1680. JOHN, Wethersfield, one of the first sett. a. 1636 ;
rem. 1642 to Stamford, there d. very soon, leav. wid. and s. John, Jonathan, and Joseph, all liv. 1666, when his will was brot. in 6 Nov. tho.
his wid. had m. Obadiah Seely, bore him three ch. and was at the same
time call. to make inv. for her latter h. JOHN, Easthampton, L. I. 1650.
Thompson. JOHN, Stamford 1662, s. of John of the same, had a ch. b.
that yr. and was grant. ld. 1667, propos. for freem. 1669, and in 1687
was rated for good est. But in 1697 he with his brs. Jonathan and
Joseph, are enum. in the patent of Bedford, set off from S. to the N. Y.
jurisdict. by the new line of boundary, wh. in 1701, left no Miller in S.
Jonathan had been in 1672 a resid. of S. A John who came passeng.
in the Speedwell, from London, 1656, aged 24, may have been that gent.
of Yarmouth with whose yrs. he precise. agrees, or the inhab. of Cape
Porpus 1680, wh. was rep. in 1685, at that Court held under auth. of
Mass. by Presid. Danforth. JOHN, Springfield, freem. 1690. JOHN,
Yarmouth, s. of John of the same, gr.s. of Rev. John, m. 23 Jan. 1707,
Thankful Howes. JONATHAN, Springfield 1678. JOSEPH, came in the
Hopewell, capt. Babb, 1635, from London, aged 15, perhaps s. of some
one that had come bef. may have been of Dover 1647, and may be
the same as the next. JOSEPH, Newbury, had w. Mary, who, Coffin
says, had been wid. of capt. John Cutting, and d. 6 Mar. 1663, but in
ano. place, 6 May 1664; and he d. 21 July 1681. JOSEPH, Marlborough, freem. 1685, may be the man of Cambridge, who m. Mary,
only d. of Walter Pope, had Thomas, b. 9 Apr. 1675 ; Samuel, 24 Sept.
1678 ; and prob. Joseph of Newton, wh. d. 1711; and Jane, wh. d.
1719. He d. 1697, and his wid. d. 1711. Perhaps he was s. of Richard. JOSIAH, Yarmouth, s. of the sec. John of the same, d. 15 Apr.
1729, and his wid. Mary d. at Pembroke, 15 Feb. 1772, " aged 94 yrs.
wanting a few days," says fam. rec. prob. with some exagger. LAZARUS,
Springfield, s. of Obadiah, took o. of alleg. 1678, as did at the same
time, OBADIAH, and OBADIAH, jr. Of the former, were Lazarus, b.
1655; Obadiah, 1658 ; and Joanna, 1659 ; his w. Joanna d. 1695.
NICHOLAS, Plymouth, whose will of 24 Oct. 1665 bears the name
Hodges, also, may therefore be the same person borne on the list of
those able to bear arms, 1643. PAUL, Boston, by w. Eliz. had Sarah, b.
21 Feb. 1692 ; and he liv. not long aft. RICHARD, Charlestown, came,
perhaps, in 1637, and had gr. of a lot, it is said, in 1638 ; but as neither
Frothingham, in the Hist. of the town, nor Budington, in that of the ch.
ment. him, we may suppose he d. early. Elinor, who join. the ch. 4
Nov. 1643, may have been his w. or wid. She m. Henry Herbert, and
d. 17 Nov. 1667 ; and her d. Hannah M. m. 17 June 1663, Nathaniel

Dade, and aft. his d. m. 4 Oct. 1667, John Edmands, and next, m. 22
May 1684, deac. Aaron Ludkin, long outliv. him, and d. 13 Dec. 1717.
RICHARD, Kittery, had Samuel, Martha, and Mary, was d. bef. June
1694 ; and his wid. Grace m. Christopher Benfield. Mary m. Ephraim
Wentworth. But she may, as also the br. and sis. belong to Ephraim, as
claim. by the Wentworths. ROBERT, a soldier under capt. Turner 1676,
prob. present in the Falls fight, may have come from Rehoboth, certain.
from some E. part. At R. he had Solomon, b. 6 Mar. 1674; Mary, 14
June 1680. ROBERT, Boston, by w. Lydia had Lydia, b. 25 Jan. 1666 ; is
possib. the same as the preced. SAMUEL, Springfield, freem. 1690. SAMU-
EL, Rehoboth, m. 20 July 1682, Esther Bowen, had Esther, b. 4 Apr. foll.
and, perhaps, he had sec. w. Rebecca, d. of Joseph Belcher. SAMUEL,
Kittery, s. of Richard, or Ephraim. SYDRACH, Salem 1629, a cooper,
prob. came with Higginson. THOMAS, Rowley 1646, had license to sell
wines next yr. THOMAS, Boston, planter, had est. of a. three acres, adjoin.
the town common, sold in 1668, to Thomas Deane. THOMAS, Springfield, m. 1649, Sarah, d. of Thomas Marshfield, had Sarah, b. 1650;
Thomas, 1653; Samuel, 1655; John, 1657; Joseph, 1659, d. soon.;
Josiah, 1660; Deborah, 1662 ; Martha, 1664, d. soon; Martha, again,
1665 ; Ebenezer, 1667; Mehitable, 1669; Joseph, again, 1671; and
Experience, a d. 1673; and he was k. by the Ind. 5 Oct. 1675, as may
have been his s. John next yr. in the gr. Falls fight. Five ds. and four
s. were m. at S. THOMAS, Middletown, an early sett. by w. Isabel, wh.
d. 1666, had Ann, that m. a. 1653, Nathaniel Bacon ; and when above
56 yrs. old, took, 6 June 1666, sec. w. Sarah, d. of Samuel Nettleton of
Branford, a girl, prob. not older than his d. Ann ; had Thomas, b. 6
May 1666, wh. date proves that some interfer. of a judicial kind had
been invok. or was aft.; Samuel, 1 Apr. 1668 ; Joseph, 21 Aug. 1670 ;
Benjamin, 10 July 1672; John, 10 Mar. 1674; Margaret, 1 Sept. 1676;
Sarah, 7 Jan. 1679 ; and Mehitable, posthum. 28 Mar. 1681. He d. 14
Aug. 1680, and in his will, three days bef. calls hims. above 70. In the
rec. Sept. foll. these ch. on the div. of est. are nam. Thomas, aged 14;
Samuel, 12; Joseph, 10; Benjamin, 8; Margaret, 4; and Sarah, 1.
His wid. m. a Harris, perhaps Thomas ; and Sarah m. Smith Johnson
of Woodstock. THOMAS, Springfield, s. of Thomas of the same, was
in the Falls fight 1676, m. Dec. 1681, Rebecca Leonard, d. of John,
had Thomas and Rebecca, and d. 1690. THOMAS, Middletown, eldest s.
of Thomas of the same, m. 1688, Eliz. Turner, perhaps d. of Edward of
the same, had Thomas, b. 1692; Abigail, 1694; and Eliz. 1695. His
w. d. this yr. and he m. 1696, Mary Rowell, had Mary, 1697, wh. d. at
16 yrs.; Stephen, 1699 ; James, 1700; Eliz. 1702; Eunice, 1704;
Patience, 1707 ; and Deborah, 1708, wh. d. at 5 yrs.; and he d. 24
Sept. 1727. Farmer had giv. one of this baptismal name at Dorchester,

but I am confident that it was mistak. by his informer for Millet. WILLIAM, Ipswich 1648, prob. rem. with earliest sett. to Northampton, by w. Patience had Mary; Rebecca, d. young; Patience, b. 15 Sept. 1657; William, 30 Nov. 1659; Mercy, 8 Feb. 1662; Ebenezer, 7 June 1664; Mehitable, 10 July 1666; Thankful, 25 Apr. 1669; and Abraham, 20 Jan. 1672; was freem. 1690; and d. 15 July 1690. His will was of 1688, and his wid. d. 16 Mar. 1716, quite aged. Mercy m. 1687, John Fowler of Westfield. WILLIAM, Wethersfield, E. side of the riv. wh. bec. Glastonbury, s. of the preced. was a tanner, had decent est. of £348. and d. 1705, leav. William, aged 11; John, 4; Jonathan, 1; and three ds. of wh. with ret. of the inv. the names and ages appear, Mary, 8; Martha, 7; and Sarah, 6; all liv. in 1721, to claim portion as heirs of their gr.f. of cert. wild lds. in Northfield. Chapin, 192, has a slight error in giv. him a br. John. For his w.'s name, that is not ment. at Glastonbury, we may succeed in the rec. of Saybrook, by find. that he m. 19 Apr. 1693, Mary Bushnell, I suppose d. of John, and there had William, b. 9 Feb. foll. Seven of this name had, in 1834, been gr. at Harv. ten at Yale, and fifteen at other N. E. coll.

MILLERD, MILLARD, or MILWARD, BENJAMIN, JOSEPH, ROBERT, and SAMUEL, were of Rehoboth 1690. THOMAS, Gloucester, a fisherman, or mariner, was selectman 1642, rem. to Newbury, had Ann, perhaps b. there in Nov. of that yr.; Rebecca; and Eliz. aft. but did not sell his est. at G. bef. 1652. He made his will 30 Aug. 1653, and d. 2 days aft. at Boston. I think his d. Rebecca m. 27 May 1656, at Boston, Thomas Thorpe. Coffin supposes he was that mate of the Hector, ment. in Winth. I. 187; but I doubt it. W. Ann, and ch. Rebecca and Eliz. under 18 yrs. are ment. in the will.

MILLET, JOHN, Gloucester, s. of Thomas of the same, m. 3 July 1663, Sarah Leach, had John, b. 23 Oct. 1665, d. soon; Hannah, 9 Mar. 1667; John, again, 22 Apr. 1669; Thomas, 23 Nov. 1671; Sarah, 1 July 1674, d. next yr.; Andrew, 9 May 1676, d. in few days; and Eliz. 24 Oct. 1677; and he d. 3 Nov. 1678. NATHANIEL, Gloucester, br. of the preced. m. 3 May 1670, Ann, d. of Andrew Lester, had Mary, b. 29 June 1671, d. young; Daniel, 31 July 1673, d. next day; Thomas, 9 Mar. 1675; Nathaniel, 2 Mar. 1677; Abigail, 12 Oct. 1679; Andrew, 6 July 1681; and his w. d. 5 June foll. RICHARD, prob. came in the fleet with Winth. but no more of him is kn. than that he req. adm. 19 Oct. 1630, when his name is spelled Myllett, and was sw. freem. 11 June 1633. THOMAS, Dorchester, came in the Elizabeth, from London, 1635, aged 30, with w. Mary, 29, and ch. Thomas, 2; had here, John, b. 8 July 1635; Jonathan, 27 July 1638, d. next mo.; Mary, 21 Aug. 1639; and Mehitable, 14 Mar. 1642; perhaps also

Bethia, wh. m. 3 Aug. 1666, Moses Eyres or Ayres (as Mr. Drake, in Geneal. Reg. V. 402, says), and d. 15 Apr. 1669. He was freem. 17 May 1637, and his w. m. in Eng. was d. of John Greenoway. Farmer had giv. the two s. b. at D. to a suppositit. Miller; but more curious was the error of Dagget (who usually is very scrupulous in correctness), for his Hist. of Attleborough gives all the childr. of Millet from our rec. to Willett, the capt. of Rehoboth, who was first mayor of New York, aft. its conq. As the mistake had not then been detected, Bliss foll. it in his Hist. of Rehoboth. When Millet or his w. d. is not ascert. THOMAS, Gloucester 1642, had John, Nathaniel, and Thomas, who were of adult age in 1664. In 1655, Mary, d. of Sylvester Eveleth, m. Thomas Millet, perhaps as sec. w. but more prob. as w. of the s. who was a preacher 1663, and d. bef. 1680; the w. surv. and s. Thomas d. at Manchester, 18 June 1707.

MILLING, SIMON, Watertown, an old man, had five ch. Simon, Richard, Mary, James, and John, all bapt. 5 Dec. 1686; but it is not told who was their mo. Perhaps she was d. and he had late. rem. thither, wh. conject. may be favor. by the ment. of bapt. of a young man, Thomas M. on 17 Oct. preced. Rare will be the occur. of such a name.

MILLINGTON, JOHN, Windsor, m. 1668, Sarah Smith, rem. to Suffield, there had John, b. 1675; Henry, 1679; prob. others. His s. John was at Coventry 1716, and aft.

MILLS, BENJAMIN, Dedham 1677, had liv. there, I suppose, more than 30 yrs. but nothing definite can be found. EDWARD, Boston, adm. to be inhab. 1645. EDWARD, Dorchester, s. of John of Braintree, m. Mehitable, d. of Stephen Minot, wid. of the younger Henry Messinger, wh. d. 16 Aug. 1690, aged 25; had Stephen. He taught the sch. in D. fr. 1687 to 92, and aft. a sch. in Boston, partly under the patronage of the London Soc. for propagat. the Gospel, and d. 7 Nov. 1732. JAMES, Lynn, may have come from Southold, L. I. where in 1663, was one of this name, m. 1 Apr. 1671, Martha, d. of Hugh Alley, had Martha, b. 14 June 1672; James, 9 Sept. 1674, d. young; Sarah, 27 Feb. 1676; James, again, 11 Oct. 1678; and Dorothy, 21 Apr. 1681. Lewis calls him the first perman. inhab. at Nahant. JOHN, Boston, came prob. in the fleet with Winth. for among the memb. of the first ch. his name is No. 33, and his w. Susanna next, desir. adm. as freem. 19 Oct. 1630, and was sw. 6 Mar. 1632. His ds. Joy, and Recompense, were bapt. in Oct. 1630, being the first on our ch. rec.; John, 3 June 1632; Jonathan, 30 Aug. 1635; and James, 3 June 1638. Vinton, 341, gives him, also, Susanna, b. in Eng. and Mary b. a. 1640. He soon rem. to Braintree, and with w. was recom. 5 Dec. 1641, to the ch. there, was town clk. 1653. Susanna, his w. d. 10 Dec. 1675, in her 80th yr. He made his will 12 Jan. 1678, pro. 10 Sept. foll. in wh. he names ds. Mary Hawkins and Susanna Dawes, and his only s. John is charged to bring up one of his s. unto learning, that he may be fit for the min. wh. was, he says, the employm. of my predecess. to 3d if not 4th generat. The gr.s. Edward, H. C. 1685, seems not to have obeyed the will of his ancest. tho. he liv. to 1732; but perhaps the fourth generat. was more regardful, at least Jonathan, H. C. 1723, was a min. JOHN, Scarborough, had John, James, Sarah, and Mary, who were all charg. with neglect of public worship; and Sarah's defence subject. her to stripes. JOHN, Braintree, s. of the first John, m. 26 Apr. 1653, Eliz. Shove, prob. sis. of Rev. George, who d. 18 Aug. 1711, in 81st yr. had Eliz. b. 5 Mar. or 1 July (as the first numeral is count. for mo. or for day) by differ. read. 1654; Sarah, 9 June 1656; John, 13 Apr. 1660; Jonathan, 9 Sept. 1662; Edward, 29 June 1665, H. C. 1685; Joanna or Susanna, 12 Mar. 1668, d. next yr.; Mary, 1 Apr. 1670; Nathaniel, 22 Apr. 1672; and Susanna, 23 Sept. 1675. His s. John and Nathaniel liv. at B. and both had fams. There was a John Mills, hav. fam. at Dedham 1676, perhaps br. of Benjamin. JOHN, of Boston, whose will, of 22 Oct. 1651, is abstr. in Geneal. Reg. IV. 285, tho. his inv. shows a good amount of prop. was prob. only a transient trader; at least, he names no w. or ch. but aft. a few trifling gifts, directs the bulk of the est. to go to his friends in the Canaries. JOHN, Simsbury, s. of Simon the sec. by w. Sarah had John, b. a. 1690; Joseph, and Benjamin, a. 1694; and Sarah, a. 1696; and he d. 11 Mar. 1698. JOSEPH, Kittery 1647, call. a planter. PETER, Windsor, in a tradit. of very light esteem, prob. a modern exercise of wit, said to have come from Holland, a tailor, with the name of Van Molyn (turn. into Eng. Mills), when relations betw. the two nations had long been hostile, strange. said to have been b. so late as 1666, m. bef. 1672, Dorcas, d. of Edward Messenger, wh. d. 18 May 1688, had Peter, and prob. other ch. perhaps Samuel, certain. Ebenezer, wh. d. 8 Feb. 1687; Return, d. 12 July 1689; and Eleazer, d. 1698, all prob. young, but date of b. of neither is seen; and m. 10 Dec. 1691, a sec. w. Jane Warren, or Fannin, of Hartford, as ano. statem. is; and he d. 12 Apr. 1702. PETER, Windsor, s. of the preced. m. 21 July 1692, Joan Porter, had Pelatiah, b. 27 Apr. 1693, wh. was a lawyer; Gideon, 3 Feb. 1695, d. soon; Jedediah, 23 May 1697, Y. C. 1722; Peter, 22 Apr. 1700, d. soon, and Peter, again, 12 Apr. 1701; Ann, 1703; John, 1706; David, 1709; Ebenezer, 1712; and Gideon, again, 15 Aug. 1715, Y. C. 1737. But Stiles omits, 704, the two last, as well as Ann, and varies in John and David. RICHARD, Stratford, and aft. 1653, at Stamford, rem. 1663 to West Chester. ROBERT, Kittery, perhaps br. of Joseph, d. 1647, leav. w. Dorothy, wh. m. John Harker of York, and four ch. SAMUEL, Windsor, m. 18 Oct. 1639, w. Joanna, wh. d. 5 July 1659, and he d. 19

May 1661. But I fear the same incid. may be ascrib. to Simon or Simeon by easy confus. of names. SAMUEL, Dedham 1642, had w. Frances, and ch. Samuel, bapt. 29 Mar. 1646, d. next mo.; Benjamin, 13 Apr. 1651; Eliz. 5 Dec. 1652; and Rebecca, 17 May 1657; yet the parents of this last, not being ment. at the time, on ch. rec. she may have been d. of Benjamin Miles, whose surname is not unfrequent. giv. as Mills. SAMUEL, Stratford 1668, rem. to L. I. and d. 1685, at Southampton. SIMON, Windsor 1639, m. that yr. prob. sec. w. Joan, wh. d. childless, July 1659. Date of his d. is unkn. SIMON, Windsor, perhaps s. of the preced. b. in Eng. tho. he may possib. be the same, but not likely, m. 23 Feb. 1660, Mary, d. of William Buell, had Samuel and Simon, tw. b. 23 Apr. 1661, both d. next mo.; Mary, 8 Dec. 1662; Hannah, 1665; Simon, again, 1 May 1667; John, 2 Jan. 1669; Sarah, 16 Sept. 1670; rem. to Simsbury, and had Abigail, 1672; Eliz. 1674; Prudence, 1676; and Simon, again, 1678. The first two and the fourth ch. d. bef. him, and he d. 6 July 1683. Both the s. liv. at Simsbury. THOMAS, Wells, freem. 1653, was constable 1664. Three of this name had, in 1834, been gr. at Harv. eighteen at Yale, and two at other N. E. coll.

MILNER, MICHAEL, Lynn, came in the James, from London, 1635, aged 23, rem. to L. I. 1640, says Lewis.

MILOM. See Mylam.

MILTON, GEORGE, New London 1663.

MILWARD. See Millerd.

MINARD, THOMAS, Hingham 1636. Lincoln.

MINGAY, * JEFFREY, Hampton, freem. 13 May 1640, rep. 1650, d. 11 July 1658. Ann, prob. his wid. m. Christopher Hussey, and d. 24 June 1680.

MINGO, ROBERT, Newbury, by w. Eliz. had Thomas, b. 2 June 1689; and Robert, 11 Oct. 1697. Coffin affords no derivat. of this person, and I indulge the conject. that the name is identic. with the last preced. and possib. that man was f. of this.

MINOR, or MINER, CLEMENT, New London 1666, s. of Thomas, adm. freem. that yr. m. 1662, Frances, wid. of young Isaac Willey, had Mary, b. 19 Jan. 1665; Joseph, 6 Aug. 1666; Clement, 6 Oct. 1668; William, 6 Nov. 1670; and Ann, 30 Nov. 1672; his w. d. 6 Jan. foll. and he m. Martha, d. of William Wellman, had Phebe, 13 Apr. 1679. This sec. w. d. 5 July 1681, and he had third w. Joanna, wh. d. Oct. 1700. He was a deac. and d. very near the same time with his last w. * EPHRAIM, Stonington 1666, s. of Thomas, was one of the found. of the ch. in June 1674, prob. had w. Hannah, and d. Eliz. freem. that yr. and was rep. 1676. * JOHN, Stratford 1659, eldest s. of Thomas of

New London, wh. the Commissnrs. of the Unit. Col. of N. E. desir. in
1654, to have qualif. at Hartford to be an instruct. of the natives, was
town clk. of S. and rep. 1667 and 76, and of the new town of Woodbury very many yrs.; m. 19 Oct. 1658, Eliz. d. of Richard Booth, had
John, b. 9 Sept. 1659; Thomas, 29 May 1662; Hannah, 2 Aug. 1664;
Eliz. 16 Jan. 1667; Grace, 20 Sept. 1670; Joseph, 4 Mar. 1673;
Ephraim, 24 Oct. 1675; Sarah, 19 June 1678; Abigail, 6 Feb. 1681;
and Joanna, bapt. July 1683; and he d. 17 Sept. 1719, but the wid. liv.
to 24 Oct. 1732, prob. 92 or 3 yrs. old. JOSEPH, Stonington, br. of
Ephraim, freem. 1666, had w. Mary. Prob. he and John were of
Woodbury 1690. MANASSEH, New London 1671, s. of Thomas of the
same, said to be the first male white, b. in that town, had Hannah, b. 3
Nov. 1677; and Thomas, 1683; was deac. and d. 29 Apr. 1728,
aged 81. * THOMAS, Charlestown 1632, s. of William of Chew Magna,
in Co. Somerset, one of the found. of the ch. in Frothingham, 70, as
well as Budington, 184, said to be dism. for that purpose from Boston
ch. 14 Oct. of that yr. but tho. the rec. at C. supports them, his name is
not in the list of Boston mem. in the surv. copy of our first ch.; freem.
4 Mar. 1634, rem. to New London soon aft. 1645, had m. 23 Apr. 1634,
Grace, eldest d. of Walter Palmer, had sev. ch. if not all, bef. rem.
They were John, bapt. 30 Aug. 1635; Thomas; Clement, b. 27 Apr.
1642; Manasseh; Ephraim; Joseph; Judah; Samuel; Ann; Eliz.;
Eunice; and Mary. He was a very valua. man, rep. 1650 and 1, perhaps 65, 70, and 3, for Stonington, but I doubt, some of the latter
honors belong to his s. of the same name, and prob. Hinman, who makes
him town clk. of Woodbury for 30 yrs. from 1674, makes the same mistake in pp. 54, 153, and 222. The f. as the oldest gr.stone at Stonington
shows, d. 1690, aged 83. A diary kept by him for sev. yrs. furnish.
some good informat. Sometimes in Conn. this name is Myner; and in
1834, nine of the fam. had been gr. at Yale.

MINORD, JAMES, Boston, by w. Mary had Amander, a s. b. Sept.
1645.

MINOT, * GEORGE, Dorchester, s. of Thomas, b. 4 Aug. 1594, at
Saffron Walden, Co. Essex, was an early sett. tho. not of 1630, as
Harris gives, freem. 1 Apr. 1634, rep. 1635 and 6, rul. elder 30 yrs. d.
24 Dec. 1671. By w. Martha he had John, b. 2 Apr. 1626; James, 31
Dec. 1628; Stephen, 2 May 1631; all b. in Eng.; and Samuel, 18
Dec. 1635. His w. d. 23 Dec. 1657, aged a. 60. GEORGE, Dorchester,
s. of James, freem. 1690, was capt. 1688 in com. of one of the comps.
at Pemaquid 1689. JAMES, Dorchester, s. of the first George, b. in
Eng. m. 9 Dec. 1653, Hannah, d. of Israel Stoughton, had Israel, b. 18
Oct. 1654, d. young; George, 14 Nov. 1655, bef. ment.; Hannah, 1657,

d. young; James, 2 Apr. 1659; William, 18 Sept. 1662; Eliz. 27 Dec. 1663; and Mehitable, 17 Sept. 1668; was freem. 1665. His w. d. 12 Mar. 1670, says Shattuck, in Genealog. Reg. I. 172, but the gr.stone says 27; and he m. 21 May 1673, Hepzibah, d. of famous Elijah Corlet, and d. 30 Mar. 1676. His wid. m. 4 June 1684, Daniel Champney. Eliz m. 21 Nov. 1682, Rev. John Danforth; and Mehitable m. first, Thomas Cooper, and next, 19 Dec. 1706, Peter Sargent, Esquire, and third, 12 May 1715, Simeon Stoddard, Esq. outliv. him, and d. 23 Sept. 1738. JAMES, Dorchester, s. of John, taught the gram. sch. for some yrs. rem. to Concord, preach. and stud. physic, m. a. 1684, Rebecca, d. of Timothy Wheeler, had Rebecca, b. 9 Feb. 1685; Lydia, 12 Mar. 1687; Mary, 16 Nov. 1689; Timothy, 18 June 1692; James, 17 Oct. 1694; Eliz. 29 Jan. 1697; Martha, 3 Apr. 1699; Lucy and Mercy, tw. 15 Apr. 1702; and Samuel, 25 Mar. 1706; freem. 1690, when the name is spell. Minerd. His w. d. 23 Sept. 1734, and he d. 20 Sept. foll. JAMES, Concord, s. of the first James, m. 9 Feb. 1686 or 1688, for both dates are giv. Rebecca, d. of John Jones, had only ch. Jonathan; and his wid. m. 9 Mar. 1696, capt. Joseph Bulkeley. JOHN, Dorchester, s. of the first George, b. in Eng. m. 19 May 1647, Lydia, d. of Nicholas Butler, had John, b. 22 Jan. 1648; James, 14 Sept. 1653, bef. ment. H. C. 1675; Martha, 22 Sept. 1657; Stephen, 10 Aug. 1662; Samuel, 3 July 1665; and a ch. d. inf. He had sec. w. Mary, wid. of John Biggs, d. of John Dassett; was freem. 1665; a capt. d. 12 Aug. 1669. In applica. to him of the anecdote from Hutch. I. 288, relat. in Dwight's Travels, the writer of the Genealogy mistakes by forgetting that he had been in his grave six yrs. bef. the occurrence. The only d. Martha d. 23 Nov. 1678, betroth. to John Morgan, jr. to whom in her will she made affecting reference. His wid. d. 1676, her will of 5 June in that yr. was pro. 27 July foll. JOHN, Boston, d. 1659, leav. wid. Eliz. JOHN, Dorchester, s. of John of the same, m. 11 Mar. 1670, Eliz. d. of Edward Breck, had John, b. 10 Oct. 1672; Israel, 23 Aug. 1676; Josiah, 27 Dec. 1677; Jerusha, 28 Jan. 1680; and George, 16 Aug. 1682; was a town officer 1690, and freem. the same yr.; his w. d. 6 Apr. 1690, and he d. 26 Jan. foll. SAMUEL, Boston, s. of the first George, m. 23 June 1670, Hannah, d. of Robert Howard, had Samuel, b. 26 Apr. 1672, d. soon; Samuel, again, 31 Mar. 1673, d. young; rem. to Dorchester, there had George, 1675; and Samuel, again, 23 Nov. 1688, d. next June. SAMUEL, Concord, s. of the first John, m. Hannah Jones, had only ch. Jonathan, and Shattuck adds d. young. STEPHEN, Dorchester, s. of the first George, b. I think, in Eng. m. 10 Nov. 1654, Truecross, d. of capt. Richard Davenport, had Martha, b. 22 Sept. 1656, wh. d. unm. 11 Oct. 1683; Jonathan, 11 Sept. 1658, d. at 2 mos.; Eliz.

wh. d. young; Mehitable, 4, bapt. 18 June 1665; and Eliz. again,
posthum. 10 June 1672. He was freem. 1665, and d. 16 Feb. 1672, yet
the gr.stone careless. says 1662. Mehitable m. Henry Messenger, wh.
d. soon, and she m. Edward Mills of Boston, and d. 16 Aug. 1690; and
Eliz. with Stephen Mills, s. of Mehitable, were only heirs of the wid.
wh. d. 3 Aug. 1692. STEPHEN, Boston, s. of the first John, m. 1 Dec.
1686, Mary, d. of Christopher Clark, had Rebecca, b. 20 Aug. 1687, d.
in few days; Stephen, 27 Oct. 1688; John, 27 Dec. 1690; Mehitable,
6 Dec. 1692; Lydia, 15 May 1695; Rebecca, again, 6 Nov. 1697;
George, 21 Jan. 1700, d. young; Peter, 4 Mar. 1702, d. in few mos.;
George, again, 29 Jan. 1704; Christopher, H. C. 1725; Peter; and
James. He was one of the founders of Brattle str. ch. and d. 1732, his
will of 30 Oct. being pro. 13 Nov. foll. The reputa. of his gr. gr.s.
George R. M. H. C. 1778, is fixed in one generat. by most amiab.
character, and for the succeed. by his works on our history. Twelve of
the name had, in 1834, been gr. at Harv. and two at other N. E. coll.

MINTER, TOBIAS, New London, s. of Ezer, came from Newfoundland
1672, d. next yr. TRISTRAM, New London, d. bef. 1674, when his wid.
m. Joshua Baker.

MIRABLE, ... Charlestown 1651, had w. Eliz. wh. was one of
the friends of Matthews. But perhaps the true name was Marble,
wh. see. Yet in the will of George Knower, Mary Mirable is call.
his d.

MIRIAM, JOHN, Boston, was a selectman 1691. See Meriam.

MIRICK, or MYRICK, BENJAMIN, Charlestown, s. of John, by w.
Sarah had Benjamin, and Sarah, bapt. 30 Jan. 1687. JAMES, Newbury
1656, had Hannah, b. 6 Feb. 1657; Abigail, 5 Sept. 1658; Joseph, 27
Apr. 1661; Isaac, 6 Jan. 1665; Timothy, 28 Sept. 1666; and Susanna,
20 Aug. 1670. Coffin says he was b. 1612; but it would have better
pleased us to learn the time of his d. JAMES, Newbury, s. of the preced.
perhaps, yet not so indicat. by Coffin, who says, by w. Hannah he had
Benjamin, b. 16 Apr. 1683; James, 16 July 1684; but in the former
line he had him 16 Apr. 1683; and John, 10 Sept. 1686. JOHN,
Charlestown, by w. Judith, unless this be, as I suspect, error for Hopestill, had Hopestill, b. 20 Feb. 1643; Benjamin, 22 June 1644; and,
perhaps, others. By sec. w. Hopestill (unless it be the first, as I suspect,
for Hopestill M. is adm. of the ch. in Charlestown, 10 Sept. 1644), he had
Sarah, 1 May 1657; Mercy, 30 Dec. 1658; and Abigail, bapt. 17 Feb.
1661. His d. Ann m. John Walker, bef. 3 Oct. 1675, when she join. the
ch. unless his w. were d. of Jacob Leager. JOHN, Newton, perhaps s. of
the preced. m. 1682, Eliz. d. of deac. James Trowbridge, had Thankful,
b. 24 Apr. 1685; Rebecca, 20 Apr. 1687; Lydia, 18 Feb. 1689, d.

young; Samuel, 1 Mar. 1691; John, 30 Nov. 1694; Margaret; James, 26 Oct. 1696; Deborah; Eliz. Aug. 1699; Elisha, 5 Mar. 1701; and Lydia, again, 7 July 1704; in the order giv. by Jackson; but Bond substitutes for Deborah, Sarah, 6 Mar. 1695, add. that she m. Jonathan Fuller, with wh. Jackson, 280, concurs. He was freem. 1685, k. at Groton, by the Ind. 21 July 1706, unless Butler in his Hist. be mistak. as Jackson, 366, renders prob. That very careful collector, p. 96, refers to Penhallow for his extract; but in that writer I do not discov. the passage. Yet Homer, in his Hist. of N. had print. the same passage, 1 Mass. Hist. Coll. V. 273. It is curious, that both the other sufferers at G. on that day, were of N. I suppose they were part of a garrison at G. But this John d. 11 July 1706, and had made his will 29 Apr. preced. "under a languish. sickness." Some mistake of the town was made. TIMOTHY, Newbury, youngest s. of the first James, m. 1696, Mary Lancaster, had Ezra, b. 31 Mar. 1697; Abigail, 26 Nov. 1698; and, perhaps, more.

MITCHELL, ANDREW, Charlestown, had Mary, bapt. 2 Dec. 1688; Abigail, 17 Feb. 1689; Sarah; Eliz. 7 Jan. 1694; and Andrew, 28 Jan. 1695. His w. was Abigail. DAVID, Stratford, br. of Jonathan, came prob. with his f. 1635, in the James from Bristol, arr. at Boston 16 Aug. and accomp. his f. to Saybrook, thence to Wethersfield for some yrs. and Stamford, taught the sch. at Watertown, perhaps Dec. 1649, at least was invit. for that object, and soon aft. rem. to Stratford, where certain. he was in 1665, when he had two s. but who was the mo. or when the f. d. are all unkn. Cothren, 634, names four s. Matthew, John, Nathan, and Abraham, and tho. the d. of the f. name of the mo. or b. of either of the four is sought in vain, he permits us to infer that the two ment. in 1665 may have been Abraham and Matthew, but that John was older than Abraham. In Nov. 1675 he was entrust. by the Council of war with import. affairs. EDWARD, Hingham, came in the Diligent, 1638, but we kn. no more of him, exc. that he was from Old Hingham. EDWARD, Bridgewater, s. of Experience, m. Mary, d. of Thomas Hayward, and in 40 yrs. by her had no ch. m. next, 1708, Alice, d. of major John Bradford, had Mary, b. 1709; Alice, 1714; and Edward, 7 Feb. 1716, wh. d. 23 Dec. 1801, the gr.f. of Nahum, H. C. 1789. He d. 1717, and his wid. m. deac. Joshua Hersey of Hingham. EXPERIENCE, Plymouth, a youth, came in the Ann, 1623, had been one of the goodly comp. at Leyden, where he left a br. Thomas, who d. there. Perhaps he was under the care of Francis Cook, at least, he is of his comp. in partak. sh. of cattle 1627, and soon aft. m. his d. Jane, was of Duxbury aft. 1631, and long aft. rem. to Bridgewater, there d. 1689, aged above 80 yrs. His ch. were Eliz. wh. m. 1645,

John Washburn; Thomas; Mary, m. 24 Dec. 1652, James Shaw, and d. 1679; Edward; Sarah; Jacob; John; and Hannah, but the order of b. is uncert. and so may be the mo. for he had sec. w. Mary. Sarah m. John Hayward; and Hannah m. Joseph Hayward, as his third w. GEORGE, Boston 1644, carpenter, by w. Mary had Eliz. b. 26 Aug. 1645; Mary, 25 Aug. 1648; John, 3 June 1650; and Sarah, 8 Dec. 1652. JACOB, Dartmouth, s. of Experience, m. 7 Nov. 1666, Susanna, d. of Thomas Pope, had Jacob, Thomas, and Mary, all brot. up by their uncle Edward, aft. hims. and w. were k. 1675, in Philip's war, by the Ind. ⸗ JOHN, Kittery, seems by his inv. 28 May 1664, to have large prop. £784; but I kn. no more, exc. that his admor. was Elias Stileman. JOHN, Hartford 1660, freem. 1667, d. 28 July 1683, leav. ch. Mary, aged 28; John, 25; Sarah, 21; Margaret, 19; Mabel, 17; and Miriam, 15. JOHN, Duxbury, youngest s. of Experience, m. 14 Dec. 1675, Mary, d. of Thomas Bonney, had Experience, b. 1676; and his w. d. the yr. foll. Next, 14 Jan. 1679, he m. Mary Lothrop, wh. d. 13 Feb. 1680; and he m. 24 May 1682, Mary Prior, had Mary, 28 Feb. 1683; Hannah, 13 Feb. 1684; Joseph, 23 Mar. 1684; Eliz. 25 Mar. 1685, d. soon; Eliz. again, 29 May 1686; John, 13 Jan. 1689; Sarah, 9 May 1690; and Esther, 22 Jan. 1692. Gladly would I learn wh. this third w. was, and espec. the more prob. dates of one or two of the ch. JOHN, Woodbury, s. of David, by w. Eliz. wh. d. 1730, had David, bapt. Nov. 1679, d. soon; David, again, Apr. 1681; Eliz. Nov. 1683, d. young; Elnathan, Oct. 1686; John, Feb. 1689; Knell, Apr. 1691; Eliz. again, May 1693; and Martha, Mar. 1697; as Cothren gives them, and says he d. 3 Jan. 1732. JOHN, Newbury, s. of William of the same, m. 20 May 1680, Hannah Spofford, had Hannah, b. 12 Apr. 1681; Sarah, 26 Sept. 1682; John, 17 June 1685; and Sarah, again, 10 Apr. 1689. His w. d. in two wks. aft.; and he m. 15 Nov. 1697, Constance Moores, and d. 17 Dec. 1731. *JONATHAN*, Cambridge, came with his f. Matthew, in the James, from Bristol, 1635, being then a. 9 or 10 yrs. old, was bred at H. C. where 1647, he had his A. B. ord. 21 Aug. 1650, m. 19 Nov. foll. Margaret, wid. of Rev. Thomas Shepard, his predecess. but was bef. betrothed to Sarah, d. of Rev. John Cotton, wh. d. in Jan. preced. had Margaret, b. 26 Feb. 1653, d. next yr.; Nathaniel, 4 Mar. 1656, d. at 17 yrs.; John, 16 Mar. 1658, d. next yr.; Samuel, 14, bapt. 21 Oct. 1660, H. C. 1681, whose d. is not found in the catal. and he is the latest of the childr. in the ch. reg. of his f. Yet he certain. had Jonathan, H. C. 1687, wh. d. 14 Mar. 1695; and Margaret, again, wh. m. 13 June 1682, Stephen Sewall of Salem, and only thro. her, is the blood of the disting. ancest. come down. He d. 9 July 1668, in the "forty-third yr. of his age," says the Magnalia, IV. 184, yet as Mather could not avoid an occasion of blunder, even for so famous a man, whom he calls *match-less*, he had on p. 166 of the same Book, told us he was b. 1624, at Halifax, in the W. riding of Yorksh. In 1662, he, with Gookin, were made first licensers of the press in Mass. He had good est. the inv. being £786, 17, 9. Every writer who has ment. the famous men of the early days of our country, has told of Mitchell, and the oversight of call. his f. Jonathan, instead of Matthew, by Sprague, in Annals of the American Pulpit, would seem too trivial to be noticed here, did not the minute statem. of his m. require correction: "Margaret S. daur. of his predecessor, by his first m." seems to bear on its face, the stamp of exact truth. But as accura. relat. is always desira. it may be told, the only d. of Shepard by his first w. d. inf. and this Margaret who m. Mitchell was the third w. of S. not his ch. * MATTHEW, Charlestown, came 1635, with Rev. Richard Mather, in the James, of Bristol, bring. w. and ch. David, and Jonathan, perhaps more, rem. to Concord, and soon to Springfield, there sign. compact with Pynchon and others in May 1636, soon aft. to Saybrook for short time, where, in the Pequot war, he was protect. by Lyon Gardiner, but he says the Ind. took one of the "old man's s. and roasted him alive." He was in 1639 at Wethersfield a short time, and next yr. made their town clk. but soon went to Stamford, and in 1643, with Rev. Richard Denton, to Hempstead, L. I. perhaps back again, soon to Stamford, there d. in 1645. He was rep. in 1637, but not, as Mather makes him, one of the Assist. of the Col. that yr. MATTHEW, Stratford, s. of David of the same, rem. to Southbury, by Mary, youngest d. of John Thompson the first of Stratford, who d. 18 Jan. 1711, had Mary, bapt. Feb. 1679; Jonathan, July 1683; Mary, again, July 1687; and David, Oct. 1692. He was deac. and d. 1736. THOMAS, New Haven, had Eliz. bapt. 22 Feb. 1652, who d. bef. him: and in his will, 1 Oct. 1659, nam. w. Eliz. who was prob. sec. and her d. Eliz.; his only ch. ment. is Hannah, but she may have been adult. He d. late in 1659, or early in 1660, the inv. being of 2 Mar. in this yr. The wid. m. Jeremiah Whitnell, prob. in 1662. THOMAS, Malden, m. Nov. 1655, Mary Moulton. THOMAS, Boston, by w. Ann, had Eliz. b. 19 Oct. 1664. THOMAS, Block Island 1684, was troubled by a French invasion, 1689, as Niles, a fellow-sufferer, tells in his Ind. wars, 3 Mass. Hist. Coll. VI. 272. He liv. there many yrs. WILLIAM, Newbury, m. 7 Nov. 1648, Mary Sawyer, had Mary, b. 31 Aug. 1649; John, 21 May 1651; William, 1 Mar. 1653; and Eliz. posthum. 15 Mar. 1655. He d. 6 July 1654; and his wid. m. 8 Dec. 1656, Robert Savory. WIL-LIAM, Charlestown, d. 23 Jan. 1678. Nine of this name had been gr. at Harv. in 1826, and seventeen at Yale.

MITCHELSON, oftener MICHELSON or MITCHENSON (as the vulgar
19 *

made it), ‖ EDWARD, Cambridge 1636, ar. co. 1639, marshal-gen. of the Col. 1654, at salary of £50, for many yrs. had the sad office of execut. the Quakers, tho. he was, by Mitchell's reg. in full commun. with the ch. yet not found in the list of freem.; d. 7 Mar. 1682, aged 77. By w. Ruth Bushell, who came 1635, aged 23, in the Abigail, had Thomas, b. Sept. 1637, d. soon; Ruth, 9 Nov. 1638, wh. m. 20 Oct. 1656, John Green; Bethia, 6 Dec. 1642, wh. m. Daniel Weld; Edward, 11 Nov. 1644, H. C. 1665, lost on voyage to Eng. next yr.; and Eliz. 29 Aug. 1646, wh. m. Theodore Atkinson, jr. and on 15 Nov. 1676, Henry Deering. WILLIAM, Cambridge, m. 26 Mar. 1654, Mary Bradshaw, had Mary, b. 15 Jan. 1655; Thomas, 8 Jan. 1657; and Alice; all bapt. 5 Apr. 1663; Ruth, 4 Oct. 1663; and Abigail, 11 Mar. 1666; and he d. 18 Dec. 1668.

MITTEN, MICHAEL, Falmouth 1637, then assoc. with George Cleves, whose only ch. Eliz. he m. had Ann, wh. m. Anthony Brackett; Eliz. b. 1644, m. Thaddeus Clarke; Mary, m. Thomas Brackett; Sarah, m. James Andrews; and Martha m. John Graves, wh. rem. from Kittery to Little Compton; beside only s. Nathaniel, wh. was k. by the Ind. 11 Aug. 1676, unm. He was constable in 1640, freem. 1658; but is unhappi. at an earlier day, commemo. by Winth. II. 302. He d. 1660. See also Folsom, 54, and especial. Willis, I. 96 and 173. His wid. m. a Harvey, and d. his wid. 1682.

MIX, or MEEKS, CALEB, DANIEL, JOHN, and NATHANIEL, proprs. of New Haven 1685, tho. Daniel, wh. m. Ruth, d. of John Rockwell, liv. at Wallingford, were all s. of Thomas, but my means furnish account only of John, wh. was the oldest. He m. Eliz. d. of sec. Benjamin Wilmot, had John, b. 25 Aug. 1676; Esther, 25 Dec. 1678; Eliz. 18 Feb. 1681; Joseph, 18 Dec. 1684; Abigail; and Mercy. He d. Jan. 1712, his will being of the 19th, and all the six ch. within ten days aft. agreed as to the est. STEPHEN, Wethersfield, youngest s. of Thomas the first, ord. 1694, m. 1 Dec. 1696, Mary, d. of Rev. Solomon Stoddard of Northampton, had Sarah, b. early in 1698; Mary, 1700; Rebecca, 1702; Esther, 1704; Elisha, 1706; and Christian, 1709; and he d. 28 Aug. 1738. THOMAS, New Haven 1643, m. 1649, Rebecca, d. of capt. Nathaniel Turner, had John, the eldest, b. 1649; Nathaniel, 14 Sept. 1651; Daniel, 8 Sept. 1653; Thomas, 30 Aug. 1655; Rebecca, 4 Jan. 1658, all bapt. 23 May 1658; Abigail, 1659, bapt. 22 Jan. 1660; Caleb, bapt. 15 Dec. 1661; Samuel, b. 11 Jan. 1664, bapt. 21 Feb. foll.; Hannah, 30 June 1666, bapt. 12 Aug. foll.; Esther, 30 Nov. 1668, d. within 2 yrs.; and Stephen, 1 Nov. 1672, H. C. 1690. He d. early in 1691, his inv. wh. shows good est. being of 9 June, nam. all the ten liv. ch. in his will of Apr. preced. made s. John and Stephen excors. THOMAS, New

Haven.s. of the preced.m.30 June 1677,Hannah,d.of Rev.
James Fitch of Norwich,rem.thither,and had Daniel,b.23
April.1678; Abigail,10 Mar.1680; James,29 Dec.1683;Hannah,
13 Apr.1685; Deborah,14 Apr.1687; Eliz.15 Apr.1689; Dorothy,23 Nov.1691; Ann,7 May 1694; and Zebediah,12 Dec.
1697.   WILLIAM, New Haven,perhaps br.of the first Thomas,
m. Sarah, d.of William Preston, had Benjamin,b.1650; Nathaniel,1651; Sarah,1654; Mary, 1656; Thomas,1659; and
prob.others; and d.we presume,bef.1685. The name was first
writ. Meekes.

MIXER, oft.call. MIXTER,BENJAMIN, Marlborough, s.of the
sec. Isaac, m.27 Nov.1711, Rebecca Newton,had Phineas,b.
26 Dec.1712; Benjamin,23 Mar.1715; Isaac,26 Nov.1716;
David,22 Dec.1718; Joseph,1724,d.soon; and Ebenezer,
posthum.23 May 1729; and he d.no long time bef.and his wit
m.Oct.1743, Moses Newton. DANIEL, Framingham,or.of Benjamin,by w.Judith had Daniel,b.in Groton,28 Aug.1701,d,
young; Eliz.12 Oct.1704; Daniel,again,4 June 1706,d.at 15
yrs.; John,4 Nov.1711; and Isaac; was constable and
selectman,liv.to old age. ISAAC, Watertown, came in the
Elizabeth from Ipswich,1634,aged 31, with w.Sarah,33 and
Isaac,4; was freem.2 May 1638; had b.here Sarah,wh.m.John
Stearns,and d.4 June 1656. He was selectman 1651 and 5,
prob.d.soon aft.date of his will,8 May 1655,and his wid.
d.24 Nov.1681. ISAAC, Watertown, only s.of the preced.b.
in Eng.came with his parents in the Elizabeth,1634,sw.
fidel.1652,m.19 Sept.1655, Mary,d.of John Coolidge,as San
gives it, but Cooke in Barry,had Mary,b.18 May 1656; Sara
29 Nov.1657; that w.d.(tho.the rec.calls her Sarah) 2 Mar
or 2 Nov.(both giv.by Bond)or as Barry says,2 July 1660;
and he m.10 Jan.foll.Rebecca,d.of Edward Garfield,had Rebecca,9 Mar.1662; Isaac; Eliz.18 June 1665,d.at 20 yrs.;
Joanna,14 Dec.1866; John,1 Mar.1868; George,12 Dec.1670;
Abigail,4 Nov.1672; Joseph,7 Aug.1674; Daniel,21 Feb 1676
bef.ment.; Mehitable,25 Jan.1678,d.young; Benjamin,23 May
1679; Dorothy,2 Sept.1680; and David,6 Aug.1683,d.young.

His sec.w.d.16 Mar.1684, but Bond makes it five mos.bef.
the b.of last ch. and he took third w.29 June 1687,Mary,
wid.of William French,as she had been of John Stearns of
Billerica,d.of Thomas Lothrop; and d.27 Nov.1716. Mary m.
1680,says Bond,George Munnings,jr.,Manning,says Barry;
Sarah m.Samuel Hagar; Rebecca m.13 or 23 Nov.1683,Samuel
Kendall; Joanna m.7 Nov.1688,Joseph Harrington,and next,
20 Dec.1693,Obadiah Ward; Abigail m.11 Dec.1690,Samuel
Howe; and Dorothy m.12 Jan.1710,William Davis,prob.third
of the name,of Roxbury. ISAAC, Watertown,eldest s.of the
sec.

Page 224.

Isaac of the same,m.17 Oct.1684,Eliz.d.of Daniel Pierce,
but had no ch. His will was pro.Jan.1726. JOHN,Watertown
br.of the preced.a tanner,m.15 Aug.1695,Abigail,d.of John
Fiske,had Abigail,b.26 June 1696;John,22 Jan.1699;Eliz.
30 Dec.1702; and George,27 Dec.1704. JOSEPH, Watertown,br
of the preced.m.Ann,d.of Josiah Jones,had Rebecca,b.22
Feb.1704,d.next mo.; Joseph,14 Dec.1705; Sarah,12 Mar.170
Lydia,10 June 1710; David,July 1713,d.soon; Mary,25 Oct.
1714; Josiah,10 Nov.1716; Ann,14 Aug.1719; and Abigail,26
June 1721; was deac.d.10 Dec.1723. His wid.d.a.1736.

    MODESLY. See Maudsley.

    MOGER,JOHN,Brookhaven,L.I.1655. Thompson.

    MOHONAS,TEAGUE,Boston,perhaps a fisherman,appoint.
admor.Mar.1651,on est.of Matthew Collane,wh.d.at Isle of
Shoals.

    MOISES,HENRY,Salem 1676;a householder.

    MOKUM,ROBERT,Boston,by w.Hannah had William,b.14 Mar.
1668; may be the same as MOKEY,wh.Mr.Felt found at Ipswich 1639.

    MOLT,JAMES,a soldier in Philip's war,under capt.Turne
at Hatfield 1676.

    MONK,CHRISTOPHER,Boston,by w.Mary had Christopher,b.1
Dec.1686,perhaps d.soon; Thomas,bapt.2 Feb.1690; Ebenezer
31 Jan.1692; Susanna,17 May 1696; and Mary,25 June 1700.

had been a mariner,was a neighbor of Mather,who in his
gn.VI.7,has wisely giv.the relation of capture by Alger-
es in Aug.1681,and recapture next mo. GEORGE,Boston,vint
r,at the sign of the blue anchor,by w.Lucy,who was d.of
omas Gardner,and wid.of John Turner,had George,b.7 Nov.
33; and William,17 Aug.1636. By sec.w.Eliz.wid.of John
odmansey,wh.surv.he had prob.no ch. and d.5 Sept.1698.
 his will of 5 Mar.preced.he gave George,beside portion
 his est.here,the messuage,call.Navestock,4 miles fr.
mford,in Co.Essex,that was his f.William's,and to d-in-
w Margaret Woodmansey,£50. Dunton,in his visit to Bos-
n 1686,duly honors his genial disposition. See 2 Mass.
st. Coll.II. 103.

MONTAGUE, or MOUNTAGUE,GRIFFIN, Brookline 1635,then a
.of Boston,call.Muddy river,was of Cape Porpoise in 1653,
en he sw.fidel.to Mass. By his will of 7 July 1671,pro.
Apr.foll.he gave all to w.Margaret. JOHN, Hadley,s.of
chard,had John,b.31 Dec.1681; Richard,13 Mar.1684; Hannah
Aug.1687; Hannah,again,21 Mar.1689,both d.young; Peter,
y 1690; William,16 Dec.1692; Samuel,2 Apr.1695; Hannah,
 May 1697; Luke,4 Oct.1699; and Nathaniel,1 or 6 Oct.
704. He m.23 Mar.1681,Hannah, d.of Samuel Smith. These
even s.were not scatter.far; John and

athaniel liv.at Hadley; Richard at Wethersfield; Peter,
illiam,and Luke,at South Hadley;and Samuel at Sunderland.
PETER, Hadley,br.of the preced.freem.1690,was rep.4 yrs.
ad three ws.first,Sept.1679,Mary Smith,wh.d.20 May 1680;
nd 18 Sept.foll.he m.Mary,d.of John Crow,wid.of Noah Col-
an; and his third w.was Mary,wid.of Preserved Smith. But
e had no ch,and d.27 Mar.1725,leav.good est.to relat.
ICHARD, Boston,said to be s.of Peter,of the parish of Burn
am,Co.Bucks,by w.Abigail Downing had Sarah,b.by the town
ec.15 June 1646,and d.4 Days aft.but the ch.rec.says,bapt.
8,a.2 days old,in right of her mo.who had join.4 Apr.pre-
d. and Martha,20 June 1647,a.4 days old; ren.to Wethers-

field,there had Peter,8 or 18 July 1651; thence to Hadley,
a.1659,in a depon.of 1671,calls hims.57 yrs. old,was freem
of 1681,and d.14 Dec.of that yr. His wid.liv.to 8 Nov.169
In the will,he names ch.Peter; John; Mary,prob.the oldest
ch.w.of Joseph Warriner,m.25 Nov.1668; Martha,wh.m.1 Dec.
1671,Isaac Harrison,and next,3 Apr.1677,Henry White; and
Abigail,m.8 Dec.1671,Mark Warner.

MOODIE,THOMAS, Boston 1684,one of the Scot's Charit.Soc

MOODY,MOODEY,* CALEB, Newberry,s.of William,m.24 Aug.
1659,Sarah Pierce,wh.d.25 Aug.1665,and he m.9 Nov.foll.
Judith,d.of capt.Thomas Bradbury of Salisbury,had Daniel,b
4 Apr.1662; Sarah,23 July,1664;Caleb,9 Sept.1666; Thomas,20
Oct.1668; Judith,23 Sept.1669,d.at 9 yrs.; Joshua,8 Nov.16
William,15 Dec.1673; Samuel,4 Jan.1676,H.C.1697; Mary,23 O
1678; and Judith,again,13 Feb.1683. He d.25 Aug.1698,aged
61; had been freem.1666,rep.1677 and 8,and was a confessor
prison,under the tyranny of Andros,1689. See Coffin,150.
wid.d.24 Jan.1700. The s.Samuel,min.of York,ord.20 Dec.1700
wh.d.13 Nov.1747,was f.of Joseph,H.C.1718,min.of ano.ch.at
York,wh.was f.of the celebr.Samuel, H.C. 1746,preceptor of
Dummer school,a bachelor,who produced for many yrs.the fin-
est classical students of N. E. DANIEL, Salisbury,s.of
Caleb,by w.Eliz.had Daniel,b.16 Feb.1684; Joshua,20 Oct,168
Sarah,8 May 1689; Abigail,10 Dec.1691; Mary,1 July 1694;
Eliz.11 Feb.1697; and Hannah,2 Jan.1700. DEBORAH,the lady
who purch.1640,the planta.of John Hunfrey at Lynn,was a mem
of Salem ch.wh.admonish.her for error as to bapt.of inf.mak
ing her life so uncomforta.that she rem.a.1643,to the Dutch
Col.and sett.on L.I.where Sir Henry M.liv.who may have been
her s. but more certain. in Wood's Hist.is call.one of the
orig.patentees. There she resid.long,had from Gov.Stuyve-
sant,allowance to nomin.magistr.in 1654,for Gravesend,as
Increase Mather had from king William to dictate for Mass.
in her new Charter. ELEAZER, Boston,freem. 1690. JOHN,Rox
bury,came in 1633, says the ch.

rec.with w. Sarah,but no ch. He was s. of George of
Moulton,Co.Suffolk,freem.5 Nov.1635, with prefix of respect, suffer.loss of two serv. as Winth.I.106, tells,rem.
soon to Hartford, had Samuel,perhaps only ch.unless Eliz.
Seger,to whom by his will of 25 July 1655, he gave £25,
tho.not so call.in it, were his d. His wid.Sarah d.1671,
at Hadley. JOSHUA, Portsmouth,s.of William,b.in Eng.H.C.
1653,was first min.of the first ch.ord. July 1671, tho.he
had preach. there 1658, was call.to preach the Gen.Elect.
sermon of Mass.1675; and by strange tyranny of Gov. Cranfield, he was aft.3 mos.imprison.driv.to Boston, and was
sett. in May 1684 at first ch.the same yr.was offer.the
station of Presid.of the Coll.wh.he declined. Of his
humane boldness,in the delusion of 1692, extraor.instance
is preserv. in Eliot's Biog. Dict. Back he went to his
former service in 1692 at P. but on a visit to Boston,d.
4 July 1697. Allen, in Biog. Dict. says that "his zeal
against the witchcraft delus.occasion.his dism.from the
ch. where he was   preach." Sorry should we feel to find
the proof of this,however honora. to him. Much detail on
this subject is in Essex Inst.valua. Vol.I. His w.was d.
of Edward Collins of Cambridge, prob. Martha, wh. d.bef.
Aug. 1674. See Hutch.Coll.465. His d.Martha m.a. 1680,
Jonathan Russell; and Sarah m. 5 May 1681, Rev. John Pike,
and d.2 Mar. 1688. Of other ch. only Samuel, H.C. 1689;
is known. SAMUEL, Hartford, s. of John of the same, rem.
to Hadley, a. 1660, by w. Sarah, prob. d. of first John
Dening,had Sarah, b.a. 1660; John, 24 July 1661; Hannah,
5 Mar. 1668; Mary; Samuel, 28 Nov. 1670; and Ebenezer,
23 Oct. 1675; d. 1389. His wid. Sarah d. 1714. Goodwin
suppos. he had first w. Hannah; but if so, she must have
d. young. Of the s. John had nine ch. and d. at Hartford,
1732; Samuel d.at Hadley,1745, leav. six ch.; and Ebenezer
d. at South Hadley, 11 nov. 1757,leav. eight ch.; SAMUEL,
Newbury, s. of William,freem. 1666, m.9 Nov.1657, Mary, or
perhaps Mercy, d.of capt.John Cutting,had Mary,b.16 Nov.
1658;

William, 22 July 1661, perhaps d. young; William, again,
20 June 1663; Mary,18 Feb.1665; Lydia, 5 Aug. 1667; Hannah,
4 Jan.1670; Samuel, Dec. 1671: Cutting, 9 Apr. 1674; beside
John, and Sarah, whose dates are not ment. by Coffin, wh.
tells us that he d. 4 Apr. 1675. SAMUEL, Newcastle, s. of
Rev. Joshua, m. 4 Apr.1695, Esther Green of Boston, had
Joshua, b. 11 Feb. 1696, d. at 3 mos.; Joshua, again, 31
Oct. 1697, prob. H. C. 1716; Samuel, 29 Oct. 1699, H. C.
1718; and Mary, 16 Nov. 1701; rem. to Boston. WILLIAM,
Newbury, came in 1634, a saddler, from Ipswich, Co. Suffolk, and first sat down at Ipswich, freen. 6 May 1635;
had w. Sarah, and ch. Joshua, wh. it has been agreed,
was b. in Eng. Caleb, and Samuel, bef. ment. was prob. a
propr. of Salisbury 1650,

                    Continued on Page 227.

and d. 25 Oct. 1673. Twenty-eight of this name had, in 1834, been gr. at the N. E. coll. one half at Harv. alone.

MOONE, ROBERT, Boston, tailor, by w. Dorothy had Ebenezer, b. 7 Oct. 1645.

MOORCOCK, or MORECOCK, NICHOLAS, Wethersfield, prob. came 1635, in the Elizabeth and Ann, from London to Boston, aged 14, with Bennett, 16, and Mary, 10, who may have been br. and sis. certif. by the min. of Beninden, in Co. Kent. One of this name m. a d. of Thomas Burnham of Windsor.

MOORE, or MORE, ABEL, New London, s. of Miles, was constable 1675, and again 1685, d. sudden. at Dedham, 1689, on his way home from Boston. ABRAHAM, Andover, m. 14 Dec. 1687, Priscilla Poor, but it is not cert. that she liv. at A. only that there he was m. ANDREW, Windsor, m. Sarah Phelps, perhaps d. of William, had Sarah, b. Dec. 1672; Andrew, 15 Feb. 1675; Deborah, 31 May 1677; Jonathan, 26 Feb. 1680; Abigail, 1682; Rachel, 1691; Benjamin, 1693; and Amos, 1698. CALEB, Salem 1668. ENOCH, Charlestown 1675, had w. Rebecca, wh. d. 3 Jan. 1733, in 83d yr. had Enoch, b. 28 Feb. 1678, at Woburn, and at C. James, bapt. 12 June 1681; Rebecca, 25 Feb. 1683; Susanna, 27 July 1684; James and William, tw. 29 Apr. 1688; and Ruth, 27 Oct. 1689. FRANCIS, Cambridge, freem. 22 May 1639, brot. w. Catharine, wh. d. 28 Dec. 1648, had ch. Francis, Samuel, John, and Ann, first two b. in Eng. but John, certain. b. 20 Mar. 1645, and, perhaps, Ann, were bapt. in ch. of C. and Sarah, b. there 3 Apr. 1643, and prob. Thomas, nam. with John in the will of br. Francis, m. sec. w. 6 Dec. 1653, Eliz. wid. perhaps of Thomas Periman. He d. 20 Aug. 1671, aged 85, and his wid. d. 5 Nov. 1683, aged 84. Ann m. James Kidder. FRANCIS, Cambridge, s. of the preced. b. in Eng. by w. Catharine had John, b. 20 Mar. 1645, and m. 7 Sept. 1650, Abby Eaton, prob. had no ch. at least none to live until he made his will, freem. 1652, selectman 1674–81, and some yrs. aft. d. 23 Feb. 1689, aged 69. FRANCIS, Salem, m. 31 Aug. 1666, Eliz. Woodbury. GEORGE, Scituate, had been a serv. of Edward Dotey, at Plymouth 1630, kept the ferry on Jones riv. in Kingston 1633–8, in S. had much land 1642, fell distracted in 1664, when guardians had power to sell some of his est. and d. 1677, suddenly. Deane, 313. It does not appear that he had fam. GEORGE, Lynn, had Dorothy, b. 8 Jan. 1659. GOLDIN, Cambridge 1636, freem. 2 June 1641, m. Joan, wid. of John Champney, had Hannah, b. 15 May 1643; Lydia; and Ruth; all b. and bapt. at C.; was a sett. at the farms, 1642, now Lexington, rem. to Billerica, there d. 3 Sept. 1698, in 89th yr. Hannah m. 1 Mar. 1666, John Hastings, and d. 10 June 1667; Ruth m. 5 July 1670, Daniel Shed. * ISAAC, Norwalk, one of the first sett. had first been of Farmington, m. at Hartford, 5 Dec.

1645, Ruth, d. of John Stanley, a serg. in 1649, may be that youth·of 13, who came in the Increase, 1635, from London to Boston, was rep. for N. 1657, had Ruth, b. 5 Jan. 1657; Sarah, 12 Feb. 1662; Mary, 15 Sept. 1664; and Phebe, 25 Apr. 1669; the first bapt. at Norwalk, the others at F. but no s.; went back to F. a. 1660, was a deac. m. very late in life, Dorothy, d. of Rev. Henry Smith, who had been wid. of three husbands, and liv. in 1705. JACOB, Sudbury, s. of John of the same. JAMES, Salem, perhaps br. of Richard or George, or both, in his will, of 5 July 1659, pro. Nov. foll. calls hims. of Hammersmith, in wh. he ment. w. Ruth, and little d. Deborah, may be the one, wh. m. at Lynn, 28 Dec. 1657, Ruth Pinion, wh. perhaps, was d. of Nicholas of New Haven. JAMES, Boston, "a Scottish man" as rec. of his m. 6 Feb. 1657, with Mary Both, or Booth, calls him, may have been (tho. it seems to me unlikely, as he was one of the found. of the Scot's Charit. Soc.) one of the few outcasts of the civil war, sold here, that had health or heart eno. to form a fam. JASPER, Plymouth, serv. boy of Gov. Carver, wh. d. very soon aft. arr. of the Mayflower, by careless read. oft. suppos. to be s. of the Gov. who however had no ch. tho. many thousands have prid. themselves on being his descend. JEREMY, Hingham, came in 1638, by the Diligent, was from Wymondham, a large town in Co. Norfolk, adj. old Hingham, rem. to Boston 1643, was freem. 1645, d. bef. 1669, leav. Jeremiah, Samuel, and Mary, wh. m. John Cotton. * JOHN, Dorchester 1630, came in the Mary and John, prob. for he was freem. 18 May 1631, a deac. went with Warham 1635 or 6, to Windsor, was there a chief man, rep. not as Hist. of W. 705, tells, in 1643, but 1665, 7, and oft. aft. d. 18 Sept. 1677. He had Abigail, b. 1639*; Mindwell, 10 July 1643; and John, 5 Dec. 1645; but he had also, prob. elder ds. Hannah, wh. m. 30 Nov. 1648, John Drake; and Eliz. wh. m. 24 Nov. 1654, Nathaniel Loomis. Abigail m. 11 Oct. 1655, Thomas Bissell; and Mindwell m. 25 Sept. 1662, Nathaniel Bissell. JOHN, Roxbury, freem. 3 July 1632, but perhaps he first liv. in some other town, for his name is not found early at R. nor does Mr. Ellis in his Hist. give it; but the ch. rec. has "old John Moore of 99 yrs. d. 27 Oct. 1679." JOHN, Cambridge, perhaps the freem. of 8 Dec. 1636. JOHN, Salem, had there bapt. Jerusha, 25 Dec. 1636; Abigail, 10 June 1638; Benjamin, 18 July 1641; and Ephraim, 10 Dec. 1643. Perhaps his w. was Hannah, and he may have been freem. but not, as Felt puts him, in 1633. JOHN, Newport, receiv. as an inhab. 16 Nov. 1638, may have been of Warwick 1655, had d. Mary, wh. m. Job Almy. JOHN, Lynn 1641. JOHN, Braintree, whose w. Bridget d. 1643, was liv. there 1658, and in 1660 was one of the purch. of Medway. JOHN, Sudbury 1643, perhaps he who came in the Planter, 1635, aged 24, from London, may have been of ar. co. 1638, by w. Eliz. had Mary;

Lydia, b. 24 June 1643; Jacob, 28 Apr. 1645; perhaps Joseph; and
Eliz.; m. sec. w. 16 Nov. 1654, Ann, d. of John Smith. Mary m. 8
Sept. 1661, Richard Ward; and Lydia m. 1664, Samuel Wright.
JOHN, Newtown, L. I. 1656, was their first min. says Riker's Hist.
JOHN, Roxbury, of wh. I find nothing but his insert. in list of freem.
1666. JOHN, Boston, shipwright, d. in Virginia, and admin. was giv. 15
Jan. 1683, to his wid. Mary. JOHN, Windsor, only s. of John of the
same, m. 21 Sept. 1664, Hannah, d. of Edward Goffe of Cambridge,
had John, b. 26 June 1665; Thomas, 25 July 1667; Samuel, 24 Dec.
1669; Nathaniel, 20 Sept. 1672; Edward, 2 Mar. 1675; and Josiah
and Joseph, tw. 5 July 1679. His w. Hannah d. 4 Apr. 1697; and he
m. 17 Dec. 1701, Martha Flamsworth, unless Mr. Stiles misspell. the
name, had Martha, 24 Sept. 1705; and d. 21 June 1718. * JOHN,
Lancaster, perhaps of Boston, and freem. 1669, was rep. 1689 and 90,
call. sen. JOHN, Boston, by w. Lydia had Sarah, b. 19 July 1673;
Hannah, 1675, d. soon; Hannah, again, 25 July 1676; John, Feb. 1678;
Thomas, 26 Nov. 1679; Catharine, 5 Feb. 1681; Rachel, Feb. 1682;
Francis, Nov. 1684; Catharine, again, Mar. 1686, and Francis, again, 8
Apr. 1687. He was, perhaps, the freem. of 1671, and d. 1693. He
was a brewer, had good est. of wh. admin. was giv. to his w. Lydia, 13
July. JOHN, Lynn, m. 21 July 1673, Susanna, perhaps d. of Thomas
Marshall, had Thomas, b. 20 Apr. 1674; John, 10 Feb. 1679; Richard,
22 Aug. 1680; and Susanna, 4 Mar. 1685. * JOHN, Lancaster, call.
jun. rep. 1689, perhaps s. of him who was rep. aft. JOHN, Lynn, freem.
1691. One other John, wh. came in the Susan and Ellen 1635, from
London, aged 41, I am unable to dispose of. JONATHAN, Boston,
youngest s. of Mrs. Ann, wid. of William Hibbins, the Assist. was, I
infer, only tempo. resid. here, for the will of his mo. 16 June 1656,
shortly bef. her execut. for the preposterous crime of witchcraft, wh. is
to be seen in Geneal. Reg. VI. 287, 8, speaks of him and his brs. John,
and Joseph, as if all were in Eng. and in the codic. of 19th of the same,
acknowledg. " the more than ordinary affection and pains ' of this one,'
in the time of my distress," as he had arriv. to attend the result of the
execrable fanaticism. She was prob. the richest person ever hanged in
this part; and the prejudice against witches long slumbered. JOSEPH,
Boston, m. 21 May 1656, Ruth Starr, had Joseph, b. 7 Mar. 1658.
JOSEPH, Sudbury, m. Lydia, d. of John Maynard. MILES, Milford
1646, rem. as early at least as 1657, to New London, freem. 1663, call.
old in 1680, left descend. thro. d. Miriam, w. of John Willey; beside
Abel, bef. ment. RICHARD, Plymouth, brot. by Elder Brewster, with a
br. both as serv. in the Mayflower, 1620, and the br. d. in few wks.; at
the div. of cattle 1627, when the name of every man, woman, and

ch. is giv. he was still assort. with Elder Brewster; but by Gov. Bradford's Hist. 451, we are taught that he m. and in 1651 had four or five
ch. liv. as if he had lost one or more. It is vain to regret, that the Gov.
did not mention the names of the ch. or the mo. Perhaps he rem. to
one of the newer settlem. for Winsor's Duxbury tells that he sold his
land 1637, and I am convinc. aft. long search, that he is the Richard by
Deane, in Hist. of Scituate, call. Mann, as the other four passeng. with
this bapt. name of Richard, were all then adult. See Mann. RICHARD,
Cape Porpoise, now Kennebunk, had gr. of 400 acres in 1647, and less
than 20 yrs. aft. was of Scarborough, had w. Bridget, became pauper
1679, and d. 1681. See Southgate, 77. RICHARD, Salem 1642, to wh.
says Felt, was made gr. of land 1638, freem: 28 Feb. 1643, tho. this
man may have come in the Blessing, from London 1635, aged 20. He,
or perhaps a s. of the same name, in a town office there, was liv. 1682;
and in 1668 his name, with that of Richard jun. is sign. to the petitn.
against imposts. RICHARD, Lynn, by w. Alice, wh. d. 29 May 1661,
had Mary, b. 15 Jan. preced. and he m. 6 Nov. 1662, Eliz. Wildes.
ROBERT, Boston 1651, tailor, rem. next yr. ROBERT, Boston, by w.
Ann had Susanna, b. 6 Aug. 1686. SAMUEL, Salem, freem. 6 Mar.
1632, perhaps, therefore, came in Nov. preced. in the Lion, had Samuel,
bapt. 25 Dec. 1636; and Remember, 9 Dec. 1638. SAMUEL, Boston,
prob. s. of Jeremy, m. 1 May 1660, Abigail, d. of capt. Thomas
Hawkins, had Mary, b. 2 May 1661; he d. in short time, and his wid.
m. Thomas Kellond, and 3d h. Hon. John Foster. SAMUEL, Boston, by
w. Naomi had Francis, b. 15 July 1670; and Edward, 5 July 1674.
SAMUEL, Lynn, had Mary, b. early in June 1676, d. soon; Rebecca, 9
Nov. 1677, d. soon; Abigail, 26 Sept. 1678; and Ephraim, 17 June
1681; was freem. 1691. THOMAS, Dorchester, came in the Mary and
John 1630, and prob. was br. of John of the same, freem. 18 May 1631,
rem. 1635 or 6 to Windsor, perhaps rem. to Southold, L. I. where was
one of this name 1662. THOMAS, Portsmouth, one of the first sett. sent
by John Mason, the patentee, 1631. THOMAS, Salem 1636, prob. s. of
Thomas, to whose wid. Ann, a midwife, was next yr. gr. of ld. made, by
w. Martha had Thomas, and Martha, both bapt. 21 Oct. 1639, soon aft.
the parents were rec. of the ch.; Benjamin, 2 Aug. 1640; Nathaniel, 3
July 1642; Hannah, 29 Dec. 1644; Eliz. 31 Jan. 1647; Jonathan, 3
June 1649; and Mary, 15 Dec. 1650; was freem. 27 Dec. 1642, and in
few yrs. rem. THOMAS, Boston, mariner, m. at Cambridge, 9 Nov.
1653, Sarah Hodges, had Sarah, b. 26 Apr. 1655, d. next yr.; Sarah,
again, 5 May 1660; Hannah, 26 Apr. 1662; Rachel, 25 May 1664;
Eliz. 27 Apr. 1667; and Thomas, 2 Sept. 1669, d. 1690. THOMAS,
Roxbury, freem. 1690, says the Col. rec. but I have some doubt. WIL-

LIAM, Salem 1639, may have been of Ipswich 1665, and d. 1671.
*WILLIAM, Exeter 1645, was, says Farmer, a rep. in the assemb. of
N. H. WILLIAM, York 1652, when he subm. to the Mass. governm. to
1680, when he took the o. of alleg. to his Majesty. WILLIAM, Westerly
1669, may be the same, who at Norwich m. Aug. 1677, Mary, wid. of
Thomas Howard, wh. was k. at the gr. battle of Philip's war, 19 Dec.
1675, d. of William Wellman, had Eliz. b. 20 July 1678 ; Experience,
12 May 1680; Martha, 22 Feb. 1682 ; Joshua, 1683 ; William, 1685 ;
and Abigail, 1687. His w. d. 3 Apr. 1700, and he m. 17 July foll.
Mary, wid. of Joshua Allen of Windham, wh. d. 18 Sept. 1727 ; and
he m. 10 June 1728, Tamison Simmons, and d. Apr. 1729. WILLIAM,
Amesbury 1670, a milit. officer, wh. m. as I presume, 7 Oct. 1673, Mary
Veazie, perhaps d. of George of Dover. Seven of this name had, in
1829, been gr. at Harv. six at Yale, six at Dart. and twelve at other
N. E. coll.

MOORES, EDMUND, Newbury, Coffin says, came 1640, aged 26, by w.
Ann, wh. d. 7 June 1676, had Martha, b. 12 Dec. 1643 ; Jonathan, 23
Apr. 1646 ; Mary, 30 Nov. 1648 ; Edmund, wh. d. 8 Nov. 1656 ; Rich-
ard, 3 Nov. 1653 ; and Sarah, 1 Apr. 1661. EDMUND, Newbury, call.
jun. perhaps not s. of the preced. m. 3 Jan. 1677, Sarah Cooper, had
Edmund, b. 5 Dec. foll. prob. d. young; Sarah, 9 Dec. 1681 ; Mark, 9
Feb. 1689 ; Martha, 20 Aug. 1691 ; and Edmund, again, 3 Apr. 1693.
JONATHAN, Newbury, s. of first Edmund, m. as Coffin says, 10 May
1670 [1680?], Constance Langhorne, had Jonathan, b. 3 Apr. 1681 ;
Richard, 24 July 1683 ; Samuel, 20 Feb. 1686 ; Thomas, 6 Nov. 1688 ;
and Dorothy, 8 Dec. 1690. MATTHEW, Newbury, m. 27 Mar. 1662,
Sarah Savory, had Sarah, b. 15 Dec. 1663 ; and William, 10 Feb.
1666 ; but an intermed. William was b. to wh. Coffin assigns impossib.
date. SAMUEL, Newbury, m. 3 May 1653, Hannah Plummer, wh. d. 8
Dec. 1654, and he m. 12 Dec. 1656, Mary Ilsley, d. of William of
the same.

MORE. See Moore. HENRY, Dorchester 1675, had supplied a substit.
in the comp. of capt. Johnson, Dec. of that yr. as may be read in the
list, print. in Geneal. Reg. VIII. 242, tho. his name is copied Mare.
Many of the fam. have the name, as it were, interchangeable ; the same
person on one page of the rec. spelling each way.

MOREHOUSE, or MOOREHOUSE, JOHN, Fairfield, ensign in 1676.
JONATHAN, Fairfield, m. Mary, d. of Edward Wilson of the same, bef.
1684. SAMUEL, Fairfield, perhaps s. of Thomas, freem. 1664, liv. 1670.
THOMAS, Wethersfield 1640, perhaps was at Stamford next yr. but in
1653 at Fairfield.

MORFIELD, or MOORFIELD, JOHN, Hingham, came in the Diligent,
1638, from old Hingham.

MORELL, WILLIAM, came in Sept. 1623, with Robert Gorges, sat down at Weymouth, but soon went to Plymouth, aft. Gorges left him, and home within a yr. His verses, Latin and translat. into Eng. show he was a fair scholar; and his prudence was pro. by not producing the ecclesiast. commission he had to rule on this side of the water.

MOREY, BENJAMIN, Wickford 1674, was some relat. prob. of Isaac Heath of Roxbury, who names Mary and Benjamin in his will of Jan. 1661. GEORGE, Duxbury 1640, d. that yr. may be the passeng. 1635, from London, aged 23, by the Truelove. FRANCIS, Salem 1686. JOHN, came in the Blessing, 1635, aged 19, from London, but I kn. no more of him. JONATHAN, Plymouth, m. 8 July 1659, Mary, wid. of Richard Foster, d. of Robert Bartlett. JOSEPH, Wickford 1674. NATHANIEL, Providence, m. July 1666, Joanna Inman, perhaps d. of the first Edward, had John, and prob. Joanna. ROGER, Providence 1649, had early been one of Salem ch. by w. Mary had Bethia; Mehitable; Roger, b. 8 May 1649; Thomas, 19 July 1652; and Hannah, 28 Sept. 1656; and he d. 5 Jan. 1668. ROGER, may have liv. at Milton, and, perhaps, m. Mary, d. of John Johnson, and had Abigail, bapt. at Roxbury, in her mo.'s right, 8 Aug. 1680. THOMAS, Roxbury, m. 6 Sept. 1673, Susanna, d. of the sec. Abraham Newell, had Thomas, b. 15 May 1678, d. very soon; Abigail, bapt. 4 Apr. 1680, perhaps d. soon; Abigail, b. 30 Mar. 1681; Mary, 11, bapt. 20 Aug. 1682; Susanna, 27 Apr. bapt. 17 May 1685; John, 13, bapt. 27 July 1687; Eliz. 14 Dec. 1689; and Nathaniel, 28 May 1694. He was freem. 1685, and d. 25 Dec. 1717; but I do not find the date of d. of w. Abigail m. 2 Apr. 1697, Timothy Harris.

MORGAN, BENNETT, Plymouth, came in the Fortune, 1621, but he had not sh. in the div. of cattle 1627, and so we may be sure he was gone, but whither is unkn. DAVID, Springfield, s. of Miles, freem. 1690, d. 1731, leav. Pelatiah, David, John, Ebenezer, Benjamin, and Mary. FRANCIS, Kittery 1664, was next yr. appoint. admor. on the gr. est. of capt. John Mitchell. ISAAC, Springfield 1678, br. of David, was in the Falls fight in Philip's war, rem. to Enfield, d. 1706, hav. had five ch. of wh. Abigail alone surv. * JAMES, Roxbury 1640, m. 6 Aug. of that yr. Margery Hill, had Hannah, b. 18 July, bapt. 18 Dec. 1642; James, bapt. 3 Mar. 1644; John, 30 Mar. 1645, tho. rec. of b. is 30 Sept.; Joseph, 29 Nov. 1646; Abraham, 3 Sept. 1648, d. in Aug. foll.; and a d. 17 Nov. 1650, wh. d. next week; but the town rec. omits the four last; was freem. 10 May 1643, rem. to New London, was rep. 1657, when he sw. he was fifty yrs. old, and rep. for the last time 1670. JAMES, New London, s. of the preced. was adm. freem. 1669, d. 8 Dec. 1671. JAMES, Boston, had David, b. 10 Nov. 1676; and Jonathan, 19

Nov. 1680, may have serv. in Moseley's comp. Dec. 1675, and, perhaps, was not that JAMES of Boston, whose story is in the Magnalia, book VI. 40–43, execut. for murder, 11 Mar. 1686. JOHN, New London, s. of the first James, m. 16 Nov. 1665, Rachel, d. of John Deming, had, says Miss Caulkins, seven ch. by her, and six more by sec. w. Eliz. made freem. 1669; was a lieut. and d. 1712. JONATHAN, Springfield, s. of Miles, was in the Falls fight 1676, freem. 1690, d. 1714, leav. Jonathan, and four ds. JOSEPH, Lynn, m. 12 July 1669, Deborah Hart. JOSEPH, Greenwich, ment. in Mather's Hecatompolis, as the min. may have been s. of the first James. MILES, Springfield, by fam. tradit. said to have arr. at Boston in Apr. 1636, with two brs. from Bristol, by w. Prudence had Mary, b. 1645; Jonathan, 1646; David, 1648; Pelatiah, 1650; Isaac, 1652; Lydia, 1654; Hannah, 1656; Mercy, 1658; and his w. d. 1661. He m. next, 15 Feb. 1670, Eliz. Bliss, d. of Thomas, had Nathaniel, 1671; and d. 28 May 1699. Lydia m. 1677, John Pierce. MOSES, a soldier under capt. Turner 1676, at Hadley, was prob. from E. part of the Col. NATHANIEL, Springfield, prob. youngest s. of Miles, had Nathaniel, Samuel, Ebenezer, Miles, Joseph, James, Isaac, Hannah, and Eliz. OWEN, New Haven, m. 1650, wid. Joan Bryan. Hall finds his name in 1656, at Norwalk; and a wid. M. was propr. 1655, as by his valua. Hist. but no clue is kn. to the name of her h. or the time of his d. RICHARD, Dover 1659, was prob. of Exeter 1684. ROBERT, Saco 1636, may be he of Kennebeck 1665, nam. in Sullivan, 287. ROBERT, Salem 1637, adm. of the ch. 1650, and on 23 June of that yr. had bapt. Samuel, Luke, Joseph, and Benjamin, and on 15 Dec. foll. Robert; Bethia, 29 May 1653; and Aaron, 24 May 1663; was one of the found. of the ch. at Beverly 1667. His will, of 14 Oct. 1672, pro. 24 June foll. names w. Margaret, s. Samuel, w.'s f. Norman (but wh. he was is not clear), s. Benjamin, Robert, Bethia, s. Joseph, and Moses. His inv. was of 10 Nov. 1672. ROGER, Charlestown, d. 23 Dec. 1675. SAMUEL, Marblehead 1674. WILLIAM, Amesbury 1677, perhaps twelve yrs. later liv. in New Hampsh.

MORLEY, JOHN, Braintree, freem. 1645, rem. 1658 to Charlestown, he and his w. being rec. into this ch. 29 Aug. of that yr. there d. 24 Jan. 1661; and his wid. Constant, wh. was first of the ch. at Dorchester, d. 1669. Yet Frothingham, 80, names her as wid. inhab. of 1631, tho. perhaps he means Catherine, wh. may have been his mo. in the will of Morley, made a week bef. his d. referred to as then dec. He also names in it sis. Ann Farmer. He gave to his wid. Constant, all his est. in N. E. and his lds. and tenem. at Cheshunt, in Co. Herts, O. E. In her will is more instruct. for the genealog. as she rememb. her br. Joye (perhaps meaning Joseph) Starr, her sis. Ann Farmer, her sis. Suretrust

Rous, her cous. i. e. neph. John Starr sen. her cous. Mercy Swett, her cous. Simon Eyre, and gives to cous. Eliz. w. of John Ferniside, and Eliz. w. of Joshua Edmunds, but the gr. residue of her est. to William and Eliz. childr. of said Eliz. Edmunds. No doubt, she was sis. of the first Comfort Starr. THOMAS, Westfield. See Marlo.

MORRILL, ‖ ABRAHAM, Cambridge 1632, perhaps came in the Lion, with br. Isaac, ar. co. 1638, rem. with orig. proprs. to Salisbury, where, in 1650, only four men were tax. higher, d. at Roxbury, on a visit, 20 June 1662. He had m. 10 June 1645, Sarah, d. of Robert Clement of Haverhill, had Isaac, b. 10 July 1646; Jacob, 24 Aug. 1648; Sarah, 14 Oct. 1650; Abraham, 14 Nov. 1652; Moses, 28 Dec. 1655; Aaron, 9 Aug. 1658; Richard, 6 Feb. 1660, d. soon; Lydia, 8 Mar. 1661; and Hepzibah, posthum. Jan. 1663. His will, made the yr. of his d. pro. 14 Oct. names w. Sarah, ch. Isaac, the eldest, Abraham, Jacob, Moses, Lydia, and Sarah, beside br. Job Clement. His est. was £507. Lydia m. 9 Nov. 1682, Ephraim Severence. ABRAHAM, Salisbury 1677, s. of the preced. m. 1688, Sarah Bradbury, had Bradbury, b. 22 Mar. 1693, d. young; and Sarah, 18 Dec. 1696. EZEKIEL, Reading, perhaps br. of the first Abraham, or s. of him, or his br. Isaac, had w. Mary, and d. on a visit at Roxbury, 22 May 1663. His will, of 31 May preced. ment. f.-in-law, and mo. without name of either. His wid. prob. m. 12 Aug. foll. Thomas Hodgman of R. prob. bore no ch. to either h. HENRY, New Haven, had Sarah, b. 1650, and he d. 1665. ‖ ISAAC, Roxbury, br. of Abraham, said to have been b. 1588, came in the Lion, arr. 16 Sept. 1632, bring. w. and prob. Sarah and Catharine; freem. 4 Mar. 1633, ar. co. 1638, by w. Sarah, had here, Isaac, b. 26 or 7 Nov. 1632, d. in Jan. foll.; Isaac, again, 5 Feb. 1634, d. young; Hannah, 12 or 16 Sept. 1636; Eliz. May 1638, d. same mo.; Abraham, 6 June 1640, wh. d. at 21 yrs. a "hopeful young man," says Eliot in his ch. reg. and the f. d. 20 Dec. 1661. Sarah m. 1646, Tobias Davis, and d. 23 Jan. 1649; Catherine m. 1 Aug. 1647, John Smith; and ∤Hannah m. 5 Nov. 1652, Daniel Brewer, His will, print. in Geneal. Reg. XI. 35, made a few days bef. his d. gave est. to w. for her life, names gr. ch. John, Isaac, Francis, Mary, and Abraham Smith, and Sarah Davis. His wid. d. 9 Jan. 1673, aged 72. ISAAC, Charlestown, freem. 1682, of wh. it is very vexatious to be unable to tell more than that he was prob. br. of the first Abraham. ISAAC, Salisbury, s. of Abraham the first, perhaps had two ws. by Phebe, had Abraham, b. 22 Aug. 1671; and Isaac; by Susanna, had Mary, 1 Feb. 1674; Sarah, 29 May 1675; Jacob, 25 May 1677; Rachel, 18 Feb. 1682, d. soon; Daniel, 18 Feb. 1683; Jemima, 9 Oct. 1685; Mary, again, 10 Sept. 1689; and Rachel, 24 Aug. 1692. JACOB, Salisbury, br. of the preced. by w. Susanna had Ezekiel, b. 29 Sept.

1675 or 85; Hannah; Ruth, 9 Oct. 1686; Jacob, 2 May 1689; Susanna, 14 June 1696; and Israel, 1 Mar. 1699; was freem. 1690.
JEREMIAH, Boston, by w. Sarah had Jeremiah, b. 22 Aug. 1652; Sarah
14 Aug. 1655; Mary, 5 Jan. 1658; Lydia, 30 Mar. 1659, d. soon;
Lydia, again, 14 Oct. 1661; and Hosea, 25 July 1665. MOSES, Amesbury, br. of Jacob, freem. 1690, m. Rebecca, d. of William Barnes of
the same, had William Barnes M. so nam. (bef. the custom of doub.
names so common and uncomfort. was introduc.) to preserve memo. of
his gr.f. RICHARD, New Hampsh. 1640. THOMAS, Gravesend 1650,
Newtown, L. I. 1655. Thompson. Six of this name had, in 1834,
been gr. at Harv. and four at other N. E. coll. Early this is call.
Morrell, in town rec. Murrells.

MORRIS, DANIEL, Hampton 1640. DORMAN, Boston, by w. Elinor
had Daniel, b. 13 Feb. 1672; and Honor, 1 Apr. 1674. EDMUND,
came in the Confidence, 1638, from Southampton. He was a carpenter, of Dorsetsh. perhaps the parish of Kington Magna, near Shaftes-
bury, but I hear nothing later of him. * EDWARD, Roxbury, m. 29
Nov. 1655, Grace Burr, but in Boston rec. as cop. in Geneal. Reg. XI.
201, the name is giv. Bett, wh. seems less likely to be correct surname,
had Isaac, b. 16 Sept. 1656, bapt. 19 Sept. 1658; Edward, bapt. 13
Mar. 1659; Grace, 17 Feb. 1661; Ebenezer, b. 14, bapt. 17 Apr.
1664; Eliz. bapt. 26 Mar. 1666; Margaret, 27 Sept. 1668; Samuel, 9
Apr. 1671; and Martha, 3 Jan. 1675; was rep. 1678 and to 1686.
His wid. Grace d. 6 June 1705, says the rec. but his own dec. is not
ment. there. He had rem. to New Roxbury, since call. Woodstock, and
was d. 27 Jan. 1692, when admin. on his est. was gr. Grace, his d. m.
7 Mar. 1683, Benjamin Child; and Eliz. m. 9 May 1685, Joshua Child;
and Margaret m. 4 Apr. 1689, John Johnson. EDWARD, Roxbury, s.
of the preced. m. 24 May 1683, Eliz. Brown, had Eliz. b. 12 Feb.
1685, d. soon; Eliz. again, 3 Feb. 1686; Edward, 9 Nov. 1688.
ELEAZER, New Haven, s. of Thomas, by w. Ann had Rebecca, b. 20
June 1682; John, 8 Oct. 1684; James; Eleazer; Adonijah; and Ann.
ISAAC, Roxbury, eldest s. of Edward the first, was a soldier in Johnson's
comp. in the gr. Narraganset fight, m. 2 Mar. 1680, Hannah, d. of John
Mayo, had prob. no ch. perhaps rem. to Woodstock, as he was admor. on
est. of his f. but came back to R. where his w. d. 5 Nov. 1701; and he
m. 3 Nov. 1702, Mary, wid. of Ebenezer Pierpont, and d. 21 Oct. 1715.
JOHN, Hartford 1640, d. bef. Mar. 1669, in his will names ch. John,
Joshua, and Mary. His wid. Martha m. Roger Jepson of Saybrook;
and d. Mary m. 25 Nov. 1680, John Tillotson of S. JOHN, New Haven,
s. of Thomas, perhaps b. in Eng. had w. Ann, wh. d. early; m. wid.
Eliz. Lamson, had John, wh. d. soon, and she d. bef. long. He m. 12

Aug. 1669, Hannah Bishop, and by this third w. had Mary, June 1670, d. soon; Hannah, 10 Aug. 1671; Mary, again, 9 Sept. 1673; Eliz. 1675; Thomas, Apr. 1679, d. young; Abigail, 22 Aug. 1683; and Desire, 25 Mar. 1687. JOSEPH, New Haven, br. of the preced. m. 2 June 1680, Esther Winstone, had Thomas, b. 23 Mar. 1682; Esther, 3 Sept. 1684; Sarah, 1686; Joseph, 1688; Ephraim, 1694; Dorothy, Sept. 1695; Benjamin, Apr. 1699; Mary, June 1702; and Samuel, July 1705. RICE, Charlestown, by w. Esther had Hannah, bapt. 29 Nov. 1634; and Esther, b. 6, bapt. 14 Mar. 1641; perhaps more, and d. 25 Apr. 1647. But the name appears Morus in Geneal. Reg. IX. 170. * ‖ RICHARD, Boston 1630, came prob. in the fleet with Winth. as he and w. Lenora were very early of the ch. Nos. 64 and 5, and he was made freem. 18 May 1631, with the title of serj. and so perhaps a hired officer, bec. lieut. at Roxbury soon aft. and was rep. 1635, ar. co. 1637, but favoring the cause of Rev. John Wheelwright, was disarm. and with that heresiarch went to Exeter, 1638. The name is first on our ch. rec. writ. Maurice, and when, 6 Jan. 1639, dismiss. was gr. to Wheelwright and eight others, includ. him, "unto the ch. of Christ at the falls of Paschataqua, if they be rightly gathered and ordered," the spelling is Morrys. It is wrong in Drake's diligent Hist. 224, as it was first in Belknap, wh. Farmer did not correct. RICHARD, Portsmouth, R. I. 1643, then among the freem. 1655, seems to me the same as preced. ROBERT, Rehoboth 1640, d. bef. 1647. Baylies, II. 200, 203. ROBERT, Hartford, br. of John, was divorc. from w. had no ch. d. 19 Nov. 1684. giv. est. to relat. SAMUEL, Roxbury, s. of Edward the first, by w. Mehitable had Samuel, b. 13 Aug. 1695; Benjamin, 18 Oct. 1696; Mehitable, 25 June 1698; Rebecca, 15 Sept. 1699; Hannah, 9 Nov. 1700; Dorothy, 1 Feb. 1702; and Prudence, 31 Jan. 1703; and his w. d. 8 Feb. foll. THOMAS, New Haven 1639, by w. Eliz. had John; Hannah, b. 14 Mar. 1642, bapt. 18 June 1643; Eliz. perhaps bapt. 10 Dec. foll.; John; Eleazer, bapt. 29 Oct. 1648; Thomas and Ephraim, tw. b. 3, bapt. 5 Oct. 1651, of wh. Ephraim d. soon; and Joseph, bapt. 25 May 1656. His w. Eliz. d. 1668, and he d. 21 July 1673. His will, of 11 July preced. gives est. to the ds. and John, Eleazer, and Joseph, wh. were proprs. 1685. Hannah m. 1652, Thomas Lupton. THOMAS, Boston, of wh. no more is kn. than that he d. quite early, for his will *was* on p. 18 now missing of our *first* vol. of Pro. Rec. if we may trust the index. THOMAS, Casco 1652, perhaps next yr. at Dover. WILLIAM, Portsmouth, R. I. 1655, was, perhaps, br. of Richard, may have liv. 1671, at Westerly. WILLIAM, Charlestown 1658, perhaps of Boston, there by w. Dorcas had William, b. 18 Dec. 1665, rem. prob. to Wethersfield, and was freem. of Conn. 1669, and d. 1697.

MORRISON, ANDREW, New Haven 1690. DANIEL, Newbury, by w. Hannah, wh. d. 9 Oct. 1700, had Daniel, b. 1 Aug. 1691; John, 28 Mar. 1693; Hannah, 27 Jan. 1696; Ebenezer, 6 Oct. 1697; and Mary, 20 Mar. but Coffin omits yr.

MORSE, ABRAHAM, Newbury, s. of Robert, b. perhaps in Eng. by his w. Eliz. bef. he left Marlborough, in Wilts, if his f. may be presum. br. of Anthony, rem. it is said, to New Jersey. ANTHONY, Newbury, a shoemaker of Marlborough, Wiltsh. arr. at Boston, 3 June 1635, in the James from Southampton, said to have been b. 9 May 1606, freem. 25 May 1636, by w. Mary had Anthony; Benjamin, b. 4 Mar. 1640; Sarah, 1 May 1641; Hannah, 1642; Lydia, May 1645, d. soon; Lydia, again, 7 Oct. 1647, d. in few mos.; Mary, 9 Apr. 1649, d. at 13 yrs.; Esther, 3 May 1651; Joshua, 24 July 1653; and the Fam. Genealog. adds Mary, prob. but I doubt; Coffin gives him also, Joseph, John, and Peter; yet he has confus. the marriages and deaths of f. and s. and has prob. done the same with ch. He was freem. 25 May 1636, had a sec. w. Ann, wh. d. 9 Mar. 1680, and he d. 12 Oct. 1686. Sarah m. 24 June 1663, Amos Stickney; and Esther m. 26 Feb. 1669, Robert Holmes. ANTHONY, Newbury, s. of the preced. m. 8 May 1660, Eliz. Knight, had Ruth, b. 20 May 1661, d. in few wks. Anthony, 1 Jan. 1663; Joseph, 29 July 1665; Eliz. 29 July 1667, when her mo. d. and she d. at 10 yrs. He next m. 10 Nov. 1669, Mary Barnard, perhaps d. of Thomas of Salisbury, had John, 13 Sept. 1670; Mary, 31 Aug. 1672; Peter, 14 Nov. 1674; and Sarah, 23 Nov. 1676; made his will 23 Feb. 1678, and d. two days aft. His wid. perhaps m. 22 Aug. foll. Philip Eastman; and his d. Mary m. 1692, Jabez Corbin. BENJAMIN, Newbury, s. of the first Anthony, freem. 1673, m. 27 Aug. 1667, Ruth Sawyer, had Benjamin, b. 24 Aug. 1668; Ruth, 8 Dec. 1669; Joseph, 5 or 10 Feb. 1672; William, 23 Jan. 1674; Sarah, 13 Jan. 1676, d. at 3 yrs.; Philip, 19 Oct. 1677; Sarah, again, 19 Jan. 1680; Ann, 27 Mar. 1681; Mary, 15 May 1686; and Samuel, 7 Dec. 1688. CHRISTOPHER, Boston, mariner, by w. Prudence had Sarah, b. 28 Mar. 1662; Margaret, 23 May 1663, d. soon; Prudence, 6 Feb. 1665; and Margaret, again, 19 May 1668. DANIEL, Watertown, s. of Samuel, b. in Eng. 1613, as is said, was freem. 6 May 1635, rem. to Dedham, there by w. Lydia Fisher had Obadiah, b. 8 Aug. 1639; Daniel, 31 Jan. bapt. 7 Feb. 1641; Jonathan, 8, bapt. 12 Mar. 1643; Lydia, bapt. 13 Apr. 1645; Bethia, 24 Mar. bapt. 2 Apr. 1648; Mary, bapt. 29 Sept. 1650; at Medfield had Bathshua, b. 20 July 1653; Nathaniel, 20 Jan. 1658; and Samuel, 12 May 1661. His orig. parchm. deed, convey. with assent of w. Lydia, to John Hull, part of his est. in M. 7 June 1666, was in my poss. and giv. to my friend Nathaniel I. Bowditch, Esq. and his last resid. was in Sherborn, where he d. 1688, and wid. d. 29 Jan. 1691, aged 70, at Sherborn. DANIEL, Sherborn, s. of the preced. m. at Medfield, Eliz. Barber, perhaps d. of George, had Eliz. b. Aug. 1670; Daniel, 10 July 1672 ; Esther, 21 May 1674; Eliz. again, 29 Oct. 1677 ; John, 27 Aug. 1679 ; Noah, 20 Apr. 1681 ; Margaret, 30 Sept. 1683; Hannah, 15 Dec. 1685 ; Mary, 23 Jan. 1688, d. young; Sarah, 5 June 1689 ; and David, 10 Dec. 1692, d. soon. He d. 29 Sept. 1702, and his wid. d. 1714. EDMUND, Newbury, in the Genealog. is call. tenth ch. of William, and it is said, had Edmund, bapt. at N. 24 Feb. 1678 ; but Coffin is silent as to both f. and s. EPHRAIM, Newtown, L. I. s. of the first John, prob. was of Boston 1677. EZRA, Dedham 1639, was, perhaps, br. of Samuel. EZRA, Dedham, s. of John of the same, a great mill holder, m. Joanna Hoar, had, beside other ch. John, b. 31 Mar. 1674, H. C. 1692, min. of Newtown, L. I. wh. d. 1700; and d. 1697. FRANCIS, Boston, by w. Eliz. had Eliz. b. 23 July 1667 ; and by w. Ann had Mary and Hannah, tw. b. 26 Sept. 1669 ; John, 6 June 1672; and Huldah, 7 Mar. 1674. JEREMIAH, Boston, s. of Samuel, it is said, b. in Eng. had Samuel, bapt. 29 Aug. 1647; and Jeremiah, 17 Dec. 1648; perhaps rem. to the E. JEREMIAH, Newton, s. of Joseph the sec. had liv. with his f. at Groton, rem. thence, aft. d. of f. with his mo. to Watertown, m. 13 Jan. 1682, Abigail, d. of John Woodward, wh. d. next yr. hav. had John, b. 28 Mar. 1683, d. in few wks. and he m. again w. Sarah, but prob. had only ch. James, bapt. 24 Apr. 1689 ; and d. 27 Sept. 1719. JEREMIAH, Medfield, s. of Joseph of Dedham, by w. Eliz. had Eliz. b. 22 June 1678, d. soon ; Jeremiah, 31 Oct. 1679; Eliz. again, 24 Feb. 1681, d. young perhaps ; Mary, 5 Mar. 1685 ; Timothy, 27 Dec. 1687 ; Benjamin, 31 Aug. 1692 ; Samuel, 24 Sept. 1694 ; Abigail, 18 Oct. 1696, d. young perhaps ; Jedediah, 1700 ; and John, 1704, and d. 19 Feb. 1716, and his wid. Eliz. d. 25 Apr. 1733, aged 74. JOHN, Dedham, tailor, eldest s. of Samuel, b. in Eng. it is said, 1611, may have come bef. his f. freem. 13 May 1640, by w. Annis had Ruth, b. 3 June 1637 ; John, 8 June 1639 ; Samuel and Rachel, tw. bapt. 15 (not as Genealog. says 5) Mar. 1640, both d. young ; Joseph, b. 3 Feb. bapt. 6 July 1641 ; Ezra, bapt. 4, but rec. b. 5 Feb. 1644 ; Dorcas, b. 24 Aug. 1645, prob. d. young ; Abigail, 2, bapt. 8 Mar. 1647 ; Ephraim, 19, bapt. 30 July 1648 ; Bethia, 28 Mar. bapt. 6 Apr. 1651 ; and Nathaniel, 2 May 1653 ; rem. to Boston next yr. and d. 26 May 1657. His will, of 18 Dec. 1655, made in contempla. of a voyage to Eng. pro. 18 June 1657, by the Notary wh. witness. it, names w. Annis, and the eight ch. JOHN, Charlestown 1637, perhaps rem. next yr. to Ipswich. JOHN, Boston, tailor, m. 24 Dec. 1652, Mary Jupe, niece of Robert Keayne, had Mary, b. 20 Apr. 1654 ; was, prob. the freem. of 1654, and went home, but came back in the Speedwell, July 1656, aged 40; and may be the person, whose d. is ment. 26 May 1657. In that ship, at that time, came the first Quakers to our country. JOHN, Ipswich, s. of Joseph first of the same, by w. Dinah had Eliz. b. 29 Mar. 1657, d. at 2 yrs.; and Mary, 15 Jan. 1661, wh. m. perhaps, John Shattuck; and d. 1697, leav. wid. Dinah. He was town clk. of Groton. JOHN, Watertown, sec. s. of sec. Joseph, went early to Lancaster, there m. Ann, d. of John Smith, had Lydia, b. 6 Apr. 1660; and John, 7 Apr. 1662, wh. d. soon, as did also his w. He ret. to Watertown, and m. 27 Apr. 1666, Abigail, youngest d. of first Isaac Stearns, had John, b. 10 May 1667, d. soon; James, 25 Nov. 1668; John, again, 15 Mar. 1670; Joseph, 25 Aug. 1671; Abigail, 23 Dec. 1673, d. in few wks.; Abigail, again, 6 Aug. 1677, d. says the Genealog. in Apr. 1683, but Dr. Bond says she m. John Parkhurst, liv. above 70 yrs. and had s. and ds.; Isaac, 5 Jan. 1679, d. at 15 yrs.; Samuel, 21 June 1682, d. prob. bef. 20 yrs.; and Nathaniel, bapt. 29 Jan. 1688; was deac. 1697. His w. d. 16 Oct. 1690, and a third w. was Sarah. He d. 23 or 28 July 1702. JOHN, Boston, s. of the first John, by w. Eliz. d. of Zaccheus Bosworth, had Eliz. b. 22 Jan. 1661; Ruth, 18 Dec. 1662, d. at 18 mos.; Hannah, Feb. 1665; Abigail, 30 Mar. 1667; Ruth, again, 13 Jan. 1669; Bethia, 13 or 15 Jan. 1671; John, 28 Aug. 1673; Samuel, 13 Nov. 1676, prob. d. soon; and Sarah, 24 Nov. 1677. He was freem. 1669, serv. as a commissary in Philip's war, and d. says the Genealog. 25 Oct. 1678, but in the Appendix makes that event on the same day of next yr. leav. wid. Eliz. who applied to governm. for compensat. on acco. of his serv. JONATHAN, Sherborn, s. of Daniel the first, m. 8 Sept. 1666, Mary Barber, perhaps d. of George, wh. d. 1700, had Jonathan, b. 11 July 1667; Mary, Aug. 1670; Nathan, 3 Jan. 1673; Samuel, 10 Aug. 1676; Lydia, 9 May 1682; Eliz. 10 Dec. 1684; and Ebenezer, 26 Sept. 1689; liv. at Medfield, was freem. 1677 or 72, and d. 30 Aug. 1727. JONATHAN, Watertown, s. of the sec. Joseph, m. 17 Oct. 1678, Abigail, youngest d. of William Shattuck the first, had Abigail, b. 5 or 15 Dec. 1679; Hannah, 3 Sept. or Dec. 1682; Ruth, 15 Apr. 1684; and Jonathan, 23 Jan. 1687, posthum. for his f. d. 31 July preced. perhaps at Groton, where he was freem. 1672, of whose proprs. he was clk. JONATHAN, Newbury, prob. s. of William of the same, m. 3 May 1671, Mary Clark, rem. to Beverly, there had bapt. Jonathan, 16 Nov. 1673; Mary, bapt. at N. 4 June 1676; Joshua, perhaps; and Jonathan, bapt. at N. 29 June 1681; was aft. of Middleborough, and one of the found. of first ch. there; d. 9 July 1709. JOSEPH, Ipswich 1642, prob. from Co. Suffolk, Eng. had w. Dorothy, and s. Joseph and John, of wh. one, if not both, came over bef. him, and d. Hannah, made his will 24 Apr. 1646, and d. Sept. foll.

JOSEPH, Watertown, eldest s. of the preced. came in the Elizabeth 1634, aged 24, from Ipswich, Co. Suffolk, prob. sent by his f. was freem. 6 May 1635, m. Esther, d. of John Pierce of W. had Joseph, b. 30 Apr. 1637; John, 28 Feb. 1639; Jonathan, wh. d. May 1643; Jonathan, again, 7 Nov. 1643; Esther, 7 Mar. 1646; Sarah, wh. m. 2 June 1669, Timothy Cooper of Groton; Jeremiah; and Isaac. He d. 4 Mar. 1691. Esther m. 9 Dec. 1669, Jonathan Bullard. JOSEPH, Dedham, s. of Samuel, b. in Eng. came in the Increase, from London, 1635, aged 20, with f. and mo. m. 1 Sept. 1638, Hannah or Ann Phillips of Watertown, perhaps sis. of Rev. George, had Samuel, b. 10 Jan. 1640; Hannah, 8 Aug. 1641; Sarah, 16 Sept. 1643; Dorcas, 24 Aug. 1645; Eliz. 1 Sept. 1647; Joseph, 26 Sept. 1649; Jeremiah, 10 June 1651; and ano. ch. shortly bef. his d. He d. 20 June (or at least his inv. has that date) bef. the will of his f. Dec. 1654. His wid. m. 3 Nov. 1658, Thomas Boyden of Watertown. JOSEPH, Watertown, s. of Joseph of the same, m. 12 Apr. 1661, Susanna, d. of William Shattuck, had Susanna, b. 11 Jan. 1663; Esther, 11 Sept. 1664; rem. to Groton, there was freem. 1672, and had Joseph, 11 Nov. 1667; Samuel, 4 Sept. 1670; Mary, 11 Feb. 1672; and Hannah, 7 Apr. 1674, to wh. Dr. Bond adds Jonathan, without a date, and the assiduous genealogist of the name adds that he was b. a. 1680, while on the same page he makes the f. d. 1677, wh. is right, for the wid. m. 5 July 1678, John Fay, wherefore I doubt, unless the Morse genealog. be wrong here. JOSEPH, Medfield, s. of John first of that name, m. 12 Nov. 1668, Priscilla Colburn, had John, b. 18 Aug. 1669, d. young; Joseph, 25 May 1671, or 10 Feb. 1672, H. C. 1695, min. by Mather's Hecatompolis at some Ind. town in Conn. but aft. of Dorchester, that part wh. bec. Stoughton, now Canton; John, again, 29 June 1673; Priscilla, 1675; Maria, 23 Sept. 1677; Moses, 1680; Deborah, 26 Nov. 1681; Israel, 30 Nov. 1683; Nathaniel, 23 Jan. 1686; and Aaron, 10 June 1688; was freem. 1672, and d. 1689; and his wid. d. 3 Feb. 1731. JOSEPH, Newbury, s. of William, by w. Mary had Benjamin; Joseph; Joshua; Sarah, b. 7 July 1677; and Mary, 21 Jan. 1679, her f. d. six days bef. and she was bapt. 18 May foll.
* JOSEPH, Dedham, s. of Joseph of the same, m. 17 Oct. 1671, Mehitable, d. of Nicholas Wood, liv. at Sherborn, had Mehitable, b. 25 Apr. 1673, d. young; Joseph, 3 Apr. 1676, d. soon; Elisha, 12 Dec. 1677, prob. d. young; Joseph, again, 25 Mar. 1679; Mehitable, again, 2 Nov. 1681. The mo. d. ten days aft. and he m. 11 Apr. 1683, Hannah Badcock, had James, b. 1 July 1686; Hannah, 5 Apr. 1689; Sarah, 12 Apr. 1692; David, 31 Dec. 1694; Isaac, 14 Sept. 1697; Keziah, 30 June 1700; and Asa, 24 Aug. 1703. This w. d. 9 Nov. 1711, and he m. 17 May 1713, Hannah, wid. of Joseph Dyer, and d. 19 Feb. 1718;

and his wid. d. 4 Sept. 1727, aged 67. JOSHUA, Newbury, s. of the first Anthony, by w. Joanna had Hannah, b. 15 Feb. 1681; Joshua, 11 Apr. 1686, d. in few wks.; and Anthony, 15 Apr. 1688. He d. 28 Mar. 1691, says Coffin; but the Geneal. wh. agrees with C. that his w. d. 10 Apr. 1691, gives him sec. w. Mary. JOSHUA, came to R. I. says the Geneal. and serv. as chaplain in king William's war with the French, had gr.s. of the same name, wh. was a preach. NATHANIEL, Sherborn, s. of Daniel, first of the name, by w. Mary had Nathaniel, b. 1680, d. soon; Nathaniel, again, 1682; Joseph, 1683; Benjamin, 1684, prob. d. soon; Aaron, 5 Mar. 1686; Mary and Rachel, tw. 2 Apr. 1687; Ruth, 21 Oct. 1688; Dorothy, 1695; and Obadiah, 1698; was a deac. and d. 17 Oct. 1728. * OBADIAH, Sherborn, eldest br. of the preced. freem. 1672 or 7, being so ent. in ea. yr. m. Martha Johnson, had only Obadiah, wh. d. young, was first clk. of the town, and deac. d. 4 Mar. 1704, and his wid. d. 1714. An OBADIAH, among freem. 1674, is call. of Portsmouth in the rec. but I fear, he can have no more told of him, but that in Feb. 1690, with majority of N. H. people, he desir. jurisdict. of Mass. ROBERT, Boston, perhaps br. of the first Anthony, brot. from Eng. w. Eliz. and prob. s. Abraham, had James, b. at B. 1644, rem. to Newbury, perhaps bef. his w. d. but more likely aft.; m. 30 Oct. 1654, Ann Lewis, had Eliz. b. 25 Sept. 1655, d. in 6 mos.; Robert, 1 Feb. 1657; Mary, 25 Feb. 1658, d. in 8 mos.; a d. 16 Dec. 1660, wh. liv. not to obt. a name; Lydia, 13 July 1662; and Sarah, 28 Apr. 1665, but Coffin makes it a yr. later; liv. some time at Rowley, there, perhaps, had Peter, and at last rem. to N. J. SAMUEL, Dedham, perhaps br. of Daniel, came in the Increase, from London, 1635, aged 50, with w. Eliz. 48, and s. Joseph, bef. ment. but how the other childr. came or when, is uncert.; freem. 8 Oct. 1640; d. says the Geneal. 20 June 1654; but either that date or one of his will is wrong, as pub. in Geneal. Reg. V. 299, where the test. is 2 Dec. 1654. I presume the d. of his s. Joseph was intend. for June. Farmer says he d. 3 days aft. and agrees with town rec. therein. It gives w. Eliz. all his est. but aft. her life to be div. among ch. John, Daniel, and Mary, w. of Samuel Bullen, beside Ann, wid. of Joseph, for his childr. equal. and no more; so that I doubt the other names giv. in the Geneal. may not be all correct, especially as Abigail is said, therein, to m. Daniel Fisher, the speaker, whose w. was, I think, Abigail, d. of Thomas Marrett. Geneal. Reg. IX. 141, gives the inv. by wid. Eliz. 10 July 1654. Perhaps the dates are confus. by the numerals for mos. and days in one of the transact. being interchang. The wid. d. 20 June 1655. SAMUEL, perhaps s. of the preced. liv. at Dedham, says the Geneal. there by w. Mary Bullen had Mary, b. 20 June 1642; and Samuel; but it could tell no more, and guesses that he rem. to E. SAMUEL, Dedham, in the part wh. bec. Medfield, eldest s. of Joseph of the same, m. 10 Feb. 1665, Eliz. Moore, had Samuel, b. 8 Feb. 1666; Eliz. 28 Mar. 1668; Hannah, 30 Aug. 1669, d. soon; Hannah, again, 9 Nov. 1670, d. soon; Ruth, 21 Mar. 1672; Joseph, 16 Jan. 1674, both these d. young; Joshua, 7 Apr. 1679; Eleazer, 10 Aug. 1680; and Benoni, 19 June 1682; and in one week aft. his w. d. He m. 29 Apr. 1684, Sarah Thurston, had Solomon, 5 Jan. 1685; and Sarah, 11 July 1686; and this w. d. 29 Apr. 1688; and he d. 28 Feb. 1718. SAMUEL, Sherborn, youngest s. of the first Daniel, by w. Deborah had Samuel, b. 4 June 1687; Eleazer, 22 Oct. 1688; Deborah, 1690; Mehitable, 1695, d. soon; Martha and Sarah, perhaps tw. 1696; Bethia, 1698; Miriam, 30 June 1700; Tabitha, 1702; and Benjamin, 1703, d. next yr. and the f. d. 2 Mar. 1704, and his wid. d. 5 Oct. 1719. THOMAS, Dedham, adm. of the ch. 28 June 1640, but I find not his name in the great Geneal. in the preparat. of wh. Rev. Abner, in our days, spent over thirty yrs. WALTER, Boston, I suppose of Muddy riv. for bef. 1667, James Clark of that planta. in his will provides for the d. who m. him; yet his name is not includ. with the innumera. Morses. WILLIAM, Newbury, br. of Anthony, came with him 1635, in the James, from Southampton, hav. been a shoemaker at Marlborough, by w. Eliz. had Eliz. wh. d. 18 Mar. 1655; Ann, perhaps bef. her, yet may be the d. nam. by Coffin, 6 Mar. 1641; perhaps John or Jonathan; Joseph; Timothy, 10 June 1647 or 8, d. young; Abigail, 14 Feb. 1652; and prob. Edmund; d. says Coffin, 29 Nov. 1683, aged 69. Ann m. 5 Feb. 1655, Francis Thorla of N. Mather, Magn. VI. 68, exults in the wondrous, diabolical operations, within, around, and against his dwelling, of wh. all were traceable to a roguish gr.son. It was Increase Mather that first publish. the full relation of those follies as wonders. Much of the evidence how the devil was played in 1679, for wh. Eliz. the poor tormented gr.mo. of young scapegrace was sentenced to be hanged, but happily pardoned, bef. the gr. adversary's full triumph, was gather. by Coffin in his Hist. of N. and is well giv. in the Memorial of the Morses. Thirteen of this name in sev. forms of spelling, had, in 1834, been gr. at Harv. six at Dart. four at Yale, and three at other N. E. coll.

MORTIMER, MORTIMORE, or MALTIMORE, EDWARD, Boston, merch. by w. Jane had Dorcas, b. 28 Nov. 1674; Edward, 20 June 1676; Eliz. 19 Aug. 1678; Richard, 10 Aug. 1680; Jane, 12 July 1686; and Robert, 31 July 1688. He is highly commend. by John Dunton, wh. says he came from Ireland. RICHARD, Boston, perhaps br. of the preced. by w. Ann had Mary, b. 28 May 1664. THOMAS, New London, was constable 1680, had w. Eliz. and two ds. Mary, wh. m. Robert Stoddard, and Eliz. m. Abraham Willey. He d. 11 Mar. 1710.

MORTON, *CHARLES*, Charlestown, eldest s. of Rev. Nicholas, wh. d. at Southwark, near London, there hav. a parish, descend. of an anc. fam. at Morton, in Co. Notts, where was the seat of Thomas Morton, says Farmer, secr. of Edward III. was b. 1626, in Cornwall, bred at Wadham Coll. Oxford, and sett. at Blisland, in his native Co. as a min. thence eject. in 1662, he liv. sev. yrs. at Newington Green, near London, and was wholly engag. in teach. a private semin. until 1686, when he emb. for Boston, and 5 Nov. of this yr. was ord. at C. His neph. Charles, an M. D., came with him, but went home in July of next yr. ; ano. neph. Nicholas, H. C. 1686, wh. d. at Charlestown, 3 Nov. 1689, had come a yr. earlier than his uncle. An aged wid. Ann, says the rec. d. 20 Dec. 1690 ; but she may not have been relat. Some reports still circulate a. the design of mak. him head of our college, but there can be no founda. for the idea, that such an inducem. caus. his com. for Increase Mather was chos. near. a yr. bef. his leav. Eng. and some jealousy was rais. against him for teach. matters of high rank in the college curriculum. Vice President he was indeed chos. being the first in such rank, and, I suppose, the last who acted *under* a presid. officer, for when the Inst. was reliev. from the rule of Mather, and nobody was to be found fit to be his successor, with condition of resid. on inadequ. salary, Willard was made real head of the Coll. with the inferior title that Morton had enjoy. yet not held to resid. M. was too old to succeed Mather, when this latter was sent to Eng. and d. some yrs. bef. the office was vacat. by him. It is rather strange, that his d. wh. was on 11 Apr. 1698, by Penhallow, who was his pupil in Eng. and came over with him, is mark. 1696, see 2 Mass. Hist. Coll. I. 162, and by Dr. Bartlett, in the next Vol. of Coll. 171, noted 1706, aged 80. * EPHRAIM, Plymouth, s. of George, came with his f. in the Ann, 1623 ; but Judge Davis, in the preface to the Memorial, says, he was b. on the passage. Cotton's Plymouth ch. hist. in 1 Hist. Coll. IV. 126, marks his d. 7 Sept. 1693, in 70th yr. of his age, wh. implies that he was b. aft. the arr. of the sh. in July. Perhaps the differ. may be explain. by error in Cotton's use of the Latin word, as very frequent. occurs in careless mod. writers. He m. 18 Nov. 1644, Ann Cooper, wh. d. 1 Sept. 1691, had Ephraim, b. 27 Jan. 1648 ; Rebecca, 15 Mar. 1651 ; Josiah, 1653 ; George ; Nathaniel ; Eleazer ; Thomas ; and Patience ; who were all m. and ea. s. had issue. He had sec. w. Mary, wid. of William Harlow, d. of Robert Shelly of Scituate, was a man of much serv. in the council of war, a col. and rep. 28 yrs. from 1657, and again under the new chart. 1692, also a deac. in wh. office his s. George succeed. Nathaniel was in the milit. a lieut. He is by Judge Davis nam. anc. of Perez, late Att.-Gen. GEORGE, Plymouth, not the s. of Thomas, b. at Austerfield, in Yorksh.

bapt. 12 Feb. 1599, yet, no doubt, a relat. of that num. fam. perhaps br. of the sec. Thomas, came in the Ann, 1623, with w. m. at Leyden, 23 July 1612, Julian, d. of Alexander Carpenter, and four or five ch. counted with Experience Mitchell for 8 in the div. 1624, of lds. and d. in June the same yr. leav. wid. Julian, wh. m. Manasseh Kempton, and is thot. to have been sis. of Gov. Bradford, and d. 19 Feb. 1665, aged 81, beside ch. Nathaniel; Patience, wh. m. 1633, a fellow-passeng. John Faunce, f. of the celebr. Elder; John, b. 1616; Sarah, 1618, m. 20 Dec. 1644, George Bonham; and Ephraim, bef. ment. By sagac. conject. he is presum. to be the Editor of the valua. tract, usual. call. Mourt's Relation. See Dr. Young, Chron. of Pilgr. 113. Dr. Felt, Ann. of Salem, I. 228, differs from Dr. Young, and speaks of Mourt as visiting Naumkeag in 1621; but his addr. "to the reader" seems to imply of necessity, that *he* had never visited our country, tho. he hoped to. GEORGE, Plymouth, perhaps s. of the preced. at least, how the rec. of P. that ment. d. of Phebe, w. of George, 22 May 1663, can otherwise be explain. I do not discov. and thé elucidat. must be wait. for. GEORGE, Plymouth, s. perhaps eldest, of Ephraim of the same, m. 22 Dec. 1664, Joanna Kempton, d. of Ephraim, was one of the first purch. of Dartmouth, 1652, tho. then an inf. if his f. prefers to have the right in his name. He had Hannah, b. 27 Nov. 1668, if the Col. Rec. be right, wh. is very improb.; Manasseh, 3 Feb. 1669; Ephraim, 12 Apr. 1670; Joanna, 27 June 1673; Ruth, 20 Dec. 1676; George, 8 July 1678; Timothy, 12 Mar. 1682. * JOHN, Plymouth, s. of the first George, came with his f. by w. Lettice had John, b. 11 Dec. 1649, d. soon; John, again, 21 Dec. 1650; Deborah; Mary; Martha; Hannah; Esther; and Manasseh and Ephraim, tw. 7 June 1653; rep. 1662, rem. to Middleborough, of wh. he was rep. 1672, and d. 3 Oct. 1673. His wid. m. Andrew Ring, and d. 22 Feb. 1691. He is, by Judge Davis, reput. to be anc. of Gov. Marcus. JOHN, Boston, by w. Martha had John, b. 13 Jan. 1649. JOHN, Salem, petitnr. against imposts 1668. NATHANIEL, Plymouth, eldest s. of George the first, b. in Eng. a. 1613, came with his f. freem. 1635, and that yr. m. Lydia Cooper, had Remember, b. 1637; Mercy; Lydia; Eliz. 3 May 1652; Joanna, 9 Nov. 1654; and Hannah; beside Eliezer, and Nathaniel, wh. both d. in early youth, so that descend. in male line fail. He was secr. of the Col. from 1645 till he d. 29 June 1685. The first w. d. 23 Sept. 1673, and he m. 29 Apr. 1674, Ann, wid. of Richard Templar of Charlestown, wh. surv. him, and d. at C. 26 Dec. 1690, aged 66. Remember m. 18 Nov. 1657, Abraham Jackson; Mercy m. at the same time, Joseph Dunham, and d. bef. her f.; Hannah m. 27 Nov. 1666, Benjamin Bosworth of Hull; Lydia m. George Ellison; Joanna m. 7 Dec. 1670, Joseph Prince of

Hull; and Eliz. m. 7 Dec. 1670, Benjamin Bosworth. He had the benefit of all the MSS. of his uncle, Gov. Bradford, and compiled the well kn. Memorial, of wh. the fifth Ed. was illustrat. by Judge Davis. RICHARD, Hartford, blacksmith, was freem. there 1669, had Richard and Thomas, rem. 1670 to Hatfield, there had John, b. 1670, d. soon; Joseph, 1672; John, again, 1674, d. young; Abraham, 1676; Eliz. 1680; Ebenezer, 1682; and Jonathan, 1684; was freem. 1690, and d. 1710. His wid. Ruth d. 1714. All his s. exc. Thomas, liv. at Hatfield. RICHARD, Hatfield, s. of the preced. m. 1690, Mehitable, d. of Isaac Graves of the same, d. next yr. and his wid. m. William Worthington of Hartford. THOMAS, Plymouth, came in the Fortune, Nov. 1621, and either d. or went home soon aft. the div. of lds. in wh. he had part, and bef. the div. of cattle 1627, in wh. he had none. See Davis's Morton, 378. THOMAS, Braintree, the pettifogger of Clifford's Inn, London, came June 1622, and seems much to have displeas. all the sett. in other planta. perhaps in no small degree for calling his planta. Merry Mount; was seiz. and sent home, June 1628, for causes well set down by Gov. Bradford in 1 Hist. Coll. III. 62; soon came back, and foll. similar courses, and by Gov. Winthrop, in 1630, was sent off; still he was infatuat. with love of N. E. and a third time got here, and a third time was punish. and d. in poverty at York, a. 1646. See Winth. II. 192. He publish. New English Canaan, one of the most amusing, and not least valua. of the books descript. of our country. He prob. had no w. THOMAS, Plymouth, came in the Ann 1623, in co. with George, who may have been his br. is call. junr. in the div. of cattle 1627, tho. other Thomas is not nam. was still resid. there 1641. See Davis's Morton, 379, 382, 403. He was an orig. purch. of Dartmouth in 1652. WILLIAM, New London, one of the first sett. in 1646, constable 1658 and aft. d. prob. 1668, without ch. WILLIAM, Windsor, freem. 1669, d. a. 1670, had William, wh. d. bef. his f.; John; Thomas, wh. d. bef. his f. leav. ch. Five of this name had, in 1834, been gr. of Harv. and six at other N. E. coll.

MOSELEY. See Maudsley. Twelve of this name had been gr. in 1829, at Yale, one at Harv. and five at other N. E. coll.

MOSES, AARON, New Hampsh. 1690, perhaps s. of John, crav. jurisdict. of Mass. that yr. HENRY, Salem, m. 1 Apr. 1659, Remember, d. of Edward Gyles, had Hannah, b. 20 Jan. 1660, d. next yr.; Henry, 8 Feb. 1662; Eliz. 8 Feb. 1664; John, 19 Nov. 1666; Remember, 14 Nov. 1668; Edward, 10 Nov. 1670; Eleazer, 23 Mar. 1673; and Samuel, 24 June 1677. JOHN, Windsor 1647, m. 18 May 1653, Mary Brown, had John, b. 15 June 1654; William, 1 Sept. 1655; Thomas, 19 Feb. 1659, both the last d. bef. the f.; Mary, 2 Dec. 1661; Sarah, 2

Feb. 1663; Margaret, 2 Dec. 1666; Timothy, Feb. 1670; Martha, 3 Mar. 1672; and Mindwell, 13 Dec. 1676. He d. 14 Oct. 1683; and his wid. d. 14 Sept. 1689; and his d. Mary m. 1685, as his sec. w. Samuel Farnsworth. The name is perpet. in the neighb. JOHN, New Hampsh. 1658. Farmer says the name is still in the E. part of the State.

MOSIER, or MOSHIER, ARTHUR, Boston, by w. Rebecca had Lydia, b. 25 Feb. 1678; Thomas, 22 Sept. 1679; and Samuel, 21 Jan. 1683. Perhaps it is bec. Mosher. HUGH, Falmouth 1640, came, perhaps, in the Jane, from London, in eight wks. pass. arr. at Boston 12 June 1632, was inhab. of Newport 1660, engag. in the purch. of Misquamicut, d. bef. 1666, leav. James and John, says Willis, I. 37. He had not then acquir. the knowl. of resid. of Hugh in R. I. where he m. Rebecca, d. of John Harndel of Newport, as sec. w. prob. unless ano. Hugh be intend. in the will of her f. 9 Feb. 1685. See also, 4 Mass. Hist. Coll. I. 93, in notes. Of James, we kn. only that he was admor. 1666, appoint. at the July Ct. on est. of his f. and of John, that in 1683, he was of Brookhaven, L. I. and gave conveyance of ld. in Casco Bay.

MOSMAN, James, Wrentham, by w. Ann had Eliz. b. 24 May 1675, d. 6 Mar. foll. He prob. rem. to Roxbury, there had Timothy, b. 17 Nov. 1679; and Eliz. 18 Dec. 1696; but it is not sure that it was by the same w. or whether other ch. had not been b. perhaps in ano. town.

MOSS, * JOHN, New Haven 1639, sign. the orig. comp. 4 June 1643, had John, bapt. prob. 5 Jan. 1640, d. young; Samuel, 4 Apr. 1641; Abigail, 10 Apr. 1642; Joseph, prob. 5 Nov. 1643; Ephraim, 16 Nov. 1645; Mary, 11 Apr. 1647; Mercy, male, 1 Apr. 1649; John, again, b. 12, bapt. 20 Oct. 1650; Eliz. 3, bapt. 7 Oct. 1652; Esther, 2 Jan. 1654; and Isaac, 21, bapt. 30 Nov. 1655; as the print. in Geneal. Reg. IX. 361, gives the bapt. wh. may be a mistake for Dec. The rec. of b. may be trust. that of bapt. is certain. wrong. He was rep. 1667–70, and then rem. to Wallingford 1670, of wh. he was rep. 1671–3, yet contin. propr. at New Haven, d. 1707, aged 103, perhaps with slight exagg. yet thot. to be the oldest that ever d. in Conn. See Dana, Cent. disc. 1770. Mary m. 3 Nov. 1664, John Peck; and Eliz. m. 1670, Nathaniel Hitchcock. JOHN, Boston. See Morse. JOHN, Woburn, m. 5 Mar. 1686, Dinah Knight. JOHN, Salisbury, by w. Sarah had Joseph, b. 11 Jan. 1694; Abiel, 19 Aug. 1695; Mary, 4 Mar. 1697; and Benjamin, 24 Oct. 1698. He may have been a Morse. JOSEPH, Portsmouth 1665. JOSEPH, New Haven, s. of John of the same, m. 11 Apr. 1667, Mary, d. of Roger Alling, had, beside prob. others, Samuel, b. 27 Jan. 1675, d. next yr.; Joseph, 7 Apr. 1679, H. C. 1699, a min. of reputa. at Derby, ord. 1706; and Samuel, again,

18 Mar. 1681. JOSEPH, Boston, by w. Mary had Joseph, b. 22 Mar. 1687; and Joseph, again, 18 Jan. 1689. MERCY, New Haven, s. of John, by w. Eliz. had John; and William, b. 28 June 1682; but perhaps John was not the elder. He d. not long aft. for his inv. was of 3 Mar. 1685, and only the wid. and two s. to have int. in it. In no other case have I seen this female name enjoy. by a man. The surname is sometimes writ. by mistake for Morse.

MOTT, ADAM, Hingham, a tailor, from Cambridge, Eng. came in the Defence 1635, aged 39, with w. Sarah, 31, and ch. John, 14; Adam, 12; Jonathan, 9; Eliz. 6; and Mary, 4; was first of Roxbury, freem. 25 May 1636; perhaps dissatisf. as a friend of Hutchinson, went 1638 to Rh. Island with fam. there had, perhaps, more ch. and was with Adam jr. John, and Jonathan, perhaps his s. liv. at Portsmouth, as freem. 1655. ADAM, 'Portsmouth, R. I. s. of the preced. m. Oct. 1647, Mary Lott, had Adam, b. Sept. 1650; Mary, 1 Jan. 1656; Sarah, 11 Oct. 1657; Eliz. 9 Aug. 1659; Phebe, 20 Aug. 1661; Bethia, 1 Apr. 1664; Abigail, 3 May 1666; and John, 1 Jan. 1671, JACOB, Newport, perhaps s. of the first Adam, by w. Joanna had Hannah, b. Nov. 1663; Mercy, 8 Jan. 1666; Sarah, 3 Feb. 1670; Eliz. 12 Sept. 1672; and Samuel, 4 Sept. 1678. JOHN, Newport, perhaps br. of the first Adam, sign. the compact at the same time with him, July 1638, was of Block isl. or one of the same name, 1684. NATHANIEL, Scituate, able to bear arms 1643, rem. to Braintree, m. 1656, Hannah Shooter, had Nathaniel, b. 28 Dec. 1657. A Margaret M. came in the Speedwell, 1656, aged 12.

MOULD, HUGH, New London 1660, sh. builder, m. 11 June 1662, Martha, d. of John Coit, had been prob. first at Barnstable, d. 1692, leav. wid. Martha, and six ds. of wh. Susanna m. Mar. 1683, Daniel White; and Mary m. 1693, Joseph White, and the mo. of the girls m. the f. of their hs. as his sec. w. SAMUEL, Charlestown, by w. Mary had Mary, bapt. 30 Mar. 1689, the mo. hav. been bapt. 13 Feb. 1687, aged 20.

MOULDER, NICHOLAS, Boston 1671, merch. by w. Christian had Nicholas, b. 21 June 1672. He was abus. as a Quaker, by Gov. Bellingham, and rem. to whence he came. But ano. kind of abuse was practis. in the change of his Christian name at Boston, for the Friend's rec. prove that it was EDWARD, and that at Newport, by w. Christian, he had Edward, b. 24 Mar. 1669; and at Boston, Nicholas, 29 May 1671, wh. prob. d. soon; and Nicholas, again, agreea. to Boston rec. 21 June 1672.

MOULTHROP, or MOULTROP, JOHN, New Haven, s. of the sec. Matthew, m. 29 June 1692, Abigail Bradley, d. of Joseph, had Abigail, b.

12 Aug. 1693 ; John, 17 Mar. 1696; Mary, 1698, d. young; Sarah, 1701; Dan, 1 Dec. 1703; Israel, 7 June 1706; Joseph; and Timothy. MATTHEW, New Haven 1639, by w. Jane had Matthew, Eliz. and Mary, perhaps the first two b. in Eng. certain. Eliz. b. in 1638 ; and Mary, in 1641, were bapt. in 1642. He d. 22 Dec. 1668, and his wid. d. May 1672. Eliz. m. 1663, John Gregory. MATTHEW, New Haven, s. of the preced. m. 26 June 1662, Hannah, d. of the first John Thompson, had Hannah, b. 2 Nov. 1663, d. soon ; Hannah, again, 20 Apr. 1665, wh. m. 17 Aug. 1687, John Russell ; John, 5 Feb. 1668; Matthew, 18 July 1670; a ch. 1673, d. soon ; Lydia, 8 Aug. 1674; Samuel, 24 June 1677, d. soon ; Samuel, again, 13 Apr. 1679 ; and Keziah, 12 Apr. 1682 ; was freem. 1669 ; a propr. 1685, and d. 1 Feb. 1692, aged 53.

MOULTON, BENJAMIN, Hampton, s. of William, took o. of fidel. 1678, and was liv. in 1690 to desire jurisdict. of Mass. HENRY, Hampton 1640, prob. s. of John, b. in Eng. His will in 1654, names w. Mary, I think a d. of Edward Hilton, ch. Jonathan and David. JACOB, Charlestown 1663, says Barry. JAMES, Salem, join. the ch. 31 Dec. 1637, as did his w. Mary next yr.; had there bapt. James, 7 Jan. 1638 ; and Samuel, 25 Dec. 1642, beside d. Mary, wh. may have been b. aft. rem. from S.; was freem. Mar. 1638, liv. at Wenham 1667, and there d. His will of 1679, names the two s. and d. Mary Friend. JAMES, Wenham, s. of the preced. was freem. 1666. ‡ * JEREMIAH, York, perhaps s. of Thomas, took o. of alleg. 1681, rep. 1692, and aft. of the counc. d. 22 Oct. 1727, in 77th yr. JOHN, Newbury, came from Ormsby, in Co. Norfolk, near Great Yarmouth, emb. Apr. 1637, call. husbandman, aged 38, with w. Ann of same age, five ch. Henry, Mary, Ann, Jane, and Bridget, two serv. Adam Goodwin, 20, and Alice Eden, 19 ; had John, bapt. Mar. 1638 ; rem. to Hampton 1639, there had Ruth, bapt. 7 May 1640, d. 1651, says Coffin, who also informs us that he had other ch. William, and Thomas, and the Jane and Bridget were tw. wh. d. on the same day, 19 Mar. 1699, aged 64. Of the case of the tw. Cotton Mather took advantage to write to Woodward of the Royal Soc. a memoir on those maidens that may be read in N. H. Hist. Coll. III. 122. His will of 1650, names w. Ann; s. Henry, John, and Thomas; ds. Mary Sanborn, Ann, Jane, Bridget; and s. Sanborn. In the same ship came a wid. from Ormsby, Mary M. aged 38 yrs. with two serv. John Maston, aged 20, and Marian Moulton, 23 ; as also Ruth M. a maiden of 20. JOHN, Hampton 1678, may have been s. of the preced. or of ano. and prob. m. 23 Mar. 1666, Lydia, d. of the first Anthony Taylor, had Martha, b. 16 Nov. foll. ; s. John, wh. took o. of fidel. the same yr. call. jun. JOHN, Salem, had m. a d. of Giles Corey, who bef. suffering d. by horrid form of the old com. law, made his will July 1692, in favor of two s.-in-law, giv. all lds. stock, and other prop. to them, as by our law conviction did not work forfeit. JOSEPH, Hampton 1678, s. of William of the same, or of sec. Robert, in 1690 req. jurisdict. of Mass. JOSEPH, York 1680, perhaps br. of Jeremiah, sw. alleg. 1681. JOSIAH, Hampton 1678, is not kn. to be s. of any sett. there. * ROBERT, Salem, a shipbuilder, came 1629, in the fleet with Higginson, but went to Charlestown soon, freem. 18 May 1631, was one of the first selectmen, and rep. at the first Court, 1634, and for Salem, to wh. he had rem. in 1637, and was that yr. disarm. as a friend of Wheelwright, d. 1655, leav. Robert, and Dorothy, w. of one Edwards, both nam. as also gr.s. Robert, in his will of 20 Feb. pro. 20 June foll. See Young's Chron. of Mass. 161. ROBERT, Salem, s. of the preced. b. in Eng. rec. of the ch. 1640, had Robert, bapt. 23 June 1644; Abigail; Samuel; Hannah; John; Joseph; Miriam; and Mary; some, perhaps, bef. Robert; Samuel, d. in aut. of 1665. Miriam m. 8 Oct. 1677, Joseph Bachiler. ROBERT, Salem, m. 1672, Mary Cook, had Mary; Robert, 1675; Ebenezer, 1678; and Abigail, 1682; may have liv. at Hampton 1678, was prob. s. of the preced. THOMAS, Charlestown 1631, perhaps br. of the first Robert, liv. on Malden side, had w. Jane, and ch. John, bapt. 16 Mar. 1633; Martha, 24 July 1637; Hannah, 20 Dec. 1641; Eliz. 24 Apr. 1642; beside Jacob, whose bapt. is not kn. wh. d. Dec. 1657. A d. Mary, I think, m. Nov. 1655, Thomas Mitchell. THOMAS, Newbury 1637, rem. with Rev. Mr. Bachilor, in 1639, to Hampton, by w. Martha had Thomas, bapt. 24 Nov. 1639; and Daniel, 13 Feb. 1641; was freem. 13 Mar. 1639, and d. 18 Feb. 1665. THOMAS, York, constable 1661. WILLIAM, Hampton, came 1637, aged 20, as serv. of Robert Page of Ormsby, Co. Norf.'k and m. his d. Margaret, had Joseph, Benjamin, Hannah, Mary, Robert, and Sarah, wh. was b. 17 Dec. 1656; all ment. in his will of 8 Mar. 1664, pro. Oct. foll. beside provision for unb. ch. perhaps call. Ruth. Mary m. 1 Jan. 1674, it is said, Jonathan Haynes of H. wh. d. soon, and he next m. 30 Dec. of the same yr. Sarah, d. of W. Moulton, and I presume, sis. of the first w. tho. the acco. in Geneal. Reg. IX. 349, does not pledge itself to any parentage of the first w. WILLIAM, Newbury, perhaps s. of John, m. 27 May 1685, Abigail, d. of John Webster, had Abigail, b. 13 June 1686; Batt, 4 July 1688; Jonathan, 7 Sept. 1692; Joseph, 25 Nov. 1694; Margaret, 21 Feb. 1699, d. at 2 yrs.; Sarah, 4 July 1701; and Mary, 2 Aug. 1705.

MOUNTAIN, RICHARD, Boston, had w. Abigail, wh. join. the ch. 4 Apr. 1646.

MOUNTFORT, MUNFORD, or MUMFORD, ‖ BENJAMIN, Boston, merch. came, it is said, 1675, in the Dove, from London, aged 30, ar. co. 1679,

was one of the wardens of King's Chapel 1690, and d. 1714. EBEN-
EZER, Boston, in Mar. 1676, when the sec. ch. was burnt, his ho. was
also burned; perhaps was f. of Ebenezer, H. C. 1702. EDMUND, Boston, tailor, by w. Eliz. had Edmund, b. 11 July 1664; Henry, 7 Mar.
1666; Benjamin, 19 Feb. 1668; John, 28 Mar. 1670; Sarah, 22 Apr.
1672; Hannah, 14 Apr. 1673; Joshua, 6 Feb. 1675; and Jonathan, 15
June 1678. His will, of 8 Aug. 1690, was pro. 20 Mar. next. HENRY,
Boston, br. of the preced. by w. Ruth, perhaps d. of Elder John Wiswall,
had Henry, b. 12 Feb. 1688, d. young; and in his will of 20 May 1691,
nam. Ebenezer, then minor, as only ch. yet rememb. two sis. in Eng.
Hannah and Sarah. JOHN, Providence, took o. of alleg. in May 1671.
‖ JOHN, Boston, s. of Benjamin, ar. co. 1697, had Edmund, bapt. 21 Oct.
1694; Benjamin, 5 Apr. 1696; Eliz. 27 Feb. 1698; Mary, 6 Oct.
1700; John, 7 Mar. 1703; Joanna, 11 June 1704; Susanna, 1 Apr.
1705; Joshua, 22 Sept. 1706; Jonathan, 26 Sept. 1708; Hannah, 21
Jan. 1711; Joseph, 19 Apr. 1713; and Edmund, again, 26 May 1717.
JONATHAN, Boston, s. prob. of Edmund, m. 7 Jan. 1702, Hannah
Nichols. WILLIAM, Boston, mason, by w. Ruth had Ruth, b. 26 Mar.
1671; Lydia, 17 Nov. 1672; William, 2 June 1677; Eliz. 2 Sept.
1679; and Naomi, 18 Aug. 1681; perhaps one, not rec. in Philip's war.

MOUNTJOY, BENJAMIN, Salem, d. 1659. WALTER, Salem, m. 18
Jan. 1672, wid. Eliz. Owen. See Munjoy.

MOUSALL, * ‖ JOHN, Charlestown 1634, with w. join. the ch. 23 Aug.
freem. 3 Sept. of that yr. rep. 1635, ar. co. 1641, deac. and selectman
1642, rem. to Woburn, and d. 27 Mar. 1665. Possib. he was tempt. to
Salem, for Felt prints Mousar John as hav. gr. of ld. there 1639, and
among ch. memb. 1646, prints Ruth Monsall, both so very closely
resembling this name, may be mistak. for it. His d. Eunice m. 1 Nov.
1649, John Brooks. His will, of 9 June 1660, pro. 4 Apr. 1665, names
w. Joanna, makes s. John and John Brooks excors. with remem. of
Sarah, Eunice, and Joanna Brooks, gr.ch. of testa. JOHN, Woburn, s.
of the preced. m. 13 May 1650, Sarah Brooks. JOHN, Charlestown, s.
prob. of Ralph, b. in Eng. by w. Eliz. wh. d. 16 Aug. 1685, aged 51,
had Eliz. b. 16 July 1659; was, I suppose, that soldier of Moseley's
comp. in Dec. 1675, in Geneal. Reg. VIII. 242, print. Monsall, d. 1
Feb. 1704, aged 74.   * RALPH, Charlestown, br. of the first John, came,
I doubt not, in the fleet with Winth. he being no. 72 and w. Alice 73 in
the list of Boston ch. memb. desir. adm. as freem. 19 Oct. 1630, and 18
May foll. was sworn, when the name appears Mashell, and in Geneal.
Reg. VII. 30, Moushole. He was one of the founders of the ch. at C.
rep. 1636, 7, and 8, but being a favorer of Wheelwright, was eject. yet
aft. hold. his tongue and recov. his reputa. was deac. d. 30 Apr. 1657,

leav. John, wh. was prob. b. in Eng.; Thomas, bapt. 25 May 1633; Mary Goble; Ruth Wood; and Eliz. His will, of 13 Apr. preced. besides w. and ch. names cous. Nathaniel Ball, and Mary Wayne, and in a codic. ten days aft. ment. s. Thomas hav. a s. born. His wid. d. 1667. THOMAS, Charlestown, s. of the preced. by w. Mary, perhaps d. of Samuel Richardson, had Thomas, b. 5 Apr. 1655, d. soon; Joseph, 10 Apr. 1657, d. in few wks.; Mary, 26 July 1659, bapt. as also, Ralph, 21 June 1668; Joseph and Benjamin, tw. bapt. 21 Feb. 1669; Samuel, 23 Apr. 1671; Mercy, 28 Sept. 1673; and Thomas, again, 22 Nov. 1674. His w. d. 13 Sept. 1677, and he had sec. w. and d. 16 Apr. 1713, in 81st yr. and his wid. Ann d. 25 Aug. 1742, in 82d yr. The s. Ralph d. at C. 7 June 1718.

MOUSSETT, THOMAS, Boston, by w. Catharine had Peter, b. 18 Oct. 1687; was prob. a Huguenot, and one of the four rul. elders of that communion. But the name is not found in Boston any more, tho. I discover that he own. ld. in Roxbury 1698, and had liv. at Braintree.

MOWER, RICHARD, Salem 1638, was prob. passeng. in the Blessing from London, 1635, aged 20, a mariner, join. the ch. 1642, and had Samuel and Thomas, bapt. 6 Mar. in that yr.; Caleb, 31 Mar. 1644; Joshua, 3 May 1646; Richard, 2 Jan. 1648; Susanna, 12 May 1650; and Christian, 5 Sept. 1652; was freem. 28 Feb. 1643, employ. by governm. 1654, had Mary, b. so late as 15 Jan. 1662, and was liv. 1696. See Moore, with wh. spell. Felt names him.

MOWRY, JOHN, may be writ. Morey, wh. see, or, as at the London custom-ho. Mory, a passeng. aged 19, in the Blessing from London 1635. Spell. with a *w*, was he of Providence 1676, who did not rem. for the war. ROGER, Providence 1655.

MOXON, *GEORGE*, Springfield 1637, the first min. came from Yorksh. had been bred at Sidney Coll. in the Univ. of Cambridge, there took his A. B. 1623, and here, with w. Ann, sat down at Dorchester first, but aft. being made freem. 7 Sept. 1637, was attract. to S. by his former neighb. Pynchon, with whom he was very intimate; had there s. Union, b. 16 Feb. 1642; Samuel, 1645; and ano. s. 1647, whose name is not ment. in the rec. but elder childr. Martha and Rebecca were, in 1651, said to be bewitched by Mary, w. of Hugh Parsons, who was, on trial, found not guilty. The f. was, perhaps, more influenced by the writing or conversa. of Pynchon, whom he follow. to their native land 1653. Johnson, in Wonderwork. Provid. Lib. III. ch. 2, speaks largely of his ability, and suggests no misgiving about the soundness of his faith; yet we can hardly doubt, that he was drawn home by sympathy with Pynchon to partake the greater freedom then enjoy. in Eng. and there d. 15 Sept. 1687, aged 85. Calamy, II. 313, names his s. George among the min. eject. 1662.

MOYSE, JOSEPH, Salisbury. His w. Hannah d. 1655.

MUDDLE, or MUDDLES, HENRY, Gloucester, d. bef. June 1663, when inv. of small prop. was tak. PHILIP, Gloucester, perhaps s. or br. of the preced. petitn. against imposts 1668.

MUDGE, JAMES, one of the "flower of Essex" under capt. Lothrop, k. by the Ind. 18 Sept. 1675, at Bloody brook. JERVIS, Wethersfield 1643, m. 1649, the wid. of Abraham Elsen, but aft. rem. to New London, and there d. early in 1652, leav. that wid. and two s. prob. b. of a former w. JOHN, Malden, perhaps s. of Thomas, was a soldier of Moseley's comp. Dec. 1675, freem. 1690, by w. Ruth had John, b. 15 Oct. 1685, prob. d. soon; John, again, 21 Nov. 1686; Martha, 25 Oct. 1691. His w. d. 17 Oct. 1733, and he d. twelve days aft. MICAH, Northampton 1670, s. of Jervis, m. that yr. Mary, d. of George Alexander, rem. to Northfield, among early proprs. thence driven, 1675, and again, 1690, in the Ind. wars, rem. to Lebanon, a. 1698 again to Hebron ; had Ebenezer ; Moses ; Eliz. ; Mary ; Thankful ; Susanna ; and Sarah, not all liv. to 1721, when he made his will. MOSES, Sharon 1696, br. of the preced. Caulkins, Hist. of N. L. 269. THOMAS, Malden 1658, had Samuel, b. in May of that yr. and, perhaps, Martha, w. of Rev. Michael Wigglesworth. A George M. d. 25 Nov. 1685, at M. or Charlestown.

MUDGET, THOMAS, Salisbury, m. perhaps for sec. w. 8 Oct. 1665, Sarah Morrell, eldest d. of Abraham the first, had Mary, b. 30 Apr. 1667 ; and Temperance, 16 Oct. 1670 ; was freem. 1690. Ano. THOMAS, Salisbury, s. of the preced. or, perhaps, the same, by w. Ann had William, b. 16 Oct. 1696; Thomas, 3 Jan. 1699, prob. d. soon; and Thomas, again, 17 Dec. 1700.

MULFORD, JOHN, Easthampton, L. I. 1650, one of the first sett. says Wood, 44, perhaps went home for some time, and came again in the Speedwell, 1656, from London, when the name appears Mulfoot; was chos. Assist. 1658, had commiss. from Conn. in 1664 as a magistr. and 1674, as a judge. JOHN, Eastham, s. prob. of Thomas, m. 1 Nov. 1699, Jemima Higgins. THOMAS, Eastham, by w. Hannah had John, b. July 1670 ; Patience, 17 Aug. 1674 ; Ann, 23 Mar. 1677 ; and prob. older than either, Thomas. His wid. d. 10 Feb. 1718. THOMAS, Eastham, perhaps s. of the preced. m. 28 Oct. 1690, Mary Bassett, had Ann, b. 28 July 1691 ; Dorcas, 6 Mar. 1693 ; Mary, 26 June 1695 ; Hannah, 1 Sept. 1698 ; Eliz. 30 June 1701 ; Thomas, 20 Oct. 1703 ; and Jemima, 13 Oct. 1706. WILLIAM, Easthampton, L. I. 1650. Thompson.

MULLIGAN, MULLEGIN, or MULLEKIN, HUGH, Boston, by w. Elinor had Robert, b. 9 Aug. 1681, in 1684 was adm. memb. of the Scot's Charit. Soc. ROBERT, Rowley, perhaps br. of the preced. by w. Rebecca had Robert, b. 9 Dec. 1688; John, 26 July 1690; Mary, 26 Sept. 1692; and others. One Robert, prob. the f. d. there 11 June 1741, and ano. Robert, perhaps his s. d. 19 June 1756.

MULLERY, JOHN, Boston, by w. Abigail had Eliz. b. 16 Nov. 1672; John, 28 Jan. 1674; Ann, 26 Aug. 1677; Abigail, 8 Jan. 1681; Susanna, 3 Apr. 1684; Robert, 17 Nov. 1686; and Joseph, 16 May 1688; beside Sarah, bapt. 5 Jan. 1690; and Benjamin, 29 Nov. 1691.

MULLINER, THOMAS, New Haven 1640, was a gr. purchas. of Branford, by its Ind. name of Totoket, in that yr. had div. of lds. there in 1646 and 8. THOMAS, New Haven, prob. s. of the preced. sold out his lds. at Branford 1651, by w. Martha had Martha, b. 4 July 1656; and Eliz. 10 June 1658, rem. a. 1658 to West Chester, and there was liv. in 1691 with w. Martha.

MULLINS, or MOLINES, WILLIAM, Plymouth, came in the Mayflower 1620, with w. two ch. Joseph and Priscilla, and a serv. Robert Carter; but the w. d. a few days bef. or aft. him, who d. 21 Feb. 1621; and the s. and serv. d. the same season; but his d. Priscilla m. John Alden, and had eleven ch. WILLIAM, Duxbury 1642, may have been s. of the preced. left by his f. in Eng. or Holland, and aft. came to join the surviv. friends. He had lds. in Middleborough 1664. Good est. as well as charact. is told of the pilgrim. WILLIAM, Boston, m. 7 May 1656, Ann, wid. of Thomas Bell.

MUMFORD, EDMUND, Boston, m. Eliz. wid. of Joshua Carwithy of the same, a. 1663; but I kn. no more. PELEG, Kingstown, s. of Thomas the first, had two ws. it is said, Mary, d. of Ephraim Bull, and Mary, perhaps d. of the sec. John Coggeshall, yet there is some uncertain. a. this, for his s. Peleg is also said to have m. that d. of Ephraim Bull. In the will of the f. however, pro. 1741, are nam. his ch. Peleg; Mary Hanson; Sarah Barber; Eliz. Foster; and Hannah Hopkins; beside gr.ch. Samuel, Peleg, Thomas, Abigail, and Content. His kinsman, William Mumford, was made excor. STEPHEN, Newport, came from London 1664, and was the first preach. of the sect of seventh day Bapt. wh. prevails in a part of the State. I presume he had descend. THOMAS, Newport, had Thomas, b. 1656; Peleg, 1659; George; and Abigail, wh. m. 1 May 1682, Daniel Fish. Yet he does not appear a constant resid. at N. tho. he join. with Brenton, John Hull, and others in purch. and settlem. of Pettaquamscuck. Possib. the name is the same as Mountfort. The name of his w. is not kn. nor the time of his d. but it was bef. 1692. THOMAS, prob. of Kingstown, eldest s. of the preced. by w. Abigail (whose surname is not told), had Thomas, b. 1 Apr. 1687; George, 15 July 1689; Joseph, 17 Sept. 1691; William, 18 Feb. 1694; Benjamin, 10 Apr. 1696; and Richard, 6 Sept.

1698; wh. six s. were popular. call. the thirty-six feet Mumfords. His w. d. 1707, in her 38th yr. Perhaps he had ano. w. Esther Tefft, in 1708, and by her, John, Sarah, Tabitha, and Esther, and he d. 1726. WILLIAM, a Quaker, whip. at Boston 1677, where, I presume, he staid not long.

MUN, or MUNN, BENJAMIN, Hartford, serv. in the war with the Pequots, 1637, rem. to Springfield, m. 1649, Abigail, wid. of Francis Ball, d. of Henry Burt, had Abigail, b. 1650; John, 1652; Benjamin, 1655; James, 1657; and Nathaniel, 1661; and d. Nov. 1675. His wid. m. lieut. Thomas Stebbins, and his d. Abigail m. Thomas Stebbins jr. DANIEL, Milford, d. 1666, leav. will. Inv. of his est. was £42. JAMES, Springfield, s. of Benjamin, was in the fight at Turner's falls, 1676, and sett. at Colchester. JOHN, Westfield, eldest br. of the preced. was in the great fight of Turner's falls, m. 23 Dec. 1680, Abigail Parsons, and d. at Springfield, 16 Sept. 1684, leav. John, b. 16 Mar. 1682, and Benjamin. NATHANIEL, Springfield, youngest br. of the preced. may have had fam. SAMUEL, Woodbury 1680, wheelwright, may well seem to be of a differ. fam. from any of the preced. as Cothren says he came in from Milford, and his f. is unkn. had Jane, and Amy, bapt. Oct. 1680; Mary, Nov. 1681; Daniel, Feb. 1684; and Samuel, Apr. 1687. In mod. times the name has double n.

MUNDAY, or MONDAY, HENRY, Salisbury, freem. 13 May 1640, was rated in 1652, higher than any other inhab. but one. Farmer, from the rec. says his w. d. 22 July 1654. The spell. is sometimes Monde or Munde. He has prefix of respect in town rec. WILLIAM, passeng. in the Mary and John, 1634, may have been f. of the preced. at least we kn. that sev. of the early sett. at Salisbury came in that voyage.

MUNDEN, ABRAHAM, Springfield, m. 16 May 1644, Ann Munson, had Mary, b. 8 Aug. 1645, and he was drown. 29 Oct. at Enfield Falls, the same yr. This d. was complain. against, in 1676, at Northampton, for " wearing silk, and that in a flaunting manner; " the enormity of her offence was aggravat. perhaps, by the disaster of her f. thirty yrs. bef.

MUNGER, JOHN, Guilford, s. of Nicholas, m. 1684, Mary Everts, d. of James, had Mary, b. 1686, d. young; John, 1687; Mary, again, 1689; Abigail, 1691; Ebenezer, 4 July 1693; Caleb, 1695; Jonathan, 1697; Josiah, 20 July 1704; and Rachel, 1706; and he d. 3 Nov. 1732; and his wid. d. 1734. NICHOLAS, Guilford, m. 2 June 1659, Sarah Hull, had John, b. 26 Apr. 1660; and Samuel; d. 16 Oct. 1668. SAMUEL, Guilford, younger s. of the preced. by w. Sarah had Samuel, b. 1689; Joseph, 1693; Sarah, 1695; Deliverance, a d. 1697; Nathaniel, 1699; James, 1701; Ann, 1703; and Jane 1705; and he d. 5 Nov. 1717.

MUNJOY, or MUNGY, BENJAMIN, of Boston, perhaps was a mariner in 1655, but of him no more is kn. exc. that admin. on his est. was giv. in Essex Co. 28 June 1659, to his w. wh. brot. in inv. of £19, 2, 5. Perhaps he was br. of George. GEORGE, Boston, master mariner, or sh. carpent. 1647, s. of John of Abbotsham, near Biddeford, Devonsh. adm. of the ch. 15 May, and same mo. freem. m. Mary, only d. of John Philips of Boston, had John, b. 17, bapt. 24 Apr. 1653; George, 21, bapt. 27 Apr. 1656, when ch. rec. calls him John; and Josiah, 4 Apr. 1658; next yr. bot. the Noah's Ark tavern in B. but rem. soon to Casco, to have charge of the great purch. from Cleves, by his f.-in-law, had at Falmouth, Mary, brot. up to B. for bapt. 9 July 1665; and Hepzibah, beside s. Phillips, Benjamin, Pelatiah, and Gershom; all liv. 1675, when the Ind. war began. He d. 1681, leav. wid. Mary and most of the ch. so bef. ment. but only three had fams. Mary m. John Palmer of F.; Hepzibah m. a Mortimore; and the wid. m. Robert Lawrence, and in 1690, Stephen Cross. GEORGE, Braintree, s. of the preced. by w. Mary had Josiah, wh. d. without ch.; Mary; and ano. d. b. aft. he made his will, 25 Feb. 1697; and he d. next yr. JOHN, Falmouth, br. of the preced. was k. by the Ind. in their assault, 11 Aug. 1676, and left wid. and only ch. Huldah, so that the name was soon extinct, exc. as it is preserv. in the hill on wh. stands the observatory in the beautiful city of Portland. See Willis, I. 93, 170. Munjoy was easily adopt. from the sound of old Mountjoy; but the ancestor in our country always used the shorter form. WALTER, Marblehead 1668, petitnr. against imposts.

MUNNINGS, or MULLINGS, EDMUND, Dorchester, came in the Abigail, 1635, aged 40, with w. Mary, 30; and ch. Mary, 9; Ann, 6; and Mahalaleel, 3. At D. had Hopestill, b. 15 Apr. 1637; Returned, 7 Sept. 1640; and Takeheed, 20 Oct. 1642. He was a propr. late as 1658, but had prob. gone home, I think, to Malden, Co. Essex, there, at least, was somehow connect. with Joseph Hills, who bef. com. over had given M. £11 in a bill for bring. one bullock for the use of H. GEORGE, Watertown, came from Ipswich, Co. Suff'k in the Elizabeth, 1634, aged 37, with w. Eliz. 41; and ch. Eliz. 12; and Abigail, 7; freem. 4 Mar. 1635; perhaps had Rebecca, wh. m. 14 Jan. 1652, Edmund Maddocks at Boston; was active in ch. and town, lost an eye in serv. of the Pequot war 1637; was an orig. propr. of Sudbury, but resid. at Boston 1645, sev. yrs. kept the gaol, and d. at B. 24 Aug. 1658. His will, made the day bef. names w. Johanna, to wh. he gave his est. She had, I judge, been wid. of Simon Boyer. See Geneal. Reg. VIII. 354. Farmer has noted the misprint of his name in the Christian Examiner for 1828, p. 501. GEORGE, Boston, s. prob. of the preced. by w. Hannah had George, b. 24 Nov. 1655; Eliz. 19 Mar. 1657; Elisha,

15 Dec. 1659 ; Eliz. again, 13 Oct. 1661; James, 6 Mar. 1663 ; Hannah, 20 Apr. 1665 ; Mary, 3 Nov. 1666 ; Sarah, 19 Mar. 1668; John, 11 Oct. 1671 ; and Joseph, 6 Nov. 1674. MAHALALEEL, Dorchester, s. of Edmund, went home, perhaps, with his f. but came again in the Speedwell 1656, m. that yr. Hannah, d. of John Wiswall of Boston, had Hannah, b. 23 Sept. 1657, rem. soon to Boston, here was adm. of the sec. ch. 27 Nov. 1659, and was drown. 27 Feb. foll. hav. call. by the same *un*christian name, a s. who d. 22 Nov. preced. His est. was insolv. The wid. m. Thomas Overman, and his d. Hannah m. Josiah Willis. At the London custom-ho. the names of his fam. are Monnings.

MUNROE, or MONROE, ALEXANDER, whose place of resid. in N. E. is not sure, had bef. May 1651, lawsuit in Mass. with Elias Parkman. See Col. Rec. IV. pt. I. 52 and 114. Prob. he was a Scotch merch. trans. certain. not a prisoner, sent here for sale. BENJAMIN, Lexington, youngest s. of William, by w. Abigail, had Lydia, b. 7 Mar. 1718 ; Abigail, 5 Oct. 1719 ; Benjamin, 24 Jan. 1723 ; Rebecca, 21 Aug. 1725 ; Sarah, 26 July 1727 ; Martha and Mary, tw. 18 Mar. 1729 ; Ann, 4 Mar. 1732 ; Eunice, 9 Apr. 1734 ; and Kezia, 22 Apr. 1736. He had sec. w. Prudence Estabrook, prob. a wid. m. Dec. 1748, at Weston, and there d. 6 Apr. 1766. DANIEL, Lexington, s. of William, by w. Dorothy had Daniel, b. 27 Jan. 1717 ; Jedediah, 20 May 1721 ; Sarah, 14 July 1724; Dorothy, 21 June 1728 ; and John, 1731. GEORGE, Lexington, s. youngest by the first w. of William the first, by w. Sarah had William, b. 6 Jan. 1700 ; Sarah, 17 Oct. 1701 ; Dorothy, 19 Nov. 1703 ; Lydia, 13 Dec. 1705 ; George, 17 Oct. 1707 ; Robert, 4 May 1712 ; Samuel, 23 Oct. 1714 ; Andrew, 4 Feb. or June 1718 ; and Lucy, 20 Aug. 1720. JOHN, Lexington, eldest s. of the first William, by w. Hannah had John, Hannah, Constance, and Nathan, all bapt. early in 1699 ; William, b. 1 Feb. 1701 ; Eliz. 5 Mar. 1703 ; Susanna, bapt. 1 July 1705 ; Jonas, b. 22 Nov. 1707 ; and Marrett, 6 Dec. 1713. He was lieut. and had gr. of ld. for serv. in the fight at Lamprey riv. 1690. JOSEPH, Lexington, br. of the preced. by w. Eliz. had Joseph, b. 23 May 1713 ; perhaps Eliz. 12 Jan. 1715 ; Nathan, 11 Sept. 1716 ; Joshua, 22 Dec. 1717 ; Nathaniel, 17 Nov. 1720 ; Abigail, 21 Jan. 1723 ; Mary, 21 Jan. 1726 ; Kezia, 16 Oct. 1731 ; Hannah, 29 Nov. 1733. WILLIAM, Cambridge, in the part now Lexington, freem. 1690, by w. Martha had John, b. 10 Mar. 1666; Martha, 2 Nov. 1667 ; William, 10 Oct. 1669 ; and George. By sec. w. Mary he had Daniel, b. 12 Aug. 1673 ; Hannah ; Eliz.; Mary, 24 June 1678 ; David, 6 Oct. 1680 ; Eleanor, 24 Feb. 1683 ; Sarah, 18 Mar. 1685 ; Joseph, 16 Aug. 1687 ; and Benjamin, 16 Aug. 1690. He d. 27 Jan. 1717, call. 92 yrs. old. It has been conject. that he was a prisoner, tak. by Cromwell at the decisive battle of Worcester 1651, ship. in Nov. to be sold here, where the 272 unhappy men arr. in May foll. but I see little reason for the conject. exc. that Hugh, John, Robert, and ano. without bapt. name, all Monrows, form. part of the sad freight. See Geneal. Reg. I. 378, 9. Of his ds. Martha m. 21 Jan. 1688, John Come of Concord; Hannah m. 21 Dec. 1692, Joseph Pierce, as his sec. w.; Eliz. m. a Rugg; Mary m. perhaps, a Farwell; Eleanor m. 21 Aug. 1707, William Burgess of Charlestown; and Sarah m. a Blanchard. WILLIAM, Lexington, sec. s. of the preced. by w. Mary had Mary, b. 3 Apr. 1699; Abigail, 28 June 1701; William, 19 Dec. 1703; Thomas, 19 Mar. or May 1706; David, 28 Sept. 1708; Ruth, 16 Mar. 1711; Hannah, 19 Mar. 1713; and by sec. w. Joanna, d. of Philip Russell, had Philip, 26 Feb. 1717; and Joanna, 21 Oct. 1726.

MUNSON, or MONSON, RICHARD, New Hampsh. was one of the petitnrs. in the winter of 1689–90 for Mass. jurisdict. SAMUEL, New Haven, only s. of Thomas, m. 26 Oct. 1665, Martha, d. of William Bradley, had Martha, b. 6 May 1667; Samuel, 28 Feb. 1669; Thomas, 12 Mar. 1671; John, 26 Jan. 1673; Theophilus, 1 Sept. 1675; Joseph; Stephen, perhaps b. at Wallingford; Caleb, at New Haven, 19 Nov. 1682; and Joshua, 7 Feb. 1684; all liv. in 1698; was freem. 1669; ensign at Wallingford 1675, yet contin. propr. 1685, and d. at N. H. 1692, or 3. His wid. m. a Preston. *THOMAS, Hartford 1641, rem. next yr. to New Haven, had Samuel, bapt. prob. 6 Aug. (but not 7, as print. in Geneal. Reg. IX. 361), 1643; and Hannah, 11 June 1648; was rep. 1666, 9, 70–5, and serv. in the Ind. war. He d. 1685, and in the div. of his est. we find ano. ch. Eliz. w. of Richard Higginbotham. Hannah m. 2 Mar. 1667, Joseph Tuttle. Susan, who came in the Eliz. to Boston, 1634, aged 25, was, perhaps, his w.

MUNT, or MOUNT, THOMAS, Boston 1635, mason. His w. Dorothy d. 28 Feb. 1640, and by w. Elinor he had Faith, wh. d. soon; and Faith, again, 24 Apr. 1645; beside two more ds. whose names are not seen. He d. early in July 1664, and his wid. m. bef. Mar. 1668, Thomas Hill. Faith m. 21 Nov. 1660, Clement Short.

MURDOCK, ROBERT, Roxbury, m. 28 Apr. 1692, Hannah Stedman, had Hannah, b. 22 Jan. 1693; Robert, 1 Feb. 1695; John, 25 Mar. 1696; Samuel, 24 Mar. 1698; and Benjamin, 4 Mar. 1701; rem. 1703, to Newton, there had Hannah, 22 May 1705. He is by Jackson, suppos. to have come from Plymouth Col. and from his page we learn that the w. d. 1727, that he had sec. w. Abigail, and d. 1754, aged 89.

MURPHY, BRYAN, Boston, an Irishman, m. 20 July 1661, wid. Margaret Mahone.

MURRY, JAMES, Dover 1658.

MUSGROVE, JABEZ, a soldier under capt. Turner 1676, at Hatfield, shot by an Ind. with a ball "in at his ear, and out at his eye," as told in Remark. Providences of Increase Mather; may have come from Concord, for one Mary M. d. there, 25 Dec. 1649; but in 1680 he was of Newbury.

MUSHAMORE, ..., Portsmouth 1677. Mary, perhaps his d. m. 4 Dec. of that yr. Christopher Kenniston.

MUSSELWHITE, JOHN, Newbury, came in the James, 1635, from Southampton, call. in the custom-ho. rec. of Longford, wh. is near Salisbury, Wilts, laborer, was first of Ipswich, freem. 22 May 1639, d. 30 Jan. 1671, leav. est. in Laverstock, close to Salisbury, to brs. Thomas, John, and sis. Eda.

MUSSEY, or MUZZEY, ABRAHAM, a passeng. who took the o. of supremacy and alleg. to pass for N. E. 26 Mar. 1634, in the John and Mary that yr. with John, perhaps his br. but no acco. is obtain. of him. BENJAMIN, Malden, perhaps liv. some time in that part of Boston call. Rumney Marsh, m. Alice, d. of Richard Dexter, had Benjamin, b. 16 Apr. 1657; Joseph, 1 Mar. 1659; perhaps others; was prob. s. of Robert, b. a. 1635, freem. 1665. Perhaps Sarah, wh. m. 12 June 1674, John Waite of M. was his d. BENJAMIN, Cambridge Farms, or Lexington, s. of the preced. by w. Sarah had Mary, b. 1683; Benjamin, 20 Feb. 1689; Amos, 6 Jan. 1700; and Bethia, 1701; and he d. 17 May 1732. JOHN, Ipswich 1635, perhaps br. of Abraham, with wh. he came 1634, rem. to Salisbury, d. ·12 Apr. 1690. JOSEPH, Newbury, s. of Robert, m. 9 Feb. 1671, Esther, d. of James Jackman, had Mary, b. 25 Nov. 1672; Esther, 8 Jan. 1675; Joseph, 21 Dec. 1677; and Benjamin, 17 Aug. 1680, wh. d. at 16 yrs.; and d. 30 Dec. 1680. Mary m. 7 Dec. 1694, Henry Dow. ROBERT, Ipswich, one of the first sett. freem. 3 Sept. 1634, d. a. 1644. THOMAS, Cape Porpus, 1663–81, in wh. last yr. he sw. alleg. to the k. Among Cambridge proprs. 1632, appears Esther M. a wid. wh. m. 1635 or 6, William Rusco, Rosco, or Rescue, prob. his sec. w. He sold part of her est. as her h. 24 Mar. 1636. Often this is spelled Muzzy or Muzzey.

MUSSILLOWAY, DANIEL, Newbury, an Irishman, had been, 1665, serv. to Joseph Plummer, m. 14 June 1672, Ann, wid. of Aquila Chase, wh. d. 21 Apr. 1687; and by sec. w. Mary had Daniel, b. 16 May 1688, d. in 3 days; Daniel, again, 9 Sept. 1690; and John, 13 Feb. 1693; and d. 18 Jan. 1711. Coffin thinks this name has become Siloway, and was easi. mistak. for Musselwhite.

MUSTE, EDWARD, Mass. of whom no more is found than that he was adm. freem. 14 May 1634.

MYCALL, JAMES, Braintree, m. as Geneal. Reg. XII. 347 shows, 11

Dec. 1657, or 10 Jan. 1658 (as we read the numerals for mo. bef. or aft. those for days) Mary Farr, had James, b. 22 Jan. 1659; and tw. sis. Rebecca, wh. m. 16 July 1679, Richard Thayer.

MYGATE, MYGATT, sometimes MAYGOTT or MEGGOTT, JACOB, Hartford, s. of Joseph, b. prob. in Eng. for he calls hims. in 1667, 34 yrs. old, m. a. the end of 1654, Sarah, d. of William Whiting, had only two ch. Joseph, and Sarah; d. a. mid. age, and his wid. m. 1683, John King of Northampton, and d. 1706. Sarah m. first, John Webster, and next, Benjamin Graham. * JOSEPH, Cambridge, came in the Griffin, with famous Cotton and Hooker 1633, freem. 6 May 1635, rem. in the great migrat. to Hartford, was rep. 1658, and oft. aft. deac. call. his age 70, in 1666, had only two ch. Jacob, b. it is thot. in 1633; and Mary, 1637. His wid. Ann, wh. was b. 1602, surv. him some yrs. yet he liv. to 7 Dec. 1680, aged 84. Mary m. 20 Sept. or 12 Dec. 1657, John Deming the sec. JOSEPH, Hartford, s. of Jacob, m. 5 or 15 Nov. 1677, Sarah, d. of Robert Webster, had Joseph, b. 23 Oct. 1678; Susanna, 3 Oct. 1680; Mary, 4 Dec. 1682; two, nam. Jacob, d. early; Thomas, 11 Sept. 1688; Sarah, 9 Mar. 1692; Zebulon, 3 Nov. 1693; and Dorothy, 26 Jan. 1696; and the f. d. 1698. His wid. m. 12 Dec. 1722, as his sec. w. Bevil Waters, then 92 yrs. old, long outliv. him, and d. Feb. 1744, aged 89.

MYLAM, or MILOM, HUMPHREY, Boston 1648, by w. Mary, d. I think, of John Gore of Roxbury, had Mary, b. 23 May 1652; Constance, 15 Dec. 1653; Abigail, 10 Oct. 1660; Hannah, 27 June 1663; and Ruth, 26 Apr. 1666; beside Mary and Sarah; was a cooper, in his will of 14 Feb. 1667, pro. 3 May foll. names w. Mary and five ds. of wh. Constance m. John Alcock. One of his ws. if he had two, was d. of John Gore. JOHN, Boston, br. of the preced. prob. elder, a cooper, freem. 25 May 1636, by w. Christian had Benjamin, bapt. 10 Jan. 1636, d. at 4 yrs.; Constance, 16 Sept. 1638, tho. rec. of town says he was b. 28 Dec. of that yr.; John, 13 Sept. 1640, but town rec. says b. 18 Sept.; Eliasaph, b. 30 Sept. 1642, wisely bapt. Eleazer, 2 Oct. a. 4 days old; Samuel, 18 Oct. 1644, a. 3 days old; Ebenezer, 6, bapt. 10 May 1646; Samson, bapt. 12 Aug. 1649; and Joseph and Mary, tw. b. 26 Feb. 1652; rem. that yr. but if the rec. is true, wh. I distrust, he came back, and by ano. w. Mary had Sarah, 6 Apr. 1656.

MYLES, JOHN, Swanzey, came from Swansea, in Wales, a. 1662, first formed his ch. at Rehoboth 1663, rem. to S. 1667, and d. 3 Feb. 1683, leav. wid. Ann, d. of John Humphrey, and ch. John, Susanna, and Samuel, then, says his will, at coll. H. C. 1684. JOHN, Swansey, s. of the preced. had James, b. 26 Dec. 1674. SAMUEL, Boston, s. of the first John, aft. grad. went. to Eng. there was ord. by a Bp. of the estab. ch.

and came back to be instit. rector of the King's Chapel in B. 29 June 1689, had degr. of A. M. conf. by the Univ. of Oxford 1693, d. 4 Mar. 1729.

MYRICK. See Mirick.

NALY, RICHARD, Kittery, disfranchis. 1669, as a Quaker.

NANEY, or NANNY, ROBERT, Boston, sent by Robert Cordell, a goldsmith of Lombard street, London, in the Increase, 1635, aged 22, was first at Dover, perhaps, or Saco, had good charact. bef. com. in 1652, to B. by w. Catharine, d. of Rev. John Wheelwright, had John, b. 16 Feb. 1654, d. soon ; John, again, 12 Aug. 1655, d. soon ; John, again, 12 Aug. 1656 ; Joseph, 1 June 1658 ; James, 27 Aug. 1659 ; Mary, 22 June 1661 ; and Eliz. 2 Jan. 1663 ; and he d. 27 Aug. foll. His will, made 5 days preced. names w. and ch. only Samuel, who was b. bef. his f. came from the E. and Mary, and one anticip. ; so that prob. Joseph, James, and Eliz. beside the three Johns d. early. He was a merch. own. est. in Barbadoes, perhaps in comp. with Richard Hutchinson of London, wh. he calls uncle, and by inv. shows £1089, 14, 1¼ ; and his wid. m. Edward Naylor.

NARRAMORE, RICHARD, Mass. master of the ketch Sparrow, in Aug. 1687, brot. persons from the Bahamas, suspected of piracy by Sir E. Andros, our Gov. See 3 Mass. Hist. Coll. VII. 185. THOMAS, Dorchester 1664, a fisherman, perhaps br. of the preced. rem. to Boston, where w. Hannah join. the sec. ch. 29 May 1681, by her had Hannah, b. 23 Sept. 1671 ; Sarah, 26 Sept. 1672 ; James, 4 May 1674 ; John, 10 Sept. 1676 ; and Sarah, again, 10 Aug. 1686. Prob. he rem. to New Hampsh. and early in 1690 pray. for jurisdict. of Mass.

NASH, DANIEL, Northampton, s. of Timothy, m. 1 June 1710, Experience, d. of John Clark, had Sylvanus, b. 11 Jan. 1712 ; Zeruiah, 2 Nov. 1713 ; Daniel, 13 Sept. 1715 ; Experience, 26 Dec. 1716 ; Joseph, 23 Apr. 1718 ; rem. to Hadley, there had Onesimus ; Jonathan, 3 Dec. 1721 ; Rebecca ; Josiah ; and Phineas ; was deac. rem. a. 1739, over the mountains to Housatonic, now Great Barrington, and d. 10 Mar. 1760, aged 84, says the gr.stone. EDWARD, Norwalk 1654, in 1672 had two ch. in his fam. but prob. others. He is not in the list of freem. 1669, tho. accept. conditionally 1664, yet had good est. EBENEZER, Suffield, s. of Timothy, m. July 1701, Mary, d. of John Scott, had Jonathan, b. 30 May 1702, d. at 2 yrs. ; Mary, 29 Oct. 1704 ; and Miriam, 27 Jan. 1710. EPHRAIM, Hadley, youngest br. of the preced. m. 10 Jan. 1705, Joanna, d. of John Smith, had Timothy, b. 26 Jan. 1707 ; Ephraim, 16 Jan. 1710 ; Aaron, 23 Feb. 1712 ; Joanna, 4 July 1715, d. soon ; Joanna, again, 28 Aug. 1716, d. at 2 yrs ; Martin, 19 Jan. 1718 ; Eleazer, 10 Feb. 1720 ; and Elisha, 8 Oct. 1729. FRANCIS,

Braintree, a soldier of capt. Johnson's comp. Dec. 1675. GREGORY, Charlestown 1630, came prob. in the fleet with Winth. and he and his w. d. in Feb. foll. ISAAC, Dover 1657, perhaps rem. to York, there d. bef. July 1662. His wid. Phebe m. John Pierce. * JACOB, Weymouth, s. of James, by w. Abigail had Joseph, b. 11 Oct. 1669; John, 8 Oct. 1671; Abigail, 7 Aug. 1673; Thomas, 11 Jan. 1682; Alice and Benjamin, tw. 24 Mar. 1685; Sarah, 7 June 1688; beside Alice, and, perhaps, more, of wh. the rec. is imperf.; was freem. 1666, rep. in 1689 and 90. JACOB, Weymouth, prob. s. of James, was freem. 1686. * JAMES, Weymouth, fondly thot. to have been a sett. there in 1628, but very prob. may have been of 1638, freem. 1645, had James, Jacob, and, perhaps, other ch. was rep. 1655, 62, and 7. JAMES, Boston, carpenter in 1651, prob. s. of the preced. went to Weymouth, was freem. 1666. ‡ * JOHN, New Haven 1642, s. of Thomas, b. in Eng. had by w. Eliz. (d. prob. of Edmund Tapp of Milford) wh. d. 1 May 1676, Eliz. bapt. 3 Jan. 1647; Sarah, 29 July 1649; Mary, b. 13 Dec. 1652, bapt. prob. 16 Jan. foll.; Hannah, 24 July 1655, bapt. 4 days aft.; and prob. no s.; was lieut. 1652, rep. 1665, at the first Ct. aft. the union, and in 1672 chos. an Assist. in wh. place he was cont. acc. the custom of ann. elect. to his d. 3 July 1687. Eliz. m. 2 Dec. 1676, capt. Aaron Cook, and d. 3 Sept. 1687; Sarah m. 8 Feb. 1689, Thomas Yale; Mary m. 1679, Philip Paine; and Hannah m. 13 Feb. 1673, Eliphalet Ball, and next, 2 Apr. 1689, Thomas Trowbridge. JOHN, Branford, prob. s. of the first Joseph, m. 22 Aug. 1677, Eliz. wid. of Anthony Howe, had Joseph, b. 1 Aug. 1678; Thomas, 28 Jan. 1680; and Eliz. 15 Apr. 1681; and he d. next yr. JOHN, Norwalk, perhaps s. of Edward, said to be the first Eng. ch. b. in the town, m. 1 May 1684, Mary, d. of John Combs of Boston, not (as the valua. Hist. of Hall says) of Thomas Barlow, or Barley, of Fairfield, whose wid. had m. Combs, had John, b. 25 Dec. 1688; Nathan, 26 June 1693, beside Joseph, and four ds. who are not ment. in Hall's Hist. Hall makes the ws. dec. 2 Sept. 1711, but ano. acco. says 1698. JOHN, Salisbury 1660, had prob. been 8 yrs. bef. at Newbury. JOHN, Boston, cooper, m. Rebecca, d. of Laurence Smith of Dorchester, had Mary, b. 26 Nov. 1667; and John, 9 Mar. 1672. JOHN, Hadley, s. of Timothy, m. 29 Mar. 1689, Hannah, d. of Samuel Porter, who d. within 2 mos. and he m. 27 Nov. 1691, Eliz. d. of Joseph Kellogg, had Rebecca, b. 27 Feb. 1693; John, 2 July 1694; Moses, 2 July 1696; Eliz. 15 Dec. 1698, d. in few days; Timothy, 13 Nov. 1699; Abigail, 10 Apr. 1702; Stephen, 20 Sept. 1704; Daniel, 8 Dec. 1706; Samuel, 29 Jan. 1709; Phineas, 18 Jan. 1713, d. at 2 mos.; and Enos, 21 Apr. 1714. JOSEPH, New Haven, s. of Thomas, by w. Mary, wh. d. 25 Dec. 1654, had John, b. 12, bapt. 14 July 1650; Hannah, 21

Jan. 1652, bapt. 4 days aft. not 2, as the rec. in Geneal. Reg. IX. 361, has it; perhaps ano. d. wh. d. a few wks. aft. her mo.; was freem. of that Col. 1657, and rem. to Hartford, made freem. of this Col. 1658, and d. 1678, leav. good est. to wid. Margaret, and d. Sarah. His will, of 19 Jan. 1676, pro. 17 Oct. 1678, made br. John excor. and left to him his est. if d. Sarah d. without issue, of wh. conting. we are uninform. JOSEPH, Weymouth, by w. Eliz. d. prob. of John Holbrook, had Joseph, b. 8 June 1674, and prob. d. young, if, as Deane says, he rem. to Boston, there had Joseph, b. 1678, and had est. at Scituate in 1670, but Deane prob. was in error, for JOSEPH, Scituate, s. of the preced. m. 1700, Hannah, d. prob. of John Curtis, had Joseph, b. 1701; John, 1703; Hannah, 1705; James, 1708; Eliz. 1709; David, 1712; Mary, 1713, d. soon; Ephraim, 1715; Mercy, 1718; Simeon, 1720; Elisha, 1722; and Mary, 1724; and he d. 23 May 1732, aged 58, says the gr.stone. JOSHUA, Boston, m. 23 Feb. 1659, Eliz. d. of Edward Porter, had Thomas, b. 21 Apr. 1660; Eliz. 23 Feb. 1662; Sarah, 20 Feb. 1664; Robert, 3 Dec. 1666; and Joseph, 14 Feb. 1672. PETER, Charlestown 1658, s. of William, was, perhaps, of Rowley 1660. ROBERT, Boston, butcher, in 1643, had been of Charlestown, d. 13 Sept. 1661. His w. was Sarah; and d. Eliz. m. 20 June 1654, John Conney. * SAMUEL, Plymouth 1630 perhaps, but certain. in 1632, for the beginning of next yr. he was taxed half as high as capt. Standish; in 1643 was of Duxbury, was sheriff of the Col. 1652, rep. 1653, and in his 89th yr. was liv. 1682. His d. Martha m. William Clark; ano. d. m. Abraham Sampson. THOMAS, New Haven 1643, or earlier, had, in 1639, been at Guilford, d. 12 May 1658. His w. Margary, d. of Nicholas Baker of Herts, d. 11 Feb. 1656, and his will, made 1 Aug. 1657, names eldest s. John; Joseph; Mary, w. of Roger Allen; Sarah, w. of Robert Talmage; and Timothy, all brot. from Eng. THOMAS, Hatfield, eldest surv. ch. of Timothy, was of age to take the o. of alleg. 8 Feb. 1679, m. Aug. 1685, Hannah, d. of John Coleman, had John, b. at Hadley 28 Oct. 1686; Hannah, 2 Sept. 1689; Thomas, 26 Feb. 1693; Rebecca, 20 Apr. 1699; and Sarah, 9 July 1704. His w. d. 1 July 1722, and he d. 19 Jan. 1728. TIMOTHY, Hartford, youngest s. of the first Thomas, b. in Eng. m. a. 1657, Rebecca, d. of Rev. Samuel Stone, had Rebecca, b. 12 Mar. 1658, at New Haven, d. young; Samuel, 8 Feb. 1660, k. at Hadley, by a horse, at 8 yrs.; and Thomas, 1661; rem. to Hadley 1663, there had Joseph, 27 Jan. 1664; Timothy, 1665; John, 21 Aug. 1667; Samuel, again, 17 June 1669; Hope, 20 Nov. 1670; Ebenezer, 25 Oct. 1673; Daniel, 1676; Ephraim, 1682; and Mary, 1684, wh. d. 1687; was freem. of Mass. 1678, a lieut. and man of large influence, rep. 1690, 1, and 5, d. 13 Mar. 1699. His wid. d.

Mar. or Apr. 1709. All the last eight s. are provid. for in the will of the f. 10 Mar. three days preced. his dec. as also the d. Hope, w. of Isaac Warner; but the will of his wid. 18 Apr. 1707, names seven s. omitt. Timothy, who had d. at Deerfield; and aft. gift to d. Hope Warner, names d. Mary Nash, and Joanna N. wh. as to these, means, perhaps, ws. of two s. WILLIAM, Charlestown, possib. s. of Gregory, with w. Mary join. the ch. 31 Aug. 1634, and three days aft. sw. as freem. was prob. d. bef. 1658, when wid. N. alone of householders is found. Her will, of 20 Apr. 1674, pro. 3 July foll. names s. Peter, d. Mary, w. of Thomas Hale, and gr.ch. John and Mary H. and her next kinswoman Hannah Edenden, but how relat. is not ascert.

NASON, BENJAMIN, Dover, perhaps s. of Richard, m. 30 June 1687, Martha Kenny. JOHN, Dover, prob. br. of the preced. m. 6 Nov. 1674, Hannah, d. of John Heard. JOSEPH, Dover 1671, and there the fam. has cont. RICHARD, Kittery 1649, submit. 1652, to Mass. was ensign 1653, and in 1656 chos. rep. but disallow. by the Gen. Ct. and 3 yrs. later was fined for receiv. Quakers, and disfranch. He had John, Joseph, Benjamin, and Baker, nam. in his will of 14 July 1694, pro. 1696, in wh. he names his w. wh. had been wid. of Nicholas Follett, and was not mo. of these ch.

NAYLOR, EDWARD, Boston, merch. perhaps came not bef. 1665, m. Catharine, wid. of Robert Nanney, d. of Rev. John Wheelwright, had Tabitha, b. 2 July 1667; and Lydia, 26 July 1668. Perhaps he rem. but certain. his est. in 1673, was taken in execu. for debt to John Freake.

NAZITER, MICHAEL, Saco 1666, had Michael, b. 1664; and John, 1666; and Jane, prob. his d. m. 1669, Richard Peard. Folsom, 187.

NEAL, ANDREW, Boston 1664, a taverner, by w. Milicent had Sarah, b. 1 Apr. 1665; Mary, 6 June 1666; Andrew, 25 Nov. 1668; Eliz. 2 Aug. 1670, d. soon; Eliz. again, 11 Dec. 1671; and Mary, again, 11 June 1674. BENJAMIN, Braintree, youngest s. of the first Henry of the same, m. 20 Jan. 1689, Lydia, youngest d. of Stephen Paine of the same, had Lydia, b. 9 Feb. 1690; Hannah, 15 Mar. 1692; Benjamin, 3 Mar. 1694; Joseph, 17 Nov. 1695; Henry, 4 Aug. 1697; Abigail, 20 Aug. 1698; Jonathan, 13 Oct. 1700; Jerusha, 2 Oct. 1703; and Abijah, 22 Dec. 1709; and d. 12 Jan. 1746. EDWARD, Weymouth 1662, may have rem. to Westfield, there, by w. Martha, d. of Edmund Hart, had Deborah, b. 1670; Abigail, 23 Apr. 1672; Mary, 24 July 1675; Martha, 8 May 1677; Edward, 8 Feb. 1679; Esther, 8 Nov. 1680; and Eliz. 26 Feb. 1683; and he d. 1698. His d. Abigail m. 1694, Ephraim Stiles the sec. * FRANCIS, Falmouth, m. a d. of Arthur Macworth, had Francis, wh. d. 1693; and Samuel, who surv. was great propr. at Scarborough 1657, rep. 1670, rem. from the Ind. devast. to

Salem, and d. 1696, leav. wid. HENRY, Braintree 1640, by w. Martha had Martha, b. 16 Jan. 1643 ; Samuel, 31 July 1647 ; Henry, 19 Mar. 1650 ; and by a sec. w. Hannah Pray, perhaps sis. of John of the same, m. 14 Feb. 1656, had Abigail, 14 Feb. 1657 ; Hannah ; Joseph, 8 Aug. 1660; Sarah, 20 Dec. 1661; Mary, 11 May 1664; Rachel, Feb. 1666 ; Deborah, 1 Sept. 1667 ; Benjamin, 7 Mar. 1669 ; Ruth, 25 Dec. 1670 ; Lydia ; Eliz. 28 June 1675 ; Joanna, 27 May 1680 ; Rebecca, of unkn. date, and five more of unkn. names. Ruth m. 2 Aug. 1688, Ebenezer Thayer. In the will of 11 Aug. 1688, pro. 20 Feb. 1691, is provision for the four s. for w. Hannah, and for eleven ds. Abigail Scott, Hannah, w. of Nehemiah Hayden, Sarah Mansfield, Mary Thayer, Ruth Thayer, Deborah, Lydia, Rebecca, Rachel, Eliz. and Joanna ; but to the last six, perhaps ch. of the surv. w. only £50 ea. are giv. The boast on his gr.stone is, that he was f. of 21 ch. but far better is it thot. to provide for 15. HENRY, Braintree, s. of the preced. m. it is said, 14 Feb. 1666, Hannah Pray ; and nothing more is told, but that he d. 26 July 1717. JEREMIAH, Easthampton, L. I. 1649. JEREMIAH, Salem, s. of the first John of the same, m. 15 June 1668, Sarah Hart, had John, b. 16 Apr. 1669 ; Mary, 11 May 1670; and Sarah, 1 Nov. 1671 ; and his w. d. 28 Sept. 1672. He m. next, Mary, d. of Robert Buffum, had Jeremiah, 25 Sept. 1674 ; Abigail ; Lydia ; Robert ; Deborah ; and Hannah, by her ; and m. next, 31 Oct. 1707, Dorothy Lord ; was lieut. and d. July 1722. His wid. d. bef. May 1735. JOHN, Salem, freem. 18 May 1642, but Felt does not incl. his name with ch. memb. wh. may be conjectural. expl. by guess, that he had unit. with some other ch. bef. going thither ; yet he had bapt. there, John, 22 May 1642 ; John, again, 24 Mar. 1644 ; Jeremiah, 18 Jan. 1646 ; Lydia, 7 Apr. 1650 ; Jonathan, 15 Aug. 1652 ; Mary, b. 14 Mar. bapt. 29 Apr. 1655 ; and John, again, bapt. 24 June 1658, tho. we may be confident that he was b. several yrs. bef. and I should prefer to make his day of bapt. 24 Jan. 1647 ; beside Sarah, wh. d. 22 July 1658, perhaps quite young ; and Joseph, b. as the fam. tradit. goes, 1663, and d. 12 May 1672. As Mary is among ch. memb. 1647, I presume she was his w. only ch. of Francis Lawes, and she m. next, Andrew Mansfield. JOHN, Salem, s. of the preced. m. Ann Nichols, had John, b. 15 Apr. 1673 ; Thomas, 14 Feb. 1675; Joseph, 4 Dec. 1677 ; and Rebecca, 23 Feb. 1679 ; and he d. 11 Nov. foll. His wid. m. William Sterling of Haverhill. JOSEPH, Salem, br. of the preced. m. Judith, d. of Richard Croad of the same, had Judith, b. 1682, d. at 16 yrs. ; Joseph, 1690 ; Lydia ; and Hannah. His w. d. bef. 1689, and he rem. to Pennsylv. JOSEPH, Braintree, s. of the first Henry, by w. Mary had Mary, b. 4 Sept. 1689 ; Hannah, 6 Dec. 1691 ; and Eliz. 12 May 1695 ; and he d. 23 Dec. 1737. His wid. d. 18 Apr. 1747, aged

83 yrs. SAMUEL, a soldier on Conn. riv. under capt. Turner in 1676, was from Braintree, s. of Henry, m. 18 Apr. 1678, Abigail, d. of James Penniman, and, perhaps liv. in New Hampsh. in 1690, pray. for jurisdict. of Mass. WALTER, Portsmouth, came early in 1630, by the Warwick, as Gov. of the planta. of Gorges and Mason, went home in Aug. 1633, sail. from Boston 13th of that mo. aft. being above ten days there. Both his coming and going, therefore, from this shore, is to a sober man satisfact. proof of the falsity of the gr. Ind. deed to Wheelwright of 17 May 1629, seven yrs. bef. the grantee came, and one yr. bef. this witness arr. Much stronger, even, is the evid. of forgery of a letter, pretend. to be of Neal and Wiggin, to the patentee John Mason, 13 Aug. 1633, wh. was, by the managers of the fraud, intend. for a buttress of the splendid grant. That letter purports to be writ. at Northam, wh. was the complimenta. name some yrs. later, for Dover, on the Piscataqua, when we kn. from p. 107 of Vol. I. of the Hist. by Gov. Winth. that on that same day Neal was at Boston, and had been above a week, with a comp. of eight friends, to embark in the Elizabeth Bonadventure, that sail. for Eng. on 15 of that month; and from p. 115 of the same Vol. that Wiggin was in London on the date of that forgery of the preposter. letter, embarking at Gravesend for Salem, the very day that Neal left Boston for Eng. In the assiduity of Farmer no further acco. is reach. but he thinks WALTER of N. H. 1660, who by w. Mary had Samuel, b. 14 June 1661, and was in 1673, lieut. in the comp. of wh. James Pendleton was capt. might have been his s. He join. most of his neighb. in desir. jurisdict. of Mass. 1690.

NEAVE, MARGARET, Salem, came from Yarmouth, in Co. Norf'k 1637, a wid. aged 58, with gr.ch. Rachel Dickson, in the Mary Ann, and ten yrs. aft. join. the ch.

NEEDHAM, ANTHONY, Salem, with w. Ann, only ch. of Humphrey Potter, charg. as Quakers 1658, he then 30 yrs. old, and the w. aft. being oft. fined for abs. from publ. worsh. in vain, was in June 1660, sentenc. to be whip. twelve stripes. Yet these perverse worshippers have no small claims on our kind regard, at least for their long contin. lives, both acting in 1696, and he in 1705, beside good success in rear. ch. for we see by deed of 1 Jan. 1730, that Anthony, Isaac, Thomas, Rebecca, Hannah, Eliz. Mary, Abigail, and Rachel should enjoy the est. of their mo. DANIEL, Lynn, perhaps s. of Edmund, m. 24 Feb. 1659 (Lewis strange. says 1673) Ruth Chadwell, had Daniel, b. 19 Feb. 1665; Judith, 24 June 1667; Ezekiel, 13 May 1670; Mary, 28 Nov. 1672; Eliz. 1 Feb. 1675; Edmund, 17 Sept. 1677; Daniel and Ruth, tw. 23 Feb. 1680, of wh. Ruth d. at 2 mos.; was freem. 1691. EDMUND, Lynn 1639, one of the grantees of Southampton next yr. but prob. went not there, d. at L. 16 May 1677. Perhaps his w. Joan d. 24 Oct. 1674, aged a. 65. EZEKIEL, Lynn, perhaps s. of the preced. m. 27 Oct. 1669, Sarah, d. of Daniel King, had Edmund, b. 2 Aug. 1670; one in Apr. 1673, d. soon; Sarah, 27 May 1674; Ezekiel, Dec. 1676, d. soon; Ezekiel, again, 17 Nov. 1677; Daniel, 15 Mar. 1680; and Ralph, 26 Aug. 1682. JOHN, Boston, by w. Eliz. d. of Zechariah Hicks, m. 10 Oct. 1679, wh. d. 4 Feb. 1691, and was bur. at Cambridge, had Eliz. b. 23 Nov. 1680; Margaret, 8 Nov. 1683; Zechariah, 1 Oct. 1685; Mehitable, 17 Dec. 1687; and by sec. w. Keziah, had John, 22 Dec. 1692; and, perhaps, others. Ano. JOHN of Boston, left s. William and John, to be rememb. by-a kinsman to wh. he was indebt. when he d. 1690. NATHANIEL, Lynn, perhaps s. of Edmund, had Ruth, b. 22 Aug. 1682. NICHOLAS, Exeter 1638, one of the 35 who form. the orig. compact there, was a witness to the *true* deed from Ind. sachems, made to Wheelwright and others, not the *spurious* one, bearing date 7 or 8 yrs. bef. W. came from Eng.; was liv. in 1652. WILLIAM, Braintree, may have been of Newport 1638, and came aft. to Mass. freem. 1648, rem. I think, to Boston, had prob. no w. or ch. for in his will of 10 June 1690, he freely gives one third of his est. to Old South ch. opposite to wh. was his resid. and two thirds to William, and John, s. of his kinsman John N. late of Boston, dec. and he minutely disposes of his furnit. and d. 30 Dec. aft.

NEFF, WILLIAM, Newbury, rem. to Haverhill, m. 23 Jan. 1665, Mary, d. of George Corless, d. on serv. at Pemaquid, as a soldier, Feb. 1689, aged 47. His wid. was tak. by the Ind. in the assault on H. 15 Mar. 1697, and carried towards Canada, in co. with the celebr. Mrs. Duston, in whose remarka. rescue she particip. and d. 22 Oct. 1722. See Mirick, Hist. of H. 87, and Magn. VII. art. 25.

NEGUS, NEGOS, or NEGOOS, BENJAMIN, Boston, shopkeeper, by w. Eliz. had Eliz. b. 14 Apr. 1640; Benjamin, Sept. 1641; both bapt. 11 June 1643; Mary, 1, bapt. 8 Oct. 1643; Samuel, 17 Dec. 1645, bapt. 4 Jan. foll.; and Hannah, 2 Oct. 1653; was freem. 1648. Eliz. m. 2 Mar. 1659, Richard Barnard. ISAAC, Taunton 1675, cooper, styles hims. sole heir of Jonathan N. late of Boston, m. 7 Apr. 1679, Hannah Andrews. JABEZ, Boston 1673, carpenter, was freem. 1691. JONATHAN, Boston 1634, is said to have been at Lynn 1630, freem. 3 Sept. 1634, by w. Jane had Mary, b. 6 July 1653, wh. prob. d. young. He was clk. of the writs 1651, and sev. yrs. aft. and seems to have been faithful in mak. returns of bs. ds. and ms. as the law requir. and much must we lament that the county recorder did not scrupulously compare these transcripts from the several rec. of the respective towns in his jurisdict. wh. have long been universal. lost; or that the first copies in most instances are lost, so that an inquirer is compel. to rely on a copy of a copy. Negus had est. at Muddy riv. and his sis. Grace m. Barnabas Fawer.

NEIGHBORS, or NABORS, JAMES, Boston, cooper, by w. Lettice had Rebecca, b. 30 Mar. 1657, but she prob. d. young, for in his will of 27 Jan. pro. 19 June at B. on acco. of est. here 1672, he gave est. to five elder ds. Mary, w. of Daniel Matthews; Sarah Johnson; Eliz. w. of William Wills in Carolina; Rachel, w. of Peter Codner; and Martha, wh. he calls youngest, who soon bec. w. of John Hunt; and to a gr.d. Mercy. He liv. sev. yrs. at Huntington, L. I. and d. there. Robert Gibbs had in Court recov. large damages against him in Aug. 1661.

NELSON, FRANCIS, Rowley, s. of the sec. Thomas, m. Mary Ray, had Solomon, b. 1703; Daniel, 1707; and Jonathan, 1713. Gage's Hist. of Rowley. JOHN, Middleborough, perhaps s. of William, m. Lydia, wid. of James Barnaby, d. of Robert Bartlett of Plymouth. But she was, I judge, his sec. w. and that he first m. 28 Nov. 1667, Sarah, d. of Henry Wood, wh. d. 4 Mar. 1676, hav. had John, wh. d. 5 June 1676; and Martha, wh. d. 19 Feb. preced. ‖ JOHN, Boston, a relat. of Sir Thomas Temple, ar. co. 1680, capt. of the same, one of the chief actors in the revo. against Andros, 1689, tak. by Fr. and Ind. long impris. at Quebec and in France. Hutch. I. 376-80. He d. prob. 4 Dec. 1721. In right of his w. Eliz. was heir and excor. with others, of lieut.-gov. Stoughton. He was s. of William, to wh. Sir Thomas, wh. he calls his uncle, had made lease of his patent rights in Nova Scotia. See a very valua. letter from Paris, while he was a prisoner, 1698, in 3 Mass. Hist. Coll. I. 196. MATTHEW, Portsmouth 1684, had w. Jane, in 1690 solicit. for jurisdict. of Mass. PHILIP, Rowley, eldest s. of Thomas, came with his f. 1638, H. C. 1654, m. 24 June 1657, Sarah, d. of the first Joseph Jewett, had Philip, b. 1659, and one d.; was freem. 1665; and by sec. w. Eliz. d. of John Lowell of Newbury, m. 1 Jan. 1667, had John, 1668; and by third w. Mary, wid. of John Hobson, had, perhaps, Joseph, 1682; and Jeremiah, 1686, beside four ds. Coffin, wh. says he d. 20 Aug. 1691, tells a sad story a. his delusion as to power of working miracles, that Farmer abstract. but I prefer to omit. PHILIP, Rowley 1691, s. of the preced. * THOMAS, Rowley 1638, prob. arr. that yr. freem. 23 May 1639, rep. 1641; brot. from Eng. Philip, and Thomas, and by w. Joanna had Mercy, and Samuel, went home in 1647 or 8, as we learn from his will, made in contemplat. of the voyage so early as 24 Dec. 1645, with codic. made in Eng. designing to return hither, 6 Aug. 1648, wherein his uncle, Rich. Dummer and Gov. Bellingham have trusts as excors. and also care of the ch. Abst. is in the Geneal. Reg. III. 267. I suppose he d. bef. coming back. THOMAS, Rowley, s. of the preced. m. Ann, d. of Francis Lambert, had Thomas, b. 1661;

Jonathan, 1667; Gershom, 1672; and Francis, 1676; beside three ds.; and by sec. w. Mary Hunt, had Ephraim, 1682; and d. 5 Apr. 1712, in his 77th yr. WILLIAM, Plymouth, m. 27 Oct. 1640, Martha Ford, d. of the wid. passeng. in the Fortune 1621; one of the purch. in 1662 of Middleborough, had, perhaps, John, b. 8 June 1647; Jane, or Joan, 28 Feb. 1651. In 1668 the wife of a William of Plymouth was Martha. His d. Jane m. 13 Dec. 1672, Thomas Faunce. Seventeen of this name had, in 1834, been gr. at the N. E. coll. of wh. three only at Harv.

NEST, JOSEPH, New London 1678, had w. Sarah, wh. d. bef. him, and d. Susanna, wh. m. George Way. He d. 8 Dec. 1711.

NETHERLAND, WILLIAM, in the list of freem. 4 Mar. 1635, and of the jury of inq. on Peter Fitchew's body, found drown. 18 May 1639, I judge must be that Lytherland, a well kn. memb. of Boston ch. See that name.

NETTLETON, JOHN, Killingworth 1663, propound. to be made free, 1670, may have been s. of Samuel, and liv. at Milford 1713. SAMUEL, Milford in 1639 or soon aft. had Hannah, wh. m. 10 July 1656, Thomas Smith; Martha, wh. m. 1656, John Ufford; and, perhaps, other ch.; was propr. there 1713, unless ano. Samuel, were the man, as seems to me almost cert.

NEVERS, RICHARD, Woburn, by w. Martha had Samuel, b. 16 Dec. 1689; Mary, 9 July 1694; and Martha, 20 July 1698.

NEVINSON, JOHN, Watertown 1670, came a. 2 yrs. bef. from East Horsley, in Co. Surry, s. of Rev. Roger, by w. Eliz. m. prob. in Eng. had John; Sarah, b. 22 July 1672; Eliz. 22 Oct. 1675; Ann, 2 Oct. 1678; William, 26 June 1681; and Mary, wh. was the oldest ch. b. in Eng.; and d. 24 Jan. 1695. Soon aft. the wid. m. William Bond. Both s. d. unm. the elder on 23 Feb. 1692; the younger in 1711; and so the name fail. Sarah m. 29 Oct. 1713, Nathaniel Stearns, and next, Samuel Livermore; Eliz. m. 24 Apr. 1694, Samuel Hastings; Ann m. 30 Aug. 1716, Joshua Grant; and Mary m. Samuel Hastings soon aft. early d. of her sis. his first w.

NEWBERRY, ‡* BENJAMIN, Windsor, s. of Thomas of Dorchester, b. in Eng. m. 11 June 1646, Mary, only d. of Matthew Allyn, had Mary, b. 10 Mar. 1648; Sarah, 15 June 1650; Hannah, 22 Dec. 1652, d. at 11 yrs.; Rebecca, 2 May 1655; Thomas, 1 Sept. 1657; Abigail, 14 May 1659; Margaret, 23 Oct. 1662; Benjamin, 20 Apr. 1669; Hannah, again, 1 July 1673; and he d. 11 Sept. 1689; his w. d. 29 July preced. tho. Stiles, 720, makes it 14 Dec. 1703. An idle tradit. reports that he m. Abigail, wid. of Rev. John Warham, and had two ds. He was rep. at 22 sess. and an Assist. 1685, a capt. in the war with k. Philip, and memb. of the Council of war. His eldest d. m. 10 Dec. 1664, John Maudsley, as Stiles correct. says, 703, yet 721, under Newberry, calls him Marshall; Sarah m. 4 June 1668, Preserved Clap; Abigail m. 8 Jan. 1684, Ephraim Howard; Margaret m. 23 May 1689, Return Strong; and Hannah m. 17 Dec. 1703, John Wolcott. BENJAMIN, Windsor, youngest s. of the preced. m. 3 Mar. 1690, Hannah, d. of Thomas Dewey of Westfield, had Benjamin, b. 31 Jan. 1692; Roger, 4 June 1706; Marah, 3 Feb. 1710; and the f. d. 3 Nov. foll. JOHN, Windsor, an early sett. prob. rem. or d. bef. mid. age, was br. of the preced. JOSEPH, Windsor, br. of the preced. d. early or rem. perhaps; but one of the s. of his f. was call. prob. to go home to look aft. prop. of the testator. RICHARD, Weymouth, freem. 1645, by w. Sarah had Tryal, Joseph, and Dorcas, beside Benjamin, b. 22 May 1660. In this yr. he purch. ld. at Malden, and rem. thither, made his imperfect will 20 Mar. 1685, and his inv. has date of 7 Apr. foll. Benjamin was prob. d. long bef. his f. as also was d. Martha, wh. d. May 1676. Of the three nam. in the will, Joseph was d. bef. 1702, when the wid. Sarah was liv. and Tryal, and Dorcas, wh. m. I think, Joseph Burrill, and she had been adminx. hav. by will of the f. most of his prop. but charg. to take care of her mo. * THOMAS, Dorchester, may have come in the Mary and John 1630, freem. 3 Sept. 1634, rep. 1635, was engag. to go with Warham and most of his cong. to plant Windsor, but d. bef. the migrat. by his will of 1 Dec. 1635, of wh. abstr. is in Geneal. Reg. VII. 29, leav. large prop. of wh. £200 to w. Jane, beside what she brot. at m. and residue equally to childr. exc. that the three youngest ds. should ea. have £50 less than the others. Instead of £50, as I had read some yrs. bef. Mr. Trask, who usually is a careful copier of the old writings, gives 50s. in that abstr. wh. might, in case of some petty estate, seem large enough. This may have affected his eyesight, as the fact of great prop. on my reëxamination, wh. led to conforming my first transcript, possib. may have influenced me to judge, that so rich a man would not make so poor a differ. betw. his ds. The inv. tak. 28 Jan. foll. (includ. ld. in Eng. at £300) was of £1520, 4, 7. Sarah m. 8 Nov. 1640, Henry Wolcott; Mary m. 13 June 1644, Daniel Clarke; Rebecca was sec. w. of Rev. John Russell of Hadley; and Hannah m. Rev. Thomas Hanford, and d. early. THOMAS, Windsor, perhaps s. of the preced. d. 12 June 1644. THOMAS, Dover 1671. THOMAS, Windsor, s. of Benjamin, m. 12 Mar. 1677 (but Stiles says, 12 May 1676) Ann Ford, perhaps d. of Thomas, had Thomas, b. 20 Jan. 1678; Hannah, 10 Feb. 1680; Thomas, again, 22 Mar. 1683; Joseph, 24 Oct. 1684; and Benjamin, 18 Feb. 1687; and d. 20 (30, acc. Stiles) Apr. 1688. TRYAL, Malden, s. prob. eldest, of Richard, was a soldier in Turner's comp.

1676, at Hadley, and in the Falls fight, by w. Priscilla had Nathaniel; John, b. 28 Mar. 1686; Mehitable, 7 Sept. 1688; and Mary, 13 Mar. 1690; in wh. yr. he was made freem. and he d. 9 Dec. 1705. Nathaniel had admin. of the est. ‡ WALTER, Newport, m. 13 Apr. 1675, Ann Collins of London, had Sankey, b. 19 Jan. 1676, prob. d. young; Samuel, 3 Mar. 1677; Sarah, 4 Sept. 1680; Walter, 21 Dec. 1682; Sankey, again, 29 June 1684; Eliz. and Martha, tw. 16 Nov. 1686, of wh. the latter prob. d. soon; Martha, again, 7 Jan. 1689; and Mary, Feb. 1691; one of the Counc. 1687 to Sir E. Andros. Hutch. I. 354. Prob. he was not an oppressor.

NEWBY, GEORGE, Boston, by w. Mary had John, b. 25 Dec. 1680. I think he had sec. w. Eliz. WILLIAM, a passeng. in the Mary and John from London 1634, wh. took the o. of supremacy and alleg. 16 Apr. 1634, bound for N. E. but where he pitched his tent first or last, is unkn.

NEWCOMB, or NEWCOME, ANDREW, Boston, mariner, m. Grace, wid. of William Rix, had Grace, b. 20 Oct. 1664. By his will of 31 Jan. 1683, pro. 8 Dec. 1686, his w. and d. Grace Butler and gr.ch. Newcomb Blake were cared for. FRANCIS, Boston 1635, came in the Planter, aged 30, that yr. with w. Rachel, 20, and two ch. Rachel, $2\frac{1}{2}$ yrs. and John, 9 mos.; liv. aft. at Braintree, and d. 27 May 1692, "upwards of 100 yrs. old," as was fondly told, tho. the gr.st. more moderate in its exaggera. says aged 100 yrs. but prob. only 87; had Hannah, bapt. 15 Oct. 1637; Mary, b. 31 Mar. 1640; Sarah, 24 May 1643; Judith, 16 Jan. 1646; Peter, 16 May 1648; Abigail, 16 July 1651; Leah, 30 July 1654; and Eliz. 26 Aug. 1658, when the folly of tradit. would make her mo. over 66 yrs. old. Mary m. 10 Nov. 1657, Samuel Dearing. PETER, Braintree, s. of the preced. m. 2 June 1672, Susanna, d. of Richard Cutting. Four of this name had, in 1834, been gr. at Harv. and as many at other N. E. coll.

NEWCOMEN, ELIAS, Isle of Shoals, constable in 1650. JOHN, Plymouth, a youth waylaid and k. by John Billington, for wh. he was execut. Oct. 1630.

NEWELL, ABRAHAM, Roxbury, came in the Francis, 1634, aged 50, from Ipswich, says the custom-ho. rec. with w. Frances, 40, and ch. Faith, who in the rec. of the ch. is nam. Ruth, 14; Grace, 13; Abraham, 8; John, 5; Isaac, 2; and Jacob, b. on the passage; freem. 4 Mar. 1635, d. 13, bur. 15 June 1672, aged, says the rec. of ch. 91; and his wid. Frances d. 13 Jan. 1683, aged 100, says the rec. of the town, with greater exaggera. Ruth m. a Bennett, for whose ch. John, the gr.f. liberal. provid.; Grace m. 14 Sept. 1644, William Tay of Boston, and d. 11 Apr. 1712, aged 91, as the town rec. says correct. ABRAHAM,

Roxbury, s. of the preced. brot. from Eng. by his f. freem. 1653, by a w. whose name is not found, nor date of her d. had Joseph, b. 30 Oct. 1651, d. in six wks. if the town rec. of d. and b. be good ; and he m. 8 Feb. 1652, Susanna, d. of Robert Rand of Charlestown, had Abraham, b. 30 Mar. 1654; Susanna, 30 Mar. bapt. 6 Apr. 1656 ; Joseph, bapt. 25 July 1658; Mary, 10, bapt. 14 Apr. 1661 ; Thomas, 24 June, bapt. 19 July 1663, d. at 11 yrs. ; Eliz. bapt. 12 Aug. 1666 ; Rebecca, b. 15 July 1667 ; Ruth, 28 Feb. 1669, but in careless rec. of town b. 29th ; John, 6, bapt. 9 June 1672 ; Robert, 2, bapt. 7 June 1674; and d. 17 Aug. 1692. Susanna m. 6 Sept. 1673, Thomas Morey. ABRAHAM, Roxbury, s. of the preced. m. 21 July 1681, Abigail Rhoades, had Abigail, wh. d. 3 Apr. 1682 ; Eliz. b. 14 Mar. 1683, and d. in 6 days; and his w. d. 12 May 1686. He d. 9 Oct. 1726. ANDREW, Charlestown, a merch. from Bristol, whose wid. d. 26 Sept. 1684, in her 78th yr. says the gr.st. EBENEZER, Roxbury, s. of the first Isaac, by w. Mary had Experience, wh. d. Dec. 1706; Nathaniel, b. 24 June 1707 ; Eliz. 11 Sept. 1709 ; Ebenezer, 28 Nov. 1711; and d. 16 Oct. 1746. ISAAC, Roxbury, brot. by his f. Abraham from Eng.; by w. Eliz. d. of William Curtis, m. 14 Dec. 1658, tho. the rec. then calls him John, I think, had Isaac, b. 11 Dec. 1660; Josiah, 1, bapt. 7 Dec. 1662, d. at 16 yrs. ; Sarah, 22, bapt. 26 Mar. 1665; Abraham, 28 Feb. bapt. 3 Mar. 1667, d. at 11 yrs. ; Eliz. 6, bapt. 24 Jan. 1669 ; Hannah, 4, bapt. 19 Feb. 1671 ; Ebenezer, 29 Nov. 1673, bapt. 1 Feb. foll. ; Experience, 29 Jan. 1678 ; and Josiah, again, 6, bapt. 14 Mar. 1680. The f. d. 8 Dec. 1707. Hannah m. 9 Apr. 1690, John Holmes ; and the same rec. says her sis. Eliz. was m. the same day, but it does not give the import. informat. of the name of the h. ; and Experience m. 23 May 1700, Samuel Willis. ISAAC, Roxbury, s. prob. of the preced. by w. Sarah had Isaac, b. 1 Feb. 1688 ; Philip, 26 Mar. 1693; Mehitable, 2 Apr. 1695 ; Abigail, 15 Nov. 1697, d. soon ; Jonathan, 10 Oct. 1701. JACOB, Roxbury, s. of the first Abraham, b. on the voyage, m. 3 Nov. 1657, Martha, d. of John Gibson of Cambridge, had Jacob, b. 23 Oct. 1658; Martha, 15 May 1661, both bapt. 12 Apr. 1663 ; Rebecca, 14 Apr. bapt. 31 May 1663 ; Mary, by town rec. 30 May, bapt. as Mercy, 2 July 1665 ; Samuel, bapt. 4 Aug. 1667; Faith, 14 Oct. bapt. 5 Dec. 1669 ; Mary, bapt. 18 Aug. 1672 ; and Grace, b. 8 Aug. bapt. 20 Sept. 1674; and he was bur. 30 Dec. 1678. Rebecca m. 24 May 1686, William Cheney. JACOB, Roxbury, s. of the preced. freem. 1690, m. 23 May 1700, Joyce, d. of Joseph Gleason of Sudbury, had Thankful, b. 1 Sept. 1702 ; Jacob, 5 June 1704; Joseph, 19 Jan. 1708; and Elisha, 21 Mar. 1713. JOHN, Roxbury, s. of the first Abraham, who came 1634, with his f. d. 1673, perhaps unm. JOHN, Charlestown, m. 15 Feb. 1665, Hannah, d. of John

Larkin, and d. 14 Oct. 1704, in 71st yr. His wid. Hannah d. 10 Dec. foll. aged 62. JOHN, Roxbury, freem. 1690, was prob. s. of the sec. Abraham. JOHN, Charlestown, prob. s. of John of the same, d. 7 Apr. 1747, in 83d yr. says the gr.st. by w. Hannah had Hannah, bapt. 23 Dec. 1688; Andrew, 20 Mar. 1692; Ann, 27 Aug. 1693; William, 7 Oct. 1694; Edward, 30 Oct. 1698; Abigail, 18 Apr. 1702; Eliphalet, 11 Feb. 1705; and Abigail, 25 Jan. 1708. JOSEPH, Charlestown, had w. Hannah, who unit. with the ch. 26 June 1681, and, perhaps, ano. w. Margaret, who d. 7 Dec. 1689, in her 23d yr. and he by w. Eliz. had Thomas, bapt. 20 Aug. 1699; Andrew, 1 Mar. 1702; and David, 10 Sept. 1704; and he d. 25 Apr. 1709, aged a. 58. Ano. JOSEPH, Charlestown, by w. Sarah, d. of John Tuttle, had Mary, wh. d. young, 2 May 1683; Joseph, bapt. 4 Mar. 1688; John, 30 June 1689, d. soon; and John, again, 31 Jan. 1692; and the mo. d. 1 Feb. 1719, aged 63. ROBERT, Roxbury, s. of the sec. Abraham, m. 29 Dec. 1704, Mehitable Jones, but has no ch. on town rec. down to 1721; yet from the inscript. on gr.st. Geneal. Reg. VII. 331, we learn that his w. d. 4 Nov. 1739, aged a. 70 yrs. and he d. 17 Feb. 1741, in 68th yr. SAMUEL, Farmington, s. of Thomas, had Samuel, bapt. 19 June 1687; Thomas, 2 Mar. 1690; John, 29 Jan. 1693. SAMUEL, Roxbury, s. of the first Jacob, was engag. in the sad expedit. of Sir William Phips against Quebec, shipwreck. on return. from the abortive serv. in the lower part of the St. Lawrence, tak. prison. by the Ind. and kept one yr. got among the Christian enemy, and was near five yrs. abs. from home; by w. Mary had Mary, b. 30 Sept. 1697; Martha, 29 Apr. 1699; Mercy, 16 Sept. 1700; Samuel, 10 Dec. 1702; Sarah, 8 May 1705; and Eunice, 18 Sept. 1707. THOMAS, Farmington 1652, m. Rebecca Olmstead, sis. of John and Richard O. had nine ch. to partake div. of his est. 1689, Rebecca Woodford, then aged 46; Mary, w. of Thomas Bascom of Northampton, 44; John, 42; Thomas, 39; Esther Stanley, 37; Sarah Smith, 34, wh. was bapt. 18 Feb. 1655; Hannah North, 31, bapt. 11 Apr. 1658; Samuel, bapt. 5 Dec. 1660; and Joseph, 20 Apr. 1664, wh. d. bef. Nov. 1689, but aft. the yr. came in. THOMAS, Waterbury, s. of the preced. m. 5 Nov. 1679, Eliz. d. of Simon Wrotham; had Thomas, bapt. 14 May 1682, when his w. join. the ch.; Simon, 24 June 1683; Susanna, 24 Apr. 1687; Joseph, 2 June 1689; and Eliz. 31 Dec. 1693; in 1686 was one of the petitnrs. for estab. that plantâ. call. Matatock. Seven of this name had been gr. in 1834 at Harv. and twelve at Yale.

NEWGATE, or NEWDIGATE, * JOHN, Boston 1632, merch. b. 1580, in Southwark, near London bridge, brot. w. Ann with childr. b. in Eng. here had Hannah, b. 1, bapt. 6 Aug. 1633, d. at 5 mos.; Hannah, again, bapt. 19 July 1635, tho. blunder in town rec. makes her b. 1 Aug. aft.; was freem. 4 Mar. 1635, constable, rep. 1638, oft. a selectman, d. 1665.

Of his ch. we can hardly speak with certainty. Prob. Joshua, wh. d. 12 Nov. 1658, at Boston, was the oldest, and h. of that Eliz. N. call. on adm. to our ch. 30 Mar. 1634, "d.-in-law to our sis. Ann N." Eliz. prob. the eldest d. m. John Oliver, and aft. his d. m. 14 Mar. 1649, Edward Jackson; Sarah, ano. d. m. Peter Oliver, br. of the h. of her sis. and d. Oct. 1692; Nathaniel, b. a. 1627; and Hannah, the youngest, m. 22 Feb. 1653, Simon Lynde, was nam. in the will of her mo. 6 Aug. 1676, pro. 8 Apr. 1679; but her gr.ch. Eliz. and Nathaniel Lynde, and Nathaniel N. of London are ment. His will, of 25 Nov. 1664, with codic. of 8 May foll. is in Geneal. Reg. XIII. 333. NATHANIEL, Boston, s. of the preced. b. in Eng. ar. co. 1646, went home, prob. bef. m. there had Nathaniel, a merch. in London, by his w. Isabel, wh. surv. him, and in 1671, was w. of John Johnson of London. Farmer says some of the descend. write the name Newdigate, as was here done occasionally.

NEWGROVE, JOHN, Dover 1648.

NEWHALL, ANTHONY, oft. confus. with Newell, Lynn 1636, some time of Salem, d. 31 Jan. 1657, had John, and, perhaps, other childr. for his will of 14 Jan. pro. 31 Mar. 1657, ment. gr.ch. Richard and Eliz. Hood. JOHN, Lynn, s. of Anthony, m. 31 Dec. 1656, Eliz. Normanton, had, perhaps, issue, but ano. JOHN, of Lynn, m. 3 Feb. 1657, Eliz. Payton, wh. d. 22 Oct. 1677, had Nathaniel, b. 3 Apr. 1658; Sarah, 22 Aug. 1662; John, 11 Oct. 1664, perhaps d. young; Rebecca, 6 Dec. 1670; Mary, 27 Sept. 1673; Priscilla, 24 Nov. 1676; and a ch. 9 Oct. 1677, d. same day; and by ano. w. it is said, had Hannah, 6 Mar. 1680; and John, again, 13 Oct. 1681, d. in 3 wks. so that one is daunted at the proximity of the two Johns and Eliz. Sarah m. 3 Mar. 1680, Timothy Breed. A third JOHN, of Lynn, m. 18 June 1677, Esther, d. of William Bartram, had Eliz. b. 12 May 1678; Sarah, 15 Feb. 1680, d. in few days; Jonathan, 25 Dec. 1681; Sarah, again, 23 Jan. 1683; and Jeremiah, 12 Feb. 1685. One of these Johns was freem. 1684, and two in 1691, of wh. one is mark. sen. and the other ens. But Lewis provides for a JOHN, of Lynn, much earlier, s. of Thomas, b. in Eng. to m. 10 Apr. 1646, Sarah Lewis. Some doubt rises in my mind bec. I kn. not whose d. she was or could be. JOSEPH, Lynn, freem. 1690, had Jemima, b. Dec. 1678; and Thomas, 16 Jan. 1681. He was, perhaps, s. of the first Thomas, and may be that Joseph who perish. in the gr. snow storm 29 and 30 Jan. 1705. Jemima m. Benjamin Very of Salem. NATHANIEL, Lynn, s. of Thomas, is prob. the freem. of 1691, call. junr. but NATHANIEL, s. of John, is prob. that freem. 1691, call. sen. THOMAS, Lynn 1630, Mr. Lewis thinks, brot. John, had Thomas, the first Eng. ch. b. in that town. His w. d. 25 Sept. 1665, and he d. 25

May 1674. His will, of 1 Apr. 1668, pro. 1 July 1674, names two s. John, and Thomas, ds. Susanna, w. of Richard Haven, and her five ch. Joseph, Richard, Sarah, Nathaniel, and Moses ; and Mary, w. of Thomas Brown, and her ch. not nam. them. THOMAS, Lynn, s. of the preced. m. says Lewis, 29 Sept. 1652, Eliz. d. of Robert Potter, had Joseph, b. 22 Sept. 1658; Nathaniel, 17 Mar. 1660 ; Eliz. 21 Mar. 1662, d. at 3 yrs.; Elisha, 3 Nov. 1665; Eliz. again, 22 Oct. 1667 ; Mary, 18 Feb. 1670 ; Samuel, 19 Nov. 1672 ; and Rebecca, 17 July 1675 ; and he was bur. 1 Apr. 1687, in 57th yr. More descend. remain of this than any other fam. in the town. THOMAS, Malden, by w. Rebecca, wh. d. 26 May 1725, had Lydia, b. 17 Apr. 1687 ; Samuel, 26 Apr. 1689 ; and he d. 13 July 1728.

NEWLAND, ANTHONY, Salisbury 1650, soon rem. prob. for the name is not aft. seen there, and may be the foll. ANTHONY, Taunton, s. of Jeremiah, m. 16 Dec. 1682, Esther Austin. HENRY, Taunton 1666. JEREMIAH, Taunton, had Anthony, b. 1 Aug. 1657. JOHN, Sandwich 1643, perhaps s. of William. * WILLIAM, Sandwich, had rem. thither from Lynn 1637, was freem. of the Col. 1641, rep. 1642, 3, and 4, but 3 Oct. 1659 disfranch. for abetting Quakers ; m. 19 May 1648, Rose Holloway, had Mary, b. 16 Apr. 1649 ; John ; and Mercy, wh. m. an Edwards, and had admin. of the est. of her f. 26 June 1694. One William is enumerat. among the soldiers of Gallup's comp. in the sad expedit. of Phips against Quebec, 1690, in Geneal. Reg. IX. 354, but the more correct roll in XIII. has it not.

NEWMAN, ANTIPAS, Wenham, s. of Rev. Samuel, b. prob. in Eng. began to pr. 1657, but was not ord. until Dec. 1663, m. 1658, Eliz. d. of the younger Gov. John Winth. had John, b. 7 Dec. 1660 ; Samuel, 7 Sept. 1666 ; Eliz. 15 June 1668 ; Sybel, 10 Mar. 1670 ; and Waitstill, 13 Dec. 1671 ; and d. 15 Oct. 1672. He was one of those min. who sustain. the erection of Boston 3d ch. by separat. from the first, for the deception practis. in obtain. Davenport from New Haven. Hutch. I. 273. The wid. m. Zerubbabel Endicott ; and Sybel m. John Edwards of Boston. BENJAMIN, Ipswich 1678, s. of Thomas. DANIEL, Stamford 1670. § ‡ FRANCIS, New Haven 1638, an Assist. 1653 and aft. until made Gov. 1658, to his d. 18 Nov. 1660. He also serv. in the import. place of Commr. of the Unit. Col. 1654 and 8, and in the troublesome relations with the Dutch of New Netherlands. In his barn was form. the compact, June 1639, or civil const. by wh. the Col. many yrs. was ruled. His wid. m. says Emery, Rev. Nicholas Street, yet we are ign. who was her f. or what was her name. Of ch. I find only Eliz. wh. m. Thomas Knowles, and next, Nicholas Knell. JOHN, perhaps br. of Thomas, came in the Mary and John, 1634, but at what place he sett. is unkn.

yet conject. favors Ipswich ; but he was of Wenham 1690. JOHN, Ipswich 1648, s. of Thomas, b. in Eng. had come 1634, with his f. in the Mary and John, and may be the same as the preced. JOHN, Gloucester, s. of Antipas, a physician, m. Ruth, eldest d. of Rev. John Emerson, had issue, but details are unkn. JOHN, a serj. in capt. Turner's comp. 1676, station. at Hadley, must have come from the E. and prob. from Ipswich, at least, a John N. junr. was there 1679, owning commons. JOHN, Oyster Bay, L. I. 1685, may have been a propr. at New Haven 1669, and again in 1685, possib. a s. of the Gov. *NOAH*, Rehoboth, s. of Rev. Samuel, wh. he succeed. m. 30 Dec. 1669, Joanna, d. of Rev. Henry Flint, had Sybel, b. 31 Mar. 1675, d. in few mos. ; beside Samuel, wh. was bur. 2 Oct. 1677 ; and Henry, H. C. 1687, librarian at the coll. and agent in Eng. for the Prov. of N. H. and d. 26 Apr. 1678, but Col. Rec. says, bur. 18. The wid. by her will of 7 Nov. 1678, pro. 24 Feb. 1680, gave her est. to Henry, but in case of his d. to childr. of her br. Rev. George Shove, who had m. Hopestill Newman, sis. of Noah. RICH-ARD, New Haven 1656, possib. a s. of the Gov. had Samuel, b. that yr. ; John ; Sarah ; both bapt. 1665, tho. the officer wh. kept that unsatisfact. rec. gives no day, nor mo. ; and Mercy, b. 7 Dec. 1665, bapt. prob. 28 Jan. foll. tho. the rec. names wrong day, we are sure ; may have been some time at Stamford, a. 1666, and was propr. at New Haven 1685. ROBERT, came in the Mary and John, 1634, to Boston, but in what part of Mass. he sett. is unkn. ; rem. to New Haven, in 1638 or 9, was a man of good est. one of the seven pillars at gather. of the ch. and a deac. ; had Bethia, bapt. 2 Oct. 1642 ; and Grace, prob. 25 Oct. (a wrong day being giv. in Geneal. Reg. IX. 361) 1646 ; went home bef. 1660, it is believed. *SAMUEL*, Rehoboth, b. at Banbury, Oxfordsh. bapt. 24 May 1602, s. of Richard, was matricul. of Trinity Coll. Oxford, 3 Mar. 1620 in his 17th yr. but on proceed. A. B. 17 Oct. of that yr. is titled in Wood's Fasti, I. 392, of St. Edmund Hall, had a very small benefice, 1625, at Midhope, part of the parish of Ecclesfield, in the W. Riding of Yorksh. to wh. his successor was presented ten yrs. aft. He came to N. E. perhaps in 1636, tho. Eliz. aged 24, who may have been his w. or sis. came in the James from London 1635 ; yet Mather, III. c. 15, who, in three whole folio pages of double column, by his multifarious nothingness, gives less than six lines of facts, makes him come in 1638, spend a yr. and a half at Dorchester, five yrs. at Weymouth, and nineteen at R. Dr. Harris did not find his name at Dorchester, but he was adm. freem. 13 Mar. 1639 (yet casual. as is plain, without prefix of respect), no doubt then of Weymouth, where his d. Hope was b. 29 Aug. or Nov. 1641, as we believe discordant rec. in Geneal. Reg. VIII. 348, or IX. 171 ; and, perhaps, other ch. Greatly does he deserve esteem for his serv. in framing the Concordance, said to have been writ. by light of burning pine knots. He suffer. more than his temper could bear, by the spreading of the antipædobapt. in his diocese, and d. 5 July 1663, aged 61; in the will of 18 Nov. 1661, names w. Sybel, s. Samuel, Antipas, Noah, to wh. he gave his libr. and d. Hopestill, or Hope, wh. m. 12 July 1664, Rev. John Shove, and d. 7 Mar. 1674. Patience, an elder d. m. 3 Oct. 1649, Nathaniel Sparhawk of Cambridge. For those who have not easy access to the Magn. Dr. Allen furnishes the wondrous story of Newman's predict. of the hour of his own d. with happy exactness, and Dr. Eliot, in his Biog. Dict. has fully vindica. Mather from the discredit that might be attach. to his page by this. Now to prove what Eliot tells of the acco. being sent to Eng. as well as spread thro. our country, no doubt (when the immortal author of the Magnalia was but few mos. old) we may look into the Diary of Samuel Pepys, and find the "good story of Mr. Newman" to be matter of conversat. in Jan. 1667–8, bef. our N. E. ecclesiast. hist. had filled his six yrs. See p. 354 of Lord Braybrook's Pepys, Vol. III. Ed. 4th.

* SAMUEL, Rehoboth, s. prob. the eldest, of the preced. b. perhaps, in Eng. m. 6 Dec. 1659, Bethia, d. of Francis Chickering of Dedham, had Samuel, b. 1662; Antipas, 29 Mar. 1673, d. in few mos.; and prob. other ch.; m. for sec. w. 2 May 1689, Hannah, d. of John Bunker, and for third w. aft. 1690, Theodosia, wid. of capt. Noah Wiswall, d. of John Jackson, was deac. and rep. for Swanzey 1692. THOMAS, Ipswich 1639, had come 1634, in the Mary and John, hav. tak. o. of supremacy and alleg. 16 Apr. d. 1676, leav. wid. wh. d. 19 Nov. 1679, and s. Thomas, John, and Benjamin. WILLIAM, Stamford 1665, may have rem. to Narragansett aft. 1669. Five of this name had, in 1834, been gr. at Harv. and two at other N. E. coll.

NEWMARCH, JOHN, Ipswich 1638, at Rowley perhaps 1643, and back to I. 1648; m. Martha, d. of Zaccheus Gould, had, as is learn. from his will of 14 Feb. 1696, pro. 26 Apr. 1697, John, Thomas, Zaccheus, Martha, wh. m. 1675, Samuel Balch, Phebe Pennywell, and Sarah Berry. It made w. Martha extrix. and nam. gr.ch. Thomas Gould, and Martha Balch, tho. it might be hard to find the gr.ch. Thomas Gould. JOHN, Kittery, H. C. 1690, wh. d. 1754, was, perhaps, a gr.s. and it may be that Joseph, H. C. 1728, wh. d. 1765, a couns. of N. H. in 1754, was s. of this min. Sometimes it is Newmarsh.

NEWPORT, RICHARD, Boston, by w. Ruth had Ruth, b. 27 Apr. 1668.

NEWTON, ANTHONY, Dorchester, of Braintree 1640, engag. 1652 in sett. of Lancaster, was freem. 1671. BRYAN, Jamaica, L. I. 1656. DANIEL, Marlborough, s. of Richard, had Daniel, Benjamin, Susanna, Isaac, Abraham, Mary, Samuel, Nathaniel, Lydia, and Mercy; and

d. 29 Nov. 1739. EDWARD, New Haven, took o. of fidel. 1645.
EZEKIEL, Milford, s. of Roger, was liv. 1700. GEORGE, Ipswich, a.
1676 or 7. HENRY, Newtown, L. I. 1655, perhaps s. or br. of Bryan
of the adj. town. JOHN, Dorchester, 1632, freem. 4 Mar. 1633, rem. to
Dedham, was kinsman of Edward Alleyn of Dedham, who, dying
sudden. at Boston, where he was a rep. 1642, by nuncup. will gave his
est. to him, and ano. relat.; had Henry, bapt. 1 Mar. 1643. JOHN,
Dedham, perhaps s. of the preced. freem. 1643. JOHN, Marlborough,
s. of Richard, by w. Eliz. m. 1666, had John, b. 1667; Samuel, 1668;
Zechary, 1671; Eliz. 1672; Thomas; Sarah, 1679; and Silence; was
freem. 1690. JOHN, Boston, by w. Mehitable had Samuel, b. 23 Jan.
1678. JOHN, Milford, s. of Roger, d. 1699, leav. wid. Lydia, ch. Prudence, aged 18; Thomas, 17; Ezekiel, 12; and Joseph, 2. JOSEPH,
Marlborough, s. of Richard, freem. 1685, perhaps sworn again, 1691;
had w. Catharine. MOSES, Marlborough, br. of the preced. m. 28 Oct.
1668, Joanna, prob. d. of Edward Larkin, had Moses; David, b. 1672;
Jonathan, 1679; James; Josiah; Edward; Hannah; Mercy; Jacob;
and Ebenezer; was freem. 1690; and d. 23 May 1736. RICHARD,
Sudbury 1640, by w. Ann or Hannah had John, b. 20 Oct. 1641;
Mary, 12 or 22 June 1644; Moses, 26 Mar. 1646; Joseph; Daniel, 21
Dec. 1665; Eliz.; Sarah; Isaac; and Hannah, wh. d. 13 Apr. 1654.
He took the freeman's oath 1645, and again, I suppose, in 1647, for no
other Richard is heard of, but aft. 1656, rem. to S. part of Marlborough,
now Southborough, was liv. Oct. 1675. Mary m. Jonathan Johnson;
Eliz. m. a Dingley; and Sarah m. a Taylor, as says Barry. ROGER,
Farmington, the first min. m. at Hartford, Mary, eldest d. of Rev.
Thomas Hooker, wh. d. 4 Feb. 1676, had at H. Samuel, bapt. 20 Oct.
1646; was ord. the day the ch. was form. 13 Oct. 1652, there had John,
bapt. June 1656, but not 6, as print. in Geneal. Reg. XI. 324; and prob.
other ch. bef. or aft. or both. He was dism. 1657, came to Boston, in
Oct. to emb. for Eng. The ship in wh. he had tak. pass. was with ano.
for the same destinat. detain. sev. days by head winds in the outer
harbor, and he was invit. by letter to town on a special serv. A
lamentab. superstit. encourag. the shipmaster and some others, as in
Hull's Diary, p. 185, is told, to consent to his leav. the voyage, "as
think. his presence some cause of the cross wind." I hope he got passage, without contra. wind, in a later ship, and aft. return, he went to
Milford, there was inst. 22 Aug. 1660, and d. 7 June 1683. His will, of
12 Mar. bef. names Samuel, Roger, Susanna, John, Ezekiel, bapt. 1660;
Sarah, 1662; Alice, 1664; and Mary; but in some· cases the order of
success. is not ascert. His d. Susanna m. John Stone of M.; and Sarah
m. 4 July 1683, John Wilson of New Haven. ROGER, Milford, s. of

the preced. d. 1690, leav. wid. Abigail, guard. of a s. and a d. not nam.
Among the proprs. in 1713 at M. were seven of his name. SAMUEL,
Milford, s. of the preced. was ens. 1673, m. 14 Mar. 1669, Martha, d. of
the first Benjamin Fenn, had Martha, b. 1671; and Thomas, 1675;
and d. 1708. *THOMAS, Fairfield, one of the five first sett. a man of
conseq. chos. rep. to Apr. sess. 1645; had freq. suits at law with his
neighb. and in 1652 charg. with a cap. crime, prob. witchcraft, or other
imagin. offence, he escap. from prison, took refuge with the Dutch, who
believed him innoc. He liv. at Newtown, on L. I. 1656, a purchaser that
yr. of Middleburg, and was a capt. under Stuyvesant. By compact with
the Unit. Cols. of N. E. the Dutch were bound to extradit. of fugit. as
were the members of the Un. among thems. by art. VIII. of the confed.
and in the rec. of the Commissnrs. Haz. II. 229, may be read the instruct.
by Congr. to Newman, Leverett, and Davis, to proceed to New York
and demand his body, and Ib. 236, their claim " of the body of Thomas
Newton, some time a capit. offender in one of the Cols. of N. E." War
was then raging betw. Eng. and Holland, but amicab. relat. wisely were
preserv. on our side of the water; and Stuyvesant issued a warrant, Ib.
238, on the same day; but we may be glad that either cunning or common sense prevent. its execut. THOMAS, Boston 1688, came from New
Hampsh. is supposed to have been b. 10 Jan. 1661, and was Sect. of
that Prov. until 1690, was controller of the customs at B. judge of the
admir. and Atty.-Gen. in the witchcraft prosecut. and aft. d. 28 May
1721. His opinion must have led to the cure of the infernal delusion,
for in Jan. 1693 he wrote to Sir Wm. Phips, the Gov. that of the 52
charg. at Salem that court, the three convicts should have been acquit.
like the rest. Twelve of this name had, in 1827, been gr. at N. E. coll.
exc. Harv. where none.

NICHOLET, *CHARLES*, Salem, came, 1672, from Virg. contin. preach.
to 20 Apr. 1676, by vote of the town, with dissatisf. of both the ch. and
its pastor, went to Eng. See Felt, II. 588.

NICHOLS, ABRAHAM, Woodbury, s. of the first Caleb, m. Dec. 1684,
Rachel Kellogg, sec. d. of the first Daniel of Stratford, in 1706 was
excor. of his br. Caleb; but his fam. is not giv. by Cothren. ADAM,
New Haven 1645 or earlier, m. Ann, d. of John Wakeman, had John,
bapt. 10 Aug. 1645; Barachiah, 14 Feb. 1647; Esther, 10 Mar. 1650;
and Lydia, b. 28 Feb. 1652; in 1655 was of Hartford, rem. 1661 to
Hadley, where his s. John was drown. next yr. His f.-in-law, in his will,
pro. 16 Oct. 1661, ment. these ch. of his d. Ann N. viz: John, Hannah,
Sarah, and Ebenezer, the last three prob. b. at Hartford, and some time
later he had Esther. Next he was of Boston, freem. 1670, if our Secr.
is to be accept. in his Col. Rec. ret. to Hartford, and d. 25 Aug. 1682,

when his only ch. was Esther Ellis. ALLEN or ALLYN, Barnstable, m. 12 Apr. 1670, Abigail, d. of Austin Bearse, had Nathaniel, b. 12 Oct. 1671; Mary, 12 Feb. 1673; a s. 1 Jan. 1675, d. soon; Josiah, 23 Apr. 1676, d. at 2 yrs.; Joseph, 11 Apr. 1678; Abigail, 11 Feb. 1681; Priscilla, 28 June 1682, d. next Mar.; Experience, 8 Jan. 1684, wh. was bapt. with Nathaniel, Mary, and Joseph, on 1 Jan. 1688; and James, b. 1 Apr. 1689, bapt. with Abigail, 12 May foll. CALEB, Stratford, s. of Francis, b. in Eng. was among the freem. 1669, by w. Ann had Sarah, b. 1 Dec. 1651; Ann, 5 Mar. 1653; Esther, 18 Feb. 1655; Joseph, 25 Dec. 1656; Samuel, 29 Mar. 1658; Andrew, 28 Nov. 1659; Abraham, 19 Jan. 1662; Abigail, Feb. 1664; Hannah, Aug. 1667; Caleb, Feb. 1669; Phebe, 12 Nov. 1671; and John, Nov. 1676; rem. to Woodbury, and d. 1690. In his will of 6 Aug. in that yr. he names Samuel, John, Caleb, and Abraham, of his six s. and three ds. Mary, Ann, and Phebe, beside Moses Wheeler, John Prentiss, and William Martin, call. by him s.-in-law. Wheeler had m. 20 Oct. 1674, the d. Sarah, but this Sarah was long and erron. call. w.' of Daniel Brinsmead, to wh. in better acco. is giv. for w. Sarah, d. of Daniel Kellogg the first. CALEB, Woodbury, s. of the preced. prob. d. unm. for his will, of 6 Mar. 1706, pro. 1 Jan. foll. makes br. Abraham excor. and gives prop. to him and br. John, and sis. Abigail Martin, w. of William, Mary Hull, Phebe Knell, and Hannah N. He d. 14 Apr. CYPRIAN, call. Siborn in the rec. of Hartford 1668, made freem. next yr.; was from Witham, Co. Essex, and had bot. bef. com. est. of William Whiting, merch. of London, 6 Apr. 1664, gent. that was prop. of the f. of W. in our country, perhaps came with s. Cyprian in 1667, was nomin. 1668 for freem. with prefix of respect, was selectman 1670, 5, and 6, and in other town offices, yet the date of his d. is unkn. CYPRIAN, Hartford, s. of the preced. b. in Eng. was a capt. had Cyprian, b. 1672; James; William; and perhaps Sarah, wh. m. 1700, William Webster; and Mary, wh. m. 1700, Ephraim Turner. His w. Helen d. 12 May 1702. CYPRIAN, Hartford, s. of the preced. by w. Helen, d. of John Talcott, had only ch. Eliz. bapt. 14 Jan. 1700; and his w. d. a. 1703. He m. 24 May 1705, as sec. w. Mary, d. of Samuel Spencer, had Cyprian, bapt. Feb. 1706; James, Feb. 1708; William, Jan. 1710; Mary, 1713; and prob. others, and d. 2 Jan. 1756, aged 84; and his wid. d. 15 Feb. foll. DANIEL, Charlestown, d. there 2 July 1659, but was prob. only a trans. visitor. DAVID, d. at Boston, 13 Mar. 1653, but whether an inhab. or not is unkn. EPHRAIM, Hingham, freem. 1684, was s. of Thomas. EPHRAIM, Stratford, s. of Isaac of the same, m. Sept. 1682, Esther, wid. of Ebenezer Hawley, was ens. and d. a. 1690, leav. ch. not kn. to us, and his wid. m. Eliphalet Hill. FRANCIS, Stratford, d. 1650, was f. of Isaac,

Caleb, and John, who were all b. in Eng. His est. was small; and neither will nor inv. is of rec. in Pro. FRANCIS, Falmouth 1680, perhaps s. of Robert. Willis, I. 160. HUGH, Salem, m. 26 Apr. 1694, Priscilla Shattuck, d. of Samuel of the same, and d. bef. Nov. 1701. * ISAAC, Stratford 1639, s. of Francis, b. in Eng. one of the first sett. I think was that serj. appoint. to train the men in milit. discip. this yr. as in Trumbull, Col. Rec. of Conn. I. 36 is told; was rep. 1664 at the Oct. sess.; had Mary, b. 2 Feb. 1648, wh. m. 8 Jan. 1667, Israel Chauncy, the min. of the town; Sarah, 1 Nov. 1649; Josiah, 29 Jan. 1652; Isaac, 12 Mar. 1654; Jonathan, 20 Dec. 1655; Ephraim, 16 Dec. 1657; Patience, 2 Feb. 1660; Temperance, 17 May 1662; Margery, 30 Nov. 1663; Benjamin, 2 Feb. 1666; and Eliz. 2 Apr. 1668. He was a soapboiler, had good est. made his will 28 Sept. 1694, and his inv. was brot. in Sept. of next yr. He names w. Margaret, and all the ch. but Josiah, who had d. 1691, leav. wid. but no ch. Yet three other s. Isaac, Jonathan, and Ephraim were also d. but to the childr. of ea. was small legacy, direct by that instrum. bec. ea. f. had been portion. Sarah m. 8 Jan. 1674, Stephen Burritt; and Eliz. m. 1691, Rev. Joseph Webb. ISAAC, Stratford, s. of John of Fairfield, being by his uncle Isaac brot. up, is usual. call. on the rec. cous.; m. 15 Aug. 1672, Esther Clark, had Grace, b. 6 June 1673; Alice, 25 Oct. 1674; John 10 Oct. 1676; Samuel, 6 Dec. 1678; and he perhaps rem. to Derby. ISAAC, Stratford, s. of Isaac of the same, d. 1690, leav. wid. Mary, and ch. Francis, b. June 1676; Richard, Nov. 1678; and Joseph, Nov. 1680. ISRAEL, Hingham, s. of Thomas, it is said m. 10 June 1688, Mary, third d. of Roger Sumner of Dorchester. JAMES, Malden, m. Apr. 1660, Mary, d. of George Felt, had Mary, b. 1 Mar. foll.; James, Dec. 1662; Eliz.; Nathaniel, 1666; Ann; Samuel; and Caleb; was freem. 1668; and d. 1694, prob. in Apr. certain. bef. 5 Nov. JAMES, Malden, s. of the preced. perhaps was one of sev. grantees in 1685, for services in the late Ind. war, of tract of 8 miles sq. in the Nipmug country; by w. Hannah Whittemore, m. 15 Nov. 1686, had Hannah, b. 22 Nov. 1687; James, 28 Jan. 1689; by sec. w. Abigail had Esther, b. 5 Jan. 1691, misprint. 1692, in Geneal. Reg. X. 163; Abigail, Aug. perhaps 25, 1692; James, again, 22 Oct. 1694; Joshua, 5 Jan. 1697; Caleb, 27 Apr. 1699; and Jemima, 4 Nov. 1702. One of these Jameses d. Farmer says, 30 May 1695, and prob. it was the eldest, with error of a yr. for the sec. James d. 22 Mar. 1726. JAMES, Reading, s. of Richard, freem. 1691. JOHN, Watertown, a propr. 1636 or 7, says Bond. He may well seem to be the man of Fairfield, buying ld. bef. 1653, perhaps reaching that final resid. aft. a tempora. one at Wethersfield, and the br. of Isaac and Caleb. By w. Grace he had Isaac, Sarah, and John, nam. on ret. of his inv. 19 June 1655, with hope of ano. wh. was the Samuel, prob. nam. by the wid. 4 June 1659, when, giv. deed to her s. Isaac, she requires him to pay her childr. Sarah, John, and Samuel certain sums. This seems to compel us to think, Esther, Eliz. Hannah, the three elder ch. nam. on giv. the inv. of f. were by a former w. The wid. m. Richard Perry of the same, who was d. in 1658. His s. John serv. in Philip's war, and d. in the first yr. of it unm. JOHN, Topsfield, s. of William of the same, by w. Lydia had William, b. 25 Aug. 1663; Ann, 24 Aug. 1665; John, 14 Jan. 1668; Thomas, 20 Jan. 1670; Isaac, 6 Feb. 1673; Lydia, 16 Apr. 1675; Rachel, 3 Nov. 1677; Eliz. 16 Mar. 1680; Ebenezer, 9 Nov. 1685; beside Margaret, ment. in his will of 12 Oct. 1700, pro. 11 Nov. foll. in wh. all the ch. are nam. exc. Isaac, wh. perhaps, was d. JOHN, Reading, s. of Richard, freem. 1691, by w. Abigail, had John, b. 1677; Richard, 1679, d. soon; Richard, again, 1682; Thomas; Kendall, 1686; James, 1688; Nathaniel, 1691; Abigail, 1694; Samuel, 1696; Benjamin, 1699; and Joseph, 1702. JOHN, Boston, a joiner, perhaps s. of Mordecai, freem. 1690, had w. Sarah, wh. d. at Charlestown, 13 Sept. 1678, in her 21st yr. JOHN, Greenwich, R. I. 1687. JONATHAN, a soldier of Moseley's comp. Dec. 1675, and next yr. under capt. Turner on Conn. riv. in Philip's war, was, of course, from the E. JONATHAN, Stratford, s. of the first Isaac, d. 1689, leav. wid. who is not nam. and ch. Josiah, aged 7; Mary, 4; and Jonathan, 2, on ret. of the inv. 28 Oct. of that yr. His est. was good. JOSIAH, Stratford, br. of the preced. m. 13 Dec. 1678, Hannah, d. of Joseph Hawley, prob. had no ch. d. 1691. MORDECAI, Boston, mariner, m. 1652, Alice, d. of Richard Hallet, had John, b. 18 Aug. 1653; and Samuel, 9 Dec. 1658, wh. d. young. He d. not long aft. for 29 Apr. 1664, his wid. gave inv. and 3 Feb. foll. provision for the only ch. John was made in Court, for the reason, says the rec. of the wid. "being ready to dispose of herself." She soon m. Thomas Clark of Plymouth. NATHANIEL, Charlestown, d. bef. 21 Aug. 1687, when his wid. Joanna brot. says the ch. rec. to bapt. her ch. Eliz. and Hannah. But perhaps he had liv. in ano. town. One of the name from Hingham was in Johnson's comp. Dec. 1675, may have outliv. the hard serv. His wid. who was, I infer, d. of Richard Shute, m. Joseph Buckley of Boston. Hannah m. 7 Jan. 1702, Jonathan Mountford. NATHANIEL, Malden, s. of the first James of the same, by w. Sarah had Nathaniel, b. 30 July 1692; Samuel, 12 Oct. 1696; Sarah, 24 Apr. 1699; Josiah, 18 Feb. 1704; Eliz. 27 Oct. 1706; John, 21 June 1709; Mary, 23 Sept. 1712; and Ann, 12 Sept. 1715; and he d. 10 May 1725. RANDOLPH, or RANDAL, Charlestown, had w. Eliz. d. I think, of Thomas Pierce, senr. and ch. Sarah, b. 27 Jan. 1643; Eliz.; Hannah, 4 Apr.

1647; John, 16 Jan. 1654; Nathaniel, 10 Nov. 1655; William, 2 Aug. 1657; and Daniel, 21 Nov. 1658; perhaps others; was liv. 1678, a householder at C. His d. Sarah, in the will of Nicholas Shapleigh of C. 21 Jan. 1662, his s. Joseph was advised to m. or at least a beq. was made to him on condit. that he should do so. Eliz. m. Thomas Tuck. RICHARD, Ipswich 1648, may be the man who liv. long at Reading, there d. 22 Nov. 1674, in his will, three days bef. of wh. s. John was excor. names w. Ann, other s. Thomas, and James, and ds. Mary and Hannah. ROBERT, Watertown, m. 1644 or 5, Sarah, wid. of John Goss, may be the man, to wh. with many others, our Col. governm. in 1680, made gr. of ld. at the bot. of Casco Bay five miles sq. and two of the islds. adj. ROBERT, Saybrook 1664–73. ROBERT, Falmouth 1670, perhaps s. of the first Robert, was k. by the Ind. Sept. 1675, at Scarborough. SAMUEL, Reading, nam. an early sett. by Eaton, but I find no other ment. of him; unless he were that s. of the first James of Malden, wh. had d. Eliz. to rec. in right of her f. dec. on settlem. of her gr.f.'s est. in 1706. SAMUEL, Stratford, s. of Caleb of the same, rem. early to Derby, thence, perhaps, to Woodbury, there d. 1691, leav. wid. Susanna, and only ch. Josiah, aged 4. THOMAS, Hingham 1637, rem. prob. to Scituate, aft. m. with Rebecca, d. of Thomas Josselyn or Jostlin, but in few yrs. back to H. had Rebecca, Ephraim, Israel, and Thomas, beside Martha and Mary, tw. b. 3 July 1653; and Sarah, 20 July 1655. Rebecca m. 1664, Samuel House, the sec. THOMAS, Sandwich 1643. THOMAS, Malden, m. Sept. 1655, Mary Moulton, may be he who at Salisbury, by w. Mary had Ebenezer, b. 3 Aug. 1664; and, perhaps, of Amesbury in 1677. That ch. Ebenezer was, perhaps, fem. for the same rec. makes Benoni Tucker m. June 1686, Ebenezer N. THOMAS, Reading, s. of Richard, freem. 1684, was deac. THOMAS, Scituate, s. of the first Thomas, m. 1663, Sarah, d. of John Whiston, had Sarah, b. 1668; Rebecca, 1670; Joseph, 1673; Susanna, 1676; Mary, 1679; Bathsheba, 1681; Israel, 1683; Patience, 1685; and Eliz. 1690. Deane. THOMAS, Reading, freem. 1691, was prob. s. of deac. Thomas. WALTER, Charlestown 1638, had been of some other ch. if he be as I think prob. that freem. of 7 Dec. 1636, whose name in the appendix to Winth. is print. Nicholas, and by Paige's list, Nicoles, wh. was very freq. spell. of this surname in old rec. An Eliz. N. emb. at London 1635, aged 25, in the Susan and Ellen, at the same time with Richard Saltonstall, and that Penelope Pelham, who some yrs. aft. m. Gov. Bellingham; but whether she was w. of any of the preced. is unkn. WILLIAM, Salem 1638, had then gr. of ld. rem. to New London, perhaps in co. with Robert Isbell, wh. d. a. 1655, and N. m. his wid. Ann. He was a substantial man in business of the town, had no ch. and d. 4 Sept. 1673. His wid.

d. 15 Sept. 1689. WILLIAM, Topsfield, in his will of 26 Apr. 1693, pro. 17 Feb. 1696, ment. w. Mary, ch. John, Mary, w. of Thomas Cove, and Hannah, w. of Thomas Wilkins, and from this docum. is our best informat. He gave a depon. 14 May 1694, "*aged upwards of* 100 *yrs.*" bef. Judge Curwin, that he had liv. upwards of 42 yrs. on a farm he bot. of Henry Bartholomew, lying betw. the bounds of Salem and Ipswich riv. paid rates to S. sev. yrs. and Topsfield, aft. the run of the line betw. the towns, claim. and enforc. paym. See Geneal. Reg. IX. 377. How many yrs. should be subtract. from the date fix. by this centenary, can easi. be ascertain. at Salem, to a high probabil. or perhaps certain. as his descend. have confid. that he was b. 1599 ; for he sw. 24 June 1662, that he was 63 yrs. old. Six of this name had, in 1834, been gr. at Harv. and seventeen at other N. E. coll.

NICHOLSON, CHRISTOPHER, Lynn, s. of Edmund, m. 22 Oct. 1662, Hannah Redknap, prob. d. of Joseph. EDMUND, Marblehead, 1648, d. 1660, it is presum. for his inv. tak. 22 Nov. of that yr. was brot. in six days aft. by Eliz. his wid. wh. was persecut. as a Quaker the same yr. His ch. then were aged as the rec. shows, respectiv. Christopher, 22 ; Joseph, 20 ; Samuel, 16 ; John, 14 ; Eliz. 11 ; and Thomas, 7 ; Joseph, Thomas, and Eliz. then w. of Nicholas Andrews, all unit. in a deed, 1672, to their br. Samuel. JAMES, Charlestown, d. Jan. 1668. JOHN, and ROBERT, are count. 1675, at Falmouth ; JOSEPH, and SAMUEL, at Marblehead 1668, s. of Edmund ; and a JOHN in Conn. had desert. his w. Mercy more than five yrs. for wh. she obt. divorce. But one JOSEPH, Portsmouth, R. I. seems happier, if we can judge by his will 1693, describ. his ch. as Joseph, wh. was b. 2 Nov. 1650 ; Sarah, b. 1 Feb. 1653, w. of John Ward ; Rebecca, 1 Feb. 1656, w. of Nicholas Carr ; Rachel, b. at Bootle, 22 Apr. 1658, w. of John Peabody ; Dinah, w. of James Burrill, b. at Salem, 21 Mar. 1660 ; Benjamin, in Barbados, 6 July 1665 ; Eliz. at Martinico, 8 June 1667 ; and Jane, in R. I. 29 Sept. 1669. He was, we may believe, s. of Edmund of Marblehead, and his w. was Jane. WILLIAM, Yarmouth 1641, fin. for disrespect to relig. next yr. had William, bapt. at Barnstable 1 June 1646.

NICK, or NECK, CHRISTOPHER, Marblehead 1668. JOHN, Lynn, m. 22 Mar. 1676, Mary Richards, had William, b. 21 Dec. 1676, d. next yr. ; Bathsheba, 24 Dec. 1678, d. soon ; and Bathsheba, again, 11 May 1682. If this be the same name with Nicks, he may have been s. of that *Matthew* Nicks, wh. had, Felt says, gr. of ld. at Salem 1639 ; but the same yr. he ment. Matthew Nixon, as grantee of ld. from the town, and prob. he was the same. WILLIAM, Marblehead, 1674, may have been br. of John ; but possib. tho. not prob. it is only abbrev. for Nicholson.

NICKERSON, WILLIAM, Boston, weaver, from Norwich, Eng. aged 33, with w. Ann, eldest d. of Nicholas Busby (who came in the same ship), aged 28, and four ch. Nicholas, Robert, Eliz. and Ann, emb. at Ipswich, or Yarmouth, 8 Apr. 1637, arr. 20 June at Boston, proceed. with f.-in-law, I presume, first to Watertown, where he might be allow. to join the ch. for in Boston there exist. nothing but contention among the memb. to drive out, and nobody was rec. until long aft. N. had been adm. freem. 2 May 1638. But he is aft. found at Yarmouth where he had Joseph, b. Dec. 1647; and Eliz. m. Oct. 1649, Robert Eldred. WILLIAM, Eastham, m. 22 Jan. 1691, Mary Snow, had Mercy, b. 17 Mar. 1692; and Nicholas, 19 Mar. 1694. Perhaps the spell. was Neck.

NICKISON, JOHN, Salisbury 1650, prob. only a misprint for Dickinson.

NICHOLSON, ROBERT, Scarborough, had Robert, and John. His inv. is of 1 July 1676.

NIGHTINGALE, BENJAMIN, Braintree 1689. JOSEPH, Braintree, per- haps s. of William, by w. Hannah had Joseph, wh. d. young; and the mo. d. 11 Oct. 1718, aged 26; and the f. d. 1726, aged 48. WILLIAM, Braintree 1689, or earlier, d. 10 May 1714, aged a. 77. WILLIAM, jun. Braintree, s. perhaps of the preced. was freem. 1690.

NILES, BENJAMIN, Block Isl. 1684, was s. of John, and I kn. no more. INCREASE, Braintree, s. of John, was a soldier of Johnson's comp. Dec. 1675, m. 4 Dec. 1677, Mary Purchas, had John, b. 10 Oct. 1678; Increase, 9 Mar. 1680; Ebenezer; and Mary; and d. 1 Sept. 1693. JOHN, Dorchester 1634, Braintree 1636, freem. 1647, had w. Jane, and ch. Hannah, b. 16 Feb. 1637; John, 4 Mar. 1639; Joseph, 15 Aug. 1640; Nathaniel, 16 Aug. 1642; Samuel, 12 May 1644; Increase, 16 Dec. 1646; Benjamin, 11 Mar. 1651; and his w. d. 15 May 1654. He went to Block isl. perhaps, but bef. rem. by w. Hannah, had, prob. Isaac, b. 2 Apr. 1658. It is not cert. that he went to Block. isl. as that John wh. liv. there may have been the s. of this, wh. d. at Braintree, 8 Feb. 1694, aged a. 91 yrs. and his wid. d. 31 Jan. 1703. JONATHAN, Hull, freem. 1680. JOSEPH, Braintree, sec. s. of John, m. 2 Nov. 1662, Mary Mycall, had Hannah, b. 15 Feb. 1664; Joseph, 21 Sept. 1666; Mary, 8 Jan. 1669; John; and Benjamin, 2 Jan. 1675. NATHANIEL, Block isl. 1670, s. of John, had m. Sarah, d. of James Sands, perhaps in 1671, and beside Jeremiah, and Nathaniel, one older, one younger, as Vinton suppos. had Samuel, min. of Braintree, a disting. controversial writer, b. 1 May 1674, H. C. 1699, wh. compil. the Narrative of wars in N. E. with Fr. and Ind. partly print. in 3 Mass. Hist. Coll. VI. 154, et seq. and d. 1 May 1762; was f. of Samuel, H. C. 1731, and gr.f. of Rev. Samuel of Abington, wh. d. 16 June 1814. SAMUEL, Braintree, third s. of John, m. 20 Apr. 1680, Vinton says, wid. Mary Belcher, and I wish his industr. research had ascertain. of wh. she was wid. so that we might not be left to conject. that she was d. of Roger Billings, wh. m. Samuel Belcher. By her he had Sarah, b. Jan. 1681; Hannah, 1682; and Samuel, 15 June 1686; was a lieut. 1697. Eleven of this name had, in 1634, been gr. at N. E. coll. of wh. four were of Dart. three of Harv. and two of Yale.

NIMS, EBENEZER, Deerfield, s. of Godfrey, in the assault, 29 Feb. 1704, by the Fr. and Ind. when most of the fam. were destroy. was tak. carr. to Canada, adopt. by an Ind. squaw, had there a w. and one ch. but was liberat. 1714, and came home. I hear nothing of the w. and ch. GODFREY, Northampton 1668, was a soldier in Philip's war, m. Margaret, wid. of Zebediah Williams, had Rebecca, b. 1678, d. soon; John and Rebecca, tw. 1679; Henry, 1682; rem. to Deerfield, there had Thankful, 1684; and Ebenezer, 1687; his w. d. next yr. and he m. 1692, Mehitable, wid. of Jeremiah Hull, d. of William Smead, had Thomas, 1693, wh. d. at 4 yrs.; Mehitable, 1696; Mary and Mercy, tw. 1699; and Abigail, 1701. Henry was k. 29 Feb. 1704, at the surprise of the town by Fr. and Ind. Mehitable, Mary, and Mercy were at the same time burn to d. in the cellar of his ho. and his w. carr. off, but k. on the road to Canada, whither John, Ebenezer, and Abigail were carr. John fail. to escape in his first attempt, but got free in the sec. from Montreal, 1705; and Abigail was prob. never heard of aft. His d. Rebecca had m. Philip Mattoon, and was k. with him, and their only ch. at the same time, so that of all his fam. only John, Thankful, and Ebenezer were liv. and the youngest a captive for nine yrs. aft. the f. d. 1705. But the name is well perpet.

NIXON, or NICKSON, JOHN, R. I. 1663. Knowles, 421. MATTHEW, Salem 1639, was petitnr. 1668, against imposts, sign. for self and comp. See Nick.

NOAKES, or NOAKE, ROBERT, Boston, by w. Mary, perhaps d. of Robert Wright, wh. in his will calls Noakes his s. had Arthur, b. 17 Mar. 1665; Mary, 5 Dec. 1667; Robert, 10 July 1670; Joseph, 16 Oct. 1671; and Robert, again, 13 Oct. 1676. I suppose he was liv. 1701.

NOBLE, JOHN, Westfield, prob. s. of the first Thomas, m. 13 Sept. 1682, Abigail, d. of John Sacket, had Abigail, b. 30 June 1683, and his w. d. in 3 days; by sec. w. had John, 15 Feb. 1685; Stephen, 15 Aug. 1688; William, d. young; David, 25 Jan. 1695; Hannah, 2 Nov. 1697; Sarah, 22 Mar. 1699; and Mabel, 28 Feb. 1705. He d. at New Milford, 17 Aug. 1714. MARK, Westfield, prob. br. of the preced. m. 10 Dec. 1690, Hannah, d. of the sec. Thomas Dewey, had Joseph, b. 8 Oct. 1691; Hezekiah, 14 May 1694; Matthew, 19 Sept. 1698; Solomon, 23 Dec. 1700; Elisha, 9 Feb. 1703; Obadiah, 19 Oct. 1705; Hannah, 11

Oct. 1707 ; Esther, 6 June 1710 ; and Rhoda, 17 Apr. 1717. *THOMAS, Boston 1652, rem. to Springfield, m. 1 Nov. 1660, Hannah, only d. of William Warriner, rem. to Westfield, 1669, freem. 1681, rep. 1692, bef. going thither had John, b. 1662, bef. ment.; Hannah, 24 Feb. 1664, wh. m. John Goodman of Hadley, and next, 12 Oct. 1728, Nathaniel Edwards of Northampton ; and Thomas, 14 Jan. 1667. He had at W. Eliz. b. 9 Feb. 1673 ; Luke, 15 July 1675 ; James, 1 Oct. 1677 ; Mary, 29 June 1680 ; and Rebecca, 4 Jan. 1683 ; but when or whence he came is unkn. His d. was 20 Jan. 1704, and the wid. Hannah m. deac. Medad Pomeroy. THOMAS, Westfield, prob. s. of the preced. m. 19 Dec. 1695, Eliz. d. of the sec. Thomas Dewey, had Thomas, b. 10 Sept. 1696 ; Job, 28 Jan. 1699, d. at 5 mos.; Jonathan, 1 May 1700, d. at 19 yrs.; Seth, 30 Oct. 1702, d. in few wks.; Israel, 20 Sept. 1703 ; Eliz. 3 Sept. 1705 ; Lois, 4 July 1708 ; Ebenezer, 11 Oct. 1711 ; Thankful, 31 May 1714 ; Ann, 30 Oct. 1716 ; and Jonathan, 23 May 1721 ; was deac. and d. 29 July 1750 ; and his wid. d. 2 Oct. 1757. WILLIAM, Flushing, L. I. was, in 1664, employ. by the Conn. Col. Six of this name had been gr. at Yale, and nine at the other N. E. coll. in 1834, says Farmer's MS. wh. is the more observ. bec. none was of Harv. or Dart.

NOCK, HENRY, Dover, youngest s. of Thomas of the same, m. 10 Jan. 1692, Sarah, d. of Charles Adams. SYLVANUS, br. of the preced. m. 20 Apr. 1677, Eliz. Emery, had Eliz. b. 12 Feb. 1678 ; Sarah, 4 May 1680 ; and others. THOMAS, Dover 1655, by w. Rebecca, prob. d. of Henry Tibbets, had Eliz. b. 21 Nov. 1663, d. at 5 yrs.; Henry, posthum. 8 Feb. 1667 ; beside others earlier, as Sylvanus, and Rebecca, and d. 29 Oct. 1666. His wid. m. 28 Sept. 1669, Philip Benmore, outliv. him, and d. 30 Mar. 1680. It is said this name has bec. Knox in some branches.

NODDLE, WILLIAM, Salem, came prob. in the fleet with Winth. freem. 18 May 1631, was drown. in June 1632. Winth. I. 80. Prince, II. 29, thinks Noddle's isl. was nam. for him.

NORCROSS, JEREMIAH, Watertown 1642, perhaps the freem. 1653, whose bapt. name is not giv. on the rec. d. in Eng. 1657 ; in his will, made 15 Sept. 1654, pro. 6 Oct. 1657, beside s. Nathaniel, and Richard, he names d. Sarah, w. of Francis Macy, tho. Bond, 376, reads the name Merry or Massey, s. Richard, d. Mary, and John Smith, s. of his w. Adrean, and speaks of gr.childr. in Eng. JEREMIAH, a soldier in Philip's war, under capt. Turner, 1676, was s. of Richard, and gr.s. of the preced.; d. says Bond, 30 Nov. 1717. JOHN, Cambridge 1642, Bond thinks was br. of the preced. and refer. to in his will; but no more is heard of him. NATHANIEL, Salem 1639, join. the ch. there

1641, freem. 10 May 1643, was, Bond says, that s. of the first Jeremiah, b. in Eng. bred at Catharine Hall in the Univ. of Cambridge, where he had his A. B. 1636–7, liv. 1647 at Watertown, and prob. preach. a little, hav. declin. the request of the first sett. of Lancaster, two or three yrs. bef. and prob. went back to Eng. to exercise his faculties, may have had a ch. at Walsingham, in Norf'k. whence, says Calamy, he was eject. at the great day of triumph aft. the restorat. Winth. II. 161. NA-THANIEL, Watertown, s. of Richard the first, m. 20 June 1687, Mehitable, d. of William Hagar, had Mehitable, b. 4 Feb. 1691. His w. d. 5 Apr. foll. and by sec. w. Susanna, d. of Philip Shattuck, of course gr.d. of his mo.-in-law, he had Nathaniel, 20 Dec. 1695; Philip, 5 Mar. 1698; and Susanna, 26 Feb. 1701. He d. perhaps bef. his f. RICHARD, Watertown, s. of Jeremiah, b. in Eng. a. 1621, m. 24 June 1650, Mary Brooks, had Mary, b. 27 Aug. 1652, who d. 19 Oct. 1661; Jeremiah, 3 Mar. 1655; Sarah, 28 Dec. 1657; Richard, 4 Aug. 1660; Mary, again, 10 July 1663; Nathaniel, 18 Dec. 1665; and Samuel, 4 May 1671; was freem. 1652, but Bond calls the yr. 1653, taught a town sch. says Bond, 49 yrs. at least. His w. d. 24 Feb. 1672; and he m. 18 Nov. 1673, Susanna, wid. of William Shattuck, who d. 11 Dec. 1686, and he had 3d w. Mary, and d. 1709. His will ment. s. Richard, Samuel, and Jeremiah, d. Mary, unm. and 6 ch. of his dec. d. Sarah. Sarah m. 23 Sept. 1680, Joseph Child; and Mary m. 2 Apr. 1713, John Stearns as sec. w. RICHARD, Watertown, s. of the preced. m. 10 Aug. 1686, Rose, d. of the first John Woodward, had Richard, b. 30 Dec. 1687; Samuel, 14 Oct. 1689; and Abigail, 11 July 1692. By sec. w. m. 6 Aug. 1695, Hannah Sanders, he had John, 28 Dec. 1696; Hannah, 16 Feb. 1699; Joseph, 1 July 1701; Jeremiah, 2 July, 1703; George, 22 Aug. 1705; Rose, or Ruth, 20 Mar. 1708; Peter, 28 Sept. 1710; and Wil-liam, 14 Mar. 1715. He was sch.master, like his f. and like him, liv. to good old age.

NORCUT, or NORCOTT, DANIEL, Boston, sail. in the Pied Cow, 1635, for Eng. and bec. she was not heard of next yr. admin. of his est. was giv. to John Coggan, who prob. was a creditor, Jan. 1637. WILLIAM, Marshfield, m. Sarah Chapman, had William, b. 20 Feb. 1663; John, 1 Aug. 1664; Thomas, 1 June 1670; Ralph, 5 Oct. 1673; Isaac, 10 June 1675; Ephraim, 4 Nov. 1683; and Ebenezer, 1 Mar. 1691; beside four or five ds.; and d. 18 Sept. 1693. Possib. he was of Boston 1650, to witness the will of Robert Saltonstall.

NORDEN, * NATHANIEL, Marblehead, a capt. and freem. 1690, also rep. same yr. and the former. SAMUEL, Boston, shoemaker, perhaps br. of the preced. by w. Joanna, had Samuel, b. 8 Nov. 1651; Nathaniel, 27 Nov. 1653; and Benjamin, 15 June 1656; and his w. d. 29 June;

but by sec. w. m. 1656, Eliz. d. of Philemon Pormort, had Eliz. 2 Sept. 1657 ; Susanna, 26 Nov. 1659 ; Joseph, 28 Feb. 1664; Joshua, 3 July 1666; Mary, 22 Mar. 1669 ; and Isaac, 8 Mar. 1672 ; was freem. 1666.

NORMAN, HUGH, Plymouth, m. 8 Oct. 1639, Mary White ; rem. to Yarmouth bef. 1643, had Eliz. wh. was drown. 28 May 1648, aged 6 yrs.; rem. again to Barnstable. JOHN, Salem 1631, by w. Arabella had John, b. Aug. 1637, bapt. 4 Mar. 1638; Lydia, 15 Jan. bapt. 23 Feb. 1640; Ann or Hannah, 15 Jan. bapt. 1 May 1642; Arabella, 14 Feb. bapt. Apr. 1644; Martha, May 1646; Richard 12 Oct. 1651; Joseph, 8 Sept. 1653, d. soon; and Joseph, again, 7 Sept. 1656; was in 1640, at Jeffrey's creek, now Manchester, of Marblehead 1648, and back again to Salem; d. 1673, in his 60th yr. and his wid. d. 1679. His d. Arabella, m. Sept. 1664, John Baldwin. JOHN, Salem, s. of Richard, m. Abigail, d. of George Ropes, had, perhaps, by a former w. John, b. a. 1660, and prob. is the man wh. was tak. in the Dutch war, 1667. He d. 6 May 1713, aged 76, says the gr.st. rec. and his wid. Mary, I suppose d. 24 Oct. 1713, aged 67. Ano. JOHN, perhaps s. of the first John, m. Sarah, youngest d. of Moses Maverick. RICHARD, Salem, perhaps br. of John the first, came in 1626, as Felt thinks, prob. from Dorchester in Eng. with s. Richard, to ea. of wh. he assigns that yr. but John, wh. was elder, may have been left in Eng. Farmer thinks he had also William, liv. at Marblehead 1648; and says the elder Richard d. 1683, tho. it may seem as prob. that it was the s. of that name, who, he says, was b. 1623, and liv. 1672 at Marblehead. It seems to me, that the elder d. prob. bef. this last date, and that sec. RICHARD was the freem. of 1680. SAMUEL, Barnstable, perhaps s. of Hugh, m. 24 Nov. 1697, by Mr. Hamblen's extr. from the rec. wid. Casley, but of wh. she was wid. is not kn. THOMAS, Boston 1674, prob. rem. to Topsfield, where he was liv. when made freem. 1681.

NORRIS, EDWARD, Salem, fourth min. at that ch. ord. 18 Mar. 1640, had join. the Boston ch. 21 July 1639, as did next mo. his w. Elinor ; yet his d. Mary unit. with the ch. of Roxbury soon aft.; freem. 13 May 1640; d. as Farmer has it, 10 Apr. 1659, aged a. 70 ; but 23 Dec. on more prob. auth. of John Hull, who calls the age a. "fourscore." His will, of 9 Dec. 1657, was pro. 27 June 1660. Mather includes him in his first classis, yet omits his name of bapt. He was ord. by a Bp. we may be sure in the last days of Eliz. or first of James, but we have no report of his cure. EDWARD, SALEM 1639, s. of the preced. sch.master 1640 to 1676, d. 1684, in 70th yr.; by w. Dorothy had Edward, bapt. 18 Oct. 1657 ; and Eliz. ; perhaps more, but these outliv. him. EDWARD, Salem, s. of the preced. m. 3 Dec. 1685, Mary Symonds, and perpet. the name, the eighth Edward being recent. an active man. NICHOLAS, Exeter

1666, of wh. I kn. nothing, but that he took, 30 Nov. 1677, the o. of alleg. and in 1690 desir. jurisdict. of Mass.

NORTH, JAMES, Northampton 1677, s. of John, d. 25 July 1689, leav. ch. Sarah, b. 1679; and Mary, 1687. JOHN, Farmington, an early sett. prob. he who came 1635, aged 20, in the Susan and Ellen, to Boston, was freem. of Conn. 1657; had Thomas; John, b. a. 1641; Samuel and Mary, tw. 1643; James, 1647; Sarah, bapt. 1653; Nathaniel, 29 June 1656; Lydia, 9 May 1658; and Joseph, 1660; d. late in 1691, or early in 1692, his inv. being of 12 Feb. in this yr. Mary m. John Searle; and Sarah m. the sec. Matthew Woodruff of Farmington. JOHN, Wethersfield, prob. s. of the preced. d. 1682, leav. John, aged 10; Mary, 8; and Susanna, 6. Miss Caulkins gives reason for presuming he practis. physic, in 1662, at New London. JOSEPH, Farmington 1690, s. of the first John. RICHARD, Salisbury 1640, one of the first proprs. freem. 2 June 1641; rem. to Salem, there made his will 1649, in wh. w. Ursula, ch. Mary, Sarah, wh. m. an Oldham, and Susanna, are ment. Mary was w. of Thomas Jones of Gloucester, and d. 4 Feb. 1682, as his wid.; and Susanna, of George Martin of S. SAMUEL, Farmington, s. of the first John, d. 1682, leav. John, aged 13; Samuel, 10; Thomas, 8; and Hannah, 4. THOMAS, New Haven 1644, had by w. Mary, d. of Walter Price of Newington Butts, near London, wh. had been wid. of Philip Petersfield of Holborn, three ch. Thomas, John, and Bathshua. She outliv. him, and m. Thomas Dunck of Saybrook, and d. in Eng. whither she went 1670, to recover est. descend. to her, leav. D. to get ano. w. bef. 10 July 1677. THOMAS, Hadley 1678, took o. of alleg. 8 Feb. next.

NORTHAM, JAMES, Hartford 1655, may have been, 10 yrs. bef. at Wethersfield, freem. 1658, was engag. next yr. with the seceders, who would rem. to Hadley, but he was not able to fulfil his design, and d. bef. 1662. He m. wid. Isabel Catlin, had only Samuel, yet it may be he was by a former w. His wid. rem. to New Jersey, but aft. to Hadley, where she m. Joseph Baldwin. SAMUEL, Hatfield 1674, s. of the preced. m. that yr. Mary, d. of John Dickinson, had Samuel, b. 4 May 1675; Mary, 7 Jan. 1677; Eliz. 1 Apr. 1680; and Jonathan, 18 May 1682; rem. to Deerfield, but in 1715, with s. Jonathan, was of Colchester, where he d.

NORTHCUT, WILLIAM, Yarmouth 1643, then able to bear arms, may have been f. of bef. ment. W. Norcut; but in my guess, was the same person.

NORTHEND, EZEKIEL, Rowley 1645; was b. a. 1622, m. Edna, wid. of Richard Bailey, had beside four ds. John, b. 1658; and Ezekiel, 1666; was selectman 1691. His d. Eliz. m. Humphrey Hobson, and next, Thomas Gage; Edna m. Thomas Lambert. * EZEKIEL, Rowley, perhaps s. of the preced. a corpo. in 1691, when he was the richest man in town; m. 10 Sept. of that yr. Dorothy, d. of Henry Sewall of New-bury, had John, b. 1692; Ezekiel, 1697; Samuel, 1707; beside six ds. Possib. some were by sec. w. He was rep. 1715–17. JOHN, Wethers-field, one of the first sett. rem. prob. to Stamford, where final *s* was added.

NORTHEY, JOHN, Marblehead 1648, was b. a. 1607, and prob. f. of that JOHN of Scituate, wh. serv. in Philip's war, became a Quaker, and m. 1675, Sarah, d. of Henry Ewell, had James, b. 1687, of wh. is still a line of descend. at S.

NORTHROP, NORTHRUP, NORTROP, or NORTHUP, JOSEPH, Milford, an early sett. d. 1669, prob. for his will is of that yr. JOSEPH, Milford, perhaps s. of the preced. prop. for freem. 1670. SAMUEL, Milford, prob. br. of the preced. prop. for freem. 1671. Twelve proprs. of this name were counted in 1713, at that place, includ. two or three wids. STEPHEN, Providence 1645, adm. freem. 1658, and, perhaps, of Wick-ford 1674.

NORTON, BONUS, Ipswich, s. of William, had w. Mary Goodhue, d. of Joseph, m. bef. 1690, who outliv. him, and ch. John; Mary; Sarah; William, b. 9 May 1691; Joseph, 17 Nov. 1695; Samuel, 12 Sept. 1699; Eliz.; Lucy; and Ann; but the order is unkn. for the most. He rem. to Hingham in his mid. life, went last to Hampton, there d. 30 Apr. 1718, aged 61, as the gr.st. tells. * ‖ FRANCIS, Portsmouth 1631, a steward, sent by Mason and other patentees, rem. to Charles-town, says Frothingham, as erly as 1637, was freem. 18 May 1642, ar. co. 1643, a capt. and rep. many yrs. betw. 1647 and 61, d. 11 July 1667. His wid. Mary m. 27 Aug. 1670, deac. William Stitson; prob. he had no s. but of ds. Abigail m. John Long; Mary m. 30 Oct. 1656, Joseph Noyes; Eliz. m. 21 Sept. 1671, Timothy Symmes; Deborah m. Zechary Hill, and next, Matthew Griffin; and Sarah was unm. FRANCIS, Wethersfield, one of the first sett. but was of Milford 1660, thence rem. 1662, to New Haven, where he was drown. 1667, leav. no ch. but in his will of 1666, names cous. i. e. neph. John N. FREEGRACE, Saco, eldest s. of George of Salem, serv. on the gr. jury 1662, but soon aft. rem. to Ipswich, was a serj. in Philip's war, of capt. Appleton's comp. k. by the Ind. 19 Oct. 1675, at Hatfield, then 40 yrs. old; had m. a d. of Roger Spencer, the capt. of S. perhaps had ch. but nothing is kn. * GEORGE, Salem, was prob. that carpenter, who came in the fleet with Higginson, Apr. 1629, from London, freem. 14 May 1634, by w. Mary had Freegrace, b. prob. 1635, but whose bapt. I find not; John, bapt. Oct. 1637; Nathaniel, May 1639; George, 28 Mar. 1641; rem. to

Gloucester, was there selectman 1642, 3, and rep. 1642–4; and there Mary was b. 28 Feb. 1643; unless this were mistake, as to me seems prob. for Henry; Mehitable; Sarah; Hannah; and Abigail, 1651; rem. again, perhaps for short time, to Ipswich, but soon to Wenham, where was bapt. his d. Sarah, 14 Feb. 1647; and Eliz. 7 Aug. 1653; and he d. 1659; leav. wid. Mary and those ten ch. His wid. m. Philip Fowler. * GEORGE, Suffield, s. of the preced. prob. may have first been of Ipswich, but more prob. at Salem, and rem. to I. where first five ch. were b. by w. Sarah, who d. 23 June 1682; he had George; Thomas, b. 1670; Nathaniel; Sarah; and Alice; but aft. gett. est. at S. then part of Springfield, 1674, rem. thither, and had Samuel, b. 22 Jan. 1680, d. soon; Samuel, again, 9 Apr. 1681, d. soon; and John, 12 June 1682, d. soon; he m. 20 June 1683, Mary or Mercy, wid. of John Gillett of Windsor, d. of the first Thomas Barker, had Mary, b. 18 Jan. 1685; Abigail, 14 Jan. 1687; Freegrace, 1 Jan. 1689; Joanna, 17 Mar. 1693; Eliz. 31 Aug. 1695, d. young; and Eliz. again, posthum. when nine others were liv. 19 Mar. 1697. He was freem. 1681, and selectman, and rep. 1693, and d. 15 Nov. 1696, and his wid. d. 31 Dec. 1725. GEORGE, York 1680, perhaps s. of Henry, m. Mary, d. of Richard Foxwell of Scarborough; sw. alleg. 1680. HENRY, York 1656, was marshal of the Col. had, four yrs. earlier, sw. alleg. to Mass. but prob. went home next yr. His s. George had admin. 1679; yet the f. d. early in 1659, as in the inv. show. £103, 18, of date 2 Mar. HUMPHREY, Plymouth 1657, a Quaker, who prob. had come but few mos. bef. he was expel. from the Col. in Oct. being "found guilty of divers horrid errors," and driv. to R. I. There the quiet of tolerat. could not be long endur. and in the spring foll. he went back to court persecution, and at the June Court had the advantage of attract. attention eno. to be whip. imprison. and made to pay fees therefor; but the severity of that minor jurisdict. even aft. the death of Gov. Bradford, rose not to the sublime of folly exhibit. by Mass. and, I suppose, Humphrey went home in 1658, to avoid what he had first sought. Yet the infection was malign. eno. at Plymouth to drive Hatherly and Cudworth from their high places of serv. Prob. he was no relat. of Rev. John, whose extreme virulence against this sect, was better suit. to the majority of our people than the new form of worship of the disciples. JAMES, New Haven 1640. JOHN, Charlestown, may have come in 1629, but certain. was here next yr. had gone to York, where Stone, on a trading voyage along shore, took him up in 1633, for a companion to Virginia, but near the mouth of Connecticut, the Pequots, in a quarrel, cut off the whole party. He was call. capt. in Charlestown. Winth. I. 123. JOHN, Ipswich, an eminent divine, s. of William, b. 6 May 1606, says Mather, at Starford, meaning, I think, Bishop Stortford, in Herts, bred at Peter House, in the Univ. of Cambridge, where I saw his subscriptions on tak. his A. B. 1623–4, and A. M. 1627, tho. by the Magn. it is said (with unusual confid. even for that work) he left the Univ. on occasion of a disaster to his f.'s est. and bec. an usher to a sch. and curate at Starford. He was domestic chaplain to Sir William Masham in the neighb. Co. Essex, but could obt. no preferm. and dissatisf. with the formalities demand. in the ch. serv. emb. in 1634, to come to our country with Shepard, but they were compel. by a storm to go back, and he came later than S. next yr. reaching Plymouth aft. ano. terrible storm in ship with Gov. Winslow, being the Hopewell, capt. Babb, prob. in Oct. 1635; but he could not be content there, aft. teach. some mos. tho. earnest. desir. by the people. At Ipswich he was ord. 1636, freem. yet without prefix of resp. 17 May 1637, not long aft. d. of famous John Cotton was call. to make good his place in Boston, and instal. 23 July 1656. In Feb. 1662 was sent with Bradstreet to make fair weather for our Col. in London, fulfill. his mission with skill, and came back in Sept. but was less kindly rec. here, especially by those who had desir. no such result, and d. 5 Apr. 1663, leav. w. Mary but no ch. in his will, pro. 16 Apr. foll. ment. br. William of Ipswich, br. Thomas of London, mo. sis. Eliz. and his w. Mary. His wid. d. 17 Jan. 1678. Her will, of 20 Aug. 1677, ment. neph. John, wh. bec. min. of Hingham, brs. Thomas and William, sis. Eliz. and Mary, beside sis. Lucy, w. of William. JOHN, Branford 1645, perhaps s. of Thomas of Saybrook, had there sev. ch. by w. Hannah Clark, rem. to Hartford, and soon to Farmington, there had Samuel, bapt. 20 May 1659, d. soon; in Oct. 1661, brot. for bapt. his ch. Hannah, aged a. 12; Dorothy, 10; John, 8; and Thomas, a. 13 mos.; was freem. 1657 or 1664, and d. 1711. |JOHN, Guilford, s. of Thomas, freem. 1667, m. Hannah, d. of William Stone of the same, and sec. w. Eliz. Hubbard, had John, b. 18 Nov. 1666, d. in few wks.; John, again, 29 May 1668; Samuel, 4 Oct. 1672; Thomas, 4 Mar. 1675; Hannah, 4 Feb. 1678; and Mary, 1680; but whether all by first w. tho. prob. is not distinct. told. He d. 5 Mar. 1704. His will of 24 Feb. 1701, names three s. and two ds. JOHN, Hingham, third min. s. of William of Ipswich, ord. 27 Nov. 1678, m. the same week, Mary, d. of Arthur Mason of Boston, had Eliz. and John, and d. 3 Oct. 1716. JOHN, Springfield, m. 1678, Lydia, d. of deac. Samuel Wright, wid. of Lawrence Bliss, had no ch. by her. JOHN, Salem, a carpenter, was call. 56 yrs. old in 1693, m. 3 Apr. 1660, Mary, perhaps d. of Elder Samuel Sharp, had Mary, b. 4 Jan. 1662, d. in one mo.; Mary, again, 26 Apr. 1664; Hannah, 17 Oct. 1668; Abigail, 30 Jan. 1671; George, 20 Apr. 1672; Eliz. 30 Aug. 1674; and John, 30 Oct. 1679. JOHN,

Farmington, s. of John of the same, had John, bapt. 6 Apr. 1684; Mary, 21 Nov. 1686; Sarah, prob. 31 Mar. but rec. says 1 Apr. (the fool's day that yr. being Monday) 1689; Hannah, 15 May 1692; Dorcas, 20 Jan. 1695; and three or four others, whose names and dates are not seen. JOSEPH, Salisbury, m. 10 Mar. 1662, Susanna, d. of Samuel Getchell, had s. b. 1662, d. soon; Samuel, 11 Oct. 1663; Joseph, 14 Aug. 1665; Priscilla, 16 Dec. 1667; Solomon, 31 Jan. 1670; Benjamin, 24 Mar. 1672; Caleb, June 1675; Flower, a d. 21 Nov. 1677; and Joshua, 13 Oct. 1680. NICHOLAS, Weymouth, had Isaac, b. 3 May 1641; and Jacob, 1 Mar. 1644. NICHOLAS, Edgartown 1669, perhaps s. of the preced. had w. Eliz. and eleven ch. of wh. 4 were s. and one of them, Joseph, was head of a long line of descend. He and w. d. a. 1690, he a. 80 yrs. old. RICHARD, Boston 1648, a cooper, by w. Dorothy had Richard, b. perhaps 10 Feb. 1650, d. on the same; and the f. d. bef. 8 Aug. 1657, when his est. was apprais. SAMUEL, Boston, wh. d. 28 June 1654, may have been only trans. visitor. THOMAS, Guilford, one of the signers of the first compact, 1 June 1639, d. 1648, bef. mid. life, leav. w. Grace, s. Thomas, and John; ds. Ann; Grace; Mary; and Abigail, wh. m. 1667, Ananias Trians; Ann m. John Warner at Hartford; Grace m. 2 Apr. 1651, William Seward; and Mary m. 7 Apr. 1660, Samuel Rockwell of Windsor. THOMAS, Salem 1654, made by George Williams first of the overseers of his will that yr. THOMAS, Saybrook, s. of the first Thomas, m. 8 May 1671, Eliz. d. of John Mason, had Eliz. b. 13 Oct. 1674, d. young; Thomas, 1 June 1677; Eliz. again, 26 Dec. 1679; Joseph and Samuel, tw. 6 Nov. 1681; Abigail and Ebenezer, tw. 16 Oct. 1683; and John, 3 Oct. 1686. His w. d. 31 Jan. 1699; he rem. to Durham, and d. late in 1712. WALTER, a capt. desir. adm. as freem. 19 Oct. 1630, and 18 May foll. was rec. but very uncert. is it, when, or whence he came, whither he went, or where resid. exc. that Charlestown may seem better entitled than any other town, for a capt. N. was very early sett. there, and it has been guessed that this was the capt. k. by the Pequots 1633, who by me is in the Index to Winthrop's Hist. call. John, on what authority, however, in the lapse of above thirty yrs. is forgotten. WILLIAM, Ipswich, strange. call. rev. in Geneal. Reg. XIII. 229, was younger br. of Rev. John, came in the Hopewell, capt. Babb, late in 1635, aged 25, from London, tho. he had prob. come in 1632, with Edward Winslow, in the William and Francis, arr. at Boston 5 June; freem. 3 Mar. 1636, then, perhaps, of Hingham, yet it is not easy to find where he liv. bef. going to I. nor when or wh. he m. He d. 30 Apr. 1694, and by his will of two days preced. pro. 15 May foll. we gain positive knowledge, and find his w. Lucy, d. of Emmanuel Downing, as is said, ch. Rev. John, H. C. 1671; and Bonus, bef. ment.; Eliz.

w. of John Wainwright, Esq. aft. w. of Hon. Isaac Addington. Other younger ch. William, b. 12 Feb. 1661; and Lucy, 25 Jan. 1662, were prob. d. bef. the will. The wid. d. 5 Feb. 1698. WILLIAM, Boston 1658, m. 14 Dec. 1659, Susanna, d. of Ralph Mason, had John, b. 22 Aug. 1660; William, 14 Sept. 1662; David, 31 May 1664; Mary, 5 Feb. 1668; William, again, 8 July 1670; Mary, again, 15 Dec. 1671; and Susanna, 25 June 1676. Twelve of this name had, in 1834, been gr. at Yale, seven at Harv. and four at other N. E. coll.

NORWICH, JOHN, freem. 13 May 1640, of wh. we kn. no more, and have no clue even to his resid. exc. that the freemen's list has his name betw. a Brown of Newbury and a Pitts of Hingham.

NORWOOD, CALEB, Gloucester, youngest s. of Francis, m. Alice, d. prob. of Hon. Samuel Donnell, had sev. ch. rem. to Boston, there kept an inn, made his will 29 Nov. 1735, nam. s. Gustavus, and five ds. FRANCIS, Gloucester, m. 15 Oct. 1663, Eliz. Coldum, prob. d. of Clement the sec. had Thomas, b. 10 Dec. 1664; Francis, 9 Dec. 1666; Eliz. 17 Feb. 1669; Mary, 7 Jan. 1672; Stephen, 24 Nov. 1674; Deborah, 14 Sept. 1677; Hannah, 8 Nov. 1679; Joshua, 1683; Caleb, 1685; and Abigail, 1689; and he d. 4 Mar. 1709. FRANCIS, Gloucester, s. of the preced. m. 24 Jan. 1693, Mary, d. of James Stevens, had William, and Jonathan, wh. both liv. long. JOSHUA, Gloucester, br. of the preced. m. 25 Sept. 1704, Eliz. d. of William Andrews of Ipswich, had four s. and eleven ds. says Babson in his valua. Hist. of G. and d. 1762. RICHARD, Cambridge, d. 13 May 1644. STEPHEN, Gloucester, s. of the first Francis, m. Feb. 1702, Eliz. Ingleby, and d. 7 Jan. foll. THOMAS, Gloucester, s. of Francis, m. 24 Aug. 1685, Mary, d. of Thomas Brown of Lynn, and Lewis tells of six ch. Francis, Ebenezer, Mary, Thomas, Mary, and Jonathan, without dates of any.

NOSEWORTHY, ROBERT, Boston 1675, mariner.

NOTT, * JOHN, Wethersfield 1640, or earlier, had Hannah, b. 10 June 1649; John, 10 Jan. 1651; and Eliz. who was eldest; was oft. a rep. from 1665, in 19 sess. d. 25 Jan. 1682, leav. as in his will two yrs. preced. ment. wid. Ann, and those ch. of wh. Hannah m. John Hale; and Eliz. m. Robert Reeves. From him in fourth generat. was the late Rev. Dr. Samuel, Y. C. 1780, wh. d. in 99th yr. on 26 May 1852. JOHN, Wethersfield, s. of the preced. m. 28 Mar. 1683, Patience, d. of William Miller, had John, b. 23 Nov. 1683; Jonathan, 4 June 1685; William, 19 Nov. 1686; Thomas, 1 Oct. 1688; Nathaniel, 18 Apr. 1691; Gershom, 19 Mar. 1693; Thankful, 6 Jan. 1695; Abraham, 29 Jan. 1697; and Ann, 29 July 1699; and he d. 21 Mar. 1710. His wid. outliv. 1745.

NOWELL, ALEXANDER, Charlestown, s. of Increase, freem. 1671, compos. sev. almanacs, but d. 13 July 1672, prob. unm. ‖ GEORGE, Boston, blacksmith, ar. co. 1662. ‡ INCREASE, Charlestown, came 1630, in the fleet with Winth. prob. in the Arbella, was one of the founders of first ch. in Boston, his being the fifth name on the list of memb. and w. Parnell the fourteenth, had here Increase, b. 19, bapt. 21 Nov. 1630, d. young; Abigail, b. 27 Apr. bapt. 3 June 1632, being the very next bapt. to that of Increase, because intermed. Wilson the min. had been gone to Eng. and she d. young; was one of the founders of the new ch. at Charlestown by setting off from Boston, had Samuel, b. 12, bapt. 22 Nov. 1634, H. C. 1653; Eleazer, b. 16 Nov. 1636, d. soon; Mehitable, b. 2 Feb. 1638; Increase, again, 23 May 1640, prob. error for 13, as he was bapt. 19 of that mo.; Mary, 26 May 1643; and Alexander, a. 1645, H. C. 1664. His w. was Parnell Gray, d. of wid. Catharine Coytemore, who came over with the fam. of N. and elder sis. of capt. Thomas Coytemore, but the w. of N. was by her first h. Gray; and the prop. of Coytemore, bef. the law made half blood to be heirs, was adjudged to descend. of Coytemore alone. He was always in pub. serv. hav. early giv. up the place of ch. elder, was Secr. of the Col. many yrs. and Assist. from the elect. in Eng. bef. the royal chart. to his d. 1 Nov. 1655. His wid. d. 25 Mar. 1687, aged 84. Mehitable m. William Hilton, and next, deac. John Cutler, and d. 1711; Mary m. 14 Aug. 1666, Isaac Winslow, and next, 16 Sept. 1674, John Long. PHILIP, Salem, mariner, drown. 15 Nov. 1675. ROBERT, Salem, m. 1 Jan. 1668, Mary Tatchell, unless this be, as I conject. an impossib. name, had William and Robert, tw. both d. in few days; Mary, b. 27 Feb. 1670; and Robert, 5 Nov. 1672. ‡ SAMUEL, Charlestown, eldest surv. s. of Increase, a preach. but never a sett. min. was chaplain in Philip's war, both on Conn. riv. and in the gr. Narraganset fight, where his bravery is much applaud. in Magn. VII. cap. 6, sec. 10, and Mather wishes us to suppose, that he used other than spiritual weapons; freem. 1677, Assist. 1680, and in Oct. 1685, chos. Treasr. of the Col. from wh. the royal commiss. to Dudley next yr. reliev. him; went to Eng. to act with Mather at Court, in favor of the country, but d. at London, in Sept. 1688. His wid. Mary, by wh. he had no ch. d. 14 Aug. 1693. She was d. of William Alford, and was first w. of Peter Butler, third w. of Hezekiah Usher, and first of N. This fam. was of repute in Eng. Alexander, dean of St. Paul's in Queen Eliz. day, a learned puritan, s. of John of Great Mearly, near Clitheroe, in Lancashire, on the edge of Yorksh. d. 13 Feb. 1601, aged 90, says Wood's Athenæ. THOMAS, Windsor, an early sett. tho. it is not thot. that he had been at Dorchester, had w. Eliz. but no ch. and in his will of 3 Nov. 1648, aft. small gifts to his kindr. Rob-

ert Wilson, and Isabel Phelps, devises a compet. est. to w. for life, remaind. in fee to Christopher Nowell, s. of Edward of Wakefield, Yorksh.
yet he calls neither his br. Both the will and inv. of 22 Feb. foll. are
in J. H. Trumbull's Conn. Col. Rec. I. 506, 8. A reasonable conject.
may arise, from the moderate distance betw. Wakefield and Clitheroe,
less than 40 miles, that the stock of this Windsor wayfarer and our
Secr. of Mass. was in the sixteenth cent. the same, tho. we find no evid.
of their ever meet. in our country. Farmer says the name is still found
in both the States of New Hampsh. and Mass. and I should be very
glad to see the deduction from first comer.

NOYES, NOYCE, or NOISE, CUTTING, Newbury, s. of Nicholas, freem.
1674, m. 25 Feb. 1674, Eliz. d. of John Knight, had John, b. 15 Dec.
1674; Cutting, 28 Jan. 1677; Eliz. 2 Jan. 1679; Nicholas, 22 May
1681, d. at 14 yrs.; Joseph, 21 Jan. 1689; and Mary, 27 Mar. 1693.
JAMES, Newbury, one of the two first min. b. 1608, at Choulderton, in
Wilts, near the edge of Hants, betw. Amesbury in W. and Andover in
H. s. of Rev. William, who was instit. I find by the registry of that
diocese, in 1602 as rector, but in 1621, resign. in favor of Nathan Noyes.
His mo. was sis. of Robert Parker a very learned Puritan, driv. to
Holland for his heterodoxy a. forms; and he was bred at Brazen Nose,
Oxford, as his nephew, Rev. Nicholas in his acco. for Magn. III.
cap. 25, Append. writes, and was call. away by his cous. Thomas
Parker to assist him at the sch. of Newbury, in Berksh. He m. 1634,
Sarah, eldest d. of Mr. Joseph Brown of Southampton, and in Mar. of
that yr. emb. for N. E. in co. with his br. Nicholas and cous. Thomas
Parker, in the Mary and John of London, preach. some short time at
Medford, was freem. 3 Sept. 1634, and invit. to Watertown ch. but in
1635 went to Newbury, and tho. younger than his collea. cous. d. first,
22 Oct. 1656. His will, made five days bef. ment. w. Sarah and ch. br.
Rev. Nicholas N. and cous. Rev. Thomas Parker; the inv. show. good
est. and ch. were Joseph, b. 15 Oct. 1637; James, 11 Mar. 1640, H. C.
1659; Sarah, 12 Aug. 1641, d. young; Moses, 6 Dec. 1643, H. C.
1659; John, 3 June 1645; Thomas, 10 Aug. 1648; Rebecca, 1 Apr.
1651; William, 22 Sept. 1653; Sarah, again, 25 Mar. 1656; and his
wid. d. 13 Sept. 1691. Sarah m. 31 Mar. 1684, Rev. John Hale of
Beverly. We owe gratitude to Mather for rare modesty in being
content with the faithful and judic. contrib. of the Salem kinsman, of
wh. in our day Eliot's Biogr. Dict. has well abbrev. the charact. *JAMES*,
Stonington, s. of the preced. began there to preach 1664, yet was not
ord. bef. 10 Sept. 1674, m. next day Dorothy, d. of Thomas Stanton
(who d. 19 Jan. 1743, in her 91st yr.) had Dorothy, b. 20 June foll. tho.
in ano. place the date is 16 Jan. 1676; James, 2 Aug. 1677; Thomas,

15 Aug. 1679; Ann, 16 Apr. 1682, d. at 12 yrs.; John, 13 Jan. 1685; Joseph, 16 Oct. 1688, Y. C. 1709; and Moses, 19 Mar. 1692, d. next mo. He preach. 55 yrs. d. 30 Dec. 1719. Much honor attach. to his name for so long faithful fulfilm. of his ministry, as in a most judicious fun. serm. by Adams of New London, is shown; and equal. so for serv. in the foundat. of Yale Coll. stand. there as the first on the list of Fellows. JAMES, Newbury, s. of Nicholas, m. 31 Mar. 1684, Hannah, d. of John Knight, whose two elder ds. had m. his two elder brs. had Rebecca, b. 12 Jan. 1685; Joseph, 20 Sept. 1686; Hannah, 13 Mar. 1688; Nicholas, 9 Feb. 1690; Nathan, 5 Feb. 1692; Ephraim, 20 Nov. 1694, d. in 3 wks.; Lydia, 30 Nov. 1695; Ephraim, again, 25 Dec. 1698; Benjamin, 22 Feb. 1701; Mary, 13 Mar. 1703; and James, 19 Aug. 1705. JOHN, Newbury, s. of Nicholas, m. 23 Nov. 1668, Mary, d. of John Poor, had Nicholas, b. 18 May 1671; Daniel, 23 Oct. 1673; Mary, 10 Dec. 1675; John, 15 Feb. 1678; Martha, 24 Dec. 1679, d. soon; Martha, again, 19 Dec. 1680; Nathaniel, 28 Oct. 1681; Eliz. 15 Nov. 1684; Moses, 22 May 1688; and Samuel, 9 Feb. 1692. He was freem. 1674. JOHN, Boston, freem. 1676, was that yr. constable, m. Sarah, d. of Peter Oliver, had Sarah; John; and Oliver, b. 1675, bapt. 22 Oct. 1676, H. C. 1695. JOSEPH, Salisbury 1640, had, perhaps, Mary, wh. m. 23 Mar. 1651, John French of Ipswich; but this name in Geneal. Reg. III. 55 and 6, is Moys. JOSEPH, ·Charlestown, m. 30 Oct. 1656, Mary, d. of Francis Norton, and she d. 10 Nov. 1657, being bound on a voyage when he made his will, 21 Dec. 1659, wh. was pro. 2 Apr. 1661, in wh. he calls Peter and Thomas of Sudbury, his brs. and "father Norton's four ds." his sis. gives land in Eng. all wh. may indicate him as s. of the first Peter. JOSEPH, Sudbury, perhaps s. of the first Thomas, m. 1662, Mary, d. of Robert Darvell, had Joseph, b. 1663; James, 1664; Moses, 1667; and five more, one of wh. was John, 1674, bef. she d. 1677. He next m. 14 July 1680, Mary, wid. of maj. Simon Willard, wh. d. 28 Dec. 1715, and he d. 16 Nov. 1717. Shattuck, in Farmer, says he was selectman 28 yrs. from 1662, yet we find not his name among the freem. of the Col. *MOSES*, Lyme, s. of the first James, was the first min. at that place, where he serv. 60 yrs.; m. Ruth, d. of John Picket, but of the issue I kn. nothing. * NICHOLAS, Newbury, younger br. of the first James, b. a. 1616, came with him, freem. 17 May 1637, m. Mary, d. of capt. John Cutting had Mary, b. 15 Oct. 1641; Hannah, 30 Oct. 1643; John, 20 Jan. 1646; Nicholas, 22 Dec. 1647, H. C. 1667; Cutting, 23 Sept. 1649; Sarah, 13 Sept. 1651, d. soon; Sarah, again, 22 Aug. 1653; Timothy, 23 June 1655; James, 16 May 1657; Abigail, 11 Apr. 1659; Rachel, 10 May 1661; Thomas, 20 June 1663; and Rebecca, 18 May 1665, wh. d. at 18 yrs. He was rep. 1660, 79, and 80, and d. 9 Nov.

1701. Hannah m. 14 May 1663, Peter Cheney; and Sarah m. 13 Sept. 1674, Matthew Pettingell. NICHOLAS, Salem, s. of the preced. preach. many yrs. at Haddam, but having in 1682 a call to S. to assist the venera. John Higginson, he became his collea. ord. 14 Nov. 1683, was one of the promoters of the horrible delusion of 1692, and yet a d. of his noble collea. was one of the accused. He did not altogether lose his faculties, as his let. to Mather of the character of his uncle, wh. is certain. one of the best parts of the strange. compound of materials in the Magnalia; as also a good epistle to John Higginson in London, preserv. in 3 Mass. Hist. Coll. VII. 212, will prove. He d. 13 Dec. 1717, unm. * OLIVER, Boston, s. of John of B. m. Ann, d. of Hon. Andrew Belcher, had Ann, b. 17 Apr. 1704; Oliver, 4 July 1705, d. in few days; Oliver, again, 1 Sept. 1707, d. at 7 mos.; Belcher, 10 Oct. 1709, H. C. 1727; Sarah, 21 Oct. 1710; John, 12 Aug. 1713, d. young; and John, again, 8 Aug. 1718, d. in few weeks; was rep. 1714, oft. aft. took sec. w. 6 Feb. 1719, Catharine, wid. of sec. David Jeffries; and d. 16 Mar. 1721. Hutchinson, wh. well kn. him, gives character, II. 249. * PETER, Sudbury 1639, came in the Confidence, 1638, from Southampton, latter part of Apr. aged 47, with s. Thomas, 15; d. Eliz. and three serv. is call. yeoman in the custom-ho. rec. but aft. arr. gentleman. He was of Penton, in Co. Hants, wh. is near Andover; went home aft. short visit or explorat. here, well pleased with what he saw at Watertown, and next yr. came again in the Jonathan, with sev. friends, and Nicholas, Dorothy, Abigail, and Peter, all prob. his ch. beside John Waterman, Richard Barnes, William Street, Agnes Bent, Eliz. Plimpton, and Agnes Blanchard, wh. I judge to be his serv. as he paid for their passages; but such was not Agnes Bent, for she paid for herself, for d. Agnes, Thomas Blanchard's w. with her h. and Richard Barnes, s. of said Blanchard's w. and prob. Eliz. Plimpton. Blanchard's w. with inf. d. on the passage, 15 days out, and Barnes's gr.mo. d. this side of the Banks. He had share in the first div. of lds. in his town, and again in the 2d and 3d, made 1640, was freem. 13 May 1640, selectman 18 yrs. rep. 1640, 1, and 50, deac. of the ch. and d. 23 Sept. 1657. Three yrs. bef. he gave his est. in Old Eng. to his eldest s. Thomas, and in his will, of wh. Thomas was made excor. made the day bef. his d. he names other ch. Peter, Joseph, Eliz. w. of Josiah Haynes, Dorothy, w. of John Haynes, Abigail, w. of Thomas Plympton, d.-in-law Mary, w. of his s. Thomas, and kinsm. Shadrach Hapgood. * PETER, Sudbury, s. of the preced. m. 30 Nov. 1654, Eliz. d. of Robert Darvell, had Eliz. b. 26 Aug. 1655, wh. m. 21 Aug. 1677, Thomas Hammond; Peter, 12 Feb. 1657; and, perhaps, more, freem. 1672, rep. 1679, 90, and 1. RICHARD, Newbury 1647. * THOMAS, Sudbury, eldest s. of Peter the first, had share in the first, sec. and third grants of lds. or divisions on sett. 1639 and 1640; and his f.'s est. in Eng. to wh. he had been sent some yrs. aft. he was brot. in 1638 at the age of 15, came again in the Speedwell, arr. 27 July 1656, m. Mary, d. of Walter Haynes, who had been his fell. passeng. in early youth, by the Confidence, was twelve yrs. a selectman, and rep. at the sec. sess. 1664; d. 7 Dec. 1666. His will, of 20 May 1664, names w. Mary, but no ch. ment. sis. Eliz. Dorothy, and Abigail, and two eldest ds. of Josiah Tredaway, whose w. Sufferance was sis. of his w. He had est. at Foxcote, near Andover, Eng. and was interest. in iron works at Concord, also in those of the Leonards at Taunton. * THOMAS, Newbury, s. of the first James, m. 28 Dec. 1669, Martha Pierce, and for sec. w. 24 Sept. 1677, Eliz. d. of Stephen Greenleaf, had Sarah, b. 14 Sept. 1670; Martha, 24 Feb. 1673; Daniel, 30 Aug. 1674, by the first w. and by the next, James, 3 July 1678; Thomas, 2 Oct. 1679; Parker, 29 Oct. 1681; Eliz. 29 Feb. 1684; Joseph, 5 Aug. 1688; Moses, 29 Jan. 1692; Rebecca, 19 Apr. 1700; and Judith, 17 Apr. 1702; freem. 1671, and capt. 1690 in war with E. Ind. and rep. 1689, 90, and 2. THOMAS, Newbury, youngest s. of Nicholas the first, by w. Sarah had Bethia, b. 20 Oct. 1691; and Rebecca, 20 Jan. 1694, d. in few days. TIMOTHY, Newbury, s. of the first Nicholas, m. 13 Jan. 1681, Mary, d. of John Knight, had James, b. 12 Mar. 1684; Abigail, 28 Feb. 1685; Mary, 28 Dec. 1686; Sarah, 26 Mar. 1689; Timothy, 25 Jan. 1691; Rachel, 8 Feb. 1694; John, 19 Feb. 1696; Martha, 14 Mar. 1697; and Nicholas, 7 Mar. 1701; was freem. 1684, and d. 1718. WILLIAM, Newbury, s. of James the first, m. 6 Nov. 1685, Sarah Cogswell, had John, b. 27 July 1686; William, 11 Sept. 1688; Sarah, 10 May 1691, d. young; Moses, 27 Jan. 1694, d. in 3 wks.; Susanna, 25 Feb. 1696; Mary, 24 May 1699, d. young; Sarah, again, 5 Dec. 1703; and Parker, 17 Jan. 1705. Considering the very short distance betw. the resid. of the two progenit. of this widely diffus. name, in the W. border of Hants, and the E. frontier of Wilts, where ea. stood in favora. social position in the latter days of Queen Eliz. no doubt can be felt of their common origin. Fifteen of this name had, in 1834, been gr. at Harv. twelve at Yale (all descend. of Stonington James), and eleven at other N. E. coll.

NUDD, JOSEPH, Hampton 1678, was prob. s. of Thomas. THOMAS, Hampton, s. it is said, of Roger, was a minor with his wid. mo. at Watertown, wh. bef. 1645, bec. third w. of Henry Dow, and rem. from W. to H.; m. 9 Dec. 1659, Sarah, d. of Godfrey Dearborn, and had seven ch. says fam. tradit. of wh. one was Samuel, and, perhaps, ano. Joseph.

NUNN, RICHARD, a passeng. in the Increase, from London to Boston, 1635, aged 19, but no more is heard.

NURSE, BENJAMIN, Framingham, s. of Francis, by w. Thomasine had Thomasine, b. 13 Nov. 1691; Benjamin, 20 Jan. 1694; William, 8 Mar. 1696; Eliz. 18 Sept. 1698 ; Ebenezer, 27 Mar. 1701; Margaret, 24 Apr. 1703 ; Moses, Mar. 1705; and Aaron, 11 Jan. 1708. He m. sec. w. 16 Feb. 1714, Eliz. wid. of Joseph Morse ; and prob. d. late in 1747, or early in 1748, for Barry found his will pro. 13 Feb. 1748. FRANCIS, Salem, in that part now Danvers, by w. Rebecca, d. of William Towne, had John ; Samuel; Rebecca ; Mary; Francis, b. 3 Feb. 1661; Benjamin, 26 Jan. 1666 ; Michael ; and ano. d. who m. William Russell. Rebecca m. 15 Apr. 1669, Thomas Preston ; and Mary m. 1678, John Tarbell. The unhappy mo. of these ch. suffer. death in the stupendous fanaticism of 1692, wh. began the investig. of her case, 24 Mar. tho. twice the jury fail. to find a verdict, to wh. at last they assent. from her not giv. satisfact. answers to their questions in open Court, that from her deafness she fail. to understand. Sir William Phips, the Gov. upon hearing this, prepar. a reprieve, but by solicit. of those who had less responsibility, weak. withheld it, and the dreadful sentence was execut. on 19th July; and he surv. until 22 Nov. 1695, aged 77. Her sis. Sarah Cloyce, not less guilty, perhaps, aft. long suffer. having better hearing, escaped with life. Felt, in Ann. of Salem, I. 484, well sums up the cases. She was excommunica. bef. trial, but that opprobrious deed was cancell. 20 yrs. aft. the sufferer was hang. FRANCIS, Reading, s. of the preced. by w. Sarah had Francis, b. 1686, d. early ; Benjamin, 28 Jan. 1690 ; Jonathan, 1692, d. at 25 yrs. ; Josiah, 1694, d. at 24 yrs. ; Joshua ; Caleb ; Nathaniel, 1697, who all d. bef. mid. age ; and Abigail. His est. was sett. says Barry, in 1716. This name is commonly made Nourse. JOHN, Salem, br. of the first Francis, m. 1 Nov. 1672, Eliz. Smith, had John, b. 12 Oct. 1673 ; and he m. sec. w. 17 Aug. 1677, Eliz. Very, had Eliz. 18 Mar. 1678 ; Samuel, 20 Aug. 1679 ; Sarah, 10 Nov. 1680; Jonathan, 3 May 1682; Joseph, 20 Sept. 1683; Benjamin, 20 Feb. 1686; Hannah, 22 Jan. 1687 ; and Deborah ; and he d. 1719. SAMUEL, Salem, br. of the preced. m. 5 Apr. 1677, Mary Smith, had Samuel, b. 7 Jan. 1678; Margaret, 24 Feb. 1680; George, 29 July 1682; Mary, 25 May 1685 ; Rebecca, 15 Sept. 1688 ; and Ebenezer. He was freem. 1690 ; but suffer. some disability in the Christian ch. prob. bec. he was s. of his mo.

NUTBROWNE, FRANCIS, a youth of 16, passeng. 1635, in the Defence, from London for Boston, wh. is not again heard of.

NUTE, ABRAHAM, Dover 1666, prob. s. of James the first, had w. Joanna and s. Abraham, b. 9 Mar. 1706. JAMES, Dover 1631, one of the men sent by Mason and other patentees, was still there 1659, had James, b. 1643 ; and Abraham, 1644. JAMES, Dover, s. prob. of the preced. m. Eliz. d. of John Heard, had James, b. 27 July 1687; Samuel, 1689; and two other ch. as the indefatiga. Mr. Quint shows in Geneal. Reg. VII. 258; but he makes his wid. in 1691 Mary.

NUTT, MILES, Watertown, freem. 17 May 1637, brot. from Eng. d. Sarah, who m. 5 Nov. 1644, at Woburn, where he then resid. John Wyman, and next, 25 Aug. 1684, Thomas Fuller; but he d. at Malden, 2 July 1671. There he had liv. sev. yrs.; was one of the petitnrs. in favor of freedom in the ch. made contr. of m. 4 Jan. 1659 with wid. Sibell Bibble, wh. was for benefit of herself and her d. Ann, w. of Robert Jones of Hull, aft. of Lancaster, pro. 15 Dec. 1674, by James Cary and Thomas Carter, who had, with Solomon Phipps, been witn. of his will, 1 Feb. 1661, in wh. said contr. was design. to be fulfil. In that will he made John Wyman sen. excor. provides for the sec. w. names d. Sarah, her s. John, and, perhaps, others of the ch. Inv. of the est. was with the vol. of rec. burned. The wid. m. 30 Oct. 1674, John Doolittle, of that part of Boston call. Rumney marsh, who d. 1681, and she d. 23 Sept. 1690, aged 82.

NUTTER, ‡* ANTHONY, Dover, s. of Hatevil, had John, b. 27 Dec. 1662, perhaps other ch. was freem. 1666, rep. in Mass. 1674 and 6, of the Counc. N. H. 1682, d. 19 Feb. 1686. HATEVIL, Dover 1641, was in 1649 of the gr. jury in Maine, but soon back on the W. side of the river; much betrust. a rul. elder, active against the Quakers, as says Sewall, I. 564, wh. perverts his good name to Nutwell, had beside Anthony and, perhaps, other childr. a d. who m. Thomas Laighton; Mary, wh. m. John Wingate; and he d. 1675, aged 71.

NUTTING, JAMES, Groton, prob. s. of John, by w. Lydia, d. of William Longley, had Sarah, b. 11 Mar. 1681; Lydia, 3 June 1686; Joanna, 21 Feb. 1691; Ruth, 17 Apr. 1693; Eliz. 5 Nov. 1698; and William, betw. Lydia and Joanna, who d. 12 Apr. 1712. JOHN, Groton, m. at Woburn, 28 Aug. 1650, Sarah Eggleton or Eggleden, or Iggleden, perhaps d. of Stephen, there had a s. b. 1651, who may have been John, and prob. other ch. certain. at Chelmsford, Mary, 16 Jan. 1656; and John, James, and Mary were bapt. 3 Aug. 1656; Sarah, b. 7 Jan. 1660, d. soon; but at G. the rec. gives these names: Sarah, 29 May 1663; Ebenezer, 23 Oct. 1666; and Jonathan, 17 Oct. 1668; was freem. 1660. JOHN, Groton, prob. s. of the preced. had two ws. both nam. Mary, of wh. the first, m. 11 Dec. 1674, was mo. of all his ch. but the dispersion of king Philip's war next yr. and long enduring perils of Ind. hostil. prevent. his return, account for deficiency of their rec.

NYE, BENJAMIN, Lynn, rem. to Sandwich 1637, where he was progenit. of a very numer. line, yet of a single s. only, Jonathan, b. 20 Nov. 1649, is the date of b. kn. and of Mary, 8 Apr. 1652. EBENEZER,

Sandwich, s. prob. of Benjamin, m. 17 Dec. 1675, Sarah Gibbes, and I suspect error in Col. Rec. wh. tells that his d. Bethia was b. 5 Oct. 1675. JOHN, Sandwich, perhaps br. of Ebenezer, had Benjamin, b. 25 Nov. 1673; John, 22 Nov. 1675; Abigail, 18 Apr. 1678; Experience, 16 Dec. 1682; Hannah, ‘19 June 1685; Ebenezer, 23 Sept. 1687; and Peleg, 12 Nov. 1689. Of this last, Esther was mo. and may have been of the preced. NATHAN, Sandwich, perhaps s. of Benjamin, had Remembrance, b. 28 Feb. 1687.

OAKES, * EDWARD, Cambridge, freem. 18 May 1642, brot. from Eng. w. Jane and ch. Urian, H. C. 1649 ; and Edward; had here Mary; and Thomas, H. C. 1662, this last b. 18 June 1644, both bapt. at C. was lieut. of Prentice's comp. in Philip's war, selectman 26 yrs. betw. 1643 and 78, rep. 15 yrs. betw. 1659 and 82, and of Concord 1684, where he d. 13 Oct. 1689. EDWARD, Cambridge, prob. s. of Urian, H. C. 1679, preach. a yr. aft. 1683 at Branford and New London, but bef. Sept. 1685, withdrew, as we learn from Caulkins's Hist. and no more, not even the yr. of his d. is kn. but he was d. bef. the Catal. of 1698, pr. in the Magn. GEORGE, Lynn 1654, had George; John, b. 30 July 1664; Mary, 18 Oct. 1666; Richard, 16 Dec. 1668 ; Sarah, 15 Mar. 1671 ; and Eliz. 25 Jan. 1674; and d. July 1688. Lewis gives the name of w. Jennet, but counts the number of ch. five, yet is liberal eno. to give the six names. NATHANIEL, Marlborough 1686, m. Mehitable, d. of John Rediat. RICHARD, Boston, had gr. of a lot a. 1635, wh. he did not improve, perhaps went home. SAMUEL, Boston, freem. 1690. SIMON, nam. in Hist. of Cambridge, by Dr. Holmes, as a propr. in 1632, is prob. mistak. for ano. person. THOMAS, Cambridge, br. of the first Edward, freem. 18 May 1642, by w. Eliz. had Eliz. b. 3 Nov. 1646, d. young ; Thomas, 5 Nov. 1648, d. at 2 mos. ; Eliz. again, 26 May 1650; Hannah, 4 May 1657 ; prob. Mary, wh. d. Aug. 1659 ; and Thomas, posthum. 18, bapt. 20 Mar. 1659, to wh. the f. in his will of 12 Sept. 1658, left double portion ; and made his wid. extrix. and d. bef. pro. (of course) of his will, 23 Dec. 1658, tho. town rec. says Aug. 1659. She m. Apr. 1661, Seth Sweetzer of Charlestown, and next, m. Samuel Hayward of Malden, wh. she outliv. and in her will of 11 May 1686, pro. 5 May 1687, takes notice of the portion of personal est. that came to her from her first h. wh. she gives to d. Abigail that she bore to Hayward, with condition that if it be more than £20, Samuel, s. of her late h. by former w. should have 20s. Eliz. m. 12 July 1670, Lemuel Jenkins ; and Hannah m. 7 Aug. 1672, Joseph Waite, both of Malden. ‡ * THOMAS, Boston, s. of the first Edward, a physician, by w. Martha had James, b. 30 Oct. 1687 ; and Josiah, 3 May 1689, H. C. 1708, min. of Eastham, was rep. 1689, speaker the same yr. an Assist. next yr. and until the new Chart. when

William and Mary, under dictation of Increase Mather, left him out, as he was sent, with Elisha Cooke to London, agents for the Col. to vindicate their rights under the old chart. He was speaker of the Ho. again, 1705 and 6, but rem. prob. to gratify his s. Josiah, to Cape Cod ; yet at Boston, his w. Martha d. 19 Apr. 1719, aged 70 ; and he d. 15 July foll. at Eastham. Perhaps that Urian O. wh. Judge Sewall bur. 5 Oct. 1694, with prefix of respect, may have been his s. John Dunton speaks very highly of him. THOMAS, Malden, s. of the first Thomas, carr. to M. by his mo. when she m. Samuel Hayward, m. 22 May 1689, Sarah d. of Peter Tufts, had Thomas, b. 2 Apr. 1690 ; Sarah, 23 May 1694 ; Lydia, 27 Nov. 1697 ; Uriah, 22 June 1700 ; Mary, 14 May 1702 ; Hannah, 28 Feb. 1705 ; Eliz. 20 May 1707 ; Jonathan, 6 Oct. 1709 ; and Abigail, 24 Dec. 1714 ; was freem. 1690, and d. Sept. 1732. His wid. d. July 1749. URIAN, Cambridge, s. of the first Edward, b. in Eng. a. 1631 or 2, pub. an Almanac for 1650, went home, and óbt. a situat. in the ch. the fine liv. of Titchfield, in Hants, 78 miles from London, m. as is said, Ruth, d. of famous William Ames, aft. eject. in 1662, and his w. d. 1669, he came again to C. but not bef. 1671, and was install. 8 Nov. 1671, to fill the place of matchless Mitchell, freem. 1672, and in Apr. 1675, chos. presid. of the coll. as success. to Dr. Hoar. How to construe the dark sayings of Cotton Mather in Book IV. 129 of the Magn. without indulg. of some suspicion against O. puzzled the late Presid. Quincy in his great Hist. of the Univ. and when we rememb. that a very short interval aft. the d. of Oakes, the greater Mather was call. to stand in his place, and that the lesser Mather was under Hoar and Oakes at the time of their academic. rule, we may suppose that the oracle was, as often happened, ambiguously inspired. Some tenderness may, however, be yield. to the Ecclesiast. Histor. for he did not feel as if call. by a Ct. of justice, under oath, to tell the whole truth. Silence was safety to hims. and superiors. What the learned s. of Increase meant by his phrase, about new election, 2 Feb. 1680, is of little consequence, for the presid. d. 25 July 1681, under 50 yrs. of age. Some obscurity also attaches to our kn. of his fam. Prob. he m. in Eng. and there had ch. two, three, four, or more ; but when b. who was the mo. how many were brot. over the ocean, whether his w. d. bef. or aft. are unansw. questions. That his d. Hannah m. 2 Sept. 1680, Rev. Samuel Angier, and was his only d. seems clear ; but the town rec. helps to incr. our vexation, as it tells the d. of Lawrence O. *bachelor of arts*, 13 June 1679, aged 18, and of Urian O. 3 Nov. foll. for we kn. there was no such bach. and are left to conject. that the honora. title belongs to Urian, H. C. 1678, who d. at 22 yrs. that Lawrence was an undergrad. and that both were s. of the presid. Of the gr. of 1679, Edward, too, doubts on more than one point would at this late day be not easy of solution.

OAKLEY, was the name of a wid. prob. Sarah, at Charlestown, wh. unit. with the ch. 30 Aug. 1634, but who was her h. or whether he d. on the voyage, or this side of the water, is unkn. yet Frothingham, 84, shows her resid. was allow. and on 14 Feb. 1654, an Eliz. Oakley, perhaps her d. m. at Boston, Edmund Brown.

OAKMAN, ELIAS, Scarborough 1666, perhaps s. of Samuel, m. Joanna, d. of Andrew Alger, had Elias, b. 21 Apr. 1680, as is rec. in Boston. His wid. m. John Mills. SAMUEL, Scarborough, on 13 July 1658, acknowl. alleg. to Mass. under his hand (by affix. his mark); had Samuel, and, perhaps, Elias, was selectman 1679, and d. next yr. It is print. Gakman in Geneal. Reg. V. 264.

OATES, JOHN, is the name of a soldier in Moseley's comp. Sept. 1675, k. by the Ind.

OBBINSON, WILLIAM, Boston 1675, a tanner, is of unkn. derivat. may have been that yr. driven in by the Ind. war from some outlying settlem. had w. Mary but no ch. and he with his w. 11 May 1704, gave their est. to Paul, then call. eldest surv. s. of the Gov. Joseph Dudley; but I can assign no cause for such generosity.

OBER, RICHARD, Salem 1668, Beverly 1679, m. Abigail, d. of Nicholas Woodbury of B. had Hezekiah, b. 1681; Ann; Richard, 1684; and Nicholas, 1686. Farmer says this name, writ. sometimes Obear, prevails near Beverly, and is found in New Hampsh. In the Watertown rec. Dr. Bond finds a name Orbear, THOMAS, with variations, Obear, and Ober, for wh. he suggests Hobart, with which I cannot agree, but this sett. by w. Mary had Samuel, b. 8 Aug. 1640; and Judith, 15 Mar. 1643.

OCKINGTON, or OKINGTON, SAMUEL, Watertown, may have been f. of that Mary O. wh. m. 30 Mar. 1692, Edward Harrington, but nothing is kn. of him. WILLIAM, Boston, by w. Mary had Matthias, b. 1 Jan. 1667; and Mary, 7 Sept. 1669.

ODELL, or ODLE, JOHN, Fairfield 1664, perhaps s. of William the first, freem. 1665. REGINALD, Boston, by w. Priscilla had Reginald, b. 20 Jan. 1687; Samuel, 29 Jan. 1688, d. soon; Thomas, 8 Apr. 1690; Samuel, again, 20 Aug. 1695; and William, 19 July 1697. WILLIAM, Concord 1639, prob. brot. w. and ch. from Eng. had here James, b. 2 Jan. 1640, d. next yr.; and Rebecca, 17 July 1642, rem. to Southampton, L. I. that yr. and soon aft. to Fairfield, in 1670 was call. sen. WILLIAM, Greenwich, perhaps s. of the preced. in 1681 was aged 47.

ODERIC, JOHN, Salem, d. 30 Dec. 1660, was, perhaps, only trans. visit. for his inv. of £41, 5, 11, was tak. 12 Dec. foll. and no relat. is nam.

ODIORNE, JOHN, Newcastle 1660, of gr. jury 1686, d. 1707. ‡Jo-

THAM, Newcastle, a counsel. who d. 16 Aug. 1748, aged 73, Farmer thinks was s. of the preced.

ODLIN, ODLYN, original. AUDLEY or AUDLIN, ELISHA, Boston, s. of John, m. Aug. 1659, Abigail, d. of deac. Henry Bright of Watertown, had Hannah, b. 3 Sept. 1666 ; Margaret, 26 Feb. 1669, d. soon; Abigail, 5 Apr. 1670; and Margaret, again, 5 Aug. 1672; John, 25, bapt. 28 May 1678; John, again, 18, bapt. 20 Nov. 1681, H. C. 1702 (min. of Exeter, who was f. of Elisha, H. C. 1731, min. of Amesbury, and of Woodbridge, H. C. 1738, min. at Exeter) ; and d. a. 1724. JOHN, Boston, one of the early sett. No. 139 on the ch. list, was a cutler or armorer, disfranchis. Nov. 1637 as an antinomian, by w. Margaret had·John, b. 3 June 1635, d. soon aft. says the town rec. but in the ch. bapt. 28 ; Hannah, 9 Feb. 1638, d. soon aft. says the town rec. but by the ch. bapt. 4 Mar. foll. ; Elisha, b. 1, bapt. 5 July 1640 ; John, again, 3, bapt. 13 Feb. 1642; Hannah, again, bapt. 29 Oct. 1643, a. 8 days old ; and Peter, bapt. 12 July 1646, a. 9 days old (while town rec. asserts his b. 2 Aug.) ; and d. 18 Dec. 1685, aged 83. His will, of 6 Mar. 1685, pro. 11 Jan. foll. of wh. Elisha was excor. names the three s. and gr.ch. Hannah Bumstead, but whose d. she was is not kn.

OFFITT, JOHN, Milford, s. of the first Thomas of the same, b. in Eng. had w. Hannah Hawley, who claim. divorce from him, and obtain. her desire, m. again, John Beard. He next m. 1656 or 7, Martha, d. of Samuel Nettleton of Branford, had Thomas, b. 20 Aug. 1657, d. young; Martha, 12 Aug. 1659 ; Mary, 20 June 1661; John, 3 Feb. 1665, d. soon ; John, again, 21 Jan. 1667 ; Samuel, 21 Jan. 1670 ; Eliz. 19 Feb. 1673 ; and Lydia. He was propound. for freem. 1670 ; and d. early in 1692, prob. as his inv. was tak. 4 May. By his will, of 29 July 1689, the two s. and four ds. are nam. as liv. Martha, w. of Peter Carrow ; Mary, w. of Daniel Picket ; and the two unm. Eliz. d. 1699, her prop. was distrib. to the five brs. and sis. and the name seems to be Uffet in one place, and Uffert in ano. THOMAS, Roxbury 1632, came in the Lion, arr. at Boston 16 Sept. with w. Isabel and ch. Thomas, John, and a d. wh. m. Roger Terrill, but whose name is not seen. This uncommon name is spelled Uffitt as the ch. rec. of R. exhibits it, or Uskitt, perhaps in despair of getting the letters into a more common shape, in the rec. of his qualifica. at London, adm. freem. 4 Mar. 1633, rem. 1635, with Pynchon to Springfield, where the name is Ufford, as the descend. now write it, but passing into Conn. at Milford 1639, where he and w. join. the ch. 1645, it bec. Uffoote. Chapin confus. the f. with s. of the same name, makes him an early propr. of Wethersfield, and aft. of Stratford 1644, whereas he was never an inhab. of either of those towns. A yr. or two bef. his d. he m. at Stamford, Eliz. wid. of Nicholas Thele, wh. outliv. him very little time, and d. 27 Dec. 1660. Of the day of his d. we are ign. but are sure that it was bef. 20 Aug. 1660, when his est. was div. tho. Lambert says he d. at Milford, 1691. THOMAS, Stratford, s. of the preced. b. in Eng. and prob. well gro. bef. his f. came over, for in 1641 he had ld. in Wethersfield, and there m. Frances, d. of the first Thomas Kilborne, who outliv. him but few wks. and in Jan. 1684 her est. was div. equal. among her br. John K. of W. and sis. Margaret, w. of Richard Law of Stamford, Lydia, w. of Robert Howard of Windsor, and Mary, w. of the first John Root of Farmington. He had large est. but no ch. and his name was, no doubt, in high esteem at S. yet the selectmen and constable, in return of their list of freem. give it Ufoth. The inv. of his prop. 26 Dec. 1683, show. £1,834, wh. by his will of 17 May preced. was giv. in a large proport. to Samuel, s. of his br. John, and good sh. to childr. of his br. Roger Terrill, to his br. John, and his childr. beside adeq. provis. for the wid.

OFFLEY, ‖ DAVID, Boston, ar. co. 1638, rem. to Plymouth 1643, but by letter of Gov. Bradford to Gov. Winthrop as to complts. of Ind. against O. dated 11 Dec. 1645, we may infer that he had come back to B. See 4 Mass. Hist. Coll. II. 119. THOMAS, Salem, collector of the port 1686-9.

OFIELD, THOMAS, Boston 1669, mariner, had w. Maudline, and sev. ch. yet in his will of 29 Sept. 1677, pro. 14 Oct. 1679, tho. he ment. w. and childr. gives the name of w. only.

OGDEN, ‡ * JOHN, Stamford 1641, agreed next yr. with Gov. Kieft of New York to build a stone ch. for 2,500 guilders, in 1644 was a patentee of Hempstead, L. I. liv. 1651 at Southampton, L. I. in 1656 was chos. an Assist. reëlect. to 1660, is nam. in the royal chart. of 1662, and chos. again that yr. an Assist. but went soon to New Jersey, and with Gov. Carteret made large purch.; was rep. for Elizabethtown in the first assemb. of that prov. 1668. * JOHN, Rye, perhaps s. of the preced. rep. 1674. RICHARD, Fairfield 1667, br. of the first John, had been partner with him in the contr. 1642 with Kieft. See O'Callaghan, Hist. of New Netherlands, I. 262, when he was of Stamford, was freem. 1668, and a large propr. of F. 1670; had descend. and most honorab. has been the name perpet.

OGLEBY, JAMES, Scarborough, 1676.

OKEY, JOHN, Boston, by w. Mary had Mary, b. 8 Oct. 1686; and Tacey, 9 May 1688.

OLCOTT, JOHN, Hartford 1676, youngest s. of Thomas the first, m. 1695, Mary, d. of John Blackleach, wid. of Mr. Thomas Welles, had Samuel, b. 16, bapt. 23 Aug. 1696; Mary, b. 1, bapt. 7 Aug. 1698; Rachel, b. 28 Oct. 1701; and Abigail, 15 Feb. 1704; and d. 1712. His wid. m. Joseph Wadsworth, and as his only s. did not m. the line bec. ext. at his d. SAMUEL, Hartford, br. of the preced. freem. 1664, m. Sarah, d. of George Stocking, d. Mar. 1704, in his will of 13th of that mo. pro. 12 Apr. foll. names ch. Thomas, George, Sarah, Mary, and Eliz. THOMAS, Hartford, an orig. propr. whose lot in 1640, is exhibit. on the ground plan with his name writ. Alcock, and oft. it appears Alcot, was a merch. who d. late in 1654 or early in 1655, his inv. of large est. for that day being of 13 Feb.; had Thomas; Samuel; Eliz. bapt. 7 Dec. 1645; John, 3 Feb. 1650; and Hannah. His wid. Abigail made her will 12 Jan. and d. 26 May 1693, aged 78. Hannah d. perhaps young, certain. bef. her mo. Eliz. m. Timothy Hyde of Wethersfield. THOMAS, Hartford, eldest s. of the preced. perhaps b. in Eng. freem. 1658, d. in advanced yrs. and his wid. Mary d. 3 May 1721. He had Abigail, Mary, Thomas, Samuel, John, drown. 25 May 1685; and Timothy, b. 1677. THOMAS, Hartford, s. of the preced. m. Nov. 1691, Sarah, d. of Nathaniel Foote, third of this name, had Abigail, b. 4 Aug. 1692; Sarah, 12 Dec. 1694; Mary, 21 Nov. 1696; Cullick, 18 Apr. 1699; Nathaniel, 11 Sept. 1701; Josiah, 2 Mar. 1703; Margaret, 12 Apr. 1705; Hannah, 4 Aug. 1707; Eliz. 17 Nov. 1709; one b. and d. 1712; and Thomas, 1713. TIMOTHY, Colchester, br. of the preced. by first w. whose name is unkn. had Timothy, b. 1703; Titus, 1705; James; Margaret, 1714; and Benoni, 1716. For sec. w. he took Mary, wid. of Ebenezer Field, wh. d. 20 Apr. 1740; and a third w. Eliz. outliv. him more than 20 yrs. He was a deac. and d. 5 Apr. 1754. Thirteen of this name had, in 1834, been gr. at N. E. coll. exclus. of Harv. of wh. Peter, judge of the Sup. Ct. of Vermt. d. Sept. 1808.

OLD, ROBERT, Windsor, m. Susanna Hanford (but Stiles, 728, calls her Hosford), had Robert, b. 9 Oct. 1670; and Jonathan, 24 Dec. 1672, or 4 Jan. 1673, at Windsor; rem. to Suffield, there had Mindwell, 1675; Hanford, 1678; William, 1680; Susanna, 1683; and Ebenezer, 1688; in wh. yr. his w. d. and he m. Dorothy Granger, had John, 1691, and, perhaps, more. Of the ch. Robert was of Springfield; Hanford of Westfield.

OLDAGE, OLDIGE, OLDRIDGE, or OLDERIGE, RICHARD, Windsor, bef. 1640, possib. went from Dorchester, but was not kn. there to Dr. Harris, d. 27 Jan. 1661, and the name is extinct. His only ch. Ann m. 19 May 1645, John Osborn.

OLDEN, JOHN, Boston, by w. Eliz. had Nathaniel, b. 9 July 1668. Perhaps it may be Holden.

OLDFIELDS, JOHN, Southampton, L. I. 1641, and Jamaica, L. I. 1686. Thompson.

OLDHAM, ISAAC, Scituate, s. of Thomas, m. Mary, d. of Josiah Keen, had Isaac, and two ds. rem. to Pembroke a. 1703. * JOHN, Plymouth, came in the Ann 1623 with a comp. so that in div. of lds. next yr. he was reckon. for ten heads; in less than two yrs. gave offence by siding with Rev. Mr. Lyford, and was punish. with more contempt than severity, driven to Nantasket, thence, with Conant, to Cape Ann, home in 1628, so well reconciled to the Plymouth governm. as to be trusted by them with their prisoner, mischief-making Morton, back to N. E. late in 1629, or early in 1630, freem. 18 May 1631, with prefix of respect, liv. at Watertown, much engag. in trade with the Ind. especial. by water, rep. in the first Gen. Court 1634, was k. by the Ind. in his shallop, July 1636, off the mouth of Narraganset Bay. Admin. of his est. was, of course, had in Mass. but in the noble Conn. Rec. by J. H. Trumbull, I. 43, we see that ancillary process was had in that Col. the earliest action being at their Court, 1 Sept. held at Watertown, now Wethersfield, and next, in Oct. at Newtown, now Hartford. Of the largest creditors there were Gov. Cradock of London, Gov. Hopkins of Hartford, and Clement Chaplin of Wethersfield, wh. certain. vouch from large opportunity of acquaint. for his good conduct. Hinman, in his first Ed. 127, mistook the side of the acco. or inv. in the rec. making Gov. C. a debtor to O. We may conject. that he had w. and childr. but certain. is not attaina. In 1635 the Elizabeth and Ann brot. from London two youths of this name, John, aged 12, and Thomas, 10, neither of wh. was likely to be his s. JOHN, Cambridge, s. of Richard, m. 22 July 1675, Abigail Wood, had John, b. 20 July 1676; Abigail, 28 Nov. 1679; and was freem. 1690; selectman, 1694 and oft. aft.; d. 14 Oct. 1719, in 67th yr. Harris, Epit. 62. RICHARD, Cambridge, perhaps s. of John the first, b. in Eng. freem. 1651, m. Martha, d. of William Eaton of Watertown, had Samuel, and John, the latter b. a. 1652; and d. Dec. 1658, leav. by his will of 8 July preced. his wid. and Samuel Hyde excors. His wid. m. Thomas Brown of Concord. SAMUEL, Cambridge, s. of the preced. by w. Hannah had Samuel, wh. d. 16 Jan. 1673; Samuel, again, d. 24 Aug. 1675; Hannah, d. 9 July 1676; Andrew, d. 12 July 1677; and Nathaniel, d. 3 May 1678. Harris, Epit. 170 and 1. He was freem. 1690. Three ds. liv. long eno. to be ment. in his will of 13 July 1727, Hannah, w. of Amos Gates; Mary, w. of James Read; and Ann, unm. THOMAS, Scituate, was of Duxbury 1643, perhaps that youth who came from London 1635, in the Elizabeth and Ann, and may have been br. of John, his fellow-passeng. m. 20 Nov. 1656, Mary, d. of Rev. William Wetherell, had Mary, b. 20 Aug. 1658; Thomas, 30 Oct. 1660; Sarah; Hannah; Grace; Isaac; Ruth; Eliz.; and Lydia; all bef. 1679; and d. 1711. THOMAS, Scituate, s. of the preced. m. 1683, Mercy, d. of Robert Sproat, had Joshua and Mary, tw. b. 1684; Mercy; and Desire.

OLIN, HENRY, Greenwich, s. of John of the same, had, it is said, tho. his ws. name is not seen, nor the date of b. of either, Justin, and Caleb, both of wh. rem. bef. the revolut. war, to Vermont, and the latter, hav. seven s. d. in St. Lawrence Co. N. Y. Of such infirm material few N. E. fam. are compel. to build. JOHN, West Greenwich, R. I. said to have come a. 1678, in his youth, from Wales, had by w. unkn. John, Henry, and, perhaps, Justin, and Joseph ; but of the last two, in the fam. geneal. no acco. is render. nor is the date of m. or d. of f. or either of the other s. giv. JOHN, East Greenwich, R. I. s. of the preced.

OLIVER, ‡ DANIEL, Boston, youngest s. of Peter the first, m. 23 Apr. 1696, Eliz. d. of Hon. Andrew Belcher, sis. of Gov. Jonathan, had Daniel, b. 14 Jan. 1704, H. C. 1722, wh. d. of smallpox, at London, 5 July 1727 ; Andrew, 28 Mar. 1706, H. C. 1724, who was lieut.-gov. of the Prov. and d. 3 Mar. 1774 ; and Peter, 17 Mar. 1713, H. C. 1730, the Ch. Justice of the Sup. Ct. of Mass. who was impeach. and d. at Birmingham, Oct. 1791 ; was freem. 1690, and d. 23 July 1732. His wid. d. 1735. DAVID, Pemaquid, took the o. of fidel. to Mass. 23 July 1674. ‖ JAMES, Boston, s. of Thomas, the rul. Elder, brot. by his f. from Bristol, in Co. Somerset, 1632, in the William and Francis, freem. 12 Oct. 1640, an emin. merch. ar. co. 1637, capt. of it 1656, and 66, serv. in Philip's war, as a capt. in the gr. fight of 19 Dec. 1675, and d. 1682, without issue. JAMES, Cambridge, s. of Peter, a physician, freem. 1690, m. Mercy, d. of Samuel Bradstreet, had Mercy, b. 1695 ; and Sarah, 4 Sept. bapt. 20 Dec. 1696 ; and he d. 8 Apr. 1703, and his wid. d. 29 Mar. 1710, in her 43d yr. * JOHN, Boston 1632, younger br. or per- haps neph. of Elder Thomas, came with him in the William and Francis, disarm. in Nov. 1637, was chos. rep. 1638, but reject. by the ho. as a support. of the cause of Wheelwright, rem. to Newbury, was freem. 13 May 1640, m. Joanna Goodale, prob. d. of Eliz. and sis. of Richard the first, had only Mary, b. 7 June 1640, and he d. 1642. Very frequent has been the confus. betw. him and John, the s. of the rul. Elder, but a careful comparison will find in our rec. three or four un- failing points in assist. him to discrimin. In the beautiful Appleton Memor. p. 22, the will of John Oliver of Boston, wh. d. a few yrs. later, of wh. abstr. is in Geneal. Reg. III. 266, from Vol. I. of Pro. Rec. is erron. assum. to be the act of the Newbury man, who was, I think, his uncle. His d. Mary m. 8 Dec. 1656, Samuel Appleton, the sec. of Ips- wich, I believe, as his sec. w. His wid. m. capt. William Gerrish. ‖ JOHN, Boston, s. of the Elder Thomas, so distinct. call. at his adm. into the ch. 1633, freem. 14 May 1634, m. Eliz. d. of John Newgate, had John, bapt. 29 July 1638, tho. the town rec. strange. makes his b. 21 Nov. aft. d. Mar. foll. ; Eliz. b. 28 Feb. bapt. 8 Mar. 1640 ; Hannah, 3,

bapt. 6 Mar. 1642, d. young ; John, again, 15, bapt. 21 Apr. 1644 ; and
Thomas, 10 Feb. bapt. 8 Mar. 1646, d. young. He was of ar. co. 1638,
call. serj. a skilful surveyor, yet took up the duty of a preacher, for
success in wh. he ent. the college, had his A. B. 1645, odd as such a
course seems for a mar. man, d. 12 Apr. 1646, very deep. lament. See
Winth. II. 257. His wid. 14 Mar. 1649, bec. sec. w. of Edward Jackson of Cambridge ; and the d. Eliz. m. 25 Nov. 1657, Enoch Wiswall
of Dorchester. ‖ JOHN, Boston, s. of the preced. by w. Susanna, d. of
John Sweet, had s. Sweet, b. 1668 ; was of ar. co. 1680 ; freem. 1681,
of the sec. ch. with prefix of respect, and d. 1683. JOHN, Boston,
memb. of the first ch. freem. 1683, but he is not thot. to have derived
his blood from the venerable Elder. JOSEPH, Scarborough 1676. NA-
THANIEL, Boston 1651, a tailor, of wh. I find no more. NATHANIEL,
Boston, s. of Peter, m. 3 Jan. 1677, Eliz. d. of Thomas Brattle, was one
of the Committee of safety aft. overthrow of Andros, 1689, freem. 1690
with prefix of respect, among the earliest mem. of Brattle st. ch. and
d. 15 Apr. 1704, leav. wid. who d. May 1719, and ch. Eliz. Nathaniel,
Sarah, James, Brattle, Peter, and Mary. ‖ PETER, Boston, s. of the
Elder Thomas, b. in Eng. a. 1618, freem. 13 May 1640, an emin. trader,
one of the founders of the 3d or Old South ch. wh. honor, in the valua.
Hist. of Boston, by Mr. Drake, is inadv. giv. p. 591, to his fourth s.
Hon. Daniel, then only five yrs. old. He m. Sarah, d. of John Newgate,
had Sarah, bapt. 7 Jan. 1644 ; Mary, 1 Mar. 1646, a. 8 days old ; Na-
thaniel, b. 8 Mar. 1652 ; Peter, 3 Mar. 1655, H. C. 1675 ; James, 19
Mar. 1659, H. C. 1680 ; and Daniel, 28 Feb. 1664 ; was of ar. co.
1643, its capt. 1669, and d. 11 Apr. 1670. His wid. Sarah was bur. 11
Oct. 1692. His will, of 8 Apr. 1670, was pro. 5 May foll. His d.
Sarah m. John Noyes, and d. 19 Mar. 1707. Mary m. a. 1666, Jonathan Shrimpton, wh. d. 1673, and she next yr. m. Nathaniel Williams.
PETER, Boston, s. of the preced. of wh. no more is told, not even the
yr. of his d. in the Catal. of H. C. but we kn. that ano. PETER of Boston, a goldsmith, s. of John, m. 8 Mar. 1710, Jerusha, d. of Increase
Mather, had Jerusha, wh. d. 4 Jan. next, as had her mo. five days bef.
and he m. 1 Mar. 1712, Hopestill Wensley, made his will 24th of next
mo. and d. very soon. RICHARD, Salem 1668, a petitnr. against imposts,
may be he in Maine wh. sw. fidel. to Mass. in 1674, with prefix of
respect, was the same yr. made clk. of one of the tempor. div. of that
Province call. Devonshire, liv. some time in Monhegin, was lieut. in the
early part of Philip's war, and is oft. nam. by Hubbard. ‖ SAMUEL,
Boston, s. of the Elder Thomas, b. in Eng. adm. of the ch. 21 May
1643, yet never made freem. ar. co. 1648, had w. Lydia adm. of the ch.
Nov. 1647, and s. Vigilant, bapt. 27 June preced. ; Patience, wh. d. 26

Nov. 1653 ; and Deborah, bapt. 1 Feb. 1652; was drown. 27 Mar. 1652 leav. wid. Lydia, wh. m. 16 Feb. 1654, Joshua Fisher sec. of Dedham. THOMAS, Boston 1632, s. of John, and gr.s. of Thomas of Bristol, Eng.; came in the William and Francis, 9 Mar. from London, arr. 5 June 1632 at B. bring. w. Ann, wh. d. May 1635, d. Abigail, and certain. six s. scil. the four bef. ment.; and Nathaniel, k. at 15 yrs. by fall of a tree on Boston neck, 9 Jan. 1633, as Winth. I. 98, relates; and Daniel, wh. d. June 1637. He was from Bristol, freem. 1632, selectman oft. a most useful citizen, had in old age sec. w. Ann, who was of Dorchester; and d. 1 June 1658, "being ninety yrs. old," says the diary of John Hull. His d. Abigail m. James Johnson; and ano. d. m. Richard Wolfall. Our first Vol. of Prob. Rec. has his will of 13 Mar. 1653. THOMAS, Salem, a calender, from Norwich, came, at the age of 36, in the Mary Ann of Yarmouth, 1637, with w. Mary, 34, two ch. Thomas, and John, and two serv. Thomas Doged, 30, and Mary Sape, 12. The w. had the faculty of speech to an unpleasant excess, had suffer. in Eng. for neglect of some custom of trifling import. in the solemnities of the ch. and was punish. here for siding with Roger Williams, in 1638, and for berating our elders, as late as 1646. See Felt, II. 457, 576, and Winth. I. 281, 2. The h. as well as the state, seem to have suffer. for he was driven to go home in 1648 or 9, but came back in few yrs. and was in office 1670, as measurer of wood. A Bridget O. of Salem, charged with witchcraft, 1680, perhaps was d. of the free speaking woman. THOMAS, Fairfield 1660-70. ‡ * THOMAS, Cambridge, s. of John, the scholar, freem. 1672, m. 27 Nov. 1667, Grace, d. of capt. Thomas Prentice, had Grace, b. 15 Nov. 1668, d. at 12 yrs.; Eliz. 11 Apr. 1670, d. at 4 yrs.; John, 22 Nov. 1671, d. at 2 yrs.; Hannah, 16 Aug. 1674; Thomas, 22 Aug. 1676; and Samuel, 18 May 1679, both d. young; his w. d. 30 Sept. 1681, and he m. 19 Apr. 1682, Mary, d. of Nathaniel Wilson, had John, again, 9 July 1683, d. at two mos.; Nathaniel, 1 Feb. 1685; Mary, 20 Mar. 1688; Sarah, 14 Nov. 1690; Thomas, again, 17 July 1700, H. C. 1719 ; and Samuel, again, 12 Jan. 1702. He was deac. aft. many yrs. being capt. a rep. and of the Counc. honor. for integr. and piety, d. 31 Oct. 1715, hav. made his will the day preced. Twenty-five of this name had, in 1828, been gr. at Harv. Coll. the greater part, says Farmer, descend. of the rul. Elder of Boston first ch. But Eliot's Biog. Dict. wh. is very discriminat. in giv. the charact. of more than one of this progeny, says the last royal lieut. gov. of Mass. Thomas O. was of a dif. fam. from most of the foregoing.

OLMSTEAD, JAMES, Cambridge, came to Boston 16 Sept. 1632, in the Lion, from London, with two ch. and others, was rec. as freem. 6 Nov. foll. constable some yrs. at C. but rem. with earliest sett. to Hartford

1636, of wh. he was an orig. propr. with large lots of ld. and d. 1640. His will, of 28 Sept. of that yr. with inv. show. comfortab. prop. is found in Trumbull's Coll. Rec. I. 446–9. It names only two ch. Nicholas, and Nehemiah; but niece Rebecca O. wh. he brot. over, has also a small provis. and his kinsmen Richard, and John O. perhaps brs. of Rebecca, by the overseers of his will, with concur. of the s. rec. too, a small portion of the est. Yet prob. it was their own prop. held by him in tr. and they may have come with her. It also provides for his serv. William Corbee or Corby. * JAMES, Norwalk, s. of Richard of the same, had (tho. Hall's rec. gives not the name of w.) James, b. 10 Mar. 1677; perhaps Nathan, 27 Apr. 1678; Samuel, 13 May 1683; and John, 14 Aug. 1692; was rep. 1691, 2, 3, and 9. JOHN, Hartford 1640, neph. prob. of the first James, rem. soon to Saybrook, thence, a. 1660, to Norwich, was freem. 1662, surg. of part of the forces in Philip's war, had w. Eliz. d. of Matthew Marvin, but nam. no ch. in his will, pro. 22 Sept. 1686, made not long bef. tho. he calls hims. only 60, wh. no doubt, was by several yrs. too small a reckon.; left most of his good est. to ch. of his br. and sis. JOHN, Norwalk, s. of Richard of the same, m. 17 July 1673, Mary, d. of Thomas Benedict the first, but in his valua. Hist. Hall has not giv. any issue; was ens. 1674. In the list of proprs. 1687, he shows fair est. NEHEMIAH, Fairfield 1649, s. of James the first, was a serj. in 1657; of him no more is heard, but that his wid. Eliz. m. Obadiah Gilbert, and, perhaps, he had d. Sarah. * NICHOLAS, Hartford, br. of the preced. b. in Eng. serv. 1637 in the Pequot war, aft. sowing his wild oats, bec. a good citizen, freem. 1669, ens. and rep. 1672 and 3, capt. in 1675, and d. 31 Aug. 1684. He had early m. bef. his f.'s will of 28 Sept. 1640, a d. of Joseph Loomis of Windsor, had Sarah; Mary or Mabel, b. 20 Nov. 1646; Rebecca, Mar. 1648; John, 3 Feb. 1650; and left s. Joseph, Samuel, and Thomas, beside ds. Sarah Gates, prob. w. of George, m. early in 1662; Mabel Butler; and Rebecca Bigelow. * RICHARD, Hartford 1639, neph. of James the first, an orig. propr. had John, bapt. there 30 Dec. 1649; rem. to Norwalk of wh. he was one of the first purch. 1650, made serj. 1653, and rep. at May sess. of that yr. and a dozen other sess. to 1679; d. a. 1686, left only s. James, and John, wh. had div. of prop. of their uncle John, and, perhaps, one or more ds. SAMUEL, freem. of Conn. 1677, was prob. of Hartford, s. of Nicholas, and d. 13 Jan. 1726, in 73d yr. of his age. THOMAS, Hartford, prob. s. of Nicholas, m. 25 June 1691, Hannah Mix, perhaps d. of the first Thomas of New Haven, had prob. Thomas, and, perhaps, other ch. Five of this name, says Farmer, MS. had been gr. at Yale in 1834, and six are add. since. This fam. was from Suff k. Eng.

OLNEY, EPENETUS, Providence, s. of Thomas the first, b. in Eng. m.

9 Mar. 1666, Mary, sec. d. of John Whipple of the same, had Mary, b. 13 July 1668; James, 9 Nov. 1670; Sarah, 10 Sept. 1672; Epenetus, 18 Jan. 1675; John; Thomas, 18 May 1686; and Lydia, 20 Jan. 1689. He took o. of alleg. to k. Charles II. in May 1666; and d. July 1698. EPENETUS, Providence, s. of the preced. m. Mercy Williams, had James, Charles, Joseph, Anthony, Mary, Amy, Ann, Martha, and Freeborn. He had rem. to Gloucester, R. I. and d. 18 Sept. 1740. Perhaps at G. the dates of b. of these ch. or some of them may be ascertain. JAMES, Providence, br. of the preced. sw. alleg. June 1667; rem. not from P. dur. Philip's war. He d. bef. Feb. 1677, prob. unm. JAMES, Providence, eldest s. of Epenetus the first, m. 31 Aug. 1702, Hallelujah Brown, had James, b. 18 Sept. 1703, wh. d. soon; Mary, 30 Sept. 1704; Joseph, 6 June 1706; James, 28 Dec. 1708, d. in few wks.; Jonathan, 9 Mar. 1710; Jeremiah, 20 Mar. 1711; and Lydia, 1 Nov. 1716; and he d. 5 or 6 Oct. 1744. JOHN, Providence, s. of the first Epenetus, m. 11 Aug. 1699, Rachel Coggeshall, had John, b. 27 May 1701; William, 22 Feb. 1706; Jeremiah, 4 Nov. 1708; Freelove, 29 Nov. 1711; and Nebadiah, 10 Feb. 1715. ‡ THOMAS, Salem, shoemaker, of Hertford, Eng. came in the Planter to Boston, 1635, from London, aged 35; with w. Mary, 30; s. Thomas, 3; and Epenetus, 1; was freem. 17 May 1637, had Nebadiah, bapt. Aug. foll. wh. d. young; soon aft. went to Providence, and join. 1638, with Roger Williams in purch. of Providence and in found. the first bapt. ch. on our contin. There he prob. had Stephen, Mary, James, and Lydia; took the o. of alleg. May 1666, and d. 1682. Of his ds. Mary m. 4 Dec. 1663, John Whipple; and Lydia m. 17 Dec. 1669, Joseph Williams. Hutch. I. 421, prints the act of excommunica. of him and others for their fall from the ch. as verified by Hugh Peter; and Felt, Ann. II. 576, rec. the excision of both him and his w. tho. the name of neither appears among his ch. memb. A s. of his, prob. Stephen, but may have been Nebadiah, d. early in 1659–60, as a let. of Williams to J. Winth. in 3 Mass. Hist. Coll. X. 28, tells. He was made Treasr. in 1638, the only officer wh. is nam. on the rec. and in 1649 an Assist. THOMAS, Providence, eldest s. of the preced. b. at Hertford, Co. Herts, a. 1632, was memb. of the Bapt. ch. took the o. of alleg. the same day as his f.; m. 31 July 1660, Eliz. Marsh of Newport, had Thomas, b. 7 May 1661; William, 25 June 1663; Eliz. 31 Jan. 1667; Ann, 13 Jan. 1669; and Phebe, 15 Sept. 1675. Benedict, Hist. I. 478. He d. 11 June 1722, in his will, of 20 Feb. preced. pro. 9 July foll. ment. s. William, gr.ch. Thomas and Obadiah, s. of Thomas, dec. and William, Thomas and William, s. of William, and John Waterman, wh. was h. of his d. Ann. THOMAS, Providence, eldest s. of the preced. sw. alleg. May 1682, by w.

Lydia, m. 13 July 1687, had Lydia, b. 30 Apr. 1688; Phebe, 29 Oct. 1689; Sarah, 26 Aug. 1693; Thomas, 18 Jan. 1696; Eliz. 29 Jan. 1698; Ann, 26 Mar. 1700; Mary, 25 Feb. 1702; and Obadiah, 14 Feb. 1710; and d. 1 Mar. 1718. THOMAS, Providence, s. of the first Epenetus, by w. Patience, m. 18 May 1686, had Lydia, and Esther. His w. d. 8 Aug. 1746, and he d. 28 July 1752. WILLIAM, Providence, br. of sec. Thomas of the same, took the o. of alleg. to k. Charles II. on the same day with him, m. 28 Dec. 1692, Catharine Sayles, d. prob. of the first John, had William, b. 6 Oct. 1694; John, 7 May 1699; Catharine, 11 Aug. 1701; Thomas, 26 Apr. 1706; Deborah, 30 July 1708; and Richard, 4 Nov. 1711. His w. d. 21 Feb. 1753, aged 81 yrs.

OLT, JOHN, Dover 1655. See Ault.

OLVERTON, WILLIAM, is the strange name of one, prob. a soldier, k. 19 Oct. 1675, by the Ind. at Hatfield.

ONGE, FRANCIS, Watertown, came with w. and childr. in the Lion, arr. at Boston 5 Feb. 1631, hav. 1 Dec. bef. sail. from Bristol, prob. d. in few yrs. and Frances O. wh. in the Watertown rec. of bur. 12 Nov. 1838, is nam. wid. was, perhaps, mo. of his ch. to wh. in 1643 a mortg. is found. Simon, in 1646, and Isaac, in 1649, wh. m. 18 May 1670, Mary, d. of Joseph Underwood, were of W. but Simon got across the river to Newton 1676; and Jacob, in 1678, was of Groton. Mary, aged 27, a passeng. 1634, from Ipswich, in the Francis, may have been sis. or d. tho. the embarca. on opposite side of the kingdom seems to be inconsist.

ONION, BENJAMIN, Dedham, prob. s. of Robert of the same, m. at Rehoboth, 24 May 1683, Deborah Woodcock. JOHN, Braintree 1640. ROBERT, Roxbury, came in the Blessing, from London 1635, aged 26, m. at R. but his w. Mary d. with her first ch. Apr. 1643; rem. to Dedham 1645, freem. 1646, had sec. w. Grace, wh. d. 16 Feb. 1647; and he m. Sarah, d. of Michael Metcalf, had Susanna, b. 27 May 1649; Mary, 16 Feb. 1651; Hannah, 6 July 1656; Joseph, 10, bapt. 22 Mar. 1663; Grace, 25 Mar. 1666; and possib. others.

ONTHANK, CHRISTOPHER, one of the Warwick freem. 1655, more oft. is writ. Unthank.

ORCHARD, ROBERT, Boston, merch. by w. Sarah had Mary, b. 26 Mar. 1668; was involv. in controv. at the admiralty 1666, and complain. to the king, 1682, against the Col. See Snow, 169.

ORCUTT, JOHN, Bridgewater, s. of William, had Hannah, b. 1695; Samuel, 1697; and John, 1700; but as Mitchell says Hannah was call. 2d ch. we may believe that an earlier one d. soon. WILLIAM, Scituate, had, perhaps, b. at Weymouth, William, in 1664; and Andrew; but at S. had John, b. 1669; Martha, 1671; Joseph, 1672; Mary and Hannah, tw. 1674; Thomas, 1675; Benjamin, 1679; Eliz. 1682; and Deborah, 1683. However, Mitchell adds Susanna, b. prob. aft. his rem. to Bridgewater, and says, that all the ch. exc. Eliz. and Deborah, perhaps then not liv. were nam. in his will of 1694. Mary m. 1697, Daniel Hudson. WILLIAM, Bridgewater, s. of the preced. m. Jane, d. of John Washburn, had Moses; Caleb; Joanna; Eliz.; Jane; Deliverance, b. 1712; and Martha; and d. 1739.

ORDWAY, ABNER, Watertown 1643, m. perhaps as sec. w. 15 Aug. 1656, Sarah, wid. of Edward Dennis of Boston. EDWARD, Newbury, s. of James, m. 12 Dec. 1678, Mary Wood, had Joanna, b. 28 Nov. 1685; Rachel, 14 Jan. 1688; Jacob, 14 Jan. 1690; Isaiah, 28 Jan. 1692; and Daniel, 13 Jan. 1694. HANANIAH, Newbury, youngest br. of the preced. by w. Abigail had Rebecca, b. 22 Dec. 1690; Abigail, 2 Aug. 1693; Nathaniel, 3 July 1695; Joanna, 15 Apr. 1698; and Eliz. 15 Feb. 1702. JAMES, Dover, b. it is said, in Wales, a. 1620, rem. to Newbury, m. 23 Nov. 1648, Ann Emery, perhaps d. of Anthony, was tax. 1649 at Dover, where E. had liv. the former yr.; had Ephraim, b. 25 Apr. 1650; James, 16 Apr. 1651; Edward, 17 Sept. 1653; Sarah, 14 Sept. 1656; John, 17 Nov. 1658; Isaac, 4 Dec. 1660, d. at 8 yrs.; Jane, 22 Nov. 1663; Hananiah, 2 Dec. 1665; Ann, 12 Feb. 1670; Mary, 5 Apr. 1673; his w. d. 31 Mar. 1687; was freem. 1668, and d. aft. 1702. JAMES, Newbury, s. of the preced. m. Tirzah, wid. of Thomas Bartlett, had a ch. that d. soon; and Lydia, b. 12 July 1693, d. young; he m. sec. w. May 1696, Sarah Clark, had Lydia, b. 14 July 1696; Joanna, 22 May 1697; John, 22 June 1699; and Mary, 28 Apr. 1703, if Coffin has correct. giv. the dates. JOHN, Newbury, br. of the preced. m. 5 Dec. 1681, Mary, d. of Peter Godfrey, had Mary, b. 18 Sept. 1682; John, 29 Oct. 1684; James, 4 July 1687; Esther, Aug. 1689; Peter, 15 Sept. 1691; Hannah, 20 Nov. 1693, d. in two wks.; Hannah, again, 6 Mar. 1695; Stephen, 8 Apr. 1697; Ann, 15 May 1699; and Nathan, 28 Apr. 1703. SAMUEL, Newbury, had Isaac, b. 4 Feb. 1680.

ORMES, JOHN, Salem, by w. Mary had Mary, b. 26 Oct. 1656; John, 28 Nov. 1658; Eliz. 24 Dec. 1660; Joseph, 15 Mar. 1663; Benjamin and Jonathan, tw. 14 July 1665, of wh. the latter d. next yr.; Edonia, 1 June 1668; and James 14 July 1670; and this last was d. when his mo. took admin. of his est. 14 Nov. 1693. JOHN, Salem, s. of the preced. by w. Ann had John, b. 15 Mar. 1687. RICHARD, Boston, by w. Rebecca had John, b. 17 Nov. 1682; and Richard, 17 Aug. 1685.

ORMSBY, or ORMSBEE, EDWARD, Boston, perhaps s. of that wid. Ann who was adm. of our ch. 28 Aug. 1634, had gr. of ld. 1637, and in Sept. 1639 was recom. to ch. of Dedham, whither she had, no doubt, rem.

JACOB, Rehoboth, s. of Richard, was a propr. 1668, had Jacob, b. 23 Aug. 1674, wh. d. 16 Feb. 1678, and he d. two wks. aft. JOHN, Rehoboth, a propr. 1668, may have been br. of the preced. had Eliz. b. 27 Nov. 1674; Mary, 4 Apr. 1677; Jonathan, 26 Aug. 1678; Martha, 7 May 1680; Jacob, 16 Mar. 1682; was one of Gallup's comp. 1690 in Phips's expedit. against Quebec. RICHARD, Saco 1641, acc. Willis, I. 36, rem. to Salisbury, there, by w. Sarah, had Thomas, b. 11 Nov. 1645; Jacob, 6 Mar. 1647; and prob. John, bef. either of these, may have been b. at Saco ; was at Haverhill 1653, and prob. d. at Rehoboth 1664, where his inv. was tak. 3 July of that yr. THOMAS, Rehoboth, s. of the preced. was a propr. 1668, had Jeremiah, b. 25 Nov. 1672 ; Hannah, 23 Sept. 1678; Jacob, 13 Sept. 1680 ; Bethia, 15 Apr. 1682.

ORNE. See Horne. Of this mod. spell. are found eight names of gr. at Harv. and two at Bowd. in 1834.

ORRIS, ORIS, or ORRICE, GEORGE, Boston, blacksmith, came, 1635, aged 21, in the Elizabeth and Ann, by w. Eliz. wh. join. our ch. 15 Mar. 1645, had Mary, bapt. 23 of same, a. a yr. and 7 mos. old; John, b. 1 Mar. 1647 ; Sarah, 1653 ; Jonathan, 1656 ; Samuel, 20 Dec. 1659 ; Nathaniel, 27 Apr. 1664 ; and Experience; and his w. d. 1673. Experience was of Braintree 1690, but I hear no more of him. JOHN, Boston, s. of the preced. by w. Sarah had John, b. 5 Aug. 1672 ; Sarah, 14 Aug. 1676; and by sec. w. Hannah had Samuel, 2 Nov. 1684; Martha, 15 Oct. 1686, d. soon; and Martha, again, 26 Nov. 1688; and he d. 19 Dec. 1699. Another Hannah O. of the sec. ch. of Boston, perhaps w. of Samuel or of Nathaniel, being adm. 1 Jan. 1691, brot. for bapt. Eliz. Hannah, and Joseph, all on 1 Feb. foll. JONATHAN, a soldier of Turner's comp. in Philip's war, prob. s. of George, liv. aft. 1680 at Falmouth; but in 1691 was of Gloucester. Willis, I. 212, says his br. Nathaniel liv. at Barnstable.

ORTON, EBENEZER, Charlestown, s. of Thomas of the same, had w. prob. liv. at Hingham, and was going thither with her on 7 Aug. 1694, when he was knock. overboard by the boom and drown. He had that morn. sign. contr. for build. a barque at H. and had in his pocket one hundred good pieces of eight, as part of the price. JOHN, Farmington, only s. of Thomas of the same, had two ws. Hannah, whose surname is not found, and Mary, d. prob. of Owen Tudor, had three s. and ds. Mary, bapt. 20 May 1688 ; Mary, again, 16 Feb. 1690, and Margaret; d. 1695, leav. Thomas ; John, bapt. 4 Dec. 1692 ; Samuel, 11 Nov. 1694 ; and two ds. but wh. ch. came of the first w. is not told. * JOSEPH, Rye 1669, propound. next yr. for freem. with the spell. Horten, was rep. 1671, a lieut. and seems to have serv. much as a surveyor. See Trumbull, Col. Rec. II. THOMAS, Windsor, m. 16 June 1641, Margaret Pall, or Paul, not, as the copy in Geneal. Reg. V. 230 has it (with addit. mistake of the man's name, Josias for Thomas), had John, b. 17 Feb. 1648; Mary, 16 May 1650; Sarah, 22 Aug. 1652; and Eliz. 1 Oct. 1654; rem. a. 1655 to Farmington, there had Hannah, bapt. 28, not 29 Dec. 1656, as print. in Geneal. Reg. XI. 324, wh. d. soon. In 1688, to avoid the extortiona. rule of Andros, requir. wills to be rec. at Boston for all the parts of N. E. he div. his est. among the four ch. John; Mary Root; Sarah Dewey; and Eliz. Lewis. THOMAS, Charlestown 1642, by w. Mary, who join. the ch. 12 Apr. 1650, had Mary, b. 27 Aug. 1648; and he was a householder 1658 and 77; d. 19 May 1687. His ch. bapt. there were William, 5 Feb. 1660; Samuel, 10 Nov. 1661; Ebenezer, 17 Jan. 1664; Thomas, 7 May 1665; Amie, 5 Aug. 1666; and Abigail, 19 Sept. 1669; but possib. others. From Cothren it would be thot. that he presumed the Windsor and Charlestown man the same, to wh. there appears insurmounta. objection.

ORVIS, GEORGE, Farmington, m. a. 1652, Eliz. wid. of David Carpenter, had Samuel, b. May 1653; Hannah, Apr. 1655; Roger, June 1657; Ebenezer, Feb. 1660; Margaret, June 1661; and Mary, June 1663, wh. all were bapt. at unkn. times; was freem. 1658, and d. 27 Apr. 1664. His wid. m. Richard Bronson. ROGER, Farmington, s. of the preced. was a soldier in Philip's war, under capt. Newberry, and wound. at Hatfield, May 1676. SAMUEL, Farmington, br. of the preced. had w. Deborah, wh. join. the ch. 7 May 1682, and d. Deborah, bapt. 14 May foll. wh. was b. a. 17 Apr. 1681; Martha, bapt. 6 May 1683; Samuel, 25 Oct. 1685; Margaret, 17 Apr. 1687, not as print. in Geneal. Reg. XII. 149; Sarah, 12 Oct. 1690; and Ann, 11 Nov. 1694. ROGER, Farmington, s. of George, m. 15 Dec. 1692, Eliz. Harrison of Hartford, had Eliz. b. 1 Oct. 1693; Ebenezer, 3 Oct. 1695; David, Mar. 1697; Bethia, 3 Jan. 1699; Abiah, 2 Nov. 1702; and Mary, 18 Oct. 1707.

OSBILL, JOHN, New Haven, freem. 1669. Among proprs. 1685, no such name appears.

OSBORN, or OSBURN, CHRISTOPHER, Duxbury 1638. DAVID, Fairfield, s. of Richard of the same, m. Abigail, d. of Philip Pinckney of East Chester, then claim. as of Conn. jurisdict. whither he rem. and d. 1679; had Richard, and prob. no more ch. Yet he made up by the length of his life for one or two more, if the fact be clear, that he d. not bef. 1779, at Ridgefield. JAMES, Springfield, m. 1646, Joyce Smith, had Eliz. b. 1647; Mary, 16 Mar. 1650; James, 1654; Sarah, 1658; and Samuel, 1664; rem. to Hartford, there d. 1676, all those ch. then liv. * JEREMIAH, New Haven, perhaps br. of Richard, tanner, by w. Mary had Rebecca, bapt. 23 Oct. 1642; Increase, 5 Feb. 1643; Benjamin, 3 Jan. 1647; Jeremiah, 1652, d. soon; Mary, b. 29 Mar. 1653;

Eliz. 5 Jan. 1655; both bapt. 21 Oct. 1655; Jeremiah, again, 28 Nov. 1656, bapt. 2 days aft.; Joanna, 8 Dec. 1658, bapt. 30 Jan. foll.; Thomas, b. and prob. d. 1660; and Eliz. again, 9 Dec. 1665, bapt. 14 Jan. foll. but of sev. of these ch. it may be thot. that some were b. to Richard, or Thomas, the entry on the rec. of the ch. oft. nam. not f. but the rite being admin. only for sis. O. at least, in the case of not a few other names, such was the custom. He was rep. 1672–4, d. 1676. His wid. s. Jeremiah, and other heirs were proprs. 1685. JOHN, Braintree, had Matthew, wh. d. May 1641. JOHN, Weymouth, by w. Mary had John, b. 2 Feb. 1640; and Ephraim, 11 Aug. 1657; but how many or wh. intermediate, is not found; yet his d. Mary m. 7 May 1659, John Ross. JOHN, Windsor, m. 19 May 1645, Ann, only ch. of Richard Oldage, had John, b. 10 Jan. 1646; Ann, 15 Jan. 1648; Nathaniel, 10 Mar. 1650; Samuel, 25 July 1652, d. soon; Mary, 16 Apr. 1655; Hannah, 18 Dec. 1657; Samuel, again, 8 May 1660; Esther, 9 Aug. 1662; Isaac, 28 Sept. 1664, d. at 9 yrs.; and Sarah, 8 Feb. 1667. He d. 27 Oct. 1686, when were liv. beside John, Nathaniel, and Samuel, all the ds. exc. Ann, wh. m. 12 Nov. 1663, Humphrey Prior, and had left two s.; Mary, m. 22 Oct. 1674, Josiah Owen; Hannah m. Elias Shadduck, and next, m. 6 Mar. 1678, Benjamin Eggleston. JOHN, Southampton, L. I. 1650, was, perhaps, s. of Thomas. JOHN, Westfield, s. of John of Windsor, m. 14 Oct. 1669, Abigail, d. of Bagot Eggleston, had John, b. 25 Aug. 1670; rem. to Windsor, there had Abigail, 2 Mar. 1672; Mindwell, 2 Jan. 1674; Ann, Jan. 1676; Mary, Jan. 1678; Hannah, 14 June 1680; Sarah, 12 Aug. 1682, both d. young; Eliz. 19 Dec. 1684; Martha, 10 Apr. 1687; tw. s. b. and d. 3 Feb. 1692; Isaac, 6 June 1694; and fam. tradit. says, he rem. to L. I. there had Mary, again, 10 Feb. 1696; and Jacob, 4 Jan. 1698. JOHN, Boston, by w. Eliz. had John and Thomas, tw. b. 11 June 1670; and Eliz. 25 Dec. 1673, in wh. yr. he was freem. being of 2d ch. JOHN, Fairfield, s. of Richard, m. Sarah, d. of James Bennett, had Samuel, John, David, Joseph, and Eliz. but dates of either m. or b. are unheard of, and he d. 1709. NICHOLAS, Pemaquid, took the o. of fidel. to Mass. 22 July 1674. RECOMPENSE, New Haven, was by the late lamented Professor Kingsley, thot. to be s. of Thomas, H. C. 1661, tho. it is less prob. from Geneal. Reg. XI. 345, than that he was s. of William, and aft. leav. coll. taught the sch. at New Haven, until he rem. to East Hampton, on L. I. The coll. catal. has never yet been advis. of the yr. of his d. tho. it was bef. the Magnalia of 1698. RICHARD, Hingham, one of the first sett. 1635, rem. soon to Conn. serv. in the Pequot war 1637; next, to New Haven bef. 1640, where he had one ch. as early as 1643. Thence he rem. to Fairfield 1653, and had there in 1671, a gr. of 80 acres for his serv. in the old war. Yet he had in 1666 int. in the lds. at Newtown, L. I. and some yrs. bef. his d. liv. at West Chester that was then thot. to belong to Conn. Of the time of his m. or name of his w. inq. has been fruitless; yet his descend. in our age, has confid. that he had five ch. at least, John, Daniel, Eliz. Priscilla, and ano. ch. he calls his "oldest d." SAMUEL, Windsor, s. of the first John of the same, by w. Mary had Samuel, b. 19 Oct. 1684; Rebecca, 20 Apr. 1687. His w. d. 3 Aug. 1690; and by Abigail perhaps had Rebecca, 9 July 1691; but very confus. is the statem. in Stiles, 729–30. THOMAS, Charlestown 1644, freem. 10 May 1648, by w. Hannah had Sarah, b. 29 Mar. 1647; Thomas, 26 June 1649; Mary, 11 Mar. 1652; ano. ch. 30 Apr. 1654; and Martha, 8 Oct. 1656; beside John, bapt. 19 Feb. 1660. He liv. on Malden side, there had w. Sarah, who, in Oct. 1651, stood up manfully, with her sisterhood, in defence of Rev. Mr. Matthews against the Gen. Court. In Feb. 1662, he and his w. were rec. into the ch. of Charlestown, by dismiss. from M. but prob. he had a hankering for heresy, as he next yr. united with Gould, as a Bapt. having embraced the opinions of that sect as early as 1658, tho. their ch. was not formed until May 1665. See Budington, 56; Frothingham, 126, 166–170; and Hutch. Coll. 399. Oft. the name is Ozban in rec. of Middlesex. THOMAS, New Haven 1639, perhaps br. of Richard, with far better est.; counted a fam. of six in few yrs.; rem. to East Hampton, L. I. 1650, there, perhaps, had Thomas, Jeremiah, and John, yet most of them may have been b. bef. rem. or even in Eng. WILLIAM, Salem 1630, freem. 22 May 1639, by w. call. in Felt's list of ch. memb. 1641, Frezwith or Freesweed, had there, I think, no ch. rem. to Dorchester, and there town rec. ment. by Frodiswerd his w. had Recompense, b. 26 May 1644, a. "six o'clock P. M." H. C. 1661, at Braintree had Hannah, 24 Aug. 1646; Bezaleel, 8 Mar. 1650; and some yrs. aft. at Boston, by prob. the same w. call. Fredeswith and in Prov. rec. Freesweed, had Joseph, b. 6 Apr. 1652; and Jonathan, 16 Nov. 1656. He was a merch. and he d. a. mid. life; his inv. of 29 Apr. 1662 shows over £1000; well for that time. His wid. m. John Mulford of South Hampton, Yorksh. E. Riding, and in 1670 sold to Rev. Antipas Newman of Wenham, that 110 acres granted to O. Ano. O. there was, unhappi. at Salem, Sarah, impris. at Boston from 7 Mar. to 10 May 1692, on charge of witchcraft, wh. was not brot. to trial bec. she d. in gaol. How tenderly alleviat. was the suffer. of her latest hours, is nowhere told. She was, perhaps, w. of that WILLIAM of Salem vill. freem. 1690. WILLIAM, Braintree, had Bezaleel, b. 1650. WILLIAM, Newtown, L. I. 1656–86. Riker. WILLIAM, New Haven, d. 1662. His inv. of 29 Apr. is there. Five of this name at Harv. and fifteen at other N. E. coll. had been gr. in 1834.

OSGOOD, CHRISTOPHER, Ipswich, came in the Mary and John, 1634, freem. 6 May 1635, d. 1650, leav. w. Margery, wh. was d. of Philip Fowler, and ch. Mary; Abigail; Eliz.; Deborah; Christopher, b. 1643; and Thomas, prob. posthum. Mary m. 1 June 1651, John Lovejoy; and Abigail m. 9 Apr. 1657, as seems prob. Shoreborn Wilson of I. * CHRISTOPHER, Andover, s. of the preced. m. 6 Dec. 1663, Hannah Belknap, perhaps d. of Abraham, wh. d. 21 Nov. 1679, and he m. 27 May 1680, Hannah, d. of Richard Barker, wh. d. 6 Apr. 1687, as did Mary, her d. 9 days aft. and, perhaps he had 3d w. Sarah, wh. d. 8 July 1689, bring. him no ch. and he had fourth w. Sarah; was freem. 1676, an ardent patriot, a capt. imprison. some days by Andros, without warrant, and rep. 1690; d. 1723, in his 80th yr. He had by the first w. Mary, b. 5 July 1665; Hannah, 19 Oct. 1668; Dorothy, 4 July 1671; Abigail, 29 Aug. 1673; Christopher, 28 June 1675; and Ezekiel, 5 Nov. 1679; by the sec. w. had Priscilla, 1 Apr. 1681; Sarah, 19 Feb. 1683; Esther, 31 Oct. 1684; and Ann, 8 Mar. 1687; and the fourth w. brot. him Rebecca, 3 May 1692; Lydia, 14 June 1694, d. soon; Lydia, again, 1 Sept. 1695; Martha, 14 Dec. 1698; Jeremiah, 1702; and Mary, again, 1705. Yet he was unhappy with most of the peop. of his town, and forc. to petitn. in Oct. 1692 in behalf of his first ch. Mary Marston, w. of John, imprison. on the ludicrous, if it were not execra. charge of witchcr. * JOHN, Ipswich, perhaps br. of Christopher the first, came from Andover, in Hampsh. Eng. where he was b. 23 July 1595, wh. in the open. line of his will of 12 Apr. 1650, pro. 25 Nov. 1651, he plain. assert.; rem. soon to Newbury, freem. 22 May 1639, thence to Andover, where he was one of the found. of the ch. Oct. 1645, and the first rep. of the town, 1651; d. 24 Oct. of that yr. A wid. Sarah O. d. at A. 8 Apr. 1667. His ch. were Sarah; John, b. in Eng. a. 1631; Stephen, a. 1638; Mary; Eliz.; all bef. he went to A. and there had Hannah, 1644; and prob. Deborah. Sarah m. 1 June 1648, John Clement; Mary m. 6 July 1653, Henry Ingalls; Eliz. m. 12 Oct. 1659, John Brown of Reading; Hannah m. 21 May 1660, Samuel Archer; and Deborah m. 28 Aug. 1663, John Russ. * JOHN, Andover, s. of the preced. b. in Eng. oft. a selectman, was capt. and rep. 1666, 9, 89, and 90, with high popularity, as he had been imprison. by Andros. He m. at Haverhill, 15 Nov. 1653, Mary, d. of Robert Clements, had John, b. 3 Sept. 1654; Mary, 27 Nov. 1656; Timothy, 10 Aug. 1659; Lydia, 12 Aug. 1661; Peter, 30 Aug. 1663; Samuel, 10 Mar. 1665; Sarah, 7 Apr. 1667; Mehitable, 4 Mar. 1671; Hannah, 30 May 1674; Sarah, 4 Nov. 1675; Ebenezer, 4 Oct. 1678; Clement, 12 Oct. 1680, d. soon. He d. 21 Aug. 1693, no doubt in some degree, from the torment inflict. on his w. by accusa. of witchcraft in the damnable delusion of 1692, tho.

she saved her life by confess. of impossib. guilt. See Abbot, Calef, and Hutchinson, II. 31. Charming page is that in 1 Mass. Hist. Coll. VII. 241, wh. gives her indictm. the gist of it being, that she "a covenant with the devil did make, and signed the devil's book, and took the devil to be her God, and consented to serve and worship him, and was bapt. by the devil, and renounc. her former Christian bapt. and promised to be the devil's, both body and soul forever, and to serve him." I rejoice, that, aft. the evaporation of the infernal spirit, she had energy eno. to acknowledge, 19 Oct. 1692, bef. the venerab. Increase Mather (not Cotton M. as in Geneal. Reg. XIII. 118, told) the falsehood of her confess. for surely most of the charges in that indictm. would be better laid against the judges in the oyer and terminer. They served, if they did not worship the devil, and took him to be their God, whether they signed his book or not. Had that book been brot. into Court, as it ought to have been, or the governm. call. on to show at least, what means they had used to get the precious rec. to the open view of the jury, the name of William Stoughton, and more than one of his assoc. judges, I doubt not, as clear. as that of Mary Osgood, would have flared in the sapphire blaze. Hard is it to decide, whether prisoners or judges were under stronger delusion. Sarah d. 22 Apr. 1667; Hannah d. 3 Aug. 1674. Lydia m. 20 Jan. 1680, James Frye; Mary m. 8 July 1680, John Aslett. Clement d. 18 Nov. 1680. JOHN, Salisbury, s. of William, m. 5 Nov. 1668, Mary Stephens, had Mary, b. 7 May 1669; Joseph, 12 Apr. 1671; William, 30 July 1673; John, 1 July 1677; Timothy, 2 May 1680; and Hannah, 19 Oct. 1682. JOHN, Andover, eldest s. of John, sec. of the same, m. 17 Oct. 1681, Hannah Ayres, had John, b. 28 June 1683; Ebenezer, 16 Mar. 1685; Nathaniel, 6 Jan. 1687; Jeremiah, 16 Jan. 1689, d. 7 Apr. foll.; Jeremiah, again, 11 July 1691; Daniel, 19 July 1693; William, 1697; Hannah, 24 June 1699; Benjamin, 28 Aug. 1700, d. young; Samuel, 8 July 1704, d. young; and Josiah, 13 July 1706; was freem. 1691, and d. 1725, aged 71. * PETER, Salem, br. of the preced. a tanner, m. 19 May 1690, Martha Ayres of Haverhill, had Mary, b. 15 Apr. 1691; Samuel, 6 Nov. 1695; Peter, 2 June 1697; John, 16 June 1700; William, 23 Dec. 1702, H. C. 1721; James, 6 Aug. 1705, H. C. 1724; was rep. 1714, and some yrs. more to 23, deac. of the first ch. but when he was 70 was involv. in the distract. of that body, and with others form. a new ch.; d. 24 Sept. 1753, and his wid. Martha d. 10 Sept. 1760, aged 92. SAMUEL, Andover, br. of the preced. m. 1702, Hannah Dane, had Samuel, b. 1702; Hannah, 1704; Mary, 1706; James, 1707; Sarah, 1709; Mehitable, 1711; Dean, 27 July 1714; and Lydia, 20 Oct. 1716; and he d. 1717. STEPHEN, Andover, s. of John first of the same, m. 24 Oct. 1663, Mary Hooker, but I can hardly guess who was her f. had Stephen, b. 11 Mar. 1665, wh. d. 1 Oct. 1667; Hooker, 24 June 1668; Stephen, again, 16 Aug. 1670; Joseph, 1 June 1673; and Mary, 4 Mar. 1678, wh. prob. d. bef. her f.; was freem. 1669, and d. of smallpox, 15 Jan. 1691. THOMAS, Andover, youngest ch. prob. posthum. of the first Christopher, freem. 1676, by w. Susanna had Mary, b. 14 Feb. 1675; Sarah, 6 Feb. 1677; Hannah, 29 Nov. 1679; Thomas, 17 Dec. 1680; Josiah, 1 Mar. 1682, d. soon; Judith, 8 Feb. 1683; Deborah, 26 Feb. 1685; Josiah, again, 31 May 1688; Abigail, 11 Aug. 1690; and Susanna, 29 Oct. 1692, d. soon. TIMOTHY, Andover, s. of the second John, m. 29 May 1689, Deborah Poor, perhaps d. of Daniel, had Mary, b. 8 Aug. 1690; Timothy, 22 Aug. 1693; Sarah, 8 Aug. 1697; Peter, 31 May 1699; Deborah; and Isaac, 1708; of wh. the three eldest were liv. and the three youngest were d. when the f. d. 18 Sept. 1748. He was freem. 1691; and sec. w. was Mary Poole. WILLIAM, Salisbury 1640, a propr. of that date, b. a. 1605, may earlier have had progeny than kn. to me, but at S. by rec. I find John and William, tw. b. 8 Oct. 1648; Mary, 3 Mar. 1650; Joseph, 18 Mar. 1651, d. soon; Sarah, 2 Feb. 1653; and Joseph, again, 2 Dec. 1656. Not connect. with him, however, in near consanguin. I discover in the Confidence, at Southampton, 24 Apr. 1638, there emb. Sarah O. with four ch. under eleven yrs. old, of wh. one was William Jones, one William Osgood. They were from Herrell, or Wherwell, near Andover, in Hants; but who was the h. and f. is beyond my reach. Robert Quimby of Salisbury m. Eliz. O. and Robert Jones of Salisbury m. a. 1658, Joan O. WILLIAM, Salisbury, s. of the preced. freem. 1690, by w. Abigail, d. of John Severance, m. Oct. 1672 (but in the Geneal. Reg. VIII. 160, a very diligent contrib. calls her Ambrose, and it will be found that she was d. of the w. of Severance by a former h.) had Nathaniel, b. 17 Dec. 1674; John, 27 Oct. 1676; Jonathan, 2 Apr. 1678; Abigail, 15 Feb. 1681; Sarah, 24 Apr. 1684; Richard, 13 Jan. 1686; Eliz. 9 Sept. 1688; and Joseph, 9 Aug. 1691. Not a few hours of sev. days have been giv. to the details of this geneal. in wh. my own gather. were constant. compar. with those of an assidu. contrib. C. M. Endicott, Esq. and usual. similar results have foll. our inquir. Nineteen of this name had, in 1834, swell. the Catal. of gr. at Harv. and eight at the various other N. E. coll.

OSIER, or OSYER, ABEL, a soldier of capt. Lothrop's comp. call. " the flower of Essex," k. at Bloody brook, 18 Sept. 1675. His inv. of 28 June foll. show. £3, 1, 10, that was giv. to his br. by order of Ct.

OSLAND, HUMPHREY, Cambridge vill. or Newton, shoemaker, m. 7 Mar. 1667, Eliz. d. of Samuel Hyde, had Eliz. b. 25 Jan. foll.; John, 1 Oct. 1669; Hannah; and Sarah, 23 Nov. 1683; and d. 19 June 1720.

His wid. d. 13 Mar. 1723.   Eliz. m. 11 Mar. 1693, Nathanael Wilson,
as his sec. w.; Hannah m. 1696, John Prentice; and Sarah m. Edward
Prentice.   JOHN, Newton, s. of the preced. m.   Sarah, d. of Jonathan
Hyde the first of the same, had Mary, b. 6 June 1699; Sarah; Esther,
8 Mar. 1704, d. at 21 yrs.; Jonathan, 30 Jan. 1706; Lydia; Eliz.;
and Thankful; and d. 1740.   His wid. d. 1753.

OTIS, or OTTIS, JAMES, Weymouth, s. of John the sec. was in the
wild advent. of Sir William Phips against Quebec, serv. in capt.
Ephraim Hunt's comp. 1690, where he was k.   Bef. enlist. he made his
will, 3 Aug. of that yr. pro. 27 Jan. foll. of wh. his br. Stephen was
excor. and to him he gave most of his est. a portion "to youngest br.
Job, when he comes of age," and a small sum to William Chard, the
sch.master.   It is in Vol. VIII. 21.   JOB, Scituate, br. of the preced. m.
Mary Little, d. 1758, was a shipbuilder.   JOHN, Hingham, came some
wks. bef. Rev. Peter Hobart and comp. with wh. he assoc. in sett. of that
town, 1635, b. a. 1581, at Glastonbury, Co. Somerset, perhaps s. of
Richard, had bef. leav. Eng. three ch. there bur. beside Richard, bapt.
27 Feb. 1617, and John, 14 Jan. 1622; and ds. older as well as younger,
brot. over, exc. that Richard prob. staid at home, perhaps all by w.
Margaret, wh. d. 28 June 1653; was adm. freem. 3 Mar. 1636, selectman oft.   Aft. d. of his w. rem. to Weymouth, there took sec. w. whose
name prob. was Eliz. Streame, a wid. mo. of Thomas and Benjamin
Streame, as in Geneal. Reg. XI. 173, from our Prob. rec. appears (who
in her will of 22 Sept. 1672, pro. 17 July 1676, names a s. John S. giv.
him £80, speaks of s.-in-law John Holbrook, who should pay that sum;
and d. Eliz. H. and her ch. Ichabod); and d. 31 May 1657, had his will
made one day bef. and sign. it by mark, tho. usual. in health, he wrote
plain. pro. 28 July foll. in wh. beside provid. for w. and s. John, he gives
to d. Margaret, w. of Thomas Burton, and her three ch. to d. Hannah,
w. of Thomas Gill, and two only of her many ch. Mary, and Thomas,
and to his ds. Ann, and Alice, wh. were prob. unm.   JOHN, Hingham, s.
of the preced. brot. prob. by his f. 1635, m. 1652, or earlier, Mary, d. of
Nicholas Jacob, had Mary, bapt. 1 May 1653, prob. d. soon; Mary,
again, b. 14 Mar. 1654; Eliz.; John, b. 21 Nov. 1657; a d. perhaps
Hannah, 1660; Stephen, 1661; James, 1663; Joseph, bapt. 3 June
1666; rem. to Scituate, there had Job, 20 Mar. 1677; the next yr. rem.
to Barnstable, from wh. he came back to S. and d. 16 Jan. 1684, leav.
good est. in ea. of the three towns of H. S. and B.   Mary m. 24 Feb.
1676, John Gorham of B.; and Eliz. m. 9 Oct. 1688, Thomas Allyn,
and next, 20 July 1699, David Loring.   ‡ * JOHN, Barnstable, eldest
s. of the preced. m. 18 July 1683, Mercy, youngest d. of Nathanael
Bacon, had Mary, b. 10 Dec. 1685; John, 14 Jan. 1688, H. C. 1707;

Nathaniel, 28 May 1690, bapt. 6 Sept. 1691; Mercy, 15 Oct. bapt. 13 Nov. 1692; Solomon, 13 Oct. bapt. 20 Dec. 1696, H. C. 1717; and James, 14 June 1702, the gr. politician, f. of the eloq. James, H. C. 1743, the prime mover of the Americ. revo. He was rep. 20 yrs. and aft. that, 21 yrs. of the Counc. and d. 23 Sept. 1727. JOSEPH, Scituate, br. of the ·preced. m. 20 Nov. 1688, Dorothy Thomas, d. of Nathaniel, had Nathaniel, b. 30 Jan. 1690; James, 21 Jan. 1693; Deborah, 24 Apr. 1694; Mary, 20 Mar. 1696; Dorothy, 24 Apr. 1698; Eliz. 2 Sept. 1700; Ann, 21 Sept. 1702; Bethia, 20 Nov. 1703; Delight, 19 Dec. 1706; Hannah, 10 Dec. 1709, d. at 16 yrs.; Joseph, 1 Oct. 1712; and Rachel, 1 Dec. 1713; rem. to New London a. 1716, was in gr. esteem, and d. 11 June 1754, hav. made his will 9 Jan. preced. NICHO-LAS, Dover, s. of Richard, had Nicholas, but his w. is not kn. He was k. by the Ind. in assault of the town, 26 July 1696, when his s. was tak. carr. off to Penobscot, and in short time releas. but liv. not long. RICH-ARD, Dover 1656, had been first at Boston, there, in May 1655, when adm. to be an inhab. call. a smith, prob. was only s. b. a. 1626, of Stephen of Glastonbury, Co. Somerset, who seems to have been elder br. of the first John; had in Nov. 1655 ld. at D. was selectman 1660, and had three ws. the first, Rose Stoughton, m. some yrs. bef. he was at D. From a MS. in the Brit. Museum, marked No. 6174 in the catal. of those call. " Additional," writ. by Sir Nicholas S. in wh. the latest date perceiv. is 1672, I found, she was his elder sis. b. a. 1629, and d. of Anthony, sent by his and her f. 1643, by capt. S. (no doubt our' Israel), to America, and the MS. adds, " now liv. there, the w. of —— Otis, with sev. ch." Of these ch. we learn not, for most, the exact date of b. and must not be confid. of the order; the names were Stephen, b. 1652; Rose; Richard; Nicholas; Solomon, 15 Oct. 1663, d. next yr.; Experience, 7 Nov. 1666; and Judith. Bef. 5 Nov. 1677, he had sec. w. Shuah, wid. of James Heard, on whose est. he was then admor. but no ch. of this m. is heard of. By third w. Grizzle, a young d. of James Warren, he had Hannah, b. 1689; and a d. 6 Mar. 1689, the subject of romantic story. He was k. by the Ind. 28 June 1689, with his d. Hannah, when his w. and the ch. of 3 mos. were tak. away to Canada. The ch. was bapt. by the French, who purch. her, and the mo. aft. m. a Frenchman, having two ch. and being left a wid. she came back to N. E. m. capt. Thomas Baker of Brookfield, for wh. and her suffer. the town made her gr. of ld. if she would not go again to Canada. Her former ghostly father wrote to preserve or recover his convert, but our Gov. Burnet took up the spiritual controversy, and the Romish priest failed. She liv. to 23 Feb. 1773. The mo. m. a Mr. Robitail at Montreal, and liv. to great age. The three elder ds. had been tak. at the same time,

but were recapt. by fresh pursuit at Conway, on their route to Canada.
Rose m. John Pinkham, had ten ch.; Experience m. Samuel Heard;
and Judith m. John Tuttle, wh. was k. by the Ind. In the first, sec. and
third generat. no fam. in N. E. I think, could match this of Richard O.
for measure of calam. from war. RICHARD, Dover, s. of the preced.
dissatisf. with the ch. as his f. had been 1663, proceed. further in dissent,
bec. a Quaker, yet was wound. by the·Ind. 26 July 1696, when his br.
Nicholas was k.; had w. Susanna, and ch. Rose; Richard; Rebecca, b.
11 July 1695; Stephen, 22 Aug. 1698; and Nicholas, 8 Apr. 1701;
and d. that yr. His wid. m. 1703, John Varney. STEPHEN, Dover, br.
of the preced. perhaps older, m. 16 Apr. 1674, Mary, d. of William
Pitman, had Stephen, Nathaniel, and Mary; was k. by the Ind. 28 June
1689, the same time with his f. and the s. were both carr. to Canada,
there liv. and d. as good Catholics. STEPHEN, Scituate, s. of John the
sec. m. 1685, Hannah, wh. d. 1 May 1729, only ch. of that John Ensign
who gave her all his est. aft. d. of his mo. by will made the evening bef.
he fell in the great battle of Rehoboth, 26 Mar. 1676; had Hannah, b.
16 May 1686; Mary, 7 July 1689; Ensign, 1691; John, 1694; Stephen,
3 Nov. 1697; Isaac, 1699; Joseph, 1709; and Joshua, 1711; was a
capt. d. 26 May or Aug. as the gr.st. may have var. read. 1733. His
will was of 1729. Sixteen of this name had, in 1825, been gr. at Harv.
as Farmer notes, and none at other N. E. coll. all descend. of John the
sec. I believe. Mr. Otis, the assiduous antiquary of Yarmouth, from
wh. I have gain. much knowl. of Scituate, Barnstable, and Yarmouth
early sett. is deriv. from ano. stock, emigr. at least eighty yrs. later than
the Hingham pioneer, and coming from a part of Eng. widely remote
from the first.

OTLEY, ABRAHAM, Lynn 1641. ‖ ADAM, Lynn 1641, perhaps br. of
the preced. ar. co. 1641, m. a d. of John Humfrey, Esquire, says Lewis.
Hutch. Coll. 121. Perhaps it is the same as Utley.

OTWAY, JOHN, Boston 1657, own. ld. in Lynn, and may be of the
same fam. as the last. WILLIAM, Taunton 1654.

OVELL, NATHANIEL, a cordwainer, from Dover, Co. Kent, came with
a serv. a. 1636, as by an authent. docum. I read in the Hist. of Sandwich, Eng. appears; but where he sett. is unkn.

OVERMAN, THOMAS, Boston, m. Hannah, wid. of Mahalaleel Munnings, d. of John Wiswall, was freem. 1671, d. bef. 1675. Of his wid.
Hannah, admin. was giv. 5 June 1694, to Matthew Johnson of Woburn.

OVERTON, ROBERT, Boston, had w. and s. John, and d. at sea 3 Sept.
1673, hav. made his will 27 Aug. preced. aboard ship, in lat. a. 24° pro.
5 Nov. foll. by those who saw him die.

OVIAT, or OVIETT, THOMAS, Milford 1665, propos. for freem. 1673.

OWDIE, JOHN, a youth of 17, came in the Increase, 1635, to Boston from London, but more is not kn.

OWEN, DANIEL, Braintree, eldest s. of William, m. Hannah, prob. d. of Samuel Lincoln of Taunton. EBENEZER, Braintree, s. of William, was of the comp. of brave capt. Johnson, Dec. 1675. ISAAC, Windsor, youngest s. of John, m. 20 Dec. 1694, Sarah Holcomb, perhaps d. of Benajah, had Sarah, b. 17 Feb. foll. Eunice, 8 Aug. 1696; Rebecca, 2 Mar. 1698; Ann, 12 June 1700; Isaac, 7 Nov. 1702; and Elijah, 7 Oct. 1706. JOHN, Windsor, said to be b. 25 Dec. 1624, m. 3 Oct. 1650, Rebecca Wade, perhaps d. of Robert of Hartford, had Josias, b. 8 Sept. 1651; John, 5 Nov. 1652; d. soon; John, again, 23 Apr. 1654, d. at 16 yrs.; Nathaniel, 9 Apr. 1656; Daniel, 28 Mar. 1658; Joseph, 23 Oct. 1660; Mary, 5 Dec. 1662; Benjamin, 20 Sept. 1664, d. soon; Rebecca, 28 Mar. 1666; Obadiah, 12 Dec. 1667; and Isaac, 27 May 1670; was freem. 1667, and rem. to Simsbury, and d. 1 Feb. 1699. Mary m. 1681, Nathaniel Williams of W. JOSIAH, Windsor or Simsbury, s. of the preced. m. 22 Oct. 1674, Mary, d. of John Osborn, had Josiah, b. 6 June 1675; Isaac, 4 June 1678, but Stiles, 731, is very differ.; Mary, 15 Feb. 1680; and Eliz. NATHANIEL, Windsor, s. of John, m. 2 Feb. 1698, Sarah, d. of Timothy Palmer, had Sarah, b. 3 May 1700; Nathaniel, 31 Dec. 1702; Ann, 17 July 1705; Abner, 17 Mar. 1707, both d. soon; and Ann, again, 31 July 1709. OBADIAH, Windsor, br. of the preced. had Obadiah, b. 8 July 1694, d. in few days; Martha, 31 Aug. 1697; Jemima, 18 Nov. 1700; Christian, 10 Jan. 1703; Obadiah, 8 June 1705, d. at 23 yrs.; Samuel, 3 Aug. 1707; Tabitha, 6 Feb. 1710; Jedediah, 22 May 1712, both d. young; and Jedediah, again, 21 Apr. 1715. RICHARD, Newtown, L. I. 1656–86. Thompson, and Riker. SAMUEL, Springfield, m. 1681, Ann, wid. of John Pettee, had Sarah, b. 1682; Abigail, 1685; Samuel, 1688; rem. to Brookfield, there kept an inn. ‖ THOMAS, Boston, ar. co. 1639, imprison. 1641, perhaps unjustly, for Samuel Maverick befriend. him. Winth. II. 51. WILLIAM, Braintree, freem. 1657, call. by Charles Grice, in his will, s.-in-law, in 1661, had Daniel, b. 1 Aug. 1651; Deliverance, 15 Feb. 1655, wh. m. 1 May 1672, John Eddy, as his sec. w.; and Ebenezer, bef. ment. 1 May 1657. TIMOTHY, Marblehead, d. a. 1670.

OXENBRIDGE, JOHN, Boston, s. of Daniel, wh. was a Doctor of Physic, b. 1606, at Daventry, Co. Northampton, matricul. at Lincoln Coll. Oxford, 20 June 1623, in his 18th yr. aft. was of Magdalen Hall, and contin. there a tutor some time, but disquiet. with the increas. stringency of ch. ceremon. he went, 1634, to Bermuda and preached, in few yrs. went home again, but being eject. on the act of uniform. 1662, took depart. for Surinam; thence, in short time, to Barbados, and in 1669 came hither;

was install. 10 Apr. as collea. with Allen in the first ch. a few days aft. the loss of Davenport, adm. freem. 1670, and d. 28 Dec. 1674. He had three ws. first, Jane Butler, wh. d. 22 Apr. 1655; next, m. 1656, Frances, only d. of Rev. Hezekiah Woodward, vicar of Bray, in Co. Berks, d. next yr.; and the third is kn. from her will to have been nam. Susanna. His d. Bathshua, w. of Richard Scott, Esq. of Jamaica, was sole extrix. and had good est. by the will. A younger d. Theodora, m. 21 Nov. 1677, Rev. Peter Thacher of Milton. Calamy. Wood's Athenæ.

OXMAN, WILLIAM, Salem 1668, then 35 yrs. of age.

PACEY, or PACYE, NICHOLAS, Salem 1639, when Felt says he had gr. of ld.; join. the ch. 1650. Perhaps Catharine, of the same ch. 1641, was his w. Who was the unfortun. man procured to be unit. with Sarah, d. of Gov. Thomas Dudley, aft. her h. Benjamin Keayne had cast her off, neither Dudley nor capt. K. informs us, tho. both in their wills ment. her, as does also, in his will, young Thomas D. speak. of his aunt P. as if ignorant of her slender claims on his regard. Possib. it was Thomas P. named in the inv. of John Mills, as one of his debtors 1651.

PACKARD, JOHN, Bridgewater, s. of the first Samuel of the same, had Joseph, who sett. his old f.'s est. 1741; and Mitchell tells no more, but that his wid. d. 1761, very aged. NATHANIEL, Bridgewater, br. of the preced. by w. d. prob. of John Kingman, had Samuel, Zechariah, George, Fearnot, Margaret, Sarah, Lydia, Faithful, Hannah, Deliverance, Eliz. Mary, and Deborah. His will is of 1720. SAMUEL, Hingham 1638, came in the Diligent, with w. prob. Eliz. and one ch. arr. 10 Aug. had been of Wymondham, in Co. Norfk. rem. to Weymouth, first, perhaps, where he had John, b. 20 July 1655, thence to Bridgewater by 1664,· had elder ch. Samuel, Zaccheus, Eliz. Mary, beside Hannah, Thomas, Jael, Israel, Deborah, Deliverance, and Nathaniel; but the order is not exact. indicat. for the most. Eliz. m. 14 Nov. 1665, Thomas Alger of Taunton; Mary m. Richard Phillips of Weymouth; Hannah m. Thomas Randall; Jael m. 15 Nov. 1672, John Smith; Deborah m. Samuel Washburn; and Deliverance m. Thomas Washburn. SAMUEL, Bridgewater, s. of the preced. m. Eliz. d. of Mark Lothrop, had Samuel, Daniel, Joseph, Eliz. Mary, and Susanna. His est. was sett. 1698. ZACCHEUS, Bridgewater, br. of the preced. m. Sarah, d. of John Howard, had Israel, b. 1680; Sarah, 1682; Jonathan, 1684; David, 1687; Solomon, 1689; James, 1691; Zaccheus, 1693; John, 1695; and Abiel, 1699; and d. 1723. This name was first writ. as pronounc. Packer.

PACKER, BENJAMIN, New London, s. of the first John, impress. for serv. in the French war, 1709, made his will, giv. his brs. James, Joseph, and sis. Rebecca, his est. and prob. d. soon aft. GEORGE, Portsmouth,

R. I. 1655. JAMES, New London, br. of Benjamin, was a capt. d. 1764. JOHN, New London 1655, by first w. Eliz. wh. d. 4 May 1674, had prob. John, Samuel, and Richard; by sec. w. Rebecca, wid. of Thomas Latham, d. of Hugh Wells, m. 24 June 1676, who surv. him, had James, bapt. 11 Sept. 1681; beside Joseph, Benjamin, and Rebecca, as Miss Caulkins in her Hist. judges. He d. 1689, and his wid. m. a Watson of Kingston, R. I. JOHN, New London, s. of the preced. m. Lydia, d. of Cary Latham, and d. 1701. SAMUEL, New London, s. prob. of the first John, m. Mary, d. of William Williams of the same. THOMAS, Salem, whose w. Hepzibah d. 22 Jan. 1685, aged 25 yrs. ‡ THOMAS, Portsmouth 1686, a physician, from London, was col. judge of pro. and a counsel. in 1719, d. 1728. His w. Eliz. m. 7 Aug. 1687, d. 4 Aug. 1717, in 62d yr.

PADDLEFORD, PADELFORD, sometimes PADDLEFOOT, JONATHAN, Cambridge, in rec. spelt Padlfoote, m. 5 Oct. 1652, Mary Blandford, prob. d. of John of Sudbury, had Jonathan, b. 6 July 1653, d. soon; Mary, 22 Aug. 1654; Jonathan, again, 13 Aug. 1656; Zechariah, 16 Dec. 1657, these three bapt. 6 Nov. 1659; and Edward, 13 June, bapt. 8 July foll. His wid. m. 1662, Thomas Eames of Sherburne, and 1 Feb. 1676, she was k. by the Ind. and at the same time nine of his ch. whereof most were hers also, were either k. or tak. See Barry, 27. JONATHAN, Braintree, s. of the preced. by w. Hannah had Jonathan, b. 15 Mar. 1680, rem. to Taunton a. 1700, and there, thro. his said s. Jonathan, perpet. the fam. name even to our days. ZECHARIAH, Framingham, s. of the preced. d. 7 July 1737, as Mr. Barry thinks. The name is frequent at Providence and the vicinity; and four had, in 1834, says Farmer, been gr. at Brown and Yale coll.

PADDOCK, ICHABOD, the subj. of a trifl. tradit. that he was invit. 1690 from Cape Cod to Nantucket to tea. the art of k. whales [Macy, Hist. of Nant. 30], when 18 yrs. earlier James Loper had there been so engaged. It is strange, that neither name was of perman. resid. bef. the last was certain. at N. JOHN, Swansey, s. of Robert, m. 21 Dec. 1673, Ann Jones. ROBERT, Plymouth 1643, and prob. some yrs. bef. perhaps was never a freem. of the col. had Robert, b. 1634; Zechariah, 20 Mar. 1636; Mary, 10 Mar. 1638; Alice, 7 Mar. 1640; John, 1 Apr. 1643, and Susanna, 1649; but his w. is not kn. He d. 25 July 1650. Mary m. 24 Mar. 1651, Thomas Roberts; Alice m. 7 May 1663, Zechariah Eddy; and Susanna m. 12 or 30 Nov. 1665, John Eddy, and d. 14 Mar. 1670. ZECHARIAH, Barnstable, s. of Robert, m. 1659, Deborah Sears, liv. at Yarmouth, and d. 1 May 1727, in 88th yr. leav. wid. and very numer. descend. See N. E. Weekly Journal of 5 June in that yr.

PADDY, THOMAS, Boston, s. of "*blessed*" William, m. Deborah Waite, d. 3 Feb. 1690, and his wid. d. 22 Mar. 1697. * ‖ WILLIAM, Plymouth,

came in the James, 1635, from Southampton, emb. 6 Apr. arr. at Boston
3 June, call. in the custom-ho. clearance, skinner, late of London, wh.
precision makes me suspect, that he was of the comp. or guild of the
skinners, and a liveryman of the metrop. who could not at London have
obtain. liberty to leave home, as he prob. was a subsidy man, that would
not be spared; m. 24 Nov. 1639, Alice, d. of Edmund Freeman, had
Eliz. b. 12 Nov. 1641; John, 25 Nov. 1643, d. at 18 yrs.; Samuel, 1
Aug. 1645; Thomas, 6 Sept. 1647; Joseph, 10 Sept. 1649, d. in few
mos.; and Mercy; was one of four rep. from his town in the first gen.
Court of dep. for that Col. June 1639. His w. d. 24 Apr. 1651, and he
m. at Boston, 3 Dec. foll. Mary, wid. of Bezaleel Payton, sis. of William Greenough the first, had William, a. 16 Sept. 1652, d. under 20
yrs.; rem. to Boston, was ar. co. 1652, here had Nathaniel, b. 5, bapt. 9
Nov. 1653, d. under 19 yrs.; Hannah, 8 Jan. 1656; Benjamin, 23 Feb.
1658; and Rebecca, posthum. bapt. 3 Apr. 1659, whose b. in the town
rec. is strange. put 3 Aug. of that yr. when her f. d. 24 Aug. preced.
aged 58. His will of 20 Aug. pro. 9 Sept. foll. (abstr. in Geneal. Reg.
VIII. 355), names all his 9 ch. besides the two Paytons, and provides
for the expected one. His wid. d. 21 Oct. 1675, aged a. 60. Eliz. m.
John Wensley; and Mercy m. Leonard Dowden. Nathaniel, who was
prob. unm. d. soon aft. mak. his will, 16 Sept. 1680, in wh. he gave est.
to his sis. Mary Shore, aunts Sarah Phillips, and Eliz. Greenough, cous.
Eliz. Greenough, and others. Farmer was led into a striking error in
giving from Boston rec. death of William P. 11 Nov. 1653, by omission
in his correspondent's transcr. of the words that precede, for the orig. is
thus: "Susan, the d. of Edward Breck of Dorchester, serv. to Mr.
William Paddy, d. 11 Nov. 1653." In his Appendix he made stranger
explanat. wh. would have been avoid. had the rec. been scrutiniz.
More preposterous than either of these two mistakes was the supposit.
started some 20 yrs. since, on finding a gr.st. with his name and descript.
laid in the common sewer, near the old town ho. in State str. that this
was the spot of his interm. as if so excellent a pub. officer had been bur.
in the highway. It had, prob. been reject. for its coarseness. To correct ano. error wh. comprehends sev. is almost indispensa. needful, on
account of the authority it might carry from its place in 3 Mass. Hist.
Coll. VII. 286, where upon the first described of the Portraits of the
Winslow fam. that of Mrs. Alice Wensley is strange. call. of the d. of
Edmund Freeman, who, aft the d. of her h. deac. William Paddy, bec.
the w. of Samuel Wensley, Esq. and then to extend the confusion
thorough. wh. was deep eno. bef. a d. of hers by her last h. was made
w. of the Hon. Isaac Winslow, only s. of Gov. Josiah. Whose portrait
that canvas exhibits, whether the mo. or gr.mo. of the w. of Isaac

Winslow, may be uncert. but as the wid. of Paddy did not m. at all, and as the d. of the w. of Samuel Wensley did not m. Winslow, the picture may be of Eliz. w. of John Wensley, or of Sarah, her d. who was w. of Winslow.

PADNER, EZEKIEL, Boston, by w. Ruth had Ruth, b. 12 Sept. 1668.

PAGE, ABRAHAM, Boston 1645, a tailor, from Great Baddow, in Essex, by w. Mary, of Braintree ch. had Abraham, b. 7, bapt. 8 Mar. 1646, at Boston, d. same mo. and, perhaps, he rem. ANTHONY, Dover 1662-6. BENJAMIN, Haverhill, m. 21 Sept. 1666, Mary, prob. d. of Thomas Whittier, had 9 ch. says Barry, but perhaps he could not name one. CORNELIUS, Haverhill 1677, may have been br. of the preced. ‖ EDWARD, Boston, cooper, by w. Eliz. d. of William Beamsley, had Eliz. wh. d. 19 Nov. 1653; Sarah, b. 13 Apr. 1656; Edward, 20 Mar. 1658; Jonathan, 31 July 1660; Penuel, 2 May 1663; Eliz. 12 Sept. 1666; and Humility, 7 June 1673; was of ar. co. 1661. FRANCIS, Hampton 1678, oldest s. of deac. Robert, may be that deac. wh. d. 15 Nov. 1706, aged 76. GEORGE, Saco 1653, m. Mary, d. of Nicholas Edgecomb; and she m. next, John Ashton of Scarborough. GEORGE, Branford 1667, may be the same who was an ens. and d. at Boston, where in Aug. 1675 his inv. was tak. HENRY, Hampton, freem. 1666. ISAAC, Boston, m. 30 Sept. 1653, Damaris Shattuck; was prob. the bricklayer at Salem 1658. JOHN, Watertown, came in the fleet with Winth. made constable 19 Oct. 1630, when he req. to be freem. and was adm. 18 May foll.; was from Dedham, Co. Essex, with w. and two ch. whose suffer. in the first winter were duly thot. of by his former min. blessed John Rogers. See Winth. I. 47. His w. was Phebe, sis. of William Paine and of the w. of William Hammond of W. nam. Eliz. who d. 25 Sept. 1677, in 87th yr.; he d. 18 Dec. preced. aged a. 90; and their ch. were John, prob. one of the two brot. from Eng.; Samuel, b. 20 Aug. 1633; Daniel, 10 Aug. 1634, d. very soon; and Eliz. Mary and Phebe, of wh. one may have been b. in Eng. Phebe was third w. of James Cutler. JOHN, Dedham, freem. 8 Oct. 1640. * JOHN, Watertown, s. of John of the same, perhaps brot. from Eng. sw. fidel. 1652, may be he who m. 12 May 1664, Faith Dunster, prob. niece of the Presid. of the coll. rem. to Groton, had, perhaps, Joseph; John, b. 10 Dec. 1669; Samuel, 4 June 1672; Mary, 9 June 1675, wh. perhaps m. a Boardman; went back to W. had Jonathan, b. 24 June 1677, and was selectman 1695-8, rep. 1700. His w. d. 1699, and he m. 5 Sept. 1699, Emory Lamb of Boston, but was d. bef. 1712. JOHN, Haverhill 1646, d. Nov. 1687, and his wid. d. says Barry, Nov. 1697. JOHN, Haverhill, s. of the preced. m. 18 June 1663, Sarah, d. of James Davis, had Sarah, b. 7 July 1680, and prob. others bef. or aft. or both. JOHN,

Groton, 1711, s. of sec. John of Watertown, and I kn. no more. JONA-
THAN, Groton, br. of the preced. by w. Mary had a d. b. 28 Dec. 1706,
d. very soon; Faith, 6 Nov. 1707; Jonathan, 5 June 1710; John, 30
Jan. 1712; Joseph, 22 Oct. 1714; Mary, 20 Feb. 1717; Benjamin, 19
July 1719; Simeon, 23 Jan. 1722; and Sarah, 10 Dec. 1724; and he
d. 10 Oct. 1751. JOSEPH, Haverhill 1669, m. Martha, wid. of Joseph
Heath of the same aft. 1672. JOSEPH, Salisbury, s. of the first Onesiphorus, m. 12 Mar. 1691, Sarah Smith, had Sarah, b. 12 Oct. 1691;
Judith, 22 Oct. 1692, d. young; John, 17 June 1696; Joseph, 3 Sept.
1698; and Joshua, 15 Nov. 1700. JOSEPH, Watertown 1714, s. of sec.
John of the same, of wh. no more can be learned even from Bond. ONESI-
PHORUS, Salisbury, m. 22 Nov. 1664, Mary, d. of Thomas Hawksworth,
had Mary, b. 29 Oct. 1666; Joseph, 3 Apr. 1670; Abigail, 23 June
1672; Mary, again, 18 Nov. 1674; Sarah, 7 July 1677; Onesiphorus,
10 Feb. 1679; Cornelius, wh. d. 1683; and Mary, again, 29 Sept.
1686. His w. d. 8 May 1695; and he m. 31 July foll. Sarah Rowell,
had John, b. 21 Feb. 1697; and d. 28 June 1706. ONESIPHORUS,
Salisbury, s. of the preced. 21 Nov. 1711, Mehitable, d. of Isaac
Green, wid. of Simon Dow. * ROBERT, Salem, from Ormsby, near
Yarmouth, Co. Norfk. came 1637, aged 33, with w. Lucy, 30; three
ch. Francis, Margaret, and Susanna; and two serv. William Moulton,
20, and Ann Wadd, 15; freem. 18 May 1642, rem. to Hampton, rep.
in 1657, 1668, and d. 22 Sept. 1679. His will, of 9 Sept. in that
yr. names oldest s. Francis, d. Margaret, wh. m. William Moul-
ton, no doubt the fellow-passeng.; Mary, w. of Samuel Fogg;
Thomas; Rebecca, w. of John Smith; Hannah, w. of Henry Dow;
Robert, s. of his s. Thomas; and a gr.s. John; beside s.-in-law William
Marston. Prob. he had s. Robert. SAMUEL, Concord, s. of first John,
by w. Hannah had Hannah, b. 10 Feb. 1668; Samuel, 5 Jan. 1671;
Ebenezer, 17 Jan. 1676; Mildred; Mercy; Eliz.; Sarah; and Ex-
perience; and d. at Watertown. All the ch. exc. Samuel, wh. was in
S. C. agreed with their wid. mo. in 1704 on div. of est. SAMUEL,
Groton, s. of the sec. John, by w. Martha had Eliz. b. 23 Mar. 1719;
and Daniel, 10 Aug. 1722. THOMAS, Saco 1636, came prob. in the
Increase to Boston from the parish of All Saints Staynings, Marklane,
London, a tailor, aged 29, with w. Eliz. 28, and ch. Thomas, 2, and
Catharine, 1. He was of gr. jury 1640, and, perhaps, rem. to Casco.
See Folsom, 33. WILLIAM, Watertown, prob. s. of first John, b. in
Eng. by w. Ann had John, b. 7 Sept. 1642, d. in few days, and he d. 19
Feb. 1665. His will, of 16 Dec. preced. names no ch. calls w. Hannah,
and the wid. m. Nicholas Wood of Medfield. Eight of this name had, as
Farmer's MS. marks, in 1834, been gr. at Harv. two at Yale, and eight
at the other N. E. coll.

PAIGE, JOHN, Saybrook 1684. NATHANIEL, Roxbury 1686, had sev. ch. b. prob. in Eng. and here had James, bapt. 28 Nov. 1686, d. at 8 mos. tho. town rec. ment. neither b. nor d.; rem. 1688 to Billerica, was freem. 1690; had Christopher, b. 10 Feb. 1691. By Joseph Dudley, as Presid. he was made, 1686, marshal of the Co. of Suff'k. he d. 12 Apr. 1692 ; but tho. descend. are num. eno. it is not ascert. from what part of Eng. or when he came. His will names w. Joanna ; his d. Eliz. m. 2 Dec. 1698, John Simpkins of Boston; Sarah m. 7 Jan. 1699, Samuel Hill, jr. of Billerica. His s. Nathaniel d. at Bedford, 2 Mar. 1755, aged 75 ; and Christopher was the first deac. at Hardwick, where he d. 10 Mar. 1774. ‖ NICHOLAS, Boston 1665, perhaps br. of the preced. came from Plymouth, Co. Devon, m. Ann, wid. of Edward Lane, d. of Benjamin Keayne, was on serv. in Philip's war 1675, was capt. and later a col. ar. co. 1693, and its com. His w. d. 30 June 1704, and he d. prob. late in 1717, for his will was pro. 3 Jan. foll. Hutch. 295, and 375, where is strange mistake in call. his w. sis. of Gov. Joseph Dudley, when she was d. of that unhappy sis. In the weakness of that parent, she was suspect. of inherit. a melancholy share, was indict. and aft. disagreem. of the jury, was at the Gen. Court in May 1666, found " guilty of much wickedness " ; but great lenity was exhibit. towards her, and on acknowledgm. of her offences she was discharg. See in Mass. Rec. IV. part 2, page 309, a brief of the very strange process.

PAINE, ANTHONY, Portsmouth, R. I. rec. to be an inhab. 6 Dec. 1638, had w. Rose, who m. a Weeden, and may seem to have had fam. from his release, of 1650, to share of property of P. wh. d. a. 1640. ARTHUR, Portsmouth, R. I. 1655, in the list of freem. BENJAMIN, Bristol, youngest and fifth s. of the sec. Stephen of Rehoboth, d. in the spring of 1698, his will of 18 Apr. pro. 3 May foll. in that yr. giv. his est. to brs. and sis. shows he' was unm. and for so young a man his inv. was large, but chief. it was deriv. from his f. and gr.f. EDWARD, Lynn 1637, Charlestown 1638, rem. prob. 1643 to Exeter or Dover, and bef. 1649 went home. ELISHA, Eastham, s. of Thomas of the same, m. 21 Jan. 1687, Rebecca, d. of John Doane, had Abigail, b. 5 Jan. and bapt. 21 Oct. 1688 ; Elisha, b. 29 Dec. 1693 ; Mary, 1 Feb. 1696 ; Solomon, 16 May 1698 ; and Dorcas, 24 Feb. 1700. Four or five more ch. are assign. to him in the Fam. Geneal. but without dates, and it is said he rem. to Canterbury, Conn. and d. 7 Feb. 1735. JAMES, Newport, by w. Amy had Amy, b. 18 Jan. 1660. JAMES, Barnstable, s. of Thomas of Eastham, m. 9 Apr. 1691, Bethia, d. of John Thacher of Yarmouth, had James, b. 24, bapt. 27 Mar. 1692, d. at 19 yrs.; Thomas, bapt. 8 Apr. 1694 ; Bethia, 22 Feb. bapt. 8 Mar. 1696, d. next yr.; Bethia, again, 23, bapt. 29 May 1698 ; Mary, 13, bapt. 18 Aug. 1700 ; Experience, b. 17

Mar. 1703; and Rebecca, 8 Apr. 1705, d. at 21 yrs. JOHN, Southold, L. I. perhaps s. of Thomas of Salem, was freem. of Conn. 1662, and may have been a propr. of New Haven 1685; tho. JOHN, of New Haven 1670, seems to me to be ano. person. JOHN, Ipswich, s. of Robert, ar. co. 1666, went to Nantucket, there d. 13 July 1677, says Farmer; but I feel some distrust of it. JOHN, Middletown, d. 1681, leav. wid. an eldest s. aged 20; Job, aged 4 yrs.; Patience, 3; and Abigail, 1. One of this name, wh. I kn. not how to appropriate, was passeng. at 14 yrs. of age, in the Abigail, 1635, from London. JOHN, Boston, s. of William, m. Mar. 1659, Sarah, d. of Richard Parker; but if the tradit. be good, that he d. at sea, aft. convey. 29 Dec. 1674, some est. to his niece, Hannah, d. of Samuel Appleton, w. of William Downes, he had prob. lost his w. By her he had Sarah, b. 14 Aug. 1660; Hannah, 31 Mar. 1662, both d. young; William, 15 Mar. 1664; Ann, 24 Mar. 1665; and Eliz. 19 Feb. 1666. JOHN, Dedham, s. prob. of Thomas the first of the same, m. 7 Feb. 1677, Mary, d. of Ralph Day, had Rebecca, b. 7 June 1678; Mary, 11 July 1680; Susanna, 17 Aug. 1682; John, 28 Feb. 1685; Thomas, 8 Jan. 1687; and Sarah, 17 Nov. 1689. Prob. his w. d. 25 Oct. 1694. JOHN, Rehoboth, s. of Stephen of the same, had Eliz. b. 12 July 1682. JOHN, Braintree, s. of the sec. Stephen of the same, m. 20 Jan. 1689, Deborah, d. of Henry Neal, had John, b. 13 Aug. 1690, casual. k. at 16 yrs.; Deborah, 28 Sept. 1692, d. young; Stephen, 19 Jan. 1694; Joseph, 26 Oct. 1695; Moses, 7 Nov. 1697, d. soon; Benjamin, 6 Mar. 1700; Seth, 16 Jan. 1702; and James and Deborah, tw. 27 July 1704. JOHN, Eastham, prob. s. of Thomas of the same, by first w. said to have been a Bennett, who d. 20 May 1716, had John, b. 18 Sept. 1690; Mary, 28 Jan. 1693; William, 6 June 1695; Benjamin, 22 Feb. 1697, d. young; Sarah, 14 Apr. 1699; Eliz. 2 June 1702; Theophilus, 7 Feb. 1704; Josiah, 8 Mar. 1706; Nathaniel, 18 Nov. 1707; Rebecca, 30 Oct. 1709; Mercy, 3 Apr. 1712; and Benjamin, 18 May 1714, d. young; and he m. 3 Mar. 1720, Alice Mayo, had Hannah, 11 Jan. 1721, d. young; James, 17 Dec. 1723, d. young; Thomas, 6 Apr. 1725; and Alice, 4 Dec. 1728. He d. 18 Oct. 1731. JOSEPH, Charlestown 1649, was s. of Edward, bef. ment. who had est. at Wapping, near London, wh. this s. sold, and went home, prob. JOSEPH, Eastham, s. of Thomas of the same, m. 27 May 1691, Patience Sparrow, perhaps d. of Jonathan, had Ebenezer, b. 8 Apr. 1692; Hannah, 5 July 1694; Joseph, 27 Mar. 1697; and Richard, 25 Mar. 1699. MOSES, Braintree, freem. 2 June 1641, had est. in Cambridge, Concord, and at Piscataqua, as well as Braintree, and three ch. to wh. by will of 17 June 1643, he div. his prop. half to Moses, made excor. one quarter to d. Eliz. and the other to s. Stephen, who was to be under Moses' governm. until 23 yrs. old. These were all b. in Eng. Besides he adds codic. three days later, one day bef. his d. giv. w. Judith twenty shill. to be paid within a cert. time. The will was pro. 30 Oct. 1643, and his inv. ret. the same day, shows rather large est. yet without the sums due to him from Eng. Of the four appraisers, half were Guilford men, wh. appears strange, but the provision for his wid. seems more strange. She had been not long his w. hav. been wid. of the first Edmund Quincy, brot. him no ch. and in few yrs. m. Robert Hull. Eliz. m. 17 Nov. 1643, Henry Adams, and was casual. k. 21 Feb. 1676 in few hours aft. her h. was shot. * ‖ MOSES, Braintree, elder s. of the preced. b. in Eng. by w. Eliz. had nine or ten ch. of wh. Moses, b. 16 July 1646, d. young; Eliz. 5 Aug. 1648; Sarah, 30 Jan. 1651, d. young; Moses, again, 26 June 1652, d. young; Mary, 12 Mar. 1656; William, 1 Apr. 1657; John, 12 Oct. 1659, d. soon; Sarah, again, 2 May 1662; and Margaret, 20 Dec. 1664. He was ar. co. 1644, freem. 1647, lieut. and a rep. 1666 and 8, rem. to Boston, there had Hannah, 20 Apr. 1671, and Lydia, 23 Aug. 1674; was constable 1673, and d. 15 Dec. 1690. MOSES, Braintree, s. of the first Stephen of the same, was deac. and d. 22 June 1746. By w. Mary he had Mary, b. 4 May 1689; Hannah, 2 Apr. 1692; Moses, 21 Oct. 1694, d. within 3 yrs.; Sarah, 3 July 1697; Moses, again, 13 June 1700; and Aaron, 8 Nov. 1703, d. young. * NATHANIEL, Rehoboth, younger s. of the first Stephen, b. in Eng. a merch. partner with his f. was rep. 1670-1, and liv. at Boston; but d. bef. his f. leav. Nathaniel, his only ch. b. 18 Oct. 1661, and wid. Eliz. or Alice. NATHANIEL, Rehoboth, s. of the preced. by w. Dorothy had Dorothy, b. 3 Feb. 1696; Nathaniel, 24 May 1697; Abigail, 28 July 1699; Jonathan, 2 July 1701; perhaps Mary of unkn. date; Rachel, 13 July 1705; and Eliz. 15 Apr. 1712; and he d. 1718. NATHANIEL, Rehoboth, s. of the sec. Stephen of the same, prob. rem. to Bristol, had s. Nathaniel, thot. to be ancest. of the gr. fam. at Worcester, and was, perhaps, f. of Stephen, H. C. 1721; and six ds. Eliz. Sarah, Mary, Hannah, Martha, and Dorothy. NICHOLAS, Eastham, s. of Thomas of the same, by w. Hannah had Thankful, b. 14 Mar. 1700; Priscilla, 16 Oct. 1701; Philip, 18 Nov. 1704, d. under 21 yrs.; Lois, 29 Sept. 1705; Abigail, 3 Aug. 1707; and Hannah, 24 Sept. 1709; and his w. d. 24 Jan. 1732. PHILIP, New Haven, m. 1679, Mary, d. of capt. John Nash, rem. to Northampton, freem. 1690, and liv. some yrs. there, and Seth, wh. d. 12 Aug. 1689, may have been his ch.; had Mary, b. 1690, but rem. again to Conn. and part of his days was of Windham. * ROBERT, Ipswich, b. a. 1601, was prob. from Co. Suffolk, as his w. Ann was d. of John Whiting of Hadleigh in that shire, freem. 2 June 1641, rep. 1647-9, had good est. and was liberal in distrib. of it, was rul. elder, Treasr. of Essex Co. eighteen yrs. had sec. w. Dorcas, wh. d. 23 Feb. 1681; and he d. 1684, leav. s. John, and Robert, H. C. 1656. ROBERT, Ipswich, s. of the preced. freem. 1685, was liv. 1704. SAMUEL, Boston, by w. Eliz. had Samuel, b. 26 Aug. 1670. SAMUEL, Braintree, s. of Stephen first of the same, freem. 1690, m. 4 Apr. 1678, Mary, d. of James Penniman, had Mary, b. 27 Oct. 1680; Lydia, 6 Jan. 1682; Samuel, 26 Nov. 1684; Hannah, 1 Feb. 1687; Joseph, 3 Aug. 1689; Mehitable, 8 Dec. 1693; and Benjamin, 28 Dec. 1696; and d. 10 Dec. 1739. SAMUEL, Eastham, s. of Thomas of the same, m. 31 Jan. 1683, Patience Freeman, had Samuel, b. 30 Oct. 1683; Mercy, 5 Aug. 1686; Nathaniel, 9 July 1689, d. young; Ebenezer, 17 June 1692; Eliz. 11 June 1694; Joshua, 20 May 1696; Isaac, 3 Jan. 1699; Mary, 24 Feb. 1704; and Seth, 5 Oct. 1706, d. young. SAMUEL, Rehoboth, s. of the sec. Stephen of the same, m. it is said, Abigail Frissell, but whose ch. she was, is unkn. had Samuel, b. 13 Sept. 1686; Ann, 15 Sept. 1688; Seth, 20 Aug. 1690; Sarah, 11 Dec. 1692; Judith, 18 Feb. 1695; Noah, 28 May 1696; Stephen, 21 June 1699; Daniel, 22 Feb. 1703; Joshua; and Rebecca; and he rem. to Woodstock 1710, and d. 11 May 1735. His wid. d. 13 Jan. 1752, aged 79, acc. Fam. Geneal. * STEPHEN, Hingham 1638, from Great Ellingham, near Attleburgh, Co. Norfk. miller, came that yr. in the Diligent, with w. Rose, three ch. and four serv. freem. 6 June 1639, rep. 1641, rem. 1645 to Rehoboth, rep. 1647, and 18 yrs. more. His w. d. 20 Jan. 1661, and next yr. he m. Alice, wid. of William Parker, I presume, of Taunton, wh. outliv. him, and he d. 24 June 1678, or as I read Col. Rec. 24 Jan. foll. but neither can be true for him, tho. one may be for his s. of the same name, since the rec. bears "S. P. sen. was bur. 21 Aug. 1679." His will was of 18 July in that yr. and inv. of very large est. was tak. 11 Sept. foll. ‖ STEPHEN, Braintree, younger s. of Moses the first, b. in Eng. ar. co. 1649, freem. 1653, m. 15 Nov. 1651, Hannah, d. of deac. Samuel Bass, had Stephen, b. 8 Mar. 1653; Samuel, 10 June 1654; Hannah, 28 Jan. 1656; Sarah, 1 Nov. 1657; Moses, 26 Mar. 1660; John, 21 Sept. 1666; and Lydia, 20 Sept. 1670. He d. 29 July 1691. Sarah m. 22 Jan. 1678, Roger Billings; and Lydia, his youngest ch. m. 20 Jan. 1689, Benjamin Neale, the same day that her br. m. his sis. STEPHEN, Rehoboth, s. of the first Stephen, b. prob. in Eng. a tanner, had est. at Watertown in 1654, but liv. not long there, and at R. had Stephen, b. 23 Nov. 1654; Rebecca, 20 Dec. 1656; John, 3 Apr. 1658; Mary, 11 July 1660; Samuel, 12 Aug. 1662; Eliz. 27 Oct. 1664; Sarah, 12 Oct. 1666; Nathaniel, 20 Nov. 1667; and Benjamin, 9 Mar. 1675, wh. d. unm. at 23 yrs. The other ch. were all m. and he d. bef. his f. Rebecca m. 24 Dec. 1673, Peter Hunt, and 21 Nov. 1677,

Samuel Peck; Mary m. Daniel Aldis, as says the Fam. Geneal. but it may be a mistake, for D. Aldis m. Sarah, and I believe her to have been d. of the sec. Moses of Braintree; Eliz. m. 10 Feb. 1685, Jacob Pepper; and Sarah m. Enoch Hunt, if the Fam. Geneal. be foll. but my research makes E. Hunt m. 29 Oct. 1678, Mary Paine. Into such errors it is much easier to fall than to recover from them. STEPHEN, Dedham, m. 3 Nov. 1652, Ann, d. of Francis Chickering, of wh. aft. hard search I can find no more, unless he be the Rehoboth man, and his wid. m. 2 Dec. 1679, Thomas Metcalf of D. STEPHEN, Charlestown, or Malden, freem. 1665, by w. Eliz. had Mary, b. 15 Nov. 1658, was tythingman 1679, at C. adj. M. STEPHEN, Braintree, eldest s. of Stephen of the same, freem. 1678, m. 20 Feb. 1682, Ellen, d. of William Veazie, had Stephen, b. 7 Nov. foll.; Ellen, bapt. 12 Oct. 1684; Samuel, 13 Feb. 1687, d. at 2 yrs.; Samuel, again, 14 Apr. 1689; and d. 24 May 1690. His wid. m. 5 Oct. 1693, Joseph Crosby. STEPHEN, Rehoboth, eldest s. of the sec. Stephen of the same, by first w. Eliz. had, it is thot. no ch. but by sec. w. m. 12 Aug. 1707, Mary Brintnall, had Stephen, b. 30 Apr. 1708; and Edward, 22 Jan. 1710; and the f. d. 12 Mar. foll. His wid. it is said, rem. to Conn. THOMAS, Salem, a weaver, from Wrentham, in Co. Suffk. came 1637, aged 50, in the Mary Ann of Yarmouth, with w. Eliz. 53; and six ch. Mary, b. 12 Oct. 1611; Thomas, 18 Jan. 1613; Eliz. 20 Jan. 1615; Dorothy, 6 Dec. 1618; John, 26 Aug. 1620; and Sarah, 7 Mar. 1622; as by a very trustworthy anc. docum. appears, in wh. he (call. s. of Thomas and Catharine of Cooklie, near Halesworth, in Co. Suffk.) is said to be b. 11 Dec. 1586, m. this w. 22 Nov. 1610, and, beside the six ch. brot. over, had Peter, 14 Mar. 1617, wh. prob. d. young; and Nathaniel, 21 July 1626, wh. d. under 10 yrs. He had, says Felt, gr. of ld. 1637, was freem. 2 June 1641, unless it was his s. then adm. wh. seems much more prob.; made his will 10 Apr. 1638, and by the bef. ment. docum. is supposed to have d. 1640. Mary m. Philemon Dickinson. THOMAS, Dedham, s. of the preced. b. in Eng. prob. the freem. of 2 June 1641, by w. Rebecca had Rebecca, b. 19 Sept. 1642; Thomas, 19, bapt. 24 Mar. 1644; John, b. 27 Apr. 1646; and Eliz. 6, bapt. 12 Mar. 1648, and he d. 3 Aug. 1686. His will was made 26 July preced. in wh. beside w. Rebecca, he provides for s.-in-law Thomas Patten, whose w. Rebecca his d. m. 1 Apr. 1662, had d. leav. Rebecca, and for Eliz. Hunting, w. of John, m. 18 Apr. 1671; and devises ld. to s. Thomas, gives resid. of est. equal. between s. Thomas and John. The wid. made her will 3 Mar. 1688. * THOMAS, Yarmouth 1643, had been there certainly four yrs. for he was rep. 1639 (tho. no respect is due to report of his com. 1621), rem. to Eastham, of wh. he was rep. 1671 and six yrs. more, had, beside Eleazer, b. 10 Mar. 1659, wh. d. young,

Thomas; Joseph; Nicholas; Samuel; Elisha; John; James, 6 July 1665; Mary; and Dorcas. Mary m. 11 Jan. 1670, James Rogers, jr. and next, 24 Apr. 1679, Isaiah Cole; and Dorcas m. Benjamin Vickery. The will of the f. was of 12 May 1705, pro. 2 Oct. 1706, unless there be confus. betw. f. and s. of the same bapt. name, wh. seems very prob. THOMAS, Boston, m. 25 Aug. 1659, Hannah, d. of Thomas Bray of New Haven, had Thomas, b. 19 Feb. 1665. He was, perhaps, that s. of Thomas of London, b. 8 Feb. 1632, wh. 1647, chose for his guardian, Thomas Mayhew, wh. had m. in London his mo. Jane. THOMAS, Newtown, L. I. 1656. Riker, 43. THOMAS, York, sw. alleg. 1680. THOMAS, Dover 1659, constable 1687, made his will 17 Oct. 1694, pro. 1700, ment. w. Eliz. wh. was nam. extrix. and ch. Thomas, Jane, Eliz. Catharine, and Ann, said to be all minors. THOMAS, Dedham, s. of Thomas sec. of the same, m. 25 Apr. 1671, Rebecca Peck, had no ch. His w. d. 28 Nov. 1682; and he had sec. w. Margaret, wh. prob. brot. him that Thomas wh. d. 6 Sept. 1686; Margaret, wh. d. ten days aft. her br. 16 Sept. 1686; and Thomas, again, b. 5 Sept. 1687, wh. d. at 10 yrs. his mo. hav. d. some yrs. preced.; and he m. next, 20 Aug. 1689, Mary Lawson, had Mary, b. 16 Aug. 1698, and his third w. d. 5 Apr. 1718. He made his will 24 Jan. 1726, pro. 25 Feb. foll. THOMAS, Eastham, prob. s. of Thomas of the same, m. 5 Aug. 1678, Hannah Shaw, had Hannah, b. 6 Apr. 1679, d. young; Hugh, 5 July 1680, d. next yr.; Thomas, 28 Feb. 1682; Hannah, again, 12 May 1684; Jonathan, 1 Feb. 1686; Abigail, 4 Mar. 1688, d. next winter; Abigail, again, 10 Nov. 1689; Phebe, 14 Mar. 1691, d. young; Elkanah, 1 Feb. 1693; Moses, 28 Sept. 1695; Joshua, 28 Aug. 1697; Phebe, again, 11 Feb. 1699; Lydia, 4 Dec. 1700; and Barnabas, 13 Nov. 1705. THOMAS, Newport 1683, very active as capt. of a privateer many yrs. and one of the found. of the Episcop. ch. in that place, of wh. much may be seen in the valua. Hist. of Arnold, I. 471, and aft. TOBIAS, Boston, came from Jamaica, m. 1665, Sarah, wid. of Miles Standish, jr. d. of John Winslow, had William, b. 21 Jan. 1669, H. C. 1689, and he d. 12 Sept. 1669, with so short notice, that his will was nuncup. In it he provides only for this s. and the wid. wh. obtain. 3d h. Richard Middlecot. WILLIAM, Ipswich, came in the Increase from London, 1635, aged 37, with Ann, prob. his w. 40; beside Susan, 11; William, 10; Ann, 5; John, 3; and Daniel, 8 wks.; freem. 13 May 1640, may have been first at Watertown some few yrs. had large est. and used it in a publ. spirit, rem. to Boston, and d. 10 Oct. 1660, leav. only s. John, bef. ment. His will, made 8 days bef. pro. 14 Nov. foll. in our Vol. of rec. I. 345, provides £200 to his w. Hannah, and the dwel.-ho. for life; £1,500 to the 3 ch. of his d. Hannah, w. of Samuel Appleton, viz.: Hannah, 600; Samuel, 500; and

Judith, 400, a lib. allow. for s. John, to six ch. of Simon Eyre, dec. viz. : Benjamin, Mary, Rebecca, Christian, Ann, and Dorothy, £5 ea. and to Simon, wh. was older than most of them, £5. (from this I conject. as also from being fellow-passeng. that the w. of Eyre was sis. of this testator) ; to my sis. Page £3 per an. and to her ch. John, Samuel, Eliz. Mary, and Phebe, £5 ea.; to ch. of my sis. Hammond, John, Eliz. and Hannah, £5. ea.; to my kinswo. Eliz. d. of Samuel Howse, £10, to two ds. of my cous. John Tall, 40s. ea.; s.-in-law Samuel Appleton, £10.; William Howard, £15.; Jeremiah Belcher, 40s.; Anthony Stoddard, £10.; Christopher Clark, £10.; Joseph Taintor, £10.; Oliver Purchase, £10.; to an Ind. serv. 40s. yearly; to the free sch. at Ipswich his ld. at Jeffrys neck; to the coll. at Cambr. £20. as a stock forever, and to friends in the min. Norton, Wilson, Sherman, Brown, Cobbett, Fiske, Phillips, and Mayo, 40s. ea. WILLIAM, Salem, shoemaker, may be that passeng. in the Abigail, 1635, aged·15, and at S. to Eliz. perhaps his w. or mo. Felt says gr. of ld. was made 1640, and he was prob. the freem. of 1650, d. a. 1660. WILLIAM, New Haven 1667, perhaps br. of John, was freem. 1669. WILLIAM, Boston s. of Tobias, by w. Mary had William, bapt. 24 Nov. 1695; Tobiah, 27 June 1697; and Sarah, 16 July 1699, at the 2d ch. that of the Mathers; but as he was next winter one of the found. of the Brattle st. ch. perhaps others were bapt. there. He d. 11 June 1735. Twenty of this name had been in 1827 gr. at Harv. and above half as many more at other N. E. coll. beside not a small number, spelling Payne; but I could not discrimin. the fams. and had it been in my power, there would have no benefit foll. because sev. have used both forms. Of ARTHUR, ment. by Farmer, as rec. into Boston ch. 1639, I have the utmost confidence that it belongs to Perry, only one Arthur occurr. in adm. of memb. in that yr.

PAINTER, SHUBAEL, Westerly, perhaps s. of Thomas, with him among earliest sett. there 1661. THOMAS, Hingham 1637, rem. perhaps to Providence, at least Roger Williams gives him deed of a lot there, among home lots; but he was aft. at Boston, by w. Catharine, wh. d. 1641, had Eliz. William, and Thomas, wh. all d. betw. 30 Sept. 1639 and 24 Apr. foll. says the town rec. wh. may so far be true, but ano. Thomas was by the ch. rec. bapt. 13 Sept. 1640, the f. being adm. 5 preced. and freem. 12 Oct. 1640, rem. to Charlestown, New Haven, Rowley, and back to Hingham bef. 1644, there had ano. w. and ch. and suffered severely for unwilling. to bring the ch. to bapt. as told in Winth. II. 174. So I think he rem. next to Providence, thence again to Newport, bef. 1655, when his name is enroll. among the freem. and prob. his last rem. was to Westerly with its first sett. in 1661. THOMAS, Westerly 1669, perhaps s. of the preced. and one of the name was drown. 25 Mar. 1706, whether that being new yrs. day gave any occasion for the casualty is not heard. WILLIAM, Charlestown, a sea capt. and merch. d. 28 Aug. 1666. His will, made 4 days preced. names w. Eliz. speaks of est. in Barbados and Carolina.

PALFREY, PALFERY, PALFRY, or PALFRAY, JOHN, Cambridge, brot. from Eng. perhaps by his mo. who m. George Willis, sometimes writ. Willowes; by w. Rebecca, d. of William Bordman, m. 4 Aug. 1664, had Rebecca, b. 15, bapt. 17 Sept. 1665; John, 12, bapt. 14 Apr. 1667, d. in few wks.; Eliz. bapt. 24 May 1668; Martha, b. 18 May 1670; Thomas, 7 May 1672, wh. d. 21 Nov. 1677; Ruth, 1 Nov. 1677, wh. d. unm. at Medford, aged 60; John, early in 1689, wh. d. 1 Dec. 1759, says Cambr. Epit. in 71st yr. and unm. There were two or three ds. more, of wh. one was Mary, wh. m. 1 Dec. 1700, Ebenezer Williams. He d. 1689; in his will of 18 Feb. pro. 17 Dec. of that yr. he provides for the new b. John, and six ds. but does not name them. Rebecca bec. sec. w. 24 Nov. 1716, of Joseph Hicks; and Martha m. 30 May 1689, Benjamin Goddard. * PETER, Salem 1626, came, perhaps, with Conant, or soon aft. req. adm. as freem. 19 Oct. 1630, and took 18 May foll. the oath, was much betrusted, rep. 1635; by w. Edith had Jonathan, bapt. 25 Dec. 1636; Jehoiadan, d. early; Remember, bapt. 16 Sept. 1638; Mary, 15 Dec. 1639; and at least two ds. more; rem. to Reading, there d. strick. in yrs. 15 Sept. 1663. He m. for sec. w. Eliz. wid. of John Fairfield, and had 3d w. Alice, nam. in his will of 21 Oct. 1662, with codic. of 19 May foll. He names no s. but prob. had bef. giv. most of his est. the inv. of resid. being small. The wid. liv. to 21 Mar. 1677, far strick. in yrs. Remember m. 12 Feb. 1662, Peter Aspenwall, beside wh. he names other s.-in-law Matthew Johnson, who had m. 12 Nov. 1656, his d. Hannah, wh. d. 1 Aug. 1662; Samuel Pickman; and Benjamin Smith, who alone of the four liv. at R. and d. Mary, prob. then unm. We fail to gain kn. of the m. of s. Descent, however, from this patriarch is claimed by many, of wh. one is the learned Professor P. the dilig. hist. of N. E.

PALGRAVE, or PALSGRAVE, JOHN, Boston, s. of Richard, m. 8 Feb. 1656, Mary, d. of Samuel Maverick of Noddles isl. He d. early, and his wid. m. 20 Sept. 1660, Mr. Francis Hooke of Kittery. See Geneal. Reg. VIII. 334. RICHARD, Charlestown, a physician, came in the fleet with Winth. from Stepney, Co. Middlesex, adjoin. London, with w. Ann, and ds. Mary, Sarah, and, perhaps, other ch.; had here Rebecca, b. 25 July 1631; John, 6, bapt. 9 Mar. 1634; Lydia, 15, bapt. 17 Jan. 1636; and Bethia, bapt. 8 July 1638; all these bapt. were in Boston ch. of wh. the f. and mo. were both mem. Nos. 105 and 6, and did not transfer their relat. to the Charlestown ch. This last ch. d. 21 Aug. aft.

says the town rec. of Charlestown, in wh. it may be more correct than the date of its b. wh. is two days aft. its bapt. He req. adm. as freem. 19 Oct. 1630, and took the o. 18 May foll. d. says Frothingham, a. 1656, and his wid. rem. to Roxbury, there was bur. 17 Mar. 1669, aged 75, says Roxbury rec.; in her will, made six days bef. names eldest d. Mary, w. of Roger Wellington, the ch. of her dec. s. and d. John and Sarah Alcock, with wh. she had liv. since the d. of her h. and John Heylet, or Aylet, s. of her d. Lydia, who was w. of Edmund of Stepney, near London.

PALMER, * ABRAHAM, Charlestown, a merch. from London, wh. there had join. the comp. of the faithful patentees of Mass. 1628, gave £50. to promote its obj. and emb. hims. 1629, prob. with Higginson, was most act. and intellig. town offic. req. adm. 19 Oct. 1630, and was made freem. 18 May foll. of Boston ch. with w. Grace, No. 68 and 9, and of the found. of ch. at Charlestown, was in first assemb. of rep. 1634, and serj. in the Pequot war, went to Barbados 1652, in the Mayflower of Boston, in wh. his sh. of adventure was ⅗, and that of Edward Burt ⅔, to be account. for in London; there d. 1653; yet prob. he intend. to come back. His wid. Grace d. Dec. 1660, and lieut. Thomas Lathrop had admin. perhaps as a creditor. BENJAMIN, Stonington 1665, s. of Walter, freem. 1666, liv. on the disput. border of R. I. was capt. much involv. in controv. and d. 10 Apr. 1716, and from that time no generat. has failed to have, as is said, both Joseph and Benjamin. CHRISTOPHER, Hampton, s. of William of the same, m. a d. of Edward Hilton. EDWARD, Boston 1639, put in the stocks of his own mak. for charg. too high a price. See Hubbard, 248. Prob. he rem. to Hampton. ELIHU, Stonington 1658, s. of Walter, was not an inhab. in 1670. ELNATHAN, Scituate, s. of John of the same, m. 1695, Mary, d. of Thomas Clark. EPHRAIM, Greenwich 1672. FRANCIS, Rowley 1691, may have been s. of John. GEORGE, Boston, wine cooper 1640, ar. co. 1641, rem. to the E. bef. 1660, and he or ano. of the name was at Warwick, R. I. bef. 1655, tho. the place of his resid. is not told, and d. a. 1669. In Apr. 1670, a Boston creditor, James Neighbors, had gr. of admin. GEORGE, Warwick, may be the same as preced. among freem. 1655, m. Bethia, d. of Roger Morey of Providence, a. 1660. GERSHOM, Stonington 1665, br. of Benjamin, freem. 1666, m. 28 Nov. 1667, Ann, d. of capt. George Denison, had Gershom, Ichabod, William, George, Walter, Elihu, Mary, Rebecca, and Mercy. * HENRY, Newbury 1637, freem. 22 June 1642, rem. to Haverhill, from wh. he was rep. 1667, 74, 6–9, and d. 15 July 1680. Perhaps he was of Hampton in his latter days. His d. Eliz. m. 1659, Robert Ayer of Haverhill, and Mehitable m. 1676, Samuel Dalton. HENRY, Wethersfield, by w. Catharine had Deborah,

b. 1642; Hannah, 1645; a s. whose name is not disting. in the rec. 1648; Dorcas, 1650; freem. 1657, and liv. 1663. HENRY, Pemaquid, sw. fidel. to Mass. 1674. JOHN, Hingham, came in Sept. 1635, freem. 13 Mar. 1639; rem. perhaps to Scituate; at least Deane makes him, in Hist. 319, to be freem. of Plymouth Col. 1657, to have ch. then John and Elnathan, afterwards Josiah and Bezaleel. JOHN, Charlestown, perhaps came in the Elizabeth, 1634, from Ipswich, aged 24, was freem. 2 June 1641, and d. 24 Aug. 1677, aged 62, unless the gr.st. be wrong, or misread. JOHN, Portsmouth, by Mr. Wentworth copied from list of mem. of the ch. May 1640, but prob. many yrs. too early. He serv. in Philip's war, then being inhab. of Hampton. JOHN, Boston, carpenter, adm. townsman 30 Mar. 1640, perhaps rem. to Rowley 1647; or may have been br. of Henry, and with him at Wethersfield, freem. 1657. JOHN, Stonington, s. of Walter, prob. eldest, and by first w. b. in Eng. of wh. no more is kn. JOHN, Fairfield, may have been first at Wethersfield, and, perhaps, br. of Henry, freem. of Conn. 1657, had possib. been many yrs. in trade to Virg. and may be was at Greenwich 1672. JOHN, Scituate, s. of the first John of the same, had Elnathan, b. 1666; John, 1667; Hannah, 1671; Eliz. 1673; Bezaleel, 1675; Experience, 1679; and Samuel, 1683. JOHN, Pemaquid, with JOHN, jr. perhaps his s. took o. of fidel. to Mass. 1674. JOHN, Scarborough 1676, m. Eliz. d. of Andrew Alger, and rem. 1680, to Boston, and spent there the residue of his life, says Southgate, 82. JOHN, Falmouth 1689, consult. by the council of war for def. of that town 1689, was wound. 21 Sept.; had m. Mary, d. of George Munjoy. JOHN, Boston 1689, took side against the inhab. for rising against Andros, of whose council he had been, and was suspect. to have come from Eng. just bef. with a commiss. to be ch. just. Hutch. I. 371. JONAS, or JONATHAN, Rehoboth 1668, s. of Walter. JOSEPH, Newbury, m. 18 Mar. 1665, Sarah, d. of James Jackman, had Sarah, b. 5 Dec. 1665; James, 18 Dec. 1667; and Joseph, 8 July 1670. He was youngest s. of William. His s. Joseph had at Newbury two ws. and s. Joseph. JOSIAH, Scituate, s. of first John of the same, had Josiah, b. 1685; Joshua, 1687; and Ruth. MICHAEL, Branford 1667, an orig. signer of the planta. covenant 20 Jan. 1668, freem. 1669. MOSES, Stonington 1658, s. of Walter, by w. Dorothy had Moses, b. 29 Oct. 1673; and John, 1 Sept. 1677; perhaps others bef. or aft. or both. Bond says he m. Abigail, d. of Daniel Allen of Watertown. * NEHE-MIAH, Stonington, s. of Walter, m. 20 Nov. 1662, Hannah, d. of Thomas Stanton, the younger, had Joseph, b. 1663; Elihu, 1665, d. soon; Jonathan, 1668; Daniel, 12 Nov. 1672; was a man of trust, rep. 1668 and 9, and d. 17 Feb. 1718, aged 80. NICHOLAS, Windsor, freem. 1669, was an early sett. had Mary, b. 3 May 1637; Hannah, bapt. 11 Oct.

1640; Timothy, 20 Mar. 1642; and Eliz. b. 7 Aug. 1644. His sec. w. Joan, wid. of John Purchase, m. 29 Oct. 1646, d. 16 Apr. 1683, and he d. 30 Aug. 1689. RICHARD, Salem, m. 24 Nov. 1672, Mary, d. of Humphrey Gilbert, had Mary, b. 8 Sept. 1673; Richard, 6 Dec. 1675; Martha, 21 Aug. 1678; and Samuel, 7 Apr. 1683. RICHARD, Saco, or Wells, 1676, may be the passeng. of 1635, aged 29, in the James from London to Boston. SAMUEL, Rehoboth, m. 12 Jan. 1681, Eliz. Kingsley, perhaps d. of John of Milton, had John, b. 25 Mar. 1682, wh. was bur. 15 July 1683; Samuel and John, tw. 4 Jan. 1684, of wh. John was bur. next day. THOMAS, of Rowley 1648, and SAMUEL, in 1691, perhaps were s. of John. STEPHEN, Cambridge, perhaps s. of William, m. Eliz. d. of Daniel Cheever. SAMUEL, Rowley, freem. 1684, was of Salem, prob. two or three yrs. later, where one of the name acted for John Dunton in sale of his books. THOMAS, Rowley 1643, d. says Farmer, 1669. THOMAS, Scituate, s. of William, held the est. of his f. 1680. THOMAS, Boston, merch. one of the found. of Brattle st. ch. TIMOTHY, Windsor, s. of Nicholas, freem. 1667, m. 17 Sept. 1663, Hannah, d. of William Buell, had Timothy, b. 25 Aug. foll.; Hannah, 3 Oct. 1666; Mary, 14 May 1669; Sarah, 25 Feb. 1672, d. soon; John, 13 Apr. 1673; Sarah, again, 12 Apr. 1675; Samuel, 7 Sept. 1677; Martha, 29 Dec. 1679, d. at 3 yrs.; Benjamin, 1682; and Stephen, 1687. The time of his d. is unkn. TIMOTHY, Suffield, had, bef. going thither, w. Eliz. and s. Timothy, and b. there Esther, 1676; beside two wh. d. young; and Thomas, 1682. He d. 1697, leav. Timothy, Esther, and Thomas. * WALTER, Charlestown 1629, prob. younger br. of Abraham, charg. in Sept. 1630, with k. Austin Bratcher, freem. 18 May 1631, was constable 1633, on 1 June of wh. yr. he, with new w. Rebecca, and d. Grace, unit. with the ch. so that it is plain that the d. was by a former w.; had Hannah, bapt. 15 June 1634; Elihu, 24 Jan. 1636; Nehemiah, b. 23 Nov. 1637; Moses, 6 Apr. 1640; Benjamin, 30 May, bapt. 5 June 1642; all by Rebecca Short, a mem. of Roxbury ch. who came in 1632, as a serv. says the rec. of R. ch. rem. to Rehoboth, was rep. 1646 and 7, being the first from that town, had more ch. and rem. again, to Stonington, 1653. His will, of 19 May 1658, made at S. pro. 11 May 1662, cont. in Suff'k. reg. (for S. then call. Southerton, was claim. as pt. of our Co. strange as such civil geography now seems), names w. Rebecca and eleven ch. John; Grace; Jonas; William; Gershom; Elihu; Nehemiah; Moses; Benjamin; Hannah, w. of Thomas Huet; and Eliz. and omits to name d. Rebecca, wh. m. 20 Apr. 1665, Elisha Cheesbrough; and was, perhaps, unable to count the gr.ch. WILLIAM, Plymouth, came in the Fortune 1621, with s. William, and his w. Frances, came in the next ship, the Ann, 1623, had sh. in the div. of cattle 1627, rem.

to Duxbury, m. a young w. had Henry and Bridget, but perhaps by former w. both nam. in the will, and gr.ch. Rebecca; and d. prob. early in 1638, as his will of 4 Dec. 1637 was pro. 5 Mar. foll. WILLIAM, Watertown 1636, Newbury 1637, own. ld. at Great Ormsby, Co. Norfk. freem. 13 Mar. 1639, rem. to Hampton, had by first w. s. Edward, Christopher, and Stephen, beside d. Martha, who m. as said, I think, capt. John Sherman of Watertown. For sec. w. he had Grace, wid. of Thomas Rogers, wh. surv. him, and m. Roger Porter. WILLIAM, Wethersfield, an early sett. sold his est. 1644, and, perhaps, rem. yet may have come back, for in 1660, W. P. sen. was freed from milit. serv. WILLIAM, Kittery 1652, constable 1661, may have been s. of William of Hampton. * WILLIAM, Scituate 1633, s. of William, the first comer, brot. by him, m. 27 Mar. of that yr. Eliz. Hodgkins, had William, b. 27 June 1634; Thomas; and prob. others; rem. to Yarmouth bef. 1643, was a lieut. and rep. 1644, and three yrs. aft.; was one of the purch. of Dartmouth 1652, but rem. to Newtown, L. I. 1656, d. bef. 1661, in high esteem. Riker, I suspect, confus. the f. and s. of the same name, for we are told that the wid. of William Palmer jun, m. deac. John Willis of Bridgewater, and Mitchell enum. a goodly progeny, of wh. some ds. were m. in few yrs. aft. R. permits her to be a wid. Possib. she may have been sec. w. and not mo. of half his ch. Yet some explanat. may arise from WILLIAM, s. of the preced. being in Col. Rec. designat. as s.-in-law of Robert Paddock. Still Riker must be content with ano. WILLIAM than our Dartmouth man in 1670. WILLIAM, Charlestown 1640, may have been s. of Walter, and of Stonington 1666, of Killingworth, then call. Kenilworth, as in all decency it should contin. to be, in 1670. Ten of this name had, in 1834, been gr. at Harv. six at Yale, and six at the other N. E. coll.

PALMERLY, JOHN, a passeng. in the Elizabeth and Ann from London 1635, aged 20; may be the same as Parmely or Parmarly of Guilford, sw. as freem. of Conn. 1665. See Parmelee.

PALMES, ANDREW, New London, s. of Edward, had Guy, Bryan, Edward, Andrew, and Sarah, and d. 1721. * EDWARD, New Haven 1659, a merch. rem. next yr. to New London, m. Lucy, d. of Gov. John Winthrop, freem. 1667, rep. 1671-4 and 7, was a major in the great Ind. war. By first w. wh. d. 24 Nov. 1676, six mos. aft. her f. he had no ch. and next yr. he m. Sarah Davis, wid. of capt. William of Boston, as Miss Caulkins thinks, had Guy, bapt. 17 Nov. 1678; Andrew, 1 Oct. 1682, H. C. 1703; and Lucy. He d. 21 Mar. 1715, in 78th yr. leav. good est. in his will to only Lucy, and Andrew. Lucy m. Samuel Gray, who d. 1713; and next m. Samuel Lynde of Saybrook. Caulkins. He was nam. in the royal commiss. 1683 to adjust claims in the King's

Province, or Narraganset country.   See Trumbull, Hist. I. 358, wh. gives his name without *e*, and it is found in print as Palmer.   See also 1 Mass. Hist. Coll. V. 232.   WILLIAM, Salem, m. Ann, eldest d. of John Humfrey, Esq. who aft. his d. m. Rev. Samuel Myles.

PALMETER, NATHANIEL, Killingworth 1667, then call. Kenilworth, freem. 1668, whose name is spelt Palmerley in the return of the officers of the town ; possib. the same as Palmerly.

PANNLY, ALEXANDER, is in Paige's list of freem. of Mass. 1660 ; but I doubt the name was pervert. by Mr. Secr. or some clk.

PANTON, RICHARD, Westchester 1656, a man of influence, who d. aft. 1700 ; took the side of Conn. 1662 against the Dutch at Newtown, L. I. Riker, 59.

PANTRY, or PANTREE, JOHN, Hartford, s. of William, b. in Eng. freem. 1650, m. Hannah Tuttle of Boston, who was prob. d. of Richard, had beside Mary and Hannah, John, bapt. 17 Mar. 1650; and d. prob. 1653.   His wid. m. 23 June 1654, Thomas Welles.   Hannah d. 1672, unm.   JOHN, Hartford, s. of the preced. had John (who d. bef. his f. leav. only ch. Abigail) ; and ds. Abigail, b. 11 Jan. 1679 ; Hannah ; and Rebecca.   He d. 4 Apr. 1736, and so the name ceased in that quarter. WILLIAM, Cambridge 1634, came in May by the same ship with Simon Willard, excus. from milit. duty by reason of age, freem. 4 Mar. 1635, rem. next yr. with Hooker's friends to Hartford, where he was among the chief proprs.

PAPILLANS, or PAPILLON, PETER, Boston 1679, by w. Joan had Mary, b. 29 Jan. 1680 ; and Peter, b. Mar. 1681 ; he was one of that comp. wh. broke off from the New North ch. when Rev. Peter Thacher was brot. in 1718 to be collea. with their first min. and in 1722 had command of a ship employ. against pirates on the coast.   He came into Boston 28 June from his cruise, hav. seen nothing of the great object of his outfit, the famous pirate, Low, who long harassed the trade of N. E. but brot. in a brigantine, that had been in possessn. of the foe.   When he d. is not seen.   PETER, Boston, perhaps s. of the preced. by w. Catharine had Mary, wh. d. 30 July 1721, aged 17 ; Catharine, b. a. 1715; Martha, a. 1718 ; Mercy, 20 Jan. 1720 ; Samuel, 11 Sept. 1721, the last two d. young; and Mary, 25 Oct. 1722 ; and he d. early in 1733 ; admin. to his wid. and John Wallcot of Salem was giv. 10 May in that yr.   I suppose this was a Huguenot name.

PARD, SAMUEL, Boston, by w. Mary had Samuel, b. 25 Sept. 1671.

PARDEE, GEORGE, New Haven, a youth, apprent. 1644 to Francis Brown, of whose orig. or coming nothing is kn. m. 20 Oct. 1650, Martha, d. of Richard Miles, had John, b. 20 Aug. 1651, d. young ; John, again, 2 Sept. 1653, d. bef. his f. George, 15 Jan. 1656; Mary, 18 Apr. 1658 ;

Eliz. 10 June 1660, the last three bapt. 18 May 1662, I presume; and he m. sec. w. 29 Dec. 1662, Dodd says, Rebecca (but Catharine, reads ano.) Lane, had Joseph, b. 27 Apr. 1664; Rebecca, 18 Apr. 1666, bapt. I judge, four days aft. but surely not, as the ch. rec. in Geneal. Reg. IX. 361, says, Monday, 23; Sarah, b. 2 Feb. 1668; and Hannah, 7 July 1672; and he d. Apr. 1700, aged 71. His will, of 14 of that mo. names all the ds. and s. George and Joseph. Mary m. 1677, Joshua Hotchkiss; Eliz. m. 25 Dec. 1679, Thomas Gregory, and in the will of her f. is call. an Olmstead; Rebecca m. 1699, Samuel Alling; and Hannah m. Edward Vickers. GEORGE, New Haven, s. of the preced. m. 10 Feb. 1676, Mercy Ball, perhaps d. of Alling, had Mercy, b. 16 Jan. 1677; Eliphalet, 26 Dec. 1678; Martha, 18 Mar. 1681; and John, 4 Nov. 1683; his w. d. 13 Aug. foll. and he m. 11 Feb. next, Mary Denison, perhaps d. of James, had Stephen, 1686; Ebenezer; George, Jan. 1691; James; Mary; Sarah; and Eliz. and he d. 22 Nov. 1723. JOHN, New Haven, whose inv. of 12 Nov. 1683 is foll. by remarks a. his childr. JOSEPH, New Haven, br. of the preced. m. 30 July 1688, or 30 Jan. 1689, Eliz. Yale, d. of the first Thomas, had John, wh. d. 27 Oct. of same yr.; Joseph, 9 Aug. 1693; Thomas, 26 Oct. 1695; John, again, 6 Feb. 1698; and Mary, 9 Apr. 1700; his w. d. 19 Sept. 1701, and he m. sec. w. 2 Dec. 1703, Eliz. Paine, had Eliz. 16 Sept. 1704; Daniel, 28 Nov. 1706; Rebecca, 26 Mar. 1708; Josiah, 14 Sept. 1711; Ebenezer, 4 Nov. 1714; Samuel, 3 Aug. 1718; and Sarah, 1 Aug. 1721. The name is wide. spread.

PARDON, WILLIAM, Mass. freem. 1645, of wh. I kn. no more, not even his resid.

PARENTS, JOHN, Haddam, sett. a. 1662, d. 1686, leav. two ds.

PARIS, or PARRIS, CHRISTOPHER, Boston 1649. JOHN, Braintree, m. 30 Sept. 1664, says Farmer, Mary Jewell, prob. d. of Thomas. NICHOLAS, Salem 1648, witness to the will of John Balch. SAMUEL, Salem, s. of Thomas of London, the unhappy promoter of the sad tragedy of the witchcraft, 1692, was educ. at Harv. but left bef. gr. was of the first ch. at Boston, freem. 1683, and preach. at the Salem vil. now Danvers, in 1689, and bec. the first min. of the society that he reduced to such misery, ord. 15 Nov. of that yr. left his place by compulsion June 1696, and was two or three yrs. preach. at Stow, but in 1700, of Watertown, hav. license as a retailer, soon aft. sat down at Concord, there contin. 1705 engag. in trade unprofitably, but preached a few mos. at Dunstable 1711. His w. Dorothy d. 6 Sept. 1719; and he d. 29 Feb. foll. at Sudbury. In his will, pro. 28 Mar. 1720, he ment. f. Thomas; uncle John; ds. Eliz. w. of Benjamin Barnard; Dorothy, b. 28 Aug. 1700, w. of Hopestill Brown; and Mary, b. 1703, m. 1727,

Peter Bent; beside two s. Samuel, b. at W. 9 Jan. bapt. 1 Mar. 1702; and Noyes, b. 22 Aug. 1699, H. C. 1721, both minors. SAMUEL, Boston, by w. Eliz. had Thomas, b. 25 Oct. 1681; Eliz. 28 Nov. 1682; and Susanna, 9 Jan. 1688; perhaps he rem. and may have been that unhap. min. of Salem. THOMAS, Newbury 1685, s. of John, a dissent. clerg. of Ugborough, in Co. Devon, had come two yrs. bef. to Long Island, rem. to S. part of Mass. perhaps Plymouth, had Thomas, gr.f. of Rev. Martin of Marshfield, and ancest. of Gov. Albion K. of Maine. THOMAS, Boston, perhaps br. of sec. Samuel, by w. Mary had Mary, b. 27 May 1686, d. soon; Mary, again, 25 Sept. 1687; and Eliz. 10 July 1693; and prob. rem. Frequent spelling is with two r's.

PARISH, * JOHN, Groton, perhaps s. of Thomas the first, or a br. as seems more likely, was, says Butler, an orig. propr. and in 1683, serv. on a com. with Page and Lawrence, others of the earliest sett. to prove the ld. rights of the town bef. its destruct. in Philip's war; rep. 1690. JOHN, Groton, prob. s. of the preced. by w. Mary had Lydia, b. 20 Apr. 1687; and Eliz. 19 Mar. 1691. * ROBERT, Groton, perhaps s. of the first Thomas, by w. Mary, prob. d. of John Blanchard, had Mary, b. 5 Jan. 1668; Ann, 2 Sept. 1669; Robert, 20 Nov. 1670; Ann, again, 10 Sept. 1672; and Mary, again, 8 Sept. 1674; rep. 1689, at the Dec. session for the neighb. town of Dunstable. THOMAS, Cambridge, came in the Increase, 1635, aged 22, was a physician, tho. in the custom-ho. rec. call. possib. for decept. a clothier, freem. 18 Apr. 1637, by w. Mary had Mary, b. 3 Apr. 1638; Thomas, 21 July 1641, H. C. 1659; and Mary, again, 3 Apr. 1643. Prob. he went home, liv. at Nayland, Co. Suffk. as his atty. Thomas Danforth calls him. THOMAS, Groton, s. of the preced. had w. Mary, wh. d. 8 Oct. 1674, aged 23. The coll. catal. of 1698 did not mark him as dead, and Farmer thot. he liv. to 12 Sept. 1707.

PARKE, or PARKS, EDWARD, Guilford 1685, d. 11 Aug. 1690; and there the name contin. 20 yrs. EDWARD, Newton, s. of Thomas of the same, m. 13 Mar. 1695, Martha, d. of Nathan Fiske of Cambridge, had Martha, b. 16 May 1699; Edward, 18 Apr. 1701; Thomas, 1703; and Nathan; d. 1 Mar. 1745, near 84 yrs. old. JACOB, Mass. freem. 1657, may have been of Concord, or possib. of Rowley, for his name stands in Paige's list between those of inhabs. of these towns. JOHN, Newton 1678, s. of Thomas of the same, serv. in Philip's war under capt. Beers, and was allow. pension for wound; by first w. had George, bapt. 24 Oct. 1686; and Ann, 17 May 1691, both d. prob. young, at Watertown; m. next, 5 Apr. 1694, Eliz. Miller, had Eliz. b. 24 Feb. 1695, d. young; John, 20 Dec. 1696; Solomon, 16 Oct. 1699; Eliz. 27 Feb. 1701; Abigail, 20 Apr. 1702; Joseph, 12 Mar. 1705, H. C. 1724;

and Mary, 17 Mar. 1708; and he d. 21 Mar. 1718. JOHN, Norwich 1680, s. of Thomas of New London, liv. in that pt. wh. bec. Preston. He is common. call. capt. John of P. and d. 1716, leav. w. Mary, and d. Dorothy, w. of Ebenezer Avery, but in his will rememb. four ch. of his only other d. Abigail, w. of Christopher Avery, wh. was d. JONATHAN, Newton, br. of John of the same, m. 18 Mar. 1691, Ann, d. of Henry Spring, wh. d. the same yr.; and by w. Eliz. had Jonathan, b. 30 Mar. 1695; Jonas, 1 Jan. 1697, d. soon; Lydia; Mindwell; Margery; Eunice; and no more in Bond's list, but Jackson adds Hannah. His w. d. 10 Apr. 1713, and he took 3d w. 27 Apr. says Bond (but Jackson makes it June) 1715, Hannah, d. of John Kimball, had Hannah, again, says Jackson, 25 Feb. (tho. Bond says Oct.) 1718. He d. 23 Jan. foll. (wh. by Jackson is agreed, tho. he makes the will in Feb. 1719), in his will of 11 days preced. names w. and six ch. making w. and Jonathan excors. NATHANIEL, Norwich 1680, s. of Thomas, was of Preston. He d. 1718, leav. w. Sarah, and ch. Nathaniel, Ezekiel, Joseph, John, Isaac, Jacob, Phebe, w. of Thomas Beman, and Margaret, w. of Jabez Spicer, all adult. RICHARD, Cambridge 1636, a propr. at the Farms, now Lexington, 1642; d. at Cambridge vill. (where he had liv. 18 yrs.) 1665, leav. will of 12 July in that yr. provid. for w. Sarah, wh. had been wid. of Love Brewster, and was liv. at Duxbury 1678; two ds. and only s. Thomas. The inv. of 19 Aug. show. good est. Isabel, one of his ds. m. Francis Whittemore; and Sarah, the other, d. 1699. *RICHARD, Newton, gr.s. of the preced. and s. of Thomas, by w. Sarah Cutter, had William; Thomas, 7 Feb. 1690, both d. young; prob. Abigail, 25 July 1693; Richard, 1 Mar. 1696; and Sarah, 11 May 1699, d. soon; all b. at N.; rem. to Concord, m. 1699, Eliz. d. prob. of John Billings, had Joseph; Eliz.; Sarah; Josiah; Abigail; Jonathan; Isaac; Rebecca; Ephraim; Daniel; and Zaccheus; tho. Jackson counts only ten for the sec. w.; was lieut. rep. and d. 19 June 1725. His will, made 11 days bef. names w. Eliz. and her seven s. and four ds. *ROBERT, Wethersfield 1639, freem. Apr. 1640, may have sent ano. beside his eldest s. William some yrs. bef. he came to our shore, as permanent resid. for I have the best reason for think. he had come in 1630, and went back the same yr. carrying an order by our Gov. to his s. John in Eng. to pay money, wh. is in my possess. and may be the earliest bill of exchange dr. on our side of the water, but was not guid. by the decision of the s. as to his planta. rep. first in Aug. 1642, rem. 1649 to New London, where his barn was the first place of worship, selectman 1651, rep. 1652, call. an aged man 1662, d. 1665. His will, of 14 May 1660, pro. Mar. 1665, names only three ch. William, Samuel, and Thomas; but perhaps a d. Ann had accomp. her br. William early to Roxbury, there m. 20

Aug. 1640, Edward Payson, and d. 10 Sept. of foll. yr. In his favor, I suppose, was the curious order of 30 May 1644, by our Gen. Ct. that he might "proceed in m. with Alice Tompson, without further publishment." ROBERT, New London, s. of Thomas the first, m. 24 Nov. 1681, Rachel, eldest d. of Thomas Leffingwell, had Rebecca, b. 7 Sept. foll.; James, 1684; and eight more ch. and d. bef. Sept. 1707. SAMUEL, Stonington, s. of Robert, had Robert, William, and prob. other ch. THOMAS, Wethersfield, s. of Robert, b. in Eng. by w. Dorothy had Martha, b. 1646; Thomas, 1648; rem. to Stonington, thence to New London, had Robert, Nathaniel, William, Dorothy, Alice, and John, of whose dates of b. we are ignor. Provid. for w. Dorothy, for ch. John, Nathaniel, William, Martha, Dorothy, and Alice, for gr.s. Samuel, s. of Thomas, and James, s. of Robert, he made his will 5 Sept. 1707, and d. 30 July 1709. He was of the new town of Preston 1686, and first deac. of the ch. there gather. 1698. His d. Martha m. 16 Jan. 1668, Isaac Wheeler of S.; Dorothy m. Apr. 1670, Joseph Morgan; and Alice m. Mar. 16, 1673, Greenfield Larrabee. THOMAS, Newton, s. of Richard the first, prob. b. in Eng. m. 1 Dec. 1653, Abigail, d. of Edward Dix, had Thomas, b. 2 Nov. 1654; John, 6 Sept. 1656; Abigail, 3 Mar. 1658; Edward, 8 Apr. 1661; Richard, 21 Dec. 1663; Sarah, 21 Mar. 1666; Rebecca, 13 Apr. 1668; Jonathan, 27 Aug. 1670; and Eliz. 28 July 1679; was freem. 1671, and d. 1690. Abigail m. 9 Dec. 1679, John Fiske; Sarah m. 4 Aug. 1686, John Knapp 2d; Rebecca m. 1686, John Sanger; and Eliz. m. John Holland. THOMAS, New London, s. of Thomas of the same, m. 4 Jan. 1672, Mary, d. of Robert Allyn, had Samuel, b. 26 Nov. 1673; Thomas, 20 Jan. 1676; Mary, 28 Jan. 1678; Jonathan, 6 Apr. 1679; and Deborah, Dec. 1680; and d. bef. his f. THOMAS, Newton, s. of Thomas of the same, freem. 1680, d. 28 Aug. 1681. * ‖ WILLIAM, Roxbury, eldest s. of Robert, came in the Lion, arr. at Boston, Feb. 1631, with Roger Williams, was, perhaps, sent by his f. to look out good spot for planta. one of the earliest memb. of the ch. freem. 18 May 1631, m. Martha, d. of John Holgrave of Salem, had Theoda, b. 26 July 1637; Hannah, 28 Aug. 1639; d. 24, bur. 26 June 1655; Martha, 2, bapt. 13 Mar. 1642; Sarah, bapt. 19 Nov. 1643, who d. says the town rec. 8 Sept. foll.; John, 30 June, bapt. 6 July 1645, d. next June; Deborah, bapt. 16 Jan. 1647, whose b. the town rec. omits, but ins. her d. Aug. 1649; John, again, 13 May 1649, d. at 14 yrs.; Deborah, again, b. 26 Mar. bapt. 6 Apr. 1651; s. and d. tw. unbapt. bur. 1 June 1653; William, bapt. 8 Oct. 1654, d. young; and Hannah, again, 26 Sept. 1658; ar. co. 1638, was rep. 1635, and 32 various yrs. aft. the longest term of serv. in that rank under the old chart. Johnson, in his "Wonderwork. Providence" &c. calls him "a man of a pregnant understanding," and he kn. well, for he sat 21 yrs. with him. He was many yrs. deac. and d. 11 May 1685; hav. made his will 20 July preced. with codic. of 4 Apr. in wh. he provides for the w. of his youth, ment. two surv. ds. and many gr. ch. besides brs. Thomas, dec. and Samuel. But gr. stone in Geneal. Reg. makes the d. 10 May 1683. The wid. Martha d. 25 Aug. 1708, aged 94, Theoda m. 2 Mar. 1654, Samuel Williams, and so was mo. of Rev. John, H. C. 1683, of Deerfield, the famous " Redeemed Captive ; " ano. d. Martha, m. Isaac Williams, whose s. William, H. C. 1683, min. of Hatfield, the gr. f. says he had taken charge of from the age of 3 yrs. beside part of Stonington land to other s. and ano. d. m. John Smith, and to them he gives part of his Stonington ld. Five of this name, in its sev. spellings had been gr. at Harv. in 1834 and thirteen at other N. E. coll.

PARKER, ABRAHAM, Woburn, m. 18 Nov. 1644, Rose Whitlock, had Ann, b. 29 Oct. 1645 ; John, 30 Oct. 1647; Abraham, 8 Mar. 1650, d. next yr.; Abraham, again, Aug. 1652; rem. to Chelmsford, there had Mary, 20 Nov. 1655, bapt. 20 Apr. foll.; Moses ; Isaac, b. 13 Sept. 1660 ; Eliz. 10 Apr. 1663 ; Lydia; and Jacob, 24 Mar. 1669. He was freem. 1645, and d. 12 Aug. 1685 ; and his wid. d. 13 Nov. 1691. ABRAHAM, Chelmsford, s. of the preced. freem. 1682. Ano. Abraham of Chelmsford was freem. 1690, unless as I suspect, he had been sworn some yrs. bef. and was really the preced. but ano. of this name was of York 1680, and sw. alleg. next yr. AZRIKAM, Boston 1662, mariner. BASIL, York 1649, recorder of the Province, and made by Gorges one of the counc. was d. bef. 18 Oct. 1651, when admin. was giv. to John Alcock. BENJAMIN, Billerica, s. of Robert, m. 18 Apr. 1661, Sarah, d. of William Hartwell, had Benjamin, and John ; and d. 17 Jan. 1672. made his will two days bef. ment. childr. but gives not names, made w. extrix. DANIEL, Charlestown, s. of sec. John of Kennebeck, by w. Ann had Ann, John, and Isaac, and d. 18 Oct. 1694, aged only 27 yrs. Isaac was gr. f. of my admira. friend, the late Isaac, Ch. Just. of the Commonw. DANIEL, Barnstable, s. of Robert of the same, m. 11 Dec. 1689. Mary, perhaps d. of Benjamin, perhaps of Thomas, Lombard, had Patience, b. 1690; Abigail, 27 May 1692; Experience, 7, bapt. 17 Feb. 1695, d. soon; Daniel, 20 Feb. bapt. 15 Mar. 1696, d. under 21 yrs. : Rebecca, 1, bapt. 24 Apr. 1698 ; David, 17 Feb. bapt. 17 Mar. 1700 : Hannah, 5, bapt. 19 Apr. 1702 ; d. at 13 yrs.; Samuel, 5 Feb. 1704 : Jonathan, Jan. 1706; Nehemiah, Oct. 1708; and Mary, 15 Aug. 1710 : and he d. 23 Dec. 1728. EDMUND, Roxbury, m. 31 May 1647, Eliz. prob. d. of the first Abraham Howe, had there bapt. Eliz. 2 Apr. 1648, d. soon; Eliz. again, 29 Apr. 1649; Abraham, 5 Sept. 1652 ; Mary, Esther, and Deborah, 22 June 1656, perhaps not all b. in one day; for he may have rem. to Lancaster, where he was propr. 1654, and there brought these ch. to bapt. and possib. had others later. Roxbury rec. of b. or d. has nothing of him, unless death of Abraham, 17 Sept. 1693 means of his s. EDWARD, New Haven 1644, m. Eliz. wid. of John Potter, had Mary, bapt. 27 Aug. not as print. Apr. 1648, being one or two yrs. old; John, 8 Oct. 1648; Hope, b. 26 Apr. bapt. 26 May 1650; and Lydia, b. 14 Apr. bapt. soon, 1652; and he d. 1662. In 1666 Mary m. John Hall; in 1667 Hope m. Samuel Cooke; and Lydia m. 1671, John Thomas. ELISHA, Barnstable, m. 15 July 1657, Eliz. Hinckley, sis. of Gov. Thomas, had Thomas, b. 15 May 1658; Elisha, Nov. 1660; and Sarah, May 1662. GEORGE, Portsmouth R. I. 1638, may be that carpenter from London, who came 1635, in the Elizabeth and Ann, aged 23, was serj. gen. d. 1656, leav. wid. and d. Frances, wh. m. 27 July 1676, Benjamin Hall, beside Mary, wh. m. Ichabod Sheffield. GEORGE, York, freem. 1652, was constable there 1659. HANANIAH, Reading, s. perhaps eldest, of Thomas of the same, m. 30 Sept. 1663, Eliz. d. I presume of Nicholas Brown, wh. ten yrs. aft. made him an overseer of his will, had John, b. 3 Aug. 1664; Samuel, 24 Oct. 1666; Eliz. June 1668; Sarah, 20 Feb. 1672, d. next yr.; Hananiah, 2 Nov. 1674, d. in few mos.; Ebenezer, 13 Feb. 1676; Hananiah, again, 30 Apr. 1681, d. in few mos.; and Mary. He was freem. 1679; lost his w. 27 Feb. 1698; and m. 12 Dec. 1700 sec. w. Mary, d. of William Barsham, and wid. of deac. John Bright, who surv. him, and he d. 10 Mar. 1724, aged 85. ISAAC, Newton, s. of the first John of the same, m. 4 May 1687, Mary Parker, had Mary, b. 4 Feb. 1689, d. soon; Benjamin, 8 Oct. 1702; Martha, and perhaps others bef. or aft. he rem. to Needham. JACOB, Chelmsford, by w. Sarah had Sarah, b. 14 Jan. or Apr. 1654; Thomas, 28 Mar. 1656; both with elder br. Jacob, bapt. 20 Apr. 1656; Tabitha, 28 Feb. 1658; Rebecca, 29 May 1661; Rachel, 9 May 1665; and Mary, 8 Sept. 1667; perhaps others. He d. in few mos. and wid. Sarah present. inv. 6 Apr. 1669. JACOB, Malden, perhaps s. of the preced. freem. 1690, d. 13 Oct. 1694, aged 42. His wid. Joanna m. John Stearns. JACOB, Roxbury, m. 3 May 1687, Thankful, d. of John Hemmenway, had Thankful, d. 19 Feb. 1688, few days old; Sarah, b. 8 Apr. 1689; Jacob, d. 26 Apr. 1691, soon aft. b. Thankful, again, 9 May 1692; Jacob, again, 19 Jan. 1697; Mary, 2 Mar. 1699; Eliz. 25 July 1700; and Experience, 25 Mar. 1705. *JAMES, Dorchester, early, perhaps, as 1630, freem. 14 May 1634, rem. to Weymouth, and was rep. 1639–42, thence to Portsmouth, where he was invit. to be their min. but prefer. to contin. in trade, tho. he preach. a few yrs. went to Barbados, whence a good letter to Gov. Winth. from him is giv. by Hutch. Coll. 155 d. on a visit to Boston, 1666. JAMES, Woburn,

1640, m. 23 May 1643, Eliz. d. of Robert Long of Charlestown, had Eliz. b. 12 Mar. 1645; Ann, 5 Mar. 1647; John, 18 Feb. 1649; Sarah, 29 Aug. 1650, d. next yr. Joseph, 1651; James, 15 Apr. 1652, (wh. was k. by the Ind. 27 July 1694); was freem. 1644; and a grantee of Billerica, rem. to Chelmsford and had Josiah, 1655; Samuel, 1656; Joshua, 13 Mar. 1658; Zechariah, 14 Jan. 1659; and Eleazer, 9 Nov. 1660; was capt. rem. to Groton, and, perhaps, by sec. w. Eunice, had, very late in life, Sarah, again, 12 Dec. 1697; and he d. 1701 in 84th yr. Butler, Hist. 282, refers to the will in proof. JAMES, Groton, s. of the preced. by w. Mary, m. 14 Dec. 1678, had five ch. all b. bef. their aunt Sarah, as also were 13 or 14 of their cousins. See Butler. He was town clk. 20 yrs. a deac. and after overthr. of Andros, 1689, of the Comte. of Safety. Hutch. I. 382. Was k. by the Ind. when all his fam. were tak. by them. JAMES, Andover, s. of the first Nathan, was k. by the Ind. 29 June 1677, being on serv. as a soldier at Scarborough. JAMES, Kennebeck, s. of John, with his f. was by the Ind. driv. from his isl. and at Falmouth, where they took refuge, were both k. by the Ind. at the sec. destruct. of that town, May 1690. Willis, I. 65. JOHN, Boston 1635, a carpenter of Marlborough, Co. Wilts, came that yr. in the James. arr. 3 June from Southampton, with w. Jane, had Thomas, b. 2 Oct. 1635, bapt. 22 Jan. 1637, his w. hav. unit. with the ch. two weeks bef. Noah, 3, bapt. 8 Apr. 1638; beside John, and Margaret, who may have been brot. from Eng. He liv. at Muddy riv. now Brookline, and d. in few yrs. for in 1656 his wid. Jane had m. Richard Tare, and then sold her ho. and gard. in Boston to Stephen Greenleaf, who came from Newbury. JOHN, Saco 1636, the purch. of Parker's isl. now Georgetown, on E. side of Kennebec riv. near the mo. is by Williamson fondly thought to have first sett. in 1629 on the W. side of the riv. but his purch. was in 1650. Tradit. says he was from Bideford, Co. Devon, and d. bef. June 1661. By w. Mary he had Thomas, John, and Mary, but all may have been b. in Eng. tho. tradit. makes John b. at Saco 1634. Mary m. Thomas Webber, it is said, who d. at Charlestown bef. 1695. She was wid. on join. the ch. that yr. *JOHN, Hingham 1636, says Lincoln, p. 45, rem. to Taunton, of wh. with William, prob. elder br. he was a purch. 1637, was rep. 1642, and d. 14 Feb. 1668. Baylies, II. 2 and 282. JOHN, Boston 1644, shoemaker, had w. Sarah, who join. our ch. in Aug. of that yr. and prob. d. Sarah, who m. 22 June 1653, Isaac Bull. Perhaps he was the freem. of 1650. JOHN, Woburn 1653, rem. prob. to Billerica, was there first town clk. d. at Charlestown, 14 June 1669. But a JOHN of Billerica, the serj. who d. Sept. 1668, leav. wid. but no ch. and good est. may in 1652 have been of Cambridge, s. of Robert, and then took sh. of his f. in the Shawshin lds. wh. was the beginning of sett. at B. JOHN, Cambridge, in the part which bec. Newton, had come from Hingham, with Druce, Hammond, and Winchester, induc. to rem. by Nicholas Hodgdon, was, perhaps, the freem. of 1654; by w. Joanna had Mary, b. 28 Jan. 1648; Martha, 1 May 1649; John, 15 Feb. 1652; Joanna, 16 Jan. 1654; Jeremiah, 16 Feb. 1656, d. early; Thomas, 1 Feb. 1658, d. at 21 yrs.; Sarah, 6 Jan. 1660; Isaac, 15 Mar. 1663; Jonathan, 6 Nov. 1665; and Lydia, 15 May 1667; but the first two were brot. from H. and he d. 1686, aged 71, hav. made his will 7 Sept. of that yr. The wid. d. 14 Mar. 1688. Mary m. Peter Hanchett of Roxbury; Martha m. James Horsley; Sarah m. Sept. 1686, Samuel Snow of Woburn; and Joanna, m. a Stone. JOHN, York, freem. 1652, kept the prison in 1678, was excus. from milit. serv. by reason of age, still liv. in 1681, when he took o. of alleg. to the k. as ano. JOHN, perhaps his s. had in 1680. JOHN, Kennebeck, s. of John of Saco, perhaps b. in Eng. came to Boston to m. 20 Aug. 1660, Mary, d. of Daniel Fairfield, having the yr. bef. bot. of the Ind. a large tract on the W. side of the Kennebeck opposite his f's. isl. now Phipsburg, had, beside four ds. Daniel and James. He, who may be the one who sw. fidel. at Pemaquid 1674, with James, was k. by the Ind. in May 1690 at Falmouth, to wh. they had resort. for safety. JOHN, Newport, in the list of freem. 1655. JOHN, Saybrook, s. of William, m. 24 Dec. 1666, Mary Buckingham, prob. d. of Thomas the first, had John, b. 6 Oct. 1667; Deborah, 31 Aug. 1671; Ebenezer, 18 Aug. 1674; and Samuel, 24 Jan. 1677. JOHN, Reading, br. of Hananiah, m. 13 Nov. 1667, Hannah, d. prob. of Thomas Kendall, who d. 8 July 1689, had John, b. 16 Dec. 1668; Thomas, 9 Nov. 1670; Hannah, 25 Feb. 1672; Rebecca, 18 Feb. 1675; wh. last three ch. d. 17 and 19 June 1689; Kendall, 15 Nov. 1677; Abigail, 10 Oct. 1679, d. in few wks.; Jonathan, 18 July 1681; Daniel, 30 Oct. 1686; and Abigail, again, 24 Dec. 1688, d. at 6 mos. By sec. w. Thankful, m. 28 Jan. 1690, he had Hannah, again, 28 Jan. 1691; Rebecca, again, 13 Feb. 1693; Thomas, again, 17 Mar. 1695; and Eliz. 27 Mar. 1698; and he d. 21 Feb. foll. JOHN, New Haven 1668, s. of Edward, m. 8 Nov. 1670, Hannah, d. of William Bassett, had Hannah, b. 20 Aug. 1671; John, 26 Mar. 1675; and Abiah, 26 Mar. 1677; rem. to Wallingford, and very likely had more. JOHN, whose w. Alice suff. by hang. as a witch, in the horrible delusion, at Salem, 22 Sept. 1692, was not of that town, but I think, possib. of Andover, yet Felt, II. 480, has not specif. JOHN, Andover, s. of Joseph, k. by the Ind. 29 June 1677, at Scarborough, on serv. as a soldier under Capt. Swett. JOHN, Malden, freem. 1678. JOHN, Newton, may have been that s. of Robert, wh. Cambridge rec. says, d. 15 May 1682; but, as there was two JOHNS at N. acc. Jackson, p. 10, one disting. as South, the other as East, it may be hard to determ. Yet of the Newton John, s. of the first John of the same, Jackson teach. that by w. Mary, he had John, b. 17 Aug. 1687; Mary, 3 Mar. 1690; Deborah, 11 Feb. 1693; Sarah, 24 Mar. 1695; and Thomas, 9 Jan. 1700; and d. Oct. 1713. His wid. d. Mar. 1715. JOHN, came from London 1671, in the Arabella, but it is altogether doubtful where he sat down, or whether he had not bef. liv. on this side and gone home on business. JOHN, Andover, s. of Nathan, m. 24 May 1687, Hannah Brown, but I feel uncert. as ano. JOHN was of Andover, s. of Joseph, and neither of these, s. of Joseph or Nathan, was likely to be h. of that Alice, old enough to be hanged for a witch in the fanaticism of 1692. However, the s. of Nathan, named John, had John, Nathan, Benjamin, and James, of whom the last three says Farmer, were proprs. of Concord N. H. 1726, and he d. 1738. JOHN, Reading, s. of Hananiah, by w. Deliverance, had Hananiah, b. 10 Oct. 1691, d. on. serv. at Port Royal, 1711; Andrew, 14 Feb. 1693; Josiah, 11 Apr. 1694; Mary, 4 Dec. 1695, d. at 14 yrs.; a s. whose name is not plain, 19 Aug. 1697, wh. d. at 12 yrs.; and John, 8 Nov. 1703. Prob. he was freem. 1691, liv. late at Lexington, where his w. d. 10 Mar. 1718, and he d. 22 Jan. 1741. JONATHAN, Boston, s. of Ralph, had Thomas, was a merch. mariner, and d. bef. 1706. JONATHAN, Newton, youngest s. of the first John of the same, by w. Deliverance, had Mary, b. 25 Sept. 1701; rem. to Needham, there had Jonathan, 21 July 1711, and perhaps others bef. or after, and ano. w. Sarah. JOSEPH, Newbury, came in the Confidence from Southampton 1638, aged 24, was a tanner of Newbury, Co. Berks, had Joseph, b. 15 May 1642, rem. to Andover where he was one of the founders of the ch. Oct. 1645, and had more ch. of wh. were Stephen, b. 1651, and Samuel, Thomas, non compos, and ds. Sarah, Mary, and Ruth, who all outliv. him, also John k. by the Ind. 1678; and he d. 5 Nov. 1678. All his est. in Rumsey, Co. Hants, a. 8 ms. from Southampton, he devis. to his w. by the last will, made 4 Nov. of that yr. her name was Mary, and a wid. of that name d. 2 Oct. 1695. JOSEPH, Chelmsford, m. 24 June 1655, Rebecca Read, had Ann, b. 7 Feb. 1656; Mary, 28 Oct. 1657; John, 31 July 1659; and John, 24 Nov. 1660; but the rec. gives not mo. of the first two, and for the third names Mary; and Margaret for fourth. Yet it may seem prob. that one w. either Mary or Margaret brought all; and perhaps there were more. JOSEPH, Dunstable, is altogether unkn. to me, unless he were of ano. town, and tho. a propr. only a tempor. resid. he had by w. Margaret, as on the rec. of Chelmsford is to be seen, Joseph, b. 30 Mar. 1653; Ann, 2 Feb. 1655, bapt. 20 Apr. foll. d. young; Mary, 28 Oct. 1657; John, 4 Nov. 1660,

d. 8 Oct. foll.; Ann, 16 Nov. 1663 ; and Sarah, 16 Nov. 1666; as shown in Shattuck's Memorials; yet I can hardly doubt that confus. betw. husbands of Rebecca and of Margaret, in the rec. of their ch. must have occurr. especial. as ea. has Mary b. on one day. JOSEPH, Groton, prob. s. of James the first, had two ws. Eliz. and Hannah, the latter m. 19 Nov. 1684, and by them had Sarah, b. 16 Nov. 1666 or 1676 ; Eliz. 31 Aug. 1679 ; Simon, 27 Aug. 1687 ; Joseph, 1 Mar. 1689 ; Benjamin, 3 Dec. 1691 ; and John, 26 Aug. 1695. In the excel. Hist. of Groton by Butler, five pages are filled with descend. of James and Joseph. But Shattuck's Memorials, page 376, does not contain the name of the first ch. as above giv. yet supplies two, Nehemiah and Isaac, bef. Simon. JOSEPH, Saybrook, s. of William, m. 3 June 1673, Hannah Gilbert, had Joseph, b. 3 July 1674; Jonathan, 15 July 1675 ; d. at 8 yrs.; Sarah and Hannah, tw. 15 Feb. 1677, both d. very soon; Hannah, 18 July 1679 ; Margery, 22 June 1681, d. in few mos. ; Margery, again, 12 Mar. 1683, d. at 1 yr.; Matthew; and Jonathan, again, 6 Oct. 1686. JOSEPH, Scituate, s. of William of the same, had, says Deane, from 1684 to 1702, Alice, Mary, Joseph, Judith, and Miles, but he does not fix the date of any. JOSEPH, Andover, s. prob. of Joseph the first, m. 7 Oct. 1680, Eliz. Bridges, wid. of Obadiah, and prob. d. 6 Apr. 1684; and perhaps his wid. m. 26 Apr. 1686, Samuel Hutchinson. JOSHUA, Groton, s. of Capt. James of the same, m. 22 Sept. 1690, Abigail, youngest d. of the first William Shattuck, and wid. of Jonathan Morse, had Abiel, a d. JOSIAH, Groton, s. of James the first, m. 8 May 1678, Eliz. Saxton of Boston, prob. d. of Thomas, had Eliz. b. 31 Aug. 1679 ; John, 13 Apr. 1681 ; and Sarah, 1 May 1683; rem. to Chelmsford, Watertown, and last to Cambridge, in one or more of wh. resid. he had Josiah ; Joshua ; and Thomas, H. C. 1718, the min. of Dracut, to wh. by his will of 26 July 1731 he gave his Groton homestead, and made him excor. MATTHEW, Boston, d. 19 Sept. 1652. MOSES, Chelmsford, s. of Abraham of the same, m. Abigail, d. of Richard Hildreth, had Moses, who was k. by lightning; Abigail, b. 8 May 1685 ; Aaron, 9 Apr. 1689 ; Eliz. 26 Dec. 1691; Joseph, 25 Mar. 1694 ; Benjamin, 14 Apr. 1696 ; and Mary, 6 Sept. 1698. NATHAN, Newbury, an early sett. rem. to Andover, was br. of Joseph of the same, m. 10 Nov. 1648, Sarah, or Susan, Short, wh. d. at A. 26 Aug. 1651; but by ano. w. Mary he had John, b. 1653 ; James ; Robert; and Peter ; and d. 25 June 1685. Perhaps this man may be he who was ent. as Nathaniel, of London, a baker, aged 20, in 1638, when Stephen Dummer brought him in the Bevis from Southampton. NATHAN, Newbury, prob. s. of the preced. m. 15 Dec. 1675, Mary Brown, d. of John, says one acco. in the Geneal. Reg. VI. 232, by ano. corrected report, IX. 221, of Francis, but both describ. as

of Hampton, and the latter acco. makes her to have sec. h. Eliot. NA-
THANIEL, Reading, br. of Hananiah, by w. Bethia had Bethia, b. 23 July
1678, d. in few wks.; Nathaniel, 4 Dec. 1679; Stephen, 14 June 1684,
d. in few mos.; Bethia, again, 6 Sept. 1685; Susanna, 29 Dec. 1687;
Ebenezer, 28 Dec. 1689; Stephen, again, 21 Apr. 1692; Caleb, 22
Feb. 1694; Timothy, 24 Feb. 1696; Obadiah, 13 Jan. 1698; Abigail,
25 Sept. 1699; Amy, 1 June 1701, d. soon; Amy, again, 8 Nov. 1702;
and Phineas, 27 Sept. 1704; was freem. 1691. His w. d. 23 Aug. 1748,
in 90th yr. NATHANIEL, Newton, youngest s. of Samuel of Dedham,
m. 1694, Margaret, d. of Capt. Noah Wiswall, had Noah, b. 20 Jan.
1695; Caleb, 9 Nov. 1696; and his w. d. 30 July 1736. In Dec. foll.
he m. Mary, wid. of Joseph Hovey, d. prob. of John Marrett of Cambridge; and d. 28 Feb. 1747. His wid. d. 10 Sept. 1758. NICHOLAS,
Roxbury, came in 1633, either with Cotton in the Griffin, or in the Bird
(both of wh. arr. 4 Sept.), with w. Ann, ch. Mary, and Nicholas; freem.
4 Mar. 1634, had Johanna, b. 1 June 1635, says the Roxbury ch. rec.
rem. soon aft. to Boston, had a ch. b. 14 June 1637, d. very soon; Jonathan 1, bapt. 2 Feb. 1640; Abiel, 15 Jan. bapt. 27 Mar. 1642; Joseph,
26 Mar. bapt. 14 May 1643; but when or where he d. I see not. His
d. Mary m. William Davis; Joanna m. 5 July 1655, Arthur Mason, the
stout patriot. constable; and Jonathan liv. in London. RALPH, Gloucester 1647, rem. to New London 1651, had Mary by a former w. and
by Susanna, d. of William Keeny, had Susanna; Jonathan; Ralph, b.
29 Aug. 1670; Thomas; Hannah; Mehitable; and Rebecca, was a
master mariner and merch. and d. 1683; Mary m. a. 1663, William
Condy; Susanna m. 27 Mar. 1666, Thomas Forster; Hannah m. Richard Wyatt, it is said; Mehitable m. William Pendall; and Rebecca m.
1685 John Prentiss, as his sec. w. RICHARD, Boston, merch. by w.
Ann had Joseph, b. 1 Aug. 1638, d. in few mos.; Sarah, 8, bapt. 11
July 1641, was freem. 2 June 1641, and prob. he d. soon aft. but may
have had sec. w. for in the book of possessns. Jane, wid. of Richard,
had an est. His d. Ann b. prob. in Eng. m. a. 1651 John Manning, as
sec. w. and their d. Ann m. 1669, John Sands; and Sarah m. Mar.
1659, John Paine. ROBERT, Boston, call. on adm. to the ch. 9 Mar.
1634, "serv. to our br. William Aspenwall," was a butcher, possib. came
from Woolpit, near Bury St. Edmunds, Co. Suffk. freem. 4 Mar. foll.
rem. early to Cambridge, m. Judith, wid. of Richard Bugby of Roxbury,
had Benjamin, b. June 1636; Sarah, Apr. 1640; John, bapt. at Roxbury, in right of his w. 27 Mar. 1642, and I judge him to be the H. C. gr.
1661; Nathanael, 28 July 1643, d. young; and Rachel, wh. d. bef. her
f. His w. d. 8 May 1682, aged 80; and in his will, of 21 Mar. 1684,
pro. 7 Apr. 1685, he calls hims. a. 82 yrs. The s. Benjamin, and John,

he says, had full sh. and are d. so that he names sole heir, his d. Sarah,
w. of Thomas Foster, m. 15 Oct. 1652, and to her ch. after her, with
provision for doub. portion to the s. Thomas. See 3 Mass. Hist. Coll.
X. 168. ROBERT, Barnstable, m. 28 Jan. 1657, Sarah James, had
Mary, b. 1 Apr. 1658; Samuel, 30 June 1660; Alice, 20 Jan. 1662;
and Jane, Mar. 1664; he m. a sec. w. Aug. 1667, Patience, d. of Henry
Cobb, had Thomas, 24 Aug. 1669; Daniel, 18 Apr. 1670; Joseph, Feb.
1672; Benjamin, 15 Mar. 1674; Hannah, Apr. 1676; Sarah, 1678;
Elisha, Apr. 1680; and Alice, again, 15 Sept. 1681; both bapt. 1684;
but an erron. date of his d. is given, Sept. 1680. SAMUEL, Hingham
1638, may have been of Haverhill 1677; but owned ld. in 1682 at Weymouth. SAMUEL, Dedham, m. 9 Apr. 1657, Sarah, d. of William Holman of Cambridge, had Sarah, b. 23 Jan. 1658, d. next yr.; Samuel, 5
May 1659; Ann, 10 Jan. 1661; Sarah, again, 21 May 1662; Nathaniel, 1 Mar. 1664, d. at 3 mos.; Susanna, 19 Jan. 1667; Margaret, 3 Sept. 1668; Nathaniel, again, 26 Mar. 1670; and Mary, 1675;
and his w. d. 19 Nov. foll. and he d. 31 Dec. 1678. Admin. was giv. on
his est. 9 Nov. 1680, to Capt. Thomas Prentice and Mr. Timothy
Dwight. STEPHEN, Andover, s. of the first Joseph of the same, m. 1
Dec. 1680, Mary, prob. d. of John Marston, wh. d. 12 Apr. 1693, as did
her s. Stephen, 15 Dec. preced. and he m. 10 Jan. 1695, Susanna Dever-
eux. *THOMAS*, Newbury, only s. of Rev. Robert, wh. was one of the earliest Eng. puritans, b. June 1595, bred part. at Magdalen Coll. Oxford, part.
under Archbp. Usher at Dublin, also part. under William Ames in Holland, where he took his A. M. 1617 at Franequer. His f. enjoy. gr. fa-
vour in the days of Eliz. as in 1591 the Bp. of Winchester present. him
to the ch. of Putney, in Co. Wilts, while we find that the Earl of Pembroke had bef. giv. him the liv. of the Hospital of St. Nicholas at Salisbury, and aft. on surrender of these places, present. him, 1593, to the ch.
of St. Mary of Wilts, with the chapel of Bulbridge anxd. and in 1594
the Queen gave him that liv. of Stanton Barnard, where he, ten yrs.
later, appoint. his own vicar. But from the Reg. of Sir Thomas Phil-
lipps I learn, that seven yrs. aft. he was depriv. no doubt from showing
kindness to those wh. like his s. thot. more of k. Jesus than k. James.
This s. serv. short time at the altar in Newbury, Eng. and came in the
Mary and John, May 1634, with his neph. Rev. James Noyes, was made
freem. 3 Sept. of that yr. preach. at Ipswich, and the yr. foll. was fix. at
N. to devote a bach. life for instruct. an affectio. but dissatisf. people,
to his d. 24 Apr. 1677. The Magn. III. c. 25 is rather brief in his
biogr. THOMAS, Lynn, came in the Susan and Ellen 1635, aged 30,
young Richard Saltonstall, with his w. and ch. being fellow passeng.
freem. 17 May 1637, rem. to Reading, had Hananiah, b. a. 1638;

Thomas; Joseph, 1642, d. soon; Joseph, again, 24 Dec. 1645, d. at 4 mos.; Mary, 11 Mar. or (as ano. acco. has it) 12 Dec. 1647; Martha, 14 Mar. 1649; Nathaniel, 16 May 1651; Sarah, 30 Sept. 1653, prob. d. young; Jonathan, 18 May 1656; and Sarah, again, 23 May 1658; beside John; was there one of the founders of the ch. and many yrs. deac. till his d. 12 Aug. 1683. His will of 3 Apr. pro. 18 Dec. of that yr. provides for w. Amy, s. John, Thomas, Nathaniel, ds. Mary and Martha, beside gr.ch. Samuel, and Sarah, and makes Hananiah sole excor. His wid. d. 15 Jan. 1690. THOMAS, Kennebeck, s. prob. eldest, of John, the first propr. of Parker's isl. now Georgetown, may have visit. Pemaquid, there to take o. of fidel. 1674; had John, Jacob, and five ds. and d. at the isl. John his s. rem. to Boston. and there was a shipwright. THOMAS, Reading, s. of Thomas of the same, had Sarah, b. 9 Aug. 1668; Samuel, 26 Mar. 1670; Sarah, again, 28 Feb. 1672; Deborah, 15 Aug. 1674; Jonathan, 4 Nov. 1678, d. young; Eliz. 25 June 1681; Abigail, 11 Aug. 1683; and Ruth, 22 Apr. 1686; and he d. 9 June 1699. THOMAS, Newton, sec. s. of John of the same, had w. Margaret, but d. at 22 yrs. and his wid. m. an Atkinson. * WILLIAM, Hartford, an orig. propr. 1636, rem. to Saybrook, after hav. sev. ch. Sarah, b. Oct. 1637; Joseph, d. in few weeks; John, 1 Feb. 1642; Ruth, 15 June 1643; William, 1645; Joseph, again, a. mid. Feb. 1647; Margaret; Jonathan, Feb. 1653; David, Feb. 1656; and Deborah, Mar. 1658; but wh. were b. at H. and wh. at S. can hardly be told; was rep. 1672; his w. Margery d. 6 Dec. 1680; and he d. 21 Dec. 1686. WILLIAM, Taunton 1643, perhaps elder br. of John of the same, a purch. in 1637, in his will of 15 Mar. 1660, being 60 yrs. old, names w. Alice, but no ch. and gave small legacy to his neph. James Phillips. His wid. m. 1662, the first Stephen Paine of Rehoboth. WILLIAM, Newport 1639, possib. the same as preced. but the name is so common, it is very easy to fall into error a. the resid. WILLIAM, Watertown, by w. Eliz. had Ephraim, of wh. the rec. says, he was bur. 12 Aug. 1640 at six mos. old; and Ruhamah, 19 Sept. 1641; was freem. 2 June 1641. He was one of the orig. proprs. of Sudbury. WILLIAM, Scituate, m. Apr. 1639, Mary, d. of Thomas Rawlyns, had Mary, b. 1 Jan. 1640; William, Dec. 1643; and Patience, Feb. 1649; and his w. d. Aug. 1651; he m. 13 Nov. 1651, Mary, d. of Humphrey Turner, had Lydia, 9 May 1653; Miles, 25 June 1655; Joseph, 4 Oct. 1658; and Nathanael, 8 Mar. 1661, who perish. in Phips's expedit. against Quebec, 1690; and d. 1684. Mary m. Theophilus Wetherell; Patience m. a Randall; one d. m. Thomas Totman; and in his will are also named ds. Lydia and Judith; and this Lydia prob. was sec. w. of Theophilus Wetherell, and d. 7 Sept. 1719, aged 67. WILLIAM, Scituate, s. of the preced. m. 1693, Mary Clark, perhaps for sec. w. had

Alexander, Joshua, and Elisha, who, Deane says all rem. WILLIAM, Saybrook, s. of William of the same, by w. Hannah, wh. d. 27 Jan. 1673, had William, b. 15 of same mo. Of WILLIAM of Portsmouth Farmer indulg. good Mr. Adams, the annalist of P. with tell. that he m. 26 Feb. 1703, Zurviah Stanley, d. of the Earl of Derby, an absurdity that I ought not to expose by assert. of no *such* name of a d. being found in that ho. without suggest. also, that the maiden's f. might by the rude boys of the village hav. in the way of joke, been thus titled, and the simplicity of the modest histor. made to prolong the frolic; while the genealogist felt that nothing print. in a book could be false. Such a canon of criticism has, indeed, never been promulg. as binding, but too often passes as sacred tradit. with some, long after rejection by the majority. Forty-one of this name had in 1834, been gr. at Harv. alone, and thirty-eight at all other N. E. coll.

PARKHURST, GEORGE, Watertown, freem. 10 May 1643, brought from Eng. s. George, d. Phebe, and perhaps other ch. Barry says his w. was Susanna, and I kn. that in 1643 he m. sec. w. Susanna, wid. of John Simpson, sold his est. at W. 1645, and rem. to Boston, there was liv. in 1655. Phebe m. Thomas Arnold. GEORGE, Watertown, s. of the preced. b. in Eng. a. 1618, m. 16 Dec. 1643, Sarah, perhaps d. of John Brown, had John, b. 10 June 1644; Daniel, bapt. in Boston 10 June 1649; Sarah, b. 14 Sept. 1649; and he m. sec. w. 24 Sept. 1650, Mary, perhaps d. of William Pheese or Veazie wh. d. 9 Mar. 1681; and he d. 16 Mar. 1699. GEORGE, Boston, s. prob. of the preced. by w. Eliz. had Eliz. b. 16 May 1678; and Sarah, 1 Apr. 1680. JOHN, Watertown, s. of the sec. George, by w. Abigail, d. of sec. Edward Garfield, had John, b. 26 Feb. 1672; Abigail, 10 Sept. 1674; Sarah, 26 Nov. 1676; Rachel, 30 Dec. 1678; Eliz. 18 Sept. 1681; Mary, 23 Dec. 1683; George, 3, by Bond, but Barry gives 17 Jan. 1686; Samuel, 11 Apr. 1688; and Hannah, 17 Apr. 1690. He was freem. 1690, and d. 12 Sept. 1725; and his wid. d. 18 Oct. 1726. JOSEPH, Chelmsford, perhaps s. of George the first, by w. Rebecca had Mary, b. 10 Aug. 1657; Rebecca, 14 Aug. 1659; and Joseph, 12 Jan. 1661; was freem. 1690. Prob. his s. Joseph was one of the first sett. of Plainfield a. 1700. In the early rec. the name is Parkis, or Perkis.

PARKINSON, WILLIAM, Dover 1684.

PARKMAN, DELIVERANCE, Salem, s. of Elias, a merch. m. 9 Dec. 1673, Sarah, d. of William Verin, had Deliverance, b. 10 Jan. 1676, d. at 5 yrs.; Sarah, 29 July 1678; and Verin, 15 Feb. 1681. His w. d. 14 Jan. 1682, and he m. Mehitable, d. of John Waite of Malden, the speaker of the ho. had only Mehitable; and m. third w. Margaret Gardner, had Deliverance, again, 1686; Samuel, 24 June 1687; and Marga-

ret, 7 Oct. 1688; wh. all d. young; and his w. d. 25 Mar. 1689 aged
24. His fourth w. was Susanna, wid. of John Gedney, jr. but she had by
this union no ch. and he d. 15 Nov. 1715. ELIAS, Dorchester 1633,
freem. 6 May 1635, rem. to Windsor early, there had Elias; Rebecca;
Samuel, b. 1644; and George, who d. 1645; he prob. had an estab-
lishm. for trade at New Haven 1640, but finally rem. to Boston, there
had Mary, bapt. 24 Sept. 1648; Deliverance, b. 3, bapt. 10 Aug. 1651;
and Nathaniel, b. 24 June, bapt. 8 July 1655. His w. was Bridget.
He was a mariner, traded from Boston to Conn. riv. and perhaps on
longer voyages, in one of wh. he was prob. lost, for his w. present. inv. 2
July 1662, made two days bef. recit. that he was "suppos. to be d.;" and
as it amount. to only £37, 15, we may well think that most of his prop.
was lost at the same time. Rebecca m. 18 Sept. 1661, John Jarvis; and
perhaps his wid. m. 6 Sept. 1672, Sylvester Eveleth of Gloucester.
ELIAS, Boston 1665, mariner, s. of the preced. by w. Sarah had Elias,
b. 13 Nov. 1665; John, 20 Jan. 1669; and Eliz. 29 Dec. 1670; beside
William and Sarah; all, exc. John, who prob. d. young, nam. in his will
of 8 Aug. 1691, made in London, brot. for pro. by his w. 6 Mar. 1693.
Rev. Ebenezer, H. C. 1721, min. of Westborough, ord. 28 Oct. 1724,
who d. 9 Dec. 1782, tenth ch. of that William, b. 5 Sept. 1703, was
f. of Samuel, a promin. merch. of Boston in the last age; and of his descend. beside many by fem. lines, in the regular male line fourteen had
been in 1846, gr. at Harv. Of these my friend, Rev. Francis, H. C.
1807, will be long remem. for his urbanity, learning, and benevolence.
NATHANIEL, Boston, s. of Elias the first, by w. Hannah had Hannah, b.
30 Mar. 1686; Nathaniel, 29 Oct. 1688; Rebecca, 6 June 1696; and
Nathaniel, again.

PARMELEE, JOHN, Guilford 1639, was of New Haven 1659, when he
made his will 8 Nov. and d. short time aft. To his only s. large part
of his prop. was giv. resid. to gr.ch. Nathaniel, and Hannah, w. of John
Johnson, after provid. for his own w. Eliz. wh. m. John Evarts. JOHN,
Guilford 1650, s. of the preced. the only one who outliv. him and may
be the only one he ever had, was propr. 1685 with s. John, but prob. he
had others. Sometimes this name is Parmelin, but the mod. spell. prevails. See Palmerly.

PARMENTER, often in old rec. PARMITER, BENJAMIN, Salem 1637,
when Felt says, he had gr. of ld. but perhaps he did not live there, exc. on
Marblehead side. Yet called of S. when freem. 1678, many yrs. bef. had
w. Mary, and d. Mary, and was of Gloucester 1684, said to have been b.
a. 1610. BENJAMIN, Sudbury, s. of John the sec. of the same, m. 1680,
Thomas Rice, had Lydia, b. 29 Sept. 1681; Benjamin, 21 Jan. 1683;
David, 1685, l. soon; David, again, 12 Apr. 1686; Mercy, 8 Dec.

1687; Thankful; and sev. without name who d. soon, beside Jonathan, 15 Jan. 1703; and d. 1737. GEORGE, Sudbury, br. of the preced. m. 1679, Hannah Johnson, perhaps d. of Solomon, had George, b. 5 May 1679; Joseph, 19 May 1681; Solomon, 17 June 1683; John, 17 Apr. 1685; Daniel, 3 Aug. 1688; Amos, 12 May 1694; Hannah, 17 July 1696; and Abigail, 17 Feb. 1703; and d. 1727. JAMES, Hull 1669, may be he who d. at Sudbury, 21 Nov. 1678, unless this were a ch. JOHN, Watertown 1638, one of the first sett. of Sudbury 1639, freem. 13 May 1640, selectman and deac. had brought from Eng. s. John, and perhaps other ch. with w. Bridget, who d. 6 Apr. 1660, and he rem. to Roxbury, there m. 9 Aug. 1660, Ann, or Annis, wid. of John Dane, who had bef. been wid. of William Chandler; and he d. 1 May 1671, aged 83. In his will, he names this w. and s.-in-law John Woods, h. of his d. Mary, and gr. s. John, his s. of that name being some yrs. d. and this gr. s. made one of the excors. The will of his wid. 1 Nov. 1672, pro. eleven yrs. after, names her first h.'s childr. John, Thomas, and William Chandler, Hannah, w. of George Abbot, and Sarah, w. of William Cleaves. JOHN, Sudbury, s. of the preced. b. in Eng. freem. 10 May 1643, had by w. Amy, who d. 1681, John, b. a. 1639; Joseph, 12 Mar. 1642; Mary, 10 June 1644; George; Benjamin; and Lydia, 16 Oct. 1655, who d. bef. her f. and he d. as Barry says, tho. I think, with slight error, 12 Apr. 1666; Mary, m. 1670, Richard Burk; and Lydia m. 5 June 1681, Thomas Pratt. JOHN, Boston, housewright, by w. Judith, had Judith, b. 14 Feb. 1667, d. soon; Eliz. 8 Feb. 1668; John, 31 Oct. 1670, d. soon; Judith, again, 17 July 1672; John, again, 17 Nov. 1674; and Lydia, Jan. 1677; and by sec. w. Hannah, d. prob. of Richard Williams of Taunton, had Eliz. again, 3 Sept. 1688. JOHN, Sudbury, s. of the sec. John of the same, by w. Eliz. had Sarah, b. 29 Aug. 1668; Mary, 15 Oct. 1670; Eliz. 9 Dec. 1672; John, 9 Apr. 1678; Joseph, 24 Aug. 1685; and d. prob. 1719, at least Barry says his will was pro. 10 Nov. of that yr. Confus. of this last John, with ano. seems to have attend. the dilig. collector in Geneal. Reg. VI. 390. JOSEPH, Braintree, s. of Robert, m. Sarah, d. of Edmund Sheffield, freem. 1678, was town clk. 1699–1709, d. 20 Feb. 1737. ROBERT, Braintree, freem. 1650, by w. Leah, had John, b. 23 Oct. 1653, d. next mo.; Joseph, 20 Dec. 1655; Eliz. 22 Oct. 1657; and Hannah, 17 Jan. 1659; was deac. and d. 27 June 1696, in his 74th yr. The name is sometimes pronounced Parmiter.

PARNELL, JOHN, Dover 1666–8, perhaps had w. Mary d. of Henry Stacy. THOMAS, Pemaquid, sw. fidel. to Mass. 1674. A capt. Francis P. d. at Boston, Oct. 1724.

PARR, Abel, Boston, freem. 2 June 1641. I think it possib. that Porter was meant, instead of Parr. JAMES, one of the soldiers sent to seize Gorton, and his comp. was of unkn. resid. SAMUEL, Salem 1665.

PARROTT, PAROTE, or PARRETT, * FRANCIS, Rowley, freem. 13 May 1640, was town clk. 14 yrs. rep. 1640 and 2, being the earliest from that town, went home, and d. a. 1656. His will ment. w. Eliz. and six ch. One was prob. that Faith, who m. Ezekiel Jewett. JOHN, Rowley 1643, perhaps was s. of the preced.

PARRY, EDWARD, came from London in the Truelove, 1634, aged 24, but where he sett. is unkn.

PARSONS, BENJAMIN, Springfield, said to have come, perhaps was brot. in his childhood, from Torrington, a. 30 miles from Exeter, in the N. W. part of Devonsh. m. 1653 Sarah, d. of Richard Vore, of Windsor, had Sarah, b. 18 Aug. 1656; Benjamin, 15 Sept. 1658; Mary, 10 Dec. 1660, d. young; Abigail, 6 Jan. 1663; Samuel, 10 Oct. 1666; Ebenezer, 17 Nov. 1668; Mary, again, 17 Dec. 1670; Hezekiah, 24 Nov. 1673; and Joseph, Dec. 1675. His w. d. 1 Jan. 1676 or 7, and he m. next the wid. of John Leonard, who took after his d. third h. Hon. Peter Tilton; was deac. and d. 24 Aug. 1689. Sarah m. James Dorchester; Abigail m. 23 Dec. 1680, John Mun, and next 7 Oct. 1686 John Richards; and Mary m. 21 Oct. 1691, Thomas Richards. BENJAMIN, Springfield, s. of the preced. m. 17 Jan. 1684, Sarah, d. of John Keep, rem. to Enfield, had John, b. 19 Nov. 1684; Benjamin, 1 Mar. 1688; Christopher, 28 Jan. 1691; and Sarah, perhaps; and he d. 28 Dec. 1728. His wid. d. 8 July foll. EBENEZER, Springfield, s. of the first Benjamin, liv. on W. side of the riv. m. Margaret, d. of Samuel Marshfield, had Ebenezer, b. 12 Jan. 1692; Margaret, 19 Sept. 1693; Jonathan, 15 July 1695, drown. at 8 yrs.; Benjamin, 15 Dec. 1696; Caleb, 27 Dec. 1699; Sarah, 4 Feb. 1703; Jonathan, 30 Nov. 1705, Y. C. 1729, a min. of distinct. ord. 17 Mar. 1730 at Lyme, and thence to Newbury; Abigail, 21 Oct. 1708; and Catharine, 16 Oct. 1715. He was deac. 52 yrs. and d. 23 Sept. 1752; and his wid. d. 12 June 1758, aged 87. EBENEZER, Windsor, s. of Thomas, had Abigail, b. 1 Aug. 1675; Ebenezer, 16 Apr. 1677; and John, 29 July 1678. EBENEZER, Gloucester, youngest s. of the first Jeffery, m. Lydia, d. prob. youngest of the sec. William Haskell, had Ebenezer, Jacob, Isaac, and perhaps sev. other ch. but certain, the youngest s. Moses, b. 20 June 1716, H. C. 1736, the min. of Byfield, wh. was f. of a disting. fam. ELIHU, York, s. of John, by w. Ruth, d. of Joseph Wilson, had Ruth, b. 5 Nov. 1711; Hannah, 21 May 1713; John, 26 June 1715; Eliz. 11 Sept. 1717; Joseph, 20 Feb. 1720; Elihu, 3 June 1722; Josiah, 13 June 1724, d. young; Mary, 21 Dec. 1726; and Susanna, 15 Jan. 1730. GEORGE, Boston, by w. Eliz. d. I feel sure, of Rev. John Wheelwright, had Joseph, b. 18 Aug. 1667; and Wheelwright, 10 Apr. 1674. HEZEKIAH, Springfield, s. of Benjamin the first, m. 20 Feb. 1702, Hannah, d. of Eliakim Cooley, rem. to East Windsor, and d. 11 July 1748. HUGH, Springfield, m. 1645, Mary Lewis from Wales, had Hannah, b. 7 Aug. 1646; Samuel, 8 Jan. 1648, d. next yr.; and Joshua, 26 Oct. 1650, k. by his mo. 4 Mar. foll. and she plead. guilty in May, aft. hav. been just bef. acq. of the absurd charge of witchcraft on a ch. of the Rev. Mr. Moxon. The unhap. woman had, in her native ld. suffer. abuse by a former h. who sev. yrs. bef. she came hither, abandon. her, and her charact. was so fair, that we must believe undoubt. she was insane. But the h. was less lucky in his jury, who convict. him of a sim. crime, when, in 1652, the sentence of death was refused by the court, and the Gen. Court had sense eno. to discharge the prisoner. See Hutch. I. 179. Soon after both of the sad harmless felons rem. to Watertown. There he d. 18 June 1675, and his wid. Ruth d. 8 Aug. 1676. The first w. I fear, suffer. death for murder of her ch. but see Col. Rec. III. 229 and 273. In Drake's Hist. of Boston 322 et seq. is a valua. portion of the evid. JAMES, Gloucester, eldest ch. of Jeffery, was freem. 1682, m. 18 Dec. 1688, Hannah Younglove, had James, b. 1690; Eliezer; and Joseph; and d. 1 Oct. 1733, and the w. or wid. d. a few mos. bef. or aft. See Babson, 121. JEFFERY, Gloucester, m. 11 Nov. 1657, Sarah, d. of William Vinson, had James, b. 18 Dec. 1658; Jeffery, 25 Jan. 1661; Sarah, 19 Apr. 1663; John, 24 May 1666; Eliz. 22 Mar. 1669; Jeremiah, 28 May 1672; Nathaniel, 16 Mar. 1675; Abigail, 25 Mar. 1678; Ebenezer, 5 Jan. 1681, d. soon; and Ebenezer, again, 28 Jan. 1682. He was, it is said, b. a. 1631, at Alphington, near Exeter, adj. Topsham, Co. Devon (and we know that in the E. part of that sh. the name is extens. diffus.), and d. 16 or 19 Aug. 1689; and his wid. d. 12 Jan. 1708. His gr.-s. Moses, min. of Byfield parish in Newbury, wh. d. 14 Dec. 1783, was f. of Theophilus, H. C. 1769, Ch. Just. of Mass. one of the princip. framers of the Constit. of this Comwth. for whose successf. concoction, after many yrs. of anarchy, the way was chiefly prepared by his "Essex Result," the quintessence of our free Instit. He was the most learned lawyer in the gen. opin. of his contempo. that ever appear. on our side of the Atlantic. JEFFERY, Gloucester, s. of the preced. freem. 1690; m. 5 May 1686, Abigail Younglove, perhaps d. of the sec. Samuel of Ipswich, had Jonathan, Samuel, and Jeremiah, liv. to be nam. in his will of 1734, and all bless. with fams. JOHN, York, had John, b. 31 July 1677; Eliz. 9 Feb. 1680; Mary, 13 Oct. 1682; Elihu; Rachel; Christian; and Mercy. He took o. of alleg. 1681. Eliz. m. 12 Apr. 1698, Peter Hinkson; and Mary m. Nicholas Cane. JOHN, Northampton, s. of Joseph the first, m. 23 Dec. 1675,

Sarah, d. of William Clarke, had Sarah, b. 1678; Mary, 1681; Samuel, 1685; William, 1690; Experience, 1692; and Joseph, 1695. He was a capt. freem. 1690, and d. 1728, as did his w. The s. Samuel and Joseph were k. by the Ind. 9 July 1708. JOHN, Gloucester, s. of the first Jeffery, m. 19 Jan. 1693, Isabella Haynes, had John, Josiah, Thomas, Daniel, and Solomon, beside others, nine in all; but perhaps two, three or more of the latest were by sec. w. m. 29 July 1701, Sarah Norton, wh. d. 25 July 1726, aged 56, and he d. 1 Dec. 1714. JONATHAN, Northampton, br. of John of the same, m. Mary Clark, had Jonathan, b. 1683, d. soon; Jonathan, again, 1684, d. young; Nathanael, 1686; Mary, 1688; Hannah, 1690; Jonathan, again, 1693; and Lydia, 1695, posthum. the f. who. was freem. 1684, hav. d. 19 Oct. 1694. JOSEPH, Springfield, br. of the first Benjamin, witness to the deed from the Ind. to Pynchon, 15 July 1636, m. 26 Nov. 1646, Mary, d. of Thomas Bliss of Hartford, had Joseph, b. 1647; Benjamin, bur. 22 June 1649; John, 1649, d. soon; John, again, 1650; and Samuel, 1653; rem. to Northampton, there had Ebenezer, 1 May 1655, who is said to be the first white b. there, and was k. by the Ind. at Northfield, 2 Sept. 1675; Jonathan, 6 June 1657; David, 30 Apr. 1659, d. young; Mary, 27 June 1661; Hannah, 1663; Abigail, 3 Sept. 1666; and Esther, 24 Dec. 1672. His w. charg. with witchcraft 1674, was sent to Boston, tr. in May 1675, and acquit. by the jury, liv. to 29 Jan. 1712. He was freem. 1669, cornet of the horse, one of the richest men in the town, rem. 1679 back to Springfield, and d. 9 Oct. 1683. Mary m. 1685, Joseph Ashley, and, next, 2 Mar. 1699, Joseph Williston; Hannah m. 6 Jan. 1688, Pelatiah Glover, jr. not his f. (as the Geneal. Reg. I. 266, says); Abigail, m. 19 Feb. 1690, John Colton; and Esther m. 15 Sept. 1698, Rev. Joseph Smith, aft. of Middletown. * JOSEPH, Northampton, eldest ch. of the preced. m. 17 Mar. or 11 May 1669, Eliz. d. of Elder John Strong, had Joseph, b. 28 June 1671, H. C. 1697, first of this surname in the Catal.; John, 11 Jan. 1674; Ebenezer, 11 Dec. 1675; Eliz. 3 Feb. 1678; David, 1 Feb. 1680, H. C. 1705; Josiah, 2 Jan. 1682; Daniel, Aug. 1685; Moses, 15 Jan. 1687; Abigail, 1 Jan. 1690; and Noah, 15 Aug. 1692. He was freem. 1676, judge of the County Ct. rep. 1693, and sev. yrs. more, rem. to Springfield, was rep. 1706 and 8 for that town, back to N. and was rep. 8 yrs. more, last in 1724, but not in sequence, in all 14 yrs. and d. 21 or 29 Nov. 1729; and his wid. mo. of all those ten ch. ea. of wh. had fam. d. 12 May 1736. JOSEPH, Boston, by w. Bethia, d. of Thomas Brattle, had William, b. 29 Dec. 1685; Bethia, 1 Jan. 1687, d. soon; and Thomas, 11 Aug. 1689, d. soon; was of the patriot counc. of war for overthrow of Andros, 1689, freem. in Mar. 1690, and his w. d. 4 July 1690, of small pox; as had her first b. 24 June bef. MARK, Kennebeck 1665. See Sullivan, 287. NATHANIEL, Gloucester, s. of the first Jeffery, m. 27 Dec. 1697, Abigail, d. prob. eldest of the sec. William Haskell, had Nathaniel, William, Stephen, and d. of small pox, 21 May 1722. RICHARD, Windsor 1640, there made freem. in Apr. so he had been there, no doubt, a good season, was soon after at Hartford, prob. went home. ROBERT, Lynn, freem. 14 Mar. 1639, of wh. no more is kn. unless he were the man who d. at New Haven a. 1648, or earlier. SAMUEL, East Hampton, L. I. 1650. SAMUEL, Northampton, s. of Joseph the first, freem. 1690, had two ws. Eliz. perhaps d. of Capt. Aaron Cook, who d. 2 Sept. 1690, and Rhoda Tayler, had Samuel, b. 1678, d. soon; Samuel, again, 1680, d. at 3 yrs.; Eliz. 1684; Jemima, 1691; Rhoda, 1694; Timothy, 1696; Hannah, 1699; Simeon, 1701; Phineas, 1704; and Ithamar, 1707. This last was b. at Durham, Conn. THOMAS, Boston, seems to have, by the old book of possessns. an est. bound. E. by Elder Thomas Leverett, and this bef. 1639, but we kn. no more, unless he be the man by Worthington named of Dedham and Medfield, and this is all. THOMAS, Windsor, was soldier in the Pequot war 1637, for wh. some of his ch. had gr. of ld. many yrs. aft. m. 28 June 1641, Lydia Brown, had Bethia, b. 21 May 1642; Abigail, 21 Jan. 1644; Thomas, 9 Aug. 1645; John, 13 Nov. 1647; Mary, 23 July 1652; Ebenezer, 14 May 1655; Samuel, 18 July 1657; and Joseph, 1 May 1661; beside William in some earlier yr. not specif. and d. 23 Sept. 1661. His wid. m. Eltweed Pomeroy. Of these ch. Ebenezer, Samuel, William, and Joseph liv. at Simsbury, and some, if not all, had fams. but I kn. not the details. Bethia m. 10 May 1660, Thomas Mascall; and next, 18 Aug. 1672, John Williams of W. THOMAS, Windsor, s. of the preced. m. 24 Dec. 1668, Sarah Dare, if this name be well giv. rem. to Brookfield 1666, had Sarah, b. 12 Oct. 1669; Hannah, 3 Oct. 1671; and Thomas, 2 Jan. 1674, who d. bef. his f. and his w. d. 14 June 1674; and he rem. to Springfield, may have ret. to B. aft. the war, and d. 14 Dec. 1680. THOMAS, Suffield 1679, had w. Priscilla, but no ch. and in advanced age, they adopt. 1700, Nathaniel Austin. ‖ WILLIAM, Boston, came prob. in the James from Southampton, 1635, then by the custom ho. clearance describ. as a tailor of Salisbury, tho. call. a joiner on his adm. of the ch. 20 Apr. 1644, by w. Ruth, had Ruth, b. 3, bapt. 12 Oct. 1645, was freem. 1645, ar. co. 1646, and d. 29 Jan. 1702 in 87th yr. WILLIAM, Windsor, s. of Thomas the first, m. 26 Oct. 1666, Hannah Parker, had William, b. 27 July 1669; and Hannah, 3 Nov. 1678. Ano. William serv. 1676, under Capt. Turner, on Conn. riv. but was, of course, as the rest of his comp. from E. part of the Col. and he ret. safe. Thirty-nine of this name had been gr. in 1834, at the N. E. coll. says Farmer, of wh. 17 were clerg. and of these eighteen were at Harv. of wh. the first 8 were clerg.

PARTRIDGE, ALEXANDER, came 1645, with w. and fam. to Boston, and was found to be dangerous by his opinions, wh. he had imbib. in the Parliam. or rather Cromwell's army, so that he could not be permit. to reside here, but was forced away bef. the first winter, to Rhode Isl. Winth. II. 251. He was made chief capt. of the force in that Col. 1648, and was liv. at Newport 1655. Hutch. Coll. 226, Knowles, 213, 229. ELEAZER, Medfield, s. of John the first of the same, had perhaps by first w. Eliz. Joseph, b. 1706; David, 1708; and Benjamin, 1713; and by sec. w. Sarah, Elisha, 1716; Eleazer, 1717; Sarah, 1719; Peter, 16 May 1722; and Zechariah, tho. in Morse's Geneal. the order of success. may slightly be erron. GEORGE, Duxbury, perhaps br. of Rev. Ralph, being ment. in the rec. 1636, the same yr. that Ralph came, m. Nov. 1638, Sarah, d. of Stephen Tracy of Plymouth, had Sarah, b. 1639; Mercy; Tryphosa; Ruth; Lydia; John, b. 29 Nov. 1657; and James, who liv. to 20 Jan. 1745, but had prob. no ch. was prop. 1645 of Bridgewater, and one of the orig. purchas. of Middleborough in 1662. His d. Sarah m. a. 1658, Samuel Allen of Bridgewater; Tryphosa m. 26 Sept. 1668, Samuel West; Ruth m. 12 Jan. 1670, Rodolphus Thacher; and Lydia m. 2 Jan. 1672, William Brewster. JOHN, Portsmouth, s. of William of the same, m. 11 Dec. 1660, Mary Fernald, had Hannah, b. 14 Oct. 1661; John, 3 Jan. 1663; Mary, 26 Feb. 1665; Sarah, 3 Sept. 1668; Rachel, 4 Mar. 1671; Eliz. 4 July 1673; Abigail, 2 Feb. 1675; and Patience, 4 July 1678. JOHN, Duxbury, s. of George of the same, m. 24 Dec. 1684, Hannah Seabury, d. of Samuel, had Sarah, b. 21 Sept. 1685, d. in two mos.; Samuel, 10 Mar. 1687; George, 17 Aug. 1690; Mary, 2 May 1693; John, 27 Dec. 1697; and by sec. w. m. 23 May 1700, Mary Brewster, perhaps wid. of Wrestling, had Benjamin, b. 5 Mar. 1701; and Isaac, 2 Mar. 1705. JOHN, Medfield 1654, was s. perhaps, of William of the same, but more prob. his br. m. 18 Dec. 1655, Magdalen Bullard, had John, b. 21 Sept. 1656; Hannah, 15 Apr. 1658; Eleazer, 1664; Abiel, 1667; Experience; Rachel, 1669; Samuel, 1671; Zechariah, 1674; and Eliz. 1679. JOHN, Kingston, s. prob. of George of Duxbury, had w. Mary, who d. says her gr. stone "12 Nov. 1742, aged 80 yrs. 11 mos. and 29 days." I presume he had been many yrs d. Ano. JOHN is found at Medfield, by Morse, call. jun. but whether s. of the preced. or of William of the same is very diffic. to conject. He m. a. 1680, Eliz. Rocket or Rockwood, d. of Nicholas of the same, had Mary, b. 1681; Benoni, 1687; Jonathan, 1693; Hannah, 1696; and Deborah, 1698; and prob. by sec. w. Ann had James Oct. 1700; Sarah, 1702; Stephen, 16 Apr. 1706; and Ann, 1709. MICHAEL, Salem, mariner, drown. Apr. 1674. NATHANIEL, Boston, tailor, had w. Ellen, who join. to our ch. 23 Apr. 1643, and he, also, 4 wks. aft. was freem.

1644. OLIVER, Dorchester 1636, was mem. of the ch. with w. Sarah, bef. 1639. *RALPH*, first min. of Duxbury, arr. at Boston in a half yrs. pass. from London, Nov. 1636, eighteen wks. from land to land, in comp. with blessed Nathaniel Rogers. He had been well instruct. tho. we kn. not the place, and was many yrs. a preach. at Sutton, Co. Kent, near Dover, as is learn. from a bond and conveyance of ld. therewith by John Marshall of Lenham, Nov. 1631, made in consid. of m. by him intend. with Mary, d. of P. wh. with Jervase P. (prob. his br.) citizen and cordwainer of London, were made trustees. Yet these papers are rec. here aft. 30 yrs. It is remarkable, how little has been told of him, beside this transact. Chap. 11 of Book III. in the Magnalia could be condensed into two lines without loss of one fact. His own will, 29 Sept. 1655, pro. 4 May 1658, a few days aft. his d. names d. Eliz. w. of Rev. Thomas Thacher, m. 11 May 1643, her s. Thomas, Ralph, and Peter, beside her eldest d. Patience Kemp; also his eldest d. Mary M. and her s. Robert and John. His w. Patience was d. and in the inv. his library is count. 400 vols. wh. for that time, on this side of the sea, was very respectab. ‡ * SAMUEL, Hadley, s. of William of the same, m. 24 Sept. 1668, Mehitable, d. of John Crow, had William, b. 1669, H. C. 1689, made reg. of prob. ct. 1692, a preach. a. 1693, rem. to Hatfield, had Samuel, 1672; Mehitable, 1675; Mary, 1678; Jonathan, 1681, d. at 3 yrs.; Edward, 1683; Jonathan, again, 1685, d. next yr.; John, 1686, H. C. 1705; and Eliz. 1688. He was rep. 1685 and 6, m. 1695, the young wid. of John Atwater of Salem, d. of Rev. Seaborn Cotton; was col. of the reg. Judge of Pro. one of his Majesty's Council, &c. &c. the most import. man after d. of Col. Pynchon, 1703, in all the W. part of the Prov. and d. 25 Dec. 1740, aged 95 yrs. 2 mos. and 10 days. For some yrs. his name was by hims. writ. like his f's. Partrigg and in sev. old rec. it is Partridges, or even Patrick; but he adopt. the present spell. Mehitable m. 1693, Nathaniel Dwight; Mary m. 1695, Josiah Dwight; and Eliz. had four hs. two Hamlins, a Johnson, and a Payson. SAMUEL, Medfield, s. of John the first of the same, by w. Hannah, had Hannah, b. 1702; Thankful, 1703; Samuel, 1704; Ebenezer, 1706; Abigail, 1707; Benjamin, 1709; Silence, perhaps tw. with preced. 1709, d. young; Mehitable, 1710; Joshua, 27 July 1713; Caleb, 17 Mar. 1717; and Silence, again, 5 Mar. 1719. WILLIAM, Salisbury 1638, freem. 14 Mar. 1639, is said to be s. of John of Olney in Co. Bucks, d. 1654, left wid. Ann, perhaps mo. of the ch. John; Hannah; Eliz. b. 14 Feb. 1643; Nehemiah, 5 May 1645; Sarah, 24 Aug. 1647; Rachel, 19 June 1650; and possib. William, posthum. His wid. m. 1 Jan. 1656, Anthony Stanion, and d. 10 July 1689. Eliz. m. 26 June 1661, Joseph Shaw of Hampton; Sarah m. 14 Nov. 1666, John Heath of Haverhill;

and Rachel m. 31 Jan. 1671, Joseph Chase of Hampton, and d. 27 Oct. 1718. WILLIAM, Hartford, came, it is tradit. said, from Berwick on Tweed, m. 10 Dec. 1644, Mary Smith, only sis. of four brs. who are Christopher of Northampton, Joseph of Hartford, Simon of Hartford, and nameless one, d. 20 July 1680, had Samuel, b. 15 Oct. 1645 ; was one of the two constables 1655, rem. to Hadley 1660; there d. 27 June 1668. His name unif. ends *rigg.* His d. Mary, whose date of b. is not found, m. 12 Nov. 1663, John Smith. WILLIAM, Medfield 1649, freem. 1653, m. 23 Nov. 1654, Sarah Pierce, who had Eleazer, b. 3 days only bef. she d. 16 May 1656 ; and 19 Nov. foll. he m. Sarah Colburn, had Nathaniel, bapt. at Dedham, 18 Nov. 1660 ; John, b. 1662 ; Elisha, 1665 ; Joseph, 13 Mar. 1668 ; William, 1669 ; Priscilla, 1672 ; Sarah, 1674 ; and Mary, 1682. WILLIAM, Medfield, s. of the preced. by w. Hannah, had William, b. 1695 ; Joseph, 1699 ; Hannah, 24 Dec. 1702 ; Seth, 1706 ; and Mary, 1709. †‡WILLIAM, Portsmouth, s. possib. of William of Salisbury, m. 8 Dec. 1680, Mary Brown, prob. d. of Richard of Newbury, had Richard, b. 9 Dec. 1681; Nehemiah, 9 Mar. 1683 ; Mary, 19 Oct. 1685 ; William, 1 May 1687 ; and Eliz. 23 Sept. 1692. He was of the Counc. and Lieut. Gov. of that Prov. rem. to Newbury, there d. 3 Jan. 1729, in 75th yr. His wid. d. 10 June 1739. ZECHA-RIAH, Medfield, by w. Eliz. had Mary, b. 1702 ; Magdalen, 1703 ; Sa-rah, 1706 ; Zechariah, 1709, d. young; Asa, 1712 ; and a d. 27 Aug. 1714; and he d. 23 Sept. 1716. Three of this name had been gr. at Harv. in 1834, and nine at other N. E. colls.

PARUM, WILLIAM, Boston, by w. Frances, had John, b. 24 Aug. 1657, says the substitute rec. that we are compell. to use in place of the orig. that may have been lost near two hundred yrs. I doubt the exactness of the surname.

PARY, or PARRY, WILLIAM, adm. freem. of Mass. 1646, of wh. no more is kn. but that he was of Watertown 1642, and Bond thinks he came in from Scituate. See Perry.

PASCO, HUGH, Salem 1668. JOHN, Boston, by w. Rachel, had Dor-othy, b. 19 July 1685 ; John, 1 Apr. 1687 ; and Thomas, 4 Dec. 1688 ; in 1696, or perhaps later, rem. to Enfield, there d. 1706. JOHN, En-field, s. of the preced. m. 1713, Rebecca Terry. Of ano. JOHN of Boston, mariner, who left wid. Eliz. admin. was giv. 29 Mar. 1697 to a creditor.

PASMORE, PASMER, or PASMERE, BARTHOLOMEW, Boston, an early propr. whose est. is descr. in the book of possessns. had Abigail, b. June 1641. JAMES, Concord, by w. Alice, had Stephen, b. 13 Nov. 1642 ; and Hannah, 16 Aug. 1644. RICHARD, Ipswich 1674. Felt. WIL-LIAM, Boston, by w. Rebecca had Robert, b. 29 June 1674 ; and Re-becca, 26 Oct. 1679.

PASSAM, PASSANT, or PASSON, HUGH, Watertown 1649, d. 13 June 1675, aged a. 63, had w. Ruth, who d. 28 Aug. 1676, but prob. no ch. They were very poor, and rec. relief, as paupers. But the real name was Parsons; which see.

PATCH, ABRAHAM, Ipswich 1667, s. of Edmund, m. 13 Mar. 1671, Eunice, d. of George Fraile of Lynn, had Abraham, b. 17 May 1672; and Edmund; but bef. the b. of this latter, he ran away with the w. of ano. leav. says Col. Rec. V. 39, "his aged f. debilit. in body and mind." BENJAMIN, Salem, youngest s. of the first John of the same, m. 16 July 1694, Susanna, d. of Nicholas Legrove, had Priscilla, b. 28 Nov. foll.; John, 31 Mar. 1696; Nicholas, 10 Aug. 1698; Eliz. 4 Sept. 1700; Benjamin, 20 Sept. 1702; Brackenbury, 17 May 1705; Freeborn, 10 Oct. 1708; and Hannah, 15 June 1711. He d. 1730, and his wid. d. 2 Nov. 1733. EDMUND, Salem, 1639, had Abraham, bapt. 5 Aug. 1649; d. 10 Nov. 1680. JAMES, Salem 1646, liv. on Beverly side, by w. Hannah, had Mary, b. 21 May 1647, d. at two yrs.; Mary, again, 6 Apr. 1650; prob. James, wh. d. 10 Aug. 1653; Eliz. 16 June 1654; James, again, 21 June 1655; and Nicholas, 21 Oct. 1657, who d. Jan. foll.; d. 10 Aug. 1658; in his will of 7 Aug. in this yr. names w. Hannah, s. James; ds. Mary, and Eliz; brs. Nicholas Woodbury and John P. His d. Mary m. 28 Apr. 1688, Paul Thorndike; and Eliz. m. Richard Thistle. The wid. d. 1703, at Ipswich. JAMES, Salem, s. of the preced. rem. to Ipswich, by first w. whose name is not seen, had James; John, b. 1699; Mary; Bethia; and Hannah; took sec. w. 1707 or 17, Mary, wid. of David Thompson, but had no more ch. and d. 1733. JOHN, Salem, br. of the first James, liv. on Beverly side, freem. 1678, by w. Eliz. d. of Richard Brackenbury, had Richard, b. 30 Apr. 1648; Sarah, 28 July 1650; Eliz. 12 Aug. 1652; Ellen, 20 Sept. 1656, d. young; John, 1 Mar. 1659; and Benjamin. Eliz. m. 16 Nov. 1674, Jonathan Byles. JOHN, Salem, s. of the preced. by w. Priscilla, had Ambrose, Nicholas, and Susanna, and d. Nov. 1734. NICHOLAS, Salem, had gr. of ld. 1639, says Felt, was one of the founders of ch. at Beverly 1667, with Eliz. prob. his w. who was, says a wild tradit. the first girl of Eng. parents, b. in the Col. of Mass. and d. 14 Jan. 1715, aged 86. He d. Nov. 1673, leav. s. John, and Thomas. Hutch. II. 216 and 3 Mass. Hist. Coll. VII. 256. Felt, in a note on Ann. I. 175, informs us, "a Patch fam. was in Salem as early as 1629;" but it is thot. by many that is ten yrs. too soon. RICHARD, Salem, eldest s. of the first John, freem. 1678, m. 8 Feb. 1673, Mary Goldsmith, had Eleanor, Richard, Robert, John, and John, again. He m. 12 June, 1704, Hannah Eaton, but had no more ch. *THOMAS, Wenham, s. of Nicholas, b. a. 1638, freem. 1670, rep. 1689; m. Mary Scott of Ipswich, d. of Thomas, had Thomas, b. 19 July

1674; Stephen, 12 Apr. 1680; Isaac, a. 1682; Ephraim; Timothy; and Simon; beside two elder ds. Sarah, 8 Dec. 1666; and Marah, 3 Feb. 1669. Isaac was of Groton. WILLIAM, Scituate 1640.

PATCHIN, or PATCHING, JOSEPH, Roxbury, m. 18 Apr. 1642, Eliz. wid. of Stephen Iggleden, had Joseph, b. 14 Apr. 1643; John, 20 Dec. 1644; ano. ch. d. in May 1649; and aft. one of the parents join. to the ch. Joseph and John were bapt. 24 Mar. 1650. He rem. to Fairfield, and, in 1666, call. his age 56 yrs.

PATEFIELD, or PEATFIELD, JOHN, Charlestown, by w. Amy had Mary, b. 2 Dec. 1654; and Rebecca, 1 Nov. 1657; was there liv. 1678. His w. d. 15 Aug. 1691, aged a. 76.

PATESHALL, PATTESHALL, or PADDESHALL, EDMUND, Pemaquid 1665, sw. fidel. to Mass. 1674, may be he whose depon. is refer. to by Chalmers, 504. RICHARD, Boston 1665, freem. 1678, by w. Abigail had Edward, b. 27 Apr. 1670; and by w. Martha, had Martha, b. 31 Jan. 1674; Ann, 11 Dec. 1678; Edmund, 31 Mar. 1683; and Robert, 26 Mar. 1685. Of ano. RICHARD of Boston, mariner, who. d. at Pemaquid, 1701, admin. was gr. to his sis. Frances, 9 Oct. in that yr. ROBERT, Boston 1652, merch. was capt. and magistr. in the tempora. co. of Devonshire, Me. perhaps was the man k. by the Ind. 1689, at Pemaquid, as told in the Magn. by Mather VII. apx. art. IV.

PATIE, PETER, Haverhill, took o. of alleg. Nov. 1677.

PATRICK, DANIEL, Watertown, one of the two capt. in regular pay, brot. in the fleet by Winth. 1630, freem. 18 May 1631, was short time of Cambridge, but at W. selectman 1638; rem. to Conn. had a Dutch w. and was k. by a Dutchman 1643, at Stamford. See Winth. I. 74, and II. 151. WILLIAM, Hartford, had Samuel, b. 15 Oct. 1645.

PATTEN, NATHANIEL, Dorchester 1640, d. 31 Jan. 1661, leav. wid. Justine, and large est. on wh. the wid. admin. and d. 28 Dec. 1675. I suppose he left no ch. for his br. and heir John, from Crewkerne in Co. Somerset, sent his s. Thomas to dispose of est. in Boston, and its neighb. NATHANIEL, Cambridge, s. of William, m. 24 Nov. 1669, Rebecca, d. of John Adams, who d. 18 Dec. 1677, and he m. 8 Oct. 1678, Sarah Cooper; had Nathaniel, and prob. more ch. wás freem. 1677, and d. 12 June 1725, aged, says the gr.st. a. 80 yrs. and I think he was very near 82. THOMAS, Salem 1643. THOMAS, Boston 1671, came from Bristol, was s. of John, sent by his f. to look after the est. of Nathaniel the first, as bef. said, and prob. went home again. THOMAS, Billerica, s. of William, m. 1 Apr. 1662, Rebecca, d. of Thomas Paine of Dedham, had Rebecca, and four s. whose names and dates I find not. He was freem. 1678. WILLIAM, Cambridge, brot. from Eng. w. Mary, by wh. he had Mary, bapt. in Eng.; Thomas, b. Oct. 1636; Sarah, 27 Jan. 1638; Nathaniel, 28 July 1643; William, bur. 22 Mar. 1646, quite young, we may be sure; besides prob. a former Nathaniel, who d. Jan. 1640; freem. 1645; one of the orig. proprs. of Billerica 1658, and d. 10 Dec. 1668. Twelve of this name had, in 1834, been gr. at the N. E. coll. of wh. two were at Harv.

PATTERSON or PATTISON, ANDREW, Stratford, came from Scotland, it is said, in 1685, by the Henry and Francis, to Perth Amboy. He was accomp. by Robert McEwen and ten other passeng. wh. fled from the severities of the admin. against the covenanters, as McEwen writes in his journal of his sh. in the fight of Bothwell Bridge, a few yrs. bef. and he is careful to note the day of sail. 5 Sept. the day of land. 18 Dec. of that yr. and the day of reach. Stratford, to wh. they came on foot, 18 Feb. foll. as feeling confid. of more security in Conn. than could be expect. under the proprieta. governm. of East Jersey. No battle in ancient or mod. times is more exactly describ. than this, from wh. the friends of the sufferers escap. to New Eng. as the fervid pen of Sir Walter Scott exhibits it. Patterson m. 19 Feb. 1691, Eliz. Peat, had Sarah, b. 17 Mar. 1694; Charles 4 Apr. 1696; William, 2 July 1698; Eliz. 28 Jan. 1701; Hannah, 18 Apr. 1703; Mary, 27 Mar. 1706; and John, 24 June 1711, Y. C. 1728, wh. liv. to 20 Jan. 1806; and his name is ment. in the town rec. of S. so late as Mar. 1735. ANDREW, Billerica, s. of James the first, m. 1697, Eliz. Kibbee of Charlestown, had James, b. 13 Aug. 1707, or as Whitmore in his accurate Medford Geneal. says, 5 Oct. of that yr. Perhaps in Mar. preced. he went on a voyage and was lost at sea. CHARLES, Stratford, s. of Andrew the first, m. 29 Jan. 1719, Eunice Nicolls or Nichols, had Andrew and Abraham, tw. b. 25 Oct. foll.; Sarah, 3 June 1721; Eliz. 19 Nov. 1722; James 24, bapt. 26 July 1724; and Elnathan, 25 Jan. 1726. DAVID is the name of one of those wretched Scotch prisoners, from Worcester fight, sent out by the John and Sarah from London, Nov. 1651, to be sold in Boston, where they arr. in May foll. Of him, as of nineteen twentieths, or a greater proportion, of his fellow sufferers, no more is ever heard. EDWARD, New Haven 1639, prob. the man nam. by Mason, in his Hist. as one of his soldiers in the Pequot war, 1637, in wh. he did much serv. and perhaps the passeng. in the Christian from London 1635, aged 33, had w. in 1647, but only ch. ment. were Eliz. bapt. July 1644, who m. Thomas Smith of the same, and John in Jan. foll. obt. a gr. of ld. in 1670, sixty acres, "where he can find it," but he prob. d. without sight of it. See 3 Mass. Hist. Coll. VI. 164. EDWARD, Rehoboth 1643; Hingham 1652, where he had Faith, b. 20 Jan. 1656; Dover, 1657, may be the same person, or more than one, at Hingham call. carpenter. JAMES, Billerica, perhaps, but not very likely, br. of David, came prob. in the sad freight list of the John and Sarah from London, Nov. 1651, and if so, he is one of only four or five that prosper. here, among the great crowd of romantic young followers in Scotland of Charles II. wh. in the bloody days of 3 Sept. of the success. yrs. 1650 and 1651, were capt. on the fields of Cromwell's glory at Dunbar and Worcester, and transport. to the colonies to be sold in the shambles like other cattle, of wh. the cargoes to Boston would amount to as many hundreds. He was of B. perhaps carr. by his owner 1659, freem. 1690, and m. 29 May 1662, Rebecca. d. of Andrew Stevenson of Cambridge, had Mary, b. 22 Aug. 1666; James, 28 Feb. 1669, d. young; Andrew, 4 Apr. 1672; John, 8 Apr. 1675; Joseph, 1 Jan. 1678; Rebecca, 18 July 1680, d. young; James, again, 13 Apr. 1683; and Jonathan, 31 Jan. 1686. He serv. in the great war with the Ind. 1675, and with other soldiers, when his merits were duly consid. near. sixty yrs. aft. was reward. with gr. of ld. Narraganset, No. 6, and his gr.s. drew the proper share. His will pro. 1701, names br. in law, Andrew Stevenson. It is by hims. confident. mark. in his descript. or otherwise might have been noted with a slur as that of "a Scotchman." Mary, the eldest ch. m. 30 Jan. 1689, Peter Proctor of Chelmsford. JAMES, Billerica, s. of the preced. rem. to Dunstable, there had w. Mary, prob. brot. from B. s. John, b. 10 Apr. 1711; and a. 1718 rem. to Groton, there d. 1737. No doubt he had other ch. and James of G. Jonathan, Hezekiah, and Mary were their names, but the order or dates of birth for all are unkn. JOHN, Billerica, br. of the preced. m. at Concord, 29 Dec. 1702, Joanna Hall, had Keziah, b. 5 Feb. 1704; Rebecca, 15 Jan. 1706; Hannah, 9 July 1710; Mary, 19 Mar. 1714; and Eliz. 24 Feb. 1723. JOHN, Stratford, s. of the first Andrew, by w. Mary, had Parthenia, b. 29 Nov. 1730, bapt. 28 Mar. foll.; Josiah, 25 Mar. 1732, bapt. 1 Apr. of next yr.; John, 11 Dec. 1734; Ashbel, 3 Apr. bapt. same mo. 1737; Ephraim, 22 Mar. 1739; Stephen, bapt. 3 May 1741; Mary, 16 Jan. 1743; Matthew, 17 Mar. 1745; Isaac, 24 June 1747; and Parthenia, again, 7 May 1749. JONATHAN, br. of the first John, liv. at Watertown, 1707, was a tailor, perhaps connect. with his br. Joseph, rem. perhaps to Deerfield, there m. a. 1713, Mary, d. of deac. Eliezur Hawks, had Jonathan, b. 18 Dec. 1714, d. at 7 yrs.; and Eliezur, 1 Sept. 1716; rem. to Northfield, and d. 1718. His wid. d. 1757, aged 61. JOSEPH, Watertown, tailor, br. of the preced. m. at. Sudbury, 22 Sept. 1701, Mercy, the youngest ch. prob. of John Goodnow the sec. tho. her name by Barry is Mary, had Mercy, b. 1 Sept. 1702; Mary, 16 Aug. 1704; Lydia, 9 Oct. 1706, d. young; Eunice, 19 Apr. 1708; Joseph, 27 Aug. 1710; Hepzibah, 7 Dec. 1713; Sybil, bapt. 27 Nov. 1715; Lydia, again, b. 12 Oct. 1718; and Eliz. 27 Sept. 1727, but this by third w. m. 19 Nov. 1724, Rebecca, wid. of James Livermore, d. of John

Myrick; as the three preced. were by sec. w. Mary; as the first d. 1 Sept. 1710, after b. of Joseph. PETER, Saybrook, m. 11 June 1678, Eliz. Rithway. Geneal. Reg. IV. 140. Judd thot. the surname was Peterson. WILLIAM, Boston 1665, merch. WILLIAM, Stratford, s. of Andrew the first, by w. Ann had Joseph, b. 18 Apr. 1724; Beulah, 4 Aug. 1725; Ann, 8 Sept. bapt. 11 Dec. 1726; Charles, 8, bapt. 14 Apr. 1728; William, 4, bapt. 8 Feb. 1730; Ann, again, 3 July bapt. 1 Aug. 1731; Eunice, 10, bapt. 13 Jan. 1734; Thomas, 24 Oct. 1736, bapt. same day; and Abigail, 6 Apr. 1739. Seven of this name had been gr. at N. E. coll. in 1834, of wh. one was at Harv.

PAUL, BENJAMIN, New Haven 1639, may be the man ment. by Felt, at Salem 1647 with a final *y* added to his name. DANIEL, New Haven 1643, perhaps br. of Benjamin, may be the man who liv. at Kittery 1652, when he acknowl. the governm. of Mass. and was of the gr. jury. EDWARD, Taunton, s. perhaps youngest, of William of the same, m. 23 Aug. 1693, Esther Bobbit. JOHN, Malden, m. 3 May 1657, Lydia, d. of Joel Jenkins, had John, b. 25 Aug. 1658, d. soon; and Lydia, 9 Mar. 1660; perhaps others, certain. Eliz. Dec. 1668; and Joel, Oct. 1676, d. next mo. JOHN, Freetown, s. of William of Taunton, m. 26 May 1692, Dorothy Walker, had Dorothy, and d. 23 Mar. 1718, says the gr.st. and I kn. no more. RICHARD, Boston, a soldier, hired in 1636, for the castle, as in Winth. II. 346, was two yrs. aft. one of the proprs. of Taunton. See Baylies I. 286 and II. 267. Perhaps Hannah, b. at T. 4 Oct. 1657 was his ch. SAMUEL, Dorchester, m. 9 Jan. 1667, Mary, d. of Edward Breck, had Samuel, b. 13 Nov. 1670; Hannah, 8 Nov. 1672; Mary, 27 Mar. 1675; Eliz. 10 Oct. 1677; Ebenezer, 1 May 1680; Priscilla, 11 June 1682; and Susanna, 15 July 1685; was constable 1672, chos. clk. 1689, and he d. 3 Nov. 1690. His wid. m. 15 June 1692, John Tolman, d. 25 Aug. 1720. Samuel, his s. d. 25 Aug. 1726; and Ebenezer d. 13 Oct. 1737. A Hannah P. perhaps his w. d. of sis. Woodie, d. at Roxbury, 10 Nov. 1658, bur. 12 foll. STEPHEN, Kittery, on behalf of his w. a d. of Antipas Maverick, admin. on est. of M. was giv. to him with Edward Gilman 24 Apr. 1682. WILLIAM, Taunton, had James, b. 7 Apr. 1657; John, 10 July 1660; Edward, 7 Feb. 1665; Mary, 8 Feb. 1667; Sarah, 5 July 1668; and Abigail, 15 May 1673; and he d. 9 Nov. 1704.

PAYBODY, or PABODIE. See Peabody.

PAYNE. See Paine.

PAYSON, EDWARD, Roxbury, freem. 13 May 1640, m. 20 Aug. 1640, Ann Parke, perhaps sis. of William, and she d. 10 Sept. of the yr. foll. hav. b. Mary, 8 days bef. who prob. d. young. He m. 1 Jan. 1642, Mary Eliot, d. I presume, of Philip, had John, b. 11, bapt. 18 June

1643; Jonathan, 19, bapt. 22 Dec. 1644; Ann, 26 Apr. bapt. 2 May 1647, d. at 3 yrs.; Joanna, 5 Feb. bapt. 25 Mar. 1649 ; Ann, again, 3, bapt. 30 Nov. 1651 ; Susanna, bapt. 28 Aug. 1653, d. next yr.; Susanna, again, 27 June, bapt. 2 July 1655; Edward, 20, bapt. 28 June 1657, H. C. 1677; Ephraim, bapt. 20 Feb. 1659; Samuel, 21 Sept. 1662 ; and Mary, 19 Mar. 1665; the last three are not in the town rec. as he had rem. to Dorchester. His w. or wid. d. 24 Mar. 1697. Susanna m. 9 Apr. 1673, Samuel Capen; and Mary m. 16 May 1682, Preserved Capen, and she d. 20 Oct. 1708. EDWARD, Rowley, s. of the preced. freem. 1680, ord. 25 Oct. 1682, m. 7 Nov. 1683, Eliz. d. of Rev. Samuel Phillips, with wh. he was colleag. had twenty ch. of wh. the names and dates of seventeen are kn. but one half d. bef. him, and some of the s. were Samuel, H. C. 1716; Edward; Eliot; Stephen; David; and Phillips, of wh. this last d. young. His w. d. 1 Oct. 1724 in her 60th yr. and he m. 1726, Eliz. d. of William Whittingham, wid. of Hon. Samuel Appleton; and d. 22 Aug. 1732. EPHRAIM, Dover, freem. 1685, unless there be error, as I suspect, in the rec. EPHRAIM, Dorchester, s. of Edward the first, freem. 1690, m. 29 May 1684, Catharine, d. of Henry Leadbetter of the same, had Mary, b. 23 July 1685 ; Sarah, 22 Oct. 1686; Ruth, 2 Mar. 1689, prob. d. soon ; Ephraim, 26 Mar. 1693; Ruth, again, 7 Apr. 1697; Jonathan, 19 Aug. 1699; and Susanna, 28 June 1703 ; and he took, as sec. w. Judith, d. of Desire Clap. He d. 18 Oct. 1732, not so old by one yr. as his gr.st. made him. GILES, Roxbury, came in the Hopewell, capt. Bundock, from London 1635, aged 26, with many others of those who sat down there, prob. an Essex man, and perhaps br. of the first Edward, was freem. 18 Apr. 1637, and in that mo. m. Eliz. Dowell, had Eliz. b. 3 Feb. 1640, d. in few days; Samuel, 7 Nov. 1641 ; Eliz. again, 4, bapt. 9 Feb. 1645 ; Sarah, bapt. 16 July 1648; and possib. others, but not ment. in town or ch. rec. as indeed is not in the town rec. this last, bec. he rem. to Dorchester, where the rec. were destroy. by fire. Yet he was deac. at R. and d. 28 Jan. 1689, aged 78. Sarah m. 10 Apr. 1678, Elisha Foster, and next, 26 Mar. 1685, Ebenezer Wiswall, and d. 21 June 1714. Eliz. m. 15 Feb. 1667, Hopestill Foster, and next Edmund Brown. JOHN, Dorchester, freem. 1680. Prob. he was eldest s. of Edward, may have m. Bathsheba, d. of Thomas Tileston, and liv. in Roxbury, there by sec. w. Hannah, had Edward, b. 26 June 1685; Joseph, 24 Feb. 1687; and Benjamin, 25 Oct. 1688. SAMUEL, Roxbury, s. of Giles, m. 31 Mar. 1677, Prudence Lincoln, had no issue, was freem. 1690, d. 12 Apr. 1697. SAMUEL, Dorchester, youngest s. of Edward the first, was freem. 1690, and d. 24 Nov. 1721; by w. Mary, d. of Elder Thomas Wiswall, had Mary, b. 9 Mar. 1689, prob. d. soon ; Samuel, 4 Sept. 1693 ; Mary, again, 9 Apr. 1697 ; and others, as we learn from his will, in Vol. XXII. 150, made 21 Nov. 1721, pro. 4 Dec. foll. five ds. Sarah, Mary, Dorcas, Eliz. and Ann, to ea. of wh. it gives £80, and s. Edward and George, beside Phillips, b. 29 Feb. bapt. 12 Mar. 1704, H. C. 1724, min. of Walpole, ancest. of many disting. clerg. In the Catal. of H. C. the name was erron. print. as I thought, and that he was call. for his gr. gr.f. Philip Eliot; and it was prob. the connex. of his gr. uncle, Rev. Edward of Rowley with Rev. Samuel Phillips, that in the later generat. brought the surname into use for the bapt. name. Misled by the copy of his will, in that public rec. Vol. XXII. wherein the name is plain. giv. in three places, Philip, I long felt confid. of the desir. correction; but on turning to the orig. in the handwriting of the testator, not found without some hours' search, it is just as plain, if not as elegant, chirogr. Phillips in ea. of those three places. How earnest would have been the malediction of Judge Sewall, had he kn. the negligence of his Register. For him the will provid. that part of his sh. of the est. was to be paid after his tak. the sec. degree at the Coll. Samuel's wid. d. 25 May 1727, in her 59th yr. and this is hardly consist. with her being d. of Elder Thomas Wiswall, as Jackson makes her. Of the eldest s. Phillips, H. C. 1754, D. D. a well drawn charact. is in Eliot's Biogr. Dict. and of a younger s. Seth, H. C. 1777, D. D. it will be honor eno. that he was f. of the celebr. Edward, H. C. 1803, D. D. min. of Portland. As this celebr. evangelist was my partic. friend at the univ. and afterwards, I am anxious to correct a petty mistake, by wh. Farmer would magnify his reput. calling him of the fifth descent, the whole line being clerg. from the Rowley min. Out of such a mixt. of falsehood and truth is tradition common. engend. He was sec. in desc. from Philip, and only f. and gr. f. were clerg. In 1834, twenty-two of this name, says Farmer, had been gr. at Harv. Yale and Dart. Seven of the thirteen from Harv. were clerg.

PAYTON, BEZALEEL, Boston 1642, mariner, m. 19 Oct. of that yr. Mary Greenough of Sandwich, sis. of William of Boston, had Sarah, b. 9, bapt. 13 Aug. 1643; Mary, 7, bapt. 17 May 1646; perhaps also Bezaleel; but d. prob. in distant ld. for his inv. was rend. 24 Nov. 1651, and his wid. m. 3 of next mo. William Paddy. Sarah m. 1661 Hudson Leverett; and Mary m. Sampson Shore. ROBERT, Lynn 1639. Lewis.

PEABODY, PAYBODY or PABODIE, FRANCIS, Hampton 1638, perhaps s. of John, came in the Planter, 1635, aged 21, was freem. 18 May 1642, m. Mary, d. of Renold Foster, had John, b. 1643; Joseph, 1644; William, 1646; Isaac, 1648; Sarah, 1650; Hepzibah, 1652; Lydia, 1654; Mary, 1656; Ruth, 22 May 1658, d. bef. her f.; Damaris, 21 Jan. 1660, d. same yr.; Samuel, 4 Jan. 1662, d. at 15 yrs.; Jacob, 28 July 1664; Hannah, 28 May 1668, d. soon; and Nathaniel, 29 July 1669; and d.

19 Feb. 1698. His wid. d. 9 Apr. 1705. The Genealog. Reg. II. 155, from wh. the foregoing is deriv. says, Sarah m. a How, prob. Ephraim or John, of Topsfield, whither the f. rem. bef. 1657. Hepzibah m. a Rea of Salem ; Lydia m. Jacob Perley, wh. may be error for a sec. or third generat. ; and Mary m. John Death of Sudbury or Framingham. ISAAC, Topsfield, s. of the preced. by w. Sarah, had Francis, b. 1 Dec. 1694 ; Mary, 5 Feb. 1696 ; Isaac, 15 Mar. 1697 ; Philadelphia, 28 Sept. 1698 ; Matthew, 10 Dec. 1699 ; William, 26 Jan. 1701, d. young ; Estes, 28 Sept. 1702 ; Joseph, 14 June 1704 ; Sarah, 10 Mar. 1706 ; Ann, 31 May 1707 ; Hepzibah, 25 May 1709 ; and Samuel, 3 Jan. 1711, d. in few days. His will of 21 Oct. 1726, was pro. 2 Jan. foll. JACOB, Topsfield, br. of the preced. m. 12 Jan. 1686, Abigail Towne, had Keziah ; Mercy ; and Jacob, this last b. 9 Nov. 1689 ; and the f. d. 24 of the same mo. The wid. m. 14 Jan. 1696, Thomas Perley. JOHN, Duxbury, one of the proprs. of Bridgewater 1645, made his will 16 July 1649, names his w. Isabel ; eldest s. Thomas ; sec. Francis ; youngest, William ; d. Annis Rouse ; John, s. of John Rouse ; and John, s. of William. * JOHN, Boxford, eldest s. of Francis, m. 23 Nov. 1665, Hannah Andrews ; and had a sec. w. Sarah, but we kn. not, except for the first, wh. was mo. of these ch. John, b. 28 Aug. 1666, d. young ; Hannah ; Thomas, 22 July 1670, d. young ; Mary, 6 Apr. 1672 ; Lydia, 9 Mar. 1674 ; David, 12 July 1678 ; Eliz. 13 Aug. 1680 ; Nathan, 20 July 1682 ; Ruth, 13 Nov. 1684 ; and Moses, 27 Feb. 1687, d. bef. his f. who was freem. 1674, rep. 1689–91, made his will 27 Oct. 1719, and it was pro. Aug. foll. JOSEPH, Boxford, s. of Francis, m. 26 Oct. 1668, Bethia, d. of Edmund Bridges, had Joseph, b. 16 Apr. 1671 ; Jonathan, 1673 ; Sarah, 4 Sept. 1676 ; Samuel, 8 Apr. 1678 ; Bethia, 8 Apr. 1681 ; Lydia, 4 Feb. 1683 ; and Alice, 4 Jan. 1685 ; was freem. 1690, not 1677, as the fam. geneal. has it, made his will 20 Mar. 1721, and d. soon. * WILLIAM, Duxbury, perhaps br. of Francis, m. 26 Dec. 1644, Eliz. eldest d. of John Alden, who d. at Little Compton, 31 May 1717, aged 93, and he d. 13 Dec. 1707 in his 88th yr. Of their ch. we have less exact report than is desir. Bradford says there were five in 1650. His s. John, nam. in the will of his uncle John, was k. by casualty 1669, but he must have had other s. Eliz. his d. m. Nov. 1666, John Rogers of Duxbury. Of his ds. Hannah m. Samuel Bartlett ; Martha m. Samuel Seabury ; and Priscilla m. the Rev. patriot Ichabod Wiswall, who was indignant at Increase Mather's abolition of the independ. of Plymouth Col. He had been rep. 1659, most of the yrs. to 1678. WILLIAM, Little Compton, had two ws. perhaps Judith, who d. 20 July 1714 ; and it may be Ruth, who d. 14 Dec. 1717 ; and he d. 17 Sept. 1744, in his 80th yr. all these at Little Compton, whither his f. the first William had rem. 1680. Descend. of this patri-

arch, it is said, uniform. spell their name Pabodie. WILLIAM, Boxford, s. of Francis may be he who Coffin says m. 8 Dec. 1680, Mary, perhaps d. of Richard Browne, but she prob. liv. not long, and he m. 14 Aug. 1684, Hannah Hale, d. of Thomas the sec. of Newbury, had Stephen, b. 5 Aug. 1685; Mary, 11 Apr. 1687; Ephraim, 23 Apr. 1689; Richard, 7 Feb. 1691; Hannah, Aug. 1693; John, 1 Aug. 1695; Abiel, 1697; and Oliver, 7 May 1698, H. C. 1721, the earliest of the fam. in the Catal. He was freem. 1685, d. Mar. 1699; and his wid. d. 23 Feb. 1733. In 1834, says Farmer, thirteen of the name had been gr. at Harv. and Dart.

PEACH, ARTHUR, Plymouth, a young Irishman, wh. came from Virg. 1636, whither he had gone the yr. preced. aged 20, in the Plain Joan from London, serv. in the Pequot war, tho. "of good parentage and fair conditioned," as Winth. I. 269, tells, was, with exempla. justice, hang. for a very cowardly murder, with two assoc. in detect. of wh. Roger Williams gained much credit. See 3 Mass. Hist. Coll. I. 171–6. Farmer refers to Increase Mather's Ind. Wars, p. 55, and I can add that Baylies, I. 245–8 is equal. full and judicious. But in the contempo. hist. of Gov. Bradford 362–5, the proper study of the case must be sought. GEORGE, Marblehead 1674, may have been s. of John. See Peache. JOHN, Salem or Marblehead 1648–79, said to be b. 1612, of wh. Felt finds ment. 1630, may have been f. of John jr. of M. freem. 1683.

PEACHE or PEACHY, JOHN, Marblehead 1648, may be the same as Peach. THOMAS, Charlestown 1678. Mary perhaps his w. d. 6 Jan. 1691, in 59th yr.

PEACOCK, JOHN, New Haven 1638, at Milford early, perhaps even in 1639, certain. 1646, bef. 1650 rem. to Stratford, there d. 1670, in his will names w. Joyce, no s. and ds. Phebe, w. of Richard Burgess, Mary, who m. 1673, Benjamin Beach; and Deborah, w. of James Clark. RICHARD, Roxbury, a glazier, freem. 22 May 1639, by w. Jane had Samuel, b. 18 Feb. 1640; and Caleb, 1, bapt. 13 Mar. 1642; rem. to Boston, where his w. d. 29 July 1653; and he sold his dwell. ho. at R. to Daniel Weld. He m. 17 Aug. 1654, wid. Margery Shove, who was mo. of Rev. George, and bur. from the ho. of her s. 17 Apr. 1680. SAMUEL, Boston, glazier, s. of the preced. by w. Mary, had Samuel, b. 2 Jan. 1667; Richard, 22 Jan. 1669; Samuel, again, 26 Mar. 1670; Hannah, 20 July 1672; Jonathan, 15 Oct. 1673; and Jane, 19 Dec. 1681; and he d. 1691. Admin. of Richard, perhaps s. of Samuel, was gr. 12 Aug. 1697. WILLIAM, Roxbury 1652, came prob. in the Hopewell, capt. Bundock, from London, 1635, aged 12 yrs. with such a comp. of Eliots and Ruggleses, that he may be well thought to have sprung from Nazing or some neighb. parish to Stanstead in the border of Hertfordsh. m. 12 Apr. 1653, Mary Willis, had William, b. 24 Aug. 1655, d. soon; William, again, 6 July 1657; and Samuel, 24 Aug. 1659; and d. prob. Jan. 1661. WILLIAM, Roxbury, s. of the preced. m. 3 Aug. 1681, Sarah Edsall, had Mary, b. 3 Feb. 1682, d. soon; Sarah, 26 Nov. 1683; Eliz. 16 Aug. 1686; William, 1688; and Samuel, 8 Apr. 1691.

PEAKE, BENJAMIN, Stratford, freem. of Conn. 1669, prob. s. of John. CHRISTOPHER, Roxbury, freem. 4 Mar. 1635, m. 3 Jan. 1637, Dorcas French, had Jonathan, b. 17 Dec. 1637; Dorcas, 1 Mar. 1640; Hannah, 25 Jan. bapt. 12 Feb. 1643, d. at 17 yrs.; Joseph, 12 or 15 Feb. bapt. 23 Mar. 1645; one, unbapt. d. 13 Apr. says the ch. rec. but the town rec. has it, bur. 30 Mar. 1647; ano. bur. 6 Apr. 1648 says the rec. of town; Ephraim, b. 16 Mar. bapt. 11 Apr. 1652; and Sarah, 9 Jan. bapt. 9 Mar. 1656; and he d. 22 May 1666. JOHN, Stratford 1650, with John jr. perhaps his s. in the list freem. 1669. Possib. this name may have been otherwise spelt. JOHN, New London, s. of William, by w. Eliz. had John, b. 1690; Samuel, 1693; William, 1695; and Ruth, 1699; and he d. 25 Oct. of the same yr. JONATHAN, Roxbury, s. of Christopher, m. 15 Aug. 1660, Sarah French, had Hannah, b. 10 June 1661, bapt. 15 June 1662; Jonathan, 10, bapt. 18 Oct. 1663; John, 9 Apr. 1665, d. at 3 mos.; Christopher, d. Oct. 1666; Christopher, again, 9 Feb. bapt. 1 Mar. 1668; John, 13, bapt. 24 Apr. 1670; Joseph, 20, bapt. 24 Dec. 1671, d. at 6 mos.; Sarah, 18, bapt. 25 May 1673; William, 12, bapt. 17 Jan. 1675; and Eliz. 9, bapt. 15 Aug. 1680; was freem. 1690; and he d. 2 June 1700. I suppose his w. d. 14 Oct. 1694. WILLIAM, Scituate 1643, m. 1650, Judith, wid. of Lawrence Litchfield, had Israel, b. 1655; Eleazer, 1657; and William, 1662. The s. Israel, and William, had fam. Deane, 321, gives this name Peaks. WILLIAM, New London 1660, had Sarah, who m. 27 Dec. 1671, Abraham Deane or Dayne; William; and John; Caulkins thinks he d. a. 1685. WILLIAM, Lyme, s. of the preced. m. 24 June 1679, Abigail, d. of John Comstock. In the Hopewell, capt. Bundock, from London, emb. Mary Peak, aged 15; but whether she was relat. to any of the foregoing or to John Peak, who was a fellow passeng. aged 38, is beyond conject.

PEAKEN, JOHN, New Haven, d. 1658. His inv. was tak. 1 Feb. in that yr.

PEALE, Daniel, Marblehead 1651. Felt MS.

PEAPES. See Pepys.

PEARCE. See Pierce.

PEARD, RICHARD, Saco, m. 1669, Jane Naziter, perhaps d. of Michael. Folsom, 187.

PEARSALL, JOHN, Newtown, L. I. 1656. Thompson; but Riker, 83, spells Parcell.

PEARSON, BENJAMIN, Newbury, s. of John of Rowley, m. 20 Jan. 1680, Hannah, d. of Daniel Thurston, had Hannah, b. 3 or 5 Apr. 1681; Phebe, 14 July 1682; Daniel, 25 Dec. 1684; Ruth, 2 Aug. 1687; Abigail, 1 Mar. 1689; Benjamin, 12 Aug. 1690; Sarah, 10 Dec. 1691; Jedediah, Apr. 1694; Mehitable, 18 May 1695; Jonathan, 14 or 25 Dec. 1699; David, 18 Jan. 1702; Oliver, 14 Aug. 1704, d. at 16 yrs.; and Bartholomew; yet all but the last two were b. at Rowley. He d. 16 June 1731, and his wid. foll. him within ten weeks. GEORGE, Boston, merch. See Parsons. JEREMIAH, Rowley 1691, s. of the first John, m. 21 July 1681, Priscilla Hazen, perhaps d. of Edward, had Priscilla, b. 30 Dec. 1682; Miriam, 19 July 1685, d. at 4 yrs.; Hannah, 22 Apr. 1688; John, 10 Apr. 1690; Hepzibah, 10 Dec. 1692; Miriam, again, 8 Feb. 1694; Moses, 26 Mar. 1697; Jeremiah, 12 Sept. 1699; Amos, 5 Jan. 1702; and Hannah, 12 May 1704. He d. 23 Feb. 1737, and his wid. d. 25 Apr. 1752, aged 88 yrs. JOHN, Lynn 1637, had Mary, b. 20 June 1643; Bethia, 15 Sept. 1645; Sarah, 20 Jan. 1648; rem. to Reading, had John, 22 June 1650; and James, 2 Nov. 1652. He d. 17 Apr. 1679, aged a. 64. His will of that mo. ment. w. Maudlin, s. John, ds. Mary Burnap, Bethia Carter, and Sarah Townsend. Mary m. 3 Dec. 1663, Thomas Burnap; Bethia m. a Carter; and Sarah prob. m. 27 Jan. 1669, John Townsend. *JOHN, Rowley 1643, then set up the earliest fulling mill in America, by w. Dorcas, had Mary, b. 21 May 1643, d. young; John, 27 Dec. 1644; Eliz. 14 Oct. 1646; Samuel, 29 July 1648; Dorcas, 21 Apr. 1650; Mary, again, 14 Feb. 1652; Jeremiah, 21 Oct. 1653; Sarah, 3 May 1655, d. in few mos.; Joseph, 21 Oct. 1656, wh. was of Lothrop's comp. and fell in bat. 25 Aug. 1725, near Hatfield; Benjamin, 1 Apr. 1658; Phebe, 13 Apr. 1660; Stephen, 1663; and Sarah, May 1666, d. in few mos. prob. was the freem. of 1647, rep. 1678 and sev. yrs. later, espec. after overthrow of Andros and the anxious ones bef. his com. deac. 24 Oct. 1686, and d. 22 Dec. 1693. His wid. d. 12 Jan. 1703. In the Col. Rec. the name of the rep. is more common. giv. Peirson, but the descend. have spell. with a. Mary m. 20 Dec. 1671, Samuel Palmer; Eliz. m. 8 June 1676, John Hopkinson; and Phebe m. 24 Aug. 1682, Timothy Harris. JOHN, Rowley, s. of the preced. m. 14 Feb. 1671, Mary, d. of John Pickard, had Sarah, b. Apr. 1672; John, 1 Dec. 1674; Joseph, 22 Oct. 1677; Dorcas, 18 Mar. 1680; Jane, 21 Aug. 1684; Hepzibah, 7 Apr. 1689; and Rebecca, 16 Mar. 1693. He d. 19 Mar. 1723, and his wid. d. 13 Apr. 1728. *JOHN, Reading, s. of John of the same, m. Tabitha Kendall, youngest d. of Thomas, had James, b. 20 Nov. 1678; Tabitha, 16 Oct. 1681; John, 6 Dec. 1682; Rebecca, 12 Apr. 1686; Kendall, 3 May 1688; Susanna, 10 Aug. 1690; Mary, 10 Nov. 1692; Thomas, 3 Nov. 1694;

Ebenezer, 29 Dec. 1696; Sarah, 26 Feb. 1699; Abigail, 30 Dec. 1700, d. under 4 mos.; Abigail, again, 16 Feb. 1702; and Eliz. 4 May 1704; but the last eight were b. at Lynn, where he was deac. capt. and rep. 1703 and aft. and his w. d. 17 Oct. 1711. He had sec. w. Martha, and d. 1720. SAMUEL, s. of John of Rowley, m. 6 Dec. 1670, Mary, d. of John Poor of Newbury, had Mary, b. 27 Oct. 1671; and his w. d. the same day. He next m. 16 Apr. 1672, Dorcas Johnson of Haverhill, whose f. I see not, had there, Samuel, 22 Jan. 1673; Salathiel, 17 Jan. 1675, d. in few days; Eliz. 25 Apr. 1677; Peter, 13 Mar. 1679, d. at two mos.; John, 1 Mar. 1680; James, 28 Jan. 1682, d. at two days; Stephen, 21 Apr. 1683; Peter, again, 17 June 1686; and Sarah, 26 Dec. 1688. He rem. from H. to Newbury, after the Ind. destroy. the town. STEPHEN, Rowley, youngest s. of John the first of the same, m. 11 Nov. 1684, Mary French, had Eliz. b. 5 Aug. 1685; Stephen, 9 June 1687; Martha, 6 July 1689; Mary, 7 Jan. 1691; Jonathan, 27 Oct. 1693; Patience, 26 July 1697; and Hepzibah, 20 Jan. 1699; and he d. 25 Jan. 1706. His wid. d. 28 Sept. 1730.

PEASE, HENRY, Boston 1630, came that yr. no doubt, in the fleet, with w. Susan, and d. Susan, who was old eno. to join with the ch. 16 Aug. 1635, f. and mo. being earlier, freem. 3 Sept. 1634. His w. was bur. 25 Dec. 1645, and he had sec. w. Bridget, adm. of our ch. May 1647, and he d. 7 Aug. 1648, as his old master says. Winth. II. 355. JOHN, Salem, came in the Francis from Ipswich, Co. Suff. 1634, aged 27, with ch. Robert, 3, and two serv. in co. with his br. Robert. They were prob. from Great Baddow, near Chelmsford in Co. Essex. He perhaps, had gr. of ld. 1637; was not, we may safely judge, one of the first four sett. of Martha's Vineyard, as by doubtf. tradit. report. d. a. 1639. His wid. Margaret wh. unit. with the ch. 1639, had come with his s. John prob. in a later sh. d. 1644, and in her will of 1 Sept. in that yr. ment. br. Robert, and s. Robert. ‖ JOHN, Salem, s. of the preced. by w. Mary had John, b. 30 Mar. 1654; Robert, 14 Mar. 1656; Mary, 8 Oct. 1658; Abraham, 5 Apr. 1662; and Jonathan, 2 Jan. 1668. His w. d. 3 days aft. and he m. 8 Oct. 1669, Ann Cummings, prob. d. of Isaac the first of Ipswich, had James, 23 Oct. 1670; Isaac, 15 July 1672; and Abigail, 15 Oct. 1675. He was of ar. co. 1661, freem. 1668, was a capt. and with many neighb. obt. gr. of ld. at Springfield a. 1681, that part wh. bec. Enfield 1683; there his w. d. 29 June 1689, and he d. 8 July foll. and his d. Abigail, d. the next day. All the six s. outliv. him, and descend. are very num. Ano. John, and Lucy, perhaps his w. are ment. by Felt, II. 578, as favorers of Gorton in 1644. To this John belongs the earlier distinct. for a worse heresy, as the Court's order in Nov. 1635, proves, "that he shall be whipt, and bound to his good behav. for strik. his mo. Mrs. Weston, and deriding of her, and other ill carriage." See Col. Rec. I. 155. JOHN, Norwich, was complain. of 1672, for liv. alone, not going to ch. ROBERT, Salem. br. of John the first, came in the same sh. 1634, aged 27, by the custom ho. list, wh. gives the same age to his br. of wh. therefore we may doubt one; and to me it seems prob. that this was the elder. He join. to the ch. 1643, and 15 Oct. had bapt. his ch. Nathaniel, Sarah, and Mary, was liv. in 1655, being keeper of the cattle, 100 cows, in one part of the town. Felt, I. 278. ROBERT, Salem, perhaps s. of John, with w. Sarah, was charg. with witchcraft in 1692, and Mary P. also, who plead. guilty of the nonsense. SAMUEL, Boston, had command of a vessel, fitted out to pursue a pirate, and in the vineyard sound succeed. in mak. her his prize, tho. mortal. wound. 4 Oct. 1689, in the conflict. See the acco. by Benjamin Gallop and others. Genealog. Reg. II. 393.

PEASLEE, JOSEPH, Newbury 1641, freem. 22 June 1642, beside ch. brot. prob. from Eng. of wh. Jane wh. m. 10 Dec. 1646, John Davis, was one, had Sarah, b. 20 Sept. 1642; Joseph, 9 Sept. 1646; and Eliz. rem. to Haverhill and Salisbury; at one time was the gifted br. in lieu of a min. to the ch. at Amesbury; d. 3 Nov. 1661; in his will of 11 Nov. preced. names w. Mary, and ch. Mary, beside those three, and gr.d. Sarah. Mary m. Joseph Whittier of H. In Geneal. Reg. VIII. 161, date of his d. is 3 Dec. 1660. JOSEPH, Haverhill 1677, s. of the preced. a physician, m. Ruth Barnard, had Nathaniel, b. 25 June 1682; and Ruth; perhaps others.

PEAT, JOHN, a husbandman from Duffill parish in Co. Derby, came in the Hopewell, capt. Bundock, from London, 1635, aged 38; but where he sett. is unkn. unless he was of Stratford, and there d. early in 1678, leav. w. Sarah, and ch. Samuel, John, Joseph, Sarah, Eliz. and Jane. At S. 19 Feb. 1691, Eliz. Peat m. Andrew Patterson, a refugee from tyranny in Scotland five yrs. bef.

PECK, BENJAMIN, New Haven 1686, s. of Henry, m. 29 Mar. 1670, Mary, prob. d. of Richard Sperry of the same, had Benjamin, b. 4 Jan. foll.; Mary, 23 Sept. 1672; Joseph, 26 Feb. 1676; Esther, 1679; Ebenezer, 5 Jan. 1684; was a propr. 1685, and may have had more ch. CALEB, Greenwich, sec. s. of Rev. Jeremiah, rem. a. 1700 to Concord, Mass. there d. 10 Mar. 1725, without ch. prob. never m. ELEAZER, Wallingford 1670, s. of Henry of New Haven, m. 10 May 1709, Hannah, d. of Joshua Hotchkiss; but whether he had ch. is unkn. HENRY, New Haven, by w. Joan had Eleazer, b. prob. 10 Mar. 1644, d. soon; Joseph, and Benjamin, tw. 5 Sept. 1647; Eleazer, again; and Eliz. b. 16, bapt. 24 Mar. 1650. He d. soon, for his will was made 30 Oct 1651, and his inv. is found next mo. The prop. was giv. to w. and four ch. of wh. only Joseph is nam. Wrong parent is assign. to the tw. in Geneal. Reg. IX. 362. ICHABOD, Rehoboth, was of Gallup's comp. 1690, in the expedit. of Sir William Phips against Quebeck. ISRAEL, Rehoboth, 1668, was prob. s. of Richard, and brot. by him in the Defence, 1635, then aged 7 yrs. had Israel, b. 18 Dec. 1674 ; and by w. Bethia, says Col. rec. had Bethia, 2 Jan. 1684. *JEREMIAH*, Saybrook, s. of William, b. in London, prob. in 1623, says the fam. geneal. was brot. a. 1637, and in Mather's Hecatompolis is mark. H. C. but without any support from the Catal. kept a sch. at Guilford 1656 to 60. He m. 12 Nov. 1656, Joanna, d. of Robert Kitchell, taught the gr. sch. at New Haven 1660, and next yr. was min. at S. but in 1667 rem. to Newark, N. J. there resid. to 1674, and at Elizabethtown to 1678, aft. wh. he rem. to Greenwich, where he was min. to 1689, and then went to Waterbury as the first min. and there d. 7 June 1699, aged 76. His ch. were Samuel, b. at G. 18 Jan. 1659 ; Ruth, at N. H. 3 Apr. 1661 ; Caleb, at S. 1663 ; Ann, at S. 1665 ; Jeremiah, at Newark, or G. 1667 ; and Joshua, at N. 1673. His wid. d. 1711. Ruth m. 1 June 1681, Jonathan Atwater ; and Ann m. May 1690, Thomas Stanley of Farmington ; and Joshua d. at W. unm. 14 Feb. 1736. *JEREMIAH, Waterbury, s. of the preced. m. 14 June 1704, Rachel, youngest d. of Obadiah Richards, was constable 1713, rep. 1720, deac. at new ch. in W. 1739, and d. 1751. His ch. were Joanna, b. 12 Apr. 1705 ; Jeremiah, 9 Nov. 1706 ; Rachel, 10 May 1709 ; Ann, 10 Mar. 1713 ; Mary, 1 Oct. 1715 ; Phebe, 26 Jan. 1717 ; Ruth, 8 Feb. 1719 ; Esther, 27 June 1721 ; and Martha, 4 May 1725. JOHN, Hartford, s. of Paul, as may be thot. yet must seem very young to have first b. John, 17 May 1661, even if we be so bold as to add two yrs. to that count ; but the rec. proceeds to enrich him with Eliz. 7 Oct. 1664 ; Sarah, 20 June 1668 ; Joseph, 6 Mar. 1671 ; Ruth, 21 Dec. 1677 ; Susanna, Oct. 1680 ; and Jonathan, 6 Oct. 1683. Wh. was his w. or when he d. is not seen. JOHN, New Haven, s. of William of the same, freem. 1669, m. 3 Nov. 1664, Mary, d. of John Moss, had Mary, b. 4 Mar. 1666 ; Eliz. 1668, d. soon ; John, 16 Mar. 1670, d. in few ds. ; John, again, Aug. 1671 ; Eliz. 29 Dec. 1673 ; Lydia, 1 May 1677 ; Ruth, 20 July 1679 ; Abigail, 16 Mar. 1682 ; Ann, 3 Nov. 1684, d. soon ; and Ann, again, Mar. 1686 ; but the last six were b. at Wallingford, where his w. d. 16 Nov. 1725. JOHN, Rehoboth, prob. s. of Joseph of the same, m. a d. of John Smith of Dedham, had Rebecca, b. 5 Apr. 1674 ; Ann, 17 July 1677 ; Nathaniel, 6 July 1680 ; Abigail, 12 Mar. 1683 ; beside Esther, rememb. in the will of her gr.mo. and prob. the eldest ch. wh. m. 29 Dec. 1680, Jonathan Wilmarth. JOHN, Hadley 1669, may be that soldier k. by the Ind. 2 Sept. 1675, at Northfield. *JOSEPH, Hingham, came in the Diligent, arr. at Boston 10 Aug. 1638, from Ipswich in

Suffk. with w. three ch. two men and three maid serv. freem. 13 Mar. 1639, rep. 1639–42, rem. 1645 to Rehoboth, there d. 22 Dec. 1663. Prob. he had liv. at Hingham in Norf. for his suppos. br. Robert was min. in that pleasant town many yrs. See Lincolns' Hist. of H. and Centu. Disc. JOSEPH, New Haven, perhaps br. of Henry, resid. from 1643–9, then adm. freem. and next yr. rem. to Milford, there m. Alice, wid. of John Burwell, had Eliz. bapt. 1651; Joseph, 1653; and John, b. 4 Mar. 1655. His w. d. 19 Dec. 1666, and he m. 1669, Mary, d. of a wid. Richards, but the name of her f. is not seen, had Mary, b. 1670. He was liv. 1687 at M. as was also s. Joseph. JOSEPH, Lyme, youngest s. of William, by w. Sarah had Sarah, b. 4 Aug. 1663; Joseph, 12 Mar. 1667, d. at 10 yrs.; Eliz. 9 Sept. 1669; Deborah, 31 July 1672; Hannah, 14 Sept. 1674; Ruth, 19 Aug. 1676; Samuel, 29 July 1678; and Joseph, 20 Mar. 1680. He was a valu. citiz. town clk. and deac. d. 25 Nov. 1718; and his wid. d. 14 Sept. 1726, aged 90. JOSEPH, New Haven, s. of Henry, m. 28 Nov. 1672, Sarah, d. of Roger Alling, had Sarah, b. 11 Sept. foll.; Joseph, 9 Oct. 1675; Samuel, 29 Dec. 1677; James, 17 Feb. 1680; John, 6 Oct. 1682; Eliphalet, 12 May 1685; Abigail, 2 May 1686; Mary, 6 Oct. 1689; and Ebenezer, 2 May 1693. JOSEPH, Hartford, youngest s. of Paul, by w. Ruth had Eliz. b. 1686; Ruth, 1692; both d. young; Joseph, 1694; and Ruth, again, 1696; and he d. 26 June 1698. His wid. m. 1699, John Hoskins, as his sec. w. NATHANIEL, Hingham, perhaps s. of Joseph, may have been sent by his f. from Eng. bef. he brot. resid. of his fam. in 1635, rem. to Rehoboth, there had sh. in div. of ld. 1668; by w. Deliverance had Elisha, b. 19 Apr. 1675, and she d. 30 Apr. foll. He d. 25 Aug. 1676. NATHANIEL, Boston, requir. to give security, 11 Jan. 1687, to Sect. Randolph, for license to be m. during the governm. of Sir E. Andros that was, if possib. more contempt. than odious. See 3 Mass. Hist. Coll. VII. 170. *NICHOLAS, Rehoboth, prob. s. of Joseph, had fam. of wh. we kn. only, that a young ch. d. in Aug. 1676; and that Elisha was b. 4 Apr. 1683. He was rep. 1669, and 10 yrs. more, and a lieut. The milit. spirit was, I suppose, perpet. for two of the name, perhaps his s. Nicholas and Ichabod partook in the wild expedit. against Quebec 1690, and Nicholas was a corpo. of Gallop's comp. Perhaps neither came safe home. PAUL, Hartford 1639, was not an orig. propr. nor is it kn. from what town in Mass. he went. More do we regret, that no light can be found to indicate from what part of Eng. or in what sh. he came; but the name of his w. was Martha, and of ch. Paul, b. 1639; Martha, 1641; Eliz. 1643; John, 22 Dec. 1645; Samuel, 1647; Joseph, 22 Dec. 1650; Sarah, 1653; Hannah, 1656; and Mary, 1662, wh. m. John Andrew, and liv. to 1752. His will of 25 June 1695, was pro. 15 Jan. foll. he hav. d. 23

Dec. aged 87 yrs. Martha m. 8 June 1665, John Cornwell. Eliz. m. it is said, a House of Wallingford; Sarah m. Thomas Clark of Hartford; and Hannah m. 12 May 1680, John Shepherd of Hartford. Two more ds. are by some tradit. giv. to this first Paul, one, without a name of bapt. is said to have m. Joseph Benton of Tolland; and the other call. Ruth, wh. is made to m. 12 May 1680, Thomas Beach of Wallingford; but neither is very prob. PAUL, Hartford, s. of the preced. m. Eliz. d. of John Baysey, had Paul, b. in 1666; John, 1672; Martha, 1676; Samuel, 1680; Hannah, 1681; William, 1686; and Ruth, 1688; and he d. 1725. RICHARD, came in the Defence from London, 1635, emb. Saturday, 11 July; and no doubt sailing next week, aged 33, with Margery, perhaps his w. aged 40, and Israel, 7 with Eliz. 4, both likely eno. to be his ch. See 3 Mass. Hist. Coll. VIII. 269. How long, after arr. at Boston, he contin. there, or whither he rem. is uncert. My conject. is that he short. aft. liv. at Rehoboth. In the Geneal. Reg. XIV. 320 this name is by Mr. Drake writ. Perk; and his eyes engag. on the same ancient MS. as mine, might seem more trustworthy, as younger. But since my reading was not chang. by the skilful keeper of her Majesty's rec. in his exquisite collat. 3 Mass. Hist. Coll. X. 130, I may trust the punctilious student to follow wh. seems to him more correct. ROBERT, Hingham, prob. br. of Joseph, was bred at Magdalen Coll. Cambr. where he had his degr. of A. B. and A. M. the latter 1603, was min. over 30 yrs. at Hingham, Co. Norfk. yet was harass. for nonconform. to some of the ceremon. by Bp. Harsnet, his diocesan, whose imprudence in honor of the ch. was so gr. as to excite complaint from the peop. of Norwich in 1623 to the Ho. of Commons in Parl. Two successors in that see were milder, White and Corbet, especial. the latter, but when Wren, that bird of ill omen, came to the cathedral, no puritan could long serve at the altar. Mather gains the delight of tell. in his Magn. how this Peck was put under a bushel, III. 214. He came with w. two ch. and two serv. in the Diligent, 1638, and on 28 Nov. of that yr. was ord. freem. 13 Mar. foll. but soon aft. the overthr. of the absol. rule by the Long Parliam. he emb. 27 Oct. 1641, with w. and s. Joseph, for home, and went back to his old parsonage, there d. 1656. Brook's Purit. III. 263–5. SAMUEL, Hartford, s. of Paul, had Samuel, b. 1672, but I know not whether he had more, or wh. was his w. He d. 1696. SAMUEL, Greenwich, eldest s. of Rev. Jeremiah, m. 27 Nov. 1686, Ruth Ferris, perhaps d. of Peter of Stamford, had Samuel, b. Mar. 1688; Jeremiah, 29 Dec. 1690; Joseph, 1 May 1692; David, 15 Dec. 1694; Nathaniel, 15 Aug. 1697; Eliphalet, a. 1699; Theophilus, Mar. 1702; Peter, a. 1704; and Robert, a. 1706. He was long in high esteem, and his w. d. 17 Sept. 1745, aged 83, and he d. 28 Apr. 1746. *SAMUEL, Rehoboth, perhaps s. of Joseph of the same, was rep. 1689, at Plymouth, and 1692, under new chart. at Boston. He had w. Sarah, wh. was bur. 27 Oct. 1673 ; and he m. 21 Nov. 1677, Rebecca Hunt, wid. of Peter, d. of sec. Stephen Paine of R. had Noah, b. 21 Aug. 1678 ; d. Jael, 14 June 1680, bur. next mo.; Rebecca, 22 Oct. 1681, d. next yr.; beside Judith, wh. was bur. 20 Feb. 1682.   SIMON, Hingham 1657, perhaps s. of Robert, m. Hannah, d. of Joseph Farnsworth, had Joseph, wh. prob. d. young; and she d. 16 Apr. 1659.   He m. 1 Feb. 1661, Prudence, d. of Edward Clap of Dorchester, had Joseph, again, perhaps bapt. 15 Feb. 1663, and d. young ; John, b. 20 Apr. 1667 ; Sarah, 4 June 1669 ; and Joseph, again, 2 July 1670, prob. d. in few days. His name is misprint. Peke in the Sumner Geneal.   Geneal. Reg. VIII.   THOMAS, Boston 1652, shipwright, constable 1673, by w. Eliz. had Eliz. b. 19 Jan. 1653 ; Rachel, 21 Jan. 1655 ; and Joseph, 11 Dec. 1656 ; beside THOMAS, elder than either, wh. was a shipwright aft. his f.   Possib. John, who was a skilful shipbuild. f. of the late emin. naturalist, William D. Peck, H. C. 1782, of wh. good memoir is found in 2 Mass. Hist. Coll. X. 161, may have been of this fam.   WILLIAM, New Haven, a merch. from London, b. 1601, with w. Eliz. and s. Jeremiah, came prob. in the Hector, as compan. with Govs. Eaton and Hopkins, Rev. John Davenport, and the s. of the Earl of Marlborough, arr. at Boston 26 June 1637, was one of the first compact for N. H. in June 1639, an orig. propr. freem. 29 Oct. 1640, deac. from 1659 to his d. had John ; Joseph, bapt. 17 June 1641 ; and Eliz. 7 May 1643, not 6, as pr. in Geneal. Reg. IX. 262, for that was Saturday.   The harvest of blunders in that list of bapt. is not chargeab. to the very careful transcr. Henry White, Esq. but I fear the names assign. for parents by conject. in that docum. may sometimes be erron. as in this instance, for the ch. Eleazar and 2d Eliz. are neither in fam. geneal. allow. to the deac.   His w. d. 5 Dec. 1683, on a visit to her s. at Lyme, and he m. Sarah, wid. of William Holt, and d. 4 Oct. 1694.   His gr.st. is still to be seen in the cemet.   By the rec. of Lyme (where he d. at the ho. of his s. Joseph) the age is 83 ; but New Haven says, at the reput. age of 90.   As a gen. rule, the shorter term of a prolong. life, when two or more dates are report. must be prefer. but, in this instance, to ascertain the exact truth we may safe. presume, that the s. at whose ho. the f. d. wrote the acco. and the greater number may be adopt.   The only d. his youngest ch. Eliz. m. 1661, Samuel Andrews.   In his will, of 9 Mar. 1689, made at N. H. the sec. w. and his four ch. are ment. but no more.   Sixteen of this name had in 1834 been gr. at the N. E. coll. of wh. four were of Yale, three of Harv.

PECKER, JAMES, Charlestown 1658, said to have been b. 1622, perhaps had w. Eliz. d. of John Friend of Salem, was aft. at Haverhill, and last, a. 1682 at Boston.

PECKHAM, or PECKUM, JOHN, Newport 1639, prob. the same person, by Farmer called Joseph, wh. was one of the found. of the Bapt. ch. He is in the list of freem. 1655. STEPHEN, Dartmouth 1686, perhaps s. of the preced.

PECKIT, JOHN, Stratford 1670. Perhaps the name was obscure in the MS.

PEDINGTON. See Redington.

PEDRICK, JOHN, Marblehead 1674, had been there many yrs. His will was of 2 Aug. 1686, and ment. w. Meriam, eldest s. John, and eight more ch. Benjamin, Agnes, Mary, Ann, Sarah, Meriam, Eliz. and Joanna. One of these ds. was prob. w. of John Stacy; one of John Parrot; and ano. of Henry Prentall, as he calls ea. of these his s.-in-law. A John *Pedick* is nam. of Marblehead at the same time, but of him I kn. nothing.

PEEK, GEORGE, Marblehead 1674.

PELHAM, EDWARD, Newport, s. of Herbert, had w. Freelove, as Barry, 155, says, tho. Jackson, 387, wh. acknowledges her, makes the first w. Godsgift, d. of Gov. Benedict Arnold, wh. also had Freelove, and it may well be that Pelham took both. Jackson adds that he d. 20 Sept. 1730, and names the ch. Eliz. Edward, and Thomas. ‡∥ HERBERT, Cambridge, brot. in 1638, d. Penelope, when he came over, aft. befriend. our cause ten yrs. as a mem. of the comp. in London, where he may have been a lawyer, m. sec. w. Eliz. wid. of Roger Harlakenden, d. of Godfrey Basseville Esq. of Co. York, here had Mary, b. prob. 12 Nov. 1640; Frances, prob. 9 Nov. 1643; but in the Geneal. Reg. IV. 182, Mr. Pilsbury's copy of the rec. that is, I think, exact, gives the same yr. for both, and one must be wrong; beside Herbert, 3 Oct. 1645; wh. d. or was bur. 2 Jan. 1646. He was a gent. from Co. Lincoln, matric. at Magdalen Hall, Oxford, 12 Nov. 1619, in his 18th yr. and Gov. Hutchinson says, he was of that fam. wh. attain. the highest rank in the peerage one hundred yrs. ago, as Duke of Newcastle. He was much engag. in public serv. promoting planta. of Sudbury, where he had gr. of ld. 1644, ar. co. 1639, was chos. an Assist. 1645, being made a freem. at the same time; first treas. of Harv. Coll. 1643, and went home in 1649, liv. at Buer's hamlet, Co. Essex, but was bur. in Suffk. 1 July 1673. His will of 1 Jan. preced. names ch. Waldegrave, Edward, Henry, and Penelope, perhaps all, certain. first and last, by his first w. wh. was a Waldegrave. His wid. d. 1 Apr. 1706, in her 84th yr. and was bur. at Marshfield. Penelope m. 1657, Gov. Josiah Winslow. JOHN, perhaps br. of Herbert, came in the Susan and Ellen, from London, 1635, aged 20, with Penelope, 16, " she being to pass to her br's planta." as the custom ho. rec. says. Possib. both were under care of Saltonstall, wh. with w. and ch. were in the same sh. See Hutch. Coll. 59. The young lady unit. with the ch. of Boston, 24 Mar. 1639, and in 1641, m. the Gov. Bellingham, wh. prevail. on her to give up ano. engagem. as in Winth. II. 43, relat.; but of the jilt. man we hear no more. NATHANIEL, a scholar, H. C. 1651, perhaps s. of William, lost in the voyage to London of the sh. of James Garrett with fellow passeng. Thomas Mayhew, John Davis, and Jonathan Ince, other scholars. *WILLIAM, Sudbury, perhaps br. of John, came in the fleet with Winth. losing his passage with the Gov. s. Henry, by going on shore at Cowes, from the Arbella, and trusting fortune for ano. sh. req. adm. as freem. 19 Oct. 1630, tho. I do not see evid. of his taking the oath; was capt. of the milit. 1644, selectman 1645 and 6, and rep. 1647, was in Eng. 1652, when Johnson wrote his book.

PELL, JOHN, Fairfield, s. of Rev. Dr. John of London, came in 1670, to rec. the est. wh. his uncle Thomas left him at F. but no more is kn. of him. A letter of introd. for him to Gov. Winth. by his friend William, Lord Brereton, from London, 23 June 1670, is in my possess. JOSEPH, Lynn, freem. 14 Mar. 1639, of wh. it seems strange that we kn. no more, exc. from our Prob. rec. where his inv. 25 Apr. 1650, makes him butcher of Boston, leav. small prop. with wid. and childr. to divide it. See Geneal. Reg. VII. 234. *THOMAS, New Haven, came from London in the Hopewell, capt. Bundock, 1635, aged 22, call. in the custom ho. paper, a tailor, he, of course, sat down somewhere in Mass. but the town is unkn. Perhaps he went early to Saybrook; in the Pequot war, 1637, serv. under Mason; and prob. in 3 or 4 yrs. he foll. the attract. of Gov. Eaton, after 1646 m. the wid. of Francis Brewster, in June or July 1650 rem. to Fairfield, was made freem. 1662, rep. 1665, d. soon after the date of his will, 21 Sept. 1669. It gave most of his est. to his neph. John, s. of his only br. Rev. John of London, D. D. WILLIAM, Boston 1634, tallow chandler, freem. 6 May 1635, disarm. for his dangerous opinions, 1637, had Mary, b. 30 June bapt. 14 Sept. 1634, wh. m. 1 Nov. 1655, Richard George of B.; Nathaniel, bapt. 29 Apr. 1638, d. in few mos.; Hannah, 7 days old, 20 Dec. 1640; Deborah, 2 June 1644; and perhaps more. He may have taken, as sec. w. Eliz. wid. of Nathaniel Heaton. If so, she had third h. John Maynard, and outliv. him.

PELLET, or PELLATE, DANIEL, Concord, perhaps s. of Thomas, was freem. 1690. THOMAS, Concord, m. 5 Mar. 1660, Mary Dane or Deane, perhaps d. of Thomas, was freem. 1690.

PELTON, JOHN, Boston, very early, had est. describ. in the book of possns. rem. to Dorchester, his eld. s. John was bapt. 2 Mar. 1645. In his will of 3 Jan. 1681, pro. 10 Mar. foll. he names w. Susanna, s.

John, Samuel, and Robert, the youngest, beside d. Mary. To Samuel was gr. admin. of Robert, lost at sea, July 1683.

PEMBER, THOMAS, New London 1686, had there bapt. in 1692, Mercy, Thomas, and Eliz.; in 1694, Ann; and in 1696, John; but only four of these with w. Agnes, were liv. at his d. by drown. 27 Sept. 1711.

PEMBERTON, BENJAMIN, Boston, s. of James, was freem. 1690. His will of 8, pro. 27 Mar. 1709, ment. w. Eliz. and four ch. but names only eldest s. Benjamin, then under 17 yrs. EBENEZER, Boston, s. of James the sec. was min. of the O. S. or third ch. of wh. his f. was one of the found. ord. collea. with Willard, 28 Aug. 1700, d. 13 Feb. 1717; was f. of Ebenezer, H. C. 1721. JAMES, Charlestown, came prob. in the fleet with Winth. req. adm. as freem. 19 Oct. 1630, but that he ever took the o. does not appear; by w. Alice, wh. join. the ch. Aug. 1633, had James, bapt. 14 Sept. of that yr. prob. d. young; Mary, 3 Apr. 1636; Sarah, 30 Dec. 1638; and John, 24 Apr. 1642; perhaps rem. to Hull for short time, a. 1647; but d. at Malden, 5 Feb. 1662. His will of 23 Mar. 1661, made at M. mentions w. s. John and his w. Margaret, ds. Sarah, and Mary, with her h. Edward Barlow, and their childr. Sarah m. 30 Oct. 1668, Samuel Gibson. JAMES, Newbury 1646, freem. 1648, had John, b. 16 Feb. 1648, rem. to Boston, bec. one of the found. of O. S. ch. by w. Sarah had Thomas, b. 17 Feb. 1653; Joseph, 2 July 1655; Benjamin, 26 Apr. 1660; Mary, 13 July 1662; Benjamin, again, 11 Mar. 1666; Jonathan, 28 Aug. 1668; Elinor, 3 Feb. 1672, prob. the same as that Ebenezer, bapt. 11 Feb. 1672, H. C. 1691, bef. ment. and d. 10 Oct. 1696. JOHN, Boston, 1632, freem. 1 Apr. 1634, rem. to Newbury; and Coffin says his w. d. 1646. Perhaps he ret. to Boston, m. Sarah, d. of Thomas Marshall, the shoemaker, and in 1662 liv. at that part call. Winnesemet. JOSEPH, New London, s. of James, had liv. some time at Westerly bef. 1679, had two s. James and Joseph, who, aft. his d. 14 Oct. 1702, were taken by the wid. Mary to Boston, as Caulkins, 345, tells; while two ds. Mary, w. of Alexander Baker, and Eliz. w. of Jonathan Rogers, contin. to liv. at that part of New London, now Montville. But the wid. went back to Boston, as from the will of her s. James, Mar. 1712, is kn. THOMAS, Boston, s. of James, by w. Hannah had Eliz. b. 17, bapt. 23 June 1678; James, 4 June 1680, d. very soon; Mehitable, bapt. 17 July 1681; James, again, 3, bapt. 10 Sept. 1682; Thomas, 17, bapt. 22 Mar. 1685; Jane, b. 18 Mar. 1686; and Mary, 26 Oct. 1688; was a surgeon in that unhappy exped. of Phips against Quebec, 1690, and d. 26 July 1693.

PEMBROKE, ELKANAH, Boston, one of the found. of Brattle street ch. may have sprung from Dedham, where in 1643 was one with this surname.

PENDALL, WILLIAM, New London 1676, shipwright, m. Mehitable, d. of Ralph Parker.

PENDLETON, * ‖ BRYAN, Watertown, an early sett. freem. 3 Sept. 1634, help. to sett. Sudbury, of wh. he was selectman some yrs. but rep. bef. and aft. for W. betw. 1636 and 48 six yrs. rem. to Ipswich perhaps, certain. to Portsmouth, of wh. he was rep. some yrs. then rem. to Saco, Winter harbour, thence after near a dozen yrs. driv. by the Ind. war, Aug. 1676, went again to Portsmouth, there made his will 9 Aug. 1677, wh. was pro. 5 Apr. 1681. He was capt. and major many yrs. left w. Eleanor, s. James and d. Mary, wh. m. Seth Fletcher. CALEB, Westerly 1679. JAMES, Watertown, s. of Bryan, by w. Mary had James, b. 1 Nov. 1650; she d. 7 Nov. 1655; and he m. sec. w. 29 Apr. 1656, at Sudbury, Hannah, d. of Edmund Goodenow, had Bryan, b. 27 Sept. 1659; Joseph, Dec. 1661; Edmund, prob. 24 June 1664; Ann, 12 Nov. 1667; Caleb, 8 Aug. 1669; and James, older or younger, nam. in the will of his gr.f. He was one of the found. of the first ch. at Portsnouth 1671, but perhaps had his f's. love of rem. and liv. at Stonington 1674-8, then call. capt. and serv. in the war against Philip 1676; was at Westerly 1686 to 1700. JOSEPH, Boston 1651, witness that yr. to the will of Robert Turner, may have been s. of Bryan.

PENFIELD, SAMUEL, Lynn 1650, m. 30 Nov. 1675, Mary Lewis, had Samuel, b. 17 Sept. 1676; and Mary, 24 Oct. 1678; and at Rehoboth, John, 30 May 1681 or after; in 1688 liv. at Bristol with w. and five ch. Mary m. at Taunton 14 Apr. 1698, Jeremiah Fairbanks. THOMAS, Rehoboth, had Sarah, b. 20 Feb. 1681. WILLIAM, Middletown 1663. Hinman 62.

PENGILLY, JOHN, Springfield, had been made freem. 1678 at Ipswich, and rem. to S. that yr. liv. in that part call. now Suffield, was liv. 1728. No doubt he was Welsh or Cornish, but the print. Col. Rec. V. 539 makes the surname Bengilley. I prefer the reading of Paige, yet admit the usual correctn. of the State chirogr. Pulsifer.

PENHALLOW, ‡SAMUEL, Portsmouth, b. 2 July 1665, at St. Mabyn, near Bodmin, in Cornwall, as he tells us, and verifying the jingle of Camden's Remains:

By Tre, Ros, Pol, Lan, Caer, and *Pen*
You may know the most Cornish men.

He came with Rev. Charles Morton, under wh. he had prob. stud. at Newington Green, arr. at Charlestown 1686, join. the ch. there late in Feb. 1687, went soon to Portsmouth, m. 1 July 1687, Mary, d. of Pres. John Cutt, was counsellor, secr. and many yrs. treasr. of the Prov. judge of the Sup. Ct. 1714, and Ch. J. 1717 to his d. 2 Dec. 1726; yet in our day most thot. of as the histor. of the later Ind. Wars. His ch. were JOHN, wh. m. Ann, d. of Hon. Jacob Wendell, was capt. and d. bef. 1736;

Eliz. Joseph, Richard, Susanna, and Benjamin, H. C. 1723, d. young; and descend. are still found at P.

PENINGTON, EPHRAIM, New Haven, sw. alleg. 1644, had Ephraim, b. 1645; and Mary, 1646, both bapt. 22 Oct. 1648; and he d. 1660, leav. wid. and these two ch. EPHRAIM, New Haven, s. of the preced. m. at Milford, 25 Oct. 1667, Mary, d. of John Brockett.

PENLEY, SAMSON, Falmouth 1658, was liv. after the first destruct. of the town 1676, left wid. Rachel, and three ds. Jane, Dorcas, and Mary.

PENN, *JAMES, Boston, came in the fleet with Winth. req. 19 Oct. 1630, to be made freem. tho. it does not appear that he took the o. was rep. 1648 and 9, beadle first, and marshal aft. rul. elder, as his ch. distinct. d. 30 Sept. 1671, but John Hull says 7 Oct. Hutch. I. 269. In his will of 29 Sept. pro. 23 Oct. his w. Catharine, wh. had very early been mem. of the ch. but no ch. is nam. yet perhaps that Mary whose name is the 152d in our list of the first ch. mem. may have been a d. tho. more prob. a sis. with sis. Hannah, Mary, and other relat. WILLIAM, Charlestown 1630, came, no doubt, in the fleet with Winth. sett. at Braintree, late in his days rem. to Boston; yet in the will of 18 Dec. 1688, pro. 14 Feb. foll. directs his bur. to be at Braintree, giv. lega. to ch. and sch. there, to sev. Thompsons, Stephen Paine and their childr. but chiefly to cousin Hannah Hill, and Edward Hill, jr. and Hannah Hill and Edward Hill senr. and Sarah Hill, having, he says, sent for his kinswoman, Deborah, w. of said Edward, senr. out of Eng. promising to make her his heir, so we may be sure his w. and ch. if any he ever had, were d. Who was the Christian Penn, a passeng. in the Ann, to Plymouth, 1623, who soon after m. Francis Eaton, is, perhaps, beyond the reach of all but conject.

PENNELL, WALTER, Saco, freem. 1653, m. 1647, Mary, d. of Robert Booth, had Walter and perhaps others; in the Ind. war, 1675, rem. to Salem. WALTER, York, s. of the preced. was in 70th yr. 1719. Folsom, 181.

PENNIMAN, JAMES, Boston, came prob. in the Lion, 1631, with John Winth. jr. for he, with w. Lydia, wh. surv. him, were adm. of the ch. bef. the s. but after the w. of the Gov. freem. 6 Mar. 1632, the same day with John and Jacob Eliot, whom I reckon as fellow passeng. had James, bapt. 26 Mar. 1633; Lydia, 22 Feb. 1635; John, 15 Jan. 1637; rem. to Braintree, there had Joseph, b. 1 Aug. bapt. 29 Sept. 1639; and Sarah, b. 6 May 1641; Samuel, 14 Nov. 1645; Hannah, 26 Mar. 1648; Abigail, 27 Dec. 1651; and Mary, 29 Sept. 1653; all by w. Lydia; and he d. 26 Dec. 1664. Abigail, m. 18 Apr. 1678, Samuel Neal; and Mary m. 4 Apr. 1678, Samuel Paine of the same. ‖ JAMES, Boston, eldest s. of the preced. feltmaker, m. 10 May 1659, Mary Cross, d. of the

w. of deac. Robert Sanderson, had James, b. 27 Sept. 1661 or 2; Mary, 17 Sept. 1668; and Joseph, 8 Oct. 1674; was of ar. co. 1673. JOHN, Braintree, sec. s. of the first James, freem. 1671, m. 24 Feb. 1665, Hannah, d. of Roger Billings of Dorchester, had James, b. 7 Feb. 1666, d. at 12 yrs.; John, 23 Feb. 1668, d. young; Joseph, 15 Mar. 1671; Samuel, 18 June 1672; Jonathan, 5 Apr. 1674; Hannah, 23 Jan. 1676, d. at 2 yrs.; and John, again, 5 Jan. 1678. His w. d. 9 Feb. foll. JOSEPH, Braintree, br. of the preced. by w. Waiting, d. of William Robinson of Dorchester, had Joseph, b. 20 Feb. 1670, d. at 20 yrs of the fever contract. in Phips's crusade against Canada; Moses, 15 Mar. 1671, d. soon; Mary, a. 1674; Moses, again, 14 Feb. 1678; Deborah, 27 Feb. 1680; James, 11 Feb. 1683; and his w. d. 21 Aug. 1690; was freem. 1678, deac. and 10 May 1693 m. Sarah, wid. of deac. John Stone of Watertown, d. of deac. Samuel Bass of Braintree, and d. 5 Nov. 1705. SAMUEL, Braintree, br. of the preced. was freem. 1678, m. 6 Jan. 1674, Eliz. d. of Robert Parmenter, had Eliz. b. Jan. 1675; Samuel, 15 Mar. 1676, d. soon; Samuel, again, 5 Nov. 1677; Josiah, 21 Nov. 1678, d. soon; Hannah, 12 Feb. 1683; Jonathan, 17 Feb. 1686; and James, 29 Mar. 1695; was lieut. and d. 16 Jan. 1705. Of this name in 1834, five had been gr. at Harv. one at Yale, and four at other N. E. coll.

PENNINGTON, EPHRAIM, New Haven. See Penington. EPHRAIM, New Haven, s. of the preced. m. Mary, eldest d. of John Brocket of the same.

PENNY, HENRY, New Hampsh. secr. of the Prov. 1683, and a capt. d. 16 Mar. 1709, leav. s. Henry in Eng. Adams, 106. ROBERT, Salem, had gr. of ld. 1638. THOMAS, Gloucester 1652, of wh. our kn. is incomplete, as that his w. Ann d. 26 Apr. 1667, and he m. 15 June 1668, Agnes Clark, wh. d. 23 Feb. 1682; and he m. 17 May foll. Joan Brabrook, perhaps wid. of Richard. But when he took the first w. what was her surname, or how many ch. they had, is untold; and, tho. the name was cont. in the town to a third and fourth generat. we see in his will a. 1692, only one ment. that Joan, wh. had m. so early, Babson says, as 28 Mar. 1658, Thomas Kent.

PENOYER, or PENNYER, ROBERT, emb. in the Hopewell, capt. Babb, 8 Sept. 1635, aged 21, with Thomas, 10, perhaps br. or cousin, at London, where Mr. Somerby, from the custom ho. rec. found the name Pennaire, but I know, that he wrote it Penoire. Where he first sat down, after land. at Boston, is uncert. Yet in Col. Rec. I find he was sentenc. to be whip. in 1639, for some failure, and that, perhaps, made him rem. but, to whatever part of Mass. it was, he had left in ten yrs. being then near Gravesend on L. I. and not long after at Stamford where he m. prob. not first w. the wid. of Richard Scofield, and in Oct. 1671, giv. capt. Jon-

athan Sellick power to act for him in Eng. he calls hims. of Rye. He
was br. of William, a merch. of London, wh. was liberal in his benefact.
to H. C. by whose will, May 1670, a bequest to him was made. He or
Thomas, or perhaps both, left issue; and the benefit of his relative's gen-
eros. was, in our day, more than a century and a half since the donor's
d. partaken, by an undergr. of the univ. on claim of blood relationsh.

PENTICUS, JOHN, Charlestown 1638 or earlier, freem. 13 May 1640,
by w. Joanna, wh. was wid. of Edward Larkin, had John, b. 6 May
1659, and d. 19 Oct. 1687, aged near 90. Perhaps he had former w.
He and w. Joanna join. the ch. 16 Sept. 1639. See Budington's Hist.
Often in rec. of town and ch. the name is Penticost.

PENTLAND, NATHANIEL, Lynn.

PENWELL, or PENEWELL, JOSEPH, Saco, d. early. WALTER, Saco, d.
Mar. 1683, leav. wid. Mary, prob. d. of Robert Booth, and s. Walter, br.
of Joseph, of wh. he had been admor.

PEPPER, FRANCIS, Springfield 1645, d. 5 Dec. 1685, had prob. no w.
nor ch. ISAAC, Eastham, s. prob. of Robert of Roxbury, m. 7 Oct.
1685, Apphia, d. of Samuel Freeman, had Apphia, b. 24 Feb. 1687;
Mary, 7 Aug. 1690; Isaac, 29 July 1693; Robert, 15 Feb. 1696; Eliz.
11 July 1698; Joseph, 1 Nov. 1700, d. young; Solomon, 15 Jan. 1703;
and Joseph, again, 24 Feb. 1705. JACOB, Roxbury, s. of Robert, m. 10
Feb. 1685, Eliz. d. of Stephen Paine the sec. of Rehoboth, had Robert,
b. 27 Dec. foll. d. soon; Robert, again, 16 Mar. 1687, d. in few wks.;
and the next on rec. is Rebecca, 11 July 1702, after more than fifteen
yrs. interval; Ann, 1 Apr. 1705; Mary, 16 Nov. 1707, d. in few mos.;
and Benjamin, wh. d. 17 Feb. 1713, prob. quite young. JOHN, Roxbury, br. of the preced. m. 1669, Bethia Fisher, of Dedham, wh. d. the
same yr. and he d. 18 Mar. 1670. JOSEPH, Roxbury, br. of the preced.
by w. Mary had Bethia, b. 6 Nov. 1676, posthum. he being k. by the Ind.
21 Apr. preced. at Sudbury fight. His wid. m. 28 Feb. 1678, Joshua
Sever. RICHARD, Roxbury, came in the Francis from Ipswich, 1634,
aged 27, with w. Mary, 30, and d. Mary, $3\frac{1}{2}$, beside Stephen Beckett, of
11 yrs. unit. with the ch. early, as did his w. freem. 4 Mar. 1635; but
of f. mo. or ch. nothing is kn. beyond that, only I have a meagre note,
that he was liv. in 1648. He may have rem. to long distance in Conn.
Mr. Drake gave this man the name of Pepy in his transcript for Geneal.
Reg. XIV. 331 and 2, but on the latter p. has it both ways. I had nine
yrs. bef. print. in 3 Mass. Hist. Coll. X. 143 and 4 the copy sent me by
our countryman, Henry Stephens, the accomplish. assist. at the British
Museum, and perhaps his reading may seem equal. prob. ROBERT,
Roxbury, perhaps br. of the preced. m. 14 Mar. 1643, Eliz. Johnson, had
Eliz. bapt. 3 Mar. 1644, d. in few days; Eliz. again, b. 25 May, bapt. 1

June 1645 ; John, 8, bapt. 11 Apr. 1647 ; Joseph, 18 Mar. 1649 ; Mary,
27 Apr. 1651 ; Benjamin, 15 May 1653, d. young ; Robert, 21, bapt. 29
Apr. 1655 ; Sarah, b. 28 Apr. 1657, whose bapt. is lost from the rec.;
Isaac, 26 Apr. bapt. 1 May 1659 ; and Jacob, 28 July, bapt. 4 Aug.
1661. He was freem. 10 May 1643 ; his w. d. 5 Jan. 1684 ; and he,
the " aged Christian," as the ch. rec. calls him, d. 7 July foll. having,
three days bef. made his will, in wh. he ment. s. Isaac, and Jacob, ds.
Eliz. wh. had m. 13 May 1662, John Everett ; Mary, wh. had m. 28
Oct. 1669, Samuel Everett, both of Dedham ; Sarah, w. of John Mason
of Boston, and Bethia, sole ch. of Joseph, who was k. in service, with
many others of his townsmen under Wadsworth at Sudbury. His s.
Robert had been tak. by the Ind. at Squakheag fight, 4 Sept. 1675, under capt. Beers, when report said he was k. but Mrs. Rowlandson saw
him in the foll. winter, and he prob. d. in captiv.

PEPPERELL, ANDREW, Newcastle, s. of the first William, a merch. m.
1707, Jane, d. of Robert Eliot, had Sarah, and Margery, and d. a. 1713.
The wid. m. 25 Nov. 1714, Charles Frost of Kittery. WILLIAM, Kittery, came from Cornwall, or Devonsh. a fisherman, a. 1676, to Isle of
Shoals, thence in 3 or 4 yrs. rem. to K. m. Margery, d. of John Bray of
K. had Andrew, b. 1 July 1681 ; Mary, 5 Sept. 1685 ; Margery, 1689 ;
Joanna, 22 June 1692 ; Meriam, 3 Sept. 1694 ; Dorothy, 23 July 1698 ;
and Jane, 1701 ; beside the famous Sir William, 27 June 1696. He
was a wealthy merch. prud. magistr. and d. 15 Feb. 1734, at the age of
85, says Farmer. His wid. d. 24 Apr. 1741. Mary m. 4 Sept. 1702,
John Frost, bore him seventeen ch. bec. third w. 12 Aug. 1745, of Rev.
Benjamin Colman, of Boston ; and for third h. a. three yrs. aft. m. Benjamin Prescott of Danvers, and d. 1766 ; Margery m. Pelatiah Whittemore, wh. had by her four ch. and was drown. near Isle of Shoals, and
she m. Elihu Gunnison ; Joanna m. Dr. George Jackson ; Meriam m.
Andrew Tyler of Boston ; Dorothy m. Andrew Watkins, and next, Joseph Newmarch ; and Jane m. Benjamin Clark, and next, William Tyler of Boston.   ‡* WILLIAM, Kittery, s. of the preced. was a merch. of
great skill, energy and affluence, rep. 1726, of the counc. 1727 thirty-two
yrs. command. of the land forces in the happy expedit. 1745, against
Cape Breton, for conq. of wh. he was created baronet, and d. 6 July
1759, aged 63 ; so that his only s. Andrew, H. C. 1743, wh. d. 1 Mar.
1751, could not enjoy the title. This was, however, reviv. in favor of
William Sparhawk, H. C. 1766, the gr.s. of Sir William, by his sovereign, with the name and arms of Pepperell, in 1774, but again became
extinct, on his d. 17 Dec. 1816. The wid. of first baronet, d. 26 Nov.
1789 ; but his only surv. d. Eliz. had m. 1 May 1742, Hon. Nathaniel
Sparhawk of Portsmouth, and was mo. of the next baronet. He m. 21

Feb. 1723, unless the fam. report of 16 Mar. be more trustworthy, Mary, d. of Grove Hirst, gr.d. of Ch. Just. Sewall, had Eliz. b. 29 Dec. 1723 ; Andrew, 4 Jan. 1726; William, 26 May 1729, d. in few mos.; and Margery, 4 Sept. 1732, d. soon. The revo. of 1775 was not honor. by confiscat. of his prop. nor am I aware of the amount of the patriotic plunder, or the benefit enjoy. by partakers. Like most of the other adher. of the crown from N. E. of wh. the number was not large, he showed a gr. affection for the land of his birth, and bestow. attent. when in his power, on prisoners wh. fought against his cause, and in later yrs. on travellers from the home of his love.

PEPYS, RICHARD, Boston 1642, or earlier, took the est. that was of William Blaxton, by purch. and desir. to buy more, as in the rec. I find, that the Selectmen, 27 Feb. 1643, appoint. Colbron and Eliot, a comtee. " to view a parcel of land toward Mr. Blaxton's beach, wh. Richard Peapes desires to purchase of the town, whether it may be conveniently sold unto him." Of him I kn. no more ; but prob. he was from Cottenham in Cambridgesh. for the pronunciat. we see, in one syllab. as also his own spell. of the name, both quite rare, are the same as that of the late Lord Cottenham, the Chancellor of Great Britain, and of Samuel Pepys, F. R. S. the Diarymaker, of whose m. the certif. pub. by Lord Braybrook, spells the name Peps, acc. the common pronunciat.

PERCIVAL, PASSEVIL, PASSAVIL, or PARCYFULL, and in Col. Rec. PURSUALL, JAMES, Sandwich, had Eliz. b. 10 Sept. 1675. JAMES, Haddam, possib. s. of the preced. had John, b. 17 Oct. 1706; and Timothy (by w. Abigail), 2 Oct. 1712. JOHN, Barnstable, had Eliz. b. 22 Feb. 1704 ; and James, 5 Dec. 1711. Perhaps he was br. of the preced.

PERCY, PEERCE, PIERCY, or PERCIE, JOHN, Gloucester, m. 17 July 1673, Jane, wid. of Philip Stanwood. MARMADUKE, Salem, 1637, came the yr. bef. from Sandwich, Co. Kent, a tailor, with w. Mary, and one serv. ROBERT, New London, bought a ho. 1678, says Caulkins, and sold it next yr.

PERHAM, PERRUM, or PERAM, ABRAHAM, Rehoboth, had Sarah and Rebecca, tw. b. 11 Oct. 1679, and the latter d. in 3 ds. JOHN, Rehoboth 1643, supposed by Farmer to be an early sett. at Chelmsford, but the contin. resid. of him and descend. at R. as shown by Baylies, II. 199, 203, 8, 16 and IV. 85, satisfy me of the contra. He had Noah, b. 24 Dec. 1679. JOHN, Chelmsford 1666, freem. 1690. In the same yr. JOHN of Roxbury appears in the list of freem. but I suspect an error of the rec. as that name is not found in R. near that time. Possib. John Perry may have been ment.

PERIGO, EZEKIEL, Saybrook, prob. s. of Robert, said to be b. 22 June 1658, went as a soldier to Northampton, 1707, and that yr. m.

Mary Webb. ROBERT, Saybrook, had suit, 1665, in Ct. of Assist. in Mass.

PERIT, BENJAMIN, Stratford 1669.

PERKINS, ABRAHAM, Hampton, by w. Mary, wh. d. 29 May 1706, aged 88, had Mary, and Abraham, b. 2 Sept. both bapt. 15 Dec. 1639, was freem. 13 May 1640. Other ch. were Humphrey, b. 22 Jan. 1642, d. young; James, 11 Apr. 1644 ; Timothy, July 1646 ; both d. young; James, again, 5 Oct. 1647 ; Jonathan, May 1650 ; David, 1653 ; Abigail, 2 or 12 Apr. 1655 ; Timothy, 2 or 29 June 1657, d. in few mos. as told in Geneal. Reg. XII. 79 ; Sarah, 7 or 26 July 1659 ; and Humphrey, 17 May 1661 ; beside Caleb, and Luke of doubtful date. His will of 22 Aug. 1683 was pro. 18 Sept. foll. Abigail m. 10 Nov. 1675, John Folsom the sec. of Hampton. ABRAHAM, Hampton, s. prob. of the preced. m. Eliz. d. of Thomas Sleeper of the same, was k. by the Ind. 13 June 1677, leav. ds. Mercy, b. 3 July 1671 ; Mary, 20 Nov. 1673 ; and Eliz. 9 Apr. 1676. ABRAHAM, Ipswich, s. of John sec. of the same, freem. 1685, m. 16 Oct. 1661, Hannah, d. of William Beamsley of Boston, then a young wid. Bushnell, had Hannah, b. 7 Aug. 1662 ; Beamsley, 7 Apr. 1673 ; John, 23 Aug. 1676, H. C. 1695 ; Stephen, 1683 ; and Abraham, 22 Dec. 1685 ; and d. 27 Apr. 1722 ; and his wid. d. 16 Oct. 1732, aged 91. BENJAMIN, Newbury, had Daniel, b. 18 Dec. 1684. CALEB, Hampton, s. of Abraham the first of the same, or of Isaac of the same, as is said, m. Bethia, d. of James Philbrick, had Rhoda, b. 24 June 1677 ; Benjamin, 11 May 1680; and Ann, 19 Mar. 1682. EBENEZER, Hampton, s. of Isaac of the same, by w. Mercy, had Daniel, b. June 1685 ; Abigail, 11 Aug. 1687 ; and Jonathan 10 May 1691. EDMUND, Boston 1675, m. Susanna, wid. of John Howlett, d. of Francis Hudson, had Edmund, b. 8 May 1678, d. young ; John, 14 Oct. 1680 ; Edmund, again, 6 Sept. 1683 ; and Jane, 25 Feb. 1687. Of his d. I find not rec. but his w. was nam. 1697, in the will of her f. EDMUND, Boston, s. of the preced. m. 1709, Mary Farris, had Edmund, William, and Mary. He took sec. w. 8 Mar. 1722, Esther Frothingham, and had John ; Esther ; Edmund, again ; Susanna, wh. d. young ; James, b. 1733 ; Samuel; and Susanna, again ; and d. 1761. James was a merch. and f. of the late Thomas H. P. one of the most disting. merch. of the U. S. but Sabine, in his Loyalists, confus. ano. James with this, as one of the address. to Gov. Hutchinson, wh. was imposs. for the f. of Col. T. H. P. d. 1773. EDWARD, New Haven, m. 1650, Eliz. Butcher, had John, b. 1651 ; Mehitable, 1652 ; Jonathan, 1653 ; David, 1656 ; and perhaps others. He and the three s. were proprs. in 1685. ELEAZER, Hampton 1678. ELISHA, Topsfield, s. of deac. Thomas of the same, m. 23 Feb. 1681, Catharine, d. of Jacob Towne of the same, had Thomas, b. 15 Oct. 1681, whose

descend. have been disting. at Kennebunk, whither this ch. on m. rem.
*HUMPHREY, Hampton 1678, perhaps youngest s. of Abraham first of
the same, by w. Martha had John, b. 12 Mar. 1688; Humphrey, Mar.
1690; Jonathan, 24 Nov. 1691; Mary, 28 Nov. 1693; James, 9 Sept.
1695; Martha; Sarah; Abigail; and these last three were bapt. 7 Dec.
1712, sev. mos. after d. of f.; but the sequence of b. is not kn. ISAAC,
Hampton, prob. br. of first Abraham, freem. 18 May 1642, by w. Susanna had perhaps Lydia; Isaac, bapt. 8 Dec. 1639; Jacob, 24 May
1640; Lydia; and Rebecca, both of wh. may have been elder; Daniel,
wh. d. young; Caleb; Benjamin, b. 17 Feb. 1650; Susanna, 21 Aug.
1652; Hannah, 24 Feb. 1656; Mary, 23 July 1658; Ebenezer, 9 Dec.
1659; and Joseph, 9 Apr. 1661; and the time of his d. is uncert. Mary
m. Isaac Chase of H. ISAAC, Ipswich, s. of John sec. of the same, by w.
Hannah had John, b. 1 July 1670; Abraham, Sept. 1671; Hannah,
1673; Isaac, 1676; Jacob, 1678; Sarah, 28 Mar. 1683; and Mary,
1684. JABEZ, Norwich, s. of the first Jacob, m. 30 June 1698, Hannah
Lothrop, perhaps d. of Samuel, wh. d. 1721, had Jabez, b. 3 June 1699;
Hannah, 1701; Eliz. 1703; Mary; Jacob, 1705; Lucy, or Luke, 1709;
and Judith, 1714. He took sec. w. 1722, Charity Leonard, and d. 15
Jan. 1742. JACOB, Ipswich, youngest s. of first John of the same, b. in
Eng. by w. Eliz. had Eliz. b. 1 Apr. 1650; John, 3 July 1654; Judith,
11 July 1655; Mary, 14 May 1658; Jacob, 3 Aug. 1662; Matthew, 23
June 1665; Joseph; and Jabez; is usual. call. serg. and has very large
line of descend. His w. d. 12 Feb. 1686, and he d. 29 Jan. 1701, aged
76. JACOB, Ipswich, s. of John the sec. m. Sarah, d. of Francis Wainwright, had Phillis, b. 1667; John, 1668; Hannah, 1670; Francis, 1672;
Wensley, 1674; Sarah, 1679; Mary, 1685; Eliz. 1689; Jacob, 1690;
Eunice, 1691; and John, again, 1693. JACOB, Hampton, s. of the first
Isaac, m. 30 Dec. 1669, Mary Philbrook, had Isaac, b. 18 Dec.
1671; Jacob, 24 Dec. 1674; Alice, perhaps; Mary, 10 Aug. 1678;
and Benjamin, 12 Aug. 1693; but some hesitat. attends this statem.
in Geneal. Reg. XII. 82, tho. concur. exact. with X. 216. Prob.
differ. generat. may reconcile. JACOB, Edgartown 1674-85. JACOB,
Ipswich, s. of the first Jacob of the same, m. 15 Oct. 1684, Eliz.
d. of John Sparks of the same, had Jacob, b. 15 Feb. 1686; John;
Eliz. 18 Mar. 1691; and perhaps ano. ch. when she d. 10 Apr.
1692. Great uncertainty occurs in the subdivis. of both these Ipswich families, as the names are too oft. repeat. JAMES, Hampton, s.
of Abraham the first of the same, by first w. Mary had Jonathan, b. 6
May 1675; and by sec. w. m. 13 Dec. 1681, Leah, d. of Moses Cox of
the same, wh. d. 19 Feb. 1749, aged 88, had Sarah, 3 Oct. 1682; Mary,
2 Dec. 1686; Lydia, 30 Jan. 1689; Hannah, 18 Aug. 1691; Eliz. 1694;

James, 17 Mar. 1696; Moses, 13 or 30 July 1698; and David, 30 Nov. 1701. His will of 8 May 1723, was pro. 9 Dec. 1731. JAMES, Exeter 1677. *JOHN, Ipswich, b. a. 1590, it is said, at Newent in Co. Glouces- ter, came, prob. in the Lion to Boston, Feb. 1631, with Roger Williams, bring. also, w. Judith, s. John, b. a. 1614; and prob. other ch. certain. Mary, wh. m. perhaps 1636, Thomas Bradbury; and Eliz. wh. bec. w. of William Sargent. He with his w. soon join. our ch. had Lydia, bapt. 3 June 1632, was freem. 18 May 1631, and in 1633 went to I. with John Winth. the younger, rep. in 1636, d. 1654, leav. John, Thomas, b. a. 1616; and Jacob, a. 1624, b. in Eng.; Lydia m. a Bennet. JOHN, Ipswich, eldest s. of the preced. wh. may have been adm. freem. 18 May 1637, had John; Abraham, b. 1641; and others, Jacob; Luke; Isaac; Nathaniel; Samuel; and perhaps Thomas; of some of wh. very little is kn. of none the date of b. JOHN, Ipswich, s. of the preced. by w. Judith, had two ch. of unkn. names, and d. 1659. JOHN, Ipswich, eldest s. of deac. Thomas, m. 28 Nov. 1666, Deborah, d. of Thomas Browning of Topsfield, had Thomas, b. 4 Nov. 1667; and d. 19 May foll. His inv. of next mo. was of £48.15; and the wid. m. 26 Dec. 1669, Isaac Meacham. JOHN, Topsfield, youngest br. of the preced. by w. Mary wh. d. 22 June 1750, had Elisha, b. 1714; Isaac, 1717; John, 1719; Thomas, 1723; and Moses, 1732. JOHN, New Haven, 1688. JOHN, Lynn, s. of Rev. William, m. 29 Aug. 1695, Ann Hutchinson, and had Ann, b. 28 Dec. 1696; John, 9 Mar. 1698; Eliz. 9 Mar. 1700; Mary, 20 Aug. 1702; and William, 10 Aug. 1704. He d. 12 Jan. 1712, and his wid. d. 1717. JOHN, Boston, s. of Edmund, m. 17 June 1708, Remember, d. of Wil- liam Hewes, had John, b. 4 Aug. 1711; and Remember, 30 July 1714. JONATHAN, Norwalk 1671-7. JONATHAN, Hampton 1678, s. of the first Abraham of the same, by w. Sarah had Abraham, b. a. 1684; and Abi- gail, 30 Apr. 1687; and he d. Dec. foll. JOSEPH, Hampton 1678, young- est s. of Isaac of the same, by w. Martha had Joseph, b. 28 July 1689; John, 4 June 1691; and Caleb, 8 July 1693. JOSEPH, Norwich, s. of Jacob the first, m. 22 May 1700, Martha Morgan, perhaps d. of John, had Eliz. b. 5 Nov. 1701; Joseph, 25 Oct. 1704; Martha, 21 Aug. 1705; John, 5 Oct. 1709; Jerusha, 1 Sept. 1711; Matthew, 31 Aug. 1713; Deborah, and Ann, tw. 20 July 1715; Hannah, 1717; Simon, 1720; and William, 1722; and d. Sept. 1726. His wid. d. Oct. 1754. LUKE, Charlestown 1666, by w. Hannah had Henry, John, and Luke, all bapt. 13 Jan. 1667; Luke, again, 24 Mar. 1667; Eliz. 21 Mar. 1669; John, again, 19 June 1670; Abraham, 28 July 1672; Hannah, 14 Dec. 1673; and Mary, 9 Apr. 1676. LUKE, Ipswich, s. of the first John of the same, m. 26 Apr. 1677, Eliz. Jaques, says Geneal. Reg. X. 214; but it says no more. MATTHEW, Ipswich, youngest s. of the first Jacob of the same, went early to Norwich with brs. Jabez and Joseph, but soon back to I. m. a d. of lieut. Burnham, had Abraham, Matthew and others, and d. aged 90. NATHANIEL, Ipswich, s. of the first John of the same, by w. Judith had Nathaniel, b. 1685; and Jemima, 29 June 1686. SAMUEL, Ipswich, br. of the preced. m. 1677, Hannah West, had Samuel, b. 1679; Ebenezer, 1681; Eliz. 13 June 1685; and John, 12 May 1692. THOMAS, Ipswich 1648, s. of John the first, brot. no doubt, from Eng. by his f. was the deac. whose d. Phebe m. Joseph Towne of Topsfield; ano. m. a Lamson; and a third, Judith, was b. 28 Jan. 1658. His s. were John, Thomas, Elisha, Timothy and Zaccheus, and John, again, b. 2 Aug. 1685. He had m. Phebe, d. prob. eldest, of Zaccheus Gould, sett. in Topsfield, and d. 7 May 1686. His will of 11 Dec. preced. pro. Sept. foll. dispos. of large est. THOMAS, Topsfield, s. of the preced. m. 1683, Sarah Wallis, had Sarah; Phebe; Hannah; Martha, b. 1695; Robert, 1697; Samuel, 1699; and d. 1719. THOMAS, Dover 1665, b. it is said, in 1628, took o. of fidel. 1669, and gave land, 25 Apr. 1693, to s. Nathaniel. TIMOTHY, Topsfield, youngest s. of Rev. William of the same, m. 2 Aug. 1686, Edna Hazen of Rowley, had Timothy, b. 21 Sept. 1687; Nathaniel, 13, bapt. 22 Sept. 1689; John, 2, bapt. 4 Sept. 1692; Richard, b. 23 Sept. 1694; Jacob, 11, bapt. 18 Oct. 1696; William, b. 11 Nov. 1698; Hepzibah, 6 Oct. 1702; and Hannah, 14 Nov. 1703; was freem. 1690. *TOBIJAH, Topsfield, br. of the preced. m. 4 Nov. 1680, Sarah Denison, d. perhaps of John, gr.d. of Daniel, the maj. Gen. had Priscilla, b. 21, bapt. 28 Apr. 1689; Mary, 19, bapt. 25 Jan. 1691; Tobijah, b. 8 Jan. 1693; Joseph, 1 Apr. 1695; Daniel, 15 June 1697, H. C. 1717, min. of Bridgewater, was freem. 1685, capt. and rep. 1694, and d. 30 Apr. 1723. *‖ WILLIAM, Roxbury, a min. but where educ. is unheard, s. of William of London, a merch. tailor (wh. was s. of George of Co. Warwick), was b. 25 Aug. 1607, and his s. hav. giv. to the company for our planta. £50, was a member, and to this s. gr. of 400 acres was made. He came in the William and Francis, leav. London 9 Mar. 1632, was freem. 3 Sept. 1634, ar. co. 1638, m. 30 Aug. 1636, Eliz. Wootton, had William, b. 12 Oct. 1639, d. in few wks.; William, again, 25 Feb. 1642; rem. in 1643 to Weymouth, there had Eliz. 18 June 1643; Tobijah, 20 Oct. 1646; and Catharine, 29 Oct. 1648; was rep. 1644, a capt. 1645, rem. again, I suppose, to Gloucester, there had Mary, 17 May 1652; preach. 1651-5, and bec. sec. min. of Topsfield, there had John, 2 Apr. 1655; Sarah, 2 Mar. 1657; Timothy, 11 Aug. 1658; and Rebecca, 4 May 1662. He d. 21 May 1682, leav. these nine ch. wh. all were m. Eliz. m. 31 May 1671, John Ramsdell; Catharine m. 13 May 1667, John Baker; Mary m. 17 Sept. 1672, Oliver Purchis of Lynn, as his sec. w.; Sarah m. one report says 11 June 1677, or as ano. has it, 17 June 1679, John Bradstreet; and Rebecca m. 3 Nov. 1678, Thomas Fiske of Wenham. Dr. Bentley, the diligent antiq. of Salem, in a letter to me, conject. that he was the fellow-passeng. with Williams; but Farmer gave that honor, with greater prob. to John, and I have since received from London, the custom ho. certific. mak. his voyage begin there, more than a yr. later than Roger Williams's arr. here. WILLIAM, Dover 1662, took o. of fidel. 1669, was b. says tradit. in 1616, and d. at Newmarket 1732. If we allow for considera. exagger. a large depreciat. is mark. in his gr. gr.s. Thomas, wh. d. at Wakefield, 1824, aged only 91. WILLIAM, Topsfield, s. of William the first, m. 24 Oct. 1669, Eliz. d. of Daniel Clark, had Eliz. b. 21 July 1670; Mary, 4 Apr. 1672; William; John, 20 Feb. 1676; Dorothy, 30 Apr. 1678; Timothy, 23 Feb. 1681; Nathan, 24 Apr. 1683; and Rebecca, 4 Sept. 1685. He was freem. 1690, and d. 30 Oct. 1695. Twenty-four of this name had, in 1834, been gr. at Yale, fifteen at Harv. and thirteen at other N. E. coll.

PERLEY, ALLEN, Ipswich, came in the Planter from London, 1635, aged 27, freem. 18 May 1642; and Coffin says, he was from Wales. He had, beside Nathaniel, wh. d. 29 Apr. 1668, aged 24, John; Thomas; both of wh. were older than him; Samuel; Sarah; Martha; and Timothy. He d. 28 Dec. 1675, leav. wid. Susanna, wh. d. 11 Feb. 1692; but whether she was mo. of all the ch. or part only, is not kn. His will of 23 June 1670, aft. ment. that his three eldest s. had left him on com. of age, yet that he had giv. them pieces of ld. beside Nathaniel's pt. provides for the wid. and the other three ch. and a codic. of 16 Nov. 1671 is add. *JOHN, Boxford, perhaps s. of the preced. b. in Eng. was freem. 1690, and Farmer says, rep. 1689–91. One John at Ipswich, by w. Jane had Hannah, b. 1 Sept. 1699; but he was not prob. the rep. and may be gr.s. of Allen. SAMUEL, Ipswich, s. of Allen, freem. 1669, may have liv. short time at Newbury, m. 15 July 1664, Ruth, perhaps d. of John Trumbull of Rowley, had Sarah, b. 7 June 1665; Samuel, 28 May 1667; John, 28 Sept. 1669; Hannah, 8 June 1671; Ruth, 4 June 1675; and Hepzibah, 28 Sept. 1679. THOMAS, Rowley, perhaps br. of the preced. in 1670 was of that part made Boxford, and in 1677, I suppose, of Newbury, when he was made freem. TIMOTHY, Ipswich, youngest s. of Allen, took o. of alleg. 1678, by w. Dorothy had Patience, b. 28 Mar. 1682; Stephen, 15 June 1684; Allen, 1 Mar. 1688; and Joseph, 3 June 1695; and d. 25 Jan. 1719, aged 64. Of WILLIAM, Marlborough, whose ho. was a garrison in Oct. 1675, I kn. no more.

PERMET. See Portmort.

PERRIMAN, THOMAS, Weymouth 1652, an indent. apprent. of Dorothy Hunt. At Cambridge, Frances P. m. Isaac Amsden, 8 June 1654, and

Rebecca P. m. 27 Mar. 1660, Daniel Farrabas, but I kn. not wh. they were. Perhaps these maidens were sis. of the apprent. and they may have been brot. from Eng. after d. of f.

PERRIN, PERRAN, or PERING, ABRAHAM, Rehoboth, perhaps s. of the first John, m. 27 Dec. 1677, Sarah, eldest d. of Philip Walker, wh. d. Aug. 1693, and he d. May foll. He had Eliz. b. 3 Dec. 1681; Daniel, 18 Mar. 1683; and Nathaniel, 9 Feb. 1685. HENRY, Newport 1656, Brookhaven, L. I. 1657, says Thompson, and may have been adm. freem. of Conn. 1664, but his name does not appear in the list of 1669. JOHN, Braintree, had Mary, b. 22 Feb. 1641, rem. perhaps to Rehoboth. It would seem that a JOHN, sen. should be look. for in the same town, whether f. of Abraham or not, for on Col. Rec. is seen that John, sen. was bur. 13 Sept. 1674. Ann, I suppose his d. m. 16 June 1675, Thomas Read of Rehoboth. JOHN, Rehoboth, call. jun. had Mary, b. 16 Apr. 1673; Nathaniel, 3 Sept. 1675, d. young; Mehitable, 19 Apr. 1677. THOMAS, Ipswich, m. bef. 1669, Susanna, wid. of Robert Roberts, was liv. 1679.

PERRY, or PURY, * ANTHONY, Rehoboth 1658-78, was rep. 1674, says Baylies, IV. 85. Perhaps he had Jariel and Mehitable, both d. by Col. Rec. Sept. 1676, and he d. 1 Mar. 1683. ‖ ARTHUR, Boston 1638, a tailor, by w. Eliz. had Elishua, a d. b. 20 Dec. 1637, d. in few mos.; Seth, 7 Mar. 1639, bapt. 15 Mar. 1640; John, 26 Apr. bapt. 1 May 1642; and Eliz. b. 28 Jan. 1647; ar. co. 1638; Sarah, bapt. 15 Dec. 1647; Deborah, aged a. 4 days, bapt. 1 July 1649; was the town drummer, freem. 13 May 1640, and d. 9 Oct. 1652. Both of the s. foll. the trade of their f. EDWARD, Sandwich, from being nam. as s. in the will of Edmund Freeman, it may be thot. he had m. a d. of that gent. but more prob. his mo. had bec. sec. w. of Freeman; by w. Mary, wh. may have been d. of that Edmund Freeman or of Edward Freeman, he had Samuel, b. a. 1664; and prob. others. EZRA, Sandwich, m. 12 Feb. 1652, Eliz. only d. of Thomas Burge of the same, had Ezra, b. 11 Feb. foll.; Deborah, 28 Nov. 1654; John, 1 Jan. 1657; Samuel, 15 Mar. 1667; Benjamin, 15 Jan. 1670; and Remembrance, 1 Jan. 1676 or 7. FRANCIS, Salem 1631, a wheelwright, b. a. 1608, had w. Jane wh. join. the ch. 1641, and had bapt. Sarah, and Benjamin, 8 July of that yr.; David, 1 Aug. 1641; Samuel, 10 Apr. 1642; and Elisha, 11 Aug. 1644; he rem. but I kn. not whither. HENRY, Salem 1652, as the diligence of Coffin picked out of rec. of County, but the equal dilig. of Felt discern. not in rec. of town or ch. ISAAC, Boston 1631, prob. arr. Nov. with apostle Eliot in the Lion, and ent. on ch. list soon after, freem. 6 Mar. 1632; but no more is kn. of him. JOHN, Roxbury, perhaps br. of Isaac, came prob. in the Lion, 1632, very early of the ch. there, being No. 17

on the list, freem. 4 Mar. 1633, had Eliz. b. 25 Jan. 1638 ; John, 7 Sept. 1639 ; and Samuel, 1 Mar. 1641, bapt. 6 Mar. 1642, unless error of a yr. either in rec. of the town or ch. interven. He d. of consumpt. and same day was bur. 21 Sept. 1642, hav. made his will 4 June preced. pro. 7 Mar. 1643 in wh. provis. is contain. for the w. and three ch. JOHN, Newbury 1651, had w. Damaris. He may be the man nam. in Felt's list 1637. JOHN, Medfield 1678, perhaps s. of Roxbury John, m. 23 May 1665, Bethia, d. of Daniel Morse the first, had John, b. Sept. or 24 Dec. 1667 ; Samuel and Joseph, tw. 25 Aug. 1674 ; Nathaniel, 18 May 1671, d. under 10 yrs. ; Nathaniel, again ; Bethia, 1685 ; Eleazer, 1 June 1680, acc. the order of Morse, wh. I do not understand. JOHN, New Haven, a propr. 1685. JOHN, Taunton 1643. JOHN, Watertown 1674, then aged 61, may have been f. of that JOHN, Watertown, who m. 13 Dec. 1667, Sarah, d. of John Clary, had John, b. 1 Oct. 1668, d. in few wks. ; John, again, 3 Mar. 1670 ; Joanna, 8 Nov. 1672 ; Sarah, 11 July 1675 ; Josiah, 7 Dec. 1677, d. young ; Eliz. 2 Oct. 1681 ; Josiah, again, 28 Nov. 1684 ; Joseph, 17 Jan. 1691 ; and Sarah, 30 Apr. 1694. JOSEPH, Seacunk, i. e. Rehoboth, 1651, perhaps was br. of Anthony of the same, or of Thomas of Scituate. NATHANIEL, Rehoboth, m. 17 May 1683, Sarah Carpenter, d. of Samuel of the same, as I presume. OBADIAH, Dunstable, s. of William, freem. 1678, one of the found. of the ch. m. 21 Aug. 1667, Esther, d. of Richard Hassell, had Obadiah, b. 11 Oct. 1669 ; Ebenezer, 20 Nov. 1671 ; Esther, 11 Aug. 1674 ; John, 31 Jan. 1682 ; and Eliz. 7 Apr. 1683 ; perhaps others ; was k. by the Ind. 28 Sept. 1691. Bond mistakes about him. RICHARD, New Haven 1640, had Mary, bapt. 4 Oct. of that yr. ; Micajah, 31 Oct. 1641 ; Samuel, 8 June 1645 ; John, 11 July 1647 ; and Grace, 2 Sept. 1649 ; perhaps rem. 1651, and was at Fairfield 1650. Share in div. of ld. there is giv. to Nathaniel, but not to Richard, wh. may have d. bef. and this have been his heir. Perhaps he was adm. as an inhab. 1637 at Charlestown, wh. is not long found resid. there ; and at Fairfield m. Grace, wid. of John Nichols aft. June 1653, and was d. in 1658 ; but the identity is uncert. for in 1655 one of the name was at Providence, it is said. This, too, was the name of a merch. at London, one of the Assist. nam. in the royal chart. 1629, wh. aided our cause by money, but never came over. SAMUEL, Roxbury, s. of John of the same, was apprent. of John Ruggles as ment. in his will, Geneal. Reg. XII. 343, m. 28 Jan. 1669, Sarah Stedman, prob. d. of John of Cambridge, had Sarah, b. 11 Jan. 1670, d. at 13 yrs. ; Samuel, 23 Feb. 1672 ; Eliz. 7 June 1674 ; John, 12 Apr. 1677 ; Thomas, 1 Sept. 1680 ; Nathaniel, 27 Aug. 1685, d. soon ; Nathaniel, again, 3 Jan. 1687 ; and Joseph, 20 Dec. 1688 ; and d. 16 Apr. 1706. SAMUEL, Newport, s. of Edward of Sandwich, m. 12

Dec. 1678, Mary Miller, had Mehitable, b. 30 Apr. 1680; Jaciel, 6 May 1682; m. 9 May 1690, Mary, d. of Henry Tucker of Sandwich, as I read in tho. Friends' rec. at N. tho. fam. geneal. calls her of Dartmouth, had James; Edward; Samuel, b. 1695; Simon; and Benjamin; and d. at Kingston 1716. Benjamin was gr. gr.f. of the disting. commodore O. H. P. SETH, Boston, s. of Arthur, a tailor, freem. 1666. THOMAS, Scituate 1643, m. Sarah, d. of Isaac Stedman, had Thomas, William, Henry, Joseph, John, and perhaps more. THOMAS, Ipswich 1648. THOMAS, Scituate, s. of Thomas, m. 1671, Susanna, d. of John Whiston, had Thomas; James, 12 Mar. 1673 or 4; John; and David. WILLIAM, Scituate 1638, perhaps br. of the first Thomas, may have rem. to Watertown 1640, by w. Ann had Eliz. b. 12 Aug. 1641; and sev. more ch. of wh. he names five others in his will made a. 1681, when 75 yrs. old, pro. 3 Oct. 1683, Obadiah, Samuel, Sarah, Ann, and Abia. He d. 9 Sept. 1683. Abia m. 3 Jan. 1674, William Bull. Farmer thot. him to be the freem. of 1646, spelt Pary; and for that opinion I see good ground. WILLIAM, Scituate, s. of the first Thomas, m. 1681, Eliz. Lobdell, and had twelve ch. says Deane. Of this name seven at Yale, five at Harv. and fourteen at other N. E. coll. had been gr. in 1834, by Farmer's count.

PERSON, GEORGE, Reading, d. 17 Apr. 1679, as Eaton cites the gr.-st. aged 64. See Parsons. JOHN, Lynn, prob. s. of the preced. by w. Tabitha, had James, b. 28 Nov. 1680; Tabitha; John; Rebecca; Kendall; Susanna; Mary; Thomas; Ebenezer; Sarah; and Abigail; as they are rank. by Lewis.

PERWIDGE, or PERWYDGE, WILLIAM, an odd name, found 1644, at Hartford or the neighb.

PESTER, or PESTOR, WILLIAM, Salem 1637, when with a gr. of ld. he had the prefix of respect, yet abandon. the country in 1642, and 10 yrs. later not being heard of, his w. Dorothy had leave to m. again.

PETCOCK. See Pidcock.

PETERS, ANDREW, Boston 1659, a distiller, m. Mercy, wid. of Michael Wilborne, d. of William Beamsley, rem. to Ipswich 1665, thence to Andover, where, 14 Aug. 1689, his s. Andrew and John, were k. by the Ind. and other ch. were Mercy, wh. m. 22 May 1686, John Allen; Mary, wh. m. on same day, Thomas Chandler; and Eliz. wh. m. 26 Apr. 1692, James Johnson; William; and Samuel; and he d. at the age of 77. Curious it must appear to this later generat. that his name, in one deed, is Peters, and in ano. relat. to the same est. it is writ. Peterson. ANDREW, Andover, s. of the preced. m. 8 Feb. 1686, Eliz. prob. d. of Thomas Farnham, may have had issue, but early was k. by the Ind. Rev. Andrew, H. C. 1723, min. of Middletown, wh. d. 1756, may have been gr.s. GILBERT, Salem 1689, mariner. *HUGH*, Salem, the fourth min. there, was b. 1599, at the parish of St. Ewe, or, as commonly said, in the town of Fowey, Cornwall, bred at Trinity Coll. Cambridge, where he had his degrees, 1617, and 22, preach. in London with gr. success, until he was driv. to Holland, there taught, with famous William Ames, the Eng. ch. at Rotterdam, and for some two yrs. after d. of Ames. He came, I presume, in the Abigail, 1635, tho. his name, for good reason, does not appear at the London custom ho. and perhaps he got on board in the Downs, arr. 6 Oct. in comp. with sec. John Winth. the mo. of whose first w. he had m. as it seems, was freem. 3 Mar. 1636, sett. in the ch. at S. 21 Dec. foll. in Aug. 1641, with Hibbins and Welde, as agents for the Col. he went home, by way of Newfoundland, in the sh. with John Winth. the younger, and Lechford, the lawyer, engag. with great zeal, in the civil war, and partook largely in the triumphs of this cause and for the detesta. felt at his violence was execut. soon after the restor. 16 Oct. 1660, being, I think, the only clerg. of sev. thousand, who thus suffer. He had not, prob. brot. over his first w. by wh. he had no ch. but m. here Deliverence Sheffield, one of the ch. of Boston, by wh. he had Eliz. bapt. 8 Mar. 1640, the only ch. to wh. his dying legacy was addressed. The w. was many yrs. bef. his d. insane, and to some extent this may palliate his ill carriage and violence, that caus. him so many enemies. She was depend. on private charity in London 1677. Hutch. Coll. 514. He usually wrote his name without final s. A question of slight value is raised, wh. was Ann Peters, on the list of Boston ch. mem. No. 104 " rec. from the ch. of Salem " bef. Nov. 1631. A curious extr. from a fugitive tract, call. " Fresh Discovery of New Wandering Blazing Stars and Firebrands " 1646, by that famous William Prynne (wh. suffer. so cruelly from sentence of the Star Chamber) in p. 33 of Ed. 2, gives the subscript. 17 Aug. 1627, of Hugh Peter to the Bp. of London, setting forth his submiss. to the Ch. of Eng. and for the governm. thereof by Archbps. and Bps. and the ceremonies in use, granting his full approbat. and allowance, and for the Bk. of Com. Prayer, the Liturgy, and what is in them cont. " subscribe with my heart and hand," and submit myself to your Lordship's pleasure. To wh. the learned barrister of Lincoln's Inn adds, " If master Peter be now of ano. judgment, it manifests either his gross ignorance, or temporizing then, or his levity now, and that he is as unsteady in his opinions, as in his eccentrick motion from place to place." Peter denied his master, and was not frightened by such animadversion. JOHN, Gravesend, L. I. 1650. Thompson. SAMUEL, Andover, s. prob. youngest of Andrew, m. 15 Dec. 1696, Phebe Frye, d. prob. of Samuel of the same, but I kn. no more. THOMAS, New London, younger br. of Hugh, of far milder temper, said to have been bred at Oxford, but on uncert. authty. was a min. in his native shire of Cornwall, whence driv. in 1643, by the royalist forces, he came next yr. to this country, assisted the younger Winth. in his planta. 1646, hav. serv. bef. at Saybrook in the ch. yet contin. but short time, hav. been invited home by former parish, in 1646, and went next yr. Hinman, p. 61, mistakes Hugh for this br. as being with Col. Fenwick, at his *first* coming to Saybrook, whereas Thomas was not there so early as four yrs. aft. his *sec.* visit. But he obey. the guidance of Dr. Trumbull, common. safe. In the life of Hugh Peter (a work wh. for its perpet. indifference to truth, and frequent bold violations of it, Farmer thought it hazardous to quote), the oldest br. of Hugh call. WILLIAM, is said to have liv. at Boston, and to have had s. John, Andrew, Thomas, William, Samuel, and Joseph. After very diligent search, no William is found, either in Boston, or its vicinity; and I suppose this may be regarded as one of the many inventions of that book. WILLIAM, Andover, s. of Andrew, prob. was k. by the Ind. 13 Aug. 1696. Six of this name had, in 1834, been gr. at Yale and four at Harv. Coll.

PETERSON, CORNELIUS, Boston 1685. HENRY, and JOHN of Lyme, were of the train band 1678, and no more is kn. of either, exc. that John was aft. of Duxbury, and m. Mary, d. of George Soule; and that Henry by w. Marah, m. 15 Apr. 1683, had Sarah, b. 20 Oct. 1686.

PETTIFORD, PETFORD, or PITTFORD, PETER, Salem 1641, Mr. Felt found ment. of, but nothing is told of him, exc. that he resid. at Marblehead 1648. Among Charlestown bapt. is Samuel, s. of Mary Pettiford, br. Baker's d. on 12 Sept. 1669.

PETTELL, ANTHONY, Marblehead 1653, a fisherman, perhaps from Guernsey.

PETTIBONE, JOHN, Windsor, freem. 1658, m. 15 Feb. 1665, Sarah, d. of Bigot Egglestone, had John, b. 15 Dec. 1665; Sarah, 24 Sept. 1667, d. young; Stephen, 3 Oct. 1669; besides Samuel, and sev. ds. of wh. was ano. Sarah, of uncert. date. He had est. in that part made Simsbury, was one of the first sett. and there with John, Stephen, and Samuel, was liv. 1712. Three of the name have been gr. at Yale.

PETTENGELL, or PATTINGGELL, MATTHEW, Newbury, s. of Richard, m. 13 Sept. 1674, Sarah, d. of Nicholas Noyes, had Nathaniel, b. 21 Jan. 1676; Matthew, 18 Sept. 1678; Joanna, 27 Jan. 1681; Nicholas, 15 Nov. 1685; Sarah, 19 Apr. 1688; John, 16 Feb. 1694; Abraham, 23 Sept. 1696; Abigail, 17 Oct. 1699; beside Mary, wh. d. 3 Mar. 1698, prob. b. bef. Nicholas. He m. sec. w. 1703, wid. Jemima French, it is said, d. of Peter Cheney, but perhaps that is wrong, or Coffin has confus. two names of bapt. RICHARD, Newbury, came from Staffordsh. tradit. says, was first at Salem, there m. Joanna, d. of Richard Ingersoll, had Samuel, bapt. 9 Feb. 1645; freem. 2 June 1641, was some yrs. at Wenham; and at N. had Mary, b. 6 July 1652; and Nathaniel, 24 Sept. 1654; beside Matthew and Nathaniel, bef. or aft. Mary m. 10 Nov.

1670, Abraham Adams. SAMUEL, Newbury, s. of the preced. m. 16 Feb. 1674, Sarah Poor, perhaps d. of John, had Samuel, b. 3 Feb. 1676; Richard, 26 Aug. 1677, d. soon; Richard, again, 24 Jan. 1679; John, 20 Sept. 1680; Mary and Sarah, tw. 20 Jan. 1686; Joanna, 10 Feb. 1689; and Benjamin, 18 Dec. 1692.

PETTES, or PETTIT, GILBERT, Salem 1668. JOHN, Roxbury 1639, of wh. Mr. Ellis in his Hist. says nothing, but the name occurs, yet with fam. of sev. heads, rem. prob. to Stamford, or Long Island, where I find at Newtown, Thomas in 1660; Nathaniel, 1667; and John, in 1686. Yet it may well be that his s. John, wh. m. Sarah, d. of Daniel Scofield, was of Stamford 1669. THOMAS, Exeter 1639, a signer of the orig. combina. in 1647 was the chief milit. man.

PETTS, JOHN, a soldier k. by the Ind. 19 Oct. 1675, at Hatfield.

PETTY, or PETTEE, JOHN, Springfield, had liv. at Windsor, but m. at Boston 30 Mar. 1662, Ann Canning, had at W. James, b. same yr.; and at S. Hannah, 1666, d. soon; John, 1667; Mary, 1670; Joseph, 1672; Ann, 1675; and Ebenezer, 1678; and d. 8 Mar. 1680. His wid. m. Samuel Owen. James and John ea. had fams. at S. JOSEPH, Deerfield, s. of the preced. was with w. tak. by the Ind. and Fr. 29 Feb. 1704, carr. to Canada, safe got back next yr. and sett. at Northfield, where the name is bec. very common. PETER, sail. from Salem on fishing voyage, k. by the Ind. in the autumn of 1677. Felt II. 213. PETER, Haverhill 1680. Mirick, 85. It may be the same name as Pattee, wh. is seen in New Hampsh.

PETYGOOD, or PETGOOD, PETER, Marblehead 1641. RICHARD, Ipswich 1641.

PEVERLY, JOHN, Portsmouth, one of the men sent over, 1631, by Mason, the Patentee. THOMAS, Portsmouth, perhaps s. of the preced. d. aft. 1670, leav. by w. wh. may have been a d. of Thomas Walford, s. John, Thomas, Lazarus, Samuel, and Jeremiah.

PHELPS, ABRAHAM, Windsor, s. of George, liv. with his uncle, Abraham Randall, wh. had no ch. and gave him his est. was freem. 1668, m. 6 July 1665, Mary, d. of Humphrey Pinney, had Abraham, b. 6 Mar. 1666; Isaac, 5 Aug. 1673; Benjamin, 1 Oct. 1683; and perhaps others; his w. d. 2 July 1725, aged above 81; and he d. 28 Jan. 1728, aged 85. CHRISTOPHER, Salem, m. 9 July 1658, Eliz. Sharp, and I kn. no more, but that he sign. petitn. against imposts 1668. EDWARD, Newbury, rem. to Andover, by w. Eliz. d. of Robert Adams, had, beside others, John, b. at N. 15 Dec. 1657, wh. was k. by the Ind. on serv. at Scarborough, 29 June 1677; and he d. 3 Oct. 1689. EDWARD, Andover, prob. s. of the preced. m. 9 Mar. 1682, Ruth Andrews, had prob. others beside Edward and Bathsheba, wh. d. 24 Feb. 1694; and Eliz. b. 27

Jan. 1690; rem. to Lancaster, and d. 30 Nov. of uncert. yr. and there
Eliz. m. Samuel Willard of L. EPHRAIM, Simsbury, s. of Edward, m.
11 May 1691, Mary Jaggers, and d. 1697. GEORGE, Dorchester, freem.
6 May 1635, rem. with Warham to Windsor, by first w. said to be nam.
Philbury, d. of Philip Randall, wh. d. 29 Apr. 1648, had Isaac, b. 20
Aug. 1638; Abraham, 22 Jan. 1643; and Joseph, 24 June 1647, wh. d.
soon, as did Abraham in the same yr. He m. 2, or as ano. acco. is,
30 Nov. 1648, Frances, wh. had been wid. Clark, and then was wid.
of Thomas Dewey, and had Jacob, 7 Feb. 1650; John, 15 Feb. 1652;
and Nathaniel, 7 Dec. 1653; rem. to Westfield, there had more ch. and
d. 8 May 1687, but Stiles in Hist. 743, says 9 July 1678. Six s. were
then liv. no d. is nam. His wid. d. 27 Sept. 1690. HENRY, Salem,
from London, came in the Hercules 1634, m. 1652, Hannah Bassett, but
as sec. w. in my opin. for there is some prob. that he had m. a d. of
Thomas Tresler, by wh. he had s. John, rememb. in the will of his gr.mo.
Perhaps he was a Quaker, at least, Felt II. 582 tells how Hannah P. in
Oct. 1659, was admonish. But she may have been w. of Nicholas P.
ISAAC, Windsor, eldest s. of George of the same, m. 11 May 1663, or 11
Mar. 1664 (Parsons gives both dates only six lines apart in Geneal.
Reg. V. 369, so that it is quite doubtful wh. day we should prefer, but
Stiles takes the earlier), Ann, d. of the sec. William Gaylord, had Isaac,
b. 18 Sept. 1666, wh. had 3 ch. yet d. at 32 yrs.; Sarah, bapt. 4 July
1670; and rem. to Westfield, there was freem. 1671, had John, b. 27
Dec. 1672, bapt. 29 June 1673; Hannah, 5 Nov. 1674; Hezekiah, 9
July 1677; Joseph, 28 Nov. 1679; Noah, 14 Oct. 1684; and Ebenezer, 6 June 1687; beside Daniel, and ano. both d. young. His w. d. Sept.
1690, and he d. 8 May 1687, or 21 Sept. 1725. Why so gr. interval betw.
var. dates is seen, I have no explanat. JACOB, Westfield, br. of the preced. m. 2 May 1672, Dorothy, sec. d. of John Ingersoll, had Dorothy, b.
as one tells, 18 Oct. but Goodwin says Dec. 1673, d. in few wks.; Dorothy,
again, 10 May 1675; Hannah, 26 Nov. 1677; Israel, 3 Apr. 1681;
Benjamin, 8 Jan. 1684; Joseph, 5 Aug. 1686; and Jedediah, 7 Dec.
1688; and d. 6 Oct. 1689. His wid. m. a Root. JAMES, Boston 1657.
JOHN, Charlestown, by w. Catharine had Catharine, b. 8 May 1659, says
the Middlesex rec. and the same authty. adds that Catharine Phelps, d.
19 June foll. But I find no Phelps in Charlestown, for a long time bef.
or aft. and John Phillips at that time had w. Catharine wh. may have
had that ch. In some rec. the name is plain Philps, and this shows how
easily one may be converted to the other. JOHN, Salem, perhaps s. of
Henry, by w. Abigail had Abigail, b. 21 Apr. 1669; John, 6 Feb. 1671;
Henry, 3 Apr. 1673; Joseph, 7 Dec. 1675; Abigail, 7 Jan. 1678; Samuel, 6 Jan. 1680; and Hannah, 12 Apr. 1683. JOHN, Windsor, br. of

Jacob, m. Sarah, d. prob. of Thomas Buckland, had Enoch, b. 21 Jan. 1676; John, 12 Apr. 1678; Josiah, 17 Feb. 1680; Sarah, but Stiles says Samuel, 2 Mar. 1682; Francis, Stiles prints Frances, Dec. 1683; Thomas, 21 Aug. 1687; David, 17 Jan. 1690; Job, 27 Apr. 1692, d. soon; Job, again, 2 May or Aug. 1693. JOHN, Reading, s. prob. of John of Salem, m. 12 Mar. 1701, Eliz. Putnam, prob. d. of John. JOSEPH, Windsor, s. of William, perhaps b. in Eng. freem. 1664, m. 20 Sept. 1660, Hannah Newton, not d. of Rev. Roger, nor prob. of any man on our side of the water, but sis. of Joan, it is said, wh. m. Benedict Alvord, had Joseph, b. 27 Aug. 1667; Hannah, 2 Feb. 1669; rem. to Simsbury, there had Timothy, Sarah, and William, in 1676 m. sec. w. Mary, wid. of Thomas Salmon, and d. 1684. JOSEPH, Windsor, s. of George, m. 26 June 1673, Mary, d. of John Porter, had Mary, b. 13 Jan. 1675; Sarah, 4 Apr. 1677; Joseph, 30 Dec. 1678; Hannah, 1681; Mindwell, 1683; Esther, 1691; Abigail, 1693; and Benoni, 1695. JOSEPH, Simsbury, s. of first Joseph, by w. Mary, d. of Joseph Collier, had Joseph, b. 9 Oct. 1689; Hannah, 25 Oct. 1693; and Mary, 17 Nov. 1696; and his w. d. 1697. He m. again, 6 Nov. 1699, Sarah, d. of the first John Case, had Sarah, b. 11 Aug. 1700, d. bef. 14 yrs.; and Damaris, 5 Mar. 1702. This w. d. 2 May 1704; and he d. 20 Jan. 1750. JOSIAH, Simsbury, youngest ch. of Samuel of the same, m. 26 Apr. 1690, Sarah Winchell. ⟨ NATHANIEL, Northampton, s. of William, b. in Eng. had liv. at Windsor, m. 17 Sept. 1650, wid. Eliz. Copley, had Mary, b. 21 June 1651; Nathaniel, 2 Apr. 1653; Abigail, 5 Apr. 1655; all b. at W. but at N. had William, 22 June 1657; and Mercy, 1662; was freem. 1681, a deac. and d. 27 May 1702; and his wid. d. 6 Dec. 1712. Mary, m. 1670, Matthew Clesson, and Abigail, wh. m. John Alvord, d. 26 Aug. 1756, therefore, allow. for the correct. of old style 4 yrs. bef. aged 101 yrs. 4 mos. and ten days, the oldest person that ever d. at N. NATHANIEL, Northampton s. of the preced. m. 1676, Grace Martin, had Grace, b. 11 Nov. 1676, wh. d. soon; Nathaniel, 1 Nov. 1678, d. at 12 yrs.; Samuel, 9 Dec. 1680; Lydia, 7 Jan. 1683; Grace, again, 10 Nov. 1685; Eliz. 19 Feb. 1688; Abigail, 3 Nov. 1690; Nathaniel, again, 13 Feb. 1693; Sarah, 8 May 1695; and Timothy, 1697. A well deriv. tradit. a. the mo. of these ch. is worth insert. Her lover in Eng. was false and m. ano. She left her native ld. came to our country to relatives, the respectab. fam. of Marsh of Hadley, but in ignor. of their resid. or want of funds or both, on reach. Boston, was in danger of being sold for her passage, bef. relief came from her friends. One version of the story goes further, that she was sold; but it is good eno. without this. Descend. are very num. among wh. was my disting. antiquar. friend, Sylvester Judd. NATHANIEL, Westfield, s.

of George, by w. Eunice, had Nathaniel, b. 10 Oct. 1678; Eunice, 29 May 1680, d. at 6 yrs.; Jonathan, 28 Dec. 1682; Thomas, 15 May 1685, d. next yr.; Eunice, again, 12 Oct. 1688; and Lois, 7 Sept. 1691. He d. June 1723; and his wid. d. 17 Dec. 1738. NICHOLAS, Salem 1658, a quaker, whose w. was censur. that yr. and in 1661 fined for misuse of her tongue. Felt II. 581, 3. RICHARD, Dorchester 1633, of wh. no more is kn. and conject. is useless. SAMUEL, Dorchester, rem. to Windsor, was s. of William, b. prob. in Eng. m. 10 Nov. 1650, Sarah, d. of Edward Griswold, had Samuel, bapt. 5 Sept. 1652; Sarah, b. 16 Mar. 1654; Timothy, 26 Oct. 1656; Mary, Oct. 1658; William, 3 Nov. 1660; John, 7 July 1662; Ephraim, 1 Nov. 1663; Abigail, 16 May 1666; and Josiah, 15 Dec. 1667; and d. 15 May 1669. In latter days he was of Simsbury. His wid. m. 21 July 1670, Nathaniel Pinney; Sarah m. 13 Dec. 1683, John Mansfield. SAMUEL, Boston, by w. Eliz. had Eliz. b. 5 Sept. 1681; and Grace, 5 Apr. 1687. SAMUEL, Andover, perhaps s. of Edward the first, m. 29 May 1682, Sarah Chandler, had Sarah, b. 10 Oct. foll.; Samuel, 22 Nov. 1684; John, 28 Sept. 1686; Joseph, 8 Feb. 1689; Hannah, 18 May 1691, d. young; Henry, 24 Sept. 1693; Thomas, 5 Nov. 1695; Eliz. 6 Sept. 1698; Annis, 22 Feb. 1701; and Deborah, 1703. TIMOTHY, Windsor, s. of William, freem. 1664, m. 19 May 1661, Mary, d. of Edward Griswold, had Timothy, b. 1 Nov. 1663; Joseph, 27 Sept. 1666; William, 4 Feb. 1669; Cornelius, 26 Apr. 1671; Mary, 14 Aug. 1673, d. young; Samuel, 29 Jan. 1676; Nathaniel, 7 Jan. 1678; Sarah, 27 Dec. 1679; Abigail, 3 June 1682; Hannah, 4 Aug. 1684; Ann, 2 Oct. 1686; and Martha, 12 Nov. 1688. He was lieut. and d. 1719, in his will, of 1717, names all these ch. except Mary, tho. two others of the ds. were d. but had left ch. TIMOTHY, Simsbury, s. of Samuel, m. 18 Nov. 1680, Sarah, prob. d. of Samuel Gaylord, and sec. w. 13 Nov. 1690, Sarah Pratt; and he d. 1712. ‡*WILLIAM, Dorchester, came, prob. in the Mary and John, 1630, from Plymouth, and may well be thot. a Devonsh. man, and perhaps br. of George, tho. more prob. his f. req. to be adm. freem. 19 Oct. of that yr. and was sw. 18 May foll. brot. w. whose name is not found, and ch. William, Samuel, Nathaniel, Joseph, and Sarah, yet one or two of these may have been b. at D. was rep. at the first gen. ct. of Mass. 1634, and Selectman 1634 and 5, went next yr. with Warham to Windsor, there had Timothy, b. Aug. 1639; and Mary, Mar. 1644. He was of the earliest Assist. 1636–42, a rep. 1645–57, Assist. again, 1658 to 1662, but not under the new chart. and d. 14 July 1672. Sarah m. 1658, William Wade; and Mary m. Dec. 1665, Thomas Barber. WILLIAM, Windsor, s. of the preced. b. in Eng. freem. 1669, m. 4 June 1646 (one report is 1645), Isabel Wilson, and sec. w. 20 Dec. 1676, Sarah, d. of

Humphrey Pinney, had no ch. by either, and d. 1682. WILLIAM, Boston, mariner, whose first w. is unkn. but for sec. w. he m. Jane, wid. of Henry Butterfield, wh. hav. power of dispos. gave her est. by will of 10 Feb. 1692, to him for life, remaind. to John and William P. s. of her present h. so that it may be infer. that she had no ch. by either of her hs. WILLIAM, Northampton, s. of deac. Nathaniel, m. 30 May 1678, Abigail, d. of John Stebbins, had Abigail, b. Aug. 1679; Eliz. 4 Feb. 1682; William, Apr. 1684; Mary, 3 June 1688; Nathaniel, 5 Oct. 1690; Deborah, 17 Mar. 1694; Ebenezer, 1697; Joseph, 5 Dec. 1699; and Mercy, 4 Mar. 1703. He was freem. 1690, and d. 1 June 1745, and his wid. d. Dec. 1748, ea. aged 88. Nineteen of this name had, in 1834, been gr. at Yale, four at Harv. and three at other N. E. coll.

PHENIX, ALEXANDER, Wickford 1674.

PHESE, or PHESEY, SAMUEL, a soldier from the E. part of the Col. in Mar. 1676, sent up to Conn. river, in the Ind. war, was prob. from Braintree, and s. of William. WILLIAM, Braintree, or possib. Watertown, freem. 10 May 1643, may be indebted to a careless clk. for this spelling of a name, that I should prob. write Veazie, with confidence.

PHILBRICK, or PHILBROOK, sometimes FILBRICK, JAMES, Hampton 1644, prob. s. of Thomas, was first perhaps at Watertown, had w. Ann, d. of Thomas Roberts of Dover, and by her had Bethia, wh. m. 24 Apr. 1677, Caleb Perkins; James; and perhaps others; was perhaps a mariner, and drown. 1 Nov. 1674. JAMES, Hampton, s. of the preced. m. 1 Dec. 1674, Hannah, d. of Isaac Perkins, had Joseph, b. 1693; and prob. more ch. JOHN, Hampton 1639, wh. may have been br. of the first James, had Hannah, Sarah, John, but dates are not seen; was lost 20 Oct. 1657, with seven others, of wh. were his w. Ann, and d. Sarah, in a boat going out of the harb. JOHN, Hampton, s. of the preced. perhaps, b. a. 1624, was liv. 1697, perhaps at Greenland, and was f. of Elias. JONATHAN, Hampton, prob. s. of Thomas, took o. of alleg. and fidel. 1678. JOSEPH, Hampton, perhaps br. of James the sec. had Joseph, b. 14 Dec. 1686, d. soon; prob. Joseph, again, and perhaps more. ROBERT, Ipswich 1639, perhaps earlier, was a soldier in the Pequot war, 1636, but after 1648 may have rem. The town rec. has Filbrick. SAMUEL, Hampton 1678, was prob. s. of Thomas the first, and ano. Samuel, the same yr. took o. of alleg. there. THOMAS, Watertown 1636, where the rec. gives the spell. Filbrick, rem. early to Hampton, sold his est. at W. 1646, had many ch. that he brot. from Eng. by w. Ann, d. of William Knapp, but none prob. b. here, d. 1667. His will of Mar. 1664 calls hims. very aged, ment. s. James, gr.s. John, s. Thomas, ds. Eliz. Garland, Hannah, Mary, and Martha, gr.childr. James Chase, and Martha, w. of John Cass. His d. Eliz. prob. the eldest, had bef. 1643, m. Thomas

Chase, after whose d. leav. 5 ch. by her, she m. 26 Oct. 1654, John Garland, and again, 19 Feb. 1674, m. Henry Roby; Mary m. a. 1647, Edward Tucke; and Martha m. John Cass, the ancest. of the disting. diplomatist, Lewis Cass. THOMAS, Hampton, prob. s. of the preced. b. in Eng. a. 1624, freem. 1668, had perhaps Thomas (as a jr. is nam. for tak. o. of alleg. 1678, some mos. bef. Thomas senr.), and prob. sev. others, as I think he had sec. w. Hannah, d. of Edward French, young wid. of John White, and by her had Hannah, wh. m. Joseph Walker of Portsmouth, and next, 29 July 1686, John Seavey. THOMAS, Hampton, perhaps s. of the preced. by w. Mehitable, had Eliz. b. 17 Oct. 1686. WILLIAM, Hampton, may have been s. of Thomas the sec. by w. Mary had Walter, b. 10 Nov. 1690; and Mary, 20 May 1692. Of many under this surname I fail to find connex.

PHILLIPS, ANDREW, Charlestown, by w. Eliz. had Andrew; Eliz. b. 29 May 1657; and Ephraim, 31 Mar. 1659; perhaps others. ANDREW, Charlestown, s. prob. of the preced. m. 11 Nov. 1683, Sarah, d. of Michael Smith of Malden, had Andrew, b. 23 July 1687; Ebenezer, 17 Aug. 1695; Joanna, 8 Sept. 1697; and perhaps more. BENJAMIN, Charlestown 1681, s. of deac. Nicholas of Weymouth, by w. Ann had Benjamin, bapt. 17 Apr. 1681, d. young; Benjamin and Joshua, b. 14 Apr. 1685; and posthum. d. Abiah, 18 Aug. 1688. He d. 13 Feb. preced. and his wid. m. 3 Feb. 1696, Benjamin Lawrence. BENJAMIN, Marshfield, m. 12 Jan. 1682, Sarah Thomas, prob. d. of Nathaniel. CALEB, Roxbury, by w. Eliz. had Caleb, bapt. 9 July 1682; John, b. 25 Jan. bapt. 3 Feb. 1684, d. in few wks.; Eliz. 25 Oct. 1685; Mary, 28, bapt. 29 Apr. 1688; and Ebenezer, 11 July 1690. CHARLES, Lynn, had David, b. 17 Mar. 1656, d. at 5 mos.; Abigail, perhaps, 29 Oct. 1657, but the rec. is doubtful; John, 15 Aug. 1658, d. young; George, 20 Dec. 1663; and John, again, 27 June, 1667. DANIEL, Newtown, L. I. 1686, by Riker call. br. of Theophilus, was town clk. superseded on the revo. 1689, and may have been of Gallup's comp. 1690, against Quebec. DAVID, Milford 1655–60. ELEAZER, Charlestown, s. of Henry, by first w. Ann, d. of capt. William Foster, had Henry, b. 28 Dec. 1680, d. soon; Eleazer, 23 Apr. 1682; Ann, 26 Aug. 1684; William, 31 Mar. bapt. 10 Apr. 1687, d. soon; Nathaniel, 24, bapt. 27 Apr. 1688, d. in 4 mos.; Isaac, 3, bapt. 7 July 1689, d. soon; Joseph, 17, bapt. 20 July 1690; Eliz. bapt. 23 Oct. 1692; and Jonathan, 19, bapt. 24 Nov. 1695. His w. d. 1 Dec. foll. and he m. 10 Feb. 1696, Sarah Cutler, perhaps d. of deac. John, wh. d. 11 Jan. 1705; and he m. 22 Mar. 1706, wid. Eliz. Bill. He was a capt. and d. 29 Apr. 1709. The will of 20 Mar. 1708 names his new w. and his three s. and one d. only liv. GEORGE, Watertown, the first min. came in the Arbella, the admiral sh. of the fleet, with

Winth. 1630, bring. s. Samuel, and w. beside Eliz. and perhaps Abigail, an only ch. sis. by ano. f. of John Hayward of Watertown and Charlestown, wh. d. soon after land. at Salem. He was s. of Christopher, b. 1593, at Rainham St. Martins near Rougham, in the hundr. of Gallow, Co. Norfolk, not Raymond, as says Mather III. cap. 4, but Brook, in Lives of Puritans II. 493, says Roudham in the same Co. yet Dr. Fuller, writ. to Gov. Bradford, particularly calls him a Suffolk man (refer. no doubt, to the exercise of his min. for more prob. is the deriv. from Norfolk); however, more import. is it, that he was bred at Gonville and Caius Coll. Cambridge, matricula. 20 Apr. 1610, as from its rec. Mr. Somerby certified me, and there, I found, he took his degr. 1613 and 1617, was sett. in Boxted, Co. Essex, as the dilig. inq. of a descend. in our day has estab. tho. Prince's Ann. II. 45, with minute knowledge, prefer. a differ. but not dist. parish. Hubbard, wh. ought to have kn. calls him "faithful min. of the gospel at Bocksted, near Groton in Suff'lk." By a sec. w. m. prob. 1631, Eliz. by Bond, with happy conject. thot. to be wid. of capt. Robert Welden, he had Zorobabel, b. 5 Apr. 1632; Jonathan, 16 Nov. 1633; Theophilus, 28 May 1636; Amabel, Dec. 1637, d. Apr. foll.; Ephraim, bur. 12 June 1640, very young; Obadiah, b. 5 Apr. 1641; and a d. Abiel, perhaps that Abigail, wh. m. 8 Oct. 1666, James Barnard. He had req. on 19 Oct. to be made freem. took the o. with the earliest, 18 May foll. d. Monday 1 July 1644, and was bur. the next day. His wid. d. 27 Jan. 1681. GEORGE, Dorchester, freem. 18 May 1631, may be presum. to have come, in the Mary and John, the yr. bef. rem. early to Windsor, for his slender health in 1648 and 55, was excus. from milit. watch. His w. d. 1662, leav. him no ch. and he was so unfortun. 1676, as to be involv. in a wordy controv. with the authority of the col. wh. disfranch. him next yr. of wh. some acco. is in Trumbull's Rec. II. 307; but lucki. for him, he d. 9 July 1678. His est. was disput. for by remote heirs. GEORGE, Brookhaven, s. of Samuel the first, was min. there 42 yrs. m. Sarah, eldest d. of William Hallet, the sec. had George, William, John, H. C. 1725, and three ds. but of only one, Mary, is the name told. He d. 3 Apr. 1739. * || HENRY, Dedham, freem. 13 Mar. 1639, ar. co. 1640, had w. Eliz. Brock, wh. d. 1 Aug. 1640, and m. 1 May 1641, Ann Hunting, prob. sis. of Elder John, had Eleazur, b. 30 Jan. bapt. 6 Feb. 1642, d. in few days; Hannah, 25, bapt. 28 May 1643; Abigail, 20 Oct. 1645; and by third w. Mary, d. of John Dwight, had Nathaniel, bapt. 3 Apr. 1653, d. bef. his f.; and Eleazur, 8 Oct. 1654; was ens. of the milit. comp. 1648; rem. to Boston to follow his trade of a butcher; there had Henry, b. 1, bapt. 26 Oct. 1656, d. bef. his f.; Timothy, 15, bapt. 19 Sept. 1658; Mary, 28 Nov. bapt. 2 Dec. 1660; Samuel, bapt. 2 Nov. 1662; Elisha, 12, bapt. 15 May 1665; Jonathan, 12 Sept. 1666, bapt. uncert. day;

Mehitable, bapt. 21 July 1667; John, 22, bapt. 24 Jan. 1669, d. soon; John, again, 9, bapt. 10 July 1670; and Eliz. 9, bapt. 18 Aug. 1672. In this yr. he was made deac. of the first ch. and rep. for Hadley. Judge Sewall, in his diary, chronicles his bur. 3 Feb. 1686. His will of 7 Aug. 1682, with codic. 4 Dec. 1685, pro. 18 Feb. foll. disposes of good est. names w. s. Eleazer, Timothy, Samuel, and John, direct. this last for college, ds. Hannah Negus, Abigail East, Mehitable, and Eliz. also notices Henry and Nathaniel as dec. so that prob. both had reach. mature yrs. A Mary P. wh. may have been his mo. or ch. d. 2 July 1640. He was much esteemed; and his youngest s. John might have made good the place of Christian min. (that his f. was desir. to undertake, as Farmer tells), had he obt. the educat. intend. but prob. he d. early. Eliz. m. a Ruggles. HENRY, New London, on the tax list of 1667, but never again on any rec. there, says Miss Caulkins. HENRY, Charlestown, may have been s. of Henry of Dedham, tho. it is not very prob. for by w. Mary, he had Joseph, b. 19 Feb. 1675, of course less than 18 and $\frac{1}{2}$ yrs. younger than his f. Contra. to this suppos. also is the will of deac. Henry speak. of est. of s. Henry dec. in his hands, as belong. to other of his own ch. HENRY, Charlestown, s. of col. John, m. 27 May 1708, Joanna, d. of col. Joseph Lynd, wid. of Samuel Everton, and d. 14 Dec. 1729, prob. without issue. JAMES, Taunton 1659, s. of William of the same, neph. of William Parker, wh. left him small legacy. He had James, b. 1 Jan. 1662; Nathaniel, 25 Mar. 1664; Sarah, 17 Mar. 1667; William, 21 Aug. 1669. Perhaps he rem. to Providence, where one of this name took the o. of alleg. to Charles II. in May 1682. JOHN, Dover, or Portsmouth, d. 1642. JOHN, Dedham 1638, a famous min. of Wrentham (wh. is a. 30 ms. N. E. from Ipswich, Eng.), where he obt. his living as rector, 1609, and m. 6 Jan. 1612, Eliz. a sis. of famous Dr. Ames, wh. gave him favor in the eyes of puritans, was desired to accept office here in sev. places, espec. Cambridge, perhaps in connex. with the newly begun coll. but prefer. to go home in the autumn of 1641. Felt I. 212, thinks, he was made townsman of Salem, but the prob. is at least equal, that ano. man was thus honored. He was accomp. to Eng. by John Humphrey, Esq. and then honored in the triumph of the cause, made one of the assembly of divines at Westminster; was founder of the Congreg. ch. 1650, after the N. E. pattern, and d. 2 Sept. 1660, aged 78. Calamy, Cont. II. 797. Winth. II. 86. Lamson. Lechford, 38, refers to him shortly bef. he sailed. His name he wrote without final s. His w. Eliz. was bur. 22 Jan. 1659. He was bred at the Univ. of Cambridge, having his A. B. at Catharine Hall, 1596, and taking his A. M. 1600 and B. D. 1608 at Clare Hall as the Registrar of the Univ. certif. to me. JOHN, Dorchester, a baker, came prob. in the Mary and John, 1630, desired

19 Oct. of that yr. to be made freem. but was not sw. until 7 Aug. 1632, by w. Joanna, had Mary, b. Apr. 1633, d. at 7 yrs.; John, 22 Apr. 1635; Martha, Apr. 1636, d. soon; Mary, again; Israel, 3 June 1642, d. next yr. by the Gen. Ct. appoint. constable 1636; rem. to Boston, bec. one of the found. and a deac. of sec. ch. 5 June 1650. His w. d. 22 Oct. 1675, says the rec. and gr-st. 24 Oct. aged 80 yrs. but perhaps exagger. or copied wrong. In Jan. foll. he m. wid. Sarah Minor, and d. 16 Dec. 1682, aged 77. His only ch. that reach. matur. Mary, m. George Munjoy of Falmouth, and after him Robert Lawrence of the same. JOHN, Plymouth 1640, aft. of Marshfield, had John and other ch. b. in Eng. m. for sec. w. 14 Mar. 1667, Faith, wid. of Edward Dotey, wh. d. the same yr. says Miss Thomas, p. 83, and he d. 1677, says Winsor. But Shurtleff, who gives a full memoir of him, says he was of Duxbury 1643, by first w. whose name is unkn. had John, Samuel, Jeremiah, and Mary; the eldest, prob. John, was k. by lightning, 31 July 1658, as by the Coroner's inq. four days after, is shown; that his sec. w. was Grace, m. 1654, wid. of William Holloway, and she, with his s. Jeremiah was k. by lightning 23 June 1666, when William Shurtleff, ancest. of the disting. antiq. was k. by the same bolt; and that the third w. Faith d. 1667, by wh. he had no ch. but by the sec. had Hannah; Grace; Joseph, b. 1655, wh. was, says Miss Thomas, k. at Rehoboth fight, 1676; and Benjamin; and that he prob. d. Oct. 1691, almost 90 yrs. old, leav. Samuel, Benjamin, and Mary. Both of these s. had fams. See also, Thomas's Memo. of Marshfield. JOHN, Duxbury 1643, may be that apprent. wh. went from Boston 1631, but there is no certainty as to that apprent. JOHN, Wenham 1647, nam. in the will of Christopher Young as trustee with charge to take his s. JOHN, called a Welshman, Casco 1642, perhaps freem. of 1658, rem. to Kittery, was liv. 1684, aged 77. Willis I. 69. JOHN, Boston, by w. Mary had Mary, b. 13 July 1652; Sarah, 29 June 1654, d. same day; and Mary, again, 5 Aug. 1658; and the same, or ano. of the same name, by w. Sarah had John, 4 Mar. 1662. ‡*‖ JOHN, Charlestown, perhaps br. of Henry, was a master mariner, m. 19 July 1655, Catharine, d. of John Anderson, had Catharine, b. 30, bapt. 31 Aug. 1662; Samuel, 16, bapt. 21 Feb. 1664; both d. early; Mehitable, 1, bapt. 2 July 1668; Abigail, 19 June 1670; Catharine, again, 23, bapt. 25 June 1672; John, 18, bapt. 23 Mar. 1673, d. at 2 yrs.; Mary, bapt. 14 Mar. 1675; Anderson, 11 July 1680; and Henry, 4 Dec. 1681. He was freem. 1677, ar. co. 1680, its capt. 1685, rep. 1683–6, of the Comtee. of safety on the revo. against Andros, nam. in the new chart. of the Council, but by pop. vote chos. bef. and so contin. to 1716, col. of the milit. treas. of the Prov. judge of the County Ct. and such serv. were successiv. enjoy. by him. His w. d. 24 Feb. and was bur. 2 Mar. 1699,

aged 59; and soon after he bec. h. of Sarah, d. of John Stedman of Cambridge, wh. had successiv. been wid. of John Brackett, Samuel Alcock, and Thomas Graves; and she outliv. him, tho. he did not d. until 20 Mar. 1726, aged 93 yrs. 9 mos. Abigail m. 4 May 1686, Cotton Mather, and d. 28 Nov. 1702. JOHN, Marshfield, m. 3 Apr. 1677, Ann Torry. JOHN, Lynn, may have been s. of Charles of the same, by w. Hannah had John, b. 3 Dec. 1689; and Hannah, 6 June 1694; and he d. 29 Sept. foll. Lewis says, others of this fam. perhaps earlier, had sett. at Lynn. JOHN, Charlestown, s. of col. John, I think bapt. Anderson, was a mariner, m. 15 Aug. 1694, Mary, d. of Samuel Hayman, had Samuel, b. 18 Nov. 1695, d. soon; John, 15 Jan. 1697; Samuel, again, 21 Dec. 1699. His w. d. 6 Jan. 1702, and he m. 11 Sept. foll. Ann, d. of col. Joseph Lynde, wid. of Isaac Greenwood, had Abigail, b. 19 Apr. 1712, d. young; Anderson, 5 Feb. 1715; and Abigail, again, 31 Dec. 1716. JONATHAN, Watertown, s. of Rev. George of the same, m. 26 Jan. 1681, Sarah Holland, perhaps d. of Nathaniel, had Sarah, b. 14 Sept. 1682, d. at 6 yrs.; Eliz. 27 Nov. 1684; Ruth, 28 Mar. 1687; Sarah, again, bapt. 4 Aug. 1689; Abigail, b. 22 Apr. 1693, d. young; Jonathan, bapt. 20 June 1697; Hannah, 23 Apr. 1699; George, 23 Feb. 1701; Nathaniel, 2 May 1703; and Benjamin, 8 Apr. 1705; perhaps posthum. for the f. d. 1704. His wid. m. 1 Jan. 1717, John Bemis. JOSEPH, Newtown, L. I. 1686, then nam. by Gov. Dongan in his gr. of chart. but he had been a freeholder there for 20 yrs. Riker. He may have been br. of Theophilus, but wh. shall discover their f. will be fortunate. JOSEPH, Providence, took o. of alleg. in May 1682. JOSEPH, Boston, by w. Bridget had Joseph, b. 7 May 1684; Benjamin, 18 Oct. 1685; and Nathaniel, 30 Mar. 1689; perhaps others. JOSHUA, Weymouth, s. of Nicholas, was a soldier, 1676, serv. on Conn. river under capt. Turner, perhaps then ruin. his health, made his will 10 Apr. 1679, calling hims. 32 yrs. old, pro. 2 May next, in wh. he names br. Richard, and gives to sis. Experience King and Hannah White only, so that he left no w. nor ch. MARTIN, Medfield 1664. NICHOLAS, Dedham 1638, br. of Henry, rem. to Weymouth perhaps late in life, freem. 13 May 1640, had Experience, b. 8 May 1641; Caleb, 22 Jan. 1644; was deac. and d. Sept. 1672. His will of 2 June 1671, pro. 3 Oct. 1672, makes Richard his eldest s. excor. but wishes br. Henry to act as overseer, divides est. to his ch. Richard, Joshua, and Benjamin, Alice or Eliz. Shaw, Experience King, Hannah White and Abigail P. NICHOLAS, Boston, m. 4 Dec. 1651, Hannah Salter, had Eliz. b. 24 Feb. 1653; Hannah, 25 Nov. 1654; Nicholas, 26 Feb. 1657, d. 1 Aug. foll.; Nicholas, again, 12 May 1660; Abigail, 20 Feb. 1662; Sarah, 13 Apr. 1665; and Thomas 19 Oct. 1667. He d. I imagine, in Apr. 1670, for Hannah, his wid. renders

inv. 24th of that mo. He seems to have been a shopkeeper. Nicholas, Boston, butcher, by w. Philippa had Nicholas, b. 30 Nov. 1665;
John, 3 May 1667, d. soon; John, again, 21 June 1669; Joseph and
Benjamin, tw. 14 May 1671; and Mary, 23 June 1674. Nicholas,
Weymouth, s. of the last preced. prob. but possib. of the last but one, by
w. Mary had Mary, b. 29 Nov. 1690, d. soon; Mary, again, 24 Aug.
1692; Nicholas and Hannah, tw. 23 May 1697. Philip, Boston, may
be that youth of 15 yrs. from Olney, Co. Bucks, arr. in the Hopewell, capt. Bundock, 1635, serv. to John Cooper, wh. sat down, prob. at
Lynn, and went to L. I. had by w. Rachel at B. Susanna, wh. d. 14 Dec.
1651; Susanna, wh. d. 15 Aug. 1656; and David, b. 1 Mar. 1660; d. Oct.
1669, and admin. was giv. the mo. foll. to William Dennison of Milton
in behalf of the eldest s. John and two other s. perhaps b. bef. he came to
B. but his inv. was only £2. 16. Richard, Weymouth, eldest s. of the
first Nicholas of the same, by w. Mary, d. of Samuel Packard, had one
ch. b. 7 Dec. 1657, not nam. in the rec. and may therefore be supposed to
have d. soon; Mary, 21 May 1660, d. soon; Mary, again, 24 May 1661;
Joshua, 10 May 1662; Nicholas, 30 Mar. 1664; Eliz. 27 Nov. 1665;
Richard, 20 Oct. 1667; and Samuel, 7 May 1670; was freem. 1678.
Mitchell, in Hist. of Bridgewater, gives him w. Eliz. d. of deac. Samuel
Edson, besides Mary Packard. If he be correct, perhaps the sec. w. was
Edson. Samuel, Taunton, m. 15 May 1676, a wid. Cobb, had Mehitable,
b. 9 Jan. foll. Samuel, Rowley, s. of the first George, b. in Eng. 1625,
at Boxted in Essex, if Prince II. 45, seem better authority, as usual, than
Mather, who calls it Boxford, H. C. 1651, ord. June 1652, collea. with
Ezekiel Rogers, m. Oct. foll. Sarah, d. of Samuel Appleton of Ipswich,
had Samuel, b. Mar. 1654, d. young; Sarah, 7 Feb. or 14 Mar. 1656,
wh. m. Stephen Mighill; Samuel, again, 13 or 23 Mar. 1658; George,
23 Nov. 1659; Eliz. 16 Nov. 1661; Ezekiel, Feb. 1663; all three d.
soon; George, again, 3 June 1664, H. C. 1686, bef. ment.; Eliz. 2 Aug.
1665, wh. m. 7 Nov. 1683, Rev. Edward Payson, and d. 1724; Dorcas,
1667; Mary, Feb. 1668; and John, 23 Oct. 1670. The last three also
d. soon. He d. 22 Apr. 1696, and his wid. d. 15 July 1713, aged 85.
Samuel, Boston 1681, disting. as a bookseller, in Thomas, Hist. of Print.
II. 411, and John Dunton in the curious book of his Life and Errors;
m. Hannah, d. of capt. Benjamin Gillam, had Hannah, b. 8, bapt. 12
Mar. 1682; Gillam, b. 25 Sept. 1686, but not bapt. bef. 6 Oct. 1695;
Faith; Samuel, bapt. 28 May 1693; Ann, 30 Nov. 1701; and Henry,
25 Feb. 1706, prob. H. C. 1724; and he d. Oct. 1720, aged 58. Hannah, the eldest ch. m. 4 Jan. 1700, David Anderson of Charlestown, and
next, 8 July 1703, Habijah Savage of Boston; Gillam m. Mary Faneuil;
Faith m. June 1710, Arthur Savage; Samuel was drown. near home,

on return from London; Ann m. Peter Butler; and Henry d. 1729, at Rochelle in France, confident. thot. to be that unhappy man, wh. k. his intimate compan. Benjamin Woodbridge on Boston common in a private duel. SAMUEL, Boston, by w. Sarah had Sarah, b. 21 Mar. 1682; Ann, 20 May 1685; William, 1 Apr. 1688; and Bridget, 4 Feb. 1692. SAMUEL, Salem, s. of Rev. Samuel of Rowley, a goldsmith, m. 26 May 1687, Mary, d. of Rev. John Emerson of Gloucester, had, beside three ds. Samuel, b. 28 Feb. 1690, H. C. 1708, min. of Andover; and John, 22 June 1701. His w. d. 24 Oct. 1703, and he m. 27 Apr. foll. Sarah Mayfield, a wid. and had only Patience, 8 Aug. 1706. THEOPHILUS, Newtown, L. I. 1672, had prob. been sev. yrs. on the isl. perhaps as early as 1663, gr.s. of Rev. George, as Riker thot. but wh. could be his f. I have sought in vain for sev. yrs. m. Ann, d. of Ralph Hunt, had Theophilus, b. 15 May 1673; William, 28 June 1676; and Philip, 27 Dec. 1678. Riker says he had two more ws. but he names no issue. He was a very useful man; in 1676 chos. to one town office, and next yr. town clk. to his d. 26 Jan. 1689. To me it once seemed highly prob. that he was s. of Rev. George, the first, but Riker 105, suppos. him gr.ch. of wh. tho. improb. is very great, yet greater do I reckon the improb. of his being the s. For THEOPHILUS, s. of George the first, by fam. tradit. of wh. I have transcript, and feel almost certain that it is correct, m. 3 Nov. 1666, Bethia Bedell (or some other name exceeding. hard to be made out from the fugitive memoranda of fam. tradit. in conjunct. with the indistinct chirogr. of the old rec. that in this m. perhaps gives the name Keedell), by wh. he had Bethia, b. 21 Dec. 1668. His w. d. 15 Mar. foll. and he m. 21 Nov. 1677, Mary Bennett, had Samuel, 20 Feb. 1680; Benjamin, no date; Mary, 16 Sept. 1684, d. soon; Mary, again, 15 Nov. 1685; Theophilus, 24 June 1688; Jonathan, bapt. 13 July 1690; John, b. 10 Dec. 1692; Eliz. no date; Lydia, 20 June 1695; Obadiah, 22 Feb. 1698; Joseph, 4 Dec. 1702; and David, 15 Dec. 1707; and d. 1717. His wid. Mary liv. at Hopkinton, with her s. Theophilus, and d. 3 Dec. 1730. THOMAS, Pemaquid 1674, and perhaps his s. of the same name, there took o. of fidel. or one may have been br. ano. s. of William. THOMAS, Boston, perhaps s. of Nicholas of the same, by w. Hannah had Hannah, b. 7 Sept. 1690. TIMOTHY, Charlestown, freem. 1690, was s. of Henry of Dedham, m. 18 Apr. 1681, wid. Mary Smith, had Mary, bapt. 12 Oct. 1682; Timothy, b. 24 Dec. 1686, bapt. 22 Jan. foll.; Ann, 24 Mar. 1689; Sarah, 30 Aug. 1691; John, 14 July 1694; and Mary; and he d. 7 May 1712. Perhaps he liv. in Boston, but had est. in C. giv. by his f.'s will. WALTER, Wiscasset 1661, b. it is said, a. 1619, was at Salem 1689, perhaps driv. from the E. by the Ind. hostil. is call. sen. when made freem. 1690; resid. at the vill. now Danvers, and was liv. 1700. WILLIAM, Taunton 1643, and prob. some yrs. earlier, as he was among purch. 1637, in his will of 16 Apr. 1654, calls hims. "threescore yrs. and ten at the least," out of his small est. gives w. Eliz. and s. James, who was excor. but if he d. without issue, then to childr. of his d. Eliz. w. of James Walker. Baylies II. 267, 282; and Geneal. Reg. V. 260 comp. with VI. 93 and 95. WILLIAM, Hartford 1639, perhaps earlier, but not an orig. propr. d. aft. May 1653, leav. wid. Ann, but no ch. as is thot. for in her will of 31 Mar. 1668, pro. 6 Nov. 1669, she disposes of est. of wh. the val. was £391, to her br. John Rogers, as well as br. Samuel Young, both in Eng. £100 ea. to Mr. John Hooker (I suppose he was br. of Rev. Thomas), liv. in Old Eng. £10 if he come to liv. in N. E. to Mr. Samuel Hooker £10, and to his sis. w. of Rev. John Wilson of Medfield, £10. Without doubt she or her h. was relat. of famous Hooker. WILLIAM, Charlestown, with w. Mary adm. of the ch. 23 Sept. 1639, freem. 13 May 1640, had Phebe, b. 7 Apr. 1640; Nathaniel, 5 Feb. 1642; Mary, 17 Feb. 1644. His w. d. 1 May 1646, and he rem. to Boston, m. Susanna, wid. of Christopher Stanley, and by her, wh. d. 16 June 1655, had there prob. William, Eliz. and Sarah. On 10 Sept. 1650, he and his w. made separ. wills, and hers was pro. 2 Aug. 1655, in wh. reciting, that he had confirmed to her for sole dispos. what was her h. Stanley's, she gives to her d.-in-law, Mary Field (by me conject. to be w. of Robert, and d. of Stanley by a former w.), to d. Martha, or Mary Thurston, w. of Richard; d. Rebecca Lord, w. of Robert; to William, Nathaniel, Eliz. Phebe, and Sarah Phillips, called her s. and ds. tho. part were by the former w. and to Eliz. w. of William Aspinwall, prob. some relat. beside provid. if any childr. of her br. or sis. come over, £6 ea. and all the resid. to her h. The s. William prob. d. young. By a third w. Bridget he had John, b. 18, bapt. 21 Sept. 1656, d. next Aug.; Samuel, 16 Mar. 1658; and William, again, 28 Jan. bapt. 5 Feb. 1660. He had large prop. in lands and mills at Saco, liv. there many yrs. was made an officer in the milit. and magistr. in 1663, confirm. in the same by royal commissnrs. 1665, a major in 1675, when he well defend. his place against assault by Ind. wh. however burnt the ho. came back to Boston to reside; made his will, 29 Sept. 1683, pro. 13 Nov. foll. recites, that hav. portioned four ds. little est. but land was left, however, as w. Bridget had brot. him good est. that to William, her younger s. who had been then four yrs. in captiv. with the Spaniards, and to her elder Samuel, three fourths of the Saco lands and mills, were devis. His d. Eliz. m. 6 July, Abiel Everitt; and next, 1 Apr. 1660, John Alden; Phebe had m. 26 July 1659, Zechariah Gillam. WILLIAM, Boston, a mariner, called jr. to disting. him from the lieut. preced. tho. prob. not s. m. 24

Oct. 1650, Martha Franklin, had William, b. 13 Jan. 1652, wh. may
have d. young; and Martha, 10 Mar. 1654. Prob. his w. d. bef. long,
and by ano. w. Joan, he may have had William, again, 8 Aug. 1671, wh.
was a butcher, and the same or ano. WILLIAM, of Boston, possib. s. of
the major, by w. Deborah had William, b. 17 Nov. 1690; and Sarah, 28
Dec. 1692. ‖ZECHARIAH, Boston, ar. co. 1660, by w. Eliz. had (if we
accept the truth of the rec.) Zechariah, wh. d. 2 Sept. 1652; Zechariah, wh. d. 4 Sept. 1652; Zechariah, again, d. 24 July 1654; Zechariah, again, b. 5 Mar. 1657, d. young; Eliz. 29 June 1661; Sarah, 7
Sept. 1662; Zechariah, again, 22 Oct. 1664; Joseph, 4 Sept. 1669; and
Hannah, 31 July 1671. He was k. by the Ind. 2 Aug. 1675, when the
party under capt. Edward Hutchinson, going by appointm. to treat a.
peace, was treacherous. as our side said, cut off. ZOROBABEL, Southampton, L. I. 1663–73, I judge to be the eldest s. by sec. w. of George the
first, tho. fam. geneal. does not indicate his resid. nor give any thing of
him but the b. He m. at S. Ann, wid. of John White, who had been of
Lynn bef. the sett. there. I once presum. that the two uncles, Zorobabel
and Theophilus, being of L. I. drew thither Rev. George, their neph. but
some facts appear irreconcil. with this presumpt. Twenty of this name
had, twenty yrs. since, been gr. at Harv. and very few at other N. E. coll.

PHILPOT, THOMAS, Watertown 1642, fell insane 1647, but liv. at Salem 1668, well eno. to petitn. against taxes, and was, says Bond, a pauper
in 1674. WILLIAM, Boston 1645, called saltmaker, on adm. to the ch.
29 Nov. of that yr. m. 16 or 26 Dec. 1651, Ann, wid. of George Hunn.

PHINNEY, FINNEY, or FENNYE, ISAAC, Medfield 1657. JOHN, Plymouth, by w, Christian, wh. d. 9 Sept. 1649, had John, b. 24 Dec. 1638,
bapt. at Barnstable 31 July 1653, and perhaps others, rem. to Barnstable,
m. 10 June 1650, Abigail, wid. of Henry Coggin, wh. d. 6 May 1653, and
for third w. 26 June 1654, Eliz. Bayley, had Jonathan, 14 Aug. 1655;
Robert, 13 Aug. 1656; Hannah, 2 Sept. 1657; Eliz. 15 Mar. 1659;
Josiah, 11 Jan. 1661; Jeremiah, 15 Aug. 1662; and Joshua, Dec. 1665.
Hannah m. the sec. Ephraim Morton. JOHN, Barnstable, s. of the preced. m. 10 Aug. 1664, Mary Rogers, had John, b. 5 May 1665; Mela-
tiah, Oct. 1666, d. next yr.; Joseph, 28 Jan. 1668; Thomas, Jan. 1672;
Ebenezer, 8 Feb. 1674; Samuel, 4 Nov. 1676; Mary, 3 Sept. 1678;
Mercy, 10 July 1679; Reliance, 27 Aug. 1681; Benjamin, 18 June
1682, bapt. 16 Sept. 1683; Jonathan, 30 July 1684, bapt. 26 July 1685;
Hannah, 28 Mar. 1687, bapt. 7 Apr. 1689, d. young; and Eliz. bapt.
10 May 1691. JOSIAH, Barnstable, br. of the preced. m. 19 Jan. 1688,
Eliz. d. of the first Joseph Warren. ROBERT, Plymouth, prob. br. of
John the first, and perhaps elder, came with his mo. I suppose, for the
rec. says " mo. Feney d. 22 Apr. 1650, aged upwards of 80," m. 1 Sept.

1641, Phebe Ripley, was deac. 1667, and d. 7 Jan. 1688, near 80, and
his wid. d. 9 Dec. 1710, "suppos. 92 yrs. old." ROBERT, Barnstable, s.
of John the first, d. 1690, in the wild crusade of Phips against Quebec.

PHIPPEN, FITZPEN, FIPPEN, FIPPENNY, or PHIPPENNEY, BENJAMIN,
Boston, blockmaker, s. of David, b. in Eng. by w. Wilmot had David, b.
6 Nov. 1651; Sarah; Benjamin, 6 Apr. 1654, d. soon; Benjamin, again,
15 July 1656; James; Rebecca; Mary; Thomas; John; and Joseph.
He had sec. w. Elinor, and d. a. 1678. Tradit. says his ch. all rem. to
Stratford, and at least, James, Sarah, Rebecca, and Mary were there.
DAVID, Hingham 1635, was from Weymouth, or Melcombe Regis in
Co. Dorset, and s. of Robert, perhaps br. of George the rector of St. Mary's, Truro, who in that ch. set up a tablet in honor of his oldest br.
Owen, for rescuing hims. with great boldness from slavery, after seven
yrs. serv. in an Algerine corsair, and d. 17 Mar. 1637, as may be read
in the vol. of Cornwall in Lyson's Magna Britannia. He brot. w. Sarah, ch. Joseph, Rebecca, Benjamin, Gamaliel, Sarah and George; and
here had John, b. July 1637, d. soon; John, again, July 1640, d. soon;
was freem. 3 Mar. 1636, rem. to Boston 1641, and d. bef. 31 Oct. 1650,
when his will was pro. His wid. m. George Hull of Fairfield. Rebecca
m. George Vickary; the other d. m. Thomas Yeo. Geneal. Reg. VII.
233, has abstr. of his will. Whether Judith, a maid of 16, wh. came in
the Planter, 1635, from Stepney parish, London, were a relat. is not to
be suggest. with any grounds of conject. DAVID, Salem, s. of Joseph
the first, a shipwright, m. 26 June 1672, Ann, d. of Thomas Cromwell of
Salem, wid. of Benjamin Auger, had David, b. 14 Apr. 1673, d. bef. his
f.; Thomas, bapt. Aug. 1675; Ann, 19 May 1678; Cromwell, 5 Oct.
1679; Joseph, Aug. 1681; Jane, 7 Oct. 1683; and the last three d. bef.
the f.; Abigail, 2 Aug. 1685; and Eliz. May 1689. Bef. 1700 he rem.
to Boston, and soon after to Casco Bay, where he had made great purch.
of ld. E. of Presumscot riv. and was k. by the Ind. Aug. 1703. GAMA-
LIEL, Boston, br. of Benjamin, by w. Sarah Purchase, had Sarah, bapt.
30 Dec. 1649, at 6 days old; Gamaliel, b. 12 Mar. 1652, d. in few mos.;
Hannah, bapt. 31 July 1653, of whose b. the surv. copy of town rec. in
one place gives the date 25, ano. 29 of that mo. (such are the vexatious
incongru. of official doucum.); Rebecca, b. 12 Feb. 1657; Eliz. 10 Aug.
1659; Ann, 28 Apr. 1666; and Mehitable; beside a sixth d. and two s.
wh. d. young. He d. bef. 1670. Sarah m. first Robert Haughton, and
next, Benjamin Smith; Hannah m. William Gibson; Rebecca m. Job
Prince; Eliz. m. a Spencer; Ann m. 16 May 1686, William Wheeler;
and Mehitable m. Thomas Ford. GEORGE, Boston 1659, a mariner,
youngest br. of the preced. m. in London, and by w. Eliz. had two s. four
ds. in 1683 was liv. at Hull in Boston bay. JAMES, Stratford, s. of Ben-

jamin of Boston, had Benjamin, James, and a d. wh. all had fam. JAMES, Hull, s. of George, had ds. Sarah, Eliz. and Joanna. * JOSEPH, Hingham 1637, s. of David, prob. the eldest, b. in Eng. m. Dorcas Wood, had a ch. bur. 27 Apr. 1642; Joseph, bapt. Aug. 1642; Mary, 5 Mar. 1644; rem. to Boston and was made freem. that yr. had Sarah, b. 4, bapt. 9 Feb. 1645; David, bapt. 4 Apr. 1647, a. 7 wks. old; Samuel, 6 May 1649, 7 days old; and Eliz. b. 10, bapt. 20 June 1652, d. next yr. He had been, a yr. or two bef. at Falmouth very active, constable 1661, yet in 1658 had a quarrel at Scarborough with Foxwell; and was rep. but sett. 1665 at Salem where he was in good repute, made his will 21 July 1687, in wh. his w. and five ch. are nam. and d. soon aft. Willis I. 140. His d. Sarah m. 24 Sept. 1669, George Hodges of Salem; and had Sarah, as in Essex Inst. II. 151. JOSEPH, Falmouth, s. of the preced. m. Mary Standford, had Joseph. His w. d. early, and he took sec. w. Seaborn, or Sibborn, Gooding, or Goodwin, 22 Dec. 1670, had Daniel, b. 20 Dec. 1671; Samuel, 20 Sept. 1674; Sarah, 8 Oct. 1676; Dorcas and John, tw. 22 Dec. 1678; Israel, 17 July 1681; Rachel; and Ann. He prob. had been driv. by Ind. hostil. some yrs. bef. to Salem, or Lynn, of wh. last place he is titled, when freem. 1680. By third w. m. 14 Apr. 1686, Damaris, wid. of Thomas Searle, he had three more ch. of wh. the last was Benjamin, b. 29 Sept. 1688; and d. 1710. Willis II. 8. SAMUEL, Salem, s. of Joseph the first, m. 1 Feb. 1677, Rachel Guppy, had Samuel, b. 12 Dec. 1677; John, 4 Oct. 1679; Stephen, 9 May 1681; Rachel, 5 Aug. 1683; John, again, 25 Dec. 1685; Nathaniel, 4 Aug. 1687; Sarah, May 1691; Rachel, again, 11 Sept. 1693; and Joseph, 9 Feb. 1697; and d. Feb. 1718. THOMAS, Salem, s. of Benjamin prob. or perhaps of the sec. David, tho. less likely, m. Mary, eldest d. of Timothy Lindall. One Judith P. aged 16, came in the Planter from London 1635, with James Hayward, wh. m. her. Both were serv. of Nicholas Davis of Charlestown.

PHIPS, or, in mod. days, PHIPPS, JAMES, from Bristol, Eng. a gunsmith, sat down near the mouth of the Kennebeck riv. bef. 1649, hav. had very many ch. by the same w. 21 s. and 5 ds. in all, if credulity be sufficiently dilated to embrace the story, one of the youngest, the celebr. Sir William (equival. to all the s. in the opin. of his biogr.), being b. 2 Feb. 1651, this latter fact being more prob. than the numb. wh. however Mather asserts in two places, Magn. II. 38 and III. 165, tho. in this sec. place, we are naturally led to distrust his assert. by the manner of its introduct. to the support of his enormous marvel of John Sherman's felicity. Had he once more declared it, he would perhaps have accompan. his story with some incident to compel disbelief. Whether ten or twenty of the boys were b. on the other side of the water, he d. when William

was young, and his mo. liv. yet the name of no other s. exc. John, or d.
exc. Mary, Margaret, and Ann, was ever told. Of twenty-one s. the regard for males in nine cases out of ten, so greatly exceed. that for females,
we are justif. in looking for the names of more than two, especial. as
three out of the five ds. count. by Mather, find place in the will of their
br. the Gov. JOHN, Reading, by Eaton classed among the early sett. of
wh. it is desira. to kn. more, that something might be said beyond guess.
that he was b. at Charlestown. Had any date been affix. we should be
able to conject. that he was, or was not, that JOHN, s. of James, wh. had
John, prob. b. near the mo. of Kennebeck wh. accomp. his uncle William
1686, in search of the treasure ship. No more is kn. of him. But some
amus. tradit. as to the defeat of testamenta. benefact. to the s. by Sir William, may be read in Morse, who would make up for such injustice, by
giv. to his s. Jedediah near ten yrs. longer life than belong. to him.
Such is the tendency to magnify old age. * SAMUEL, Charlestown, s. of
Solomon of the same, taught the gr.sch. m. 8 Aug. 1676, Mary Phillips,
d. of Henry, wh. d. early; and by sec. w. Catharine had Samuel, bapt.
21 May 1682, d. soon; and Samuel, again, 10 Feb. 1684; was rep.
1692, at the first sess. under new chart. Reg. of deeds, and Clk. of the
County, and d. at the age of 70, Aug. 1725. Very strange seems the error of Farmer, in his Memoir of Grad. of H. C. making Gov. Danforth's
d. Mary his w. when she belong. to his br. Solomon. SOLOMON, Charlestown 1641, carpenter, was adm. of the ch. 15 Jan. and freem. 18 May
1642, by w. Eliz. had Eliz. b. 23 Apr. 1643; Solomon; Samuel, H. C.
1671, bef. ment.; Mehitable, wh. d. 15 July 1657; Mehitable, again, 10
Dec. 1657; and Mehitable, again, 6 June 1659, if my transcript. of rec.
be right; Joseph, bapt. 13 Oct. 1661; and perhaps others; d. 25 July
1671, aged 52. His will of 4 May 1670 makes w. Eliz. extrix. provides
for the s. Samuel at coll. Solomon, and Joseph, beside d. Eliz. Ray
and her ch. d. Mary, mean. perhaps Solomon's w. and her ch. yet unb.
The wid. d. 1 Nov. 1688. SOLOMON, Charlestown, s. of the preced. m.
Mary, d. of Dept. Gov. Thomas Danforth, and they join. the ch. 3 Apr.
1670, was freem. 11 May foll. had Mary, b. 3 July 1670; Solomon, 10
Jan. 1675; Thomas, 22 Nov. 1676, H. C. 1695, I think (tho. Farmer
gave him to Samuel, as he had also his mo.); Eliz. 27 Feb. 1681; Jonathan, 7 Jan. 1683; Eliz. again, 5 Jan. 1684; and it is observ. that this
fam. used pp. in its name punctiliously, while single p. served for the
Gov. He d. suddenly, tho. I see not the date. Opposite causes may be
read in Morse, 195, who makes the Bapt. regard it as a judgm. upon him
for purch. ld. taken from one of their commun. for paym. of a fine; but
Phipps hims. said "he was bewitched," and his opin. is equally to be re-
spected in our days. §‡ WILLIAM, Boston, s. of James, b. says his pan-

egyrist, "at a despicable planta. on the riv. Kennebeck," wh. is by Folsom, a soberer writer, said to be on the W. side, now Phipsburg, m. Mary, wid. of John Hull (not the mint-master), d. of Roger Spencer of Saco, but had no ch. was driv. by Ind. hostil. to Boston 1676, and I discov. him there in command of a trading vessel, 1677; he prevail. by his earnest desire to hunt up a Spanish wreck, in getting, 1683, a king's ship, the Algier Rose, and in a contempo. Memoir of Sir John Brampston (s. of the old judge, who sat in the immortal cause of John Hampden for the ship money), I find this condensed descript. of him, as " a sea capt. who was well skill. in mathemat. and had acquaint. hims. in India with some that had the art of diving; having some guess where the ship perished, apprehend. he could recov. the treas." Good luck attend. his undertak. but a mod. Eng. author of distinct. wh. ascrib. to him the invent. of a diving-bell for his purpose, ought to know that Edward Bendall had used his diving-bell successful. in Boston harbor, near eight yrs. bef. Sir William was b. and may read in Winth. Hist. of N. E. that the noble machine was next yr. employed at St. Kitts. For his success he was knight. by James II. 28 June 1687, and after his return here, was made, by Andros, Sheriff of N. E. Happi. he join. the ch. of Cotton Mather 8 Mar. 1690, was freem. a fortnight later, and, as his spiritual guide exulting. tells, was bapt. 23d of that mo. this being almost a yr. after the revo. against that power that made him sheriff, and in May 1690 he conducted the little attack, by only seven hundred men, on the French of Nova Scotia, with success, and was chos. an Assist. at the ensuing elect. The great expedit. that sail. in Aug. foll. against Quebec, was project. by him, " as well formed an enterprise," says Mather, " as perhaps was ever made by the N. E." tho. in this, the world's opinion has not concur. He was not content to have the nautical control merely, in wh. his experience could have been useful, but, with greater generosity than skill or propriety, assum. the direction of the land forces, thereby saving the reputa. of Walley, our ch. milit. officer, to the injury of his own. On the failure of this Quixotic campaign, he went to London, 1691, with intent. to seek aid from the new king in ano. attempt upon the bulwark of French empire in the new world; but was most lucki. divert. from that pursuit, by the appointm. as Gov. in the new chart. on the recommend. of Increase Mather to the king. With Mather and the chart. he arr. at Boston 14 May 1692, but his incapac. was soon discern. and in two yrs. for indecent or boisterous conduct he was recall. from the Prov. to London, and there d. 18 Feb. 1695. A monum. to his mem. stands in the ch. of St. Mary Woolnoth. In Mass. the history of his admin. is the melancholy monum. for his public breach of the peace was a scandal that never befel any other ch. magistr. and the horrible delusion of the witchcraft tragedy, tho. not imputab. to him, might by him have been partially restrain. if not effect. counteract. As he never had a ch. the preposterous fable never heard of bef. this generat. that Sir Constantine Phips, the Tory lawyer, Lord Chancellor of Ireland, was his s. and the progenit. of Lord Mulgrave of the last century, may be duly esteem. It must be regret. that so respectab. an author as Smiles in his enumerat. of disting. mem. of the peerage, should have adopt. so fabulous an origin for the Normanby fam. See Self Help, p. 169. With his com. in May 1692, I have prefer. to close the enumerat. of N. E. early sett. because he brot. new people to fill offices, and succeed. emigr. may too much be thot. to have come for the same purpose. The sturdy puritan race may almost universal. be count. as earlier inhab. See Gillingham, as perhaps the latest of the prior sett. His wid. m. 9 Oct. 1701, Peter Sargent. Her neph. Spencer Bennett, H. C. 1703, took the name of Phips, had William, H. C. 1728, and was lieut. Gov. of the Province, d. 4 Apr. 1757, aged 71. Nine of this name, of single and double *p*. had, in 1832, been gr. at Harv.

PICKARD, * JOHN, Rowley 1645, m. Jane Crosby, had John, b. 1653; Samuel, 1663, and three, or, by ano. story, six ds. was rep. 1661 and 95, unless this last yr. belongs to his s. and d. 1697, aged 75. His wid. d. 20 Feb. 1716, in 89th yr. Mary, one of his ds. m. 14 Feb. 1671, John Pearson, the sec. * JOHN, Rowley, s. of the preced. freem. 1683, was perhaps rep. 1695. * SAMUEL, Rowley, br. of the preced. m. Eliz. Bradstreet, had a d. and his w. d. early. He next m. Eliz. d. of Thomas Hale, had Samuel, b. 1689; Thomas, 1691; Moses, 1694; Joseph, 1701; beside three ds. He was rep. 1723 and 4. Descend. at R. have been numer. and respect. Farmer ment. an Edmund P. from Northam in Devonsh. at Piscataqua, a. 1661.

PICKE, JOHN, Cambridge, by w. Mary had Abigail, b. 22 Apr. 1642. Perhaps it is spelt otherwise in some places.

PICKERAM or PICKRAM, GEORGE, Watertown, prob. s. of John, brot. by his f. from Eng. 1630; unit. with his wid. mo. Esther, 1 Sept. 1646, in sale of est. JOHN, Watertown, d. 10 Dec. 1630. He prob. came in the fleet with Winthrop, had, by w. Esther, s. George, beside John, who was bur. 6 July 1639, and d. Joan, wh. d. 3 days aft. her f. None of this name is found in div. of Shawshin lds. 1652, among people of Cambridge and W. I think it may be the same as Pickering.

PICKERING, JOHN, Ipswich 1634, a carpenter, rem. to Salem 1637, had there gr. of ld. by w. Eliz. had John, prob. b. that yr.; Jonathan, 1639; Eliz. bapt. 3 Mar. 1644, d. soon; and Eliz. again, perhaps b. 3, bapt. 17 Aug. 1645, prob. d. young; and he d. 1655 or 1657. The will of 30 July 1655 was pro. 1 July 1657. His wid. m. 25 Dec. of the latter yr. John Deacon of Lynn. JOHN, Portsmouth 1635, perhaps had been as early as 1630, may have rem. to Cambridge, by w. Mary had Lydia, b. 5 Nov. 1638; rem. to Portsmouth, prob. there d. 18 Jan. 1669; but one of this name is by Lewis claim. for his town of Lynn 1639, who, if transient resid. may be either of these first two. JOHN, Salem, s. of the first John of the same, freem. 1669, m. 1657, Alice, d. of William Flint, had John, b. 10 Sept. 1658; Jonathan, 27 Sept. 1660, d. young; Joseph, 9 Sept. 1663, d. young; Benjamin, 11 or 15 Jan. 1666; Edward, d. soon; Sarah, 7 Sept. 1668; William, 11 Jan. 1671; Eliz. 7 Sept. 1674; and Hannah, 2 July, 1677. In the regular descent from one John to ano. est. in Salem (perhaps got by the first John, 1642, from Emanuel Downing under power to his w. as a reasona. tradit. gives, to pay for his s. George's commencem. dinner), is now, in part, enjoy. by John of the seventh generat. He was ancest. of the disting. Timothy, H. C. 1763, whose s. and gr.s. have been gr. at the same; was lieut. and d. 5 May 1694, aged 56; and his wid. Sarah d. 27 Dec. 1714. *JOHN, Portsmouth, s. of the first John of the same, m. 10 Jan. 1665, Mary Stanyan, had John, b. 1 Dec. 1666; Mary, 18 July 1668; Thomas, 6 Apr. 1679, d. next yr.; two Sarahs wh. d. 1671 and 3, and perhaps others; was capt. rep. to Boston 1691; and in N. H. was speaker of the assemb. as was his namesake, the elder br. of Timothy in that of Mass. at a later day. He was liv. 1718, and ancest. of Hon. John of Portsmouth, H. C. 1761, wh. d. 11 Apr. 1805; and prob. William of Concord, H. C. 1797. His d. Mary m. John Plaisted. JONATHAN, Salem, s. of John the first of the same, ship-carpenter, m. 19 Mar. 1666, Jane, d. of doctor Thomas Cromwell, had Jane, b. last week of Nov. 1667, d. young; Eliz. 2 or 4 June 1669; Mary, 1 Dec. 1670; Ann, Aug. 1672; Jonathan, 11 May 1674; Sarah, 25 Jan. 1676; John, bapt. 19 May 1678; but these five last ment. all d. young; Hannah, bapt. 28 May 1682; and Mercy. Thirteen of this name, had, in 1831, been gr. at Harv.

PICKES, JOHN, Piscataqua, i. e. prob. Dover or Kittery 1640; but Mr. Judd, on examin. of the original rec. presum. the name to intend Pike.

PICKET, ADAM, New London, youngest s. of John of the same, m. 16 May 1680, Hannah, d. of Daniel Wetherell, had Adam, b. 1681; and John, 1685; and d. 1691. His bros. d. unm. and s. Adam. d. without issue. CHRISTOPHER, Boston, in that part call. Muddy riv. now Brookline, m. June 1647, Eliz. Stow, d. of John, had John, b. 6 Sept. 1657; was liv. at B. 1661; and 14 Oct. 1675, at Scarborough, prob. a soldier, witness to nuncup. will of Arthur Alger. DANIEL, Stratford, youngest s. of the first John of the same, m. 13 Sept. 1683, Mary, d. of John

Offit, had Samuel, b. 23 Nov. 1684, d. young; Margaret, 14 Aug. 1686;
Daniel, 27 Feb. 1688, prob. d. soon; Samuel, again, 31 Oct. 1689;
Daniel, again, 1 Oct. 1691; Mary, 15 Jan. 1693; Comfort, a d. 6 Sept.
1694; and Rebecca, 5 Mar. 1701. JAMES, Stratford 1669, br. of the
preced. went to Norwalk 1673, m. 17 July of that yr. Rebecca, d. of
Ralph Keeler, had James, b. 7 May 1674; and perhaps rem. *JOHN,
Salem 1648, had John, James, Thomas, and Sarah, in Nov. of that yr.
bapt. together; Rebecca, 30 June 1650; and Daniel, 25 Jan. 1652. I
do not find the name of w. among ch. mem. and his is by Felt copied
Pigket, follow. the sound. He rem. 1660 to Stratford, there was constable 1667, one of the selectmen in 1669, and rep. 1673 and 5. His w.
Margaret d. 6 Oct. 1683, and he d. 11 Apr. foll. Sarah m. 19 Dec.
1665, Robert Lane of S. and Rebecca m. 31 Dec. 1673, James Sention
of Norwalk. JOHN, Boston, whose s. John, by w. Eliz. d. 14 Aug.
1657, may be the same as the preced. JOHN, New London, m. Ruth, d.
of Jonathan Brewster, had Mary; Ruth; William; John, b. 25 July
1656; Adam, 15 Nov. 1658; and Mercy, 16 Jan. 1661. He was an
active merch. had good est. and d. 16 Aug. 1667; and his wid. m. 18
July foll. Charles Hill, who, in 1670, obtain. from the Col. confirmat.
of a grant of 600 acres, made by Uncas to P.; Mary m. 10 Apr. 1672,
Benjamin Shapley; Ruth m. Rev. Moses Noyes of Lyme; and Mercy
m. 1 Nov. 1682, Samuel Fosdick, and next, John Arnold. JOHN, Stratford, s. of John of the same, freem. 1670, m. 19 Jan. 1673, Mary Cross,
or some such name, had Rebecca, b. 31 Dec. foll.; John, 5 Jan. 1678;
Sarah, 8 Mar. 1681; and James, 5 Jan. 1686. His w. d. 7 Oct. 1687.
THOMAS, Stratford, br. of the preced. m. 16 Nov. 1676, Abigail, d. of
Thomas Seymour of Norwalk, had Abigail, b. 30 July 1678; Hannah,
20 May 1680; and Jacob, 15 Feb. 1682.

PICKLES, JONAS, Scituate 1650, m. 1657, Alice, d. of William Hatch,
had Jonas, b. 5 Feb. 1659; Mary, 1660; Nathan, 1661; Lydia, 1662;
and Jonas, 1663; next yr. he d. suddenly, I presume, for his will was
nuncup. 15 Dec. and pro. by two females. NATHAN, Scituate, s. of
the preced. m. 1687, Miriam, d. of John Turner, had Mary, b. 1688;
Alice, 1691; Nathan, 1693; David, 1695; and Nathan, again, 1699.
Deane.

PICKMAN, oft. writ. PITMAN, as sound. BENJAMIN, Salem, third s. of
Nathaniel of Bristol, Eng. bapt. at Lewen's Mead, Bristol, the ch. seat
of the dissent. interest in that city, 1645, m. 27 July 1667, Eliz. d. of
Capt. Joseph Hardy, had Joseph, b. 11 June 1668; Benjamin, 30 Jan.
1672; Susanna, 3 Feb. 1674; Martha, 3 June 1677; John, 12 Sept.
1679; Joshua, 28 Aug. 1681; William, 10 June 1684; and Nicholas,
call. a d. 18 Aug. 1687; and he d. 1708. His wid. d. 19 Dec. 1727,

aged 77. Susanna m. John Viall; Martha m. Edmund Batter; and
Nicholas m. Richard Pike, and d. in her 90th yr. BENJAMIN, Salem, s.
of the preced. by first w. Miss Hasket, had only John; he next m. 26
Oct. 1704, Abigail, sec. d. of Timothy Lindall, had Abigail, b. 9 Feb.
1706; Benjamin, 28 Jan. 1708, an honorable counsellor, wh. was gr.f. of
the late Benjamin Pickman, H. C. 1784, mem. of U. S. Congr. and d. 2
Aug. 1773; William, 1 Oct. 1710; Samuel, 19 Jan. 1712; Eliz. 22
Jan. 1714; Caleb, 10 June 1715; Rachel, 25 July 1717; and Sarah, 1
Dec. 1718; and he d. next yr. on 26 Apr. NATHANIEL, Salem 1654,
came from Bristol with w. Tabitha, wh. d. 10 Sept. 1668, and ch. Nathaniel, John, Benjamin, William, Samuel, and perhaps Tabitha, and Mary,
beside Bethia, wh. all m. the last, 15 Feb. 1673, with John Silsbee;
Mary, 22 June 1665, with Robert Hodges; and Tabitha, 30 Aug. 1664,
with Edmund Feveryear. NATHANIEL, Salem, s. of the preced. had
Tabitha, b. Nov. 1670, d. in few wks.; Tabitha, again, 4 Nov. 1671;
Eliz. 25 Dec. 1673; and Nathaniel, 13 Apr. 1676. SAMUEL, Salem,
br. of the preced. by w. Lydia, perhaps d. of Peter Palfrey, had Sarah,
wh. d. 4 Dec. 1659; Samuel, wh. d. 24 May 1660; Sarah, again, 7
Feb. 1662, perhaps b. at Lynn; Samuel, again, 21 Nov. 1664; Peter,
14 Aug. 1667, d. at 13 mos.; Peter, again, 27 Nov. 1669; Lydia, 7
Dec. 1672; and Joshua, 19 Aug. 1675. WILLIAM, Salem, br. of the
preced. m. 24 June 1673, Eliz. Eastwick, had William, b. 7 Sept. 1676,
posthum. and d. prob. 1676, for to her was admin. giv. 28 June of that yr.

PICKTON, THOMAS, Salem, had, says Felt, gr. of ld. 1639, was on
Beverly side, by will of 19 Oct. pro. 28 Nov. 1677, gave all his est. to
w. Ann, who. d. in 1683, aged 83.

PICKWORTH, AMARIAH, Salem, had, says very good autho. d. Rachel,
who m. the sec. John Sibley, but I feel no small degree of hesitat. bec.
the first John S. m. Rachel Pickworth, as is said. BENJAMIN, Salem, s. of
John, had w. Eliz. nam. in his will, 20 Aug. 1681. JOHN, Salem 1637,
had gone from some part of the Bay to Plymouth 1631, got a w. and
went back, says Gov. Bradford in letter of Feb. 1632. His w. Ann join.
the ch. 1638, and had bapt. Ruth, Hannah, and John, 14 Oct. that yr.;
Samuel; Joseph, 12 Feb. 1643; Rachel, 3 May 1646; Benjamin, 2 July
1648; Sarah, 6 Oct. 1650; Abigail, Oct. 1652; and Jacob, 3 Sept.
1654. He had gr. of ld. at New London 1651, but forfeit. for non resid.
Ruth m. Nathaniel Masters; Rachel m. John Sibley; and Sarah m. 25
Mar. 1680, Joseph Mazury. His will of 27 June 1663, was pro. 25
Nov. foll. names 4 s. the first ment. and 3 ds. but inv. had been tak.
three mos. Elias, of Beverly 1687, may have been ano. s. or perhaps a
gr.s. SAMUEL, Salem, a soldier, k. in Philip's war, 15 Dec. 1675, was
s. of John, m. 3 Nov. 1667, Sarah, d. prob. of the first John Marston,

had Sarah, b. 17 July 1668; Hannah, 3 May 1670; Samuel, 3 Sept. 1672; and Mary, 30 July 1675. He left wid. Sarah. See Geneal. Reg. II. 243. I regret to add, that young Samuel was an unhappy witness in 1692, at some of the witch trials, and, of course, was led to swear to more than was true.

PID, RICHARD, freem. of Mass. 22 June 1642, is wholly unkn. to me.

PIDDELL, CORBITT, of Conn. as strange a name as the preced. had a suit in Court 1649.

PIDCOCK, or PIDCOKE, GEORGE, Scituate, m. 1640, Sarah Richards, was liv. 1670, and Deane, 324, says no fam. is heard of. In the Col. Rec. it is found, that he gave to the town that yr. both hims. and his propr. as being too feeble to manage his affairs.

PIDGE. See Pigg.

PIERCE, PEARSE, PEARS, PEIRSE, or PEARCE, ABRAHAM, Plymouth 1629, had sh. in div. of cattle that yr. of Duxbury 1643, was a propr. of Bridgewater 1645, by w. Rebecca had Abraham, b. Jan. 1638; Isaac; and three ds. of wh. Alice was bapt. at Barnstable, 21 July 1650; and d. at D. 1673. Haz. I. 326; Baylies II. 254. ABRAHAM, Duxbury, s. of the preced. by w. Hannah had Abraham; John; and Samuel; and d. Jan. 1718. ANTHONY, Watertown, eldest s. of John of the same, b. in Eng. freem. 3 Sept. 1634, but by Felt is claim. for Salem that yr. yet perhaps against the stronger right of W. for here the rec. says by w. Sarah or Ann (for he had two, but Ann was the surv.) was b. Mary, 28 Dec. 1633; John, eldest s. whose date is not kn.; Mary, again, 1636; Jacob, 15 Sept. 1637; Daniel, 1 Jan. 1640; Martha, 24 Apr. 1641; Joseph; Benjamin, 1649; and Judith, 18 July 1650; and he d. 9 May 1678. Mary m. Ralph Read of Woburn; and Judith m. 16 Feb. 1667, John Sawin. AZERIKAM, or AZRAKIM, Warwick, is suppos. to have come in from Rehoboth, or Swanzey, had ch. Samuel and Tabitha, perhaps others. BENJAMIN, Scituate, s. of Michael, m. 1678, Martha, d. of James Adams, had Martha, Jerusha, Benjamin, Ebenezer, Persis, Caleb, Thomas, Adams, Jeremiah, and Elisha, b. betw. 1679 and 99. Deane. BENJAMIN, Watertown, s. of Anthony, m. 15 Jan. 1678, Hannah, d. of Joshua Brooks of Concord; had eight ch. says Bond, but he names only Hannah, b. 25 Dec. 1679; Benjamin, 29 Apr. 1682; Grace, 4 June 1685; Sarah, 1 Jan. 1688; Samuel, 22 Aug. 1689; Lydia, 3 Oct. 1692; and Hannah, again, 2 Jan. 1700; was freem. 1690; but the time of d. is not ment. BENJAMIN, Woburn, s. perhaps of Robert, more prob. of Thomas of the same, by w. Mary had Benjamin, b. 28 Aug. 1689; Mary, 29 Jan. 1692; Esther, 25 Oct. 1696; Rebecca, Oct. 1698; Deborah, 5 Dec. 1700; Thomas, 23 Nov. 1702; and Zurishaddai, 22 June 1705. DANIEL, Watertown, blacksmith, came in the

Elizabeth from Ipswich, Co. Suff. (but call. of London by Coffin) 1634,
aged 23; freem. 2 May 1638, rem. to Newbury, by w. Sarah had Dan-
iel, b. 15 May 1642; Joshua, 15 May 1643; and Martha, 14 Feb.
1648. He sw. fidel. 1652, and m. 26 Dec. 1654, Ann, perhaps wid. of
Thomas Millerd, and d. 27 Nov. 1677, leav. good est. His wid. d. 27
Nov. 1690; and his d. m. perhaps a Thorpe. DANIEL, Groton, s. of
Anthony, as from Butler's Hist. we learn, by w. Eliz. had Eliz. b. 16
May 1665; Daniel, 28 Nov. 1666; John, 18 Aug. 1668; Ephraim, 15
Oct. 1673; and Josiah, 2 May 1675. Of course the Ind. hostil. drove
him away; and Bond fixes him at Watertown, and says he had Joseph;
Abigail, b. 3 Jan. 1682; Hannah, bapt. 16 Jan. 1687; and Benjamin,
the same day; the last three at W. ‡* DANIEL, Newbury, s. of Daniel
of the same, by w. Joanna had Joanna; Daniel, b. 20 Dec. 1663; Ann,
22 May 1666; Benjamin, 26 Feb. 1669; Joshua, 16 Oct. 1671;
Thomas, 1 May 1674; Martha, 26 Feb. 1677; Sarah, 3 Oct. 1679;
George, 5 Mar. 1682; Mary, 14 Apr. 1685; John, 16 Oct. 1687; and
Catharine, 18 Sept. 1690; was a capt. rep. 1682 and 3, of the council
of safety on the revo. 1689, col. of one of the Essex reg. rep. under the
new chart. in the import. yr. 1692; and d. 22 Jan. tho. Hutch. II. 48,
makes it 4 Apr. 1704. His w. d. 26 Sept. 1690, and Daniel and Joanna,
the eldest two ch. a few days bef. DAVID, Dorchester, freem. 7 Dec.
1636; but Mr. Paige, in his very careful list, Geneal. Reg. III. 94, read
it Price. EDWARD, Watertown 1639, says Bond, wh. thinks he went
to Wethersfield, but nothing certain is kn. of the man. EPHRAIM,
Weymouth, perhaps s. of Michael, by w. Hannah, d. of John Holbrook
of the same, had Azrikam, b. 4 Jan. 1672; prob. Ephraim; and perhaps others. GEORGE, Boston, a smith, m. Mary, d. of Richard Woodhouse, had Mary, b. 20 June 1660, and he d. 7 Dec. 1661. GEORGE,
Portsmouth, R. I. m. 7 Apr. 1687, Alice, d. of Richard Hart, had Susanna, b. 21 Aug. 1688; and perhaps more. GILES, Greenwich, R. I.
1687. ISAAC, Boston, tailor, m. Grace, d. of Lewis Tucker of Casco.
JAMES, Boston, k. in youth, by lightning, at Plymouth 1660. JAMES,
Woburn, s. of Thomas, by w. Eliz. had Eliz. b. 11 Oct. 1688; James,
28 Feb. 1690; and perhaps rem. JOHN, the patentee under the Pres.
and Counc. of N. E. 1620 and 1, tho. connect. with the pilgr. of Plymouth, never came, in my opin. to this shore, yet Willis seems contra.
I. 13. After most respectful consider. of the docum. refer. to in his
note, I am constrain. to express a confidence, that the London cloth-
worker never succeed. in accomplish. tho. he did undertake, a voyage
to Plymouth, the ship being put back in distress. My judgment
seems to have confirmat. by what is read in Bradford, 140. * JOHN,
Dorchester, came perhaps in the Mary and John, 1630, or in the Lion,

Feb. 1631, is call. mariner from Stepney, one of the modern London parishes, freem. 18 May 1631, by w. Parnell had Joseph, b. 30
Oct. 1631; Abia, 17 July 1633; John, 3 Mar. 1635, d. the same mo.;
Nehemiah, 12 July 1637, d. Oct. 1639; and his w. d. the same mo.   He
was selectman 1636 and 41; rep. Mar. 1639; rem. 1642 to Boston, m.
sec. w. 10 Aug. 1654, Rebecca, wid. of Thomas Wheeler, and d. 17
Sept. 1661.   His will made the day bef. ment. w. Rebecca, s. Samuel,
and Nehemiah, ds. Mehitable, the w. of Jeremiah Rogers, prob. eldest,
and her three ch. beside Mary, Mercy, and Exercise, as may be read in
Geneal. Reg. X. 359, 60.   In the Hist. of Dorchester, 71, Samuel is supposed to be elder than Nehemiah, "as he is ment. first;" but it seems
clear, that he was younger, no doubt, by the sec. w.   JOHN, Watertown,
freem. Mar. 1638, a man of very good est. project. settlem. at Sudbury
and Lancaster, d. 19 Aug. 1661; and his will of 4 Mar. 1658 was pro.
1 Oct. foll.   In it he provides for w. Eliz. eldest s. Anthony, and other
childr. without naming; but his wid. in her will of 15 Mar. 1667, in wh.
mo. she d. aged 79, supplies the defic. naming ch. Anthony, John, Robert,
Esther Morse, w. of Joseph, Mary Coldam, whose h. is not of my
acquaint. beside gr.childr. Mary Ball, and ano. Ball, Esther Morse, and
the childr. of Anthony and Robert.   He had also d. Eliz. wh. m. 30
Jan. 1645, Francis Wyman, but she d. bef. her f.   JOHN, Boston, by w.
Eliz. had John and Eliz. tw. b. 16 June 1643; and of him nothing more
is kn. unless he may be that man call. John Peirse, to whose *four* ch.
John Mills of Boston, in his will, Oct. 1651, made gift.   *JOHN, Woburn, prob. s. of John of Watertown, and b. in Eng. had John, b. 23
Nov. 1644; Joseph, 12 Sept. 1646; and Thomas, 3 May 1649; perhaps
others bef. or aft. was freem. in Apr. and rep. May 1690.   JOHN, Gloucester, husbandman, freem. 1651, m. 4 Nov. 1643 w. Eliz. had Mary, b.
Sept. 1650; and John, 14 July 1653.   His w. d. 3 July 1673, and he
m. 12 Sept. foll. Jane Stanwood, and d. 15 Dec. 1695.   His wid. d. 18
Aug. 1706.   JOHN, Boston, s. of Anthony of Watertown, adm. as inhab.
28 Feb. 1643, freem. 1648, m. 15 Apr. 1656, Ruth, d. of Nathaniel
Bishop; had Hannah, b. 30 June 1660; Ruth, 22 Nov. 1662; Hannah,
again, 1 Mar. 1665 (as to me seems, tho. in the infirm town rec. she is
call. d. of John Pease, and w. Ruth, neither of wh. is seen elsewhere);
beside Nathaniel, 10 Apr. 1678; and Rebecca, 15 Feb. 1680.   Perhaps
betw. the earliest and latest pair he was resid. in some other town.   His
will of 21 Oct. 1682, pro. 7 Nov. foll. gives to his w. Ruth all his est. to
bring up the childr. withal, as it lay in Boston or was giv. by his f. at
W. or as may be inher. from gr.f. as this testat. was eldest s. of his f.
JOHN, Hartford 1640, a youth who prob. rem. soon.   JOHN, Charlestown 1652, may have rem. to Kittery, and d. 1673, leav. wid. Elinor.

His inv. of £154 is dat. 5 Dec. by Francis Hooke, and Hubertus Mattoon. He may have been the witness to will of Thomas Coytmore, Aug. 1642. JOHN, Boston, a mariner, in 1654, was perhaps he who m. 15 Apr. 1656, Ruth, d. of Nathaniel Bishop, had Hannah, b. 30 June 1660; may have been adm. an inhab. 1657. Ano. JOHN of Boston, perhaps by w. Isabel had Samuel, b. 14 Jan. 1660; and d. 17 Sept. 1661. JOHN, Sudbury, perhaps br. of Anthony, had w. Eliz. wh. d. 12 June 1655. One JOHN, a weaver, came from Norwich, Co. Norf. 1637, aged 49, with w. Eliz. 36, and four ch. John, Barbara, Eliz. and Judith, and one serv. John Gedney, 19, may have been this Sudbury man or not, as the commonness of the name prevents distinct. JOHN, Woburn, s. perhaps eldest, of John of the same, m. 1 July 1663, Deborah, d. of James Converse, had Deborah, b. 30 Oct. 1666; John, 26 Jan. 1671; Thomas, 23 Dec. 1672; James, 6 Aug. 1674, d. at 11 yrs.; Daniel, 7 Nov. 1676; James, again, 8 Oct. 1686; and Joseph, 24 Aug. 1688. JOHN, Salem 1675, was then chos. lieut. of capt. Gardner's comp. of wh. therefore more ought to be kn. Felt II. 497. JOHN, Boston 1670, a bricklayer; a d. of his had m. William Talmage. JOHN, Springfield, m. 1677, Lydia, d. of Miles Morgan, had Nathaniel, b. 1679; John, 1683; Jonathan; rem. to Enfield, there had Lydia 1693, and he d. Sept. 1696, leav. the w. and these ch. JOHN, York 1680, took o. of alleg. next yr. had sev. yrs. bef. m. Phebe Nash, wid. of Isaac. JOHN, Gloucester, s. of John of the same, m. Mary, d. of Robert Ratchell of Boston, had, beside the Stephen and Silas, ment. by Babson, 126, without dates, John, b. 17 Jan. 1679; and Stephen, 25 Jan. 1681; and rem. prob. next yr. JOHN, Woodbury, by Cothren suppos. to be s. of John of Wethersfield, yet wh. he was is not ment. m. the defraud. orphan Ann, sis. of John Hathwit, had John, bapt. Sept. 1683; and Eliz. Aug. 1685; and he d. 19 Nov. 1731. JOHN, Scituate, s. of Michael, m. 1683, Patience, d. of Anthony Dodson, had (says Deane, 325) Michael, John, Jonathan, Ruth, Jael, David, and Clothier, b. betw. 1684 and 98. JONATHAN, Woburn, s. of Robert of the same, m. 19 Nov. 1689, Hannah Wilson, had Hannah, b. 8 Mar. 1691, d. young; Jonathan, 11 May 1693, d. next yr. as did the f. 17 June 1694. JOSEPH, Woburn, prob. s. of Thomas of the same, m. 24 June 1681, Mary Richardson, was freem. 1684. JOSEPH, Watertown, s. prob. of Anthony, by w. Martha, had Joseph, b. 2 Oct. 1669; Francis, 27 July 1671; John, 27 May 1673; Mary, 26 Nov. 1674; Benjamin, 25 Mar. 1677; Jacob, 26 Dec. 1678; Martha, 24 Dec. 1681; Stephen, Oct. 1683; Israel, 7 Oct. 1685; and Eliz. 9 Sept. 1687. He was freem. 1690, and took sec. w. 15 June 1698, Eliz. Winship of Cambridge, wid. of Ephraim, d. of Francis Kendall. JOSHUA, Newbury, s. of the first Daniel of the same, m. 7 May 1668, Dorothy, d. of maj. Robert Pike, had Joshua, and perhaps other ch. but no dates are giv. LAUNCELOT, Pegypscot, m. a d. of Thomas Stevens, had William. Willis I. 163. MARK, Cambridge 1642, rem. next yr. to New Haven. MARMADUKE, Salem 1639, charged with k. his apprent. See Winth. I. 318, 9, where the surname seems Percy or Perry. He came 1637 from Sandwich, in Kent, with w. Mary and a serv. In Boys's Hist. of Sandwich, p. 752, it is spelled Peerce, and in Felt I. 169, Percie, but in Ib. II. 458, Pierce. MICHAEL, Hingham 1646, had there bapt. that yr. Persis; other ch. were Benjamin, John, Ephraim, Eliz. Deborah, Ann, Abia, and Ruth, all nam. in his will, beside prob. Abigail, b. 1662, when his w. d. Soon aft. he rem. to Scituate, took sec. w. Ann; was a capt. of great bravery, in command of 50 Eng. and 20 friend. Ind. from Cape Cod, in Philip's war, and was with most of them k. 26 Mar. 1676, at Pawtucket fight in Rehoboth. Deane, 122, 325. NATHANIEL, Woburn, s. of Robert of the same, was a soldier in Philip's war, and engag. in the memo. Falls fight, 19 May 1676, wh. he long surv. m. 27 Dec. 1677, Hannah Convers, had Nathaniel, b. 2 Feb. 1679; and his w. d. 23 Mar. foll. He m. 23 Mar. 1680, Eliz. Foster, perhaps wid. of Hopestill of Charlestown, had Robert, wh. d. 14 May 1689. ‖ NEHEMIAH, Boston 1661, a cooper, ar. co. 1671, m. perhaps sec. w. 1684, Ann, wid. of capt. Samuel Mosely, eldest d. of Isaac Addington, and d. 1691. Admin. was giv. 28 Apr. of that yr. to his wid. RICHARD, Portsmouth, R. I. had perhaps other ch. beside that Susanna wh. m. 4 Dec. 1673, George Brownell. RICHARD, Pemaquid, a carpenter, I think is the man to wh. in Jan. 1642, an Ind. sagamore made large gr. of lds. and islds. as may be seen in Geneal. Reg. XIII. 365; took o. of fidel. 1674. RICHARD, Boston, printer, m. 27 Aug. 1680, Sarah, d. of Rev. Seaborn Cotton. Thomas, Hist. I. 282. For Benjamin Harris, bookseller, he publish. 25 Sept. 1690, the *first* No. of a newspaper, of wh. the *sec.* never appeared. See Felt II. 14. ROBERT, Dorchester, perhaps 1630, but not very likely, may have been br. of John, the mariner, by w. Ann, d. of John Greenway, had Deborah, b. Feb. 1640, d. in few wks. was freem. 18 May 1642, and d. 6 Jan. 1665, leav. only s. Thomas, and Mary, wh. m. Thomas Herring, not (as oft. said) Haven, of Dedham; and his wid. d. 31 Dec. 1695, "the oldest person, prob. that ever liv. in D." says the Hist. 261, aged "about 104 yrs." unless we suppose some exagger. in Blake's Ann. as may be reasona. if not unavoida. Of his will, good abstr. is in Geneal. Reg. XIII. 154. Some of the *bread* brot. over the ocean by him, tradit. fondly reports to be still in possess. of descend. and so, by more than 165 yrs. older even than her. It may as well keep many centuries more. ROBERT, Ipswich, m. Abigail, d. of Mark Symonds of the same. ROBERT, Watertown 1646, s. of John of the same, rem. prob. to

Woburn, was freem. 1650, by w. Mary, had Judith, b. 30 Sept. 1651;
Mary, 21 Jan. 1653; Nathaniel, 4 Dec. 1655; Eliz. 6 Mar. 1658; Jonathan, 2 Feb. 1663; and Joseph, 1 May 1672. Farmer assum. that
he might be the ancest. of Gov. Benjamin, a native of Chelmsford,
assigning, in a way not common with that scrupul. antiquary, as a reason,
that the Chelmsford Pierces were from Woburn. ROBERT, Charlestown, m. 18 Feb. 1657, Sarah Eyre. SAMUEL, Malden, whose w.'s
name I find not, had Mary, b. 20 Aug. 1656; Thomas, 7 Jan. 1658;
John, and perhaps Joseph, Aug. 1659; of wh. John d. very soon; and
Eliz. Oct. 1666; prob. more, for I suppose he rem. to Charlestown, and
may be the person whose w. Mary join. the Charlestown ch. 27 Mar.
1670, he hav. done so 5 Dec. preced. and brot. to bapt. Samuel, Thomas,
Joseph, Jonathan, John, Mary, Eliz. and Persis, all 16 Jan. 1670; Abigail, 29 May 1670; Hannah, 31 Dec. 1671; and Benjamin, 15 Aug.
1675. SAMUEL, Boston 1672, cooper, prob. s. of John of the same, may
have rem. 1677, to Charlestown. SAMUEL, Woburn, s. of Thomas of the
same, freem. 1684, m. 9 Dec. 1680, Lydia Bacon, had Samuel, b. 25
Nov. 1681; Lydia, 25 May 1683; Joseph, 28 Mar. 1685; Isaac, 22
Mar. 1687; Abigail, 27 Feb. 1689; Sarah, 22 Jan. 1691; Tabitha, 28
Aug. 1697, d. next mo.; and Tabitha, again, 19 Mar. 1700. STEPHEN,
fifth s. of Thomas the sec. set. at Chelmsford, by w. Tabitha had Stephen, whose s. Benjamin was gr.f. of the late Presid. of the U. S. says
the memoir of Gov. Benjamin in Geneal. Reg. VII. 10; but the writer has perhaps sunk one generat. by confus. of one Thomas with ano.
of the same name, prob. the emigr. ancest. THOMAS, Charlestown
1634, freem. 6 May 1635, by w. Eliz. had Abigail, bapt. 17 June 1639,
unless she were ch. of ano. Thomas, as seems not unlikely; for no other
is ascrib. to this one, wh. d. 7 Oct. 1666, and in his will of 7 Nov. preced.
ment. his age of 82 yrs. his w. Eliz. aged a. 71, s. John, Randall Nichols,
beside gr.ch. Mary Bridge and Eliz. Jeffts; and gave legacy to the coll.
His wid. Eliz. mo. of Mary, w. of Peter Tufts, was perhaps his sec. w.
THOMAS, Woburn 1643, may not improb. seem to be s. of the preced. b.
in Eng. liv. first at Charleston, and may have been f. of that Abigail;
but at W. had John, b. 7 Mar. 1644, d. prob. soon; Thomas, 21 Jan.
1645; Eliz. 25 Dec. 1646; Joseph, 22 Sept. 1648, d. soon; Joseph,
again, 13 Aug. 1649; Stephen, 16 July 1651; Samuel, 20 Feb. 1654,
d. at 2 yrs.; Samuel, again, 7 Apr. 1656; William, 7 Mar. 1658;
James, 7 May 1659; and Abigail, 20 Nov. 1660. He was freem. 1677
and 13 Nov. of that yr. sold ld. in Charlestown. Thomas, f. of Stephen,
could not be, as the biogr. suppos. the same Thomas that d. 7 Oct. 1666,
aged 83 yrs. THOMAS, Setauket, L. I. 1661, had that yr. a commiss. as
a magistr. of Conn. THOMAS, Dorchester, only s. of Robert, m. Mary, d.

of George Proctor, had nine ch. of wh. were Thomas, bapt. 26 Oct. 1662; Mary, b. Apr. 1665; John, 26 Oct. 1668; beside Samuel, k. 16 Dec. 1698, by fall of a tree. His w. d. 22 Mar. 1704, aged 62, and he d. 26 Oct. 1706, aged 71. He was ancest. of the late well beloved Rev. Dr. John of Brookline, H. C. 1793. THOMAS, Gloucester, had w. Ann, wh. d. 26 Jan. 1668, perhaps d. Eliz. d. 3 July 1673. WILLIAM, Boston, a disting. shipmaster, made more voyages than any other person in the same yrs. to and from Boston, was k. by the Spaniards at Providence in the Bahamas, 13 July 1641. Winth. II. 33. Prince says in Ann. II. 69, he was ancest. of Rev. James, a disting. theolog. of Exeter, Eng. wh. d. 1730. WILLIAM, Boston, came in the Griffin, arr. 4 Sept. 1633, with Cotton, Hooker, Gov. Haynes, and other ch. men, was made freem. 14 May foll. oft. a selectman, d. 1661. He had early m. Sarah, d. of William Colbron, had d. Sarah nam. Sarah Colpit in the will of her gr.f. But I fear that name is wrong, at least, such name is not kn. in Boston. See the note in Winth. I. 109. WILLIAM, Barnstable 1643. WILLIAM, Boston 1653, a mariner, d. 1669, leav. small prop. to his wid. By w. Esther, I suppose, he had Mary, b. 10 Dec. 1656; Martha and Mary, tw. b. 26 May 1659. WILLIAM, Falmouth 1680, on the sec. destruct. of the town, 1690, rem. to Milton. Willis I. 163. WILLIAM, Suffield, m. 1688, Esther Spencer, had Thomas, b. 1688. WILLIAM, Woburn, perhaps s. of Thomas of the same, m. 8 Apr. 1690, Abigail Somers, alias Warren. Fifteen of this name, in its various forms, had, in 1834, been gr. at Harv. five at Yale, and ten at other N. E. coll.

PIERPONT, EBENEZER, Roxbury, s. of John of the same, m. 20 Oct. 1692, Mary, d. of Samuel Ruggles, had John, b. 20 Sept. 1693; Ebenezer, 14 Sept. 1694; and Mary, 21 Sept. 1696, d. Feb. foll.; and he d. 11 Dec. foll. His wid. m. 3 Nov. 1702, Isaac Morris. JAMES, Ipswich, had w. Margaret, left s. John and Robert, wh. he brot. from Eng. JAMES, New Haven, s. of John of Roxbury, ord. 2 July 1685, m. 27 Oct. 1691, Abigail, d. of John Davenport sec. wh. d. within four mos. and his sec. w. 1694, was Sarah, d. of Rev. Joseph Haynes, and by her he had only Abigail; his third w. 1698, was Mary, d. of Rev. Samuel Hooker. Whether he was promin. as divine, or what issue he had by this last, I am not able to discover (yet Edward C. Herrick, Esq. Libr. can tell), but his wonderful story of the apparition of the ship in the sky, at New Haven, many yrs. bef. he was b. that worthi. adorns the Magnalia, Book I. ch. 6, § 6, is evidence of his felicity of fancy. It may be compar. with the contempo. acco. of the prodigy in Winth. II. 328. He d. 22 Nov. 1714. JOHN, Roxbury, s. of James of Ipswich, b. in Eng. m. Thankful, d. of John Stow, had Thankful, b. 26 Nov. bapt. 2 Dec. 1649, d. in few days; John, 22 July

1651, d. in few days unbapt.; John, again, 28, bapt. 31 Oct. 1652; Experience, 4 Jan. bapt. 18 Feb. 1655; one, 4 Aug. 1657, d. in very few days unbapt.; James, 4, bapt. 8 Jan. 1660, H. C. 1681; Ebenezer, 21, bapt. 22 Dec. 1661; Thankful, again, 18 Nov. 1663; Joseph, 8 Apr. 1666; and Benjamin, 26 July 1668, H. C. 1689, wh. was a min. that d. 1698 at Charleston, S. C. He was freem. 1652, and d. 7 Dec. 1682, aged 64. His s. John d. 30 Dec. 1690 unm. I think; and Joseph, prob. a stud. at coll. at least bur. at Cambridge, d. 25 Feb. 1687. JONATHAN, s. of Robert of Roxbury, was fourth min. of Reading, ord. 26 June 1689, m. 29 Oct. 1691, Eliz. d. of Edmund Angier of Cambridge, had Eliz. b. 25 Feb. 1693; Jonathan, 14 Sept. 1695, H. C. 1714; Joseph, 13 Oct. 1706; Mary, 11 Feb. 1708; and he d. 2 June 1709. ROBERT, Ipswich 1648, br. prob. of James the first, may, I suppose, be regard. as f. of that ROBERT of I. who was adm. freem. 1676; but no good report of either has reached me. ROBERT, Roxbury, s. of the first James, b. in Eng. m. at Charlestown 18 Feb. 1657, tho. Frothingham says 1666, Sarah, d. of Thomas Lynde, had James, b. 30 Nov. 1657, d. very soon; Margaret, 13 Mar. 1659, d. in few days; Margaret, again, 14 Mar. 1661, d. in few days; Jonathan, 8 Oct. 1663, d. in few days; Jonathan, again, 11 June 1665, H. C. 1685; Thomas, 7 July 1667; Ezra, 30 July 1669, d. soon; Sarah, 29 Nov. 1671, d. very soon; Margaret, again, 30 Apr. 1672; James, again, 28 Oct. 1675, d. next yr.; James, again, 27 Aug. 1677; Robert, 31 Dec. 1678, d. in few wks.; and Sarah, again, 24 May 1680; and he d. 16 May 1694. His wid. gave a depon. it is said, at the age of 85 yrs. wh. illustrates much the genealog. tho. her mem. was infirm eno. to magnify the number of her days, by reckon. six or seven yrs. too many, or in the shorter term of Farmer, four or five. So dangerous is an oath taken under the burden of age. Eight of this name, includ. the spelling of Pierrepont, the noble fam. in Eng. had in 1834 been gr. at Harv. and six at Yale.

PIERSON, PEARSON, PORSUNE, or PERSON, ABRAHAM, Branford, was of Yorksh. came to Boston 1640, join. the ch. 5 Sept. of that yr. when he is call. "a studient," of wh. we may doubt the meaning, as we kn. he was bred at Trinity Coll. Cambridge, where he took his A. B. 1632, and he is in Mather's first Classis as a min. bef. coming over, tho. this may well seem incorrect; bec. min. of the ch. gather. in Lynn Nov. 1640 to go to sett. at Southampton, L. I. thence a. 1647 went to Branford, and thence in the autumn of 1667, with a part of his congreg. to Newark, N. J. See his letter to John Winthrop, 3 Mass. Hist. Coll. X. 69 and 84. He had Abraham, b. at Lynn 1641, H. C. 1668; Thomas, John, and Abigail, bef. his rem. from S. and at B. were b. Grace, 13 June 1650; Susanna, 10 Dec. 1652; Rebecca, 10 Dec. 1654; and Theophi-

lus, 15 Mar. or May 1659; beside Isaac; and Mary. Abigail m. 27
Nov. 1663, John Davenport the younger; Susanna m. 1672, Jonathan
Bell of Stamford, as his sec. w.; Grace was sec. w. of Samuel Kitchell;
and Rebecca m. Joseph Johnson, and d. 8 Nov. 1732. But much of the
details belong to Newark. He d. 9 Aug. 1678. Descend. are in Conn.
N. Y. and N. J. of wh. Farmer says twelve had in 1829, been gr. at the
coll. of those three States. Lechford, in Plain Dealing, 43, calls him
Pridgeon. Of his will, I have large abstr. furnish. by Samuel H. Con-
gar, Esq. It bears date 10 Aug. 1671, provides out of good est. for four
s. Abraham, Thomas, Theophilus, and Isaac; four ds. beside his "choice
and precious d. Davenport," so that we may be sure John was d. bef.
that date. ABRAHAM, Killingworth, s. of the preced. had been ord. as
collea. with his f. at Newark, 4 Mar. 1672, in 1692 came to Conn. and
in 1694 was sett. at K. m. Abigail, d. of George Clark of Milford; in
1701, was made the first head of Yale coll. and serv. until he d. 5
May 1707. He had ch. Abraham, Sarah, Susannah, Mary, Hannah,
Ruth, James, and Abigail, beside John, Y. C. 1711, min. of Woodbridge, N. J. BARTHOLOMEW, Watertown 1639, by w. Ursula, writ.
Azlee, Uzlah, Uzlee in the rec. had Bartholomew, b. Sept. 1640, d. next
mo.; Bartholomew, again, 26 Feb. 1642, d. in few mos.; Martha, 17
Sept. 1643; perhaps Mary; Jonathan, 12 Aug. 1648; Joseph, 8 Nov.
1650; Sarah, 7 May 1653; and Bartholomew, again, wh. d. in few yrs.
In 1648 he was made freem. spell. Porsune in the rec. and in 1653 he
rem. to Woburn, was selectman 1665 and 6, and d. 12 Mar. 1687. His
wid. d. 28 May 1694. HENRY, Hempstead, L. I. 1686. HUGH,
Watertown 1649, had, in 1654, w. Alice and d. Ruth, then 9 yrs. old,
and he d. 13 June 1675, very poor, as he had liv. JOHN, Middletown,
d. July 1677, leav. w. and s. three yrs. old. PETER, Boston, a quaker,
to be whipp. at the cart's tail 1660, thro. Boston, Roxbury, and Dedham.
Hutch. I. 203. It is not relat. in any book how this tended to his con-
version. STEPHEN, Derby 1679, had prob. other ch. beside Stephen
and Sarah; for the name of Abraham is found in the list of est. 1717,
and this may lead to the presumption that Stephen was s. of the first
Abraham. THOMAS, Branford 1668, not (as oft. he is call.) s. of Rev.
Abraham the first, m. 27 Nov. 1662, Mary, d. of Richard Harrison, had
Samuel, b. a. 1663, rem. to Newark, and d. there. He sw. alleg. to the
Dutch in 1673. He was prob. br. possib. neph. of the first Rev. Abraham, and his will of 12 Jan. 1698, with codic. of 3 Mar. 1701, was pro.
in May foll. It names s. Samuel and Thomas, ds. Hannah and Eliz.
THOMAS, Branford, s. of the first Abraham, m. Mary Harrison, went to
Newark from Branford with his f. was call. jun. was in good esteem, but
was d. bef. 1684.

PIGG, PIDGE, or PIGGE, JOHN, Dedham, prob. s. of Thomas, freem. 1690, print. in the list Pidg, as the name of his mo. in the Metcalf genealog. is spelt Pidge, wh. may show the sound. ROBERT, New Haven 1644, d. 1660, or very early next yr. his inv. being of 23 Jan. foll. and his will of .28 Mar. preced. In it he names w. Margaret, wh. m. 1662, William Tharpe or Thorpe, d. Alice, mean. w. of John Jenner, perhaps, her s. Thomas "and her other childr." Possib. he was br. of THOMAS of Roxbury, freem. 14 May 1634, wh. brot. from Eng. w. Mary, and sev. ch. had here Martha, bapt. 12 Mar. 1643, and he d. 30 Dec. foll. His will, pro. 12 Sept. 1644, gives Thomas, John, Hannah, Sarah, and Martha, propty. in R. and to d. Mary, w. I think of Nicholas Wood, his allotm. in Dedham. His wid. m. 13 Aug. 1645, Michael Metcalf. THOMAS, Dedham, s. of the preced. d. early in Sept. 1660, prob. never m. at least his br. John and sis. had his prop. Geneal. Reg. X. 180.

PIGDEN, THOMAS, Lynn 1647. Lewis.

PIGGOT, CHRISTOPHER, Boston 1655, on 27 Apr. of wh. yr. an order was passed, that his w. shall be forthwith sent to him at Muddy riv. by the constable.

PIGHOGG, Mr. Boston, adm. a townsman 28 Feb. 1652, with prefix of respect, and entitled a "churrergeon." See Rec. I. 103, wh. gives no name of bapt.

PIGROM, WILLIAM, Dorchester 1653, perhaps only transient.

PIKE, GEORGE, Marblehead 1668. HUGH, Newbury, a soldier under Turner, at Hatfield, in Apr. 1676, m. 17 June 1685, Sarah, d. of Francis Brown, had Hugh, b. 28 May 1686, and Joseph. JAMES, Charlestown 1647, then adm. of the ch. and made freem. rem. to Reading, had two ws. Naomi, and Sarah, two s. John, b. 1 Jan. 1654; and Zechariah, 8 Oct. 1658; but of wh. w. either was s. or whether there were more ch. or their names if there were more, as is prob. exc. Jeremiah, or when either of the ws. or the ch. d. I have not heard. He d. 1699. JEREMIAH, Reading, prob. s. of the preced. had Jeremiah, b. 15 Jan. 1674; James, 2 May 1676, d. soon; as did Eliezer or Ebenezer, b. next yr.; Michael, 7 Apr. 1678; James, again, 7 Nov. 1679, d. young; Rachel, 14 Dec. 1681; James, again, 15 Sept. 1682; Nathaniel, 4 May 1685; William, 14 Mar. 1687; Naomi, 14 Feb. 1689; was of Framingham, a selectman 1700, and d. 9 Jan. 1711. JOHN, Newbury, came in the James, 1635, from Southampton, call. in the clearance from the custom-ho. laborer of Langford, with ch. was at Ipswich first, in 1640 of Piscataqua, and rem. perhaps early to Salisbury, but more prob. only estab. there on his est. sec. s. d. 26 May 1654, leav. will, made two days bef. in wh. he provides for gr.s. John, s. of John, and gr.s. John, s. of Robert, three ds. Dorothy, w. of Daniel Hendrick, by wh. we discov. the error of Genealog. Reg. VI. 342, where she is call. d. instead of sis. of Robert; Israel, w. of Henry True; and Ann. I presume all these ch. and Sarah, not found in the will, were brot. from Eng. or Coffin would have giv. us the date of b. here, as well as the name of the w. as yet unkn. *JOHN, Newbury, s. of the preced. b. in Eng. by w. Mary had Joseph, b. 26 Dec. 1638; John, 12 Jan. 1641, d. at 8 yrs.; Hannah, 26 Apr. 1643; Mary, 11 Nov. 1647; John, again, 20 Mar. 1650; Ruth, 17 July 1652; Sarah, 13 Sept. 1655; Thomas, 7 Dec. 1657; and Samuel; was rep. 1657 and 8, tho. as freem. his name is not found; rem. to Woodbridge, N. J. 1669, among the first sett. there, and was some yrs. a magistr. JOHN, Newbury, s. of the preced. m. 18 Mar. 1695, Lydia, wid. of Moses Little, d. of Tristram Coffin, had Judith, b. 4 Dec. foll.; Susanna, 3 Apr. 1697; Lydia, 23 Dec. 1698; Joanna, 17 Dec. 1700; and Dorothy, 23 Sept. 1702; and he d. 13 Aug. 1714. JOHN, Roxbury, had Jessie, b. 26 Feb. 1685. JOHN, Dover, s. of Robert, freem. 1676, ord. success. to sec. John Rayner, 31 Aug. 1681, m. 5 May preced. Sarah, d. of Rev. Joshua Moody; had Robert, b. 6 Feb. 1685; Abigail, 1688, d. at 6 yrs.; Hannah and Mary, tw. 1691; Joshua, 1693; Margaret, 1699; and Solomon, 1700; and his w. d. 24 Jan. 1703. He rem. 1689 to Portsmouth when D. was destr. by the Ind. next yr. to Hampton, next yr. to Newbury, next yr. to Portsmouth to emb. for Pemaquid as chapl. to the garris. back to Portsmouth in July 1695, and to Dover 1698, and in less than four yrs. to Salisbury, where he was b. but in a yr. or two went last to Dover again, there d. 10 Mar. 1710. All inquirers for minute statements about his neighb. are much indebted to his Journal in Vol. III. of N. H. Hist. Coll. His will of 6 Mar. bef. names ch. Nathaniel, Robert, Joshua, Solomon, Hannah, and Mary. *JOSEPH, Newbury, s. of John of the same, rep. 1690–2, by w. Susanna, d. of Henry Kingsbury the sec. m. 29 Jan. 1663, had Sarah, Mary, John, Thomas, Joseph, Hannah, and Benjamin; was k. by the Ind. betw. Amesbury and Haverhill, 4 Sept. 1694. JOSEPH, Charlestown 1683, had w. Susanna, k. by the Ind. 4 Sept. 1694, near Dover. MOSES, Salisbury, youngest ch. of Robert, by w. Susanna, had Moses, b. 16 Aug. 1688; Elias, 10 July 1692; Mary, 27 Apr. 1695; and Sarah, 27 Oct. 1698. RICHARD, Newbury 1655, was sett. at Falmouth 1675. Willis, I. 140, 3. ‡*ROBERT, Salisbury, s. of John the first, brot. from Eng. was first at Newbury, freem. 17 May 1637, m. 3 Apr. 1641, Sarah Sanders, perhaps d. of John or his sis. had Sarah, b. 24 Feb. 1642; Mary, 22 Feb. 1644, d. young; Dorothy, 11 Nov. 1645; Mary, again, 5 Aug. 1647; Eliz. 24 June 1650; John, 13 May 1653, H. C. 1675; Robert, 26 June 1655; and Moses, 15 Mar. 1659; was early one of the ch. mem. at S. rep. 1648 and some yrs. foll. lieut. capt.

major in comm. of one of the Essex regim. an Assist. 1682 to the sub-vers. of the chart. one of the counc. of safety on the overthrow of Andros, 1689, and in William and Mary's Chart. 1691, again made one of the council. His w. d. 1 Nov. 1679, and he d. 12 Dec. 1706 in his 91st yr. Sarah m. 7 May 1661, Wymond Bradbury; and next, 10 May 1671, John Stockman; Dorothy m. Joshua Pierce; and Eliz. m. 20 Aug. 1672, William Carr. ROBERT, Providence 1645, may have been only trans. inhab. ROBERT, Salisbury, s. of Robert of the same, m. 30 Oct. 1684, Martha Goldwyer, perhaps d. of George, had Robert, b. 3 Sept. 1687; and Sarah, 3 Feb. 1690; was freem. that yr. and d. 22 Aug. of the same. SAMUEL, Falmouth, 1688, s. of Richard. Willis I. 143, 190. Four of this name had, in 1829, been gr. at Harv. and two at Dartm. coll.

PILE, WILLIAM, Salisbury 1659, rem. to Nantucket, thence to Dover, bef. July 1663.

PILLING, or PILLEN, JOHN, Kittery 1639, a fisherman, was prob. of Dover 1653.

PILSBURY, ABEL, Newbury, s. of William, by w. Mary had Joshua, b. 12 Apr. 1679; John, 13 Sept. 1682; Jacob, 20 Mar. 1687; Abel, 12 Apr. 1690; and Eliz. 20 Mar. 1694. CALEB and INCREASE, brs. of the preced. were of Newbury 1678, but we kn. no more of either exc. that the former d. 4 July 1680, acc. Coffin, wh. says nothing of the latter aft. his b. JOB, Newbury, eldest br. of the preced. freem. 1670, m. 5 Apr. 1677, Catharine Gavett, had Daniel, b. 20 Sept. 1678; and Josiah, 17 Apr. 1686. MOSES, Newbury, br. of the preced. freem. 1673, m. 1668, Susanna, wid. of Lionel Worth, d. of John Whipple, had Joseph, b. 6 June 1670; Dorothy, 9 Apr. 1675; Susanna, 5 Feb. 1677; Judith, 16 Mar. 1679; Caleb, 27 July 1681; and Hannah, 3 May 1686; but I doubt that the last five must have been by a sec. w. Coffin's page does not allude to d. of the first. Yet as w. of Worth she had brot. a number. WILLIAM, Dorchester 1641, m. that yr. prob. Dorothy Crosby, had Deborah, b. 16 Apr. 1642; Job, 26 Oct. 1643; Moses; Abel; rem. to Newbury, there had Caleb, 28 Jan. 1654; William, 27 July 1656; Experience, 10 Apr. 1658; Increase, 10 Oct. 1660; Thankful, 22 Apr. 1662; and Joshua, 20 June 1671; freem. 1668, d. 19 June 1686, aged 71. WILLIAM, Newbury, s. of the preced. m. 13 Dec. 1677, Mary Kenny, had William, b. 22 Mar. 1680, prob. d. soon; Experience, 16 Apr. 1682; William, again, 7 July 1687; Lydia, 25 Dec. 1689; Increase, 5 Jan. 1695; and Apphia, 8 May 1700. Nine of this name had, in 1834, been gr. at N. E. coll.

PIMORE, THOMAS, New Haven, a propr. 1685.

PINCKNEY, PHILIP, Fairfield 1650, perhaps he was not there much aft. 1653, certain. was at East Chester, 1665. His s. John liv. there 1690, and perhaps he had other ch. beside Abigail, wh. m. David Osborn.

PINDAR, PINDER, PYNDER, or PINTER, HENRY, Ipswich 1642, perhaps was f. of Mary, wh. m. 21 Mar. 1643, Solomon Martin, and of Joanna, wh. m. 14 Nov. 1643, Valentine Rowell. He had come prob. as early as 1635 at least, for in that yr. emb. at London, in the Susan and Ellen, to come hither, were Mary, aged 53, with six ch.; Francis, 20; Mary, 17; Joanna, 14; Ann, 12; Catharine, 10; and John, 8. JOHN, Ipswich 1648, may have been s. of the preced. m. a d. of Theophilus Wilson, and had s. Thomas; and perhaps rem. to Watertown, there d. 14 Apr. 1662. SAMUEL, Ipswich 1683.

PINGRY, PINGREW, PINGREE, or PENGRY, AARON, Ipswich 1648. *MOSES, Ipswich 1642, perhaps br. of the preced. a saltmaker, m. Abigail, d. of first Robert Clement, was rep. 1665, and deac. d. 1695, aged prob. 85 yrs. JOHN, prob. s. of Aaron or Moses, took lease of the sch. farm in 1680, m. Faith, perhaps d. of the first Joseph Jewett.

PINION, NICHOLAS, Lynn 1647, perhaps worked at the iron mine, rem. to New Haven, there wrought at the iron works, by w. Eliz. wh. d. 1667, had Ruth, Hannah, Mary, Thomas, and Robert; and d. Apr. 1676. His inv. amount. only to £43; but that was a season of extreme depression. The spelling is Dodd's, but Sylvester Judd read the rec. Pineon. Ruth m. at Lynn, 28 Dec. 1657, James Moore. ROBERT, Lynn 1647, may have been s. of the preced. THOMAS, Sudbury 1661, may have been s. of Nicholas, sett. at New Haven, by w. Mary had Christiana, Mercy, and Abigail, and d. 10 Oct. 1710. Doubts as to this name have been express. in Conn. for it might easily be read Pineon, or Pineo, and the sound of either is not much unlike the others, it is said, and was seldom uttered in public.

PINKHAM, JOHN, Dover 1665, s. of Richard, in 1671 had gr. from his f. of most of his prop. on condit. of support. him for life, and m. Rose, d. of the first Richard Otis, had Richard, Thomas, Amos, Otis, Solomon, James, Rose, Eliz. Sarah, and John; 7 s. 3 ds. RICHARD, Dover 1648, hir. to call the people to ch. by beat. the drum. RICHARD, Dover, s. of the preced. m. Eliz. d. of Thomas Layton the sec. had Richard, Tristram, and John, this last b. 19 Aug. 1696. RICHARD, Nantucket, had Jonathan, b. 12 Nov. 1684; Shubael, 7 June 1691; Nathaniel, 22 Jan. 1693; Deborah, 28 Feb. 1695; Daniel, 8 Dec. 1697; Barnabas, 3 Jan. 1700; Peleg, 5 Feb. 1702; Theophilus, 14 Mar. 1706; and James, 19 Feb. 1708; but the name of w. is not seen in Geneal. Reg. VII. 263. THOMAS, Dover 1665, perhaps br. of John.

PINNEY, or PYNNY, HUMPHREY, Dorchester, b. in Somertsh. came, as once was thot. in the Mary and John, 1630, but Stiles, in Hist. of Windsor, 745, shows that in 1631 he was engag. in Eng. on will of his uncle Edmund, freem. 14 May 1634, m. at Dorchester, Mary, d. of George Hull, had Samuel; rem. to Windsor, there had Nathaniel, b. Dec. 1641, bapt. 2 Jan. 1642; Mary, bapt. 16 June 1644; Sarah, 19 Nov. bapt. 3 Dec. 1648; John, bapt. 19 Oct. 1651; Abigail, 26 Nov. 1654; and Isaac 24, bapt. 28 Feb. 1664. All these ch. were liv. when he made his will, June 1682. He d. 20 Aug. 1683; and his wid. wh. d. 18 Aug. 1684, names in her will 12 Sept. bef. all her ch. but of Abigail only her three ch. leav. the inference that she was d. Mary m. 6 July, 1665, Abraham Phelps; Sarah was sec. w. 20 Dec. 1676, of the sec. William Phelps; and Abigail m. (23 Dec. 1667, acc. Stiles, 746, but, as she was then only 13 yrs. 10 days old, I prefer my earlier informat. as to date) 1677, John Adams. ISAAC, Windsor, youngest s. of the preced. m. a. 1685, Sarah, d. of Daniel Clark, had Isaac, b. 17 Jan. 1687; Jonathan, 23 Oct. 1688; Mary, 4 Mar. 1690; Sarah, 7 Mar. 1692 or 3; Humphrey, 5 Sept. 1694; Eliz. 6 Jan. 1697; and Noah, 24 Jan. 1703; beside Hannah, and Daniel, whose dates are unkn. to Goodwin. JOHN, Charlestown, m. 4 July 1682, Eliz. d. of Thomas Rand, had John, Edmund, and Eliz. all bapt. 11 Sept. 1687; yet I ⁊ ᵃ not inform. in whose right the ordinance was perform. nor is any thing more kn. of him, the w. or ch. at C. That he was not the s. of Humphrey, is well inferr. from what is told me, that the Windsor John d. 1697, without ch. NATHANIEL, Windsor, s. of Humphrey, freem. 1667, m. 21 July, 1670, Sarah Phelps, wid. of Samuel, d. of Edward Griswold, had Nathaniel, b. 11 May 1671; and Sarah, 11 Oct. 1673; and d. 7 Aug. 1676. His wid. d. 6 Nov. 1715. SAMUEL, Windsor, eldest br. of the preced. b. at Dorchester, made freem. 1658, m. 17 Nov. 1665, Joyce, d. of John Bissell, had Mary, b. 16 June 1667; Samuel, 20 Nov. 1668; rem. to Simsbury, and there had Josiah, 3 Nov. 1681. THOMAS, Gloucester 1671, freem. 1672, and was there ten yrs. aft.

PINSON, PINCHIN, or PINCIN, ANDREW, Wethersfield, d. 7 May 1697, aft. more than thirty yrs. inhab. aged 74, and prob. without ever w. or ch. EDMUND, Cambridge 1665, m. Ann, d. of John Cooper, had Ann, wh. d. 8 May, 1666, inf. He had sec. w. Sarah, d. of Richard Dexter. THOMAS, Scituate 1636, m. 1639, Jane, d. of Richard Standlake, had Thomas, b. 15 May 1640; Hannah, 4 Dec. 1642; Waitstill, 1650; John, 1655; and Joshua, 1658. Hannah m. 15 Jan. 1662, George Young. THOMAS, Scituate, s. of the preced. m. 18 Sept. 1662, Eliz. perhaps d. of Gawin White, had Thomas, b. 1662; Ebenezer, 1668; and perhaps others; he had sec. w. Sarah Turner. Deane.

PIPER, JONATHAN, Ipswich, youngest s. of Nathaniel, had w. Sarah, wh. d. 6 May 1700, and next m. the same yr. Alice Darby, rem. 1731 to Concord, there d. 11 May 1752, and his wid. d. 23 Apr. 1758. Of eight ch. Jonathan, Nathaniel, Josiah, John, Alice, Sarah, Mary, and Joseph, the last, b. 1718, is the only one to whom date is affix. nor can we discern by wh. w. they respectively came. NATHANIEL, Ipswich 1665, is thot. to have come from Dartmouth in Devonsh. His will of 7 Mar. 1676, names w. Sarah, and ch. Sarah, Nathaniel, Josiah, John, Thomas, Mary, Margaret, Samuel, and Jonathan. * RICHARD, Haddam 1669, was then constable, in 1674 rep. d. 3 Apr. 1678, in his will names no w. nor ch. but gives prop. to relat. and friends.

PIPON, JOHN, master of a ship at Salem, 1673, was prob. that capt. in the forces to wh. Andros gave comm. at the castle. Felt I. 359. Perhaps Andros's officer in 1687 command. at Pemaquid was Joshua. See 3 Mass. Hist. Coll. VII. 180.

PITCHER, ANDREW, Dorchester 1634, freem. 2 June 1641, by w. Margaret had, beside eldest s. Samuel, John, Jonathan and Nathaniel nam. in his will, Experience, bapt. 25 Sept. 1642; Mary, 25 Nov. 1644; Ruth, 25 July 1647; and ano. s. 18 Apr. 1652, wh. d. young, as prob. did Mary; neither being ment. in his will; d. 19 Feb. 1661, having made his will 4 Dec. preced. dwelt in that part wh. next yr. bec. Milton. Experience m. Joseph Bugby of Roxbury; and Mary m. Mills. JOHN, Bridgewater 1666, serv. of Francis Godfrey, wh. names him in his will. NATHANIEL, Milton, s. of Andrew, m. 8 July 1684, Mary, d. of Ezra Clap. SAMUEL, Milton, br. of the preced. was freem. 1683, and prob. f. of Rev. Nathaniel, b. 1685, H. C. 1703, wh. d. 27 Sept. 1723, a well belov. min. of Scituate.

PITHOUSE. See Pittice.

PITKIN, NATHANIEL, Hartford, s. of William the first, m. Esther, d. of Stephen Hosmer, had Nathaniel, b. 1699; Esther, 1701; Ann, 1703; Dorothy, 1705; Hannah, 1707; and Deborah; by sec. w. Eliz. d. of Rev. John Whiting, had Eliz. and d. 20 Feb. 1733; and his wid. m. Moses Porter of Hadley, and d. 20 yrs. aft. OZIAS, Hartford, youngest br. of the preced. wh. d. 30 Jan. 1747, in his will of Nov. bef. names w. Esther, s. Samuel; Ozias, b. 10 May 1710; Isaac; Daniel; and James; ds. Abigail, w. of William Bidwell; Eliz. w. of William Olmstead; Mary, w. of Daniel Pratt; Hannah, w. of Asahel Olmstead; Martha, w. of Rev. John Eels; and Ruth, then under age, as were two of the s. The last nam. d. and last three s. were ch. of the sec. w. Esther Cadwell; but the other five ds. and two s. were of former w. who was Eliz. Green of Boston. ROGER, Hartford, eldest br. of the preced. m. 1683, Hannah, d. of Caleb Stanley, had Hannah, b. 30 May 1684; Caleb, 19 July 1687; Mary, 30 Dec. 1689; Rachel, 14 Dec. 1692; Mabel, 1695,

d. soon; Jonathan, 1 Mar. 1696; Mabel, again, 23 Mar. 1700; and Roger, 29 Oct. 1703; and three days aft. the w. d. He made his will, 1 Jan. 1734; but it was not pro. bef. 15 yrs. for he liv. to 24 Nov. 1748. ‡ * WILLIAM, Hartford 1660, freem: 1662, was s. of Roger wh. was of London in 1666, tho. fam. tradit. brings him from the city of Norwich, had prob. been bred a lawyer in Eng. here first taught a sch. was soon made Atty. for the Col. rep. 1675, treasr. 1676, m. Hannah, only d. of Ozias Goodwin, had Roger, b. 1662; William, 1664; John; Nathaniel; George, 1675; Ozias, 1679; Hannah; and Eliz. 1677; all nam. in his will, as also is br. Roger; was an Assist. sev. yrs. and d. 15 Dec. 1694, aged 58; and his wid. d. 12 Feb. 1724, aged 86. His s. George d. 23 Dec. 1702, and John in 1705 or 6, both without ch. Hannah m. Timothy Cowles; and Eliz. m. John Marsh, jr. He brot. from Eng. or she follow. him, as tradit. says, sis. Martha wh. m. 17 Oct. 1661, Simon Wolcott, was mo. of the first Gov. W. who, in the funer. sermon upon him, is said to have never gone to any sch. but to have been solely educat. by her at home, and aft. m. Daniel Clark. ‡ * WILLIAM, Hartford, s. of the preced. m. 1686, Eliz. d. of Caleb Stanley, had Eliz. b. 30 Aug. 1687, d. soon; Eliz. again, 18 Aug. 1689; Martha, 28 Feb. 1692; William, 30 Apr. 1694; Joseph, 26 May 1696; Sarah, 26 Mar. 1698, d. soon; Thomas, 18 June 1700; Sarah, again, 28 Nov. 1702; John, 18 July 1706, d. soon; John, again, 18 Dec. 1707; and Jerusha, 22 June 1710; was rep. 1696, next yr. Assist. and he d. 5 Apr. 1723, in his will of Oct. preced. naming w. and the eight liv. ch. Nine of this name have been gr. at Yale.

PITMAN, oft. PITNAM, EZEKIEL, New Hampsh. 1683. JOHN, Salem, a capt. freem. 1690, liv. in what bec. Danvers. JONATHAN, Stratford, m. 21 Nov. 1681, Temperance, elder d. of John Welles of the same, had Jonathan, b. 4 Nov. 1682, d. soon; Jonathan, again, 21 May 1687; Robert, 16 Oct. 1689; and Samuel, 1 Feb. 1692; and d. a. 1727. JOSEPH, Charlestown, d. 27 Oct. 1658; says Farmer; but a doubt is rais. whether he were not casual resid. for neither as townsman nor ch. man does the name appear. JOSEPH, Dover, in serv. of William Tasket, disch. by the Court, 1686, for cruelty of the master, k. by the Ind. 19 Aug. 1704. MARK, Marblehead 1674, call. 50 yrs. old, was, I suppose, a soldier, k. next yr. 25 Aug. at Hatfield. NATHANIEL, Salem 1639, had then, says Felt, gr. of ld. He is usual. nam. Pickman. SAMUEL, Salem 1670. THOMAS, Marblehead 1648, perhaps had s. Thomas. THOMAS, Marblehead, call. jun. aged 17 in 1669 may be the man titled sen. in 1683 when made freem. WILLIAM, Dover, m. at Boston, 29 Nov. 1653, Barbara Evans, had prob. that Mary wh. m. 16 Apr. 1674, Stephen Otis; and he may have liv. 1677 at Boston.

PITNEY, JAMES, Boston 1652, had been of Ipswich 1639. His w. Sarah, had come in the Planter, 1635, from London, aged 22, with Margaret, 22, who perhaps was his sis. and two ch. Sarah, 7, and Samuel, 1 and ½. He was of Marshfield 1643, and aft. d. of his w. 14 Aug. 1658, rem. to M. again, for there his d. Sarah m. 21 Dec. 1648, John Thomas, and there he d. 14 Mar. 1663, by nuncup. will giv. his little prop. to his ch. James, Abigail, and John, and Sarah Thomas and her childr. He was then 80 yrs. old, it is said. The s. James is prob. not that youth ment. in a let. of Roger Williams to John Winthrop, Apr. 1655, as having run away from his master, James Bill of Boston, steering for New London.

PITT, WILLIAM, Plymouth, came, Nov. 1621, in the Fortune, had sh. in the div. of ld. Mar. 1624, but was not present at the div. of cattle 1627; and may have rem. to the N. shore of the Bay. He was possib. of Marblehead in 1674; at least, one Hugh Latimer, of M. seems to have m. 1669, Mary, d. of a man of this name, wh. liv. there in May 1665. See Morton's Memo. by Davis, 378; and Baylies I. 85.

PITTEE, PITTY, or PITTEY, JOSEPH, Ipswich, freem. 1680. JOSEPH, Weymouth, prob. s. of William of the same, tho. the rec. of his b. has a false date, freem. 1681, by w. Sarah had Mary, b. 27 Dec. 1672; Sarah, 11 June 1674; John 7 Nov. 1679; William, 17 Mar. 1682; Benjamin, 27 Apr. 1687; Ebenezer, 9 Sept. 1689; and Nathaniel, 14 June 1691; perhaps one or two more, as rec. are partial. lost. SAMUEL, Weymouth, s. of William, by w. Mary had Samuel, b. 24 Oct. 1685; James, 1 Apr. 1692; and perhaps others. WILLIAM, Weymouth, an early sett. by w. Mary, had, as I conject. (tho. rec. makes Samuel the f.) Samuel, b. 12 Aug. 1657; and William, 12 May 1661; others, also, much earlier; John, b. 28 Jan. 1639, wh. was drown. 28 May 1659; and Mary, 13 June 1643, wh. m. 10 May 1660, Henry Adams. WILLIAM, Weymouth, s. of the preced. by w. Mary had James, b. 16 Nov. 1686; and perhaps others not ment. on rec.

PITTICE, JOHN, Ipswich 1648, may be, I think, the passeng. in the James from Southampton, 1635, who was of Marlborough in Wilts, says the custom-ho. rec. spelling it Pithouse, and possib. the Pettis or Pittis populat. may thus be deriv.

PITTS, EDMUND, Hingham, from Hingham in Eng. came with w. and ch. was a weaver, freem. 13 May 1640, and had br. Leonard in comp. had s. John, b. 27 Nov. 1653; and Jeremy, 25 Jan. 1657. Deborah, wh. m. May 1672 to Daniel Howard; Mary m. Nov. 1672 to John Bull or Bullen; and Eliz. m. Dec. 1673, Thomas Jones, were his ds. or they or some may have come of ano. fam. Coffin inf. Farmer, that, a John P. d. at Ipswich, 20 May 1653; and I find an Eliz. at Gloucester, 1639.

Peter, Taunton 1643–60, had, perhaps, m. Mary, d. of Henry Andrews, wid. of William Hodges or Hedges, wh. in her will aft. 2 Apr. 1654, provid. that Peter P. should perform its conditions "in case I make him my husband." Samuel, Taunton, m. 25 Mar. 1680, Sarah Bobbett, d. of Edward of the same. William, Hingham, came in the Diligent, 1638, from Old Hingham, may be the man of wh. Winth. II. 305 tells, and may have been at Marblehead, 1654, but 7 Dec. of next yr. m. Susanna, wid. of Philip Alley, was a trader, and prob. liv. at Boston; but his w. Susanna d. at M. on a visit 28 Sept. 1668. See Essex Inst. Coll. II. 69.

Pittums, or Pittoms, John, Boston, by w. Mary had Nathaniel, b. 8 July 1678; Mary, 18 May 1680, bapt. 26 June 1681; and Eliz. whose b. is not seen, but bapt. 22 Nov. 1685.

Pixley, Ebenezer, Westfield, s. of William of the same, m. 1711, Mary Strong, prob. d. of Jedediah, had only Elijah, b. 1714; and d. 1716. Joseph, Westfield, s. of William, m. 23 Aug. 1699, Abigail, one of the nine ds. of John Clark of Farmington, had Jonah, b. 3 Mar. 1701; Joseph, 4 Mar. 1703; Abigail, 29 May 1705; Moses, 9 June 1707; John, 22 Oct. 1709; Jonathan, 17 Jan. 1712; David, 21 Mar. 1714; and Clark, 3 Oct. 1724; rem. to Sheffield. Thomas, Westfield, br. of the preced. m. 1699, Lydia Dibble, d. of Abraham, had Sarah, b. 1699; Noah, 1706; and d. 1731. William, Hadley, m. 24 Nov. 1663, Sarah Lawrence, had Sarah, b. 11 Jan. 1665; Thomas, 6 June 1667; rem. to Northampton, there had William, 27 June 1669; Joseph, 18 Nov. 1671, d. young; Joseph, again, 9 Mar. 1676; Ebenezer, 13 May 1678; rem. to Westfield, there had Anthony, 4 July 1681, wh. d. 25 Apr. 1697; beside Mary, wh. d. 1735, at Westfield, unm. the date of whose b. is not kn. and he d. 9 Oct. 1689; and his wid. d. 25 Nov. 1713. Sarah m. 9 Dec. 1680, John Lee. Thomas, and Ebenezer, as well as Joseph, bef. ment. had ch. in W. but their names have not been learned. The name is still found.

Place, sometimes Plaise, Enoch, Kingstown, R. I. from whose will, May 1695, I learn that he was 64 yrs. old, and had w. Sarah, m. Nov. 1657, at Dorchester, as in Geneal. Rec. XI. 332 is seen, without her surname, and ch. Enoch, Peter, Thomas, and Joseph, the youngest, beside Sarah, w. of * * * Cook. The same Dorchester rec. ment. that Dinah P. d. 28 July of that yr. Peter, Boston, came in the Truelove, 1635, from London, aged 20, freem. 1646, by w. Alice had Hannah, b. 20 Jan. bapt. 19 Mar. 1643; Eliz. 29 Sept. bapt. 6 Oct. 1644; Joseph, b. 19 Oct. 1646; Peter, bapt. 17 June 1649, a. 3 days old; Eliz. again, 21 Oct. 1652, wh. d. young.; Sarah, 3 Sept. 1657. Peter, Providence, perhaps s. of the preced. sw. alleg. to Charles II. May 1682. Thomas,

Braintree or Dorchester, freem. 13 May 1640. WILLIAM, Salem, blacksmith, had gr. of ld. 1637, when Felt notes he was called "old Mr. William P." He had w. but no ch. and d. 14 Apr. 1646.

PLAISTED, or PLAYSTEAD, ‡ICHABOD, Portsmouth, s. of Roger, one of the counc. of the Prov. of Mass. d. 16 Nov. 1715 in 52d yr. Hutch. II. 212. He m. 5 Jan. 1693, Mary, youngest ch. of Christopher Jose, had Samuel, b. 10 June 1696, H. C. 1715; Ichabod, 21 July 1700; Mary, 6 Oct. 1702; and prob. others. *JOHN, New Hamp. 1679, speaker 1695, and oft. aft. judge of sup. ct. 1699, and ch. just. 1716, m. Mary, d. of John Pickering, had John, b. 2 Jan. 1683; Joshua, 20 Sept. 1685; and Mary, 29 Mar. 1687. *ROGER, Kittery, br. of the preced. very loyal to Mass. in 1667; was betrust. with civil commiss. as early as 1661, a brave and trustworthy officer, made a lieut. under autho. of Mass. 1668, had been rep. 1663 and 4, and again in 1673, k. by the Ind. 16 Oct. 1675, aged 48, with s. Roger, and ano. s. mortally wound. at the same time. His wid. Olive, eldest s. William, and s. James, were appoint. admors. 30 Nov. 1675, inv. was £567 15s. Hutch. I. 266, 308; Hubbard, Ind. Wars, 22, 3, and 4; Sullivan, 250; Belkn. I. 73; Geneal. Reg. III. 255. ROGER, Kittery, s. of the preced. left w. Hannah and childr.

PLANE, or PLAIN, WILLIAM, Guilford 1639, execut. 1646, at New Haven, for monstrous crimes. Winth. II. 265.

PLASTOW, JOSIAH, Boston 1631, banish. Winth. I. 52, 61, 2. It is said he d. bef. 5 June 1632.

PLATT, ABEL, Rowley 1678. ISAAC, Huntington, L. I. adm. freem. of Conn. 1664. JAMES, Rowley 1691. JOHN, Norwalk 1663, freem. 1668, by w. Hannah, d. of George Clark the first of Milford, had John, b. June 1664; Josiah, 28 Dec. 1667; Samuel, 26 Jan. 1671; Joseph, 14, by ano. report 17, Feb. 1673; Hannah, 15 Dec. 1674; and Sarah, 21 May 1678. He was deac. Hall. JOHN, Rowley 1691, prob. s. of Jonathan. JOHN, Norwalk, s. of the first John, m. May 1695, Sarah, d. of Ephraim Lockwood, had Sarah, b. 30 Mar. 1697; Eliz. 11 June 1699; John, 2 Apr. 1702; and Abigail, 12 Feb. 1708. JONAS, Rowley 1691. JONATHAN, Rowley, m. 1 Dec. 1655, Eliz. Johnson, made his will, 24 July 1680, nam. w. Sarah, and s. JOSEPH, Milford, youngest s. of Richard of the same, m. 1680, Mary, eldest d. of Daniel Kellogg. JOSEPH, Norwalk, s. of John the first, m. 6 Nov. 1700, Eliz. d. of Matthew Marvin the sec. had Eliz. b. 2 Dec. 1701; his w. d. 9 Apr. 1703, and he m. 26 Jan. 1704, Hannah, d. of Rev. Thomas Hanford, had Hannah, b. 29 Oct. 1704; and Joseph, 9 Sept. 1716, if there be not mistake of ten yrs. as I suspect. RICHARD, Milford 1639, then mem. of the ch. where he had lds. 1646, in the list of freem. 1669, was deac.

and d. 1684 or 5; had prob. brot. from Eng. Mary, John, Isaac, and Sarah, and at M. had bapt. Epenetus, prob. 12 July 1640; Hannah, 1 Oct. 1643; Josiah, 1645; Joseph, 1649; and his w. Mary d. or was bur. 24 Jan. 1676. In his will of 4 Aug. 1683 he names all the s. beside childr. of Mary his d. by her sec. h. Thomas Wetmore; of Sarah, by two hs. Thomas Beach, and Miles Merwin, both of these ds. being d. also Hannah, w. of Christopher Comstock. Mary m. 1 May 1651, Luke Atkinson of New Haven, and next, 3 Jan. 1667, T. W. Six of the name were liv. there. *SAMUEL, Rowley, rep. 1681, perhaps the freem. of 1684, prob. had fam. SAMUEL, Rowley, perhaps s. of the preced. was town clk. 19 yrs. and d. 24 Mar. 1726. SAMUEL, Norwalk, s. of deac. John, m. 18 June, 1712, Rebecca, d. of Samuel Benedict of Danbury, had Rebecca, b. 9 Apr. foll. and he d. 4 Dec. 1713. THOMAS, Boston 1669, a butcher. Oft. the name is found with final s.

PLATTS, JAMES. See Platt.

PLAYES, ENOCH. Wickford 1674.

PLIMPTON. See Plympton.

PLOTT, JOSIAH, Milford 1671, as print. in Trumbull, Col. Rec. II. I think may be s. of Richard Platt.

PLUMBE, or PLUM, *JOHN, Dorchester, rem. to Wethersfield bef. Sept. 1636, and bef. deputs. to Gen. Ct. were introd. in Conn. was a sort of ruler in 1637, rep. 1641, 2, and 3, had Samuel, and Dorcas, wh. m. 12 Jan. 1655, John Lyman, was nomina. 1643 for elect. as Assist. but did not succeed. in the choice, made custom-ho. officer 1644, sold his est. and rem. to Branford bef. 1646, and there d. His will was pro. 1 Aug. 1648. Yet is it not kn. where he first land. in our country, or whence he came. Perhaps he was f. of JOHN, New London, b. a. 1621, where aft. 1665 he seems much connect. tho. prob. liv. at Hartford, a mariner wh. traded up and down the riv. freem. 1669, yet bef. 1677 establ. at N. L. where he had Mercy, bapt. 1677; George, 1679; and Sarah, 1682. Miss Caulkins is confid. that he had elder ch. John, Samuel, of wh. one thinks he was b. 1659, Joseph, and Greene. His w. was fin. 1671 for sale of liquor to Ind. but at N. L. he was constable 1680, and an innhold. and d. 1696. John, Samuel, and Joseph, were at Milford, but John came back to N. L. and was deac. many yrs. says Caulkins, wh. sends George to Stonington. JOHN, Milford, s. of Robert, m. 24 Nov. 1668, Eliz. Norton, had Eliz. b. 1669; John, 1671; and Mary, 1673; prob. more, for in 1676 and some yrs. aft. rec. of b. is want. He was a man of distinct. One JOHN was a soldier in Lothrop's comp. k. by the Ind. at Deerfield, 18 Sept. 1675; but ano. JOHN, Dorchester, is only ment. as partak. of bounty to the poor in 1680. See Hist. of D. 239. But prob. he had long liv. there, and had d. Waiting, b. 14 Nov. 1657. JOSEPH, New London, s. of John of the same, rem. a. 1700 to Milford. ROBERT, Milford 1639, m. Mary, d. of Sylvester Baldwin, had Mary, bapt. 1645, wh. m. 16 June 1668, the sec. Matthew Woodruff; John, 1646; Robert, 1648; Samuel, 1650, d. young; Samuel, again, 1653; and Joseph, posthum. 10 July 1655; and d. 12 May 1655. His wid. m. 1676, William East, and d. 1708. Of the ch. only John is kn. to have had issue. SAMUEL, Branford, s. of the first John, took freeman's o. 1666, and was there in 1667, and next yr. rem. to Newark, N. J. Tho. name of his w. is not seen, Mr. Judd gave me names and dates of ch. Eliz. b. 6 Jan. 1650; Mary, 1 Apr. 1653; Samuel, 2 May 1654; John, 28 Oct. 1657; Dorothy, 26 May 1660; Josiah, 3 Aug. 1662; and Joshua, 11 Mar. 1665. SAMUEL, New London, s. of John of the same, rem. with his br. Joseph to Milford; but it seems impossib. to pick all these Plums.

PLUMLY, ALEXANDER, Braintree, by w. Esther had s. Submit, b. 8 Jan. 1654. He was one of the promoters of settlem. at Mendon, 1663.

PLUMMER, BENJAMIN, Rowley, s. prob. of the first Joseph, m. Mary, d. of Thomas Wood, had Joseph, b. 1680; Benjamin, 1682; Thomas, 1684; Stephen, 1688; and Nathan, 1702; beside four ds. EPHRAIM, Newbury, third s. of Samuel the first, m. 15 Jan. 1680, Hannah, d. of Henry Jacques, had Mary, b. 19 Feb. 1681; Hannah, 12 Oct. 1682; Samuel, 27 Oct. 1684; Eliz. 21 Nov. 1686; John, 7 Nov. 1688; Ruth, 5 Nov. 1690; Daniel, 10 Mar. 1693; Richard, 3 Aug. 1695; Bitfield, 12 June 1697; Sarah, 26 July 1699; and Emma, 21 June 1704. FRANCIS, Newbury 1635, linen weaver, came in 1633, says one tradit. from Woolwich, near London, but ano. says from Wales; we kn. not in wh. town he first inhab. but he was freem. 14 May 1634, brot. w. Ruth, wh. d. 18 Aug. 1647, and sev. ch. certain. Samuel and Joseph. He m. 31 Mar. 1648, wid. Ann Palmer, wh. d. 18 Oct. 1665; and he m. third, 29 Nov. foll. Beatrice wid. of William Cantlebury, and d. 17 Jan. 1673. His d. Mary m. 20 May 1660, John Cheney the sec. FRANCIS, Newbury, s. of Joseph, m. Mary Elithorp, perhaps d. of Nathaniel, had Mary, b. 15 May 1701. JOHN, at Hatfield, k. by the Ind. 25 Aug. 1675, may have been a soldier, not inhab. of H. but come from Dorchester in Johnson's comp. JONATHAN, Newbury, youngest s. of Joseph the first, m. 16 June 1696, Sarah Pearson, perhaps d. of John of Rowley, had John, b. 25 Mar. 1697; Daniel, 7 Jan. 1699; Mary, 6 Dec. 1701; and Jonathan, 14 Aug. 1705; and d. 27 Sept. 1726. JOSEPH, Newbury, s. of the first Francis, b. in Eng. a. 1630, m. 23 Dec. 1652, Sarah, d. of John Cheney the elder, rem. to Rowley, perhaps late, had Joseph, b. 11 Sept. 1654; Benjamin, 23 Oct. 1656; Sarah, 13 May 1660; Francis, 23 Apr. 1662, d. young; Francis, again, 25 Feb. 1664;

Nathaniel, 31 Jan. 1666; Jonathan, 13 May, 1668; and Abigail, 15 July 1669, d. under 15 yrs.; was freem. 1670. JOSEPH, Newbury, s. of the preced. m. 1685, Hannah, d. of capt. Benjamin Swett, had Samuel, b. 4 May 1686; Abigail, 11 Dec. 1687; Miriam, 16 Jan. 1691; Aaron, 16 Jan. 1693; Eleanor, 29 Jan. 1694; Joseph, 12 Jan. 1695; David, 16 Mar. 1696; Samson, 14 Mar. 1699; Hannah, 17 July 1700; Sarah, 17 Apr. 1702; Deborah, 19 Dec. 1703; and Eliphalet, 1 Apr. 1705. JOSHUA, Newbury, youngest s. of Samuel the first, m. 6 Nov. 1699, Eliz. d. of Richard Dole the sec. had Samuel, b. 3 Sept. 1700; Stephen, 7 Dec. 1702; Joshua, 22 Aug. 1705; Nathaniel, 19 June 1708; Enoch, 3 Dec. 1711; and Eliz. 22 Mar. 1716. * SAMUEL, Newbury, eldest ch. of John, b. in Eng. a. 1619, freem. 2 June 1641, by w. Mary had Samuel, b. 20 Apr. 1647; Mary, 8 Feb. 1650; John, 11 May 1652; Ephraim, 16 Sept. 1655; Hannah, 16 Feb. 1657; Sylvanus, 22 Feb. 1658; Ruth, 7 Aug. 1660; Eliz. 19 Oct. 1662; Deborah, 13 Mar. 1665; Joshua; Lydia, 2 July 1668; and Bathshua, 31 July 1670. He kept the ferry over the Merrimac, was rep. 1676, and d. 1702. SAMUEL, Newbury, eldest s. of the preced. m. 1670, Joanna, d. of Nicholas Woodbury of Beverly, had not any ch. ment. by Coffin in Hist. or by the f. of his w. in the will. SYLVANUS, Newbury, fourth s. of the first Samuel of the same, freem. 1690, m. 1682, Sarah Moody, prob. d. of Samuel, had Mary, b. 22 Oct. 1683; Samuel, 12 Nov. 1684, d. next yr.; Samuel, again; Lydia; Sarah; and Benjamin. This Samuel's sec. s. Samuel, b. 14 Jan. 1722, was f. of William, Gov. of New Hampsh. and wrote his name, according to the old abbrev. with single m.

PLYMPTON, or PLIMPTON, HENRY, Boston, d. prob. early in 1653, for his inv. was brot. in 3 Feb. of that yr. JOHN, Dedham 1642, perhaps br. of the preced. came prob. some yrs. bef. for Dr. George Alcock of Roxbury, in his will of 22 Dec. 1640, calls him his serv. meaning apprent. may be the freem. of 10 May 1643, printed Plunton; by w. Jane (prob. d. of Richard Dummer, brot. from Eng. m. 13 Mar. 1644) had Hannah, b. 1, bapt. 16 Mar. 1645; John, 21 Mar. bapt. 5 Apr. 1646, d. soon; Mary, 9, bapt. 16 Apr. 1648; John, again, 16, bapt. 23 June 1650; Peter, bapt. Mar. 1652; and the foll. at Medfield of wh. only dates of b. appear: Joseph, 7 Oct. 1653; Mehitable, 15 Sept. 1655; Jonathan, 23 Nov. 1657; Eleazer, 20 Feb. 1660, d. soon; Eleazer, again, 3 or 7 May 1661; Rhoda, 2 Feb. 1663, d. soon; Jane, 2 or 3 June 1664, d. soon; and Henry, 9 Jan. 1666, wh. d. 4 Jan. 1668; but they were no doubt bapt. like the earlier. He rem. aft. the gr. war began, I suppose, to Deerfield, where he was serj.; his s. Jonathan was k. by the Ind. 18 Sept. 1675, at Bloody Brook, and the f. was tak. two yrs. and one day aft. d. of Jonathan, by the Ind. carr. towards Canada, and k. one report says, by burn. at the stake. The Hampsh. Prob. rec. take notice 1678 of his wid. Jane, and that the ch. were to have the lds. all rem. in few yrs. to the old settlem. near Boston. His wid. m. 16 Mar. 1679, Nicholas Hide; Hannah m. 31 Jan. 1665, Nathaniel Sutliffe; Mary m. 14 Nov. 1671, Nathaniel Johnson; Mehitable m. 28 Sept. 1676, Ephraim Hinsdale. JOHN, Medfield, s. of the preced. was of Moseley's comp. Dec. 1675, m. 2 Jan. 1678, Eliz. Fisher, d. of John, and had John, b. 17 Mar. 1680; Henry, 20 Jan. 1685; his w. d. 13 May 1694, and he for sec. w. m. 28 Feb. 1696, Sarah Turner, and had Sarah, b. 28 Dec. 1700; and Eliz. 29 Sept. 1702. The f. d. 13 Jan. 1704. JOSEPH, Medfield, br. of the preced. m. 3 Nov. 1675, Mary Morse, perhaps d. of Daniel, and had Joseph, b. 15 Mar. 1677; Jonathan, 28 Apr. 1680; Jeremiah, 8 Nov. 1683; and Mary, July 1692. The f. d. 20 June 1702. PETER, Hatfield 1679, br. of the preced. aft. 1677 had abandon. Deerfield, m. at Hadley 1677, Mary Mundan or Munden, d. of Abraham; had Hannah, b. 1679; and Mary, 1681; and he d. at Marlborough 27 Mar. 1717. PETER, Sudbury, s. of Thomas, m. 8 Nov. 1720, Abigail Thompson, and had Abigail, b. 23 Oct. 1721; Thomas, 17 Apr. 1723; and Jane, 11 Apr. 1725. The f. d. 14 Sept. 1743. ROBERT, New London, was chos. to office 24 Feb. 1681, and d. bef. 13 July 1686. THOMAS, Sudbury 1643, by w. Abigail, d. of Peter Noyes, had Abigail, b. 30 Sept. 1653; Jane, 18 Aug. 1655; Mary, 20 Nov. 1656; Eliz. 23 Dec. 1658; Thomas, 12 May 1661; Dorothy, 3 Oct. 1664; and Peter, 4 Jan. 1667, and was k. at Sudbury fight, 21 Apr. 1676. His d. Jane m. 14 Jan. 1677, Joseph Derby; Mary m. Matthew Stone; and Eliz. m. 29 or 31 May 1683, John Locke. Eliz. perhaps sis. of Thomas, as both were legatees of her grand m. Agnes Bent, came with Peter Noyes, f. of Abigail, w. of Thomas Plimpton, from London to Boston, 12 Apr. 1639, in the Jonathan, bef. 8 July 1652 was w. of John Rutter of Sudbury, and d. so 15 May 1689.

POCHER, GEORGE, Braintree, d. 29 Sept. 1639.

POCOCK, JOHN, a soldier in the list of k. by the Ind. at Hadley, 19 Oct. 1675, may be misspell. of Peacock.

POD, DANIEL, Ipswich 1642. SAMUEL, Ipswich, came in the Susan and Ellen, aged 25, from London.

POLE, GEORGE, Plymouth, or perhaps Yarmouth 1646, with Anthony Thacher, was, as Drake, Book of the Ind. p. 20, tells, on a committee against tobacco. Possib. the name had double o.

POLLARD, GEORGE, Salem, bef. 1646, says Felt. In his will of 13 May, pro. 31 Dec. 1646, he is call. of Marblehead. JOHN, Boston, eldest s. of William the first of the same, by w. Deliverance, had Hannah, b. 15 Aug. 1668; William, 1 Feb. 1671 and perhaps by sec. w. Mary, d. of Solomon Leonard of Bridgewater, m. at Taunton 24 Dec. 1673, had John, 20 Mar. 1676; Mary, 8 Mar. 1678; Samuel, 16 Jan. 1680; but no more is to be learn. JONATHAN, Boston, br. of the preced. m. Mary, d. of Edward Winslow of the same, had Benjamin, b. 6 Jan. 1696; and Ann, 22 Jan. 1698; but the rec. tells no more. SAMUEL, Boston, br. of the preced. by w. Mary, had Mary, b. 22 Nov. 1673, and nothing more is seen. THOMAS, Billerica, s. of William of Coventry, Co. Warwick, m. Nov. 1692, his cous. Sarah, d. of Edward Farmer of the same, had ten s. and five ds. and d. 4 Apr. 1724, and his wid. d. 3 May 1725. The ch. were Mary, Edward, Barbara, Thomas, William, John, Sarah, Joseph, Oliver, Sarah, again, Nathaniel, James, Walter, Eliz. and Benjamin, and we must in vain regr. that dates are not giv. WILLIAM, Boston, innholder, by w. Ann had John, b. 4 June 1644; Samuel, 24 Jan. 1646; Hannah, 10 Jan. 1649; William, 20 Mar. 1653; Eliz. 13 Jan. 1655; Joseph, 15 Mar. 1657; Sarah, 20 Oct. 1659; Benjamin, 22 Apr. 1663; Ann, 18 Oct. 1664; Jonathan, 12 Apr. 1666; and David, 18 Apr. 1668; the last with eight others were bapt. at one time in O. S. ch. 26 June 1670. He made his will, 15 Oct. 1678, republ. it 16 Apr. 1686, pro. 3 June foll. in wh. he names eldest s. John, but to other s. and ds. gives £10 ea. without naming, and appoints w. Ann, with Arthur Mason Excors. One Ann P. at Boston prob. his wid. d. Monday, 6 Dec. 1725 in 105th yr. it is said, in Franklin's N. E. Courant of Saturday foll. tho. something exagger. as we kn. from her testim. less than twelve yrs. bef. that she was 89. Aft. this age, and even bef. people are too apt to grow old. She was wont to tell, that she went over in the first boat that cross. Charles river, in 1630, to what is now Boston, that she was the first that jump. ashore, etc. Of the exact truth of this pleasant myth, the possib. is not to be denied; but I would fully learn three points — the name of the sh. in wh. she arr. and wh. brot. her; and still more import. is her maiden name. Tradit. has not ascertain. the fact, and possib. it was not worth adding, whether she was the only one of her sex, that cross. from Charlestown in the first boat. Small deduct. from the full tale of 105 yrs. will anybody make on looking at the portrait tak. (when she is call. 100 yrs. 3 mos.) in 1721, preserv. in the Historical Society's Collect. tho. to have liv. near 58 yrs. aft. her eleventh ch. was b. ought to have satisf. the appetite of any decent worshipper of tradit. without bring. her over in Gov. Winthrop's comp. Still a dozen or two of yrs. could easily be spared, if the circumstance of the young maiden's jumping from the boat on approach. the shore in Boston harbor, had made stronger impression on her mind, than the petty concomit. of time and fellow-passeng. in cross.

the sea or the river. ‖ WILLIAM, Boston, s. of the preced. ar. co. 1679, by w. Margaret had William, b. 21 Dec. 1687, prob. d. soon; and William, again, 2 Apr. 1690. He was gr.f. of col. Benjamin, Sheriff of the Co.

POLLY, or POLLEY, GEORGE, Woburn, m. 21 May 1649, Eliz. Winn, perhaps d. of Edward, had John, b. 16 Dec. 1650; Joseph, 25 Dec. 1652; George, 4 Jan. 1656; Eliz. 14 Apr. 1657; Samuel, 24 Jan. 1661, d. in 2 wks.; Hannah, 6 Apr. 1662, d. same day; Hannah, again, 28 June 1663; and he d. 22 Dec. 1683. GEORGE, Woburn, s. of the preced. m. 24 Oct. 1677, Mary Knight, prob. d. of John of the ch. of Charlestown, had George, b. 11 Oct. 1678; Joseph, 24 Aug. 1680; Mary, 25 Nov. 1682; Eliz. 5 Aug. 1684; Sarah, 30 Oct. 1686; Abigail, 17 Mar. 1689; Hannah, 21 Mar. 1691; Ebenezer, 20 Oct. 1693; Miriam, 31 Oct. 1695; and Mercy, 21 Feb. 1698. JOHN, Roxbury, perhaps br. of the first George, had Mary and Sarah, tw. bapt. 2 June 1650; Hannah, 15 Feb. 1652; Abigail, 4 June 1654; Bethia, b. 12, bapt. 20 Feb. 1659; and Susanna, 22 Dec. 1661. His w. Susanna d. 30 Apr. 1664; and he by sec. w. Hannah had Rebecca, b. 7 Aug. 1668; and Joanna, 7 Mar. 1670. This w. d. 8 June 1684, and he m. 3d w. Jane Walter, wh. d. 24 Oct. 1701. He d. 2 Apr. 1689, aged 71. Hannah m. 10 May 1670, Isaac Curtis; Abigail, on the same day, m. John Lyon; and Susanna m. 23 June 1683, Samuel Weld. JOHN, Woburn, s. of the first George, by w. Mary had John, b. 21 May 1686; Matthew, Mar. 1689; Abigail, 29 Apr. 1692; Thomas, 13 Oct. 1694, d. at 6 mos. Thomas, again, 10 Oct. 1696; and Sarah, 12 Oct. 1702. SAMUEL, Woburn, br. of the preced. by w. Priscilla had Samuel, b. 3 Oct. 1689; Jonathan, 16 July 1691; Jacob, 23 Feb. 1694; and Priscilla, 11 Dec. 1696.

POMEROY, POMROY, PUMMERY, or PUMRY, CALEB, Northampton, s. of Eltweed, m. 8 Mar. 1665, Hepzibah, d. of Jeffery Baker, had Hepzibah, b. at Windsor, 27 July 1666, d. young; and at N. had Samuel, 29 May 1669; Abigail, 26 Oct. 1671; Hepzibah, again, bapt. 19 Jan. 1673; Ebenezer, 15 Mar. 1674, d. at 25 yrs.; Caleb, 3 May 1677, d. young; Eldad, 6 Dec. 1679; Hannah, 4 July 1682; Mercy, 20 Sept. 1684; and Sarah, 6 Aug. 1687; was freem. 1674, printed Pumbrey in Paige's list, and he d. 18 Nov. 1691. His wid. m. 1705, Walter Lee. ELTWEED, Dorchester, by Dr. Harris mark. as of 1630, and if so, came prob. in the Mary and John, freem. 4 Mar. 1633, rem. a. 1636 or 7 to Windsor, carr. Mary wh. d. 1640; John, wh. d. 1647; and Eldad, all b. prob. at D. of wh. the two former d. at W.; had at W. Medad, bapt. 19 Aug. 1638; Caleb, 6 Mar. 1642; Mary, again, 21 Apr. 1644, d. under 15 yrs.; Joshua, 22 Nov. 1646; and Joseph, 20 June 1652. His

w. d. 1655, and he m. Lydia, wid. of Thomas Parsons, rem. 1672 to live with his s. Medad at Northampton, there d. in Mar. 1673. His s. Eldad d. unm. 1662, hav. been adm. freem. of Conn. 1658, and betroth. to Susanna, only ch. of Henry Cunliffe. Whence the ancest. came is uncert. Tradit. long assert. the birthright of Devonsh. but a less gen. tradit. offers the claim to a hamlet far distant in the N. within two miles of Burnley, Co. Lancaster, and some claim is put forth in favor of Wales. The Christian name is variously distort. Some make this s. to have the same name as his f. or rather call the f. Eldad. Others write it Eldred, wh. might easily be mistak. in the old engrossing hand. Edward sometimes is proposed, and Eltweed more commonly appears than any other, but to me it seems the double *e* was meant for *oo*. JOHN, Boston, shipwright, made his will 14 Apr. 1690, bound to sea, and gave his prop. to Mary Brookings, prob. d. of John, wh. prov. it 13 Nov. 1691. He was, no doubt, a young, unm. man, prob. engag. to m. the devisee. JOSEPH, Westfield, youngest s. of Eltweed, m. 20 June 1677, Hannah, d. of Richard Lyman, of Northampton, had Joseph, b. 1 Sept. 1678, d. in few wks.; Hannah, 13 Dec. 1679, d. in few days; Hannah, again, Jan. 1681, d. young; Eliz. 7 Feb. 1682, d. next yr.; Abigail, 5 Feb. 1684; Medad, 4 Nov. 1686; John, 11 July 1688, d. in few days; Hannah, again, 22 Apr. 1694; beside sec. Joseph, Noah, and Sarah, of wh. one or more may have been b. at Colchester, or come bef. Hannah. He was freem. 1680, but rem. to Colchester, where are descend. JOSHUA, Northampton, br. of the preced. m. 20 Aug. 1672, Eliz. d. of Richard Lyman, wh. d. 22 May 1676, had John, b. 2 May 1674, d. soon; Joshua, 24 Sept. 1675; Eliz. 1677, d. young; Nathaniel, 9 Mar. 1680; Abigail, 23 July 1682, d. young; Lydia, 3 Mar. 1684; and John, 1688, d. young; all exc. the first two by sec. w. Abigail, youngest d. of Nathaniel Cook of Windsor, m. 9 Jan. 1677. He rem. 1683 to Deerfield, and d. 16 Oct. 1689. His wid. m. David Hoyt, suffer. in the destr. of D. 29 Feb. 1704, was carr. to Canada, but came back, and had third h. Lydia, the d. also came back from Canada, m. Nathaniel Ponder of Westfield; and both the s. were sufferers, tho. in diff. degr. Nathaniel was k. by the Ind. 16 July 1698; and Joshua was carr. from D. with his sec. w. Esther, wh. was k. by the Ind. the day aft. capt. on their way to Canada, whence he got back, and liv. at Dorchester, had third w. Repent, wh. d. 22 July 1714, and he got a fourth w. *MEDAD, Northampton, br. of the preced. m. 21 Nov. 1661, Experience, d. of Henry Woodward, had John, b. 24 Aug. 1662; Joseph, 24 Dec. 1664, d. next yr.; Mehitable, 3 July 1666; Ebenezer, 30 May 1669; Joseph, again, 26 June 1672; Medad, 19 June, 1674, d. soon; Eliakim, 10 Aug. 1675, d. next yr.; Mindwell, July 1677; Thankful, 31 May 1679; Mary, 15

Feb. 1684; and John, again, 30 May 1686, d. with his mo. 8 June foll. He m. the next 8 Sept. Abigail, d. of Elder John Strong, wid. of Rev. Nathaniel Chauncy, had Samuel, 16 Aug. or Sept. 1687, Y. C. 1705; and his w. d. 15 Apr. 1704. For third w. he had 24 Jan. 1705, Hannah, wid. of Thomas Noble the first of Westfield. He was a blacksmith, freem. 1671, many yrs. town clk. deac. and rep. 1677, 83, 4, 6, 90, and 2, and d. 30 Dec. 1716. Distinc. for public serv. attach. to most of the s. Samuel, the youngest, was min. of Newtown, L. I. join. the Presbyt. commun. and was active in extend. the influence of that name; as fully told in Riker's Hist. Joseph was f. of Rev. Benjamin, Y. C. 1733, of Hebron; Ebenezer, the Sheriff of Hampsh. one of his Majesty's Counc. for the Prov. foll. the trade of a blacksmith, as did his s. Col. Seth, a hero of the early day of our Revo. who, in his will, 1777, gave "to my s. Quartus my bick iron, wh. his gr.gr.f. made 105 yrs. ago. He is the fourth smith in the fam. and Quartus is his name." THOMAS, whose name is writ. Pummery, was of Portsmouth, m. bef. 1679, Rebecca, d. of William Brooking of the same. Eight of this name, had in 1834, been gr. at Yale, one at Harv. and ten at other N. E. coll.

POMFRET, WILLIAM, Dover 1640, was early town clk. and lieut. d. 7 Aug. 1680. His d. Martha m. William Dame; and ano. d. m. Thomas Whitehouse.

POND, DANIEL, Dedham, perhaps s. of the first Robert, may have been b. in Eng. freem. 1690, d. Feb. 1698. His first w. was Abigail, d. of Edward Shepard of Cambridge, prob. had sev. ch. but by ano. w. Ann, wh. surv. some of the foll. may have come: John; Ephraim, bapt. 6 July 1656; William; Daniel, both, 26 Apr. 1663; Robert, 11 Aug. 1667; Caleb; and Jabez; seven s. beside Abigail, wh. m. Ralph Day; Hannah Devotion, prob. w. of John; Rachel Stow dec.; and Sarah, unm. at the d. of f. EPHRAIM, Wrentham, s. of the preced. m. 6 Jan. 1686, Deborah Hawes, had Ephraim, b. 21 Oct. 1686; Daniel, 22 Sept. 1689; Deborah, 13 Sept. 1693; and Samuel, 29 Dec. 1695; and d. 22 Dec. 1704. ISAAC, Windsor, prob. s. of Samuel of the same, m. 10 or 20 May 1667, Hannah, d. of John Griffin, had Hannah, b. 10 Feb. 1688; and he d. 15 Nov. next yr. JOHN, s. of one of Winth.'s old neighb. came 1630 with the Gov. as also did a br. whose name is not ment. when the Gov. in the first letter aft. arr. to his eldest s. at Groton, directs him to tell "old Pond" both his s. are well, and remember their duty. JOHN, Wrentham, s. of Daniel of Dedham, by w. Hannah, wh. d. 2 Jan. 1692, had Daniel, b. 2 Apr. 1690; and by w. Rachel, had Hannah, 16 Mar. 1694; and Rachel, 19 Oct. 1695. ROBERT, Dorchester, tho. not found in the list of Dr. Harris, was there to partake, 1638, in div. of Cow commons, d. 1637; his inv. is dat. 27 Dec. of that yr. and his wid. m. Edward Shepard of Cambridge. His derivat. was from Co. Suffk. and he may have been that br. of John, ment. in one of the first lett. of Gov. Winth. His d. Mary was call. eleven yrs. of age when her mo. join. Cambridge ch. wh. may be an ascert. day. She m. John Blackman. ROBERT, Milton, s. prob. of the preced. b. in Eng. adm. freem. 18 May 1642, by w. Mary Ball from Bury St. Edmunds, Co. Suffk. had Mary, b. 14 July 1657; Martha, 13 Apr. 1660; and ano. ch. possib. that Sarah wh. m. Desire Clap; and he d. bef. mid. life. His wid. m. 3 July 1663, Nicholas Allen or Ellen, outliv. him, and m. Daniel Henshaw. ROBERT, Wrentham, s. of Daniel, by w. Joanna had Ann, b. 2 Oct. 1689; Sarah, 30 Sept. 1692; Robert, wh. d. 28 May 1694; and Robert, again, 18 May 1695. SAMUEL, Windsor, by w. Sarah, m. 18 Nov. 1642, had Isaac, b. 16 Mar. 1646; Samuel, 4 Mar. 1648; Nathaniel, 21 Sept. 1650; and Sarah, 11 Feb. 1653; and he d. 14 Mar. 1655. His. s. Nathaniel was k. with his capt. Marshall in the great Narraganset fight, 19 Dec. 1675. Sarah m. Jonathan Hayt or Hoyt, wh. sett. at Guilford. SAMUEL, Branford 1668, sign. the planta. and ch. covenant, and may therefore be thot. of ano. fam. or possib. was s. of the preced. He m. 1670, Miriam, d. of Thomas Blatchley of B. THOMAS, perhaps, for the surname is doubtful on the rec. of the custom-ho. and by Mr. Hunter thot. as near to Pount as Pond, a passeng. in the Elizabeth and Ann, from London, 1635, aged 21. See the later read. of Geneal. Reg. XIV. 313. WILLIAM, Dorchester 1648, perhaps s. of the first Robert of the same, b. in Eng. m. Mary, d. of George Dyer, had Samuel, wh. d. 2 Oct. 1657; Eliz. and Martha, tw. 17 Feb. 1658, both d. in few days; Judith, 16 Oct. 1659; Thankful, 15 Jan. 1662; George, 20 Jan. 1666; and Mindwell, 24 Aug. 1667; and perhaps William; was constable 1659, and d. 4 Apr. 1690, call. serg. and Judge Sewall says he d. suddenly. His wid. it is said, d. 16 Feb. 1711. Thankful m. 17 Nov. 1682, Philip Withington, and d. 23 Dec. 1711. Rebecca P. aged 18, came in the Bevis from Southampton, 1638, one of the serv. of Christopher Batt of the city of Salisbury. Of this name two had been gr. at Harv. one at Yale, and six at other N. E. coll. in 1826.

PONDER, JOHN, Westfield, m. 26 June 1668, Temperance, d. of Thomas Buckland, had Susanna, b. 11 Mar. 1669; John, Nov. 1670, d. young; Mary, 30 Sept. 1672; Eliz. 3 Feb. 1675; Nathaniel, 3 Sept. 1677; John, again, 11 Mar. 1680; Thomas, 5 Mar. 1682; Martha, 27 Feb. 1684; and Sarah, 28 July 1686, d. at 4 yrs. He d. 1712, and his wid. d. 27 Oct. 1732.

PONTON, or PONTING, RICHARD, Boston, a husbandman, adm. of the ch. 28 Dec. 1649, had been bound, 1 Jan. 1641, for eight yrs. with his own assent, to John Read of Braintree, rem. to Hartford 1662, freem. 1663, d. or rem. bef. 1669.

PONTUS, WILLIAM, Plymouth 1633, in 1643 not in the list of those able to bear arms, i. e. under the age of 60, d. 9 Feb. 1653, hav. made his will 9 Sept. 1650, leav. two ch. only, with very small est. Mary wh. had m. 31 Oct. 1645, James Glass, and next, 1657, Philip Delano; and Hannah, wh. had m. 18 Dec. 1644, John Churchill, and next, 25 June 1669, Giles Rickard, and d. 22 Dec. 1690.

POOLE, POOL, or POLE, BENJAMIN, Weymouth, s. of Edward, was a soldier on Conn. riv. in Philip's war, 1676, and of him I hear no more. EDWARD, Newport 1638, prob. was of Weymouth most of his days, had Samuel, Isaac, Joseph, Benjamin, John, Sarah, and Jacob, nam. in this order in his will of 22 Aug. 1664, of wh. his w. was Extrix. pro. 16 Sept. foll. of wh. the three last were minors, and prob. Samuel the eldest. See Geneal. Reg. XII. 12 and 13. The w.'s name is not seen. ELIZABETH, Taunton 1637, the chief cause of build. at T. was maiden sis. of William, and elder than him, of a good fam. in heraldry, as well as religion, may be regard. as one of the most decid. proofs of the deep roots that puritanism had attain. in Eng. She d. 21 May 1654, aged 65, hav. made her will four days bef. in wh. John, eldest s. of her br. was nam. Excor. Abstr. of it is in Geneal. Reg. V. 262. See Winth. I. 252. HENRY, Boston, d. 14 Sept. 1643; may have been inf. ISAAC, Weymouth, s. of Edward, by w. Elishama had Margaret, b. 24 Aug. 1669; and perhaps others not on rec. or he may have rem. JOHN, Cambridge 1632, went to Lynn bef. 1638, when he had there 200 acres, and last of Reading, where his w. Margaret d. 29 Apr. 1662, and he d. 1 Apr. 1667. His will of 14 Feb. preced. made Jonathan his s. Excor. names other ch. Mary, and her h. Matthew Edwards, and her ch. Mary, Sarah, and Eliz. also s.-in-law, William Barrett, whose w. Sarah (d. not of testat. but of Richard Champney) was d. also her ch. John and Lydia; also gr.ch. John, Sarah, and Mary P. wh. I presume to be ch. of his s. Jonathan; and lastly br. Armitage, and his three s. sis. Armitage and cous. Godfrey Armitage, and his w. and two ch. beside Mr. Dane of Andover, and his w. whose relationship is less appar. JOHN, Boston 1670, s. of William, merch. freem. 1673, with prefix of respect, was disting. says Baylies I. 287, as an officer in Philip's war, yet possib. by that author mistak. for the Reading gent. He m. 28 Mar. 1672, Eliz. d. of Gov. Brenton, not Benton, as in Geneal. Reg. V. 402. His w. was bapt. as the O. S. ch. rec. shows " at a ch. meeting at her ho." a very uncommon favor, if not unexampl. bef. that, in our country, and John, Eliz. and Courtney, his and her ch. were bapt. some days aft.; William, 11 Jan. 1680; and Jane, 12 Nov. 1682. Bef. that time no ch.

in N. E. had been bapt. exc. on the Lord's day, as Sunday was call. in law and popul. usage. JOHN, Weymouth, s. of Edward of the same, by w. Eliz. had Susanna, b. 17 Dec. 1679 ; and by w. Joanna had Hannah, 24 Oct. 1687 ; and Joanna, 21 Dec. 1688. JOHN, Beverly, a carpenter, m. Sarah, wid. of Richard Woodbury, wh. d. 13 Nov. 1716, had Jonathan, b. 1694; Miriam, 1695; Robert, 1697; Ebenezer, 1699; and Joshua, 1700; rem. to Gloucester, and had Caleb, 1701; and John, 1703. For sec. w. he had Deborah Dodge, d. prob. of Samuel, but she d. 1 Feb. 1718; and his third w. Eliz. Holmes, perhaps d. of John of Salem, d. 13 July 1720; and he took fourth w. in May 1721, Abigail Ballard of Lynn, says Babson, and had Return in 1722; and Abigail, 1725; and he d. 19 May 1727. *JONATHAN, Reading, s. of the first John, had Sarah, b. 11 July 1656; Judah, a d. 1 Sept. 1658, prob. d. young; Mary, 21 Aug. 1660, d. next yr.; Mary, again, 14 Nov. 1662; and prob. a John; was much valu. in Philip's war, a capt. under major Appleton at Hadley, and Presid. of the counc. of war in the winter of 1675–6, rep. 1677, d. 24 Dec. 1678 aged 44. JOSEPH, Weymouth, s. of Edward, by w. Eliz. had Eliz. b. 6 Dec. 1674; Mary, 20 Jan. 1681; Benjamin, 9 Feb. 1683; Margaret, 22 Apr. 1688; and by w. Mary had Abigail, 30 June 1690. RICHARD, New London, d. a. 20 Apr. 1662, without w. or ch. gave his est. to w. and childr. of George Tongue. SAMUEL, Boston, adm. of the ch. 19 June 1642, call. merch. with prefix of respect, had Ann, bapt. 7 Aug. next a. 8 days old; yet I kn. nothing more of him, unless he were that capt. wh. m. Silence, d. of Rev. Peter Saxton of Scituate, wh. d. bef. 1 Oct. 1651; or perhaps of Reading, where Eaton calls one early sett. by his name. SAMUEL, Weymouth, s. prob. eldest of Edward, by w. Mercy had Mary, b. 20 Nov. 1668. *WILLIAM, Dorchester, perhaps as early as 1630, yet most remarkable is it, that he was at Taunton sev. yrs. aft. 1637, there call. capt. rep. 1641, being br. of the patron saint of that newer town, but in rec. of D. describ. as town clk. ten yrs. and oft. sch. master, while we do not learn whether these functions were fulfill. bef. he went or aft. his return, or partly both. My opinion is that not long aft. the d. of his sis. from whose will we learn more than by all other means a. his fam. he came back to D. and pass. the last 18 or 20 yrs. Certain. at D. he had Theophilus, b. 27 May, bapt. 3 June 1660, and this may render prob. that his elder s. and ds. John, Nathaniel, Timothy, Mary, and Bethesda, were b. at T. He d. at D. 24 Feb. 1675, aged 81; and his wid. wh. had been m. as early, I judge, as June 1638, perhaps Mary, d. of John Richmond, d. near the end of 1690. Timothy was drown. at T. 15 Dec. 1667; of Nathaniel nothing is heard exc. in the will of his aunt Eliz. and it may be that he d. young; nor is more told of Theophilus than his b. and bapt.; Mary was sec. w. of Daniel Henchman, and Bethesda Poole (whose f. show. his relig. we may regret, more than his judgm. in taking for the d.'s name that of the intermit. fountain, of wh. the power is so beautiful. told in the narrat. of the evangelist) m. 1686 John Filer, as his sec. w. He had s. William, wh. was bapt. 20 June 1658 at Roxbury. Baylies derives the fam. from Taunton in Co. Somerset. WILLIAM, Brookhaven, L. I. 1680, perhaps was s. of the preced. Thompson.

POOR, or POORE, BENJAMIN, Newbury, s. of Samuel the first, m. 13 Apr. 1696, Mary, wid. of George Hardy, who d. 8 Aug. 1707, had Sarah, b. 6 Sept. 1697; and Ann, 31 Oct. 1700. DANIEL, Andover, is that youth, I suppose, aged 14, whose name on the list of passeng. in the Bevis from Southampton, 1638, is Dayell, coming with Alce or Alice P. aged 20, prob. his sis. and Samuel P. 18, perhaps their br. and others, under the designat. of serv. of Richard Dummer, m. 20 Oct. 1650, Mary Farnum, perhaps d. of Ralph; and d. 1713, it is said, aged 85, wh. is one of the very few instances of under estimate. Only s. Daniel, and John, are nam.; and of John the d. is so early as 24 Dec. 1690, that perhaps he was never m. But seven fem. Poors are as early found to m. and all may have been his ds. viz. Martha, with John Granger, 9 Feb. 1680; Hannah, with Francis Dane, jr. 16 Nov. 1681; Eliz. with Jacob Marston, 7 Apr. 1686; Priscilla, with Abraham Moore, 14 Dec. 1687; Deborah, with Timothy Osgood, 29 May 1689; Ruth, with John Stevens, 20 Dec. 1689; and Lucy, with Samuel Austin, 11 Oct. 1691. DANIEL, Andover, s. of the preced. by w. Mehitable had Daniel, Mehitable, John, Samuel, Joseph, and Thomas; yet the dates of b. are not kn. of either, and from the rec. is kn. that Mehitable d. 14 Jan. 1691, prob. quite young; while of Thomas, we doubt whether it be this s. of Daniel, or ano. whose d. is ment. 7 Feb. 1695. He d. 1735, aged 79. EDWARD, Newbury, s. of John the first, or perhaps of Samuel, by w. Eliz. had Stephen, b. 20 Apr. 1688; Eliz. 21 Mar. 1690; and Joseph, 15 Apr. 1704. HENRY, Newbury, s. of John, m. 12 Sept. 1679, Abigail, d. of sec. Thomas Hale, had Abigail, b. 9 Sept. 1680; Henry, 31 Jan. 1682; Jeremiah, 10 Jan. 1684; Mary, 10 Apr. 1686, d. soon; Mary, again, 20 Sept. 1687; Hannah, 19 July 1692; Sarah, 18 Jan. 1694; Benjamin, 1696; and Daniel, 1700; was taxed in Rowley 1691. JOHN, Newbury, an early sett. said to have emigr. from Co. Wilts, was, I think, elder br. of Daniel and Samuel; had Jonathan; John, b. 21 June 1642; Hannah, 14 Oct. 1645, d. young; Eliz. 8 Nov. 1647; Hannah, again, 25 Mar. 1649; Henry, 13 Dec. 1650; Mary, 6 Mar. 1652, d. at 6 mos.; Joseph, 4 Oct. 1653; Mary, again, 12 Dec. 1654, wh. m. 6 Dec. 1670, Samuel Pearson; Lydia, 5 Dec. 1656; Edward, 4 Apr.

1658; Abigail, 23 Mar. 1660, d. soon; and Abigail, again, 5 Aug. 1661; and he d. 23 Nov. 1684, aged 69. His wid. d. says Coffin, 3 Dec. 1702. JOHN, Hampton, m. 13 Mar. 1661, Sarah, d. of John Brown of the same, had Sarah, b. 10 Dec. 1661; John, 3 Apr. 1664; Richard, 28 Oct. 1666; John, again, 30 Sept. 1668; Sarah, again, 3 Apr. 1671; Mary, 6 June 1673; and Deborah, 13 Nov. 1675. He was a mariner of Charlestown, where all but two of these ch. were b. and his w. d. 28 Dec. 1678 of smallpox, and there he m. 12 Aug. 1680, Eliz. d. of John Burrage, wid. of Thomas Dean, had Thomas, b. 27 Dec. 1682; Bethia, 1684; and Silence, posthum. 20 Sept. 1686; but the last two d. soon; and he d. 19 May 1686. JOHN, Newbury, s. of John the first, m. 27 Feb. 1667, Mary, d. of William Titcomb, had John, b. 7 May 1668, d. at 5 mos.; Mary, 9 Aug. 1669; Sarah, 27 Oct. 1671; Eliz. 26 July 1674; Hannah, 16 Aug. 1677; Jonathan, 5 Feb. 1679; Judith, 22 May 1681; and John, again, 26 June 1683; was freem. 1670, and d. 15 Feb. 1701. JOSEPH, Newbury, br. of the preced. m. 6 Aug. 1680, Mary, d. prob. of Nicholas Wellington, had Joseph, b. 25 Apr. 1685; Benjamin, 7 Nov. 1687; Sarah, 12 May 1690; Mary, 12 Aug. 1692; Abigail, 1 Aug. 1695; Hannah, 3 Apr. 1698; John, 1 Aug. 1701; and Lydia, 14 Mar. 1704. JOSEPH, Newbury, s. of Samuel, m. 1698, Ann Johnson, had Catharine, b. 18 Feb. 1699; and Joseph, 9 Apr. 1701. NICHOLAS, Lynn 1637. Lewis. SAMUEL, Newbury, prob. that passeng. in the Bevis from Southampton, 1638, aged 18, wh. may be br. of Daniel, Alce, and John, fellow-passeng. had Rebecca, b. 7 Feb. 1649; Mary, 21 Mar. 1651; Samuel, 14 Oct. 1653; Edward, 27 May 1656; Eliz. 21 Jan. 1659; Joseph, 10 June 1661; Sarah, 4 June 1664; Benjamin 22 Feb. 1667; and Mary, 21 Feb. 1671; and he was freem. 1673, d. 31 Dec. 1683, by Coffin call. 60 yrs. old, but prob. was 3 yrs. more. SAMUEL, Newbury, s. of the preced. m. 16 Feb. 1680, Rachel, d. of John Bailey, had Rebecca, b. 18 Jan. 1681; Samuel, 3 June 1682, wh. liv. to 11 July 1769; Judith, d. soon; Sarah, 12 July 1686; Eleanor, 25 Dec. 1689; and Rebecca, again, 1 Mar. 1694. THOMAS, Andover 1645, may be he whose d. is on rec. 1695.

POPE, BENJAMIN, Salem, s. of Joseph the first, m. Damaris Shattuck, d. of Samuel of Salem, had Benjamin, to wh. was giv. 13 Apr. 1702, admin. on est. of his f.; Samuel; Ebenezer; and Jerome; and their mo. having their proport. EPHRAIM, Boston, d. 1677, in his will of 27 June 1676, names only Ephraim, and Eliz. as his ch. The s. d. of smallpox, Nov. 1678. JOHN, Dorchester, came prob. 1633, with w. Jane, was a shoemaker, freem. 3 Sept. 1634, perhaps brot. two or three ch. and here had John, b. 30 June 1635; Nathan, wh. was b. as is said, but certain. d. 1641; and by w. Alice had Thomas, 27 Dec. 1643; and perhaps that

Margaret, w. of John P. whose gr.-st. says she d. 20 Oct. 1702, or 1672, as sometimes read, aged 74, was his third w. He was one of the founders of the new ch. for Richard Mather, 1636; d. 12 Apr. 1646. Of his will the abstr. may be seen in Geneal. Reg. VII. 229; yet why it was not pro. bef. 5 June 1649 and inv. delay. to four days preced. would be difficult to guess, unless we suppose the last fig. to be erron. It ment. w. and a d. but no s. four serv. br. Thomas, and Joshua, my sis.'s h. We might by this docum. judge the testator to have been a weaver, rather than a shoemaker. But early acco. is sadly confus. of all the Dorchester Popes; and the most patient of their inquir. cannot wholly unravel. One Jane, wh. d. 12 Jan. 1663, in her will of 18 Apr. preced. gives to her d. Patience, w. of Edward Blake; but whether she was w. of this John, or when that d. was b. I find not. See Geneal. Reg. XI. 339. JOHN, Dorchester, perhaps s. of the preced. by w. Beatrice had John, b. 1 July 1658; Jane, 23 May 1677; and Joseph, 17 Oct. 1680, d. in one wk. as says Geneal. Reg. V. 465, and adds that his wid. Beatrice was at Lancaster, 1700. In Hist. of D. 74, John P. sen. d. 19 Oct. 1686, but this may not of necessity deny a former John, any more than it would make Margaret w. of John wh. d. Oct. 1672, as it declares, the same Margaret left wid. of John 19 Oct. 1686. JOHN, Springfield 1678, prob. rem. to Windsor 1683, there d. that yr. unm. it is thot. JOSEPH, Salem, came in the Mary and John of London, 1634, freem. 17 May 1637, there by w. Gertrude, had Damaris, bapt. 23 Apr. 1643; Hannah, 20 July 1645, d. young; Hannah, again, 26 Mar. 1648; George, 8 July 1649, wh. prob. d. young; Joseph, 27 Oct. 1650; Benjamin, Apr. 1653; and Samuel, 18 May 1656; beside Enos, not bapt.; in 1658, was punish. for going to Quaker meet. and d. a. 1667. His will of 11 Sept. 1666, pro. 27 June foll. made w. Gertrude extrix. and nam. the two ds. and four s. last ment. Damaris m. Joshua Buffum; and Hannah m. Caleb Buffum. Joseph, Salem, s. of the preced. liv. at the vill. wh. was made Danvers, freem. 1690, m. Bathshua Folger, had Nathaniel, b. 20 Nov. 1679; Joseph, wh. d. young; Bathshua, 9 Apr. 1683; Gertrude, 27 Aug. 1685; Joseph, again, 16 June 1687; Enos, 6 June 1690; Eleazer, 4 Dec. 1693; and Jerusha, 1 Apr. 1695; and he d. 1712. His will of 25 Jan. pro. 3 Mar. of that yr. names all the ch. but the first two, and notes that the eldest d. was infirm of mind. as prob. had been her mo. at least she was much afflict. in the withcraft days; also names Mary, and Sarah, ch. of his s. Nathaniel, dec. bef. 1711. RICHARD, Dorchester 1635, but Mr. Clap thinks was not long there, and he is call. br. by Joseph in his will. SAMUEL, Salem, br. of the preced. m. 28 Jan. 1686, Exercise Smith, had Damaris, b. Feb. 1687, d. in few mos.; Samuel, 11 June 1689; Margaret, 21 Oct. 1691; Enos, 1 Feb. 1695;

Hannah, 17 Feb. 1697 ; Eliz. 23 May 1698; Eunice, 12 Aug. 1700; and Ruth, 11 Mar. 1705, d. soon. SETH, Dartmouth 1686. THOMAS, Plymouth 1631, m. 28 July 1637, Ann, d. of Gabriel Fallowell, had Hannah, wh. m. Joseph Bartlett, and d. 12 Mar. 1710, aged 71. When this w. d. is not told, but he m. sec. w. 29 May 1646, Sarah, d. of John Jenney, had Seth, b. 13 Jan. 1648; Thomas, 25 Mar. 1651 ; John, 15 Mar. 1653 ; and Susanna, wh. m. 7 Nov. 1666, Jacob Mitchell, and being call. in 1663 *eldest* d. of said P. by w. Sarah requires us to believe that ano. d. foll. In 1675, he was 67 yrs. old. THOMAS, Dorchester, perhaps br. of John of the same, had Thomas, b. 26 Dec. 1670 ; and Alice, 23 Dec. 1676 ; as says Geneal. Reg. V. 465, where it adds that he m. 18 Nov. 1681, Margaret Long. THOMAS, Suffield, by w. Margaret, had Mindwell, b. 1687 ; and his w. d. next yr. at Springfield. One of these two Thomases prob. tho. wh. of them may be hard to guess, was of Hempstead on L. I. WALTER, Charlestown 1634, d. bef. 1640, leav. one ch. to wh. the town made a gr. Frothingham, 80. WALTER, Charlestown, had Mary, wh. m. Joseph Miller. Five of this name at Harv. three at Yale, and two at other N. E. coll. had been gr. 1834.

PORTAGE, GEORGE, Boston, merch. by w. Eliz. d. of Simon Lynde, had Judith, b. 26 Feb. 1685, d. young; Hannah, 13 Feb. 1687 ; Samuel, 15 Apr. 1689 ; Judith, again, 16 Sept. 1691 ; Eliz. 16 May 1696, d. next yr. and George, wh. d. without ch. I think he rem. from Boston, prob. from the Prov. Hannah m. 16 Sept. 1714, James Bowdoin of Boston, was mo. of James, H. C. 1745, the disting. Presid. of the Convent. 1780, that framed our Mass. Const. first Presid. of A. A. S. and sec. Gov. of the Commonwealth.

PORTER, ABEL, Boston, was unm. when adm. of the ch. 23 Jan. 1641, by w. Ann, wh. had been wid. of William Simmons, had John, bapt. 19 Nov. a. 7 days old, but by the rec. of town, b. 27 Nov. 1643 ; prob. also, Abel, and perhaps others. He may have been adm. freem. 2 June 1641, and the name writ. Parr, d. 10 Mar. 1685, aged 73, says the gr.-st. ABEL, Boston, perhaps s. of the preced. freem. 1672, then call. junr. was one of a new milit. comp. Sept. 1677. BENJAMIN, Salem, s. of John of the same, d. 1701. But he had been murder. nine yrs. bef. as a witness sw. 31 May 1692, was confess. to her by a witch. DANIEL, Farmington, a surgeon, for sev. yrs. had pay from the Col. by w. Mary had Daniel, b. 2 Feb. 1653 ; Mary, 5 Feb. 1655 ; Nehemiah, 24 Oct. 1656 ; Richard, 24 Mar. 1658 ; Ann, 1661 ; John, 14 Nov. 1662 ; and Samuel, 24 Oct. 1665 ; all exc. Mary, in 1688, provid. for by deed in Aug. of that yr. to avoid making a will under Andros's admin.; he d. 1690. Of the descend. some went to Waterbury. Mary

m. Eleazer Knowles; and Ann d. unm. DANIEL, Waterbury, s. of the preced. had Daniel, b. 5 Mar. 1699; James, 20 Apr. 1700; Thomas, 1 Apr. 1702; Deborah, 6 Mar. 1704; Ebenezer, 24 Dec. 1708; and Ann, 28 Apr. 1712. He d. 18 Jan. 1727; and his wid. Deborah, prob. mo. of all the ch. d. 14 May 1765. EDWARD, Roxbury, came 1636, with two ch. John, a. 3 yrs. old; and William a. 1 yr.; and by w. Eliz. here had Eliz. bapt. 25 Dec. 1637; Hannah, b. 18 Oct. 1639; Mary, bapt. 29 May 1642; Joseph, 25 May 1644; Deborah, b. 26 Apr. bapt. 3 May 1646; was freem. 17 May 1637, rem. to Boston; there Eliz. m. 23 Feb. 1659, Joshua Nash; Hannah m. Apr. 1663, Fathergone Dinely; and Mary m. Peter Bennett. EXPERIENCE, Hadley, s. of the first Samuel of the same, m. Abigail, youngest d. of Samuel Williams of Roxbury, had there ten ch. and rem. 1725 to Mansfield. GEORGE, Salem 1647. Felt. HEZE-KIAH, Hadley, freem. 1690, was s. of Samuel of the same, had ten ch. there, rem. to Hartford, and had two more. HEZEKIAH, Windsor, s. of the sec. John of the same, m. 27 June 1700, Mary Bissell, had, as Stiles says, 704, Hezekiah, b. 7 July 1699; Deborah, 1 Mar. 1703; James, 11 May 1706; Lois, 19 Mar. 1708; and Samuel, 23 Mar. 1709. In the list of Errata, I see no correction of suspicious dates. ISRAEL, Salem, d. 30 Jan. 1678, aged 32. ISRAEL, Salem, s. of John of the same, m. 20 Nov. 1672, Eliz. d. of William Hathorne, had Eliz. b. 2 Oct. 1673; Sarah, 24 Aug. 1675; John, 24 Sept. 1677; Gingen, a d. 8 Dec. 1679; Mary, 22 Sept. 1681, d. at 9 mos.; Israel, 4 Apr. 1683; Benjamin, 4 Sept. 1685, d. at 6 yrs.; Ann, 17 June 1687; William, 12 Feb. 1689; and Benjamin, again, 17 May 1693; was selectman 1686, and freem. 1690, then of the vill. now Danvers. ISRAEL, Hadley, freem. 1684. JAMES, Windsor, sec. s. of the sec. John of the same, m. 15 Jan. 1679, Sarah, eldest d. of Owen Tudor, had James, b. 13 Oct. 1680, d. soon; Mary, 4 June 1682, d. at 2 yrs.; Isaac, 13 July 1683, d. in four mos.; Mary, 23 Sept. 1684; and Sarah, 31 May 1686; went to Eng. was in 1690 a merch. of distinct. in London, wh. declin. the office of agent for the Col. *JOHN, Windsor, among the earliest sett. 1638, and so it is by some presumed that he went from Dorchester, but more prob. is it, that he had been short time only in Mass. and accomp. Rev. Ephraim Hew-ett, bring. beside the six ch. ment. in his will, Sarah and Joseph, nam. by Goodwin, was constable 1640, rep. 1646 and 7; and add. to ch. by w. Rose, b. prob. in Eng. at W. had Nathaniel, b. 19 July 1640; and Ann, sometimes call. Hannah, 4 Sept. 1642; and Parsons, in Geneal. Reg. V. 359, says he d. 21 Apr. 1648, and was bur. next day. But his will of the day preced. was not carr. to Court bef. June of next yr. It gives eldest s. John, £100; sec. James, £60; Samuel, Nathaniel, Re-becca, Rose, Mary, and Ann, ea. £30. His wid. was bur. 20 days aft.

him. Sarah m. 24 Oct. 1644, Joseph Judson. ‡JOHN, Roxbury, freem. 5 Nov. 1633, had w. Margaret, rem. to Boston, there a supporter of Wheelwright, and disarmed 1637, soon rem. to R. I. signed their compact 1638, was an Assist. 1641 and aft. for some yrs. liv. at Portsmouth, R. I. 1655, and Wickford, 1674. Haz. II. 612. He had a d. perhaps nam. Hannah, wh. m. the sec. Samuel Wilbor. *JOHN, Hingham 1635, was rep. 1644, and that yr. rem. to Salem, had Sarah, bapt. there 5 June 1649, had many elder ch. as is shown by his will of 25 Apr. 1673, pro. 26 Sept. 1676, in 20 days aft. his d. aged 80. To his eldest s. John, wh. had been in prison at Boston, 1665, for abuse of his parents (whose case tak. up against the Col.'by the royal commrs. that yr. made such a stir among our people), wh. d. 16 Mar. 1684, he gave only £150, he having wasted much (and this is not a fifteenth part of the f.'s est.); to Joseph; Benjamin, wh. d. without ch.; Samuel, wh. was d. long bef.; and Israel; beside ds. Mary, w. of Thomas Gardner, with her three ch. and Sarah, prob. unm. adequate provis. almost naming Samuel's s. John. He was rep. 1668. His w. Mary surv. to 6 Feb. 1684, but whether she be that Mary, wh. join. the ch. 1639, or in 1644, I see not. JOHN, Windsor, eldest s. of John of the same, b. in Eng. m. Mary, d. of Thomas Standley, had John, b. 3 June 1651; Mary, 17 July 1653; Sarah, 5 Sept. 1655; James, 22 Dec. 1657; Nathaniel, 20 Apr. 1660; Hannah, 1 Jan. 1663; Samuel, 5 Mar. 1665; Rebecca, 8 Mar. 1667; Esther, 8 May 1669; Ruth, 7 Aug. 1671; Hezekiah, 7 Nov. 1673; and Joseph, 7 Feb. 1675; of wh. all exc. Esther were liv. at the date of his d. 2 Aug. 1688; and his wid. d. 13 Sept. foll. To James is giv. by Parsons the honor of being agent for Conn. but he was too young, and his uncle, the London merch. was the man. JOHN, Weymouth, by w. Deliverance, had Mary, b. 12 Oct. 1663; Susanna, 2 June 1665; John, 12 July 1667; one, whose name is not giv. 11 Apr. 1672; and Ruth, 18 Sept. 1675. JOHN, Windsor, eldest s. of John the sec. of the same, freem. 1672, m. 16 Dec. 1669 (rather early in his days), Joanna, d. of Walter Gaylord, had Joanna, b. 7 Feb. 1671; Mary, 20 Nov. 1672; John, 17 Jan. 1675; Sarah, 1 June 1677; Ann, 26 Aug. 1679; Daniel, 13 Nov. 1683; David, 3 Oct. 1685; and, if we believe Stiles, one s. and four more ds. and d. 1699. JOHN, Farmington, eldest s. of Robert, was a propr. 1673, but not at d. of his f. for he d. first. JOHN, Wenham, freem. 1690. JOHN, Hadley, freem. 1690. JOHN, Farmington, s. of the first Daniel, m. 2 Jan. 1696, Rebecca, d. of Joseph Woodford, had sec. w. Martha North, and d. 1740. JONATHAN, Salem 1637, then had gr. of ld. freem. 2 June 1641, had Mary, bapt. 12 Oct. 1645; and Jonathan, 12 Mar. 1648, was of Beverly side. Mary m. 22 Apr. 1669, Thomas Gardner. JONATHAN, Salem 1636, a sergeant in 1647, and in

Sept. of that yr. had gr. of 200 acres, was selectman 1653 and 4, but late in that yr. convey. his est. at S. to James Chichester, on condition that he should provide for his wid. Eunice if she outliv. him and rem. to Huntington, L. I. had d. bef. 1660, when Eunice sued for her right in Nov. of that yr. and in 1670 est. was div. to the heirs, wh. were all fem. His three ds. m. respectiv. James Chichester, Edward Harnett, and Stephen Jarvis; and the wid. Eunice m. Giles Smith of Fairfield. JOSEPH, Salem, s. of John of the same, freem. 1665, m. 27 Jan. 1665, Ann, eldest d. of William Hathorne, had Joseph, b. 23 Oct. foll.; Ann, 5 Sept. 1667; Samuel, 4 Aug. 1669; Nathaniel, 8 Mar. 1671; Mary, 18 Dec. 1672; William, 30 Aug. 1674; Eleazer, and Abigail, tw. 23 May 1676; Hepzibah, 11 Apr. 1678; Ruth; and Mehitable; and he d. 12 Dec. 1714. His will of 15 July 1713, pro. 27 Dec. 1714, names all the six ds. and the first four s. as liv. JOSEPH, Windsor, youngest s. of the sec. John of the same, m. 5 Dec. 1699, Hannah, d. of Samuel Buel, had Joseph, b. 14 Sept. 1700, d. in few mos.; Joseph, again, 20 Jan. 1701; Mehitable, 27 June 1707; Nathaniel, 14 June 1709; Mary, 25 May 1712, d. young. NATHANIEL, Salem 1638, had liv. elsewhere, for he was freem. 17 Apr. 1637, and is not in Felt's fine list of ch. mem. NATHANIEL, Windsor, youngest s. of John the first of the same, and the only one, prob. b. on this side of the ocean, in 1669 is among the freem. of Stratford, where he m. Hannah, d. of Philip Groves, had Hannah, b. 1665; Sarah, 1667; Ruth, 1669; and Nathaniel, 1672. By sec. w. Eliz. sis. of his former w. he had John, b. 1674; Samuel, 1675, d. soon; and Mary, 1677. He had good est. d. Jan. 1680, in his will naming w. Eliz. and the six liv. ch. NEHEMIAH, Farmington, sec. s. of the first Daniel, m. Hannah Lum, perhaps d. of John, and d. 1722. RICHARD, Weymouth, had Ruth, b. 3 Oct. 1639; was freem. 1653. RICHARD, Waterbury, s. of the first Daniel, by w. Ruth had Daniel, b. prob. at Farmington, but at W. had Joshua, 7 Aug. 1688; Mary, 14 Jan. 1691; Ruth, Oct. 1692; Samuel, 30 Mar. 1695; Hezekiah, 29 Jan. 1697, d. young; John, 11 June 1700; Timothy, 21 Dec. 1701; Hezekiah, again, 27 July 1704; and his w. d. 9 Jan. 1710. By sec. w. he had Joshua, 5 Nov. 1718, at New Haven, whither he had rem.; Richard, 22 Aug. 1722; and Lydia; and d. 1740, prob. as his will, of 13 Nov. 1738, was pro. Feb. 1740. ROBERT, Farmington, one of the first sett. m. 1644, Mary, d. of Thomas Scott of Hartford, had Mary, b. 24 Feb. 1646; John, 12 Nov. 1648; Thomas, 29 Oct. 1650; Robert, 12 Nov. 1652, d. young; Eliz. 11 Jan. 1654; Joanna, bapt. 6 Jan. 1656; Sarah, 20 Dec. 1657; Benjamin, 18 Mar. 1660; Ann, Apr. 1664; and Hepzibah, b. 4, bapt. 11 Mar. 1666. He took sec. w. Hannah Freeman, a wid. and d. 1689, for inv. was giv. 18 Sept. of that yr. Sarah m. Abraham Andrews of the same; and his br. Thomas m. ano. d. Eliz. ROBERT, Northampton, m. 1688, Sarah Burt, had John, b. 1689, wh. with his mo. d. soon. In 1691, he m. Eliz. Rising, had John, again, 1692; Eliz. 1695; James, 1698; William, 1702; and Thomas, 1705. Both William and his f. d. 1712. ROGER, Watertown, went home prob. in 1637, and again came in the Confidence, from Southampton, 1638, aged 55, a husbandman of Long Sutton, Hants, with Joan, Susan, Mary, and Rose, his ds. was freem. 22 May 1639, selectman, 1648, and d. 3 Apr. 1654, aged 71. His wid. Grace, wh. had been wid. of William and first of Thomas Rogers, d. 3 June 1662, in her will naming gr.ch. Daniel Smith, and John, Martha, Mary, Sarah, and Joseph Sherman. These last were part of the ch. of capt. John Sherman, wh. had m. her d. Martha; and ano. d. Eliz. had m. Daniel Smith. Hereby we discov. that P. had been with part of his fam. at W. for this d. Eliz. is not nam. among passeng. in the Confidence; nor is the w. Grace, wh. was left, no doubt, at W. in her h.'s absence to gov. the fam. but this is made more cert. from our kn. that Sherman's w. had her first ch. b. here, less than five mos. aft. the arr. of that ship. SAMUEL, Salem, d. a. 1659, had not long bef. m. Hannah, d. of William Dodge. His will of 10 Feb. in that yr. made in anticipat. of a voyage to Barbadoes, and the inv. of 22 June 1660, by the wid. names s. John. Perhaps, then, Hannah was sec. w. His wid. m. Thomas Woodbury. SAMUEL, Windsor, s. of the first John of the same, b. prob. in Eng. m. Hannah, d. of Thomas Stanley, rem. to Hadley 1659, had there, Samuel, b. 6 Apr. 1660, said to be the first b. of that town; one b. and d. 26 Apr. 1662; Thomas, 17 Apr. 1663; Hezekiah, 7 Jan. 1665; John, 12 Dec. 1666; Hannah 1670; Mehitable, 15 Sept. 1673; Experience, 5 Aug. 1676; Ichabod, 17 June 1678; and Nathaniel, 1680; Hannah m. 29 Mar. 1689, John Nash, and d. within two mos. All the other eight ch. were liv. at his d. 6 Sept. foll. and also at the time his wid. d. 18 Dec. 1708. Mehitable m. Nathaniel Goodwin. He was freem. 1684, much engag. in trade, owned part of the sh. Northern Adventure, and left good est. Of his seven s. Experience, and Hezekiah, are bef. ment. Thomas, John, and perhaps Nathaniel, sett. in Lebanon; Ichabod in Hatfield, and Samuel only cont. at Hadley. SAMUEL, Farmington, youngest s. of the first Thomas, had w. in 1686 to join with him in ch. commun. and had Stephen, bapt. 10 Apr. 1687; Hannah, 17 June 1688; Samuel, 20 Sept. 1691; Sarah, 19 Nov. 1693; and Martha, 5 July 1696. *SAMUEL, Hadley, eldest s. of the first Samuel of the same, at one time rep. an extensive trader with Eng. after judge, and sheriff of the Co. in wh. he was the wealthiest man at his d. 29 July 1722. He m. 22 Feb. 1684, Joanna Cook, d. of Aaron, had fourteen ch. but only seven outliv. him, four ds. out of eight, and these s. Samuel, b. 25 May 1685; Aaron, 19 July 1689, H. C. 1708, the first min. of Medford; and Eleazer, 25 Feb. 1698. To bring up his gr.s. Samuel to coll. he left £100, and he was gr. of H. C. 1730, bec. third min. of Shirborn. SAMUEL, Farmington, s. of the first Thomas of the same, was a deac. had Samuel, and Joseph. The artic. in Geneal. Reg. IX. 54, on the Porter fam. is eminent. for its merit in withhold. dates. STEPHEN, Andover, freem. 1691. THOMAS, Hartford, m. 1644, Sarah, d. of Stephen Hart, rem. to Farmington, had Sarah, b. 1646; Thomas, 1648; Joanna, 1652; wh. all were bapt. 24 July 1653, prob. but not, as in Geneal. Reg. XI. 323, 29; Dorothy, bapt. Nov. 1654; Thomas, again, 1656; Samuel; and Ruth, wh. m. 24 Mar. 1687, Samuel Smith, and next, Joseph Root. He d. 1697, and his will of 3 Mar. 1691, names only Thomas, Dorothy, and Samuel. Perhaps his d. Sarah m. Apr. 1664, Nathaniel Winchell; and Joanna m. 1676, Stephen Taylor. THOMAS, Weymouth, had Thomas, posthum. b. 3 Feb. 1673. THOMAS, Farmington, s. of Thomas of the same, m. Lois, d. of Timothy Stanley, had Lois, b. 1670; and only s. Timothy, Nov. 1672; was a deac. and d. 1711. Some of these fams. have been mark. for longev. Rev. Nehemiah, H. C. 1745, of Ashfield, d. 29 Feb. 1820, in his 100th yr. Col. Joshua, Y. C. 1754, d. 1825, in 95th yr. and Rev. Nathaniel, b. 16 Jan. 1745, H. C. 1768, of Conway, N. H. d. 1836. THOMAS, Farmington, 1682, s. of Robert, m. May 1678, Abigail, d. of Samuel Cowles, and by her had Abigail, b. 24 June 1680; William, bapt. 29 Oct. 1682; John, 18 July 1686; Mary, 2 June 1689; Nathaniel, 27 Mar. 1692, prob. not 28, as Geneal. Reg. XII. 150, says, for that was Monday; Abigail, 8 July 1694; Robert, 16 May 1697; and Eliz. b. 1 June 1703. Seventy-four of this name, of wh. sixteen were clerg. Farmer says, had been gr. in 1834 at the N. E. coll. of these twenty-three, includ. six clerg. were of Yale alone, and twenty, includ. seven clerg. at Harv. leav. only three clerg. among the thirty-one scholars at all the other N. E. coll. of wh. Dart. had fourteen.

PORTIS, or PORTOUS, ROBERT, Boston 1645, m. 3 Nov. 1659, Alice Greenwood.

PORTMORT, PORMONT, PURMONT, or PERMONT, LAZARUS, Dover, eldest ch. of Philemon, b. on our side of the water, there was taxed 1659. He was, I imagine, f. of Joseph, of Newcastle 1685. PHILEMON, Boston, adm. of the ch. with w. Susan, near the end of Aug. 1634, prob. brot. one ch. if not more, was freem. 6 May 1635, and the first gram. sch.-master, had Lazarus, b. 28 Feb. bapt. 6 Mar. 1636; Ann, 5, bapt. 15 Apr. 1638; favored the cause of Wheelwright, and followed him to Exeter and aft. to Wells, hav. letters of dism. from our ch. Jan. 1639; but prob. came back, aft. prob. not a few yrs. had Pedaiah, b. 3 June

1640; his w. d. 29 Dec. 1642; and by sec. w. Eliz. had Martha, bapt. 29 May, but town rec. says b. 16 June 1653. His d. Eliz. b. prob. in Eng. m. 24 Nov. 1652, Nathaniel Adams; but ano. pretend. rec. says Samuel Norden, in Geneal. Reg. XI. 202. Great variety is found in the letters or sound of this first sch.-master's name, as Porment, Pormet, Purmount, etc. In Allen's Biogr. Dict. the trouble is avoid. but not in a satisfactory manner.

POST, ABRAHAM, Saybrook 1664, s. prob. of Stephen, freem. 1665, ensign 1667, had Stephen, b. 3 Dec. 1664; Ann, 4 May 1667; Abraham, 9 June 1669; James, 14 Mar. 1671; Esther, 14 Dec. 1672, d. in few days; Daniel, 28 Nov. 1673; Gurdon, 27 May 1676; Joseph, 6 Feb. 1678; Mary, 21 Feb. 1680; and Elinor, 10 Feb. 1682; and his w. d. 23 Mar. 1684. In the will of Uncas, four thousand acres were devis. to him, yet in Geneal. Reg. XIII. 234, his name is Past. ISAAC, Huntington, L. I. 1666. Thompson. JOHN, Woburn, m. 27 Feb. 1650, Susanna Sutton; but whether she had ch. or how long she liv. is not told; yet I find he m. sec. w. 18 Nov. 1662, Mary Tyler, and had Mary, b. 29 Sept. 1664; Joanna, 13 Sept. 1666; and John, 14 Apr. 1669. JOHN, Saybrook, s. of Stephen, b. prob. in Eng. m. in the last of Mar. 1652, Esther, d. of William Hyde, had Margaret, b. 21 Feb. 1653; Eliz. 22 Feb. 1655; John, 12 Apr. 1657; and Sarah, 6 Nov. 1659; rem. with first sett. to Norwich, there had Abigail, 6 Nov. 1664, d. at 11 yrs.; Samuel, 8 Mar. 1668; Hannah, Oct. 1671; and Lydia, 11 Mar. 1674; was in 1663, accept. to be made free, yet seems to have missed for sev. yrs. of taking the o. wh. the Dept. Gov. was requested to admin. in 1666 and again in 1668. In the list of 1669 he is includ. and his w. d. 13 Nov. 1703. He d. 27 Nov. 1710. Lydia m. Abel Moore, and next, Joseph Harris, both of New London. JOHN, Norwich, eldest s. of the preced. m. 24 Dec. 1685, Sarah, eldest d. of John Reynolds, had Sarah, b. 1 Dec. 1686; John, 14 July 1689; and d. 15 July of next yr. His wid. d. 11 May 1703. RICHARD, Southampton, L. I. 1640, nam. by Thompson, may easily be thot. the same as that one of the first sett. of New London 1646 or 7, a blacksmith, wh. sold his est. 1651 or 2 to Amos Richardson, and rem. but whither is not heard, nor whether he had ch. or not. STEPHEN, Cambridge 1634, rem. 1636 to Hartford, an orig. propr. had John, Thomas, and Abraham, prob. Catharine, wh. m. Alexander Chalker, in 1649 was of Saybrook, where he d. 16 Aug. 1659. THOMAS, Saybrook, s. prob. of the preced. m. Jan. 1656, Mary Andrews, had Sarah, b. Nov. 1657; and a. 1660 rem. to Norwich, where his w. d. 1661; and he m. 2 Sept. 1663, Rebecca, d. of Obadiah Bruen, had Thomas, Dec. 1664; Hannah, Feb. 1666; Mary, June 1669; Obadiah; and Joseph. He d. 5 Sept. 1701, and his wid. d. 15 Apr. 1721.

POSTER, ABEL, is the name giv. to a freem. of Mass. 1674, but where he liv. is unkn. and error is suspect.

POTTER, ABEL, Dartmouth, m. 16 Nov. 1669, Rachel, youngest d. of John Warner, rem. to Warwick, in his will of 1692, names eldest s. George, youngest Stephen, and other ch. Abel, Benjamin, and Mary. ANTHONY, Ipswich 1648, m. Eliz. prob. d. of deac. John Whipple of the same, had sev. ch. wh. with w. outliv. him, as John, Edmund, Eliz. Kimball, Lydia Putnam, prob. w. of Jonathan, beside Thomas and Anthony. GEORGE, Newport 1638. HUMFREY, Salem, had only ch. Ann, who m. 10 Jan. 1656, Anthony Needham. ICHABOD, Portsmouth, R. I. perhaps s. of Robert, the friend of Gorton, m. Martha, d. of Thomas Hazard. INDIGO, or perhaps INIGO, Charlestown, m. 25 Aug. 1663, Mary Lawrence, d. of John of Groton, may have liv. in some other town, for without find. adm. of him s. or w. to the ch. there, I see that his ch. by w. Mary, viz. Mary, John, Richard, Indigo, Margaret, were all bapt. at C. 24 Apr. 1681, and Margaret, again, 9 July 1682. JOHN was a grantee of Sudbury in 1640, but I ask in vain, where he resid. or any thing else a. him. JOHN, New Haven, perhaps 1639, had John, and Samuel, bapt. (not 7, as in Geneal. Reg. IX. 362, but) prob. 17 Oct. 1641; perhaps d. bef. 1643, as a wid. P. with fam. of two is that yr. ment. She may also have m. again, for Eliz. Rose, in 1677, by her will ment. her s. John and Samuel P. beside sev. ds. Coffin made the surname Polter. JOHN, New Haven, s. of the preced. m. 1661, Hannah, d. of John Cooper, had Hannah, b. 1661, d. soon; John, June 1663, d. soon; Hannah, again, 26 June 1665; John, again, 4 Aug. 1667; Samuel, July 1669, d. soon; one, without name, Feb. 1671, d. soon; Mary, Mar. 1673, d. soon; and Samuel, again, 2 Jan. 1675; and by sec w. m. 29 Dec. 1679, Mary, wid. of Ralph Russell, had Abigail, was serg. and propr. 1685, and d. Dec. 1707, aged 70. JOHN, Warwick, was s. of Robert, freem. 1660; m. 2 June 1664, Ruth, d. of Edward Fisher of Portsmouth, R. I. had Robert, b. 5 Mar. 1666; Fisher, 12 July 1667; John, 21 Nov. 1668; William, 23 May 1671; Samuel, 10 Jan. 1673; Isabel, 17 Oct. 1674, wh. bec. sec. w. of William Burton, and long surv. him; Ruth, 29 Nov. 1676; and Content, 2 Oct. 1680. JOSEPH, New Haven, prob. s. of William, was recom. 1668 for freem. but d. 17 Aug. next yr. JUDAH, Concord, s. prob. of Luke, freem. 1690. LUKE, Concord, freem. 13 Mar. 1639, by w. Mary, wh. d. 8 Apr. 1644, had Eunice, b. 2 Mar. 1641; and Rebecca, 2 Aug. 1643, d. at 2 mos. He m. 19 Oct. 1644, Mary, d. of Walter Edmands, had Luke, 30 May 1646, d. at 15 yrs.; Samuel, 1 Apr. 1648; Dorothy, 9 Apr. 1650; Judah; Frances, wh. d. 17 Nov. 1661; and Bethia, 4 Nov. 1659; was deac. and d. 13 Oct. 1697. Eunice m. 4 Oct. 1660, John Frye of Andover. MATTHIAS, Braintree 1661. NATHANIEL, New Haven, s. prob. of William, a propr. 1685. NATHANIEL, Portsmouth, s. of that wid. Dorothy wh. m. John Albro, d. 20 Oct. 1704. NICHOLAS, Lynn, 1651, much engag. in the iron works, rem. to Salem, 1660, there call. a bricklayer, had Hannah, bapt. 25 Mar. 1661; and Mary, 15 Nov. 1663; Samuel, b. 9 Jan. 1665, d. at one yr.; Hannah, again, 27 Mar. 1666; Lydia, 26 Feb. 1667, d. next yr.; Bethia, 23 May 1668; Samuel, 22 Apr. 1669; Lydia, again, 16 July 1670, d. in Apr. foll.; Benjamin, 6 Nov. 1671; and Joseph, 9 June 1673. His w. Mary d. soon aft. and he d. 18 Oct. 1677. His inv. was tak. 25, and his will made 10 of that mo. That he had ch. by two ws. is infer. and that sec. w. Mary was d. of John Gedney appears in Essex Inst. II. 275; but for the bapt. name of the mo. of the ch. Robert, Eliz. Sarah, wh. were prob. b. at Lynn by first w. certainty is unattain. tho. from the transcr. of the will it may seem, that ea. w. brot. both Samuel and Benjamin. A flickering of light comes from p. 301, indicat. that the first w. was Alice, wh. d. 26 Jan. 1659. ROBERT, Lynn 1630, freem. 3 Sept. 1634, rem. to Newport, where in July 1638, he was adm. an inhab. and in 1641 unit. with Gorton in settlem. of Shaomet, wh. they call. Warwick, and two yrs. later was seized with the whole comp. and brot. prisoner to Boston, where the governm. sentenc. them to be confin. in various places, enjoin. them not to preach their monstr. absurd doctr. on pain of death. Soon, however, as sympathy for such suffer. was unavoidab. excit. they all were banish. and he went to Eng. and obt. justice by restorat. to their est. He kept an inn at W. in 1649, and d. in the autumn of 1655, or betw. that and the spring foll. leav. s. John, b. a. 1639, and ds. Deliverance, w. of James Greene; Eliz. wh. m. Richard Harcutt of the same; beside wid. Sarah, not. mo. of either of the ch. wh. bec. w. 19 Feb. 1657 of John Sandford, the sch.-master of Boston. Of his first w. the name is not kn. but Gorton in his narrat. of the invasion and assault by the Mass. forces upon the new settlem. of W. tells that she d. at that time, perhaps of trepidat. ROBERT, Roxbury 1634, on join. the ch. had w. Isabel, of neither of wh. do I find any other ment. in rec. of town or ch. but that he was bur. 17 Jan. 1654; yet in Boston ch. he had his d. Deliverance bapt. 5 Mar. 1637, and in the rec. of d. is error, no doubt, of Robert for William. Prob. he rem. ROBERT, Lynn, perhaps s. of the first Robert, b. in Eng. had Samuel, b. 28 May 1657; and his w. whose name is not giv. must have d. soon after; for he m. 25 Jan. 1660, Ruth Driver, perhaps d. of Robert the first, had Robert, b. 18 Mar. 1661; Nathaniel, 14 Apr. 1663; John, 13 Sept. 1665; Eliz. 9 Feb. 1668, d. soon; Eliz. again, 15 Aug. 1670; Ruth, 27 Feb. 1674; Joseph, 25 Dec. 1676; Benjamin, 11 Apr. 1680; and Samuel, 8 May 1682.

ROBERT, Lynn, s. of the preced. m. 9 Jan. 1682, Martha Hall, had Martha, b. 21 June 1685, was freem. 1691. THOMAS, Portsmouth, R. I. br. perhaps of the preced. m. 20 Jan. 1687, Susanna, d. of John Tripp, had Susanna, b. 28 June 1688; Sarah, 25 July 1690; and Ichabod, 23 Sept. 1692. VINCENT, Boston, came in the Elizabeth and Ann from London, 1635, aged 21, was next yr. a soldier at the castle [Winth. II. 346]; went home in 1639, in the same sh. with John Josselyn, wh. ment. p. 30, that he was afterwards question. for a Regicide. He was prob. one of the madcap millenarians with Venner of Salem, but not of sufficient importance to be put to death. WILLIAM, Watertown, came prob. in the Abigail from London, 1635, aged 27, with w. Frances, 26, and ch. Joseph, 20 wks. His mo. Hannah had m. bef. they came over, a Beecher, and had Isaac. He a. 1643 rem. prob. to New Haven, there had other childr. and in his will, 1662, names Nathaniel, Joseph, Hope, and Rebecca. Possib. but not prob. this is the man wh. was execut. Friday, 6 June of that yr. in the story of whose offence, being art. 3 of Appx. of Thaumaturgus, Magnalia VI. 38, Mather had gr. satisfact. and that he might defy human credulity makes the wonder, that tho. twenty yrs. a mem. of that ch. he had liv. in most infamous crimes no less than fifty yrs. together. The wretched man was perhaps s. of a wid. P. liv. at New Haven 1646. See Rec. I. 247. WILLIAM, Braintree, came perhaps in the Increase from London, 1635, aged 25, one of the early mem. of that ch. 17 Sept. 1639, freem. 13 May 1640, rem. to Roxbury, m. 2 June 1646, Judith Graves, wid. of John. He made his will 14 Jan. 1654, of wh. Geneal. Reg. V. 301, has abstr. in wh. he names no ch. but Hannah Graves, d. of his w. gives to the Rev. elders of Braintree, Tompson and Flint, £10 ea. br.'s John's and George's childr. sis. Jane's and Ann's, but all apparently in Eng. also to the sch. in R. and the coll. in Cambridge; and three days aft. was bur. tho. town rec. calls him Robert. His wid. Judith m. 13 Dec. foll. Samuel Finch. WILLIAM, New Haven, had Mary, and Sarah, prob. not tw. bapt. 22 Aug. 1641; Hope, 3 Oct. 1641; Rebecca, 1643; and Nathaniel, 22 Dec. 1644. Eight of this name, had, in 1834, been gr. at Yale, three at Harv. and nine at other N. E. coll.

POTTS, RICHARD, Kennebeck, whose w. was k. by the Ind. at Arowsic isl. Sept. 1676. Willis I. 148. THOMAS, Dover, by w. Joanna, had Mary, b. 6 July 1690, and ano. d. 28 Aug. 1693.

POTUM (if this be a possible name), CHARLES, of Cape Porpus, being d. admin. was giv. 1678 to John Barrett.

POULTER, JOHN, Billerica 1658, from Rayleigh in Co. Essex, m. 1662, Rachel Eliot of Braintree, d. of Francis, d. at Cambridge, 20 May 1676, aged 41, as the inscript. on gr.-st. is giv. by Harris. Epit. 6.

His wid. m. 1677, John Whitmore; and his sis. Hannah, perhaps, m. John Dudley, as did, 22 Nov. 1655, Eliz. with Jonathan Danforth the first; and Mary, 12 Apr. 1687, with Samuel Winship. All were, no doubt, ch. of John P. early sett. at B. but dec. bef. last date. Prob. he was driv. in by Ind. hostil. But a JOHN of Cambridge, perhaps his s. was liv. there 1698, and I suppose m. Hannah, d. of lieut. John Hammond, the richest man of Watertown. He may have rem. to Boston, and in Mar. 1713 been chos. to a town office.

POUND, THOMAS, a pirate in the Vineyard Sound, Sept. and Oct. 1689, taken and brot. in.

POUT, or POAT, WILLIAM, Marblehead 1668–74.

POW, WILLIAM, Marblehead 1674. Dana, 8. It is strange that we never find his name, especially as it bears the prefix of respect in Dana.

POWELL, ABEL, Newbury, and CALEB, his br. actors in the direful nonsense of witchcraft, 1679, against or upon William Morse and his w. Eliz. of wh. in Hist. of Newbury, 122–134, and in Essex Inst. II. 30, 31, and 212, eno. perhaps more than eno. may be read. See also a few words in this Dict. III. 242, under Morse. JOHN, Charlestown, by w. Sarah had John, bapt. 7 Mar. 1669; but the f. had d. in June preced. and the young wid. join. to the ch. 28 Feb. foll. and soon m. John Blaney. MICHAEL, Dedham 1639, by w. Abigail had perhaps that Sarah wh. m. 3 May 1653, Timothy Dwight, and may have been b. in Eng.; Eliz. b. 10 June, bapt. 5 July 1641; Dorothy, 11, bapt. 16 July 1643; and Michael, b. 12, bapt. 19 Oct. 1645; beside Margaret, bapt. 14 Apr. 1648 a. 8 days old; was freem. 2 June 1641, rem. to Boston 1647, and, without ordin. taught in the new ch. bef. sett. of a min. there, or, indeed, bef. the gather. of a ch. wh. occur. 5 June of the yr. foll. when he was ord. a rul. elder, the governm. forbid. his being min. for want of educat. had Margaret, bapt. 14 June 1649, 8 days old; and d. 28 Jan. 1673, or by gr.-st. wh. makes his age 67 yrs. 28 Dec. preced. Farmer strangely miscalls Increase Mather the first min. tho. he did, sub voce, Mayo, restore the honor to the proper man. Eliz. m. 23 Aug. 1659, Richard Hollingworth. Two of his more gifted successors, Ware and Robbins, have justly discussed the diffidence of this first instr. of their people. RALPH, Marshfield, m. 30 Oct. 1676, Martha Clement. ROBERT, Exeter, took o. of fidel. 1677. ROWLAND, Gloucester 1657, by w. Isabel had Rowland, and a d. tw. b. 9 Feb. 1658, of wh. the d. d. next day; Mary, 7 May 1660; and Stephen, 9 Nov. 1662. THOMAS, New Haven, had Hannah, b. 1641, bapt. 1643; Priscilla, Dec. 1642, bapt. 1644; Mary, bapt. 20 July 1645; Martha, 28 Jan. 1649, prob. d. soon; Martha, again, Jan. 1651; and Esther, prob. bapt. 5 June 1653;

all in right of w. Priscilla; may be the same wh. in May 1664, was of Long Isl. adm. to be sw. freem. of Conn. by Commsnrs. of Huntington. He was dissatisf. prob. with the recusancy of that Col. to the union with Conn. as by the royal chart. provid. and may have been at Springfield 1665, at least bot. ld. there, but did not cont. long, and went back to N. H. but not to be on the list of 1669, there d. 1681. Hannah m. 21 May 1660, Thomas Tuttle, and Priscilla m. 29 Mar. 1666, John Thompson. THOMAS, Saco 1670. THOMAS, Windsor, m. 25 Aug. 1676, Alce Traharen, had Ann, b. 19 Apr. 1678; Thomas, 11 July 1680; and Hannah, 1682, d. at 2 yrs. and d. 1685. WILLIAM, Charlestown 1636, by w. Eliz. had Mary, b. 30 Apr. 1637; Martha, 29 Apr. 1639; Joshua, 15 Nov. 1641, d. soon; Eliz. 22 Aug. 1642; and Joshua, again, 1644; and his w. d. 3 Dec. of that yr. He may be that man, said by Farmer to have d. at Salem 1670. WILLIAM, Taunton 1643.

POWER, JOHN, Charlestown, by w. Sarah, had Peter, b. 4 Nov. 1643. NICHOLAS, Providence, an early sett. soon aft. Roger Williams, d. 25 Aug. 1657, leav. wid. Jane, and s. Nicholas, and d. Hope, both under age. He never dwelt at Shaomet, Staples says, tho. of the number of twelve purch. of that territo. and so suffer. very slightly in the monstrous proceed. against Gorton and his comp. at Warwick 1643. Yet he is one of the signers of the declar. of their rights, 20 Nov. 1642. Tradit. has been very rich, and, as usual, very false a. this man, and his s. of the same name. The f. was here to sign the claim of rights in Nov. 1642, and was one of the purch. with Gorton and the other misbelievers of Warwick, and was next yr. brot. a prisoner to Boston, yet the mythical honor makes him to have left Drogheda, "during the siege in 1642, for Surinam, where the fam. had large estates." Authentic hist. makes the siege of Drogheda a dozen yrs. later. In favor of the sec. Nicholas, that authority makes his w. "d. of Sir Zachary R. a Cheshire baronet," but it wisely omits to tell how his title was acquir. Most curious is the docum. call. his will, made 27 May 1667 (near ten yrs. aft. his d.), by the municip. officers pub. in authentic form. R. I. Hist. Coll. II. Apx. 14. NICHOLAS, Providence, s. of the preced. freem. 1655, took engagem. of alleg. 29 Apr. 1670, m. 3 Feb. 1672, Rebecca, d. of Zachary Rhodes, had Hope wh. d. young; and col. Nicholas, b. 1673, and tradit. tells that he was k. accid. by his own friends, at the swamp fight, 19 Dec. 1675, in Philip's war. His wid. m. 1 Dec. 1676, Daniel Williams. The third Nicholas had m. one of this name, and no other s. the fourth, a fifth, and the fifth a sixth, ea. without other male issue; but the mystical number of seven was unhap. not reach. and the heredita. distinct. has expir. with the riches of Surinam. WALTER, Malden 1660, m. 11 Mar. 1661, Trial, d. of Ralph Shepard, had William; Mary; Isaac; Thomas; Daniel, b. 10 May 1669; Increase, 16 July 1671; Walter, 28 June 1674; Jacob, 15 Dec. 1679; and Sarah, 8 Feb. 1683; and d. at Littleton a. 1718.

POWES, THOMAS, Boston, of wh. I see nothing but that Sewall says, he was drown. 21 June 1684.

POWNING, or POUNDING, HENRY, Boston, freem. 1644, but he was of ano. ch. tho. of what town I am ign. had Henry, b. 28 Apr. 1654, wh. perhaps, was of ar. co. 1677; Hannah, 8 Apr. 1656, d. next yr.; and Sarah, 3 Aug. 1659. In 1695, a wid. P. was a householder in B. and Daniel P. ar. co. 1691, a deac. d. 1735.

POWSLAND, POWSLEY, POWLAND, POWLLEN, POUSLAND, POUSLIN, or POUSLY, JAMES, Salem, m. 2 Aug. 1670, Mary Barnes, wid. prob. of Thomas, 1675 was employ. as a gunner. Felt II. 486. He liv. 1674 on Marblehead side. RICHARD, Falmouth 1674–90. Willis I. 71, 133.

PRANCE, PHILIP, Salem 1689, master mariner. Felt.

PRATT, AARON, Cohasset, s. of Phineas, had Aaron, d. 25 Feb. 1735, aged 81, says the very loose statement in a newspaper, taken into the Geneal. Reg. V. 224. ABRAHAM, Charlestown, a surg. hav. in Col. rec. 19 Oct. 1630, when he req. to be made free, the prefix of respect, came, we may well infer, in the fleet with Winth. and was liv. 1631 at C. He with w. Joanna, early join. the ch. of Roxbury, but rem. again to C. and his w. d. 27 Dec. 1645; and he d. as the gr.-st. says, on the same day. BENAJAH, Plymouth, s. perhaps of Joshua or of Phineas, m. 29 Nov. 1655, Persis Dunham, prob. d. of the first John, had Abigail, b. 21 Nov. 1657. DANIEL, Hartford, s. prob. of John, freem. 1657, had Daniel, seven ds. and d. Apr. 1691, bur. 24. The ds. were Hannah, m. 1678, sec. Daniel Clark; Eliz. w. of Nathaniel Goodwin; Sarah Phelps; Mary Sanford; Rachel Skinner; Esther; and ano. whose name is not kn. Esther, in 1702, d. unm. in her will refer. to br. Daniel, and five sis. so that we infer one was d. since the f. EPHRAIM, Weymouth, by w. Phebe had Ephraim, b. 15 June 1698. EPHRAIM, Sudbury, s. of Thomas of the same, by w. Eliz. had Josiah, b. 6 Mar. 1700; Ephraim, 30 Nov. 1704; Phineas, 8 July 1706; Eliz. 25 Apr. 1711; and Mary, 2 Dec. 1718; prob. rem. to Shutesbury or Shrewsbury. Of one Ephraim, either this man or his s. is told the marvellous tale of longevity in Dwight's travels II. 358, that he was b. in Nov. 1687, and d. May 1804, could count 1500 descend. ate no animal food for forty yrs. and "was able to mow a good swarth one hundred and one yrs. in succession." Improb. crowd up against both of these Ephraims; the sen. must have been some yrs. earlier than 1687, call. by the man of sec. childhood his yr. of birth, as it is not prob. that his first ch. was b. in

wedlock bef. the f. was twelve and a half yrs. old. Dr. Dwight shoul^d
therefore, have better called him 126, than 116 yrs. old; but as part (
the same chapter in Apocrypha is, that this veteran Ephraim had
Michael wh. d. 1826, aged 103, we may adjudge the honor of the myth
to have been designed for the junr. This younger Ephraim was not
99 yrs. old, when the credulity of Pres. Dwight was instructed by the
wonder-working old man that he had mowed grass one hundred and one
yrs. in succession, and only invalided the yr. past. Dr. Dwight, tho.
not sceptical. inclined, as a juryman, on a question of this man's will,
had he made it on the day of his visit, must have decided that it was
not good, I presume, for want of disposing mind and *memory* in the testator. So easily does the false story of great age obtain belief, even
from men of sagacity, like Pres. Dwight or Mr. Ward. Next we com-
press the dimensions of Michael, tho. the day or yr. of his birth is unkn.
yet as his f. was not m. bef. 1724, he was less than one hundred; and
his f. from the last day of Nov. 1704 to any day in Mar. 1804 could
count but ninety-nine yrs. and a half. See Barry, Hist. of Framingham, for more of the fables. *JOHN, Cambridge, an expert surg. possib.
br. of Abraham, was of Hooker's ch. and freem. 14 May 1634; but
he had been so early as Mar. 1629, engag. for our comp. and came in
the Lion's Whelp, but ret. in the same sh. and when next he came, sat
down first at Braintree, in Nov. 1635 was animadvert. on for ill report
of the country, rem. to Hartford, prob. 1637, was rep. 1639–42, but not
after, excus. from watch, accord. to previous promise, in June 1644, but
went for home in Nov. foll. with his w. having no ch. and above 60 yrs.
old, and in Dec. drown. in the shipwreck on the coast of Spain. Winth.
I. 173, and II. 239, with Trumbull, Col. Rec. II. 27, 108, and 450.
JOHN, Hingham, lost his ho. by fire, 15 Mar. 1646, and perhaps rem. to
Weymouth, and may have been f. of John, Joseph, Matthew, Samuel,
and Thomas of that town, or of some of them. JOHN, Hartford, an
orig. propr. was prob. a carpenter, and was f. of John, and Daniel, d. 15
July 1655. His will of 7 Oct. preced. names w. Eliz. and the two
s. He has been sometimes confus. with the surg. wh. owned no ld.
whereas this man had sev. lots. See Trumbull, Col. Rec. I. 230. JOHN,
Dorchester, freem. 10 May 1643, had John, b. a. 1630, and Timothy,
and d. 1647, leav. wid. Mary, wh. m. William Turner. His will of 3
Mar. 1647 is abstr. in Geneal. Reg. VII. 36. Timothy sett. in Boston;
John, at Medfield. JOHN, Weymouth, s. of Matthew of the same, m.
27 Nov. 1656, Mary, d. of ens. John Whitman of the same. JOHN,
Hartford, s. of the sec. John, m. Hannah, d. of James Boosy, was
freem. 1657, had Hannah, b. 25 Nov. 1658; John, 17 May 1661; Eliz.
7 Oct. 1664; Sarah, 20 June 1668; Joseph, 6 Mar. 1671; Ruth, 21

Dec. 1677; Susanna, 2 Oct. 1680; and Jonathan, 6 Oct. 1683; and d. 1690. Perhaps some of these ch. were by his sec. w. Hepzibah, wh. m. says Porter, John Sadd, 1690, and d. 1712. JOHN, Kingstown, by w. Ann, had Deliverance, b. 13 Nov. 1664; Mary, Apr. 1666; John, Oct. 1667; Ebenezer, 31 Aug. 1669; Phineas, Apr. 1671; Joshua, 10 Jan. 1673; Jeremy, 13 Oct. 1674; and Mercy, 23 Dec. 1676. JOHN, Medfield 1666, was s. of John of Dorchester, but prob. b. in Eng. and I kn. nothing more, exc. that he had John, Mary, Priscilla, Hannah, and Sarah, and w. Rebecca, all nam. in his will of 30 Apr. 1707, from wh. we find that one d. had m. Henry Smith; ano. Timothy Clark; and that s.-in-law, Samuel Wright was made with s. John excor. JOHN, Saybrook, s. of lieut. William, m. 8 June 1665, Sarah, d. of Thomas Jones, but whether he had ch. by her, I find not. Geneal. Reg. IV. has giv. from the rec. of Saybrook *two* JOHNS, as follows: one had Thomas, b. 28 Oct. 1675; Isaac, 16 Jan. 1678; Sarah, 5 June 1680; Lydia, 18 Feb. 1682; and Mehitable, 6 Sept. 1685. He may have been s. of William. The other JOHN, call. a tailor, m. 10 Aug. 1676, Mary Andrews, had Mary, b. 24 May 1677; Martha, 16 Jan. 1679; Daniel, 13 Jan. 1680; Jonathan, 25 Dec. 1682; Hannah, 14 June 1688; and John, 19 Mar. 1691. JOHN, Malden, s. of Richard of the same, by first w. Mary had Richard; John, b. 14 June 1686; and by w. Martha, m. 18 Nov. 1686, had John, b. 24 Aug. 1687; and Martha, 1690; and he may have rem. to Reading, where Mr. Eaton sett. one of the name bef. 1700; but more prob. he was the deac. wh. d. at M. 15 Nov. 1742, aged 81 yrs. 7 mos. His wid. d. 10 May 1744, aged 83; unless she d. as his w. 20 Sept. 1742, aged 79. However, it may be, that this long liv. John was s. of Phineas, and that his w. Martha was d. of Richard Pratt. The decision is not easy upon Geneal. Reg. IX. 325. Ano. JOHN, or the same, of Malden, by w. Mary had Mary, b. 6 Mar. 1696; perhaps John, Thomas, Hannah, Ebenezer, Joseph, William, Caleb, Abigail, and Joshua, or some of them, for the ch. of this surname as the flowers of the field are spread about; but the gr.-st. in Malden, prove that one John's w. Mary, d. 17 May 1710, in 56th yr. and her h. John had d. 3 June 1708. JOHN, Weymouth, by w. Mary, wh. may have been d. of John Whitman of the same, had Samuel, b. 15 Oct. 1686, and by w. Mercy, prob. the same Mary, had John, 8 Mar. 1692; and John, again, 26 May 1696. One JOHN of Boston, m. 29 July 1691, Margaret Maverick, but of h. or w. I kn. no more. JONATHAN, Plymouth, br. perhaps of Benajah, m. 2 Nov. 1664, Abigail Wood, had Abigail, b. 16 June 1665; Bathsheba, 20 Feb. 1667; Jonathan, 20 Mar. 1669; Hannah, 28 June, 1671; Jabez, 1 Nov. 1673; Meletiah, 11 Dec. 1676; and Bethia, 8 Aug. 1679. JOSEPH, Weymouth, by w. Sarah, had Sarah, b. 31 May 1664; Joseph,

2 Feb. 1666; and John, 17 May 1668; was freem. 1672, and perhaps sw. again in 1674, when he liv. perhaps at Nantucket, and had there Mary, 16 Sept. 1675. JOSEPH, Charlestown, perhaps s. of Phineas, m. 12 Feb. 1675, Dorcas Folger, had Joseph, b. 19 Oct. 1677; Bethia, 11 Feb. 1680; Benjamin, 19 Jan. 1682, d. soon; Dorcas, 2 Apr. 1683, d. soon; Phineas, 18 Jan. 1684; Joshua, 18 June 1686; Lydia, 28 Nov. 1688; and the liv. three s. and ds. were bapt. 10 Feb. 1689, when unlucki. only Joseph is nam. in the rec. JOSEPH, Saybrook, s. of William the first, recom. for freem. 1673, by first w. had Joseph, William, Sarah, Experience, and Margaret. In Sept. 1686, he took sec. w. Sarah, youngest d. of Robert Chapman of the same, had Ann, b. 12 Aug. 1687, d. in few mos.; Ann, again, 7 Oct. 1688; Susanna, 18 Mar. 1690; Robert, 26 Oct. 1691; Caleb, a. 1693; Eliz. 6 Sept. 1695; Hannah, 27 Feb. 1699; and Temperance, 15 Feb. 1701, d. soon. JOSHUA, Plymouth, came in the Ann 1623, prob. a youth, of wh. all that is kn. seems to be, that in 1652 he was one of the purch. of Dartmouth, and d. soon aft. for inv. of his prop. present. by Bathsheba, prob. his wid. 6 Oct. 1656, was only of the amo. £18 11s. 3d. Perhaps he had ch. but the gr.s. Ephraim, by Farmer believ. to be b. Nov. 1687, and his s. Michael, wonders of old age in 1804 and 1826, are by Barry render. wholly improb. JOSHUA, Medfield 1649. MATTHEW, Weymouth, freem. 13 May 1640, had Joseph, b. 10 Aug. 1637, prob. d. soon; and perhaps others, and may have, bef. 1643, rem. to Rehoboth. MATTHEW, Weymouth, perhaps s. of the preced. by w. Sarah, had Matthew, b. 18 Sept. 1665; Mary, 1667; Hannah, 4 Nov. 1670; William, 5 May 1673; may have rem. to Boston in the war of king Philip, had s. Samuel, bapt. at 3d ch. 2 Apr. 1676, and gone again to W. there had Ann, 14 Sept. 1682; and Susanna, Sept. 1684. Prob. he was s. but may have been neph. of the preced. He bec. deaf at 12 yrs. and almost lost speech, and his w. was deaf and dumb after 3 yrs. as in the Magnalia § 12 of cap. 26 of book III. is agreeably told (extract. from Remarkab. Providences of Increase Mather, the more judicious. f. of the author), with less admixt. of nonsense than is commonly seen in that work. MICAH, Weymouth, had John, b. 4 Oct. 1691. NATHANIEL, Saybrook, s. of William first of the same, m. 2 May 1688, Sarah Beament, had Sarah, b. 6 Feb. 1689; Nathaniel, 6 Mar. 1691; Samuel, 24 Jan. 1693; Abigail, 9 Oct. 1695; Deborah, 1 Jan. 1699; Hezekiah, 9 July 1701; and Gideon, 17 Sept. 1704. PETER, Lyme, m. 5 Aug. 1679, Eliz. that d. of Matthew Griswold, wh. had been, three yrs. bef. divorc. from John Rogers for his heresy, had Peter, and d. 24 Mar. 1688, and, 1691, his wid. m. Matthew Beckwith. It is not kn. whose s. he was, tho. sometimes it has been guess. that he was William's, of

wh. the prob. is remote. PHINEAS, Plymouth, came in June 1622, as
one of capt. Weston's men, planted at Weymouth, but in Mar. foll. as
Gov. Winslow tells in Young's Chron. of the Pilgr. he went to P. had
sh. in the div. of ld. as if he had come in the Ann with Joshua, wh.
may have been a br. and so may we excuse the error of Mitchell, 279,
wh. says he came in the Ann, when it is plain he was here one yr.
earlier; m. 1630, a d. of Cuthbert Cuthbertson, it is said, rem. aft. many
yrs. to Charlestown. He address. a petition to our Gen. Ct. in 1662,
accomp. with a narrative of the first planting, whereupon they gave him
300 acres. That tract, with illustrations by the diligence of Frothingham, is print. in 4 Mass. Hist. Coll. IV. 476. He d. 19 Apr. 1680, hav.
been so reduced in est. as to need aid from the town. Frothingham, 156.
Perhaps in mak. his age a. 90 yrs. the inscript. on his gr.-st. at Charlestown may be 10 or 12 yrs. too liberal. See Prince, Ann. I. 131, or Mr.
Hale's Ed. 213. RICHARD, Charlestown, b. it is said, youngest of nine ch.
to John of Malden in Co. Essex, and there bapt. 29 June 1615, by w.
Mary, had Mary, b. 7 or 30 Sept. 1643 ; Thomas, 5 Mar. or May 1646 ;
Mercy, 15 June 1650, d. young; John, 1655 ; Eliz.; Martha, 1663;
and Hannah. He liv. on Malden side, and d. 1691. Mary m. Thomas
Skinner ; Eliz. m. Gershom Hawkes ; Martha m. 18 Nov. 1686, John
Pratt; and Hannah on slight report is call. w. of a Hovey. SAMUEL,
Weymouth, a carpenter, freem. 1666, by w. Hannah, perhaps d. of John
Rogers of the same, had Judah, b. 25 June 1661 ; ano. ch. whose name
is out, 17 Aug. 1663 ; Hannah, 21 Dec. 1665 ; Mary, 3 Mar. 1668 ;
Samuel, 15 Nov. 1670 ; Experience, 8 Jan. 1673 ; and perhaps Martha,
8 Aug. 1675. He was engag. in settlem. of Mendon 1663. SAMUEL,
Wickford 1674. SAMUEL, Weymouth, s. of Samuel of the same, by w.
Patience, had Judith, 23 Nov. 1695. THOMAS, Watertown, freem.
1647, unless, as I suspect, Barry overlooked one generat. and it was not
that freem. but his s. wh. had, partly bef. and partly aft. rem. to Framingham, after being of Sudbury, these eleven ch. Thomas, b. a. 1656 ;
John; Ebenezer; Joseph; Philip; David; Jabez; Nathaniel; Abial,
fem. Ephraim; and Jonathan; in 1682 had ld. set to him at Sherborn,
and d. a. 1692 ; at least, admin. that yr. was giv. to wid. Susanna and s.
John. All these ten s. m. and had fams. It seems prob. that the f. of
these many ch. was he wh. sw. fidel. in 1652, rather than the freem. of
1647, wh. may have been his f. THOMAS, Weymouth, had William, b.
6 Mar. 1659. A serg. Pratt of Weymouth, perhaps not this man, but
Joseph, Matthew, or Samuel, was k. by the Ind. in Philip's war, 19 Apr.
1676. THOMAS, Malden, by w. Sarah had Sarah, bapt. 6 Jan. 1661, d.
young; Eliz. 2 Feb. 1662 ; John, 29 May 1664 ; Sarah, again, 19 Aug.
1666 ; Robert, 19 Apr. 1668, d. young; Edmund, 30 Jan. 1670 ; Han-

nah, 25 Feb. 1672; William, 13 Sept. 1674; Deborah, 1 Oct. 1676; and Robert, again, 22 June 1684. THOMAS, Malden. eldest s. of Richard of the same, had, by w. unkn. to me, Richard, John, Mary, Sarah, and Thomas, b. 1700, wh. it is said, liv. to 20 Aug. 1776; but the f. d. 1718. TIMOTHY, Boston, s. of John of Dorchester, m. 9 Nov. 1659, Deborah Cooper, join. the sec. or Mather's ch. and was freem. 1683. He had sec. w. Mary, as appears in his will of 16 Aug. 1694, in wh. he ment. s. Josiah, and the Deborah, d. of his s. Timothy, dec. TIMOTHY, Charlestown, s. of the preced. m. 19 Nov. 1679, Grace, eldest d. of Thomas Shippey, had Deborah, nam. in the will of her gr.f. Pratt; Rebecca, b. 22 July 1682, d. in one yr. aft.; and he d. 25 Mar. of the same yr. He had been a barber of Boston. *WILLIAM, Hartford, an orig. propr. prob. br. of John, the sec. of the same, by w. Eliz. d. of John Clark of Milford, had Eliz. b. 1 Feb. 1642; John, 20 Feb. 1645; rem. that yr. to Saybrook, there had Joseph, 1 Aug. 1648; Sarah, 1 Apr. 1651; William, 5, but Parsons quotes 15 May 1653; Samuel, 6 Oct. 1655; Lydia, 1 Jan. 1660; and Nathaniel, perhaps bef. the last, but not nam. in rec. but by his f. in a deed to him; was lieut. in 1661, rep. 1666, and eleven yrs. more. His eldest d. m. William Backus of Norwich; Sarah m. 1670, Isaac Waterhouse; and Lydia m. 18 Nov. 1679, John Kirtland of Saybrook. WILLIAM, Weymouth, freem. 1651. WILLIAM, Saybrook, s. of the first William, m. 20 Feb. 1679, Hannah, d. of Nathaniel Kirtland, had Benjamin, b. 14 June 1680; Hannah, 24 July 1682, d. at 2 yrs.; Prudence, 11 Mar. 1685; Ebenezer, 17 Aug. 1688; and Jabez, 19 May 1691. WILLIAM, Weymouth, may have been s. of William of the same, or neph. freem. 1680, by w. Eliz. d. of Richard Baker of Dorchester, had Thankful, b. 4 Oct. 1683, and by w. Experience, had Joanna, b. 23 Sept. 1692; and William, 3 Oct. 1695. He rem. to Dorchester. Six of this name, had in 1834, been gr. at Harv. as many at Yale, and eleven at other N. E. coll.

PRAY, ELISHA, Providence,'sw. alleg. May 1682. EPHRAIM, Braintree, s. prob. eldest, of John of the same, m. Eliz. d. of John Hayden, had Ephraim, b. 14 June 1681; John, 18 Aug. 1683; Eliz. 27 Sept. 1685; Hannah, 3 June 1687; Ruth, 28 Mar. 1689; Samuel, 14 May 1692; Joseph, 14 Jan. 1695; Mary, 17 Sept. 1697; and Sarah, 16 Jan. 1700. EPHRAIM, Providence 1676, "who staid and went not away," says the rec. thro. the war. He m. the wid. of Benjamin Herendean. JOHN, Braintree, m. 7 May 1657, Joanna Dowman, had John, b. 11 Mar. foll. prob. d. bef. his f. beside Ephraim, Samuel, Joseph, and two ds. Hannah Bell, and Dorothy Furbush, to div. his est. in July 1699; but I kn. not the h.'s. JOHN, Providence, sw. alleg. 1671, another of those not frightened away in 1676. QUINTIN and RICHARD, says Lewis, were of

Lynn 1645; the former is among debtors, 1655, to est. of Joshua Foote, and the latter by Farmer is put among first sett. of R. I. and in Philip's war refus. to quit Providence. He had sw. alleg. to the king, June 1668. WILLIAM, Providence, sw. alleg. May 1682.

PREBLE, ABRAHAM, Scituate 1637, m. Judith, d. of Nathaniel Tilden, had Abraham, b. a. 1642; Nathaniel, bapt. there 1648, tho. some yrs. bef. he had rem. to York, where he perhaps had Benjamin, and others; was magistr. 1650, submit. soon to Mass. and freem. 1652, treasr. of the Co. 1659, and d. 1663, leav. wid. Judith and sev. ch. of wh. one d. was m. Willis I. 102. ABRAHAM, York, s. of the preced. prob. eldest, was made treasr. of the Co. 1678, lieut. 1680, when he took o. of alleg. to the k. He m. a. 1685, acc. fam. tradit. Hannah Kelly, wh. liv. to 9 May 1751, and had Mary, b. 8 June 1686; Abraham, 21 Aug. 1687; Caleb, 7 July 1689; Jonathan, 11 Apr. 1695; Ebenezer, 26 Mar. 1698; and Samuel, 19 Apr. 1699. He was judge and deac. d. 4 Oct. 1714 in 72d yr. "univers. faithful to the death," says gr.-st. JOHN, NATHANIEL, and STEPHEN, wh. took the o. of alleg. to his majesty at York, 1680, were prob. his bros. and his s. Abraham, Esquire, of York, d. unm. 30 Mar. 1720 in his 50th yr. Abraham the f. was appoint. admin. on est. of John 1695, Hannah, the wid. of John hav. d. 19 Aug. of that yr. Of this stock was the famous Com. P.

PRENCE, §‡THOMAS, Plymouth, came in the Fortune, 1621, was s. of Thomas of Lechlade, in Co. Gloucester, near Cricklade, in Wilts, m. 5 Aug. 1624, Patience, d. of Elder William Brewster, had Thomas, Rebecca, Hannah, Mercy, and Sarah, of none of wh. are dates of b. kn. His w. d. 1634, and he rem. to Duxbury, m. 1 Apr. 1635, Mary, d. of William Collier, and was chos. Goy. that yr. and for two or three yrs. aft. an Assist. and Gov. again in 1638, afterwards an Assist. many yrs. By this w. he had Jane, b. 1 Nov. 1637; and prob. Mary, Eliz. and Judith; in 1645 rem. to Eastham, there again chos. Gov. 1658, and there his w. d. A third w. Mary in 1662, was wid. of Samuel Freeman, sen. and he rem. again, 1663, to Plymouth, there he d. 29 Mar. 1673, aged 72, leav. wid. Mary. The s. Thomas went to Eng. m. and d. young, leav. wid. and d. Susanna. Of the ds. all were m. and we kn. the dates of all but one, and the name of her h. is obscure, even after the inquiries of Mr. Hamblen. Rebecca m. 22 Apr. 1646, Edmund Freeman, jun.; Hannah m. 13 Feb. 1650, Nathaniel Mayo, and sec. h. Jonathan Sparrow; Mercy m. 13 or 14 Feb. 1650, John Freeman; Sarah m. 1650, Jeremiah Howe of Yarmouth; Jane m. 9 Jan. 1661, Mark Snow; Mary m. John Tracy of Duxbury; Eliz. m. 9 Dec. 1667, Arthur Howland, jr.; and Judith m. 28 Dec. 1685, Isaac Barker of

Duxbury. See Morton's Mem. by Davis, 421–5; Mitchell's Bridgewater; Winsor; and Geneal. Reg. VI. 234.

PRENTICE, EDWARD, Newton, s. of the sec. Thomas of the same, by
w. Sarah, d. of Humphrey Osland, who surv. him, had only Edward, b.
19 Nov. 1706, and d. 16 Sept. 1724. Near forty yrs. aft. the wid.
join. in deed with gr.ch. convey. the est. ENOS, Newton, br. of the
preced. perhaps youngest, by w. Lydia, had Ebenezer, b. 4 Nov. 1710,
and Jackson tells no more. HENRY, Cambridge 1640, was an orig.
propri. of Sudbury, freem. 1650, d. 9 June 1654. His first w. Eliz. d.
13 May 1643, and by sec. w. Joanna, he had Mary, b. 25 Nov. 1644;
Solomon, 23 Sept. 1646; Abiah, a d. 22 May 1648; Samuel, 3 Aug.
1650; Sarah; and Henry. His wid. m. 24 July 1662, John Gibson;
and Mary m. 8 Mar. 1664, Nathaniel Hancock. HENRY, Cambridge,
prob. s. of the preced. freem. 1684, by w. Mary, had Mary, wh. d. 2
May 1685; Mary, again, d. 11 Mar. 1686; Hannah, d. 3 June 1687;
Jonathan, d. 1 May 1688; and perhaps some that liv. JAMES, Cambridge, on that side wh. bec. Newton, may have been s. of Robert of
Roxbury, b. in Eng. by w. Susanna, d. of famous capt. Edward Johnson, had James, b. 11 Mar. 1656; Susanna, 29 June 1657; Hannah, 24
Apr. 1659; Eliz. 25 Aug. 1660; Sarah, 1662; and Rose; was freem.
1690, selectman, 1694, and d. 7 Mar. 1710, aged 81. The wid. and s.
James had admin. and he and the two next ch. are rememb. in gr.f.
Johnson's will in 1671. James sold his sh. in est. of his f. to the five
sis. all singlewomen, a designat. that could, I suppose, apply to no other
five, or four, or three, sis. of their age in N. E. JAMES, Newton, s. of
Thomas, the sec. of the same, m. 8 Mar. 1709, Eliz. d. of Henry Bart-
lett of Marlborough, had Robert, b. 19 Apr. 1714; James, 1 Mar.
1715; and Mary, 19 Nov. 1716; he liv. only to 1719, and his w. surv.
JOHN, New London, s. of Valentine, b. in Eng. brot. by his f. to Rox-
bury 1631; was a blacksmith, rem. from R. 1652; by w. Esther, had
John, b. 6 Aug. 1652; Joseph, 2 Apr. 1655, d. at 21 yrs.; Jonathan, 15
July 1657; Esther, 20 July 1660; Peter, 31 July 1663, d. at 7 yrs.;
Stephen, 26 Nov. or Dec. 1666; and the five last of these were brot. to
bapt. 19 Apr. 1668, at Roxbury, more than a hundred miles, as had the
first b. been 29 Sept. 1667, into the ch. there, the f. hav. been rec. 24
Sept. 1665. Other ch. he had, Mercy, b. Dec. 1668, d. at 21 yrs.;
Hannah, June 1672; Thomas and Eliz. tw. 6 Nov. 1675; and Valen-
tine, whose date is not found. He was a prosper. man, rep. 1668 and
70, owned shipping and cultiv. ld. m. 1685, sec. w. Rebecca, d. of Ralph
Parker, had Ralph, and d. a. 1691. Often the name appears Prents.
Esther m. Benadam or Benjamin Gallop; Hannah m. lieut. John Frink
of Stonington; and Eliz. d. unm. 13 Dec. 1770. JOHN, Newton, s. of

capt. Thomas of the same, m. 28 June 1677, Eliz. d. of the first Edward
Jackson, had no ch. and d. 4 Mar. 1689. His wid. m. 13 Nov. 1699,
Jonas Bond. JOHN, New London, mariner, s. of first John of the same,
in one of whose vessels he was part owner and master, m. Sarah, d. of
Matthew Jones of Boston, had Ann, Sarah, Patience, Eliz. and Irene,
wh. all m. but no s. Perhaps he was of Stratford 1701, and d. 21 Mar.
1715. JOHN, Newton, s. of the sec. Thomas, m. 1696, Hannah, d. of
Humphrey Osland, had Hannah, b. 25 Oct. 1697; Experience, 26 Sept.
1700; and Rebecca, 27 Mar. 1704; and his w. d. 2 May next. By sec.
w. Bethia, he had Eliz.; Bethia, 16 Aug. 1713; and Ann, 17 Nov.
1717; and he d. 4 Jan. 1721. JONATHAN, New London, s. of John the
first, m. Eliz. d. of Robert Latimer, whose elder sis. Sarah Jones had
m. his elder br. John. ROBERT, Roxbury, d. or was bur. 3 Feb. 1666,
and his inv. of 7th of the same, was giv. in by his br. capt. Thomas, on
26 Apr. foll. but I can find nothing of his time of coming, or whether
he had w. or ch. SAMUEL, Newton, s. of the sec. Thomas of the same,
m. Esther Hammond, had Samuel, b. 25 Nov. 1702; Praise, 26 Jan.
1705; and Mary, 12 Apr. 1708. SOLOMON, Cambridge, s. of Henry
the first, had two ws. Eliz. wh. d. bef. 1678, and Hepzibah, wh. surv.
him, and d. 15 Jan. 1742, in her 89th yr. He had Solomon, b. 1673;
Thomas, 7 June 1674; Stephen; Nathaniel; and others, most of them
prob. by sec. w. and d. 24 July 1719. *THOMAS, Cambridge, on S. side
of the riv. now Newton, brot. from Eng. w. Grace, and d. Grace, bapt.
there, had here Thomas and Eliz. tw. b. 22 Jan. 1650; Mary; John, 2
Feb. 1654, d. next yr.; John, again, 10 July 1655; and Hannah, 1661;
was freem. 1652; rep. 1672-4, in 1675, on the first day aft. Philip
began hostil. went to the war in comm. of a troop of horse, and with
great reput. serv. through it. His influence was great in obt. separat. of
Newton, in wh. his est. was. The w. d. 9 Oct. 1692, and he d. 6 July
1710 in 89th yr. Jackson assures us that the gr.-st. says 1709, and such
error is easily believ. Grace m. 27 Nov. 1667, Thomas Oliver; and
Eliz. m. 4 May 1675, Thomas Aldrich of Dedham. The epitaph that
in Homer's Hist. of N. is said to be on his gr.-st. belongs to somebody
else, lying 45 feet from the grave of the capt. whose head and foot stone
have plain inscript. as I am assur. by the highest N. authority. THOMAS,
Cambridge, in the part now Newton, prob. br. of James, possib. neph. of
the preced. b. in Eng. it is thot. m. Rebecca, d. of Edward Jackson, sen.
had Frances, Thomas, John, Edward, James, Ebenezer, Enos, Rebecca,
and Sarah, but unhap. no date is giv. for either, was freem. 1680, selectman in 1686, and sev. yrs. aft. and d. 11 Dec. 1724, at great age, perhaps above 90. Frances m. 13 Nov. 1687, Joseph Palmer of Stonington; and Sarah m. 15 May 1707, John Hyde. THOMAS, Newton, s. of

Thomas the first, m. 20 Mar. 1676, Sarah, d. of Thomas Stanton, had Thomas, b. 13 Jan. 1677; Grace; Samuel, a. 1680; and John, 1682, H. C. 1700, the min. of Lancaster; was freem. 1680, and d. 1684. His wid. m. William Denison of Stonington. THOMAS, Newton, s. of Thomas the sec. by w. Eliz. had John, b. Mar. 1692; Rebecca, 22 Dec. 1693; Thomas; and Ebenezer, 1706, and d. 11 Dec. 1724. VALEN-TINE, Roxbury, came in 1631, prob. with Eliot in the Lion, bring. w. Alice and s. John, hav. bur. one ch. at sea, as the ch. rec. tells, was freem. 7 Aug. 1632, perhaps had one ch. b. here, but d. prob. bef. the end of next yr. for the town rec. has it, that she m. 3 Apr. 1634, John Watson. One Alice P. wh. possib. was d. of his, d. at Concord, 8 Mar. 1644. Ellis, in his Hist. of R. quotes from the ch. rec. the ment. of his sufferings and d. closing with a clause that proves how variously our ancient MS. may be read, "leaving a good *cup of gentleness* behind him," when my version of the words in Italic is "SAVOR OF GODLI-NESS." VALENTINE, Woodbury, youngest s. of John of New London, m. Abigail, d. of the sec. Zechariah Walker, had John, bapt. Oct. 1710, d. at 5 yrs.; Esther, b. 16 May 1712, d. young; Joseph, 20 Jan. 1715; Esther, again, 2 May 1717; John, again, 1 Nov. 1719; Thomas, 9 May 1722, d. soon; Thomas, again, d. at 21 yrs.; Christopher, 13 Apr. 1726; Abigail, bapt. 17 Nov. 1728; and Patience, b. 7 July 1731. A portion of the descend. of Henry, change the two last letters for *ss*, but the distinct. was not, for the first hundred yrs. uniform, and Valentine's progeny always used these. In both forms, nineteen had been gr. in 1834 at Harv. four at Yale, and five at other N. E. coll. and of ten clerg. eight were of Harv. two of Yale.

PRESBURY, JOHN, Sandwich 1643, was bur. 19 May 1648. JOHN, Saco, in 1670 was constable there, d. 1679, leav. only ch. Nathaniel.

PRESCOTT, JAMES, Hampton, by w. Mary, d. of Nathaniel Boulter, had Joshua, b. 1 Mar. 1669; James, 1 Sept. 1671; Rebecca, 15 Apr. 1673; Jonathan, 6 Aug. 1675; Mary, 11 June 1677; Abigail and Tem-perance, tw. 1 Sept. 1679; John, 19 Nov. 1681; and Nathaniel, 1683. Rebecca m. 3 Dec. 1691, Nathaniel Sanborn; Mary m. 2 Nov. 1699, Jabez Colman; and Abigail m. Richard Bounds. Descend. in N. H. are num. He took the o. of alleg. 1678. JAMES, Hampton, sec. s. of the preced. m. 6 Mar. 1695, Mary, d. of William Marston, had Jere-miah, b. 8 Dec. 1695; Samuel, 14 Mar. 1697; Elisha, 18 Mar. 1699; Sarah, 20 Jan. 1701; Lucy, 6 Feb. 1703; Ebenezer, 3 Feb. 1705; James, 12 Dec. 1708; and Rebecca, 27 Feb. 1711. He took 2d w. 17 June 1746, wid. Abigail Sanborn. JOHN, Lancaster, blacksmith, came, a. 1640, as is said with w. Mary Platts (a Yorksh. girl, while he was b. in Lancash. but liv. at Sowerby in the parish of Halifax in the W.

riding of Yorkshire) and sev. ch. sat down first at Watertown, rem. 1645 or 6 to the foundat. of new sett. at L. Childr. were Mary, Sarah, Martha, and John, all suppos. to be b. bef. com. hither; Lydia, b. 15 Aug. 1641; Jonathan; and Jonas, June 1648; the last prob. the only one at L. Difficulty and loss in his cross. Sudbury riv. on his rem. is told by Winth. II. 306. He took o. of alleg. 1652, but was not adm. freem. bef. 1669; was with his fam. rem. shortly aft. the doleful day of 10 Feb. 1676, and the town was wholly abandon. for sev. yrs. so that no white man liv. betw. the towns on Conn. riv. and those of the Concord. In 1682 the number of fams. was not more than one third so large as seven yrs. bef. But of these, Prescott's was one, and the yr. assign. for his d. tho. with some hesit. is 1683. Mary m. Thomas Sawyer; Sarah m. Richard Wheeler; Martha m. John Rugg, and d. a. 1655; and Lydia m. 28 May 1658, Jonas Fairbanks. JOHN, Lancaster, s. of the preced. b. in. Eng. blacksmith, on the destruct. of the town, sett. at Concord, freem. 1679; by w. Sarah, had Mary; John, b. a. 1672; and Ebenezer, both of wh. perpet. the name. JOHN, Hampton, fourth s. of James the first, m. 5 Aug. 1701, Abigail, d. of James Marston, had John, b. 15 Aug. 1702; Rebecca, 10 Aug. 1704; Lydia, 20 Nov. 1706; Benjamin, 18 Sept. 1708; James, 11 Apr. 1711; Abigail, 29 Apr. 1713; Nathaniel, 25 July 1715; Abraham, 20 May 1717; Jedediah, 1 June 1719; and Josiah, 2 Oct. 1721. He d. 1740; and his wid. d. at Kingston, 14 Nov. 1762. JONAS, Groton, s. prob. youngest ch. of John the first, call. of Sudbury, when he took freeman's o. 1678, m. 5 Oct. 1669, Thankful Wheeler, as one acco. says, or 14 Dec. 1670, Mary, d. of John Looker, as ano. has it, had eight ds. wh. all m. and four s. and d. 13 Dec. 1723. The youngest of the s. Benjamin, b. 4 Jan. 1696, wh. d. 3 Aug. 1738, was f. of col. William, the command. at Bunker Hill, 17 June 1775, the f. of that disting. jurist, William, H. C. 1783, wh. was f. of the more disting. historian of Ferdinand and Isabella. *JONATHAN, Concord, br. of the preced. by first w. Dorothy, m. 3 Aug. 1670, wh. d. 8 Oct. 1674, had only Samuel, b. bef. he was driv. from Lancaster; by sec. w. Eliz. d. of John Hoar, wh. d. 25 Sept. 1687, had Jonathan, b. 5 Apr. 1677; Eliz. 27 Nov. 1678; Dorothy, 31 May 1681; John, 13 July 1683; Mary, 4 Aug. 1685; and Benjamin, 16 Sept. 1687, H. C. 1709, min. of Danvers; by third w. Rebecca, wid. of Hon. Peter Bulkely, whose d. Rebecca m. his s. Jonathan, and by fourth w. Ruth Brown wh. outliv. him, and d. 9 Feb. 1740, he had no ch. was capt. freem. 1690, and rep. 1692 at first Ct. under the new chart. and his day of d. is not kn. but he was on serv. Feb. 1707. JONATHAN, Hampton, third s. of James the first, by w. Eliz. had Jonathan, b. 16 July 1696; Jeremiah, 4 Oct. 1698; Benjamin, 2 Nov. 1700; Abigail, 28 Mar. 1703; Joseph, 27

Dec. 1705; and Mary, 8 Sept. 1709. JOSHUA, Hampton, eldest br. of the preced. had, by w. whose name is unkn. Joshua, Reuben, and Edward. NATHANIEL, Hampton, youngest br. of the preced. m. 30 Dec. 1702, Ann, d. of James Marston of H. wh. d. at Kingston, 30 Dec. 1761; and he d. 26 Feb. 1771 without ch. PETER, Salem, freem. 1682, liv. in the village that bec. Danvers, and had part in the troubles of Rev. Mr. Paris. He had m. 22 May 1679, Eliz. Redington. Of this name eighteen had been gr. at Harv. bef. 1829.

PRESSIE, JOHN, Salisbury, m. 4 Dec. 1663, Mary Gage, had John, b. 1 Oct. 1664; Mary, 30 Nov. 1665; and William, 2 June 1671; bef. Dec. 1677 was of Amesbury to take o. of alleg.

PRESTON, DANIEL, Dorchester, came from London in the Elizabeth and Ann, 1635, aged 13, s. of William, sent in Apr. as the f. would follow in few mos. freem. 1665, by w. Mary, had Mary, b. a. 1645; and Daniel, 7 Oct. 1649; was chos. selectman 1675 and oft. aft. deac. and d. 10 or 12 Nov. 1707, aged 85. Mary m. 28 May 1662, Eleazer Fawer. DANIEL, Dorchester, s. of the preced. freem. 1690, was rul. Elder, had Mary, b. 1 Sept. 1675; John; Remember, 4 Nov, 1678; Abigail; Deliverance; Eliz. 5 Jan. 1687; Daniel, 15 Aug. 1689, d. soon; Relief, d. soon; Daniel, again, Dec. 1693; and d. 13 Mar. 1726 in 77th yr. His w. Abigail, d. of John Jackson of Cambridge, d. 24 Apr. 1723 in 75th yr. EDWARD, New Haven, prob. s. of William, may have been tw. br. of Daniel, sent over by his f. in the Christian, the first sh. from London in that yr. 1635, aged 13, to prepare, no doubt, for his foll. perhaps had relat. in Dorchester, or other place neighb. to Boston where all the vessels came; and aft. the f. and his fam. went off to N. H. may have cont. in this quarter, certain. in 1643, 4, and 5 was of Conn. not N. H. and at Boston, by w. Margaret, had William, b. 30 Jan. 1652; Mary, 1 Jan. 1654; Eliz. 1655; and perhaps others; was a propr. 1685. ELIASAPH, Stratford 1669, s. of William of New Haven, had perhaps liv. there some yrs. as he was then made freem. rem. to Wallingford, m. Eliz. eldest d. of John Beach of W. there was the first deac. and d. 1705, aged a. 70, said the exagger. of the new comers, when he was only 62. HACKALIAH, Woodbury, tw. br. of the preced. if Cothren, as seems almost certain, be corr. m. 20 Apr. 1676, Emma, d. of Thomas Fairchild of Stratford, had William, b. 21 Mar. 1677; Hannah, bapt. Aug. 1680; Lydia, Nov. 1682; Sarah, Nov. 1683; Jehiel, Oct. 1686; Emma, Mar. 1688; and Remember, Oct. 1691. He d. 20 Nov. 1692; and his wid. d. Feb. 1733. *JEHIEL, Stratford, may be br. of the preced. had Samuel, b. 1663, selectman, 1669, rep. 1676. JOHN, Boston, m. 28 May 1661, Susanna, wid. of Robert Read of Hampton, was liv. 1668, but Farmer ment. a JOHN of Boston, d. 6 June 1663. JOHN,

Hadley, had gone as a soldier in Turner's comp. from the E. part of the Col. in Philip's war early in Apr. 1676, was in the Falls fight of May, in 1678 m. Sarah Gardner, perhaps d. of Samuel, had eight ch. all of wh. d. under age, exc. John, b. 1686; and Sarah, 1693. JOHN, Andover, by w. Sarah, had John, and Thomas, tw. wh. d. 17 and 18 Mar. 1691, prob. soon after b. and John, again, wh. d. 17 June 1699, and perhaps others. JOSEPH, New Haven, a propr. 1685, may have been gr.s. of William, tho. it may not be kn. wh. s. was his f. or he may have been a resid. much earlier, and h. of that Mary wh. had there bapt. Hackaliah and Eliasaph, tw. 9 Apr. 1643; Joseph, 24 Jan. 1647; Mary, and Sarah, not perhaps tw. 24 July 1664. ROBERT, New Haven 1646, had been serv. of Richard Church, was single, when he made his will, 1648, in wh. no ment. of any relat. of his name is to be seen. ROGER, Ipswich 1648, a tanner, came in the Elizabeth from London 1635, aged 21, d. perhaps at Lynn, 20 Jan. 1666. SAMUEL, Andover, m. 27 May 1672, Susanna Gutterson, and tho. her d. is not ment. the same man, m. 2 Apr. 1694, Sarah Bridges. At Andover is rec. the m. of Nicholas Holt, 21 May 1666, with "wid. Preston," wh. may have been mo. of Samuel, but wh. was his f. is beyond my kn. THOMAS, Danvers, then call. Salem vill. freem. 1690, had m. 15 Apr. 1669, Rebecca, d. of Francis Nurse, had Rebecca, b. 12 May 1670; Mary, 15 Feb. 1672; John, 20 Nov. 1673; and Martha, 21 Oct. 1676; and he d. 1697. His w. was d. of that sad Rebecca, execut. as a witch; and his only s. John was early lost on a fishing voyage. WILLIAM, Dorchester 1635, came in the Truelove, the latest of seventeen sh. from London to Boston that yr. aged 44, with w. Mary, 34, and four ch. Eliz. 11; Sarah, 8; Mary, 6; and John, 3; rem. to New Haven in season to be among first subscr. of the compact, 1639; and there had Jehiel, bapt. 14 June 1640; Hackaliah, and Eliasaph, tw. 9 Apr. 1643; and Joseph, 24 Jan. 1647. I suppose the mo. of these latter ch. was a d. of Robert Seabrook, wh. gave his gr.s. Jehiel P. and Thomas Fairchild, jr. his home lot. He prob. d. not long after date of his will, 9 July 1647, in wh. he speaks of childr. of the first and sec. w. but does not enable us to disting. them, and by conject. I should make of the ch. brot. from Eng. the greater part if not all by first w. three s. and three ds. Edward, Daniel, John, Eliz. Sarah, and Mary; but of the ds. refers to one as w. of Joseph Alsop, prob. Eliz. to ano. as w. of William Meekes or Mix, prob. Sarah; and we, therefore, may well suppose that Mary was then unm. He owned est. in Giggleswick, Co. York, in the most W. part of the W. Riding. In that parish of the hill country were b. the parents of the celebr. William Paley, and of its high sch. his f. was master. Sev. towns in Eng. are call. Preston; and out of nine persons of this name gr. in 1830 at N. E. coll. three were of Yale and one of Harv.

PRETIOUS, or PRETIOSE, CHARLES, Boston, blacksmith or nailer, m. 17 Nov. 1653, Rebecca Martin, had Mary, b. 16 May 1654; and I hear of him no more, exc. as one of the debtors 1655 to est. of Joshua Foote in Geneal. Reg. IX. 137, there pervert. to Presus.

PRICE, DAVID, Dorchester, freem. 7 Dec. 1636. JAMES, Watertown, s. of William of the same, by w. Sarah, had Josiah, b. 30 Mar. 1706; Mindwell, 27 June 1708; and Abigail, 3 July 1719; and d. 4 Mar. 1756, in that part of W. now Weston. The name is oft. spell. Priest. *JOHN, Salem, s. of Walter of the same, m. Jan. 1674, Sarah, d. of Henry Wolcott of Windsor, had only s. Walter, b. 17 May 1676, H. C. 1695; was freem. 1677, rep. 1679 and aft. the revo. 1689, d. 13 Aug. 1691, and his wid. d. 1698 in her 49th yr. The s. Walter was a man of distinct. capt. in the col. service 1708. JOHN is the name of a soldier in Gallop's comp. 1690, but resid. is unkn. JOHN, Watertown, br. of James, may have sett. Bond thinks, at Lancaster. JOSEPH, Salem, k. by the Ind. 15 Dec. 1675, in the Narraganset fight, says Felt II. 505; but whose s. he was is not told; yet possib. of Walter. JOSEPH, Watertown, br. of James, m. 25 Dec. 1701, Margaret, d. of Richard Child, had Margaret, b. 3 Oct. 1702; Joseph, 4 Sept. 1704; Hannah, 20 Mar. 1707; John, 9 Dec. 1711; Joshua; James; Mehitable, 18 May 1719; and Jonas, bapt. 20 Nov. 1726; and d. 28 Apr. 1756. MATTHEW, Charlestown 1654, of wh. I kn. only that by w. Eliz. he had Joseph, b. 23 Mar. 1656, and he was a householder in 1658. Perhaps he was of Salem 1668 to sign memorial against impost with Walter and sons. ‖ RICHARD, Boston, ar. co. 1658, m. 18 Aug. 1659, Eliz. Cromwell, d. of Thomas, the prosperous privateersman, had Thomas, b. 22 July 1660; Joyliffe, 2 Mar. 1662; Eliz. 10 Feb. 1664; and Richard, 26 Mar. 1667, was freem. with prefix of respect, 1664. RICHARD, Boston, m. 6 May 1662, Grace, d. of Gamaliel Waite, had Ebenezer, b. 6 Apr. 1663; and Richard, 9 Apr. 1664. ROBERT, Northampton, had Sarah, b. 1678; Mary, 1681; Eliz. 1683; and John, 1689; rem. to Deerfield, and thence, again, 1715. THEODORE, Salem, eldest s. of Walter, m. 1 Aug. 1667, Ann Wood, had Eliz. b. 19 Jan. 1670; and Ann, 23 July 1671, in wh. yr. he was lost at sea. His inv. was taken 10 Apr. foll. His wid. m. 12 Nov. 1673, Dudley Bradstreet of Andover; and Eliz. m. 14 Dec. 1686, rev. Thomas Barnard of the same. *WALTER, Salem 1641, merch. from Bristol, Eng. brot. w. Eliz. and 6 Mar. of next yr. they unit. with the ch. freem. 27 Dec. 1642, had Eliz. bapt. 13 Mar. 1642; Theodore, Nov. 1643; John, 11 Jan. 1646; Hannah, 30 Jan. 1648; William, 24 Mar. 1650; Samuel, 12 Mar. 1654; and Walter, 16

Mar. 1656; was highly esteem. rep. 1665, and d. 5 June 1674, aged 61; yet Coffin says he was b. 16 May 1620. His will, made 21 May preced. names w. Eliz. and s. John, excors. ment. s. William, gr.ch. Eliz. and Ann P. Eliz. and John Croade, ds. Eliz. Ruck, Hannah Veren, and Ann Bradstreet, but this last was not his own ch. but had been wid. of his s. Theodore. His wid. d. 11 Nov. 1688, aged 73. Of Samuel I hear nothing. Besides Theodore, William and Walter were lost at sea. Eliz. m. 17 Mar. 1659, John Croade, and next John Ruck, misprint. Burke, in Essex Inst. Hist. Coll. II. 127; and Hannah, m. 4 May 1670, Hilliard Veren. WILLIAM, Watertown, m. 9 Apr. 1657, Mary Marplehead, had William, b. 4 May 1658; Matthew, 16 Apr. 1660; Mary, 8 Nov. 1662; John, 18 Mar. 1665; Sarah, 27 Sept. 1667; Benjamin, 22 Feb. 1670; Grace, 1 Aug. 1672; James, 15 Mar. 1675; Joseph, 2 Nov. 1677; Eliz. 20 Mar. 1680; and Hannah; and he d. 30 Oct. 1685. His will made five days bef. was pro. 15 Dec. foll. It nam. w. and s. John, excors. Hannah m. 24 Dec. 1702, Thomas Sanderson. Sometimes his name appears Priest. WILLIAM, Groton, eldest s. of the preced. of wh. Bond could tell no more, but that he sat down on ld. at G. belong. to his f.

‖ PRICHARD, or PRITCHARD, BENJAMIN, Milford, 1713, may have been s. of Roger. *‖ HUGH, Gloucester 1641–45, rem. to Roxbury, freem. 18 May 1642, had, by w. Elinor, Abigail, a d. acc. the town rec. but as I read the ch. rec. s. Abiel, bapt. 26 Dec. 1641; Zebediah, b. 17, bapt. 22 Oct. 1643, prob. d. soon; Phebe, bapt. 20 Oct. 1644, in ch. rec. call. a d. very naturally, but in the town rec. acc. to old rec. s. b. 13 Oct. without a name; and a ch. without name, bur. 10 May 1649; was of ar. co. 1643, rep. 1643, 4, and 9, capt. 1647, and went home, prob. in 1650. In giv. deed of his est. some yrs later, his attys. describe him as of Broughton, Denbighsh. wh. perhaps was the place of his nativity. Bef. the gen. introd. of surnames, the progenit. of this fam. would be represent. ap Richard, i. e. s. of Richard. JOHN, Topsfield, s. perhaps of William, was freem. 1686. JOSEPH, Milford, perhaps s. of Roger, d. a. 1676. NATHANIEL, Springfield, s. of Roger, m. 4 Feb. 1652, Hannah, d. of George Langton, wh. d. 1690, and he m. 1691, Hannah, wid. of Samuel Davis of Northampton, and rem. from S. RICHARD, Yarmouth 1643, was with w. Ann and d. Templer, adm. 29 July 1660 of the ch. at Charlestown, d. 8 Mar. 1669 at great age. His will of 22 Jan. preced. names w. Margery, d. Hannah, w. of Richard Templer, wh. was made extrix. and her ch. James, Samuel, and Deborah, gr.ch. Hannah, w. of Alexander Stewart; and her ch. James, and John; beside Richard, s. of Richard Taylor; perhaps ano. gr.ch. and possib. it was meant Templer. ROGER, Springfield 1643, freem. 13 Apr. 1648. His w. Frances d. 1651, and he rem. 1653 to Milford, m. 18 Dec. in that yr. Eliz. wid. of William Slough, d. of James Prudden, rem. thence to New Haven, there d. 1671. Alice, perhaps his d. at S. m. 18 Feb. 1645, William Bradlee of New Haven; and Joan, perhaps ano. d. m. at N. H. 1 Sept. 1647, John Lumbard of S. WILLIAM, Lynn 1645, Ipswich in 1648, bec. one of the first sett. of Brookfield, was clk. of the writs, had William, John, Joseph, and Samuel, was serg. of the mil. and with s. Samuel, at the same time that Edward Hutchinson fell, was k. by the Ind. 3 Aug. 1675. Oft. the serg.'s name is call. Joseph; it is not ment. in Wheeler's Narr. and by Coffin, 389, in a list almost offic. he is John. Inv. of his est. in Mar. 1676, is found; and Nov. 1690, John of Topsfield, and Joseph of Amesbury convey. to their br. William the est. at B. wh. was of their f. and br. Samuel, dec. WILLIAM, Suffield, s. of the preced. had two ws. nam. Eliz. and a third Rebecca, wh. in Feb. 1698 had admin. of his est. His three ch. William, b. 1684; Eliz. 1690; and William, again, 1691, all d. young.

PRIDE, JOHN, Salem 1637, there had a gr. of ld. was a brickmaker in 1641, d. a. 1647. JOHN, Pemaquid, wh. took o. of fidel. to Mass. 22 July 1674, may have been. s. of the preced.

PRIEST, DEGORY, Plymouth 1620, d. in few days aft. land. from the Mayflower, on 1 Jan. 1621; and his w. wh. was, says Gov. Bradford, sis. of Mr. Allerton, and their childr. came after. He was formerly thot. the first m. of any of the Leyden exiles, but the rec. there shows that his intent was pub. 4 Oct. 1611, and the m. with Sarah Vincent, wid. of John of London, 4 Nov. foll. and we kn. that both Isaac Allerton and his sis. had a few wks. earlier been m. I obs. on the Dutch rec. that aft. hear. of the d. of Priest so early at P. his wid. m. 13 Nov. of that same yr. one, wh. was, in my opin. the Cuthbert Cuthbertson, wh. brot. her and the ch. in the Ann. He had been adm. a cit. of Leyden 16 Nov. 1615, then call. a hatter, no other of his friends exc. Bradford and Allerton hav. enjoy. that distinct. EMANUEL, Marblehead 1668, kn. only as sign. with JOHN, perhaps his br. against impost. JAMES, Weymouth, freem. 10 May 1643, and tho. twice insert. in the list, we may be confid. as the same carelessness attaches to two other names, that only one man is intend. had James, b. 8 May 1640; and by w. Eliz. had Lydia, b. 12 Feb. 1658, d. young; and Lydia, again, 16 Mar. 1662; and d. at Salem, 1664. JOHN, Weymouth 1657. JOHN, Salem, m. 25 Feb. 1673, Eliz. Gray, had Eliz. b. 20 Jan. 1680. JOHN, Woburn, had Eliz. b. 12 Sept. 1679; John, 1 Nov. 1681; Daniel (Bond, 911, has Hannah) 19 July 1686; and perhaps others. WILLIAM, Watertown 1672, perhaps by w. Leah had William, wh. d. 3 Dec. 1688;

and William, again, b. 7 Nov. 1689. But Bond leaves it in no doubt that the name was Price, wh. see.

PRIME, JAMES, Milford a. 1654, propound. for freem. in 1669, and d. 1685, leav. wid. s. James, d. Sarah, w. of Thomas Prior, and Rebecca, wh. m. 1 Apr. 1677, Walter Smith. Among proprs. in 1713 was JAMES, s. of the preced. wh. had s. James and other ch. and perhaps Ebenezer, Y. C. 1718, min. of Huntington, L. I. wh. d. 1779, aged 79, was ano. MARK, Rowley 1643, by w. Ann had Samuel, b. 1649. SAMUEL, Rowley, s. of the preced. by w. Sarah had Samuel, b. 1675; Mark, 1680; and tw ds.

PRIMIDAYS. See Pringrydays.

PRINCE, ISAAC, Hull 1675, s. of John, of wh. we have no later knowledge than Deane gives, that he m. a. 1683, Mary, d. of John Turner. JOHN, Hull, was perhaps of Cambridge, or more prob. of Watertown, when freem. 4 Mar. 1635, s. of Rev. John, wh. had been bred at Oxford, and was min. of East Shefford, oft. called Little Shefford, a few miles from Newbury, in Co. Berks, prob. rem. to H. bef. b. of any ch. of wh. he had prob. by w. Margaret, John, b. 1638, d. 1690; Eliz. 1640; Joseph, 1642; Martha, 1645; Job, 1647; Mary, 8 Apr. 1649, says rec.; Samuel, at Boston, May 1649, says tradit.; Sarah, 1651, d. soon; Benjamin, 1652, wh. prob. d. young; Isaac, 1655; Deborah, 25 Aug. 1657; and Thomas; he took sec. w. Ann, wid. of William Barstow, was rul. eld. and d. 6 Aug. 1676, aged 66. His will of 9 May preced. names only eight ch. JOSEPH, Hull, s. of the preced. m. 7 Dec. 1670, Joanna, d. of Secretary Morton. NATHANIEL, Salem, in 1664 was of the selectmen. RICHARD, Salem 1639, a tailor, freem. 27 Dec. 1642, had there bapt. John, 20 Feb. 1642; Joseph, 10 Sept. 1643; Mary, 16 Apr. 1648; Samuel, 18 May 1651; Richard, 18 Mar. 1655; and Jonathan, 15 Mar. 1657; perhaps by w. Mary, a mem. of the ch. 1648, all exc. first two; was a deac. and d. 1675, aged 61. From his will of 21 Sept. pro. 22 Dec. foll. in that yr. we find all the ch. exc. the first b. were liv. and Mary had m. Stephen Daniel, had Stephen and Mary. RICHARD, Salem, s. of the preced. m. 25 Dec. 1677, Sarah Rix, had Richard, b. 21 Jan. 1679; Joseph, 28 Dec. 1680, wh. d. under 17 yrs.; and John, 15 Nov. 1682. ROBERT, Salem, may have been br. of the first Richard, and Felt says had gr. of ld. 1649. He m. 5 Apr. 1662, Sarah Warren, had James, b. 19 Jan. 1665, d. soon; James, again, 15 Aug. 1668; Eliz. 19 Feb. 1670; and Joseph; and d. 4 June 1674. His will of 24 May 1674, pro. 30 of next mo. made his w. extrix. and names ch. James, Joseph, and Eliz. His est. was good. *SAMUEL, Hull, s. of John, freem. 1678, rem. to Rochester, or Middleborough, of wh. he was rep. aft. the new chart. of 1692; m. 1674, Martha, d. of

William Barstow of Scituate, had three s. and two ds. of neither of wh. do I find the names. His w. d. 18 Dec. 1684, and by sec. Mary, d. of Gov. Hinckley, wh. d. 22 Oct. 1658, was f. of Rev. Thomas, b. May 1687, H. C. 1707, the assid. annalist, whose service in perpet. evidence relative to our early hist. exceeds that of any other man, since the first generat. Of written or printed matter he was a useful expounder; but the great delineator of our literary men, half a centu. ago, has well cautioned us against his credulity. See Eliot's Biog. Dict. He was also f. of Nathan, H. C. 1718, a man of talents super. to his bro.'s but of less value to society. THOMAS, Gloucester 1649, by w. Margaret had Thomas, b. 24 Dec. 1650; John, 1653; Mary, 1658; and Isaac, 7 Nov. 1663. Babson, 129, says his wid. d. 24 Feb. 1706. THOMAS, Gloucester, eldest s. of the preced. m. 27 Sept. 1676, Eliz. Harraden, and had Mary, b. 6 Dec. 1677; and Thomas, 8 Dec. 1679; beside John and Isaac, wh. surv. him; and he d. 11 Jan. 1705. THOMAS, Scituate, s. of John, m. in 1685, Ruth, d. of John Turner, had Thomas, b. 10 July 1686; Benjamin, 1693; and Job, 1695. WILLIAM, Dover 1671. One Mary P. a Quaker, came in the Speedwell, 1656, but of her no more is kn. than Hutch. I. 197 tells of her denounc. judgm. of God, from her window in the prison, against Gov. Endicott, as he went by, on Sunday, from the ch. Twice she was taken to his house, where two min. were present; and tho. I fear she suffer. worse correction than from their mouths, yet the virulence of their affections did not perhaps go beyond her banishm. Eleven of this name had, in 1834, been gr. at Harv. one at Yale, and two at other N. E. coll.

PRINDLE, JOHN, Milford 1645. Possib. the name is the same as that foll.

PRINGLE, WILLIAM, New Haven, m. 1655, Mary Desbrough, had Phebe, b. 1657; John, 1658; Mary, 1660; and perhaps others; was a propr. 1685, and so was JOSEPH, wh. may have been a s. This is now changed to Prindle, it is said.

PRINGRYDAY'S, or PRIMIDAYES, as giv. in Geneal. Reg. IX. 87, or PRIMRIDES, as by Rev. Mr. Russell in Coffin's Newbury, 390, ED-MUND, Springfield, m. 1666, Mary, d. of Miles Morgan; in the assault by the Ind. when they burned the town, 5 Oct. 1675, he was wound. and d. on 11 of the same, leav. no ch. His wid. m. 1678, Nicholas Rust.

PRIOR, or PRYOR, DANIEL, Duxbury, s. of Thomas, came late in 1635, from London, in the Hopewell, capt. Babb, aged 13, had w. Mary, and liv. at Scituate. DANIEL, Windsor, s. of Humphrey, m. 9 Feb. 1693, Sarah Eggleston, d. of Samuel of Middletown, had Sarah, b. 4 Mar. 1694. EDWARD, Kennebeck 1665. HUMPHREY, Windsor, m. 12

Nov. 1663, Ann, d. of John Osborn, had John, b. 14 Feb. 1665; and
Daniel, 18 Dec. 1667; and his w. d. bef. her f. JOHN, Scituate, br. of
Daniel, came from London with him, at the age of 15, rem. to Duxbury,
and Winsor says, in his old age, m. Eleanor Childs. JOHN, Windsor,
eldest s. of Humphrey, had Ann, b. 31 Mar. 1690; Mary, 6 Mar.
1692; and John, 16 May 1695. JOSEPH, Duxbury, br. of first John,
liv. with Rev. Ralph Partridge, when the min. made his will, 1655.
MATTHEW, Salem 1638, when he had gr. of ld. rem. to L. I. and was
of Brookhaven in 1665. His d. Sarah m. John Gould of Newport, and
next, 1711, bec. fourth w. of Gov. Walter Clark. THOMAS, Scituate,
came in 1634 from London, with Lothrop, d. 1639, bur. says Lothrop,
22 June; in his will of June in that yr. names s. Samuel, and Thomas,
ds. Eliz. and Mary, all in O. E. and his three s. here, bef. ment.

PROCTOR, BENJAMIN, Ipswich 1678, prob. s. of the first John.
GEORGE, Dorchester, freem. 17 May 1637, by w. Edith had Hannah,
b. perhaps in Eng.; Abigail, b. 24 Aug. 1637; Thomas, 16 Dec. 1638,
if we may dare to contradict the rec. wh. is 1637, or it has been thot.
that the 1637 day was that of his bur. and he may have been brot. from
Eng.; Samuel, 8 Nov. 1640; and d. 29 Jan. 1662. His wid. rem. to
Boston to live with s. Samuel, made excor. with her of the will of 27
Jan. 1662, as in Geneal. Reg. XI. 173, 4. Hannah m. 3 Mar. 1653,
John Lowell; and Abigail m. 8 Mar. 1660, Joseph Lowell of Boston.
JOHN, Ipswich, came, 1635, aged 40, from London, in the Susan and
Ellen, with w. Martha, 28; and ch. John, 3; and Mary, 1; and in few
yrs. was sett. at Salem. His w. d. 13 June 1659; but he took sec. w.
of the same bapt. name, wh. outliv. him. His will of 28 Aug. 1672,
pro. 28 Nov. foll. names w. and ch. John, Joseph, Benjamin, ds. Martha
White, Abigail Varney; Sarah Dodge; and Hannah Weeden, or some
such name. JOHN, Ipswich, s. of the preced. b. in Eng. rem. in few yrs.
to Salem, perhaps freem. 1690, m. Dec. 1662, Eliz. d. of John Thorndike, had prob. by a sec. w. Eliz. Bassett, m. 1 Apr. 1674, William, b.
6 Feb. foll.; Sarah, 28 Jan. 1677; Samuel, 11 Jan. 1686; Elisha, 28
Apr. 1687, d. next yr.; and Abigail, 27 Jan. 1692; of wh. the eldest
two were imprison. in the execrable fanaticism of 1692. These ch.
were prob. discharg. without trial; but the mo. was one of the first
accus. of witchcr. and her h. (to wh. the first w. had brot. ch. Martha, b. 4 June 1666; Mary, 26 Oct. 1667, d. soon; John, 28 Oct.
1668; Mary, again, 30 Jan. 1670; and Thorndike, 15 July 1672, and
that w. d. next mo.), for showing proper regard for her, as Hutch. II. 26
and 55 tells, fell under equal suspicion. Both were tried and condemn.
on 5th, and on him, 19 Aug. was inflict. the punishm. of death, wh. she
escap. by reason of her pregnancy, and bef. the time elaps. in wh. she

should have suffer. the power of delusion and the devil passed away. Yet four yrs. later, the wid. had to beseech the legislat. to order relief of her husband's prop. from the forfeiture. See Felt II. 484. Too brief is this statement of Mr. Felt, and slightly seems the case to have been misapprehend. by him. No doubt, Gedney, the judge of Probate, was as much bound to maintain the technical law of Eng. in opposition to that of humanity, as his superiors of the other tribunal to assert the institute of Moses against that of common sense; and she "being convict. and sentenc. of and for the detestab. crime of witchcr." was "look. upon as d.-in-law, and left out of the will of her h. and nothing giv. her therein, nor order. her upon the distrib. of the est. of said P." and the Ct. had the requisite illumina. to decree, that when she produc. the pardon she bec. alive again. The h.'s will was made 2 Aug. so three days bef. the conviction. JOSEPH, Ipswich, m. Martha, d. of Francis Wainwright, had Daniel, b. 30 Jan. 1680. PETER, Concord, s. of Robert, m. 30 Jan. 1689, Mary, d. of James Patterson of Billerica. RICHARD, Yarmouth 1643. RICHARD, Boston, freem. 1690. ROBERT, Concord, freem. 10 May 1643, m. Dec. 1645, Jane Hildreth, perhaps d. of Richard, had Sarah, b. 12 Oct. 1646; Gershom, 13 May 1648; Mary, 8 Apr. 1650; rem. to Chelmsford, had Peter; Eliz. 21 Jan. 1657; and Lydia, 19 Feb. 1660, d. at 6 mos. SAMUEL, Dorchester, s. of George, a cooper at Boston, by w. Mary had Mary, b. 22 Dec. 1671. THORNDIKE, Salem, s. of sec. John, by w. Hannah had Nathan, b. 18 Oct. 1698. Of this name in 1834, four had been gr. at Harv. one at Yale. and four at other N. E. coll.

PROSSER, ROGER, Boston 1672, bought 500 acres at Quinebaug. THOMAS, Roxbury 1649, perhaps next yr. was of Weymouth.

PROUSE, JOHN, Salisbury, by w. Hannah, perhaps d. of William Barnes, had Abigail, b. 18 Dec. 1666; was there liv. 1680. ROGER, Boston, by w. Hannah, had Peter, b. 1 May 1686.

PROUT, *EBENEZER, Concord, s. of Timothy, was a capt. and rep. 1689 and 90, and clk. of the house, was freem. 1690, m. 1678, Eliz. d. of capt. Timothy Wheeler, had Timothy. His w. d. at Charlestown, 11 Oct. 1683; and by sec. w. Grace at Watertown, had Eunice, bapt. 13 Apr. 1690; Mary, b. Apr. 1694, d. soon; John, 6 Nov. 1695, d. young; was town clk. selectman, rep. 1693. JOHN, New Haven, s. of Timothy of Boston, m. 23 Aug. 1681, Mary, wid. of Daniel Hall, d. of Henry Rutherford, propr. in 1685 with prefix of respect; had Margaret, b. 7 June 1682; Sarah, 7 Jan. 1684; John; and Mary, wh. m. 1 Sept. 1708, John Dixwell, s. of the regicide, a ruling elder at Boston, where she d. 1718. JOSEPH, Boston, br. of Ebenezer, was selectman, treasr. and many yrs. town clk. to whose careful rec. we owe much; by his will of 22 Sept. 1719, we find his w. Mary Jackson, m. 7 Nov. 1704, and Joseph, then youth, his only ch. He d. 13 Jan. 1721, aged 70. His ch. were Samuel, b. 31 Jan. 1706, d. soon; Joseph, 9 Aug. 1707; and Benjamin, 24 Sept. 1709, d. soon. * TIMOTHY, Boston, shipwright, an early inhab. adm. of the ch. 20 Apr. and freem. 29 May 1644, by w. Margaret had Timothy, b. 10, bapt. 23 Mar. 1645; Susanna, 26 Apr. bapt. 2 May 1647; John, bapt. 11 Feb. 1649, a. 8 days old; Joseph, a. 1651; William, b. 23, bapt. 29 May 1653; Benjamin, 16, bapt. 22 July 1655, wh. d. 5 Apr. 1669; Ebenezer, bef. ment. 14, bapt. 15 Mar. 1657; was rep. for sev. yrs. 1685, 9–92, and d. 3 Nov. 1702. His sec. w. Eliz. d. 19 Jan. 1694, and his will, pro. 17 Dec. foll. tho. made 7 Mar. 1699, ment. s. Timothy as long. abs. prob. d.; John; Joseph, made excor.; William; and Ebenezer; beside gr.ch. and gr.gr.childr. without names. He bec. prop. at Concord bef. 1680, and perhaps sometimes resid. there. TIMOTHY, Boston, s. of the preced. by w. Deborah had Timothy, b. 6 July 1666; Zechariah, 20 Mar. 1670; and Margaret, 11 Nov. 1674; in 1676 had striking peril in shipwreck, being master mariner, but with all his crew, after great hardships was saved, as in Hubbard, 643, may be read; and was prob. lost at a much later day. His wid. d. 13 Mar. 1716. WILLIAM, Boston, br. of the preced. by w. Love had Samuel, b. 16 Sept. 1673, and prob. d. early.

PROUTY, EDWARD, Scituate, eldest s. of Richard, by w. Eliz. Howe, had James, John, Richard, Edward, and Elisha, betw. 1711 and 1732, beside, unless Deane be mistaken, Jacob, David, Adam, and Isaac, prob. older, wh. he says, rem. to Spencer. ISAAC, Scituate, br. of the preced. m. Eliz. Merritt, had David, John, Caleb, Adam, Job, James, and Isaac, as Deane says, b. betw. 1716 and 1732. RICHARD, Scituate 1670, beside the two preced. had s. William wh. left descend. and d. Margaret, wh. d. unm. at gr. age. Descend. are num.

PROVENDER, JOHN, Charlestown, took the o. of fidel. 2 Dec. 1674.

PRUDDEN, JAMES, Milford 1639, perhaps br. of Peter, d. 1648. His d. Ann m. Samuel Coley a. 1640; and Eliz. m. William Slough. JOHN, Jamaica, L. I. s. of Peter, sett. in 1670 as min. there, rem. in 1692 to Newark, N. J. but resign. his charge 1699, and d. 11 Dec. 1725 in his 80th year. He left descend. Eliot says. PETER, Milford, arr. with famous Davenport at Boston, and at New Haven spent some time next yr. and the foll. where was gather. the ch. of M. over wh. he was sett. 18 Apr. 1640, and d. July 1656, in 56th yr. Was he ever of Wethersfield, as the diligent writer in Geneal. Reg. XI. 102 says? Mather says, he had been a successf. preacher a. Herefordsh. and near Wales; but caution is useful in receiv. the word of M. We kn. nothing of his parentage or educ. He left good est. here, beside his lds. at

Edgton in Co. York, where perhaps he was b. and certain. there m.
Joanna Boyse. We must look to Trumbull's Hist. of Conn. for not
much. He had six ds. and two s. John, bapt. 1646, H. C. 1668; and
Samuel, the eldest s. wh. prob. was the propr. at M. 1713; beside Peter,
bapt. 1652, d. soon. His wid. Joanna, wh. had m. 19 Sept. 1671, capt.
Thomas Willet, and next Rev. John Bishop, in her will of 8 Nov.
1681, names the s. and five ds. Joanna, bapt. 1640; Eliz. 4 Mar.
1643; Abigail, 1647; Sarah, 12 May 1650; and Mildred, 14 May
1653; beside Mary Walker, her d. dec. whose portion was to go to two
ch. Abigail, m. 14 Nov. 1667, Joseph Walker; Mildred m. 20 Sept.
1671, Sylvanus Baldwin; but what was the bapt. name of the h. of
Mary is yet unseen. SAMUEL, Milford, eldest s. of the preced. m. 30
Dec. 1669, Grace Judson, d. of Joseph of Stratford, had Peter, b. 28
July 1671; Samuel, 14 Aug. 1673; Joanna, bapt. 1676; and in 1685,
aft. his d. it is seen that he had Peter and four other ch. in the care of
their mo.

PUDEATER, JACOB, Salem, m. 28 Oct. 1666, Isabel Mosier, wh. d. 3
Mar. 1677, and took sec. w. Nothing is ment. of him, exc. that his wid.
Ann, was one of those innocents chged. with the preposter. offence of
witchcr. in May 1692, shut up in Boston gaol, at the same time with
Philip English and his w. tried in Sept. and with seven others execut.
on 22. See Felt II. 477–80; Essex Inst. II. 187, 8; and Hutch.
II. 58.

PUDINGTON, or PUDDINGTON, GEORGE, York 1640. Maine Hist.
Coll. I. 273, and 1 Mass. Hist. Coll. I. 101. A wid. P. I find in the
rec. of that jurisdict. 1649, licensed to sell wine. JOHN, Portsmouth
1654. Adams, 40. He may have been of York, 1680, when he sw.
alleg. and lieut. in comm. of fort, 1689, at Kennebeck. 3 Mass. Hist.
Coll. I. 86. ROBERT, Portsmouth 1640. Belkn. I. 28. Prob. it was
the same man at Newtown, L. I. 1656. See Riker, 43. But he own.
est. at P. 1660.

PUDNEY, JOHN, Salem, m. 18 Nov. 1662, Judith, d. of Henry Cooke
of the same, had John, b. 28 Sept. foll.; Judith, 24 Nov. 1665; Joanna,
29 June 1668; Samuel, 13 Oct. 1670; Joseph, 25 Aug. 1673; and
Jonathan, 18 Mar. 1678. JOHN. Salem, eldest s. of the preced. m. 1
Jan. 1684, Mary, d. of Hugh Jones, had John, b. 17 Aug. 1685; Mary,
25 Apr. 1687; Samuel, 13 July 1689; Hannah, 2 Apr. 1691; and
Abigail, 28 Apr. 1694. SAMUEL, Salem, s. of John, was of the milit.
1703.

PUFFER, or POFFER, JAMES, Braintree 1655, by w. Mary had Richard, b. 14 Mar. 1658; Martha, 28 Dec. 1658. MATTHEW, or MAT-
THIAS, Braintree, perhaps br. of James, had James, b. 4 June 1668, at

Mendon, of wh. he was one of the first sett.; and for sec. w. m. by one acco. 11 Feb. by ano. 30 Apr. 1677, Abigail, d. of Richard Everett, when, I suppose, he liv. at Wrentham. Other ch. he had, and ano. w. Mary, as by his will of 23 Apr. 1714 we learn. The ch. were John, James, Jonathan, and Esther, wh. m. 2 June 1697, William Sumner of Milton. RICHARD, Wrentham, perhaps s. of the preced. by w. Ruth had Richard, b. 17 July 1689, and one s. wh. d. 16 Jan. 1698. ROBERT, Lynn, freem. 1691, call. senr. wh. may lead to presumpt. that he had s. Robert. WILLIAM, Wrentham, by w. Ruth, d. of Joseph Farnsworth, of Dorchester, had William, b. 17 July 1686. Rev. Reuben, D. D. of Berlin, H. C. 1778, is thot. to be the only gr. of this name at any N. E. coll. and he d. Apr. 1829, aged 73.

PULLMAN, JASPER, York, took o. of alleg. to his majesty 22 Mai 1681.

PULSIFER, BENEDICT, Ipswich 1664, was in some part of the ld. aft. 1662, had d. Eliz. b. 4 Dec. 1669, but of the mo. we kn. only that she d. 16 July 1673. In Feb. foll. he m. Susanna, d. of Richard Waters of Ipswich, had Richard, b. 31 May 1675; William, 12 Dec. 1676; Susanna, 5 Sept. 1678; Joseph, 13 Nov. 1680; Benjamin, 19 May 1683; David, 27 Sept. 1685; Jonathan, 25 Sept. 1687; Joanna, 10 May 1691; and Margaret, 14 Feb. 1694. In 1688 at N. Yarmouth he was one of the first to begin hostil. with the Ind. as in his Decennium Luctuosum Mather shows, Magn. VII. 63. JOHN, Gloucester 1680, perhaps s. of Benedict, m. 31 Dec. 1684, Joanna, d. prob. of Thomas Kent of the same, had John, b. 1685, d. at 22 yrs.; Joanna, 1688; Mary, 1691; a s. 1693; Ebenezer, 1695; Mary, again, 1697; David 1701; and Jonathan, 1704.

PUNCHARD, JOHN, Salem, prob. s. of William, m. 6 Nov. 1706, Martha Hooper. WILLIAM, Salem, by tradit. said to have come from Isle of Jersey, m. 26 Oct. 1669, Abigail, d. of Richard Waters of the same, had Abigail, b. 3 Sept. 1670; Mary, 17 Jan. 1674, d. young; William, 11 Nov. 1677; John, 2 Apr. 1682; and Sarah, 27 Oct. 1685. His name is Punshin in Geneal. Reg. IX. 86.

PUNDERSON, or PONDERSON, JOHN, Boston, or the neighb. for short time only, came from Yorksh. 1637, went to New Haven, 1639, one of the pillars of the first gather. of that ch. by w. Margaret, had John, b. 1643, bapt. Oct. 1644; and Hannah, bapt. May 1642, wh. m. 27 Oct. 1670, John Gibbs; and d. 11 Feb. 1681. JOHN, New Haven, only s. of the preced. m. 5 Nov. 1667, Damaris, d. of David Atwater, had Abigail, b. 15 Sept. 1671; John, 10 Dec. 1673; Hannah, 29 July 1676; Thomas, 15 Jan. 1678; Damaris, 25 Dec. 1680; Mary, 1 Aug. 1683;

David, 3 Nov. 1686; Samuel, 20 Sept. 1691; and Ebenezer, 18 Oct. 1694. He was deac. and d. 23 Jan. 1730. Yale has furnish. five gr. bef. 1835 of this name, the first was Rev. Ebenezer, 1724, of Pittsfield.

PURCHASE, or PURKAS, ABRAHAM, Salem, 1680, by w. Ruth, d. of John Williams of the same, had Ruth, b. 10 June 1702; and Benjamin, 2 Mar. 1706. JOHN, Hartford, a. 1639, d. prob. bef. mid. age, and his will of 15 Oct. 1645 may be read in Trumbull's Coll. Rec. I. 466. His wid. Joan m. Nicholas Palmer; and his d. Mary m. Jared Speck, and d. Eliz. m. Richard Case. Whether his hope of a s. express. in the will, were prosper. is uncert. JOHN, Boston, by w. Eliz. had Sarah, wh. d. 14 Feb. 1652; Sarah, again, b. 10 Aug. 1655; John, 3 Aug. 1656; and Mary, 3 Feb. 1660. *OLIVER, Dorchester 1635, freem. 7 Dec. 1636, rem. early to Taunton, there enrol. in 1643 in the milit. was ens. 1651, and in good esteem; but few yrs. aft. rem. to Lynn, there his w. Sarah d. 21 Oct. 1671; and he m. 17 Sept. 1672, Mary, d. of Rev. William Perkins; was rep. 1660 and oft. aft. last in 1689 at four Courts; rem. to Concord a. 1691, there d. 20 Nov. 1701, in 84th yr. as one rept. gives it, or 88th as in a common desire to exagger. has been asserted. His depon. makes his yr. of b. 1613, it is said, but unless the description with circumst. be complete, it may be doubted if the true reading should not be 1618, else why was the rec. of 84th yr. ever tolerat. He was chos. one of the Assist. 1685, but refus. to take the o. prob. bec. the old chart. had been annul. I suppose that Priscilla, wh. m. 26 Oct. 1663, William Wilson, was his d. THOMAS, Kennebeck, an adventur. of good discret. and perseverance, perhaps elder br. of the preced. came first in 1628, and was princip. of the Pegypscott sett. on both sides of Androscoggin, near its mouth; appears on first leaf of Vol. I. of Maine rec. as one of the Commissnrs. at Saco, on new-year's day, 25 Mar. 1636, with the friends of Sir Ferd. Gorges, at his planta. where is now Brunswick, of wh. he sold to Mass. good part 22 July 1639, as by the Indenture in full is shown in Col. Rec. I. 272. His w. Mary d. at Boston 7 Jan. 1656. The Ind. began hostil. Sept. 1675, by plunder of his ho. and he rem. to Lynn. When he d. a few wks. bef. 11 May 1678, with usual exagger. he was said by his wid. Eliz. to be 101 yrs. old. She was prob. much younger, and m. Nov. of that yr. John Blaney of Lynn. He left s. Thomas, made excor. of his will of 2 May 1677, ds. Jane and Eliz. beside three more ch. as the wid. says. Folsom, 31, 153; Willis I. 14, 156; Sullivan, 372; Haz. I. 58; and Hubbard, Ind. Wars, 14. THOMAS, Salem, s. of the preced. in his petitn. with mo. to Pro. Ct. calls hims. "a young man," by w. Eliz. Williams, m. 3 Dec. 1679, had Thomas, b. 29 Jan. 1680; sailed on a voyage 1681, and was not heard of aft. Felt. See also Essex Inst. Coll. II. 276, and III. 14 and 15. Sometimes this is spelt Purchis.

PURDY, FRANCES, and MARY, Fairfield 1644, are witness. to the will of William Frost, 6 Jan. 1645. Possib. the first was a man.

PURPLE, EDWARD, Haddam 1674, m. Hannah Ackley, prob. d. of Nicholas. In that vicin. the name is found to our day.

PURRINGTON, BENJAMIN, is only use of a wrong surname, wh. in his case, is Parmenter, in the abstr. of will of Thomas Cawly, Essex Inst. Hist. Coll. II. 71. JOHN, Kennebunk, was clk. of the writs 1668. JOHN, Exeter, s. of Robert, rem. to Salisbury. JOHN, Salisbury, s. of the preced. perhaps, by w. Sarah had Sarah, b. 26 Jan. 1691. ROBERT, Portsmouth 1665, freem. 1672; had John, b. a. 1635; and Robert, a. 1638; perhaps both b. in Eng. may have rem. to Salisbury, and had other ch. may easily be mistaken for Pudington. The name is much diffus. and often found writ. without g but with single r.

PURRYER, WILLIAM, Ipswich, from Olney in Bucks, emb. at London, early in 1635, aged, by the custom-ho. rec. 36, in the Hopewell, with w. Alice, 37, and ch. Mary, 7; Sarah, 5; and Catharine, 1½. Oft. Felt says, the y is changed to i. I imagine he rem. to Southold, L. I. and was adm. freem. of Conn. 1662; but whether the name be perpet. is unkn.

PURY. See Perry.

PUTNAM, or PUTMAN, BENJAMIN, Salem vill. now Danvers, s. of Nathaniel of the same, freem. 1690, by w. Sarah had Nathaniel, b. 25 Aug. 1686; Tarrant, 12 Apr. 1688; Eliz. 8 Jan. 1690; Benjamin, 8 Jan. 1693; Stephen, 27 Oct. 1694; Daniel, 12 Nov. 1696; Israel, 22 Aug. 1699; and Cornelius, 3 Sept. 1702. His w. d. 21 Dec. 1705; and he m. 1 July 1706, Sarah Holton, and d. a. 1715. EDWARD, Salem vill. s. of Thomas of the same, was freem. 1690, and deac. m. 14 June 1681, Mary Holton (in Essex Inst. III. 15, call. Hale), had Edward, b. 29 Apr. 1682; Holyoke (Holbrook in Essex Inst.), 28 Sept. 1683; Elisha, 3 Nov. 1685; Joseph, 1 Nov. 1687; Mary, 14 Aug. 1689; Prudence, 25 Jan. 1692; Nehemiah, 20 Dec. 1693; Ezra, 29 Apr. 1696; and Isaac, 14 Mar. 1698; was gr.f. of an officer of gr. merit and expe-rience, Gen. Rufus, and d. 1747. ELEAZER, Danvers, s. of the sec. John, m. Hannah Boardman, had Hannah, b. 8 Dec. 1693; Eleazer, 14 Sept. 1695; Sarah, 26 Sept. 1697; Jeptha, 24 Aug. 1699; Samuel, 30 May 1707; Henry, 14 Aug. 1712; and Apphia, 8 July 1716; but pos-sib. some of the latter may have been by w. Eliz. named in his will, brot. for prob. 3 Oct. 1732. JAMES, Salem vill. br. of Eleazer, freem. 1690, had Sarah, b. Jan. 1686; Bartholomew, bapt. Oct. 1688; James, Feb. 1690; Jonathan, 1693, prob. d. young; Archelaus, bapt. July

1697, prob. d. young; Eliz. b. 4 Aug. 1700; Jethro, bapt. 2 May 1703; and Nathaniel, a mariner, wh. d. a. 1723; and d. a. 1727. JOHN, Salem 1640, is said to have come with w. Priscilla, ch. Thomas, b. it is said, a. 1618; Nathaniel, a. 1621; John, a. 1630; and Eliz. from Aston Abbots, near Aylesbury, in Co. Bucks, tho. fam. tradit. has the name of a place in Co. Warwick, where it is unkn. freem. 1647, says Farmer by mistake, tho. true it is he was that yr. rec. into the ch. as had been his w. in 1641, d. 30 Dec. 1662. *JOHN, Salem, s. prob. youngest of the preced. b. in Eng. a. 1630, m. 3 Sept. 1652, Rebecca Prince, had Rebecca, b. 28 May 1653; Sarah, 4 Sept. 1654; Priscilla, 4 Mar. 1657; Jonathan, 17 Mar. 1659; James, 4 Sept. 1661; Hannah, 2 Feb. 1663; Eleazer, 1665; John, 14 July 1667; Joanna, bapt. 4 Sept. 1670; and Ruth, Aug. 1673; was freem. 1665, a lieut. and rep. 1680, 6, and 91 and 2 bef. the new chart. Rebecca m. 22 Apr. 1672, John Fuller; and Sarah m. July foll. John Hutchinson. JOHN, Danvers, s. of Nathaniel, m. 2 Dec. 1678, Hannah Cutler, had Hannah, b. 22 Aug. 1679; Eliz. 26 Nov. 1680; Abigail, 20 Feb. 1682; Samuel, 5 Nov. 1684; Josiah, 29 Oct. 1686; Mary, 29 Sept. 1688; Susanna, 11 Apr. 1690; John, and Rebecca, tw. 16 Aug. 1691; Sarah, 5 Mar. 1693; Amos, 27 Jan. 1697; Priscilla, 7 May 1699; and Joshua. JOHN, Salem vill. s. of the sec. John, freem. 1690, by w. Hannah had Caleb, b. 14 Feb. 1694; Mehitable, 20 July 1695; Miriam, 9 Feb. 1698; Moses, 29 May 1700; Ruth, 13 July 1703; and Hannah, 7 May 1708. His will was pro. 4 Mar. 1737. *JONATHAN, Salem vill. freem. 1690, br. of the preced. by w. Lydia, prob. d. of Anthony Potter of Ipswich, had Lydia, b. 4 Oct. 1684; Eliz. 2 Feb. 1687; Ruth, 7 Apr. 1689; Jonathan, 8 May 1691; Esther, 18 Nov. 1693; and Joshua, 2 May 1696; was rep. 1710. JOSEPH, Danvers, youngest ch. of Thomas the first, m. 21 Apr. 1690, Eliz. d. of Israel Porter, had Mary, b. 2 Feb. 1691; Eliz. 12 Apr. 1695; Sarah, 26 Sept. 1697; William, 8 Feb. 1700; Rachel, 7 Aug. 1702; Ann, 26 Apr. 1705; David, 25 Oct. 1707; Eunice, 13 Apr. 1710; s. 14 Apr. 1713, d. very soon; Huldah, 29 Nov. 1716; Israel, 7 Jan. bapt. 2 Feb. 1718; and Mehitable, 13 Jan. 1720. His youngest s. oft. call. old Put, was that celebr. Gen. wh. d. at Brooklyn, Conn. 19 May 1790. *NATHANIEL, Salem vil. s. of the first John, b. in Eng. was adm. of the ch. 1648, but his name is not in freemen's list, m. 3 Sept. 1652, Eliz. Prince, had Samuel, b. 18 Feb. 1653; Nathaniel, 24 Apr. 1655; John, 26 Mar. 1657; Joseph, 29 Oct. 1659; Eliz. 11 Aug. 1662; Benjamin, 24 Dec. 1664; and Mary, 15 Sept. 1668; was rep. 1690 and 1, d. 23 July 1700, aged a. 79. His w. d. 14 June 1688, in her 60th yr. Perhaps he had sec. w. d. of John Gedney. Eliz. wh. d. bef. her f. m. a Flint, perhaps John; and Mary,

w. of John Tufts, John, and Benjamin, were the only ch. that surv. him.
SAMUEL, Salem, prob. eldest s. of the preced. had w. Eliz. and d. Eliz.
and d. early in 1676, perhaps in the war. THOMAS, Lynn, eldest s. of
first John, b. in Eng. early rem. to Salem, was freem. 18 May 1642, m.
17 Oct. 1643, Ann, d. of Edward Holyoke, had Ann, b. 25 Aug. 1645,
but at S. were bapt. Sarah, 30 July 1648; Mary, b. 17 Oct. 1649, bapt.
19 May 1650; Thomas, b. 12 Mar. bapt. 16 May 1652; Edward, 4,
bapt. 9 July 1654; Deliverance, 5 Sept. 1656, bapt. 10 May 1657;
Eliz. 30 Aug. 1659; Prudence, 25 or 28 Feb. bapt. 29 June 1662; and
Joseph, b. 1 Sept. 1665, prob. d. young. His w. d. 1 Sept. 1665; he had
sec. w. wid. Mary Veren, m. 14 Nov. 1666, and s. Joseph, 14 Sept.
1669, was a lieut. and deac. 1681, and d. 5 May 1686; and his wid.
Mary d. 16 Mar. 1695. THOMAS, Salem, s. of the preced. was freem.
1680; m. 25 Nov. 1678, Ann Carr, had Ann, b. 18 Oct. foll.; Thomas,
9 Feb. 1681; Eliz. 29 May 1683; Ebenezer, 25 July 1685; Deliverance, 8 or 11 Sept. 1687; Abigail; Timothy, bapt. 30 Oct. 1692;
Susanna, 1694; and Seth; and d. 24 May 1699. His wid. d. 8th of
next mo. Thirteen of this fam. had, in 1832, been deac. of the first ch.
of Danvers; and of the name pervert. sometimes, most flagitious. to
Putmun, as vulgar. sound. in 1828, had been twenty-five gr. at Harv.
two at Yale, and seven at other N. E. coll.

PYGAN, PYGON, PIGGIN, or PIGGON, ALEXANDER, New London
1665, perhaps earlier, from Norwich, Co. Norf. m. 17 June 1667,
Judith, d. of William Redfield, had Sarah, b. 23 Feb. 1670; and Jane,
Feb. 1671. His w. d. 30 Apr. 1678; and in short time he rem. to Saybrook, there was an innhold. m. 15 Apr. 1684, Lydia, wid. of Samuel
Boyes, had only Lydia, b. 10 Jan. 1685, and went back to N. L. bef.
her b. there he d. Sept. 1701, and the wid. d. 20 July 1734. Sarah m.
8 July 1686, Nicholas Hallam; Jane m. 29 Mar. 1694, Jonas Greene;
and Lydia m. 15 Dec. 1709, Rev. Eliphalet Adams. In the modest,
model, memoir of that clerg. by Miss Caulkins, the first artic. of 4 Mass.
Hist. Coll. I. some particulars of his f.-in-law, the only male of this
name may be read.

PYNCHON, or PINCHEON, ‡*JOHN, Springfield, only s. of William,
b. in Eng. 1625, brot. with three sis. and their mo. by his f. in the fleet
with Winth. 1630, m. 30 Oct. Hartford rec. says 6 Nov. 1645, Amy, d.
of George Wyllys of Hartford, wh. d. 9 Jan. 1699, had Joseph, b. 26
July 1646, H. C. 1664; John, 15 Oct. 1647; Mary, 28 Oct. 1650;
William, 11 Oct. 1653, d. in few mos.; and Mehitable, 22 Nov. 1661, d.
young. He was freem. 1648, rep. 1659, 62, 3, and 4, in 1665 an Assist.
and ever aft. to the abolit. of the old form of governm. 1686; next of
the Counc. to Andros, major of the Hampsh. reg. from its format. and

during the usurp. of A. call. col. and was the chief man in all the W. yet Mather unwisely dictat. to the king who took somebody else for the honor of counc. in his new chart. 1692, but the people next yr. correct. that blunder, and he was chos. until 1702, every yr. exc. 1699; and Phips made him Judge of Pro. in June 1692. He d. 17 Jan. 1703. Mary m. 6 Aug. 1670, Joseph Whiting of Westfield, as the rec. has it, but Goodwin's scrupul. Geneal. says 5 Oct. 1669. JOHN, s. of the preced. was two yrs. stud. at H. C. liv. at Boston 1673, rem. to Ipswich, there m. Margaret, d. of Rev. William Hubbard, had John, Margaret, and William, all b. there, rem. to Springfield, where his w. d. 11 Nov. 1716; was lieut. col. clk. of the Courts and Regist. of deeds, and d. 25 Apr. 1721. *JOSEPH, Springfield, br. of the preced. a physician, was rep. 1681, and 2, but in this last yr. d. 30 Dec. unm. at Boston. ‡WILLIAM, Roxbury, an Assist. came in the fleet with Winth. 1630, had been assoc. with the patentees, 1628, wh. purch. from the Plymouth comp. that yr. and named to office by the royal chart. of 4 Mar. 1629; brot. four ch. Ann, Mary, John, and Margaret, with their mo. says the rec. of Roxbury ch. of wh. his name is first. His w. d. in the first season, bef. ret. of the sh. in wh. they came; and aft. some yrs. he m. Frances Sanford, a grave matron of the ch. of Dorchester, and a. 1636, rem. to found the town of Springfield, so named, prob. from the place of his resid. near Chelmsford in Old Eng. He was a man of great enterprise, and highly honored as Treasr. bef. his leav. the seacoast, and as Couns. after, until his publicat. of the dangerous judgm. as to religion, wh. he had formed 30 yrs. bef. For this he suffered indignity in 1651, when his book was by our governm. ordered to be burned, and lest the same form of purificat. might reach to the author, he went home, as more freedom was enjoyed in his native ld. See the letter, in full, to Sir H. Vane, from our Gov. Endicott and his council of Assist. in 3 Mass. Hist. Coll. I. 35. At Wraisbury, on the Thames, near famous Runnymede, in Co. Bucks, he d. Oct. 1662, in 72d or 74th yr. his w. having d. there 10 Oct. 1657. Ann m. Henry Smith, s. by her first h. of the sec. w. of her f.; Margaret m. Dec. 6, 1644, capt. William Davis of Boston; and Mary m. 20 Nov. 1640, capt. Elizur Holyoke, and d. 26 Oct. 1657. Four of this name had been gr. at Harv. and three at Yale, 1825.

PYNE, JAMES, Hartford 1647, may have been only trans. inhab. there or at Fairfield. See Trumbull, Col. Rec. I. 150, 158. THOMAS, the freem. of Mass. 6 May 1635, was, by Farmer, thought to be the same as *Pinney*, wh. does not to me seem prob.

QUARLES, WILLIAM, Ipswich 1678, prob. came in from Salisbury, or some other town, where in 1665 he was 18 yrs. old, but no more is kn.

of him, exc. that his Inv. is found of 14 Mar. 1690. WILLIAM, Ipswich, perhaps s. of the preced. but of wh. I learn nothing exc. by his will of est. among Prob. rec. after dec. 10 Apr. 1719, when wid. Mary, eldest s. William, and other s. Robert and Francis, and other relat. are ment. It is possible from adopt. his name for one of his s. that he was of kin to Quarles, the puritan poet. Yet in Boston Joanna was m. by Gov. Bellingham to Richard Smith of Lancaster, 2 Aug. 1654; tho. no occur. of the name can be found for more than 80 yrs. after the sett. of the town, either in births, or deaths, or in the public reg. of deeds or of wills.

QUELCH, BENJAMIN, Boston, by w. Eliz. had Nathaniel, b. 9 Dec. 1692; and Benjamin, 25 Aug. 1694; prob. rem. soon, as he is not in the list of inhab. 1695.

QUELVES, ROBERT, is the impossib. name writ. by the Secreta. in our Col. Rec. for Oct. 1645 (the bungler was Increase Nowell), among the petnrs. for a new planta. that our rulers wuold have gained from R. I. or Providence jurisdict. No doubt it was Twelves, of Braintree, the freem. of 1663, and in later vols. of the rec. restitut. was made in place of the false letters.

QUICK, NATHANIEL, New Hampshire, d. 1677. Kelly. WILLIAM, Charlestown 1636, a mariner, as seems from Trumbull, Col. Rec. I. 6, rem. to Newport, where he was adm. an inhab. 27 Dec. 1638. Prob. his relig. opin. or those of his friends led to that, and he sold ho. and ld. June 1644. Ann Q. of Charlestown, perhaps his mo. sold her ho. and ld. in Apr. 1640.

QUIDDINGTON, ABRAHAM, one of the soldiers k. by the Ind. 19 Oct. 1675, at Hatfield, but of what town he had been inhab. is unkn. ABRAHAM, Boston, perhaps s. of the preced. by w. Sarah had Eliz. bapt. 31 Dec. 1682, but her b. is not found in the rec. of the town, so that I infer, he came in from the neighbor. He had also Ann, bapt. 1 Feb. 1685, and was of the 3d or O. S. ch. but he no more is heard of. His d. Ann m. 14 Oct. 1703, Thomas Holland.

QUILTER, JOSEPH, Ipswich 1679, perhaps s. of Mark the first, is ment. in the valu. pamphlet of 1689, Revo. in N. E. justif. p. 38. MARK, Ipswich 1637, came prob. with Rev. Nathaniel Rogers the yr. bef. bring. some ch. and d. perhaps, 1654, his will being of 7 Feb. in that yr. His ch. were Joseph, Mark, Mary, Rebecca, and Sarah; the two first may have been b. in Eng. His d. Mary is nam. in the will of Rev. N. Rogers, 3 July 1655, as his maid serv. MARK, Ipswich, s. of the preced. m. Frances, d. of Richard Swan of Rowley. He was b. a. 1630, and his will is of 4 Nov. 1678.

QUIMBY, or QUINBY, JOHN, Stratford 1654, had one ch. b. there, but after some yrs. rem. and was one of the patentees of West Chester in 1664, where the fam. has contin. ROBERT, Salisbury 1663, had Lydia, b. 22 Jan. 1658; William, 11 June 1660; John, 7 Sept. 1665; and Thomas, 8 Feb. 1668; and prob. d. 1677. Lydia m. 10 Apr. 1674, William Holdridge. WILLIAM, Amesbury, perhaps br. perhaps s. of the preced. took o. of fidel. 20 Dec. 1677.

QUINCY, ‖ DANIEL, Boston, goldsmith, eldest s. of Edmund the sec. ar. co. 1675, m. 9 Nov. 1682, Ann or Hannah, d. of Rev. Thomas Shepard of Charlestown, had Ann, b. 1 June 1685; and John, 21 July 1689, H. C. 1708; and d. 10 Aug. of the yr. foll. his will of 4 Apr. 1690, being pro. 18 Sept. aft. His wid. m. 7 Jan. 1701, Rev. Moses Fiske as his sec. w. and d. 24 July 1708. His d. Ann m. John Holman, wh. may have been the gr. of H. C. 1700; and his only s. was speaker of the ho. of Reps. 1729–39, many yrs. of his majesty's council, and d. 13 July 1767. *EDMUND, Boston, arr. 4 Sept. 1633 with John Cotton; making it prob. that he came from the same Co. Lincoln, tho. really he was of Wigsthorpe Co. Northampton, s. of Edmund, and bapt. 30 May 1602, and was, with w. Judith m. 14 July 1623, adm. of the ch. in Nov. 1633, and within four mos. five of his serv. joined it; freem. 4 Mar. 1634, and rep. at the first Gen. Ct. of Mass. 14 May in that yr. rec. gr. of ld. in Braintree, 1635, still enj. by his descend. and d. soon aft. in his 33d yr. His wid. m. Moses Paine, wh. d. 1643, and in few yrs. she m. Robert Hull, and d. 29 Nov. 1654, as in his Diary is told by John Hull, the mintmaster, wh. m. 11 May 1647 his d. Judith, b. in Eng. 3 Sept. 1626. *EDMUND, Braintree, only s. of the preced. b. in Eng. a. 1628, bapt. 15 Mar. of that yr. m. 26 July 1648, Joanna, d. of wid. Joanna Hoar, and sis. of Presdt. H. had Mary, b. 4 Mar. 1650; Daniel, 7 Feb. 1651, but thro. misread. of the numerals in Advertisem. to Hull's Americ. Diary, p. 117, by the scrupul. Editor of Archaeol. Amer. repeat. p. 275, is made five mos. too early, for the rec. Geneal. Reg. XI. 333, shows the truth to be not 12 (7) 1650, but 7 (12) 1650; John, 5 Apr. 1652, d. young; Joanna, 16 Apr. 1654; Judith, 25 June 1655; Eliz. 28 Sept. 1656; Edmund, 9 July 1657, d. at 4 mos.; Ruth, 29 Oct. 1658; Ann, wh. d. 3 Sept. 1676, aft. 3 days illness, aged 13, as her gr.-st. tells; and Experience. His w. d. 16 May 1680 (misprint. 1650 in letter of J. Q. Adams, Arch. Amer. III. 276), in her 55th yr. and he m. in Dec. foll. Eliz. d. of Hon. Daniel Gookin, wid. of John Eliot, jr. wh. d. 30 Nov. 1700, by her had Edmund, again, b. 21 Oct. 1681, H. C. 1699; and Mary, again, a. 1684. He was freem. 1665, major and lieut.-col. of the Suffk. regim. rep. 1670, 3, 5, 9, and last in the trying times, May 1692, and d. 7 Jan. 1698, in his 70th yr. His will of 11 Dec. preced. was pro. 31 Mar. foll. Of his ds. the first Mary m. Ephraim Savage, had four ch. and d. 7 Oct. 1676; Joanna m. David Hobart of Hingham, bore him five ch. and d. 18 May 1695; Judith m. Rev. John Rayner jr. of Dover, wh. d. soon aft. 21 Dec. 1676, and she d. 8 Mar. 1679; Eliz. m. 1681, Rev. Daniel Gookin of Shirborne; Ruth m. 19 Oct. 1686, John Hunt of Weymouth; Experience m. William Savil, surv. him, and d. late in 1706, or early in 1707, when admin. was giv. to her br. Edmund; and the sec. Mary m. Rev. Daniel Baker of Shirborne, and d. 29 Mar. 1716 in 32d yr. The geneal. in Geneal. Reg. XI. is rather imperf. ‡ * EDMUND, Braintree, youngest s. of the preced. and only one wh. outliv. the f. m. Dorothy, d. of Rev. Josiah Flynt of Dorchester, was col. of the regim. rep. 1713 and 14, of the council 1715, and 1718 one of the justices of the Sup. Ct. of the Prov. In the cause of the Prov. he was sent to the Court of the Sovereign in Dec. 1737, and d. there of smallpox 23 Feb. after. The inscript. on his monum. erect. by our Gen. Ct. in Bunhill Fields (where rest the ashes of John Milton and John Bunyan) may be read in Eliot's Biog. Dict. His will made just bef. embark. 10 Dec. 1737, pro. 18 Apr. next, names only ch. Edmund, b. 1703, H. C. 1722, Josiah, 1709, H. C. 1728, Eliz. and Dorothy, and wid. Dorothy. This Josiah was a merch. of emin. and disting. as a patriot in the Revo. f. of that fervid orator, Josiah, b. 23 Feb. 1744, H. C. 1763, wh. expended his life for the cause of his country, dying on shipboard, in sight of home, as he ret. from Eng. aft. hostil. had begun only seven days. Fourteen descend. of the first Edmund, in male line, are of the gr. at Harv. of wh. the only s. of the eloquent patriot was some yrs. Presid. and to whose honor he devot. a Hist. that for its truthfulness may put to shame most of the narratives of all Institutions under difficult combinations.

QUING, or QUIN, ARTHUR, Boston 1677.

QUOITMORE, THOMAS, a perverse spelling in some rec. of Coytmore.

RABEY, or RABBE, CATHARINE, Salem, a waterman's wid. from Yarmouth, in Co. Norf. emb. 12 Apr. 1637, aged 68, to come hither, "to remain with her s." as the official docum. in Westminster Hall or her Majesty's Remembrancer's office says. Who he was is unkn. but she unit. with the ch. of S. 1641.

RABUN, or RABONE, GEORGE, Exeter 1639, by Belkn. I. 432, spelled Rawbone.

RADDEN, THADDEUS, Marblehead 1674, as print. in Geneal. Reg. VIII. 288, wh. I presume to mean the same person as T. Reddam, Redden, and Raddin in Essex Inst. II. 279 and 280, with less prob. name in Geneal. Reg. VII. 70, Thaddeus Kidder or Kiddar.

RAGLAND, JOHN, Boston, d. 27 Nov. 1690, in his will, of 26, pro. 8 Jan. foll. gave all his est. to w. Mary.

RAINES, or RAYNES, FRANCIS, York, sw. freem. of Mass. 1652, with prefix of dignity, lieut. 1654, had a d. m. John Woodman of Dover; as a capt. sw. alleg. to the k. 1680; made his will 21 Aug. 1693. NATHANIEL, York, s. perhaps of Francis, sw. alleg. to the k. 1681. RICHARD, Edgartown 1659.

RAINSBOROW, WILLIAM, Charlestown 1639, was of ar. co. that yr. and had next yr. est. at Watertown, was prob. desirous of liv. on this side of the ocean, purchas. in the first yr. of his resid. the *old* meeting-house, as Budington, 195, has shown, but went home bef. the civil war, in wh. he acquir. distinct. He is call. br. of Stephen Winthrop (perhaps by m. of W. with sis. of R.), whose excors. conveyed to Edward R. prob. s. of William, large est. in Lynn, half of fifteen hundred acres, and also half of Prudence isle in Narraganset Bay. Edward in 1672, was of London. Clarendon in Hist. of the Rebellion, gives acco. of William's d. 1648.

RAINSFORD, oft. RANSFORD, EDWARD, Boston 1630, came in the fleet with Winth. by Hutchinson I. 260, called br. of Ch. Just. Rainsford, wh. so strongly do I suspect to be erron. that gladly would conject. be offered of its possib. cause, were it in my power, was freem. 17 Apr. 1637, a deac. and rul. elder of the first ch. and one of the founders of the third, indignant at the artifices practis. to bring Davenport from New Haven, d. 16 Aug. 1680. He by first w. had Mary and Josiah, b. 1, both bapt. 17 June 1632; the mo. d. the same mo. and Josiah d. in Sept. foll. and by sec. w. Eliz. had John, b. 30 June, bapt. 27 July 1634; Jonathan, bapt. 23 Oct. 1636; Ranis, 4, bapt. 10 June 1638; Nathan, 24 July, bapt. 1 Aug. 1641, d. bef. his f.; David, bapt. 1 Sept. 1644, d. 28 Nov. 1691; Solomon; Edward; Eliz.; and Ann, b. 1 Feb. 1652; all exc. the first s. named in the will, made 3, pro. 28 Aug. 1680, tho. Jonathan and Nathan are ment. as d. yet the latter prob. without issue, as his share is giv. to Edward and the ch. of the other are named, Jonathan, Dorothy, and Mary. His wid. Eliz. wh. d. 16 Nov. 1688, aged 81, is nam. excor. and he calls his ds. Mary Parcyfull, meaning possib. Percival, but wh. the h. was is unkn. Ranis Belcher, w. of Josiah, Eliz. Greenough, sec. w. of William and Ann Hough, w. of Samuel of Boston. EDWARD, Boston, a fisherman, came in the Abigail from London, 1635, aged 26, whom I dare not deny, tho. I must not assert, to be the same as preced. JOHN, Boston, ship carpenter, s. of the preced. m. Susanna, d. of Peter Vergoose, had Eliz. John, Mary Shute, Susanna, Edward, Hannah, and Nathan, as all are nam. legatees in the will of their gr.mo. Susanna V. He d. 5 Apr. 1698. JONATHAN, Boston, s. of the Elder, m. 29 Nov. 1656, Mary, d. of John Sunderland, had Mary, b. 2 July 1659; Jonathan, 26 July 1661; Dorothy, 11 Sept. 1663;

and Hannah, 5 Apr. 1666; d. at Barbadoes, 11 Mar. 1671, leav. his f. and Jacob Eliot excors. of his will (wh. was nuncup.) and trust. for his ch. The wid. m. Aug. 1674, Joshua Hobart. NATHAN, Charlestown, s. of the Elder, was a cooper, rem. to Boston, a merch. in 1674. SAMUEL, a soldier, under capt. Turner, k. by the Ind. May 1676 in the fight near the falls of Miller's riv.

RAM, GEORGE, came in the Abigail, from London, 1635, aged 25; but nothing more is kn. of him. In Geneal. Reg. XIV. 318, Mr. Drake is positive that this name in the custom-ho. rec. is Rum. How much his eyesight was better than mine, in copying the same page for 3 Hist. Coll. VIII. 267, I may be satisf. when next visit. London; but till then, as keep. of her majesty's rec. in his many correct. of my text in same ser. of Hist. Coll. X. 130, did not include this error, let it pass. Rum or Ram is unkn.

RAMACKE, CHRISTIAN, Kittery, of the gr. jury 1659.

RAMSDELL, or RAMSDEN, AQUILA, Lynn, s. of John, freem. 1691, had Nathaniel, b. 16 Sept. 1673; Aquila, last of Jan. 1676; John, 25 Mar. 1678; Jonathan, 23 Aug. 1679, d. next mo.; Hannah, 26 Sept. 1680; Samuel, 26 Oct. 1684; and Jonathan, again, 25 Feb. 1686. ISAAC, Lynn, prob. br. of the preced. m. 12 July 1666, Eleanor, eldest d. of John Vinton, had Dorcas and John, wh. both d. young; Nathaniel, b. last of May 1677; John, again, 29 Mar. 1680; Joseph, 17 Sept. 1683; Sarah, 8 May 1685; and Eleanor, 8 Apr. 1688. JOHN, Lynn 1630, or at least a very early sett. had John and Aquila, and d. says Lewis, 27 Oct. 1688, aged 86, whose w. Priscilla, he adds, had d. 23 Jan. 1676. His d. Eliz. I judge, bec. w. 12 Aug. 1674 of John Shaw of Malden, and the s. prob. the youngest, Jonathan, b. 31 Mar. 1657, d. next yr. JOHN, Boxford 1673, perhaps s. of the preced. m. 31 May 1671, Eliz. d. of Rev. William Perkins of Topsfield.

RAMSDEN, DANIEL, Plymouth 1665. JOHN, Newtown, L. I. 1663, selectman 1664, and same yr. made freem. of Conn. of whose jurisdict. he was strenuous support. and liv. in 1686 to be nam. in the patent from Gov. Dongan. See Riker. JOSEPH, Plymouth, m. 1646, Rachel, d. of Francis Eaton, had Daniel, b. 14 Sept. 1649. He m. again, 16 Oct. 1661, Mary Savory.

RAMSEY, JOHN, one of Moseley's comp. Dec. 1675, but where he liv. or when he d. is not kn.

RANCE, JOHN, Scituate, a quaker, wh. assist. in erect. meeting ho. was whipp. for ardent lang. 1677, and rem. to Barbadoes. Yet he had serv. in Philip's war. His wid. was at S. in 1697. Deane, 51.

RAND, FRANCIS, Portsmouth 1631, sent over by John Mason, and there liv. to serve on the jury 1656. Adams's Ann. 18. Perhaps he was at Exeter 1657. HENRY, Stow, m. 19 Sept. 1682, Mary Crane, and had ch. b. there. JAMES, Plymouth, came in the Ann, 1623, and next yr. had his share in the div. of ld. but none in the div. of cattle, 1627, so that we may conclude, he was gone. JOHN, Charlestown, perhaps s. of Robert, d. 19 Dec. 1659, prob. unm. JOHN, Braintree 1657, a mariner, there liv. 1662. JOHN, Dover, m. Remembrance, d. of John Alt, was freem. 1672, perhaps had sec. w. Eliz. wh. admin. his est. 1690. JOHN, Charlestown, s. of Thomas, m. 2 Dec. 1685, Mehitable, d. of John Call, had Mehitable, b. 27 Mar. 1687; Sarah, 5 Jan. 1688, d. very soon; John, 7 Mar. 1690; Hannah, 6 Feb. 1692; Jonathan, 27 Apr. 1694; Sarah, again, bapt. 19 July 1696; Rebecca, b. 4 Nov. 1698, d. at 2 mos.; Benjamin, 17 Mar. 1700; Thomas, 22 Mar. 1702; Caleb, 6 Dec. 1703; Isaac, and Rebecca, tw. bapt. 8 Sept. 1706, both d. next mo.; Rebecca, again, b. 31 July 1708, d. soon; Edmund, 2 July 1710; and Richard, 19 Nov. 1714. His w. d. 25 Mar. 1727, aged 58, and he m. 14 Oct. 1730, Mary Randall, and d. 24 Sept. 1737. His wid. d. 22 Sept. 1757, aged 85. NATHANIEL, Charlestown, s. perhaps youngest, of Robert, m. 2 Sept. 1664, Mary, d. of Samuel Carter of the same, had Nathaniel, b. 13 July 1665, d. in few days; Mary, 30 Dec. 1666, bapt. 5 Apr. 1668, he having been adm. of the ch. on Sunday preced. and she d. in few days after; Nathaniel, again, 12, bapt. 16 Aug. 1668, d. young; Samuel, bapt. 4 Sept. 1670, d. young; John, 17, bapt. 22 Oct. 1671, d. soon; John, again, bapt. 19 Oct. 1673; Samuel, again, 20 Feb. 1676, d. young; Mary, again, b. 16, bapt. 18 Nov. 1677; and by sec. w. Abigail, had Abigail, b. 9 Mar. bapt. 16 May 1680; Joseph, 4, bapt. 5 Feb. 1682; Thomas, b. 10 Aug. 1685, d. soon; Ebenezer, bapt. 6 May 1688; Sarah, b. 16 June 1690; Susanna and Isabel, tw. bapt. 3 June 1694, both d. in few mos. and was freem. 1668, one of the selectmen 1690, and d. 17 May 1696, his w. hav. d. 16 Oct. bef. ROBERT, Charlestown 1635, brot. from Eng. w. Alice, said to be d. of Nicholas Sharp in Eng. and sis. of Mary, w. of the first capt. Richard Sprague, with ch. Margery, Thomas, Susanna, and prob. Alice; here had Nathaniel, bapt. 3 Nov. 1636; and Eliz. 29 Dec. 1639, but he d. bef. Margery m. a. 1646, as his sec. w. Lawrence Dowse. Susanna m. 8 Feb. 1652, Abraham Newell of Roxbury; Alice m. Thomas Lord, and d. 11 Aug. 1721 in her 88th yr. and Eliz. m. a. 1662, Nathaniel Brewer of Roxbury. His wid. liv. to 29 July 1691, aged 87, and her will was pro. 17 Aug. foll. ROBERT, Lynn 1649, had Robert; Zechary; and Hannah, b. Aug. 1657; d. 8 Nov. 1694, says Lewis, in Hist. sec. ed. 112, where he says his w. Eliz. d. 29 Aug. 1693, and adds Eliz. and Mary to the number of his ch. ROBERT, Lynn, s. prob. of the preced. m. last of Jan. 1684, Tabitha, d. of sec. Thomas Ivory of Lynn.

SAMUEL, Dover, m. 14 Aug. 1679, Mary, d. of George Walton.
THOMAS, Charlestown, s. prob. eldest of Robert, b. in Eng. a. 1627,
brot. by his f. m. 12 Mar. 1656, Sarah, d. of Edmund Edenden, had
Thomas, b. 1 Feb. 1657, bapt. 6 May 1660, as f. and mo. joined the
ch. the week preced.; John b. 6 Oct. 1659, d. in few wks.; Eliz. bapt. 2
Feb. 1662; John, again, b. 25 May 1664; Sarah, 15 Aug. 1666;
Robert, bapt. 19 Apr. 1668; Edmund, b. 27 Jan. 1670, d. young; Hannah, 21 Feb. 1672; William, 11 Sept. 1674; Deborah, 28 Sept. 1676;
and Samuel, 3 May 1679; was freem. 1660, and d. 3 Aug. 1683, and
his wid. d. 1699, in her 63d yr. Eliz. m. 4 July 1682, John Pinney;
and Hannah m. 12 Apr. 1694, Nathaniel Frothingham. THOMAS,
Charlestown, s. of the preced. m. 17 June 1679, Sarah, d. of William
Longley or Langley of Groton, had Sarah, b. 27 Jan. 1680, d. soon;
Thomas, 26 Dec. 1681; Edmund, wh. d. 31 Aug. 1683; Robert, 18 June
1684; Edmund, again, 22 Aug. 1686; William, 4 May 1689; Joshua,
2 Mar. 1692; and Sarah, 1 Sept. 1694, d. next yr. He was drown. 2
Oct. 1695, and his wid. had admin. 2 Dec. foll. WILLIAM, Charlestown, br. of the preced. by w. Persis had Mary, b. 21 May 1695; Eliz.
bapt. 4 Apr. 1697; William, 1698; John, b. 11 Feb. 1701, d. soon;
Deborah, bapt. 29 Nov. 1702; Samuel, b. 27 May 1704; Thomas, 22
Aug. 1711; and Joshua, bapt. 20 Sept. 1713; and d. 19 Feb. 1747;
and his wid d. 25 June 1748, aged 80 yrs. Ten of this name had, in
1828, been gr. at Harv.

RANDALL, ABRAHAM, Dorchester, s. of Philip, rem. with his f. to
Windsor 1636, was constable 1656, m. first w. Mary, 1 Dec. 1640, and
sec. w. 27 Oct. 1681, Eliz. Kibby, but prob. had no ch. by either, or at
least left none, when he d. 21 Aug. 1690; in his will gave most of his
est. to Abraham and two other s. of George Phelps, his nephews.
ANTHONY, Salem 1688, a physician. Felt. ISAAC, Scituate, young-
est s. of William of the same, m. 19 Nov. 1684, Susanna, d. of Joseph
Barstow, and for sec. w. 1692, Deborah, d. of John Buck, had Isaac
Susanna, Jacob, Deborah, Robert, Ruth, Gideon, Rachel, Caleb, Elisha,
Mary, Abigail, Grace, and Perez; of whom we may presume that the
last eleven were by the sec. Deane says he liv. to the age of 102. JOB,
Scituate, s. of William of the same, had Mary, b. 1680; Job, 1683;
James, 1685; Nehemiah, 1688; Lydia, 1690; and Samuel, 1694.
JOHN, Watertown, by w. Susanna had Sarah, b. 7 Aug. 1659; beside
Susanna, suppos. to be first ch.; Stephen; Mary; Samuel, 20 Mar.
1669; and Eleazer, 30 Apr. 1672; all nam. in his will of 22 Apr. pro
5 Oct. 1680. His w. had d. 14 May 1673. He was prob. younger br
of Stephen, and d. 16 June 1680. Susanna m. Enoch Sawtell. JOHN
Westerly 1667, complained of by Conn. Ind. Trumbull II. 529. JOHN

Weymouth, s. of Robert, freem. 1691, by w. Mercy had Mary, b. 31 May 1668; John, 16 Apr. 1673; Eliz.; Mercy; and other ch. whose dates are not in the rec. but in his will of 28 Dec. 1715, he names w. Sarah, s. John, Mercy, w. of Thomas Kingman; Eliz. w. of Benjamin Orcut; besides w. of Benjamin Luddam; and w. of . . . . . Reed, as his ds. JOHN, Rochester, may have been s. of William of Scituate, and liv. there early, had John, b. 6 May 1677; Patience, 13 Jan. 1679; Thomas, 25 Jan. 1681; Mercy, 20 Jan. 1683; William, 6 Feb. 1685; Job, 3 Mar. 1688; Judith, 29 Apr. 1690; and Lazarus, 25 Dec. 1691. Perhaps his w. was relat. of Thomas Rollins the sec. of Boston; at least in his will of 12 Dec. 1681, she is nam. among other kin. JOHN, Watertown, m. Rachel, d. of John Waite of the same, had Mary, b. 10 June 1690; and he d. Dec. foll. JOSEPH, Scituate, eldest s. of William of the same, m. 1673, Hannah Macomber, perhaps d. of William, had Eliz. and Sarah, b. 1673; Joseph, 1675; Hannah, 1677; Sarah, again, 1680; Margaret, 1683; Mercy, 1684; and Benjamin, 1688, as Deane tells. NATHANIEL, Boston 1660, s. of John of Clerkenwell, London, that had w. Eliz. wh. was sis. of William Morton of Windsor and New London. PHILIP, Dorchester, freem. 14 May 1634, had one d. call. Philury, wh. m. George Phelps, and s. Abraham, bef. ment. and Philip, rem. 1636 to Windsor, there d. 6 Sept. 1648, unless this be date of his s. of the same name, and he, I think, liv. to 1662, but had no ch. and the name soon after was extinct at W. The wid. d. 1665, aged 87. RICHARD, Saco, had Richard, b. 1659; and Sarah, 1661; may be the same wh. was of Boston 1676, mariner, had w. Eliz. and many yrs. later was of Dover. ROBERT, Weymouth, freem. 1647, then spell. Rendell, in his will of 27 Mar. 1691, names his ch. John, Thomas, Mary, wh. was b. 20 or 30 Mar. 1642, w. of Abraham Staples, m. 17 Sept. 1660; and Hannah, w. of John Warfield, both then of Mendon. Mary, his w. was bur. 3 Sept. 1640, but his next w. is unkn. He came from Wendover, Co. Bucks, as he testif. in 1688, at the age of 80. SAMUEL, Watertown, s. of John of the same, m. 27 Jan. 1709, Eliz. Gleason of Cambridge, had Eliz. b. 22 Mar. 1710; Samuel, 12 Nov. 1711; Susanna, Dec. 1713, d. at 10 yrs.; Mary, 23 Feb. 1713; John, Jan. 1719; and Stephen, 29 Jan. 1722; and d. 24 Jan. 1730. STEPHEN, Watertown, m. 14 Dec. 1653, Susanna, d. of Ellis Barron, had Eliz. wh. m. Stephen Codman; Stephen, b. 20 Aug. 1655, wh. prob. d. young; Susanna, wh. m. William Shattuck; and Mary, 24 June 1662. He was perhaps elder s. of that wid. Eliz. wh. d. at W. 24 Dec. 1672, aged 80; and he d. 26 Feb. 1708. The will of 13 Jan. 1698, names the three ds. and Mary m. only six weeks aft. that date, Abraham Chamberlain; yet the will was not, of course, potential in the match. He left no male descend. THOMAS, Marblehead, fisherman, m. bef. Feb. 1665, Sarah, d. of John Langdon of Boston, d. soon, for his inv. was tak. 20 Nov. 1667. THOMAS, Weymouth, s. of Robert, freem. 1691, by w. Hannah had Deborah, b. 25 Sept. 1683. WILLIAM, Scituate 1640, had liv. perhaps in 1636 at R. I. certain. in 1637 at Marshfield, bef. m. and aft. had Sarah, b. 1640; Joseph, Mar. 1642; Hannah, Mar. 1644; William, Dec. 1647; John, Apr. 1650; Eliz. Oct. 1652; Job, 8 Feb. 1655; Benjamin, 1656; and Isaac, 1658. To his w. Eliz. by will of Michael Barstow of Watertown, in June 1674, was giv. a good legacy. WILLIAM, Newbury, by w. Eliz. wh. Coffin says he m. 2 Oct. 1649, had Eliz. b. 13 May 1650; William, 2 Mar. 1653; John, 5 Mar. 1655; Mary, 26 Mar. 1656; and Hannah, 7 Jan. 1659. WILLIAM, Newbury, s. of the preced. by w. Rebecca, had Enoch, b. Dec. 1676; and his w. d. 18 Feb. foll. WILLIAM, Westfield, perhaps s. of William of Scituate, by w. Mary had childr. bef. going thither, of wh. only Mary is kn. but prob. ano. was William, and there had John, b. 17 June 1682; Abigail, 26 July 1684; Hannah, 23 Nov. 1686; and Eliz. 8 Apr. 1689, d. next yr. at Enfield, whither he rem. In Mar. 1691, his d. Mary was charged with witchcr. but the murderous spirit was rebuked by the judges considerate. adm. her f. to be surety. One of the early purch. at Taunton was a wid. R. but of wh. she had been w. is not kn.

RANDOLPH, EDWARD, Boston, call. "the evil genius of N. E." from 1676, engag. in the project of overturning the rights secured by the Charter, and after its extinct. in 1684, employ. with Sir E. Andros, and other instrum. of tyranny until the glorious revo. 1689, when he, with the rest, was imprison. in few wks. aft. rejoiced to be sent home, and it is said that he d. in the W. I. See Eliot's Biog. Dict.; Hutch. I. 319; and Chalmer's Pol. Ann. 491.

RANGER, EDMUND, Boston, a stationer, or as Thomas II. 411, calls him, binder, by first w. Sarah, had Prudence, b. 5 Nov. 1672; John, 16 Apr. 1674; and by w. Mary had Samuel, 29 Mar. 1681; and Sarah, 15 Sept. 1692; was freem. 1671.

RANKIN, ANDREW, York, d. bef. 1678, leav. five ch. and wid. Martha, wh. m. Philip Frost. JOHN, Roxbury 1653, a serv. of Gov. Thomas Dudley.

RANNEY, EBENEZER, Middletown, youngest s. of Thomas the first, m. 4 Aug. 1698, Sarah Warner, perhaps d. of Robert of the same. JOHN, Middletown, br. of the preced. m. 1693, Hannah Turner. JOSEPH, Middletown, br. of the preced. m. 1693, Mary, prob. d. of Comfort Star of the same, and d. 2 Mar. 1745. THOMAS, Middletown, from Scotland, says Field, 33, m. May 1659, Mary Hubbard, d. of George, and

d. 25 June 1713, leav. good est. and four s. Thomas, b. 1 Mar. 1660; John, 14 Nov. 1662; Joseph, Sept. 1663; and Ebenezer, beside ds. Mary, b. Feb. 1665, m. 30 May 1682, John Savage; Eliz. 12 Apr. 1660, w. of Jonathan Warner, m. 4 Aug. 1698; and Esther, wh. m. 3 Nov. 1696, Nathan Savage. His wid. d. 18 Dec. 1721. THOMAS, Middletown, eldest s. of the preced. m. 1690, Rebecca, eldest d. of Nathaniel Willet, prob. had sev. ch.

RANSOM, MATTHEW, Saybrook, m. 7 Mar. 1683, Hannah Jones, had Joseph, b. 10 Jan. 1684.

RAPER, THOMAS, Boston, by w. Martha had Jeremiah, b. 27 Apr. 1685; Mercy, 8 Oct. 1686, d. young; Stephen, 16 June 1688; Martha, 18 Nov. 1689; and Mercy, again, 23 Oct. 1691.

RASHLEY, HENRY, Boston 1648, perhaps br. of Thomas, d. bef. July 1657. JOHN, charg. with murder 1679, to the E. of Kennebeck. *THOMAS*, Boston, adm. of the ch. 8 Mar. 1640, called "a studyent," meaning in theology, no doubt, and next yr. at Gloucester, as we learn from Lechford, he exercis. as they say, in a prophetical way, and there perhaps m. but his s. John "being a. six wks. old," was bapt. at B. 18 May 1645, in wh. yr. he was possib. of ar. co. and of Exeter 1646; but soon went home, was the min. at Bishop Stoke, Co. Hants, where, 4 May 1652, he bapt. Samuel Sewall, first of that name, Ch. Just. of Mass. He was after, as Farmer, in a MS. note says, sett. in Wiltsh.

RASOR, RICHARD, Boston, m. 24 Aug. 1660, Exercise, d. of John Blackleach.

RATCHELL, or RACHELL, ROBERT, Boston, m. Judith, d. of John Hart, had Mary, b. 31 Aug. 1652; Ann, 4 Feb. 1654; and Temperance, 8 June 1658; he d. 1659, when inv. of his est. was £5 4s. 8d. and his wid. m. 3 Dec. 1663, Philip Bullis. Boston rec. however, by seeming incongru. makes Thomas Reape to be m. by Gov. John Endicott, 30 Nov. 1660, to wid. Judith Ratchell. Still Bullis prevailed, possib. at a later day. Mary m. John Pierce of Gloucester; Ann m. 1677, Andrew Hall of Boston; and Temperance m. William Johnson of Boston, and was wid. 1677.

RATCLIFF, or RATLIFFE, JOHN, Boston, by w. Alice had John, b. 16 Nov. 1664; Thomas, 17 Jan. 1667; and Eliz. 1 Jan. 1670. PHILIP, agent for Gov. Cradock, prob. in the Marblehead fishery, bef. 1630, severely, even cruelly punish. for maledict. of the ch. at Salem in June 1631, as cutting off his ears, and a sort of excuse seems to be suggested that he could not have felt the indignity, bec. he was insane. He was banish. as in Winth. is told I. 56. ROBERT, Plymouth, came in the Ann, 1623, prob. with w. and ch. for in the div. of lds. next yr. he had four sh. but in the div. of cattle, 1627, his name is not found. *ROBERT*,

Boston 1686, the first Episcop. min. sett. in N. E. was induct. 15 June of that yr. and Sewall, in his Diary Notes, that on 15 Sept. Mr. David Jeffries was by him m. to Miss Betty Usher, prob. d. of John; but perhaps no edifice for worship was erect. in his time. Neither Pemberton nor Eliot give any report of him after the first yr. Dunton says he " was an emin. preach. and his Sermons were useful, and well dressed." He had come in the frigate Rose, 15 May 1686, and went home, no doubt, at the end of three yrs. when his patron Andros was overthrown. *WILLIAM, Greenwich 1669, had prob. liv. at Stamford, there m. 27 Oct. 1659, Eliz. d. of Nicholas Thele, was rep. 1670.

RATHBON, JOHN, THOMAS, THOMAS, jr. and WILLIAM, were of Block isl. 1678.

RATSTOCK, JOSHUA, Boston 1687, prayed Sir E. Andros for leave to keep a sch. at the N. end, but his success is not heard of.

RAVENSCROFT, ANTHONY, Westerly 1661, was a soldier in 1675. SAMUEL, Boston, ar. co. 1679, m. Dionysia, d. of Maj. Thomas Savage, had Dionysia, b. 12 Apr. 1681; Samuel, 12 Apr. 1682; both bapt. 7 May this yr.; George, 20, bapt. 23 Mar. 1684; Sarah, 20 Nov. 1686; and Thomas, 29 June 1688. He was one of the Wardens of the first Episcop. ch. and that prevent. the bapt. of the ch. at O. S. to wh. he had belong. and it may be thot. perhaps led to his imprison. at the revo. in Apr. 1689. Soon after, he unit. in a loyal address to King William, but prob. rem. in short time.

RAVENSDALE, JOHN, was sw. a freem. of Mass. 6 May 1635; but where liv. I find not.

RAWBONE. See Rabun.

RAWLINS, RAWLINGS, or ROLLINS, ‖ CALEB, Boston, s. of Thomas the sec. by w. Eliz. d. of Nicholas Wilmot, had Thomas, b. 15 Sept. 1673; Mary, 10 Mar. 1677; and Ann, 25 Oct. 1679. ICHABOD, Dover, perhaps s. of James, was taxed 1665. JAMES, Newbury, freem. 14 May 1634, was of Dover two yrs. after, and in 1656, fined for neglect of public worship. JASPER, Roxbury, came with w. Joan in 1632 prob. for 11 June 1633 he was adm. freem. went early to Wethersfield, soon aft. to Windsor; but back to R. bef. 1646; there m. 8 June 1651, wid. of Thomas Griggs, perhaps Hannah, to wh. by his will of 7 Jan. 1666, pro. 13 June 1667, he gave all his est. unless any of his ch. came here to sett. I believe they all contin. in Conn. He was of Boston 1654, and aft. JOHN, Boston, by w. Judah had Gershom, b. 29 Jan. 1686; and perhaps more. JOSHUA, Boston 1671, mariner, s. of sec. Thomas, by w. Abigail had Abigail, b. 25 May of that yr. wh. m. Oct. 1686, Zechariah Kirk. NATHANIEL, Scituate, s. of Thomas, came with his f. to Roxbury 1630, m. 4 Sept. 1652, Lydia, d. of Richard Sylvester, had Eliz. b. 1 Mar.

1654, d. young; Ruth, 27 Sept. 1655; Patience, 1658; Nathaniel, 1659; Eliz. again, 1661; and Nathaniel, again, 7 Sept. 1662; and d. 23 Dec. 1662. His wid. m. 25 May 1664, Edward Wright. His d. Eliz. m. 1679, James Torrey. NICHOLAS, Newbury, m. 31 Oct. 1679, Rebecca, d. of Robert Long of the same, had John, b. 1 Dec. 1680; Daniel, 21 Mar. 1682; Mary, 10 Apr. 1683; Joseph, 25 Mar. 1685; Benjamin, 2 Mar. 1687; Rebecca, 1 Oct. 1689; and Martha, 5 Nov. 1692. RICHARD, Boston 1638, a plaisterer, adm. of the ch. 1642, freem. 10 May 1643, had w. Mary. ROBERT, Amesbury, sw. alleg. 20 Dec. 1677. SAMUEL, a soldier at Hadley in 1676, was perhaps s. of Thomas the sec. of Boston. THOMAS, Roxbury 1630, perhaps br. of Jasper, "came with the first comp." says the ch. rec. that is, with Winth. bef. either Eliot or Welde, bring. with w. five ch. Thomas, Mary, Joan, Nathaniel, and John, was made freem. 18 May 1631, hav. req. that benefit 19 Oct. bef. His w. Mary d. a. 1639, and he soon rem. to Weymouth, thence to Scituate, and few yrs. later to Boston, where his w. Emma d. 27 Dec. 1655, and he m. 2 May 1656, Sarah, wid. of David Mattocks of R. and d. 15 Mar. 1660. His will of three days bef. pro. 4 Apr. foll. names only w. Sarah, and s. Thomas and Nathaniel. Mary, the d. brot. from Eng. m. Apr. 1639, William Parker, and Joan m. 28 Jan. 1646, Ephraim Kempton, both of S. but their ws. were d. bef. this will. Deane has slightly confus. the acco. THOMAS, Weymouth, mariner, s. of the preced. came 1630, with his f. freem. 3 Mar. 1636, prob. rem. after b. of Thomas his first s. and Joshua, b. 2 Dec. 1642, to Boston, there had Caleb, 8 Mar. 1645; Joseph, bapt. in right of his mo. of the ch. of W. at B. 25 June 1648, a. 11 days old; Mary, b. 24 Nov. 1652; Samuel, 1 Sept. 1655; and his w. Hannah, mo. of these ch. was admor. of the est. 1677. THOMAS, Dorchester, of wh. all we kn. comes from the gr.-st. that he d. 7 July 1693, aged a. 70 yrs. THOMAS, Boston, s. prob. of the sec. Thomas, by w. Sarah had Thomas, b. 20 Jan. 1667; but no more is found on the rec. and we may presume he d. or rem. Almost universal. this name is become Rollins.

RAWLINSON, THOMAS, Ipswich, freem. 2 May 1638. See Rowlandson.

RAWSON, * EDWARD, Newbury, b. 16 Apr. 1615, at Gillingham, Co. Dorset, near the bounds of Hants and of Wilts, from both of wh. came many of our Newbury people, arr. I suppose, in 1637, and in Mar. 1638, freem. was first clk. of the town, rep. 1638, 9, 42, 4, 6, 8, and 9, and Secr. 1650 to 86, d. 27 Aug. 1693, having rem. to Boston, 1650; was long reg. of deeds for Suff'k. Co. as well as Secr. for the Col. for wh. office the vols. of rec. exhibit strange evid. in many places of his incompetency or more wonderful neglect. One instance is specified under Adams, Joseph. He had s. Daniel, bef. 1662. He m. in Eng. Rachel, d. of Thomas Pirne, or Perne, and his first ch. a d. was b. there, and left at home; beside her, six more ds. are said to have been b. to him, and five s. Of these we can hardly be sure of the dates of more than half; Edward, H. C. 1653; and Rachel, wh. m. at Boston, 18 Jan. 1653, William Aubrey, we may suppose to have been b. in Eng. also; but the rest would prob. be b. here, though we may mistake names as well as dates. David, b. 6 May 1644; Pirne or Parnell, 1646; and Grindall, 23 Jan. 1649, wh. d. young, we may admit to have their b. at N. as Coffin gives them; tho. his Susan wh. d. in Roxbury 1654, must be rejected, since the town rec. is silent, and by inspect. of the ch. rec. it seems prob. Susanna, d. of Edward Payson, was thus read. John, wh. went to Eng. and never came back, and William, b. at B. 21, bapt. 25 May 1651; Rebecca, 19 Oct. 1654, d. soon; Rebecca, again, b. 21, bapt. 25 May 1656; Sarah; Eliz. 12 Nov. 1657; and Grindall, again, 23 Jan. 1659, H. C. 1678, will complete the number without the conjectural Susan of Roxbury. His w. had d. 11 Oct. 1677. Mary m. 15 May 1657, Rev. Samuel Torrey; Rebecca m. 1 July 1679, one Thomas Rumsey, a scoundrel, wh. pretend. to be Thomas Hale, jr. a neph. of the great jurist, Sir Matthew, Ch. J. of Eng. wh. carried her to London, and immediate. abandon. her; and Sarah m. Thomas Broughton of Boston. EDWARD, Boston, eldest s. of the preced. went home, and was a sett. min. at Horsmanden in Co. Kent, whence, after the Restor. he was eject. by the former incumbent. GRINDALL, Mendon, youngest s. of Edward the first, so nam. in honor of the puritan Archbp. of Canterbury in Elizabeth's day, was sec. min. in that town, freem. 1683, ord. 7 Apr. 1684, m. Susanna, d. of Rev. John Wilson of Medfield, had Edmund, b. 1684, d. soon; John, 26 Apr. 1685, d. next mo.; Susanna, 3 Oct. 1686; Edmund, again, 8 July 1689; Wilson, 23 June 1692; John, again, 1 Oct. 1695; Mary, 22 June 1699; Rachel, 6 Sept. 1701; David, 25 Oct. 1703, d. in 3 mos.; Grindall, 6 Sept. 1707; and Eliz. 21 Apr. 1710. He d. 6 Feb. 1715, and his wid. d. 8 July 1748, in her 84th yr. WILLIAM, Boston, br. of the preced. m. 11 July 1673, Ann, only d. of Nathaniel Glover of Dorchester, had Ann, b. 11 Apr. 1674; Wilson, 1675; Margaret, 1 Aug. 1676; Edward, 6 Sept. 1677, d. soon; Edward, again, 29 Aug. 1678; Rachel, 16 Oct. 1679; Dorothy, 8 Aug. 1681, all d. young; William, 2 or 8 Dec. 1682, H. C. 1703; David, 13 Dec. 1683; Dorothy, again, 19 June 1686, d. young; rem. to Dorchester, there had Ebenezer, 1687, d. young; Thankful, 6 Aug. 1688, d. in few days; rem. to Braintree, there had Nathaniel, 1689; Ebenezer, again, 24 July 1691, d. in few mos.; Edward, again, 27 Jan. 1692; Ann, 28 Aug. 1693, d. soon; Patience, 8 Nov. 1694, d. soon; Pelatiah,

2 July 1696; Grindall, 24 Aug. 1697; and Mary, 1698; but the last two d. soon. The names of these twenty ch. of wh. only five liv. to grow up, it is said are record. in the anc. fam. bible, and so, we presume, are the dates; one of wh. is impossible to be true.

RAY, or REA, CALEB, Boston, by w. Eliz. had Caleb, b. 19 Feb. 1683; and by w. Mary had Mary, 28 Aug. 1691. DANIEL, Plymouth 1631, rem. to Salem, and prob. was that freem. of 14 May 1634, spell. Wray in Col. Rec. and perhaps h. of Bethia, adm. of the ch. 1637, and Sept. of that yr. was on the gr. jury, liv. there 1644. He had d. Bethia wh. m. first the brave Capt. Thomas Lothrop, next Joseph Grafton, and last deac. William Goodhue. But other ch. were Joshua, Rebecca, and Sarah. JAMES, Hingham, m. in Jan. 1682, wid. Hewett, perhaps relict of Thomas. JOSHUA, Salem, s. of Daniel, may have been brot. from Eng. freem. 1665, was a taverner, 1693. He m. 26 Feb. 1652, Sarah Waters, possib. d. of Richard, wh. d. 19 May 1700, aged 70, had Daniel, b. 30 Mar. 1654, wh. serv. in Philip's war 1676; Rebecca, 4 Sept. 1656; Sarah, 10 Nov. 1658, d. soon; ano. Sarah, and Eliz. dates of whose b. are so confus. in Essex Inst. III. 16, that tho. it is clear, that one is false, we kn. not wh. besides Bethia, 3 Jan. 1663; Joshua, 6 Aug. 1664; John, 23 May 1666; and Hannah, 1 Aug. 1668. Rebecca m. that Samuel Stephens, k. Sept. 1675 at the fight of Bloody Brook, and her f. report. to the governm. that his br.-in-law, Capt. Thomas Lothrop, and his s.-in-law, Samuel Stephens, both k. by the Ind. in that serv. left fams. depend. on him. RICHARD, Warwick 1656. SIMON, Braintree, came, it is said, from Braintree, Co. Essex, and d. 30 Sept. 1641. His will was copied on one of the lost pages of our Vol. I. in Prob. Court, if we may believe the Index; and his inv. of 20 Feb. foll. shows good est. Perhaps Mary, wh. m. 15 Nov. 1651, Samuel Deering, was his d. SIMON, Block isl. s. of the preced. an orig. propr. of the isl. in 1661, m. Mary d. of the first Nathaniel Thomas of Marshfield, had Mary, b. 19 May 1667; Dorothy, 16 Oct. 1669; Simon, 9 Apr. 1672; and Sibel, 19 Mar. 1675. He liv. to see num. progeny thro. male and fem. lines, and d. 17 Mar. 1737, in 102d yr. says the gr.-stone; and from him came into the fam. by subseq. interm. the Hon. Nathaniel Ray Thomas, one of his Majesty's Counsellors of Mass. Bay 1774.

RAYMOND, perhaps oft. RAYMENT, DANIEL, Lyme, youngest s. of Richard, m. Eliz. d. of Gabriel Harris, wh. d. 10 Aug. 1683, had Eliz. and Sarah; and m. next Rebecca, d. of John Lay, had Richard, Samuel, and perhaps others, and d. 1696. His wid. m. Samuel Gager of Norwich. JOHN, Beverly 1670, perhaps the freem. of 1683, d. in 87th yr. 18 Jan. 1703. JOHN, Beverly, possib. may be thot. s. of the preced.

as in 1682. he was call. sen. JOHN, Norwalk, s. of Richard, m. 10 Dec.
1664, Mary d. of Thomas Betts, had John, b. 9 Sept. 1665; Samuel, 7
July 1673; and perhaps others; was liv. with two ch. 1694. JOSHUA,
New London 1658, eldest s. of Richard, m. 10 Dec. 1659, Eliz. d. of
Nehemiah Smith, had Joshua, b. 18 Sept. 1660; Eliz. 24 May 1662;
Ann, 12 May 1664; Hannah, 8 Aug. 1668; Mary, 12 Mar. 1672; and
Experience, 20 Jan. 1674, d. at 16 yrs. beside Richard and Mehitable,
wh. d. inf.; and he d. 1676. His wid. m. 26 Jan. 1681, George Dennis.
JOSHUA, Block isl. 1687, s. of the preced. RICHARD, Salem, perhaps
br. of the first John and of William, freem. 14 May 1634, had there
bapt. Bathsheba, 11 July 1637, wh. m. 29 July 1659, Humphrey
Coombs; Joshua, 3 Mar. 1639; Lemuel, 3 Jan. 1641; Hannah, Feb.
1643; Samuel, 13 July 1645; Richard, 2 Jan. 1648; Eliz. 28 Apr.
1650; and Daniel, 17 Apr. 1653, all prob. by w. Judith; rem. to Norwalk, thence in 1664 to Saybrook, there d. 1692. RICHARD, Saybrook,
s. of the preced. d. as early as 1680. SAMUEL, New London, s. of the
first Richard, m. Mary, d. of Nehemiah Smith, had no ch.; but he and w.
were liv. 1700. THOMAS, Salem vill. freem. 1690. WILLIAM, Portsmouth 1632, sent out by Capt. John Mason. * WILLIAM, Salem 1648,
br. perhaps of the first John and Richard, m. Hannah Bishop, and next
Ruth Hall, by both had ch. prob. one William, aged 20 in 1692, witness
a. witchcraft, was a capt. of Beverly, and with Rev. John Hale, his min.
went in the unfortunate expedit. project. by Sir William Phips, when he
was sheriff, 1690, against Quebec; freem. 1683, and rep. 1685 and 9;
and d. 29 Jan. 1709.

RAYN or RAYNES, FRANCIS, York 1649, a selectman, capt. 1659, and
magistr. 1670, owned alleg. to Mass. Hutch. I. 267, and Hubbard, 617.
JOSEPH, Portsmouth, 1685, Atty.-Gen. of the Prov. to do the pleasure
of Gov. Cranfield. NATHANIEL, York 1680, was perhaps s. of Francis.

RAYNER or REYNER, EDWARD, Hempstead, L. I. 1647, was prob. s.
of Thurston, or at least came with him, 1634, aged 10, from Ipswich, Co.
Suff. in the Elizabeth, liv. first at Watertown. HENRY, Boston, m. 9 June
1662, wid. Joanna Edwards, was a soldier on Conn. riv. 1676, under
Capt. Turner. * HUMPHREY, Rowley, b. at Gildersome, in the W. riding
of Yorksh. not far from Leeds, freem. 18 May 1642, was rep. 1649, had
beside the d. Mary, wh. m. Michael Wigglesworth, and perhaps d. bef.
her f. Ann, wh. m. William Hobson; and Martha, m. John Whipple; d.
1660, and to those ds. gave all his est. after wid. d. JACHIN, Rowley, s.
of Rev. John the first, m. 22 Nov. 1662, Eliz. prob. d. of Edward Denison, wh. d. perhaps 7 May 1672, had d. Eliz. and by ano. w. had Ann,
b. 23 July 1678; d. 8 July 1708, and perhaps his w. d. ten yrs. bef.
JOHN, Plymouth, br. of Humphrey, b. at Gildersome, was bred at Mag-

dalen Coll. Cambridge, where he had his A. B. 1625, m. one of four coheiresses named Boyes of his native parish, and Rev. Peter Prudden is kn. to have taken ano. came a. 1635, perhaps with first w. by wh. he had Jachin; and Hannah, wh. m. Sept. 1660, Job Lane of Malden; beside an elder d. wh. was once thought, but erron. the first wife of Michael Wigglesworth, m. 1642, for sec. w. Frances Clark, had John, H. C. 1663; Joseph, 15 Aug. 1650, d. at two yrs.; Eliz. Dorothy; Abigail; and Judith, wh. perhaps bec. w. of Rev. Jabez Fox of Woburn. One of the ds. whose name is lost from the Col. Rec. was b. 26 Dec. 1647. After 18 years of serv. at P. he rem. to Dover, there d. 20 Apr. 1669. He had est. at Gildersome, the place of his nativ. in the parish of Batley in the W. riding of Yorksh. near Leeds, where the celebr. Dr. Priestly was b. His will, made only one or two days bef. he d. pro. 30 June foll. directs the div. of rents from his lds. at Gildersome, provides for his w. and their five ch. having formerly provid. for ch. by first w. and in case his w. m. again, carefully devises both the Dover and Eng. est. Mr. Hunter, in Early Hist. of the Founders of New Plymouth, 4 Mass. Hist. Coll. I. 84, supposed he may be derived from Bassetlaw in Co. Notts. But he was b. at no gr. distance, as the same accurate inquirer, in his revised work, London 1854, pp. 118 and 119, proves. He made his name Reyner. JOHN, Dover, s. of the preced. ord. 12 July 1671, m. Judith, d. of Edmund Quincy sec. of Braintree, and in short time after d. at B. 21 Dec. 1676, prob. without ch. aged 33. His wid. d. 8 Mar. 1679 or 80, as the gr.-st. inscript. blindly makes it. JOHN, Charlestown, by. w. Catharine, wh. d. 22 Dec. 1682, in her 23d yr. had John, wh. d. the day bef. his mo. and he m. 31 July 1685, Abigail Hathorne, wh. d. 17 May 1714, in her 47th yr.; had Abigail, bapt. 21 June 1691, d. young, and two ds. Eliz. wh. both d. young; beside John bapt. 25 Dec. 1687, wh. reached mid. life. JOHN, Rowley 1691. JONATHAN and JOSEPH, Southampton, L. I. 1663–73, were perhaps s. of Thurston. SAMUEL, Watertown, had been of Cambridge, where by w. Mary he had Hannah, b. 2 Mar. 1654, wh. m. 7 Apr. 1670, Ephraim Winship; d. 1669, in his will 26 Sept. of that yr. names w. Mary and a. d. SAMUEL, Charlestown, by w. Mary had Sarah, bapt. 8 May 1687. THOMAS, Hempstead, L. I. 1643, acc. Wood's Hist. yet possib. the name may be mistaken for the foll. ‡ * THURSTON, Watertown, came in the Elizabeth 1634, from Ipswich, Co. Suff. aged 40, with w. Eliz. 36; Thurston, 13; Joseph, 11; Eliz. 9; Sarah, 7; and Lydia, 1; who, by the order of their names in the rec. certif. up to London, may be thot. his ch. and Edward, foll. on the same list, aged 10, may have been s. or neph. in 1636; rem. to Wethersfield, was rep. 1638, 9, and 40; rem. 1641 to Stamford, there had commiss. from New Haven jurisdict. but in few years rem. to

Southampton, L. I. under Conn. and was an assist. 1661 and 3 ; made his will 6 July, 1667, pro. same yr. In it he names w. Martha, two s. Joseph and Jonathan, beside allud. to four more ch. not nam. Jonathan was not of age. His d. Hannah m. Arthur Howell, as his sec. w. Mather in Magn. II. 33, forgot his bapt. name. WILLIAM, Marblehead, the freem. of 1670, may have been s. of that WILLIAM wh. d. 1666, having m. as Farmer says in MS. note, Eliz. wid. of Humphrey Gilbert. This was aged 45 in 1668.

RAYNGER, EDMUND, Boston, a witness to the will of Gov. Bellingham, 25 Nov. 1672, as in Geneal. Reg. XIV. 238. He was of Bristol 1688.

REA, JOSHUA, Salem. See Ray.

READ or REED, ABRAHAM, Salem, s. of the first Thomas, had Samuel, wh. went to Eng. and by deed at London, 1701, convey. to Daniel Epps part of est. of his gr.f. that fell to his f. and early in this centu. was kn. as the Derby farm. ARTHUR, perhaps of Stratford 1676. See Trumbull, Col. Rec. II. 424. BENJAMIN, Duxbury, fit to bear arms 1643. DANIEL, Rehoboth, s. of John first of the same, m. at Taunton 20 Mar. 1677, Hannah Peck, but Col. Rec. says 20 Aug. of that yr. had Hannah, b. 30 June 1678 ; Bethia, 2 Nov. 1679 ; Daniel, 20 Jan. 1681 ; John, 25 Feb. 1683, d. in few ds. prob. sev. others, and d. 17 Oct. 1710. DANIEL, Woburn, s. of Ralph, m. 17 Jan. 1699, purch. the squaw sachem farm, so call. on wh. as is said, his descend. still reside. EDWARD, Marblehead 1674. * ESDRAS, Salem 1639, had Bethia, b. a. 1637 ; and Obadiah, 1639 ; both bapt. there, 31 May 1640, b. by w. prob. named Alice ; was freem. 2 June 1641, rem. to Wenham, of wh. he was rep. 1648 and 51, and with his min. rem. 1655 to Chelmsford. ESDRAS, Boston 1661, a tailor, perhaps s. of the preced. was with his w. adm. of the sec. ch. that yr. GEORGE, Woburn, s. of William of Dorchester, b. in Eng. m. 4 Oct. 1652, Eliz. d. of Robert Jennison, (not Jennings, as oft. said), wh. d. 26 Feb. 1665, had Eliz. b. 29 July 1653 ; twins, d. 14 Nov. 1654, prob. few hours old ; Samuel, 29 Apr. 1656 ; Abigail, 27 June 1658 ; George, 14 Sept. 1660 ; William, 22 Sept. 1662 ; Sarah, 12 Feb. 1665 ; and by sec. w. of unkn. name, Hannah, 18 Feb. 1670 ; John, 18 Mar. 1672 ; Mary, 15 June 1674 ; Timothy, 20 Oct. 1678 ; and Thomas, 15 July 1682, was freem. 1684 ; Eliz. m. 15 Dec. 1675, Daniel Fiske. I presume he was s. of William of Newcastle in Northumberland, and d. 21 Feb. 1706. GEORGE, Woburn, s. of the preced. freem. 1690, by w. Abigail Pierce, m. 15 Feb. 1685, wh. d. 7 Sept. 1719, had Abigail, b. 6 Feb. 1686 ; Ebenezer, 6 Mar. 1690 ; George, 2 Aug. 1697, d. in few wks. and Eliz. 14 June 1700. He m. sec. w. 24 May 1721, Sybel Rice, prob. wid. of Isaac, and was, it is said, the first deac. in ch. of Burlington. ISRAEL, Woburn, by w. Mary, had Mary, b.

15 Oct. 1670; Sarah, 29 Aug. 1673; a d. without name on the rec. 2 June, 1679; Eliz. 22 Dec. 1681; Ruth, 6 Jan. 1684; Israel, 17 Mar. 1687; Jemima, 23 July 1689; and Patience, 3 Dec. 1697. ISRAEL, Rehoboth, youngest s. of John the first, m. 6 Nov. 1684, Rebecca, youngest d. of the third John Ruggles of Roxbury, had eleven ch. but my correspond. gives date or name to neither, and he d. 17 Nov. 1732. JACOB, Salem, s. of the first Thomas, own. est. in 1661, but prob. d. bef. his f. or at least nothing more is kn. of him. JACOB, Salem, s. of the sec. Thomas, m. Dec. 1693, Eliz. Green, had Aaron, b. June 1694; John, 26 Dec. 1695; Mary, 1697; Jacob, 1699; Jonathan, 12 Jan. 1701; Sarah, 15 May, 1703; and Eliz.·13 Mar. 1705. His will was of 5 Jan. 1741, and his w. then liv. JAMES, Taunton, s. perhaps youngest, of William of Dorchester, perhaps the soldier of Johnson's comp. in Philip's war, m. 18 Apr. 1683, Susanna Richmond, d. of John, had James, William, John, Thomas, Mary, b. 1697, Martha, Ann, and Susanna. ‖ JOHN, Dorchester, rem. to Weymouth or Braintree, freem. 13 May 1640, ar. co. 1644, had Abigail, b. at Dorchester; John, 29 Aug. 1640; and Thomas, 20 Nov. 1641; rem. to Rehoboth, 1645, there had, perhaps, William; Samuel; Moses, Oct. 1650; Mary, June 1652; Eliz. Jan. 1654; Daniel, Mar. 1655; Israel, 1657; and Mehitable, Aug. 1659; was one of good prop. and influence, whose gr.stone, still extant, it is said, shows that he d. Sept. 1685, aged 87. JOHN, jr. Rehoboth, s. of the preced. who had sh. in div. of lds. 1668, and by w. Sarah had John, b. 8 Dec. 1669; Thomas, 23 July 1672; beside Sarah bur. 19 July 1673, was k. by the Ind. at Pierce's fight, 26 Mar. 1676. JOHN, New London 1651, had then gr. of ld. wh. he forfeit. by neglect of resid. JOHN, Weymouth, s. of William first of the same, is prob. he wh. m. Bethia, d. of George Fry, rem. to Taunton, had William, Thomas, George, Mary, Ruth, and Hannah, prob. some of them bef. rem. and d. at Dighton, 13 Jan. 1721. His wid. d. 20 Oct. 1730, aged 77. He may have been of Johnson's comp. in Philip's war, and by a former w. had John, b. 5 June 1674; but neither her surname, nor bapt. name can I decipher from the MS. of my friend. correspondent. JOHN, Scituate, may be that youth bound 1653 to Michael Pierce for nine yrs. personal serv. as rec. in 1662, m. 1668, Mary, d. of Christopher Winter, had John; liv. some yrs. at Marshfield, and d. 21 May 1694. JOHN, Rye, rem. to Norwalk, prob. had John, as in 1687, he is disting. as sen. and both liv. there 1694. JOHN, Woburn, s. of Ralph, m. 21 Mar. 1682, Eliz. Holden, perhaps d. of Richard, had John, b. 22 Mar. 1684; Ralph, 6 Sept. 1686; Eliz. 25 Feb. 1691; and he took sec. w. 4 Dec. 1705, Abigail Baldwin, perhaps d. of Henry. JOHN, Woburn, s. of George the first, m. 10 Jan. 1697, Ruth Johnson, prob. d. of Matthew, but I hear no

more. JOHN, Boston, whose f. by no dilig. inquiry can be ascert. but seems to be entit. to insert. here, tho. the first ment. of him is as gr. at H. C. 1697, bec. it is so high a prob. that he was either b. on our side of the ocean, or at least had been here so many yrs. JOSEPH and JOSIAH, of Lynn, are among the freem. of 1681. The former came to Boston 1671, in the Arabella from London. JOSIAH, New London 1662, rem. to Norwich, m. at Marshfield, Nov. 1666, Grace Holloway, had Josiah, b. Apr. 1668; William, Apr. 1670; Eliz. Sept. 1672; Experience, 27 Feb. 1675; John, 15 Apr. 1679; Joseph, 12 Mar. 1681; Susanna, 20 Sept. 1685; Hannah, July 1688; and he d. 3 July 1711. His wid. d. 9 May 1727. MATTHEW, Norwalk, adm. to be an inhab. 1655, but his name is not found after. Hall's Hist. 48. MICHAEL, nam. in the will of William, pro. at London, 31 Oct. 1656, as one of three s. m. in N. E. but the name is not kn. to me as of an inhab. *MOSES, Rehoboth, s. of the first John, m. at Taunton, 6 Dec. 1677, Rebecca Fitch, had Zechariah, b. 25 Oct. 1678, d. in Jan. foll.; Zechariah again, 20 Oct. 1681; Rebecca, 14 Sept. 1683; was rep. sev. yrs. and d. 14 Dec. 1716. NICHOLAS, Danvers, apprent. of Edward Putnam, k. by the Ind. Sept. 1689, aged 18. OBADIAH, Boston, m. 19 Aug. 1664, Ann, d. of Obadiah Swift, had Eliz. b. 29 Mar. 1669; Sarah, 16 Apr. 1671, d. young; Ann, 3 Feb. 1673; Obadiah, 29 Nov. 1677, d. soon; Obadiah, again, 29 Nov. 1678, d. young; and James, 29 Feb. 1680. His w. d. 13 Sept. foll. aged 33; and by w. Eliz. he had Obadiah, again, 27 Mar. 1683; Mary, 4 May 1684; Nathaniel, 23 Aug. 1686; and Sarah, again, 26 Jan. 1688. PHILIP, Weymouth 1640, by w. Mary had Philip, b. 24 Oct. 1641; Samuel; and Mary, wh. m. 27 Nov. 1669, John Vining; was prob. the freem. of 1660, and his will of 15 Dec. 1674, was pro. 5 May 1676. PHILIP, Lynn 1669, a physician, is presum. to be that resident of Concord, wh. after liv. there 25 yrs. d. 10 May 1696. PHILIP, Weymouth, s. of Philip the first, by w. Hannah had Mary b. 21 Mar. 1669; Hannah, 18 Feb. 1672; Philip, 2 Nov. 1674; John, 16. Aug. 1676; and prob. these by w. Abigail, Samuel, 29 Sept. 1681; Prudence, 7 Oct. 1685; Stephen, 15 Oct. 1690; and Deborah, 30 Aug. 1692. RALPH, Woburn, s. of William of Dorchester, brought from Eng. by his f. in very early youth, by w. Mary, d. of Anthony Pierce of Watertown, had William, b. 1658; John, 1660; Joseph; Daniel; Timothy, b. 14 Feb. 1665; David; and Jonathan. RICHARD, Marblehead 1674, in June 1678 was witness with Samuel R. to the will of Samuel Condy. RICHARD, Boston, by w. Joanna, had Mary, b. 26 Mar. 1687, and perhaps others. ROBERT, Exeter 1638, was one of the first sett. at Hampton, but rem. to Boston, there by w. Hannah, had Rebecca, b. 29 Sept. bapt. 1 Nov. 1646, wh. prob. d. young; again went to Hampton, there had

Hannah, Mary, and Sarah; again rem. to Boston, perhaps, where he had the last ment. bapt. 1 Sept. 1650; and Samuel, 3 Apr. 1653; this s. d. the end of Mar. foll. and ano. Samuel was b. 28 Feb. 1655. His w. d. 24 June foll. and he went once more to Hampton, had ano. w. Susanna; and was drown. 20 Oct. 1657, by overset. of a boat. See Belkn. I. 58, of Farmer's ed. His wid. m. John Preston, and she join. with the childr. in convey. of est. in B. Hannah m. 11 Jan. 1661, John Senter of Boston. SAMUEL, Mendon, s. of John the first, freem. 1673, m. 1668, Hopestill Holbrook, perhaps d. of William the first, had Samuel, John, Josiah, and Ebenezer, beside Mary, w. prob. of Seth Chapin; but dates are not seen. His will was of 5 Apr. 1717. The s. John is said to be that gr. of H. C. 1697, wh. was held the greatest lawyer this country produc. bef. the Americ. Revo. exc. perhaps Judge Trowbridge. See full exhibit. of his esteem in Eliot's Biogr. Dict. SAMUEL, Marblehead 1674, perhaps br. of Richard. SAMUEL, Charlestown, s. of George the first, a physician, m. 19 June 1679, Eliz. d. of John Mousal, had Eliz. b. 3 Apr. 1680; Joanna, 16 Feb. 1681; Abigail, 10 Jan. 1683; Samuel, 16 July 1688, d. in few days; Mary, 9 Jan. 1690; Mercy, 29 Nov. 1697. THOMAS, Salem 1630, freem. 1 Apr. 1634, was made ens. 1637, had s. Thomas, Abraham, and perhaps others, and he may earlier have been of Lynn and Marblehead, at wh. latter he was a witness, 28 Sept. 1630, bef. coroner's jury. THOMAS, Salem, elder s. of the preced. by w. Mary, had Susanna, bapt. 23 Sept. 1649; John, 15 June 1651; Mary, 10 Apr. 1653; Eliz. 13 May 1655; Remember, 26 Apr. 1657; Jacob, 5 June 1659; Sarah, 15 Mar. 1661; but prob. the last two d. young, for ano. Jacob was bapt. there 7 Nov. 1663; and Sarah, again, 19 Aug. 1666. Yet here, without doubt, is some confus. and more omis. I feel sure there were two, and prob. three Thomases contempo. at Salem. The first had title of Col. and d. abroad a. 1663; left beside a sec. w. call. Elsy, two s. of wh. Abraham, the younger, was admor. By Wait Winthrop, his atty. Samuel, only s. of the other Thomas, calling hims. merch. of London, sold 28 June 1701, to Daniel Epps the farm at Salem that had belong. to his f. But Essex Inst. II. 16, gives inv. of ano. THOMAS, tak. 5 Apr. 1667. THOMAS, Milford 1646, may have been a promin. man at Newtown, L. I. 1656. THOMAS, Sudbury, may be the freem. of 1656, had Thomas, and perhaps more, d. 19 Sept. 1701, as Mr. Shattuck thinks. THOMAS, Boston, by w. Mary had Eliz. b. 28 Jan. 1657; and he d. 11 May 1661. THOMAS, Rehoboth, s. of John the first, m. 29 Mar. 1665, Eliz. Clark, bur. 23 Feb. 1675, aged 32; and m. 16 June 1675, Ann Perrin, perhaps d. of the first John, had John, wh. d. 4 Dec. 1676; Thomas, 25 Mar. 1678; Nathaniel, 30 Mar. 1680; and Hannah, 12 Apr. 1682; and he d. 6 Feb. 1696. THOMAS, Weymouth, s. of William the first, by w. Sarah had Thomas, b. 12 Sept. 1671; John, 30 Dec. 1679; Samuel, 12 Apr. 1681; Ruth, 20 Feb. 1685; William, 4 Feb. 1688; Hannah, 25 Sept. 1689; and Eliz. 9 Nov. 1694. THOMAS, Sudbury, s. of Thomas of the same, m. 30 May, 1677, Mary, d. of John Goodrich of Wethersfield, had fam. was freem. 1678, then call. jun. One THOMAS of New Hampsh. 1689, pray. for jurisdict. of Mass. THOMAS, Woburn, youngest s. of George the first, m. 1 Feb. 1704, Sarah Sawyer. TIMOTHY, Woburn, s. of Ralph, m. 27 Dec. 1688, Martha Boyden, had Martha, b. 1 Mar. 1690; William, 5 Oct. 1694, so nam. for a bro. k. by the f.; Jonathan, 15 Dec. 1701, d. young; Eliz. 1 Dec. 1706; and Mary, 25 Dec. 1709; and by sec. w. Persis, had Persis, 21 July 1711; Timothy, 27 Sept. 1713; Jacob, 31 Jan. 1716; and Jonathan again, 19 May 1718. But it must be told, that the h. of Persis, to wh. these last four ch. are giv. is, by my correspond. call. s. of George the first. WILLIAM, Boston, perhaps very early, but more prob. not, as it seems likely that most, if not all of his ch. were brot. from Eng. So far as can be gather. or reasona. conject. they were Margaret, wh. m. 3 Mar. 1659, Richard Stubbs; Susanna m. 13 Dec. 1659, Samuel Smith; Esther m. 30 July 1661, John Canney, all at B. Edward, Richard, and Samuel, all at Marblehead, and it is said Christopher, wh. d. at Charlestown 1696. Tradit. tells, that he d. at sea, on a passage, 1667, hither from Ireland. *WILLIAM, Weymouth. freem. 2 Sept. 1635, rep. 1636 and 8, had John; William, b. 15 Dec. 1639; Esther, 8 May 1641; and prob. others, certain Mary wh. d. by rec. 16 Apr. 1655. But ano. Mary, d. of one William at W. m. 11 May 1657, John Vining, by the same rec. so that some mistake may be fear. Perhaps the earlier date refers to the mo. of the m. Mary. He had also Thomas, Margaret, and James. WILLIAM, Dorchester, came prob. in the Defence 1635, aged 48, with w. Mabel, 30; 'George, 6; Ralph, 5; and Justus, 18 mos. and had at D. Abigail, bapt. 30 Dec. 1638; was freem. 14 Mar. 1639; rem. prob. first to Rehoboth, or perhaps liv. at Woburn. WILLIAM, Boston, perhaps br. of the first John, there by w. Susanna, had Susanna; and, John b. 25, bapt. 27 Sept. 1646, a. 4 days old, as the ch. rec. says. His w. d. 12 Oct. 1653, and he m. 20 May 1654, Ruth Crook, had William, 3 Feb. 1655, d. soon; Isaac, 18 Apr. 1656; Ephraim, 23 Nov. 1657; Jonathan, 23 Apr. 1659; Timothy, 11 Aug. 1660; William, again, 7 May 1662; Hezekiah, 6 July 1663; Sarah, 26 June 1665; Eliz. 22 Dec. 1666; and Eliz. again, 22 Apr. 1669. He may have been of the first proprs. of Worcester, 1674. His d. Hannah d. 25 Nov. 1656, by rec. and d. Susanna m. 13 Dec. 1659, Samuel Smith. WILLIAM, Norwalk 1654, perhaps was only a transient man, and very soon aft. of Newtown, L. I. WILLIAM, Boston, by w.

Hannah had William, b. 26 Mar. 1665, unless there be error in town
rec. wh. is not very improb. and John, 25 Apr. 1669. WILLIAM, Woburn, eldest s. of Ralph, by w. Eliz. had William, b. 23 Aug. 1682;
Mary, 12 Mar. 1685; Eliz. 23 Feb. 1687; was casual. k. by his own
bro. Timothy, 7 Nov. 1688, shooting at a deer. WILLIAM, Woburn, s.
of George, m. 24 May 1686, Abigail Kendall. WILLIAM, Weymouth,
s. of William the first of the same, not the freem. 1653, m. 1675 Esther
Thompson, had William; Esther; John, b. 21 Oct. 1680; ano. ch.
whose name is not in the rec. 24 May 1682; John, again, 10 July 1687;
so that prob. the first John d. young; Jacob, 6 Nov. 1691; and Sarah,
21 Mar. 1694; beside others, as we are confident, for his will of 26 Oct.
1705, pro. 12 Sept. foll. names w. Esther; eldest s. William; John; Jacob, and ds. Bathshua Porter; Mercy Whitmarsh; and unm. ones,
Mary; Esther; and Sarah. This name is very common, often written
Reed, and under either form likely to breed confus. betw. sev. hav. the
same bapt. title. Aft. spend. many hours of sev. days, I am unable to
reconcile and fix the habita. of all. Farmer found 60 gr. in the N. E.,
N. J., and Union Coll. 1829. Twelve at Harv. and eleven at Yale had
been gr. in 1834.

READER, JOHN, Springfield 1636, had gr. of ld. but did not long cont.ʳ
perhaps was of New Haven in 1643; Stratford 1650; but last of Newtown, L. I. 1656.

REAPE, SAMUEL, Newport, m. bef. 30 Jan. 1669, Joanna, wid. of
Zechariah Rhoades. THOMAS, Boston, m. 30 Nov. 1660, by Gov.
Endicott, to Judith, wid. of Robert Ratchell. WILLIAM, Newport, by
w. Sarah, had Sarah, b. 17 Apr. 1664; and William, 31 Dec. 1667;
and d. 6 Aug. 1670, aged 42.

RECORD, JOHN, Weymouth, was a soldier on Conn. Riv. in Philip's
war 1676, and in July 1677, m. at Hingham, Hannah, d. of Thomas
Hobart.

REDDING, RIDDAN, or READING, JOHN, Sandwich, m. 22 Oct. 1676,
Mary Bassett, perhaps d. of William the sec. JOSEPH, Boston, early
one of the ch. and prob. came in the fleet with Winth. rem. to Cambridge 1632, was freem. 14 May 1634, and at Ipswich 1637, where a
wid. R. perhaps his, was liv. 1678. MILES, Boston, perhaps br. of the
preced. a cooper, came prob. with Winth. for in the list of first ch.
mem. his No. is 81, freem. 14 May 1634, was a propr. of Billerica 1665.
THADDEUS, Lynn, by w. Eliz. had Hannah and Sarah, tw. b. 12 Aug.
1660, of wh. Hannah d. in 3 mos.; Hannah again, 11 Nov. 1662; John,
3 Feb. 1665; and Abigail, 4 June 1671; was of Marblehead 1674.
THOMAS, Saco 1652, freem. 1653. See Folsom, 183. This name,
Farmer says, is found still in N. H.

REDDOCK, HENRY, Providence 1645–55, in 1661 liv. at Warwick, was f.-in-law of Christopher Hauxhurst. JOHN, Sudbury, an orig. propr. 1640.

REDFIELD, or REDFIN, JAMES, New London, perhaps as early as 1649. One of the name is ment. at Edgartown 1671, yet he may more likely be the foll. JAMES, New London, s. of William, apprent. to a tanner 1662, but prob. bec. a weaver, m. at New Haven, Eliz. Howe, d. of Jeremiah, in May 1669, had Eliz. b. 31 May 1670; and Sarah; beside Theophilus 1682; seems to be resid. at Saybrook in 1676. He rem. to Fairfield, m. Deborah, d. of John Sturges, had Margaret, bapt. 7 Oct. 1694; and James, 25 Oct. 1696; and prob. d. aft. 1719, when he gave est. to s. James. WILLIAM, New London, soon after 1646, br. prob. of James the first, by w. Rebecca, had Rebecca, wh. m. 12 Dec. 1661, Thomas Roach; Lydia, wh. m. 10 Jan. 1656, Thomas Bayley; James, bef. ment. and Judith, wh. m. 17 June 1667, Alexander Pygan; and d. 1662. He had been of Cambridge 1639–42, in the S. part now Newton, where he sold his est. Sept. 1646, to Edward Jackson, being in my opinion, the same man call. by Jackson, in his Hist. 9 and 23 (mistak. the letter *f*, for the ancient long *s*, in his name), Redson, Redsyn, or Redsen. Prob. some of his ch. were b. in Eng. one or more at C.

REDFORD, CHARLES, Salem, merch. was capt. of the troop 1691, perhaps went home, d. 1692, Felt says.

REDIAT, RIDIAT, or RADYATE, JOHN, Sudbury, freem. 1645, by w. Ann had John, b. 19 Apr. 1644; Samuel, 22 Oct. 1653, d. in few wks. and Eliz. 12 Aug. 1657; perhaps others. Deborah R. m. at Concord, 22 May 1679, Daniel Farrabas, as sec. w. is in his will of 5 Feb. 1687, made at Marlborough, pro. 28 Apr. foll. call his d. Farrowbush, and therein favored with good part of his est. ano. part to Mehitable, his d. w. of Nathaniel Oakes, and some provis. for gr.ch. John and Mary R. s. and d. of his dec. s. John. JOHN, Sudbury, s. of the preced. by w. Susanna had John; Susanna, b. 1 Dec. 1672; and Mary, 8 Feb. 1675; and d. 1676. His wid. m. John Miles of Concord; Susanna, m. 26 Dec. 1692, Jacob Farrar; Mary, m. 1 Sept. 1696, Nathaniel Jones; and John d. 5 Aug. 1694, prob. without issue, and the name perhaps is extinct.

REDINGTON, * ABRAHAM, Rowley 1667, was rep. in 1686, for Topsfield or Boxford, freem. 1690. I suppose he m. Mary or Margaret, d. of Zacheus Gould of T. but no issue is kn. to me, unless he be (as highly prob. it seems), that man, call. in Geneal. Reg. VIII. 77, Pedington, whose s. Benjamin was b. 19 Apr. 1661. DANIEL, Topsfield, freem. 1685. THOMAS, Boxford, freem. 1690.

REDKNAP or REDNAPE, BENJAMIN, Lynn, s. of Joseph, freem. 1691, had Sarah, b. 8 Feb. 1675; Hannah, 9 Apr. 1679; Rebecca, 9 Aug.

1682; and Joseph, 20 Jan. 1684. JOSEPH, Lynn, a wine-cooper from London, came prob. in 1634, was freem. 3 Sept. of that yr. had a fam. Nathaniel and Benjamin, or d. Sarah, wh. m. 28 Dec. 1671, Thomas Laighton; certain. liv. to gr. age. Presid. Dudley pro. his will 28 Oct. 1686, that was made 20 May 1681, at Lynn. It names only s. Nathaniel, to wh. he gave ld. at Springfield; and Benjamin, mak. the latter excor. and devis. to him est. at Lynn. Hutch I. 341, says he came over at 60 (but he could be little more than 40), and d. in Boston, aged 110. He foll. authority of Judge Sewall (wh. in one place says he d. at Lynn), not doubting to draw the conclus. as to his age on arr. when S. said he liv. here a. 50 yrs. To this weight, Felt, Eccl. Hist. I. 531 offers no resistance. But as the Court rec. of Essex Co. show that giv. evidence in 1657, he was a. 60, and in 1670, he call. hims. betw. 70 and 80, we may judge with highest confidence, that when he d. 22 Jan. 1686, he had not run much beyond 90, and perhaps not reached it. Lewis, whose regard was absorbed by Boniface Burton, barely refers to Sewall's liberal allowance to Redknap, but gives no addit. to the credit of the tradit. Sewall was very apt to believe what old persons told him, often when their habits or power of mind should rather have led to distrust their evidence. He owned est. at Hampton in Co. Middlesex, called Blackbush right, near Hampton Court, wh. he sold in 1649 to Edward Tomlyns.

REDMAN, JOHN, Hampton, a blacksmith, one of the early sett. in 1685 was call. 70 yrs. old. JOHN, Hampton 1678, prob. s. of the preced. m. Martha, d. of John Cass, may have had John. RICHARD, Boston 1639, a mariner, was charged for murder, 1645, in Delaware Bay, long imprison. but acquit. for defect. of evid. See Winthr. II. 237. Yet the Court rec. seems to permit us to suppose, that his discharge was for conven. of the prison keeper. ROBERT, Dorchester, was of Milton when he made his will, 30 Dec. 1678, pro. 31 Jan. foll. wh. ment. w. Luce; eldest s. John; youngest s. Charles; ds. Mercy; Ruth wh. m. Everenden, that is an unkn. man; and s.-in-law William Delene, also unkn. so by conject. may seem h. of Ruth.

REDWAY, REDWEY, READAWAY, or REDDAWAY, JAMES, Rehoboth 1646, prob. had John, perhaps more, as Sarah, wh. m. 25 May 1660, Samuel Carpenter; and was bur. 28 Oct. 1676. JOHN, Rehoboth, prob. s. of the preced. had James, b. 10 Jan. 1679; and John, 10 Sept. 1682.

REEVE, or REEVES, HENRY, came in the Speedwell 1656, from London, aged only 8 yrs. but to whose care he was deliv. we kn. not. JOHN, Salem, came in the Christian to Boston 1635, aged 19, from London, prob. as apprent. of Francis Stiles, wh. next yr. carr. him to Windsor; but in 1643, he had gr. of ld. at S. by w. Jane, a mem. of the ch. 1640, had William; Freeborn, b. 10 Mar. 1658; and Benjamin, 30 Dec. 1661; but he had sec. w. Eliz. wh. may have been mo. of these last two. A few yrs. later, wid. Reeves was excommun. by the ch. ROBERT, Hartford, by w. Eliz. d. of John Nott of Wethersfield, had Sarah, b. 25 Dec. 1663; Mary, 31 July 1665; Eliz. Dec. 1668; Hannah, Oct. 1670; Nathaniel, Oct. 1672; Robert and Ann, tw. Apr. 1675; Abraham, Sept. 1677; and Mehitable, Mar. 1680; made his will 23 Dec. 1680, and d. in Feb. foll. One of his s. went to L. I. The venerable Dr. Stiles in " History of Three of the Judges," the regicides, gave this name Peirce, p. 352. THOMAS, Roxbury, came in the Bevis 1638, from Southampton, serv. of Henry Byley of Salisbury, at R. was serv. of John Gore until 1644, m. at R. 15 Apr. 1645, Hannah Rowe, was made freem. that yr. had Thomas, bapt. 5 July 1646; rem. that yr. to Springfield, there had Hannah, 11 Feb. 1649; and John, 12 Mar. 1651, posthum. d. next yr. was the town drummer and° d. 5 Nov. 1650. His wid. m. 4 June 1651, Richard Exell; Mary, perhaps his d. m. 17 Feb. 1670, William Webster, and was terribly troubled as a witch. THOMAS, Southampton, L. I. 1673, was prob. that goodman R. of the adjoining town of Southold, made freem. of Conn. 1662; had a d. wh. m. Peter Dickinson; perhaps other childr. and it may be that Tapping R. the learned jurisprud. of Conn. wh. was b. at Southold, deriv. blood from him. WILLIAM, Salem 1668, prob. br. of John, came in the Elizabeth and Ann, from London 1635, aged 22. WILLIAM, Medford, s. of John, m. 14 Mar. 1669, Eliz. Collins, had John, Cochran, and Eliz.

REGION, THOMAS, a soldier in Moseley's comp. Dec. 1675.

REITH, RICHARD, Lynn, m. 16 Feb. 1665, Eliz. George, as Mr. Felt copies the rec. The name is strange; but he is found at Marblehead 1674.

RELPH, RALPH, or RELF, THOMAS, Warwick, m. 1655 or 6, Mary, wid. of John Cooke of the same. But he had liv. some yrs. bef. at Guilford, there by w. Eliz. Desborough or Disbrow, had Samuel, and his w. obt. divorce from him for his fault, and m. 1 Oct. 1651, John Johnson. He had prob. liv. some time at W. bef. getting the new w. and by her had Alice, b. 13 Jan. 1657, d. young; Thomas, 12 July 1658; Sarah, 4 Dec. 1661; and Deliverance, 20 Aug. 1666; beside Benjamin, of wh. the last four with Samuel, are ment. in his will, pro. 1682. It also names gr.ch. William Fenner, and cousin Samuel Stafford.

REMICK CHRISTIAN, Kittery, freem. 1652. In Maine and New Hampsh. this name is diffus. and on Cape Cod, prob. as descend. are seen in ea. direction.

REMINGTON, or RIMMINGTON, JOHN, Newbury, 1637, freem. 22 May 1639, rem. to incorp. with Bradstreet, Denison and others as milit. comp.

1645, and was lieut. had Joseph, b. 1650; and Thomas. His w. Eliz.
d. Dec. 1657, and he rem. to Roxbury, there m. Rhoda, wid. of John
Gore, and d. or was bur. 8 June 1667. JOHN, Haverhill and Andover,
had w. Abigail, and s. Daniel, b. 18 Oct. 1661; and Hannah, 3 July
1664. JONATHAN, Cambridge, b. in Rowley 1639, perhaps s. of John
the first, m. 13 July, 1664; Martha, d. of Andrew Belcher, had Martha,
b. 18 Feb. 1667; Jonathan, 18 Mar. 1669; both d. in Apr. 1669;
Martha again, 28 Oct. 1674; Jonathan, 27 July 1677, H. C. 1696;
Samuel, 11 July 1679, d. next yr.; Ann, 30 Jan. 1681; John, wh. d. 6
Apr. 1689; and Sarah, 10 May 1688. He was selectman, town clk.
and treasur. d. 21 Apr. 1700, and his wid. Martha d. 16 July 1711.
His s. Jonathan, one of the judges of the Sup. Ct. d. 1745, had Jonathan,
H. C. 1736, wh. d. after two yrs. THOMAS, Windsor, had Thomas, John,
and Sarah, perhaps bef. he went there perhaps from Rowley, where he
perhaps had w. Mehitable, and was freem. 1672; had Joseph, b. at W.
1 Sept. 1675; rem. to Suffield, there had Benjamin 1677; took o. of
alleg. 1679, with s. Thomas and John, they being then 16 yrs. old and
upwards. Thomas d. 1683, prob. unm. John m. in 1687; and Sarah
m. 1689, Peter Rose; but when the f. d. is unkn. THOMAS, Hingham,
m. Mar. 1688, Remember Stowell. Five of the name had in 1798,
been gr. at Harv. and one at Yale.

RENDALL, JAMES, perhaps of Portsmouth 1686, m. I suppose, Martha
wid. of John Lewis, d. of William Brooking. See Randall.

REVELL, ‡ JOHN, Salem, a merch. of London, greatly engag. in the
promot. of settlem. of Mass. Bay, by the Gov. and Comp. chos. an
Assist. 20 Oct. 1629, came in the Jewell, one of Winthrop's fleet, June
1630, but went home next mo. in the Lion. THOMAS, New London 1658,
a merch. from London at Barbadoes 1660, but liv. here 1662–66. Miss
Caulkins thinks he was proscribed at the restorat. having stood for the
Commonwealth, that he is the hermit of Braintree at a later date, called
" Tom Revel," a regicide, or holy hermit gone crazy, he and his hog en-
joying their common stye, of wh. absurd tradit. in Whitney's Hist. of
Quincy is given, " that when he d. the Gov. of the Province and other
disting. men came out from Boston, and were his pall-bearers." That the
hog, being nearest relat. was chief mourner, is unaccountab. omit. Usual.
there is some slight foundation of truth, to afford appear. of support to the
wildest story; but here even that is wanting. We read the ridic. tale in
a note on p. 36. Every one knows, that there was no regicide of this name;
that no Gov. of the Prov. after 1691, could have been such a fool, nor
would any Gov. of the Col. after 1660, have shown such public honor to
a regicide; nor lastly is any such name, as Rev. W. P. Lunt, after scrutiny of Braintree rec. assures me, to be found among d. at B.

Rew, Edward, Newport 1638, was of Taunton 1643, where he m. Sarah, d. of John Richmond; and Baylies says II. 282, he d. 16 July 1678, leav. no ch. and his wid. m. 4 Nov. foll. James Walker.

Rex, William, unless the name be misspell. was a propr. of Watertown 1642, liv. at Boston aft. there by w. Grace had Elisha, b. Aug. 1645; Mary, 4 Mar. 1647; and Ezekiel, 30 Nov. 1656.

Reyner. See Rayner.

Reynolds, Renold, or Renolds, Francis, Kingstown, in the Narraganset country, 1686, was perhaps s. of James the first. Henry, Salem, had gr. of ld. 1642, was of Lynn 1647, and perhaps again of S. Henry, Kingstown, wh. m. Sarah, d. of James Greene, was br. of Francis. See 3 Mass. Hist. Coll. 183. James, Plymouth, if we may suppose his name to be carelessly spell. Renell in 1643, perhaps rem. to R. I. jurisdict. and bef. 1674, was with fam. of sev. s. estab. at Wickford, in the Narraganset ld. and in the conflict betw. Conn. and R. I. for jurisdict. was imprison. by one party. See Trumbull, Col. Rec. II. 540. James, jr. and Joseph, inhab. there 1687, as well as bef. ment. Francis and Henry, may have all been his s. of wh. James m. 19 Feb. 1685, Mary d. of James Greene; Henry m. Sarah, ano. d. of the same; and Eliz. ano. d. m. also a Reynolds. John, Watertown 1634, freem. 6 May 1635; Sarah, perhaps his w. came with many people of W. in the Elizabeth from Ipswich, Co. Suff. 1634, aged 20, rem. in two yrs. to Wethersfield, rem. again bef. 1644, to Stamford, and may have been f. of Jonathan and John, freem. in 1669, of Greenwich, where the fam. long contin. John, an early sett. at Isle of Shoals, complain. against in 1647 (when he was constable), for having a w. there, as he might have been on the mainland, for not hav. one. See 1 Mass. Hist. Coll. VII. 250. John, Saybrook, rem. to Norwich, with first sett. a. 1659, made freem. 1663, selectman 1669; had eleven ch. of wh. Caulkins in her Hist. ment. John, b. at S. Aug. 1655; Sarah, Nov. 1656; Susanna, Oct. 1658; Joseph, Mar. 1660; Mary, 1664; Eliz. 1666; Stephen, Jan. 1669; and Lydia, Feb. 1671. The s. John was k. by the Ind. 28 Jan. 1676. See Trumbull, Col. Rec. II. 403. He perhaps was of Stonington 1670, but d. at N. 1702, leav. only s. Joseph, ds. Sarah, w. of the sec. John Post, Mary Lothrop; Eliz. Lyman; and Lydia Miller. John, Weymouth, carpenter, by w. Ann had Mary, b. 15 Mar. 1660, prob. rem. soon, for in 1664, he sold his W. est. John, Wethersfield, perhaps s. of John the first, had Kezia, b. 1667; Ann, 1669; Rebina, 1671; John, 1674; Jonathan, 1677; and d. 1682. John, Providence 1676. *Jonathan, Stamford, rep. 1667, perhaps br. of first John, d. 1673, leav. ch. Rebecca, aged 17; Jonathan, 13; John, 11; Sarah, 8; Eliz. 6; and Joseph, 4¼. ‖ Nathaniel, Boston, s. of Robert the first, perhaps b. in Eng.

shoemaker, m. 30 Dec. 1657, or as ano. rec. has it, 7 Jan. 1658, Sarah, d. of John Dwight of Dedham, had Sarah, b. 26 July 1659; Mary, 20 Nov. 1660; Nathaniel, 3 Mar. 1662; and by w. Priscilla, had John, 4 Aug. 1668; Peter, 26 Jan. 1670; Philip, 15, bapt. 20 Sept. 1674, and Joseph, b. 29 Dec. 1676. He was of ar. co. 1658, freem. 1665, and I think that capt. in Philip's war on serv. at Chelmsford, 25 Feb. 1676. ˙He is in Boston tax list of 1695; but perhaps had some yrs. liv. at Bristol. His s. John was, I presume, that mem. of the sec. ch. at Newport, that Presid. Stiles, in MS. Itiner. notes the d. of at Bristol, 30 Jan. 1757, in his 90th yr. RICHARD, a passeng. in the Mary and John 1634, of wh. I kn. no more. ROBERT, Watertown 1635, shoemaker, freem. 3 Sept. 1634, was dism. by the ch. 29 Mar. 1636, to form a ch. at Wethersfield, but prob. after few yrs. rem. to Boston, had w. Mary, but no ch. is found in town or ch. rec. so that we infer that all the five ch. named in his will of 20 Apr. 1658, good abstr. of wh. is in Geneal. Reg. IX. 137, viz. Ruth Whitney, w. of John, Tabitha wid. of Matthew Abdy, Sarah Mason, and Mary Sanger, w. of Richard, beside Nathaniel, above, must have been brot. from Eng. He is ment. with remarka. kindness in the will of Capt. Robert Keayne, and d. 27 Apr. 1659. ROBERT, Boston, by w. Eliz. had Eliz. b. 2 Jan. 1669; and Ann, 11 Aug. 1670. I think he was a fisherman, may have been s. of the preced. and liv. at Pulling Point. THOMAS, New London, perhaps on the tax list of 1666, m. 11 Oct. 1683 Sarah, d. of Joseph Clark the first of Newport, and in 1680 had a lot at Westerly. WILLIAM, Duxbury 1636, m. 30 Aug. 1638, Alice Kitson, may be the same wh. was in 1634 one of Howland's men, when the dispute in Kennebeck riv. caus. d. of two men, and of Cape Porpoise 1653, then adm. freem. of Mass. to wh. gr. of 200 acres at Kennebunk 4 or 5 yrs. bef. had been made. WILLIAM, Providence, as early as May 1637. WILLIAM, Salem, in Felt's list of ch. mem. it appears that he was adm. 1640. Ten of this name had been gr. at Yale 1852, and three at Harv.

RHODES, ROADS, or RHOADS, HENRY, Lynn, b. 1608, had Eleazer, 6 Feb. 1641; Samuel, Feb. 1643; Joseph, Jan. 1645; Joshua, Apr. 1648; Josiah, Apr. 1651; Jonathan, Aug. 1654, d. bef. 23 yrs.; and Eliz. Mar. 1658. JEREMIAH, Providence, sw. alleg. in May 1671. JOHN, and JOHN jr. were at Salem 1678. JOHN, Providence, s. of Zachary, d. 1712, his will of that date, nam. w. Waite, and ch. Zachariah, John, Joseph, William, Resolved, Phebe, and Waite, of wh. all but the first were minors, but of them William and John were by a former w. Mercy, youngest d. of Roger Williams, wh. had been w. of Samuel Winsor, and bef. that of Resolved Waterman. JOHN, Boston 1659, shoemaker, may not have been of Providence 1676. JOHN, Lynn, freem.

1684, perhaps was of Marblehead 1673. JOSEPH, Lynn, prob. s. of Henry, freem. 1677 or 1684, and again took the o. 1690, as perhaps did others a sec. time, after the overthrow of Andros, m. 25 May 1674, Jane Coates, had Samuel, b. 6 Mar. 1675, d. at 4 mos.; Eliz. 22 Aug. 1676; Joseph, 14 Apr. 1678, d. at 3 mos.; Jane, 14 July 1679; John, 20 Jan. 1682; and Susanna, 18 Nov. 1684. JOSHUA, Lynn, br. of the preced. m. 12 June 1678, Ann Graves, perhaps d. of the first Samuel of the same, had Hannah, b. 28 Mar. 1679; Joseph, 19 Jan. 1681; Henry, Dec. 1682; and Thomas, 14 Feb. 1685; was freem. 1690. JOSIAH, Lynn, br. of the preced. m. 23 July 1673, Eliz. Coates, had Henry b. 1 June 1674; Eliz. 13 Aug. 1676; Mary, 21 Oct. 1677, d. soon; John, 27 May 1679, d. at 5 yrs.; Josiah, 29 Jan. 1681; and Eleazer, 8 July 1683; was freem. 1690. MALACHI, Providence, s. of Zachary, m. Mary, d. of Richard Carder, and d. 1682; his will of 17 Oct. in that yr. pro. 10 Dec. foll. names w. Mary, eldest s. Malachi, a minor, ds. Sarah and Mary, br. John, and brs.-in-law, John Low and Daniel Williams. RICHARD, Salem 1669. SAMUEL, Lynn, br. of Joshua, m. 16 Jan. 1684, Abigail Coates, had Jonathan, b. 28 Nov. 1685; and Samuel, 2 Aug. with a wrong yr. in the rec. that may have been intend. for 1687; was freem. 1691. THEOPHILUS, Boston, freem. 1683. WALTER, Providence, " gave engagem. of alleg. to his Maj. Charles II. bef. William Carpenter, Assist. in the face of the town," 1 June 1668. WILLIAM, Block Isl. 1678. ZACHARY, Providence, m. Joanna, d. of William Arnold, had John, b. a. 1658; Zechariah; and Malachi; beside a d. Rebecca, wh. m. Nicholas. Power the sec. and he d. 1668. His wid. m. Samuel Reape, of Newport, bef. the end of Jan. 1669; and the s. Zechariah, d. without issue. He had also some others. This name is oft. found without an *h*, but rarely in mod. days.

RICE, BENJAMIN, Marlborough, youngest of eight s. of the first Edmund of the same, m. a. 1662 Mary, eldest ch. of deac. William Brown of Sudbury, had only Ebenezer, b. 1 May 1671; and his w. d. 3 Jan. 1691. BENJAMIN, Marlborough, youngest of five s. of Edward, m. 1 Apr. 1691, Mary Graves, had Azariah; Lydia, b. 1695; Eliz. 1697; Simon 1699; Zerubabel 1702; Rachel 1703; Matthias 1706; Priscilla 1708; and Damaris 1711; and he d. 23 Feb. 1748. CALEB, Marlborough, s. of Joseph, m. 1696, Mary Ward, had Martha, Mary, Josiah, Jabez, Nathan, Rebecca, Sarah, Caleb, Hepzibah, and Kezia; was deac. d. 5 Jan. 1739, and his wid. d. 1742. DANIEL, Marlborough, s. of Edward the first, m. 10 Feb. 1681, Bethia, youngest d. of the first William Ward, had Bethia, b. 1682; Daniel 1684; Luke 1689; Priscilla 1692; Eleazer 1695; Deborah 1697; and Hopestill 1702; his w. d. 8 Dec. 1721, aged 63, and he d. 14 July 1737. DAVID, Framingham,

s. of Henry, m. 7 Apr. 1687, Hannah, d. of Thomas Walker, had Eliz.
b. 8 Sept. 1689; Hannah, 5 Jan. 1692; Bezaleel; Josiah, 19 Aug.
1701. He was deac. his w. d. 18 Dec. 1704; and he d. 16 Oct. 1723.
* EDMUND, Sudbury, was from Barkhamstead in Co. Herts, and of the
first sett. 1639, appoint. to lay out the planta. freem. 13 May 1640, and
among proprs. that yr. is a wid. Rice, perhaps his mo. was rep. in
Oct. foll. and 1643, deac. and selectman, b. a. 1594, brot. from Eng.
w. Thomasine, and ch. by her, Edward, b. 1618; Henry; Edmund;
Thomas; Matthew; Samuel; and Joseph; had here Benjamin, b. 31
May 1640. His w. d. 18 June 1654; and he m. 1 Mar. 1655, Mercy,
wid. of Thomas Brigham, wh. surv. him, and had Ruth b. 29 Sept. 1659;
and Ann, 19 Nov. 1661; was among early sett. of Marlborough, and he
d. 3 May 1663, all the ten ch. having div. of his est. His wid. m. William Hunt. EDMUND, Marlborough, s. of the preced. b. in Eng. m. 13
Oct. 1680, Joyce Russell, d. of William of Cambridge, had Joyce b.
1681; Edmund, 9 July 1688; and Lydia, 24 May 1690; Joyce m.
1705, Samuel Abbot. EDMUND, Sudbury, sec. s. of Edward the first,
was a deac. and d. 25 Sept. 1719, but of m. or issue I hear not. EDMUND,
Westborough, s. of Samuel, m. 15 Nov. 1692, Ruth Parker of Roxbury,
says Barry, and had at Marlborough, Dinah, b. 1693; Silas 1695; Timothy 1697; Nahor 1699, k. by the Ind. at 5 yrs; Huldah 1701; Moses
1704, d. soon; Seth 1705; Thankful 1707; Eleazer 1709; Ruth 1712;
Ebenezer 1714; and Ann 1716; d. 1726, leav. wid. Hannah. EDWARD,
Sudbury, s. of the first Edmund, prob. eldest, b. at Barkhamstead, Eng.
by first w. Agnes Bent, says Barry, he had no ch. but John Bent, in his
will of 14 Sept. 1672, speaks of his d. Agnes Rice, so that I doubt she
was not first, but sec. w. unless Agnes and Ann mean one woman.
Childr. by w. Ann, acc. Barry, were John; Lydia, b. 30 July 1648, d.
soon; Lydia, again, 10 Dec. 1649; Edmund, 9 Dec. 1653; Daniel, 8
Nov. 1655; Caleb, 8 Feb. 1658, d. soon; Ann, 9 Nov. 1661; Dorcas,
29 Jan. 1664; Benjamin, 22 Dec. 1666; and Abigail, 9 May 1671;
rem. to Marlborough, was a deac. and d. 15 Aug. 1712 at gr. age, and
his wid. Ann d. next yr. EDWARD, Marlborough, s. of Samuel, m.
25 May 1702, Lydia Fairbanks, had Gideon, and nine ds. ELISHA,
Sudbury, s. of the first Thomas, it is said, liv. to near 60 yrs. EPHRAIM,
Sudbury, s. of the first Thomas, m. 21 Feb. 1689, Hannah Livermore,
perhaps d. of John of Watertown, had Hannah, d. young; Ephraim;
Mary; Josiah; Grace d. young; Thomas; Gershom; John; Isaac; and
Hannah, again; and he d. 1732. Of course he was 65, or at most, 69
yrs. old, but the age is kind. stretched to 71, in Geneal. Reg. XIII. 140.
GERSHOM, Worcester, br. of the preced. d. 29 Dec. 1768, at the gr. age
of 101, as may be read in Geneal. Reg. XIII. 140. He had seven ch.

all then liv. HENRY, Sudbury, s. of Edmund the first, b. in Eng. m. 1 Feb. 1644, Eliz. Moore, had Mary, b. 19 Sept. 1646; Eliz. 4 Aug. 1648; Jonathan, 3 July 1654; Abigail, 17 June 1657; David, 27 Dec. 1659; Thomasine, 2 Feb. 1662; Rachel, 10 May 1664; Lydia, 4 June 1668; Mercy, 1 Jan. 1671; beside Hannah; was freem. 10 May 1648, an early propr. of Marlborough, rem. to Framingham, there his w. d. 3 Aug. 1705; and he d. 10 Feb. 1711. Eliz. m. John Brewer; Abigail m. Thomas Smith; Thomasine m. 1680, Benjamin Parmenter; Rachel m. 15 Dec. 1687, Thomas Drury; Lydia m. Samuel Wheelock; Mercy m. Elnathan Allen; and Hannah m. 5 Aug. 1675, Eleazer Ward, and next, 17 Oct. 1677, Richard Taylor. ISAAC, Framingham, s. of Matthew, by w. Sybilla, had Sybilla, b. 1691; Martha; Mary; Abigail; and Ruth; and he d. 1718. JAMES, Marlborough, s. of the first Thomas, had Jotham; Zebediah; Cyrus; Frances; James; Jaazaniah; Grace; and Berzela, if Barry is correct, who adds that he d. at Worcester 1730. His age was 61 yrs. but in Geneal. Reg. XIII. 140, made to run up to 72. Perhaps his w. was Sarah, and he had at Framingham Daniel, b. 13 Mar. 1705. JOHN, Boston, by w. Mary, had John, b. 9 May 1669. JOHN, Warwick, m. 16 July 1674, Eliz. sec. d. of the first Randall Houlden, d. 6 Jan. 1731, aged 85, had John, and Randal, perhaps others. JOHN, Marlborough, eldest s. of Edward the first, m. 2 or 27 Nov. 1674, Tabitha, d. of John Stone, had John b. 1675; Ann, 1678; Deliverance, 1681; Tabitha, 1683; Prudence, 1685; Abigail, 1687; Edward, 23 Dec. 1689; Dinah, 1691; Moses, 1694; Tamar, 1697; and Aaron, 13 Aug. 1700; and d. 5 Sept. 1719. JOHN, Warwick, s. of John of the same, m. 25 July 1695, Elnathan, sec. d. of John Whipple the sec. of Providence, had John, b. 6 Apr. 1696; Eliz. 6 May 1698; Thomas, 26 Apr. 1700; Mary, 22 Sept. 1702, d. next yr.; Nathan, 20 June 1704; Barbara, 24 Apr. 1706; William, 25 Mar. 1708; Mary, again, 24 Jan. 1710; Lydia, 30 Dec. 1711; Randall, 22 May, 1714; and Elnathan, 4 Aug. 1716; and he d. 9 Jan. 1755, aged 80. JONAS, Sudbury, s. of the first Thomas, said in the doubtful rep. to have liv. 84 yrs. JONATHAN, Norwich, m. Mar. 1661, Deborah, d. of Hugh Caulkins, had Eliz. b. Jan. 1662; and John, 1663; made freem. 1663, constable 1669. * JONATHAN, Sudbury, s. of Henry, by w. Martha had Martha, b. 27 June 1675, d. soon, as did the mo. He m. 1 Nov. 1677, Rebecca Watson, had Jonathan, 1678; David, 1680; Ann, 1683; and Henry, 1685. His w. d. 22 Dec. 1689, and he m. 3d w. 12 Feb. 1691, Eliz. Wheeler, had Martha; Hezekiah; Abraham; Ezekiel, 14 Oct. 1700; Eliz. 28 Feb. 1703; Phineas, 24 June 1705; rem. to Framingham, there had Sarah, 24 Sept. 1707; Richard, 31 Jan. 1710; and Abigail, 23 Mar. 1714; was selectman, rep. 1711 and 20,.

and d. 12 Apr. 1725. JONATHAN, Sudbury, s. of Joseph the first, m. 25
Mar. 1702, Ann Derby of Stow, as by the highest authority is told, was
deac. and d. 7 June 1772, and his wid. d. 23 Dec. 1773. So they had
liv. as h. and w. over 70 yrs. but whether any ch. came of the union is
not told yet, but may be when the fam. geneal. is publish. JOSEPH,
Sudbury, prob. youngest s. of Edmund the first, b. in Eng. m. 1658,
Mercy King, perhaps d. of Thomas of Watertown, but no issue is found
in Barry, wh. says, by w. Martha he had Martha, b. 14 Jan. 1662;
Josiah, 3 May 1663; Caleb, 1666; and this w. Martha d. 4 Jan. 1669;
by third w. Mary, by Bond thot. d. of Capt. Richard Beers, he had Joseph,
5 June 1671; Eleazer, 26 Oct. 1672; rem. to Marlborough, was freem.
1672; had there Mary, 13 Aug. 1674; perhaps driv. by the Ind. war
to Watertown, his w. d. there 13 May 1677; and there by 4th w. Sarah,
had Jonathan, 26 Mar. 1679; and Sarah, 14 Feb. 1681, wh. d. soon;
and again might have, at Marlborough, Phineas, 24 Aug. 1684. JOSEPH,
Marlborough, s. of the preced. had w. Eliz. wh. d. 13 Oct. 1733, aged
48, and he d. 3 Dec. 1745. JOSEPH, Marlborough, youngest ch. of
Samuel, had Jesse and sev. ds. JOSHUA, Boston 1663, shoemaker, s. of
Robert, by w. Bathshua, had Joshua, b. 3 May 1664. JOSHUA, Marlborough, s. perhaps eldest, of Samuel, freem. 1690, by w. Mary, had Samuel, b. 1693; Nahum, 1695; Sarah, 1698; Zephaniah, 1700; Andrew,
1703; and of him, w. or ch. I find no more in Barry. MATTHEW, Sudbury, s. prob. fifth of Edmund the first, b. in Eng. freem. 1660, m. 2
Nov. 1654, Martha Lamson, perhaps d. of Barnaby of Cambridge, had
Sarah b. 9 Sept. 1655, wh. m. a Loker; Martha, 17 Aug. 1656, m. John
Bent as his sec. w.; Deborah, 14 Feb. 1660, m. 23 Jan. 1684, Thomas
Sawin; Ruth, 2 Apr. 1662, m. 21 Nov. 1682, Joseph Hastings, and d.
two mos. aft.; Eliz. 20 May 1663, d. soon; Dorothy, 14 Feb. 1665, m.
a Ware; Isaac, 1668; and Patience, 5 Mar. 1671, m. a Leland. His
will was pro. 30 Dec. 1717. MICHAEL, New London, freem. 1663, as
in Trumbull, Col. Rec. I. 406, yet the name is not in Caulkins. NA-
THANIEL, New London, freem. 1669. NATHANIEL, Sudbury, s. of
Thomas the first, had Nathaniel, Mary, and Patience, but he had two ws.
Sarah, and next m. 1704, wid. Patience Stone, and he d. 13 Nov. 1726.
His age of 66 yrs. is swell. to 70 in Geneal. Reg. XIII. 140. NEHE-
MIAH, New London, freem. 1666. NICHOLAS, Boston 1672, hir. a farm
of Gov. Bellingham. PETER, Marlborough, s. of Thomas the first, by w.
Rebecca had Elisha, b. 1690; Zipporah, 1691; Cyprian, 1693; Pelatiah, 1694; Elnathan; Peter; Abigail; Deborah; Rebecca; and Abraham, 1709. His w. d. 1749, and he d. 28 Nov. 1753, aged 95 yrs. and
one mo. less a week, allow for change of style. By the common tendency
to exagger. he is made 97 in Geneal. Reg. XIII. 140. Sev. of his ch.
reach. old age. PHILIP, Boston 1640, is call. a tailor, on his unit. with

the ch. 21 Nov. 1641. He d. prob. in 1665. PHINEAS, Sudbury, youngest s. of Joseph first of the same, m. 2 Oct. 1707, Eliz. d. of Daniel Willard of the same, had sev. ch. by her, wh. d. 9 Mar. 1761, but I kn. neither names nor dates, and he d. 4 Sept. 1768. RANDALL, Warwick, s. of first John of the same, had childr. but no rec. is seen of them. RICHARD, Cambridge 1635, rem. to Concord 1636, freem. 2 June 1641, had Eliz. b. 27 Oct. 1641; and John, 23 Feb. 1644; d. 9 June 1709, aged, says the rec. more than 100 yrs. wh. Shattuck judicious. reduced. Farmer reports that he left 8 s. wh. liv. to gr. ages, showing how easy tradition borrowed for him the facts of Edmund, of wh. he is not kn. to be a relat. ROBERT, Boston, spelled Roys, Roise, and Royce, in dif. rec. freem. 1 Apr. 1634, had prob. come 1631, as he is No. 137 on the list of ch. mem. by w. Eliz. had Joshua, b. 14, bapt. 16 Apr. 1637; Nathaniel, bapt. 24 Mar. tho. town rec. says b. 1 Apr. 1639; and Patience, b. 1 Apr. 1642, bur. next week; Nathaniel d. young. His wid. m. I presume, Michael Tarne, for they call. Joshua R. their s. when in 1668 the three unit. to mortg. est. Perhaps there were both Rice and Roise. See Roise. ROBERT, Stratford 1656, was of New London after, freem. 1669. SAMUEL, Sudbury, s. of Edmund the first, b. in Eng. m. 8 Nov. 1655, Eliz. King, had Eliz. b. 26 Oct. 1656, wh. m. 2 Jan. 1677, Peter Haynes; Hannah, wh. m. . . . Hubbard; Joshua; Edmund; Esther, 1665, wh. m. 1 Nov. 1683, Daniel Hubbard; Samuel, 1667; Mary, 1669; Edward, 1672; Abigail, 1674; and Joseph. He had rem. to Marlborough, m. 1668, sec. w. Mary, wid. of Abraham Brown, wh. d. 18 June 1678; and he prob. d. 1684, or early next yr. for his will was pro. 7 Apr. 1685. SAMUEL, New London 1669. THOMAS, Sudbury, s. of Edmund the first, b. in Eng. by w. Mary had Grace, wh. d. 1654; Thomas b. 30 June 1654; Mary, 4 Sept. 1656, m. 1678, Joseph White; Peter, 24 Oct. 1658; Nathaniel, 3 Jan. 1660; Sarah, 15 Jan. 1662, m. John Adams; was freem. 1660, rem. to Marlborough, had there Ephraim; Gershom, said to be b. 9 May 1667; James, 1669; Jonas, 1673; Grace, 1675, m. 1702, Nathaniel Moore; perhaps Elisha; and Frances, wh. m. an Allen; and in Geneal. Reg. XIII. 140, was made to live 96 yrs. His will was pro. 1681, so that we may be sure his age was by ten yrs. magnif. by his s. as in Geneal. Reg. XIII. 140; and the will of his wid. was pro. 1715. THOMAS, Marlborough, eldest s. of the preced. by w. Ann m. 1681, had Jedediah, b. 1690; Abiel; Ann; Arthur; Adonijah; Perez; Vashti; Beriah; Jason; Thomas; and Charles. In Geneal. Reg. XIII. 140, his age is call. 94; but my doubt is so strong, that I wish to kn. the day, mo. and yr. when he d. TIMOTHY, Concord, freem. 1690, m. 27 Apr. 1687, Abigail, d. of John Marrett of Cambridge. Twenty-four of this name had been gr. at Harv. in 1849, and six at Yale.

RICH, OBADIAH, Salem 1668, had w. Bethia, to wh. admin. on his est. was giv. Jan. 1678. RICHARD, Dover 1671, mariner, m. Sarah, d. of Thomas Roberts, perhaps rem. after 1675, to Eastham, there d. 1692, had Richard. RICHARD, Eastham, s. of the preced. by w. Ann, had Sarah, b. 22 Jan. 1696; Richard, 28 Feb. 1699; Rebecca, 15 June 1701; Zaccheus, 2 Apr. 1704; Obadiah, 15 July 1707; Priscilla, 5 Feb. 1710, d. young; Huldah, July 1712; Joseph, 5 Oct. 1715; and Sylvanus, 4 Sept. 1720.

RICHARDS, BENJAMIN, Boston, merch. s. of Thomas of Weymouth, m. 10 Oct. 1661, Hannah, d. of William Hudson, jr. d. early, and prob. without ch. His wid. m. 1666 Richard Crispe. DAVID, New London, youngest s. of the first John of the same, m. 14 Dec. 1698, Eliz. Raymond, perhaps d. of Daniel of the same; but Miss Caulkins does not enlarge upon him. EDWARD, Dedham, m. 10 Sept. 1638, Susanna Hunting, perhaps sis. of the first John, had Mary, b. 29 Sept. 1639; John, 1 or 10 July 1641; Dorcas, 24 Sept. 1643; Nathaniel, 25 Jan. 1649, not bapt. as Geneal. Reg. XIV. 111, says, next day, wh. was Friday; and Sarah, 1651; was freem. 2 June 1641. From his will, 1684, shortly bef. his d. we learn, that John and Nathaniel were then liv. that Mary m. Nathaniel Bullard, and ano. d. m. a Hearsey; that a gr.d. was Mary Gay, prob. w. of Jonathan, and d. of Bullard; and that if Nathaniel would bring up one of his s. at the coll. he should have £60. EDWARD, complained of 1646, by Gerard Spencer, may have been of Lynn, a joiner in 1661, was in 40th yr. had William, b. 7 June 1663; in 1678 swore that he had liv. there 45 yrs. and d. 26 Jan. 1690, in 74th yr. it is said, leav. s. John. ISRAEL, New London, sec. s. of the first John of the same, had Israel, Jeremiah, and sev. ds. as Caulkins tells, but ment. no dates, nor name of w. nor time of his own or her d. ‡ JAMES, Boston, s. perhaps of Thomas of Dorchester, freem. 1652, rem. a. 10 yrs. later to Hartford, there made freem. of Conn. 1664, m. Sarah, only ch. of William Gibbons of H. had Sarah, b. 22 Feb. 1662; Mary, 16 Aug. 1663; Jerusha, 28 June 1665; Eliz. 19 May 1667; and Thomas, 16 Sept. 1670; all nam. as liv. in his will of 9 June 1680, where he also provid. for unb. ch. after call. Ann; beside three nam. John, and d. Abigail, wh. all d. inf. He was in the highest esteem, chosen an Assist. 1665 (and contin. I suppose, in that office till his d. 11 July, 1680), Commiss. of the Unit. Col. of N. E. 1672 and 5. His est. was of the largest. The wid. Sarah m. Humphrey Davie of Boston, and next Col. Jonathan Tyng of Dunstable, as sec w. and his d. Sarah m. Capt. Benjamin Davis; Mary m. Benjamin Alford, both of Boston; Jerusha m. Rev. Gurdon Saltonstall of New London, afterwards Gov. of the Col.; Eliz. m. John. s. of Humphrey Davie wh. bec. baronet by

desc. from his uncle Sir John, and next m. Jonathan Taylor; and Ann
d. unm. bef. 1691, so that br. and the sis. had the £700, her sh. of the
est. JAMES, Weymouth, by w. Ruth, had Benjamin, b. 22 Feb. 1684.
JAMES, Dedham, m. Hannah, d. of Jonathan Metcalf, early in the 18th
cent. ‡*‖ JOHN, Dorchester, s. of Thomas, perhaps eldest, b. in Eng. ar.
co. 1644, was establ. in 1649 at Arowsic Isl. Kennebeck, to trade with
the Ind. rem. 1653 to Boston, but had two yrs. bef. been at London, m.
3 May 1654, Eliz. wid. of Adam Winthrop, d. of Capt. Thomas Hawkins, wh. d. 1 Nov. 1691, and he m. 1 Sept. foll. Ann, d. of Gov. John
Winthrop of Conn. but he had no ch. by either; was lieut. capt. and
major, rep. 1671–3 for Newbury, 1675 for Hadley, and 1679–80 for
Boston; was speaker this last yr. and next elect. Assist. until the coming
of Andros; a high friend of liberty, named counsellor in the new chart.
bec. a judge of the Sup. Ct. and d. very suddenly, as Sewall says, 2
Apr. 1694. His wid. d. 27 June 1704. JOHN, New London, of whose
orig. or date of arr. in our country we are ign. was there bef. 1660, says
Caulkins, had eldest s. John, b. 1666; Israel; Mary; Penelope; Lydia;
Eliz.; and Hannah; but when she assures us that all the seven were bapt.
26 Mar. 1671, we necessarily deduce that most, if not all, of the ds. were
b. bef. the eldest s. and that careful writer suppos. he was m. bef. he sett.
at New London. He had also David, bapt. 27 July 1673, and d. 1687.
His d. Lydia m. 15 Nov. 1678, William Mynard. JOHN, Dedham, s. of
Edward the first, by w. Mary, had John, b. 20 July 1663, was freem.
1671. JOHN, Lynn, perhaps s. perhaps br. of Edward, m. 18 Nov.
1674, Mary Brewer, had Mary, b. 16 Oct. 1675; John, 1 May 1677;
Edward, 13 June 1679; Crispus, 20 Oct. 1681; Eliz. 1683; Joseph,
1685; William, 1688; and Abigail, 1691; was freem. 1691. JOHN,
Hartford, s. of first Thomas of the same, b. in Eng. had w. Lydia, d. of
George Stocking, and ch. John, Thomas, and Samuel; was freem. 1669,
and in 1695 was 64 yrs. old. JOHN, Weymouth, s. of William, freem.
1681, by w. Sarah, had Sarah, b. 20 June 1672; Bathshua, 16 Nov. 1674;
John, 20 Feb. 1680; William, 12 Apr. 1685; Ephraim, 30 Apr. 1687;
Grace, 16 Mar. 1689; and Lydia, 8 Nov. 1691. JOHN, Westfield, by
w. Abigail, wid. of John Mun, m. 7 Oct. 1686, had John, b. 26 July
1687; Abigail, 10 Jan. 1689; and Thomas, 7 Nov. 1691. JOHN, New
London, eldest s. of John of the same, m. Love, d. of Oliver Manwaring
of the same, had ten or more ch. of wh. four only, John, George, Samuel, and Lydia, outliv. him, wh. d. 2 Nov. 1720. JOSEPH, Weymouth,
s. of William, was prob. one of Johnson's comp. Dec. 1675, freem. 1681,
by w. Susanna had James, b. 28 Sept. 1680; and by w. Sarah had Deborah, 19 Oct. 1684; Benjamin, 7 Apr. 1686; Mary, 6 Mar. 1689; and
Daniel, 28 Feb. 1695. JUSTINIAN, New Hampsh. 1689, pray. for Mass.

jurisdict. *NATHANIEL, Cambridge, came to Boston in the Lion, 16 Sept. 1632, as pub. by me in 4 Mass. Hist. Coll. I. 94, reprint. in Geneal. Reg. XIV. 301, was freem. 6 Nov. of that yr. rem. as one of the first sett. at Hartford 1636, and early in 1652 at Norwalk, where in 1655 were but four men with larger est. and only two in 1671, was rep. at Oct. sess. 1658, prob. left no ch. for his will of 7 Oct. 1681, gives all his est. to the hs. of four ds. of his w. Rosamond, by her former h. Henry Lindall. NATHANIEL, Dedham 1642, perhaps was br. of Edward. NATHANIEL, Dedham, s. of Edward, m. 21 Feb. 1679, Mary, d. of deac. John Aldis, may be he wh. took o. of alleg. at Springfield, 1 Jan. 1679, and freem. at D. 1690, and d. very sudden. 15 Feb. 1727. OBADIAH, Farmington, s. of Thomas the sec. had perhaps by w. Hannah, d. of John Andrews of the same, John, b. 1668; Mary, Jan. 1670; Hannah, Nov. 1671; Esther, June 1673; Eliz. July 1675; Sarah, Apr. 1677; Obadiah, 1 Oct. 1679; wh. were all bapt. 21 Mar. 1680; rem. to Waterbury, and had Rachel, bapt. 6 May 1683; Thomas, 9 Aug. 1685; and Benjamin, 5 Apr. 1691, and d. 11 Nov. 1702. His wid. d. May 1725. RICHARD, Salem 1667, d. prob. June 1678. SAMUEL, made freem. of Conn. 1658, but of what town is uncert. See Trumbull, Col. Rec. I. 315; and the name is not found among the freem. of 1669, in Vol. II. Perhaps he was s. of the first Thomas, of Hartford, m. Dec. 1665, Mary Graves, and d. early without issue. THOMAS, Dorchester 1630, perhaps came in the Mary and John, with s. James and John, bef. ment. rem. to Weymouth, freem. 13 May 1640, d. soon aft. 17 Dec. 1650. His will made at Hull on that day, pro. 28 Jan. foll. names s. John, James, Samuel, Joseph, and Benjamin, calling the last two minors; and ds. Mary, Ann, Alice, and Hannah. This last ch. d. 10 Nov. foll. His wid. Welthian, mo. of these ch. in her will of July 1679, pro. Nov. foll. ment. only James, John, and Ann, w. of Ephraim Hunt, as then liv.; Mary, m. 7 Dec. 1641, Thomas Hinckley of Barnstable, after Gov. of that Col. and d. 24 June 1659; Alice m. William Bradford, the Dep. Gov. of the same Col.; and d. 12 Dec. 1671. THOMAS, Hartford 1639, d. early, leav. wid. wh. d. 1671, and ch. John, Mary Peck of Milford, perhaps w. of Joseph, beside Thomas, and Obadiah. Descend. are num. in Conn. but some of them erron. suppose they derived from James bef. ment. s. of the former Thomas, wh. had only s. Thomas that left not male issue. ‖ THOMAS, Boston, freem. 1645, ar. co. 1648, of wh. no more is kn. THOMAS, Hartford, only s. of James that grew up, m. Joanna Dodd, had Joanna b. 21 July 1702; and Mary, 14 Oct. 1703; and d. 5 Dec. 1714. His wid. m. Dr. John Cutter, as is said. WILLIAM, Plymouth 1633, Haz. I. 327, but in 1643, he is not found there. Deane thinks he rem. to Scituate; but he presumes him to have rem. also to

Weymouth, wh. may be true, and yet not be what Deane thought, the same as WILLIAM, Weymouth 1648, perhaps br. of Thomas of the same, by w. Grace, had William; James b. 1658; John; Joseph; and Benjamin, of wh. this youngest was b. 19 May 1660, all nam. with w. Grace, in his will of 18 June 1680, pro. 23 July 1682. WILLIAM, Weymouth, prob. s. of the preced. was freem. 1681. Of this name seven had been in 1834, gr. at Yale, two at Harv. and ten at other N. E. Coll.

RICHARDSON, or RICHESON, often in old rec. * AMOS, Boston, merch. tailor, perhaps one of that gr. London guild, by w. Mary, had John bapt. 26 Dec. 1647, H. C. 1666; Amos, 20 Jan. 1650, in right of their mo.; Stephen, b. 14 June 1652; Catharine, 6 Jan. 1655; Sarah, 19 July 1657; Samuel, 18 Feb. 1660; freem. 1665, rem. next yr. to Stonington, of wh. he was rep. 1676 and 7, and there d. 5 Aug. 1683. His w. Mary liv. but few weeks after him. Beside those s. he had ds. Mary, m. June 1663, Jonathan Gatline, or Gatliffe, of Braintree, and Prudence, many yrs. younger, m. 15 Mar. 1683, John Hallam, and next 17 Mar. 1703, Elnathan Miner. He had been agent of Stephen Winth. and was after of Gov. John, his br. was of gr. enterprise, and good est. one of the purchas. with Winth. Atherton, Hudson, and others of the Narraganset lds. on wh. he first sett. at Westerly, and when the claim of Conn. was subject. to R. I. jurisdict. he crossed over to S. A good letter from him to Fitz John Winthrop, at Cardross in Scotland, writ. 13 Sept. 1659, sign. Amos Richerson, as often the name is in rec. was giv. me. CALEB, Newbury, s. of Edward of the same, m. 31 July 1682, Mary Ladd, had Ruth b. 1 Mar. 1683; and Mary, 12 Jan. 1685. EDWARD, Newbury, had Edward, b. 21 Dec. 1649; Caleb, 18 Aug. 1652; Ruth, 23 Nov. 1655; Moses, 4 Apr. 1658; and Mary, 2 Sept. 1660; and he d. 14 Nov. 1685, as Coffin tells, who adds that ano. Edward R. d. there, 25 Mar. 1655; but he does not inform us, whether this were ch. or adult. One was 61 yrs. in 1678. EDWARD, Newbury, s. of the preced. m. 28 Oct. 1673, Ann, prob. d. of Christopher Bartlett, had Mary, b. says Coffin, 25 Oct. 1673, d. young; Edward, 2 Sept. 1674; Mary, again, 25 Aug. 1676; Moses, 22 Jan. 1680; and Margaret, 7 July 1682; and he d. as in Coffin, 14 Nov. foll. But there was an Edward of Rowley, a serg. in 1691. * EZEKIEL, Charlestown 1630, came prob. in the fleet of Winth. with w. Susanna. They belong. to the ch. of Boston, and were dism. with others, 11 Oct. 1632, to establish a ch. at C. freem. 18 May 1631, by the Court appoint. 1633, constable, and by the peop. rep. 1635, with many of his townsmen unit. in remonstrance against the Act of the governm. towards Wheelwright, in 1637, and, his heart failing him, in Nov. express. his contrit. and had his name crossed over. In 1640, when a selectman, he favor sett. at Woburn, and there d. 21 Oct. 1647. His will of 20 July preced. is in Geneal. Reg. VII. 172, names eldest s. Theophilus, and the wid. Excors. other ch. only Josias, James, and Phebe, and brs. Samuel and Thomas are ment. Phebe was bapt. in Boston, 3 June 1632; Theophilus, 22 Dec. 1633; Josiah, 7 Nov. 1635; John, 21 July 1638; Jonathan, 5 Feb. 1640; both d. young; James, 11 July 1641, at C. and Woburn rec. proves that his d. Ruth, b. 31 Aug. 1643, d. in a week. Phebe m. 1 Nov. 1649, Henry Baldwin. GEORGE, Watertown, came in the Susan and Ellen 1635, aged 30, from London, had small fam. in 1642, says Bond. HENRY, came from Canterbury, Co. Kent, with w. Mary and five ch. in 1635 or 6; but I kn. no more than is told in 3 Mass. Hist. Coll. VIII. 276. ISAAC, Woburn, m. 19 June 1667, Deborah, d. of Thomas Fuller, had Jonathan, b. 12 Dec. 1669; Deborah, 22 Jan. 1672; Joseph and Benjamin, tw. 25 Jan. 1674; Mercy, 27 Oct. 1676; tw. 13 May 1678, both d. very soon; David, 4 Feb. 1679, prob. d. soon; Phebe, 14 Feb. 1681; Mary, 14 July 1683; Eliz. 8 Nov. 1685; and Samuel, 2 Feb. 1687; and d. 2 Apr. 1689. JAMES, Woburn, prob. br. of Ezekiel, rem. 1659 to Chelmsford, m. 28 Nov. 1660, Bridget, d. of Thomas Henchman, had Thomas b. 26 Oct. 1660, as the rec. shows; James, 26 Oct. 1661; and sev. other ch. Farmer says. His wid. perhaps m. 8 Oct. 1679, William Chandler of Andover. JOHN, Watertown 1636, may have been at Exeter 1642. One of this name having recently m. Eliz. Tryer here, having w. in Eng. the m. was in Nov. 1644 declar. void. JOHN, Woburn, eldest s. of Samuel of the same, m. 22 Oct. 1658, Eliz. d. of Michael Bacon of the same, had John b. 24 Jan. 1661; and Joseph, 3 Jan. 1667; and m. 28 Oct. 1673, Mary Pierson, perhaps d. of Bartholomew, had Pierson, b. 29 Sept. 1674; Jacob, 15 Feb. 1676; William, 29 June 1678, d. in few weeks; and by third w. m. 25 June 1689, Margaret Willing, had Willing, 5 Oct. 1692, d. at 12 yrs.; and Job, 30 Apr. 1696; was a lieut. and d. 1 Jan. 1697. *JOHN*, Newbury, eldest s. of Amos, by w. wh. is not nam. in Coffin, and by Farmer was mistak. for w. of the preced. had Sarah, b. 9 Sept. 1674; John; Mary 22 July 1677; Eliz. 29 Apr. 1680; and Catharine, 15 Sept. 1681; was ord. 20 Oct. 1675, and Farmer says was freem. that yr. of wh. I do not see the proof. He had early been a mem. of the corpo. of Harv. Coll. and engaged, I am sorry to say, in the less reput. business of rem. Presid. Hoar, and d. 27 Apr. 1696. JOSEPH, Woburn, s. of Samuel of the same, m. 5 Nov. 1666, Hannah Green, had Hannah, b. 21 Oct. 1667; Mary, 22 Mar. 1669; Eliz. 28 June 1670; Joseph, 19 May 1672; and Stephen, 7 Feb. 1674; was freem. 1672, and d. 5 Mar. 1718. JOSEPH, Newbury, s. of William, m. 12 July 1681, Margaret, d. of Peter Godfrey, had Mary, b. 16 Apr. 1682; William, 22 Mar. 1684; Joseph, 31 Dec. 1686;

Eliz. 28 Feb. 1689 ; Daniel, 4 Apr. 1692 ; Sarah, 19 June 1694 ; Thomas, 15 Feb. 1697 ; and Caleb, 9 June 1704. JOSHUA, Newbury, m. 31 Jan. 1679, Mary Parker, had Esther, b. 15 Mar. 1683. His w. d. 7 Mar. 1685, and by sec. w. Jane, he had Judith, b. 25 June 1688 ; Hannah, 9 Oct. 1690 ; Abigail, 6 Aug. 1692 ; Eliz. 4 Nov. 1694 ; Joanna, 6 Mar. 1697 ; and Joshua, 20 May 1702. * JOSIAH, Chelmsford, s. of Ezekiel, m. 6 June 1659, Remembrance, d. of William Underwood, had Sarah, b. 1660 ; Mary, 1662 ; Josiah, 18 May 1665 ; Jonathan, 8 Oct. 1667 ; John, 14 Feb. 1669 ; Samuel, 21 Feb. 1672 ; and Remembrance, 20 Apr. 1684 ; was town clk. selectman, capt. rep. 1689 and 90, and d. 22 July 1695. Descend. are very num. and much diffus. MOSES, Rowley, or Newbury, youngest s. of Edward of N. m. Lydia, d. of Tobias Coleman ; but I kn. no more. NATHANIEL, Woburn, freem. 1690, by w. Mary, had Nathaniel, b. 27 Aug. 1673 ; James, 26 Feb. 1676 ; Mary, 10 Mar. 1679 ; Joshua, 3 June 1681 ; Martha, 1683 ; John, 25 Jan. 1685 ; Thomas, 15 Apr. 1687 ; Hannah, May 1689 ; Samuel, 24 Sept. 1691 ; Phineas, Feb. 1694 ; Phebe, 4 Mar. 1696 ; Amos, 10 Aug. 1698 ; and Benjamin, 27 Aug. 1700 ; and d. 4 Dec. 1714. His wid. d. 22 Dec. 1719. RICHARD, Boston 1654, had w. Joanna, and d. Joanna, b. 25 Feb. 1658 ; and s.-in-law Timothy Armitage. RICHARD, Lynn, m. 20 June 1665, Amy Graves, had John, b. Apr. 1670, and Thomas, 15 Apr. 1674. SAMUEL, Charlestown, prob. br. of Ezekiel, by w. Joanna, had Mary, bapt. 25 Feb. 1638, prob. m. Thomas Mousall ; John, bapt. 12 Nov. 1639 ; was freem. 2 May 1638, rem. early to Woburn, there had Hannah, b. 8 Mar. 1642, d. next mo. Joseph, 27 July 1643 ; Samuel, 22 Apr. 1646 ; Stephen, 15 Aug. 1649 ; Thomas, 31 Dec. 1651, d. bef. his f. and Eliz. was one of the founders of the ch. 24 Aug. 1642, and d. 23 Mar. 1658 or 9. His wid. Joanna, wh. d. 1666, in her will of 20 June 166, the last fig. being lost, names eldest s. John, and other ch. Samuel, Stephen, Eliz. and Mary Mousall. SAMUEL, Woburn, s. of the preced. by w. Martha, wh. d. 20 Dec. 1673, had Samuel and Thomas, tw. b. 5 Nov. 1670 ; Eliz. a. 1672 ; and Martha, 20 Dec. 1673, prob. d. very soon. On 30 Sept. 1674, he m. Hannah Kingsley, perhaps d. of Samuel of Braintree, had Hannah, wh. at the age of one wk. with her mo. and br. Thomas were k. by the Ind. it is said, 10 Apr. 1676 ; and next he m. 7 Nov. foll. Phebe, d. prob. of Henry Baldwin of W. had Zechariah, b. 21 Nov. 1677 ; and she d. 20 Oct. 1679. By fourth w. Sarah Hayward, perhaps not a maiden, m. 8 Sept. 1680, he had Thomas, b. 18 Aug. 1681, d. next mo.; Sarah, 20 Aug. 1682 ; Thomas again, 25 Sept. 1684 ; Ebenezer, 15 Mar. 1687 ; a s. 17 Aug. 1689, d. without name ; Hannah, 11 Aug. 1690 ; Eleazer, 10 Feb. 1693 ; Jonathan, 16 July 1696 ; and David, 14 Apr. 1700 ; and d. 29 Apr. 1712. His wid. d. 14 Oct. 1717.

STEPHEN, Woburn, br. of the preced. m. at Billerica, 2 Jan. 1675, Abigail Wyman, perhaps d. of Francis, had Stephen, b. 20 Feb. 1676; Francis, 19 Jan. 1678, d. in few days; William, 14 Dec. 1678; Francis, again, 15 Jan. 1681; Timothy, 6 Dec. 1682, d. in few wks; Abigail, 14 Nov. 1683; Prudence, 17 Jan. 1686; Timothy, again, 24 Jan. 1688; Seth, 16 Jan. 1690; Daniel, 16 Oct. 1691; Mary, 3 May 1696; Rebecca, 10 June 1698, d. at 13 yrs.; Solomon, 27 Mar. 1702; and Henry, 1704; was freem. 1690, and d. 22 Mar. 1718. His wid. d. 17 Sept. 1720. STEPHEN, Stonington, s. of Amos, was a man of import. 1676, and after. THEOPHILUS, Woburn, s. of Ezekiel, m. 2 May 1654, Mary, d. of John Champney of Cambridge, had Ezekiel, b. 28 Oct. 1655; Mary, 15 Jan. 1658; Sarah, 23 Apr. 1660; Abigail, 21 Oct. 1662; Hannah, 6 Apr. 1665; John, 16 Jan. 1668; Esther, 25 June 1670; Ruth, 31 Aug. 1673; and prob. Bridget; and he d. 28 Dec. 1674. THOMAS, Woburn, br. of Ezekiel, had liv. few yrs. at Charlestown, freem. 2 May 1638, one of the founders of the ch. at W. by w. Mary, had Mary, bapt. 17 Nov. 1638; Sarah, 22 Nov. 1640; both at C. but at W. had Isaac, b. 14 or 24 May 1643; Thomas, 4 Oct. 1645; Ruth, 14 Apr. 1647; Phebe, 24 Jan. 1649; and Nathaniel, 2 Jan. 1651; and d. 28 Aug. 1651. THOMAS, Farmington, perhaps came to Boston in the Speedwell, July 1656, from London, aged 19, had Mary, b. 25 Dec. 1667; Sarah, 25 Mar. 1669; John, 15 Apr. 1672; Israel; and Thomas; rem. to Waterbury, there had Rebecca, 27 Apr. 1679, the first ch. says the rec. b. there; Ruth, b. 10 May 1681; Joanna, 1 Sept. 1683, bapt. 8 Apr. 1684; Nathaniel, b. 28 May 1686; and Ebenezer, 4 Feb. 1690, bapt. 28 June 1691 and d. 1712. His w. was Mary; d. Sarah m. 1691, James Williams of Hartford; and the name common. was writ. Richason. THOMAS, Billerica, s. of Thomas the first, d. 25 Feb. 1721, says Farmer, wh. adds that he had many descend. Ano. THOMAS, was of Gallup's comp. 1690, for the adventure against Quebec; but I dare not conject. wh. was his f. WILLIAM, Newport 1638, and there liv. 1655, when the name appears Richinson. WILLIAM, Newbury, m. 23 Aug. 1654, Eliz. Wiseman, had Joseph, b. 18 May 1655; and Benjamin 13 Mar. 1657; and d. 14 Mar. 1658. WILLIAM, Newport, perhaps s. of William of the same, m. 30 Aug. 1670, Deliverance, d. of Richard Scott, but I fear she liv. not long, for I find on rec. no ment. of ch. and he, or ano. of the same name at N. m. 27 Mar. 1678, Eliz. Borden, of whose f. I am ign. and she, we may suppose, d. soon, for he m. 14 May 1679, Eliz. d. of the sec. Adam Mott, and had Rebecca, b. 14 May 1681; and John, 11 Feb. 1683. Of this name, eighteen had been gr. at Harv. in 1850, and three at Yale, beside sev. at other N. E. coll.

RICHBELL, or RIZBELL, JOHN, Charlestown 1648, merch. rem. bef. 1662, to Oyster Bay, L. I. He owned a planta. at the isl. of St. Christophers. ROBERT, Oyster Bay, L. I. wh. may have been s. or br. of the preced. was made by Conn. a commiss. (see 3 Mass. Hist. Coll. X. 86), and is call. Col. by Sewall, mark. his d. 22 July 1682, at Boston. Rev. Noadiah Russell, in his Diary, calls him Maj. Rechtill from Barbadoes, with income of £1,500 per an. and says his fun. was attend. by eight foot companies of B.

RICHELLS, RITCHELL, or RICHAL, SIGISMUND, Wethersfield 1661, then had a s. grown up ; perhaps was of Brainford after.

RICHMOND, EDWARD, Westerly, s. of the first John, purch. at Misquamicuk, the most W. part of R. I. jurisdict. 1661, had in 1667 gr. at E. Greenwich, near the centre of the Col. and Farmer thought he was of Little Compton, the most E. town. JOHN, Taunton, one of the first purchas. 1637, may be the same, wh. Folsom, 138, places in Maine. He was not of T. so late as 1643, but perhaps in R. I. where I find him 1655, yet late in life went again to T. d. 20 Mar. 1664, aged a. 70. Abstr. of his will made at T. 14 Dec. 1663, is in Geneal. Reg. VII. 180, names s. John and Edward, ds. Mary, w. of William Paul, and Sarah, w. of Edward Rew, and next, 4 Nov. 1678, James Walker, gr.ch. Edward, s. of Edward, and Thomas, s. of John. Fam. tradit. brings this John from Ashton Keynes, a parish of Wiltsh. 4½ miles West from Crichlade, where he was bapt. 1597. JOHN, Taunton, s. of the preced. perhaps b. in Eng. had Mary, b. 2 June 1654 at Bridgewater, wh. m. 1 Jan. 1680, Richard Godfrey ; John, 6 June 1656, also at B. wh. may have d. bef. the will of his gr.f. ; Thomas, at Newport, 2 Feb. 1659 ; Susanna, at B. 4 Nov. 1661, wh. m. 18 Apr. 1683, James Read ; Joseph, or Josiah, 8 Dec. 1663 ; Edward, 8 Feb. 1666 ; Samuel, 23 Sept. 1668 ; Sarah, 26 Feb. 1671 ; John, again, 5 Dec. 1673 ; Ebenezer, 12 May 1676 ; and Abigail, 26 Feb. 1679 ; all at T. exc. the last two wh. were b. at Newport, and prob. Mary, wh. may have m. the sec. Richard Godfree ; and d. 7 Oct. 1715, aged 88. Abigail, prob. his wid. d. 1 Aug. 1727, aged 86. JOSEPH, Taunton, prob. s. of the preced. m. 26 June 1685, Mary Andrews. SAMUEL, Taunton, prob. br. of the preced. m. 20 Dec. 1694, Mehitable Andrews. THOMAS, Middleborough, br. of the preced. d. 14 Dec. 1705. Of this name, in old rec. sometimes Richmand, two had been gr. in 1834 at Harv. and seven at other N. E. coll.

RICKARD, or RICKER, or RICKET, GEORGE, Dover, 1670, by w. Eleanor, had Judith, b. 1 Feb. 1681 ; John, 1 Apr. 1682 ; Mary, 22 Mar. 1685 ; Maturin, 1 Feb. 1688 ; Eliz. 8 Aug. 1690 ; Hannah, 12 May 1693 ; Ephraim, 15 Feb. 1696 ; Eleanor, 15 Feb. 1699 ; and George, 19 Feb. 1702. He was k. by the Ind. 4 June 1706. GILES, Plymouth, freem. 1637, had first w. Judith, wh. d. 6 Feb. and m. 20 May 1662, for 2d w. Joan Tilson, but had s. Giles and John, perhaps Sarah (wh. m. 1657, as is said, George Paddock), all by former, and m. 3d w. 25 June 1669, Hannah, wid. of John Churchill, d. of William Pontus ; d. 1684, aged 87 ; and his wid. d. 12 Dec. 1690. GILES, Plymouth, s. of the preced. m. 31 Oct. 1651, Hannah Dunham, perhaps d. of the first John, had John, b. the next yr. day and mo. lost from the rec. ; Samuel, 14 Jan. 1663. JOHN, Plymouth, s. of Giles the first, m. 31 Oct. 1651, Esther Barnes, had John, b. 24 Nov. 1657 ; Mary, 27 Oct. 1677 ; Lydia, 12 Dec. 1679 ; John, 29 Dec. 1681 ; and Mercy, wh. d. 12 Feb. 1683. MATURIN, Dover, br. of George, had Joseph, and was k. on the same day with his br. THOMAS, Scituate. His will of 14 Nov. 1648, names no w. or ch. THOMAS, Salem 1670, had w. and d. Sarah.

RICKETSON, WILLIAM, Dartmouth, s. of Eliz. wh. may have been a wid. resid. there, by w. Eliz. had Rebecca, b. 14 May, 1681 ; John, 11 Feb. 1683 ; Eliz. 1 Sept. 1684.; William, 26 Feb. 1686 ; Jonathan, 7 Apr. 1688 ; and Timothy, 22 Jan. 1690 ; and d. 1 Mar. 1691.

RICKMAN, ISAAC, Salem, came in the fleet with Higginson 1629 ; and perhaps went back soon, at least no more is heard of him.

RIDDAN, or RIDDAINE, THADDEUS, Lynn, merch. freem. 1672, by w. Eliz. had Hannah, wh. d. 13 Nov. 1660 ; Hannah, again, b. 11 Nov. 1662 ; John, 3 Feb. 1665 ; and Abigail, 4 June 1671. By his correspond. Farmer was inform. that this name 'was Kidder.

RIDER, BENJAMIN, Yarmouth, m. 13 June 1670, Mary, prob. d. of William Lumpkin. JAMES, Cambridge, by w. Hannah, had Hannah, b. 1 Mar. 1651 ; James, 3 Jan. 1654 ; and Thomas, 1 Mar. 1657. Perhaps he rem. JOHN, Falmouth 1665–76, was perhaps s. of Phineas of the same. See Hutch. Coll. 398, and Willis, I. 141. *PHINEAS, Falmouth 1658, had perhaps been of Gloucester 1649, was a man of import. rep. 1670. See Willis, I. SAMUEL, Yarmouth 1643, m. 23 Dec. 1656, Sarah, d. of Robert Bartlett of Plymouth, had by earlier w. Mary, b. 6 Sept. 1647 ; and Eliz. wh. m. 2 Nov. 1667, John Cole ; and by this had Samuel, 18 Nov. 1657. SAMUEL, Taunton, s. of the preced. m. 14 June 1680, Lydia Tilden, perhaps d. of Joseph of Scituate. THOMAS, Dorchester, had come in the yr. 1634, by the Hercules, m. Eliz. d. of William Lane, was perhaps a caulker, of Boston 1650, had Hannah, b. 7 Mar. 1655. THOMAS, Watertown, freem. 1690, m. Sarah Lawrence, d. of George the first, had Sarah, b. 23 Dec. 1694, d. next mo. Prob. he rem. to Framingham, in Bond's judgm. and was as likely to be at Dorchester 1709. In the will of her f. this Sarah is ment. 1707 ; and she d. at Roxbury 14 Aug. 1714, says, perhaps erron. Geneal. Reg. XIV. 53. WILLIAM, Watertown, m. 7 or 11 Aug. 1674, Hannah Lovett, had

William, b. 29 July 1675; Hannah, 4 Apr. 1678, d. young; Hannah, again, 28 May 1680; rem. to Shirborn, had Daniel; and Eleazer, 22 Jan. 1687; and d. 27 Aug. 1724.

RIDGDALE or RIGDALE, JOHN, Plymouth, one of the passeng. in the Mayflower 1620, with w. Alice, and both d. bef. Apr. 1621.

RIDGE, JOHN, Newbury, d. 30 Dec. 1666. THOMAS, of town unkn. His wid. Martha gave inv. of his est. 25 Nov. 1684.

RIDGEWAY, or RIDGAWAY, JOHN, Malden, had w. Mary, wh. d. 24 Dec. 1670.

RIDLAND, JOHN, Charlestown, of wh. no more is kn. by me but that his name is in the list of household. 1678.

RIDLEY, RICHARD, came in the Planter, a serv. of Martin Saunders, from London 1635, aged 16, but no more is kn. of him.

RIFF, RICHARD, Salem, seems a strange name, but is in the list of freem. 1678.

RIGBY, EDWARD, Lancaster 1654. JOHN, Dorchester 1637, freem. 18 May 1642, d. in Apr. 1647; was perhaps f. of Samuel, bapt. there 21 Mar. 1641, and of Abigail, wh. m. 19 Feb. 1664, Thomas Holman. SAMUEL, Dorchester 1662, perhaps s. of the preced. a shoemaker, by first w. had Eliz. wh. m. 23 Jan. 1678, Watching Atherton; and Mehitable; and by sec. w. had John and Silence.

RIGGS, ANDREW, Gloucester, s. of the first Thomas, m. 24 Jan. 1704, Mary Richardson, had s. William, Joseph, and George, besides six ds. not nam. in Babson's Hist. wh. tells that he was liv. so late as 1771. EDWARD, Roxbury 1633, brot. w. Eliz. and ch. Lydia, wh. d. Aug. 1633, being the earliest on the rec.; Eliz. wh. d. in May next; and John d. Oct. foll. and his w. d. next yr. in Oct. He m. 5 Apr. 1636, Eliz. Rooke, by wh. he had not any ch. nam. on rec. of b. and therefore it may be conclud. that he had brot. one other s. and two ds. wh. liv. to m. but all d. bef. him. The w. d. 1669, and he was bur. 5 Mar. 1672, in his will of 2 Sept. 1670, naming s. Edward as dec. leav. wid. and childr. beside Joseph, Hannah, and other childr. of his d. Mary Twitchell, and gr.ch. Eliz. Allen. He was freem. 14 May 1634. EDWARD, Milford 1640, s. prob. of the preced. b. in Eng. had perhaps John and Samuel, and was one of the early sett. at Paugusset, after nam. Derby, but d. bef. his f. JOHN, Milford, perhaps s. of the preced. d. a. 1670. JOHN, Gloucester, s. of the first Thomas, m. 1 Jan. 1690, Ruth Wheeler, had s. John, Jeremiah, and Jonathan, beside one that d. inf. and seven ds.; and d. 12 Jan. 1748. SAMUEL, Milford 1671, then propound. for freem. may have been br. of the first John, m. 1667, Sarah, d. of Richard Baldwin of the same, and rem. to Derby. STEPHEN, Marblehead 1674. * THOMAS, Gloucester, was town clk. 51 yrs. selectman 20, sometime sch.m. rep.

1700; m. 7 June 1658, Mary, d. of Thomas Millet, wh. d. 23 Jan. 1695, had Mary, b. 6 Mar. 1659; Thomas, 23 Jan. 1661, d. in few days; Sarah, 16 Jan. 1662; Ann, 27 Apr. 1664; Thomas, again, 7 Dec. 1666; John, 25 Feb. 1670; Eliz. 22 Apr. 1672; Abigail, 29 Dec. 1678; and Andrew, 8 Jan. 1682. He m. 30 Oct. 1695, Eliz. Frese, and d. 26 Feb. 1722, aged 90. His wid. d. 16 June foll. aged 80. Mary, m. 21 Nov. 1677, Benjamin Haskell; and Sarah, m. 9 May 1681, John Tucker. THOMAS, Gloucester, eldest s. of the preced. m. 22 Nov. 1687, Ann Wheeler of Salisbury, had the same number of ch. male and fem. as his br. John, call. the s. Thomas, Moses, Aaron, and Joshua, but the seven ds. go without names, and all the ch. without dates.

RIGHT, GEORGE, freem. 18 May 1642, was, I think, either of Dorchester or Weymouth; tho. more prob. with an initial W. of Braintree. JOSEPH, Woburn, freem. 1690, when jun. is affix. so that there was an elder of the same name. ROBERT, Boston, had d. Hannah, wh. m. 1669, William Hoar; but the spelling is often with initial W.

RIGMAN, EPHRAIM, a soldier in Philip's war, 1675 and 6, under Capt. Poole, on Conn. riv.

RILEY, HENRY, Rowley, d. 1710, aged 82. JOHN, Wethersfield, by w. Grace had John, b. 1646; Joseph, 1649; Jonathan, 1651; beside Mary, Grace, Sarah, Jacob, and Isaac, whose dates are unkn. but all the eight are named in this order in his will of 1671, soon after wh. he d. All exc. Jacob, wh. prob. d. earlier, div. the est. of Joseph, wh. d. without w. or ch. in 1706; and John and Jonathan d. 1711; Grace m. 22 Nov. 1680, William Goodrich the sec. JOHN, Springfield, by w. Margaret had Margaret, b. 1662; and Mary, 1665; was freem. 1671, and d. 24 Oct. 1684. His wid. d. 22 Aug. 1689. Margaret, his d. m. 1685. RICHARD, by Hinman count. as one of the early sett. at Wethersfield, is by me thought to mean Risley.

RINDGE, DANIEL, Roxbury 1639, rem. to Ipswich bef. 1648, prob. had ch. ISAAC, Ipswich, perhaps s. of the preced. m. a. 1692, Eliz. d. of John Dutch. JARVIS, Salisbury, freem. 1690. We may hardly doubt that this should be Ring, and that he was s. of Robert. JOHN, Ipswich 1664, was perhaps br. of the preced. Daniel, H. C. 1709, wh. d. 1712, may have been s. of Isaac, or other s. of first Daniel.

RING, ANDREW, Plymouth, whose wid. mo. made her will there 28 Oct. 1633, leav. him to the care of Elder Fuller, came prob. a. 1629, was freem. 1646, m. that yr. Deborah, d. of Stephen Hopkins, had William; Eleazer; Mary; Deborah; and Eliz. 19 Apr. 1652. He was one of the first sett. of Middleborough, had for sec. w. Lettys, wid. of John Morton. His sis. Eliz. wh. m. Stephen Dean, and Susanna, wh. m. Thomas Clark, were both older than A. which d. 1692, in 75th yr.

Whether his f. came or d. in Eng. is uncert. JARVIS, Salisbury, s. of Robert, m. 24 Dec. 1685, Hannah Fowler, perhaps d. of Thomas, had Jarvis, b. 2 Oct. 1686; Hannah, 3 Mar. 1689; Eliz. 3 Sept. 1692; and Oliver, 17 June 1698. JOHN, perhaps of Salisbury, came in the Bevis 1638, from Southampton, was a carpenter. JOHN, Ipswich, m. 18 Nov. 1664, Mary, eldest d. of Thomas Bray of Gloucester, rem. thither, perhaps, bef. 1697, or at least his w. there d. 11 Apr. 1725, aged 77, and they prob. had William, Daniel, and David, possib. also, John. JOHN, Salisbury, s. of Robert, by w. Priscilla had Moses, b. 30 Apr. 1692. ROBERT, Salisbury, one of the first sett. came in the Bevis, 1638, from Southampton, as serv. of Richard Austin, was perhaps br. of John, freem. 9 Oct. 1640, by w. Eliz. had Martha, b. 12 Dec. 1654; Jarvis, Feb. 1658; John, 17 Feb. 1662; and Joseph, 3 Aug. 1664. THOMAS, had been of Salem, perhaps in 1637, was after of Exeter, there d. 1667.

RIPLEY, ABRAHAM, Hingham, s. of William, brot. by his f. from Eng. freem. 1656, m. Mary, eldest d. of Joseph Farnsworth of Dorchester, wh. outliv. him, and, 1684, m. Edward Jenkins of Scituate. JOHN, Hingham, elder s. of William, b. in Eng. m. Eliz. eldest d. of Rev. Peter Hobart, was freem. 1656, and d. soon after date of his will, 31 Jan. 1684, in wh. he names ch. only, John, b. 2 Mar. 1657; Joshua, Jeremiah, Josiah, Peter, and Hezekiah. JOSHUA, Hingham, s. of the preced. m. 28 Nov. 1682, Hannah, d. of Dept. Gov. William Bradford. JOSIAH, Hingham, br. of the preced. by w. Joanna had Mary, b. 18 Feb. 1695. WILLIAM, Hingham 1638, came, as by the contempo. MS. of his townsman, Daniel Cushing, we learn, with w. and two s. and two ds. from Hingham, Co. Norfolk, Eng. was freem. 18 May, 1642, m. 29 Sept. 1654, as sec. w. Eliz. wid. of Thomas Thaxter, and d. 20 July 1656. His will of 30 June preced. abstr. in Geneal. Reg. VI. 354; is minute eno. as to the geogr. of his lds. but names no relat. exc. the two s. wh. are made excors. His d. Sarah m. 18 Oct. 1653, Jeremiah Beal, but neither she nor the other d. nor w. are ment. The latter m. 20 Jan. 1658, John Dwight of Dedham. One WILLIAM was of Gallop's comp. for the sad campaign against Quebec, 1690. Nine of this name had been, in 1834, gr. at Yale, five at Harv. and six at other N. E. coll.

RISCRAFT, RICHARD, Northampton, took the o. of alleg. 8 Feb. 1679.

RISDEN, ELISHA, Milford, 1678, s. of Robert, perhaps rem. ROBERT, Boston 1654, mariner, by w. Beatrice, had Elisha, b. 25 Jan. 1655; and Sarah, 29 May 1662, rem. to Fairfield, there with w. d. a. 1666, leav. five ch. of wh. only Elisha is nam. He own. beside prop. at F. est. at the isle of Nevis, sold by guardians of the ch. wh. in 1678, desired to abrog. the contr.

RISHWORTH, *EDWARD, Exeter 1639, Wells 1643, m. a d. of Rev.

John Wheelwright, whose name is not seen, had Edward, and a d. Mary, wh. in the will of her gr.f. W. is nam. White, d. of Edward R. was of York 1652, of Godfrey's council, to support Gorges' patent, 1649, as well as three yrs. preced. rep. for York 1653, and 12 yrs. succeed. last in 1679, after wh. yr. no more rep. came from Maine under the old chart. was in high esteem, either as republican or royalist, a magistr. of Mass. 1681, and liv. as Farmer says, in 1683. But strong reason is found in the wills of Samuel Hutchinson and of Rev. John Wheelwright for presumpt. that f. and s. were by Farmer here confus. He had, beside Edward, prob. other ch. and perhaps had m. in Eng. a sis. of the w. of W. for S. H. in his will, Apr. 1667, gives to E. R. by the descript. of " eldest s. of sis. R." and it may fairly be assumed that the f. was then d. At least, the magistr. of 1681, wh. was prob. the recorder of 1671, must be judged, after Apr. 1667, to have m. that Sarah W. the unm. d. of Rev. John, nam. in her uncle's will, and to be meant in 1679 in the will of her f. calling him "s.-in-law." Difficulty, however, attends this hypothesis, because it is said, that Richard Crisp m. 1671, Sarah, that d. of Rev. John Wheelwright. Still, R. may have m. the cousin, wid. of C.

RISING, JAMES, Boston, m. 7 July 1657, Eliz. d. of Robert Hinsdale of Medfield, rem. to Bermudas, there was of the ch. and brot. letters from their pastor, Nathaniel White, H. C. 1646, and was adm. a. 1662, of Salem ch. and rem. in few yrs. to Windsor, where his w. d. 1669, as did ano. w. 2 Apr. 1674; had James, John, and perhaps other ch. bef. his rem. kept the ferry at W. rem. to Suffield a. 1679, there d. 11 Sept. 1688. His s. James d. 1690, without ch. JOHN, Suffield, s. of the preced. m. 1684, d. 1720, leav. John, James, Josiah, Jonathan, Joseph, Aaron, and Moses, beside four ds. Rysand was the spell. at S.

RISLEY, RISLA, RYSLEY, or RISSLY, RICHARD, Hartford, 1639, liv. on E. side of the riv. d. 1648. His inv. is in Trumbull, Col. Rec. I. 486; and at the end are nam. the three ch. Sarah, betw. 7 and 8 yrs. old; Samuel, a. 2; and Richard, a. 3 mos. wh. was bapt. 20 Aug. 1648, not as the rec. reads, 21, wh. was Monday. Richard the s. had a fam. Samuel d. 1670, prob. without fam. WILLIAM, Dover, 1659.

RIST, NICHOLAS, Reading, had w. Sarah imprison. 20 yrs. aft. m. for witchcr. June 1692.

RITH, or RIETH, RICHARD, Marblehead, 1675.

RIX, JAMES, Salem, prob. s. of Thomas of the same, had come back after some yrs. abs. in 1682. JOHN, Boston, s. of William, tailor, by w. Charity had Mary, b. 3 Jan. 1674; John, 16 Aug. 1676, d. soon; Solomon, 10 Jan. 1678; Eliz. 3 Oct. 1679; Thomas, 22 Jan. 1681; William, 6 Feb. 1682; Charity, 29 Jan. 1684; John, again, 30 Aug.

1685; and Benjamin, wh. d. young, 16 June, 1693. RICHARD, Salem 1676. THOMAS, Salem 1649, barber surgeon, had there bapt. Remember, 13 Oct. 1650; Sarah, 29 June 1651; Esther, 5 June 1653; Thomas, 26 Aug. 1655; James, 18 Oct. 1657; and Theophilus, 20 Aug. 1665. THOMAS, Boston, gunsmith, br. of John of the same, d. early, hav. by w. Sarah only ch. Elisha, b. 30 Aug. 1674; and she m. after his d. Joseph Goodale. THOMAS, Wethersfield, m. Abigail, d. of John Ingersoll, and d. 21 May, 1690, leav. wid. and only ch. Abigail. His wid. m. Joshua Wills of Windsor, as his third w. a. 1696. WILLIAM, Boston, weaver, by w. Grace had Elisha, b. Aug. 1645, bapt. 8 Mar. 1646, wh. d. 19 May, 1672; Mary, 4 Mar. 1647; John, 14 Nov. 1648; Thomas, 1, ano. rec. says 11 Apr. 1654; and Ezekiel, 30 Nov. 1656, wh. d. young; and d. 13 Nov. 1657. His wid. m. 1663, Andrew Newcome. This name, oft. appearing in old rec. Rick or Ricks, is still found in New Hampsh.

ROACH, THOMAS, New London 1651, m. 12 Dec. 1661, Rebecca, d. of William Redfield, wh. d. 16 Aug. 1670; but he was liv. to testify in 1708, as Miss Caulkins tells in her Hist.

ROANES or ROANE, WILLIAM, perhaps of York a. 1672, m. Wilmott, wid. of Edward Start, d. leav. two ch. and John Parker senr. was made admor. in 1678.

ROATH, ROBERT, Norwich, m. Oct. 1668, Sarah Saxton, eldest d. of Richard of Windsor, had John b. Nov. 1669; Sarah, Aug. 1672, wh. d. 12 Mar. 1695; Mary, Nov. 1674; Eliz. Mar. 1677, d. next yr. Hannah, Apr. 1679; Daniel, 1 Feb. 1681; Peter, 17 Feb. 1684; and his w. d. 20 Mar. 1687.

ROBBINS, BENJAMIN, perhaps of Wallingford, m. 29 Aug. 1687, Sarah, d. of John Brooks. * JOHN, Wethersfield 1638, by w. Mary had Mary, b. 20 Jan. 1642; Hannah, 30 Apr. 1643; Comfort, 12 Oct. 1646; John, 29 Apr. 1649; Joshua; all liv. in 1667; and Samuel, wh. d. 1659, as did his w. was rep. 1656, 7, and 9, and d. 27 June 1660. JOHN, Branford 1667, m. 4 Nov. 1659, Mary, wid. of Robert Abbot. JOHN, Bridgewater, s. of Nicholas, m. 14 Dec. 1665, Jehosabeth Jourdaine, had Jeduthun, b. 1667. JOHN, Wethersfield, s. of the first John, perhaps was of Lyme in 1671, by w. Mary had John, b. 1676, d. in few yrs.; Joshua, 1678; Samuel, 1680; John, again 1684; and Richard, 1687; made his will 1 July 1689, and d. prob. in Nov. foll. unless Hinman, 291, be right in prolong. his days. JOSHUA, Wethersfield, br. of the preced. was in office in the town 1678, 9, 81, 2, 9, 90, 1 and 3; yet Hinman, ut sup. says he d. young, perhaps confus. the brs. or rem. and was not found there after d. of his f. But the town rec. proves that he took w. Eliz. 1680, and possib. he had childr. Frequent. the name of mem. of this fam. is with single *b.* NATHANIEL, Cambridge, prob. s. of Richard, by w. Mary had Mary, wh. d. 30 Nov. 1676; and perhaps others; was freem. 1690, d. Dec. 1719, in 71st yr. NICHOLAS, Duxbury, 1638, by w. Ann had John, Mary, Hannah, and Rebecca, all ment. in his will of 9 Feb. 1651. RICHARD, Charlestown 1639, with w. Rebecca of the ch. 24 May 1640; rem. to Boston, soon after to Cambridge, had John bapt. 31 May 1640; Samuel, b. 22 May 1643; Nathaniel; and Rebecca; of wh. the last three were bapt. at Cambridge, Mitchell's ch. reg. tells, as the first had been at Charlestown. He was liv. Apr. 1683. Rebecca m. John Woodward. ROBERT, Concord 1678. SAMUEL, Salisbury, in his will of 22 Aug. 1665, names f. John, mo. Esther, and br. Joseph of Thedingworth in Leicestersh. Eng. and therefore I suppose he was only trans. not perman. inhab. SAMUEL, Cambridge, prob. s. of Richard, was freem. 1680, when he liv. at the vill. now Newton. THOMAS, Duxbury 1643, may be he of Salem 1650, whose wid. m. Michael Spencer of Lynn. THOMAS, Salem, sw. in 1675, that he was 55 yrs. old. WILLIAM, Reading, freem. 1691, perhaps d. at Boston 1693; but Winsor names a William of Hingham, wh. m. 1665, Susanna Lane. Thirteen of this name had been gr. at Yale, nine at Harv. and seven at other N. E. coll. in 1834.

ROBERTS, DAVID, Woburn, m. 3 Oct. 1678, Joanna Brooks, had Eunice, b. 28 Oct. 1679; David, 24 Oct. 1681; Giles, 16 Jan. 1687; Joanna, 13 Feb. 1694; Sarah, 15 Jan. 1697; and perhaps he rem. ELI, New Haven, a propr. 1685. GEORGE, Exeter 1677, in 1690 desir. jurisdict. of Mass. GILES, Scarborough 1662, perhaps br. of David, had five ch. of wh. none but Abraham is nam. His will of 25 Jan. 1667, only five days bef. the inv. does not enlighten us, exc. by call. Arthur Auger, and William Sheldon, his brs.-in-law. HUGH, Gloucester, m. 8 Nov. 1649, Mary, d. of Hugh Caulkins, rem. to New London, where he was a tanner, and had Mary, b. 9 Dec. 1652; Samuel, 25 Apr. 1656; and Mehitable, 15 Apr. 1658; in 1667, with others of the oldest sett. went to Newark, N. J. JOHN, Roxbury, came, says the ch. rec. "in 1636, brought his aged mo. w. and ch. Thomas, Edward, Eliz. Margery, Jane, Alce, Lydia, Ruth, and Deborah. He was one of the first fruits of Wales that came to N. E. called to Christ by the ministry of that rev. and worthy instrument Mr. Wrath." In its proper place the rec. has this: "7 Jan. 1645/6, old mother Roberts, a Welch woman, d. in the 103d yr. of her age. She was above 90 yrs. old when she left her native country." He was freem. 22 May 1639, d. 27 Nov. 1651. Of not one of the seven ds. do I find the m. or d. JOHN, Marblehead 1668. JOHN, Dover, s. of Thomas of the same, m. Abigail, d. of Hatevil Nutter, had Joseph; prob. Hatevil; Thomas; and Abigail, wh. m. 8 Nov. 1671,

John Hall jr. of the same. He was active against the Quakers 1662, marshall 1680, mem. of a whig convention 1689, and d. 21 Jan. 1695, Belkn. in Farmer's ed. I. 91, 122. JOHN, Boston, freem. 1671. JOHN Northampton, k. by the Ind. 29 Oct. 1675. JOHN, Roxbury, a soldier k. by the Ind. at Sudbury fight, under Wadsworth, Apr. 1676. JOHN, Hartford, m. Eliz. d. of Rev. Samuel Stone, the divorc. w. of William (Goodwin, 212, says Samuel, erron.) Sedgwick, had John, to wh. in her will 1681, his gr.mo. Stone gave some est. He rem. a. 1684, to Newtown, L. I. and with w. was liv. 1695. It is not kn. wh. was his f. when he was b. or when he d. but he was an unfortun. man. JOHN, Gloucester, m. 4 Feb. 1678, Hannah, d. of Thomas Bray, had Nathaniel, b. 26 Mar. 1679; and John, 12 Dec. 1680; Samuel, 1685; Thomas, 1687; Ebenezer, 1690; Mary, 1696; and Job, 1701. He d. 10 Jan. 1714, and his wid. d. 23 Mar. 1717. JOHN, Hadley, wh. took o. of alleg. 8 Feb. 1679, was perhaps s. of John of Northampton. JOHN, Boston, by w. Experience, had Sarah, b. Jan. 1686, d. young. JOSEPH, perhaps of Portsmouth, sent by Capt. Mason 1632, in the Lion, arr. at Boston, 16 Sept. ROBERT, Boston 1640, by w. Eunice had Timothy, b. 7 Aug. 1646; was of Ipswich 1648, d. a. 19 July 1663, leav. wid. Susanna, and eight ch. of wh. the eldest was John, and the youngest two were Abigail, b. 27 Mar. 1658; and Patience, 20 Feb. 1661. His wid. m. Thomas Perrin. ROBERT, Rowley 1676, perhaps s. of the preced. SAMUEL, Ipswich, d. June 1670, prob. for his inv. is of 21 of that mo. SAMUEL, Norwich, s. of Hugh, by w. Eliz. m. 9 Dec. 1680, had Samuel, b. 20 Oct. 1682, wh. d. next mo. Hugh, 26 Oct. 1683, d. under six yrs. Mary, 22 Mar. 1685; Samuel, 9 May 1688; Eliz. 12 Oct. 1690; and his w. d. 29 Apr. 1692. SIMON, Boston, m. 18 July, 1654, Christian, d. of Alexander Baker, had John, b. 27 Apr. 1655; Simon, 22 Nov. 1656; Samuel, 18 Mar. 1658; Joseph, 18 Sept. 1662, d. young; Eliz. 28 Dec. 1665; Ann, 18 July 1669; Benjamin, 8 Jan. 1671; and Joseph, again, 24 Jan. 1673. In Geneal. Reg. X. 303, may be read a fine specim. of the wretched vanity that was exhibit. on the d. of a gr. s. 1774, wh. oft. characteriz. the obituary notices of people bearing the same surnames as memb. of the noble houses in Eng. or France. THOMAS, Dover, prob. sett. there with the Hiltons, 1623, was Presid. of the Col. chos. in oppos. to noted John Underhill, had John, b. 1629; Thomas, 1633; Esther; Ann; Eliz. and Sarah; and d. after 27 Sept. 1673, the date of his will, pro. 30 June foll. Esther m. John Martin; Ann m. James Philbrick; Eliz. m. Benjamin Heard; and Sarah m. Richard Rich. ‖ THOMAS, Boston, perhaps s. of John of Roxbury, where he first liv. and was mem. of that ch. by w. Eunice had Timothy, Eliz. Lydia, and Eunice, this last b. 18 Aug. 1653; ar. co. 1644; freem. 1645;

d. prob. July 1654; and his wid. Eunice, m. 22 Oct. 1656, Moses Maverick, as his sec. w. THOMAS, Duxbury, 1640, m. 24 Mar. 1651 (Winsor, 286), or more prob. 1656, Mary, d. of Robert Paddock, may have rem. to Eastham. THOMAS, Roxbury, a. 1645, s. prob. of John, but I presume he rem. aft. or bef. d. of his f. THOMAS, Providence 1650, is in the list of freem. there 1655, m. a sis. of William Harris, but d. at Newport, without ch. early in Apr. 1676. THOMAS, Dover, s. of Thomas the first, by w. Mary, d. of Thomas Leighton, had s. Thomas, and Nathaniel, perhaps other ch. Thomas d. unm. but the name was perpet. there by Nathaniel. THOMAS, a soldier under Capt. William Turner, k. by the Ind. at the Falls fight, 19 May 1676. WILLIAM, Milford 1645–1669. WILLIAM, Dover 1645, had a fam. and with his s.-in-law was k. by the Ind. in 1675. But whether he had s. or not, is unascert. by the indefatig. Mr. Quint, to whom, for all informat. a. Dover, antiquaries are so much indebt. WILLIAM, Charlestown 1648, may have rem. to New Haven, there been propr. 1685. Perhaps by w. Joanna, he had William; Zachariah; Alice and Lydia, tw.; Ann, and Abigail. His s. William perpet. the fam. See Dodd. WILLIAM, Boston, m. at Hingham, Oct. 1667, Eliz. Tower.

ROBERTSON, JOHN, was k. by the Ind. 21 Oct. 1676, at Salisbury, as Coffin inform. Farmer. NICHOLAS. See Robinson. WILLIAM, is nam. by Shattuck as at Concord 1670.

ROBIE, or ROBY, ANDREW, Hartford, m. 19 Nov. 1691, Abigail Curtis, perhaps had Mary, b. 4 Nov. 1692; and Eliz. 19 July 1694. EBENEZER, Sudbury, s. of William of Boston, a physician, stud. under the celebr. Boerhave, was much esteemed, and d. 1 or 4 Sept. 1772. HENRY, Hampton 1678, had been at Exeter, it is said, and Farmer had the date 1639, in wh. yr. he thought he rem. from Dorchester, but the name at D. was mistak. for Kibby; d. 1688, leav. w. Sarah, and ch. Thomas, Samuel, Ichabod, John, Judith, and Ruth. His will of 10 Jan. 1687, with codic. of 3 Apr. 1688 was pro. 5 June foll. But he had been m. 19 Feb. 1674, as 3d h. of Eliz. wid. of John Garland, d. of Thomas Philbrick, wh. had first been w. of Thomas Chase; and he may have been that man, b. as in the Bible of his br. Thomas, at Castle Dunnington, was writ. 12 Feb. 1618/9, add. that he went and liv. in N. E. JOHN, Haverhill, s. of the preced. d. prob. June 1691. JOSEPH, Boston, s. of William, by w. Priscilla had Henry, b. 3 Oct. 1722; Joseph, 12 May 1724, H. C. 1742; Hannah, 9 Jan. 1726; and William, 5 June 1727. RICHARD, Marblehead 1674. SAMUEL, in the Bible of his br. Thomas, wh. Dr. Ebenezer cop. from at Castle Dunnington, the fam. seat, is mark. b. 12 Feb. 1628/9, with the add. "went to New Eng." but I have never heard of his arr. and fear that his int. may have been defeat. by the civ. war. No more recent accounts of him have been told, unless he were the inhab. of New Hampsh. wh. prayed for jurisdict. of Mass. 1690, and perhaps br. of Henry. THOMAS, Salem, s. of William, had been librarian of the coll. and for some short time a fellow of the corpo. preached a little, but in conseq. prob. of malign. report spread about, as in a dedica. of a serm. to Presid. Leverett preach. at coll. wh. he print. "that his sermons were only heathenish discourses, no better Christianity than was in Tully," he withdrew from the pulpit and became a physician, m. Mehitable, d. of Maj. Stephen Sewall, had William, wh. d. young; Mehitable; and Thomas; both m. and d. 28 Aug. 1729. WILLIAM, Boston, s. of Thomas, b. in Eng. 26 Apr. 1648, prob. at Castle Dunnington, in the E. riding of Yorksh. came hither, perhaps at man's age, and m. Eliz. d. of William Greenough, had Mary, b. 19 Oct. 1687, d. young; Thomas, 20 Mar. 1689, H. C. 1708; William, bapt. 1 Nov. 1690; John, 6 Dec. 1691; Joseph, 20 Aug. 1693; Samuel, 1 Nov. 1694; Dorothy, 29 Mar. 1696; Mercy and Ann, tw. 19 Sept. 1697; Sarah, b. 6, bapt. 11 Dec. 1698, d. young; Ebenezer, 29 Sept. bapt. 5 Oct. 1701, H. C. 1719; Henry, 18, bapt. 21 Feb. 1703, d. at 18 yrs.; and Mercy, again, 29 Aug. bapt. 3 Sept. 1704; and perhaps more, for tradit. says, he had fifteen. Prob. one was Mary, wh. m. a Thomas; and Eliz. wh. m. James Barnard was ano. He was constable 1684, and d. 23 Jan. 1718. Mercy m. 18 Sept. 1722, John Goodwin of Boston. WILLIAM, Boston, s. of the preced. by w. Lois had William, b. 16 Feb. 1721, and his w. d. 4 days aft. and he m. 15 May 1722, Ann Pollard.

ROBINSON, ABRAHAM, Gloucester, not s. (as report. by worthless modern tradit.) of famous John of Leyden, for I can never believe that Prince, so full as well as accur. could have ment. nothing of him, and no s. of this name was b. to the gr. teach. of non-conform. had Abraham (said most improb. to be the first b. of the town, for his f.-in-law's will, Apr. 1662, calls him under 21 yrs.), and perhaps other ch. and d. 18 Feb. 1646, wh. may be the earliest preserv. rec. of d. there, yet we must presume that earlier are lost. His wid. Mary, m. 15 July 1646, William Brown, and Henry Walker, 26 Sept. 1662, d. 17 Apr. 1690. ABRAHAM, Gloucester, s. of the preced. m. 7 July 1668, Mary Harraden, d. of Edward, had Mary b. 20 Aug. 1669; Sarah, 17 Sept. 1671; Eliz. 12 Sept. 1673; Abigail, 4 Jan. 1676; Abraham, 15 Oct. 1677; Andrew, 2 Oct. 1679; Stephen, 9 Dec. 1681; Ann, 1684; Dorcas, 1685; Deborah, 1688; Hannah, 1691; and Jane, 1693. His life is traced by Mr. Babson down to 1730, so that he was old man when he d. yet it was less than the statem. of descend. wh. would make it one hundred and two yrs. Prob. he was one or two yrs. under 90.

ANTHONY, an unprofit. apprent. punish. by the Court 1636. DAVID, Exeter 1657–83, was perhaps s. of John of the same. He perhaps had s. David, wh. m. 1 Jan. 1706, Sarah, d. of Josiah Sanborn of Hampton. EDWARD, Newport, one of the freem. 1655. FRANCIS, Saco 1643, in 1645, was called on by Vines in the interest of Gorges, as a counsellor, but we learn nothing more of him. FRANCIS, Boston, freem. 1671. GEORGE, Rehoboth 1646–77, in 1668, had part in the div. of Attleborough lds. and serv. in Philip's war. Baylies II. 217, and IV. 84. GEORGE, Boston, m. 3 Oct. 1657, Mary Bushnell, perhaps d. of John of the same, had George b. 30 Mar. 1658; John, 1661; and Martha, 31 Mar. 1665; was one of the first comp. to act with fire engines, 1678. GEORGE, Swanzey, Winsor says m. 12 Nov. 1680, Eliz. Gaille (so strange a name that I think it may be a mistake of Col. Rec. and severe scrutiny might discover Cole, or ano. word), had John, b. 5 Sept. 1681; but prob. by a former w. whose name I see not, had Nathaniel, b. 1 Nov. 1673, bur. one week aft.; Samuel, 16 Nov. 1679. GEORGE, Boston, prob. s. of George the first, by w. Eliz. had George b. 28 Dec. 1680; John, 13 June 1684; and perhaps more. GEORGE, Watertown, by w. Sarah had Beriah, b. 7 Jan. 1684; George 1 July 1685; John, 4 Mar. 1688; Ebenezer, 22 Sept. 1692; Samuel, 13 Oct. 1695; and his w. d. 5 May 1703. He m. 4 Aug. foll. Sarah, d. of Peter Behoney, under fifteen yrs old, had David, 5 May 1704; and Jonathan, 4 Feb. 1706. ISAAC, Plymouth 1630, s. of blessed John, the apostle of Leyden, came prob. with his mo. in the fleet with Winth. See lett. of Sherley, 8 Mar. 1629–30, to Bradford. He was taxed 1634, when perhaps he liv. on Duxbury side, but was freem. of Scituate 1636, there m. 1636, Margaret Hanford, sis. of Rev. Thomas, niece of Timothy Hatherly, sold his est. 1639, and with Rev. John Lathrop rem. to Barnstable, had Susanna, bapt. at S. 21 Jan. 1638; and John, at B. 5 Apr. 1640; Isaac, 7 Aug. 1642; Fear 26 Jan. 1645; and Mercy, 4 July 1647, all rememb. exc. Susanna, prob. d. in the will of Timothy Hatherly in 1664. His w. was bur. 13 June 1649, with a. d. premat. b. the week bef. Fear was w. of Samuel Baker. Isaac, the younger, was m. in 1666, but drown. 6 Oct. 1668. Mercy m. 16 Mar. 1669, William Weeks. He m. a sec. w. whose name of bapt. is not, I think, giv. by the tradit. wh. calls her sis. of famous elder Faunce, but our rec. proves, that he had Israel, bapt. 5 Oct. 1651; and Jacob, 15 May 1653. Peter and Thomas are add. by Mr. Otis. By the teach. of his worthy f. as well as his experience, he gain. the wisdom thro. wh. he was oppos. to Gov. Prince's policy of severity against the Quakers, 1659, and was disfranchis. Deane says. But he would have him count. an Assist. wherein he was wrong. He may be more corr. in saying he liv. 93 yrs. In some of his latter yrs. he was of Martha's

Vineyard, Mr. Otis says. Prince is very careful (p. 238 of Hale's ed.
of the Annals, Boston, 1826), after saying that he "liv. to above 90 yrs.
of age," to add that he had often seen him, and that he "left male posterity." His greater reverence for the Leyden pastor convinces me,
that he would equally have ment. were such the opinion as to Abraham;
yet the fact, that nothing is ever seen of the wid. mo. in any earlier
writer, militates somewhat with my opinion. Still no reason thence can
be deduced in favor of Abraham being s. of the glorious John, and the
opinion or suggestion of Mr. Babson in the note of careful Mr. Deane,
Bradford, 247, as to the obscurity of Mrs. Robinson on our side of the
water, is not to be explain. by her suppos. residence at Salem, where,
in Felt's list of mem. of the ch. is a wid. Ann R. join. in 1637. The
greater probability appears to me, that she d. very soon after reach.
our shores; yet she must be inquired for, not at Cape Ann, but on the
other side of the Bay of Mass. unless some appearance of tradit. in favor
of Abraham be found, as it has not been, in the first, sec. third, or fourth
generat. of her descend. IsAAC, Lynn 1637, came in the Hopewell,
Babb, master, late in 1635, aged 15, was perhaps early d. at least Lewis
gives nothing of him. IsAAC, Tisbury, s. of the first Isaac, was bapt.
Israel, as Mr. Otis, with much sagacity argues, and that after the drown.
of his first Isaac, he call. this s. for him, as the name Israel is no more
heard aft. 1668, and Isaac d. 1728, mak. his will 5 Feb. wh. was pro. 1
Oct. foll. JACOB, New Haven, m. 1690, Sarah Hitchcock, had John, b. 3
Dec. 1691; Thomas, 5 Dec. 1693; Sarah, 24 Dec. 1695; Hannah, 24
Feb. 1698; Mary; and Eliakim, 2 Apr. 1706. JACOB, Tisbury, s. of
Isaac, d. bef. 19 Nov. 1733, when, on div. of his est. are ment. wid. Ex-
perience, and ch. Jacob, Isaac, and Mary. JAMES, Boston, m. 21 Feb.
1654, Martha Buck, had Sarah, b. 24 Mar. 1659; John, 17 Sept. 1662;
James, 21 July 1667; and Eliz.; was a mariner. I suppose both s. d.
young, for he gave his est. in 1673 to John Hull and Thomas Brattle in
tr. for hims. for life, next for w. Martha for life, and then to use of his
ds. Eliz. and Sarah. JAMES, Dorchester, m. 27 Sept. 1664, Mary, d. of
Thomas Alcock, had James, b. 8 Nov. 1665; Thomas, 15 Apr. 1668;
Samuel, 4 Sept. 1670; Mary, 17 Mar. 1673, d. young; John, 17 Apr.
1675, H. C. 1695, min. of Duxbury; Henry, 21 June 1678, d. very
soon; and Ebenezer, 5 Jan. 1682, wh. was k. 27 May 1707, at Port
Royal, in the abortive siege; was freem. 1690, and d. 18 Apr. 1694.
His wid. d. 13 Mar. 1718, aged 73. JAMES, Boston, by his will, 3 Sept.
1676, pro. 3 days aft. names no w. nor ch. but gives est. to brs. Thomas,
Joseph, and sis. Mary, *one half*, and other half to aunt Eliz. w. of Joseph
Rock, and cousin Hannah, w. of James Brading. This proves, that he
was s. of deac. Thomas of Scituate. JAMES, Newcastle 1683, then of the

gr. jury, had liv. at Scarborough 1666, there m. Lucretia, d. of Richard Foxwell, had four ds. and rem. on the Ind. hostil. 1675 to N. whence they did not return. JOHN, Salem 1639, in Felt's list of ch. mem. where also appear Ann, a wid. and Isabella, both 1637. He was prob. the freem. of 2 June 1641, may have rem. to Boston, and in a will of 2 June 1653, giv. his prop. to mo. or sis. if alive ; but this condition seems hardly consist. with the prob. that the fem. ch. mem. of Salem 1637, could be those. His inv. was ret. Nov. 1653. Ano. JOHN was of New London 1646–9, yet Caulkins could only tell of his house lot ; and he may have d. at Ipswich, 1 Mar. 1657, if Farmer have the date right ; but a JOHN of Ipswich, wheelwright, wh. in his will of 27 Feb. pro. 30 Mar. 1658, names no ch. and to swell the confus. ano. JOHN was there liv. 1660. JOHN, early at Haverhill, rem. to Exeter 1657, perhaps f. of David, Jonathan, and Stephen, was k. by the Ind. as Hubbard tells, Sept. 1675. JOHN, Salem, s. of William of the same, had w. and fam. in 1677. *JOHN, Barnstable, perhaps eldest s. of Isaac, m. May 1667, Eliz. Weeks, had John, b. 20 Mar. 1668 ; Isaac, 30 Jan. 1670 ; Timothy, 30 Oct. 1671 ; Abigail, 20 Mar. 1674 ; and Fear, 16 June 1676 ; the last three with Joseph, Mercy, and Mary, wh. were younger, all bapt. 21 Oct. 1688 ; beside a s. b. 12 Dec. 1683, and a d. 1 May 1688, ea. d. soon aft. He was rep. for Falmouth, C. C. 1689, 90, and 1, but in Apr. 1714 rem. to Conn. *JOHN, Falmouth, C. C. was rep. at Plymouth 1689 and 90, in fair presumpt. may be reckoned the same as preced. until further investigat. disproves it. A suppositit. mythical, or tradit. John, assumed by the late Professor James F. Dana to be br. of Isaac, and sett. at Gloucester, and f. of Abraham, acc. his relat. to Farmer, is not sustained by the slightest probabil. as Mr. Babson assures me, to be acq. from the rec. JOHN, Duxbury, s. of Samuel, not James, as Winsor, 184, had it, giv. also wrong date of b. prob. of Dorchester, ord. 13 Nov. 1702, m. Hannah, d. of Rev. Ichabod Wiswall, his predecessor, the patriotic agent in London, of the Plymouth Col. who was overborne or circumvent. by the cunning management of Increase Mather, the Mass. agent, had Mary, b. 23 Feb. 1706 ; Hannah, 2 Nov. 1708 ; Alithea, 26 May 1710 ; Eliz. 28 Sept. 1712 ; John, 16 Apr. 1715 ; Ichabod ; and Faith, 1718. His w. with eldest ch. Mary was drown. 22 Sept. 1722, at Nantasket, on their voyage to Boston ; and he d. 14 Nov. 1745 ; more than 7 yrs. aft. separat. from his cure, at the residence in Lebanon of the first Gov. Jonathan Trumbull, wh. had m. his youngest d. He was a man of more wit than discretion in his parish managem. JOHN, Narraganset, s. of Rowland of the same, m. Mary Hazard, had Mary, b. 1705 ; Sarah, 1707 ; Ruth, 1709 ; and prob. more. He d. bef. his f. JOHN, Newbury, s. of Robert, by w. Susanna had John, b. 6 Sept. 1690 ; Samuel, 2 Dec. 1692 ;

Daniel, 14 Mar. 1695 ; and d. Mar. 1699. JONATHAN, Exeter 1657–83, perhaps was s. of John of the same. JOSEPH, Salem, eldest s. of William, had sett. in Barbadoes bef. 1676. JOSEPH, Andover, m. 30 May 1671, Phebe, d. of Rev. Francis Dane, had Dorothy, wh. d. 23 Sept. 1675 ; Dane ; and perhaps more ; was freem. 1691. NATHANIEL, Boston, by w. Damaris, had Nathaniel, b. 29 Aug. 1655 ; Eliz. 24 Feb. 1657 ; Daniel, 10 Feb. 1667 ; Mary, 22 June, 1668 ; Robert, 28 July 1671 ; and Damaris, 29 Dec. 1674 ; was aft. of Cambridge, freem. 1673. An earlier NATHANIEL was he of Boston, wh. in his will of 2 Mar. 1667, names no w. or ch. NICHOLAS, a passeng. in the Blessing from London, 1635, aged 30, call. then Robertson, is thot. by me to mean Robinson, because in the same voyage came Eliz. 32 ; Catherine, 12 ; Mary, 7 ; John, 5 ; and Sarah, 1½ ; all spell. in the latter form, and may have been, especial. if we imagine his yrs. were two or three more, his w. and childr. PETER, Tisbury, s. of Isaac, m. a d. of John Manton, Mr. Otis says, and that he was of Chilmark in 1706, and of Norwich 1710, after at Windham, had seven s. wh. all m. and had fams. and seven ds. but no names are heard, nor dates giv. RICHARD, Charlestown, the freem. of 2 June 1641, may be suppos. to be br. of John, adm. to the o. on the same day, by w. Rebecca had John, bapt. 31 May 1640 ; but in the valua. list of ch. mem. in Budington, the name is giv. Robbins. Yet I presume one person is meant, and the Col. rec. or the ch. rec. is so far wrong. Having examin. the orig. I testify, that Robinson is as plain as any name in the vol. ROBERT, Newbury, m. 26 Oct. 1664, Mary, d. of Thomas Silver, had Mary, b. 18 Nov. 1665 ; Daniel, 9 Oct. 1667 ; John, 12 Dec. 1669 ; Samuel ; Thomas ; Sarah ; Hannah, 21 Dec. 1683 ; and Robert, 5 May 1686. Coffin says he was b. 1628, and from the births of ch. we should confident. believe, that he was not the Robert, wh. came from London in the Christian, early in 1635, aged 45, but of him no discov. is obtain. ROWLAND, Narraganset, b. says Potter, a. 1654, came 1675, m. Mary Allen, d. of John, but wh. John we ask in vain, had John ; Eliz. wh. m. 1707, William Brown ; Mary, m. 1709 a Mumford ; Sarah, m. 1704, Rufus Barton ; Mercy, wh. m. 1714, John Potter ; and William, 26 Jan. 1693. Tradit. makes him come from Longburgh or Longbrough, Co. Cumberland, a. 6 ms. from Carlisle, and he d. a. 1716. SAMUEL, Salem, may have been s. of John, but more likely of William, of the same, was a subject of fine 1669, for entertainm. of Thomas Maule, a Quaker. SAMUEL, Boston, s. of Thomas, d. 1662 ; but his est. was so small, that his f. renounc. admin. SAMUEL, Fairfield, d. 1674, leav. wid. and perhaps ch. SAMUEL, Hartford, d. 30 Aug. 1683, leav. ch. Sarah, b. 1665 ; Samuel, 1668 ; Mary, 1672 ; John, 1676 ; and Hannah, 1679 ; but whether all these were b. at H. is not kn. *SAMUEL, Dorchester, eldest s. of William, m. a d. of Richard Baker, was constable 1667, selectman 1688, freem. 1690, rep. 1701 and 2, d. 16 Sept. 1718, leav. beside John, H. C. 1695, min. of Duxbury, and gr.-gr.f. of Rev. Edward whose learn. has done so much honor to our country, elder s. Samuel, wh. d. 30 Mar. 1734, in 68th yr. STE-PHEN, Exeter, 1689. STEPHEN, Dover 1662, perhaps was f. of Timothy. THOMAS, Boston, had Samuel, wh. d. bef. his f. 1662, and I can tell no more. THOMAS, Scituate 1642, m. at Boston, for sec. w. 10 Jan. 1653, Mary, d. of John Coggan of Boston, wid. of John Woodie of Roxbury, wh. d. May preced. had James, b. 14 Mar. 1654; Thomas, 1654; Jo-seph, 1656; Mary, 1657; Mercy, 1659, wh. prob. d. young; but by his former w. had eldest John, wh. he thot. was in Eng. when he made his will. His w. d. at Boston, 26 Oct. 1661, and he took 3d w. Eliz. wid. of Richard Sherman, was a deac. and made his will 17 Mar. 1665, in wh. he ment. est. in Boston, his w. as liv. separ. from him, yet gives £10 to her (wh. d. little more than a yr. aft.), and ch. John, Thomas, James, Joseph, and Mary. Curious inq. would turn to the will of his wid. 21 Aug. 1666, pro. 16 Nov. 1667, in vol. VI. p. 9, in wh. refer. to the contract of m. with her late h. Thomas, whereby £50 was due to her, she gives half to childr. of her former h. Sherman, and half to be disp. by deac. John Wiswall and William Bartholomew; and of other est. legacies to John, s. of Edmund Brown of Dorchester; Samuel, s. of John Damon of Reading; Eliz. d. of Thomas Spaule of Boston; childr. ea. of her sis. Bridget Lock of Fausett, in Eng. and her orchard to kinsman John Greenleaf, he paying, within six mos. £20 to his sis. Mary. Deane has confus. f. and s. The Boston est. was sold by admors. 1667, for the benefit of heirs; and the tree that k. Thomas in its fall, 1676, did not, as D. thot. hit the deac. but his s. THOMAS, Boston, by w. Margaret had Jane, b. Sept. 1646. No more is heard of him, but ano. THOMAS, prob. by w. Mary, perhaps d. of William Beamsley, had James, b. 14 Mar. 1655; and his wid. m. Thomas Dennis. THOMAS, Salisbury 1652. THOMAS, Roxbury, a. 1640, had w. Silence, a mem. of the ch. had rem. to Boston bef. Nov. 1662, when he sold to John Weld his two lots of twelve acres ea. THOMAS, New London 1665–6. THOMAS, Guilford 1677, and perhaps sev. yrs. bef. had Thomas, wh. was, as well as the f. propr. in 1685; and Samuel, wh. sett. at Durham, beside sev. ds. m. at G. Descend. are respecta. THOMAS, Newtown, L. I. 1657, one of the patentees under Gov. Dongan, Nov. 1686. THOMAS, Boston, cordwainer, in his will of 11 June 1690, pro. 30 July 1700, names ch. three, Thomas, Sarah, and James, w. Sarah, to wh. he gives all est. during wid. but only half if she m. again, calls Jacob Green jr. and William Dennison brs.-in-law, making the former excor.

The s. Thomas I judge to be that in Roxbury, b. 5 Nov. 1677. THOMAS, youngest s. of Isaac, by Mr. Otis said to have own ld. in Edgartown 1700, and to have rem. to Guilford. TIMOTHY, Salem, d. 1668, his inv. being of 20 June, left wid. and a young ch. Perhaps he was s. of William. TIMOTHY, Dover, perhaps s. of Stephen, by w. Mary had Abigail, b. 23 May 1693; Mary, 10 Apr. 1695; Eliz. 14 Apr. 1700, d. at 10 yrs.; Sarah, 3 Oct. 1702; Hannah, 21 Nov. 1707; Timothy, 1 Aug. 1710; and Eliz. again, 30 July 1712. WILLIAM, Braintree 1662. ‖ WILLIAM, Dorchester 1636, freem. 18 May 1642, ar. co. 1643, had Samuel, bapt. 14 June 1640; Increase, 14 Mar. 1642; Prudence, 1643; and Waiting, 26 Apr. 1646; and he d. 6 July 1668. His will, tho. without date, was allow. 31 July foll. It names, beside his own offspr. Mary Streeter, my wife's d. His wid. Ursula wh. had been wid. of Samuel Hosier, as of Stephen Streeter at an earlier day, was not prob. mo. of these ch. m. 15 July 1673, Griffin Crafts; and this fourth h. bur. her, but suppli. his loss by ano. w. Prudence m. John Bridge of Roxbury; and Waiting m. Joseph Penniman of Braintree. WILLIAM, Salem, a tailor, by w. Isabella had Ann, bapt. 3 Dec. 1637, the mo. hav. unit. with the ch. that yr.; Samuel, 26 Jan. 1640; Mary, 12 Mar. 1643; Timothy, 28 Apr. 1644; and Esther, 28 May 1654; was freem. 27 Dec. 1642; names in his will of 9 Feb. 1677, pro. 29 Nov. 1678, s. Joseph, eldest, wh. then liv. at Barbados; Samuel, and John, wh. were made excors. d. Sarah Newbury, whose h. is not of my acquaint. and gr.ch. Timothy R. when he comes of age. WILLIAM, Boston 1659, suffer. whip. as a quaker, and soon aft. not being sufficient. enlighten. by that evangelic. discipline, on 27 Oct. was hanged, says the Diary of John Hull, with Marmaduke Stephenson, ano. youth, ea. "LITTLE ABOVE TWENTY YRS. OF AGE." We may judge of the perfect sincerity of the persecutors in their ferocious bigotry, from the same Diary, 1661, relat. that, after this execut. of R. and his three fellow martyrs, "the rest of the Quakers had liberty, if they pleased to use it, to depart the jurisdict. tho. some of them capitally guilty;" and the pious writer adds this ejacul. prayer: "The good Lord pardon this timidity of spirit to execute the sentence of God's Holy Law upon such blasphemous persons." That the delusion spread can excite no wonder, even in this day, when some pray rather for pardon of the judicial murder, than for that of the treacher. timidity that liberated the innocent. Hull was a milit. man, and felt that discipline requir. the enemy of God especial. to be put to death. No man in the Col. was held in higher esteem than John Hull. See Josselyn; Hubbard, 572; Hutch. I. 199, 200; and Sewel's Hist. 220–4. WILLIAM, Concord, by w. Eliz. had Hannah, b. 13 July 1671; rem. to Cambridge, in that part now Newton, there by w. Eliz.

had William, b. 10 July 1673; Mary, 6 Sept. 1676; David, 23 Mar. 1678; Samuel, 20 Apr. 1680; and Jeremiah, 20 Apr. 1682; and Robert; freem. 1685. WILLIAM, Lynn, had, says Lewis, three s. William, b. 7 Oct. 1683; Aquila; and John. One WILLIAM was a soldier in Gallop's comp. 1690, of the expedit. against Quebec, but where he was b. or whether he outliv. the serv. I kn. not. WILLIAM, Newton, s. of William of the same, by w. Eliz. had William; Daniel; Jeremiah, b. 22 Oct. 1705; Eliz. 11 Sept. 1707; Hannah, 16 Sept. 1709; Josiah, 17 Sept. 1711; Ichabod, 2 Sept. 1713; Thankful, 3 Sept. 1715; and John, 1722; was selectman. His w. d. 1747, and he d. 1754, leav. large est. § WILLIAM, South Kingston, youngest s. of Rowland of the same, by two ws. of wh. the first was Mary, had thirteen ch. as he says; Rowland, b. 1719; John, 1721; Margaret or Mary, 1722; Eliz. 1724; Martha, 1725; Christopher, 1727; William, 1729; Mary, 1736; James, 1738; John, again, 1742; Sylvester; Thomas; and Abigail; perhaps the last eight by sec. w. He was Gov. of the Col. and d. a. 1751. The first w. was d. of John Potter, and the next was wid. Abigail Hazard, d. of William Gardiner, both of South Kingstown. All the ch. exc. the sec. and third, wh. d. young, were m. Of this name (oft. mistak. as Robertson, wh. was exceeding. rare in N. E. bef. the last century), there had, in 1832, been gr. twelve at Yale, seven at Harv. and ten at the other N. E. coll.

ROCK, JOSEPH, Boston, by w. Eliz. d. of John Coggan, wh. brot. him good est. had Eliz. b. 5 Feb. 1652; Sarah, 17 Jan. 1653, d. next yr.; Rebecca, 16 Mar. 1655, d. at 6 mos.; John, 2 Nov. 1656, d. Aug. foll.; Joseph, 1 Feb. 1658; Benjamin, 9 Sept. 1659, d. soon; Lydia, 21 Apr. 1661; Samuel, 17 May 1662; Benjamin, again, 3 Sept. 1663; and Elisha, 16 Feb. 1667; was freem. 1652; one of the founders of the 3d or O. S. ch. In his will of 18 Jan. 1683, pro. 3 Jan. foll. he ment. d. Hannah Brading, wh. was m. 9 Oct. 1657, and her h. James; gr. ch. James and Joseph B. and gr.-gr.ch. Eliz. Bromfield. That Mary R. wh. d. 13 Sept. 1713, in her 81st yr. I presume was his sec. w. One THOMAS R. wh. d. at Weymouth, 15 July 1642, is call. serv. to Edward Smith.

ROCKETT, BENJAMIN, Medfield 1678, Wrentham 1680, perhaps s. of Nicholas, by w. Judith had Bethia, b. 4 July 1679, at M.; Judith, b. at W. 17 Mar. 1681; Mary, 2 Oct. 1683; Patience, 20 May 1686; and Hezekiah, 26 Aug. 1688, wh. d. 1689. JOHN, Dorchester 1633. JOHN, Mendon, s. perhaps of Richard, had John, b. at Braintree, 18 Aug. 1663, wh. was k. by the Ind. when they burn. the town in 1675; rem. to Medfield, there had Joseph, with perhaps two or three more; but certain. Trial, 28 Feb. 1677; and Deliverance, 31 Oct. 1678; in the interval suffer. much from Ind. and still had w. and six ch. to support. Jo-

sᴇᴘʜ, Rehoboth, m. 5 Jan. 1681, Mary Wilmouth, had Mary, b. 14 Dec.
foll. posthum. for the f. was bur. 21 July of that yr. unless the rec. be
confus. Jᴏsɪᴀʜ, Medfield, prob. s. of Nicholas, m. 9 May 1677, Mary
Twitchell, d. of Benjamin of Dorchester, had Israel, b. 25 Feb. 1678;
Mary, 3 Aug. 1681; Bethia, 21 Feb. 1684; Mehitable, 14 Oct. 1686;
Hannah, 24 Oct. 1691; and Joanna, 28 Dec. 1693. His w. d. 15 Sept.
1699, and he m. 10 Nov. 1703, Sarah Wheelock. He had serv. in Philip's war. Nɪᴄʜᴏʟᴀs, Dedham 1640, in the part made Medfield, was
freem. 1666, had by w. Jane, Samuel, b. prob. at Braintree; Benjamin,
8 Sept. 1651 at M.; Josiah; and his w. d. 15 Dec. 1654. He m. 16
July 1656, Margaret, not, as giv. Holliocke, in the copy of Medfield rec.
Geneal Reg. XIII. 217, but Holbrook, d. of John the first, had Eliz. b.
3 Apr. 1657; Joseph, a. 1659; John, 12 Feb. 1662; and Nathaniel, 3
Feb. 1665. This w. d. 23 Apr. 1670; and by third w. Silence, wh. d.
9 Nov. 1677, he had Isaac, b. 22 July preced. but wh. d. bef. his mo.
and the f. d. 26 Jan. 1680. Eliz. m. John Partridge the younger, of the
same. Rɪᴄʜᴀʀᴅ, Dorchester 1635, perhaps br. of John, rem. to Braintree, where by w. Agnes, wh. d. 9 July 1643, he had John, b. 1 Dec.
1641. Perhaps his w. was d. of Zachary Bicknell, whose est. they
sold to William Read. See Col. Rec. I. 189. Oft. this name is Rockwood.

Rᴏᴄᴋᴡᴇʟʟ, Aʙʀᴀʜᴀᴍ, Windsor, of unkn. parentage, m. 4 Dec. 1640,
Mary whose surname is unkn. and wh. d. 8 July 1677, without ch.
Jᴏʜɴ, Windsor, one of the first sett. may therefore have been first at
Dorchester, was infirm or old eno. in 1649, to be exempt from watch.
and train. d. 1662, leav. two ds. Mary, wh. m. 10 Dec. 1646, Robert
Watson, and one wh. m. Zachary Sanford of Saybrook, beside s. Simon,
wh. d. 1665, unm. and gave to his sis. his est. and possib. other s. Jᴏʜɴ,
Windsor, s. of William, prob. b. in Eng. m. 6 May 1651, Sarah Ensign,
perhaps d. of James, had Sarah, b. 12 May 1653; Ruth, 5 Mar. 1655;
and Lydia, 27 Nov. 1656. His w. d. 23 June 1659. He m. 18 Aug.
1662, Deliverance Haynes of Dorchester, rem. to Stamford, had John,
b. 6 Sept. 1663; Hannah, 30 May 1665; Joseph, 8 July 1668; and
Eliz. 5 Feb. 1671; and he d. 3 Sept. 1673, aged 46, all his ch. exc.
John, being then liv. Sarah, m. 8 Oct. 1676, John Crampton of Norwalk,
unless Hall, in his Hist. 188, be wrong. But Stiles, 762, says that she
m. David Hall; Ruth m. Daniel Mix; Lydia m. Joshua Atwater, 24
June 1680, and h. and w. d. next yr.; Eliz. m. 1 Feb. 1694, James
Ward. Jᴏʜɴ, Greenwich, or Rye, d. prob. 1676, leav. w. and ch. See
Trumbull, Col. Rec. II. 313. Jᴏɴᴀᴛʜᴀɴ, Norwalk 1687–94. Jᴏsᴇᴘʜ,
Middletown, s. of John the sec. may have first liv. at Norwalk, m. 1 Feb.
1694, Eliz. Foster, and had John and Joseph, tw. b. 1694; Edwin

and Eliz. tw. 1700; William, 1702; Hannah, 1704; was a deac.
JOSIAH, Norwich, perhaps s. of William, had liv. at New London sev. yrs.
and had there most of his ch. perhaps even the eldest, Hannah, 6 Sept.
1658, d. at 3 yrs.; Josiah, June 1662; Joseph, Mar. 1665; John, Dec.
1667; Mary, Feb. 1669; Hannah again, 23 Aug. 1672; and Samuel,
posthum. 30 Sept. 1676. He was k. by the Ind. near the end of Jan.
1676, at the same time with young John Reynolds; and his s. Josiah was
tak. by them, and soon restor. JOSIAH, Norwich, s. of the preced. m. 8
Apr. 1688, Ann, d. of Thomas Bliss, had Daniel, b. 24 Oct. 1689; John,
3 Apr. 1692; Jerusha, 6 Mar. 1695; Hannah, 6 June 1698; and Eliz.
19 Apr. 1700. His w. d. 19 Feb. 1715; and he d. 18 Mar. 1729.
SAMUEL, Windsor, s. of William, perhaps b. at Dorchester, freem. of
Conn. 1657; m. 7 Apr. 1660, Mary Norton of Saybrook, had Mary, b.
18 Jan. 1662; Abigail, 23 Aug. 1664; Samuel, 19 Oct. 1667; Joseph,
22 May 1670; John, 31 May 1673; Abigail, again, 11 Apr. 1676; and
Josiah, 10 Mar. 1678. WILLIAM, Dorchester, f. of John the first. came
prob. in the Mary and John, req. adm. as freem. 19 Oct. 1630, and was
sw. 18 May foll. was one of the first two deac. rem. to Windsor, in its
sec. yr. there d. 15 May 1640, leav. wid. Susanna (prob. sec. w. to wh.
Hist. of D. gives the surname Chapin), wh. m. Matthew Grant, and ch.
John; Samuel; Joan, wh. m. 15 Nov. 1642, Jeffrey Baker; Ruth, wh.
m. 7 Oct. 1652, Christopher Huntington; Mary; Joseph; and Sarah,
wh. m. 22 Mar. 1658, Walter Gaylord, as his sec. w. Stiles makes
Mary m. Jeffrey Mahon; but I doubt the outlandish surname, and suspect the bapt. name was borrow. from the h. of Joan. Of this name, ten
had in 1829 been gr. at Yale and one at Dart.

ROCKWOOD, SAMUEL, eldest s. of Nicholas Rockett (wh. see), Medfield, freem. 1682, m. 15 Dec. 1671, Hannah, d. of John Ellis of M. had
Hannah, b. 1 Oct. 1673; Susanna, 31 Oct. 1675; Samuel, 11 Apr.
1677, d. at seven yrs.; Abigail, 17 May 1679; Eleazer, 18 Apr. 1681;
d. at 12 yrs.; Patience, 14 May 1682; d. soon; Joseph, 8 Sept. 1686;
and Deliverance, whose b. or that of the preced. must be wrong in Morse.
His w. d. 7 May 1717, and he m. ano. w. Sarah, and d. 17 Dec. 1728.
Six of this name, in the early time oft. writ. Rockett (from wh. much
doubt is caus.) had been gr. in 1828, at Harv. Dart. and Middleb. two
at ea.

RODGERS, whose name of bapt. is unkn. a young man sent from Eng.
with Allerton early in 1628, to be min. at Plymouth, but sent back next
yr. as disord. in brain. Mass. Hist. Coll. IV. 109. It is oft. spell.
without d. *JOHN, Bristol, a selectman 1686, patriotic to resist Andros,
rep. 1689. 3 Mass. Hist. Coll. VII. 171.

RODMAN, THOMAS, Newport, br. of John, came from Barbados, a

surgeon, m. Hannah, d. of Gov. Walter Clark, but she was, I presume, sec. w. for the Friends' rec. of N. show his m. 7 June 1682, with Patience Malins, and Gov. Walter Clarke's d. was then rather too young.

ROE, ANTHONY, Falmouth or Scarborough 1663–83, of good repute in 1670, as by the court with ano. he was made conjoint. constable of both towns. EDWARD, Exeter, sw. alleg. 30 Nov. 1677. ELIAS, Charlestown, m. 17 July 1656, Rebecca, d. of Robert Long, had John, bapt. 27 Nov. 1670. He d. 18 Jan. 1687, his w. hav. d. earlier. HUGH, Hartford 1661, rem. perhaps to Salem, but, in 1669, is on the freem. list of Conn. and bef. 1678, was at Suffield, there d. 5 Aug. 1689, and his w. Abigail d. 3 Sept. foll. He had first liv. at Weymouth, and there his d. Esther d. 11 July 1655 ; and his s. Samuel was b. 14 Jan. foll. wh. d. the yr. bef. his f. and other ch. nam. in his will were Peter, Mary Denslow, Eliz. Merrill of Saybrook, and Abigail Taylor ; gr.ch. Abigail Kent ; and three Warners. JOHN, Charlestown, prob. s. of Elias, by w. Ruth, had Elias, bapt. 26 Aug. 1688, d. in few days ; John, 27 Oct. 1689 ; and Ruth, 5 Apr. 1691. MARK, York 1666, serv. that yr. on the gr. jury. PETER, Suffield, s. of Hugh, m. 1689, Sarah, d. of Thomas Remington, and had sev. ch. RICHARD, Charlestown, br. of Elias, wh. had admin. of his est. after he perish. Nov. 1666, by casual. at sea. Sometimes, but rarely, these names are enriched with a w.

ROGERS, ANDREW, a passeng. from London 1671, in the Arabella, of wh. no more is heard in our country. DANIEL, Ipswich, s. of Presid. John, m. Sarah, d. of the first John Appleton, tho. the Appleton mem. p. 16, makes her w. of Samuel R. had Sarah, wh. d. inf. ; Sarah, again, b. 27 Apr. 1694, d. soon ; Sarah, again, 29 May 1695 ; Margaret, prob. 8 Jan. 1699 ; Eliz. ; Priscilla ; Mary ; Daniel, 17 Oct. 1706, H. C. 1725, the min. of Littleton ; John, 16 Sept. 1708 ; Patience, 4 Sept. 1710 ; and Nathaniel, 6 Aug. 1712, d. in few days. He was sch.master, town clk. and reg. of probate, tho. his handwriting is ill, and he perish. in a cold snowstorm on Hampton Beach, 1 Dec. 1722. See Geneal. Reg. VI. 70. DAVID, Braintree, had Ruth, b. 3 Jan. 1641 ; and he d. 24 Sept. 1642. ELEAZER, Milford, was freem. 1669, and the name was perpet. there to 1713. EZEKIEL, Rowley, first min. there, s. of Richard, a disting. Purit. divine of Weathersfield, Co. Essex, wh. is assum. by the author of the mem. of Fam. of Nathaniel, but with slight, or, as I think, not even slight, support for his assumpt. to be s. of him burned at the stake 1555, was bred at Cambridge, where in 1604, he was of Corpus Christi, when he had his A. B. and of Christ's Coll. in 1608, on rec. his A. M. came in 1638, with his w. Sarah, d. of John Everard, citiz. of London, wh. d. in ten yrs. He had serv. long aft. 1621, with great reput. and favor of Archbp. Matthews, in that parish in Yorksh. whose name was adopt. here by the people wh. accomp. him; and in a commission out of chanc. for inquisit. into misapplica. of funds giv. by the Queen, he was includ. by her Majesty, as first among seven clerg. after the Archbp. of York, the E. of Cumberland, three baronets, six knights, and eight esqrs. See Oliver's Hist. of Beverly, 195, 6. He was freem. 23 May 1639, had for sec. w. a d. of Rev. John Wilson, wh. d. bef. giv. b. to her first ch. and the third w. Mary, wh. surv. him was wid. of Thomas Barker, m. 16 July 1651; but when he d. 23 Jan. 1661, leav. good est. there was no ch. to inherit; nor is it kn. that he ever had a s. EZEKIEL, Ipswich, s. of Rev. Nathaniel, m. Margaret, wid. of Thomas Scott, d. of William Hubbard, and sis. of the histor. had Martha; Nathaniel, b. 14 Aug. 1664; John, 12 June 1666; Ezekiel, 4 June 1667; Timothy and Samuel; and d. 5 July 1674. His wid. d. 1678, and her will of 22 June was pro. 17 Sept. of the same yr. In it she speaks of being extrix. of her s. Thomas Scott's est. and gives £40 to the s. Rogers, and d. Snelling of her d. Snelling, the name of wh. d. was, I believe, Margaret. GAMALIEL, Boston, s. of Simon, by w. Mercy, had Jane, b. 3 Jan. 1689. GEORGE, Maine, was of the jury 1650, but of what town I see not. HENRY, Springfield, took the o. of alleg. 1678. It is not kn. whether he came from Eng. or was b. here, but prob. the latter; and he m. 30 Dec. 1675, Mary, eldest d. of Richard Exell of S. had Mary, b. 23 Dec. 1676, d. within 4 yrs. John, 5 Mar. 1678; Dorothy, 5 Sept. 1679; Mary, 8 Aug. 1681; a. d. Apr. 1683, d. soon; and Henry, 28 Dec. 1687, and d. 26 Sept. 1724. His wid. d. 23 Oct. 1732. Both his s. had fams. Mary m. 1702, Samuel Cooper; and Dorothy m. 1704, James Taylor the younger. JAMES, New London, is by Miss Caulkins thought to be that passeng. in the Increase from London, 1635, aged 20, and was early at Stratford, there m. Eliz. d. of Samuel Rowland, rem. to Milford, had Samuel, b. a. 1640; Joseph, bapt. 1646; John, 1648; Bathsheba, 1650; James, a. 1652; Jonathan, b. 31 Dec. 1655; and Eliz. 1658; soon aft. he rem. to N. L. was the richest man in the settlem. after Gov. Winth. freem. 1660, rep. 1661–8 and in 1676, began to make with his childr. much opposit. to inf. bapt. and d. a. 1688. Bathsheba m. 4 Mar. 1670, Richard Smith of N. L. and next Samuel Fox as his third w. and Eliz. m. 9 Feb. 1682, the sec. Samuel Beeby. From this man, thro. his fifth s. Jonathan, is deriv. the ancient imperfect vol. contain. the Psalms and New Testam. with a ch. liturgy thot. to be of the days of Edward VI. JAMES, Newport 1638, adm. freem. 1640, and is in the list of 1655, and was gen. serg. 1661–3. JAMES, Eastham, s. of Joseph, m. 11 Jan. 1671, Mary, d. prob. of the first Thomas Paine, had James b. 30 Oct. 1673; Mary, 9 Nov. 1675; and Abigail, 2 Mar. 1678; was a lieut. and d. 13 Apr. foll. JAMES,

New London, s. of James of the same, a sea capt. m. 5 Nov. 1674, Mary, d. of Jeffrey Jordan, of wh. very pleasant tradit. is told by Caulkins, p. 202, tho. as nothing was ever heard of her f. or mo. or bro. or sis. it may fail of truth in some partic. had James, Mary, Eliz. Sarah, Samuel, Jonathan, Richard, and William. In 1677, his w. was fin. for absence from pub. worship as estab. by the governm. and soon after he and his w. were vexed for worsh. estab. by his f. and friends. He d. 8 Nov. 1713.

JEREMIAH, Dorchester, m. Mehitable, d. prob. eldest of John Pierce, and had three ch. as in the will of their gr.f. Pierce in 1661, is ment. viz. Margaret, bapt. 1653; Mehitable, b. 6 Oct. 1658; and Ichabod, bapt. 27 May 1660, brot. to D. for the ordin. from Lancaster, whither his f. had rem. beside prob. that Sarah, wh. by rec. of D. d. 21 Sept. 1657.

JOHN, Duxbury 1634, prob. of Plymouth 1631, rep. 1657, by w. Frances, had John, Joseph, Timothy, Ann, Mary, and Abigail. In his will of 1 Feb. 1661, he calls hims. of Marshfield, names w. and the six ch. beside gr.ch. George and John Russell. Ann m. John Hudson; and one of the other ds. m. the sec. George Russell. He may have been br. of the first Thomas. JOHN, Watertown 1636, freem. 17 May 1637; JOHN, Weymouth, m. 16 Apr. 1639, Ann, d. prob. of Hugh Churchman, had Lydia, b. 27 Mar. 1642, rem. 1644, to Scituate, going thither, with Rev. Mr. Witherell. This led Deane, he says, to conject. that he was a descend. of him of Smithfield, whose martyrdom was above 99 yrs. bef. and perhaps a slighter conject. never was brought in aid of a trifling tradit. A tradit. prob. equal. worthless, to sustain that, is giv. by D. that the mo. of W. was also a descend. of the martyr. He had also John, Thomas, and Samuel, prob. the first, if not more, b. in Eng. and went back to W. there d. 11 Feb. 1662. The Weymouth man was a deac. and his will of 8 Feb. 1661, pro. 30 Apr. foll. satisfied me, that Deane had confus. two if not three Johns into one. (See Geneal. Reg. X. 265–6.) It gives est. to w. Judith, s. John, ds. Mary Rane, i. e. prob. Rand, w. of John, Lydia, wh. m. 19 Sept. 1660, Joseph White; Hannah m. the same day, Samuel Pratt, and Sarah. The h. of Mary was John. So that we may be sure the Scituate man, with s. Thomas and Samuel, was ano. and that Deane misled Barry in his Hist. of Hanover; and Winsor in his Hist. of Duxbury. JOHN, Watertown, freem. 13 Mar. 1639, m. 1640, Priscilla Dawes at Boston, wh. on her join. the ch. is call. maid serv. of our Elder Thomas Oliver, had John, b. 11 Sept. 1641; Mary, 26 Oct. 1643; Thomas; Daniel; Nathaniel; and prob. sev. ds. was perhaps a baker, rem. to Billerica, there his d. Abigail m. Arthur Warren of Chelmsford; Priscilla, wh. m. 19 Jan. 1682, Simon Coolidge, as sec. w. was prob. ano. His s. John was k. by the Ind. 5 Aug. 1695, as was also, on the same day, his br.

Thomas, and his s. Thomas, aged 11 yrs. Both these s. as well as Daniel and Nathaniel, and d. Priscilla are nam. in his will, made three days aft. that date, of wh. T. and N. were excors. From this we learn also that he had sec. w. for he gives to his w.'s s. George Brown, and her d. Mary B. and he d. 25 Jan. 1686. But ano. JOHN, prob. older, was of Watertown as early perhaps as the preced. and may have been of Dedham 1636, m. so late as Nov. 1653 (but it may have not been first w.), Abigail Martin, had Abigail, b. 21 Jan. 1657; and he d. 22 Dec. 1674, aged 80. Dr. Bond suppos. he was f. of Billerica John. JOHN, Scituate, s. of John of the same, prob. b. in Eng. m. at Boston, 8 Oct. 1656, Rhoda, d. of Elder Thomas King of S. had John, and perhaps Abigail, or others, but not, I think, the Mary, or Eliz. or Hannah ascrib. to him by Deane, as they were ds. of the Weymouth deac.; Mary was sis. of her wh. m. Joseph White of S. and of the other two, prob. unless the dates for m. of the three several. were by him intend. to mean dates of b. Confus. in Deane is here evident, but what he should have said is uncert. Abigail m. 1678, Timothy White of S. JOHN, Milford 1646, d. 1684. JOHN, Huntington, L. I. adm. 1664, freem. of Conn. and in 1669, had been two yrs. perhaps of Branford, d. bef. 1676, prob. without being m. or at least without ch. for his br. Noah inherit. his est. JOHN, Ipswich, eldest s. of Rev. Nathaniel, b. in Eng. early in 1631 (not 1620, as Geneal. Reg. X. 148), prob. at Coggeshall in Essex, where liv. the f. of his mo. but Farmer says at Assington in Suff. was both physician and preacher after leav. Coll. 1649, and some yrs. I believe, was of Boston, but of so common a name, a mistake is very easy; freem. 1674; m. Eliz. only d. of Maj-Gen. Daniel Dennison, had Eliz. b. one acco. says 3, ano. 26 Feb. 1662; Margaret, 18 Feb. 1664; John, 7 July 1666, H. C. 1684; Daniel, 25 Sept. 1667, H. C. 1686; Nathaniel, 22 Feb. 1670, H. C. 1687; and Patience, 13 or 25 May, 1676; preach. occasional. as aid to Cobbett and Hubbard, was chos. Presid. to succeed Hoar, 1676, but declin. and his classmate Oakes was appoint. but aft. d. of O. he was again chos. 1683, when Mather and Torrey had declin. the offer, and d. 2 July 1684, less than one yr. from enter. on his office. His wid. d. 13 June 1723. Eliz. m. 23 Nov. 1681, John Appleton; Margaret, m. 28 Dec. 1686, Dr. Thomas Berry, and next, 25 Nov. 1697, Hon. John Leverett, and d. 7 June 1720; and Patience, m. 15 Apr. 1696, Benjamin Marston of Salem, and d. 22 May 1731. Never, I think, is heard any suggest. that he was of the stock of the martyr of Smithfield, when it might have been difficult to avoid that topic of congratula. had any of his relatives or friends believ. it. JOHN, Duxbury or Marshfield, perhaps s. of Thomas of the Mayflower, and left at home some yrs. Winsor says, had Eliz. wh. m. 17 Nov. 1668, Nathaniel Williams of Taunton;

Abigail, wh. m. a Richmond; and Hannah, m. 23 Nov. 1664, John Tisdale; beside, I presume, that Thomas, bapt. at Scituate, 6 May 1638. JOHN, Duxbury, m. Nov. 1666, Eliz. d. of William Peabody, had Hannah, b. Nov. 1668; John, 22 Sept. 1670; Ruth, 18 Apr. 1675; Sarah, 4 May 1677; and Eliz. He may be the same whose d. is rec. at Marshfield, 7 May 1717, in his 85th yr. if liberal discount be allow. for exagger. Far more prob. is it that the other John of D. was thus long lived. JOHN, Eastham, s. of Joseph, m. 19 Aug. 1669, Eliz. Twining, perhaps d. of William, had Samuel, b. 1 Nov. 1671, d. soon; John, 1 Nov. 1672; Judah, 23 Nov. 1677; Joseph, 22 Feb. 1679; Eliz. 23 Oct. 1682; Eleazer, 18 May 1685; Mehitable, 13 Mar. 1687; Hannah, 5 Aug. 1689; and Nathaniel, 3 Oct. 1693. His wid. Eliz. d. 10 Mar. 1725. JOHN, New London, s. of James the first, m. 17 Oct. 1670, Eliz. d. of Matthew Griswold, had Eliz. b. 8 Nov. 1671; and John, 20 Mar. 1674; began, bef. the end of this yr. to assert opinions and follow forms in relig. wh. disgust. his w. wh. desir. divorce next yr. and aft. 18 mos. gain. the reluct. assent of the Ct. wh. allow. her to retain both the ch. Yet as the ch. grew up, they took to their f. perhaps bec. the mo. had m. 5 Aug. 1679, Peter Pratt, and, in 1691, a third h. Matthew Beckwith. He was found. of a new sect, call. Rogerenes, but tho. he had the glory of kn. that his writings were condemn. and burn. as pestilent heresies, yet without caus. much light to be spread, the schism went off soon aft. his d. wh. was 17 Oct. 1721. A sec. w. Mary Ransford caused him more trouble than the first. JOHN, Boston, of whose est. admin. was giv. 25 Apr. 1672, to his wid. Eliz. JOHN, Weymouth, perhaps s. of John of the same, m. 8 Feb. 1663, Mary Bates, had Mary, b. 3 Apr. 1664; Lydia, 1 Mar. 1666; Experience, 29 Nov. 1667; and Hannah, 23 July 1670; was freem. 1671. JOHN, Salem 1681, a glazier. *JOHN, Bristol, was rep. 1689. *JOHN*, Ipswich, eldest s. of Presid. John, was ord. 12 Oct. 1692, as collea. with his uncle Hubbard, m. 4 Mar. 1691, Martha, d. of William Whittingham, had John, b. 19 Jan. 1692, H. C. 1711, min. of Kittery; Martha, 20 Nov. 1694; Mary; William, 19 June 1699; Nathaniel, 22 Sept. 1701, H. C. 1721, min. of Ipswich, collea. with his f.; Richard, 2 Dec. 1703; Eliz. 1705, d. young; Daniel and Eliz. tw. 28 July 1707, of wh. Daniel was H. C. 1725, min. of Exeter; and Samuel, 31 Aug. 1709, H. C. 1725. He d. 28 Dec. 1745, and his wid. d. 9 Mar. 1759. JONATHAN, Huntington, L. I. adm. freem. of Conn. 1664. JONATHAN, perhaps of Westerly bef. 1680, m. Naomi, d. of Robert Burdick. JONATHAN, New London, youngest s. of James the first, d. 1697, leav. large fam. but only s. Jonathan. JOSEPH, Plymouth, s. of Thomas, brot. by his f. in the Mayflower, 1620, had two sh. in the div. of lds. 1624, prob. on acco. of his f. wh. d. in the first six mos. but in the div. of cattle

had single sh. in the comp. with Gov. Bradford, liv. at Duxbury, there
had Sarah, b. 6 Aug. 1633, d. soon; Joseph, 19 July 1635 ; Thomas,
29 Mar. bapt. 6 May 1638; Eliz. 29 Sept. 1639; John, 3 Apr. 1642;
Mary, 22 Sept. 1644; James, 18 Oct. 1648; these six liv. says Bradford, in 1650; and Hannah, 8 Aug. 1652 ; was some time at Sandwich,
but as early as 1655 at Eastham, was lieut. and d. at E. 1678. Eliz.
m. 9 Jan. 1660, Jonathan Higgins. JOSEPH, Eastham, s. of the preced.
m. 4 Apr. 1660, or Feb. 1661, as in Geneal. Reg. VI. 235, is said, tho.
I think with mistake of the mo. by its numeral, 2, wh. in ano. and higher
auth. Coll. Rec. foll. by Geneal. Reg. III. 379, stands 4 Apr. 1660, Susanna, d. of Stephen Deane, had Joseph, perhaps posthum. for the f. d.
27 Dec. or Jan. foll. by injury in a fall. His wid. m. 28 Oct. 1663, Stephen Snow. JOSEPH, Salem, d. a. 1668. JOSEPH, Boston, s. perhaps
of Simon, by w. Eliz. had Susanna, b. 4 Dec. 1688. JOSEPH, New
London, sec. s. of James the first, d. 1697, leav. large fam. JOSHUA,
Boston, m. 12 Oct. 1653, Ann Fisen, if that be not an impossib. name,
had Joshua, b. 20 Feb. 1655, but the rec. notes his d. on 15 of that mo.
NATHANIEL, Ipswich, sec. s. of Rev. John of Dedham, Co. Essex, Eng.
fondly report. in mod. times with very little, or rather no probabil. to be
descend. of the first martyr in Queen Mary's day, was b. a. 1598 at Haverhill, where his f. was then min. bred at Cambridge Univ. where he
was matric. of Emmanuel, 1614, had his deg. 1617 and 21, first preach.
at Bocking in Essex, next at Assington in Sufflk. where were Gurdon
and other Purit. gentry, the Bp. of the diocese, after fill. by Wren,
the puritan-disturber, having comforta. respect. him five yrs. He m.
Margaret, d. of Robert Crane, a gent. with good est. of Coggeshall, Co.
Essex, at whose ho. perhaps the eldest ch. John was b. Jan. 1631, H. C.
1649 ; had also Nathaniel, b. at Assington, 30 Sept. 1632 ; Samuel, 16
Jan. 1635 ; Timothy, 9 Nov. 1638, at Ipswich ; and Ezekiel, H. C. 1659 ;
beside Margaret, wh. was, no doubt, b. in Eng. and here m. William
Hubbard, the Hist. He came from London to Boston, arr. Nov. 1636,
and on 20 Feb. 1638 was ord. as collea. with Norton, to succeed Nathaniel Ward, wh. strange. gave up his profession ; was freem. 23 May
1639, tho. the magistr. at I. had authority to adm. him 6 Sept. preced.
and d. 3 July 1655, a century after the faggot's blaze in Smithfield, and
about a hundred yrs. bef. the earliest surmise of the derivat. from the
hero of it, of the num. and honorable families here of the same name.
His will, nuncup. was pro. 26 Sept. in the hand-writ. of Ezekiel Cheever,
first master of the gram. sch. at I. He had carefully kept a Diary, but
was wise eno. to see it burned bef. his d. That he, or his kinsman, Ezekiel, were descend. of the celebr. Smithfield martyr, might seem to be
justif. by the note of Hutch. I. 190, wh. cites Hubbard, tho. the earliest

hist. says nothing like it. Into such carelessness Hutch. does not oft. fall. Hubbard, wh. m. the only d. of this Nathaniel, clearly eno. calls him s. of Rev. John of Dedham, wh. he honorab. marks as the famous preach. as if "it might be honor eno. to say" of Nathaniel, "that he was the s. of Mr. John," "yet heir of a double portion of his spirit, and worthy to have transmit. more honor to his posterity than he received from those bef. him, by reason of his emin. learning, singular piety, holy zeal, with other ministerial abilities." See Hubbard, 554. Surely the hist. could not intend a slur upon the learning, piety, holy zeal, or minist. abilities of him wh. glorified his master in the martyr's fire; and the irresistib. inference is, that he, tho. so intimately related to Nathaniel, had never heard of his descent from the protomartyr of Queen Mary. Tho. he is wholly silent as to John's progenit. hardly can it seem possible that our Ipswich Hist. should not have stated the propagat. of the martyr's seed on our side of the water, when hims. m. (as idly report.) a gr.d. and his sis. (both nam. Margaret), m. Ezekiel, a gr.s. It would have been equally sure to be ment. by him, if these two ms. had been of the fourth or fifth generat. no less than of the third as assert. Neither Johnson, who expends verse upon both of the min. of Ipswich and Rowley, then liv. nor the more judicious and equally affectionate contempor. annalist, Gov. Winth. nor garrulous Mather in his Magn. all-gathering espe- cial. of doubtful reports, nor Ch. J. Sewall, jealous for the honor of puritans, nor Prince, the pattern of accuracy in minute details, hint at any such glorious ancest. more than Hubbard. I presume the tradit. has no older origin than Hutchinson's day; and perhaps he got it, as may have also Dr. Eliot, from their common friend, Rev. Daniel of Littleton, whose f. Daniel was perhaps so nam. out of rever. to Maj.-Gen. Daniel Dennison, f. of his mo. whose only d. she was, rather than of Daniel, s. of the martyr of Smithfield, whose memory puritans would gladly forget, as he was a courtier, and did not keep the godly simplicity of the suf- ferer. My admirable friend, the late Dr. Eliot, wh. in his Biog. Dict. gave currency to the tradit. as if it were authentic, had assist. he tells us, the Rev. Daniel, some mos. in his pulpit; and the gr.st. at L. over the clerg. that d. Nov. 1782, shows how the sleeper there accept. the honor. But the four generat. of silence on our side of the ocean, add. to the prior eighty yrs. stillness of the mother country, forbid me to entertain any respect for the report first heard in the fifth age of our own history. All the evidence is indeed of a negative charact. but so many facts are ascer- tain. quite inconsist. with the assumpt. founded on the mod. tradit. that it seems a far safer conclus. may be dr. than if half a dozen pieces of positive testim. were laid for its substratum. From the silence of Giles Firmin, wh. had liv. at our Ipswich under the preaching of Nathaniel Rogers, and

wh. tells how his gr.mo. bec. w. of famous Richard Rogers, author of the
seven treatises, and father of our Ezekiel, tho. he is very copious in acco.
of both Richard and Dedham John, yet being wholly silent a. the witness
of Smithfield fire, my friend, Charles Deane, the scrupulous antiquary at
Cambridge, is strongly inclined to disbelieve, that either of these promi-
nent Essex divines could be gr.s. much less own s. of the martyr. His
valua. argument on the assum. point of genealogy may be seen in the
Cambridge Chronicle of 3 Jan. 1850. Resort is had by the diligent
writer in Geneal. Reg. V. 101, to the "identical bible wh. belong. to the
protomartyr, print. in 1549," "own. by a descend. at Lunenburg." That
volume has been oft. and once or twice with severest, not unaid. scrutiny,
examin. by me. It may be premised, that no English bible, print. in
1549, by Cawood and Jugge, printers of our Lunenburg exemplar, after
diligent search for one hundred yrs. has been discovered; and all compe-
tent judges are now agreed, that the opinion formerly thrown out, as to
such an edit. is without support. But the Lunenburg copy is very
clearly ascertain. to be of the yr. 1561, the earliest Eng. bible, indeed, of
Elizabeth's reign, yet six yrs. after Rogers was burned at Smithfield.
Infallible proof of this was furnish. by Mr. Stevens of London, and another mod. disting. biblic. bibliograph. George Offer of London, on a part
of the volume sent from this country ; and by collation, in many hours by
myself, with a sheet of the bible of 1561, sent hither from London, by Mr.
O. to his friend George Livermore, Esq. of Cambridge, the perfect. identity is exhibit. in the printer's monogram, the pictures, and the minutest
parts of single words, and letters, in the text, correct as well as erroneous.
So that this relic, however valua. in itself, affords no prop to the claim
of descent from him, any more than it does to the wild tradit. that the
noble martyr held this same precious copy in his hand, when suffering at
the stake. In proof of the fable, Geneal. Reg. III. 373, truly says the
vol. "is much burnt," and it might have add. that it better would have
pleased the partakers of the triumph to have burned the book instead of
the man. But of the burnt part, wh. very slightly affect. the print,
Queen Eliz. in her service book of 1661, suffers most, as I testify.
Many of us know of volumes, burnt in part, that never were in the
hands of martyrs in Smithfield. From very long protract. inquiry, in
order to sustain or reverse my first express. of unhesitat. belief in the
descent of our N. E. posterity of Nathaniel Rogers, the closest approach
to any exact relation with the martyr amounts only to this : the f. of
Rev. William Jenkin of London, wh. was min. of Sudbury, when William was b. 1612, and of course the predecess. of our John Wilson was
gr.s. of a d. of the sufferer of 1555, and he had stud. under the old puritan, Richard Rogers of Wethersfield. See Palmer's Non-Conform. Mem.

Vol. I. Slight indeed, and very remote will this relationship appear; but no nearer connex. can be found, I think, betw. any of our innumerable Rogerses and the glorious suffer. John, the editor of Tyndall's bible. Encouragem. to adhere to the illusion, against the strong array of Mr. Deane's logic, was felt by some of the supporters of tradit. for the holy martyr's descent, on hearing that Mr. Hunter of London was slow in deciding adverse to the claim. No judgment, on such a point, could outweigh his. He says in a letter to me, Oct. 1855, " The subject has been so long absent from my mind, that I really do not now understand, how the question rests at present, or even what I may have written about it " — " I know nothing but what I learned from America; and, on the other hand, I never saw in English docum. any evid. of the descent wh. they claim, wh. may, for any thing I kn. be correct, tho. I shd. like to see the evid. on wh. it rests. Something beyond tradit. is now demand. in all claims to ancestr. honors." Only will I add that this tradit. is very modern. In the mass of MS. gather. by Candler to illustr. the Puritan Hist. of Eng. tho. he is so copious upon the E. counties' confessors, no reference to this desc. of John of D. was perceiv. by Hunter, and this since the tradit. was first ment. within twenty yrs. The name was most widely diffus. in Eng. Perhaps there were near a hundred min. in the days of Eliz. nam. Rogers, of wh. one or more may well have been s. of the proto-martyr of the preced. reign. In the Register of the single-diocese of Salisbury by Sir Thomas Phillips, from 1297, to 1810, wh. he gave me, are rec. the institutions of Nicholas R. 1565; of Ambrose R. 1569; and of John R. 1582. So natural is it to infer that the blood of the sufferer should in the sec. and third generat. be blessed, that the writer of a Memoir of the fam. of Rev. Nathaniel, claiming to be a descend. in Geneal. Reg. V. 105, most copiously carried out, makes his f. John of Dedham, to be gr.s. of the martyr, and a student so diligent as Dr. Allen, in the Sec. Ed. of his Biog. Dict. made even Nathaniel the gr.s. whereas from the monum. inscript. on John, the Dedham min. we learn that he was not b. bef. 1571 or 2, 16 or 17 yrs. after the solemn scene of his supposed f's. martyrd. in the midst of London. In his third Ed. however, the f. of Nathaniel is made gr.s. of Smithfield John. No tradit. that the f. of Nathaniel was descend. of the hero of 1555, had ever reached his successor at the altar, or the hearers in Dedham, bef. it was told by me in 1642. See 3 Mass. Hist. Coll. VIII. 309. Good acco. is not to be any where found of the ten ch. male and fem. of the noble sufferer at Smithfield, exc. Daniel, ment. by Fox, the martyrolog. He got promotion at Court, under patronage of some civilian of Eliz. and may hardly have encourag. the puritan tendency of any relative. See Hunter's Suffolk Emigr. 3 Mass. Hist. Coll. X. 165. There was a

John R. in the ch. one generat. later than Nathaniel's f. blessed John of Dedham, so strong a purit. as to give offence to Cromwell, wh. imprison. him at Lambeth, and aft. at Windsor; but the religion of the great soldier partook little of the fierce sincerity of Queen Mary, and he was too sagacious, if not humane, to put the confessor to death. See Brook's Lives III. 326. One John R. of our own days was min. at Rendham, in Co. Suff'k. not long since, and may still be. NATHANIEL, Ipswich, s. of the preced. serv. in the cavalry in Philip's war 1676, and d. 14 June 1680, prob. unm. for the careful author of the Fam. Mem. tells, that his nuncup. will gave his prop. to neph. John, s. of his br. John. *NATHANIEL*, Portsmouth, youngest s. of Presid. John, ord. 3 May 1699, d. 3 Oct. 1723. He had by w. Sarah, eight ch. of wh. some attain. distinct. as in Geneal. Reg. V. 325. NOAH, Branford, youngest s. of John of the same, whose prop. he inherit. m. 8 Apr. 1673, Eliz. d. of the first Michael Taintor, had Mary, b. 14 Apr. 1675; John, 8 Nov. 1677; Josiah, 31 Jan. 1680; Hezekiah; Noah; Eliz.; and Ann; but the last four names are obt. from his will of 22 Dec. 1724, wh. ment. all the seven. OBADIAH, Southampton, L. I. 1673, where Thompson thinks he was in 1640, wh. would compel us to suppose, that he rem. from Lynn, to that place. In 1683, at the neighb. town of Southold are found Obadiah, and Obadiah jr. among the tax payers. RICHARD, Dover 1642. ROBERT, Newbury, by w. Susanna had Robert, b. 28 Apr. 1650; Thomas, 9 July 1652; John, 13 Mar. 1654; Susanna, 6 Feb. 1657; Joshua, 1 Aug. 1658; and d. 23 Dec. 1659; and his wid. m. William Thomas. SAMUEL, Ipswich, s. of Rev. Nathaniel, b. in Eng. prob. at Assington, brot. in inf. was town clk. 1653, m. 12 Dec. 1657, Judith, d. of the first Samuel Appleton, wh. d. July 1659; and he next m. 13 Nov. 1661, Sarah, d. of Jonathan Wade, had Sarah, wh. d. soon; John d. soon; John, again, b. 29 Apr. 1667; Susanna, 17 Mar. 1669; Jonathan, 29 Mar. 1671; Mary, 10 Sept. 1672; Margaret, 29 Oct. 1675; Eliz. 1 Oct. 1678; Abigail, 5 July, 1681; and Sarah, 30 Sept. 1682; and he d. 21 Dec. 1693. His wid. m. Henry Woodhouse of Concord. In the geneal. of Nathaniel R's. s. Samuel, Geneal. Reg. V. 316, there seem. sev. points of doubtful exactness, tho. the gr. article is a very valua. one. One of the ds. should be call. Martha, for she admin. 1696, the est. of her br. John. Samuel had charg. his prop. with annuity of £10 to his wid. SAMUEL, New London, eldest s. of James the first, had good est. by devise of his gr.-f. Samuel Rowland, m. 17 Nov. 1662, Caulkins says, p. 297, but on p. 202 says 1664, Mary, d. of Thomas Stanton the first, had perhaps a fam. tho. I find no ment. of it in the hist. but he had d. Mary, wh. m. 2 Oct. 1684, Capt. Samuel Gilbert, and d. 30 Sept. 1756, aged 90; and he d. 1 Dec. 1713. SIMON, Boston, came in the

Defence 1635, aged 20, from London, was a shoemaker, liv. first at Concord, where his w. Mary d. 1 Aug. 1640, freem. 13 May 1640, rem. to B. and by w. Susanna had Nathaniel, b. 14 Feb. bapt. 12 Mar. 1643, wh. d. bef. his f.; Lydia, 1, bapt. 7 Dec. 1645; John, bapt. 23 July 1648, a. 5 days old; Simon, 28 Apr. 1654; Gamaliel, 26 Mar. 1657; and Joseph, 29 July 1662; perhaps others; in B. was a tanner. In his will of 1 Apr. 1678, pro. 3 Jan. 1680, names w. Susanna, eldest s. Gamaliel, and Joseph, and d. Eliz. Rust. THOMAS, Plymouth, came in the Mayflower 1620, with s. Joseph, and d. early next yr. But Bradford informs us that "the rest of his childr. came over, are m. and have [1650] many ch." THOMAS, Watertown, 1636, freem. 17 May 1637, d. or was bur. 12 Nov. 1638, aged 50, says Bond, and his wid. Grace m. William Palmer. THOMAS, Scituate, s. of the first John of the same, Deane says, had a fam. of wh. are descend. to our day. THOMAS, Saco 1652, was constable 1659. His ho. was burn. by the Ind. Oct. 1676. THOMAS, Eastham, s. of Joseph the first, m. 13 Dec. 1665, Eliz. Snow, had Eliz. b. 8 Oct. 1666; Joseph, 1 Feb. 1668; Hannah, 20 Mar. 1669 or 70; Thomas, 6 Mar. 1671, d. in few days; Thomas, again, 6 May 1672; Eleazer, 3 Nov. 1673; and Nathaniel, 18 Jan. 1676. His w. d. 16 June 1678. THOMAS, Newbury, s. of Robert, perhaps in 1691 taxed at Rowley, m. 18 May 1677, Ruth Brown, had Thomas, b. 14 Aug. 1678; Ruth, 16 Apr. 1680; Susanna, 17 Mar. 1682; Robert, 5 Apr. 1684; John, 11 July 1686; Isaac, 21 June 1691; Stephen, 20 Aug. 1693; Daniel, 14 Nov. 1695; and Jonathan, 18 June 1702. TIMOTHY, Boston, s. of Rev. Nathaniel, a merch. 1665-88, was not among household. 1695. WILLIAM, York, was adm. freem. 1652. WILLIAM, Boston, Farmer says, had sev. ch. b. there, and d. 13 July 1664; but I doubt he relied on informat. that has not reached me. WILLIAM, Boston, merch. by w. Susannah, if that name be not wrong, had Mary, b. 9 Apr. 1667; perhaps had sec. w. at least m. 22 Apr. 1676, inv. of his est. was taken by his wid. Margaret, wh. had one s. by him, and wh. on 4 May foll. was appoint. admin. and she had bef. 30 Jan. foll. m. William Snelling. WILLIAM, Charlestown 1678, may have rem. to Reading. WILLIAM, Nantucket, had Experience, a d. b. 23 July 1673; Ebenezer, 5 Jan. 1676. In his MS. Farmer obs. that of this name 54 had been gr. of which 37 were of Harv. 10 of Yale; and that 15 of these were clerg. of wh. I count 12 at Harv.

ROISE or ROYCE, ISAAC, New London, s. of Robert, m. 15 Dec. 1669, Eliz. eldest d. of Samuel Lothrop, and rem. to Wallingford. His wid. m. Joseph Thompson of the same. JOHN, Willimantic 1686. JONATHAN, Norwich, s. of Robert of New London, m. June 1660, Deborah, d. of Hugh Caulkins, had Eliz. b. Jan. 1662; John, 9 Nov. 1663; Sarah, Oct. 1665;

Abigail, Sept. 1667, d. next yr.; Ruth, Apr. 1669; Hannah, Apr. 1671; Abigail, again, Apr. 1673; Jonathan, Aug. 1678; Deborah, 10 Aug. 1680; and Daniel, 19 Aug. 1682. NATHANIEL, New London, s. of Robert, freem. 1669, rem. to Wallingford bef. 1674. He m. Abigail, wid. of David Hoyt, after her ret. from captiv. in Canada. NEHEMIAH, New London, prob. br. of the preced. m. 20 Nov. 1660, Hannah, d. of James Morgan, was freem. 1666; rem. to Wallingford. * ROBERT, of Boston, as early as 1631 or 2; freem. 1 Apr. 1634, by w. Eliz. had Joshua, b. 14, bapt. 16 Apr. 1637; Nathaniel, bapt. 24 Mar. 1639, tho. town rec. has b. 1 Apr. and Patience b. 1 Apr. 1642, d. in one wk. was one of the disarmed 1637, as a supporter of Mrs. Hutchinson in her revelations, or of Wheelwright in his opinions; had rem. bef. 1657 to New London, perhaps in 1650 was of Stratford, but constable in 1660 and in 1661 rep. for N. L. where he liv. in good repute, and his d. Ruth m. 15 Dec. 1669, John Lothrop; and Sarah m. John Caulkins. Of his s. Nehemiah, Samuel, Nathaniel, Isaac, and Jonathan, the four first rem. to Wallingford, aft. m. in New London, and Lothrop also rem. to W. He d. 1676, and his wid. Mary was liv. on his est. 1688. SAMUEL, New London, s. of the preced. m. 9 Jan. 1667, Hannah, d. of Josiah Churchwood of Wethersfield, freem. 1669, rem. to Wallingford. Oft. the name appears Rise or Rice, and may have been sometimes confound. with Rose.

ROLESTONE, ROWLSTONE, or ROULSTONE, JOHN, a soldier in Philip's war, at Northampton 1676, was prob. he of Boston, wh. by w. Mary had Thomas, b. 28 July 1686; Joseph, 28 Nov. 1688; and Mary, 29 Sept. 1690.

ROLFE, BENJAMIN, Newbury, weaver, gr.s. of Henry, says Coffin, whose only s. John must then be infer. to be f. but reason is found for call. him br. of John, and s. of Henry, was b. betw. 1637 and 1640, freem. 1659, or more prob. 1670, by w. Apphia, wh. he m. 3 Nov. 1659, had John, b. 12 Oct. 1660; Benjamin, 13 Sept. 1662, H. C. 1684, chaplain to our forces at Falmouth 1689, the sec. min. of Haverhill, ord. Jan. 1694, k. by the Ind. 29 Aug. 1708; Apphia, 8 Mar. 1667; Mary, 16 Sept. 1669, d. young; Samuel, 14 Jan. 1672; Mary, again, 11 Nov. 1674, d. young; Henry, 12 Oct. 1677; Eliz. 15 Dec. 1679; Nathaniel, 12 Nov. 1681; and Abigail, 5 May 1684. His w. d. 24 Dec. 1708, and he d. 10 Aug. 1710. DANIEL, Ipswich, s. of Robert, wh. came not prob. to this country, m. Hannah, d. of Humphrey Bradstreet, had, perhaps, Daniel, Ezra, and other ch. and may have d. at Salem, June 1654. His wid. m. 12 June 1658, Nicholas Holt of Andover, and d. 20 June 1665. DANIEL, Ipswich, s. prob. of the preced. may be that s.-in-law of Robert Collins, k. in Philip's war. EZRA, Haverhill, s. prob. of Daniel the first,

m. 2 Mar. 1676, Abigail, d. of John Bond, had Abigail, b. 17 Sept. 1677; Ezra, 24 Nov. 1680; Daniel, 14 Feb. 1685; Mary and Martha, tw. 23 Nov. 1687; and he was wound. and capt. by the Ind. 17 Oct. 1689, and d. 3 days aft. HENRY, Newbury, one of the early sett. prob. from Co. Wilts, with w. and childr. of wh. John, Benjamin, and Hannah, wh. m. the first Richard Dole, are kn. d. 1 Mar. 1643; in his will of 15 Feb. preced. beside w. and ch. he names br. John and neph. John Saunders, and calls Thomas Whittier, kinsman. Perhaps his wid. was Honour, wh. d. at Charlestown, 19 Dec. 1650. JOHN, Newbury, br. of the preced. came in the Confidence 1638, from Southampton, aged 50, in the custom ho. call. husbandman of Melchit Park, Wilts, with w. Ann, d. Esther, and serv. Thomas Whittier, call. Whittle in Geneal. Reg. V. 440, and XIV. 335, was freem. 6 Sept. 1639, by our Secr. spell. Roffe, as at the Southampton custom ho. Mr. Somerby in Geneal. Reg. V. 440, assures us it was Roaf, correcting Mr. Stevens's eyesight in II. 109, Mr. Drake says, Geneal. Reg. XIV. 335, it was Roaff, vindicating the honor of Mr. Somerby's vision; in ea. of the three cases, no doubt, foll. the sound, as it reach. the ear of the subordinate official, bec. one of the earliest propr. of Salisbury, there taxed 1650 and 2; perhaps had sec. w. Esther, wh. d. 3 June 1647; in July 1663, he was one of the proprs. of Nantucket, and d. 8 Feb. 1664. His d. Esther m. John Saunders. But of ano. JOHN of Newbury, prob. s. of Henry, we hear, that he m. 4 Dec. 1656, Mary Scullard, possib. d. of Samuel, had Mary, b. 2 Nov. 1658, d. next mo.; Mary, again, 16 Jan. 1660; and Rebecca, 9 Feb. 1662; and Coffin thot. him br. of Henry, to wh. I discern obj. Ano. JOHN, Nantucket, may have gone from Newbury, but at the first nam. place had John, b. 5 Mar. 1664; Samuel, 8 Mar. 1665; Sarah, 2 Dec. 1667; Joseph, 12 Mar. 1670; and Hannah, 5 Feb. 1672; possib. may have gone back to Newbury, and been the man wh. Coffin says d. 30 Sept. 1681. Yet of ano. JOHN of Newbury, if he be not one of the preced. C. tells us that he had w. Dorothy, and s. John, b. 24 Mar. 1691; and Jonathan 2 Aug. 1695. Farmer names Thomas of Ipswich 1648, but he eludes my search, unless he be the man of Guilford, wh. had m. Eliz. Disbrow, and for some heinous offence ran off for refuge to the col. of Rhode Island, and so his w. obt. divorce, 1 Oct. 1651, by the jurisdict. of New Haven col. resum. her maiden name, and m. John Johnson of the same town, and she d. 23 Dec. 1669. Four of this name had, in 1834, been gr. at Harv. and three at the other N. E. coll.

ROLLO, ALEXANDER, Middletown, one of the earliest proprs. of East Haddam, d. 22 July 1709.

ROLLOCK, ROBERT, Sandwich, d. prob. Sept. 1669.

ROMAN, JOHN, Cambridge, d. 19 Dec. 1638. Of this solitary name no other occurrence is kn.

RONALLS, JOHN, JOSIAH, and SAMUEL, perhaps brs. at Wickford 1674, may have spelled variously.

ROOD, THOMAS, Norwich, had sev. childr. bef. liv. there; Sarah, b. Oct. 1649; Thomas, Mar. 1651; Micah, Feb. 1653; Rachel, Feb. 1655; Jóhn, Sept. 1658; Joseph, Mar. 1661; Benjamin, Feb. 1663; Mary, Mar. 1664, d. soon; and Samuel, June 1666. His w. d. happi. Mar. 1668, for his d. Sarah was whip. and he execut. 18 Oct. 1672, as in Trumbull, Col. Rec. II. 184, is detail. Perhaps the name was changed to Rudd or Rude. JOHN, with this latter spelling was a petitnr. 1686, for Preston townsh.

ROOKER, WILLIAM, Hadley, petitio. against imposts 1668, took the o. of alleg. 8 Feb. 1679.

ROOKMAN, JOHN, came in the Abigail, 1635, aged 45, with w. Eliz. 31, and s. John, 9; but the name is never found in any of our settlem.

ROOME, or ROME, JOHN, Portsmouth 1638, is among freem. 1655, and is nam. in the royal chart. 1663. See Haz. II. 612. He was from Bristol, Eng. prob. for by his will he devis. ho. and ld. in that city to his w. Ann, wh. in 1669 gave her gr.s. William Cory, power to sell it.

ROOT, CALEB, Farmington, s. of John the first of the same, m. 9 Aug. 1693, Eliz. d. of Thomas Salmon of Northampton, had Mary, b. 6 Mar. 1695, bapt. 4 Apr. 1697; Caleb, 14 Mar. 1698; Thomas, 16 Jan. 1702; Eliz. 8 Apr. 1706; and Samuel, 20 Nov. 1712; and d. 1712. HEZE-KIAH, Northampton 1678, s. of Thomas the first, freem. 1690, d. bef. his f. m. 1682, Mehitable, d. of Sampson Frary of Deerfield, had Benja-min, b. 1686; Mehitable, perhaps the sec. d. of the.name, 1688; and Mercy 1689, wh. was k. at Deerfield, with her gr.f. Frary, 29 Feb. 1704, by the Fr. and Ind. His wid. m. a. 1702, Jeremiah Alvord. JACOB, Northampton, br. of the preced. m. a. 1680, Mary or Mercy, d. of Sampson Frary, had Joanna, b. 1681; Daniel, 1684; Jacob, 1687; Mercy, 1690; Margaret, 1692; William, 1695; Hezekiah, 1697; Ruth, 1699; Nathaniel, 1702; and Jonathan, 1705; was freem. 1684, but rem. to Hebron, and d. 1731. His will, 1728, names all the ch. exc. Hezekiah, tho. some were d. leav. heirs. Of this fam. was the late Hon. Erastus R. of Albany. JOHN, Farmington, m. Mary, d. of Thomas Kil-bourne, had John; Thomas; Samuel; Joseph; Caleb; Stephen; Mary, wh. m. Isaac Bronson; and Susanna, m. Oct. 1683, Joseph Langton; was freem. 1657, and d. 1684, leav. good est. and his wid. d. 1697, aged 70. His first three s. sett. at Westfield. In the Hist. of the Kilbourne Fam. pp. 42 and 3, exhibit. the extraord. dilig. of P. K. Kilbourne, some slight differences may be found. JOHN, Farmington, perhaps s. of the preced. m. 18 Oct. 1664, Mary, d. of Richard Ashley of Springfield, and sett. at Westfield soon, there had Mary, b. 22 Sept. 1667; Sarah, 24

Sept. 1670; John, 28 Dec. 1672; Samuel, 16 Sept. 1675; Hannah, 9 Dec. 1677; Abigail, 26 June 1680; Joshua, 23 Nov. 1682; and Mercy, 15 Mar. 1684 or 5; and he d. 1687, hav. been made freem. 1669. All his ch. were liv. in 1710. JOHN, Deerfield, s. of Thomas the first, m. Mehitable, the wid. of Samuel Hinsdale, had Thankful, b. 1677, and was k. by the Ind. 19 Sept. that same yr. JOHN, Fairfield, s. or neph. of Richard, by w. Dorcas had John, Susanna, Mary, and Sarah, all bapt. Apr. 1685 at Woodbury, where prob. some of them were b. for certain. he had rem. thither three or four yrs. bef. beside Josiah, bapt. Mar. 1688; Bethia, Dec. 1691, d. under 9 yrs.; John, again, b. 9 June 1693; Joseph, bapt. June 1698; and Bethia b. 7 Feb. 1703; as Cothren, wh. has confus. in my opin. the stock, as if he were s. of the first John of Farmington, tho. he speaks only of prob. on that point. His w. d. 15 May 1720; and he d. 25 May 1723. JONATHAN, Northampton 1680, s. of Thomas of the same, freem. 1690, m. Ann, d. of William Gull of Hatfield, had Eliz. b. 1681; Esther, 1683; Hannah, 1687; Ann, 1690; and Hannah, 1695; and he d. 25 Dec. 1741. JOSEPH, Northampton, br. prob. eldest, of the preced. m. Hannah, d. of Edmund Haynes, had Hannah, b. 1662; Joseph, 1665; Thomas, 1667; John, 1669; Sarah, 1672; Hope, a s. 1675; and Hezekiah, 1677; for sec. w. had Mary Burt, wid. of Henry, and d. 19 Apr. 1711. JOSEPH, Farmington, br. of Caleb, m. 1691, Eliz. Warner, had Eliz. b. 22, bapt. 26 June 1692; Mary, 22, bapt. 28 Jan. 1694; Joseph, 27 Aug. 1699; and took sec. w. 3 Mar. 1727, Ruth, wid. of Samuel Smith, d. of Thomas Porter. JOSHUA, Salem, 1637, when he had gr. of ld. and Felt quotes the rec. of his being drummer, 1657. JOSIAH, Salem, came in the Hercules, 1635, from Kent, aft. join. the ch. 1648, had bapt. Josiah, Bethiah, John, and Susanna, 24 Sept. of that yr. and Thomas, 16 Feb. 1651; was one of the found. of Beverly ch. 1667. Susanna was imprison. in the witchcraft madness; but we may hope that her f. was d. bef. JOSIAH, Boston 1673, mariner, may have been s. of the preced. RALPH, Boston, came in the Abigail, 1635, aged 50. His w. Ann. join. our ch. 1639. But our rec. ment. d. of his w. Mary (prob. a sec. w.), 15 Nov. 1655. In 1660, he gave d. Sarah, and her h. James Balston, his ho. orchard, and garden, to secure mainten. of hims. for residue of life. Mary, aged 15, wh. came in the Abigail, was perhaps his d. RICHARD, Lynn, was of Salem ch. 1636, freem. 9 Mar. 1637, may have rem. to Fairfield, where the rec. of his name always has s final. He there d. bef. 1653, when his wid. Margaret m. Michael Fry. ROBERT, Newport 1639. SAMUEL, Westfield, s. of John the first, was freem. 1680, and d. 27 Nov. 1711, leav. wid. Mary, but no ch. STEPHEN, Farmington, br. of Caleb, m. Sarah, d. of John Wadsworth of Hartford, had Timothy, b. a. 1681;

John, a. 1685; Mary, a. 1691; all bapt. 17 May 1691; Sarah, 17 Dec. 1693; and Hannah, wh. d. unm. and perhaps others; and he d. 1717. His wid. d. 20 Mar. 1740. THOMAS, Salem 1637, when he had gr. of ld. that he prob. slighted, as he was of Hartford 1639, or earlier, had large fam. was a weaver, and rem. a. 1659, to Northampton, where he was one of the seven pillars for foundat. of the ch. 1661, and d. at gr. age, 17 July 1694, in his will naming progeny, Joseph, Thomas, John (wh. was b. 10 June 1646, and had d. but left d. Thankful), Jonathan, Jacob, Hezekiah (who was d. but left childr.), and Sarah, w. of Samuel Kellogg of Hatfield. THOMAS, Northampton, s. of the preced. m. 1666, Abigail, eldest d. of Alexander Alvord, had Thomas, b. 1667; Abigail, 1668; Samuel, 1673; and Hezekiah. 1676, wh. d. young; and aft. 1700, rem. prob. to Coventry. THOMAS, Westfield, s. of John the first, m. 1670 Mary Gridley, prob. d. of the first Thomas, had Thomas, b. 1 Sept. 1671, d. at 18 yrs.; and Mary, 21 Oct. 1673. Soon after his w. d. in that yr. m. 7 Oct. 1675, Mary Spencer, had John, b. 25 Dec. 1676; Samuel, 16 Feb. 1679; Eliz. 16 Feb. 1681; Sarah, 27 July 1683; Timothy, 3 Dec. 1685; Joseph, 16 June 1688; and this sec. w. d. 4 Nov. 1690. Early in 1693 he m. third w. Sarah, wid. of Josiah Leonard, had Thankful and Mary, tw. 12 Nov. 1693, and this w. d. 3 Jan. foll. and he d. 16 Aug. 1709. Not a few errors are seen in the acco. of his ms. and childr. in Geneal. Reg. VI. 267. THOMAS, Boston, mariner, m. Eliz. d. of Ambrose Gale of Marblehead, had Mary; and in his will 18 Sept. 1683, pro. 31 Jan. foll. in wh. he says he is bd. on voyage to Jamaica, names only that w. ch. and f.-in-law. This name oft. is spell. Rootes.

ROOTEN, or ROWTON, RICHARD, Lynn, emb. at London, in the Susan and Ellen, Apr. 1635, aged 36, with w. Ann of the same age, and ch. Edmund, 6 mos. No more is kn. of any of the fam. but that one rec. tells that he d. 20 Sept. 1663, ano. that the will of 12 June preced. pro. in Nov. names no ch. but does the w. and kinsman, Edmund, wh. d. 8 Apr. 1675. He had modera. est.

ROPER, BENJAMIN, a soldier in Philip's war, whose resid. perhaps was Dedham, k. by the Ind. 18 Sept. 1675, with the flower of Essex, under Capt. Lothrop. He may have been s. or gr.s. of Walter; though in Farmer he is made tw. br. of Ephraim. EPHRAIM, s. of John of Dedham, serv. as a soldier under Capt. Turner in Philip's war, was in the Falls fight. His first w. was k. by the Ind. and he m. 20 Nov. 1677, Hannah, prob. the wid. of Stephen Goble, had Ruth, b. 7 Mar. 1681; and Eliz. 17 Mar. 1683. He with w. and one d. was k. by the Ind. 1697. JOHN, Dedham 1639, when his w. and d. Mary, join. with the ch. was freem. 2 June 1641. JOHN, Dedham, possib. s. of the preced.

came, 1637, aged 26, with w. Alice, 23, and two ch. Alice and Eliz. a carpenter from New Bukenham, Co. Norfk. as says the rec. [See 4 Mass. Hist. Coll. I. 99.] At D. by w. Alice he had Rachel, b. 16 Mar. 1640, d. next yr.; Hannah, 5, bapt. 9 Apr. 1642; Ephraim and Benjamin, b..23 Feb. tho. the rec. of bapt. has Ephraim and Nathaniel tw. 2 Mar. 1645; and I would gladly tell more if kn. to me. An Alice R. bec. perhaps third w. of John Dickinson of Salisbury. JOHN, Charlestown 1647–58, may be he wh. rem. to Lancaster, and was k. by the Ind. early in 1676, on the same day when all the other inhab. gave up their residences to conflagr. WALTER, Hampton 1639, had Mary, bapt. 22 Aug. 1641, freem. 18 May 1642, rem. to Ipswich bef. 1666, was aft. of Andover, but d. in Ipsw. 15 July 1680, in 68th yr. His will names w. Susan, ch. John, Nathaniel, Mary, Eliz. and Sarah; beside gr.ch. Eliz. Margaret, Susan, Rose, Sarah Sparks, and John Dutch, s. of Mary, w. of Robert. John, his s. d. 27 Nov. 1709, in 60th yr.

ROPES, GEORGE, Salem 1637, by w. Mary had George, wh. may have been among the youngest, and unm. when k. by the Ind. 18 Sept. 1675, at Bloody Brook, in the flower of Essex under Lothrop; Jonathan, bapt. 5 June 1642, d. at 19 yrs; Sarah, 3 Nov. 1643, d. soon, perhaps, for the ch. rec. makes Mary, bapt. 3 Nov. 1644; John, 4 July 1647; William, 28 Dec. 1651; Abigail, 29 Oct. 1654; and Samuel, 15 Mar. 1657; was constable 1665, and d. June 1670, leav. no will. His wid. wh. had admin. d. 1691. The d. Mary m. 17 Nov. 1663 John Norman. JAMES, Boston, by w. Sarah had Sarah, b. 22 Nov. 1680 and James, 30 Jan. 1688. JOHN, Salem, s. of George, m. 25 Mar. 1669, Lydia Wells, had Benjamin, b. 22 Mar. 1670; Lydia, 26 Dec. 1672; Mary, 21 Aug. 1675; John, 3 Sept. 1678; Abigail, 20 Apr. 1681; Sarah, 23 Feb. 1685; Samuel, 24 Jan. 1687; Eliz. Nov. 1689; and Nathaniel 1692, wh. was f. of Nathaniel, H. C. 1745, Judge of the Sup. Ct. of the Prov. RICHARD, Salem, prob. br. of the preced. m. 7 June 1670, Ruth, d. of John Ingersoll, had Richard, b. 20 Apr. 1674; and John, 16 Aug. 1678. SAMUEL, Salem, perhaps br. of George, sign. petition against impost 1668. WILLIAM, Salem, br. of the preced. m. 1676, Sarah Ingersoll, d. prob. of John, had Jonathan, b. Nov. 1680; Sarah, Jan. 1683; William, Mar. 1685; George, Aug. 1688; Richard, 1690; Joseph, Jan. 1692; John, Jan. 1694; and Ruth.

ROSE, DANIEL, Wethersfield, s. of Robert, freem. 1665, m. 1664, Eliz. eldest d. of the first John Goodrich, had Eliz. b. 15 Apr. 1665; Daniel, 20 Aug. 1667; Mary, 11 Feb. 1669; Hannah, 12 Aug. 1673; Jonathan, 20 Sept. 1679; Sarah, 2 Nov. 1681; Abigail, 14 Sept. 1683; Dorothy, 3 May 1687; and Lydia, 2 Apr. 1689; was call. 66 yrs. old in 1696, and so may be presum. to have been b. in Eng. and brot. by his f.

DANIEL, Wethersfield, s. of the preced. m. at Colchester, 14 May 1706, Mary, d. of the third Nathaniel Foote, and sett. at C. GEORGE, Braintree, one of the founders of the ch. there, 17 Sept. 1639, rem. to Concord, freem. 13 May 1640,.d. 20 May 1649. GEORGE, New Haven, by w. Constance had John, bapt. May 1662 ; and Daniel, Nov. 1663 ; both in her right, but the days of both are giv. wrong in Geneal. Reg. IX. 362. GIDEON, Scituate, s. of Thomas of the same, had Jabez and Jeremiah. HENRY, came in the James from Southampton 1635 ; but no more is kn. of him. JEREMIAH, Scituate, s. of the first Thomas, m. 1698, Eliz. d. of Anthony Collamore, had only Thomas, and d. 1699. His wid. m. Timothy Symmes. JOHN, Watertown 1636, rem. to Branford, was of the jury, perhaps, in 1649, and was liv. there 1667. He may have been s. of Robert, and f. of that John, wh. the Cambridge rec. says d. 12 Dec. 1640. JOHN, Scituate, s. of Thomas, k. by the Ind. 25 Mar. 1676, in Rehoboth fight, under Capt. Pierce. JOHN, Marshfield, perish. 13 Feb. 1677, with cold, when shoot. on the beach. JONATHAN, Branford 1667, may have been s. or br. of John of the same. JONATHAN, Wethersfield, s. of Daniel the first, m. 26 Feb. 1707, Abigail, d. of Ebenezer Hale. JOSEPH, Marshfield, s. of Thomas, m. 5 June 1654, Eliz. Bumpus, perhaps d. of Edward. RICHARD, Salem 1668. * ROBERT, Wethersfield 1639, but he went it is thought, from Watertown, came in the Francis from Ipswich, Co. Suff'k. 1634, aged 40, with w. Margery, 40, and ch. John, 15 ; Robert, 15 ; Eliz. 13 ; Mary, 11 ; Samuel, 9 ; Sarah, 7 ; Daniel, 3 ; and Dorcas, 2 ; was constable 1640 ; rep. 1641, 2, and 3 ; rem. bef. 1648 to Stratford, where the list of freem. 1669 bears his name, unless it be of his s. ROBERT, wh. is more prob. for one R. (James, as Mr. Whitmore, in Geneal. Reg. XIII. 301, says), d. at Branford, leav. good est. in 1664 or 5 ; and I judge the younger was among early sett. at Easthampton, L. I. 1650. Mary, d. of the younger Robert, m. a. 1676, Moses Johnson of Stratford ; and Hannah m. Isaac Stiles jr. ROGER, Boston, 1663, a mariner, and serv. of William Hudson, m. at Watertown a. 1661, Abigail, d. of Christopher Grant, and prob. at W. spent most of his days, liv. there 1693. THOMAS, Scituate, bef. 1660, had John, Gideon, both bef. ment. Thomas, and perhaps others ; m. sec. w. 1666, Alice, wid. of Jonas Pickels, d. of Elder William Hatch, and had Jeremiah. THOMAS, New London, m. bef. 1683, Hannah, d. of Robert Allyn, was one of the grantees of Preston, 1686. THOMAS, Marblehead 1673, may be the same as the preced. or quite as likely of Billerica 1679, unless this be wrongly writ. for Ross. THOMAS, Scituate, s. of Thomas the first, had Gideon, b. 1702 ; and prob. others. At Block isl. in 1678, some Rose, with a wild spell. termed rose, in ano. place, Tormot Roosse, was a townsman, as in the diligent extr. of Geneal. Reg. XIII. 37. In the Index his name bec. Ross.

Ross, Alexander, New Hampsh. 1688. Daniel and Ezra, Ipswich 1648, of wh. no more is kn. George, New Haven, m. 1658, Constance Little, perhaps d. of Richard, was freem. 1668. Sometimes his name is Roose. James, Sudbury, by w. Mary had Mary, b. 25 Dec. 1656. He, or the succeed. may have been that soldier, whose w. Mary, in the spring of 1676, says her h. went to Narraganset, under Capt. Mosely, of course in Dec. bef. was near 70 yrs. old, was still in the serv. and his fam. suffer. so that she begg. for his release. Sudbury James had d. Dorothy, wh. m. 11 Apr. 1687, Eliezer Whitney from Watertown. James, Falmouth 1657, m. Ann, eldest d. of George Lewis, had James, b. 1662; and other ch. all taken by the Ind. 11 Aug. 1676. After 1678, with his fam. he went back to Falmouth, liv. at Back Cove; but at the sec. destruct. of the town in 1690, again was taken and carr. to Canada, whence in Oct. 1695, one of the name, prob. the s. was ransom. and aft. liv. says Willis, at Salem. John, Cambridge, m. 7 May 1659, at Boston, Mary, d. of John Osborn of Weymouth, had Sarah, b. 21 May 1660; and at Malden had Mary, 24 Apr. 1675. John prob. of Ipswich, m. 28 Aug. 1663, Deborah, d. of Christopher Osgood the first. Killecriss, or Killcross, wh. may be the same as some name nearer to a common one, perhaps Gilchrist, was of Ipswich 1678. Thomas, Cambridge 1659, m. 16 Jan. 1662, Seeth, d. of William Holman, had Thomas, wh. d. 19 Jan. 1663; Margaret, bapt. May 1665; Thomas, again, bapt. 1 July 1666; and other ch. of wh. one or more sett. at Billerica, where Seeth, his wid. was k. by the Ind. 5 Aug. 1695.

Rosseter or Rocester, Bray or Bryan, Guilford 1642, had been of Dorchester, s. prob. of Edward, and brot. by his f. in the Mary and John, 1630, freem. 18 May 1631, was the first town clk. at Windsor, 1639, and serv. as a physician many yrs. with good reputa. After some yrs. resid. at G. rem. to Killingworth, but ret. soon, and there his w. Eliz. and d. Sarah d. Aug. 1669; made his will 1672, and d. 30 Sept. of that yr. He had Joanna, wh. m. at Wethersfield, 7 Nov. 1660, Rev. John Cotton, after of Plymouth; Susanna, b. 18 Nov. 1652, wh. m. Rev. Zechariah Walker; John and Josiah, beside four wh. d. young. ‡Edward, Dorchester 1630, came in the Mary and John, arr. from Plymouth 30 May, had been chos. as an Assist. in London, 20 Oct. 1629, when Winth. was first chos. Gov. Humfrey, Dept. and Saltonstall, Johnson, Dudley, Endicott, and thirteen others Assist. of the Col. of the Mass. Bay in N. E. but was never present at any meeting, as he resid. far in the West. He had good est. prob. in Co. Somerset or Devon, for Hutch. I. 17, by wh. alone any informat. is glean. (even the exquis. dilig. of Prince fails to add any thing to his master Winth.) says his son (as if he had only one) liv. at Combe, in Devon, and his gr.s. Edward was a deac. 1682, in the dissent. ch. of Taunton in S. Faithful. he attend. the first in Aug. and Sept. sec. and third meet. at Charlestown, of the Assist. but was not present on the next 19 Oct. and d. on 23d of that mo. in the first yr. In 1685 his youngest surv. ch. wid. Jane Hart, praying aid from our governm. said she was 70 yrs. old. HUGH, Dorchester, not prob. s. of the preced. tho. he had gr. of small lot in 1635, was of Taunton 1637, among the earliest sett. [Baylies, I. 286], had Jane, wh. m. bef. 1643, Thomas Gilbert, and Baylies, II. 281, thought this the first m. in town, and 267, that he had gone to Conn. perhaps, or New Haven; but it may well be thot. as his name is not found in either Col. that he went home, or d. JOHN, Killingworth, s. perhaps eldest, of Bryan, was in 1669, one of the selectmen, m. Mary, d. of Jonathan Gilbert the first, had John, b. 12 May 1670; and d. Sept. 1670. His wid. m. Samuel Holton of Northampton. *JOSIAH, Guilford 1685, prob. s. of Bray, m. Sarah, only d. of the first Samuel Sherman, had Sarah, b. 26 Nov. 1677, d. next yr.; Eliz. 16 May 1679; Josiah, 31 May 1680; Samuel, 28 Jan. 1682, d. soon; Timothy, 5 June 1683; John, 13 Oct. 1684, d. young; Samuel, 18 Feb. 1686; David, 17 Apr. 1687, d. at one yr.; Jonathan, 3 Apr. 1688; Nathaniel, 10 Nov. 1689; Sarah, 25 Feb. 1691; Patience, 6 Apr. 1692; Joanna, 23 Apr. 1693, d. at 10 yrs.; Mary, 3 Sept. 1694; Theophilus, 12 Feb. 1696; Susanna, 13 June 1697; and Ebenezer, 4 Feb. 1699, Y. C. 1718, min. 40 yrs. of Stonington; was rep. 1701–11, and d. 31 Jan. 1716. He may be that man ordered to be adm. freem. of Killingworth 1669. Six of this name had been gr. at Yale in 1756, beside three in later yrs. spelt Rossiter.

ROSWELL or ROSEWELL, JOHN, New Haven, perhaps br. perhaps s. of Richard or of William, d. 1688. RICHARD, New Haven, s. of William, by first w. m. 22 Dec. 1681, then under 16 yrs. of age, Lydia, d. of Thomas Trowbridge, had Sarah, b. 5 Dec. 1682; Dorcas, 21 Dec. 1684; Lydia, 21 Aug. 1687; Eliz. 5 Sept. 1690; and Catharine, 26 Dec. 1695; and d. Mar. 1702, leav. good est. He was engag. with his f. in large trade to W. I. His wid. d. 10 Dec. 1731. WILLIAM, Branford, merch. rem. to Charlestown, there was inhab. 1658, and Frothingham, 145, says, m. 29 Nov. 1654 (tho. judge Smith of Guilford makes the date many yrs. later, and perhaps it should be, by ten yrs. nearly), Catharine, d. of Hon. Richard Russell of that place, but rem. soon aft. to Branford, where he, in Jan. 1668, partook in the new combinat. for ch. aft. withdrawal of Rev. Abraham Pierson to New Jersey, and very soon rem. to New Haven, and was active in business, sent in 1673 to the Dutch, after they had retaken New York, to inq. a. their further purpose, named capt. of the horse in Philip's war, but declined to accept, was a judge of the Co. bef. during, and aft. the usurp. of Andros, had turned out in 1690; and in 1692, with Edward Palmes and Gershom Bulkley, oppos. the Charter gov. and d. 19 July 1694, aged 64, as the gr.st. tells, and his wid. d. 1698. He had Maud, b. 21 Aug. 1668; and William, 16 June 1670; both at New Haven, beside the Richard, wh. prob. was b. at Charlestown; and perhaps by ano. w. Eliz. 1 Oct. 1679. This call. by Caulkins "only ch. of W. R." bec. sec. w. of Gov. Saltonstall, had five ch. and d. soon aft. b. of the last. It may be, that "only child" means only surviv. but to me it seems more prob. to refer to the only ch. of a sec. w. My informat. is deriv. chiefly from Judge R. D. Smith of Guilford, aft. dilig. scrutiny of rec.

ROTHERFORD, RUDDERFORD, or RUTHERFORD, HENRY, New Haven 1643, by w. Sarah had Sarah, b. 31 Jan. 1641; and he d. 1668, leav. wid. Sarah, wh. m. 1670, Gov. William Loete, and d. soon aft. mak. her will, 12 Feb. 1674. Mary m. 1670, Daniel Hall; and Sarah, m. 24 June 1657, Thomas Trowbridge.

ROUNDY, ROUNDEE, or ROUNDAY, PHILIP, Salem, m. Nov. 1671, Ann Bush, and d. 1678, for his inv. of est. £7.10.6 only, was tak. 24 June of that yr. Mary R. perhaps his d. m. 19 Apr. 1695, Thomas Walter. Perhaps Mark Round, one of the soldiers under Capt. Hill, against E. Ind. 1699, was his s.

ROUS, ROUSE, or ROWSE, ALEXANDER, prob. of Cambridge, bef. Groton, by w. Judith, m. 15 May 1672, had Judith and Eliz. tw. b. 2 Feb. 1673, both d. soon; Eliz. again, d. soon; and Sarah, 26 July 1686. Butler. EDWARD, Gloucester 1651. FAITHFUL, Charlestown 1641, adm. of the ch. 1 July 1643, his w. Suretrust hav. join. the yr. bef. and d. Mercy in Dec. aft. him; was freem. 1644, and d. 18 May 1664, aged 75; in his will of 9 Apr. pro. 21 June foll. names w. S. and d. M. Sweat, prob. w. of John. JOHN, Duxbury, m. Annis, d. of John Peabody, had Mary, b. 1640, wh. m. a Price; John, 1643; Simon, 1645; George, 1648; Ann, wh. m. 1678, Isaac Holmes; and Eliz. wh. m. 10 Apr. 1681, Thomas Bourne, and d. 9 Apr. 1701. His will, Winsor says, was of 1682. He liv. in Marshfield chiefly, and there d. 1684; but Deane claims him, prob. by mistake, for some time, at Scituate, where he should suffer whip. and banishm. as a quaker, but came back 1658. JOHN, Marshfield, s. prob. of the preced. m. 13 Jan. 1675, Eliz. Dotey; and d. Oct. 1717. *SIMON, Little Compton 1691, a rep. unless this distinct. belongs to S. Rowley. WILLIAM, Boston, goldsmith, by w. Sarah had Mary, b. 20 Sept. 1676; William, 25 May 1678; and d. 1705 in 65th yr. WILLIAM, Boston, prob. s. of the preced. mariner, charged, with sev. others, in 1706, for a high misdemean. in trad. with the enemy, and on imprison. was, by Ch. Just. Sewall, refus. his habeas corpus, suffer. a yr. and a half in gaol. Prob. this was to spite Gov. Dudley, against

whom bitter railing and false report were raised out of the circumstances.
See the official papers in 2 Mass. Hist. Coll. VIII. 240 ; Hutch. II.
154–162 ; and the wonderful letters of Increase and Cotton Mather to
D. with his reply in 1 Mass. Hist. Coll. III. 126–137. Sewall relates
in his Diary, that his min. the famous Ebenezer Pemberton, wh. we may
suspect that the parishioner had favored with a perusal, said to him, that
"if he were Gov. he would humble Cotton Mather, tho. it cost him his
head." In our whole Provinc. hist. nothing is more curious than the
outcry a. trad. with the enemy at this time, and the results, partly cruel,
partly ridiculous.

ROWDEN, JOHN, Salem 1652–68, m. aft. Aug. 1676, the wid. of Richard Hammond, k. at that time, with Capt. Lake, by the Ind. at Kennebeck. See petitn. of his w. to Sir Edmund Andros, for redress in the
destruct. of the prop. by Major Waldron. 3 Mass. Hist. Coll. VII. 181.

ROWE, HUGH, Gloucester, s. of John, m. 10 June 1667, Rachel
Langdon, had Rachel, b. 10 Nov. 1668 ; Ruth, 26 Jan. 1671 ; and Mary,
5 Feb. 1674. His w. d. 7 of next mo. and he m. 10 Sept. foll. Mary, d.
of Thomas Prince, had next yr. Margaret, wh. d. soon ; Abigail, 19 Dec.
1677 ; and ano. d. besides Joseph ; Benjamin ; Abraham, 26 Apr. 1689 ;
Isaac ; and Jacob. JOHN, Duxbury, early took o. of fidel. says Winsor ;
but when was early is not told, nor any thing else. I suspect the name
means Rowse. JOHN, Gloucester 1651, d. 9 Mar. 1662 ; in his will of
15 Oct. 1661, pro. 24 June foll. names w. Bridget, and s. John, and
Hugh, the latter call. 20 yrs. old in 1665. The wid. m. 14 Nov.
1662, William Colman, outliv. him a fortnight, d. 2 May 1640. JOHN,
Gloucester, elder br. of Hugh, freem. 1673, m. 27 Sept. 1663, Mary
Dickinson, d. perhaps of Philemon, had John, b. Apr. 1665 ; James,
25 Dec. 1666 ; Thomas, 26 Nov. 1668 ; Mary, 11 Feb. 1671 ; Eliz.
21 May 1673 ; Stephen, 26 Sept. 1675 ; Samuel, 26 Mar. 1678 ; Ebenezer, 19 Aug. 1680 ; and Andrew, 1683, wh. d. at 17 yrs. His w. d.
25 Apr. 1684 ; and he m. 1 Sept. foll. Sarah Redington, wh. d. 15 Feb.
1701, by wh. he had four more ch. of wh. only Rebecca outliv. youth.
The f. d. 25 Sept. 1700. JOHN, New Haven, s. of Matthew, m. 14 July
1680, Abigail, d. of Joseph Alsop, had John, b. 23 Oct. 1681 ; Matthew,
14 Feb. 1684 ; Stephen, 1 July 1687 ; Abigail, 13 Aug. 1689 ; Hannah
11 Feb. 1691 ; and Sarah, 15 Oct. 1700. MATTHEW, New Haven, had
Eliz. b. Jan. 1651 ; Daniel, Jan. 1652 ; both d. young ; John, 30 Apr.
1654 ; Hannah, Aug. 1656 ; Joseph, Nov. 1658 ; both d. young ; and
Stephen, 28 Aug. 1660 ; and d. 27 May 1662. MOSES, Boston, d. Jan.
1663, prob. unm. NICHOLAS, Portsmouth 1640, had w. Eliz. RICHARD,
Dover, 1650, had Thomas ; Edward ; and Jane, wh. m. John Dame.
THOMAS, Hampton, 1678. Prob. some of this name may be spell. Roe,
and oft. Row. A goodman R. at Bristol, 1689, had ten ch.

Rowell, Jacob, Amesbury, had Moses, b. 29 Nov. 1699. Nathaniel, Salisbury 1650. Philip, Amesbury 1677. Thomas, Ipswich 1652-8, had been of Salem 1649, Salisbury 1650, and m. Margery, wid. of the first Christopher Osgood, wh. aft. d. of R. m. Thomas Coleman of Nantucket; perhaps d. at Andover, 8 May 1662. Thomas, Boston, worsted comber, where prob. he resid. very short time, made his will, 10 Sept. 1658. Valentine, Salisbury, m. 14 Nov. 1643, Joanna Pinder, d. I presume, of Henry, had John, b. 1645, d. young; Philip, 8 Mar. 1648; Mary, 31 Jan. 1650; Sarah, 16 Nov. 1651; and John, again, wh. d. 18 Feb. 1656; was a carpenter, and d. 17 May 1662.

Rowland, Henry, Fairfield 1650-70, freem. 1669, perhaps was f. of that Eliz. wh. a. 1640, m. James Rogers; and certain. his d. Rebecca m. Eleazer Smith. In his will he names four ds. Eliz. Wheeler, wh. had been w. of James Rogers; Abigail, w. of Thomas Jones; Rebecca Smith; and Mary, w. of Daniel Frost. He d. in 1691; and Jonathan, wh. left a wid. and Henry wh. was unm. both his s. d. the same yr. John, Hingham, but possib. may be ano. spelling, for somebody, unless he were that Plymouth man of 1632, whose bapt. name in the tax of Jan. 1633, is lost. Joseph, Fairfield, s. prob. of Henry, was 43 yrs. old in Sept 1691. Richard, Salem 1648, was of Marblehead 1673 and 4. His w. was Mary, d. of James Smith, and ch. Samuel, Mary, Joseph, and two more. Samuel, Stratford, may have been f. of Henry, but possib. his d. Eliz. m. bef. 1640 James Rogers, to whose eldest s. Samuel he gave large est. Five of this name had been gr. at Yale, in 1829, and three at other N. E. coll. none at Harv.

Rowlandson, Joseph, Lancaster, s. of Thomas, b. prob. in Eng. was the first min. there, the sole grad. of 1652 at Harv. in two yrs. went to L. to preach, but was not ord. bef. 1660, tho. highly reput. m. Mary, d. of John White, a woman of uncommon discretion and firmness, as her Narrative of that doleful captivity wh. foll. the assault by the Ind. 10 Feb. 1676, when one or more of the fam. were k. and the rest taken exc. hims. wh. had gone to Boston for succor, most fully exhib. They had Joseph, wh. d. soon; Joseph, again, b. 2 Mar. 1662; Mary, 1666; Sarah, 1669; perhaps one or two more; for her distress leaves some indistinctness in the story of her fate. Aft. the utter destruct. of his town, he preach. in Boston and elsewhere, tho. unsett. until call. to Wethersfield Apr. 1677, where his time was but short, d. 23 or 24 Nov. 1678. Of the curious work of Mrs. R. usual. call. the Removes, Mr. Willard in 1828, pub. the sixth edit. with copious illustration, and some strange matter of youthful indiscret. in the h. He had, of all his fam. only w. and Joseph, and Mary, liv. at the time of his d. The books in his inv. were val. at £82, wh. must be regard. as extraord. amt. after so short a time from his loss.

JOSEPH, Wethersfield, s. of the preced. m. Hannah, d. of Phineas Wilson, had large prop. with her, wh. d. 1704, aged 29. He d. 22 Jan. 1713, leav. descend. there for above a century. THOMAS, Ipswich 1637, freem. 2 May 1638, then spell. Rawlinson, as oft. in town rec. it is Rolenson, had Thomas, Joseph, and perhaps other ch. some, if not all, b. in Eng. d. at Lancaster 17 Nov. 1657. THOMAS, Salisbury, s. of the preced. b. in Eng. m. 17 May 1653 or 4, as the rec. says, Dorothy Portland, tho. where this name was found, is quite a mystery to me, had Eliz. b. 7 June 1654, d. next yr. Thomas, 5 July 1656; Sarah, 5 Aug. 1658; Eliz. again, 26 Feb. 1661; Joseph, 18 Feb. 1664; Mary, 24 Aug. 1665; Martha, 24 Aug. 1666; John, 20 Mar. 1668; and Ann, 16 Mar. 1669. His will of 7 July 1682, just bef. his d. names s. Joseph and four ds. Sarah m. 5 Dec. 1684, Nicholas Bond.

ROWLE, RICHARD, ins. among inhab. of Newbury 1678, in Geneal. Reg. VII. 349, is by me confid. thot. to be mispr. for Lowle or Lowell, because the age is 76, wh. is the exact number of yrs. of Lowell then liv. at N. and his name does not appear in that list. ROBERT, Marblehead 1668.

ROWLEY, HENRY, Plymouth 1632, perhaps came in the Charles, with Hatherly, was of Scituate 1634, with his w. partook in gather. of first ch. there, 8 Jan. 1635, and rem. to Barnstable with Lathrop 1639, m. 17 Oct. 1633, Ann, wid. of Thomas Blossom, prob. as his sec. w. for I suppose Sarah, wh. m. 11 Apr. 1646, Jonathan Hatch, was his d. JOSEPH, Barnstable 1655, perhaps was s. of the preced. *MOSES, Barnstable, br. perhaps of the preced. m. 22 Apr. 1652, Eliz. Fuller, had Mary, b. 20 Mar. 1653; Moses, 10 Nov. 1654; a ch. b. and d. 15 Aug. 1656; Shubael and Mehitable, tw. 11 Jan. 1660; Sarah, 10 Sept. 1662; Aaron, 1 May 1666; John, 2 Oct. 1667; was rep. 1692, prob. under new chart. rem. to Haddam, there d. 1705, leav. wid. Eliz. and ch. Moses, Matthew, and Mehitable, w. of John Fuller. SHUBAEL, East Haddam, s. of Moses, d. in Mar. 1714, leav. wid. Catharine, d. of Thomas Crippin, and she, 5 Feb. 1719, in deed, calls Edward Fuller her s.-in-law. *SIMON, Little Compton, rep. 1691, by Baylies, IV. 142, call. perhaps correct. Rouse. THOMAS, Windsor, m. 5 May 1669, Mary, d. of Henry Denslow, had Mary, b. 16 Apr. 1670; Martha, 13 May 1677; John, 27 Oct. 1679; Abigail, 10 Feb. 1686; and Grace, 5 Aug. 1692; beside Thomas, and Samuel, whose dates, prob. intermed. are unkn. He was freem. 1669, and d. 4 Aug. 1708. THOMAS, Windsor, s. of the preced. m. 16 Mar. 1699, Violet Stedman, had Hannah, b. 5 July 1700, d. young; Ann, 24 Sept. 1703; Thomas, 5 Dec. 1705; Sarah, 17 Sept. 1708; Samuel, 11 Mar. 1710; Daniel, 11 Oct. 1717; and Hannah, again, 11 Feb. 1720. Sometimes the name is Rowell in the rec.

Rowton, Richard, came 1635, in the Susan and Ellen from London, aged 36, with w. Ann, 36, and ch. Edmund, 6. He is call. in the Eng. rec. husbandman, but I hear not of him on this side of the water. See 3 Mass. Hist. Coll. VIII. 260, with correct. in X. 128 ; but also in Geneal. Reg. XIV. 311.

Roy, John, Charlestown, by w. Eliz. Phipps, prob. d. of Solomon, had there bapt. Eliz. 9 Oct. 1670 ; Solomon, 16 Feb. 1673 ; Mary, 7 Mar. 1675, perhaps d. soon ; and Mary, 22 Aug. 1680.

Royal, or Ryall, Iaac, Dorchester, carpenter, m. Ruth, d. of Thomas Tolman, had Ruth, b. 2 Nov. 1668 ; Mary, 8 Sept. 1670 ; Samuel, 21 July 1677 ; and William, 17 Mar. 1680 ; built the new ch. edifice 1676, and bo. the old one for £10, tho. the new was not occup. bef. Nov. 1678 ; was freem. 1690, but the w. d. 1 May 1681, and by ano. w. he had, says Geneal. Reg. XIV. 249, Isaac, 10 May 1682 ; Jerusha, 15 Jan. 1684 ; and Robert, Jan. 1688. John, York, s. of William the first, m. Eliz. Dodd ; was there in 1680, to take o. of alleg. to the k. but in 1688 was tak. by the Ind. at North Yarmouth ; yet was liv. in Boston, 1695. Joseph, Charlestown, by w. Mary had one ch. bapt. 21 Jan. 1683, she hav. join. the ch. the wk. bef. and a d. 15 July foll. but neither of these nam. in the rec. yet one was Sarah prob. beside Phebe, 16 June 1690 ; was of Boston 1695. Sarah, m. William Tyler. Samuel, Boston 1665, br. of John, a cooper, had w. Sarah, and was rememb. in the will of Samuel Cole. William, Casco 1636, had been sent by the Gov. and Comp. to Capt. Endicott at Salem from London, as noted in their letter to him, 17 Apr. 1629, as a "cleaver of timber." See Young's Chron. of Mass. 164, or the noble first quarto of our Col. Rec. 396. Part of the town of S. was early call. Ryall side, or Ryall neck. He purch. of Gorges 1643, on E. side of Wescustogo, now Royall's riv. in North Yarmouth, and liv. near its mouth, m. perhaps at Boston, or Malden, Phebe Green, d. of that wid. Margaret, wh. bec. sec. w. of Samuel Cole of B. had William, b. 1640 ; John ; and Samuel. To this last, out of regard for his gr.mo. Cole gave, in 1653, an est. in B. and confirm. it in his will. In 1673, he convey. his E. principality to s. William and John, for support dur. life of self and w. See Willis I. 195. William, North Yarmouth, s. of the preced. was driv. by the Ind. to the W. and at Dorchester spent some yrs. freem. 1678, and d. 7 Nov. 1724. He had Isaac, b. a. 1672, and other childr. but their names are not kn. nor their fortunes, exc. that one d. m. Amos Stevens of North Yarmouth ; that Jemima, d. of William and Mary, aged 17, d. at Dorchester, 9 Nov. 1709 ; and that the eldest s. aft. near 40 yrs. resid. in Antigua, came home, July 1737, and d. at his beautiful resid. in Medford, 7 June 1739. His s. Isaac was chos. a Provinc. Counsel, and serv. a

long period as rep. but standing for the crown, on the outburst of the
revo. he went to Eng. and d. Oct. 1781. Sabine says, in Amer. Loyalists, 582, that his prop. was confiscat. If so, the claws of the harpies
employ. did not reach all, for he enjoy. a patriot gentleman's revenge,
and show. his resentment in making gift of more than 2,000 acres in
Worcester Co. to Harv. Coll. where he had not been educ. as foundat.
of the Royall Professorship of Law.

ROYCE. See Roise.

ROYLE, GABRIEL, Plymouth 1643, unless this be, as I fear, a
misprint.

RUCK, * JOHN, Salem, s. of Thomas of the same, b. in Eng. m.
Hannah, d. of Thomas Spooner of the same, had bapt. there Eliz. and
Hannah, 18 May 1655; Sarah, 17 Dec. 1656; John, 6 Sept. 1657;
Thomas, 16 June 1659; and Mary, 6 Aug. 1665; beside Rebecca, wh.
m. 1689, John Appleton; was freem. 1665, in 1684 was aged 57, rep.
1685, 90 and 1; selectman 1686. He m. for sec. w. Eliz. wid. of John
Croade, d. of Walter Price, but in Vol. II. 127 and 184 of Essex Inst.
Hist. Coll. his name is giv. Burke. Hannah m. 24 Oct. 1676, Ben-
jamin Gerrish. He had the unhap. distinct. of being foreman of that gr.
jury wh. found one of the *five* indictm. against Bridget Bishop, the first
suffer. under the infernal delusion of 1692. See Mather brief extr.
from Hale, more full in Calef, best in Essex Inst. II. 139. SAMUEL,
Boston, was freem. 1683, and possib. was again sw. 1690. THOMAS,
Charlestown 1638, rem. with w. to Salem, freem. 13 May 1640, had
Stephen, bapt. 17 Apr. 1642, and prob. others, d. 1670, as did, I suppose,
his wid. for her inv. was tak. in Nov. of that yr. THOMAS, innholder at
Boston 1651, m. 22 July 1656, Margaret Clark, and in 1675 had w. Eliz.
and ch. of these sev. ages: Eliz. 18, being b. 11 May 1657; Thomas, 16,
b. 9 July 1659; Sarah, 14; Abigail, 11; Peter, 9, wh. was H. C. 1685;
John, 6; and Margaret, 4. THOMAS, Boston, s. of Thomas of the same, d.
in Eng. a 1652, in his will made there, of wh. admin. was giv. 16 June
1653, names f. Thomas, sis. Joane, w. of George Halsey, and Samuel and
John, perhaps cous. of Salem. It is impossible, I fear, exactly to discrimin. these Rucks.

RUDD, JONATHAN, New Haven, perhaps 1640, certain. took o. of
fidel. 1 Oct. 1644, Saybrook 1646, adm. freem. 1651 at Hartford, m. in
the winter of 1647, by John Winth. of New London, wh. act. under
commis. from Mass. there, and made the young couple meet him half
way, bec. the snow was so deep, and he had no authority at S. See
Trumbull, Col. Rec. II. 558. Miss Caulkins, New London 48, tells the
story, with docum. in full, and has also commemo. it in verse. He prob.
d. 1668. His d. Patience m. 7 Oct. 1675, Samuel Bushnell. Other ch.

prob. were Mary, suppos, first b. wh. m. 12 Dec. 1666, Thomas Bingham; Jonathan; and Nathaniel. JONATHAN, Norwich, prob. s. of the preced. by w. Mercy, m. 19 Dec. 1678, had Mercy, b. 8 Oct. 1679; Jonathan, 18 Mar. 1682; Nathaniel, 22 May 1684; Mary, 15 Oct. 1686; and Abigail, 2 Feb. 1688. NATHANIEL, Norwich, prob. br. of the preced. m. 16 Apr. 1685, Mary Post, had Jonathan, b. 22 May 1693; Mary, 3 Feb. 1696; Lydia, 22 June 1697; and his w. d. Nov. 1705. By sec. w. m. 31 Jan. 1706, he had Nathaniel, 6 Apr. 1707; Joseph, 31 Oct. 1708; and eight more ch. and he d. Apr. 1727.

RUDDOCK, or RUDDYK, JOLLIFF, Boston, perhaps s. of John, d. Sept. 1649. JOHN, Sudbury, freem. 13 May 1640, one of the first sett. at Marlborough, and town clk. 1660, also deac. The Ruddock fam. I think of Trowbridge, Wilts.

RUEL, JOHN, Saco, m. 1668, Emma, d. of William Seely.

RUGG, DANIEL, Lancaster, s. of John, m. 1704, Eliz. Priest. JOHN, Maine, sw. alleg. to the king 1665. JOHN, Lancaster 1654, freem. 1669, by first w. Martha Prescott, d. of John, wh. d. soon aft. hav. 1655, two ch. wh. both d. m. 4 May 1660, sec. w. Hannah, had John, b. 4 June 1662; Mercy, 11 July 1664; Thomas, 15 Sept. 1666; Joseph, 15 Dec. 1668; Hannah, 2 Jan. 1671; Rebecca, 16 May 1673; Daniel, 15 Nov. 1678; and Jonathan, 10 Feb. 1681; d. a. 1696, at least his will was pro. that yr. and next yr. his wid. was k. by the Ind. Hannah m. 1690, John Ball; and Rebecca m. Nathaniel Hudson. JOHN, Lancaster, s. of the preced. by w. Eliz. had John, wh. d. young; Samuel; Nathaniel, b. 1701; David'; Jonathan; Benjamin; Mary; and Abigail. He d. 1712. JONATHAN, Marlborough, youngest br. of the preced. m. Sarah, d. of John Newton, had Bathsheba, b. 26 Oct. 1703; rem. to Framingham, and had Sarah, 2 Oct. 1705; Hepzibah, 18 Jan. 1708; Abraham, 27 Apr. 1710; and his w. d. 7 May foll. He m. 11 Dec. aft. Hannah, d. of Nathaniel Singletary, had Mehitable, 15 Sept. 1711; Hannah, 28 Nov. 1713; Jonathan, 27 Nov. 1716, d. young; John, 10 June 1718; Ebenezer, 22 July 1720; and Jonathan, again, a. 1722. He had third w. Eliz. liv. at his d. 25 Dec. 1753. JOSEPH, Lancaster, br. of the preced. with his w. and three ch. and his mo. Hannah, was k. by the Ind. 1697. ROBERT, Conn. 1646, of wh. no more is kn. but that he was then bound to keep the peace. Perhaps he was a trans. person. THOMAS, Lancaster, s. of John the first, by w. Eliz. had Thomas, b. 6 Dec. 1691; William, 16 Nov. 1693; Eliz. 20 Jan. 1695; Hannah, 26 Apr. 1697; Abigail, 15 Mar. 1699; Sarah, 12 Feb. 1702; Mary, 30 May 1703; Ruth, Sept. 1706; Tabitha, 10 Sept. 1708; Milicent, 11 Nov. 1710; and Martha, 10 Nov. 1713. Barry thinks he liv. at Lexington. This name belongs to an anc. fam. in Co. Norf. Eng. two of whom, says Lord Braybrooke, were aldermen of Norwich.

Ruggles, Benjamin, Suffield, s. of the fourth John, but third of Roxbury, had seven ch. to leave when he d. 7 Sept. 1708, only 32 yrs. old. George, Boston 1633, weaver, freem. 4 Mar. 1634, by w. Eliz. had Eliz. bapt. 8 Dec. 1633; Mary, 3 Jan. 1636; John, 31 Dec. 1637; rem. to Braintree, there had George, b. 5 May 1640, d. next yr.; Rachel, 15 Feb. 1643; Sarah, 29 Sept. 1645; Samuel, 3 Mar. 1649; and Mehitable, 16 July 1650; came back to Boston and d. bef. 1670, when his wid. gave her share to his d. Sarah, wid. of John Wilmot, mariner. His d. Eliz. m. 24 Apr. 1655, William Brown, and Rachel m. Philip Squire. Jeffrey, Boston, arr. in the fleet with Gov. Winth. 1630, and d. bef. the yr. end. He was from Sudbury in Co. Suff. and therefore had been a near neighb. in their native ld. had w. Margaret, wh. was No. 47 on our list of ch. mem. John, Boston 1630, freem. 3 July 1632, had w. Frances, No. 37 among ch. mem. and a d. wh. d. Jan. 1631, aged 11 yrs. of wh. Gov. Dudley writes well. See in Prince II. 17 and 69. Whether he had other ch. or when he d. are unkn. but his inv. was of 22 Jan. 1657. Perhaps he was br. of the preced. * John, Roxbury, came in the Hopewell, capt. Bundock, from London 1635, aged 44, with w. Barbara, 30, and first b. ch. John, 2; a shoemaker from Nazing in Co. Essex, a. 20 ms. from London, was freem. 18 Apr. 1637. His w. d. Jan. 1638, in giv. b. to a stillb. ch. and to a sec. w. Margaret, by wh. he had no ch. he gave half his est. was rep. 1658, 60, and 1, and d. 6 Oct. 1663. His will that names only ch. John, was pro. Jan. foll. John, Roxbury, s. of Thomas, b. in Eng. came in the Hopewell, 1635, aged 10, with his uncle John, but brot. by Philip Eliot, says the ch. rec. m. 24 Jan. 1651, Abigail, d. of Griffin Crafts, had John, b. 16 Oct. foll. d. soon; John, again, bapt. 22 Jan. 1654; Thomas, 28 Jan. 1655, H. C. 1690, and Samuel, b. 16, bapt. 23 Aug. 1657; was freem. 1654; a serg. and d. or was bur. 15 Sept, 1658. In his will of 9 Aug. preced. print. in Geríeal. Reg. IX. 139, he names the w. and three ch. His wid. m. Edward Adams. John, Roxbury, s. of the first John of the same, b. in Eng. m. 3 Apr. 1655, Mary, d. of John Gibson of Cambridge, had John, b. 19 May 1657; Mary, bapt. with her br. John, 30 Jan. 1659, the w. hav. join. to the ch. the week bef. Rebecca, b. 20, bapt. 28 Sept. 1662; Joseph, 25, bapt. 26 Dec. 1669; was freem. 1674. His w. d. 6 Dec. 1674, as with gr. minuteness Eliot tells in his ch. rec. and 15 Mar. aft. he m. Sarah Dyer of Weymouth, had Benjamin, b. 11 Aug. 1676, H. C. 1693, the min. of Suffield. His w. d. 2 May 1687, and he took third w. Ruth, wh. d. 11 Apr. 1710, and he d. 25 Feb. 1712. Perhaps his d. Mary m. 6 June 1682, John Searle. John, Boston, a butcher, s. of George, freem. 1663, rem. in his latter days to Braintree, in his will of 10 Nov. 1707, pro. 11 Nov. 1709, gave s. John his est. in Boston, and

the rest of his prop. to s. Joseph, d. Eliz. Belcher, s. in law, Jonathan
Hayward, and gr.ch. Sarah H. s. in law Jonathan Jones, and gr.ch. Sarah and Ruth J. w. Rebecca, and gr.ch. John Ruggles.   JOHN, Roxbury,
s. of John sec. of the same, a miller, m. 2 Sept. 1674, Martha, d. of Edward Devotion, had Abigail, b. 5 June, 1675; his w. d. and he m. 1
May 1679, her sis. Hannah, had John, 16 Mar. 1680; Edward, 16 Nov.
1683, d. young; Rebecca, 14 Mar. 1685; Martha, 21 Dec. 1686; or
Sarah, 28 Feb. 1687; perhaps Dorothy, 20 Feb. 1688; and Edward,
again, 2 Oct. 1691.   He d. 16 Dec. 1694; and his wid. d. 17 Dec. 1700,
but one tradit. is that she m. a Paine. Perhaps he liv. at Muddy riv.
and so the Roxbury rec. was neglect.   JOHN, Roxbury, s. of John third
of the same, m. 4 Nov. 1676, Mary, d. of John May, had Mary, b. 24
Sept. foll. d. young; Hannah, 15 July 1680; Mary, again, 23, bapt. 25
Dec. 1681; Sarah, 28 Feb. 1687, unless it should be Martha, 21 Dec.
1686; and perhaps Dorothy, 20 Feb. 1688; and I am unable to discrimin.
by the rec.   Great care was need. among the earlier Johns; but of the
last two, I kn. not wh. was the freem. of 1690.   Four, five or six differ-
ent ones are call. junrs. and sometimes both deaths and marriages are in-
adeq. guides; for I greatly fear that both Hannah and Martha, ws. of
one or the other John, as also part of their childr. respective. are here
interchangeab. confus.   NATHANIEL, Boston, a mariner, whose f. I cannot trace, unless he were s. of Samuel the first of Roxbury, in his will
of wh. I discov. not the date, but it was pro. 15 Dec. 1702, aft. commit.
his "soul into the hands of my Creator and Redeemer the Ld. Jesus
Christ," a strange confusion of terms guarded against by the creed of
St. Athanasius, he gives to his "mo. Ann and to Sarah Paine, my
intend. w. all my est. in R." and makes Joseph Belknap jr. and William
Paine excors.   * SAMUEL, Roxbury, s. of Thomas, brot. from Eng. by
his f. m. 10 Jan. 1655, Hannah, d. of George Fowle of Charlestown, had
Hannah, b. 21 Jan. 1656, d. in few wks.; Mary, 10 Jan. 1657, d. young;
Samuel, 1 Jan. bapt. 20 Feb. 1659, the f. hav. join. the ch. the wk. bef.;
Joseph, 12, bapt. 19 Feb. 1660; Hannah, again, perhaps 2, bapt. 22
Dec. 1661; Sarah, 18, bapt. 22 Nov. 1663, d. next yr.; Mary, again, 8
Dec. 1666, bapt. next day; and Sarah, again, 30 Aug. bapt. 5 Sept.
1669; in that yr. his w. d. 24 Oct. and d. Hannah d. on 6 Nov. and d.
Sarah d. on 16 Nov. of the same yr.   He m. 26 May 1670, Ann, d. of
Henry Bright of Watertown, had Thomas, b. 10, bapt. 12 Mar. 1671;
Ann, 30 Sept. bapt. 6 Oct. 1672; Nathaniel, 22, bapt. 29 Nov. 1674, d.
young; Eliz. b. 1 May, 1677; Henry, 7 July 1681 d. at 21 yrs.; and
Huldah, 4, bapt. 6 July 1684; was lieut. rep. 1689–92, and d. 15 Aug.
1692; and his wid. d. 5 Sept. 1711.   SAMUEL, Boston, s. of George,
a weaver, in his will of 22 Dec. 1689, pro. 12 June 1697, names w.

Sarah, s. John, Samuel, and Jeremiah, and sis. Mehitable Richards. SAMUEL, Roxbury, s. of Samuel of the same, m. 8 July 1680, Martha Woodbridge, d. of Rev. John, had Samuel, b. 3 Dec. 1681, H. C. 1702, min. of Billerica; Lucy, 8 Sept. 1683; Timothy, 3 Nov. 1685, H. C. 1707, min. of Rochester; Hannah, 16 Apr. 1688; Patience 9 Nov. 1689; Martha, 1 Feb. 1692; Sarah, 18 June 1694, or Jan. 1695; Joseph, 21 July 1696; Mary, 20 Sept. 1698; and Benjamin, 4 July 1700, Y. C. 1721, min. of Middleborough; and d. 25 Feb. 1716. His wid. d. 1738, at her son's in Billerica. THOMAS, Roxbury, elder br. of John first of the same, and prob. cousin of the first John of Boston, came in 1637, with w. Mary, and ch. Sarah, and Samuel; their first s. had d. in Eng. and the next, John, was brot. two yrs. bef. by Philip Eliot; freem. 22 May 1639; d. 15 Nov. 1644. His will, made six ds. bef. gives est. to w. and ch. John, Samuel, and Sarah. In his rec. of the ch. Eliot inserts his name, among the bur. next to that of John Graves, and adds, "he d. of a consumpt. These two brake the knot of the Nazing Christians that came from that town in Eng." There, he had been, prob. their spiritual guide. Mary the wid. of Thomas, m. aft. 1662, a Roote, whose name of bapt. is unkn. and of her, at the date of her bur. 14 Feb. 1675, Eliot writes thus: "Old mo. Roote, wh. was Thomas Ruggles' wid. afore. She lived not only till past use, but till more tedious than a child. She was in her 89th yr." THOMAS, Guilford, s. of John the sec. of Roxbury, ord. 1695, had Thomas, Y. C. 1723; and other ch. for this, wh. succeed his f. in that pulpit, call. hims. eldest s. d. 1 June 1728. Sixteen of this name in 1834, had been gr. at the N. E. Coll.

RUM. See Ram.

RUMBALL, DANIEL, Salem 1644–1666, blacksmith, had 80 acres of ld. laid out 5 Feb. 1644, was liv. 1681. THOMAS, Stratford, came to Boston in the Truelove, 1635, aged 22, was out in the Pequot war next yr. under Lyon Gardiner, so we may believe he was of Saybrook at that time. His d. Bethia m. 12 June 1661, Robert Stewart of Norwalk, as Hall, 186, tells.

RUMRILL, RUMERELL, or RUMMERELL, SIMON, Enfield, m. Feb. 1692, Sarah Fairman, had Sarah, b. Feb. 1693; Simon, 1696; Ebenezer, 1701; and John, 1704; perhaps more. See Hinman 18.

RUMNY, or RUMSIE, ROBERT, Fairfield, bef. 1670, had a fam. there cont. af. 1700. THOMAS, Boston 1678, an impostor, m. 1 July 1679, Rebecca, d. of our Secr. Edward Rawson, carr. her to London, and there abandon. her immed. See Coffin's Newbury, 398, or Geneal. Reg. III. 298.

RUNDLE, WILLIAM, Greenwich 1672.

RUNDLET, RUNLET, or RANLET, CHARLES, Exeter, tak. by the Ind. 1675, was permit. to esc. and was drown. 1 Aug. 1709.

Rusco, Reskie, Reskoe, or Rescue, John, Norwalk, perhaps s. of William, b. in Eng. m. at Hartford, 2 Jan. 1651, Rebecca Beebe, had in 1672 five ch. but their names or dates are unkn. exc. one, perhaps Thomas, wh. with f. was liv. 1694. Nathaniel, Hartford, br. prob. elder of the preced. b. in Eng. m. 11 Nov. 1645, Joanna Corlet, if the surname be not mistak. had Nathaniel, was freem. 1654, a surveyor 1661, d. 1673. Nathaniel, Hartford, s. of the preced. was propound. for freem. 1668. William, Cambridge, came in the Increase, 1635, aged 41, with w. Rebecca, 40; and ch. Sarah, 9; Mary, 7; Samuel, 5; and William, 1; his w. d. early, perhaps on the voyage, and in 1636 he m. wid. Esther Musse or Must, rem. early to Hartford, where he was an orig. propr. had Samuel, again, b. 12 Mar. 1648, and kept the prison in 1650. He came from Billericay in Co. Essex. His d. Sarah m. 10 Dec. 1646, Henry Cole; and Mary m. 19 Aug. 1647, Hugh Wells.

Rush, Jasper, Dorchester, freem. 1644, by w. Eliz. had Preserved, b. 24 Sept. 1651; Eliz. 24 Oct. 1653, d. at 4 yrs. and Thankful, 21 Oct. 1657, d. next mo. He m. sec. w. Judith, 24 Mar. 1664, and d. 23 Feb. 1669.

Rushmore, Thomas, Hempstead, L. I. 1663, was under jurisdict. of Conn. but would not serve as constable.

Russ, John, Newbury 1635, had perhaps Nathaniel, b. a. 1640; John, 24 June 1641; Mary, 16 Feb. 1644; rem. next yr. to Andover, there had Jonathan, Thomas, Josiah, and Joseph. His w. Margaret d. 10 July 1689, and he d. 4 Mar. 1692, aged 80. Mary m. 7 June 1662, Andrew Foster. John, Andover, s. of the preced. prob. the freem. of 1691, m. 20 Aug. 1663, Deborah Osgood, perhaps d. of John, had Joseph, wh. d. 10 June 1687; prob. Sarah, and other ch. Richard, a soldier, perhaps of Weymouth, was wound. in 1675, in the fight when Capt. Lathrop was k. and was reliev. of the bullet by a Dutch surgeon in 1678.

Russell, Benjamin, Cambridge, 1670, s. of William, by w. Rebecca had Rebecca, wh. d. 2 Feb. 1673; Jason, 10 May 1674; Benjamin, b. and d. Apr. 1676; Joyce, 14 May 1677; and Sarah, 4 July 1679; perhaps rem. soon aft. 1694. Daniel, Charlestown, sec. s. of Richard, freem. 1676, was a preach. aft. leav. coll. for a short time perhaps at New London, in 1675, where his townsman Bradstreet was the min. and invit. to sett. at his native town 1678, but d. 4 Jan. of next yr. He had m. a. 1676, Mehitable, d. of Samuel Willis of Hartford, and had only ch. Mehitable, wh. had from him good est. and m. Rev. John Hubbard of Jamaica, L. I. 12 June 1701; and aft. him m. 9 Dec. 1707, Rev. Samuel Woodbridge. Her mo. m. 1680, Rev. Isaac Foster, and next, his successor in the parish, Rev. Timothy Woodbridge as his first w.

An elegy on the d. of Daniel is preserv. ELIEZUR, Boston, goldsmith, s. of Rev. John of Hadley, d. late in 1690, unm. as we judge, for his will of 26 Dec. in that yr. names not w. or ch. but gives all to Rebecca, d. of his br. Jonathan of Barnstable, and Ch. J. Sewall notes his funeral on 2 Jan. foll. GEORGE, Hingham 1636, came in the Elizabeth from London, 1635, aged 19, was of Hawkhurst, Co. Kent, m. 14 Feb. 1640, Jane, wid. of Philip James, had Mary, bapt. 1 Apr. 1641; Eliz. Feb. 1643; and Martha, 9 Oct. 1645; rem. to Scituate next yr. had, also, George and Samuel, b. to him by first w. and he d. prob. at Hingham, says Deane, bef. 1668. GEORGE, Scituate, s. of the preced. m. a Rogers, d. of John of Duxbury, d. 1675, leav. s. George and John. GEORGE, Boston 1679, youngest s. prob. of William, fifth Earl of Bedford, and created first Duke of B. 1694, had been bred at Magdalen Col. Oxford, as Wood's Fasti shows, taking his A. M. Feb. 1667, by order of our Gen. Ct. 4 Feb. 1680, adm. freem. "if he please to accept," and the rec. says that 13 Feb. foll. he took the o. bef. the Gov. and Assist. but prob. went home bef. the execut. in 1683, of his br. the celebr. martyr, Lord William, m. Mary Pendleton, the d. of a London merch. and d. 1692, leav. s. William, who d. unm. See the note in Hutch. I. 332, and Collins's Peerage, Vol. I. 268, of Ed. 5. HENRY, Weymouth 1639, made his will 28 Jan. 1640, pro. 9 Oct. foll. names w. Jane, and only ch. Eliz. HENRY, Ipswich 1665, said then to be 55 yrs. old. He was possib. of Salisbury 1652, perhaps of Marblehead 1668–1674, tho. I think this was much younger man, the br. of John, wh. in his will, 26 Aug. 1633, gave him portion of his est. A HENRY of New Hampsh. on the gr. jury 1684, may have been his s. JAMES, New Haven 1643 or earlier, d. 1673, and his wid. Mary d. 1674. He is thot. to have had s. William, perhaps b. in Eng. the f. of Noadiah. ‡*JAMES, Charlestown, eldest s. of Hon. Richard, m. Mabel, d. of Gov. Haynes of Conn. had Mabel, b. 1 May 1665, perhaps at Hartford, and may have d. there; James, bapt. 5 Apr. 1668; Mabel, again, 23 Jan. 1670; Richard, 17 Mar. 1672, d. at 17 yrs.; John, 29 June 1673; Maud, 25 June 1676; Mary, 10 Oct. 1680; and Daniel, b. 30 Nov. 1685; but the last two were by sec. w. Mary, d. of Henry Wolcott the sec. was freem. 1668, rep. 1679, treas. of the Col. and an Assist. 1680 and onwards, named counsel. in the new chart. was a judge of Pro. and treas. of the Prov. He had third w. Abigail, d. of George Curwin, wid. of Eleazer Hathorne, and d. 28 Apr. 1709. JASON, Cambridge, s. of William, m. 27 May 1684, Mary Hubbard, had Hubbard, b. a. 1687, and perhaps more. JOHN, Dorchester, d. 26 Aug. 1633, and in his nuncup. will, gave to his brs. Henry R. and Thomas Hyatt, half his est. and half to the ch. of D. and set free his man serv. JOHN, Cambridge, freem. 3 Mar. 1636, town clk. in 1645,

constable in 1648, brought, no doubt, s. John, b. a. 1626, H. C. 1645,
rem. soon aft. to Wethersfield, where had raged a very unpleasant quarrel betw. Rev. Henry Smith and a part of his people, end. in 1648 by
his death. He next yr. m. Dorothy, the wid. of Mr. Smith, and the s.
succeed. him as min. By former w. he had also Philip, b. perhaps in
Eng. perhaps at our Cambridge; rem. 1659 to Hadley, and d. 8 May
1680, aged 83. Hinman calls him a rep. 1646–8, but tho. he says nothing else of him, p. 70, I suppose that is wrong. In neither of those yrs.
does Trumbull's Col. Rec. so honor him, indeed he was not made freem.
bef. 1655, nor was he ever so chosen. If my conjecture would benefit
the eye of a reader of those rec. he might see the name that misled H.
to be John Bissel, sometimes Byssel, wh. was more than half the time
that R. liv. in Conn. one of the reps. JOHN, Charlestown 1640, one of
the first sett. of Woburn, freem. 1644, was shoemaker and deac. had w.
Eliz. wh. d. 16 Dec. 1644, s. John, perhaps b. in Eng. and d. Mary, wh.
m. 2 Dec. 1659, Timothy Brooks; and no others are ment. in his will
of 27 May 1676, five days bef. he d. But he had m. sec. w. 13 May
1645, Eliz. Baker, perhaps d. of William of Charlestown, and she d. 17
Jan. 1690. Some distinct. is justly claim. for him as one of the founders
of the first Bapt. ch. of Boston, 1669, gather. first in Noddle's isl. some
yrs. earlier, and was its elder or deac. JOHN, Marshfield, 1643–51.
JOHN, Wethersfield, s. of John of the same, b. in Eng. m. at Hartford,
28 June 1649, Mary d. of John Talcott, had John, b. 23 Sept. 1650 (by
the false rec. in Geneal. Reg. XII. 197, said to be bapt. that day, wh.
was Monday), wh. d. at 20 yrs. and Jonathan, 1655, H. C. 1675, but
this s. may have been by sec. w. Rebecca, d. of Thomas Newberry of
Windsor, wh. d. 21 Nov. 1688, aged 57. In 1650 he was made freem.
but aft. long controv. that may seem to have been the pastor's inherit.
from his predecess. in 1659, he had rem. to Hadley, and carr. both s.
with major part of the ch. had Samuel, b. 4 Nov. 1660, H. C. 1681;
Eleazer, 8 Nov. 1663, wh. d. bef. his f. Daniel, 8 Feb. 1666, d. next yr.
and he d. 10 Dec. 1692, aged 66. At his ho. in Hadley were long conceal. the regicides, Whalley and Goffe, wh. d. there some yrs. apart, and
both corpses were bur. in his ground close to the foundat. of his ho.
where, to contradict an absurd tradit. of rem. of the bones to New Haven, the authentic remains were, a few yrs. since ascert. by rem. of the
cellar wall for the railroad. JOHN, Woburn, s. of John of the same, b. perhaps in Eng. a shoemaker, m. 31 Oct. 1661, Sarah Champney, perhaps d. of
John of Cambridge, had John, b. 1 Aug. 1662; Joseph, 15 Jan. 1664; Samuel, 3 Feb. 1667, d. at 10 mos. Sarah, 10 Feb. 1671; Eliz. 19 Feb. 1673;
Jonathan, 6 Aug. 1675; and Thomas, 5 Jan. 1678. After the loss of their
teacher, Gould, by the first Bapt. ch. in Boston, to wh. he had unit. hims.

earlier than his f. perhaps 1666, he was engag. and rem. to B. was ord. 28 July 1679, but d. 22 Dec. 1680. His wid. ret. to W. and d. 25 Apr. 1696. JOHN, Cambridge 1652, by w. Eliz. had Martha, wh. d. 7 Nov. 1675; was prob. freem. 1681, tho. as both senr. and junr. of C. were then adm. it may be uncertain, wh. of the two was the s. of William. JOHN, New Haven 1664, perhaps had been empl. in iron works at Taunton, by w. Hannah had Hannah, b. 1670; William, Sept. 1676, d. young; ano. ch. Aug. 1679, d. soon; and John, 1 Nov. 1680; and d. 1681, says Dodd, and his wid. Hannah m. Robert Dawson. * JOHN, Dartmouth, wh. serv. as rep. 1665–83. exc. 1666 and 73, and was on the import. Comtee. for distrib. the charita. contrib. from Ireland 1677, could not have been the same as the preced. for he was s. of Ralph of D. and d. 13 Feb. 1695. His w. Dorothy d. 18 Dec. 1687. By her prob. he had Joseph, b. 6 May 1650, perhaps John, for in the list of townsmen 1686, he is call. sen. JOHN, Woburn, s. of John the sec. of the same, m. 21 Dec. 1682, Eliz. Palmer, had John, b. 20 Sept. 1683, d. at 14 yrs.; Joseph, 3 Oct. 1685; Stephen, 25 Aug. 1687; Eliz. 21 June 1690; Samuel, 16 July 1692; Sarah, 15 Oct. 1694; John, again, 19 Aug. 1697; Ruth, 16 Jan. 1699; Jonathan, 7 Nov. 1700; Mary, 2 Mar. 1703; and Thomas, 26 June 1705, and d. 26 July 1717. His wid. d. a. 1723. JOHN, New Haven, s. of Ralph, m. 17 Aug. 1687, Hannah, d. of Matthew Moulthrop, had Hannah, b. 18 Feb. 1689; Lydia, 18 Sept. 1692; John, 15 Jan. 1695; Abigail, 19 May 1701; Rachel, 15 Dec. 1703; Mabel, 14 July 1706; and Sarah, 25 Feb. 1712; was a capt. and d. 13 Feb. 1724. JONATHAN, Dartmouth, perhaps br. of John senr. of the same, took o. of fidel. 1684. JONATHAN, Barnstable, s. of John of Hadley, m. Martha, d. of Rev. Joshua Moody, as is said, had Rebecca, b. at H. 7 July 1681; and at B. where he was ord. 19 Sept. had Martha, 29 Aug. as Baylies IV. 83, says, bapt. 16 Sept. 1683, d. at 3 yrs. John, 3 Nov. 1685, H. C. 1704; Abigail, 2 Oct. 1687; Jonathan, 24 Feb. bapt. 16 Mar. 1690, Y. C. 1708; Eleazer, 12, bapt. 17 Apr. 1692; Moody, 30 Aug. bapt. 2 Sept. 1694; Martha, again, bapt. 24 Jan. 1697; Samuel, 1, bapt. 7 May 1669; Joseph and Benjamin, tw. 11 Oct. 1702, both d. 12 Feb. foll. and Hannah, 12 Sept. 1707. He d. 20, or as Baylies has it, 2 Feb. 1711, and his wid. d. 28 Sept. 1729. JOSEPH, Cambridge, s. of William, b. in Eng. m. 23 June 1662, Mary d. of Jeremy (not as in Vol. I. 155 call. Andrew) Belcher, wh. d. 23 June 1691; and the d. Martha d. three days aft. He had first Mary, bapt. 8 Jan. 1665; also Abigail, bapt. 17 May 1668, sev. others, as Walter, Samuel, Jeremiah, John, and Prudence of dates unkn. and made his will 14 Nov. 1694, nam. br. Benjamin excor. His d. Abigail m. Matthew Bridge sec. of C. JOSEPH, Dartmouth, s. of John of the same, by w. Eliz. had Joseph and John, tw. b.

22 Nov. 1679. His w. d. 25 Sept. 1737; and he d. 11 Dec. 1739, aged 89. *JOSEPH, New Haven, s. of Ralph, m. 1687, Jane Blackman, had Joseph, b. 1687, d. young; and Samuel, 23 Apr. 1697. NATHANIEL, Duxbury 1657, says Winsor, wh. tells no more. NOADIAH, Middletown, s. of William of New Haven; in a few wks. after ent. at coll. the Gen. Ct. of Conn. conclud. that it was "more advantag. for the said N. that his ho. and ld. be sold, and the pay rec. be improv. for the bring. of him up in Coll. learn. than to leave his learn. and enjoy his ho. and ld. he being likely to prove a useful instrument in the wk. of God," permit the sale of est. "left him by his gr.f. and f." Trumbull Col. Rec. II. 323. After Oct. 1683, he prepar. the Cambridge Almanac, 1684, taught the gr. sch. at Ipswich, until the end of Feb. 1687, then went to M. and was ord. 24 Oct. 1688, being Wednesday, the usual day of the week for such solemnit. was one of the founders of Yale Coll. He m. 20 or 28 Feb. 1690, Mary, d. of Giles Hamlin, Esq. had William, b. 1690; Noadiah, 1692; Giles, 1693; Mary, 1695; John, 1697; Esther, 1699; Daniel, 1702; Mehitable, 1704; and Hannah, 1705; and of the value of his serv. we may be instructed by the doleful verses reprint. in the M. newspap. of 7 Feb. 1854. Of the ch. we learn by Field's Statist. Acco. of Middlesex, 44, that the eldest and the youngest, William, and Daniel, were min. bred at Yale, of wh. the former succeed. his f. at M. 1 June 1715, and d. 1 June 1761. PHILIP, Hatfield, younger br. of Rev. John of Hadley, m. 4 Feb. 1664, Joanna, d. of Rev. Henry Smith, whose wid. had m. his f. She with a d. Joanna, b. 31 Oct. d. 28 Dec. foll. and he m. 10 Jan. 1666, Eliz. d. of Stephen Terry, had John, b. 1667; Samuel, 1669; Philip, 1671; and Stephen, 1674; she was k. by the Ind. 19 Sept. 1677, with her youngest s. and Samuel was k. by them on their road to Canada. He m. 3d w. 25 Dec. 1679, Mary, d. of Edward Church, had Samuel, again, 1680; Thomas, 1683; Mary, 1685, d. soon; Mary, again, 1686; Philip, 1688; and Daniel, 1691. He was a glazier, and d. in Apr. or May 1693. His s. Thomas was k. by the Ind. 19 July 1704; when four brs. and one sis. surv. RALPH, Dartmouth, had come from Pontipool, Co. Monmouth, was one of the first sett. at Dartmouth, had been, I think, at Taunton, engag. in the iron works with the Leonards, is call. anc. of the fam. of Russells at New Bedford, wh. rec. its name, from a descend. in the fourth generat. He had s. John. RALPH, New Haven, m. 12 Oct. 1663, Mary Hitchcock, perhaps d. of Matthew, had John, b. 14 Dec. 1664; Joseph, 20 Mar. 1667; Samuel, 1671; and Edward, Feb. 1673, wh. d. soon, and he d. 1676, not 1679, as Dodd gave it to Farmer, for his inv. bears date, says Mr. Judd, 28 Feb. of the earlier yr. ‡*‖ RICHARD, Charlestown, came with newly m. w. Maud, 1640, from Hereford, as common. is told, where he was b. 1611, s. of Paul. but

apprent. 4 Oct. 1628, at Bristol. They were adm. of the ch. 22 May 1641; and he was freem. 2 June foll. had James, b. 1 Oct. 1640, bapt. 30 May foll. Daniel, H. C. 1669; Catharine; and Eliz. b. 12 Oct. 1644; but neither the b. nor bapt. of either of the two preced. is kn. His w. d. 1652; and perhaps 1655, he m. Mary, wid. of Leonard Chester of Hartford, had no ch. by her, and d. 14 May 1676, in his 65th yr. hav. by will provid. for sev. good works. The wid. d. 30 Nov. 1688, aged a. 80, says gr.st. His d. Catharine m. 29 Nov. (of the yr. wh. Frothingham 145, calls 1654, by mistake) William Roswell; and Eliz. m. 24 or 29 Aug. 1664, Nathaniel Graves or Greaves; and next, 15 Oct. 1684, Capt. John Herbert of Reading, and d. 18 Oct. 1714, aged 70 yrs. He began early to be much esteem. was selectman 1642, ar. co. 1644, rep. 1646, and many yrs. more, speaker 1648, and oft. aft. treas. of the Col. twenty yrs. and assist. 1659, to his d. ROBERT, Andover, m. 6 July 1659, Mary Marshall, freem. 1691, had Robert, wh. d. 27 May 1689, perhaps other childr. and d. 1710, in his 80th yr. having 5 s. as Farmer says; but names and dates are defic. ROGER, Marblehead, in 1674, may have been s. or br. of Henry of the same. SAMUEL, Branford, s. of Rev. John of Hadley, at Deerfield, there, I presume, serv. sev. yrs. m. Abigail, d. of John Whiting, a. 1685, had John, b. 24 Jan. 1687; Abigail, 16 Aug. 1690; Samuel, 28 Sept. 1693; Timothy, 18 Nov. 1695; Daniel, 19 June 1698; Jonathan, 21 Aug. 1700; and Ebenezer, 4 May 1703; was ord. Mar. 1687, and d. 15 June 1731, says Farmer; and his wid. d. 7 May 1733. SAMUEL, New Haven, s. of Ralph, m. 27 Feb. 1696, Esther Tuttle, had Samuel, b. 1697; Esther, 4 May, 1699; Mary, Jan. 1701, d. soon; one, d. 17 Aug. 1702; Ralph, d. Aug. 1703; Joseph, d. Dec. 1706; Daniel; and Abel; and d. 26 June 1624. THOMAS, Charlestown, a gent. with prefix of Mr. in the ch. rec. when he was adm. 23 Jan. 1676, was made freem. next mo. m. 30 Dec. 1669, Prudence, d. of Leonard Chester, had Mary, b. 27 Sept. bapt. 2 Oct. 1670, her mo. hav. join. the ch. 12 June preced. Thomas, b. 30, bapt. 31 Mar. 1672; and Prudence, bapt. 28 Mar. 1675; and he d. 20 Oct. 1676, said to be 35 yrs. old. His wid. d. 21 Oct. 1678. He is call. capt. but whose s. he was is not told, nor does his gr.st. ment. the age. As he m. the d. of Richard's sec. w. he may have been s. of R. perhaps brot. from Eng. perhaps b. here, for his adm. to the ch. was 3 mos. only bef. that of Daniel. THOMAS, Marblehead 1674. WILLIAM, Cambridge, 1645, or few yrs. earlier, a carpenter, brot. w. Martha and s. Joseph, b. a. 1636, bapt. in Eng. says the reg. of matchless Mitchell, had, perhaps, Phebe, wh. d. 8 July 1642; and prob. b. on this side of the water, Benjamin; John, 11 Sept. 1645; Martha; Philip, a. 1650; perhaps that Thomas wh. d. 21 July 1653; William, 28 Apr.

1655; Jason, 14 Nov. 1658; all but Thomas bapt. at C. Joyce, 31 Mar. bapt. 13 May 1660; and he d. 14 Feb. 1662. He made his will 13 days preced. His wid. m. 24 Mar. 1665, Humphrey Bradshaw; and next, 24 May 1683, Thomas Hall, and d. a. 1694. Joyce m. 13 Oct. 1680, Edmund Rice of Sudbury. WILLIAM, New Haven, s. prob. of James of the same, bapt. in Eng. 11 Oct. 1612, by w. Sarah, d. of William Davis, had Samuel, bapt. 16 Feb. 1645; Hannah, b. 29 July, bapt. 4 Aug. 1650; John, 1653, d. young; and Noadiah, 22, bapt. 24 July 1659 (not as print. in Geneal. Reg. IX. 362, 25 July, wh. was Monday), H. C. 1681. His w. d. 1664, and he d. next yr. tho. by one rept. he d. 24 Dec. 1664, and she soon aft. Hannah m. a Potter of Wallingford, and rem. soon to New Jersey. WILLIAM, Boston, a mason, m. 7 Sept. 1653, wid. Alice Sparrow, had Eliz. b. 22 Apr. 1659, was liv. in 1662. One of the same name was of Southampton, L. I. 1673; and Eaton makes one William to be among early sett. of Reading. WILLIAM, Cambridge, s. of William of the same, m. 18 Mar. 1683, Abigail, d. of Edward Winship, had perhaps other ch. beside Abigail, wh. d. 20 June 1710, aged 21 yrs. and ½; and Edward, wh. d. 21 Jan. 1696, aged 11 mos. In 1834, twenty-nine of this name had been gr. at Harv. fifteen at Yale, and fourteen at the other N. E. coll. among wh. Farmer reckons only 13 clerg.

RUST, EDWARD, Dedham, adm. of the ch. 1 Oct. 1665. HENRY, Hingham 1635, freem. Mar. 1638, rem. to Boston bef. 1651, on 31 Mar. of wh. yr. he was rec. to be an inhab. ISRAEL, Northampton, m. 9 Dec. 1669, Rebecca, d. of William Clark, had Nathaniel, b. 1671; Samuel, 1673, d. at 29 yrs.; Sarah, 1675; Experience, 1677; Israel, 1679; Jonathan, 1681; beside Rebecca, and John; and d. 11 Nov. 1712. *NATHANIEL, Ipswich, freem. 1674, was rep. 1690 and 1. It may seem prob. that he was br. of Israel. NICHOLAS, Springfield, took the o. of alleg. 1678. SAMUEL, Boston, a soldier under capt. Sill in Philip's war, in a memor. 15 Apr. 1676, ask. for his wages, says he had serv. 9 mos. had a w. and fam. but the name is not found in the rec. of B. and perhaps he lost his life in the war.

RUTH, VINCENT, freem. of Mass. 1645, as says the rec. wh. I do not believe. Neither can any hesitation be felt in adm. the probabil. of a conject. of Rev. L. R. Paige, that it stands for V. Druce, the Hingham man. See that name.

RUTHERFORD, or RUDDERFORD. See Rotherford.

RUTTER, JOHN, Sudbury, came 1638, in the Confidence from Southampton, aged 22, as serv. of Peter Hodges, by w. Eliz. had Eliz. b. 6 Oct. 1642; John, 7 July 1645; Joseph, 1 May 1656; and prob. others. His wid. m. that Thomas Plympton wh. was k. in Sudbury fight. JOHN, Marlborough, s. of the preced. prob. was the high whig, 1689, ment. in Revo. in N. E. justif. p. 30.

RUTTY, EDWARD, Milford 1677, rem. next yr. to Killingworth, m. 6 May 1678, Rebecca, d. of Thomas Stevens of the same, had Mercy, b. 1679; Edward, 1680; Rebecca, 1685; Phebe, 1687; Cary, 1689; Thomas, 1691; Abigail, 1696; and d. 1 May 1714. His wid. d. 26 Feb. 1737.

RYALL, WILLIAM. See Royall.

RYDEAT, JOHN. See Rediate.

RYLAND, JEREMIAH, Dorchester 1654, very poor. See Hist. 183.

MORE ADDITIONS AND CORRECTIONS

IN VOL. I.

P. 4. l. 18, aft. 1700. ins. Tho. arrest, on a warrant, with sev. other inno. persons, in Apr. 1692, for witchr. he escap. prosec. perhaps as not old eno. for the devil's prey.

P. 9. l. 15 from bot. aft. 1673. ins. ELIASHIB, Bristol, s. of Edward of Medfield, was unm. Feb. 1689.

" l. 11 from bot. for *the* aft. 1657, r. Mary,

P. 19. l. 10, aft. 1724. ins. SAMUEL, Milford, perhaps s. of Josiah by his first w. had w. Esther, and d. 1697.

" l. 11, aft. eldest, strike out "br. of the preced." and ins. s. by sec. w. of Josiah the first.

P. 22. l. 5, aft. Roxbury; add, Joanna m. Ephraim Hurd;

P. 23. l. 7, aft. Alice, add, beside Ruth.

P. 28. l. 1, bef. 1675, ins. 14 Oct.

P. 31. l. 1, at the end, add, spell. Allin,

P. 33. l. 2, aft. New Haven, erase the rest of the line.

" l. 4 from bot. bef. JOSEPH, ins. *

" l. 3 from bot. aft. 1724, add, aged 71, as Babson tells; and in his vol. we learn, that he m. 1680, Rachel Griggs, prob. d. of William, had Joseph, b. 1681; Jeremiah, 1682; and Rachel, 1684; and his w. d. 26 Apr. of that yr. In the same yr. he m. Rose Howard, and had Solomon, 1685; Benjamin, 1687; a s. without name; Thomas, 1689; Ann, 1691; John, 1692; Rose, 1694; William, 1696; Mercy, and Patience, tw. 1697; Jeremiah, again, 1698; Samuel, 1701; Zerubabel, 1703; and Moses, 1706. He was capt. and rep. 1705.

P. 34. l. 20 from bot. for Kerly r. Kirby

P. 37. l. 19, aft. 1602. ins. His will of 7 June 1678 nam. w. Eliz. and the three elder s. only; and he d. 30 Jan. foll.

P. 39. l. 17, aft. 1674. ins. His will was of 2 Jan. in that yr. and the wid. Mary took admin.

P. 40. l. 3 from bot. for Seaborn r. John — also for Hampton r. Plymouth

P. 41. l. 13, aft. m. ins. 11 Jan. 1672,

" l. 15, aft. 1683; add, Sarah, 29 Aug. 1685; Ebenezer, 22 Nov. 1687; Stephen, 4 Mar. 1690;

" l. 16, strike out "others, as is said." and ins. Susanna, 3 Oct. 1693. JOHN, New Haven, s. of the first John, m. 20 Mar. 1689, Abigail, d. of Edward Grannis, had Abigail, b. 9 Jan. foll. Mary, 26 Aug. 1693; Elijah; and Hezekiah; and had perhaps by sec. w. John, 1 Oct. 1726; and Christopher, 29 Aug. 1735.

" l. 17, erase prob.

" l. 15 from bot. aft. "will" ins. of 17 July 1682

" l. 14 from bot. erase "SAMUEL &c. to the end of the l.

" l. 7 from bot. aft. 1709. ins. SAMUEL, New Haven, s. of the first John, had Eliz. b. 19 Dec. 1691; and Joseph, 29 Mar. 1694.

P. 45. l. 16, for "is not seen" r. was Bartholomew

" l. 18, strike out "prob." — also, aft. unm. ins. He was a sea capt.

" l. 10 from bot. for "one" r. Eliz.

" l. 9 from bot. for "one perhaps the same" r. Jemima — also, aft. m. ins. 24 Mar. 1692.

" l. 2 from bot. aft. £490, ins. His wid. m. 1694, John Miles.

P. 50. l. 8, aft. 1657; ins. beside Martha, again, 23 Feb. 1660.

" l. 17 from bot. strike out, "and I kn. no more." and ins. Isaac, 29 Aug. 1680; John, 28 Dec. 1685; Thomas, 9 Jan. 1687; Jacob, 29 Feb. 1688; and Abraham, 15 Oct. 1692, as suppl. by a scrupul. writer in Geneal. Reg. XV. 21, tho. I feel compel. to change an impossib. date.

P. 52. l. 11, aft. Treat, ins. wh. d. 5 Dec. 1727, — also, aft. 1738. ins. A sec. w. Abigail, d. 9 Sept. 1742.

" l. 15 from bot. for Farmington r. Fairfield

" l. 10 from bot. for John r. Sarah

" l. 8 from bot. aft. Mary, ins. bapt. 19 May 1689; John,

P. 53. l. 4, strike out all bef. 1690, and ins. Stephen, prob. 21 Sept.

" l. 5, bef. bapt. ins. b. 7 Feb. — also, bef. 24 ins. 20, bapt. — also, strike out, "perhaps more" and ins. Joanna, b. 24 May 1698; James, 1 Aug. 1701.

" l. 13, for Thomas r. Mary

" l. 15, aft. Paul, ins. 2, not — also, aft. 1689, strike out the rest of the sentence, and ins. Ebenezer, b. 28 Aug. 1692, d. in few wks.

" l. 21, bef. EDWARD. ins. He d. 1673.

P. 54. l. 13, bef. 1643; ins. 15 Apr. — also, bef. 1645; ins. 12 Aug.

" l. 14, bef. 1647; ins. 26 Feb. — also, bef. 1648; ins. 31 Oct.

" l. 15, for 1652 r. 26 May 1651

" l. 17, aft. Benjamin, ins. June — also, aft. 1682. add, His wid. d. May 1694.

" l. 20, bef. Barnes; strike out "a" and ins. as sec. w. Thomas

" l. 18 from bot. aft. Hannah, ins. in town rec. call. Susanna, b. 12 Aug. 1659;

" l. 3 from bot. aft. Joseph, ins. Eliz. bapt. Mar. 1638; — also, aft. Ephraim, ins. 18. not, as once said 8, Oct. 1640;

P. 55. l. 9, strike out "and perhaps others." and ins. Caleb, 16 Aug. 1682, d. next yr. and Seth, 2 May 1684.

" l. 12, aft. Very. ins. Babson, wh. dates the m. 17 Nov. 1681, adds the ch. Thomas, b. 1686; Francis, 1689; Abigail, 1692; and Hannah, 1702.

" l. 17, aft. Eliz. ins. ROBERT, Rowley, call. sen. when he d. June 1668, leav. good est. for w. Grace.

P. 56. l. 17 from bot. strike out "perhaps he had others." and ins. Other ch. were

John, b. 30 Sept. 1658; Ruth, 6 Aug. 1660; Eliz. 22 Sept. 1665; Ephraim, 27 Oct. 1667, d. under two yrs. Abigail, 7 Jan. 1670; Stephen, 6 Mar. 1672; Benjamin, 4 Mar. 1676; and one b. 2 Nov. 1679, d. very soon.

P. 57. l. 1, for 1640 r. 1649

" l. 9, aft. yr. add, and Eliz. again, wh. m. Sept. 1704 Joshua Norwood.

P. 60. l. 13, aft. Martha, ins. d. of the first John Baker of Ipswich, — also, aft. sea, ins. 1664,

P. 63. l. 3, aft. m. ins. Oct. 1668, — also aft. Hutchinson, add, and d. 26 Nov. 1674.

" l. 13, erase perhaps

" l. 4 from bot. for Arsmbee r. Armsbee

P. 64. l. 3, strike out "and prob. was d."

" l. 4, aft. Windham, add, had no fam. shown on rec.

" l. 12, at the end, add, Stephen, Windham, s. of Benjamin, by w. Hannah had Hannah, b. 1 Dec. 1710, d. at 3 mos. Abigail, 1 May 1712; Hannah, again, 23 Mar. 1714; Jonathan, 26 Aug. 1715; Sarah, 21 June 1717; and Mary, 17 Feb. 1720.

P. 66. l. 19 from bot. aft. 71. add, His wid. d. 15 Feb. 1706, at Rochester.

" l. 17 from. bot. for bef. 1717 r. 11 Feb. 1709.

P. 70. l. 6 from bot. bef. Col. strike out lieut.

P. 73. l. 9 from bot. aft. told; add rem. to Bristol, there in Feb. 1689 count. four ch.

P. 75. l. 3 from bot. strike out, had a w. &c. to the end of the l. and ins. m. 24 June 1680, Lydia, d. of John Rockwell of Windsor, and both h. and w. without ch.

P. 76. l. 1, bef. 1688. ins. 22 Oct. — also, aft. 1688. ins. David, New Haven, eldest s. of the preced. had Joanna, b. 24 Feb. 1683; Abigail, 18 Jan. 1685; and Joshua, 6 Dec. 1686. Ebenezer, New Haven, br. of the preced. m. 11 Dec. 1691, Abigail, eldest d. of James Heaton, had four ch. John, br. of the preced. had ten ch.

" l. 8, strike out "prob."

" l. 13, aft. 1698; add, Lydia, again, 31 July 1701,

" l. 6 from bot. strike out "prob."

" l. 5 from bot. aft. Alling, add, had ten ch.

P. 80. l. 10, for ano. d. r. Rebecca

" l. 8 from bot. for Joshua r. David

P. 84. l. 7, for 1667 r. 1669

" l. 8, for 13 r. 18

" l. 19 from bot. aft. same, strike out down to Obadiah, and ins. had John, b. 18 Mar. 1648; Zechariah, 24 Oct. 1650; Nathaniel, 13 May 1655; Joseph, 16 Mar. 1659; and Sarah, 17 Jan. 1661. His w. d. 25 July 1662, and he m. 26 Mar. foll. Mary Wooddam, prob. d. of John of Ipswich, and there liv. 1679. John, Ipswich, m. Susanna, d. of Mark Symonds, had Edward, b. 12 Feb. 1659; Mark, 14 Dec. 1660; William, 1 May 1662; Nathaniel, 6 July 1664; and others, prob. as Sarah, John, Samuel, Thomas, and Joseph; rem. bef. 1672, to Brookfield, and was there k. by the Ind. 3 Aug. 1675. His wid. Susanna, d. 8 Feb. 1683. Moses, Dorchester, m. 3 Aug. 1666, Bethia Millet, prob. d. of Thomas, had Moses, and she d. 15 Apr. 1669. He was, I think, mariner, or merch. for, in Sept. 1684, contrib. for his redempt. from Algerine capt. was made acc. Hist. of D. 249. Moses, Dorchester, s. of the preced. by w. Eliz. had Moses, and Eliz. bef. 1704, when his w. d. He rem. to Boston, and d. bef. 1718. Nathaniel, Haverhill, prob. s. of John the first, m. 10 May 1670, Tamosin Torloar, a monstrous surname that may be Thurla, had Hannah, b. and d. 2 June 1671; Hannah, again, 19 Dec. 1672; Eliz. 19 Aug. 1674; Nathaniel, 15 Nov. 1676; Abiah, 5 Feb. 1678; Obadiah, 20 Jan. 1680; and Ruth, 30 Dec. 1681. His w. d. 13 Dec. 1700; and he d 17 Nov. 1707. Nathaniel, Boston, 1685, perhaps s. of sec. John, by w. Amy had Nathaniel, and Amy, and d. 4 Dec. 1737.

P. 84, l. 12 from bot. bef. "by" ins. br. prob. of the first Nathaniel, — also aft. Hannah, ins. d. of the sec. John Pike, — also, aft. 1663; add, Sarah, 5 Mar. 1665, d. next mo. a s. b. 1 Nov. 1666, d. in few ds.; and Samuel, 13 Sept. 1667, d. in few wks.

" l. 11 from bot. aft. Oct. ins. or 1 Nov.

" l. 9 from bot. aft. st. add, His ch. were Ruth, b. 20 Oct. 1660; Hannah, 2 Aug. 1662; Abigail, 4 July 1664; Mary, 6 Aug. 1666; Martha, 1 Mar. 1668; Samuel, 28 Sept. 1669; William, 23 Sept. 1673; Rachel, 18 Oct. 1675; and Ebenezer, 22 May 1673. The last three d. young.

" l. 8 from bot. for 1659 r. 27 Feb. 1651

" l. 7 from bot. aft. *had* ins. Eliz. b. 10 Nov. 1652; — also, aft. Samuel, add 11 Nov. 1654; Mehitable, 14 Sept. 1656; Timothy, 7 Oct. 1659; and three more, wh. d. early, unnam.

P. 85. l. 1, aft. m. strike out the next seven words, and ins. 14 Dec. 1681, Mary Johnson, d. perhaps of Thomas of Andover, — also, aft. *had* ins. Peter, b. 21 Dec. 1682, d. soon; Mehitable, 5 Feb. 1684; James, 27 Oct. 1686; — also, aft. Obadiah, ins. 9 May 1689.

" l. 2, bef. John; ins. Timothy, 9 Apr. 1692, d. soon; Lydia, 19 Dec. 1694; Hannah, 3 May 1697; Ruth, 21 Mar. 1699; Abigail, 7 Apr. 1702, d. young; and — also, aft. John, add, 7 Apr. 1705; and strike out the next two words.

" l. 8, aft. first, ins. m. 1 Apr. 1656, Eliz. d. prob. of John Hutchins,

" l. 9, aft. 1657; add Eliz. 23 Dec. 1659; Mary, 22 Mar. 1661; Love, 15 Apr. 1663; tw. s. 16 Jan. 1665, both d. soon; Thomas, 9 June 1666; and Hannah, 11 July 1671; — also, aft. 1666, add, and d. 15 July 1671.

P. 87. l. 20, aft. devil; add, beside Abigail, 1670.

" l. 21, aft. war; add, but soon d. prob. unm. JOHN, Gloucester, s. of the preced. m. 1686, Dorcas Elwell, d. of Josiah, had Eliz. b. 1687; James, 1689; John, 1691; and Josiah, 1703. He and w. d. 1737. PHILIP, Salem, br. of the preced. m. 1689, Hannah Baker, had Ann, and his w. d. 1692.

P. 88. l. 9, aft. report. add, In his will of 1673, w. Eliz. s. John, and Joseph, d. Hannah Corning, and gr.ch. John Cressy are ment.

P. 90. l. 9, strike out "perhaps"

" l. 15 from bot. aft. 1690; ins. all bapt. 26 Apr. 1691, as in Geneal. Reg. X. 347, but with wrong name, Pason, instead of Bacon;

P. 92. l. 14 from bot. bef. EBENEZER, ins. BENJAMIN, Milton, s. of George, m. 11 Feb. 1673, Hannah, d. of William Daniel, had William, b. a. 1684, and in Jan. 1692, admin. was giv. on his est.

" l. 6 from bot. aft. dates. add, His will, of 26 Sept. 1671, ment. w. Mary, s. Benjamin, Return, Enoch, and sev. ds.

P. 94. l. 8, strike out "prob. bef. 1669"

" l. 9, aft. Haddam, ins. there had Benjamin, b. 15 Nov. 1665.

P. 96. l. 18 from bot. aft. me. ins. See 4 Mass. Hist. Coll. I. 96, print. 1852, or Geneal. Reg. XIV. 324, 5, print. 1860, where this last name is var. Ipswich, John had, also, Martha, wh. m. Obadiah Antrim.

P. 97. l. 9, aft. Eliz. add, For sec. w. he m. 8 Jan. 1664, Thankful, eldest d. of Hopestill Foster, had John, b. 26 Feb. 1665; and Silence, posthum. wh. d. soon. His w. long surv. d. 27 Jan. 1698.

" l. 16, strike out the whole sent. JOHN &c. to 87 in l. 19 inclus.

" l. 19, aft. Ipswich, ins. s. of John of the same, brot. from Eng.

" l. 8 from bot. aft. foll. add, His wid. m. 1678, Thomas Lyman.

P. 98. l. 8, aft. Mary, ins. bapt. July 1639.

P. 98, l. 19, aft. yrs. add, He had Samuel, bapt. 7 Oct. 1638; John, 6 Nov. 1642; Eliz. Nov. 1644; and Deborah, 6 June 1652.

" l. 19 from bot. aft. d. ins. 4 Apr.

P. 99. l. 6 from bot. aft. Topsfield, ins. s. of the first John of Ipswich, brot. by his f. 1637

" l. 5 from bot. aft. m. ins. 26 Mar.

" l. 4 from bot. bef. "was" strike out, and prob. more ch. and ins. b. 8 Dec. 1674; Martha, 14 Oct. 1682; Rebecca, 16 Nov. 1685; Thomas, 17 Feb. 1688; John, 6 Jan. 1691; and Eliz. bapt. 17 Sept. 1693. He d. 18 Mar. 1718, aged by fam. tradit. 81 yrs. 6 mos. 5 days; so b. 13 Sept. 1636; and the wid. d. 2 Jan. 1733, aged 85. Priscilla m. Isaac Appleton.

P. 102. l. 16 from bot. for *and* r. wh.

P. 103. l. 13, aft. 1668; add, and d. Nov. 1673.

P. 104. last line, bef. SYLVANUS, ins. SAMUEL, Guilford, left w. Abigail, and ch. Abigail, aged 17; Dorothy, 12; Joanna, 10; Samuel, 7; Timothy, 5; and Nathaniel, 2; by inv. of Jan. 1696 to div. good est.

P. 105. l. 20 from bot. aft. ch. add, Abigail, aged 14; Martha, 8; Theophilus, 4; and Hezekiah, 1.   THOMAS, Newport 1651, on freem's. list 1655.

P. 106. l. 18, bef. JOHN, ins. HENRY, Salem, d. 15 May 1678.

" l. 5 from bot. aft. same, ins. by w. Mary had Sarah, b. 1673; and for sec. w.

P. 109, l. 18, aft. 1657; add, James, again, 8 Apr. 1660.

" l. 16 from bot. aft. James, ins. Eliz. 12 Aug. 1659.

P. 112. l. 12 from bot. aft. d. ins. Mary, wh. m. Benjamin Bowden;

P. 114. l. 13, aft. Lynn. add, The wid. Eliz. had admin. 29 June 1677.

P. 115. l. 5, aft. GILES, add, Gloucester 1653–5, rem. to

P. 118. l. 9, aft. Watertown, ins. rem. to Dover, and next to York, but in latter days back to W. was

" l. 10, after w. add, perhaps sec.

" l. 21 from bot. bef. John, ins. the first

P. 119. l. 13, aft. 1675, add, One JOHN was of Salem 1676, hav. a w.

" l. 16 from bot. aft. tells. add, JOSEPH, Kittery 1670, was br. of Benjamin.

" l. 13 from. bot. aft. John, ins. b. 1676,

P. 120, l. 8, at the end, add, m. 1671, Sarah Clark,

" l. 9, bef. Joseph ins. Benoni, wh. d. 1673, perhaps Daniel, wh. d. 1689, and

" l. 13 from bot. aft. Ind. add, His wid. had admin.

" l. 11 from bot. for "by w." r. m. 12 Apr. 1664, — also, aft. Sarah, add, d. of Joseph Peasley

" l. 10 from bot. for 1664 r. foll.

P. 121. l. 12, aft. 1644, strike out "perhaps" and ins. DANIEL, New Haven, s. of Thomas of the same,

" l. 13, bef. JAMES, ins. EBENEZER, Southington, s. of Thomas of the same, m. 8 Apr. 1699, Deborah Orvis, and d. 1756, leav. fifteen ch. as Mr. Porter assures me.

" l. 12 from bot. aft. same, ins. m. 8 July 1684, Abigail Gibbs, — also aft. *had* ins. Rebecca, b. June 1685, — also, aft. Abigail, ins. 18

" l. 11 from bot. aft. Eliz. add, 1 bapt. — also, aft. Mary, add, 6 bapt. — also, aft. 1695; add, Esther, b. 31 July 1697; Rachel, 19 Oct. 1699; and Joseph, 17 Aug. 1702; and d. 23 Jan. 1741 at Southington.

P. 122. l. 15 from bot. aft. 1639, ins. had Sarah, wh. m. 29 May 1666, John Scovil;

" l. 14 from bot. strike out prob.

" l. 13 from bot. aft. Jones. add, He took sec. w. Mary, eldest d. of John Andrews, had by her that Thomas, beside Ebenezer, and d. 1688.

P. 123. l. 6, bef. *had* ins. m. June 1690, Mary Jones, d. of Richard, — also, aft. 1695 ; add, Samuel, b. 4 June 1700; Martha, 8 Mar. 1703 ; Patience, Sept. 1705 ; Hannah, 6 Sept. 1708.

P. 124. l. 9, bef. Thomas, ins. Richard, Danbury, m. bef. 1696, Mary, d. of the sec. John Hurd of Stratford. Perhaps he was s. of Thomas, wh. m. the mo. of Mary.

" l. 14, at the end, add, His wid. Sarah, wh. had been prob. wid. of the sec. John Hurd, d. 24 Jan. 1718.

P. 127, l. 9, aft. early. ins. Peter, Marblehead, fisherman, made his will 28 Oct. 1675, going on serv. against Ind. and d. 26 Nov. foll.

P. 129, last line, aft. more ; add, liv. short time, a. 1657, at Gloucester ;

P. 132. l. 13 from bot. add, His wid. Ann d. the same yr.

P. 133. l. 16 from bot. aft. 1643 ; add, and he d. Nov. 1664.

P. 134. l. 15 from bot. bef. Stephen, ins. Samuel, Salem 1692, s. prob. of James, a physician, not unemploy. in the infernal cases of witcher.

P. 136. l. 6, aft. leav. ins. w. Margery, s. — also, strike out *perhaps*, and ins. in his will no — also, aft. ch. add, He and his s. were of Stratford 1674.

" l. 7, strike out *prob.*

" l. 13, strike out *perhaps* — also, for " John the first " r. William — also, aft. m. ins. 21 June 1677,

" l. 18 from bot. bef. Samuel ins. Elisha ;

" l. 15 from bot. aft. b. ins. 24 Dec. — also, aft. Samuel, ins. 15 Feb.

" l. 14 from bot. for " perhaps more " r. Phebe — also, at the end for . use ; and add, Abia m. 27 Apr. 1681, Ralph Lines ; and Phebe m. a Rose.

P. 137. l. 2, bef. *and* ins. was of Bristol, Feb. 1689, hav. one ch.

" l. 8, aft. 1657 ; add, beside Ann, 26 July 1660.

P. 138. l. 3, aft. same, ins. m. 10 Oct. 1682, Mary Leavitt, d. perhaps of John ;

" l. 8, aft. Samuel, add, bapt. 24 Mar. 1639 ; — also, for " perhaps other ch." r. Hopestill, Sept. 1644 ;

" l. 6 from bot. aft. 1649 ; add, Ruth, Sept. 1651 ;

P. 139. l. 5, aft. James, ins. b. Oct. 1666

" l. 6, aft. Hannah, ins. 7 Sept. 1668

" l. 13, aft. b. add, 8 June

" l. 14, aft. Solomon ins. , 8 Feb. — also, aft. 1680, add, My conject. is confirm. by auth. of D. Williams Patterson.

" l. 19, aft. Joshua, ins. Aug. 1671 ; — also, aft. Clement, ins. 21 Sept. 1676 ;

" l. 17 from bot. for 1666, r. 22 Feb. 1667,

" l. 16 from bot. bef. *was* ins. had Lydia, b. 2 Sept. 1669 ; Sarah, 23 Dec. 1673 ; a d. b. 12 Apr. 1676 ; ano. 17 Apr. 1678 ; Samuel, Mar. 1680 ; and David, 20 Feb. 1683 ;

P. 140. l. 19 from bot. at the end, ins. Timothy, Boston, s. prob. of Christopher, was assoc. with Penn Townsend and others, Sept. 1677, in volunt. comp. of milit. m. 3 Aug. 1699, Sarah Tudman.

P. 144. l. 10, bef. Benjamin, ins. Azariah, New Haven, s. of Richard, d. 1696, leav. 7 ch. betw. 6 and 21 yrs. of age.

" l. 11, aft. m. ins. 1673, Mary, d. of John Peacock, and next m.

" l. 13, strike out, " His wid. m. Ambrose Thompson " and ins. But his first w. had brot. him Benjamin, b. 1672 ; Bethia, 1674 ; and d. 1677. Goodwin, in Geneal. Notes, 254, led me into the error of mak. Sarah, wid. of Beach to m. A. T. whereas B. long surv. her, and the rec. of Stratford shows his third w. " Dec. 1705, Benjamin B. sen. m. wid. Mary Fairchild,"

P. 144. l. 15 from bot. aft. 1667; add, but had kept an inn at Stratford 1666

P. 146. l. 20, bef. Aug. ins 2

P. 148. l. 10, strike out 1677. and ins. , had John, b. 15 Aug. 1661, d. under 5 yrs.; Daniel; Samuel; John, again, 13 Oct. 1668; Margaret; James; Jeremy, 20 Apr. 1675; and Eliz.

" l. 13, at the end, add, But, as Beanes, he claim. as an heir of Robert Buffum, perhaps by m. of his d.

" l. 17, aft. inq. add, His inv. was tak. 27 Oct. 1681. One of his sis. was w. of Nicholas Camp; ano. Martha, m. 20 Dec. 1649, John Streame.

" l. 19, for JOHN r. *JOHN

" l. 20, bef. *had* ins. rep. 1677, and oft. aft.

" l. 18 from bot. aft. 1675. add, His est. was distrib. 18 Nov. 1690, to w. Ann, ch. John, James, Joseph, Samuel, Mary, w. of Timothy Baldwin, and Ann; and the wid. d. 1698.

P. 149. top, strike out the two lines with the last five on preced. p.

" l. 19, for "possib. BIRDSEYE" r. sound. BARESLEY

" l. 20, aft. same, add, d. 1730, aged 85.

" l. 17 from bot. aft. 1680, ins. THOMAS, Milford 1647, had Thomas.

" l. 16 from bot. aft. Stratford strike out to the end, and ins. s. of Thomas of Milford, d. 1668.

" l. 15 from bot. strike out 1644, and ins. a mason, came 1635, in the Planter from London, aged 30, with w. Mary, 26, and ch. Mary 4; John, 2; and Joseph, 6 mos. He was freem. in Mass. 7 Dec. 1636, but dwel. in wh. town is unkn. was one of the orig. proprs. of S. 1640, and there had Daniel, b. 1644; beside Samuel wh. d. 1706; prob. Sarah, wh. 'm. 1668, Obadiah Dickinson of Hatfield, and one or more other ds.

" l. 4 from bot. aft. Metcalf. ins. His d. Eliz. m. 30 June 1666, Zechariah Goodale.

P. 151. l. 17, bef. JOHN, ins. His wid. took admin. at Marblehead in June 1678.

P. 153. l. 14 from bot. bef. 1650; ins. 18 Aug.

" l. 13 from bot. bef. 1652; ins. 17 Oct. — also, bef. 1655. ins. 8 Apr. — also, aft. ch. add, John and Joseph.

" l. 10 from bot. aft. proprs. add, His will was of 26 Sept. 1689; and inv. of 28 Aug. foll.

P. 154. l. 20, strike out had a fam. &c. to the end of sent. and ins. m. Apr. 1688, Eliz. d. of John Wilcockson, had Mary, b. 5 Dec. 1689; Nathan, 1691; Josiah, Aug. 1693; and his w. d. Oct. 1694.

P. 155. l. 6 from bot. strike out Mary

" l. 4 and 3 from bot. strike out Mary m. &c. to Russell inclus.

P. 156. l. 9 from bot. after Jeremy; ins. Mary;

" l. 5 from bot. aft. 1700. add, Mary, d. of the first w. m. 23 June 1662, Joseph Russell.

" at the end of last l. add, (beside Ann and Patience)

P. 157. l. 2, aft. 1723; add, Rebecca, 12 Nov. 1671; Gill, 22 Sept. 1678;

P. 158. l. 1, bef. *had* ins. by w. Lydia, m. 24 Apr. 1657, — also, bef. 1658 ins. 12 June — also, for 1661 r. 21 June 1660

" l. 2, bef. 1663 ins. 23 Apr. — also, bef. 1666 ins. 3 Jan. — also, bef. 1668 ins. 31 Mar. — also, bef. 1670 ins. 12 Oct.

" l. 3, bef. 1673 ins. , 8 Jan. — also, aft. Margaret ins. 29 Mar.

" l. 6, bef. 1655 ins. 10 July — also, bef. 1657 ins. 6 Apr.

" l. 7, bef. 1658 ins. 28 Dec.

" l. 14, bef. 1647 ins. 20 July

P. 158. l. 15, bef. 1650 ins. 9 Jan. — also, bef. 1651 ins. 5 Nov. — also, for 1652 r. 2 Feb. 1653

" l. 16, bef. 1654 ins. 13 Nov.

P. 165. l. 8, aft. m. ins. 8 Mar.

" l. 11, aft. Joseph. add, His first w. was wid. Sarah Wilson, m. 8 Feb. 1658.

P. 166. last l. bef. Beverly, strike out *to* and ins. aft. 1671 from — also, strike out "next to Rowley" — also, at the end, add, wh. d. 26 Oct. 1733.

P. 167. l. 1, aft. 1679; add, John 1686; and Peter; and d. 12 Jan. 1691. Babson says, all the s. had fams. but gives no details.

" l. 4, aft. sis. add, of the w.

" l. 17 from bot. bef. JAMES, ins. ISAAC, perhaps of Stratford, m. 1683, Eliz. d. prob. of Daniel of Wethersfield, or perhaps of Robert of S.

" l. 13 from bot. aft. 1670 ins. James of Farmington, prob. his s. was 18 yrs. old, and there

P. 168. l. 15 from bot. aft. 1664, ins. may have been f. of Isaac, and Thomas, and freem. 1669. THOMAS, Stratford, perhaps s. of the preced. m. 1692, Mary Booth, d. perhaps of Ephraim.

" l. 14 from bot. aft. age. ins. WILLIAM, Salem, m. Mar. 1675, wid. Eliz. Smith, had Grace, b. Feb. 1677, d. soon.

P. 169. l. 19 from bot. aft. *of* ins. Peter s. of

P. 170. l. 2, aft. 1669, ins. s. of Edward of the same, d. 1672, leav. wid.

" l. 3, aft. 1669. ins. His will of 7 Mar. 1676, ment. ch. Zaccheus, a cripple, Edward, Hannah Akerly, perhaps w. of Thomas, Mary, wh. m. 6 Dec. 1666, Samuel Thorpe, Sarah Wright, Tabitha, wh. m. 27 Nov. 1684, Simon Simpson, Daniel, wh. was d. and had made Andrew resid. legatee.

P. 172. l. 20, aft. 1674. add, John sen. and John jr. were witness. in the sad witcher. trial of Ann Pudeater, wh. was hang.

" l. 17 from bot. aft. 1637, ins. had Ann, bapt. Aug. 1639. His w. d. 6 June, 1644.

P. 177. l. 1, aft 1641, add, and d. June 1666.

" l. 8 from bot. bef. Sept. ins. b. 18

P. 178. l. 3 from bot. aft. Newport ins. 1655,

P. 182. l. 1, aft. m. add, 31 Mar. 1657, — also, erase perhaps

" l. 20, aft. 1681; add, and d. 1695.

P. 183. l. 12, aft. rem. ins. with w. Philippa, bef.

" l. 13, aft. 109. ins. He d. acc. fam. rec. a. 1694, aged 73.

" l. 14, aft. Tomlinson, ins. wid. of Henry, m. Oct. 1688,

" l. 15 aft. John, ins. b. Mar. 1641; — also, aft. Joanna, ins. Nov. 1642,

" l. 16, aft. preced. add, m. 11 Dec. 1669, Phebe, d. of William Willcockson, had Hannah, b. Feb. 1671; Mary, Nov. 1675; Sarah, May 1678, d. next yr.; Abel, Nov. 1679; Joseph, Feb. 1682; and Dinah, 1688; and d. 1697. His wid. d. 20 Sept. 1743, aged 92.

P. 184. l. 10, aft. Davenport. add, His w. Patience d. 24 July 1655.

" l. 14, aft. 1691; add, but rec. says 24 June 1692.

" l. 20, aft. w. add Mary

" l. 20 from bot. aft. 1673. ins. His wid. d. 25 Oct. 1703. All the eleven ch. are nam. in his will.

" l. 16 from bot. aft. 336. ins. Hannah m. 12 Aug. 1669, John Morris;

" l. 15 from bot. aft. Giles, add, as his sec. w. Abigail m. 18 Nov. 1686, John Talmage; Ruth, m. 21 Oct. 1692, Nathaniel Yale; and Rebecca m .14 Nov. 1695, Samuel Thompson.

" l. 14 from bot. bef. JOB, ins. JAMES, New Haven, youngest s. of James the first, m.

11 Dec. 1695, Abigail Bennett, had Eliz. b. 6 Dec. foll.; Mary 11 June 1698; James, 4 Oct. 1700; Rebecca, 29 Nov. 1703; Abigail, 1 Sept. 1707; Ruth, 19 May 1709; and Joy, 28 May 1711. He prob. rem. to Stamford.

P. 185. l. 15 from bot. aft. 1689, ins. eldest s. of the first James,

" l. 14 from bot. aft. more, add, exc. as by the diligence of Mr. White taught, that he had Nathaniel, b. 15 Mar. 1691; Abigail, 5 June 1692; John, 1 Nov. 1693; Nathaniel, again, 5 Oct. 1695; Willet, 17 Oct. 1697; James, 17 Feb. 1700; Thomas, 10 Dec. 1701; Jeremiah, 7 Nov. 1703; Sarah, 19 Nov. 1705; Dinah, 1 Mar. 1708; and Ebenezer, 29 July 1710. In this yr. the f. d. and all the ch. exc. Nathaniel and Thomas, surv.

P. 186. l. 11, aft. 1681. ins. SAMUEL, New Haven, sec. s. of James the first, m. 14 Nov. 1695, Hannah, wid. prob. of Enos Talmage, had Hannah, b. 3 Sept. 1696; Samuel, 18 July 1698; Ann, 25 June 1700; Job, 6 Mar. 1702; and Eliz. 16 Apr. 1704. His w. d. 10 Feb. 1744, and he d. 12 Mar. 1748.

P. 187. l. 18, for Joseph, r. Rev. James

P. 188. l. 18, from bot. aft. Rowley ins. bef.

P. 189. l. 7 from bot. aft. old. add, He m. Dec. 1680, Abigail, eldest d. of John Hudson of New Haven, wh. d. Mar. 1713, had Richard, Jael, and Joseph. He m. 1717, a wid. wh. had two hs. bef. and he d. 1731.

P. 190. l. 10, at the end, add, and should be Blakesly.

P 194. last l. aft. 1687; add, and Hannah, 1693; by w. Hannah, and he d. 1702.

P. 195. l. 3, for "wid. Hannah" r. Jonathan.

" l. 11, bef. JOHN, ins. His wid. m. Edward Groom, wh. sett. B.'s est. 1694; but wh. he was is unkn.

" l. 20 and 21, strike out "wid. Hannah" &c. to "Goodwin" inclus. and ins. Abraham Kimberly, whose wid. m. John Curtis,

P. 199. aft. l. 12 from bot. ins. BLETSO THOMAS, Bristol, 1688, had w. and two serv. but no ch. nor is any thing more told of him.

P. 206. l. 9, aft. John, ins. 19 Oct.

P. 208. l. 3, for 1672 r. had Mary, b. 17 Oct. 1659;

P. 212. l. 9, aft. w. ins. Eliz. or

" l. 11, aft. 1680. add, His w. was oft. a witness, 1692, against witches.

" l. 20 from bot. aft. "good." add, By his first w. Mary, the posthum. d. of Hon. John Welles, he had no ch. His sec. w. Hannah, d. of John Wilcockson, brot. him Hannah, b. 1687; Robert, 1689; James, 1691; Zechariah, 1693; Joseph, 1695; David, 1697; and Nathan 1699, wh. d. at 15 yrs. and she d. 1701. Third w. he took next yr. and d. in yr. foll.

P. 213. l. 2 from bot. aft. "had" ins. Andrew, b. 22 Aug. 1671, one of emin. pub. serv. as selectman, rep. town treas. 46 yrs. and near. as long steward of the coll. beside Ruth, 28 Jan. 1673, the w. of Presid. Wadsworth, and two or three other ch.

P. 214. l. 22, aft. 1684, add, or 5

" l. 21 from bot. aft. 10, add or 19

P. 215. l. 12 from bot. strike out "Zechariah; Ephraim;" and ins. by rec. Mary, 1692; David, 1693; Martha, 1695;

" l. 10 from bot. strike out all the words, and ins. Eliz. was the name of his w.

P. 216. l. 5, aft. fam. ins. A wid. B. d. at H. 18 May 1648.

" l. 8, aft. b. ins. 9 Aug. 1668; Hannah, again,

" l. 18, aft. Hingham, add, had Eliz. bur. 18 Nov. 1638; Rebecca, bapt. Feb. 1642; Bethia, Jan. 1644; Benjamin, and Mehitable, 4 Apr. 1647; Mary, 18 Apr. 1647; Nathaniel, and Jeremiah, 29 July 1649; Hannah, 14 July 1650; Deliverance, b. 4 Aug. 1650; Joseph, bapt. June, 1652; Bellamy, 19 Nov. 1654; Edward, 29 May 1659; and Bridget, 19 Aug. 1660;

P. 216. l. 13 from bot. aft. *may* ins. have

" l. 12 from bot. at begin. ins. had Mary, bapt. 4 Oct. 1657, — also, aft. 1693. add, The s. was of Bristol 1689, a deac. with ch. and gr.ch.

P. 217. l. 20 from bot. strike out perhaps, and ins. b. at Exeter, 15 May 1648, — also, aft. Mary; add, but at H. Temperance, 8 Jan. 1650;

" l. 19 from bot. aft. Nathaniel, ins. 4 Mar. 1653

" l. 14 from bot. aft. 1678, ins. by w. Mary had Eliz. b. 8 Sept. 1688; and Mary; and d. June 1689.

P. 218. l. 16, for He r. His

P. 220. l. 16 from bot. aft. 1657; add, and Joseph, 28 Oct. 1659.

" l. 14 from bot. aft. New Haven, ins. m. Mary, d. of Edward Banister, was

" l. 5 from bot. bef. 1681, ins. Oct.

P. 224. l. 10 from bot. bef. Joseph ins. Mary;

P. 225. l. 12 from bot. bef. JOSEPH, ins. JOHN, Rowley, a. 1661; was, perhaps, s. of Matthew of the same.

P. 227. l. 15 from bot. bef. THOMAS, ins. SAMUEL, Salem, a witness in the doleful delus. a. witchcr. 1692, of wh. no more is kn.

P. 228. l. 9, aft. d. ins. Eliz. wh. m. John Patch, and d. 1716; and

P. 229. l. 1, aft. John, add, posthum.

P. 233. l. 13, for perhaps r. five — also, aft. others; add, and d. 19 Oct. 1718.

" l. 16, for prob. r. five — also, aft. others. add, He had sec. w. Mary Sacket, d. I suppose, of John.

" l. 21 from bot. aft. He ins. liv. prob. at Rowley first for sev. yrs.

" l. 20 from bot. erase " of the same "

P. 234. l. 5, at the begin. ins. br. of Daniel,

" l. 11, aft. Dorchester, add, m. 17 July 1666, Mary, d. of Richard Evans,

" l. 20, aft. Guilford, add, br. of Daniel,

" l. 15 from bot. bef. Oct. ins. 8

" l. 11 from bot. aft. Munson, ins. wh. was Martha, — also, aft. Todd, ins. m. 26 Nov. 1668

" l. 10 from bot. for Brackett r. Brockett — also, strike out, "but whether this last was Esther or" and ins. wh. was — also, aft. Sarah; strike out, "is uncert. and ins. Esther d. prob. unm. Mr. Porter thinks, this William was br. of Daniel by an elder w. of their f. and that he and other ch. were brot. by their mo. a wid. wh. was a midwife at N. H. in 1655.

P. 235. l. 13 from bot. aft. 1660. add, In Essex Inst. II. 29, Cheever says, he was prosecut. in 1652, for familiar. with the devil. Either the folly was not prov. or it was not capital.

P. 237. l. 14, aft. 45. add, JOSHUA, Haddam, br. of the preced. m. Mehitable, d. perhaps of William Dudley.

" l. 6 from bot. aft. 1711. add, Mercy m. Ebenezer Spooner.

P. 239. l. 17 from bot. aft. 1715. add, He next m. Eliz. wid. of Rev. Joseph Green, d. of Rev. Joseph Gerrish.

P. 240. l. 2, aft. 1656; ins. Sarah;

" l. 4, bef. Hannah ins. Mary m. 18 Nov. 1664, John Ring of Ipswich; Sarah m. James Sawyer;

" l. 5, aft. Roberts; add, and Esther m. 30 Oct. 1683, Philip Stanwood.

' l. 15 from bot. aft. Devon, add, or Lancash. if he came with Mather, aft. 1634, as Clap, in Hist. of D. 107, thinks,

P. 241. l. 4 from bot. aft. Bread, ins. even Broad,

P. 242. l. 1, aft. 1656, add, by w. Mary had John, b. 24 Apr. 1660; was

P. 245. l. 8, bef. and ins. Hannah m. 23 Dec. 1664, Samuel Starr;

P. 247. bef. l. 9 from bot. ins. BRIARS, JOHN, Gloucester 1652, m. that yr. Eliz. d. of John Jackson, had Grace, b. 1655; John, 1658; Benjamin, 1660; Mary, 1661, wh. d. very soon; and he rem.

P. 249. l. 2 from bot. aft. young; ins. Nathaniel, 8 Dec. 1659, prob. d. soon;

P. 252. l. 3, aft. man. add, From Hobart's Diary we find, that Hannah and Peter Briggs were bapt. 2 Aug. 1646, and John, 20 Dec. foll. but their f. is unkn.

" l. 8, aft. him. add, THOMAS, and WILLIAM, nam. in Essex Inst. II. 70, in my opin. mean Biggs.

P. 254. l. 16, aft. 1674. add, His will of 11 May 1678, pro. Nov. foll. ment. w. Tabitha, s. Philip, dr. Mary Tucker, and . . . Holman, — also, aft. br. ins. or s.

P. 257. l. 2, for Mary r. Mercy

" l. 3, bef. 1653, ins. 17 Nov. — also, bef. Brown, ins. d. of Eleazer, — also, bef. 1656, ins. 29 Jan.

" l. 6, aft. 1666; add, beside Sarah, b. 1668; Daniel, 4 May 1671; Eliz. 20 May 1674; Esther, 3 Oct. 1676; Eliphalet, 2 Oct. 1679; and Henry, 20 June 1683. Twelve of these 14 ch. surv. the f. Rebecca m. Dec. 1670, Zaccheus Candee, — also, aft. 69, ins. br. of the preced.

" l. 7, aft. same. add, Hav. no ch. he made the eldest s. of his br. heir to his est.

' l. 20, at the end, add, NATHANIEL, Newport, in the hist. of freem. 1655.

' bef. l. 21, ins. BROAD, ALLEN, mispr. oft. for Breed.

" l. 3 from bot. strike out, prob. — also, aft. m. ins. 21 Jan. 1684,

" l. 2 from bot. for Jan. r. Dec.

P. 258. l. 2, aft. Jabez, ins. b. 24 Feb.

" l. 5, aft. Joseph; ins. both m. at Milford, 25 Oct. 1667;

" l. 6, strike out, "presum. to be br. or s. of" and ins. wh. m. 22 Jan. 1673,

P. 261. l. 3, aft. 1656; ins. of wh. two were Mary, b. 5 Sept. 1654; and Eliz. 29 Sept. 1656; beside Sarah, 9 Apr. 1661;

" l. 6, erase "wh. may have been his d."

" l. 7, for or July 1674 r. 1675 — also, aft. Ford; add, and Sarah m. 29 Aug. 1687, Benjamin Robbins.

P. 264. l. 17, aft. 1657; ins. and Sarah, 6 June 1660. Ano. ABRAHAM, Boston,

P. 265. l. 21, at the end, add, CHRISTOPHER, Salem, examin. 1674, on charge of deal. with the devil.

" l. 13 from bot. bef. EBENEZER, ins. DANIEL, New Haven, s. of Eleazer, m. a. 1690, Abigail, d. of Ephraim Howe.

" l. 9 from bot. for 1684 r. 1685

" l. 6 from bot. aft. ch. ins. EDMUND, Boston, d. in the autumn of 1665, at Surinam, leav. wid. Eliz. to have all his prop.

P. 266. l. 11, aft. 1668; add, ds. Rebecca, Hannah, Eliz. and ano.

" l. 20, aft. Lydia, ins. wh. was the eldest, and m. 29 Jan. 1656, Henry Bristoll.

P. 270. l. 22, aft. eldest, ins. b. 27 Sept. 1650; — also, aft. Joseph, ins. 9 Apr. 1658; — also, aft. Nathaniel, ins. 9 June 1661; — also, aft. Lydia, ins. 6 Aug. 1656; — also, aft. Hannah, ins. 29 Jan. 1659;

" l. 6 from bot. bef. s. erase *prob.*

P. 272. l. 4, aft. capt. add, s. of John, and gr.s. of Hon. John of the same, m. 8 Nov. 1672, Ann, d. of maj. John Mason of Norwich, — also, aft. 1675; add, Lydia, 16 May 1679; Martha, 20 Nov. 1681; Daniel, 29 Oct. 1683; Ebenezer, 15 June 1685; Daniel, again, 26 Sept. 1686; Stephen, 29 Jan. 1688; and Joseph, 19 May 1690; beside Samuel, wh. may be one of two rec. Daniel.

P. 272. l. 13 from bot. aft. Salem, ins. s. of Elder John,

" 1.12 from bot. aft. Burrill, add, prob. d. soon, for inv. of his insolv. est. was giv. 16 Apr. 1667.

P. 275. l. 3 from bot. aft. "had" ins. Gideon, 12 July 1685; and

P. 276. l. 6 from bot. bef. "had," ins. d. of Thomas Newhall of the same,

P. 278. l. 1, aft. R. add, His wid. m. 26 Sept. 1662, Henry Walker as his third w. and d. Mary m. 3 July 1667, William Haskell.

" l. 17, aft. 1657; add, and Susanna, 24 Oct. 1659.

P. 279. l. 1, aft. 78. add, WILLIAM, Bristol, had in 1689 three ch. but w. was d.

" l. 13 from bot. aft. d. ins. w. of Isaac

" l. 12 from bot. at begin. ins. she was — also, for "not nam. in it" r. that — also, erase "and was d."

" l. 9 from bot. at the end, add, See Brimsmead.

P. 281. l. 1, aft. "had" ins. brot.

" l. 2, strike out "bef. com. over," — also, aft. "here" add had

" l. 15 from bot. for Brace r. Bruce

P. 284. l. 14, aft. 1639. add, He m. 4 June 1639, at Dorchester, but the w's name is not seen, had a ch. that was bur. 13 June 1640; Lydia, bapt. 3 Dec. 1643; Adam, wh. d. 24 Apr. 1646; and Abel, prob. tw. br. bapt. 26 Apr. 1646; and Lydia d. at 23 yrs.

" l. 15, aft. sh. ins. was short time at Dorchester,

P. 286. l. 12, at the end, add, STEPHEN, Bristol, in Feb. 1689, had w. and two ch.

P. 289. l. 21, aft. Salem, ins. eldest s. of Robert,

" l. 16 from bot. aft. m. ins. 22 Sept. 1673,

" l. 15 from bot. at the end, add, Inv. of his est. was tak. 15 Nov. 1669.

P. 297. l. 17, aft. mo. add, His will, 6 days bef. nam. w. Eliz. s. Thomas, gr.ch. John, s. of Henry, and d. Eliz. wh. m. 13 Jan. 1675, Richard Norman.

P. 298. l. 10, aft. Eng. ins. by w. Hannah had Hannah, b. 24 Nov. 1664; Thomas, 22 Feb. 1667; Mary, 30 May 1668; Jeremiah, 25 Nov. 1670; and Sarah, 8 Sept. 1674. By sec. w. Sarah, he had Sarah, 15 Aug. 1676; Jeremiah, 14 Oct. 1678; Abigail, 4 Nov. 1683; and Abigail, again, 12 Feb. 1685; beside Thomas, 1 Feb. 1687;

P. 300. l. 5, aft. 1685, ins. had eleven ch. names unkn. and d. 1696.

" l. 6, strike out m. and ins. had Benjamin; Nathan; Lydia; Mary, b. 4 May 1650; and Ebenezer, 25 Aug. 1653, by w.

" l. 8, aft. h. ins. with one of the ch.

P. 301. l. 2 from bot. for a. 1694 r. 4 Apr. 1690

" last l. for Philippa r. Phillis

P. 302, l. 2 from bot. bef. ROBERT, ins. RICHARD, Stratford, m. Phebe, d. of John Peacock, bef. 1679.

P. 304. l. 5, at the end, add, THOMAS, Reading, m. 3 Dec. 1663, Mary, d. of John Pearson.

P. 308. l. 5, aft. 1646; ins. all prob. by w. that d. 23 July 1647; and by ano. w. had Simon, and Hannah, both bapt. 25 Feb. 1655; Jonathan, 3 June foll. and John, b. 6 Jan. 1660;

P. 309. l. 9, aft. unkn. add, but prob. he was of Bristol, with w. and one ch. early in 1689.

" l. 9 from bot. strike out WILLIAM, &c. to the end of paragr.

P. 310. l. 7, aft. BURROWS, ins. BOROUGHS, BOROWS,

P. 311. l. 13 from bot. aft. tailor, add, rem. to Bristol, there in 1689 had w. and three ch.

P. 315. l. 19, bef. STEPHEN, ins. SOLOMON, Stratford, m. Aug. 1687, Mercy, d. of
Jeremiah Judson, had ch. whose names and dates are unkn. but descend. contin.

P. 316. l. 18, aft. print. add, Ano. SAMUEL, New Haven 1685, was younger and m.

P. 317. l. 12 from bot. aft. 1657 ; add, John, 19 Jan. 1660 ;

P. 320. l. 13 from bot. bef. JOHN, ins. JOHN, New Haven, m. 3 Jan. 1666, Eliz. Morrill,
had Mary, b. 9 Sept. 1667 ; ano. d. 1669 ; and John and James, tw. 6 Sept. 1671.

"   l. 9 from bot. aft. John. ins. Perhaps he was his s. and a. 1684 was of Stratford,
with w. Mary, wh. had admin. of his est. 1697.

P. 321. l. 16 from bot. for "to 85 " r. (, d. 1676)

"   l. 13 from bot. aft. deac. add, had, in Haddam, Samuel, b. 26 Nov. 1665 ; and Eliz.
20 Aug. 1667 ;

P. 322. bef. l. 10, ins. BUTMAN, JEREMIAH, Salem, may not be kn. exc. as a creditor
of est. of Henry Harwood, dec. 1671. See Essex Inst. II. 70. JOHN, Gloucester, m. 30 June 1690, Sarah, d. of Abraham Robinson the sec. had Jeremiah, b.
early in 1691 ; a d. 1693 ; Mary, 1697 ; Hannah, 1700 ; John, 1703 ; Jonathan,
1708 ; and Samuel, 1711.

P. 325. l. 14, aft. Sarah. add, Mary m. 28 Dec. 1672, John Cook.

P. 326. l. 8, aft. BYLES, ins. JONATHAN, Beverly, m. 16 Nov. 1674, Eliz. d. of John
Patch of Salem, had Richard, b. 3 Nov. foll. and perhaps more.

"   l. 18, at the end, add, RICHARD, Gloucester, eldest ch. of Jonathan, by w. Mary
had Charles, b. 1700 ; Mary, 1702 ; John, 1704 ; Martha, 1706 ; Sarah, 1710 ;
Eliz. 1713 ; Alexander, 1716 ; and Jonathan, 1719 ; rem. to Beverly 1727. His
w. d. Jan. 1746 ; and he d. at gr. age, 12 Feb. 1771.

P. 327. l. 5, aft. 1673. add, No ch. foll. this sec. w. prob. for in her will of 6 Feb. 1674,
Samuel B. her s. was made heir, and to her other ch. she gave 5s. ea.

P. 328. l. 5, for Edmund r. William

"   l. 15 from bot. aft. Jones, add, had Hepzibah ; Isaac, b. 1680 ; Rebecca, 1683, d.
young ; and Margaret ;

"   l. 14 from bot. for soon r. 1712

P. 332. l. 18 from bot. bef. JAMES, ins. DANIEL, Salem, m. 10 Nov. 1681, Hannah,
d. of Henry Cook, had Daniel, b. 10 Aug. foll. David, 7 July, 1683 ; Hannah, 4
Sept. 1685 ; Jonathan, 19 Jan. 1688 ; Isaac, 21 Jan. 1690 ; and Eliz. 21 Mar.
1693 ; and he d. 11 June 1695.

"   l. 17 from bot. aft. CANDE, add. CAMBEE, or KEMBEE, — also, at the end, add, m.
Dec. 1670, Rebecca, d. of Henry Bristoll.

"   bef. l. 16 from bot. ins. CANE, or CANNE, CHRISTOPHER, Cambridge, by w. Margaret had Deborah, b. 17 Jan. 1645. In Geneal. Reg. VIII. 345, is giv. the blunder of this name from copy of Boston rec. Champney.

P. 334. l. 7 from bot. at the end, add, He m. 10 Jan. 1693, Hannah, wid. of Job Coit,
and rem. to Gloucester, had Mary, b. 1693 ; William, 1696 ; Hannah, 1699 ; John,
1701 ; and Benjamin, 1710.

P. 335. l. 20, aft. rec. ins. and d. bef. his f.

"   l. 21, aft. Crosby ; add, but certain. he went home, and d. in Eng. — also, aft.
Haverhill, add, s. of the preced.

"   l. 21 from bot. aft. 1669, ins. whose wid. m. Christopher Babbage,

P. 340. l. 18, aft. 1647, add, wh. m. Peter Fowle.

"   l. 19, aft. 1648, ins. wh. m. James Fowle.

P. 344. l. 16 from bot. aft. CARY, ins. DAVID, Bristol, s. prob. of John the first, had
w. and d. there 1689.

P. 345. l. 3, aft. rem. add, to Bristol, there with w. and seven ch. was liv. in 1689,
and his w. was, prob. Hannah.

P. 349, l. 9, strike out, "was prob. f. of that" and ins. is better spell. Kirtland, wh. see.

P. 350. l. 9, aft. 1682, add, m. Mary, d. of William Nichols, had. on rec. of Topsfield, Sarah, b. 8 Mar. 1673; Hannah, 14 Mar. 1675; Abigail, 28 Mar. 1677; Thomas, 6 Mar. 1681; and Ann, 9 July, 1682.

" l. 4 from bot. aft. "His" ins. inv. was tak. 17 June 1679; and the

P. 353. l. 5 from bot. aft. 1667; add, and d. of smallpox, 26 Apr. 1668.

P. 356. l. 1, strike out the sent. begin. CHRISTOPHER,

" l. 6 from bot. aft. chart. add, In this yr. he m. Ruth, d. of Edward Michelson, wid. of John Green.

P. 359. l. 14 from bot. strike out, ,) wh. is unkn. to me

P. 360. l. 14 from bot. aft. 1668, add, m. Jan. 1676, Rebecca, eldest d. of Anthony Needham, had Michael, b. 21 Aug. 1677; Rebecca, 27 Feb. 1680; George, 5 Sept. 1682; James, 14 Sept. 1685; Anthony, 19 Sept. 1688; Isaac, 30 Mar. 1691; and d. 7 May 1692.

P. 364. l. 20, add, His will of 31 Dec. 1672, pro. June foll. nam. w. Sarah extrix. no ch. but gives to cous. Robert C. to cous. James Dennis's ch. Mary, and James, wh. I suppose were of his w. cous. Mary D. His wid. d. 21 Dec. 1676.

P. 366. bef. l. 9, ins. CHATWELL, NICHOLAS, Salem, m. 15 Feb. 1672, wid. Sarah March, had Mary, b. 24 Dec. 1673; Hannah, 22 June 1676; and Prisca, 22 Apr. 1679.

P. 368. l. 10 from bot. aft. m. ins. 8 Jan. 1667,

P. 370. l. 21 from bot. strike out, (, d. soon

P. 371. l. 16, aft. 1645, add, wh. m. 3 Sept. 1666, Samuel Goldthwait

" l. 12 from bot. aft. Danvers. add, He m. 17 June 1680, Abigail, d. of Michael Leffingwell, had Abigail, b. 22 Mar. foll. Thomas, 28 Feb. 1684; Ezekiel, 15 Mar. 1686, wh. d. young; and Samuel, 9 Feb. 1690.

P. 374. l. 5 from bot. aft. "Samuel" add first

" l. 4 from bot. aft. David, ins. b. 1 Feb. 1703; — also, aft. Mary; add, and d. 1739. His wid. d. 1744, aged 66.

P. 376. l. 17, aft. bapt. add, Mary m. 5 Sept. 1664, John Marston jr.

P. 379. l. 13, from bot. erase prob.

P. 384. exchange the posit. of CHUBB and CHRISTOPHERSON.

" l. 7 from bot. aft. young; ins. beside, prob. Alice;

P. 389. l. 8, for Samuel r. Simon — also, for Rehoboth r. Hingham, as his sec. w.

" l. 8 from bot. aft. 14 add, or 24 — also, aft. will, ins. of 11 of that mo.

" l. 4 from bot. aft. Mehitable, add, 30 Aug. 1684,

P. 390. l. 9, aft. again, ins. bapt. 11 Dec.

" l. 11, bef. PRESERVED, ins. NOAH, Sudbury, youngest s. of the preced. by first w. had Ann, b. 10 Sept. 1691; Sarah, 30 Apr. 1693; Mary, 20 Sept. 1695; and by ano. w. had Elias, 14 June 1709; and Noah; both d. young. He was town clk. and d. 1753.

P. 391. l. 22, bef. 1684. ins. 20 Apr.

P. 393. l. 2, aft. Abigail; ins. John;

" l. 3, aft. 1667. add, His wid. m. 15 June 1668, Thomas Penny.

" l. 13, aft. "had" for George, r. only s. John (excor. of his f's will, wh. d. 1693, unm.),

" l. 14, erase Aug. — also, for preced. r. pro. 20 June of that yr.

" l. 16, bef. GEORGE, ins. Other ds. were Hannah, wh. m. John Platt of Norwalk; Abigail m. Rev. Abraham Pierson; Ruth m. Robert Plumb; Rebecca m. John Brown; and Mary m. Samuel Clark. Their f. own. est. in Eng. had brs. there, John, Daniel, and Edward.

" l. 18, erase s. of George the husbandman,

P. 393. l. 19, aft. rep. strike out to the end of the sent. and ins. 1668 to 76, had Thomas, George, Samuel, and Sarah, wh. m. Jonathan Law.

P. 394. l. 2, aft. places. add, His w. was Deborah, d. of John Peacock.

"   l. 13, aft. 1660, add, at Stratford had James, b. 12 Feb. 1665; Sarah, 11 Jan. 1667; John, 17 Mar. 1669; Phebe, 15 July 1675; Isaac, 9 Jan. 1678, d. soon; Isaac, again, 25 Sept. 1679; and Mary, 10 Jan. 1687.

P. 395. l. 4 from bot. strike out, (. perhaps,

"   l. 3 from bot. aft. d. add, unm.—also, aft. Matthew; ins. Ebenezer, bapt. 10 Aug. 1690, d. soon;

P. 396. l. 1, erase sen.

"   l. 2, for Wood r. Woodruff

"   l. 4, for Martha r. Mercy

"   l. 7 and 8, erase tho. only Rebecca is nam.

"   l. 9, for 1674 r. 1676

"   l. 19, aft. ch. ins. JOHN, Newport, s. perhaps of Joseph, m. Feb. 1671 Jane Fletcher, had a d. b. 14 Feb. 1672, and the mo. d. Apr. foll. and the ch. d. Mar. 1673.

P. 399. l. 18, at the end, add, MATTHEW, Farmington, s. of John the first of same, m. Ruth, d. of John Judd, had Ruth; Matthew; wh. both d. soon; Mary; John; Ruth, again; and Matthew, again; and d. 24 Sept. 1751.

P. 402. l. 15 from bot. aft. war. ins. THOMAS, Salem, m. 4 Mar. 1676 Mary Voaker, that seems a strange name, had Thomas, b. 14 Apr. 1677.

P. 403. l. 3, aft. 80. add, He had large share in settlem. of Bristol, liv. there, 1689, with w. and five ch. and his will gave all his est. (exc. £20. to the poor of Dr. Colman's ch.) in equal sh. to his seven ch. Jonas, Sarah Paine, Mary Ruck, Margaret Fitch, Catharine Drowne, and heirs of Abigail Parrot, and of Prudence Kneeland, dec. and nam. Bryant Parrot and John Kneeland guardns. of their respective ch. mak. s. Jonas, Shem Drowne, and Joseph Fitch excors.

P. 404. l. 20 from bot. aft. ch. add, His d. Deborah d. 16 Mar. 1661.

P. 406. l. 2, aft. 1666. ins. JOHN, Salem 1676, fisherman, k. by the Ind. next yr.— also, aft. 1668, ins. m. 22 Oct. 1678, Mary Allen.

P. 409. l, 14 from bot. for 237 r. 231

P. 410. l. 13, for next yr. r. some yrs. bef.

P. 411. l. 9 from bot. for "by w." r. m. 26 July 1672,—also, aft. Eliz. add Story,— also, aft. had, add Edward, b. 27 July 1673;

P. 412. l. 11, aft. 1708. add, Hannah m. a. 1686, Daniel Eliot

"   l. 13, aft. Hannah; add, rem. to Salem, there had Mary, b. 6 July 1677; but ret. to F. and

P. 414. l. 20, aft. d. add, One of this name was of Bristol, Feb. 1689.

P. 415, l. 15, at the end, add, But at Hardwick was a Cobleigh a. 100 yrs. ago.

"   l. 18, at the end, add, Eliz. perhaps his wid. d. at S. June 1664.

P. 417. l. 6 from bot. erase and was of Stratford 1684. There his s. John m.— also, erase other

P. 418. l. 17, for "or Stratford 1650" r. with Denton,

"   l. 21, strike out "a d. b. there that yr. perhaps" and ins. Hannah, b. Sept. 1651, wh. prob. d. young;—also, aft. Susanna, ins. Apr. 1653,

"   l. 22, aft. New Haven; ins. Sarah, Apr. 1656;—also, aft. d. ins. Oct.

P. 419. l. 19 from bot. aft. Gloucester; add, but how long he resid. Mr. Babson is ign.

P. 421. l. 8, bef. JAMES, ins. BENJAMIN, Newport, s. of the sec. John, had w. Sarah, wh. d. May 1726, and he d. 16 Apr. 1739. FREEGIFT, Newport, br. of the preced. d. 27 Feb. 1728, and his w. d. 6 June 1748, aged 85,—also, erase prob.

P. 421. l. 9, for first r. sec. — also, aft. Ball; add, and he d. 2 Apr. 1712. — also erase ‡

" l. 16 and 17, erase " and one of the " to " Col." inclus.

" l. 17 and 18 erase, " aft. fill other hon. places in " — also, bef. Nov. ins. 27 — also, for " the " r. that

" l. 18 and 19 strike out, " 1680, perhaps " to " same name " inclus. and ins. aged a. 56 yrs.

" l. 22, 21, and 20 from bot. erase, " and I presume " to " dept. gov." inclus. — also, bef. JOHN, ins. ††

" l. 15 from bot. for C. r. and he

" l. 10 from bot. aft. foll. add, aged a. 36 yrs. says gr.stone. He was oft. assist. and dept. gov. bef. and aft. Andros, and d. 1 Oct. 1708, in his 90th yr.

P. 422. l. 4 from bot. bef. Abigail, ins. John, b. 1653 ; Mary, 1655 ; — also, aft. 1659, ins. beside Job, 1661 ;

" l. 3 from bot. aft. 1675, add, Babson thinks, it was sev. yrs. earlier, and that his wid. m. 3 Oct. 1667, John Fitch.

P. 423. l. 14 from bot. bef. JOHN, ins. HENRY, Salem, had w. Sarah, small prop. by his. inv. June 1676, bec. " he carr. most of his est. with him to Virg."

P. 425. l. 11, aft. COLDAM, ins. COLDOM,

" l. 20, at the end, add, But his will of 14 Mar. preced. says, aged, a. 86 yrs. no doubt he was too old to be exact. It ment. w. Joanna.

" l. 21, erase. " perhaps " — also, erase " perhaps his neph."

" l. 22, at the end, add, His will of 10 Mar. preced. nam. no w. or ch.

" l. 20 from bot. erase " perhaps " — also, for Isaac r. Thomas

P. 426. l. 15, aft. 1675. add, Perhaps he was not k. but bad. wound. for in Essex Inst. II. 183, is abstr. of his will of 8 Nov.

P. 430. l. 17, aft. 1649, add, there d. Apr. 1679. His sec. w. Ann, by her will of 1 Nov. foll. ment. s. Abraham, and John.

P. 434. last l. aft. 1685. add, He was s. of the first John, had tw. ws. and a s. by ea.

P. 435. l. 2, bef. selectman, ins. and Ann, 1649 ;

" l. 5, aft. Mary, erase prob. — also. aft. Elwell; add, had sec. h. and third, James Davis ; d. 9 Mar. 1725 ; and Ann m. 17 July 1673, Charles James, as Babson, 73, teaches.

" l. 19, aft. Henry, ins. mariner, by w. Abigail

" l. 18 from bot. aft. 1679, add, wh. d. soon. When the f. d. 22 Dec. foll. the wid. and twelve surv. ch. had a comforta. est. to div. His d. Abigail had m. 18 July 1678, Andrew Townsend.

" l. 10 from bot. aft. 1675. add, He rem. to Salem, there had Hannah, 4 Aug. 1676 ; and d. Sept. 1677.

P. 437. l. 21 from. bot. aft. 1661, ins. JOHN, Salem, d. June 1665.

" l. 16 from bot. bef. WILLIAM, ins. WILLIAM, Gloucester 1654, m. 14 Nov. 1662, Bridget, wid. of John Rowe, and d. 18 Apr. 1680, and she d. 2 May foll.

P. 439. l. 18, aft. Boston, add, was b. 26 Apr. 1644, as is said, but his f. is not kn.

" l. 20, bef. RICHARD, ins. MATTHEW, Newport, freem. 1655.

P. 440. l. 18, aft. 1659, ins. JOSHUA, Salem, gr.s. of Roger the first, but by wh. s. is not clear, m. 31 Aug. 1676, Christian, d. of Richard Mower, had Joshua, b. 12 May 1678.

" l. 21, aft. 1674, ins. when he d.

" l. 22, aft. ch. add, 5 s. 5 ds.

" l. 20 from bot. aft. d. add, but his own est. was good.

P. 441. l. 17 from bot. aft. 74, ins. by first w. Rebecca had Esther, wh. m. a Green, perhaps Charles ; and by sec. w. Ann had Ann, wh. m. a Salter, perhaps Matthew, as in his will of 9 Feb. 1678, Essex Inst. II. 277. is seen. It gives to Ann and her childr. and to Mary and Charles, ch. of Esther.

P. 446. l. 17 and 18, erase, Joseph, 27 Dec. 1643.

" l. 10 from bot. bef. ISAAC, ins. HENRY, Salem, m. Mary Hale, d. perhaps of sec. Thomas of Newbury had Mary, b. 15 July 1678.

" l. 8 from bot. aft. 1667, add, d. young — also, aft. 1668; add, Abigail, 12 July 1670 ; Hannah, 15 Oct. 1672 ; John, 23 Mar. 1674 ; Rachel, 20 Feb. 1676 ; Ebenezer, 24 Dec. 1677 ; Samuel, 1 Oct. 1679, wh. d. the same day, as did three other ch. of his b. last preced. in a few days aft. the latest. But the transcr. in Essex Inst. II. 42 may be good, and the rec. bad, as to a ch. com. betw. Abigail and Hannah.

P. 447. l. 5, aft. 1690. add, Perhaps he was the mariner, wh. m. Sarah, d. of Samuel Very of Salem, and she next m. a Stover.

" l. 21 from bot. after Mayflower; add, and d. 23 Nov. 1695. One of his ds. m. Thomas Tabor.

" l. 11 from bot. aft. 1644, add, wh. may have rem. to Stratford, and there was liv. 1667–77.

" l. 7 from bot. bef. JOHN, ins. JOHN, Salem, m. 28 Dec. 1672, Mary, prob. d. of Anthony Buxton, had Mary, b. 11 Nov. 1673 ; John, 20 Aug. 1674 ; Eliz. 7 Apr. 1676 ; Samuel, 3 Nov. 1678, d. next yr. ; Joseph, 9 Mar. 1681 ; Hannah, 9 Sept. 1684 ; Lydia, 2 Mar. 1687 ; and Isaac, 16 Apr. 1689.

" l. 4 from bot. after the sec. 1680 ; ins. beside three wh. d. inf. and Mary, b. 1688. Babson thinks his mo. was that wid. Rachel, wh. m. William Vinson, but his f. is unkn.

P. 448. l. 10, aft. ch. ins. Joseph, b. 27 Dec. 1643 ;

" l. 13, strike out " George of the same," and ins. the preced.

P. 450. l. 9, aft. d. ins. Apr. 1673, as Babson tells, or by ano. acco.

P. 451. l. 2, aft. it. ins. One Thomas, perhaps s. of the preced. was of Wethersfield 1693, and own. ld. in Stratford, until 1720.

P. 453. l. 16 from bot. aft. 1647, ins. d. Sept. 1669, prob. as this is date of inv. He left. wid. and childr. whose names I kn. not.

P. 455. l. 15, aft. John. ins. THOMAS, Salem, m. 12 June 1674, wid. Sarah Southwick, had Eliz. b. 2 Nov. of uncert. yr. Ano. THOMAS, Salem, m. 27 Dec. 1680, Deliverence, d. of William Marston.

P. 458, bef. l. 10, ins. CORNING, SAMUEL, Salem, perhaps had w. Hannah, d. of John Bachiler, as nam. in his will of 1675.

P. 459. l. 19, bef. 1707. ins. 2 Nov. — also, bef. 1708. ins. 1 Mar.

P. 460. l. 22, at the end, add, Mary m. 29 May 1673, John Parker ; Deliverance m. 5 June, 1683, Henry Crosby ; and

" l. 3 from bot. aft. preced. add, and by w. Rebecca had Rebecca, b. 2 Apr. 1660.

P. 463. l. 15 from bot. aft. Yarmouth, ins. collea. with Thornton

" l. 12 and 11 from bot. erase, " as was confidently " to " prob." inclus.

P. 464. l. 19, 20 and 21 from bot. erase, " as was once " to " Cushing " inclus.

P. 466. l. 4 from bot. aft. 1639, add, may have liv. at Salem 1672.

P. 468. l. 13, aft. Samuel, add, b. 23 Dec. 1659,

P. 469. l. 5, aft. 1671, add, liv. with w. Eliz. some yrs. later at Portsmouth.

P. 472. l. 7, aft. Mary, add, 20 Oct. 1689 ; rem. to Windham a. 1690, and had Hannah, 7 Mar. 1692 ; Isaac, 2 Apr. 1694 ; Joseph, 17 May 1696 ; Eliz. Feb. 1698, d. soon ; and Abigail, 15 Feb. 1700.

P. 472. l. 18, aft. 1674. add, He d. Nov. 1677.

" l. 21 from bot. at the end, add, ROBERT, Newport, perhaps br. of the preced. is on freem's. list 1655.

" l. 20 from bot. for "the preced." r. Gov. John,

P. 473. l. 5, aft. 1691, add, one of wh. perhaps was f. of that John, wh. by John Bachiler's will, 1675, is call. gr.s.

" l. 2 from bot. bef. 1670. ins. Nov.

" last l. erase "perhaps"

P. 474. l. 1, aft. Thomas, add, liv. at Salem, was reg. of Pro. Ct. few yrs. JOHN, Salem, s. of Richard, a mariner, d. in Eng. 19 May 1717, leav. wid. Mary.

P. 476. at top. ins. CROMPTON, SAMUEL, prob. a soldier, k. by the Ind. 1675, was, no doubt, of a town in Co. Essex, since admin. was giv. 21 Dec. of that yr. to his wid. Jane.

" l. 17 from bot. aft. 1714. add, He left to the town of S. by his will £30. for a writ. sch.

" l. 5 from bot. aft. health. add, WILLIAM, Stratford, an orig. propr. of wh. no more is kn. but that he liv. at New Haven in 1647, sold to Henry Wakelyn, his ld.

P. 477. l. 6, bef. JOSEPH, ins. HENRY, Salem, m. 5 June 1683, Deliverance, prob. d. of Giles Cory, had Henry b. 14 May 1684.

P. 478. l. 11, bef. ROBERT, ins. RICHARD, Salem, m. 24 Nov. 1670, Jane Pudeater, had Eliz. b. 17 Aug. foll. and John, 12 Apr. 1673.

P. 482. l. 12, aft. "had" ins. tak. w. in Eng. a d. of Rev. Dr. Stoughton, as is infer. from a let. in Geneal. Reg. XIV. 101, and

P. 484. l. 17, aft. CORNEY, ins. ELISHA, Gloucester, s. of John of the same, m. Rebecca, d. possib. of one of the John Smiths; and Babson says, he had a large fam. of ch.

" l. 19, aft. days; add, Mary, 1682; and Babson thinks, that ano. s. JOHN, m. 1713, Mary Cook, perhaps d. of John;

" l. 19 and 20, erase the last sent.

P. 486. l. 3, for "may" r. would

" l. 11, aft. same, ins. had Abigail, b. Oct. 1671; Sarah, Sept. 1673; William, 1675, wh. d. at 17 yrs. — also, at the end, add, Jonathan 1679.

" l. 12, erase, tho. we kn. not the names

" l. 13, aft. John. ins. His wid. m. a. 1692, Nicholas Huse, and had ano. h.

P. 487. l. 7 from bot. bef. Daniel ins. Abigail, Apr. 1650;

P. 488. l. 7, aft. 1659, add, wh. m. 19 Apr. 1677, at S. Richard Friend.

" l. 8, aft. "been" ins. of Bristol 1689, and

" l. 20, aft. d. ins. 3 or

" last l. aft. Judge ins. for trial of witches 1692, — also, aft. of add, an unlawful special, — also, aft. Saltonstall; add, succeed Leverett in 1708, in the legitim. Sup. Ct.

P. 489. l. 1, aft. 1718; add, but Essex Inst. II. 229, says, 25 July.

" l. 7, aft. John, erase, b. 6 Jan. 1672,

" l. 8, for Seaborn r. John

" l. 9, for Hampton r. Plymouth

" l. 11, erase Joanna, Mary, and Eliz.

" l. 3 from bot. at the end, add, had Jeremiah, b. 1696; Benjamin, 1700; John, 1703; and Ebenezer, 1710.

" l. 2 from bot. aft. w. ins. m. 1715, Ann Coffin,

P. 495. l. 10, bef. d. ins. had command at the fort, and

P. 498. l. 11, at the end, add, also, aft. *He*, add, spell. his name Allin,

P. 500. erase the first l.

P. 502. l. 3, at the end, add, and to save her life confess. the truth of the false charge.

P. 503. l. 22 from bot. aft. *add*, add, beside prob. Eliz. and Sarah,

" l. 17 from bot. aft. *and*, add, a ch. b. 21 Sept. 1663;

P. 506. l. 9, aft. 7, ins. from bot.

P. 507. l. 10, bef. BLETHIN, ins. BLIFFIN, or

P. 513. l. 16 from bot. for 367 r. 377

P. 514. l. 23, bef. Randall, ins. eldest ch. of Stephen

" l. 15 from bot. aft. 1674; ins. Isaac, 4 Aug. 1677; and Samuel, again, 19 May 1687.

P. 515. l. 6, aft. *add*, add, eldest

" l. 15 from bot. at the end, add, beside Sarah, 8 Nov. 1674.

" l. 12 from bot. at the end, add, also, aft. Sarah, add, b. 16 Nov. 1680 — also, aft. Jonathan, ins. 2 Feb. 1684;

P. 516. l. 9, aft. 18, add, from the bot.

MORE ADDITIONS AND CORRECTIONS

IN VOL. II.

P. 2. l. 18 from bot. aft. 52. add, THOMAS, Bristol, in Feb. 1680, had w. and two. ch.

P. 8. l. 11, aft. July, add, tho. her b. is giv. 16, in Geneal. Reg.

" l. 14, aft. 16, ins. but b. 18, — also, at the end, add, acc. Geneal. Reg. VII. 321,

P. 10. l. 11, aft. 1671. add, Ano. d. Hannah, m. 11 Feb. 1673, Benjamin Badcock. His will of 2 July 1678, ment. w. s. John, and Samuel, and d. Hannah.

" l. 20 from bot. aft. 90, add, many yrs. was of Salem

P. 16. l. 5, strike out perhaps, and ins. 1625, — also, aft. Margery, ins. d. of Richard,

P. 17. l. 22, aft. Gloucester, ins. s. of John of the same,

P. 18. l. 5, aft. 1717. add, Babson says, he was s. of John, and was third h. of Mary, d. of John Collins.

" l. 17, bef. JOHN, ins. JOHN, Gloucester, 1651, rem. aft. some yrs. to Ipswich. Of him no more is kn. exc. that he left at G. James and John.

P. 20. l. 11, from bot. for bef. 9 Aug. r. 24 July

P. 21. l. 7 from bot. bef. STEPHEN, ins. One SIMON was of Bristol, Feb. 1689, with w. and one ch.

P. 24. l. 11, aft. doubt ins. a, also, for "of some person" r. Dolor, — also, in that l. and the next, erase, "and to find" to end of the sent.

P. 25. l. 3, aft. 1657; add, and Samuel, 1 May 1660.

" l. 5, bef. *had* ins. m. Susanna, eldest d. of John Mills, — also, aft. Boston, ins. in 1652,

" l. 7, aft. rec. add, I think, he had, also, Hannah, 7 Jan. 1660; but the rec. gives her to John and Susanna, and very good reason is kn. for distrust of that vol.

" l. 6 from bot. aft. 1672; add, beside elder ones, Thomas, and Timothy, of unkn. dates.

P. 25. l. 5, from bot. erase, perhaps

" l. 4, from bot. aft. Anthony, add, m. 27 Jan. 1690, Mary, d. of Hugh Rowe, and d. 18 Feb. 1725, leav. five s. liv. Ezekiel, Pelatiah, Samuel, Nathaniel, and Jonathan. He was

P. 26. l. 18, erase perhaps

" l. 19, aft. Leach, add, wh. d. 9 Feb. 1726, aged 63;

" l. 20. bef. MATTHEW, ins. JOSEPH, Gloucester, s. prob. youngest, of Anthony, m. 15 Aug. 1695, Eliz. Gouge, says Babson, had Jeremiah, William, and sev. ds. perhaps also Joseph.

" l. 18 from bot. aft. br. add, but Mr. Paige gives strong sanction to the opin. that he was s. of William Bordman, wh. m. a niece of Day.

" l. 15 from bot. bef. RALPH, ins. NATHANIEL, Gloucester, s. of Anthony, m. 13 Feb. 1690, Ruth, d. of Hugh Rowe, had Benjamin, Nathaniel, David, and seven ds. prob. rem. bef. 1721.

P. 27. l. 18, bef. STEPHEN, ins. SAMUEL, Gloucester, s. of Anthony, m. 9 Aug. 1692, Rachel, d. of Hugh Rowe, had two ch. whose names are not seen in Babson, wh. says she d. 6 Sept. 1698, and of the h. no more is kn.

" l. 16 from bot. at the end, add, possib. but not prob.

" l. 4 from bot. aft. Laughton, add, or Langton,

" l. 3 from bot. aft. 1680. add, His w. and d. were k. by lightning in his ho. 15 July 1706; and he d. 29 Jan. 1726.

P. 28. l. 2, erase w. — also, aft. Phebe, add, Wildes, d. prob. of the sec. John, wh. d. 8 Apr. 1723, aged 70 — also, for s. b. 20 Feb. 1682. r. Timothy, Anthony, John, Joseph, Jonathan, Ebenezer, and Susanna, beside some wh. d. inf. as Babson tells.

" l. 12 from bot. aft. Pickering, add, wh. d. 30 Aug. 1662,

P. 29. l. 20 from bot. aft. 1678; add, Onesiphorus and — also, aft. Mary, add, tw. 28 Mar. both d. next mo.

" l. 19 from bot. aft. 1689. add, some confus. of names and dates is fear. in var. old MS. Even the bapt. on ch. rec. of four more ch. count wrong days for two, as Hannah, Apr. 1685; William, 6 July 1690; Nathaniel, 20 Apr. 1693; and Jonathan, Apr. 1695; the first hav. Saturday, and the last, Monday. — also, for ano. r. John

" l. 17, aft. and, add, James was

P. 31. l. 12 from bot. aft. DEARE, ins. EDMUND, Ipswich, claim. legacy, 1678, by nuncup. will of Robert Denton.

P. 33. l. 14, aft. ch. add, He was of the orig. sett. at Block isl. 1661.

P. 35. l. 14, for *Thomas* Hurlbut r. John Hurlbut

P. 36. l. 19, aft. m. strike out, I conject. Tobijah Perkins, and ins. Thomas Robinson.

P. 38. l. 3 from bot. aft. soon; add, Mary, 4 Aug. 1660; James; Amos; and Agnes;

" l. 2 from bot. aft. 1674, add, and later.

P. 40. l. 1, for RICHARD r. *RICHARD*

" l. 13, at the end, add, ROBERT, Ipswich, d. a. June 1678, prob. without heir.

P. 43. l. 7, for Saybrook ᴀ Windham

P. 45. l. 8 from bot. strike out, " was unm. 1717 " and ins. d. young

" l. 7 from bot. aft. *beside* ins. Eliz. again, 7 Apr. 1660; and

P. 47. bef. l. 6, ins. DICER. See DISER.

" l. 13, for Cook r. Cooper

" l. 14, aft. Sarah, ins. b. 28 Apr. inst. of *in*

" l. 15, aft. Ruth, ins. 5 Apr. — also, aft. Abigail, ins. 26 Sept. — also, aft. Abraham, ins. 14 Jan. 1674; inst. of 1673;

" l. 16, bef. 1677, ins. 7 Nov. — also, strike out 1679, and ins. 27 Feb. 1680

P. 47. l. 17, strike out "was w. of" and ins. m. 21 June 1677

" l. 18, aft. Sarah, strike out *of*, and ins. 2 Oct. 1683 — also, aft. Ruth, strike out *of*, and ins. 1 Mar. 1688 — also, aft. Abigail, strike out *of*, and ins. 21 Jan. 1690.

" l. 19, aft. Rebecca, strike out *of*, and ins. 1709,

P. 49. l. 16, aft. 1672. add, Perhaps his d. Eliz. m. July 1670, Morgan Owen.

P. 50. l. 4, bef. RICHARD, ins. ANTHONY, Salem, by w. Margery had Anthony, b. 24 Mar. 1666; Nathaniel, 25 Dec. 1667; Margery, 16 Aug. 1669; Jonathan, 28 Mar. 1673; Mary; and Benjamin, 22 Feb. 1680; d. 1679, and admin. 28 Nov. was gr. to his wid. Felt confus. him with Anthony Dick, ment. in Winth. Hist. I. 287, of wh. very little is ever heard.

" l. 7, aft. 1680; add, Eliz. 1683; John, 1686; Hannah, 1688; and James, 1692; and — also, bef. 1729. ins. 6 May — also, after it, add, Rebecca m. 1706 Josiah Tainer.

" l. 9, at the end, add, THOMAS, Marblehead, d. June 1668. Admin. was giv. to RICHARD, of wh. no more is kn.

P. 52. l. 5 from bot. aft. 1676. add, His will of 20 Feb. nam. s. Henry, and Edward.

" l. 3 from bot. at the end, add, It is Dispan. in Essex Inst. II. 273.

P. 54. l. 16 from bot. at the end, add, Ann m. 11 Aug. 1657, Nehemiah Howard; and Eliz. m. 15 Dec. 1658, Samuel Morgan.

P. 55. l. 12, bef. *Bathsheba*, ins. Bethia or — also, aft. How, add, d. of Jeremy,

" l. 17, for 1689 r. 1690

P. 56. l. 18 from bot. aft. 1657; add, beside Mehitable, 25 May 1660.

" l. 7 from bot. aft. Procter, add, d. of John, wh. d. 8 Feb. 1716,

P. 57. l. 17, aft. Herrick, add, and Sarah,

" l. 18, for 1672 r. 1671

" l. 9 from bot. aft. 1667. add, Roger Haskell call. him s.-in-law.

" l. 6 from bot. strike out, perhaps others; and ins. Joshua, 29 Aug. 1669; Hannah, 9 July 1671; Eliz. 26 Oct. 1673; and Sarah, 3 Mar. 1678. He m. 6 May 1685, Joanna, d. of Robert Hale, wid. of John Larkin of Charlestown, as sec. w. had Robert and Rebecca, tw. 9 Oct. 1686, of wh. Rebecca d. 22 June foll. but Robert liv. over 77 yrs. Third w. 1698, Mary, was wid. of capt. Andrew Creatty of Marblehead. He

P. 59. l. 21, aft. 7. ins. He was liv. 1672.

" l. 21 from bot. aft. Mary, ins. d. of Robert Elwell,

" l. 16 from bot. aft. *sense*, add, not her own,

P. 61. bef. l. 4, ins. DORITCH, JOHN, Salem, tho. a boy, was freq. witness in the cases of witcher. 1692, especial. against Giles Cory and George Jacobs, both of wh. suffer. d.

" l. 4, aft. DORLAND, ins. DORLAN, DARLAN,

P. 64. l. 8, aft. 1686. add, He left wid. wh. m. 21 Nov. 1711, the sec. Onesiphorus Page.

P. 65. l. 4, aft. 1657; add, and Dorothy, 31 Jan. 1659.

P. 71. l. 2 from bot. aft. Mary, ins. d. of Judah Thacher,

P. 72. l. 10 from bot. aft. Clark, add, had Eliz. b. 22 July 1660.

P. 74. l. 17, aft. matter. add, His w. was d. of Timothy Clark, in his will well provid. for.

" l. 15 from bot. aft. DRUCE, add, or DRUSE,

" l. 9 from bot. bef. VINCENT, ins. RICHARD, Boston, by w. Jane had William, b. 1 May 1660.

P. 75. bef. l. 16 from bot. ins. DUDY, MOSES, found by Mr. Babson at Gloucester, as serv. of Robert Elwell, press. into milit. serv. in Philip's war, 1676, outliv. it, and had gr. of ld. in that town.

P. 78. l. 6 from bot. aft. 1700. add, His wid. m. Richard Dart of New London.

P. 80. l. 12 from bot. aft. soon; add, Mary, 12 Nov. 1659, on rec. at Boston, wh. m. 21 June 1678, the sec. William Sargent;

P. 82. l. 19 from bot. strike out "and next yr. he m. Eliz." and ins. she was

" l. 18 from bot. aft. Glover; add, by sec. w. Eliz. he

P. 84. l. 19, aft. 82; add, and Babson names other ds. Alice, wh. m. a Meacham; Grace, wh. m. a Hodgkins; both of Ipswich, beside Mary, wh. m. 22 June 1669, Joseph Elwell.

" l. 21, aft. 1650; ins. Mary;

" l. 14 from bot. bef. SAMUEL, ins. ROBERT, Bristol, had w. and three ch. in Feb. 1689.

" l. 11 from bot. bef. THOMAS, ins. SOLOMON, Bristol, 1689, had w. and three ch.

P. 89. bef. l. 6 from bot. ins. EAGER, JONATHAN, Salem, m. 27 June 1661, Rebecca, d. of Richard Hyde, had Hannah, b. 27 July, 1662; and Jonathan, 25 Jan. 1665.

P. 92. l. 20 from bot. aft. 1683, add, H. C. 1703

P. 94. l. 2 from bot. aft. ESTY, ins. ISAAC

" last l. erase *prob.*

P. 97. l. 4, erase prob. — also, aft. w. add, Mabel, wid. of Gov. Haynes, m. 17 Nov. 1654,

P. 98. l. 21, aft. EBORNE, ins. EBBORNE,

" l. 22, for Laura r. Sarah

" l. 20 from bot. aft. Moses, ins. b. 14 Feb. 1673; — also, aft. Joseph, ins. 24 Apr. 1674; — also, for Laura r. Sarah, 26 Oct. 1676;

P. 100. l. 6, aft. EDES, ins. EADS, EADES, or EEDS, EDWARD, Boston, shipwright, s. of John the first of Charlestown, m. 26 June 1704, Martha, youngest d. of Peter Frothingham, had Edward, b. 6 June 1705; John, Nov. 1707; Jonathan, 2 Aug. 1709; and Martha, 26 May 1711. His w. d. 13 Oct. 1712, and he m. 15 July 1714, Susanna, d. of John Welch, had Thomas, 11 Apr. 1715; William, 8 Mar. 1717; and d. Sept. 1730. His wid. m. 1733, John Pinckney, and next, 1739, Erasmus Stevens.

" l. 11, aft. yr. add, Mary m. 1708, Thomas Willet; and Sarah m. 1713, Charles Wager.

" l. 14, aft. "more." add, JONATHAN, Charlestown, br. of the preced. m. 1712, Joanna Willet of Newbury. — also, aft. 1673. add, PETER, Charlestown, s. of the first John of the same, m. 1714, Martha Mudge.

P. 101. l. 3, for Perhaps he r. Thomas jr. — also, erase, "after, as sec. w."

P. 108. l. 5 from bot. aft. Oxford. add, In the doleful witchr. trials, 1692, he gave evid. with more sense than most.

P. 112. l. 16 from bot. bef. THOMAS, ins. OLIVER, Salem, had Thomas, b. 30 Sept. 1689.

" l. 15 from bot. at the end, add, THOMAS, Salem, by w. Sarah had Sarah, b. 5 June 1674; Thomas, 11 Jan. 1677; Lydia, 12 June 1679; John, 17 May 1681; Margaret, 26 Apr. 1683; Mary, 1 Dec. 1686; Magdalen, 28 Apr. 1689; Henry, 16 July 1691; and Robert, 21 Mar. 1696.

" l. 11 from bot. bef. Benjamin, ins. * — also, erase prob.

" l. 10 from bot. aft. He, add, m. 30 July 1696, Abigail, d. of John Wilkins of Boston, had nine ch. of wh. the third was William, b. at Bristol, 31 Oct. 1701, H. C. 1722, and f. of the William, signer of the declara. of Ind.

" l. 9 from bot. aft. disting. add, had large est. and his w. d. 15 Dec. 1742 — also, bef. 1746. ins. 26 July — also, aft. 1746. ins. DEPENDANCE, Gloucester, youngest br. of the preced. m. 4 Jan. 1722, Sarah Warner, had eleven ch. and d. bef. 1757.

P. 112. l. 8 from bot. at the end, add, Perhaps he was br. of the first William. JOHN, Newport, s. of the first William, and eldest by his sec. w. was a mariner, liv. 1708. NATHANIEL, Gloucester, younger br. of the preced. shipwright, m. 1 Jan. 1711, Abigail, youngest d. of Francis Norwood the first, and she d. aft. 3 mos. Next he m. 16 Feb. 1721, Ann, d. of the sec. William Sargent, had Nathaniel, Mary, William, Daniel, and Epes; and d. 30 May 1761. His wid. d. 8 Oct. 1782, aged 90.

" l. 6 from bot. for Vincent, r. Vinson,

" l. 2 from bot. aft. 1679; add, John, 1681; Nathaniel, 1683; Jemima, 1686; Elinor, 1688; William, 1694; and Dependance, 1696;

" last l. bef. 1696. ins. 9 Dec. — also, aft. 1696. add, WILLIAM, Gloucester, s. of the preced. was a mariner, had two ws. and ch. Joseph, b. a. 1740; Benjamin, and Lucy, beside sev. more not nam. by Babson, and d. 20 Sept. 1771.

P. 113. l. 20, aft. "will" ins. of 7 Jan. 1674, pro. in few mos.

" l. 21, at the end, add, RALPH, Salem, s. prob. of the preced. by w. Martha had Abigail, b. 22 Jan. 1696; and Ebenezer, 29 Aug. 1697.

" l. 13 from bot. aft. 420. add, By w. Sarah he had Francis, b. Feb. 1692; and William, 7 June 1702.

P. 116. l. 6, aft. Mehitable, add, d. of Thomas Millet,

" l. 9, aft. 1682; add, beside Joshua, and ano. d. He took sec. w. 2 Dec. 1702, wid. Mary Rowe, and d. 14 Dec. 1715.

" l. 12, aft. 1681; add, beside John, and three more ds. and d. 1710.

" l. 13, aft. Mary, ins. d. of Osmond

" l. 18, aft. 1676. add, He went to sea, and d. abroad 1679.

" l. 12 from bot. aft. 1678; add, and d. 24 Nov. 1696. His wid. d. 6 Sept. 1721, aged 82. — also, erase perhaps.

" l. 9 from bot. aft. 1682; add, beside Elisha, wh. with William, rem. from G.

P. 118. l. 3 from bot. aft. w. ins. Mary,

P. 119. l. 3 from bot. aft. Thomas, add, b. by w. Alice, 7 Jan. 1660.

P. 124. l. 8, bef. 1675, ins. 1 Sept.

P. 127. bef. l. 8, ins. ESTWICK, ESTWICH, or ESTICK, EDWARD, Salem, by w. Esther had Eliz. b. a. 1652; Sarah, 1654; Hannah, 1656; Esther, 1659; and Edward, 1662, as from his inv. June 1666, is kn.

" l. 13, at the end, add, By her he had John, b. at Boston, 8 Dec. 1659.

P. 129. l. 15, aft. 1681; add, beside Job; and — also, aft. 1684. add, His wid. m. sec. Thomas Millet, as his sec. w. surv. him, and d. 19 Mar. 1726, aged 68.

" l. 18, for possib. r. eldest — also, for "the preced. H. C. 1689" r. Joseph

" l. 20 from bot. bef. Bowman. ins. Francis

" l. 19 from bot. at the end, add, His w. d. bef. 1698.

" l. 17 from bot. aft. 1670, add, H. C. 1689

" l. 7 from bot. bef. Isaac; ins. Susanna, wh. m. 31 Dec. 1656, James Stevens;

" l. 4 from bot. bef. 1655, ins. 21 May — also, aft. Millet, erase to the end of the sent.

P. 130. l. 8 from bot. aft. Edwards, add, and d. perhaps at Salem, 22 May 1680.

P. 133. l. 18 from bot. aft. had, add, beside five ch. wh. d. young,

P. 134. l. 7, aft. "had" ins. Lydia, b. 17 Sept. 1680; — also, erase b.

" l. 8, bef. d. ins. Benjamin, 19 June 1688; and Eliz. 30 Oct. 1690; and — also, aft. d. add, at Milford.

" l. 20. aft. regret. add, Common. the name at H. was Ayer.

" l. 13 from bot. aft. London, ins. THOMAS, Boston, by w. Ann had Saville, b. 13 Dec. 1691; and Thomas, 13 July 1694. His parents are unkn.

P. 137. l. 19, for Faith r. Sarah, 19 Feb.

P. 138. l. 2, bef. JOHN, ins. JOHN, Ipswich, s. perhaps of the preced. d. Nov. 1672, leav. wid. Sarah, ch. John, Triphena, and Eliz. Next yr. the wid. m. Daniel Kilham.

P. 143. l. 5, aft. 1655; ins. and Jonathan, 13 Nov. 1659.

P. 146. l. 1, aft. 1666, add, and his wid. gave his inv. next mo.

P. 150. l. 4 and 5, erase Thomas, Hingham, d. 1678.

" l. 5 from bot. aft. Gloucester, ins. m. Hannah, d. of the first William Sargent of the same,

P. 152, l. 2, for "the preced." r. Nathaniel,

" l. 3, aft. Salem, add, m. 29 Nov. 1670, Mary, d. of John Tomkins, had Nathaniel, b. 8 June 1672; Mary, 30 Mar. 1674; John, 22 Mar. 1676, d. in few days; Hannah, 18 Apr. 1677; Eliz. 28 Feb. 1679; Samuel, 1 Jan. 1683; John, 22 Aug. 1686; and his w. d. 12 Dec. 1688. He was

" l. 5, aft. leav. ins. by w. Mary, — also, aft. Nathaniel, ins. b. 15 Aug. 1655; — also, aft. Eliz. ins. 18 Mar. 1653;

" l. 7, aft. again, ins. b. 15 Jan. bapt.

" l. 13 from bot. aft. Mehitable, add, d. of Jasper Gunn

" l. 7 from bot. for sec. s. r. br. — also, strike out 1671, and is not, &c. to the end of the l. and ins. 1691, leav. w. Esther, and s. Joseph 3 yrs old.

P. 154. bef. l. 16 from bot. ins. FERMAN, JOHN, Salem, by w. Eliz. had Eliz. b. 11 Feb. 1675. JOHN, Haddam, had Dorothy, b. 10 May 1681. THOMAS, Salem 1675.

" l. 5 from bot. aft. it; add, but he was liv. 1677.

" bef. l. 2 from bot. ins. FERNES, SAMUEL, New Haven, had Samuel, b. 2 July 1663; Eliz. 7 Dec. 1665, wh. m. 18 Nov. 1684, Thomas Sperry; and John, 3 Mar. 1668.

P. 155. l. 8 from bot. for 1666 r. 1667 — also, for 1668 r. 1669

" l. 7 from bot. for 1670 r. 1671

P. 157, l. 8, bef. THOMAS, ins. THOMAS, Salem, m. 2 Mar. 1681, Mary, d. of John Leach, had Thomas, b. 17 Jan. foll.; Mary, 4 Sept. 1683; and Samuel, 5 Dec. of uncert. yr.

P. 160. l. 13, bef. ROBERT, ins. JEREMIAH Bristol, by Dr. Stiles mark. as hav. a w. in Feb. 1689, as also, is JOSHUA, at the same time, but of either no more is told.

P. 163. l. 16, aft. ch. add, Eliz. m. 2 Jan. 1678, John Plimpton of the same.

P. 164. last l. for Michael r. Nicholas

P. 167. l. 14, aft. Eng. add, and nam. in his will of 6 Mar. 1673. He d. 7 Apr. foll.

" l. 19, aft. capt. add, was

P. 168. l. 9, bef. JABEZ, ins. DAVID, New London, s. of Rev. James, had David, Adonijah, and Mary, perhaps more. ELEAZER, Lebanon, youngest br. of the preced. m. his cous. Martha, d. of capt. John Brown, had no ch.

" l. 17 from bot. for 1667 r. 1668

" l. 13 from bot. bef. Eliz. ins. Abigail m. prob. the sec. John Mason of Norwich;

" l. 11 from bot. aft. Mix; add, Dorothy m. Nathaniel Bissell; — also, aft. m. strike out "it is said, Thomas" and ins. 5 Oct. 1698, Joseph

" l. 8 and 7 from bot. strike out "nine s." &c. to "and some" inclus. and ins. m. 1 Jan. 1676, Eliz. youngest d. of maj. John Mason own sis. of the sec. w. of his f. wh. d. 8 Oct. 1684, and by her had James, b. 1 Jan. 1678, d. soon; James, again, 7 June 1679; Jedediah, 17 Apr. 1681; Samuel, 1684; and

" l. 6 from bot. aft. Bradford, strike out wh. brot. him eight ch. and ins. m. 18 May

1687, had Abigail, 22 Feb. 1688; Ebenezer, 10 Jan. 1690; Daniel, Feb. 1693; John, 1695; Bridget, 1698; Josiah, 1699; William, 1701; and Jabez, 1703.

P. 168. l. 2 from bot. aft. Hingham, ins. had Jeremiah 5 Feb. 1660; —also, aft. 1690. add, Of his est. admin. was giv. 21 July 1692, to wid. Martha.

" last l. aft. jr. add, and Rebecca m. William Tudman.

P. 169. l. 1, bef. JOHN, ins. JEREMIAH, Lebanon, fifth s. of Rev. James, d. at Coventry 22 May 1736, teach. us by his will of 8 Mar. preced. that he left w. Ruth, ch. Jeremiah, Abner, Gideon, Elisha, James, Hannah, and Ruth.

" l. 11 at the end, add, wh. d. 7 Nov. 1692;

" l. 12, for "d." r. He d. 9 May

" l. 14, bef. JOSEPH, ins. JOHN, Windham, s. of Rev. James, m. 10 July 1695, Eliz. eldest d. of Thomas Waterman, had Eliz. b. 1 June 1696; Miriam, 17 Oct. 1699; Priscilla, 5 Feb. 1702; John, 8 Mar. 1705; was capt. and d. 24 May 1743; and his wid. d. 25 June 1751. By Stiles, 620, he is confus. with former John.

" l. 20 from bot. bef. RICHARD, ins. JOSEPH, Stonington, eighth s. of Rev. James, m. 2 Nov. 1703, his cous. Sarah, d. of Samuel Mason, had Sarah, b. 24 Jan. 1705; Mason, 11 Sept. 1708; and Joseph, 14 Feb. 1711; and he m. 29 Dec. 1721, sec. w. Ann, eldest d. of Rev. Samuel Whiting, had Samuel, 16 Jan. 1724, a disting. lawyer; Eleazer, 29 Aug. 1726; rem. to Lebanon and Windham had Asahel, 7 Nov. 1728; Ichabod, 17 May 1734; Ann, 12 July 1737; and Thomas, 11 June 1739, d. young. NATHANIEL, Lebanon, br. of the preced. m. 10 Dec. 1701, Ann, d. of Joshua Abel, had Ann, b. 5 Nov. 1702; Joshua, 13 Feb. 1704; Nathan, 29 Mar. 1705; Nehemiah, 10 Feb. 1708; James, 15 Oct. 1709; John, 7 Jan. 1712; Nathaniel, 14 May 1714; Mehitable, 3 Feb. 1717; Eliz. 26 May 1718; Rachel, Oct. 1720, d. at 6 mos.; Abel, 22 Nov. 1722; Caleb, 17 June 1725; and his w. d. 3 July 1728. He m. 17 Sept. 1729, Mindwell Tisdale, and had Jabez, 4 Oct. 1730, wh. d. young; Ezekiel, 11 Mar. 1732; and Isaac 10 May 1734; and d. 1759, his will being of 14 Feb. in that yr.

" l. 12 from bot. bef. THOMAS, ins. SAMUEL, Milford, s. of Samuel, by w. Sarah had only ch. Sarah, and d. 1690.

P. 170. l. last at the end, add, By w. Ann, he had Hannah, b. 21 Aug. 1659.

P. 174. l. 13, aft. 1665, ins. s. of William, m. Eliz. Hart, prob. d. of John, had John, b. 26 Mar. 1660; William, 12 Aug. 1661; and Thomas, 1 Feb. 1663; was

" l. 11 from bot. erase "of Edward, perhaps" — also, aft. Thomas, ins. first of the same,

" l. 8 from bot. aft. *had* ins. Samuel, b. 12 Dec. 1679; John, 8 Feb. 1682; Hannah, 4 Apr. 1685; Stephen, 29 Dec. 1687; Joshua, 28 Dec. 1689; —also, aft. 1693; ins. Lydia, 20 July 1696; Sarah, 18 Aug. 1700; and Eliz. 10 Jan. 1703.

" l. 7 from bot. aft. 1690, add, a witness against poor Jacobs in the delus. of 1692.

P. 175. l. 13 aft. wid. ins. Ann — also, aft. Eliz. ins. b. 30 June 1650; —also, aft. George, ins. 6 Mar. 1653; — also, aft. John, ins. 3 Dec. 1655;

" l. 14, aft. preced. add, m. 22 May 1666, Hannah Moulton, d. prob. of sec. Robert, had Abigail, b. 27 June 1668; and George Apr. 1672; and his w. d. 20 Mar. 1674. He m. 15 Nov. foll. Mary Downton, had Thomas, 2 Aug. 1678; Mary, 11 Nov. 1680; Ebenezer, 6 Apr. 1683; William, 17 July 1685; Eliz. 30 Aug. 1687; Jonathan, 8 Nov. 1689; Ann, 29 Sept. 1691; Samuel, 29 Sept. 1693; and Lydia, 1 June 1695;

" l. 16, aft. 1690. ins. Ano. THOMAS of Salem m. 12 Aug. 1678, Eliz. Johnson, had Ruth, b. 11 May foll.;. Timothy, 30 Sept. 1680; John, 21 June 1684; Joseph, 1 Aug. 1687; and Abigail, 8 Aug. 1692.

" l. 17, strike out May and ins. 2 Apr.

P. 175. l. 18, aft. Pickering; ins. ano. d. Hannah m. Joshua Ward.

P. 176. l. 1, aft. 1686, ins. by w. Lydia, d. of Joseph Smith of H.

P. 177. l. 8, aft. 1755. add, DAVID, Salem, prob. s. of Ralph, by w. Susanna had Susanna, b. 18 Apr. 1676. JAMES, Gloucester 1649–51.

P. 178. l. 14, aft. Salem, ins. m. 29 Nov. 1655, Persis Black, had Mary, b. 16 Mar. 1657; Robert, 20 Sept. 1659; Susanna, 1 June 1662; Hannah, 23 Dec. 1664; Ruth, 17 Dec. 1667, d. 21 May foll.; John, 10 July 1669; Abraham, 23 Dec. 1672; Isaac, and Rebecca, tw. 30 July 1674 — also, erase the resid. of sent.

P. 181. l. 6, aft. "will" ins. of 21 Sept. preced. — also, for May r. 30 June

P. 183. l. 1, for 3 Oct. r. 31 Oct.

" l. 3, for 1686 r. 26 Jan. 1687 — also, aft. 1691; add, Barnabas, 1694, posthum.

" l. 4, bef. 1694, ins. 3 Nov.

" l. 19, strike out "prob. others," and ins. Hannah, 17 Sept. 1687

P. 186. l. 14 for 1669 r. 1668

" l. 16, aft. foll. add, Andrew, 1682; Ephraim, 1683; Edward, again, 1685; Francis, 1688; and Benjamin, 1689; and d. 1689. His wid. m. Thomas Sawyer.

" l. 18, bef. CHRISTOPHER, ins. CALEB, Ipswich, youngest s. of Abraham, m. 8 June 1702, Mary, d. of John Sherwin.

" l. 17 from bot. aft. 1700. add, DAVID, Salem, s. of John of the same, by w. Hannah had David, b. 19 Mar. 1689; Jonathan, 10 Jan. 1691; Samuel, 24 Dec. 1692; Hannah, 3 Dec. 1694; Eliz. 27 Dec. 1696; and Joseph 1 Feb. 1699.

P. 187. l. 6 from bot. aft. Thankful, add, prob. eldest ch.

P. 189. l. 13, aft. 1655; add, and by w. Martha had Benjamin, b. 3 July 1658; Jonathan, 20 Dec. 1660, d. in few mos.; Jonathan, again, 22 Nov. 1662, d. young; David, 16 Oct. 1665; Eliz. 22 Nov. 1667; and Ebenezer, 5 Aug. 1677.

" l. 17, aft. he, add, 13 June 1732.

" l. 17 from bot. bef. JOSEPH, ins. JOHN, Salem, s. of John of the same, m. 18 Mar. 1673, Mary Stuard, had John, b. 27 July 1674; Mary, 12 Sept. 1675; Ann, 30 Apr. 1677; Sarah, 27 Nov. 1678; John, again, 15 Nov. 1680; Jonathan, 14 June 1683; Ebenezer, 22 Feb. 1685; Mercy, 15 July 1689; and by sec. w. Mary had James 12 Apr. 1693.

" l. 16 from bot. aft. 1690. add, JOSEPH, Salem, m. 21 Nov. 1683, Ann, wid. of Robert Wilson, had Ruth, b. 18 Oct. foll.

P. 190. l. 19 from bot. bef. STANDFAST, ins. SAMUEL, Salem, m. 14 May 1676, Sarah Stuard, had Samuel, b. 18 May 1677, d. in few mos.; John, 30 Nov. 1678; Samuel, again, 26 July 1680; Ann, 26 July 1683; Sarah, 9 Oct. 1685; Joseph, 14 Mar. 1687; Benjamin, 24 May 1689; and by w. Margery had Richard, 19 Dec. 1693; Mary, 8 Nov. 1695; Margaret, 3 Feb. 1697; Jonathan, 1699; Bartholomew, 23 Feb. 1702; and Margery, 4 Feb. 1706,

P. 191. l. 10 from bot. for 12 Aug. 1668 r. 12 Aug. 1666.

P. 192. l. 8, aft. John, ins. prob. Ann, wh. m. 10 Jan. 1655, Samuel Ruggles; and

" l. 21. aft. w. Abigail, add, d. of John Carter,

" l. 18 and 17 from bot. erase wh. m. 10 Jan. &c. to end of the sent.

" l. 7 from bot. aft. w. Mary, add, d. of John Carter,

P. 194. l. 5 and 6 strike out "was there" &c. to the last of sent. and ins. d. 1693, in will of 1 Jan. ment. w. Sarah, and s. John.

" l. 18 erase perhaps

" l. 19, for 1681 r. 1682

" l. 20, for 1683 r. 1684

P. 195. l. 11, bef. Joseph ins. as the blunder in ch. rec. says, — also, erase " or 15 "

" l. 15, for 1652 r. 1651

P. 196. l. 20 from bot. aft. 1674, add, by w. Eliz. had Nicholas, Eliz. and William; and d. 1677.

P. 198. l. 3 from bot. bef. Samuel, ins. Dorothy;

" l. 2 from bot. aft. 1689. ins. His will of 13 Nov. 1708, names Eliz. Southack as d. Dorothy, wh. m. 21 June 1705, Jonathan Armitage, beside s. John, William, Joseph, and Samuel. JOHN, Boston, s. of the preced. m. 16 Nov. 1699, Sarah Lynde, had Eliz. b. 13 June 1701. JOSEPH, Boston, mariner, br. of the preced. prob. never m. for by his will, 11 May 1730, all his prop. was giv. to ch. of br. Samuel. SAMUEL, Boston, mariner, br. of the preced. m. 26 July 1716, Eliz. Emmes, had Mary, b. 20 Aug. 1720; Joseph, 11 Sept. 1723; Dorothy, 26 May 1725; Hannah, 30 Apr. 1726, d. in few days; beside Samuel, and Eliz. nam. in the will of uncle Joseph. WILLIAM, Boston, br. of the preced. m. 5 Apr. 1716, Eliz. Campbell, had William, b. 1 Nov. foll.; John, 14 Nov. 1717, d. soon; Mary, 7 June 1720, d. soon; Mary, again, 8 Sept. 1721; John, again, 8 Feb. 1723, d. young; and Eliz. He was Treasr. of the Prov. of Mass. Bay, d. 1759.

P. 205. l. 14 from bot. aft. 1654; add, d. 1691, leav. w. Lydia, ch. Eliz. Holt, Ann Wheeler, Lydia, aged 20; Susanna, 16; Francis, 13; Jane, 11.

P. 209. l. 20, at the end, add, RICHARD, Salem, m. 19 Apr. 1677, Ann Curtis, had Mary, b. 28 Apr. 1678.

" l. 13 from bot. bef. JOHN, ins. *

" l. 12 from bot. aft. 1668; add, the former d. 1690, had John, Benoni, Jonathan, Samuel, Abigail, Josiah, Caleb, Silence, Ebenezer, and Hannah.

" l. 11 from bot. for she r. Ruth

" l. 10 from bot. at the end, add, He was rep. 1690 and 2, d. 1694; and left w. Ruth, ch. John, aged 18; Edward, 16; Rebecca, 14; Hannah, 12; Joseph, 6; Nathaniel, 4; and Lydia, 1. Prob. he was br. of Edward, and descend. of both are kn.

P. 211. l. 18 from bot. bef. JOHN, ins. JOHN, New Haven, m. 9 June 1664, Mercy Paine, had ch. b. 16 Mar. foll. d. very soon; John, 26 May 1668; Abigail, 8 Oct. 1670; Eliz. 1673; Sarah, 3 Sept. 1675; Ebenezer, 15 Aug. 1677; Mary, 5 Feb. 1679; Samuel, 5 Feb. 1682; Hannah, 2 Feb. 1686; and Rebecca, bapt. 25 May 1690.

P. 212. l. 8 from bot. aft. Greys. add, WILLIAM, Salem, by w. Mary had Mary, b. 31 July 1677.

P. 214. l. 19, aft. Eunice, add, eldest d. of Luke

P. 215. l. 4, for w. r. wid.

" l. 21, aft. Benjamin, add, b. 25 Feb. 1687.

P. 216. l. 7, bef. JOHN, ins. JOHN, Salem, s. of Thomas, m. 22 Apr. 1672, Rebecca Putnam, eldest d. of sec. John, had Eliz. b. 22 Aug. 1673; and Bethia, posthum. 22 Mar. 1676, and d. 26 Aug. preced.

P. 219. l. 8 from bot. bef. THOMAS, ins. THOMAS, Salem, by w. Ruth had Thomas, b. 3 Apr. 1671; Jonathan, 19 Sept. 1673; John, 23 Jan. 1677; Joseph, 12 Aug. 1679; and William, 30 Nov. 1685.

P. 221. l. 2 from bot. bef. 1662, ins. 25 July

P. 222. l. 1, bef. 1666 ins. 18 Nov. — also, aft. Isaac, ins. 2 July 1669 — also, aft. Jacob, ins. 15 Aug. 1671 — also, aft. Bartholomew, ins. 26 Apr. 1674 — also, aft. Daniel ins. and Mary tw. 17 Aug. 1676

P. 223. l. 14 from bot. at the end, add, He and his w. were of the ch. at Bristol in Feb. 1689.

" last l. bef. 1750 ins. 17 July — also, bef. 1652 ins. 17 June

P. 224. bef. l. 6, ins. GALT, WILLIAM, Salem, d. bef. 1669, says Essex Inst. II. 96; but as the name never appears in other place, I have doubt of the spell.

P. 225. bef. l. 11, ins. GANSON, BENJAMIN, Salem, by w. Eliz. had Eliz. b. 19 Feb. 1670; and Benjamin, 7 July 1671. As this seems very rare name, perhaps it may be var. for Jansen.

P. 226. l. 3, for 1717 r. 1707.

P. 227. l. 17, strike out "George, 24 Sept." and ins. Bethia, b. 3 June

" l. 20, for 20 Apr. perhaps 1660, r. 23 Apr. 1659 — also, aft. unbapt. ins. beside George, wh. d. 21 Aug. 1662;

" l. 12 from bot. aft. *rec.* ins. (tho. Babson has 16 June 1661)

P. 228. l. 10, aft. young; ins. George;

" l. 20, aft. preced. add, of wh. the w. was made extrix. and aft. her d. s. George. He was the only s. liv. to be nam. in it, but six ds. and three gr.s. find provis. there. See Geneal. Reg. XV. 147.

P. 229. l. 17, for 9 r. 27

" l. 18, strike out (unless this name &c. to in the rec.) and ins. d. of Roger of Hammersmith, near London, dec.

" l. 12 from bot. for Feb. r. Dec. — also, aft. 1662, ins. d. in few ds.

P. 230. l. 11, for 1663 r. 1662 — also, bef. July ins. 14

" l. 12, bef. George, ins. Samuel, 9 June 1666; — also, aft. 15, ins. or 28

" l. 13, erase "and Hannah tw." — also, aft. 1669; add, Hannah, 16 Apr. 1671;

" l. 21, bef. SAMUEL, ins. SAMUEL, Salem, s. of lieut. George, m. 24 Apr. 1673, Eliz. wid. of sec. Joseph Grafton, had George, b. 28 Jan. 1674, wh. d. the same yr. and Hannah, 4 Apr. 1676;

" l. 7 from bot. aft. *He* add, had w. Damaris, wh. d. 28 Nov. 1674, and

P. 231. l. 20, aft. Habakkuk, 25, ins. Feb. or

P. 234. l. 1, aft. Richard; add, beside Lydia, 10 Oct.

" bef. l. 17, ins. GARVEN, JOHN, Salem, was drown. 5 Feb. 1662, and his posthum. d. Eliz. was b. 26 July.

" l. 20, aft. 1648. add, Sarah, m. 24 May 1661, Peter Joy. — also, aft. preced. add, m. 30 Dec. 1662, Provided, d. of Lawrence Southwick, had Samuel, b. 23 Jan. 1664; Edward, 22 Oct. 1667; Hannah, 2 Jan. 1670; and Provided, 22 Apr. 1672.

P. 236. l. 7 from bot. at the end, add, But it may well seem, that he liv. at Salem, for there Mary, wid. of William Goult or Gott, had contr. for m. with Richard Bishop, as his sec. w. in July 1660, as in Essex Inst. II. 182, is well shown.

" l. 2 from bot. for Ebenezer r. Eleazer

" last l. aft. 1676; add, and b. in Wrentham, Lydia, 20 May 1685; and John, 25 Aug. 1687.

P. 237. l. 6, for Ebenezer r. Eleazer — also, for 21 r. 25

P. 240. l. 12 from bot. aft. *had* ins. Bartholomew, b. 4 Apr. 1664, d. at 4 mos.

" l. 11 from bot. aft. Jonathan, ins. 14 June

" l. 10 from bot. aft. Lydia, ins. 9 Mar. bapt. — also, aft. Bethia, ins. 27 May

" l. 9 from bot. bef. Jan. ins. 3 — also, for Dec. r. 2 Nov.

" l. 2 from bot. bef. 1666 ins. 18 Mar. — also, bef. 1669, ins. 2 June

P. 241. l. 13, aft. 1660; ins. Sarah, 6 July 1662, d. in few ds.

" l. 21 and 20 from bot. strike out "d. of the Rev." &c. to "Milton" inclus. and ins. Harris, m. 25 Sept. 1688.

" l. 20 from bot. at the end, add, sev. ch. beside

" l. 16 from bot. aft. 1748. ins. The first Joshua had sec. w. Eliz. d. of Judah Thacher, m. 7 Dec. 1704; and his wid. bec. third w. of Rev. Peter Thacher of Milton

P. 243. l. 15 for Thomas r. John — also, bef. freem. ins. but only four ch. by the first w. wh. d. 25 June 1685. He m. 12 Nov. foll. Ann Paine, perhaps d. of John of

Boston, by her had five ch.   She d. 1695, and he m. 24 Sept. 1696, Eliz. Turner, had two more ch. and was

P. 244. l. 11, for 1652 r. 1653

" l. 9 from bot. aft. Esther, add, bapt. 5 Mar.

" l. 8 from bot. bef. 1645 ; ins. 20 Jan.

" l. 5 from bot. aft. d. add, in few mos.

" l. 4 from bot. for 1663 r. 9 Aug. 1662

P. 249. l. 11 from bot. aft. one, ins. Mary, m. 24 Nov. 1672, Richard Palmer, and the other, June 1670,

P. 250. l. 10, aft. 1655; add, and John, 21 July 1660.

P. 251. l. 12, aft. Sarah, ins. b. 7 — also, aft. 1646, add, m. 1668, John Todd — also, aft. Rebecca, ins. bapt.

" l. 15, bef. Parker, ins. w. of Joseph.

" l. 16, erase, I suppose

" l. 17, aft. 1653. add, His w. Jane had d. 1676.

" l. 17 from bot. bef. NICHOLAS, ins. MATTHEW, New Haven, s. of the preced. by w. Sarah had Matthew, b. 1 Feb. 1685, d. very soon ; Sarah, 10 Mar. 1686 ; Matthew, again, 15 Mar. 1689 ; Joseph, 21 May 1691 ; Eliz. 14 May 1694 ; Daniel, 15 Nov. 1697 ; David, 4 July 1700 ; and d. 1711.   His wid. m. 7 July 1717, Rev. Joseph Moss.

" l. 9 from bot. bef. THOMAS, ins. SAMUEL, New Haven, youngest s. of the first Matthew, by w. Hannah had Samuel, b. 18 Nov. 1697 ; Hannah and Rebecca, tw. 19 Jan. 1700 ; Ann ; and Ebenezer, 1 July 1712 ; and d. 1721.

P. 253. l. 6, aft. John, ins. b. 15 Apr. bapt.

" l. 17, aft. Bishop, add, the Dept. Gov.

P. 255. l. 4, for 16 Feb. 1668 r. 6 Feb. 1678

" l. 9 from bot. at the end, add, had Martha, b. 2 June 1660.

P. 257. l. 10, at the end, add, Mary ;

" l. 12, aft. preced. add, His will of 20 Feb. pro. 27 June 1673, ment. w. three ch. by names, and the expect. one.

" l. 14, aft. 1637, erase Lewis, wh. possib.

" l. 16, bef. CALEB, ins. ALEXANDER, Marblehead 1670.

" l. 8 from bot. bef. EZEKIEL, ins. EDWARD, Exeter, s. prob. of the preced. m. 20 Dec. 1674, Abigail Mandrake ; but I kn. no more.

P. 259. l. 8 from bot. at the end, add, This name, I think, was Gladwin, and that he wh. bore it, rem. to Bristol, there in 1689 had w. and seven ch.

P. 260. last l. at the end, add, He may have liv. at Salem, there by w. Mary had John, b. 24 Apr. 1679.

P. 261. l. 15, bef. 1651, ins. 29 Apr. — also, aft. 1651, ins. d. soon — also, strike out bapt. and ins. Abigail, again, b. 31

" l. 20, aft. Ashley ; ins. Mercy m. 10 May 1664 Moses Mansfield ; — also, bef. 1678, ins. 11 Dec.

" l. 21, aft. Ball ; ins. and Abigail m. the same day Daniel Burr ;

" l. 3 from bot. bef. John, ins. Hannah, b. 5 Apr. 1659 ; and

" l. 2 from bot. aft. Henry, ins. yet strange.

P. 262. l. 1 and 2, strike out "it is uncert. whether " to the end of sent. and ins. tho. neither surname, nor bapt. of his w. be kn. he had Hannah, b. 10 Oct. 1672 ; John, 20 Nov. 1674 ; Eliz. 23 Feb. 1677 ; and Mehitable, 1 May 1679.

" l. 5, aft. Ebenezer, ins. 13 or

P. 270. l. 7 from bot. bef. JOSEPH, ins. ISAAC, Salem, perhaps s. of Robert, m. 25 Jan. 1669, Patience Cook, had Isaac, b. 29 May 1670 ; Esther, 17 Mar. 1672 ;

Zechariah, 15 May 1675; Abraham, 3 May 1677, d. in few days; Abigail, Nov. 1678; and ano. s. wh. d. in few. wks.

P. 271. l. 13, aft. 1645. add, ZECHARIAH, Salem, m. 30 June 1665, Eliz. d. of Edward Beacham, had Zechariah, b. 9 Feb. 1668; Samuel, 3 Dec. 1669; Joseph, 23 Sept. 1672; Mary, 27 Nov. 1674; Thomas, 30 Dec. 1676; Abraham, 7 Nov. 1678; John, 10 Aug. 1681; and Benjamin, 4 July 1687.

" l. 18, aft. Sarah, ins. w. of William,

P. 272. l. 18, bef. John, erase sec. — also, bef. Edmund erase sec.

P. 274. l. 16, aft. cov. add, and d. early in 1696, leav. w. Mary, and ch. Mary, aged 11; Abigail, 10; Eliz. 7; Bartholomew, 5; Joanna, 2; and one in hope.

P. 277. l. 5, aft. GOODWIN, ins. GOODING,

P. 278. l. 3, aft. Jones, ins. d. of Thomas,

" l. 4, bef. Eleanor, for and r. Joseph, 1677;

" l. 5, aft. 1680; ins. Daniel, 1685; Samuel, 1687; and he d. 5 Mar. 1709. His wid. d. 4 Feb. 1705, aged 80. RICHARD, Guilford, d. 1676, leav. ch. John, Mary, Eliz. and Rachel, wh. m. a Benton, as I learn from Mr. Porter, wh. could give no dates.

" l. 14 from bot. aft. same, ins. m. 26 Jan. 1683, Abigail, d. of William Gibbard, — also, for 1654 r. 1684; — also, strike out the rest of the sent. and ins. John; Nathaniel; Obadiah; Esther; Theophilus; Abigail, 1697; and Andrew. He d. 1703; and his wid. d. 1717.

" l. 13 from bot. bef. STEPHEN, ins. SAMUEL, Newport 1651, unless Stiles mistook the name.

" l. 2 from bot. aft. 1654, add, wh. m. 10 Aug. 1682, Nathan Smith.

P. 279. l. 14 from bot. erase "and by her a sec. d. Hannah."

P. 280. l. 17, aft. 1680. add, He had first m. 18 June 1665, Mary Robinson, as I suppose, at Salem, and she d. 9 Nov. foll.

" l. 19, aft. Felt. add, But his d. was ten yrs. earlier, and the town had to provide for his insane wid.

P. 281. l. 3 from bot. aft. war, ins. and bec. a propr. of Bristol, there, in Feb. 1689, hav. w. and four ch.

P. 284. l. 18 from bot. aft. Rebecca ins. Cooper, m. at Salem, 15 Aug. 1677, there had Rebecca, b. 25 Aug. 1678; and John, 31 Jan. 1680; but at G.

" l. 16 from bot. bef. CHRISTOPHER, ins. BENJAMIN, Salem, s. of Thomas of the same, was a witness to some folly in 1692.

P. 287. l. 3, aft. had, ins. Thomas, b. 27 Nov. 1659.

" l. 4, at the end, add, THOMAS, Salem, by w. Eliz. had Joseph, b. 15 Jan. 1663; Thomas, 16 Sept. 1664, d. young; James, 8 Feb. 1666; Thomas, again, 26 Feb. 1668; Benjamin, 26 Aug. 1669; and Samuel, 6 Feb. 1670.

P. 289. l. 11 from bot. at the end, ins. His wid. gave inv. 29 June 1671.

" l. 7 from bot. at the end, add, unless confus. with Joseph.

P. 290. l. 8 from bot. bef. 1690, ins. 28 Apr.

P. 292. l. 14, aft. est. ins. JOSEPH, Boston, prob. s. of Edward, m. Mary, wid. of Moses Draper.

P. 298. l. 3, bef. EDWARD, ins. ARTHUR, Salem, m. 17 Nov. 1668, Hannah, d. of Richard Hyde, had Christian, b. 1 Aug. 1670; Joseph, 26 Dec. 1672, wh. d. soon; and Mary, 26 July 1674.

" l. 6 from bot. bef. NICHOLAS, ins. JOSEPH, Salem, m. 10 Aug. 1675, Deborah Williams, had Joseph, b. 9 June 1676.

" l. 2 from bot. aft. 1659, add, and he d. 23 Jan. 1662. His wid. m. 23 June 1663, Nicholas Manning. Other ch. Thomas, as well as Edward, d. it is presum. inf.

as not nam. in his will of 1 Jan. pro. 25 June foll. That instr. ment. ano. d.
Mary, wh. was b. 3 Apr. 1661, made w. extrix. names serv. Eliz. Wicks, gives
George Hodges "a quadrant, forestaff, gunter's scale, and pair of compasses."
See Essex Inst. Hist. Coll. I. 143. One ROBERT, it is said, from Salem

P. 299. l. 6, aft. had, ins. Abigail, or by ano. call.

" l. 8, aft. Susanna, add, Langdon

" l. 10, aft. 1692; ins. Ebenezer, 31 Oct. 1697, H. C. 1716;

" l. 19, at the end, add, WILLIAM, Salem, had w. 1666, and no more is kn.

P. 303. l. 6, aft. b. ins. 26 Dec. — also, aft. 1651. ins. A wid. G. among early sett. at
N. H. was perhaps his mo.

" l. 12, aft. Peter, ins. William,

" l. 22, bef. JOHN, ins. JOHN, Salem, m. 7 Dec. 1659, Mary Warren, had Abigail, b.
22 Feb. 1661; Mary, 1 Mar. 1664; Sarah, 14 Dec. 1666; Eliz. 20 Feb. 1668;
and John, 28 June 1672.

P. 304. l. 22, aft. 1701, ins. H. C. 1719;

" l. 19 from bot. aft. 1716. ins. His wid. m. Rev. William Brattle.

" l. 17 from bot. aft. Houchin, add, had Jeremiah, b. 29 Dec. 1659; was

P. 306. l. 1, aft. s. ins. as Mr. Paige thinks, of John the marshal,

" l. 18 from bot. aft. 1656, ins. d. young

P. 310. l. 19 from bot. aft. 1668, ins. d. July 1674.

P. 311. l. 8 from bot. aft. m. ins. 28 Dec.

" l. 7 from bot. for 1694 r. 1695

P. 312. l. 13, aft. preced. ins. m. 18 Oct. 1663, Eliz. d. of Matthew Moulthrop,

P. 313. l. 14, aft. same, add, m. Esther, the posthum. d. of Thomas Thompson,

" l. 16, aft. 1694. add, He m. Dec. 1698, sec. w. Mary Humphrey, had Nathaniel, b.
Oct. 1699; Hezekiah, Aug. 1701; Mary, 17 Aug. 1708; and Daniel, 1 Oct.
1711; and d. 1712. His wid. m. 1714, John Wadsworth.

" l. 21, aft. preced. ins. m. 25 Dec. 1679, Eliz. d. of John Clark,

" l. 20 from bot. aft. 1693. add, He d. 1742, at gr. age.

" l. 14 from bot. bef. had, ins. m. 20 July 1652, Dorothy, d. of Thomas Skidmore,

" l. 13 from bot. at the begin. ins. 25 Sept. — also, aft. yr. strike out to the end of the
sent. and ins. Samuel, 22 Feb. 1656; Mary, 21 Apr. 1659; Thomas, 7 May 1662;
Joseph, 14 Nov. 1664; Sarah, 2 June 1667; Hannah, 12 Jan. 1670, wh. with her
mo. was bur. the last of Apr. foll.

P. 315. l. 11 from bot. at the end, add, WILLIAM, Boston, by w. Rachel had William, b. 2 Apr. 1640; Sarah, 6 Oct. 1642; Rachel, 13 Oct. 1644; Isaac, 5 Oct.
1646; Eliz. 3 Oct. 1648; and Jacob, Nov. 1658. On the face of the rec. as giv.
in Geneal. Reg. XV. 133, it is plain. seen, that it was all made at once; but on
p. 136 of the same vol. a contempo. rec. ins. Hannah, 12 Mar. 1659, i. e. 1660.

P. 316. l. 4, bef. 1667. ins. 12 Dec. — also, strike out, "but Dodd calls her w. of"
and ins. and 9 May 1676, Samuel

" l. 6, at the end, add, Richard liv. in Eng.

P. 318. l. 2 from bot. for 1659 r. 1660

P. 320. l. 9, aft. Salem, ins. m. 30 July 1674,

" l. 13 from bot. aft. Edmund, add, and perhaps is he wh. m. 13 May 1656, Sarah
Barney, prob. d. of the first Jacob, had Sarah, b. 28 Dec. 1659; and Hannah, 9
Nov. 1662, few days aft. wh. his w. d.

P. 321. l. 9, aft. riv. add, in wh. he d. His real surname was Legrove, and he, when
press. for the serv. was an apprent. of Elisha Ilsley.

P. 322. l. 8, aft. weaver, ins. m. Eliz. Crook, wh. is not of my acquaint. was

" l. 9, aft. Samuel, add, b. 4 Sept. 1647;

P. 322. l. 14, aft. 1675, add, m. 29 Sept. 1676, Mary, prob. d. of John Woodcock, was

P. 323. l. 7, aft. Jasper, ins. was a physician,

" l. 8, aft. Milford, add, had no ch.

" l. 16 from bot. aft. leav. ins. w. Christian, wh. d. 1690.

" l. 15 from bot. bef. JOHN, ins. JOHANNA, Milford, s. of Jasper, by w. Sarah had Abel, Nathaniel, Samuel, Christian, Eliz. and Sarah, but neither dates of b. nor bapt. are seen. JOHN, Newport 1651, of wh. I hear no more.

" l. 9 from bot. bef. SAMUEL, ins. SAMUEL, Milford, s. of Jasper, d. 1699, leav. w. Hannah, and ch. Jasper, aged 6 yrs.; Christian, 4; and Daniel, 1.

" l. 8 from bot. for the preced. r. Nathaniel

P. 324. l. 19 from bot. aft. 1680. strike out, "He had been of" and ins. JOHN, — also, for w. ins. m. 3 June 1669, — also, aft. Abigail, ins. Kitchin, perhaps d. of John,

P. 325. l. 14, at the end, add, He m. at Salem, 10 Jan. 1677, Eliz. d. of John Brown.

" l. 19 from bot. bef. had, ins. by w. Eliz.

P. 327. l. 18 from bot. bef. SAMUEL, ins. JOHN, Gloucester, 1683.

" l. 14 from bot. aft. Hutchinson, add, wh. he m. May 1658, unless the numerals in Essex Inst. II. 150 and 1, be wrong, as they prob. are — also, aft. Hannah, add, there said to be b. July 1657;

" l. 13 from bot. aft. Sarah, ins. Sept. 1659;

" l. 3 from bot. aft. had, ins. Nathaniel, b. 1677; Deborah, 1679; — also, aft. 1682; add, James, 1684; Samuel, 1687; Mary, 1696; and Benjamin, 1700; beside Joseph, and William, as Babson teaches.

P. 332. l. 18 from bot. bef. 1670, ins. 16 Nov.

" l. 17 from bot. aft. Rutherford, ins. had Daniel, b. 9 Aug. 1672, d. in few mos.; Daniel, again, 4 June 1674; and Rotherford, 21 Apr. 1675; — also, erase what follows Rutherford to m. in the next l. inclus.

" l. 16 from bot. aft. 1675. add, His wid. m. 23 Aug. 1681, John Prout.

P. 333. l. 13 from bot. aft. Adams. add, He had also, Eliz. wh. m. Edward Larkin of the same.

P. 334. l. 2. from bot. aft. will. ins. His wid. m. John Cooper sen.

P. 335. l. 20 erase perhaps

" l. 21, bef. 28 Feb. ins. 23 or

P. 337. l. 8 from bot. aft. 1683. add, He d. 9 Apr. 1727, aged 70.

P. 338. l. 3, aft. same, ins. prob. his youngest ch.

" l. 15, aft. 1733; add, but Mr. Porter says, 1697.

" l. 13 from bot. aft. Eliz. add, d. of James Fowle, wid. of Timothy Walker,

P. 339. l. 16, aft. 1639, add, call. s. of Gilbert in Eng.

P. 341. l. 4 and 5, strike out, "on marr. with" &c. to the end of sent. and ins. as by a lady of that name req. in her will devis. most of her prop. to him. They had been mut. attach. in youth, but she had m. a gent. to wh. descend. an est. held by Carew fam. from the time of Q. Eliz. Aft. H. m. a d. of Adm. Inglefield, and had sev. ch.

P. 344, l. 14, aft. 1657; ins. William, 9 Oct. 1659;

" l. 19, bef. William ins. Oct. 1673,

P. 345. l. 12, aft. 1650, ins. Mary Vincent, wh. d. 5 Aug. 1705;

" l. 21, aft. 1674. add, He d. bef. 1686, and his wid. d. 6 May 1689.

" l. 9 from bot. at the end, add, JOHN, Gloucester, s. of John of the same, m. 7 July 1686, Ruth Stanwood, wh. d. 17 Apr. 1689; and next, 20 Jan. 1691, m. Agnes Penny, and d. Jan. 1718, leav. s. John, and five ds.

P. 349. l. 14, aft. last, ins. John

" l. 21, at the end, add, 13 Mar.

P. 349. l. 22, aft. John, ins. 1 Aug. — also, aft. William, ins. 1 Mar. 1691 — also, aft. Rachel, ins. 7 Feb. 1693 — also, aft. Daniel, ins. 1 Jan. 1695

" l. 10, from bot. bef. MARK, ins. BENJAMIN, Middletown, m. 14 June 1688, Sarah, d. of William Ward, had Ann, b. 13 Jan. 1690 ; Sarah, 29 July 1697 ; Phebe, 14 July 1702 ; Benjamin, 4 Oct. 1706 ; and Ann ; and d. 8 Jan. 1740. His wid. d. 27 Apr. 1744.

P. 351. l. 2, aft. 1656 ; add, and Abigail, 8 Mar. 1660.

P. 352. l. 21, bef. had ins. m. 3 June 1669, at Salem, wid. Mary Robinson, — also, aft. had ins. Mary, b. 3 Dec. 1670.

P. 353. l. 8 from bot. bef. RICHARD, ins. JOHN, Gloucester, had liv. at Weymouth, but m. at G. 22 Apr. 1652, the wid. of Walter Tybbot, was a selectman 1664.

P. 354. l. 17 from bot. aft. Haviland, ins. had Jane, b. 1 May 1660 — also, aft. Marblehead. add, There he d. June 1679, and his will of 5 Nov. preced. names only this w. and d.

P. 355. l. 20, for Feb. 1666 r. Sept. 1665

P. 356. l. 4, bef. 1662, ins. 5 Nov.

" l. 10 at the end, add, SAMUEL, Derby, s. of Jabez, d. early in 1698, leav. w. Hannah, and ch. Joseph, 4 yrs. old ; Margaret 2 ; and Samuel, 8 mos.

" l. 3 from bot. bef. William, ins. NATHANIEL, Plymouth, s. of William first of the same, m. Abigail Buck, had Abigail, b. 27 Jan. 1693 ; Nathaniel, 27 Feb. 1696 ; and James, 1 Aug. 1698 ; and d. 19 Apr. 1721. His wid. d. 13 May 1727. SAMUEL, Plymouth, br. of the preced. by w. Priscilla had Rebecca, b. 27 Jan. 1679 ; and by w. Hannah had John, 19 Dec. 1685 ; Hannah, 15 Nov. 1689 ; Samuel, 14 Aug. 1690 ; William, 26 July 1692 ; Eleazer, 18 Apr. 1694 ; and Priscilla, 3 Oct. 1695. But in date of third ch. error of one or two yrs. prob. crept into Geneal. Reg. XIV. 229. There we learn that he and w. d. the same day 22 Mar. 1734.

P. 357. l. 3, for John r. Benjamin

" l. 7, at the end, add, He d. 26 Aug. 1691 ; and his wid. m. Ephraim Morton. WILLIAM, Plymouth, s. of the preced. m. Lydia, d. of famous Elder Thomas Cushman, had Eliz. b. 3 Feb. 1684 ; Thomas, 17 Mar. 1686 ; a d. 5 Feb. 1688, wh. d. in four wks. ; Lydia ; William ; Robert ; Mary ; Isaac ; and Rebecca.

P. 358. l. 18, bef. EDWARD, ins. BENJAMIN, Gloucester, youngest s. of the first Edward, m. 15 Jan. 1696, Deborah Norwood, d. 3 Feb. 1725, leav. s. Caleb, Joseph, and Ebenezer, but had others wh. d. young.

" l. 20, aft. 1661 ; ins. John, 1663 ; Thomas, 1665 ;

" l. 21, aft. 1671. add, He d. 17 May 1683, and his wid. d. 4 Mar. 1691. EDWARD, Gloucester, s. of the preced. m. 5 Feb. 1684, Sarah, d. of the first William Haskell, and sec. w. in 1693, Hannah York ; by the two hav. eighteen ch. not nam. in Babson. JOHN, Gloucester, br. of the preced. m. Sarah Giddings of Ipswich, whose f. is not kn. had sev. ch. of wh. Andrew alone is nam. by Babson, as d. one mo. aft. his f. and his w. d. a. two yrs. bef. her h. wh. d. 11 Nov. 1724. JOSEPH, Gloucester, br. of the preced. had two ws. but ch. is not ment. and he d. 10 May 1716.

" l. 15 from bot. aft. Miles, ins. wh. had m. Eliz. 11 Apr. 1665,

P. 362. l. 19 from bot. aft. Collins, ins. perhaps d. of Samuel,

P. 363. l. 9 aft. Dow, add, had Hannah, b. 3 Dec. 1673 ; Richard and John, tw. 3 Mar. 1675 ;

P. 364. l. 13 from bot. bef. THOMAS, ins. THOMAS, Killingworth, d. 1697, leav. ch. Mary, aged 13 ; Thomas, 8 ; Nathaniel, 3 ; and Samuel, 1.

" l. 6 from bot. bef. Phebe ins. 24 Aug. 1682,

P. 365. l. 12 from bot. for Wetmore r. Whitmore

" l. 11 from bot. for bef. 1665 r. 18 Apr. 1664

" l. 4 from bot. bef. WILLIAM, ins. WILLIAM, Middletown, s. of the first Daniel, m. 8 Jan. 1690, Martha Collins, prob. d. of Samuel, had Mary, b. 19 Feb. 1692; Sibil, 30 Apr. 1695; William, 20 May 1697; and Prudence, 1 Jan. 1701.

P. 366. l. 19, aft. 1653; ins. Ebenezer, 31 May 1660;

" l. 13 from bot. aft. John, ins. wh. d. 1675, unm.

" l. 4 from bot. aft. 1658; ins. Eliz. Jan. 1667, when her mo. d. — also, erase perhaps more

" l. 3 from bot. for 1666 r. 1667

" l. 2 from bot. bef. WILLIAM, ins. THOMAS, Branford, s. of the preced. m. Margaret Stent d. of his mo.-in-law, had Lydia, b. 1690; Jemima, 1692; Thomas, 12 Oct. 1694; Abigail, 17 Nov. 1696; Benjamin, 7 Aug. 1698; Joseph, 25 May 1700; David, 7 Feb. 1702; Aaron, 4 Mar. 1704; and Jacob, 23 Oct. 1708, as set forth in Bronson's Waterbury, p. 495. But I have had a widely differ. statem. of ch.

P. 367. l. 4, bef. JOHN, ins. JOHN, Salem, m. 4 July 1659, but his w. is not told in Essex Inst. II. 150, wh. names his ch. John, b. 10 Jan. 1661; and Jonathan, 16 Apr. 1662; both d. in few days aft. John, again, 28 Apr. 1664; Jonathan, again, 18 June 1666; David, 23 June 1668; and Alice, 28 Nov. 1672.

" l. 16 aft. parish, ins. next N. of Great Ormsby, — also, aft. vicin. add, but Mr. Drake in Geneal. Reg. XIV. 326, makes it Scratley,

" l. 18 at the end, add, ISAAC, Lynn, had w. charg. as a witch, 1692.

" l. 17 from bot. erase New Haven 1646, perhaps that — also, aft. Stephen, add, perhaps brot. from Eng. and erase *who*

" l. 14 from bot. bef. were, ins. wh. was abs. that night,

" l. 12 from bot. bef. JOSEPH, ins. JONATHAN, Salem, m. Nov. 1671, Lydia, d. of the first John Neal, had Lydia, b. 5 Jan. foll.; Jonathan, 14 Apr. 1673; and John, 6 June 1675; unless there be error in figures of Essex Inst. II. 153.

P. 368. l. 1, aft. Mary, add, prob. d. of Edmund Needham, wh. in his will, June 1677, calls H. s.-in-law, and giv. to some of the ch.

" l. 4, bef. SAMUEL, ins. But of ano. SAMUEL, wh. d. at sea, inv. was brot. into Ct. June 1671.

" l. 9, aft. Hartford, add, was deac. of Hooker's ch.

" l. 21, bef. Thomas, ins. *

" l. 21 from bot. aft. offices, add, was rep. sev. yrs. m. Ruth, d. of Anthony Hawkins,

" l. 19 from bot. aft. 1686; add, beside Mary, Benjamin, and Hawkins — also for Eliz. r. Mary, wh. d. 9 Oct. 1724.

P. 369. last l. bef. JOACHIM, ins. GEORGE, Gloucester, s. of Peter, at Salem, by w. Sarah, had Sarah, Nehemiah, Rose, and perhaps George; and at G. had Benjamin, b. 1697. His s. GEORGE at G. m. 1713, Sarah Butman, wh. d. 20 Nov. 1718; and he m. 1720, Patience York, and d. 24 Nov. 1724, aged 37, leav. s. Nehemiah.

P. 370. l. 12, for f. r. br.

" l. 20, aft. 1659. add, Perhaps he was of Salem, and his d. Sarah d. there, 26 Dec. 1659, and he had a s. b. Sept. foll.

P. 371. l. 10 from bot. bef. BENJAMIN, ins. *

" l. 9 from bot. aft. Mary, ins. d. of Thomas

" l. 8 from bot. aft. 1679; add, beside s. Benjamin, Josiah, Thomas, and William, wh. surv. him. His w. d. 29 Jan. 1698. He was deac. selectman, rep. 1706 and 7, — also, for Hampton r. Gloucester, — also at the end, add, m. 20 Nov. 1685, Mary Baker, had sev. ch. and these surv. him, Mary, Edith, Ruth, and John, wh. d. 1774, aged 79, unm.

P. 371. l. 7 from bot. strike out Feb. 1674, and ins. 2 Feb. 1718, aged 69.   His wid. d. 24 Nov. 1723, aged 58. — also for 1675 r. 1674.

"   l. 5 from bot. aft. 1681 ; add Daniel ; Ebenezer ; and others, ten in all ;

"   l. 4 from bot. bef. Roger, ins. Mark, Gloucester, youngest s. of the first William, m. 16 Dec. 1685, Eliz. Giddings, had Mark, and William, and d. 8 Sept. 1691. Babson, 102, says, his wid. m. John Denison of Ipswich ; but I much doubt.

"   last l. aft. relationsh. add, His will of 27 Mar. 1667, pro. next mo. ment. w. Eliz. sis. Jane, brs. William and Mark, and younger ch. Roger, Joseph, Samuel, Josiah, Hannah, and Sarah.

P. 372. l. 1, aft. 6, add or 16

"   l. 6, aft. G. add, Babson, 100, says Ruth m. a Grover.

"   l. 7, aft. Beverly ; add, Eleanor m. Jacob Griggs ; and Sarah m. Edward Harraden jr.

"   l. 8, aft. Mary, ins. d. of William.

"   l. 10, aft. 1681, ins. beside six other ch. — also, at the end, add, He d. 5 June 1708, leav. four s. William, Joseph, Henry, and Jacob ; and his wid. d. 12 Nov. 1715, aged 66.

"   l. 14, aft. Ellen, add, or Eliz. more prob.

"   l. 17, aft. ds. add, of wh. one was Eliz. w. of William Dana

P. 375. l. 6, bef. Charles, ins. Benjamin, Barnstable, s. of Jonathan, m. 17 Jan. 1678, Mary Hamblen, d. perhaps of the first James, had Abigail, b. 4 Aug. 1679 ; Mary, 3 Mar. 1682 ; Nathaniel, 3 Feb. 1685 ; Benjamin, 17 Oct. 1686 ; John, 16 Feb. 1690 ; Eliz. 25 Mar. 1692 ; Meletiah, 4 Oct. 1693 ; Timothy, 19 Oct. 1695 ; Hannah, 7 May 1698 ; and Solomon, 1704.

"   l. 12, for perhaps r. only

"   l. 13, for Hannah r. Sarah

"   l. 16, aft. 1662, add, or 7 Mar. 1663 — also, aft. 21, ins. or 23 Mar. 1665 ;

"   l. 17, strike out Mar. 1664, and ins. Mark, 27 Apr. 1667 ; and Lydia, 16 May 1669, the last four at Yarmouth.

"   l. 18, bef. Moses, ins. by Falmouth rec. 23 Mar. 1665.   Jonathan, Barnstable or Yarmouth, s. of the preced. m. 4 Sept. 1676, Abigail, as Falmouth rec. has it, but by Barnstable rec. 4 Dec. 1676, Eliz. Walker, had Jonathan, b. 5 Jan. 1678 ; Sarah, 17 May 1682 ; Mary, 24 June 1684 ; Nathan, 1693 ; and Ebenezer, 29 Nov. 1696.   Joseph, Falmouth, m. 7 Dec. 1683, Amy Allen, had Lydia, b. 13 Jan. 1685 ; Amy 4 July 1687 ; Joseph, 3 Aug. 1689 ; Ichabod, 21 Oct. 1691 ; Ruth, 7 Nov. 1693 ; Joanna, 2 June 1696 ; Eliz. 6 Nov. 1697 ; Bethia, 25 Jan. 1700 ; Ebenezer, 26 Mar. 1702 ; and Barnabas, 4 Feb. 1704. — also, erase youngest

"   l. 21 from bot. bef. Thomas, ins. Samuel, Falmouth, s. of the first Jonathan, had Eleazer, b. 23 Sept. 1694 ; Samuel, 28 Feb. 1696 ; James, 23 Aug. 1697 ; and Lydia, 30 May 1699.

l. 11 from bot. aft. unkn. add, Thomas, Falmouth, eldest s. of the first Jonathan m. 22 Jan. or Feb. 1679, it is said had sev. ch. of wh. only Jonathan, b. 9 Apr. 1693 ; and Nathaniel, 1698 ; are ment. in Geneal. Reg. XIV. 198.

"   l. 6 from bot. aft. and, ins. prob. first came in

P. 376. l. 20 from bot. for 1653 r. 1652

P. 377. l. 12, strike out sev. ch. and ins. Abigail, b. 14 Nov. 1665 ; George, 17 Apr. 1668 ; Eliz. 20 Feb. 1670 ; William, 9 May 1672 ; and Samuel, 23 Sept. 1674.

"   l. 17, aft. and ins. Nathaniel ; and — also, aft. 1676. add, His will of 12 Oct preced. pro. 27 June foll. ment. only the four last b. as then liv.

"   l. 21, aft. *He* add, m. 22 Mar. 1675, Ruth, d. of George Gardner,

"   l. 20 from bot. aft. John, ins. b. 10 Jan. 1676 ; — also, aft. Nathaniel, ins. 25 Nov. 1678 ;

P. 377. l. 4 from bot. at the end, add, WILLIAM, Salem, s. of the preced. was capt. and d. 1679. His wid. Sarah ret. small inv.

P. 379. l. 7, aft. Susanna, add, d. of Thomas Newhall,

" l. 12, aft. 1667. add, He was one of the petitnrs. 1655 for incorpo. of the town of Groton.

P. 381. l. 4 from bot. bef. Aug. ins. bapt. 2

P. 382. l. 10 from bot. aft. Mary, add, d. of John Mills,

P. 383. l. 2, bef. RICHARD, ins. JOSEPH, Derby, wh. d. 1682, left w. Abigail, d. of Richard Holbrook of Milford, and ch. Joseph, Eleazer, Abigail, Mary, Lois, and Agnes.

P. 384. l. 19 from bot. for Joseph r. Josia, but bef. the name ins. 1678

P. 386. l. 6 from bot. for is unkn. r. was, perhaps, Blaise,

P. 388. aft. l. 13, ins. HAYFIELD, WALTER, Wenham 1673.

" l. 22, aft. 1685. add, He was a capt. among first proprs. of Bristol, liv. there Feb. 1689, with w. and six ch.

P. 389. l. 19 from bot. aft. 1645. add, His wid. m. 17 Nov. 1654, Rev. Samuel Eaton.

P. 390. l. 19, aft. bec. ins. 30 May

" l. 20, aft. New Haven, ins. d. 7 Oct. 1696,

P. 391. l. 7 from bot. for Winsor r. Windsor

P. 396. l. 7, aft. Vinton, ins. d. of the first John,

P. 397. l. 11 from bot. aft. 1695. add, This fam. usual. spell Hurd.

P. 399. l. 2 from bot. aft. Streete, add, had Nathaniel, b. 9 Nov. 1664 ; Samuel, 4 Oct. 1667 ; James, 13 Feb. 1670, d. at 1 yr. ; James, again, 14 Jan. 1672, d. soon ; Abigail, Jan. 1674 ; Seth, 25 Mar. 1676 ; Theophilus, 12 Apr. 1680 ; Ann, 23 Dec. 1682 ; and Mr. Porter thinks he was relat. of Gov. Eaton, and in 1654 spell. so.

P. 400. l. 18 from bot. at the end, add, WILLIAM, Bristol, perhaps s. of the preced. was liv. 1689, with only one ch.

P. 401. l. 6 from bot. aft. Eliz. add, d. of Greenfield Larrabee,

P. 403. l. 12 from bot. aft. 1670, add, leav. Richard, b. a. 1667, and Caleb.

" l. 11 from bot. at the end, add, and in 1689 purch. ld. in Windham, m. 1 Mar. 1693, Sarah Smith, had Jonathan, b. 17 Mar. 1694 ; and she d. 18 of mo. foll. Next he m. 17 Oct. 1695, Eliz. Conant, had Hannah, 25 Dec. 1697 ; Sarah, 16 Apr. 1700 ; Caleb, 12 Mar. 1704, d. young ; Joshua, 25 Apr. 1707 ; Eliz. 28 Apr. 1710 ; Barzillai, 18 June 1713 ; Asa, 25 Aug. 1715 ; Nathaniel, 10 Aug. 1718 ; and Mary, 6 July 1720. He d. 6 Feb. 1743 ; and his wid. d. 23 Sept. 1762.

" l. 8 from bot. at the end, add, WILLIAM Salem, m. 12 July 1671, Eliz. Preston, had Eliz. b. 4 July foll. ; Hannah, 1674, d. in few wks. and Hannah, again, 4 Mar. 1677.

" l. 4 from bot. for 74 r. 78

P. 404. l. 5 from bot. bef. JOHN, ins. JOHN, Salem, perhaps s. of the preced. m. 15 Apr. 1672, Mary Follett, had John, b. 7 Aug. 1674.

P. 405. aft. l. 12, ins. HERMAYES, BENJAMIN, Salem, d. Nov. 1666, acc. Essex Inst. II. 15. From long acquaint. with the form of first let. in the surname, I doubt not, the same person is sometimes appear. as Fermais, and oftener as Vermayes.

" l. 20 from bot. aft. work, add, as marshal,

P. 406. l. 20 from bot. bef. Aug. ins. 5

P. 407. l. 7 from bot. at the end, add, possib. Huse,

P. 409. l. 15 from bot. for Samuel r. Joseph the first,

" l. 9 from bot. at the end, add, He next rem. to Woodbury, there d. 1687, leav. ch. Joseph, Benjamin, Mary, Eliz. and Samuel.

" l. 4 from bot. erase perhaps

P. 410. l. 5 and 6, erase wh. may have been f. of Joseph and Samuel

P. 410. l. 4 from bot. for "had w." r. m. 21 Feb. 1672, d. of Hilliard Veren senr.

P. 413. l. 2 from bot. for bapt. r. b.

P. 414. l. 1, aft. 1661, add, or 2,

" l. 7, for "long" r. only three mos.

" l. 14, aft. 1686, add, wh. d. in few mos.

" l. 13 from bot. at the end, add, Sarah m. Clark Carrington, acc. Bronson's Hist. of Waterbury p. 143; but he had, on p. 26, m. him to Mary.

P. 415. l. 5 from bot. aft. ch. add, Hannah, b. 1678; and Mary, 7 June 1686;

" l. 4, aft. 1692. add, He had sec. w. Abigail, youngest d. of William Wooden, and ch. Abigail, Sarah, Susanna,

P. 417. l. 14, aft. Salem, ins. wheelwright, m. 26 Aug. 1664, Lydia Buffum, d. prob. of Robert; had Lydia, b. 30 Mar. 1666; Eliz. 15 Dec. 1667; John, 22 Jan. 1671, and Robert, 11 Sept. 1676.

" l. 19 from bot. aft. New Haven ins. a weaver,

" l. 18 from bot. aft. ch. add, and a sec. w. m. 3 Aug. 1694, Mary.

" l. 15 from bot. bef. Jonathan, ins. Jonathan, Salem, by w. Miriam had Miriam, b. 24 Mar. 1658; and Susan, 31 July 1660; unless I mistake in read. of Essex Inst. II. 151.

P. 419. l. 18, for 1662 r. 27 Jan. 1663.

" l. 19, aft. 1663. add, His wid. m. 22 May 1666, John Scranton.

P. 420. l. 1, bef. Thomas, ins. Tahan, Guilford, s. of Robert, had w. Hannah, but no ch. and d. 1693.

P. 421 l. 6, aft. 1650, ins. m. 16 Nov. 1651, Eliz. Clark, d. prob. of Edmund,

" l. 7, aft. John; add, of wh. the sec. prob. d. young, and the third was b. 2 June 1659; — also, aft. Philip, ins. b. 24, bapt. — also, aft. Zebulon, add, Eliz. again b. 1 Feb. 1665; —

" l. 8, aft. Mary, add, 25 Jan. 1668; — also, aft. Abigail, add, 21 Sept. 1670; — also, aft. Sarah, add, 22 June 1675; — also, erase the rest of the sent.

" l. 19, aft. 1658, add, but, no doubt, the last fig. is wrong

" l. 21 at the end, add, Sometimes it is spell. Helliard. Eliz. m. 14 Sept. 1669, Gilbert Peters.

P. 426. l. 20, from bot. at the end, add, and Thomas, perhaps gr.s. of the preced. m. 18 Nov. 1684, Hannah Bristoll, d. of Henry, had Thomas, Stephen, William, Eliz. Alice, and Samuel, made, Mr. Porter informs me, resid. legatee, and his will ment. sis. Lane. But certain. most of those ch. would have been (especial. the ds. wh. bear surnames of hs.) by a former w. He d. 1698, his inv. is dat. 15 Mar. 1697, i. e. 8.

" l. 13 from bot. aft. Stratford, ins. 1653,

" l. 10 from bot. bef. *had* ins. by w. Hannah, — also, at the end, add, beside nine others.

P. 427. l. 9, aft. Barnabas, ins. b. 1667; — also, aft. Isaac, add, beside Eliz. 1672;

" l. 11, aft. preced. add, m. 28 Sept. 1676, Mary, d. of John Plimpton,

P. 428. l. 17, for 1689 r. 1688

" l. 19 from bot. aft. 1644, ins. not 16 Oct. of that yr. as by some said, for that was Wednesday.

" l. 15 from bot. aft. 196. add, His d. Mary m. 12 Oct. 1663, Ralph Russell.

" l. 11 from bot. aft. 1685. add, He d. 1704, and his wid. d. 1713.

" l. 10 from bot. aft. 1660. add, He rem. to Wallingford, m. 18 Jan. 1671, Abigail, d. of Nathaniel Merriman, had a d. b. 1671; Samuel, and Abigail, tw. 10 Apr. 1672.

P. 429. l. 7, bef. 1669. ins. Nov. and aft. it, add, His wid. Eliz. d. 1679, and his d. Eliz. m. Jan. 1673, Anthony Howd, and next, 22 Aug. 1677, John Nash.—also, for 8 Jan. 1670 r. 18 Jan. 1671.

" l. 9, for 1685 r. 1686

" l. 10, aft. 1692. add, He d. 1700, and his wid. d. 1707.

P. 430. l. 16 from bot. bef. DANIEL, ins. BENJAMIN, Bristol, s. of William, by w. Rebecca had Hannah, and he d. soon. His mo. took the ch. wh. was bapt. 26 Sept. 1708.

P. 432. l. 14 from bot. aft. 1687. add, He was of Bristol in Feb. 1689, with w. three ch. and three serv.—also, aft. Beverly, ins. a wid.

P. 434. l. 19, for Lyme r. Lynn

P. 435. l. 16 from bot. aft. sec. add, or third

P. 437. l. 13, aft. Thomas. add, WILLIAM, Topsfield, with w. Deliverance, and d. Abigail, in Apr. 1692, arrest. for witchcr. among the earliest, and their cases are not the least remarka. of that period of horrid delus. The trepidat. of the d. made her sw. to any falsehood against her f. and the w. plead guilty to any non-sense the Hon. Ct. would suggest to her.

P. 438. l. 4 from bot. aft. 1665, add, d. 1681, leav. w. Mary, and ch. John, Mary, Joseph, Thomas, and Eliz. His wid. m. 6 July 1682, Isaac Johnson.

" last l. aft. b. ins. 16 Sept.—also, bef. 1654; ins. 31 Aug.—also, bef. 1657; ins. 8 June

P. 439. l. 6, bef. WILLIAM, ins. SAMUEL, Gloucester 1684, may have been s. of William, by w. Hannah had Samuel, b. 1684; Hannah, 1686; John, 1688; Philip, 1690; William, 1691; a d. 1694; Jedediah, 1696; Patience, 1697; Abigail, 1699; Mercy, 1700; David, 1702; Martha, 1704; Ann, 1705; Jonathan, 1706; and Experience, 1708. His w. d. 28 July 1724, aged 60; and he m. 3 May 1725 Mary Stockbridge.

" l. 12, at the end, add, His will of 11 Oct. 1665 ment. w. no ch.

" l. 6 from bot. bef. THOMAS, ins. ROBERT, Salem, perhaps br. of George, m. 22 June 1665, Mary Pitman, had Mary, b. 10 Mar. foll.; Sarah, 19 Feb. 1668; Tabitha, Jan. 1670; Hannah, 23 Sept. 1672; Eliz. 15 Sept. 1674; Robert, 25 Jan. 1677; and Bethia, 23 Oct. 1678. But in Essex Inst. II. 151, the surname is giv. Hodg, and so the fam. may be diff. and prob. the w. was a Pickman, d. of Nathaniel.

P. 440. l. 19, bef. THOMAS, ins. THOMAS, Salem, m. Oct. 1661, Catharine More, says Essex Inst. II. 151, and I hear no more.

" l. 11 from bot. bef. 1651, ins. 2 Sept.—also, aft. Turner, add, d. of Nathaniel,

" l. 10 from bot. bef. 1654; ins. 25 Mar.—also, bef. 1657; ins. 5 Apr.—also, aft. 1657; add, Mary, bapt. 8 July 1660; John, 1663; both d. soon; Samuel, Sept. 1664, d. young; Mary, again, 17 Apr. 1670, d. young; Ann, Feb. 1672, d. at 1 yr.—also, erase and prob. others, beside

" l. 9 from bot. erase and John

" l. 8 from bot. aft. coll. add, He d. Oct. foll. and his wid. d. 1693.

" l. 5 from bot. aft. 1695, add, wh. d. unm. 15 Feb. 1721. The f. d. 11 Nov. 1711, leav. good est. and his wid. d. 1 Dec. foll.

" l. 3 from bot. bef. ROBERT, ins. but it was prob. a. 1701 at Stratford, at the ho. of his br.-in-law, Rev. Israel Chauncy. He left. wid. Abigail, wh. m. Richard Blackleach.

P. 441. l. 14 from bot. bef. JOHN, ins. ISRAEL, Milford, s. of Richard, had w. Mary, and one d. when he d. 1680.

P. 442. l. 10 and 9 from bot. strike out, "it is prob. many descend." and ins. w. Agnes, and ch. Abel, Israel, Pelatiah, Mary, Hannah, Patience, John, Daniel, and Abigail, w. of Joseph Hawkins.

P. 446. l. 10 from bot. at the end, add, WILLIAM, Exeter, s. of the preced. m. 10 Apr. 1674, Lydia, d. of Robert Quimby.

" l. 5 from bot. aft. Gloucester. add, There he is not ment. aft. 1653. See Babson, 105 for reason of rem.

P. 448. l. 9 from bot. aft. Powell, add, had Richard, b. 9 Aug. 1661, d. next yr.; Benjamin, 28 June 1663; John, 12 May 1665; Abigail, 1 Mar. 1668; Joseph, 4 Apr. 1670; and Caleb, 22 Dec. 1673.

" l. 6 from bot. aft. m. ins. 1 Sept. 1675,

P. 449. l. 4, at the end, add, Mr. Porter informs me, that he d. 1683, leav. w. Abigail, and ch. William, Joseph, and Abigail.

" l. 6, aft. operations, add, by w. Elinor had Susanna, b. 4 Mar. 1659 ;

" l. 7, aft. 240. add, His w. was admor. 1679.

" l. 8, erase all aft. 53

" l. 14, at the end, add, He had Eliz. b. July 1672; and Mary, 11 Dec. 1673.

" l. 21, for 1 Jan. bef. r. 3 Apr.

P. 452. l. 15 from bot. bef. JOHN, ins. JOHN, Salem, m. 21 Apr. 1672, Sarah Hone, unless the surname be wrong (as I suspect) in Essex Inst. II. 152. She was a wid. and they had Joseph, b. 14 Feb. 1673; Benjamin, 6 Oct. 1674; Sarah, 23 Feb. 1677; Eliz. 21 July 1679; and Jane, 1 June 1683.

P. 454. l. 8 from bot. bef. HENRY, ins. ELEAZER, New Haven, s. of the first William, m. 5 Nov. 1674, Tabitha, d. of John Thomas, had William, b. 25 Sept· 1675, d. soon; Thomas, 4 Nov. 1676; Sarah, 2 Apr. 1679; Susanna, 21 Oct. 1681; Tabitha, 30 Jan. 1684; Abigail, 17 Nov. 1686; Eliz. bapt. 1690; and Lydia, b. 5 Nov. 1693.

" l. 4 from bot. bef. m. ins. mariner, — also, aft. m. ins. Jan. 1674, — also, aft. Eliz. ins. d. of John — also, aft. 23 ins. or 28

" l. 2 from bot. aft. 1690. add, JOSEPH, Wallingford, s. of William, had Joseph, b. a. 1685; Daniel, 1687; Benjamin, 1690; Mary, 1694; and Eliz. 1696; but I see not the name of his w. and depend for date of his d. 1698, on conject.

P. 455. l. 17, aft. 3 ins. or 31 — also, aft. 1653, add, d. soon.

" l. 18, aft. 1657, ins. wh. d. 1690, unm.

" l. 19, aft. Mary. add, His wid. m. William Peck ; — also, aft. Wallingford, add, whither her f. rem. and there d. 1683.

" l. 17 from bot. bef. JOSEPH, ins. JOHN, Salem 1692; — also, aft. Danvers, strike out 1682, and ins. by w. Sarah had Benjamin, b. 4 Feb. 1658

" l. 16 from bot. aft. same, ins. and his f.

" l. 14 from bot. aft. 1668, ins. had w. Mary, and s. Nathaniel. He and his w. show. good courage in giv. good charact. with others of their neighb. to John Procter and his w. wh. the Ct. wish. to hang as witches.

" l. 13 from bot. bef. ROBERT, ins. RICHARD, Salem 1672.

P. 456. l. 19 from bot. aft. detail ; add, but distorts the good name Putnam of one of the s.-in-law, into an impossible Prenam

P. 457. l. 6, at the end, add, m. 23 Dec. 1669, Esther Crason, had a d. 18 Feb. preced.; John, 22 Apr. 1670; Mordecai, 3 Aug. 1673; as giv. in Essex Inst. II. 152.

P. 458. l. 2 from bot. for Eng. r. Cambridge

P. 459. l. 7, aft. 1679, add, H. C. 1700

" l. 11, aft. ds. add, of wh. Esther, 30 Nov. 1702, was one ;

" l. 5 from bot. aft. Samuel, ins. H. C. 1653,

P. 460. l. 14, aft. mariner, add, was drown. at Salem in that yr.

P. 462. l. 5, for Wait Samuel r. Samuel Wait, as Mr. Porter, wh. marks the b. 3 Aug. not 30 foll. would regard this as the *first double name* on our side of the water. I do not accept the fact; but if Wait be fasten. on the ch. it may seem rather to be nickname for his *premature* coming.

" l. 15, at the end, add, tho. she, instead of her elder sis. (by unusual inadvert. of a corresp. of extraord. accura. in Geneal. Reg. XIV. 89) is call. w. of Snow.

P. 463. l. 5, aft. was, ins. at first,

" l. 13, aft. f. ins. beside three ds. and three other s.

" l. 20 from bot. aft. John, ins. wh. m. 8 June 1676, Eliz. d. of John Pearson.

P. 464. l. 14, aft. HORN, add, or HORNE,

" l. 19, bef. 1 Aug. ins. b. 28 July, bapt.

" l. 17 from bot. bef. JOHN, ins. JOHN, Salem, prob. s. of the preced. m. 30 Oct. 1667, Mary Clark, had Mary, b. 23 Aug. foll. and d. at 1 yr. Perhaps he had by sec. w. Naomi that Jonathan, wh. d. 6 Oct. 1701.

" l. 15 from bot. bef. WILLIAM, ins. SIMON, Salem, br. of the preced. m. 28 Feb. 1676, Rebecca Stevens, wid. prob. of Samuel, had Joshua, b. mid. Sept. 1677; and Simon, 11 Jan. 1680.

P. 466. l. 19, aft. 483. add, His wid. Ann, in will, 1660, gives to her s. Thomas, his ch. John, and the w. of David Wilton,

" l. 21, aft. ch. add, He took sec. w. 1699, Ruth, wid. of Joseph Peck.

" l. 22, erase perhaps

P. 467. l. 16 from bot. aft, 1688, add, s. of Samuel (on p. 439 put under Hodgkin), m. 21 June 1683, Esther, d. of Richard Sperry, had Eliz. b. 30 Aug. 1684; Daniel, Aug. 1687; Obadiah, 20 Mar. 1690; Esther, 25 Nov. 1693; Rebecca, 14 Feb. 1698; Jemima, 26 Nov. 1702; and d. 10 Mar. 1711. His wid. d. next yr. JOHN, New Haven, br. prob. eldest of the preced. m. 2 Dec. 1672, Eliz. d. of Henry Peck, had John, b. 11 Oct. foll.; Joshua; Joseph, 8 June 1678; Josiah, 24 Jan. 1681; Caleb, 18 Oct. 1684; Eliz. 18 Jan. 1686; and ano. of unkn. name; made his will 1689. — also, bef. m. ins. br. of the preced.

" l. 15 from bot. aft. Pardee. add, He had sec. w. Esther, and third, Hannah, wh. d. 17 Feb. 1719; but when either of the former ws. d. is not kn. and so wh. was mo. of the sev. ch. is unkn. They were Mary, b. 30 Apr. 1679; Stephen, 25 Aug. 1681; Martha, 14 Dec. 1683; Joshua, wh. d. 22 Dec. 1707; Hannah; Abraham; Priscilla, 10 Dec. 1688; Abigail, 12 Oct. 1695; Isaac, June 1701; and Jacob, Feb. 1704. He was Sheriff, and d. 1722, his will being of 7 Apr. and of his good est. admin. was giv. 22 Oct. — also, for 1678 r. 18 Mar. 1679.

" l. 14 from bot. aft. Sarah, ins. d. of Robert

" l. 13 from bot. at the end, add, beside Ebenezer, and Amos, both bapt. 1690;

" l. 12 from bot. for Jan. 1705. r. 29 Dec. 1704; and his wid. Hannah d. 19 Jan. 1713, aged 41.

" l. 11 from bot. at the end, add, THOMAS, New Haven, br. of the preced. m. 27 Nov. 1677, Sarah, eldest d. of William Wilmot, then under 15 yrs. of age, had Samuel, b. 7 Sept. 1680; Sarah, 18 Feb. 1683; Ann, 12 Dec. 1684; William; Abraham; Dorcas; these three bapt. 1695; Mary, 1697; Desire, 1699, wh. d. 1702; and Lydia; and he d. 27 Dec. 1711.

P. 469. l. 17 from bot. bef. RALPH, ins. JOHN, Salem, 1692.

" l. 8 from bot. at the end, add, THOMAS, Lynn 1664.

P. 470. l. 11, at the end, add, WILLIAM, Boston, by w. Mary had d. America, b. 30 Apr. 1660.

" l. 13, from bot. at begin. erase but

P. 471. l. 20 from bot. bef. 1689; ins. 17 Sept.

" l. 19 from bot. bef. 1692; ins. 8 Mar.—also, bef. 1695; ins. 7 Aug.—also, for Esther r. Ephraim, 25 May—also, bef. 1699; ins. 3 Oct.—also, bef. 1703; ins. 3 Mar.

" l. 18 from bot. bef. 1705; ins. 3 June—also, bef. 1707; ins. 21 Dec.—also, bef. 1750, ins. aged. 84, 11 Aug.—also, bef. 1760, ins. aged 92, Feb.

P. 472. l. 6, for Samuel r. Sarah

" l. 20, bef. ROBERT, ins. NEHEMIAH, Salem, m. 11 Aug. 1657, Ann, d. of William Dixy, had Sarah, b. 3 Mar. 1659; and Hannah, 1 Aug. 1661.

P. 473. l. 4, aft. 1657; add, Mary, 15 Sept. 1659.

" l. 5, aft. 1669; add, Mary, 24 Apr. 1672; Nathan, Sept. 1673; and Solomon, 5 Aug. 1675.

" l. 16, aft. Eliz. add, d. of Matthias Hitchcock, m. Jan. 1673,

P. 474. l. 2 from bot. bef. 1653 ins. 3 Apr.—also, bef. 1655 ins. 25 Jan.—also, bef. 1657 ins. 17 Jan.

" last l. bef. 1658 ins. 1 Sept.—also, bef. Isaac, ins. Daniel, 1 Jan. 1664;—also, aft. 1666; ins. Abigail, b. 23 Apr. 1669;—also, aft. and, for prob. more r. Esther, 18 Nov. 1671;—also, bef. 1680, ins. 8 Sept.

P. 475. l. 1, aft. 1685. add, His wid. Ann d. 1712; d. Sarah m. 10 Apr. 1682, Nathaniel Tuttle; Abigail, m. Daniel Brown; and Esther m. 29 Sept. 1692, as his sec. w. James Trowbridge.

" l. 7 bef. EPHRAIM, ins. EPHRAIM, New Haven, s. of the preced. had Mary, b. 8 Dec. 1674; and I hear no more.

" l. 16 from bot. at the end, ins. 22 Oct.

" l. 14 from bot. for 1690. r. 16 Jan. 1691. His d. Eliz. m. May 1669, James Redfield; and Bethia m. 23 Oct. 1677, John Dixwell, the regicide, and outliv. him.

P. 476. l. 14 from bot. aft. 1660, ins. m. 22 Mar. 1667, Sarah, sis. of Matthew Gilbert.

" l. 13 from bot. aft. more. add, But other ch. were Zechariah, 31 Mar. 1670; Matthew and Sarah; and he d. 1703.

P. 478. l. 7 from bot. at the end, add, Such was the form for a hundred yrs. JOHN, with wh. the male line of Anthony closes, d. unm. by his will 11 Jan. 1676, express. foresight of d. in the field in the gr. Ind. war.

P. 479. l. 11 from bot. aft. John, ins. b. 24 Feb. 1627,

P. 480. l. 1, erase either—also, erase or sec.

" l. 20 from bot. aft. est. add, She was d. of Francis Hudson, had one ch. by H. and m. Edmund Perkins.

P. 481. l. 9 from bot. aft. fam. add, and d. 21 Mar. 1697, leav. wid. Mary, ch. Jonathan, then aged 24, wh. liv. but 7 yrs. aft.; Mercy, 18; Hannah, 16; and Samuel, 13.

P. 483. l. 5, aft. longitude. add, He d. 28 Oct. 1660.

" l. 11, at the end, add, 20 July

" l. 12, bef. 1678, ins. 16 Jan.—also, bef. 1681; ins. 10 Mar.—also, bef. 1683; ins. 18 Aug.

" l. 13, aft. again, ins. 23 Mar.

" l. 3 from bot. bef. Feb. ins. Jan. or

P. 485. l. 1, aft. Foster, ins. or Porter, as in Geneal. Reg. XIV. 68.

" l. 14 aft. 1660, ins. as by mistake Farmer said,

" l. 12 from bot. aft. Newport, add, br. of Benjamin,

" l. 11 from bot. aft. Watertown, add, but Bond names him not,

" l. 6 from bot. aft. age. add, He and w. Tacey m. 4 Jan. 1638, were liv. 1688.

P. 485. l. 5 from bot. for late in r. 20 Jan.

" l. 4 from bot. bef. Joseph ins. 16 Nov. 1664,

P. 487. last l. at the end, add, He rem. to Dartmouth, and d. 8 June 1727, in 99th yr. as is said.

P. 488. l. 18 from bot. aft. w. add, Susanna m. John Howlett, and next Edmund Perkins.

" l. 4 from bot. aft. 1664. add, Usual. the name is Hodgson.

P. 491. l. 17 from bot. aft. 1672, add, wh. d. 1689, as did a Rachel, but Babson does not tell, whether she were maid, wid. or w.

P. 492. l. 6, aft. *that* ins. he d. 1640, and

P. 493. l. 2, aft. m. ins. 6 May — also, at the end, add, had Jeremiah, b. 2 Jan. 1663 ; Hannah, 22 Oct. 1664; Mary, 8 Aug. 1666; John, 13 Nov. 1668; Eliz. 27 Feb. 1671, d. soon; Joseph, 11 Aug. 1672; Sarah, 4 Mar. 1675; and Martha.

P. 494. l. 2, aft. 1753. add, He prob. m. 1 Jan. 1695, Mercy Jacobs, d. of Bartholomew.

" l. 3 from bot. bef. 1662 ins. 1 Sept.

" last l. aft Mary. ins. Mary m. 1 Mar. 1654, John Jackson, and d. 26 Feb. 1665; and Hannah m. 26 Dec. 1662, Edmund Dorman.

P. 496. l. 14, for Palmes r. Palmer of Ardfinnan, Co. Tipperary in Ireland.

" l. 17, at the end, add, He d. perhaps as late as 1670 ; at least in 1671, admin. on his est. was tak. by Edmund Batter at Salem, and in 1681, Myles and his w. in her right claim. est. in Mass.

" l. 9 from bot. bef. HOPESTILL, ins. EDWARD, Marblehead 1673.

P. 499. l. 12, aft. yr. ins. John, again, 12 Feb. 1659 ; and George, 23 May 1660. He

" l. 13, aft. *but* add, d. at Salem in June 1679. Ano. NATHANIEL

P. 500. l. 15 for Thomas Holbrook the sec. r. John Alcock

P. 504. l. 18 from bot. at the end, add, d. of John

P. 505. l. 12, at the end, add, BENJAMIN, Stratford, s. of John the sec. of the same, m. Sarah, d. of Abraham Kimberly.

" l. 13 for preced. r. first Benjamin,

" l. 22, aft. *man.* add, He was prob. f. of one of the two Johns of S. in the next generat. ment. below.

" l. 15 from bot. aft. 1669, add, prob. s. of the first John, — also for 15 r. 10

" l. 13 from bot. bef. Dec. ins. 16.

" l. 12 from bot. aft. Sarah, ins. 17 — also, aft. Hannah, ins. 27 — also, aft. Isaac, ins. 2

" l. 11 from bot. aft. Jacob, ins. 16

" l. 10 from bot. aft. Mary. ins. 15 — also, aft. 1679. add, He d. 4 Feb. 1682, and Cothren makes John jr. of S. d. the same day, perhaps bec. the two cous. were m. on the same. His wid. wh. m. the first Thomas Barnum, and surv. him, d. 24 Jan. 1718, aged 76. His d. Mary m. Richard Barnum.

" l. 8 from bot. bef. Dec. ins. 10

" l. 7 from bot. aft. Benjamin, ins. 16 — also, bef. Nov. ins. 9

" l. 6 from bot. bef. Feb. ins. 12 — also, bef. Aug. ins. 17 — also, aft. 1673. ins. He early rem. to Woodbury.

P. 506. l. 1, aft. again, ins. unless Mercy, as Mr. Parsons read the rec. be the true name,

" l. 3, aft. Aug. ins. wh. Parsons calls Apr.

P. 507. l. 18, bef. THOMAS, ins. NICHOLAS, Stratford, m. a. 1692, Abigail, d. of John Thompson, wid. of Jonathan Curtis, perhaps as first, perhaps as sec. w. had no ch. and a. 1695 his wid. m. Samuel Sherman, and she d. 1731.

P. 508. l. 21 aft. Hampton ; add, and Eliz. m. 1 Apr. 1656, Thomas Ayer.

P. 508. l. 5 from bot. bef. EDWARD, ins. BENJAMIN, Salem vill. perhaps s. of Joseph, of wh. all I can find is the exploit of strik. at a spectre as in one of the witchcr. trials, 1692, was testif.

P. 511. l. 6, aft. Salem, ins. perhaps br. of Richard of the same,

" l. 9, bef. ch. ins. only one

P. 514. l. 6 from bot. aft. 1677. add, His wid. m. 3 Dec. 1680, Stephen Daniel.

P. 515. l. 5 from bot. bef. RICHARD, ins. NICHOLAS, prob. of Deerfield, m. 16 Mar. 1679, Jane, wid. of John Plympton.

" l. 2 from bot. aft. 1654. add, Rebecca m. 27 June 1661, Jonathan Eager; and Hannah m. 17 Nov. 1668, Arthur Gray.

P. 516. l. 18 from bot. for 1692 r. 1694 — also, aft. leav. ins. wid. Hannah, s. Samuel, and — also, aft. ds. add, Eliz. Hannah, Mary, and Deborah,

" l. 16 from bot. aft. Hyland. add, His wid. d. 1697.

P. 519. l. 8 from bot. bef. THOMAS, ins. STEPHEN, Salem, m. 2 Jan. 1691, Dinah Elson, had Mary, b. 6 Nov. foll.; Dinah, 24 Feb. 1694; Stephen, 16 June 1696; and Ephraim, 10 Sept. 1698.

" last l. aft. Gloucester, ins. where those ch. were b.

P. 520. l. 18, aft. two. add, by w. Judith Felton — also, aft. John, ins. 12 Sept. 1644; also, aft. Nathaniel, ins. wh. most happi. is bless. with two birthdays on the same page of Essex Inst. I. 153, viz. 10 Apr. and 2 Dec. 1647 (the same numerals being employ. in both, the day and mo. interchang.); — also, aft. Ruth, ins. 20 June 1649;

" l. 19, aft. Richard, ins. 1 Sept. 1651, as on the same page of Essex Inst. but this was Monday, and yet on the same page it is said, he was bapt. then, whereas the foregoing were — also, aft. Samuel, ins. b.

" l. 18 from bot. aft. 211. add, Other ch. were Joseph and Hannah, but both d. quite young.

P. 521. l. 5, bef. JOHN, ins. JOHN, Salem, perhaps s. of John the first, m. 17 Mar. 1670, Mary Coombs, prob. d. of Henry, had Mary, b. 10 Sept. 1671; Ruth, 2 Feb. 1674; John, bapt. 1 Sept. 1678; beside Sarah, and Eliz. both in adult age, bapt. 1702, prob. 13 Mar.

" l. 13, for a r. Sarah,

" l. 19 from bot. bef. RICHARD, ins. NATHANIEL, Salem, s. of the first John, m. 8 Oct. 1670, Mary Preston, had Eliz. b. 11 Feb. 1673; John, 17 Oct. 1674; and Nathaniel.

" l. 11, from bot. aft. £7. ins. His wid. d. 30 July 1677.

P. 522. l. 1, for 1686 r. 1687

P. 523. l. 10 from bot. aft. 1658; ins. Timothy, 2 July 1660;

P. 524. l. 21, aft. Lewis. add, His will of 26 Oct. 1674, pro. by his wid. 27 June 1676, ment. only Samuel and Ruth.

P. 525. l. 4 from bot. aft. 1668, add, m. 1 Apr. 1672, Martha, d. of Nicholas Wyeth, had Eliz. b. 8 Feb. foll. wh. d. next yr.; Thomas, 31 Mar. 1674; and Deborah, 8 Dec. 1675.

P. 526. l. 3, aft. Bassett. add, This surname is made Joes by Mr. Drake, in Geneal. Reg. XIV. 324, as by me it had been in 3 Mass. Hist. Coll. VIII. 273; but my dilig. London correspond. had correct. the name to Ives, as in 3 M. H. C. X. 130, on wh. Drake says, he cannot *torture* it into Ives, tho. to me it seems a better name than Joes. Let the New Haven readers decide.

P. 529. l. 12 from bot. aft. he; add, for the first John liv. 7 yrs. at Gloucester, there sold his est. 1662. The Ipswich John

P. 530. l. 20, at the end, add, d. of Thomas

P. 530. l. 20 from bot. aft. Mary, add, d. of Richard Hull, m. 1 Mar. 1654 — also, bef. 1665, ins. 26 Feb.

" l. 19 from bot. aft. 1655, ins. both d. soon,

" l. 18 from bot. aft. 1659, add, d. at 5 yrs.

" l. 17 from bot. aft. 1663, add, wh. d. in few days, as did ano. ch. with the mo. He m. 2 July 1668, Mary, wid. of George Smith, and d. 1683. His w. as Mr. Porter tells me, was accus. of kill. him.

" l. 16 from bot. aft. appear. add, One JOHN, perhaps s. of John of Ipswich, was a witness against poor Mrs. Easty, execut. in 1692, for a witch. How strong his evid. was, is seen in Essex Inst. II. 242.

P. 532. l. 17 from bot. aft. 1668, add, m. 20 Dec. 1666, Mercy, d. of Thomas Barnes, had a d. b. 1667; Eliz. 19 Oct. 1668; Samuel, 9 Aug. 1671; Mercy, 8 Sept. 1674; Thomas, 4 Nov. 1677; and Lydia, 3 Apr. 1681. He was

" l. 16 from bot. aft. 1685, add, and d. 1693. Mercy m. 1 Jan. 1695, John Hull.

P. 534. l. 16 from bot. aft. N. H. ins. had sec. w. Ann, wh. d. 6 Dec. 1682, giv. b. to George, and aged 18 ;

" l. 11 from bot. aft. 1702, add, m. 10 Jan. 1710, Sarah, d. of David Jeffries of Boston, had George, b. 8 Feb. 1717; Eliz. 20 July 1719; Sarah, 25 Mar. 1722; Ann, 26 Oct. 1723; and Rebecca, 23 May 1734, d. next mo. His w. d. 12 Jan. 1735; and he m. Sarah, d. of John Wentworth, wid. of Archibald McPhedris, had no ch. by her, and was

" l. 10 from bot. for 65 r. 67

P. 535. l. 9, for Frances r. Francis — also, aft. 1677; add, and d. 11 Sept. 1720, aged, says Babson, a. 69 yrs.

" l. 11 from bot. bef. GAWDY, ins. FRANCIS, Gloucester, s. of Charles, m. 1703, Eliz. the spell. of whose surname is uncert. but Babson, 107, says, tho. she had sev. ch. yet none perpet. the name.

P. 537. l. 11, at the end; add, If I understand Mr. S. the error is not on my page, for Drake's copy in Geneal. Reg. XIV. 333, agrees wholly with mine. Yet neither of us have *that* surname ; and I feel sure, that much less than half of the names of passeng. on that voyage by that sh. were report. at the custom-ho.

" l. 21, at the end, add, THOMAS, Salem 1659, wh. d. a. 1666, had James, Joseph, and Sarah, but they all liv. in Carolina, when he d.

P. 538. l. 17, for WILLIAM r. *WILLIAM*

" l. 18, aft. 1650; ins. preach. a. 1651,

P. 539. l. 9 from bot. at the end, add, It may be Jacocks, or sometimes Jackax

" l. 2 from bot. aft. 77. add, DAVID, Boston, s. of the preced. m. 18 Mar. 1713, Catharine, d. of John Eyre, had only ch. David, b. 23 Oct. 1714; next yr. he went to Eng. in his usual course of life, as a merch. and perish by shipwreck, on return, Sept. 1717.

P. 540. l. 13, bef. ROBERT, ins. JOHN, Boston, eldest s. of the first David, m. 24 Sept. 1713, Ann, d. of Thomas Clark, had only Ann, b. 25 June 1719 or 20, d. young.

" l. 18 from bot. aft. Betty, add, and her two ch. — also, aft. in ins. St. Nicholas.

P. 541. l. 9, aft. JEGGLES, ins. JEGLIS, or JIGGLES,

" l. 18, aft. 1674. ins. Abigail m. 2 Dec. 1668, Isaac Foote.

P. 545. l. 16, aft. day. add, Yet it might, from bad MS. be read Jenney.

P. 546. l. 2 from bot. aft. wks. add, and Richard, 14 June 1660.

P. 553. l. 21, for *ISAAC* r. ISAAC

P. 554. l. 3, for Sarah r. Mary — also, erase perhaps

" l. 13, at the begin. ins. the elder, 23 Nov. 1659,

P. 555. l. 13 from bot. aft. Felt. add, He m. 23 Feb. 1678, Esther Beers, perhaps d. of Philip, had John, b. 3 Aug. 1679.

P. 556. l. 18, bef. 1671, ins. 14 Nov. — also, aft. Mary. ins. d. of John

" l. 4 from bot. aft. 1666. add, His will of 20 Aug. nam. these four ch. Eliz. m. 4 Nov. 1664, the sec. Thomas Tolman.

P. 560. l. 17 and 18, strike out, Swanzey, s. of Robert of the same, and ins. Bristol, s. prob. of the first Robert, had w. Bathshua in 1688. BENJAMIN, Waterbury, among early sett. m. 2 May 1661, Hannah Spencer of Milford, had Benjamin, b. June 1662, wh. d. young; and Benjamin, again, minor at the d. of his f. 30 Dec. 1690.

" l. 20, bef. BENJAMIN, ins. BENJAMIN, Gloucester, s. of Thomas, m. 22 Jan. 1678, Eliz. Wills, says Babson, wh. adds, they had four ch. there, but he does not name them, and only says, none of the fam. were there aft. 1686.

" l. 19 from bot. bef. BENONI, ins. BENJAMIN, New Haven, s. of Benjamin of Waterbury, sold, in 1715, the ld. of his f. but contin. to reside there, and Bronson says, had Benjamin, Hannah, Ruth, Vinson, Martha, and Ebenezer betw. 1706 and 1722.

P. 561. l. 18, bef. ISAAC, ins. HUGH, Salem, m. 26 June 1660, Hannah, eldest d. of John Tompkins, had Hannah, b. 9 Feb. foll. d. next yr.; Sarah, wh. d. 12 Oct. 1662; Sarah, again, 30 Apr. 1663, d. soon; Eliz. 2 Oct. 1664; Mary, 30 Jan. 1666; John, 4 Aug. 1667; Deborah, 10 Mar. 1670; Samuel, 30 Apr. 1672; and his w. d. 10 May foll. On 31 Dec. foll. he m. Mary Foster, and had Rebecca, 15 Oct. 1673; Abigail, 7 Jan. 1675; Hannah, again, 17 May 1677; Rachel, 17 Apr. 1679; Sarah, 10 July 1681; and Lydia, 20 Feb. 1685. When he d. is not kn. but it was bef. 30 June 1692, for that day Eliz. Booth sw. on the trial for witchcr. of Eliz. Procter, that the spectre of Jones assur. the witness, that Mrs. P. k. him, " because he had a pot of cider of her, wh. he had not paid her for." Such were the nonsense stories, that the Ct. allow. to be giv. to the jury. Essex Inst. II. 198.

P. 563. l. 3 and 4, erase, or, perhaps, New Haven,

" l. 6, aft. Nevis, ins. 1657,

" l. 7, for Mary r. Joan

" l. 19, bef. JOHN, ins. JOHN, New Haven 1689, as Mr. Porter assures me, had Samuel, and John. He was prob. s. of John of Nevis.

P. 564. l. 10 from bot. aft. 1654; add, Hannah, 4 May 1659;

P. 566. l. 16 from bot. aft. 1653; add, beside Susanna, wh. m. 12 July 1659, John Jackson; ano. d. wh. m. a Kent; and ano. prob. nam. Mary, wh. m. Nathaniel Wensley, call. Winslow, of Salisbury. He

" l. 15 from bot. aft. 2 ins. or 15 — also, aft. 1671, add, aged 73. — also, erase, unless this date belong to the s. — also, for and r. d.

" l. 14 from bot. erase, be the f's. and substitute, prob. unm. — also, aft. 1682. add, Ruth m. Thomas Howard; and Remember m. Nathaniel Hadlock.

" last l. at the end, add, THOMAS, Manchester 1675.

P. 571. l. 13, for "by w." r. m. 4 June 1678, — also, aft. Bridget, ins. Day, prob. d. of Anthony,

" l. 14, for 1681 r. 1682 — also, aft. days. add, His w. d. 7 Sept. 1684, and he m. 9 Nov. 1685, Mary Lambert, perhaps d. of John of Lynn, had Ebenezer, 30 July 1686, d. in few mos.; Margaret, 1687; Mary, 1689; Constantine, 1691; Benjamin, 1695; and Mercy, 1703; and he either d. or rem. bef. 1721.

P. 572. l. 20 from bot. aft. d. strike out to the end, and ins. 1675, had brs. and sis.

" l. 5 from bot. bef. SAMUEL, ins. PETER, Salem, m. 24 May 1661, Sarah Gaskin, prob. d. of Edward, had David, b. 6 Apr. 1662; Ann, 7 Aug. 1663; Sarah, 1 Jan. 1666; Peter, 3 Dec. 1669; William, 13 Dec. 1675; and Samuel, 25 July 1678.

P. 574. l. 10 from bot. for Thomas r. William

" l. 6 from bot. bef. 12 ins. 9 or

" last l. aft. m. ins. 1658,

P. 575. l. 1, bef. Steele, ins. d. of John — also, aft. Steele, ins. wh. d. 22 May 1695, aged 56 — also, erase, bapt. 12 Oct. 1690

" l. 3, bef. 18 ins. 10 or

" l. 4 and 5, strike out, perhaps is to prob. inclus. and ins. m. 9 Feb. 1688, Sarah, d. of Stephen Freeman, wh. d. 8 Sept. 1738, aged 68 ;

" l. 13, for 1658, r. 31 Mar. 1657, — also, erase prob. — also, for sec. r. first — also, bef. 1690 ins. Nov.

" l. 14, aft. 1658; ins. Eliz. 22 July 1660 ; — also, aft. 12, ins. not (as print. in Geneal. Reg. XIV. 288) 13, wh. was Monday, — also, bef. John ins. William, 8 Jan. 1665 ;

" l. 16, aft. 1682. add, His wid. d. 27 Oct. 1718.

" l. 13 from bot. bef. 1695, ins. 23 Feb.

P. 576. l. 3, aft. 1706. add, Eliz. m. 13 Dec. 1681, Agur Tomlinson ; and Mercy m. Aug. 1687, Solomon Burton.

P. 577. l. 9 from bot. at the end, add, 1692; and, when innocence would not avail, sav. her life by false confession of guilt. On either plea, guilty or not, the father of lies was sure to triumph.

P. 578. l. 5, aft. "He" ins. took sec. w. Mary, wid. of William Wadley of Saybrook, and

" l. 24 from bot. at the end, add, beside Zechariah, 29 July 1659. But in Geneal. Reg. XV. 133, his surname is wild. turn. to *Doves*.

" l. 12 from bot. for William r. James

P. 579. l. 16 from bot. at the end, add, but he prob. was s. of Thomas.

P. 580. l. 5, for Rebexa r. Rebecca — and add, at the end, also, aft. 1686. add, Perhaps his d. Mary m. 15 Nov. 1676, Thomas Flint.

" l. 7 from bot. for 194 r. 134

P. 582. l. 6, aft. add. ins. One was, prob. Dinah, wh. m. 2 Jan. 1691, Stephen Ingalls ; and the youngest was, by w. Joanna, Benjamin, b. 20 May 1683, unless *his* f. John be thot. s. of the preced. — also, aft. James ins. SAMUEL, Salem, by w. Mary had Mary, b. 10 Nov. 1686; Samuel, 27 July 1689; and Sarah, 7 Oct. 1692. Perhaps he was s. of John

" l. 16, erase, of wh. are kn. only

" l. 17, aft. Philip, ins. b. 4 Sept. 1684 ; — also, aft. William, ins. 23 May 1679, d. young ; — also, aft. Mary, ins. 21 Feb. 1677 ; — also, aft. Susanna, ins. 5 July 1683 ; — also, aft. William, ins. again, 7 Apr. 1690, wh.

" l. 18, aft. f. ins. and Ebenezer, 21 Apr. 1694.

P. 584. l. 5, aft. 9, strike out all to the end of l. 9, and ins. aft. 1676, on 9 May, of wound rec. in the gr. battle of 19 Dec. preced. for the text at first was near. perfect on 169 p.

" l. 12, strike out all that foll. 11, and ins. aft. 1637 ins. m. 12 July 1663, Jane Eddy, had Richard, b. 13 May foll. d. soon ; James, 27 Aug. 1665; William, 5 Jan. 1668; Jane, 15 Feb. 1670; Hannah, 10 July 1672; and — also, turn to the l. in p. 174, and aft. John, ins. 28 Dec. 1674 ; and

P. 587. l. 5, at the end, add — also, aft. 1689. ins. His wid. Elinor d. 1 Mar. 1698, aged 85.

P. 592. l. 11 from bot. aft. m. strike out, a, and ins. Jan. 1670, Hannah — also, aft.

Gilbert strike out bef. 1657, and ins. had Peter, b. 10 Feb. 1671 ; David, 20 Sept. 1672 ; Hannah, 1 July 1674 ; John, 14 Apr. 1676 ; Mary, 25 Mar. 1678 ; and Sarah, 15 Apr. 1680 ; — also, aft. and, ins. he

P. 595. l. 24, aft. Holman. add, See that.

ADDITIONS AND CORRECTIONS

IN VOL. III.

P. 4. l. 4 from bot. bef. Abraham ins. Dec. 1684,

" l. 3 from bot. aft. m. ins. not, as oft. said, — also, at the end, add, but Caleb Nichols the sec.

P. 5. l. 6, aft. had ins. Eliz. b. 3 or 5 Mar. 1651 ; Joseph, 11 Aug. 1653 ; Nathaniel, bapt. 29 Oct. 1654 ; wh. all d. young ; — also, aft. bapt. ins. 28, not. as print. in Geneal. Reg. XIV. 126, mak. it Monday,

" l. 10, bef. 1662 ; ins. 28 Sept.

" l. 11, bef. 1666 ; ins. 27 Aug.

" l. 12, bef. 1668 ; ins. 9 Apr. — also, aft. Abigail, ins. 9 Oct.

" l. 13, aft. Eliz. ins. Oct. — also, aft. Prudence, ins. 14 Oct. — also, bef. 1677, ins. 22 Nov. — also, bef. 1679 ; ins. 25 Dec.

" l. 14, bef. 1682 ; ins. 23 Mar. — also, bef. 1684 ; ins. 12 May — also, bef. *and* ins. Daniel, again, 10 June 1686

" l. 16, bef. fourteen ins. of the twenty

" l. 18, aft. ch. ins. by two ws.

" l. 22, aft. ch. add, and d. 9 Sept. 1724,

" l. 3 from bot. aft. 1653, ins. prob. br. of Joseph,

" l. 2 from bot. and last, strike out, "perhaps Eliz." &c. down to "and he," and ins. w. Eliz. but no ch. and

" last. l. at the end, add, From his will of 4 June 1657, giv. all his ho. and lds. at F. to w. for life, and aft. to his br. John K. and two m. sis. all dwel. in O. E. and order, that br. and sis. shall pay cous. i. e. neph. Joseph's three ch. £6. &c. my correspond. infer. as most sound. he might, "that the fam. had an Eng. origin, rather than a Scotch one." This would correct the suggest. in Geneal. Reg. XII. 199, repeat. in XIV. 126. Even without inq. as to *first* com. we kn. that within the bounds of N. E. at the date of that will there could not be one Scottish *family* in two thousand. However, in the same Vol. XIV. 377, a more reasona. tradit. is offer. that the fam. was from Isle of Wight.

P. 6. l. 2 and 3, aft. 1693 ; strike out, and prob. others. and ins. Eleazer, 31 May 1695 ; Ezekiel, 15 Apr. 1697 ; Samuel, 4 Apr. 1699 ; Sarah, 12 Mar. 1701 ; Abigail, 19 Mar. 1703 ; Mary, 9 Mar. 1706 ; Ephraim, 2 Aug. 1709 ; and perhaps Experience.

" l. 15, at the end, add, or June

P. 8. l. 12 and 11 from bot. erase, m. 7 Nov. 1670, &c. to Faunce, inclus.

" l. 11 from bot. aft. rem. ins. bef.

P. 8. l. 10 from bot. aft. perhaps, add, aft. hav. there, by w. Mary, Ephraim, b. 14 Nov. 1674 ; Kempton (if we can believe Essex Inst. II. 25) 1 Feb. 1676 ; and Samuel, 4 Mar. 1681 ; — also, aft. his ins. s. of the same name m. 2 June 1702, Patience, d. of famous Elder Faunce ; and his

P. 10. l. 5, aft. me ; add, and Tabitha m. John Pearson.

" l. 8 from bot. bef. HENRY, ins. DANIEL, Salem, s. of Thomas, by w. Mary had Daniel, b. 19 Oct. 1705 ; — also, for 1653, r. by w. Ann — also, aft. John, add, b. Jan. 1651 — also, bef. Mary, ins. Thomas, 1 Mar. 1655 ; Hannah, 2 Mar. 1657 ; — also, aft. Mary, ins. b. May, bapt.

" l. 7 from bot. aft. Sarah, ins. b. 20 Aug. 1661, bapt. — also, strike out, and perhaps others, and ins. Eliz. b. Dec. 1662 ; Lydia, Apr. 1666 ; and Henry, 1 May 1669.

" l. 2 from bot. aft. Felt. ins. JOHN, Salem, s. of Henry, m. 17 June 1675, Eliz. Look, perhaps d. of Thomas, had John, b. 25 Mar. foll. ; and Eliz. 6 Feb. 1678 ; but by ano. w. perhaps, had John, 15 Aug. 1689 ; and Samuel, 26 Oct. 1691. — also, at the end, add, Salem, s. of Henry, m. 23 May 1677, Eliz. Knight, possib. d. of Philip, had Thomas, b. 27 July 1678 ; Joseph, 7 Sept. 1680 ; Daniel, 23 July 1682 ; and Jonathan, 27 May 1686. WILLIAM, Gloucester, had rem. bef. 1652, to New London.

P. 12. l. 2 and 3, aft. 1666, strike out down to young, inclus. and ins. m. June 1696, Jacob Tappan ; Mary, 10 Sept. 1668, wh. d. 17 Mar. 1703 ; Richard, 25 June 1670 ; Jane, wh. Mr. Coffin says, m. James Smith a. 1696 ; but I kn. not, wh. he was ; — also, in l. 3, erase, again,

" l. 4, strike out Mary &c. to 1703, and ins. William, 31 July 1682, wh. d. at 20 yrs.

" l. 5, for John r. JOHN

" l. 6 and 7, aft. had, strike out down to young, and ins. Sarah, b. 30 Aug. 1667 ; John, 23 Nov. 1668 ; — also, in l. 7, erase again, and, again, aft. Richard, and Mary

" l. 8, bef. Rebecca, ins. Judith ;

" l. 9, for 1684 r. 1685 — also, for 1686 r. 1687

" l. 10, erase prob.

" l. 11, for John r. Samuel

" last l. aft. Frances, add, Woodall, as Babson gives the name, m. 17 Jan. 1655,

P. 13. l. 15 from bot. bef. 16 ins. 6 or

P. 14. l. 7 from bot. bef. JOHN, ins. JAMES, Salem, s. of the first John, by w. Eliz. had John, and Nathaniel, tw. b. 9 Dec. 1689, of wh. John, prob. d. soon ; James, 27 Dec. 1691 ; Eliz. 19 Jan. 1694 ; and John, again, 3 July 1696 ; — also, aft. Gloucester, add, was in 1641, then a minor, charg. for breach of Sabbath &c.

" l. 6 from bot. aft. had, ins. John, b. 1654 ; William, 1656 ;

" l. 5 from bot. aft. 1665. add. He rem. and d. at Salem 12 Oct. 1685.

P. 16. l. 8 from bot. aft. KEYSER, ins. KEAZER, — also, bef. GEORGE, ins. ELIZUR, Lynn, s. of George, m. 9 Dec. 1679, Mary Collins, had Sarah, b. 6 Dec. 1686.

P. 17. l. 8, for 1660 r. 1661 — also, aft. William, add, wh. d.

" l. 10, aft. Abigail, add, wh. d. 3 Oct. 1662,

" l. 12, aft. were, ins. Eliz. 12 May 1662,

" l. 16, at the begin. for 1670 r. 1672.

" l. 17 from bot. aft. m. ins. 12 Dec. 1667,

" l. 16 from bot. for 2 r. 28

P. 21. l. 8, aft. KILLAM, ins. KILLUM,

" l. 14, aft. 1680. ins. He m. a. 1673, Sarah, wid. of John Fairfield.

" l. 15, erase 1670 — also, aft. Austin, add, m. 22 May 1666, Hannah, d. of Robert

Goodale, had Hannah, b. Mar. 1667; James, May 1669, d. soon; Ephraim, June 1672, d. soon; Ruth, Sept. 1673, d. in one day; Ruth, again, 15 Jan. 1676;

P. 21. l. 5 from bot. aft. Richard ins. the first,

P. 22. l. 3, bef. JOHN, ins. HENRY, Wenham, d. prob. early in 1676, for wid. Eliz. had admin. 30 June of that yr.

" last l. aft. Bradford, add, had eight ch. of wh. the eldest was Richard. He was

P. 23. l. 1, aft. w. ins. Mary

" l. 3, aft. foll. add, His est. was good.

" l. 6, aft. Thomas, ins. by w. Hannah, wh. was bapt. on adm. of the ch. prob. 24, certain. not (as the rec. in Geneal. Reg. IX. 360, says) 25 July 1659, wh. was Monday,—also, strike out, bapt. 24 July 1659, and ins. b. 1668; Sarah, 1672; Abraham, 1675;

" l. 8, aft. Ind. add, These ch. were all b. in Albemarle Co. of Carolina. His wid. came home, and m. John Curtis of Stratford, and there she had put on rec. the b. of ea. of the ch. Mary m. John Blakeman, and Sarah m. Benjamin Hurd. With this fam. Goodwin was quite bewilder.

" l. 6 from bot. at the end, add, This name is pervert. to Knide in Geneal. Reg. XV. 134.

P. 25. l. 14, for 1661 r. 1662

" l. 17, aft. 1687. add, Prob. he had sec. w. Ann, d. of that wid. Dorcas Hoar, wh. was long imprison. and sentenc. to d. for witchcr. but he and his w. obt. reprieve

" l. 12 from bot. aft. 1721, ins. d. Apr. foll.

" l. 11 from bot. aft. 1726, ins. wh. d. at Louisbourg, soon aft. its conq. 1745

" l. 10 from bot. aft. 280. add, His w. d. 24 Mar. 1758, aged 71, and he d. 10 June 1774. JOSEPH, one of the flower of Essex, k. with his capt. and gr. part of his comp. at Bloody Brook, may have been br. of John.

" l. 4 from bot. aft. Peter, add, ano. Richard, and was

P. 30. bef. l. 19 from bot. ins. KIPPEN or KIPPINS. See Kibby.

" l. 12 from bot. aft. 1651; add, Sarah, 1653; Joseph, 17 July 1656; Bethia, 19 Feb. 1659; Susanna, 3 May 1664; and Abigail, 6 Mar. 1666.

P. 32. l. 4 from bot. aft. 1655; add, beside, prob. Abigail, wh. m. 3 June 1669, John Guppy; and Priscilla, wh. m. Oct. 1672, Nathaniel Hum (if this be not abbrev.); but certain. Benjamin, b. 28 Aug. 1669, and d. next mo. He

P. 35. l. 8, aft. Knowles, add, d. of Francis Newman,

" l. 11, bef. Apr. ins. 2

" l. 19, at the end, add, THOMAS, Salem 1677.

" l. 11 from bot. aft. Salem, ins. m. 9 May 1667, Sarah Lemon, d. I presume of Robert, had Eliz. b. 18 May 1668; Mary, 7 Apr. 1670; and Sarah, 22 July 1673; was

" l. 10 from bot. aft. 1675. add, In Essex Inst. II. 256, this name is Knite.

P. 36. l. 18, from bot. bef. JOHN, ins. JOHN, Beverly, a mason, s. of William, brot. from Eng. by his f. bef. 1637, went home, it is said, to take part in the gr. civ. war on the side of Parliam. m. in Eng. but soon aft. came hither, had eldest s. John, beside William, Joseph, Emma, and Martha, went again to Eng. a. 1672, to obt. est. left by his f. and there d. All this was sw. by two witness. at Beverly in June 1743, ea. of the age of 85 yrs. wh. kn. him, and his eldest s. John, and the eldest s. of that John, then liv. at Manchester. It must not, then, be suppos. that he was the same as the foll. as plausib. might be suggest.

P. 39. l. 20, bef. ROBERT, ins. There was a ROBERT of Marblehead 1673.

P. 40. l. 10 from bot. at the end add, He prob. had w. Ruth.

P. 41. l. 18, aft. Mary, add. d. of the first Daniel Porter,

P. 42. l. 13 from bot. aft. Eliz. add, d. of Francis Newman,

" last l. aft. Ipswich, ins. perhaps s. of William,

P. 43. l. 1, aft. Wenham, ins. perhaps br. of the preced.

" l. 6, at the end, add, WILLIAM, Ipswich 1669, perhaps s. of the preced.

P. 45. l. 9 from bot. aft. Henry, add, m. a. Aug. 1661, Ann Stratton, had Ann, b. 1 June 1662, d. soon; Abigail, 21 Apr. 1667; Mary, 1 Feb. 1669; and William, 12 Mar. 1675; was

P. 46. l. 14, aft. came. add, Both he and Martin were engaged in planta. 1655, of Groton.

P. 48. l. 4, bef. EZRA, ins. DANIEL, Salem, eldest s. of John, m. 5 June 1682, Mary Gray, d. perhaps, of the first Robert, had Mary, b. 20 Feb. 1683; Eliz. 9 Apr. 1684; Daniel, 7 Dec. 1686; Samuel, 5 Feb. 1688, d. soon; Samuel, again, 7 Apr. 1689; Preserved, 21 Apr. 1691, d. at 5 mos. and Joseph, 12 Apr. 1692. EBENEZER, Salem, youngest s. of John, by w. Mary had Margaret, b. 26 July 1696; Mary, 26 Mar. 1703; and Eunice 3 Apr. 1706.

" l. 21. aft. 1663, ins. by w. Preserved had Daniel, b. 3 Oct. 1658; Sarah, 7 Feb. 1660; Ezekiel, 3 Mar. 1661; Samuel, wh. d. 7 July 1662, prob. very young; Samuel, again, 16 Mar. 1664; Mary, 26 Apr. 1667; Jonathan, 27 Dec. 1669; Hannah, Dec. 1671, d. in few days; and Ebenezer, 2 Apr. 1674.

" l. 17 from bot. at the end, add, He left four ch. Michael, Abigail, Moses, and Rebecca, for Mary, wh. had d. young.

" l. 10 from bot. bef. THOMAS, ins. SAMUEL, Salem, s. of John, had Margaret, b. 14 Jan. 1691; Preserved, 30 Apr. 1692; and Samuel, 2 Jan. 1694; perhaps more.

" l. 9 from bot. for "the spell. of Lombard " r. he of Boston, wh. by w. Mary had Thomas, b. 6 Nov. 1659.

P. 50. l. 5 from bot. at the end, add, JOSEPH, Bristol 1688, with no w. or ch.

P. 52. l. 11, for 1671, r. 1672.

" l. 13, bef. 29 ins. 24 or

" l. 22, bef. JOB, ins. JAMES, Malden, had John, b. a. 1653, beside Henry, Samuel, and Job, but some of these may have been b. at Falmouth on Casco Bay, whither he rem. a. 1658, says Babson, 111, and there was k. by the Ind.

P. 53. l. 6, aft. 1690, add, s. of James, was driv. to Gloucester by the Ind. hostil. aft. m. at F. Dorcas, d. of John Wallis, but at G. had Hepzibah, b. 1694; Mary, 1696; Joseph, 1698; Benjamin, 1700; Deborah, 1703; and Job, 1705; beside James, John, Dorcas, Josiah, Sarah, and David. He was liv. at age of 81, but time of his d. is unkn.

" l. 12, bef. JOSHUA, ins. JOHN, Killingworth, s. of Robert, m. 31 Dec. 1700, Lydia, d. of John Kelsey, had Sarah, b. 17 Sept. 1701; Robert, 1 July 1704, wh. d. young; Lydia, 9 June 1706; John, 20 Apr. 1708; and Daniel, 11 Apr. 1710. His w. d. 22 Apr. foll. and he m. 16 Jan. 1711, Hannah Parke, had Hannah, 14 Oct. foll. Robert, 4 Nov. 1713; Joseph, 11 Feb. 1715; Stephen, 1 Aug. 1719; and Joseph, 8 May 1723. JONATHAN, Killingworth, younger br. of the preced. m. 1 Feb. 1711, Mercy, eldest d. of William Welman, had Eliz. b. 17 Mar. 1712; Nathan, 22 July 1717; Zeruiah, 6 Sept. 1723; and his w. d. 13 Nov. 1727. He m. next 17 Sept. 1730, Patience Strong, had Jonathan, 22 Dec. 1731; Noah, 18 Jan. 1734; and d. 7 Nov. 1759. His wid. d. 18 Aug. 1773.

" l. 20, bef. ROBERT, ins. *

" l. 21 from bot. aft. Killingworth. add, He m. 19 Dec. 1665, Sarah, d. of John Picket, had Sarah, b. 24 Feb. 1667; Hannah, 26 Dec. 1668; Daniel, 27 July 1671; John, 12 July 1674; Eliz. 31 Jan. 1677; Margaret, 18, but ano. rec. says,

25 Aug. 1679; Rebecca, 7 Mar. 1682; Jonathan, 16 Oct. 1685; and Mary, 23 Sept. 1688. In 1695 he rem. to K. there d. 12 Apr. 1718; and his wid. d. 11 Mar. 1725. He was rep. for S. 1686.

P. 54. l. 21, bef. DAVID, ins. DANIEL, Bristol, in 1688 had w. and seven ch. but no more is kn.

" l. 15, from bot. bef. JOHN, ins. JOHN, Salem, when he was going to sea, in Dec. 1676, made a nuncup. will, pro. Oct. foll. show. no w. nor ch.

P. 55. l. 1, aft. Eliz. add, d. of Henry Sherburne, m. 10 June 1656,

P. 56. l. 8, aft. Pritchett, add [wh. was Hannah, w. of Nathaniel, m. 1651], also, aft. Corbee, add [prob. wid. of William of Haddam],

" l. 11, at the end, add, prob. no ch. by sec. w. wid. of deac. Thomas Gridley, but by former w.

" l. 14, aft. Eliz. add, wh. m. Luke Hayes. JOHN, Hadley, s. of John, had John, b. 1670; and d. 1683; but wh. was w. I see not. — also, bef. ROGER, ins. JOSEPH, Farmington, s. of John, m. Oct. 1683, Susanna, d. of the first John Root, had Sarah, b. Apr. 1685; Joseph, Mar. 1688; John, 3 Apr. 1691; Samuel, Dec. 1694; all bapt. 6 June 1697; Susanna, b. Oct. 1696, bapt. 29 Aug. foll. Ebenezer, b. 17 July 1701; Mary, and Mercy, tw. Apr. 1704; and Thomas, Sept. 1707. His wid. d. 5 Dec. 1712; and he m. 18 Oct. 1714, Mary, wid. of Joseph Royce, d. of Thomas Porter, and d. 30 Mar. 1736.

P. 58. l. 1, strike out, "suppos. to have been a" and ins. Phebe — also, aft. Providence. ins. wid. of Thomas Lee, wh. d. on his pass. leav. her with three ch.

" l. 3, aft. 1658. add, He was d. in Nov. 1662. Eliz. m. Joshua Hempstead, and Sarah m. 2 June 1678, John Fox, both of N. L.

" l. 4, aft. m. ins. Mar. 1673, — also, aft. New London, ins. had Thomas, b. June 1675; John, 19 June 1677; Phebe, 13 Dec. 1680; Alice, 18 Aug. 1684; Dorothy 25 Mar. 1687; Nathaniel, Jan. 1689; Eliz. Sept. 1692; Greenfield, 13 June 1696; and his w. d. 23 Nov. 1729. He liv. in that pt. of Norwich, now Preston, and d. 4 Feb. 1739, almost 91 yrs. old.

" l. 7, aft. much. ins. JOHN, Lyme, s. of the first Greenfield, d. Oct. 1725, leav. sev. ch. of wh. were John and Joseph of Coventry.

" l. 11, aft. 1639. ins. His w. d. 28 July 1658, and he

P. 59. l. 7, for 1674 r. 1675

" l. 8, bef. William, ins. Susanna, w. of

" l. 9 aft. Pitt, ins. or Pitts, prob. by Philip Alley, her former h.

" l. 19 from bot. at the end, add, He was of Lynn 1666–79, and prob. had s. Thomas, as he is call. sen. in later yrs.

P. 60. l. 7, erase senr.

P. 64. l. 6, at the end, add, Calef, wh. shows how slight was his escape from peril of the witcher. delusion, calls him Lowson.

P. 66. l. 3 from bot. aft. Lawrence, ins. b. in Eng.

P. 67. l. 3, aft. 1671, add, wh. m. 20 May 1667, Eliz. Flint, prob. d. of the first Thomas,

" l. 21, aft. rec. ins. SAMUEL, Salem, d. June 1673, and next yr. in July his wid. Alice had admin. of good est. of Robert her h. of Manchester.

" l. 11 from bot. bef. 1662 ins. 28 Apr.

" l. 10 from bot. bef. 1664 ins. 16 Oct. — also, bef. 1667 ins. 9 Apr. — also, bef. 1672 ins. 20 Jan. — also, bef. 1676 ins. 10 May

" l. 9 from bot. bef. 1678 ins. 10 Oct.

" l. 7 from bot. aft. Holland. add, But the Geneal. Reg. XIV. 248 in the fam. pedigree of Tolman, strange. makes her m. not the f. but the s. Henry, wh. was many yrs. younger than herself.

P. 68. l. 20 from bot. aft. 1727 ; add, Eliz. and ano. d.

P. 71. l. 14 from bot. bef. EDWARD, ins. DAVID, Northampton, s. of the sec. John, m. 5 Sept. 1695, Lydia, d. of Jedediah Strong.

" l. 11 from bot. aft. 1656. add, He d. Mar. 1675, at M. in his will of 12 Feb. preced. nam. w. Mary, ch. John, Samuel, Thomas, Hannah, and Sarah.

P. 72. l. 16, erase prob. — also, aft. same, add, m. 27 Dec. 1682, Eliz. Loomis, d. perhaps of Thomas of Windsor, — also, aft. John, ins. b. 7 Dec. 1683 ;

" l. 17, aft. Jonathan, ins. 20 Mar. 1686 ; — also, aft. Mary, ins. b. 15 Mar. bapt.

" l. 18, at the begin. ins. bapt. — also, aft. Samuel, ins. 23 Mar. bapt. — also, aft. Hezekiah, ins. bapt. — also, at the end, add, Eliz. b. 6 Mar. 1700 ; and Ruth, 14 Jan. 1703. He d. 24 Apr. 1723.

" l. 19, bef. JOSEPH, ins. JOHN, Lyme, eldest s. of Thomas, m. Eliz. d. of Richard Smith ; and I kn. no more of him.

P. 73. l. 21, at the end, add, STEPHEN, Kensington, s. of John of Farmington, m. 1 Oct. 1690, Eliz. Royce, perhaps d. of Isaac, had Isaac, b. 5 Sept. 1691 ; Eliz. 18 Apr. 1693, d. in few hours ; Eliz. again, 12 July 1694 ; Sarah, 8 Nov. 1696 ; Stephen, 18 Apr. 1700, k. by accid. at 18 yrs. ; Martha, 17 Feb. 1702 ; Mary, Sept. 1704 ; Ebenezer, 14 Sept. 1706, d. under 19 yrs. ; Hannah, 15 Oct. 1708 ; Josiah, 13 Aug. 1711 ; and d. 1753. His wid. d. 1760.

" l. 19 from bot. bef. THOMAS, ins. STEPHEN, Lyme, youngest s. of Thomas, m. Abigail Lord and rem. to New London.

" l. 13 from bot. for 22 Dec. 1692 r. 1702

" l. 9 from bot. aft. Eliz. ins. 20 Oct. 1681 — also, aft. Stephen, ins. 27 June 1686, d. at 8 yrs. Joseph, 14 May 1688 ; Benjamin, 8 Oct. 1690 ;

" l. 8 from bot. aft. Hannah, ins. 25 Feb. 1695 ; Stephen, again, 19 Jan. 1699 ; and Lydia, 18 Feb. 1702. — also, erase four more to young

" l. 5 from bot. aft. Saybrook. add, Of his ds. Sarah m. Daniel Buckingham ; Mary m. Joseph Beckwith, had two more hs. and in 1757, then wid. for third time, made a visit to her br. Stephen ; Eliz. m. 28 Dec. 1699, Samuel Peck ; and Hannah m. John Griswold. THOMAS, Bristol 1689, had w. and six ch. THOMAS, Lyme, s. of the sec. Thomas of the same, m. Eliz. Graham, perhaps d. of Benjamin of Hartford.

P. 74. l. 4, at the end, add, WILLIAM, Lyme, sec. s. of Thomas, m. Mary Griffing of L. I.

P. 76. l. 21, at the end, add, His will of 16 Nov. 1672, ment. w. Eliz. s. Samuel, John, and Daniel, the last being youngest, and two ch. of ea. of the other s.

" l. 21 from bot. erase perhaps

" l. 19 from bot. bef. NICHOLAS, ins. MATTHEW, a soldier, wh. d. in Philip's war, oft. call. Groe, Grove, or Groves, wh. see. — also, aft. 1668, add, by w. Hannah had Susanna, b. 8 May 1673, wh. m. 16 July 1694, Benjamin Patch.

" l. 15 from bot. at the end, add, A fam. of this name was at Bristol, in 1689, but the bapt. name of the h. is unkn. to me.

P. 78. l. 2, aft. 1643, add, wh. d. at 19 yrs.

" l. 4, aft. Looman. add, His will of 2 Aug. 1665, pro. 25 June 1667, nam. w. ds. Sarah, Hannah, Mary, Martha, wh. m. 23 July 1662, Bartholomew Gale ; and ment. Thomas, Richard, and Mary Sallows, as his creditors. His d. Sarah m. 9 May 1667, Charles Knight.

P. 86. l. 5, aft. 1662 ins. a , instead of ;

P. 87. l. 15 from bot. bef. JOHN, ins. JOHN, Lancaster 1673.

P. 88. l. 14 and 15, strike out, prob. others, down to " beside " inclus. and ins. Abigail, b. 15 Nov. 1701 ; Nathaniel, 1 Jan. 1704 ; Elisha, 3 Dec. 1705, d. young ;

—also, aft. 1708; ins. Elisha, again, 23 July 1710; Sarah, 8 May 1712; Mary, 18 Dec. 1714; Mercy, 16 Apr. 1717; Ezekiel, 19 Nov. 1718; and Phineas, 11 Apr. 1722. His w. d. 11 Apr. 1723; and he m. 4 July 1726, Thankful Lyman, and d. 24 Feb. 1752.—also, erase the residue of sent.

P. 89. l. 13 from bot. aft. Sarah, ins. 1652

" l. 11 from bot. aft. John ins. 6 May

" l. 10 from bot. bef. 1667; ins. 10 July

" l. 9 from bot. bef. 1672, ins. 20 Oct.

" l. 8 from bot. bef. 1674, ins. 7 Nov.

" l. 7 from bot. bef. 1678, ins. 19 Sept.—also, aft. 1678, add, wh. m. 10 Dec. 1696, William Wadsworth of F. and d. 1707.

" l. 2 from bot. aft. Hadley, ins. WILLIAM, Farmington, s. of the preced. m. Sarah, d. of deac. Isaac Moore, or More, had Ruth, b. 12 Sept. 1679; Sarah, 15 Apr. 1682; Isaac, 26 Apr. 1685; William, 2 Sept. 1688; Daniel, 10 Dec. 1692; Phebe, 3 Sept. 1694; Jonathan, 2 June 1697; and Mary, 31 Mar. 1700.

P. 90. l. 11 from bot. aft. 1653. add, One of this name was drown. 10 June 1669, at Pocasset.—also, aft. 210. ins. JOHN, Salem, m. May 1680, Eliz. Swasey, perhaps d. of Joseph, had Joseph, b. 14 Apr. 1681; and Samuel, 25 Oct. 1683.

P. 93. l. 16 and 17, erase, but prob. not—also, in l. 17, for or r. as

" l. 18, erase would have—also, erase so

P. 95. l. 18 from bot. aft. 1656, ins. wh. m. Ralph Keeler jun.

" l. 4 from bot. bef. Feb. ins. or 27

P. 96. l. 1, aft. 2 ins. or 12

" l. 15, for 19 r. 11

" l. 16, aft. leav. ins. d. Naomi, wh. m. 22 July 1670, Thomas Maule; and

" last l. bef. ROGER, ins. RALPH, New Haven, s. of the preced. m. 27 Apr. 1681, Abiah, d. of William Basset.

P. 98. bef. l. 12 from bot. ins. LISTON, NICHOLAS, Gloucester 1645, resid. but short period.

P. 103. l. 4 from bot. aft. 1700, add, (Geneal. Reg. XIV. 67, says 1699)

P. 105. aft. l. 16, ins. LOGEE, PHILIP, Salem, m. 11 Sept. 1673, Mary Snasher (if Essex Inst. II. 257 may be trust. for such names), had Philip, b. 27 Aug. (foll. is not the word, but preced.); Mary, 16 Aug. 1675, Abigail, 24 June 1687; and Abraham, 14 Mar. 1689. Some approach to the name of h. is giv. by Mr. Drake, to a serv. of the w. of Samuel Andrews, in Geneal. Reg. XIV. 310, emb. in the Increase at London, 1635, Ellyn Lougie, but some yrs. bef. I had copied from the same record Ellyn Longe, and in printing 3 Mass. Hist. Coll. VIII. 258, had call. it nearer to an Eng. one. We all kn. how easi. the letters n and u may change serv. but by gain of an i the Salem fam. might not be pleas.

P. 110. l. 12 from bot. aft. 1676; add, and by w. Priscilla had John, b. 11 Jan. 1681, at Salem.

P. 111. l. 10, aft. 1656, add, wh. m. 17 June 1675, John Kenny, had John, b. 25 Mar. foll. and Eliz. 6 Feb. 1678.

" l. 21 from bot. aft. LOMES, add, LOMASE,

" last l. aft. d. ins. Frances,—also, aft. m. ins. 25 Nov. 1667,—also, for Sherring r. Sherwin

P. 112. l. 19, bef. JOHN, ins. JOHN, Salem, by w. Mary had Mary, b. 16 Dec. 1659.

P. 116. l. 2, aft. clk. add, reg. of prob.

" l. 16, bef. SAMUEL, ins. ROBERT, Salem 1692, a blacksmith, prob. s. of the first Robert.

P. 117. l. 8, for perhaps r. a relat. not—also, aft. William, ins. and Abigail, wh. m. 28 Dec. 1671 Samuel Gray. But ano. WILLIAM of Salem may be the kinsm.

ment. in the will of first William; and this by w. Jane had William, b. 27 Feb. 1657; Eliz. 26 Apr. 1659; Margaret, 21 Sept. 1660; Joseph, 1 Jan. 1663; Jeremiah, 2 Apr. 1667; Jane, May 1668; Rowland, 7 Apr. 1672, d. at two yrs. and Dinah, 4 Nov. 1674.

P. 117. l. 9, for His wid. Abigail r. Abigail, wid. of the sec. William,

" l. 14, bef. WILLIAM, ins. WILLIAM, Salem, s. of the sec. William of the same m. 7 Apr. 1680, Mary Moulton, perhaps d. of the first Robert of S. had William, b. 3 Feb. foll. and Abigail, 21 Dec. 1682.

" l. 15, for the preced. r. William of Saybrook,

P. 122. l. 18, bef. SOLOMON, ins. or LOWD, FRANCIS, had made improvem. at Arowsic isl. in Kennebec riv. and thence been driv. by Ind. hostil. bef. 1679; at Ipswich by w. Sarah had Francis, b. 26 July 1700. Yet other ch. he certain. had, as Sarah, wh. was to m. Jonathan Pulsifer in Apr. 1705, and ano. prob. Deborah, m. William Start. On his petitn. the governm. allowed him, for almost 30 yrs. serv. of the Prov. to be supplied in the fort at Winter harb. at public charge. FRANCIS, Weymouth, s. of the preced. m. late in 1722, Honor, youngest ch. of Isaac Prince of Hull, and d. 2 Jan. 1774; and his wid. d. 18 Jan. 1777. Of this sec. Francis, a gr.s. is Hon. Samuel P. Loud of Dorchester. JOHN, Boston, by w. Deborah had William, wh. d. 17 Dec. 1690, aged 28 yrs. says Bridgman's Copp's Hill inscr.

" aft. l. 19, ins. LOUDER. See LOWDER.

" l. 19 and 18 from bot. strike out 23 Mar. 1678 to Salisbury, inclus. and ins. 12 Jan. 1677, Hannah Prichard,

" l. 9 from bot. strike out 12 Jan. 1677, Hannah Prichard, and ins. 23 Mar. 1678, Naomi Hoyt, d. of John the first of Salisbury,

" l. 8, from bot. aft. 1680. add, His wid. Naomi had admin. 30 Nov. foll.

P. 124. l. 12 from bot. aft. 1655, ins. wh. d. under 5 yrs.

P. 125. l. 10, aft. num. add, THOMAS, Gloucester, prob. s. of the preced. b. in Eng. d. 12 Apr. 1712, aged 80, had s. THOMAS, wh. m. Sarah, d. of Harlakenden Symonds, d. 8 Feb. 1698, leav. s. Symonds, Thomas, John, and d. Eliz.

P. 126. aft. l. 2, ins. LOWDER, or LOUDER, HENRY, Boston, by w. Mary had Henry, b. 7 Dec. 1671. JOHN, Salem, by w. Eliz. had William, b. 10 Feb. 1692; Nicholas, 31 Aug. 1693; Eliz. 1 Oct. 1695; and Jared, 1 Nov. 1697. More than usual folly was by him exhibit. in testify. against Bridget Bishop for witcher. as in Essex Inst. II. 142 and 3 is well set forth.

" l. 19, aft. b. ins. at B.

P. 127. l. 18, for 20 r. 29

P. 130. l. 7, for this last name, in Babson, 113, Abigail is substitut. and he adds Henry, 1684; and James and Eliz. tw. 1686.

P. 137. l. 21, aft. that, ins. he m. Hannah, d. of Thomas Tolman, had George, b. 16 Dec. 1662; Thomas, 10 Mar. 1665; and — also, aft. Milton. add, His wid. m. the sec. William Blake.

" l. 20 from bot. bef. JAMES, ins. JAMES, Salem, d. 30 Aug. 1661.

" l. 9 from bot. at the end, add, Mary, again, Oct. 1686;

P. 139. aft. l. 16, ins. MABER, RICHARD, Salem, m. 21 Nov. 1670, Mary Allen, had Dorcas, b. 29 July 1672; John, 1 Mar. 1675; and John, again, 15 Oct. 1679.

P. 140. bef. l. 8 from bot. ins. MACKDOWEL, ALEXANDER, Dover 1661.

P. 141. l. 7, bef. or ins. MACMILLON,

" l. 8, aft d. Eliz. add, and d. 20 June 1673.

" l. 10, at the end, add, JOHN, Salem, s. perhaps of the preced. m. 11 Dec. 1684, Mary Gilson, had John, b. 5 Sept. 1685; and Joseph, 24 Sept. 1687.

P. 141. bef. l. 6 from bot. ins. MACTAIN, JOHN, Marblehead 1677.

P. 142. l. 15, aft. Gardner, ins. had Sarah, b. 3 Apr. 1677; Deborah, 3 Mar. 1679; and Bethia, 8 Apr. 1681; and he d. 14 Oct. 1693. — also, for she next r. his wid.

" l. 21, aft. 1672, ins. or Apr. 1682, by other acco.

" l. 20 from bot. at the end, add, Thomas jr. d. 3 Dec. 1675.

P. 147. l. 6, at the end, add, OLIVER, Salem, had Eliz. b. 10 May 1685; and Sarah, 25 July 1687.

P. 147. l. 7, bef. GEORGE, ins. DENNIS, Nantucket, had Betty, b. 10 July 1679; and David 2 Apr. 1683.

" l. 14, bef. JOHN, ins. JACOB, Salem, s. of Return. was dept. marshal in the doleful service of 1692.

" l. 21 from bot. aft. Richard, add, m. 23 June 1663, Eliz. wid. of Robert Gray of Salem, had Thomas, b. 2 May 1664, d. in few mos.; Nicholas, 15 Sept. 1665, d. under 2 yrs.; Margaret, 25 Feb. 1667, d. in few days; and John, 28 May 1668. He

P. 149. l. 7, bef. 1684; ins. 13 Sept. — also, bef. 1686; ins. 5 Jan.

" l. 8, bef. 1687; ins. 16 Sept. — also, bef. 1689, ins. 16 Aug.

" l. 20, aft. 1685, ins. m. 10 May 1664, Mercy, d. of John Glover,

" l. 20 from bot. aft. 1668. add, by w. Damaris he had Damaris, b. 12 Aug. 1658; Ruth, 4 Nov. 1662; Paul, 4 Aug. 1664; Elias, 29 Mar. 1667, wh. d. in 4 mos.; Abigail, 28 June 1668; and Rebecca, 5 Mar. 1674.

" l. 17 from bot. bef. d. ins. had w. Eliz. s. Andrew, and

P. 150. l. 13 from bot. aft. NICHOLAS, ins. Ipswich, 1654,

" l. 12 from bot. aft. 1658, add, but not there sett.

P. 151. bef. l. 9 from bot. ins. MARE, JOHN, Salem, m. 18 July 1682, Joanna Brunson, but I kn. no more of either bef. or aft.

P. 152. l. 5, aft. 1643, ins. d. in 3 days

P. 154. l. 13, from bot. aft. Susanna, ins. b. one says, 23, but bapt. I think, — also, aft. Jacob, ins. b. 6 Aug. 1658, bapt.

" l. 10 from bot. bef. JOHN, ins. JOHN, Salem, prob. s. of the preced. m. 20 Mar. 1662, Sarah Young, d. perhaps of Christopher; had Sarah, b. 1 Dec. of unkn. yr.; and Ruth, Aug. 1668, and in the same mo. he d. at Barbados. On 2 Dec. 1669, his wid. took admin.

" l. 8 and 7 from bot. strike out, "d. soon; Joseph, again," and ins. Isaac, for Mr. Porter assures me, that in l. 3 of p. 197 of Geneal. Reg. XII, Boltwood, usual. so accur. is wrong.

P. 155. l. 17, bef. THOMAS, ins. SAMUEL, Salem, s. of John, m. 14 Aug. 1679, Priscilla Tompkins, youngest ch. of John, had Susanna, b. 12 May 1680; John, 1 Sept. 1681; Thomas, 18 Sept. 1683; Sarah, 18 July 1685; and Margaret, 8 Apr. 1688.

" l. 20 from bot. aft. same, ins. m. 15 Aug. 1664, Mary Silsbee, d. of Henry, had John, b. 26 Sept. 1665; Mary, 8 Dec. 1666; Zechariah; Eliz.; Jonathan, 14 Apr. 1672; and Ebenezer, 28 May 1674.

" l. 3 from bot. aft. Benjamin, ins. b. 18, bapt.

" l. 2 from bot. at begin. ins. liv. a. 1657, short time, at Gloucester,

P. 156. l. 3 from bot. aft. Boston, ins. call. "a Scottishman," — also, aft. had, add, James, b. 29 Sept. 1659;

P. 160. l. 21 from bot. for Sarah, r. 25 Nov. 1678, Abigail,

" l. 20 from bot. aft. Verin, add, had Abigail, b. 28 Aug. foll.

" l. 19 from bot. bef. EPHRAIM, ins. EPHRAIM, Salem, s. of John, by w. Eliz. had Ephraim, b. 24 May 1673; and Samuel, 2 Nov. 1676.

P. 161. l. 2, aft. 1659 ; add, beside Mary, 23 Mar. 1662. His w. was Alice.

" l. 10, for had w. r. m. 5 Sept. 1664, — also, aft. Mary, ins. Chichester, perhaps d. of William,

" l. 11, erase but I kn. no more of him than that he

" l. 12, aft. 1671, add, had John, b. 26 July, 1666, d. soon; John, again, 2 Sept. 1667 ; Mary, 14 Jan. 1670 ; James, 28 Nov. 1672 ; Sarah, 8 Oct. 1675 ; and Margaret, 25 Dec. 1677.

" l. 17, aft. 1705, add, he m. 23 Aug. 1667, Mercy Pierce, had Mercy, b. 23 June 1669, d. soon ; Benjamin, 30 July 1670 ; Samuel, 20 Dec. 1674, d. soon ; Samuel, again, 17 Mar. 1676, d. soon ; Mercy, again, 7 Aug. 1677 ; Mehitable, 14 May 1682 ; Lydia, 7 Jan. 1684 ; and Susanna, 29 Apr. 1687. But the mo. of the last two is call. Mary.

" l. 20 from bot. bef. had ins. by w. Sarah

" l. 19 from bot. aft. Hannah ins. b. 1 Sept. 1655, — also, aft. Sarah ins. (wh. d. 19 July 1665) — also, aft. 1659 ; ins. Mary, b. 2 Apr. 1661 ; — also, aft. Deliverance, ins. 15 July, bapt.

" l. 18 from bot. aft. 1663 ; ins. and William, 19 Sept. 1665 ;

" l. 15 from bot. aft. Cox. add, Deliverance m. 27 Dec. 1680, Thomas Cooper.

P. 162. l. 6, aft. Jameson, add, Of one Susanna M. (I kn. not whether this w. of George), execut. for witcher. 1692, the monstrous proceed. is well exhibit. in Essex Inst. II. 135.

l. 18, bef. JOHN, ins. JOHN, Bristol, had in 1689 w. and six ch.

" l. 18 from bot. aft. marsh, ins. had Michael, b. 10 Feb. 1660.

P. 164. l. 10, bef. 1662 ; ins. 31 July — also, bef. 1665 ; ins. 2 Jan.

P. 165. l. 5 from bot. aft. MASCALL, ins. MASCOL, — also, for there r. m. Mar. 1649, Ellen Long,

" l. 4 from bot. aft. 1651, ins. wh. was b. 25 Dec. preced. — also, aft. Stephen, ins. b. 15 Feb. bapt. — also, aft. Mehitable, ins. 15 May, bapt. — also, aft. Thomas, ins. b. 14

" l. 3 from bot. aft. James, ins. 16 Mar. bapt. — also, aft. Nicholas, ins. 14 Apr. bapt.

" l. 2 from bot. bef. ROBERT, ins. JOHN, Salem, s. of the preced. m. 6 Oct. 1674, Esther, perhaps d. of Christopher Babbage, had John, b. 5 Aug. foll. ; Stephen, 21 May 1677 ; Sarah, 20 Apr. 1687 ; and Benjamin, 15 Aug. 1699, as in Essex Inst. II. 298 is told.

P. 166. l. 18 from bot. for " a wife " r. Margaret, d. of Edward Dennison, also, erase had

" l. 16 from bot. aft. Daniel, ins. b. 26 Nov. 1674,

" l. 15 from bot. bef. Oct. ins. 10

" l. 14 from bot. bef. Hobart. ins. d. of Rev. Peter

" l. 13 from bot. aft. 1736. add, By a sec. w. he had Hezekiah, 3 May 1677, tho. the copious and exact. fam. geneal. could not furnish the name, either bapt. or surname ; yet the deficiency is well suppl. by the last, — Peter, 9 Nov. 1680 ; Rebecca, 10 Feb. 1682 ; Margaret, 21 Dec. 1683 ; Samuel, 11 Feb. 1686 ; Abigail, 3 Feb. 1689 ; Priscilla, 17 Sept. 1691 ; and Nehemiah, 24 Nov. 1693 ; all at S. His w. d. 8 Apr. 1727. See Geneal. Reg. XV. 119.

" l. 8 from bot. aft. His ins. w. Jane d. 9 Nov. 1661 ; and his

P. 168. l. 3, at the end, add, Ann m. John Brown of Swanzey, and

" l. 4 and 5, erase, and of the other, &c. to the end of sent.

" l. 18, aft. Abigail, add, prob. d. of Rev. James Fitch,

" l. 5 from bot. aft. ds. add, Prob. he had been of Hampton 20 yrs. earlier.

P. 170. l. 2, aft. 1683. add, For the name of the last d. suspicion was felt, and the fam. geneal. supplies one, Hannah, more consist. with our fathers' precision. Yet even the dilig. of Chancellor Walworth could not find the name of the first w. that bore him John, 19 Aug. 1676; Ann; and Sarah; nor give dates to the ds. The sec. w. Eliz. Peck of Rehoboth, whose f. I seek in vain, m. 4 July 1694, had Samuel, 26 Aug. 1695, d. young; Eliz. 6 May 1697; and Hannah, 14 Apr. 1699. He d. 30 Mar. 1705, and his wid. m. Gershom Palmer.

" l. 15, bef. THOMAS, ins. THOMAS, Salem, by w. Christian had Susanna, b. 22 Aug. 1687, and I see nothing more of him.

" l. 20 from bot. for 1677 r. 9 or 25 Nov. 1676

" l. 17 from bot. aft. proof. add, His w. surv. as is infer. from the ment. by the s. in June 1680, in render. admin. acco. of the est. of his f. that his mo. was d.

" l. 16 from bot. aft. 1668, ins. m. 27 Apr. 1658, Sarah Wells, — also, bef. bapt. ins. b. 14 May 1664,

" l. 15 from bot. for "perhaps elder" r. 6 Oct. 1665 — also, aft. beside ins. Thomas, 5 Dec. 1667, and Daniel, wh. both d. young; — also, for a. r. 25 July — also, aft. Ward; ins. and Thomas, again, 8 or 22 Mar. 1674, d. young.

" bef. l. 10 from bot. ins. MASSILOWAY.   See Mussilloway.

P. 171. l. 3, bef. NATHANIEL, ins. JOHN, Salem, m. 17 July 1678, Eliz. Ormes, had John, b. 24 Sept. 1681, wh. d. with his mo. in Sept. of next yr. and by w. Dores he had Eliz. last of July 1684; John, again, 15 Feb. 1687; Jonathan, 10 Nov. 1689; and Samuel, 1 Oct. 1693.

" l. 4, aft. 1659, ins. wh. m. Ruth, d. of John Pickworth,

P. 175. l. 10, from bot. aft. JOHN, ins. Boston,

P. 176. l. 20 from bot. aft. 1664. add, Prob. his w. was Sarah, d. of William Hedge.

P. 179. l. 2, bef. SAMUEL, ins. RICHARD, Boston, perhaps br. perhaps s. of Henry, m. Mary, d. of Simon Eyre the first, had only Martha, wh. it is said, m. John Ruggles, but wh. of the sev. bear. that name, or when the f. of this w. or her h. was b. is almost beyond guess.

" l. 15 from bot. bef. THOMAS, ins. EDWARD, Salem, d. 15 Nov. 1686.

" l. 13 from bot. bef. 1670 ins. 22 July

" l. 9 from bot. aft. had ins. Susanna, b. 15 Sept. 1671; Eliz. 11 Sept. 1673; Deliverance, 21 Oct. 1675, d. next yr.; Sarah, 17 Sept. 1677; Margaret, 20 Mar. 1680; Pelatiah, 10 May 1682; beside — also, aft. John, add, 9 Oct. 1684; and Joseph, 16 Feb. 1687, wh. d. next yr.

P. 183. l. 6, aft. MAXSON, ins. MAXON,

" l. 11 aft. 77. add, One of the ds. m. Hubbard Burdick.   JOHN, Westerly, s. of the preced. m. 19 Jan. 1688, Judith, d. of Joseph Clark, had Judith, b. 23 Sept. 1689; Mary, 26 Oct. 1691, d. next yr.; Bethia, 31 July 1693; Eliz. 7 Nov. 1695; Hannah, 13 June 1698; John, 21 Apr. 1701; Dorothy, 20 Oct. 1703; Susanna, 19 Oct. 1706; Joseph, Dec. 1709, d. July foll.; and Avis, 27 Dec. 1712; and the f. d. July 1747.   JONATHAN, Westerly, br. of the preced. m. 1 May 1707, Content Rogers, possib. d. of Jonathan, had Jonathan, b. 16 Jan. 1708; Content, 28 Jan. 1710; Joseph, 14 Jan. 1712; John, 2 Mar. 1714; Naomi, 6 May 1716; Samuel, 20 July 1718; Caleb, 1 Nov. 1721; and Mary, 20 Nov. 1723.   His will is of 8 June 1732.   JOSEPH, Westerly, br. of the preced. m. Tacy, d. of Robert Burdick, had Joseph, b. 10 Mar. 1692; and John, Tacy, Goodith, Mary, Ruth, and Eliz. and d. Sept. 1750.

P. 189. aft. l. 10, ins. MAZURE, or MAZURYE, BENJAMIN, Salem, m. 23 Oct. 1676, Margaret Row, had Benjamin, b. 6 July 1679.   JOSEPH, Salem, prob. br. of the preced. m. 25 Mar. 1680, Sarah, d. of John Pickworth, had Joseph, b. 25 Mar.

1681; Abigail, June 1683; Nathaniel, 23 Feb. 1687; Benjamin, 10 Nov. 1689. LAWRENCE, Salem, prob. br. of the preced. m. 25 Oct. 1670, Mary Kebbin, prob. the same as Kibby, had Mary, b. 15 Feb. 1673. I suppose in mod. days the spell. is Masury.

P. 190. l. 8, aft. Perkins, add, d. of Thomas Browning,

" l. 18, bef. 16 ins. 6 or

" l. 21 from bot. erase prob. — also, aft. 1673. add, Perhaps he rem. to Windham, and d. there 14 Apr. 1743, aged 99. His will, of 31 Dec. 1729, names w. Deborah, ch. Daniel, John, James, Joseph, and gr.s. John.

P. 191. l. 8, at the end, add, THOMAS, Salem, m. 31 Jan. 1673, Mary, perhaps wid. of Thomas Day.

P. 193. bef. l. 12, ins. MECARTER, or MACARTY, JOHN, Salem, m. 27 Jan. 1675, Rebecca, perhaps d. of Jeremiah Meacham, had John, b. 13 Jan. foll.; Rebecca, 4 Feb. 1678; Jeremiah, 9 Sept. 1679; Peter, 1 Nov. 1681; Andrew, 6 June 1684; James, 17 Nov. 1686; Isaac, 3 June 1689; and Rebecca, again, 6 Feb. 1691. The spell. of this name is from Essex Inst. II. 298.

" bef. l. 6 from bot. ins. MEGDANIEL, JOHN, Boston, by w. Eliz. had John, b. 13 Sept. 1659.

P. 197. l. 4, at the end, add, His wid. Mary, in her will of 1679, calls her d. Mary Osborn.

P. 200. l. 6, at the end, add, Abigail, m. 18 Jan. 1671, John Hitchcock.

P. 205. l. 10 from bot. bef. SAMUEL, ins. NATHANIEL, Rowley, s. of the first Thomas, was prob. a merch. and d. 13 Oct. 1677, without issue.

P. 207. l. 5, aft. down. add, He m. 18 Jan. 1662, Mary Whelan, as in Essex Inst. II. 297 is told, but I fear the ceremony was not legal. However, as his w. d. next yr. perhaps no prosecut. was had; and he was m. in a more satisfact. way, 7 Nov. 1664, to Exercise Felton, had Mary, b. 1 Apr. 1666; Susanna, 7 Oct. 1667; Abigail, 5 July 1669; and Mary, again, 27 Mar. 1671.

P. 208. l. 6, at the end, add, He m. 3 Apr. 1665, Sarah Weston, prob. d. of John, had John, b. 8 Jan. 1669; and Mary, 22 Mar. 1670.

P. 211. l. 15, aft. yr. ins. may have rem. to Middletown.

" l. 21 from bot. aft. sett. add, from Rowley,

" l. 15 from bot. bef. July ins. or 20

P. 212. l. 11 from bot. aft. 1678. add, leav. wid. Sarah.

" l. 7 from bot. strike out "and his w. d. 5 June foll." and ins. beside 5 more, of wh. one was Nathan, b. 1685. His w. d. 9 Mar. 1718, and he d. 7 Nov. 1719

" last l. aft. 1642; add, Nathaniel, 1647;

P. 213. l. 3, aft. Greenoway. add, In 1642 he rem. to Gloucester, and aft. sev. yrs. to Brookfield, there d. 1676, as did his wid. 1682.

" l. 9, strike out "When Millet or" &c. to the end of the parag. and ins. THOMAS, Gloucester, s. of the preced. m. 21 May 1655, Mary, d. of Sylvester Eveleth, wh. d. 2 July 1687, perhaps without hav. ch. and he next m. Abigail, wid. of Isaac Eveleth, d. of John Coit, and d. 18 June 1707.

" l. 3 from bot. aft. 1640, add, acc. Vinton; but I think she must be count. bef. 1630, and b. in Eng. •

P. 215. l. 20 from bot. bef. GEORGE. ins. Christopher, Ipswich 1666.

P. 226. l. 18 from bot. aft. 1689. ins. Sarah, m. 1680, Joseph Kellogg, and d. 1689.

P. 227. l. 12 from bot. aft. Woodbury add, had William, b. 9 June 1667, d. under 3 mos.; Mary, 5 Sept. 1668; Sarah, 20 Feb. 1671; Thomas, 20 Apr. 1673; Jonathan, 7 Aug. 1678; and Francis.

P. 228. l. 4, aft. 15 ins. July or

55*

P. 228. l. 5, aft. deac. add, His w. d. 26 May 1691, aged 62, and he d. a. 1694, hav.

" l. 7, aft. 1705. add, Ruth m. John Norton the sec. of F. Sarah m. William Lewis the third, and Mary m. John Hart the sec.

P. 230. l. 16 aft. imposts. add, He was a capt. and his w. d. 5 Oct. 1686.

P. 232. l. 8, for that r. next

" l. 9, aft. Truelove. add, By the Col. Ct. Jan. 1641, this strange order was pass. that Thomas Roberts of Duxbury "shall lodge no more with George M. a diseased person." GEORGE, Bristol, m. 21 Dec. 1683, Hannah Lewis, had John, b. 3 Oct. 1684; Mary, 24 Mar. 1688; Sarah, 4 Mar. 1691; Hannah, 18 May 1694; George, 31 Aug. 1696; all bapt. 13 June 1697; Martha, 12 Mar. bapt. 23 Apr. 1699; Abigail, 27 Feb. bapt. 21 June 1702; Benjamin, 18 Apr. bapt. 17 June 1705; and Thomas, 1 Jan. bapt. 20 Mar. 1709. His w. d. Dec. 1717, and he rem. to Norton. GEORGE, Norton, s. of the preced. was a capt. and d. 1784. He had George, wh. was f. of Rev. George, H. C. 1776.

" l. 11, bef. JONATHAN, ins. JOHN, Bristol, perhaps br. of the sec. George, by w. Hannah had Hannah, b. 1 Feb. 1687, wh. d. in few wks.

" l. 12, aft. Bartlett, ins. was sw. a freem. 1682.

P. 233. l. 12 from bot. aft. 1674. add, He m. 15 Dec. 1658, Eliz. d. of lieut. William Dixy.

P. 234. aft. l. 5, ins. MORRALL, PETER, Salem, m. 27 Sept. 1675, Mary Butler, both were from Isle of Jersey.

" l. 21 from bot. aft. New Haven, add 1644,

P. 247. l. 17 from bot. bef. HUGH, ins. EDWARD, Salem, by w. whose name, in Essex Inst. II. 297, seems an impossib. one, had Edward, b. 30 Oct. 1662.

" l. 14 from bot. bef. 1693, ins. 3 Apr.

P. 249. l. 14, aft. John, ins. 25 June 1655 — also, aft. Joseph, ins. 3 Jan. 1657; — also, aft. Miriam, ins. Jan. 1659 — also, aft. Mary, ins. 16 June 1661; most of these by w. Abigail, if not all;

" l. 15, aft. 1665. ins. His will of 5 Sept. was pro. Nov. foll.

" l. 16, bef. 1672, ins. 17 July — also, aft. Mary, ins. b. 2 June foll. — also, aft. Robert, ins. 3 Sept.

" l. 17, bef. 1678; ins. 28 Apr. — also, bef. 1682 ins. 28 Feb.

P. 250. l. 4, aft. Tailor, ins. perhaps br. of Benjamin,

" l. 12, for Benjamin r. Edmund — also, aft. 1697, ins. m. 17 Jan. 1694, Mary, d. of Joseph Cock.

" l. 7 from bot. aft. 74. ins. Eliz. m. 19 June 1679, Samuel Read.

P. 251. l. 22, at the end, add, Christian m. 31 Aug. 1676, Joshua Conant.

P. 252. l. 2, aft. d. ins. by shipwreck,

" l. 3, aft. tak. ins. £14 6s. 10d.

P. 254. l. 16, aft. Benjamin. add, His wid. m. 7 Oct. 1686, John Richards of Westfield.

" l. 11 from bot. at the end, add, Yet her charact. was so good as to obtain a h. next yr. Peter Plimpton.

P. 256. l. 6, aft. *here* add, had Mehitable, 20 Jan. 1659, and

P. 260. l. 11, aft. James, ins. in one rec. call. Samuel,

P. 263. l. 3 from bot. bef. FRANCIS, ins. EDWARD, Westfield, s. of the preced. m. Margaret Higason, or Higginson, d. of William.

P. 264. l. 1, bef. HENRY, ins. FRANCIS, Salem, s. of the preced. had Sarah, b. 4 Nov. 1688; and Joan, 1 June 1691.

" l. 11, aft. Mary, ins. w. of John

" l. 20, aft. next, ins. 22 Sept. 1673,

P. 264. l. 15 from bot. aft. 1655; ins. the last two d. young; Jonathan, again, 6 Sept. 1657;

" l. 11 from bot. aft. 1663, ins. (but by rec. 14 Mar. 1659, i. e. 1660); — also, aft. 1672. add, His will of 9 days preced. nam. ch. and gr.ch. in Essex Inst. II. 72.

" l. 10 from bot. aft. Francis ins. Laurie or

" l. 9 from bot. aft. Mansfield. add, Lydia m. Nov. 1671, Jonathan Hart.

P. 265. l. 15 from bot. at the end, add, I presume this is the same person, that d. 1 June 1658, at Salem, but, in Essex Inst. II. 299, call. Neare.

" l. 14 from bot. aft. Salem, ins. m. 10 Jan. 1656,

" l. 13 from bot. aft. Potter, add, had Rebecca, b. 21 Dec. foll.; Ann, 31 Aug. 1658; Eliz. 1 Dec. 1659; Provided, 12 Apr. 1661; Anthony, 11 Apr. 1663; Mary, 30 Apr. 1665; George, 26 Mar. 1667; Isaac, 15 Apr. 1669; Abigail, 31 May 1716; Thomas, 25 July 1673; Dorothy 25 Aug. 1675; and Rachel, 17 Mar. 1678. He and w. were

" l. 6 from bot. aft. mo. add, Rebecca m. Jan. 1676, Michael Chapleman. — also, erase perhaps

P. 266. l. 2, aft. 65. add, In Essex Inst. II. 234, is seen his will at large, mak. s. Ezekiel excor. and nam. legatees this s. and his two ch. s. Daniel, and his five ch. call. John, Ezekiel, Judah, Mary, and Eliz. as also d. Hannah, and her ch. Hannah, w. of Eleazer Armitage, and her last b. s. to wh. the surname is hard to find, as the source of the Nile, also, the childr. of s.-in-law, Samuel Hart, viz. Samuel, Joseph, Abigail, and Rebecca, beside Hart's d.-in-law, Eliz. Howe, also, the childr. of s.-in-law, Joseph Mansfield, viz. Joseph, John, Eliz. Wheat (whose h. is not of my acquaint.), and Deborah. Of course, the est. was good.

" l. 16, aft. 1652. add, See Appendix to Winthrop's Hist. of N. E. Vol. I. p. 499.

P. 267. l. 17 from bot. bef. PHILIP, ins. NATHANIEL, Marblehead 1675.

P. 272. l. 2, bef. JOHN, ins. JOHN, Waterbury 1674, s. of the first Thomas, rem. to Farmington a. 1694, there d. without w. or ch.

" l. 19, aft. Thomas, ins. m. 20 Dec. 1683, Mary, d. of Thomas Hart, had Samuel, b. 19 Feb. 1687; Thomas, 1 Mar. 1691; John, 17 Jan. 1693; Daniel; Mary, 23 Dec. 1697; Daniel, again, 18 Apr. 1700, Y. C. 1718; Nathaniel, 20 Feb. 1704; Sarah, 17 June 1707, His w. d. 28 Apr. 1752, aged 86; and he d. 15 Feb. 1753.

" l. 17 and 16 from bot. for Olmstead. sis. of John and Richard O. r. Adgate,

" l. 15 from bot. bef. Woodford, ins. w. of Joseph

" l. 14 from bot. bef. Stanley ins. w. of John — also, bef. Smith, r. w. of Arthur

" l. 13 from bot. bef. North ins. w. of Thomas — also, at the end, add, not as Hist. of Woodbury, 167, says, 14, wh. was Wednesday

" l. 10 from bot. aft. Thomas, ins. b. 1 Oct. 1681,

" l. 9 from bot. aft. Simon, ins. b. 1 Apr. bapt.

" l. 8 from bot. bef. 24 ins. bapt. — also, at the end, add, beside Sarah, 1 Jan. 1699; and Esther 1705. He

" l. 6 from bot. for twelve r. ten

P. 273. l. 8 from bot. aft. Lynn, add, s. of Thomas,

P. 274. l. 5, aft. Robert ins. (but I prefer Nicholas)

" l. 18, from bot.for prob. r. 15 Oct. 1627,

P. 275. l. 13, bef. 26 ins. 16 or

" l. 3 from bot. for Hope r. Hopestill

P. 276. l. 6, for John r. George

" l. 18, for perhaps r. 6 July 1625,

" l. 19 at the end, add, Mary, b. 3 Jan. 1661; Bathsheba, 19 Jan. 1662; wh. both d. young

P. 276. l. 20, for b. 1662 r. 21 Feb. 1663; David, 1 Nov. 1665; John, 1 July 1668;
Hopestill, 19 July 1669; Mary, again, 7 Nov. 1670; and

' l. 20 and 21, strike out prob. other ch. and ins. Rehoboth gr.stone calls the w's.
name Bathsheba, wh. I distrust; yet the town rec. may be wrong.

" l. 20 from bot. aft. 1692. add, He d. 14 Dec. 1710. Mary m. 2 Jan. 1699, Samuel
Woodcock. SAMUEL, Rehoboth, s. of the preced. m. 8 Oct. 1696, Hannah Ken-
rick, wh. d. 8 Apr. 1718, had Noah, b. 1 Sept. 1697; Samuel, 30 July 1699;
Hannah, 29 July 1701; Margaret, 8 Apr. 1704; Ann, 7 Apr. 1705; and John, 8
Dec. 1706; and d. 25 June 1747.

P. 279. l. 19, strike out "prob. d. unm. for," and ins. m. Sarah, d. of Daniel Kellogg,
but liv. not long, and had no ch. as

P. 283. l. 2, for Cove r. Cave

P. 288. l. 13, bef. JOHN, Salem, prob. s. of the preced. m. 17 Nov. 1663,
Mary, eldest d. of George Ropes, had John, b. 19 Nov. 1664, d. at 3 days; John,
again, 12 Dec. 1666; Mary, 14 Feb. 1669; Richard, 20 Feb. 1674; and Abigail,
10 July 1677.

" l. 17, aft. perhaps, ins. gr.

" l. 17 from bot. aft. 1680. add, He m. 13 Jan. 1675, Eliz. d. of Henry Bullock.

" l. 14 from bot. at the end, add, TIMOTHY, Salem, had Mary, b. 10 Nov. 1694.

" l. 2 from bot. aft. Symonds, add, prob. d. of James, had Mary, b. 14 Apr. 1687;

P. 289. l. 3, aft. John. ins. m. Sarah Smith,

" l. 4, aft. 1687. add, His wid. d. 1727.

" l. 7, aft. 1643, add, but one acco. makes Mary 2 yrs. later than Samuel — also,
bef. 1653, ins. 18 Dec.

" l. 8, bef. 1660 ins. 18 Mar.

" l. 11, erase prob. — also, aft. preced. ins. m. 1672, Susanna, eldest d. of Robert
Francis,

" l. 12, erase and — also, aft. 6; ins. and Sarah, 4.

" l. 14, aft. John, add, d. 1731, without issue. But his wid. Martha, d. of Thomas
Porter, m. John Porter, as sec. w.

" l. 19, aft. John, add, m. 3 Jan. 1667, Hannah, d. of John Norton,

" l. 18 from bot. bef. THOMAS, ins. THOMAS, Farmington, m. Hannah, d. of Thomas
Newall, had John, Thomas, Hannah, Nathaniel, Mary, Joseph and Rebecca, tw.
bapt. 31 Dec. 1693; Lydia, 1 Mar. 1696; Sarah, and Ebenezer.

P. 290. l. 19 from bot. bef. FRANCIS, ins. DAVID, Boston, said by tradit. to have m.
Phebe, sis. of the third Richard Templar, but I see no date. He liv. in Black-
horse lane, tho. no time is ment. yet is he among inhab. tax. 1695.

P. 291. l. 6, aft. m. ins. 27 Feb. 1660, — also, at the end, add, See Babson, 118.

P. 293. l. 1, aft. same, ins. m. Ruth, eldest d. of Isaac More or Moore,

P. 294. l. 15, erase prob.

" l. 19. aft. 1689, add, wh. m. 1 Jan. 1711, Nathaniel Ellery

" l. 21, aft. Stephens, add, wh. d. 19 Nov. 1724,

" l. 14 from bot. at the end, add, But the will of his f. ment. this s. and so prob. he
was then liv.

P. 295. l. 3, aft. 1662, ins. by w. Lydia, had Ann, b. 13 Oct. 1659.

P. 297. l. 9 from bot. aft. yrs.; add, tho. no ch. was gather. there bef. 1693. He

" l. 8 from bot. aft. nothing, add, and d. 10 Nov. 1729.

P. 300. l. 1, bef. Francis, ins. the first

" l. 9, for ano. d. r. Eliz.

" l. 16 from bot. for br. r. eldest s.

" l. 15 from bot. aft. and ins. his w. d. 10 days foll.

P. 300. l. 12 from bot. for Jan. r. June

P. 302. l. 14, aft. 1689. add, Mary m. 12 Nov. 1667, Col. John Flint of Concord.

" l. 17 from bot. aft. person, add Sacket.

P. 309. l. 5 from bot. aft. m. add, 1645,

P. 311. l. 21, at the end, add, He contin. to own est. in Eng. and here took sec. or third w. 26 July 1666, a wid. in Essex Inst. II. 300, call. Bridget Wasselbe, whose surname I take no responsib. for spell. By her he had Christian, b. 8 May 1667;

" l. 21 from bot. aft. wood, add, and d. June 1679. — also, erase A

" l. 20 from bot. erase perhaps — also, strike out, d. of the free speaking woman, and ins. tho. common. call. Bishop, with alias O. I think his wid. Prob. one was name of her f. one of her h. but it may be doubt. of both.

P. 317. l. 12, for Annie r. Amie

" l. 20, aft. Bronson. add, Mary m. Feb. 1687, Samuel Scott.

" l. 21 from bot. aft. 1676. add, He m. 15 Dec. 1692, Eliz. Harrison (unless I mistake Mr. Porter's MS.) wh. d. 26 Dec. 1747, had Eliz. b. 1 Oct. 1693; Ebenezer, 3 Oct. 1695; David, 1 Mar. 1697; Bethia, 3 Jan. 1699; Abiah, 2 Nov. 1702; Ebenezer, again, 3 Oct. 1705; and Mary, 18 Oct. 1707.

" l. 11, from bot. bef. or ins. Osbourn, — also, bef. Christopher, ins. Alexander, Salem vill. had w. Sarah, wh. was arrest. for witcher. the first day of the monstrous delus.

P. 318. l. 13, from bot. bef. John, ins. John, Salem, m. 5 Oct. 1670, Eliz. Ruck, prob. d. of John, had Eliz. and John.

" l. 2 from bot. aft. Thence ins. he rem.

P. 319. l. 19 from bot. for 1689 r. 1639

" l. 18 from bot. for 1611 r. 1641

" l. 8 from bot. bef. Ano. ins. William, Salem, m. 17 Mar. 1673, Hannah Burton, had Samuel, b. 27 Apr. 1675; John, 27 Aug. 1677; Hannah, 2 Dec. 1679; and William, 3 May 1682.

" l. 4 from bot. aft. 1690. add, Since that was print. I discov. that her h. was Alexander, as bef. herein told.

P. 320. l. 4, bef. Mary ins. The wid. m. Thomas Rowell of Ipswich, and, next, Thomas Coleman of Nantucket;

" l. 5, aft. I. ins. and Deborah, m. 28 Aug. 1663, John Ross.

" l. 2 from bot. aft. degree ins. a,

P. 321. l. 11 from bot. aft. Martha, ins. d. of Peter

" l. 10 from bot. bef. Samuel, ins. Peter, 13 Mar. 1693; — also, at the end, add, again,

" l. 8 from bot. bef. 6 ins. 1 or

P. 326. l. 19, bef. Nathaniel, ins. Morgan, Salem, m. July 1670, Eliz. Dickinson, perhaps d. of Philemon, had John, b. 10 Mar. foll. I presume he liv. not long, as two nam. Eliz. wid. of O. are seen at S. within three yrs. foll.

" l. 3 from bot. for 1634 r. 1635

P. 327. bef. l. 10 ins. Pabodie. See Peabody.

P. 328. l. 16 from bot. bef. Ichabod, ins. George, Plymouth, m. 1657, it is said, Sarah Rickard, perhaps d. of Giles the first.

" l. 9 from bot. at the end, add, George;

" l. 7 from bot. aft. 1651, add, or 1656,

P. 330. l. 16, aft. Robert, add, by w. Meribah had Joseph, b. 25 Nov. 1686;

P. 333. l. 4, aft. person, add, wh. m. 22 Jan. 1673, Abigail, youngest d. of John Brocket.

P. 334. l. 13 from bot. aft. Bristol, ins. where he had w. and four ch. in Feb. 1689,

" l. 3 from bot. bef. ROBERT, ins. RALPH, Freetown, whose f. is not kn. but he had liv. some yrs. in R. I. bef. rem. to F. and, by w. Dorothy, had John, b. 1685, and perhaps Sarah, and aft. rem. a. 1688, and later had Thomas, Joseph, and Mary, made his will 23 Apr. 1722, and d. soon.

P. 342. l. 12, aft. Rowley, ins. m. 25 Dec. 1671, Mary, d. of John Pearson,

P. 344. l. 11 from bot. aft. seen. add, But as he had w. and four ch. at Bristol in 1688, I infer that he was short time of Boston, and that the naval capt. was the foll.

P. 352. l. 2 from bot. bef. JOHN, ins. JOHN, Salem, m. 29 May 1673, Mary, d. of Giles Cory, had John, b. 30 Mar. foll.; Giles, 16 Apr. 1675; Mary, 12 Apr. 1676, d. in few days; Mary, again, 2 Feb. 1678; Joseph, 17 Sept. 1680; and Margaret, 11 Feb. 1683.

P. 355. l. 1, aft. Eliot. add, He had only ch. Mary, and d. 1 Apr. 1679.

P. 357. l. 13, aft. same, ins. by w. Deborah

P. 359. l. 5, bef. 1644; ins. 12 Aug.

" l. 15, aft. Sarah, add, d. of capt. William Trask, m. 13 Oct. 1656,

" l. 17, aft. William, add, b. at Salem, 29 Mar. 1658; Elias, 31 Aug. 1660, wh. prob. d. soon; — also, aft. Sarah, add, 19 Oct. 1662

P. 360. l. 4 from bot. bef. JOHN, ins. FRANCIS, Salem, m. 13 Jan. perhaps 1667, Mary Stacy, had Francis, b. 28 Oct. foll. wh. d. in four wks.; Mary, 6 Mar. 1669; Moses, 21 June 1670; and Joseph, 22 Nov. 1673.

P. 361. l. 8 from bot. aft. Haskell, add, wh. d. 1734,

" l. 6 from bot. aft. fam. add, He had sec. and third ws. was in high esteem, and d. 19 Dec. 1763.

P. 362. l. 18, bef. James, ins. *

" l. 20, bef. See ins. He was rep. 1710 and 4 yrs. more.

P. 367. l. 18 from bot. at the end, add, and Ruth, 5 Apr. 1660;

" l. 15 from bot. at the end, add, The name is print. Param in Geneal. Reg. XV. 137.

" l. 11 from bot. aft. 1668. add, He m. 20 Apr. 1670, Sarah, with surname unkn. had Sarah, b. 16 Oct. 1671; Margery, 3 Mar. 1674; and his w. d. 3 June 1676. Next he m. 16 Dec. 1678, Mary Pease, perhaps d. of John, had Mary, 9 Oct. 1680; Margaret, 17 Feb. 1695; and Jonathan, 11 Oct. 1696.

P. 368. l. 15 from bot. aft. 1650, ins. d. young — also, aft. 1652, add, or, by var. read. of the same numerals, 6 Feb. 1653

" l. 12 from bot. aft. Salem, add, br. of Edmund,

P. 372. l. 19 from bot. aft. ch. add, Some fam. memo. tell of his m. 8 Nov. 1638,.to Margery Tarne, of b. of s. Samuel next yr. and of the wid. m. 1662, Henry Withington, the Dorchester Elder, and of her surv. him, and d. 20 May 1676; but most of these details are uncert. — also, aft. Dorchester, ins. prob. s. of the preced.

" l. 18 from bot. aft. 13 ins. Sept. or

" l. 16 from bot. aft. 1685; ins. beside Abiel, posthum. 22 Nov. 1690, wh. d. in few wks.

" l. 10 from bot. at the end, add, perhaps br. of Richard,

P. 379. l. 12 from bot. aft. 30 for Mar. r. May — also, aft. 14 for Mar. r. May

" l. 11 from bot. for Apr. r. June

" l. 10 from bot. for Oct. r. Dec.

" l. 9 from bot. aft. 23, for Oct. r. Dec. — bef. 1675 for Oct. r. Dec.

P. 380. l. 1, at the end, add, Ano. JOHN of Salem m. 30 Jan. 1677, Margaret Adams, had John, b. 22 Apr. 1678.

" l. 8, bef. ROBERT, ins. NATHANIEL, Salem, s. of the preced. m. 15 Mar. 1667, Mary Hobbs, and no more is kn.

P. 380. l. 9, bef. John, ins. sec. — also, aft. John, ins. m. 16 Dec. 1678, Abigail Randall, had William, b. 26 Sept. foll. and Mary, 11 Mar. 1681. He or an earlier Robert of S. s. of the first John, by w. Sarah had Bethia, b. 11 June 1660, wh. d. young; Deliverance, 6 Dec. 1664; Mary, 15 Feb. 1667; Robert, 25 Mar. 1669, prob. d. soon; Robert, again, 30 Nov. 1671; Bethia, again, 18 Jan. 1674; and Nathaniel, 28 Feb. 1678. This Robert,

" l. 21 from bot. aft. 1660. add, His d. Sarah, m. 12 Apr. 1664, Thomas Barnard jr.

" l. 2 from bot. aft. 1650, add, wh. m. 2 Dec. 1672, John Hotchkiss.

P. 385. l. 9, aft. John, ins. b. by former w. Phillis, 29 Mar. 1673,

" l. 15, at the end, add, by w. Hannah had George, b. 8 Aug. 1688.

P. 389. l. 5 from bot. aft. Mar. ins. (May in Vinton, 351).

P. 390. l. 10 from bot. at the end, add, WILLIAM, Salem, m. 15 May, 1676 Sarah Greenwich.

P. 391. l. 15, at the end, add, See Pennell.

P. 401. last l. for 1689 r. 1669 — also, aft. mariner, add, m. 14 Sept. of this yr. Eliz. eldest d. of Edward Hilliard of the same, had Richard, b. 12 Jan. 1671; William, 19 June 1673; and John, 14 Mar. 1676.

P. 402. l. 6 from bot. bef. SAMUEL, ins. RICHARD, Salem, perhaps eldest s. of Gilbert, by w. Bethia, had William, b. 11 Jan. 1688; and Richard, 5 June 1690.

P. 405. l. 3, aft. 11 ins. or 21 — also, aft. Jaggers, ins. had Ephraim, b. 28 Sept. 1692; — also, aft. d. ins. 26 Nov. by rec. but, in Stiles, 739, 20 Oct.

" l. 5, for Philbury r. Phillury

P. 406. l. 21, aft. 1750. add, But Stiles gives him third w. Mary, d. of Richard Case, and ch. John, 10 Feb. 1707; and Eliz. 7 Apr. 1709; besides Amos and David by a former w.

" l. 21 from bot. aft. Winchell. add, had Samuel, b. 21 Jan. 1691; Sarah, 18 Aug. 1693; Lois, 14 July 1696; Damaris, 7 July 1699; Mary, 18 Aug. 1702; Jerusha, 8 Nov. 1705; and Josiah, 24 Aug. 1708.

P. 407. l. 19 from bot. bef. June ins. or 5

" l. 13 from bot. aft. 1712, ins. by first w. had Stephen, b. 20 Jan. 1686; and Sarah, 20 Dec. 1687; by sec. had Timothy, 22 June 1689, d. soon; but Stiles, 739, must answer for the m. being so much too late.

P. 425. l. 9, bef. NATHANIEL, ins. JOHN, Salem, s. of Nathaniel, m. 27 Aug. 1667, Hannah, d. of Thomas Weeks of the same, and she d. 23 Dec. 1670,

" l. 2 from bot. bef. SAMUEL, ins. JOHN, Salem, s. of the preced. d. 1681, prob. unm. for his br. Joseph, as admor. giv. inv. 29 Nov. in that yr. propos. div. of the prop. one third to Ann his mo. one third to him. and one third to two sis. prob. Rachel and Sarah, and we can hardly doubt that the other three were d.

P. 428. l. 3, aft. Abiah, add, or Abigail,

" l. 12, bef. JOHN, ins. Ano. JOHN of Dorchester, wh. by w. Mary had sev. ch. is so indistinguisha. as to w. or ch. by the respective names, that we must be content to call one a cooper, and one a selectman, without confidence a. either as more respect. than the other.

" l. 20, for Eliz. r. Judith,

" l. 21, aft. f. ins. By Bond he is correct. judged to be the man emb. 1637 at Yarmouth, with w. and ch. he aged 49 yrs. w. Eliz. 36, ch. John, Barbara, Eliz. and Judith, with a serv. John Gedney, 19, as had been print. in 4 Mass. Hist. Coll. I. 95, and again is giv. in Geneal. Reg. XIV. 325. He was from Norwich, a weaver.

P. 429. l. 19 from bot. for the Stephen r. Rachel

P. 431. l. 3, aft. 1672. ins. His w. d. 18 Mar. 1701, and "old Robert" d. 10 Sept. 1706.

P. 439. l. 5, aft. 1642 ins. (not 1641 as 2 Jan. in that yr. of new reckon. style was Saturday)

" l. 18, bef. Goodwin ins. either Stiles, or

P. 450. bef. l. 5, ins. POLLEN or POLAND, JOHN, Wenham, by w. Bethia had John, b. 6 Oct. 1657 ; and Joseph, 12 Dec. 1661.

P. 451. l. 12, bef. JOHN, ins. JOHN, Salem 1660, mariner, was lost at sea, says tradit. and his inv. then tak. was very small. JOHN, Salem, m. 22 July 1674, Mary Cowes, had Mary, b. 13 Oct. 1677 ; Eliz. 5 May 1680 ; Rachel, 29 Nov. 1681 ; John, 4 Nov. 1683 ; and Susanna, 20 Feb. 1686, d. in few yrs. and only one ch. was liv. in June 1691, when w. Mary admin.

P. 452. l. 16, bef. THOMAS, ins. RICHARD, Salem, 1671.

P. 458. l. 13 from bot. for Joseph r. JOSEPH

P. 460. l. 4, aft. He add, inherit. his father's *gift*, as a natural bonesetter, and

" l. 17, for 704 r. 754

" l. 16 from bot. for 1679 r. 1680

" l. 14 from bot. strike out " in four mos." and ins. 1 May foll.

P. 461. l. 20 from bot. at the end, add, or 9

" l. 6 from bot. aft. Wenham, ins. by w. Lydia had Samuel ; John, b. 21 July 1638 ; Benjamin ; Nehemiah ; Jonathan ; Lydia ; Mehitable ; Mary ; Eliz. ; Sally ; and Hannah ; was a lieut. and d. 8 Mar. 1753, yet

" l. 5 from bot. at the end, add, had Rebecca, b. 14 Oct. foll. ; Mary, 4 Apr. 1698 ; Esther, 7 Aug. 1700 ; Ann, 26 Jan. 1704 ; and Eliz. 8 July 1706.   He

" l. 4 from bot. aft. North, ins. wid. of Joseph, m. 13 Jan. 1732, — also, aft. 1740. add, His wid. d. 11 July 1749, aged 83.

P. 462. l. 16 for 1701 r. 1702

" l. 16 from bot. aft. m. ins. 21 Jan. 1687, — also, aft. John, add, had John, b. 11 Jan. foll. ; Mary, 16 Sept. 1689 ; Martha, 28 Jan. 1693 ; Hannah, 11 May 1694 ; Thomas, 25 Dec. 1697 ; Jonathan, 28 Apr. 1700 ; Samuel, 16 July 1702 ; Rachel, 28 Mar. 1704, bapt. 12 Jan. 1706 ; and Matthew, b. 1 July 1709.   His w. d. 17 May 1710, — also, aft. and ins. he

P. 463. l. 18 from bot. aft. 1663, add, wh. d. 1668, as Stiles says,

P. 463. l. 15 from bot. bef. Hannah, ins. but Stiles adds, Thomas, again, 1683 ;

" l. 8 and 7 from bot. strike out "had w. in 1686," and ins. m. 18 Feb. 1686, Martha Freeman, perhaps d. of Stephen of Newark, N. J.

" l. 6 from bot. aft. Samuel, ins. b. 7, bapt.

" l. 5 from bot. at the begin. ins. b. 15, bapt. — also, aft. Martha, ins. 1, bapt. — also, aft. 1696 ; add, Ruth, b. 26 Jan. 1699 ; Mary, Sept. 1700 ; Joseph, 12 Dec. 1702 ; Lois, 18 Mar. 1705 ; Stephen, again, 16 Jan. 1707 ; and Rachel, 3 Apr. 1710.

P. 464. l. 4 and 5, erase Samuel &c. to Joseph. inclus.

" l. 8, bef. 1644, ins. 20 Nov.

" l. 11, erase Thomas, again, 1656 ; — also, aft. Samuel ; add, Rachel, bapt. Dec. 1658, wh. m. 12 May 1685, Samuel Cowles ; Martha, wh. m. Joseph North, and next 13 Jan. 1732, John Porter, s. of Daniel ;

" l. 12, aft. next, ins. 3 May 1727, — also, aft. Root ; add, beside Mary, the youngest, wh. m. 1 Oct. 1684, Joseph Royce, and next, 18 Oct. 1714, Joseph Langdon.

" l. 13 and 14, erase Perhaps his d.

" l. 14, bef. Apr. ins. 4

" l. 15, bef. 1676, ins. Nov. — also, aft. Taylor, add, and next, 7 Feb. 1708, Samuel Tudor ; Dorothy m. Jacob Overman of Carolina.

" l. 18, bef. Nov. ins. 12

" l. 16 from bot. aft. 1703. add, THOMAS, Windsor, youngest s. of Samuel of the same, acc. Stiles, rem. to Coventry, by w. Thankful had Mary, b. 16 Nov. 1708 ; Mary 16 Nov. 1710 (I copy Stiles, wh. says both these ds. were m. but my incredul. fears mist.) ; Jonathan, 20 Mar. 1713 ; and Noah, 24 Aug. 1715. His w. d. 1736, and he had sec. w. Rebecca.

P. 467. l. 6, aft. 1666, ins. wh. m. William Roach

" l. 17, aft. 1659. add, Eliz. m. Thomas Newhall.

P. 470. l. 10, aft. yrs. ins. John, wh. d. 17 Jan. 1686 ;

P. 493. l. 9, aft. Wrentham, add, first, perhaps, at Dorchester, as certain. Richard was

" l. 16 from bot. for a s. r. Thomas,

P. 497. l. 5, at the end, add, wh. m. 18 Jan. 1667, the sec. William Trask ;

" l. 18, aft. mo. add, Sev. of this name stood in most unhap. distinct. in the melancho. witcher. delus. as witness. on one or ano. indictm. 1692, viz. Thomas, in 8 cases, Edward in 7, John in 6, ano. Thomas in 4. See Essex Inst. II. 191.

P. 503. l. 19, aft. 1680 ; ins. Jonathan, again, d. under 3 yrs.

P. 512. l. 12, bef. JAMES, ins. DANIEL, Salem, gr.s. of the preced. s. of the first Joshua, m. 10 Apr. 1678, Hepzibah Peabody, had Jemima, b. 29 Dec. 1680 ; Daniel 23 Nov. 1682 ; Zerobabel, 12 May 1687 ; Eliz. 14 Aug. 1687 (unless, as may easi. be conject. an error has crept into Essex Inst. III. 97) ; Uzziel, Mar. 1693 ; and Pilgrim, 30 Nov. 1695.

" l. 19 from bot. bef. RICHARD, ins. JOSHUA, Salem, s. of the preced. m. Eliz. Leach, had Sarah, b. 28 Apr. 1686.

P. 513. l. 1, aft. sen. add, by w. Rachel had Bethia, b. 14 June 1655, wh. d. young, as did, also, Abigail and Eliz. all in Dec. 1662 ; Rachel, b. 14 Feb. 1660 ; and Jonathan, 25 Apr. 1666 ; and his w. d. the week foll.

P. 515. last l. bef. ISRAEL, ins. ISAAC, Salem, m. 10 Mar. 1674, Joan Stone.

P. 518. l. 20 from bot. aft. 1651, add, d. at 11 yrs.

" l. 17 from bot. bef. 19 ins. 14 Oct. 1665, or

P. 523. l. 1, aft. William ; ins. prob. Mary ; and perhaps Eliz. unless she belong to sec. w. — also, aft. Mar. ins. or July

" l. 2, for may have been r. was — also, aft. two, add, wh. d. young.

" l. 3 for few r. score of — also, aft. ch. add, His will, of 1 Oct. 1677, provid. for d. Eliz. w. of Richard Richards and her d. Eliz. his own s. William, and d. Eliz. his s.-in-law Ephraim Kempton, h. of his d. Mary, and her s. John and Ephraim. But material differ. in a later will, 10 May 1681, so enlarg. the devise to K. and his w. and lessen. that to William, as to make dispute in Ct. upon its valid. Other ch. of Richards are ment. as John, Mary, and Joanna, that may be the same as Joshua.

" l. 19 from bot. for 1669 r. 1670 — also, aft. John, ins. b. 12 July 1673, by rec. of Salem.

P. 532. l. 1, aft. 1668, for had w. r. m. 6 July 1662 — also, aft. Bethia, add, d. of George Williams of the same,

" l. 2, aft. 1678. add, He had Bethia, b. 25 Jan. 1663, d. soon; Margaret, 8 Nov. 1664 ; Obadiah, 14 Jan. 1668 ; Bethia, again, 25 June 1670 ; and Mary, Dec. 1672, wh. d. within 2 yrs.

P. 533. l. 18 from bot. aft. Brewer, ins. prob. d. of Crispus,

P. 534. l. 18, strike out 1667, and ins. m. 16 Jan. 1661, Eliz. d. of John Reeves, had Eliz. b. 28 Dec. foll. d. in few mos. ; John, 25 May 1663 ; Eliz. again, Dec. 1665 ; Joshua, Mar. 1668, if the name be not Joanna ; and Mary, Dec. 1670 ; perhaps more ; and

" l. 9 from bot. aft. beside ins. Samuel, wh. d. bef. mid. age,

P. 534. l. 5 from bot. bef. THOMAS, ins. THOMAS, Waterbury, s. of Thomas of Hartford, m. 21 Oct. 1691, Mary, d. of Benjamin Parsons.

P. 535. l. 8, aft. RICHARDSON, ins. RICHASON,

" l. 17 from bot. bef. EDWARD, ins. EBENEZER, Waterbury, youngest s. of Thomas of the same, m. Margaret, d. of Thomas Warner, and Bronson, wh. says, he d. 30 June 1772, tells no more.

P. 536. l. 12, aft. Woburn, ins. s. of Thomas of the same,

" l. 14, aft. Jan. ins. (Vinton, 392, says June) — also, aft. 1676, add, d. under 2 yrs.

" l. 15, for soon r. young.

" l. 17, bef. JAMES, ins. ISRAEL, Waterbury, s. of Thomas, d. 18 Dec. 1712, with his w. and oldest ch. Mary in few weeks to foll. him, but other ch. are not nam. by Bronson.

" l. 18, aft. m. ins. prob. that yr. tho. by rec.

" l. 17 from bot. aft. 1673, ins. but 1672, acc. Vinton, 381,

" l. 16 from bot. aft. 1674, ins. Vinton r. 22 Sept. 1673

" l. 6 from bot. bef. JOSEPH, ins. JOHN, Waterbury, br. of Ebenezer, m. Ruth, d. of John Wheeler, and sec. w. Eliz. d. of Nathaniel Arnold. But the hist. gives no dates or issue of either, add, only, that he d. 17 Oct. 1712 in the gr. pestilence of that region.

" l. 5 from bot. bef. Green, ins. d. of Thomas

" l. 3 from bot. aft. 1718. add, His wid. d. 20 May 1721.

P. 537. l. 13, aft. Woburn, add, youngest s. of Thomas of the same,

" l. 19, bef. RICHARD, ins. NATHANIEL, Waterbury, s. of Thomas of the same, d. 3 Nov. 1712, unm.

" l. 21, aft. Amy ins. or Ann — also, aft. had ins. Richard, eldest s.

" l. 21 from bot. aft. 1674; ins. Francis; and Ebenezer; beside Mary, as is learn. from distrib. in Pro. Ct. aft. June 1681.

P. 538. l. 17 from bot. aft. 1691 ins. ; — also, bef. 1712 ins. 14 Nov. — also, aft. 1712. add, His w. d. a week aft. and three s. John, Israel, and Nathaniel, all sunk in the same epidem.

" l. 12 from bot. bef. WILLIAM, ins. THOMAS, Waterbury, s. of Thomas of the same, rem. to Wallingford, was liv. 1722.

P. 540. l. 21, bef. wh. ins. and Sarah, tw. b. 12 Aug. of — also, aft. wh. ins. Hannah

" l. 14 from bot. erase perhaps — also, aft. 1649 add, to 58

" l. 13 from bot. aft See ins. Babson and

P. 541. l. 21 from bot. aft. Gloucester, ins. youngest

P. 544. l. 20 ᶠrom bot. aft. John, ins. b. 14 Apr. 1661 ; — also, aft. and, ins. Hannah, 28 Feb. 1663 ; these two at S.

P. 545. l. 4, aft. 1657 ; add, all by w. Margaret, wh. d. 24 July 1660 ; — also, aft. and add, he m. 3 Nov. 1661, Bridget Fiske, wid. prob. of William, and had

" l. 18, at the end, add, WILLIAM, Lynn, m. Hannah, d. of Nicholas Potter, had William, b. 12 Aug. 1692; Hannah, 12 Oct. 1694; Eliz. 16 Apr. 1697; and Mary, 26 Oct. 1699.

P. 546. l. 16, aft. Salem, ins. had w. Isabel, wh. d. 9 Oct. 1674, and m. 11 Mar. foll. Mary Bishop, a wid.

P. 547. l. 11, aft. Gloucester, ins. prob. s. of Robert of Ipswich,

P. 551. l. 15 from bot. for 1659 r. 1660

P. 552. l. 15, aft. same, ins. m. 16 Oct. 1665, Sarah, d. of Elias Mason — also, aft. had, strike out w. and fam. and ins. Elias, b. 25 Jan. 1667 ; John, 25 Nov. 1668; Joseph, 27 Sept. 1670; and Sarah, 18 Feb. 1673; was liv.

P. 553. l. 7 from bot. for "may have been," r. eldest — also, erase of John, but more likely

" l. 6 from bot. aft. same, ins. m. 15 Aug. 1664, Martha, d. of Job Hawkins, had Samuel, b. 19 Dec. 1665 ; Thomas, 6 July 1667 ; Mary, Oct. 1669, d. Aug. foll. ; William, 29 July 1671 ; Job, Nov. 1672, d. in few wks. ; and Martha, 20 Jan. 1674. He

P. 554. l. 13 from bot. aft. prob. ins. of Boston,

P. 555. l. 3, aft. Salem, add, wh. m. 20 Feb. 1666, Mary, d. of John Kitchen,

" l. 4, strike out "a young ch. Perhaps he" and ins. Timothy, b. 15 Mar. preced.

P. 563. l. 15 from bot. aft. Salem, ins. m. 29 Oct. 1674, Eliz. d. perhaps of Daniel Baxter, was, in

P. 567. l. 6 from bot. for 1642 r. 1842

P. 568. l. 21, bef. RICHARD, ins. PETER, Windsor, d. 13 June 1651, as Stiles, 767, tells, but adds no more, subtract. final s. Of him, or John, or Joseph, both of Salem, it would be good to learn the f.

P. 573. l. 8 from bot. aft. life; add, but he had two other ds. to ea. of wh. a few shillings were giv. and he d. Feb. 1666.

" l. 4 from bot. for Fry r. Try

P. 575. l. 13 from bot. aft. Prov. ins. Some of the dates vary from those in the Essex Inst.

l. 11 from bot. aft. 1678. ins. The preced. sent. in Essex Inst. III. 96, is whol. giv. to R. Ross, wh. would be an easy mistake for Ropes in old chirogr. but I hardly dare to suppose such an error in a Salem man.

" l. 10 from bot. bef. 1676, ins. 26 July

" l. 9 from bot. bef. Nov. ins. 4

" l. 8 from bot. for Jan. 1683 r. 9 Jan. 1685 — also, for Mar. 1685 r. 5 Mar. 1686 — also, bef. Aug. ins. 12

" l. 7 from bot. for Jan. 1692 r. 11 Jan. 1693 — also, for Jan. 1694 r. 24 Jan. 1695.

P. 577. l. 2, aft. kn. add, but m. of a Daniel with Mary Knight, youngest d. of Philip of Topsfield, 5 June 1677, is rec. at Salem.

P. 579. l. 14, bef. 1670, ins. 16 Nov.

P. 581. l. 1, aft. Amesbury, ins. only s. of Thomas of Ipswich,

" l. 5, erase perhaps

P. 584. l. 12, erase bapt. there — also, aft. Eliz. ins. b. 1 Feb. 1653 ;

" l. 13, aft. Hannah, ins. 17 Mar. 1654, both bapt. — also, bef. Sarah, ins. John, 1 Apr. 1655, d. in few days ; — also, aft. Sarah, ins. 12 Aug. bapt. — also, aft. John, ins. again, 30 Aug. bapt.

" l. 14, aft. Thomas, ins. 23 Oct. 1658, bapt. — also, aft. and, ins. his w. d. 29 Jan. 1661. He m. 17 Sept. foll. Sarah Flint, perhaps d. of William, had Abigail, 28 Oct. 1662 ; — also, aft. Mary, ins. 30 July prob. tho. Essex Inst. III. 95, gives Aug. but she was bapt. — also, aft. 1665 ; ins. Bethia, 8 Apr. 1668 ; — also, aft. Rebecca, ins. Sept. 1671,

" l. 16, aft. 1686. add, His w. d. 4 May 1672. — also, aft. m. ins. 26 Dec. foll. — also, for sec. r. third

" l. 17, aft. Price, ins. had Ruth, 20 Oct. foll. ; John, again, 20 May 1675 ; and Samuel, 24 June 1676.

P. 593. l. 6 from bot. erase perhaps

P. 595. l. 15, bef. WILLIAM, ins. WILLIAM, Salem, m. 25 Oct. 1678, Eliz. d. of the first Francis Russell, had Mary, b. 22 Oct. 1680; and John, 9 Aug. 1682.

P. 620. l. 11, from bot. at the end, add, also, — aft. Joseph. add, The div. of his est. June 1680, betw. only Thomas and Joseph, under order of Ct. leads us to infer, that both of the other s. d. bef. mid. age.

P. 625. l. 2, at the end, add, prob. posthum. for the f. d. in Oct. 1679.

P. 630. l. 7 from bot. aft. ch. add, to inf. inclus.

" aft. last l. add

" l. 8 from bot. aft. yr. add, His will of 17 Feb. 1680 made w. Ann extrix. provid. for ch. of his s. Eleazur (wh. was d.) viz. William, Samuel, and Abigail; for Sarah, wid. of his s. William ; for a gr.ch. in Europe, if he come here, if not, then that devise to other gr.ch. viz. two eldest s. of his d. Coker, w. I presume of Joseph.

P. 632. l. 14, at the end, But by former w. Miriam he had Miriam and Susanna.

P. 637. l. 7, at the end, add, Abigail m. 1680 Richard Blackleach of Stratford.

P. 638. l. 6, aft. His ins. inv. was tak. 13 Nov. and the

P. 643. l. 1, aft. Mary, ins. d. of John Reeves of S.

" l. 2, aft. 25) ins. but I suppose his name was John,

END OF VOL. III.